THE
IMMORTAL
IRON
FIST

W9-ARU-685

THE IMMORTAL IRON FIST

Collection Editor: Jennifer Grünwald • Assistant Editors: Alex Starbuck & Nelson Ribeiro
Editor, Special Projects: Mark D. Beazley • Senior Editor, Special Projects: Jeff Youngquist
SVP of Print & Digital Publishing Sales: David Gabriel

Editor in Chief: Axel Alonso • Chief Creative Officer: Joe Quesada
Publisher: Dan Buckley • Executive Producer: Alan Fine

IMMORTAL IRON FIST: THE COMPLETE COLLECTION VOL. 1. Contains material originally published in magazine form as IMMORTAL IRON FIST #1-16 and ANNUAL #1, IMMORTAL IRON FIST: ORSON RANDALL AND THE GREEN MIST OF DEATH #1, IMMORTAL IRON FIST: THE ORIGIN OF DANNY RAND #1, and CIVIL WAR: CHOOSING SIDES #1. First printing 2013. ISBN# 978-0-7851-8542-0. Published by MARVEL WORLDWIDE, INC., a subsidiary of MARVEL ENTERTAINMENT, LLC. OFFICE OF PUBLICATION: 135 West 50th Street, New York, NY 10020. Copyright © 2006, 2007, 2008 and 2013 Marvel Characters, Inc. All rights reserved. All characters featured in this issue and the distinctive names and likenesses thereof, and all related indicia are trademarks of Marvel Characters, Inc. No similarity between any of the names, characters, persons, and/or institutions in this magazine with those of any living or dead person or institution is intended, and any such similarity which may exist is purely coincidental. Printed in the U.S.A. ALAN FINE, EVP - Office of the President, Marvel Worldwide, Inc. and EVP & CMO Marvel Characters B.V.; DAN BUCKLEY, Publisher & President - Print, Animation & Digital Divisions; JOE QUESADA, Chief Creative Officer; TOM BREVOORT, SVP of Publishing; DAVID BOGART, SVP of Operations & Procurement, Publishing; C.B. CEBULSKI, SVP of Creator & Content Development; DAVID GABRIEL, SVP of Print & Digital Publishing Sales; JIM O'KEEFE, VP of Operations & Logistics; DAN CARR, Executive Director of Publishing Technology; SUSAN CRESPI, Editorial Operations Manager; ALEX MORALES, Publishing Operations Manager; STAN LEE, Chairman Emeritus. For information regarding advertising in Marvel Comics or on Marvel.com, please contact Niza Disla, Director of Marvel Partnerships, at ndisla@marvel.com. For Marvel subscription inquiries, please call 800-217-9158. Manufactured between 10/18/2013 and 11/25/2013 by R.R. DONNELLEY, INC., SALEM, VA, USA.

Writers: Matt Fraction & Ed Brubaker
Artists, #1-13 & #16: David Aja
with Travel Foreman & Derek Friedolfs (#1-5), John Severin (#2), Russ Heath (#3 & #6), Sal Buscema & Tom Palmer (#4), Roy Allan Martinez (#8-9), Scott Koblish (#9), Kano (#10-13), Javier Pulido (#12) and Tonci Zonjic (#13)
Colorists: Matt Hollingsworth
with Dean White (#2), Laura Martin (#6), June Chung (#8-9), David Aja (#10), Kano (#10), Javier Rodriguez (#11-14) and Paul Mounts (#14)
Cover Art: David Aja & Matt Hollingsworth (#1-6, #8-9 & #16); Jelena Kevic Djurdjevic (#10); Travel Foreman, Mark Morales & Paul Mounts (#11); and Kaare Andrews (#12-13)

Issue #7
Artists: Travel Foreman & Derek Friedolfs, Leandro Fernandez & Francisco Paronzini and Khari Evans & Victor Olazaba
Colorist: Dan Brown
Cover Art: Travel Foreman & Len O'Grady

Orson Randall & The Green Mist of Death #1
Artists: Nick Dragotta, Mike Allred, Russ Heath, Lewis LaRosa & Stefano Gaudiano and Mitch Breitweiser
Colorists: Laura Allred, Russ Heath and Matt Hollingsworth
Cover Art: Kaare Andrews

Issue #15
Penciler: Khari Evans
Inker: Victor Olazaba
Colorists: Jelena Kevic Djurdjevic and Paul Mounts
Cover Art: Khari Evans, Victor Olazaba & Matt Hollingsworth

Annual #1
Artists: Howard Chaykin, Dan Brereton and Jelena Kevic Djurdjevic
Colorists: Edgar Delgado and Jelena Kevic Djurdjevic
Cover Art: Dan Brereton

Issue #14
Pencilers: Tonci Zonjic with Clay Mann
Inker: Stefano Gaudiano
Additional Art: Kano and Jelena Kevic Djurdjevic
Cover Art: Kaare Andrews

The Origin of Danny Rand #1 framing sequence
Artist: Kano
Cover Art: Gil Kane, Larry Hama & Rain Beredo

Civil War: Choosing Sides #1
Artist: David Aja
Cover Art: Leinil Francis Yu & Dave McCaig

Letterers: Dave Lanphear & Artmonkeys Studios
Assistant Editor: Alejandro Arbona
Editor: Warren Simons

1
鐵拳

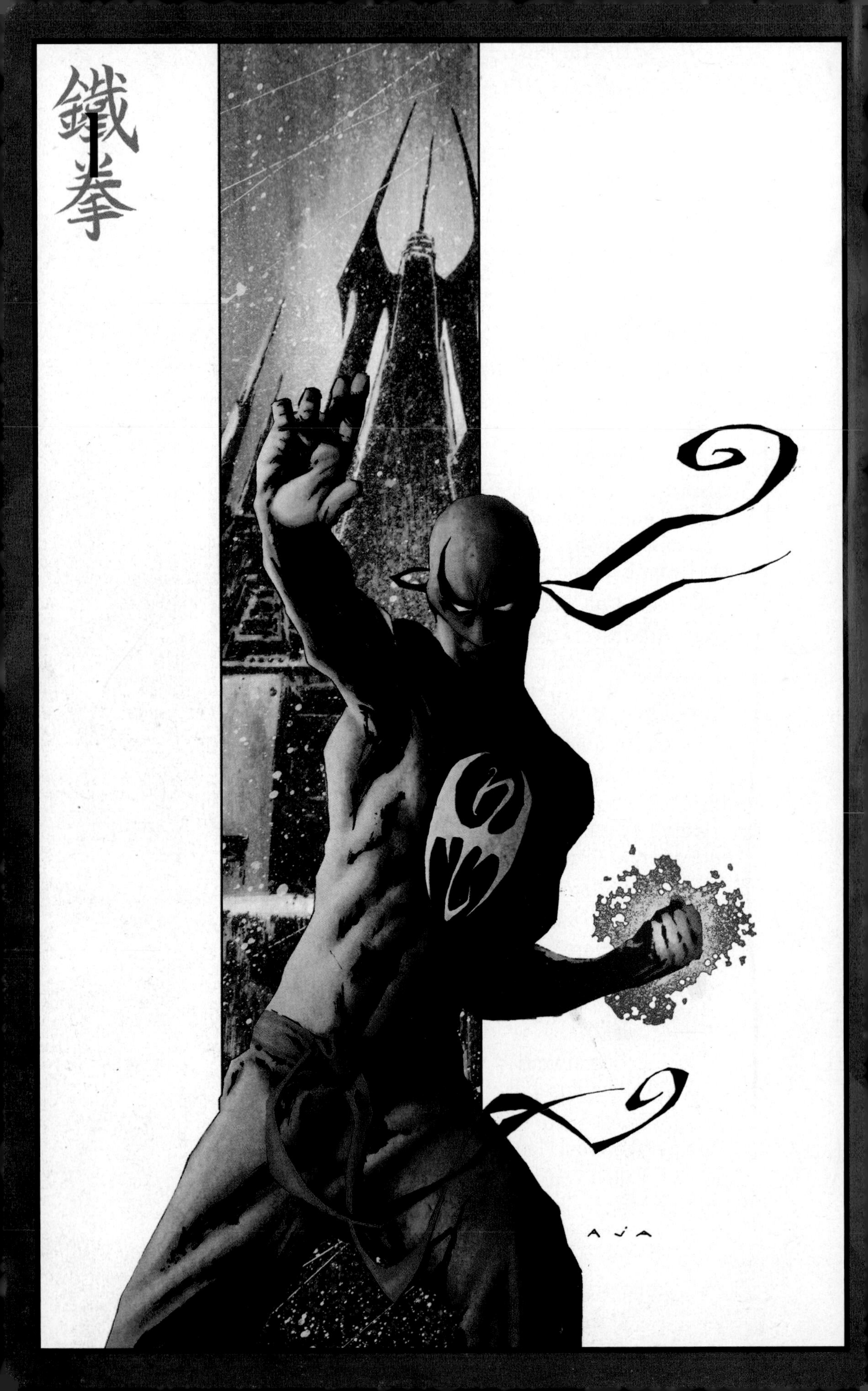
AJA

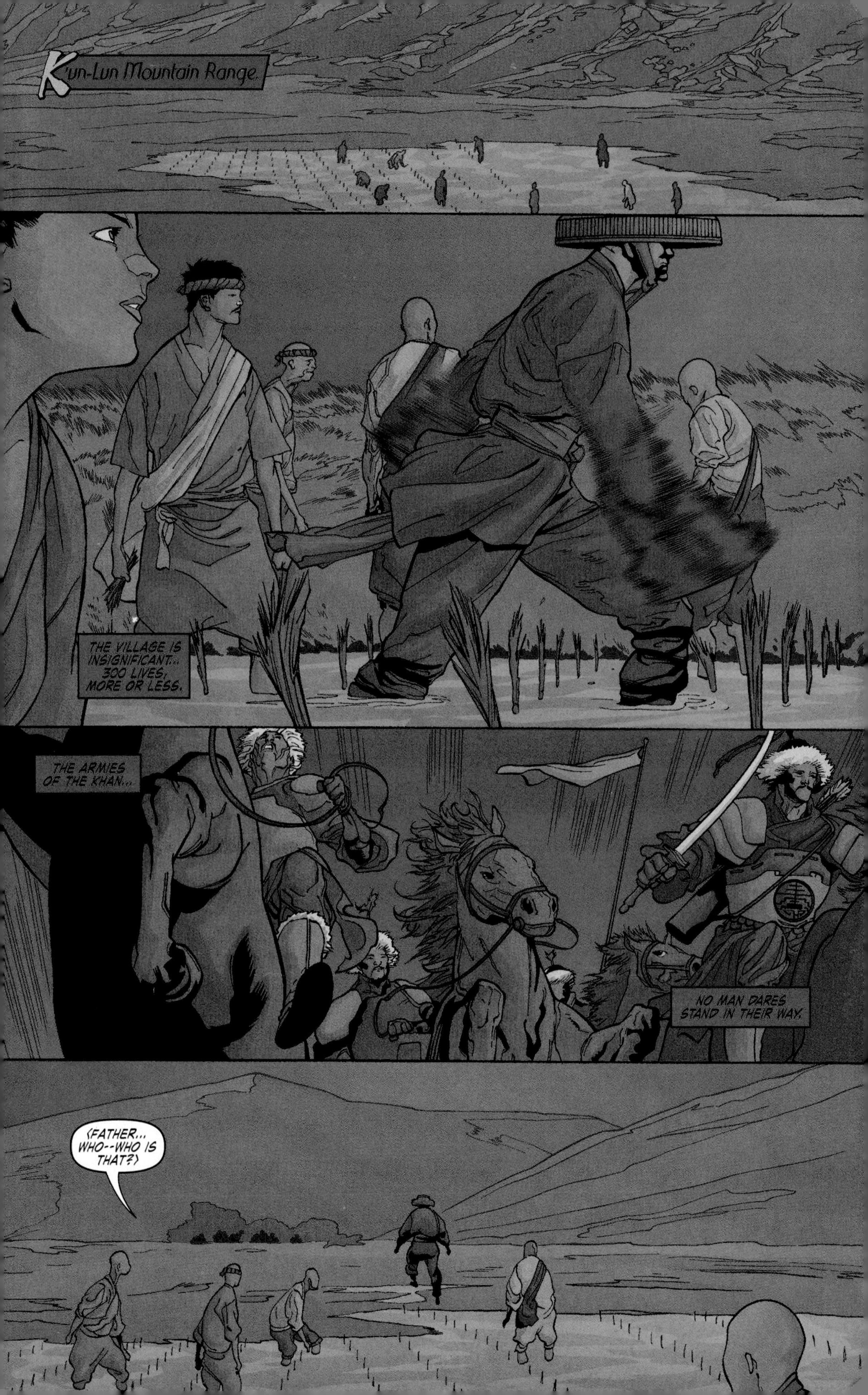
K'un-Lun Mountain Range.
THE VILLAGE IS INSIGNIFICANT.. 300 LIVES, MORE OR LESS.
THE ARMIES OF THE KHAN...
NO MAN DARES STAND IN THEIR WAY.
<FATHER... WHO--WHO IS THAT?>

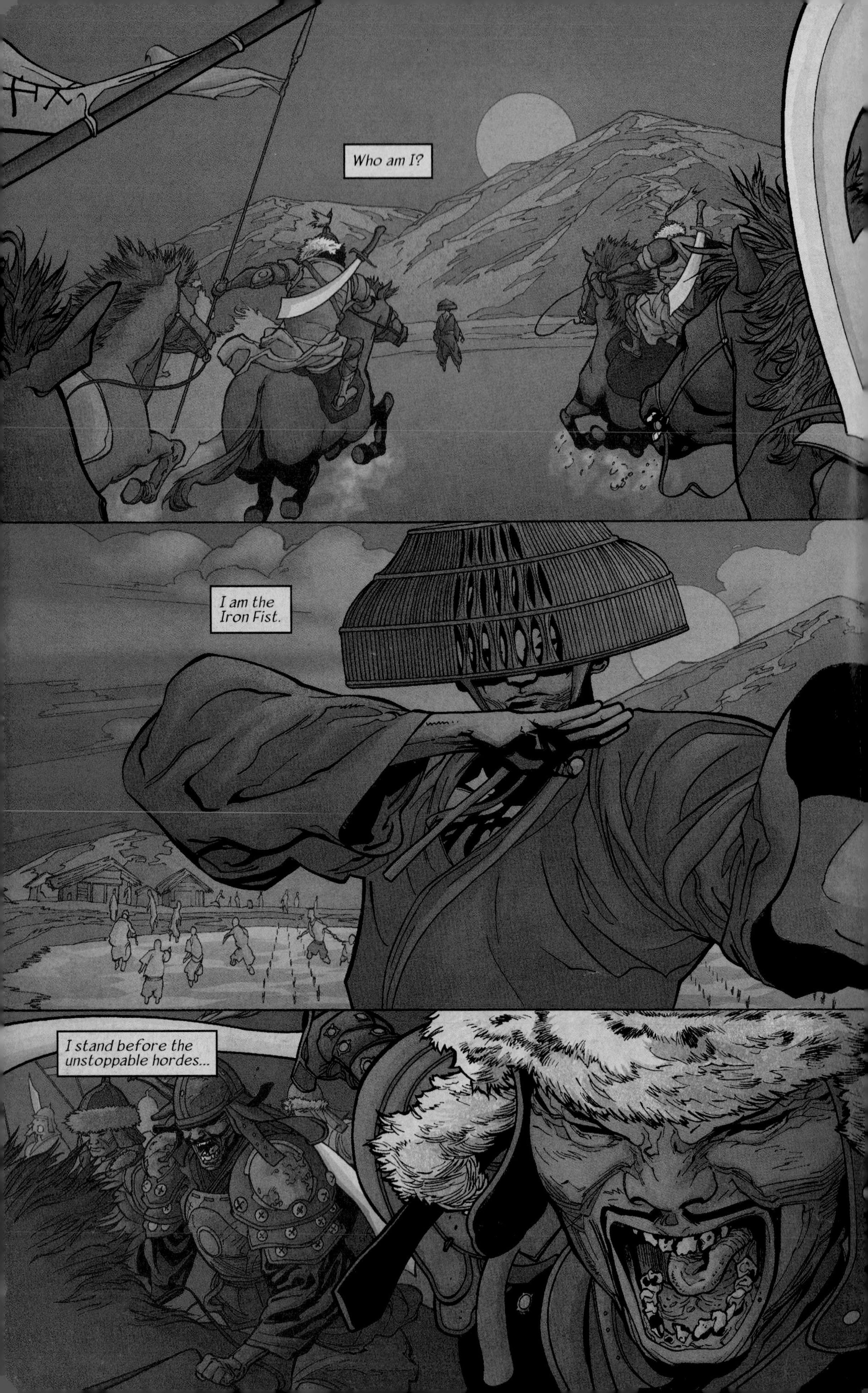
Who am I?
I am the Iron Fist.
I stand before the unstoppable hordes...

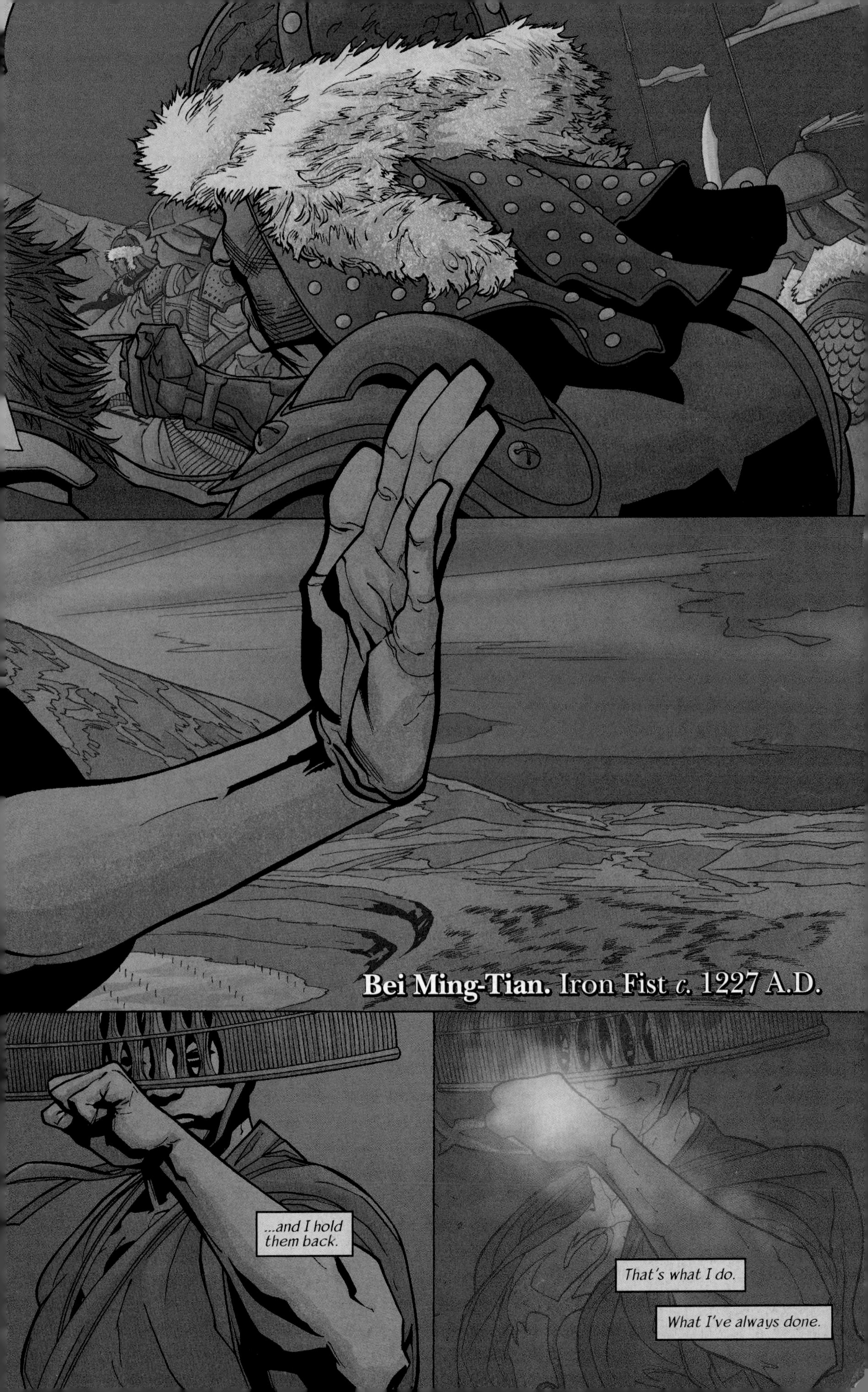
Bei Ming-Tian. Iron Fist c. 1227 A.D.
...and I hold them back.
That's what I do.
What I've always done.

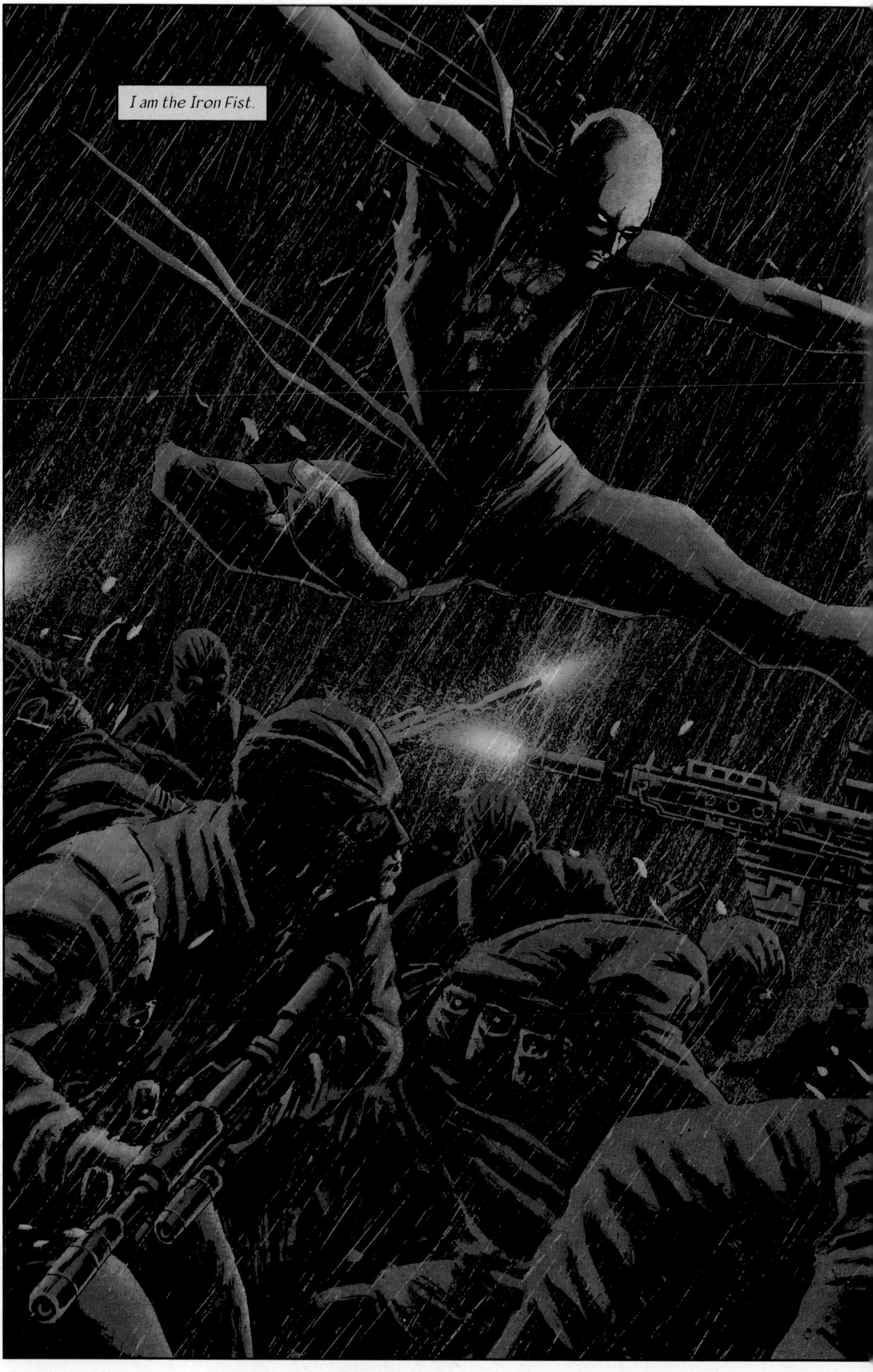
I am the Iron Fist.

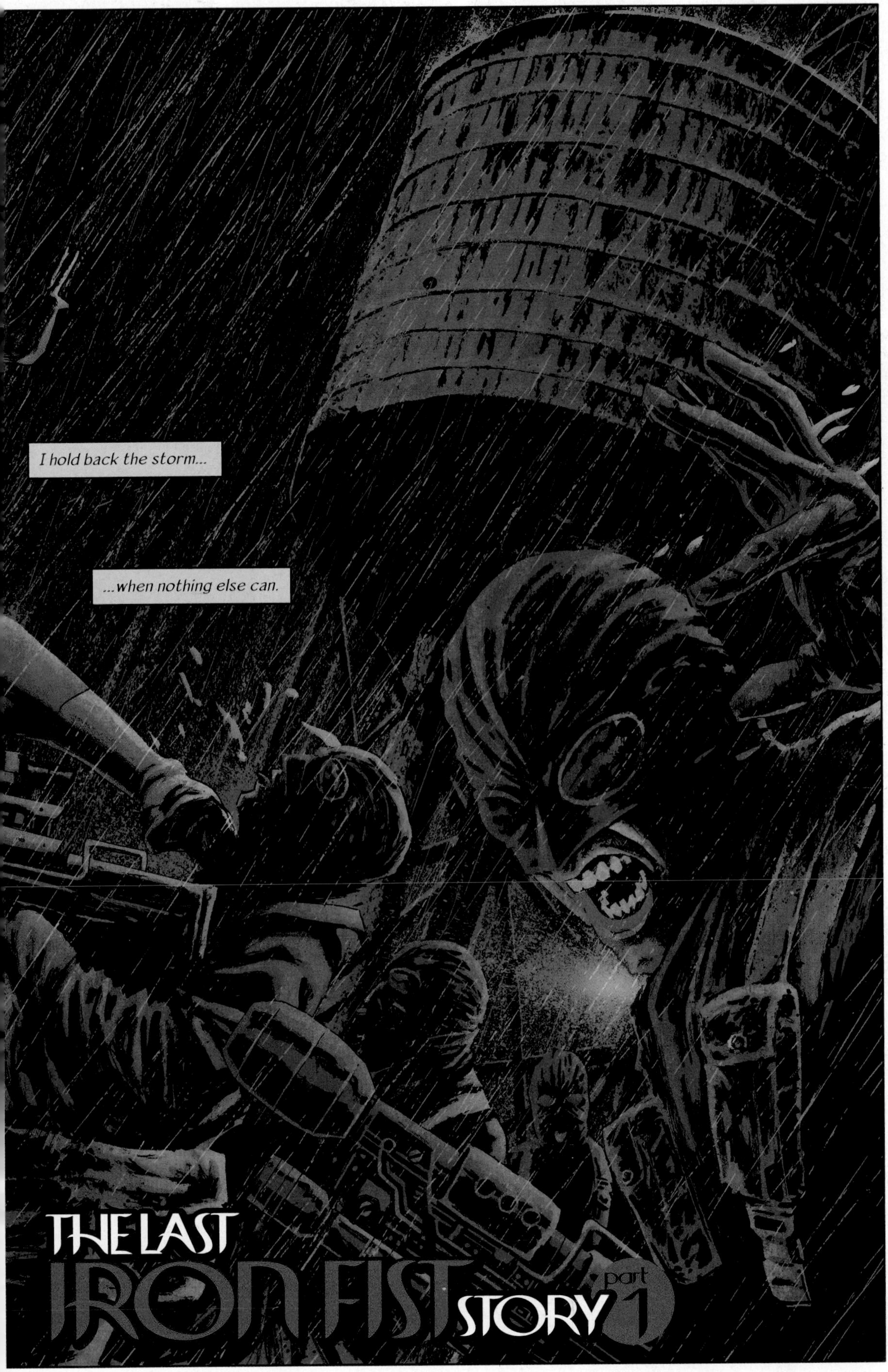
I hold back the storm...
...when nothing else can.
THE LAST IRON FIST STORY part 1

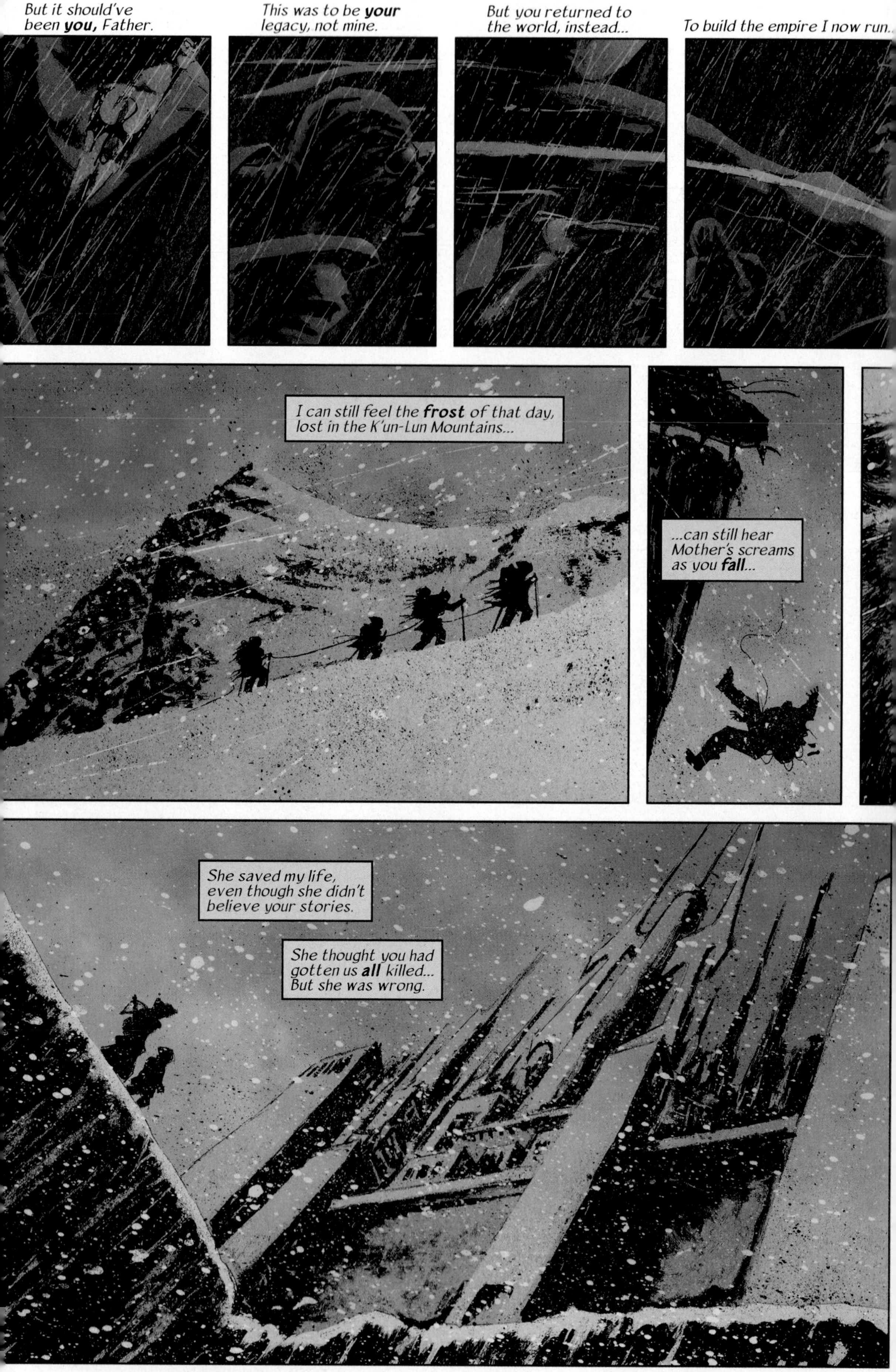
But it should've been **you,** Father.
This was to be **your** legacy, not mine.
But you returned to the world, instead...
To build the empire I now run...
I can still feel the **frost** of that day, lost in the K'un-Lun Mountains...
...can still hear Mother's screams as you **fall**...
She saved my life, even though she didn't believe your stories.
She thought you had gotten us **all** killed... But she was wrong.

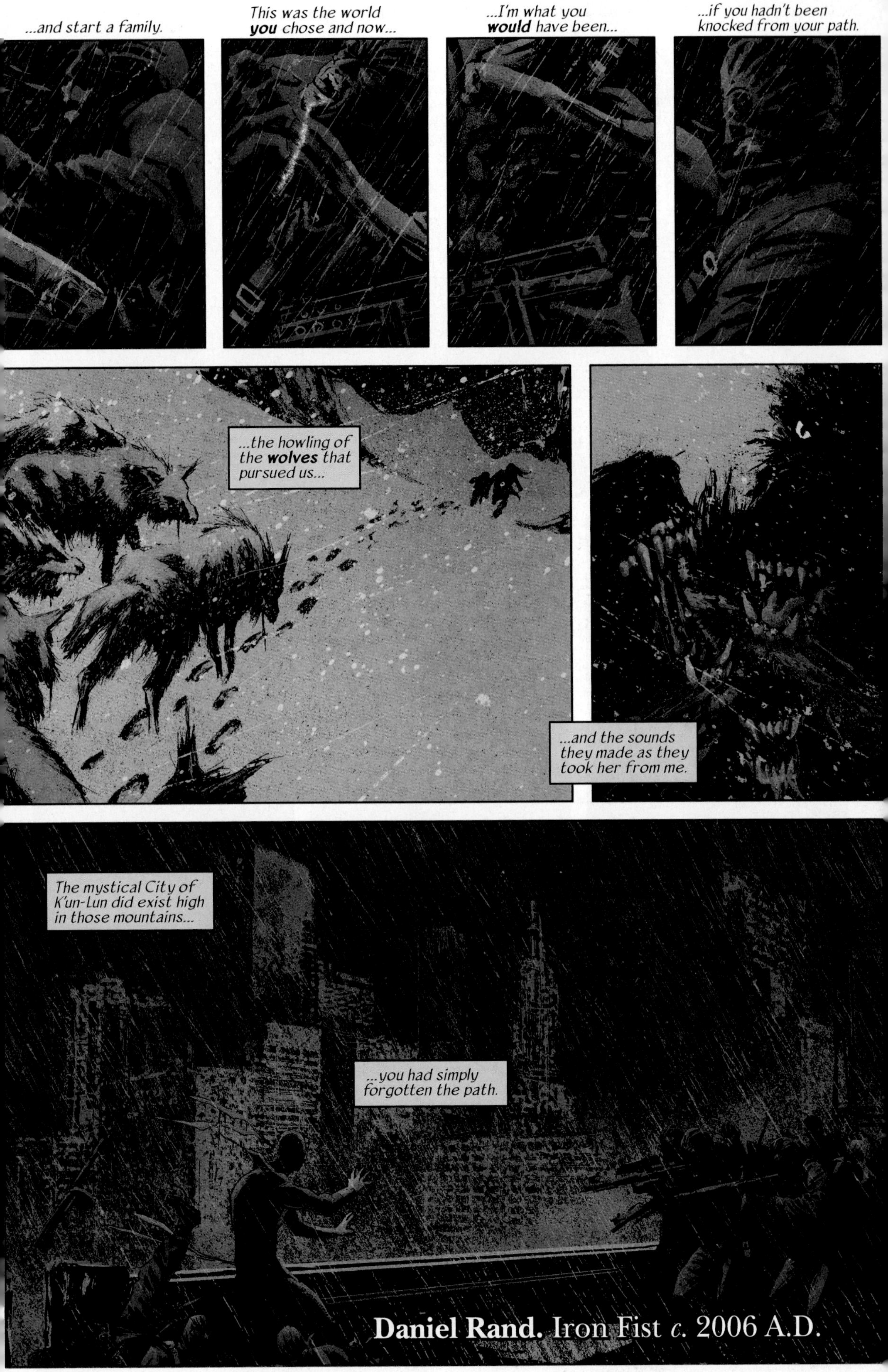
...and start a family.
This was the world **you** chose and now...
...I'm what you **would** have been...
...if you hadn't been knocked from your path.
...the howling of the **wolves** that pursued us...
...and the sounds they made as they took her from me.
The mystical City of K'un-Lun did exist high in those mountains...
...you had simply forgotten the path.
Daniel Rand. Iron Fist c. 2006 A.D.

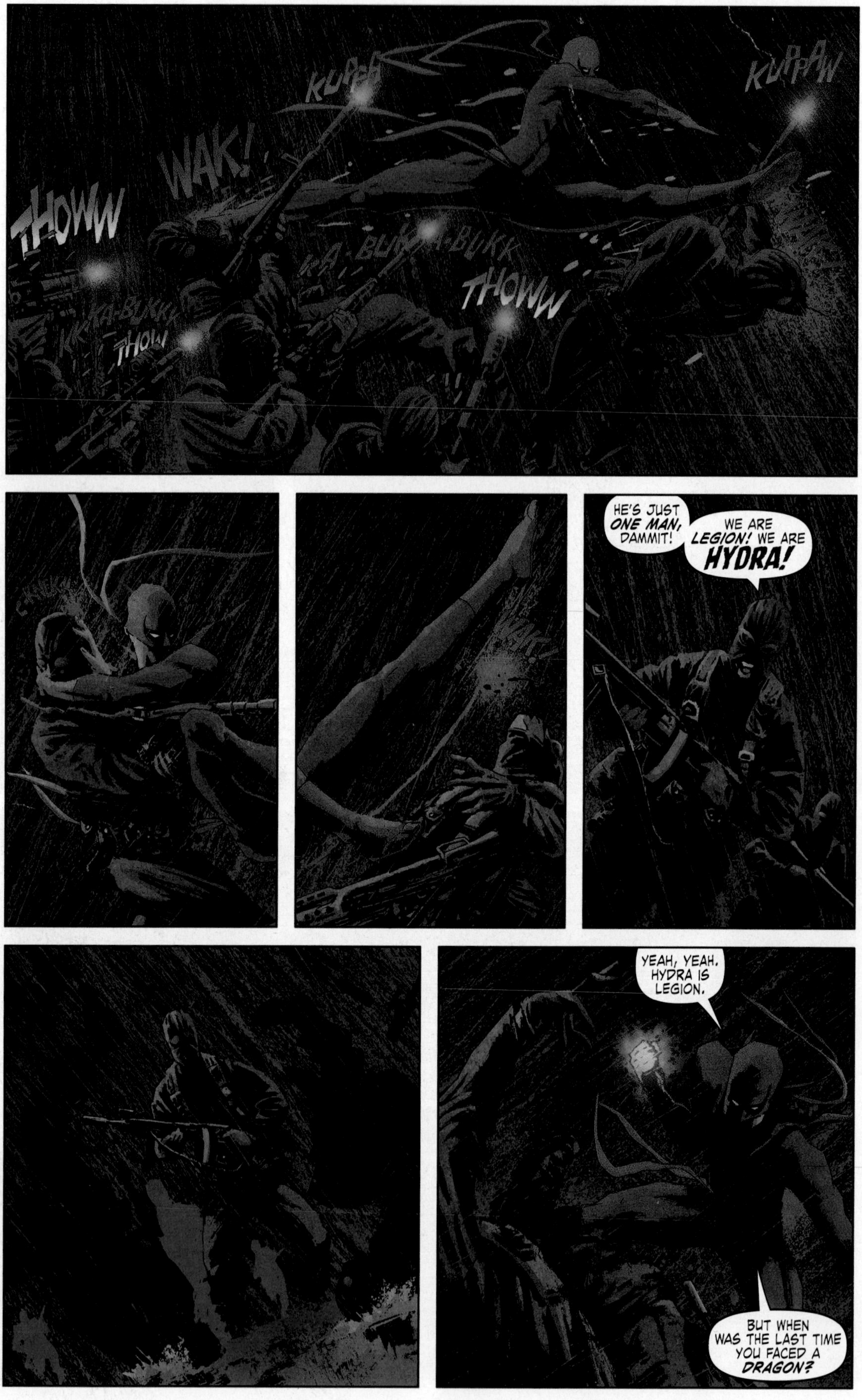
THOWW
WAK!
KUPPAW
THOWW
THOW
HE'S JUST *ONE MAN,* DAMMIT!
WE ARE *LEGION!* WE ARE **HYDRA!**
YEAH, YEAH. HYDRA IS LEGION.
BUT WHEN WAS THE LAST TIME YOU FACED A *DRAGON?*

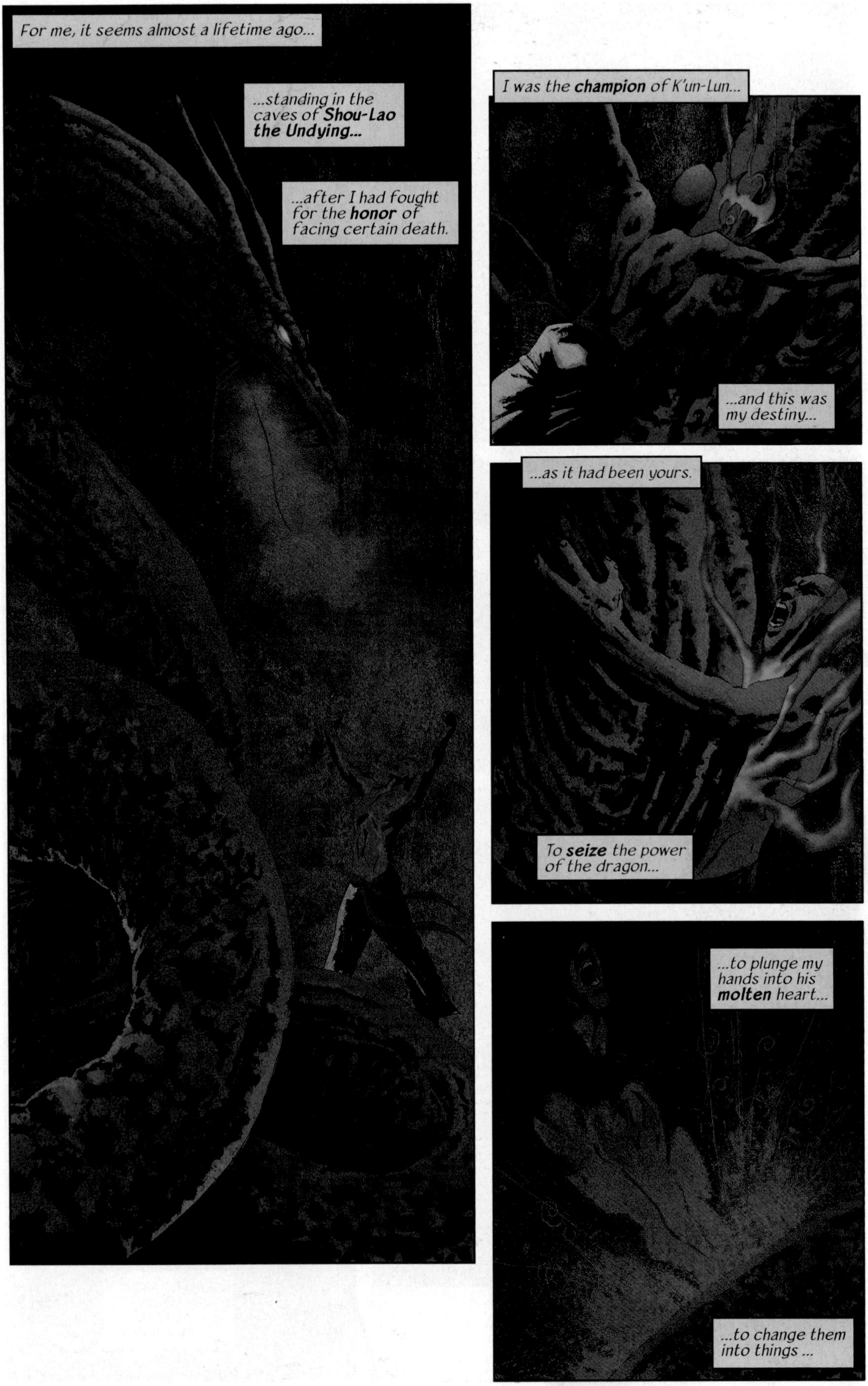
For me, it seems almost a lifetime ago...
...standing in the caves of **Shou-Lao the Undying...**
...after I had fought for the **honor** of facing certain death.
I was the **champion** of K'un-Lun...
...and this was my destiny...
...as it had been yours.
To **seize** the power of the dragon...
...to plunge my hands into his **molten** heart...
...to change them into things ...

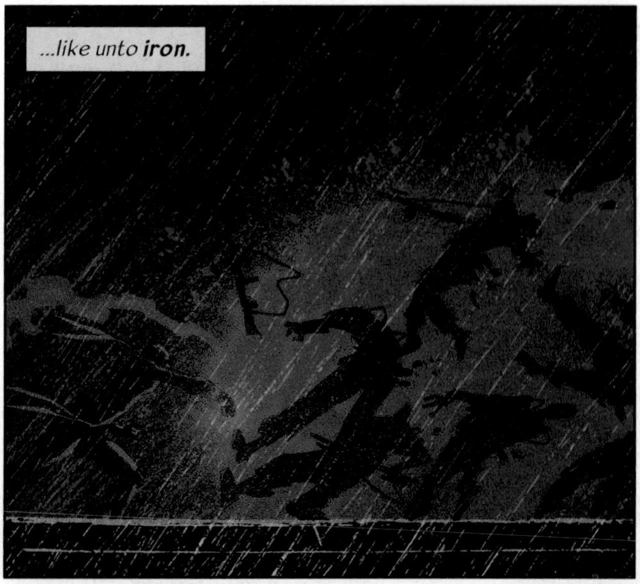
...like unto **iron.**

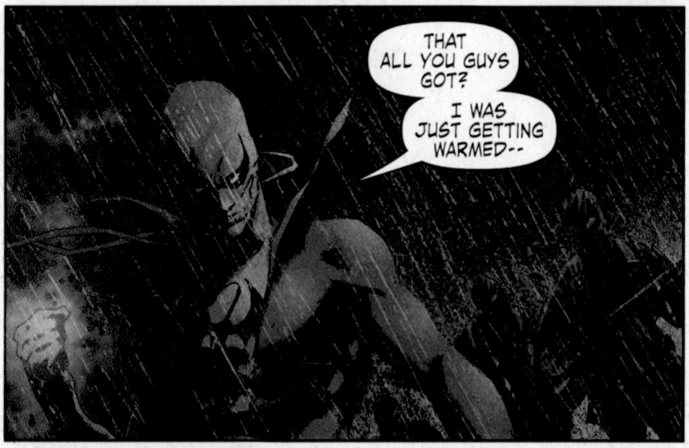
THAT ALL YOU GUYS GOT?
I WAS JUST GETTING WARMED--

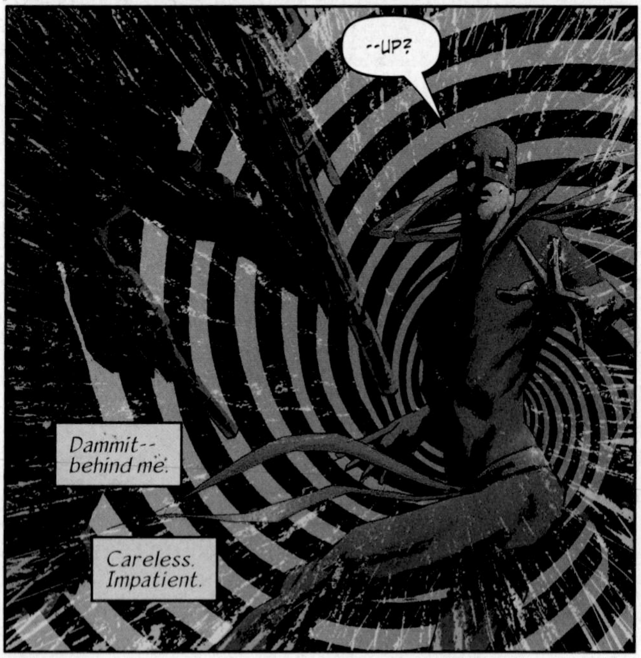
--UP?
Dammit-- behind me.
Careless. Impatient.

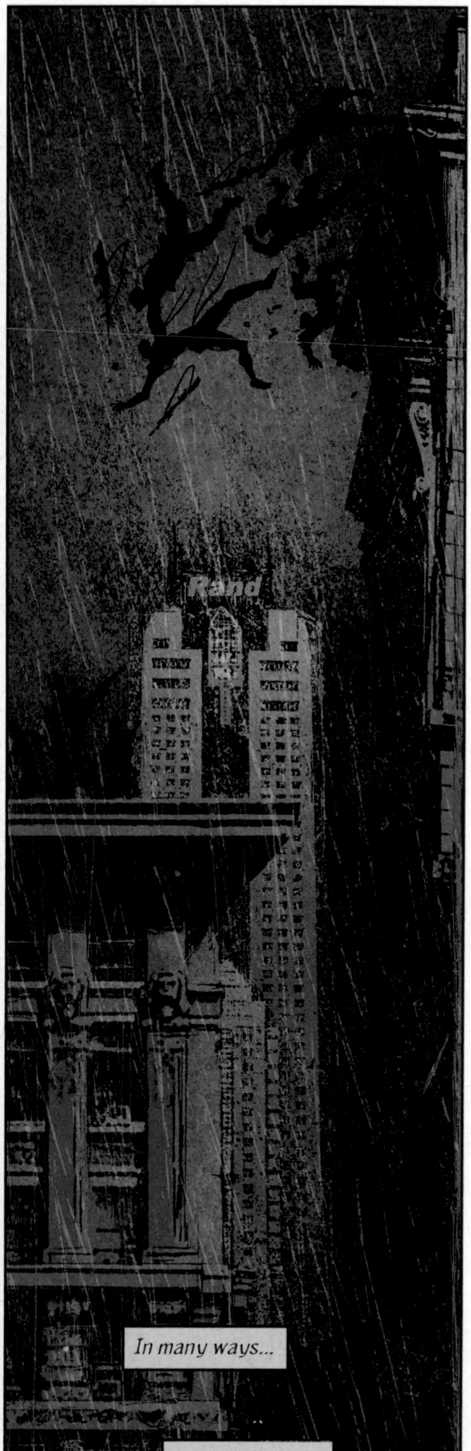
Rand
In many ways...
...I'm the same careless and impatient boy you left behind.

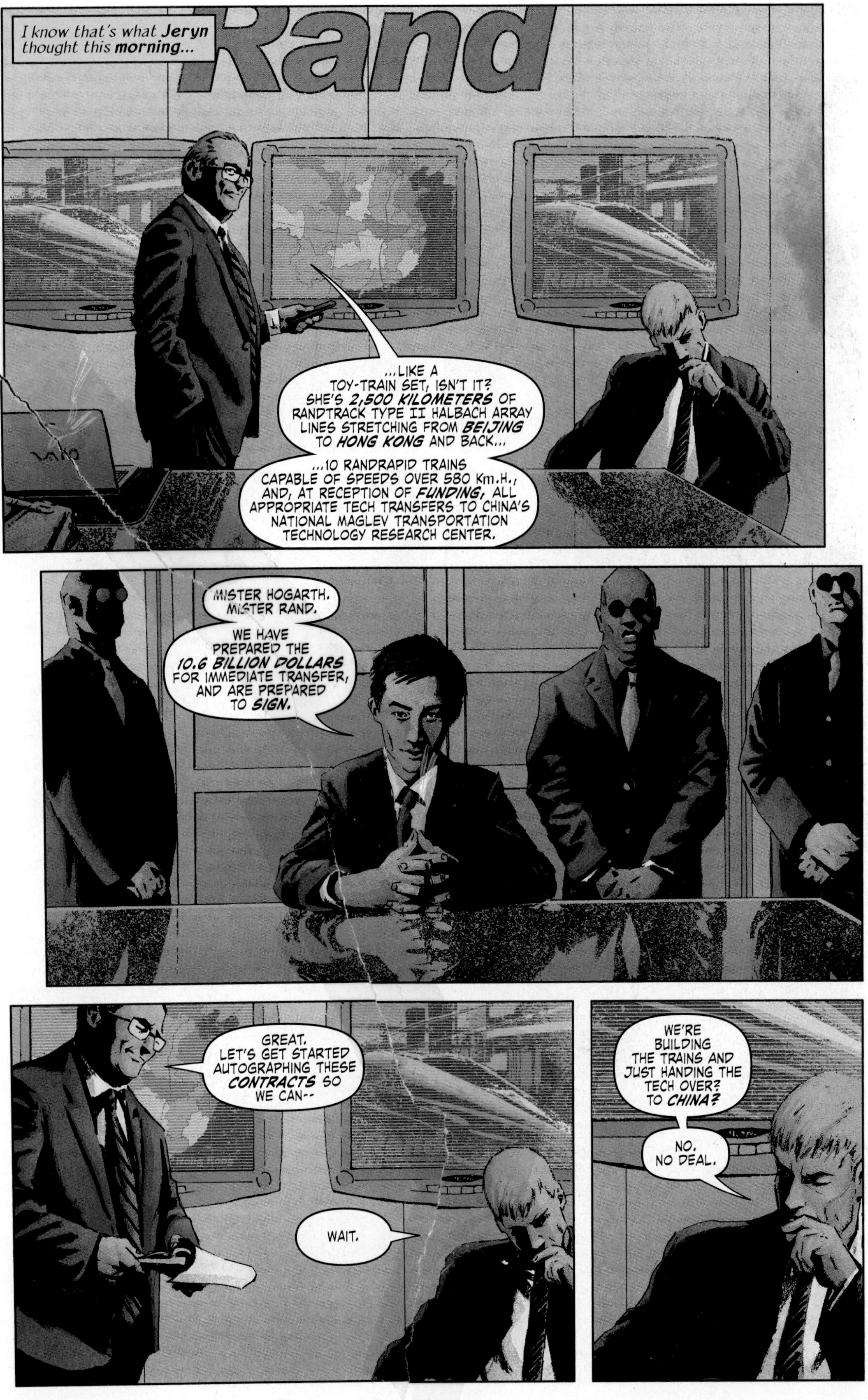
I know that's what Jeryn thought this morning...
Rand
...LIKE A TOY-TRAIN SET, ISN'T IT? SHE'S 2,500 KILOMETERS OF RANDTRACK TYPE II HALBACH ARRAY LINES STRETCHING FROM BEIJING TO HONG KONG AND BACK...
...10 RANDRAPID TRAINS CAPABLE OF SPEEDS OVER 580 Km.H., AND, AT RECEPTION OF FUNDING, ALL APPROPRIATE TECH TRANSFERS TO CHINA'S NATIONAL MAGLEV TRANSPORTATION TECHNOLOGY RESEARCH CENTER.
MISTER HOGARTH. MISTER RAND.
WE HAVE PREPARED THE 10.6 BILLION DOLLARS FOR IMMEDIATE TRANSFER, AND ARE PREPARED TO SIGN.
GREAT. LET'S GET STARTED AUTOGRAPHING THESE CONTRACTS SO WE CAN--
WAIT.
WE'RE BUILDING THE TRAINS AND JUST HANDING THE TECH OVER? TO CHINA?
NO. NO DEAL.

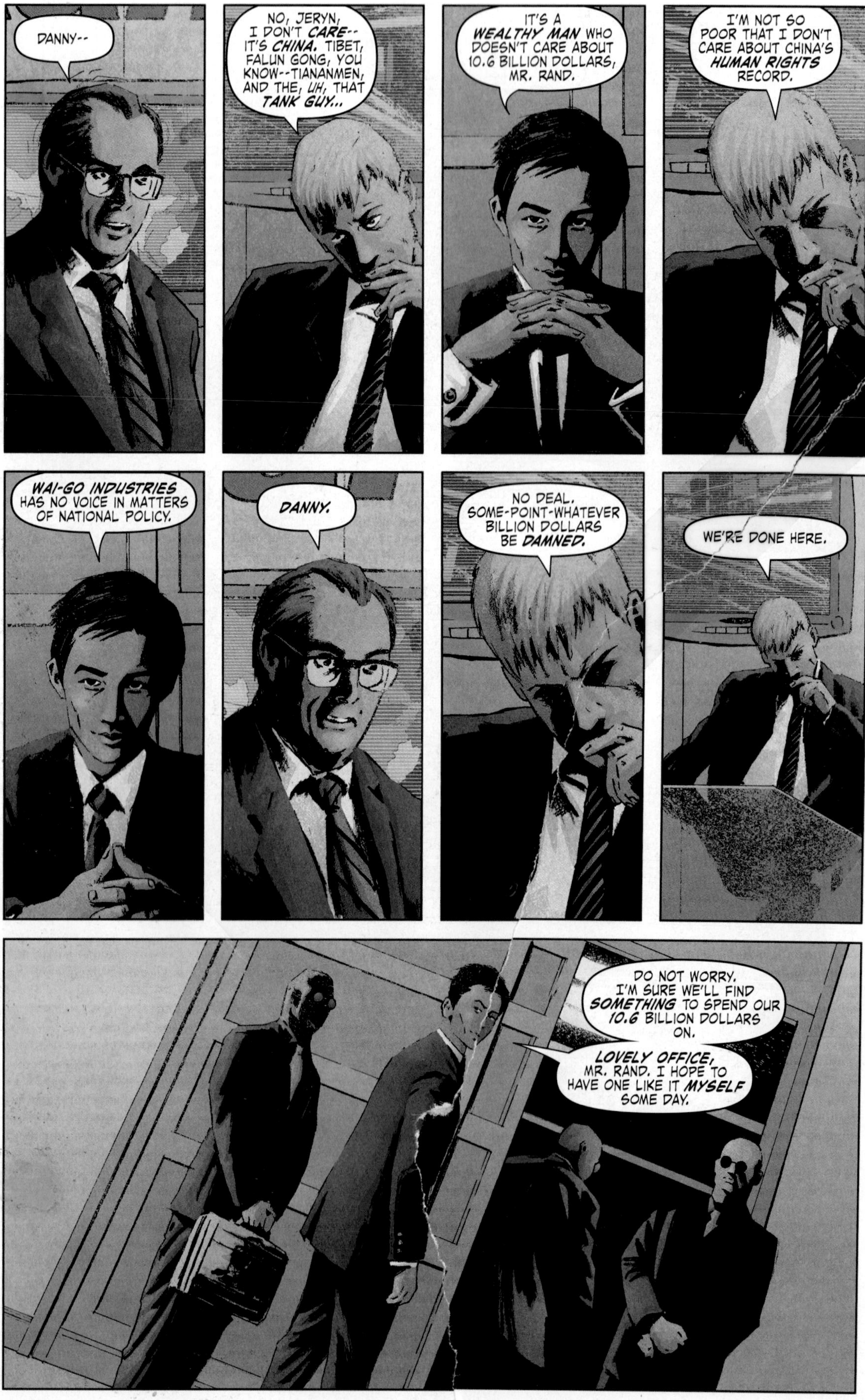
DANNY--
NO, JERYN, I DON'T CARE-- IT'S CHINA. TIBET, FALUN GONG, YOU KNOW--TIANANMEN, AND THE, UH, THAT TANK GUY...
IT'S A WEALTHY MAN WHO DOESN'T CARE ABOUT 10.6 BILLION DOLLARS, MR. RAND.
I'M NOT SO POOR THAT I DON'T CARE ABOUT CHINA'S HUMAN RIGHTS RECORD.
WAI-GO INDUSTRIES HAS NO VOICE IN MATTERS OF NATIONAL POLICY.
DANNY.
NO DEAL. SOME-POINT-WHATEVER BILLION DOLLARS BE DAMNED.
WE'RE DONE HERE.
DO NOT WORRY. I'M SURE WE'LL FIND SOMETHING TO SPEND OUR 10.6 BILLION DOLLARS ON.
LOVELY OFFICE, MR. RAND. I HOPE TO HAVE ONE LIKE IT MYSELF SOME DAY.

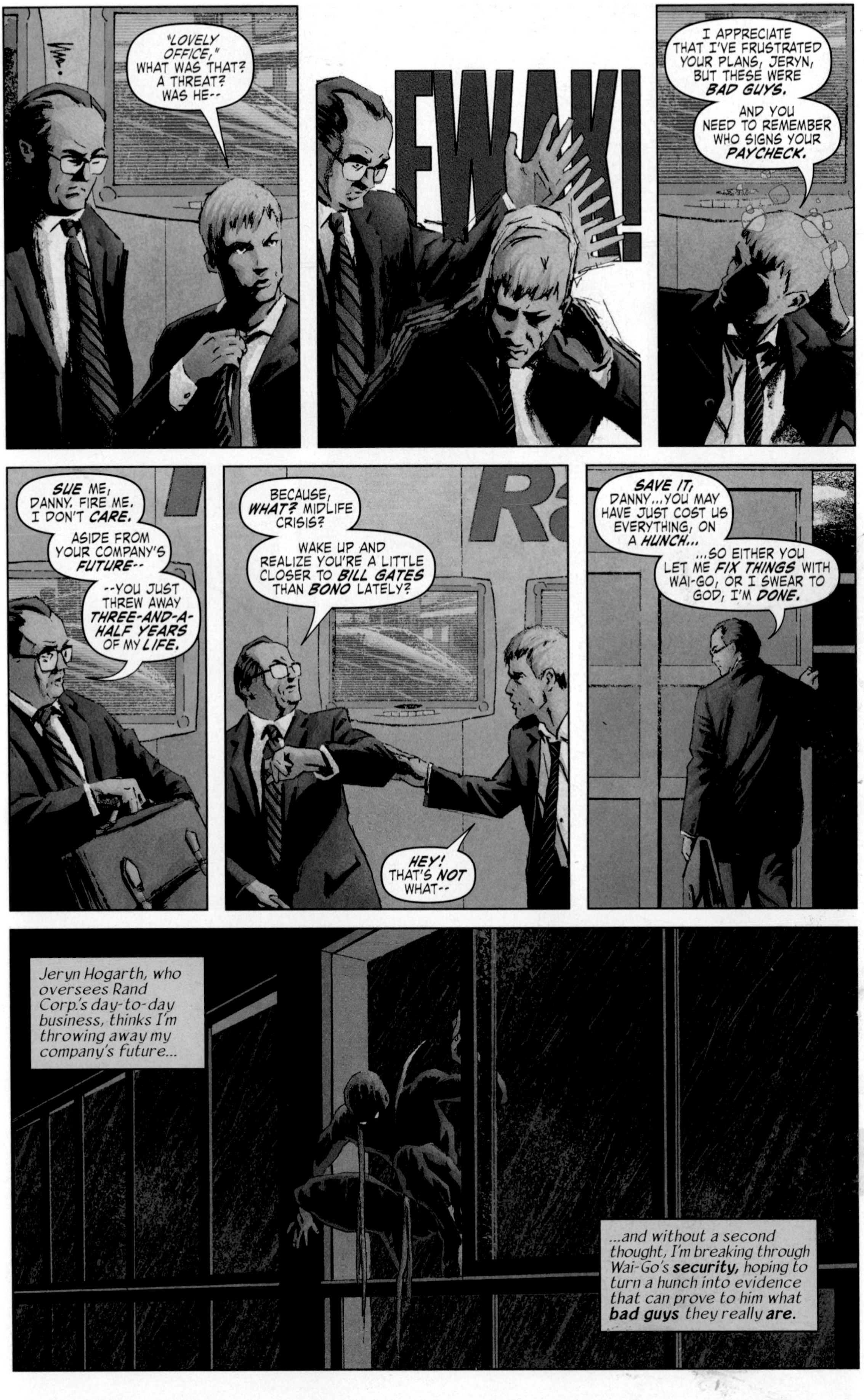
"LOVELY OFFICE," WHAT WAS THAT? A THREAT? WAS HE--
FWAK!
I APPRECIATE THAT I'VE FRUSTRATED YOUR PLANS, JERYN, BUT THESE WERE BAD GUYS.
AND YOU NEED TO REMEMBER WHO SIGNS YOUR PAYCHECK.
SUE ME, DANNY. FIRE ME. I DON'T CARE.
ASIDE FROM YOUR COMPANY'S FUTURE--
--YOU JUST THREW AWAY THREE-AND-A-HALF YEARS OF MY LIFE.
BECAUSE, WHAT? MIDLIFE CRISIS?
WAKE UP AND REALIZE YOU'RE A LITTLE CLOSER TO BILL GATES THAN BONO LATELY?
HEY! THAT'S NOT WHAT--
SAVE IT, DANNY...YOU MAY HAVE JUST COST US EVERYTHING, ON A HUNCH...
...SO EITHER YOU LET ME FIX THINGS WITH WAI-GO, OR I SWEAR TO GOD, I'M DONE.
Jeryn Hogarth, who oversees Rand Corp.'s day-to-day business, thinks I'm throwing away my company's future...
...and without a second thought, I'm breaking through Wai-Go's security, hoping to turn a hunch into evidence that can prove to him what bad guys they really are.

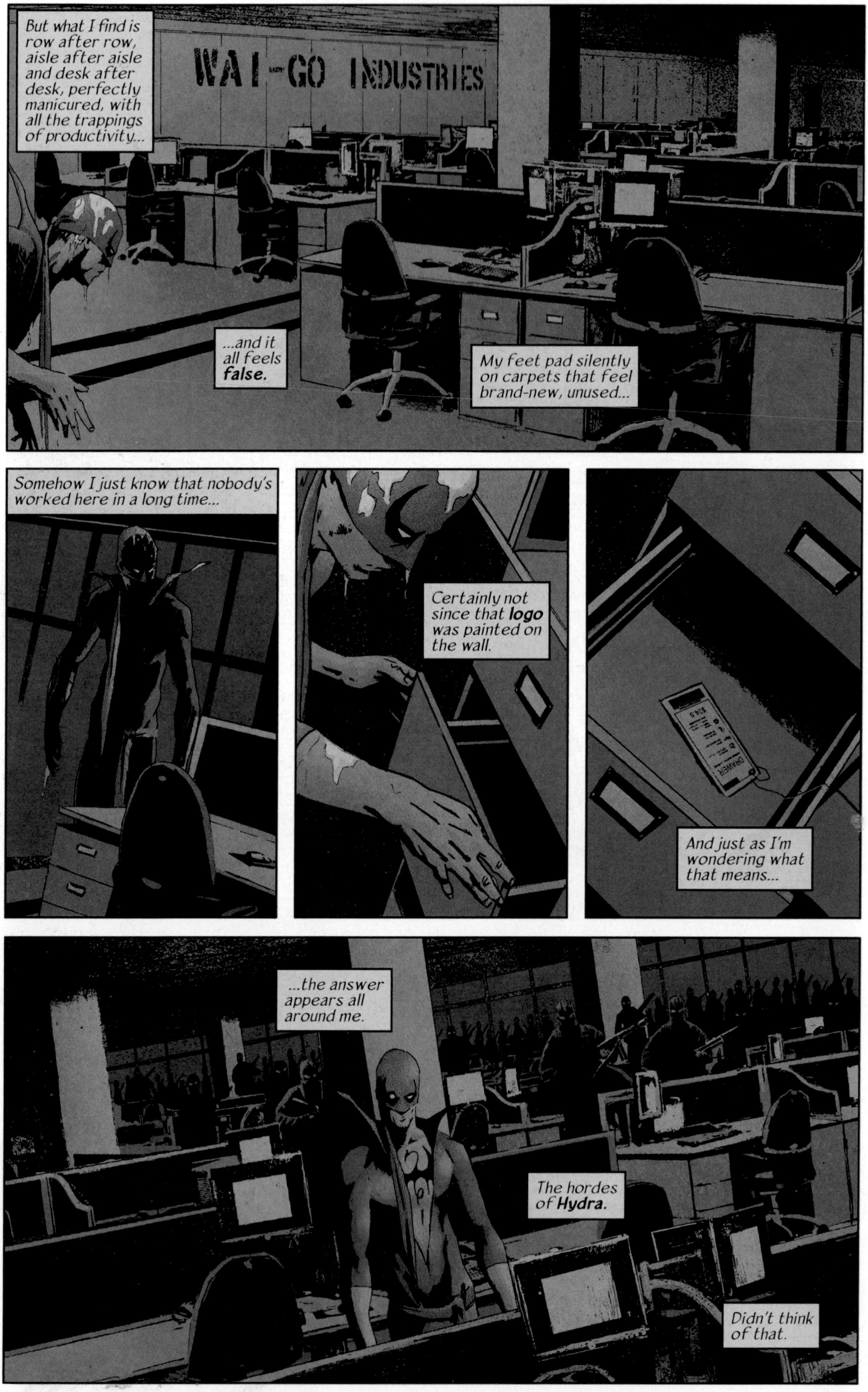

But what I find is row after row, aisle after aisle and desk after desk, perfectly manicured, with all the trappings of productivity...
WAI-GO INDUSTRIES
...and it all feels **false.**
My feet pad silently on carpets that feel brand-new, unused...
Somehow I just know that nobody's worked here in a long time...
Certainly not since that **logo** was painted on the wall.
DRAWER
And just as I'm wondering what that means...
...the answer appears all around me.
The hordes of **Hydra.**
Didn't think of that.

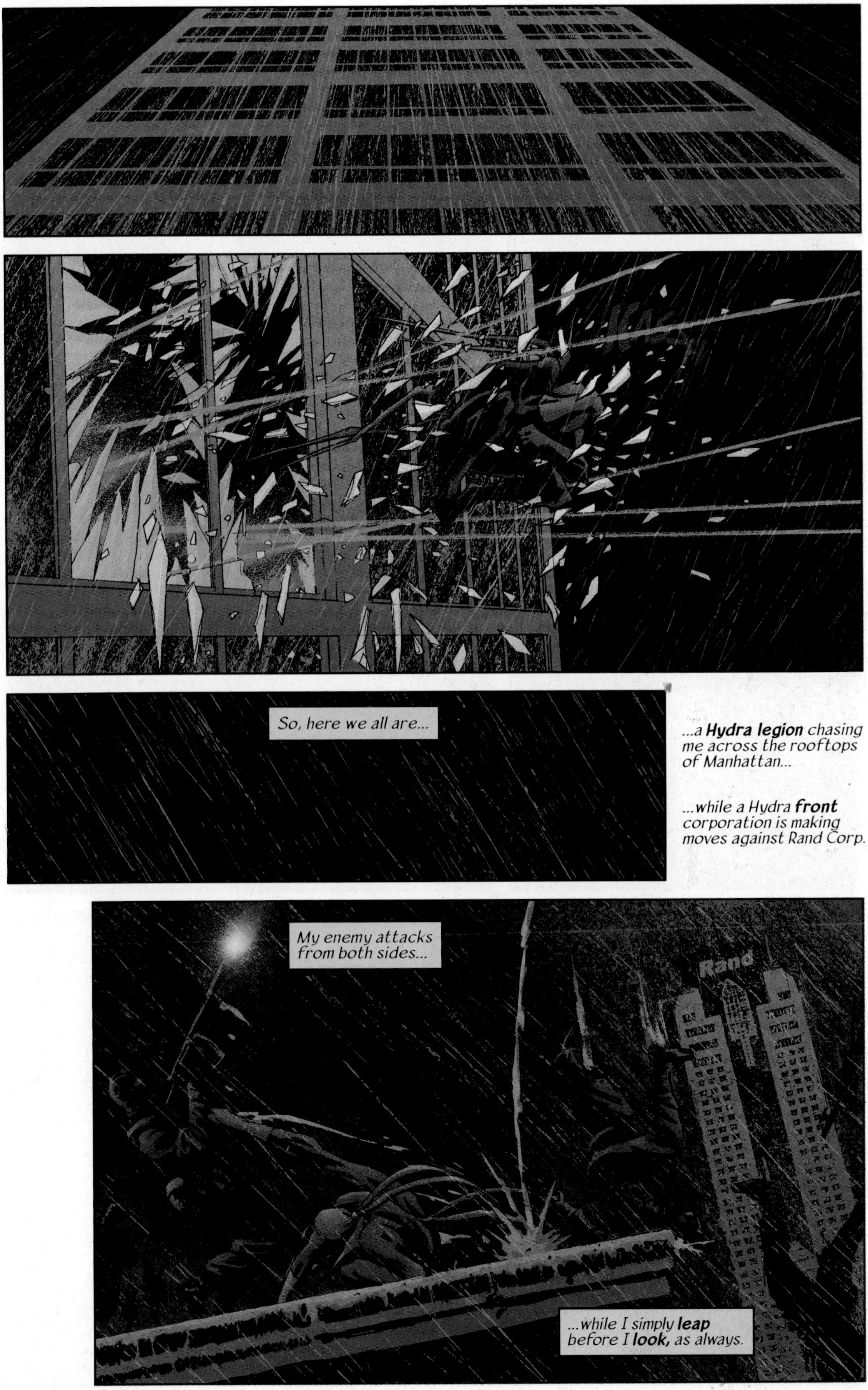
So, here we all are...
...a **Hydra legion** chasing me across the rooftops of Manhattan...
...while a Hydra **front** corporation is making moves against Rand Corp.
My enemy attacks from both sides...
Rand
...while I simply **leap** before I **look,** as always.

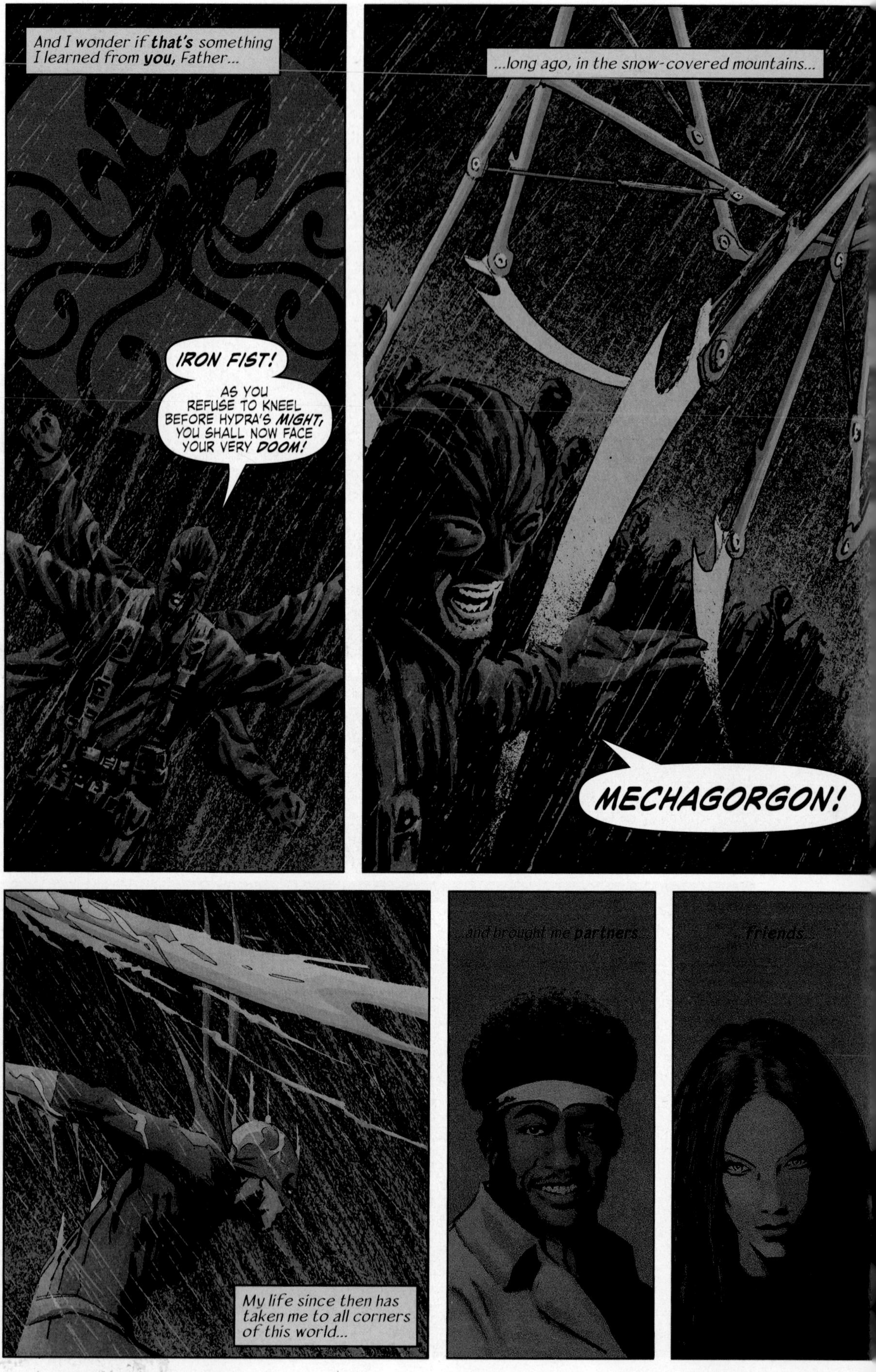

And I wonder if **that's** something I learned from **you,** Father...
IRON FIST!
AS YOU REFUSE TO KNEEL BEFORE HYDRA'S ***MIGHT,*** YOU SHALL NOW FACE YOUR VERY ***DOOM!***
...long ago, in the snow-covered mountains...
MECHAGORGON!
My life since then has taken me to all corners of this world...
...and brought me **partners**...
...**friends**...

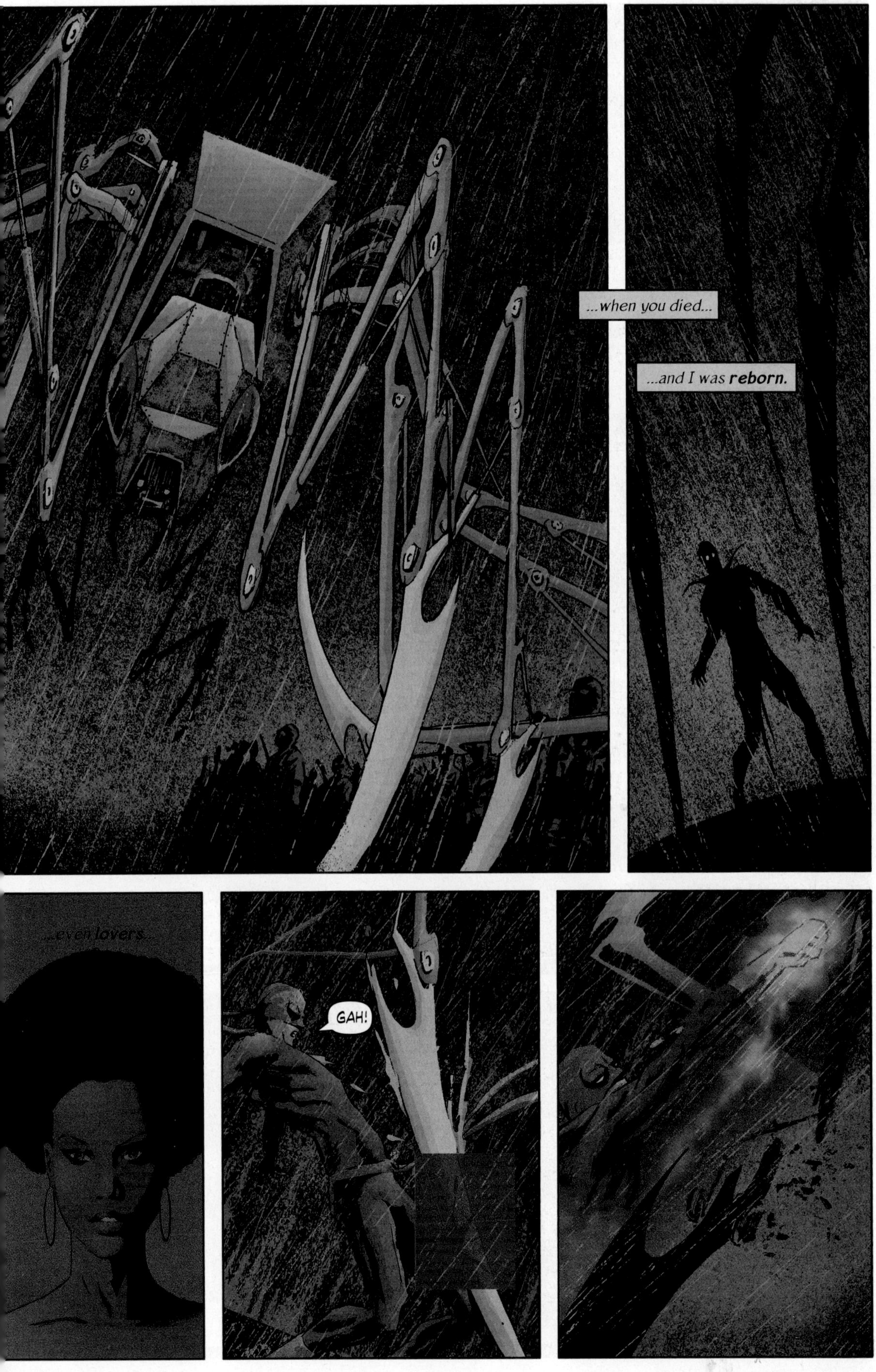
...when you died...
...and I was **reborn.**
...even lovers...
GAH!

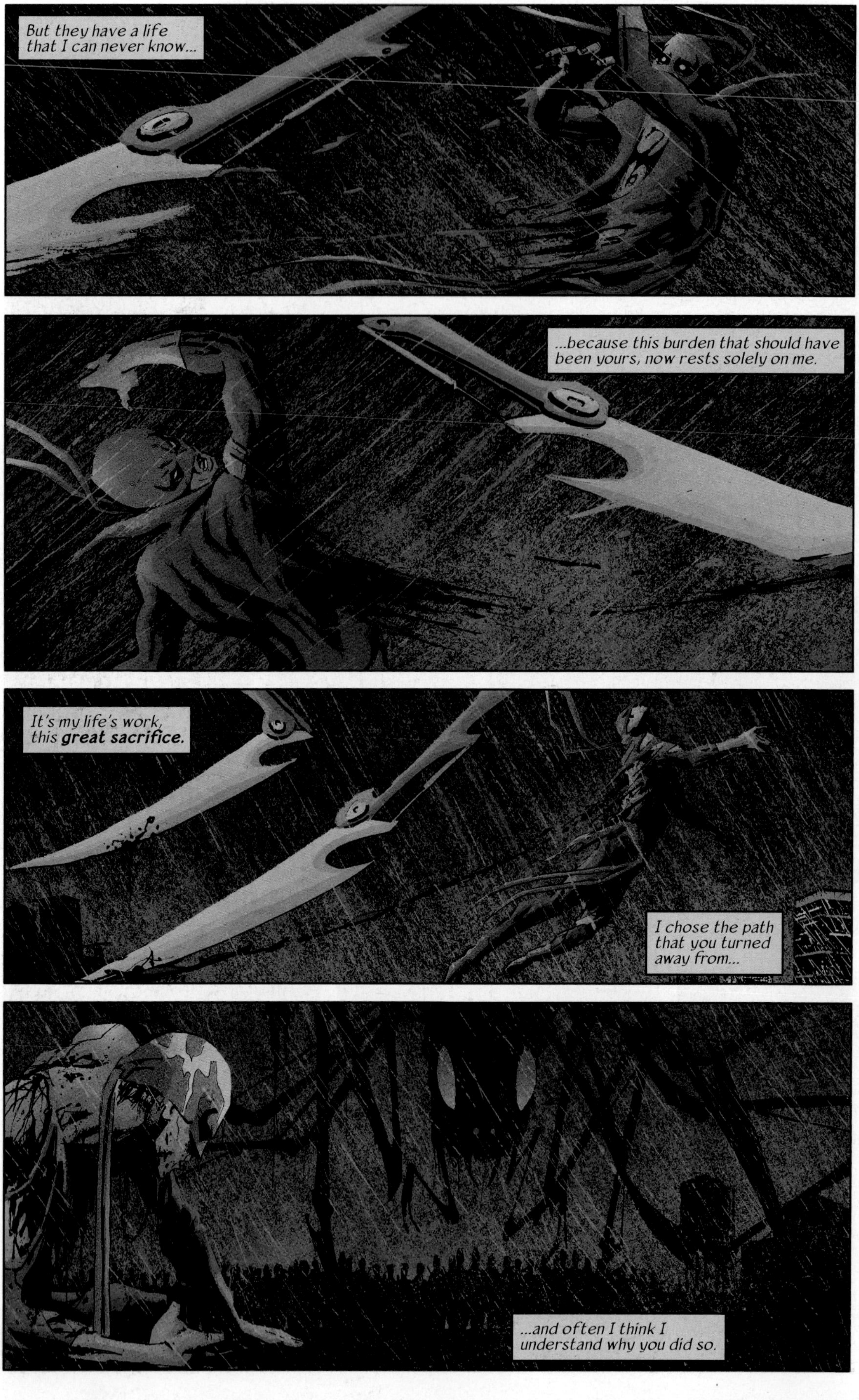
But they have a life that I can never know...
...because this burden that should have been yours, now rests solely on me.
It's my life's work, this **great sacrifice.**
I chose the path that you turned away from...
...and often I think I understand why you did so.

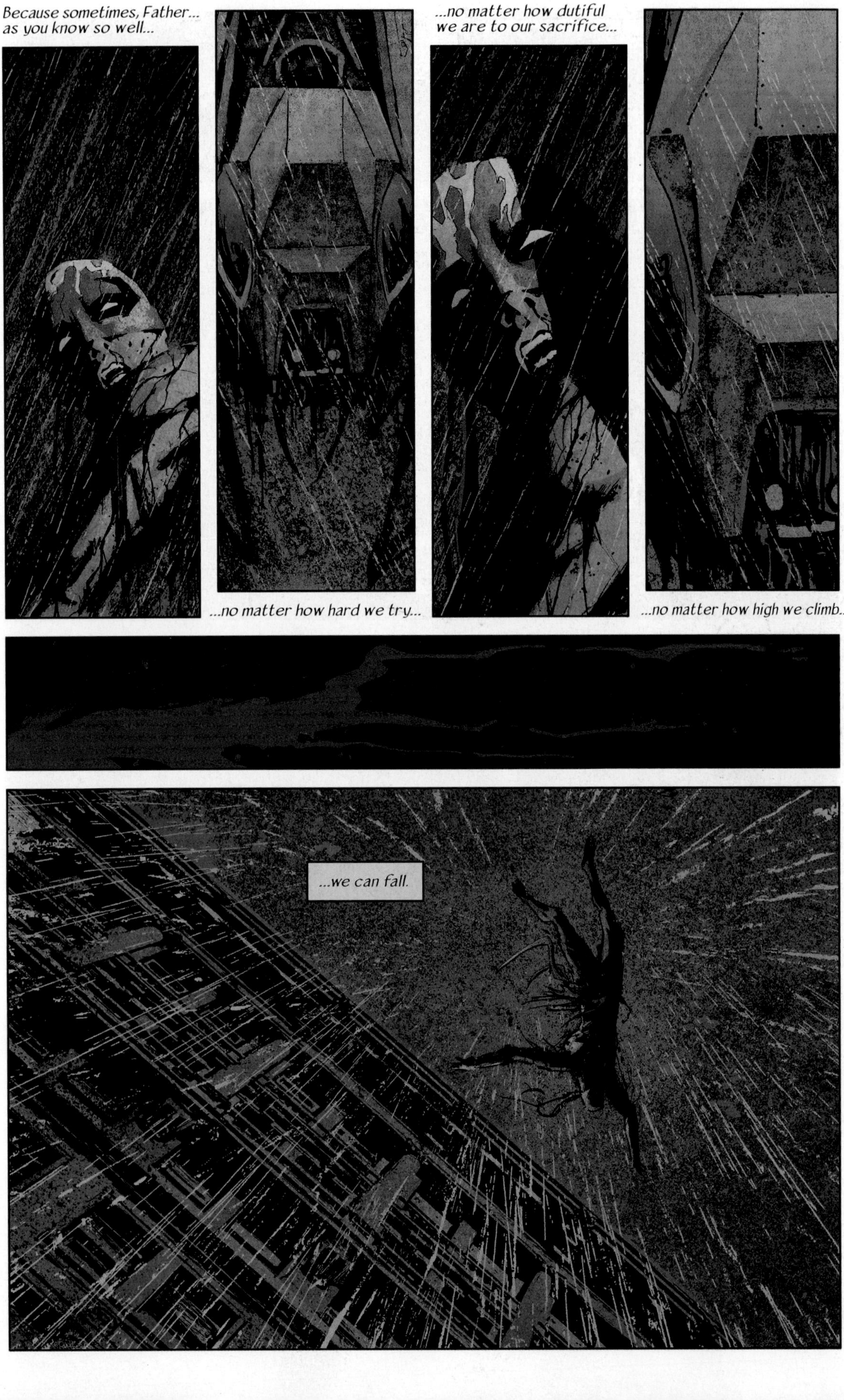
Because sometimes, Father... as you know so well...
...no matter how hard we try...
...no matter how dutiful we are to our sacrifice...
...no matter how high we climb...
...we can fall.

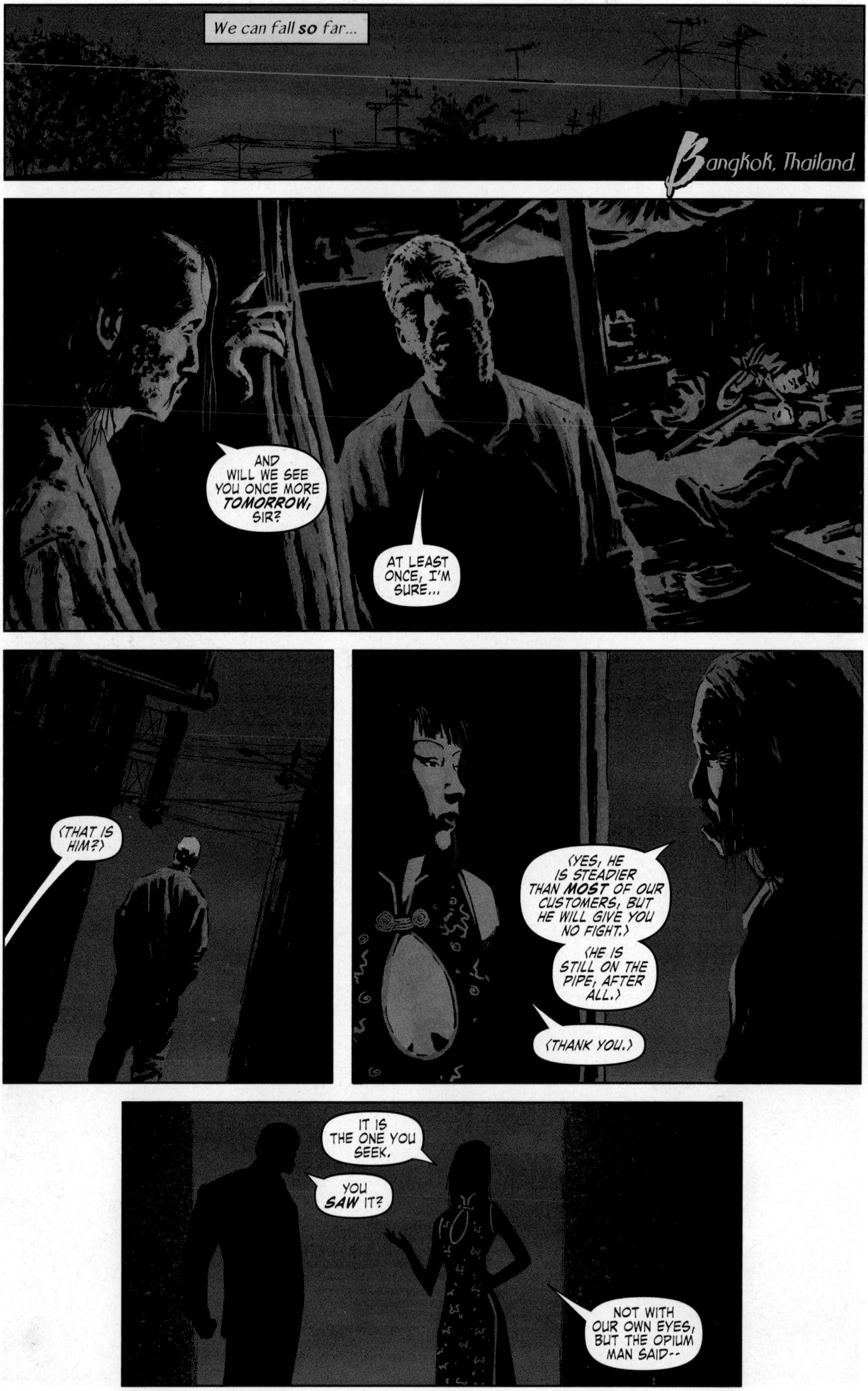
We can fall **so** far...
Bangkok, Thailand.
AND WILL WE SEE YOU ONCE MORE ***TOMORROW,*** SIR?
AT LEAST ONCE, I'M SURE...
‹THAT IS HIM?›
‹YES, HE IS STEADIER THAN **MOST** OF OUR CUSTOMERS, BUT HE WILL GIVE YOU NO FIGHT.›
‹HE IS STILL ON THE PIPE, AFTER ALL.›
‹THANK YOU.›
IT IS THE ONE YOU SEEK.
YOU ***SAW*** IT?
NOT WITH OUR OWN EYES, BUT THE OPIUM MAN SAID--

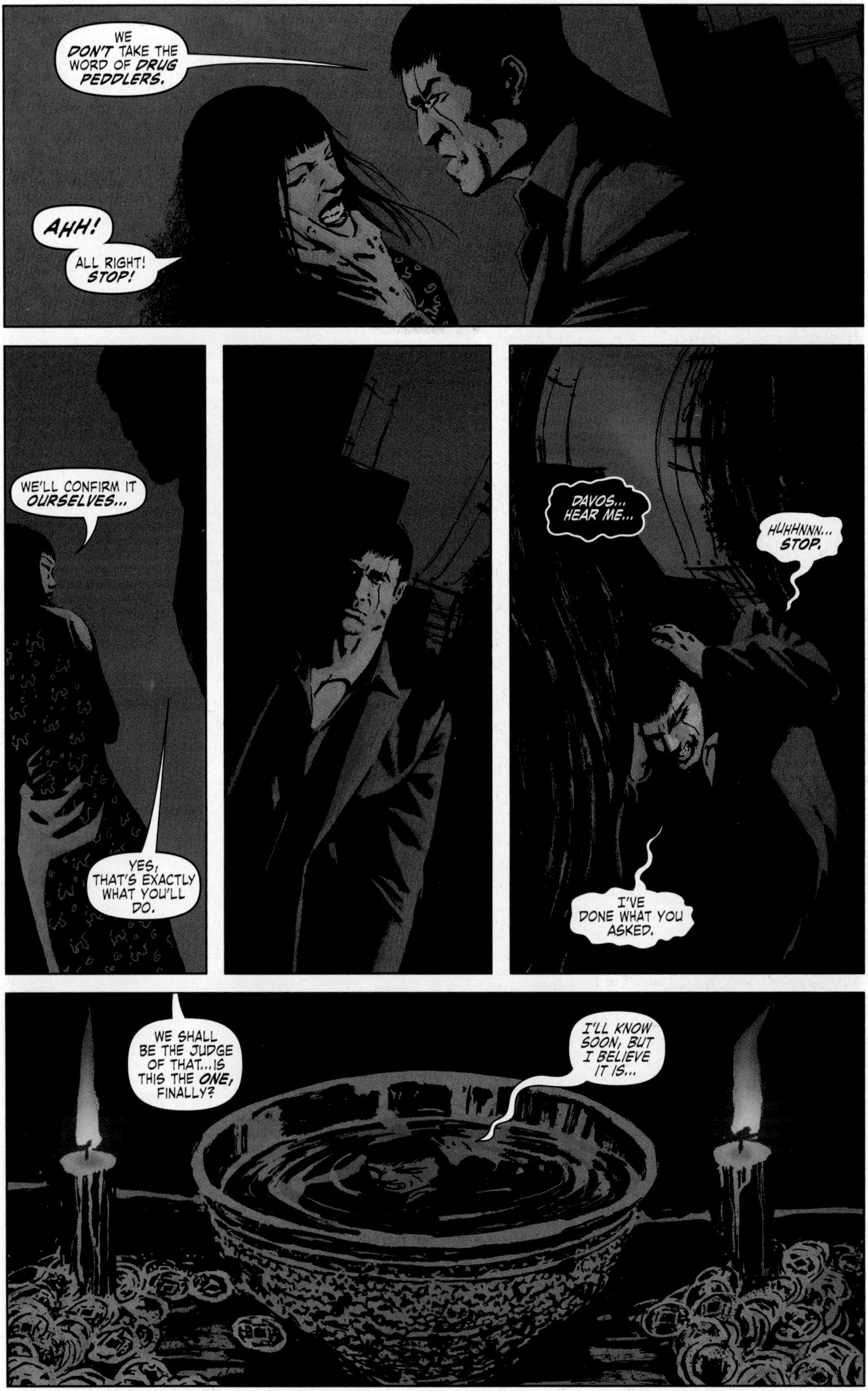
WE DON'T TAKE THE WORD OF DRUG PEDDLERS.
AHH!
ALL RIGHT! STOP!
WE'LL CONFIRM IT OURSELVES...
YES, THAT'S EXACTLY WHAT YOU'LL DO.
DAVOS... HEAR ME...
HUHHNNN... STOP.
I'VE DONE WHAT YOU ASKED.
WE SHALL BE THE JUDGE OF THAT...IS THIS THE ONE, FINALLY?
I'LL KNOW SOON, BUT I BELIEVE IT IS...

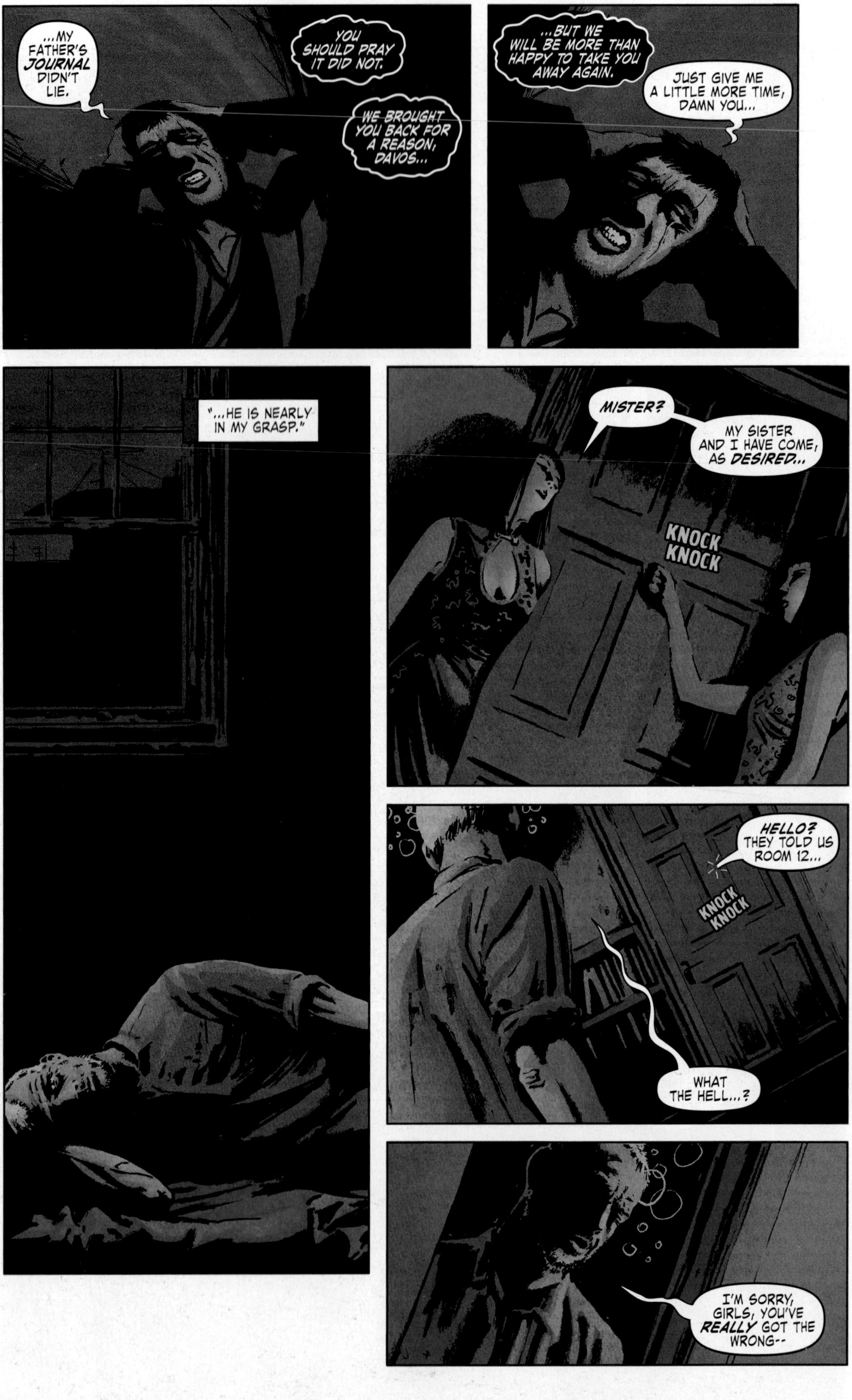
...MY FATHER'S JOURNAL DIDN'T LIE.
YOU SHOULD PRAY IT DID NOT.
WE BROUGHT YOU BACK FOR A REASON, DAVOS...
...BUT WE WILL BE MORE THAN HAPPY TO TAKE YOU AWAY AGAIN.
JUST GIVE ME A LITTLE MORE TIME, DAMN YOU...
"...HE IS NEARLY IN MY GRASP."
MISTER?
MY SISTER AND I HAVE COME, AS DESIRED...
KNOCK KNOCK
HELLO? THEY TOLD US ROOM 12...
KNOCK KNOCK
WHAT THE HELL...?
I'M SORRY, GIRLS, YOU'VE REALLY GOT THE WRONG--

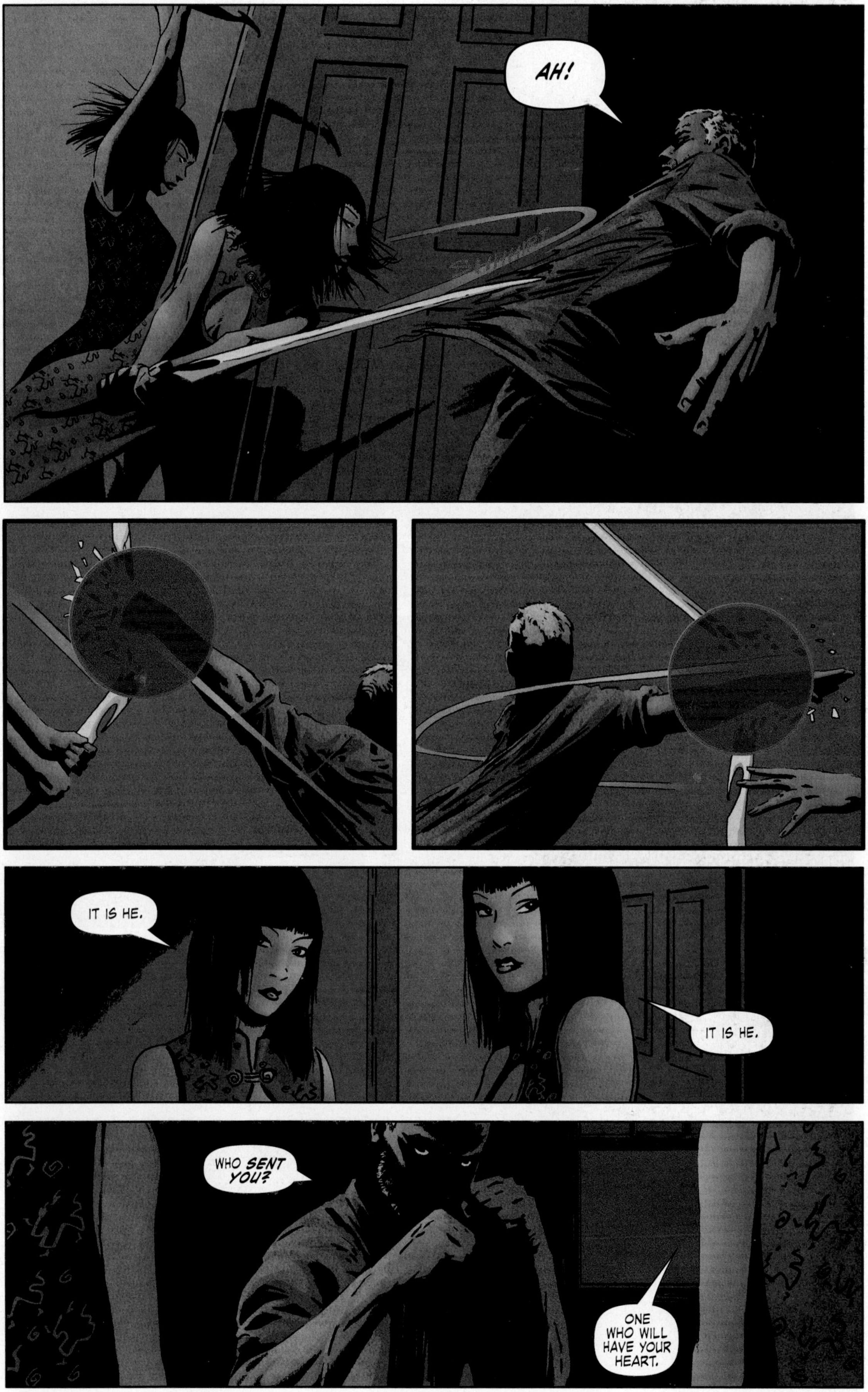
AH!
IT IS HE.
IT IS HE.
WHO *SENT* YOU?
ONE WHO WILL HAVE YOUR HEART.

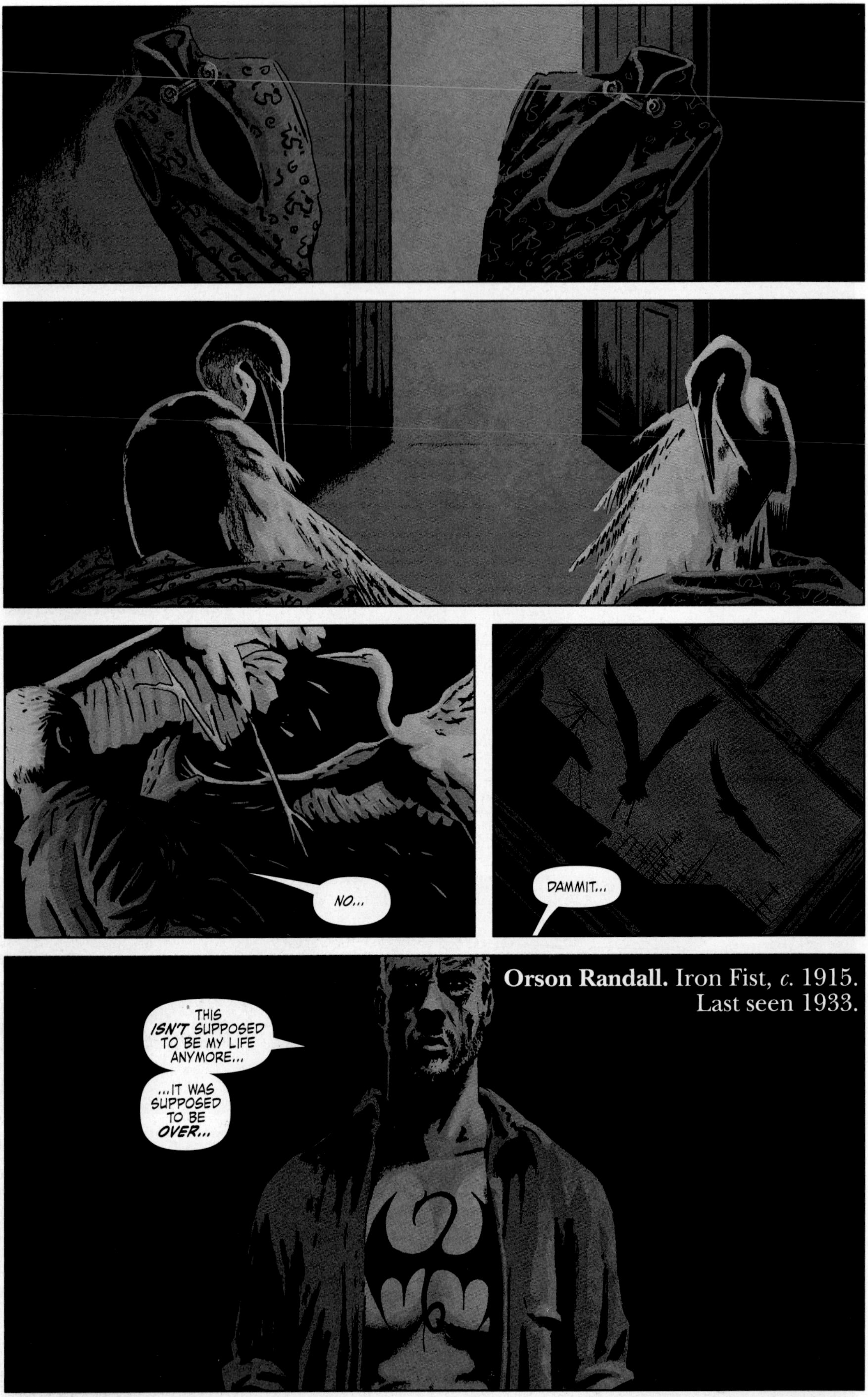
NO...
DAMMIT...
Orson Randall. Iron Fist, c. 1915.
Last seen 1933.
THIS ISN'T SUPPOSED TO BE MY LIFE ANYMORE...
...IT WAS SUPPOSED TO BE OVER...

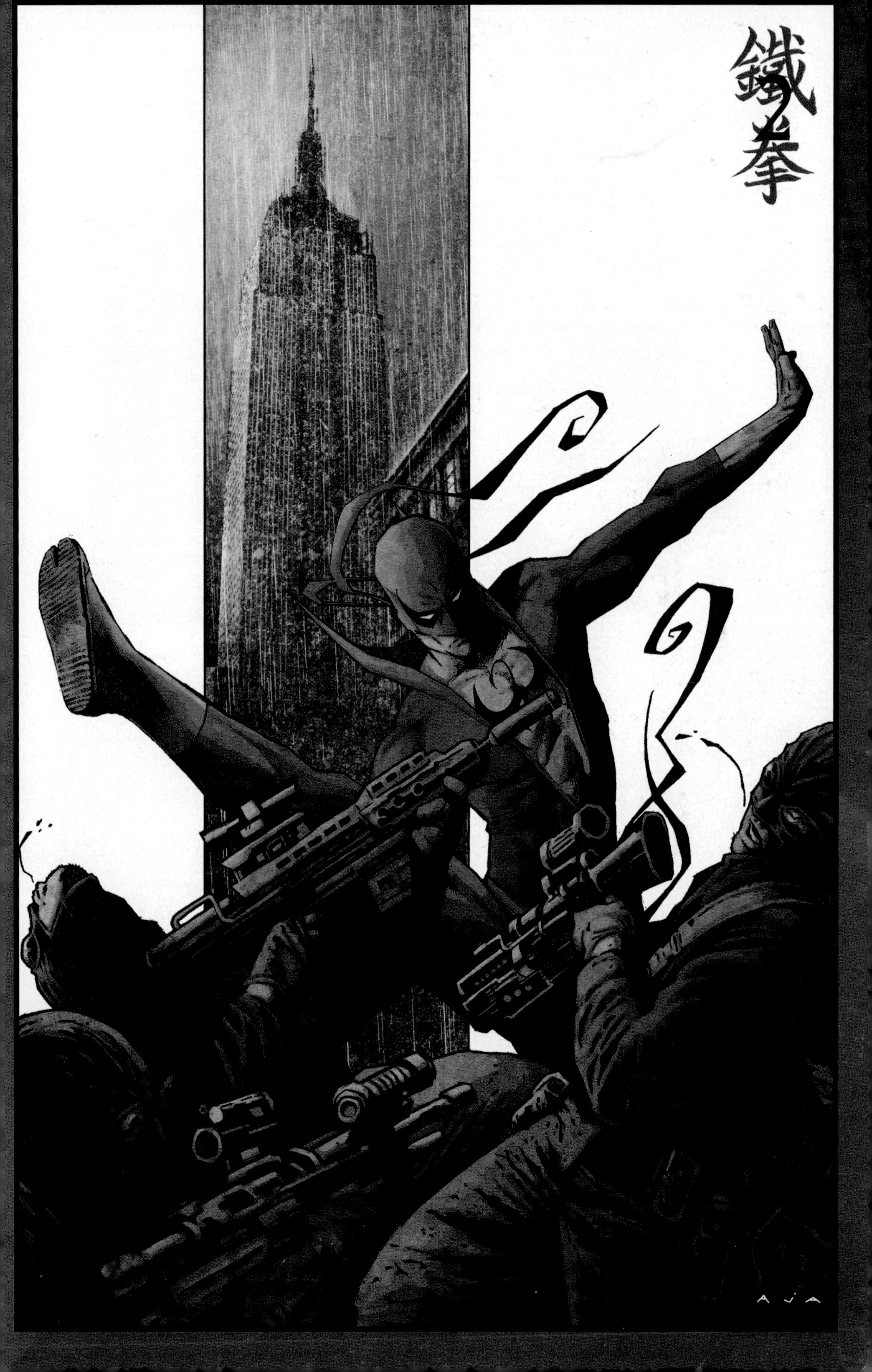
鐵拳
AJA

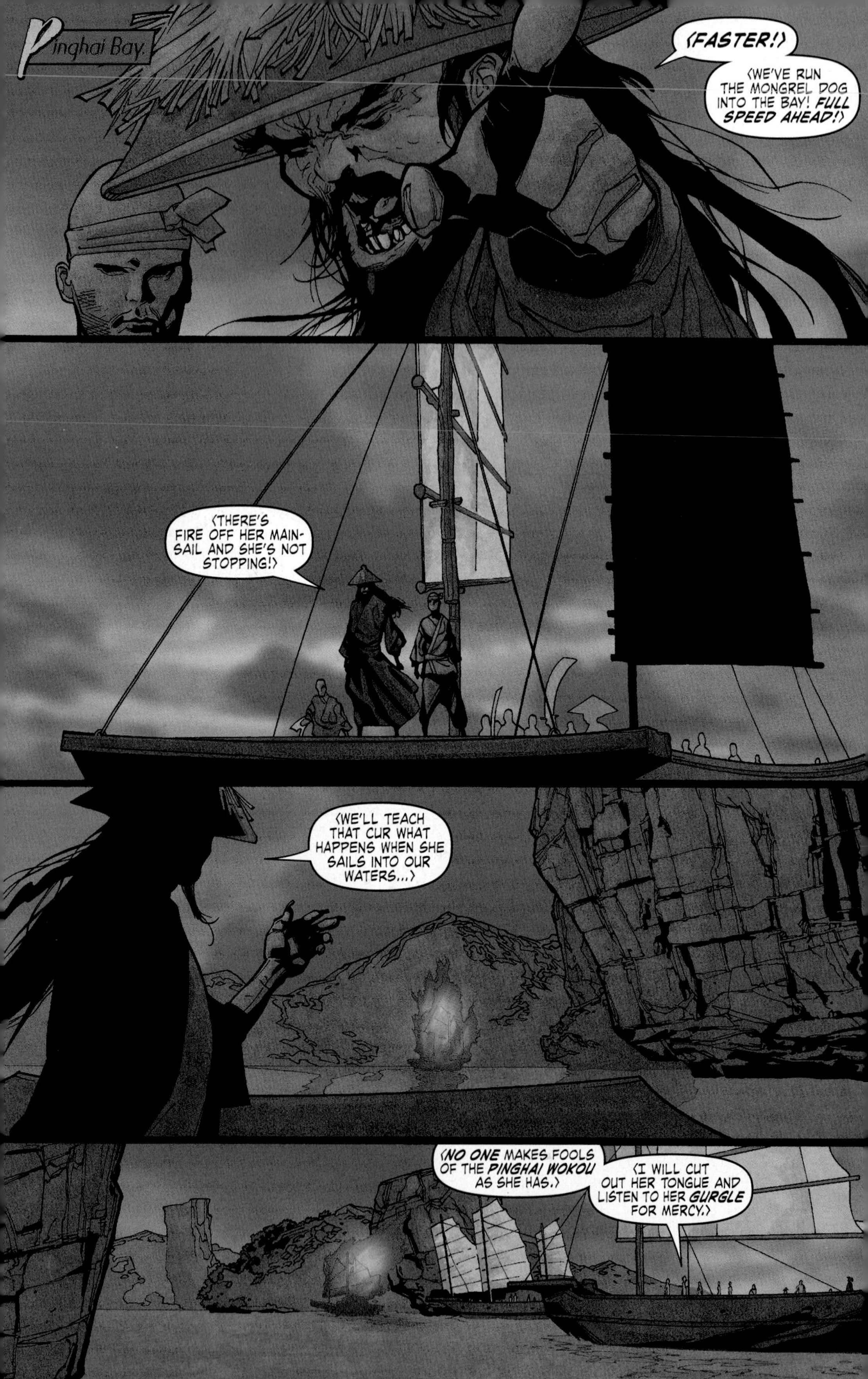
Pinghai Bay.
‹FASTER!›
‹WE'VE RUN THE MONGREL DOG INTO THE BAY! FULL SPEED AHEAD!›
‹THERE'S FIRE OFF HER MAIN-SAIL AND SHE'S NOT STOPPING!›
‹WE'LL TEACH THAT CUR WHAT HAPPENS WHEN SHE SAILS INTO OUR WATERS...›
‹NO ONE MAKES FOOLS OF THE PINGHAI WOKOU AS SHE HAS.›
‹I WILL CUT OUT HER TONGUE AND LISTEN TO HER GURGLE FOR MERCY.›

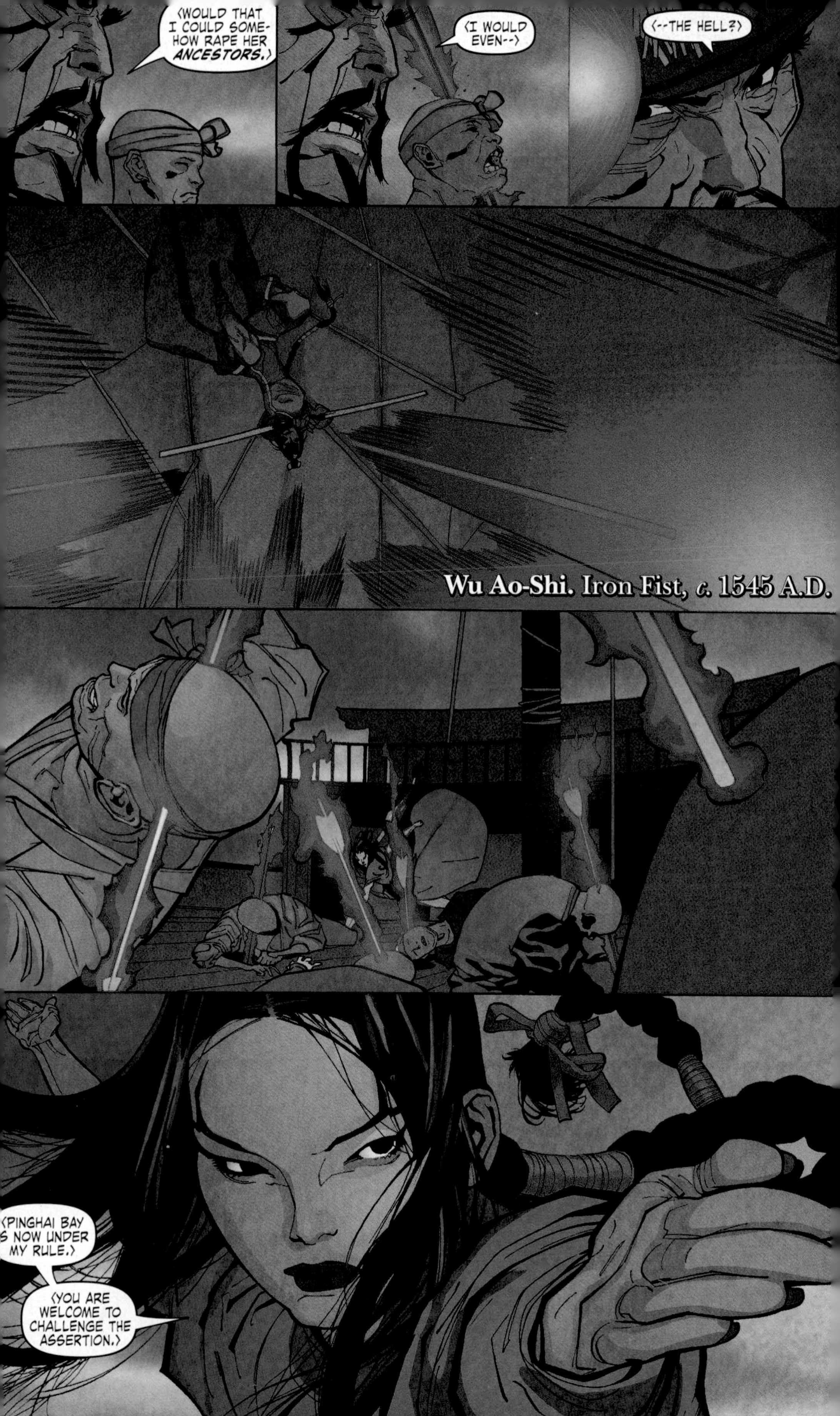
‹WOULD THAT I COULD SOMEHOW RAPE HER ANCESTORS.›
‹I WOULD EVEN--›
‹--THE HELL?›
Wu Ao-Shi. Iron Fist, c. 1545 A.D.
‹PINGHAI BAY IS NOW UNDER MY RULE.›
‹YOU ARE WELCOME TO CHALLENGE THE ASSERTION.›

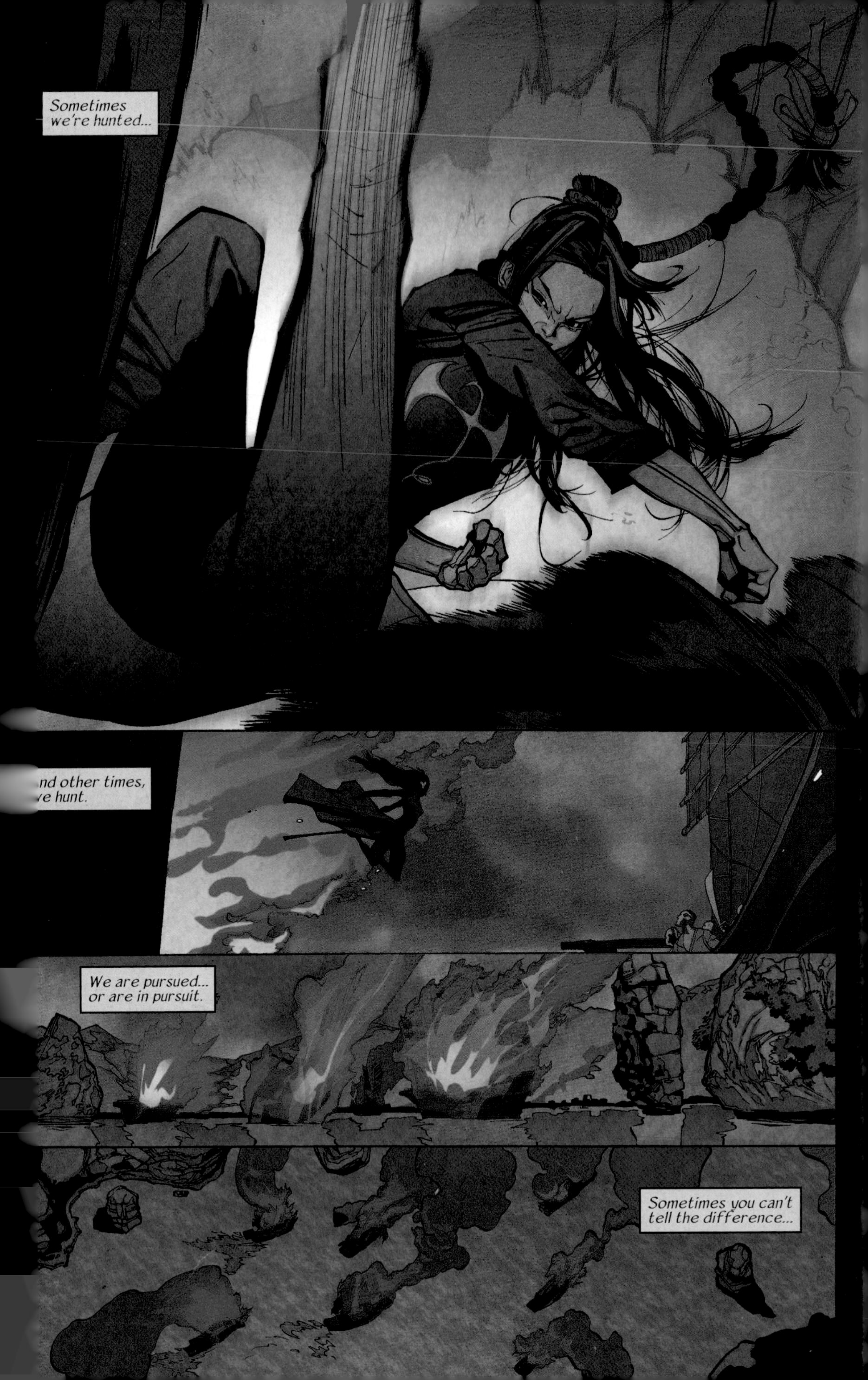
Sometimes we're hunted...
nd other times, ve hunt.
We are pursued... or are in pursuit.
Sometimes you can't tell the difference...

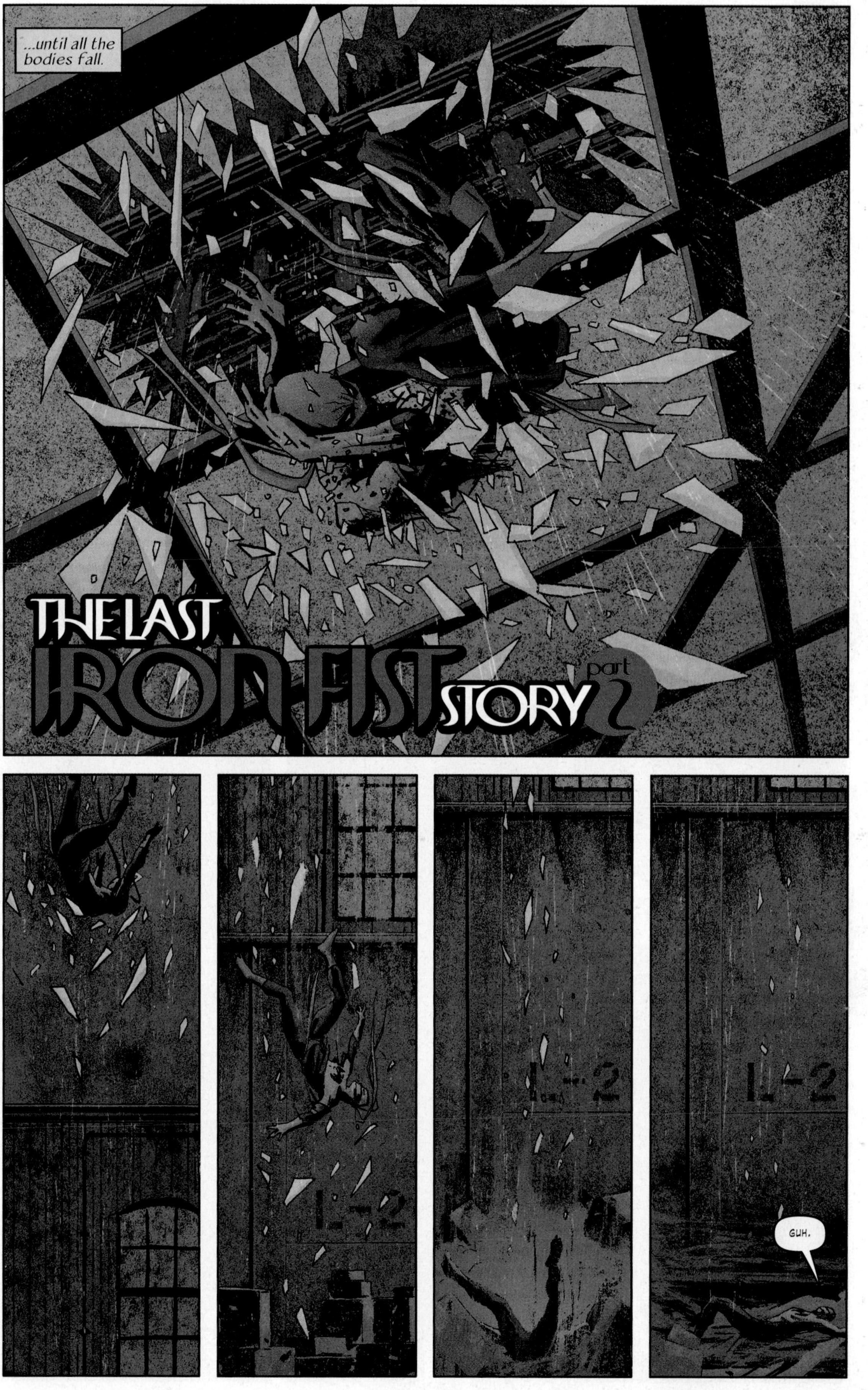
...until all the bodies fall.
THE LAST IRON FIST STORY part 2
GUH.

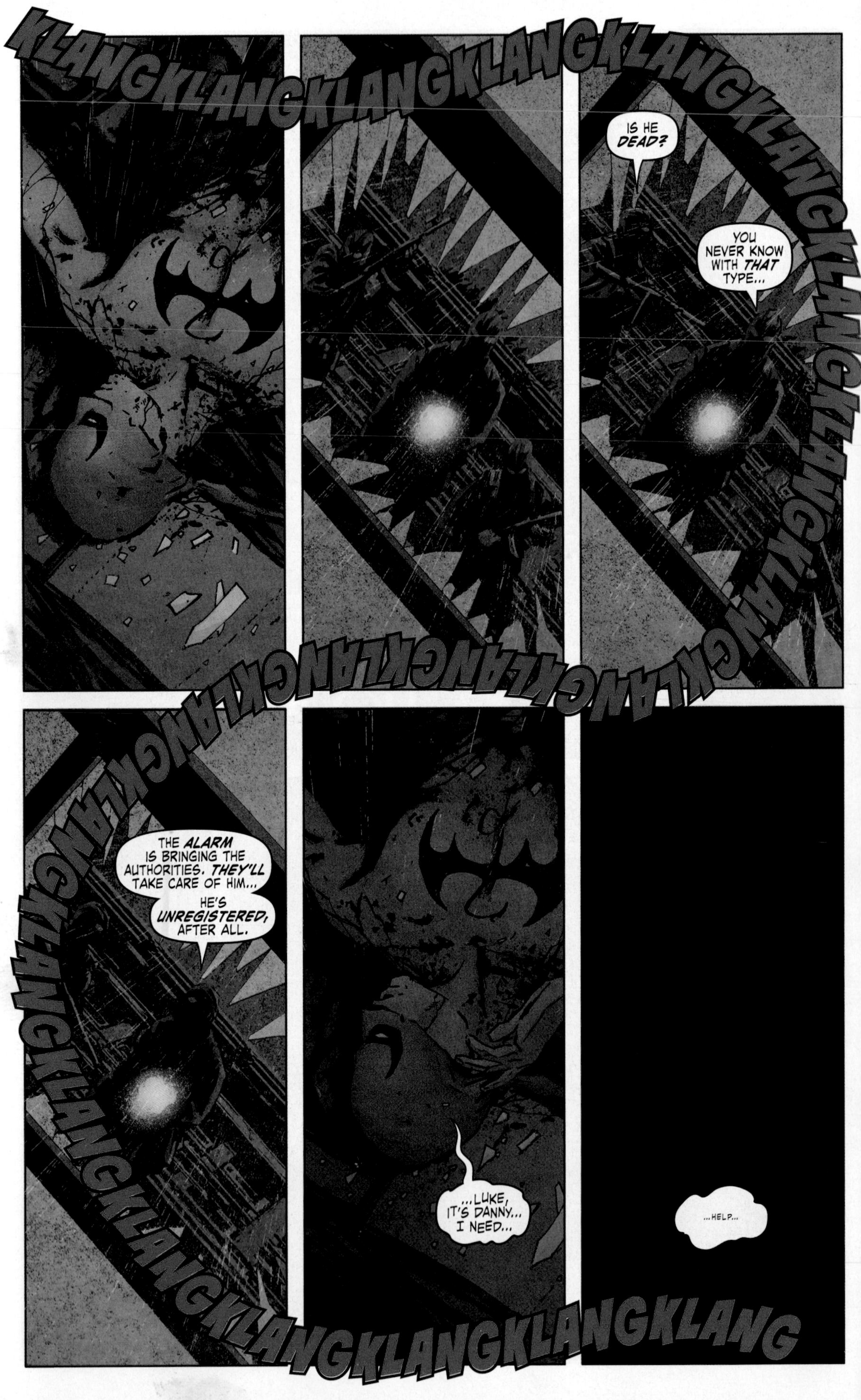
KLANGKLANGKLANGKLANGKLANGKLANG
IS HE DEAD?
YOU NEVER KNOW WITH THAT TYPE...
THE ALARM IS BRINGING THE AUTHORITIES. THEY'LL TAKE CARE OF HIM...
HE'S UNREGISTERED, AFTER ALL.
...LUKE, IT'S DANNY... I NEED...
...HELP...
KLANGKLANGKLANGKLANG

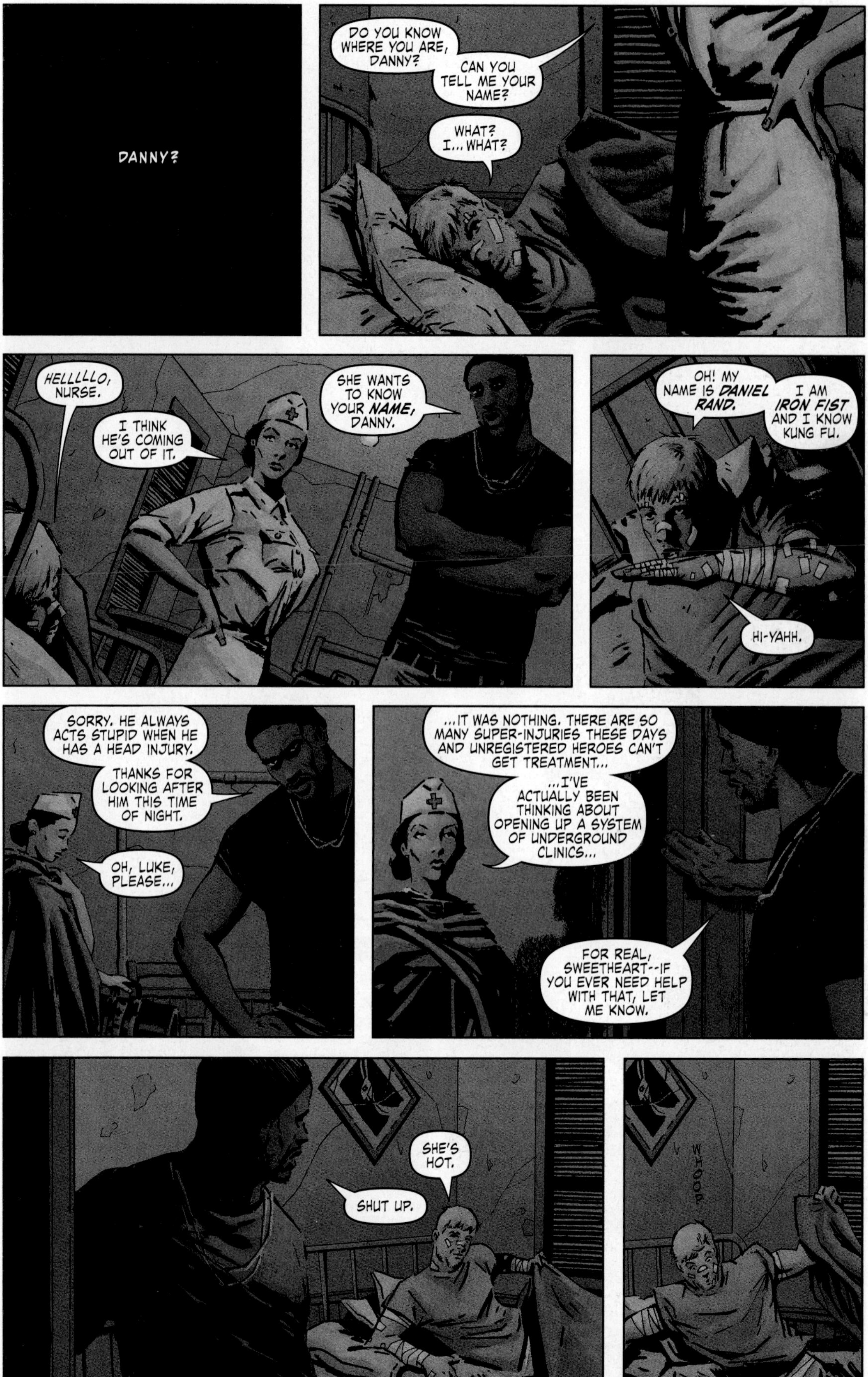
DANNY?
DO YOU KNOW WHERE YOU ARE, DANNY?
CAN YOU TELL ME YOUR NAME?
WHAT? I... WHAT?
HELLLLLO, NURSE.
I THINK HE'S COMING OUT OF IT.
SHE WANTS TO KNOW YOUR NAME, DANNY.
OH! MY NAME IS DANIEL RAND.
I AM IRON FIST AND I KNOW KUNG FU.
HI-YAHH.
SORRY. HE ALWAYS ACTS STUPID WHEN HE HAS A HEAD INJURY.
THANKS FOR LOOKING AFTER HIM THIS TIME OF NIGHT.
OH, LUKE, PLEASE...
...IT WAS NOTHING. THERE ARE SO MANY SUPER-INJURIES THESE DAYS AND UNREGISTERED HEROES CAN'T GET TREATMENT...
...I'VE ACTUALLY BEEN THINKING ABOUT OPENING UP A SYSTEM OF UNDERGROUND CLINICS...
FOR REAL, SWEETHEART--IF YOU EVER NEED HELP WITH THAT, LET ME KNOW.
SHE'S HOT.
SHUT UP.
WHOOP

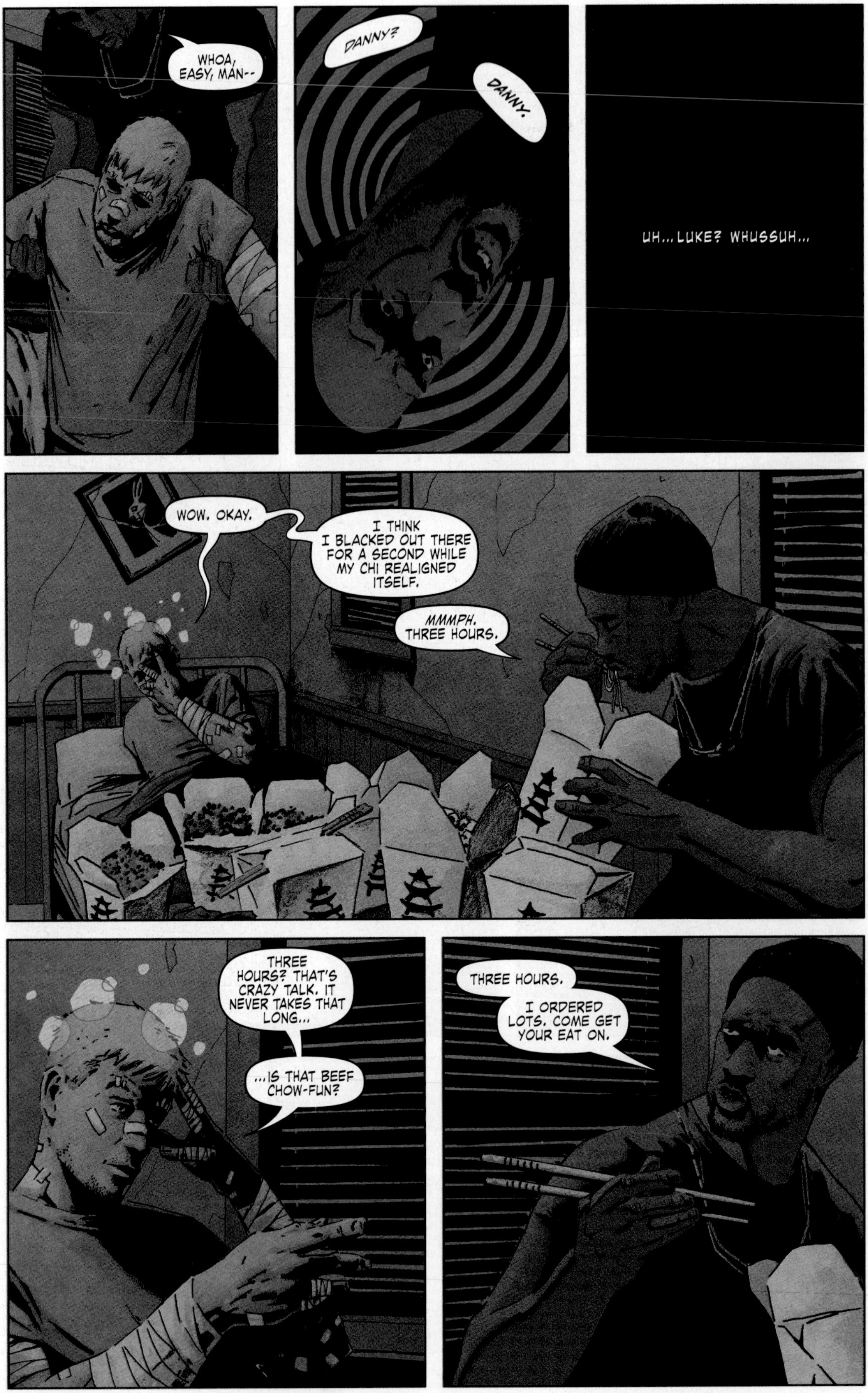
WHOA, EASY, MAN--
DANNY?
DANNY.
UH... LUKE? WHUSSUH...
WOW. OKAY.
I THINK I BLACKED OUT THERE FOR A SECOND WHILE MY CHI REALIGNED ITSELF.
MMMPH. THREE HOURS.
THREE HOURS? THAT'S CRAZY TALK. IT NEVER TAKES THAT LONG...
...IS THAT BEEF CHOW-FUN?
THREE HOURS.
I ORDERED LOTS. COME GET YOUR EAT ON.

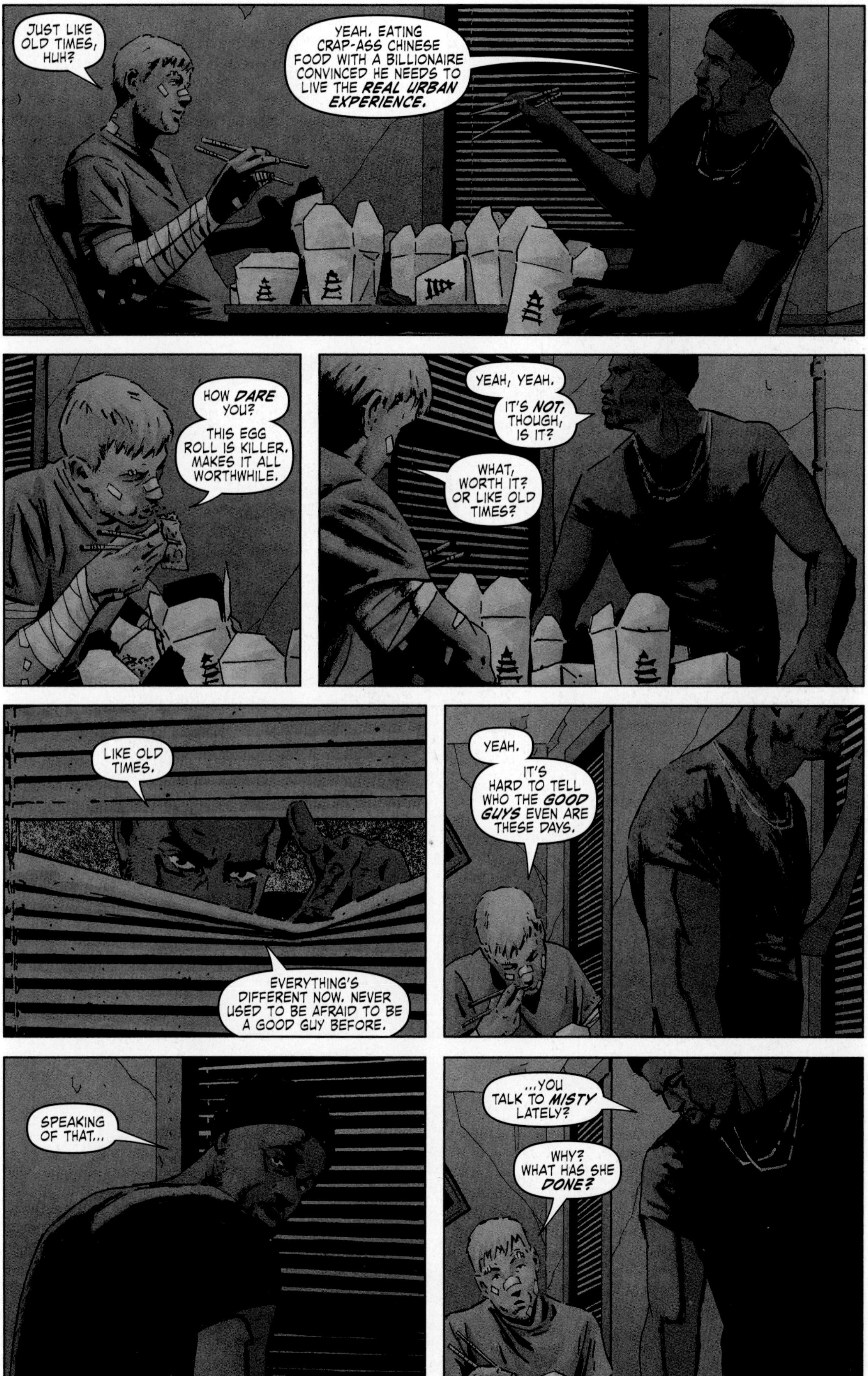
JUST LIKE OLD TIMES, HUH?
YEAH. EATING CRAP-ASS CHINESE FOOD WITH A BILLIONAIRE CONVINCED HE NEEDS TO LIVE THE REAL URBAN EXPERIENCE.
HOW DARE YOU?
THIS EGG ROLL IS KILLER. MAKES IT ALL WORTHWHILE.
YEAH, YEAH.
IT'S NOT, THOUGH, IS IT?
WHAT, WORTH IT? OR LIKE OLD TIMES?
LIKE OLD TIMES.
EVERYTHING'S DIFFERENT NOW. NEVER USED TO BE AFRAID TO BE A GOOD GUY BEFORE.
YEAH.
IT'S HARD TO TELL WHO THE GOOD GUYS EVEN ARE THESE DAYS.
SPEAKING OF THAT...
...YOU TALK TO MISTY LATELY?
WHY? WHAT HAS SHE DONE?

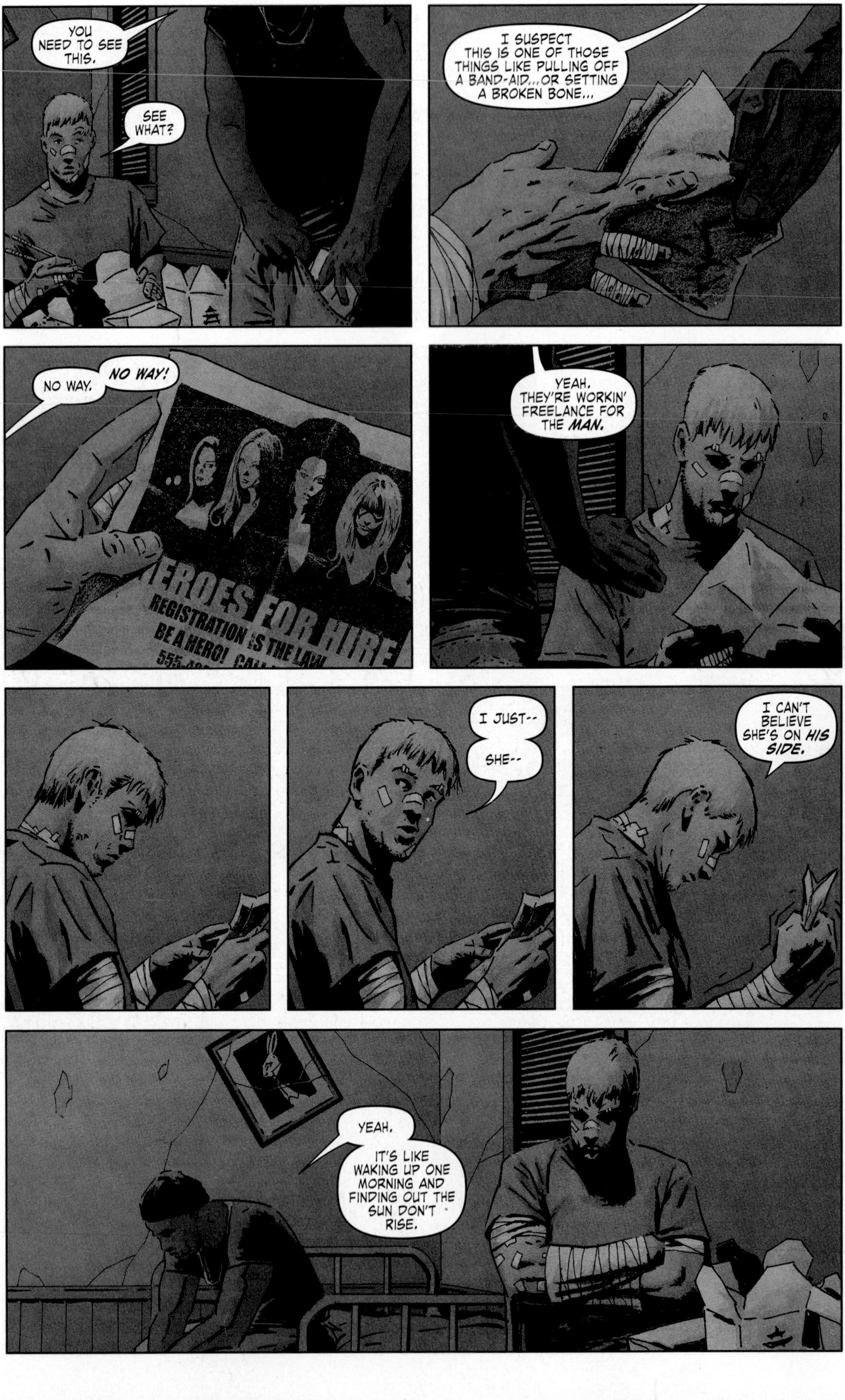
YOU NEED TO SEE THIS.
SEE WHAT?
I SUSPECT THIS IS ONE OF THOSE THINGS LIKE PULLING OFF A BAND-AID...OR SETTING A BROKEN BONE...
NO WAY.
NO WAY!
REGISTRATION IS THE LAW
BE A HERO!
YEAH. THEY'RE WORKIN' FREELANCE FOR THE *MAN.*
I JUST--
SHE--
I CAN'T BELIEVE SHE'S ON *HIS SIDE.*
YEAH.
IT'S LIKE WAKING UP ONE MORNING AND FINDING OUT THE SUN DON'T RISE.

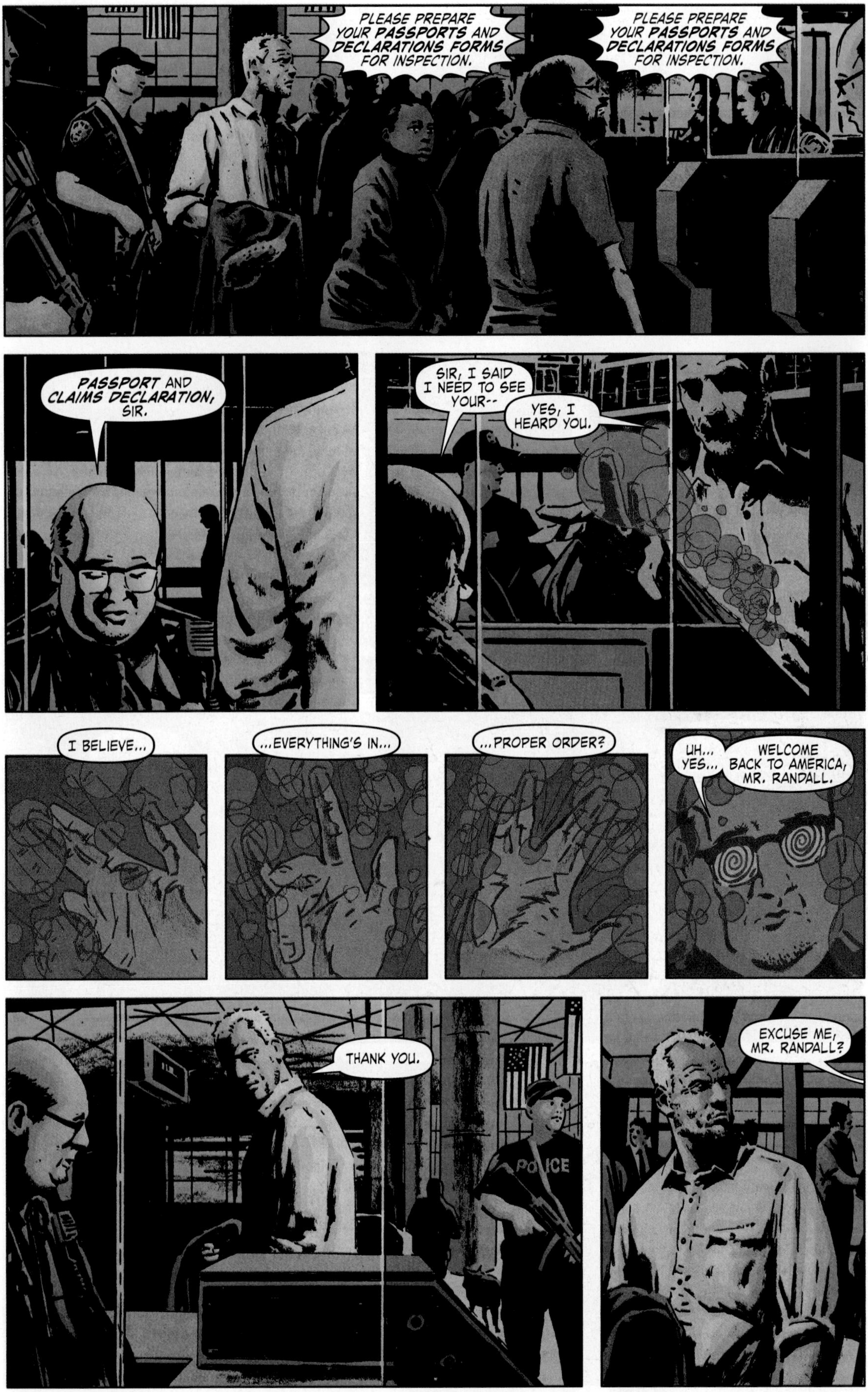
PLEASE PREPARE YOUR **PASSPORTS** AND **DECLARATIONS FORMS** FOR INSPECTION.
PLEASE PREPARE YOUR **PASSPORTS** AND **DECLARATIONS FORMS** FOR INSPECTION.
PASSPORT AND **CLAIMS DECLARATION,** SIR.
SIR, I SAID I NEED TO SEE YOUR--
YES, I HEARD YOU.
I BELIEVE...
...EVERYTHING'S IN...
...PROPER ORDER?
UH... YES...
WELCOME BACK TO AMERICA, MR. RANDALL.
THANK YOU.
EXCUSE ME, MR. RANDALL?

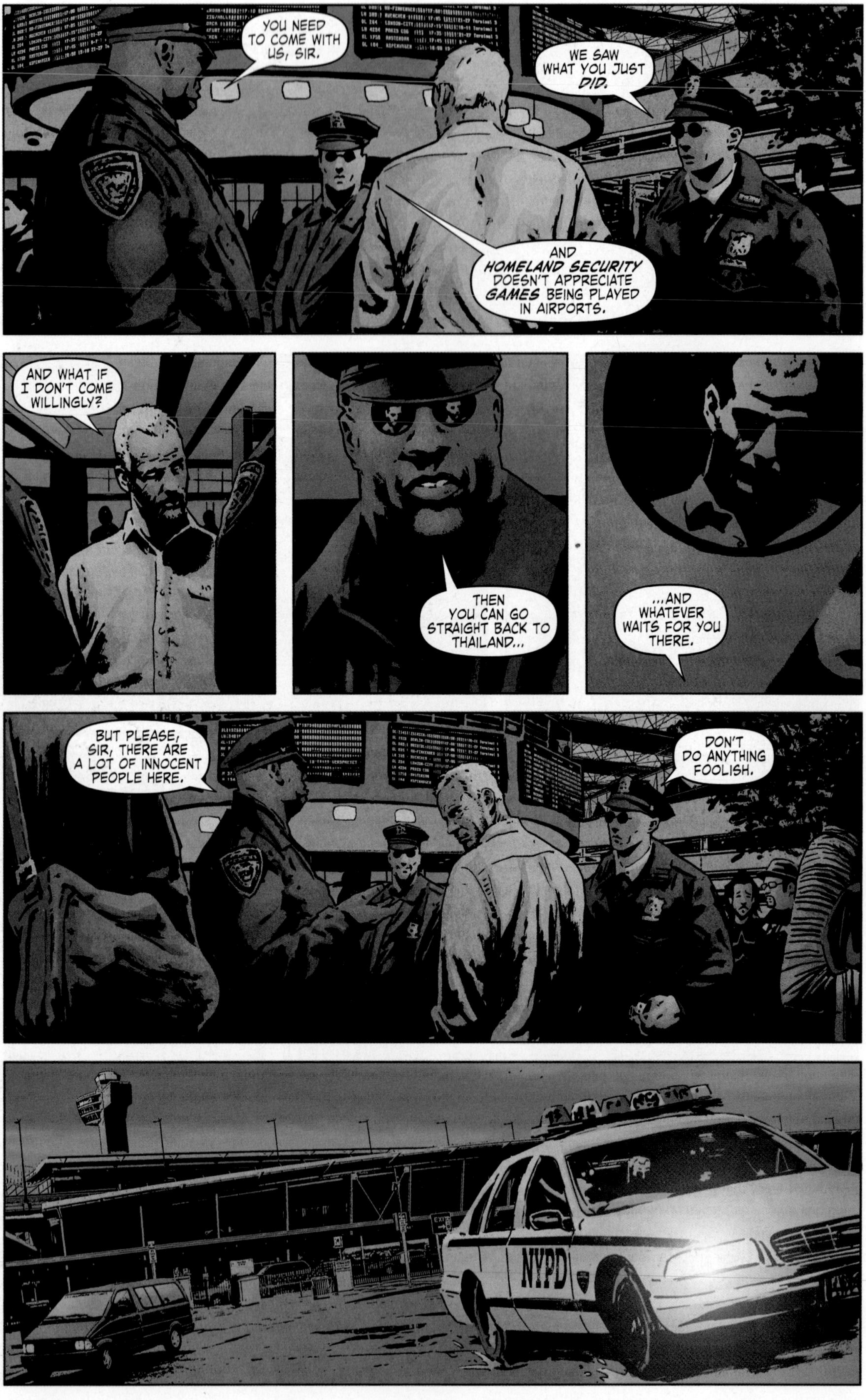
YOU NEED TO COME WITH US, SIR.
WE SAW WHAT YOU JUST DID.
AND HOMELAND SECURITY DOESN'T APPRECIATE GAMES BEING PLAYED IN AIRPORTS.
AND WHAT IF I DON'T COME WILLINGLY?
THEN YOU CAN GO STRAIGHT BACK TO THAILAND...
...AND WHATEVER WAITS FOR YOU THERE.
BUT PLEASE, SIR, THERE ARE A LOT OF INNOCENT PEOPLE HERE.
DON'T DO ANYTHING FOOLISH.
NYPD

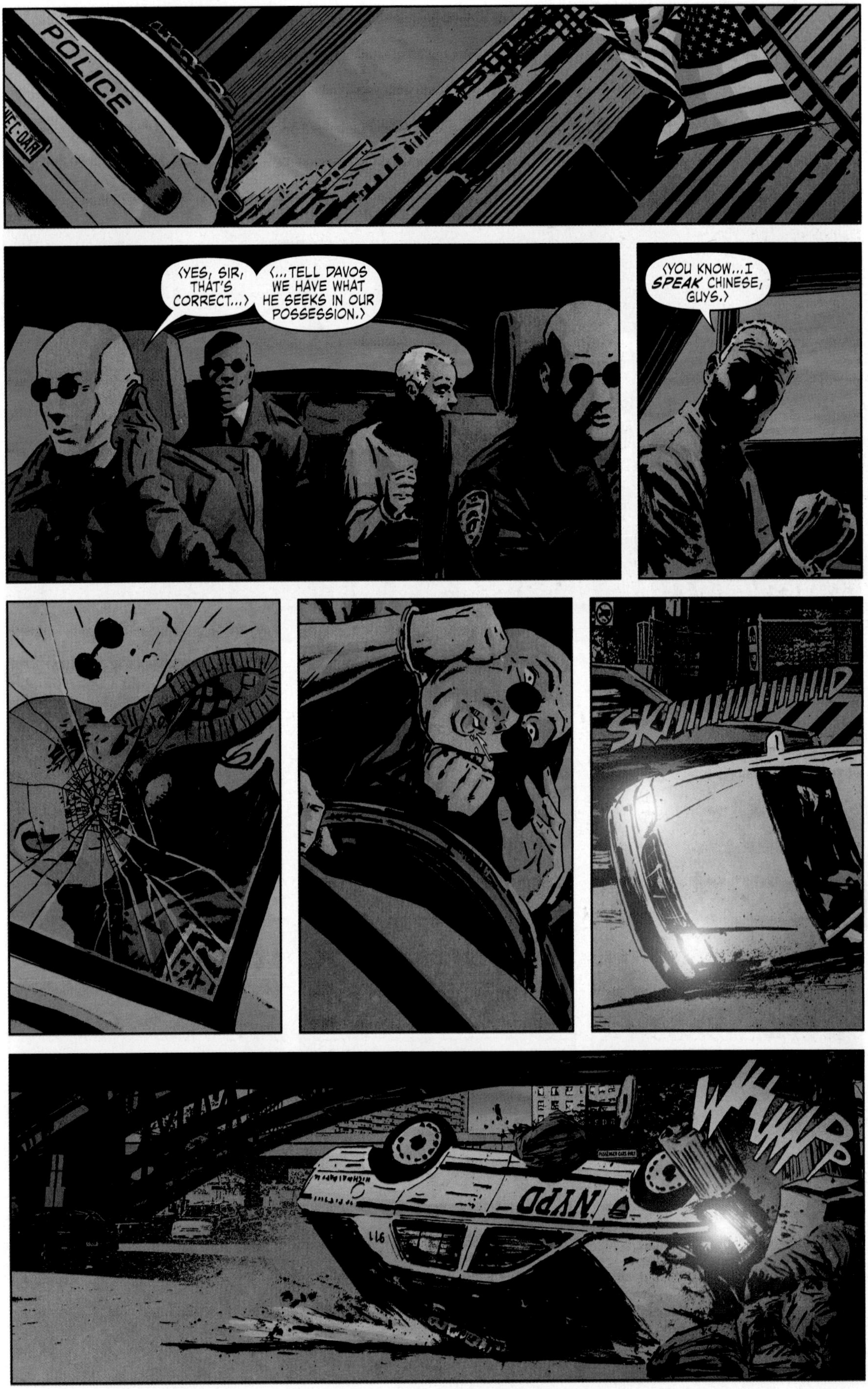
POLICE
‹YES, SIR, THAT'S CORRECT...›
‹...TELL DAVOS WE HAVE WHAT HE SEEKS IN OUR POSSESSION.›
‹YOU KNOW...I **SPEAK** CHINESE, GUYS.›
SKIIIIIIIIIIIIID
NYPD
911
WHUMP

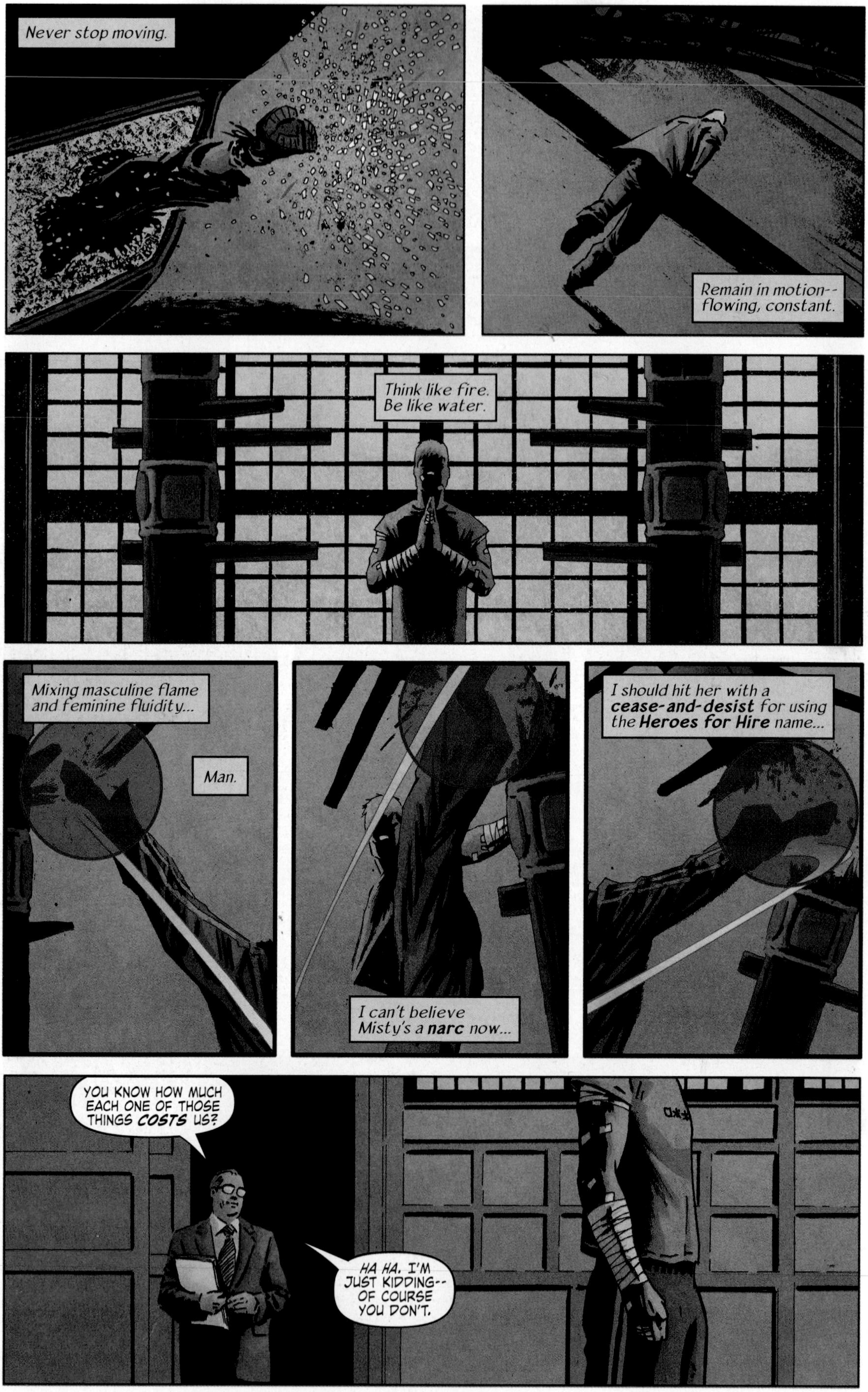
Never stop moving.
Remain in motion--flowing, constant.
Think like fire. Be like water.
Mixing masculine flame and feminine fluidity...
Man.
I can't believe Misty's a **narc** now...
I should hit her with a **cease-and-desist** for using the **Heroes for Hire** name...
YOU KNOW HOW MUCH EACH ONE OF THOSE THINGS ***COSTS*** US?
HA HA. I'M JUST KIDDING--OF COURSE YOU DON'T.

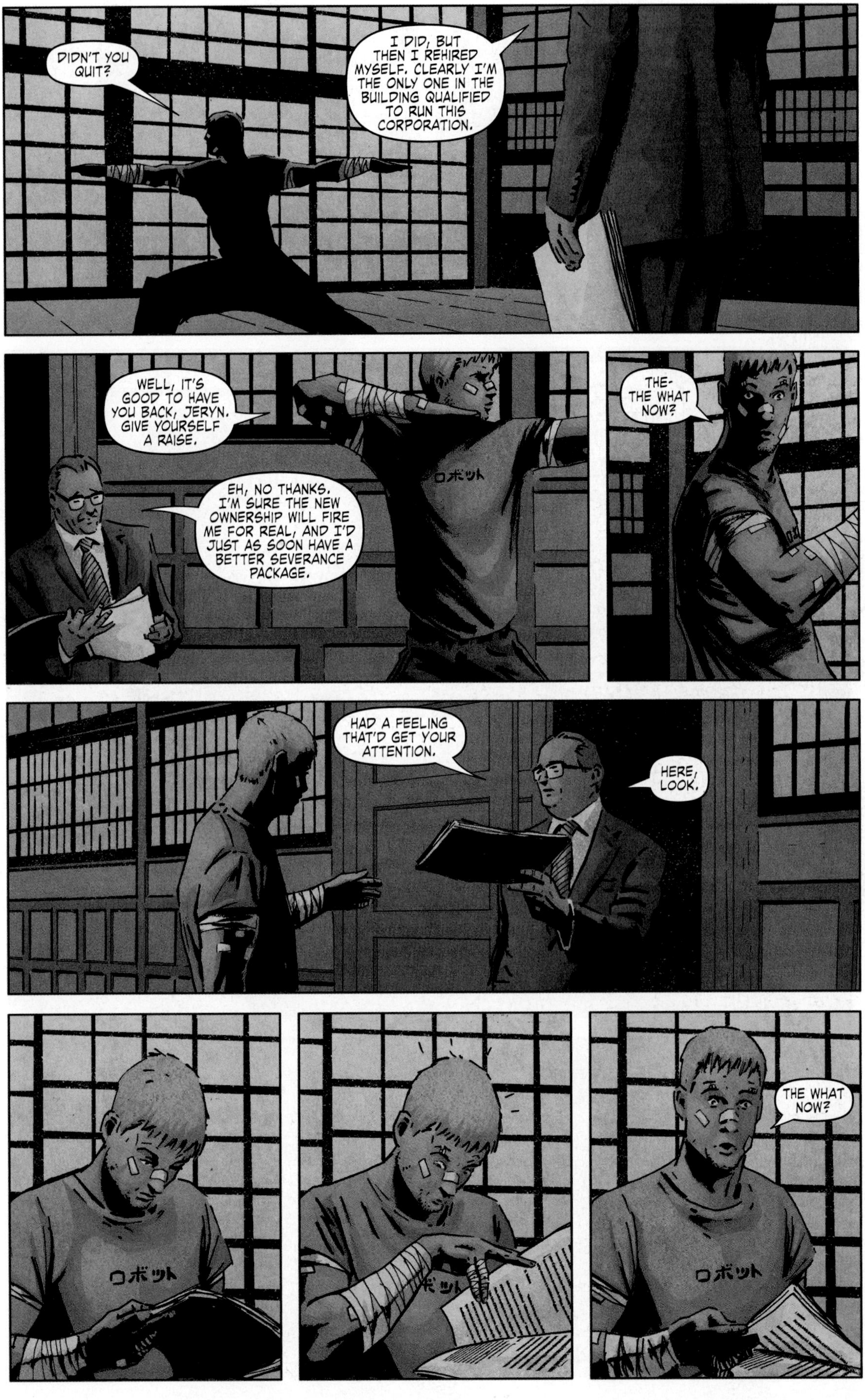
DIDN'T YOU QUIT?
I DID, BUT THEN I REHIRED MYSELF. CLEARLY I'M THE ONLY ONE IN THE BUILDING QUALIFIED TO RUN THIS CORPORATION.
WELL, IT'S GOOD TO HAVE YOU BACK, JERYN. GIVE YOURSELF A RAISE.
ロボット
EH, NO THANKS. I'M SURE THE NEW OWNERSHIP WILL FIRE ME FOR REAL, AND I'D JUST AS SOON HAVE A BETTER SEVERANCE PACKAGE.
THE-THE WHAT NOW?
HAD A FEELING THAT'D GET YOUR ATTENTION.
HERE, LOOK.
ロボット
ロボット
THE WHAT NOW?

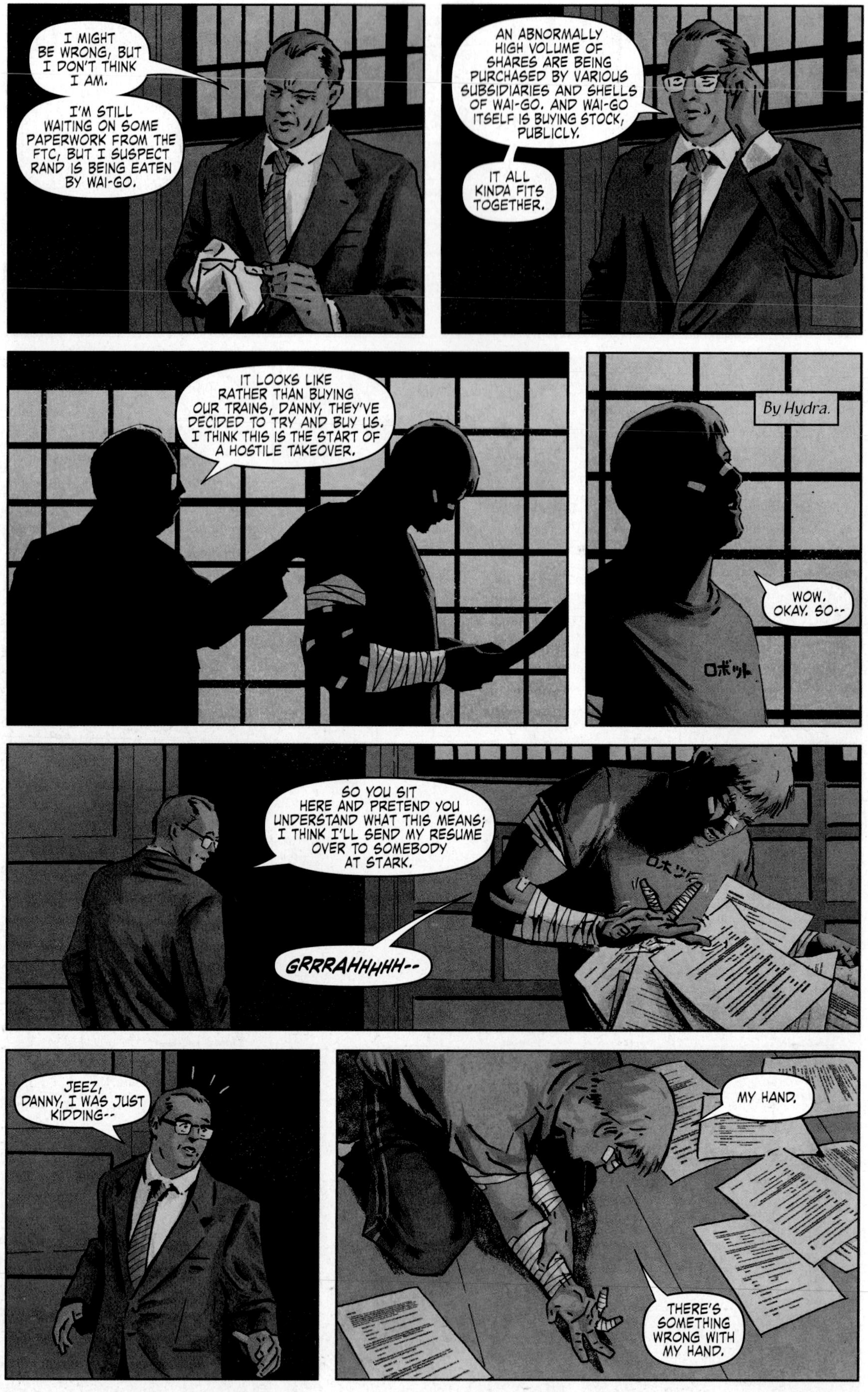
I MIGHT BE WRONG, BUT I DON'T THINK I AM.
I'M STILL WAITING ON SOME PAPERWORK FROM THE FTC, BUT I SUSPECT RAND IS BEING EATEN BY WAI-GO.
AN ABNORMALLY HIGH VOLUME OF SHARES ARE BEING PURCHASED BY VARIOUS SUBSIDIARIES AND SHELLS OF WAI-GO. AND WAI-GO ITSELF IS BUYING STOCK, PUBLICLY.
IT ALL KINDA FITS TOGETHER.
IT LOOKS LIKE RATHER THAN BUYING OUR TRAINS, DANNY, THEY'VE DECIDED TO TRY AND BUY US. I THINK THIS IS THE START OF A HOSTILE TAKEOVER.
By Hydra.
WOW. OKAY. SO--
ロボット
SO YOU SIT HERE AND PRETEND YOU UNDERSTAND WHAT THIS MEANS; I THINK I'LL SEND MY RESUME OVER TO SOMEBODY AT STARK.
GRRRAHHHHH--
JEEZ, DANNY, I WAS JUST KIDDING--
MY HAND.
THERE'S SOMETHING WRONG WITH MY HAND.

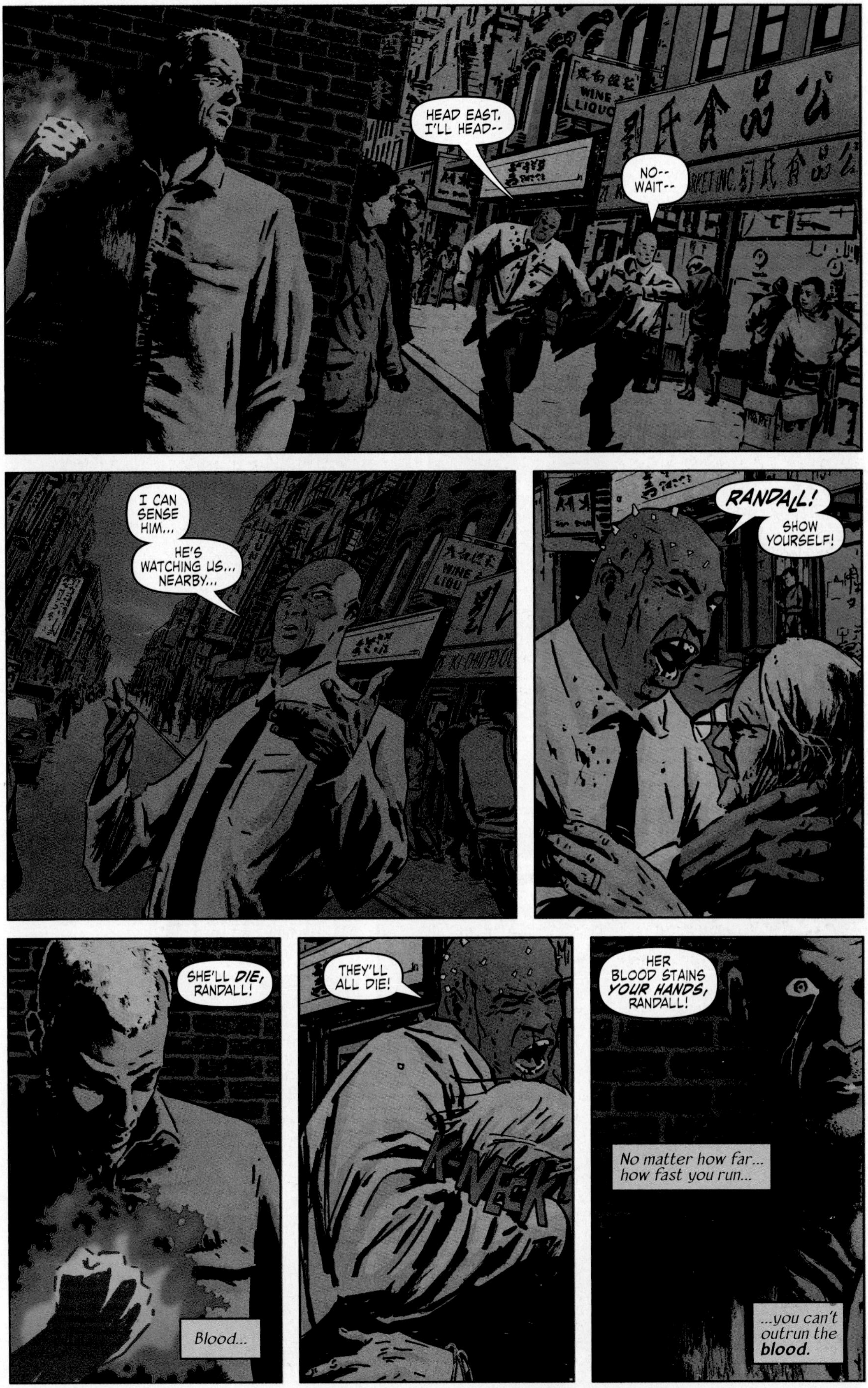
HEAD EAST. I'LL HEAD--
NO-- WAIT--
I CAN SENSE HIM...
HE'S WATCHING US... NEARBY...
RANDALL!
SHOW YOURSELF!
SHE'LL DIE, RANDALL!
Blood...
THEY'LL ALL DIE!
K-NECK
HER BLOOD STAINS YOUR HANDS, RANDALL!
No matter how far... how fast you run...
...you can't outrun the blood.

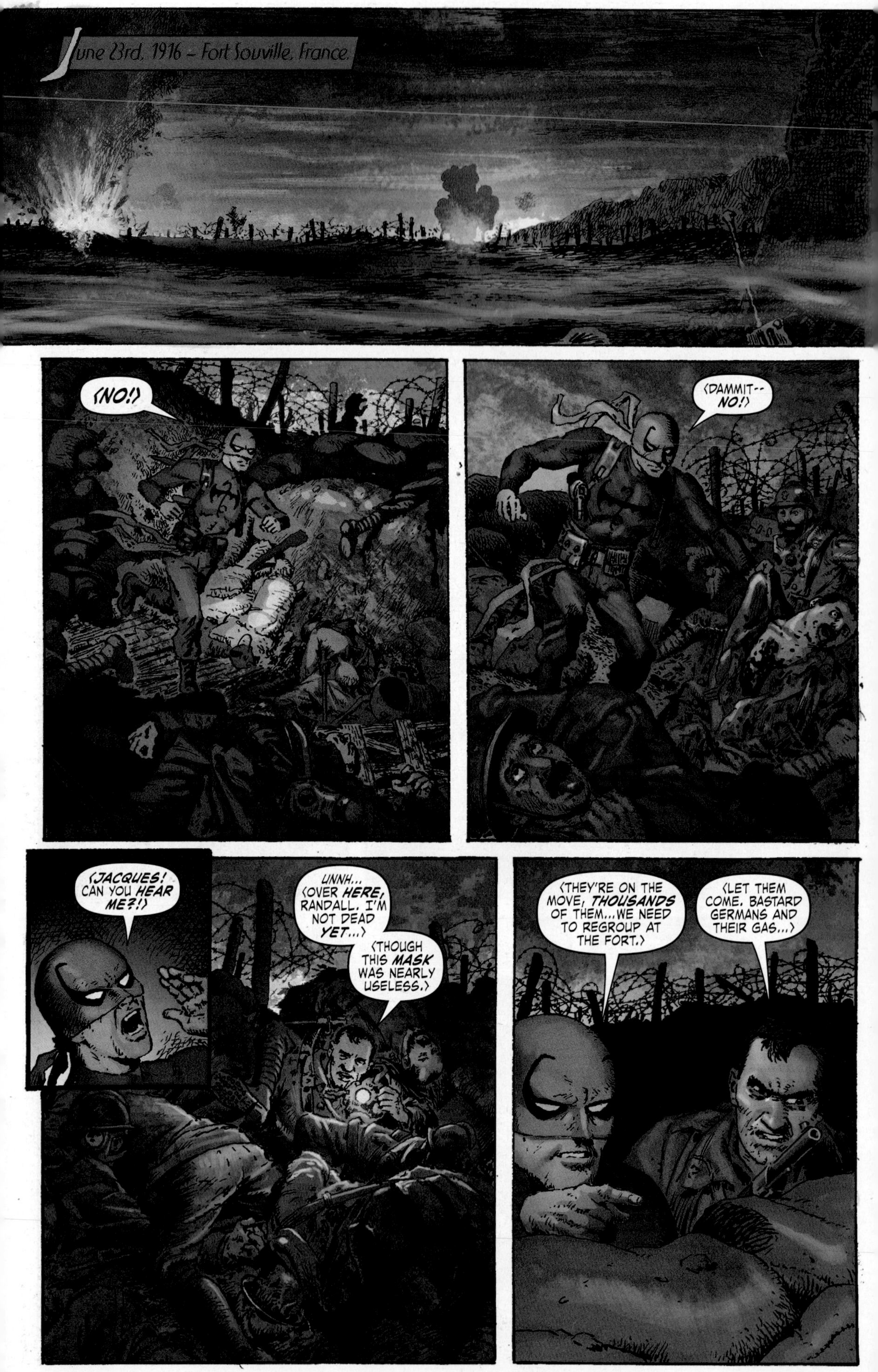
June 23rd, 1916 – Fort Souville, France.
‹NO!›
‹DAMMIT-- NO!›
‹JACQUES! CAN YOU HEAR ME?!›
UNNH... ‹OVER HERE, RANDALL. I'M NOT DEAD YET...›
‹THOUGH THIS MASK WAS NEARLY USELESS.›
‹THEY'RE ON THE MOVE, THOUSANDS OF THEM...WE NEED TO REGROUP AT THE FORT.›
‹LET THEM COME. BASTARD GERMANS AND THEIR GAS...›

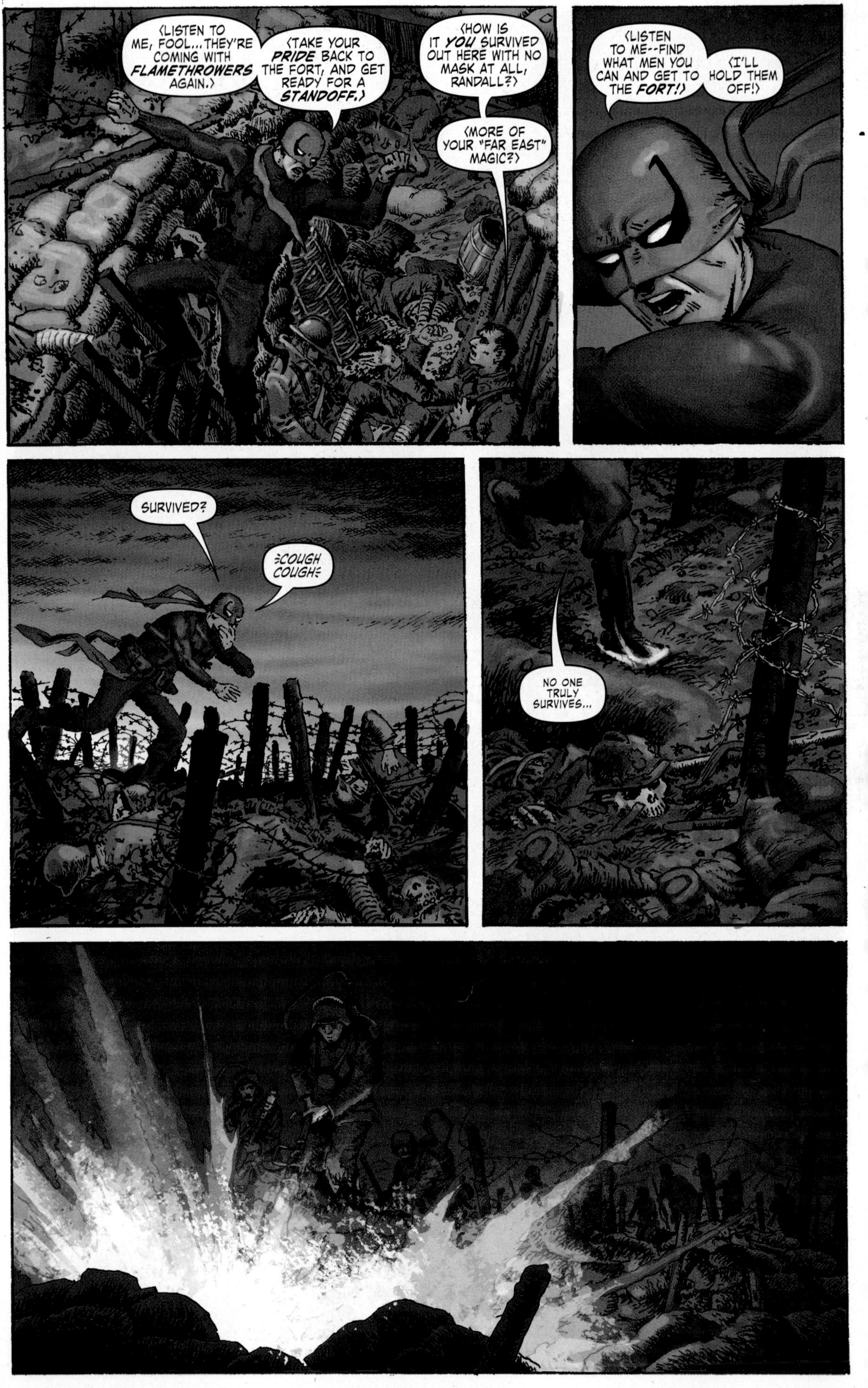
〈LISTEN TO ME, FOOL...THEY'RE COMING WITH FLAMETHROWERS AGAIN.〉
〈TAKE YOUR PRIDE BACK TO THE FORT, AND GET READY FOR A STANDOFF.〉
〈HOW IS IT YOU SURVIVED OUT HERE WITH NO MASK AT ALL, RANDALL?〉
〈MORE OF YOUR "FAR EAST" MAGIC?〉
〈LISTEN TO ME--FIND WHAT MEN YOU CAN AND GET TO THE FORT!〉
〈I'LL HOLD THEM OFF!〉
SURVIVED?
COUGH COUGH
NO ONE TRULY SURVIVES...

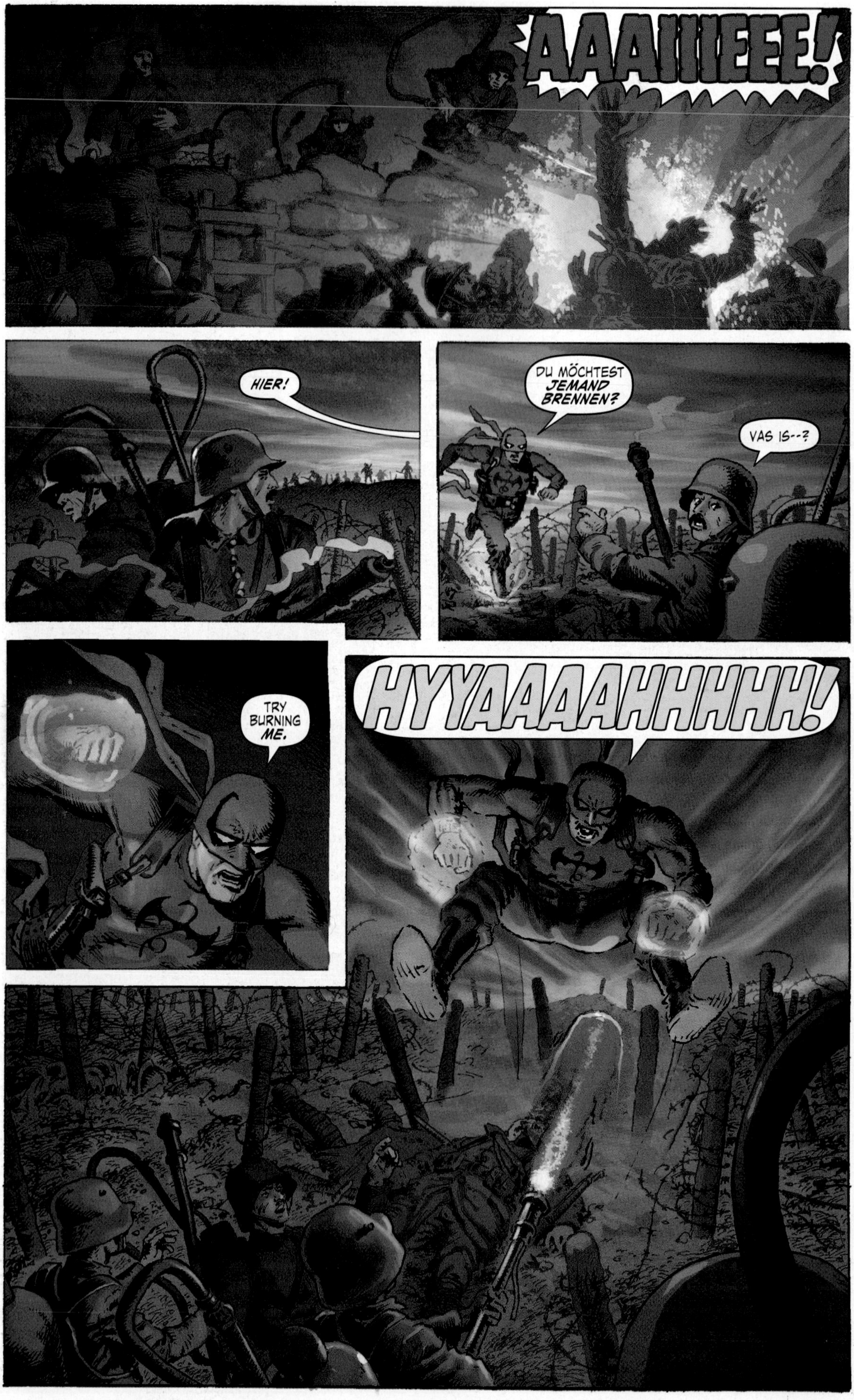
AAAIIIEEEE!
HIER!
DU MÖCHTEST JEMAND BRENNEN?
VAS IS--?
TRY BURNING ME.
HYYAAAAAHHHHH!

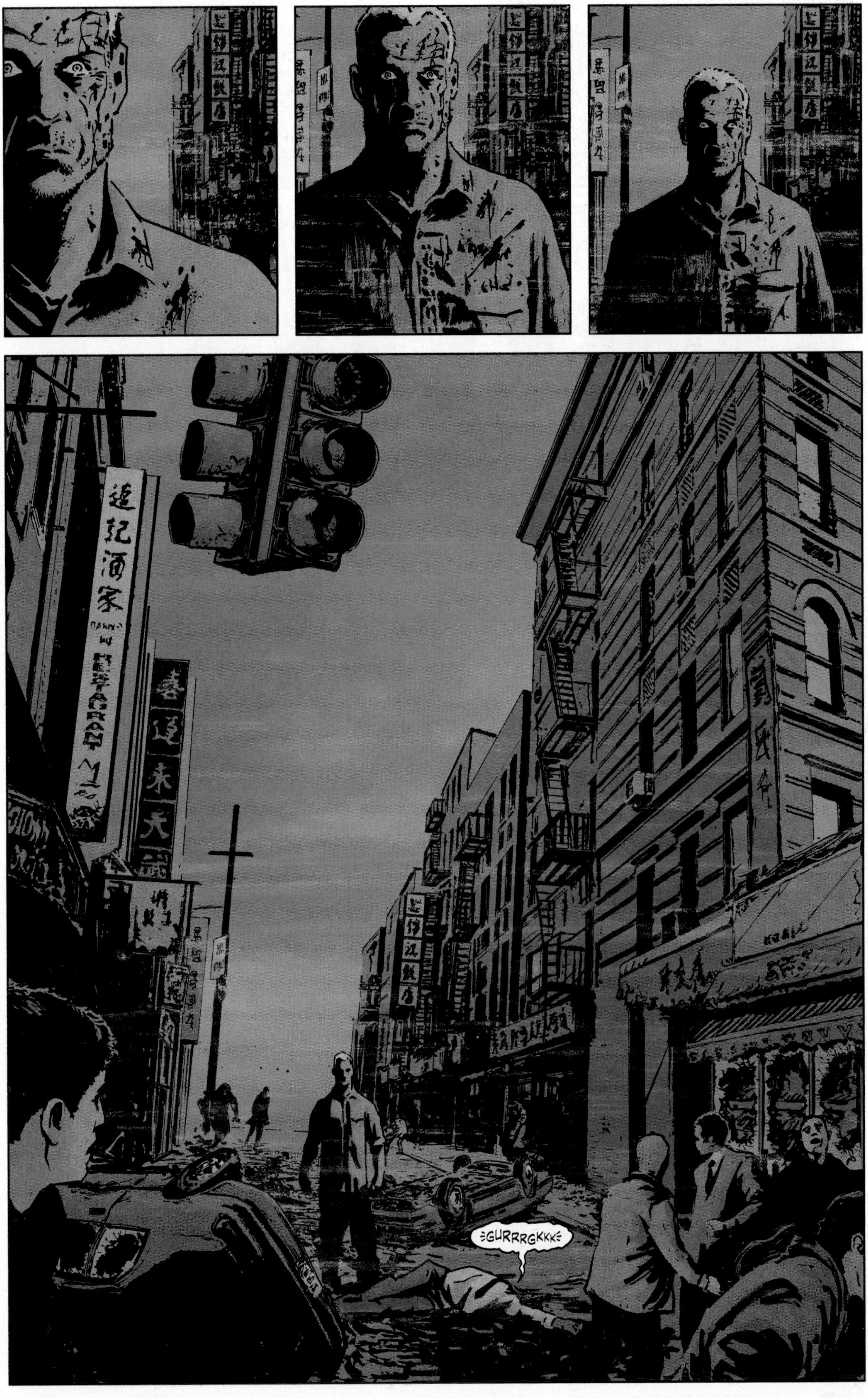
GURRRGKKK

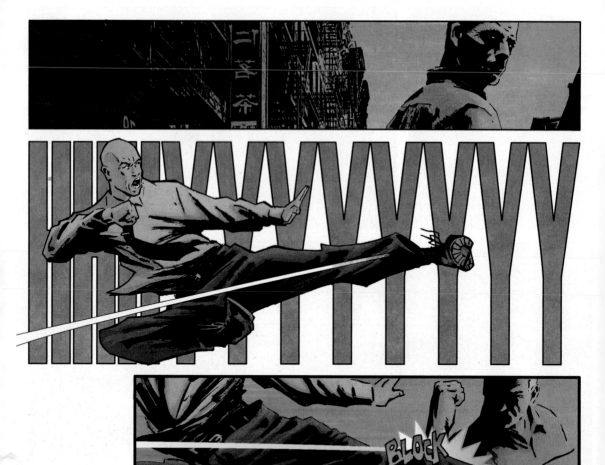

The sound of the assassin's heart bursting in his chest brings me back...

...out of the tidal wave of blood that is my past...

...and into the moment where there is nothing but the blood and me...

The immortal Iron Fist.

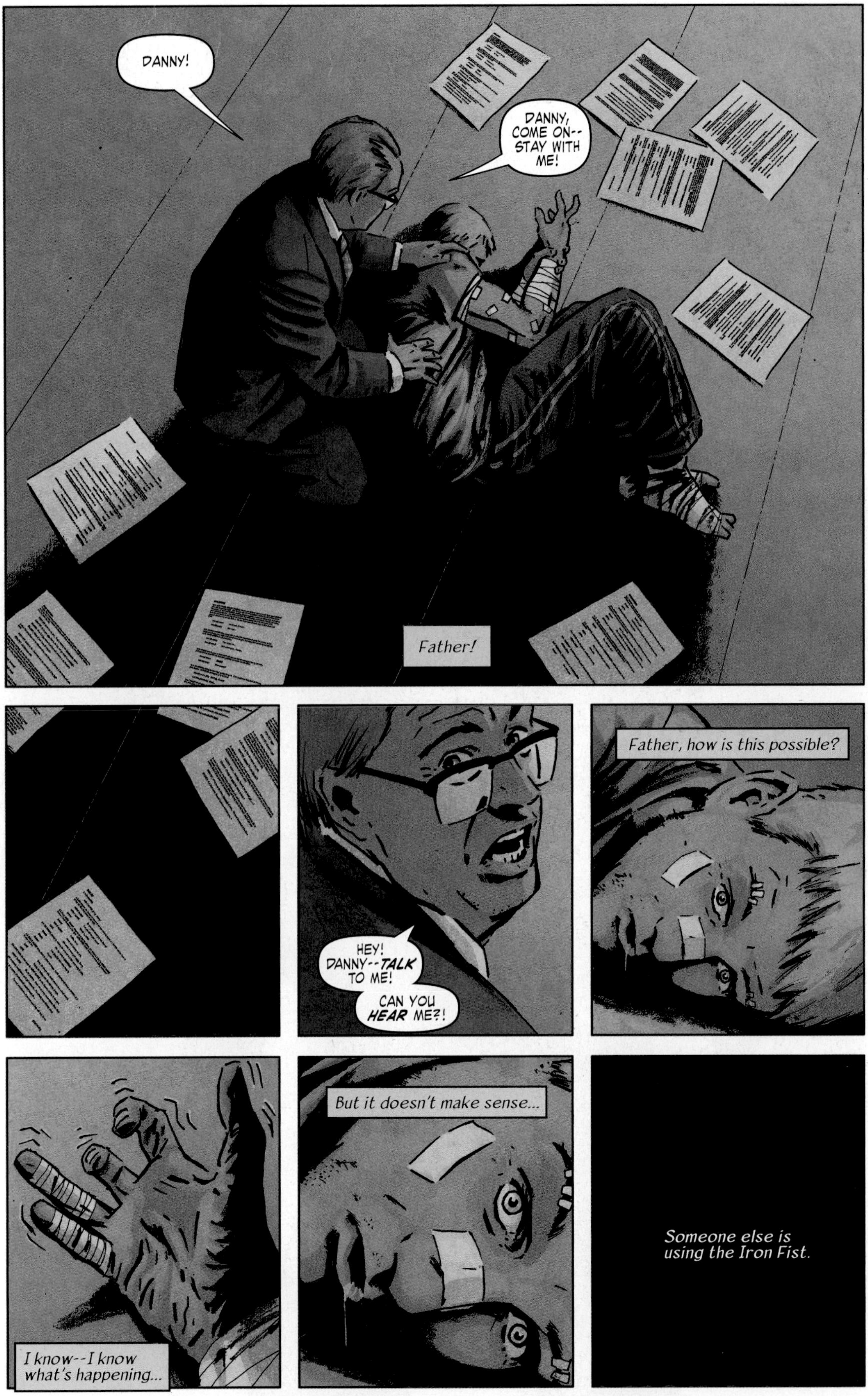
DANNY!
DANNY, COME ON-- STAY WITH ME!
Father!
HEY! DANNY--TALK TO ME!
CAN YOU HEAR ME?!
Father, how is this possible?
I know--I know what's happening...
But it doesn't make sense...
Someone else is using the Iron Fist.

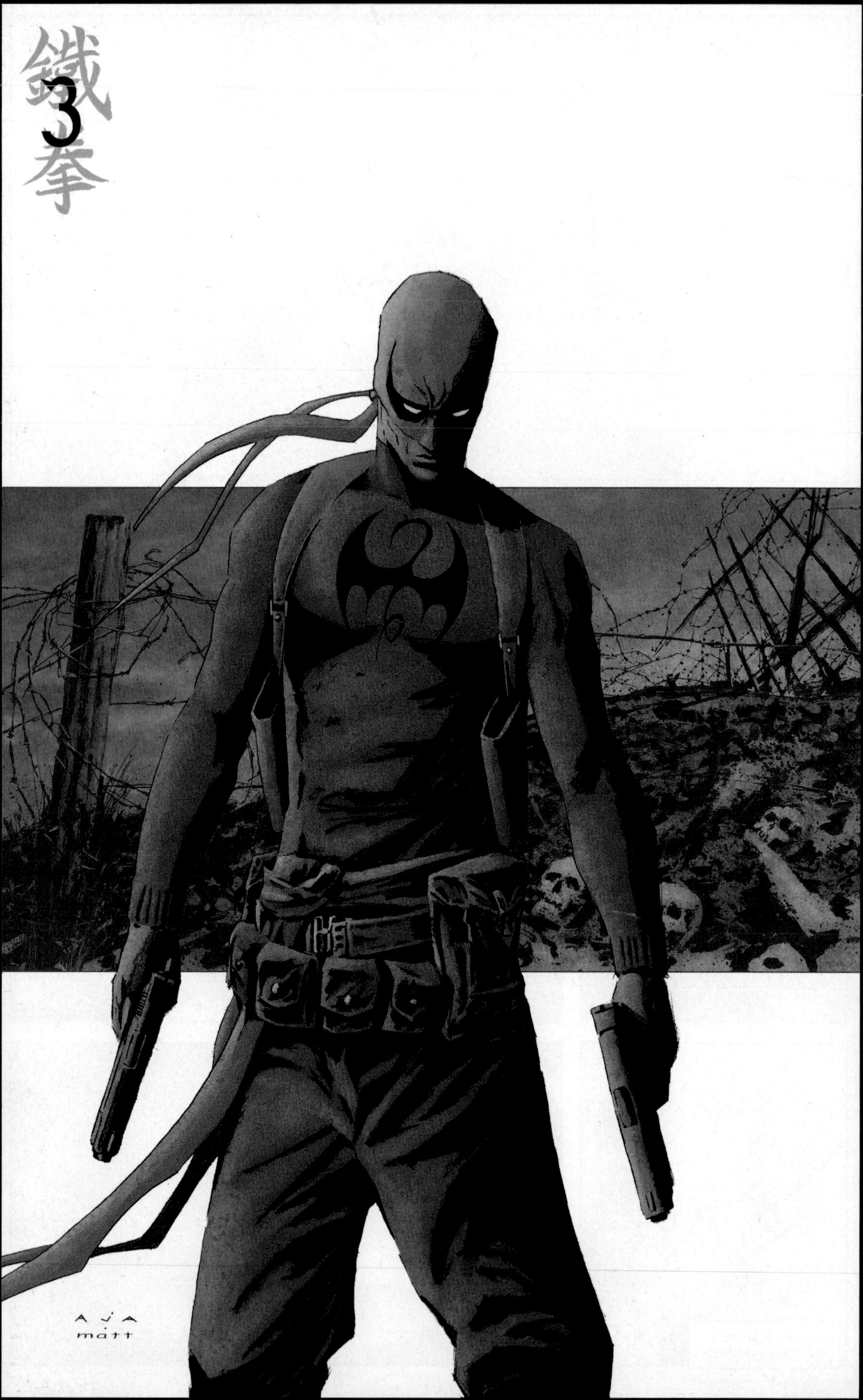

鐵拳
3
AJA
matt

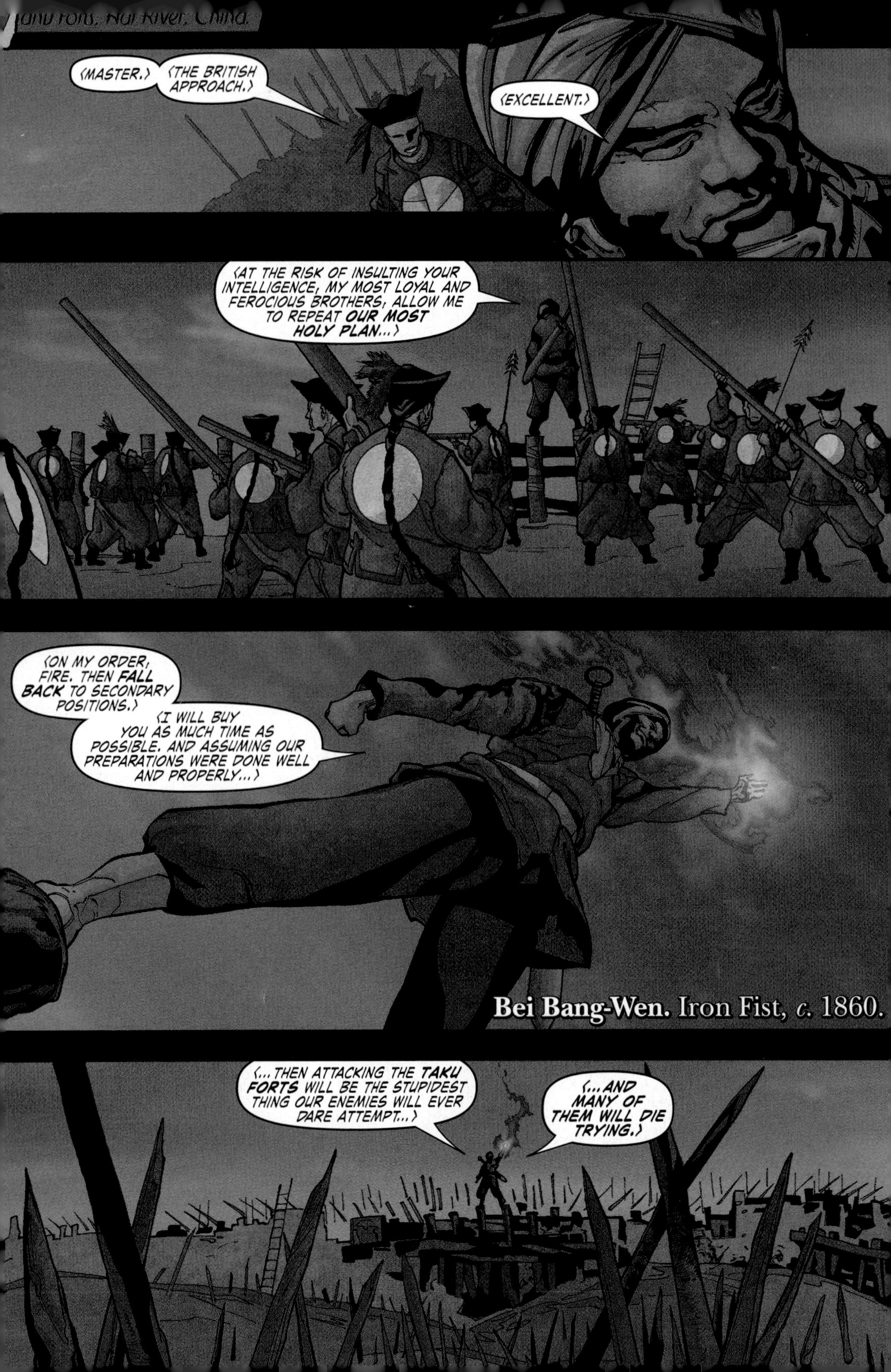
Forts, Hai River, China.
<MASTER.>
<THE BRITISH APPROACH.>
<EXCELLENT.>
<AT THE RISK OF INSULTING YOUR INTELLIGENCE, MY MOST LOYAL AND FEROCIOUS BROTHERS, ALLOW ME TO REPEAT **OUR MOST HOLY PLAN**...>
<ON MY ORDER, FIRE. THEN **FALL BACK** TO SECONDARY POSITIONS.>
<I WILL BUY YOU AS MUCH TIME AS POSSIBLE. AND ASSUMING OUR PREPARATIONS WERE DONE WELL AND PROPERLY...>
Bei Bang-Wen. Iron Fist, *c.* 1860.
<...THEN ATTACKING THE **TAKU FORTS** WILL BE THE STUPIDEST THING OUR ENEMIES WILL EVER DARE ATTEMPT...>
<**...AND MANY OF THEM WILL DIE TRYING.**>

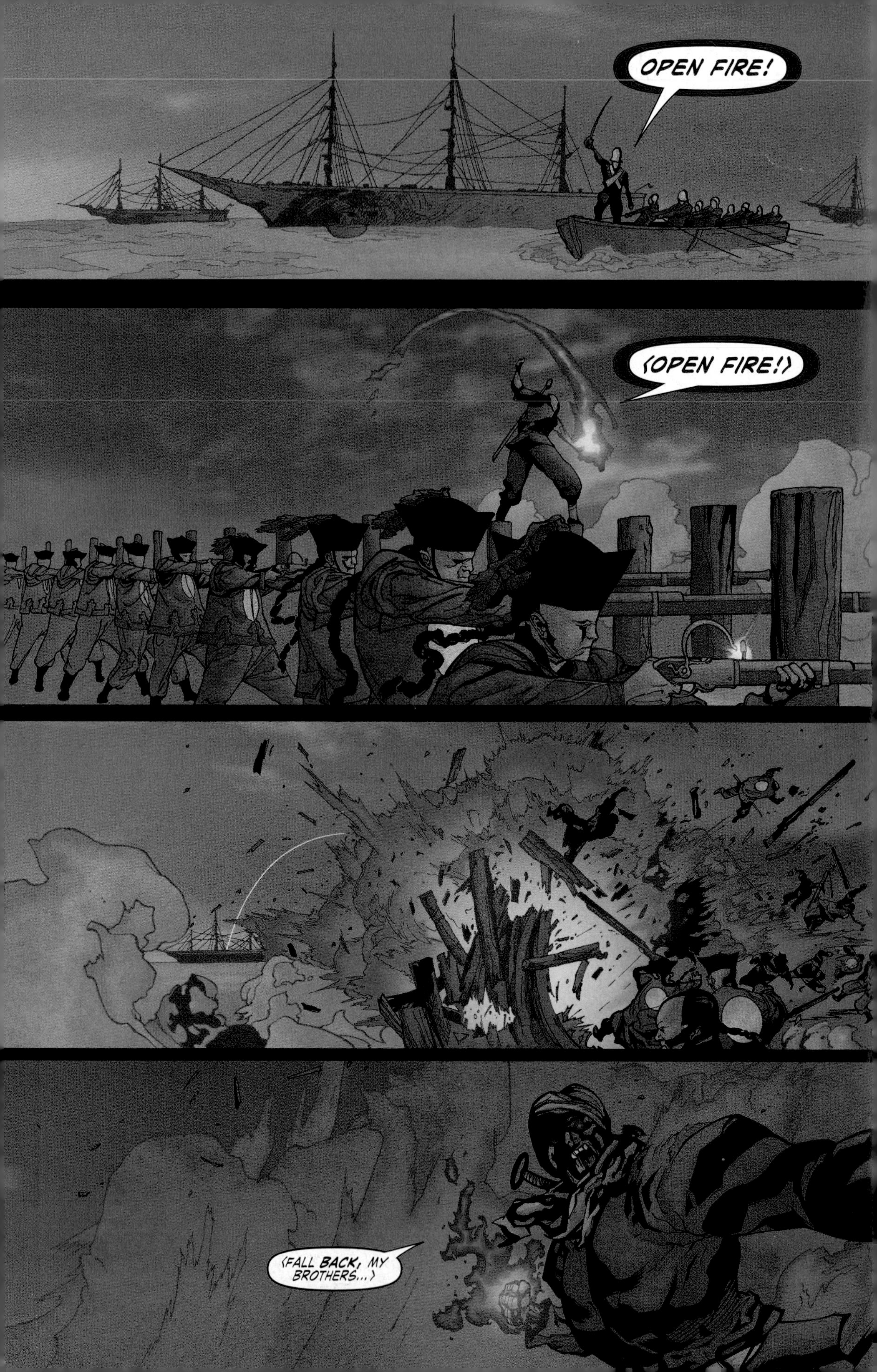
OPEN FIRE!
⟨OPEN FIRE!⟩
⟨FALL BACK, MY BROTHERS...⟩

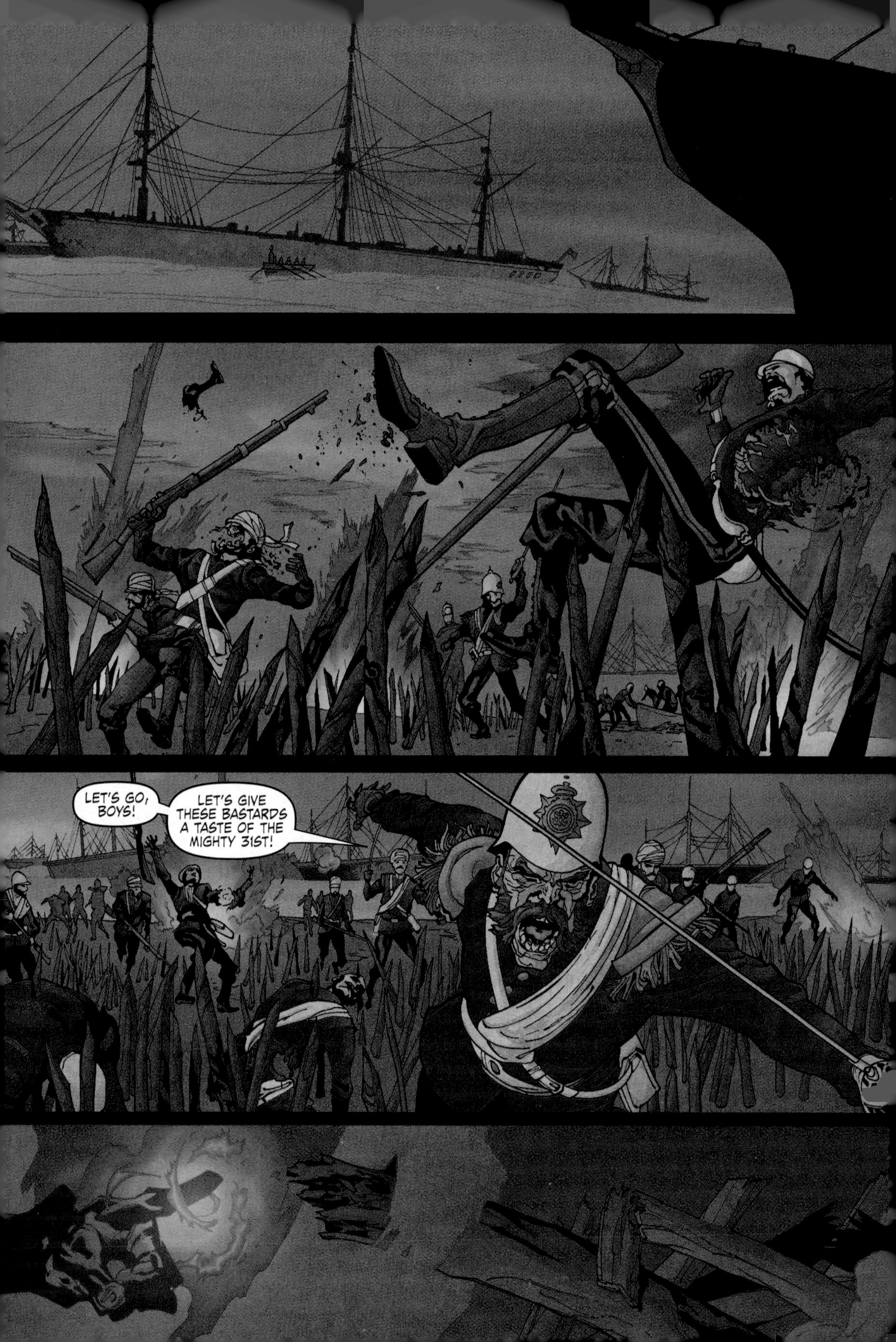
LET'S GO, BOYS!
LET'S GIVE THESE BASTARDS A TASTE OF THE MIGHTY 31ST!

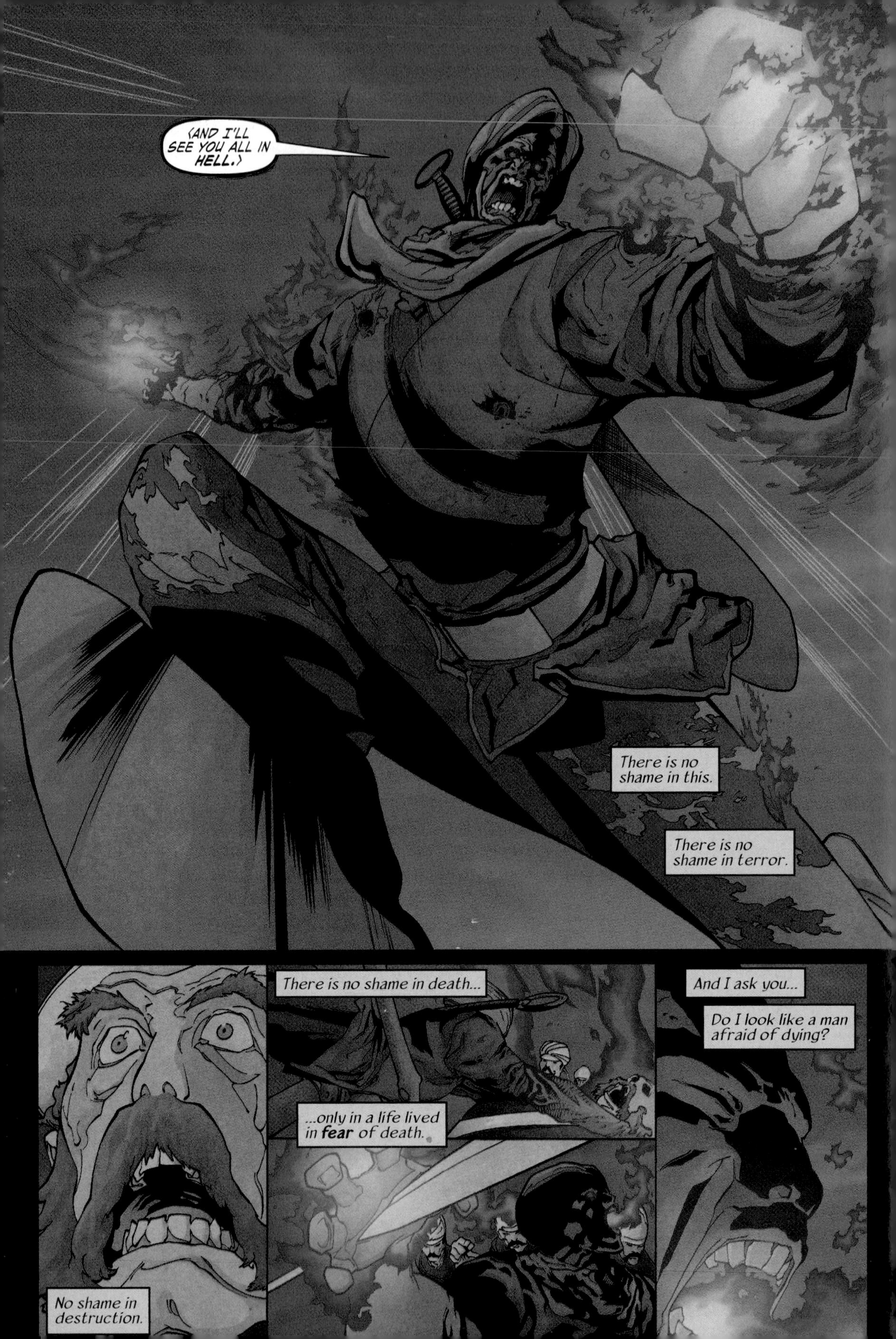
‹AND I'LL SEE YOU ALL IN HELL.›
There is no shame in this.
There is no shame in terror.
No shame in destruction.
There is no shame in death...
...only in a life lived in fear of death.
And I ask you...
Do I look like a man afraid of dying?

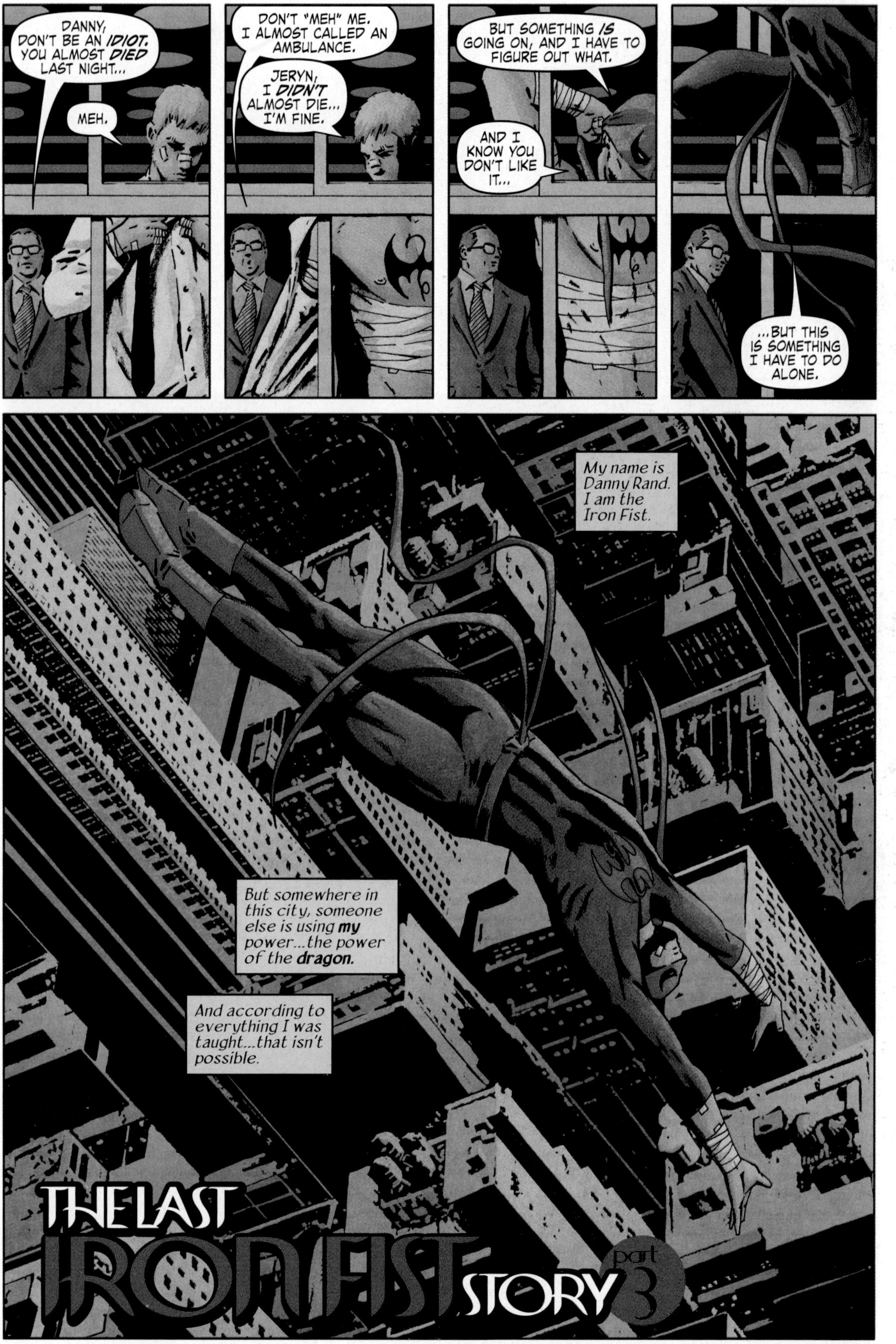
DANNY, DON'T BE AN *IDIOT.* YOU ALMOST *DIED* LAST NIGHT...
MEH.
DON'T "MEH" ME. I ALMOST CALLED AN AMBULANCE.
JERYN, I *DIDN'T* ALMOST DIE... I'M FINE.
BUT SOMETHING *IS* GOING ON, AND I HAVE TO FIGURE OUT WHAT.
AND I KNOW YOU DON'T LIKE IT...
...BUT THIS IS SOMETHING I HAVE TO DO ALONE.
My name is Danny Rand. I am the Iron Fist.
But somewhere in this city, someone else is using **my** power...the power of the **dragon.**
And according to everything I was taught...that isn't possible.
THE LAST IRON FIST STORY part 3

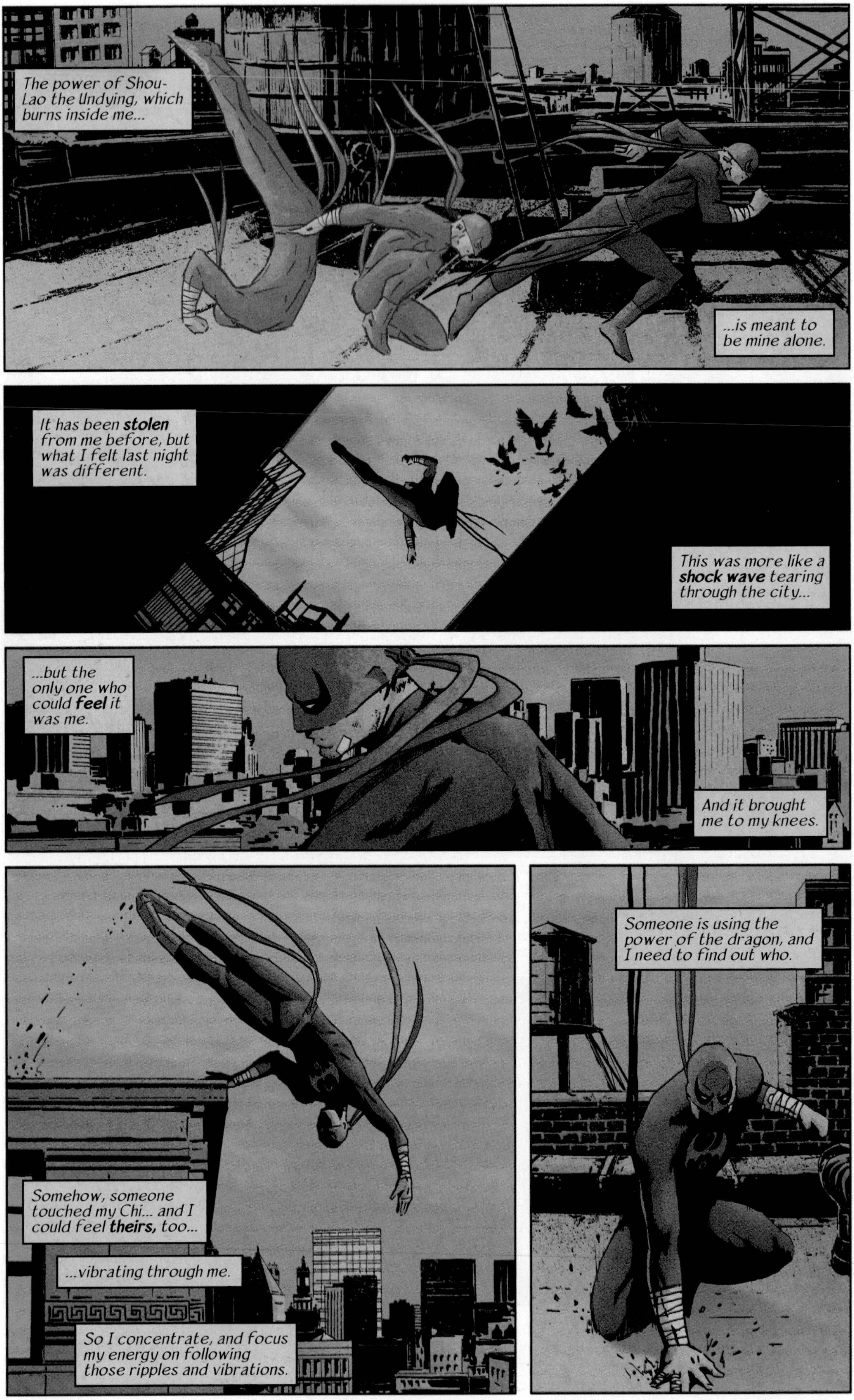

The power of Shou-Lao the Undying, which burns inside me...
...is meant to be mine alone.
It has been **stolen** from me before, but what I felt last night was different.
This was more like a **shock wave** tearing through the city...
...but the only one who could **feel** it was me.
And it brought me to my knees.
Somehow, someone touched my Chi... and I could feel **theirs,** too...
...vibrating through me.
So I concentrate, and focus my energy on following those ripples and vibrations.
Someone is using the power of the dragon, and I need to find out who.

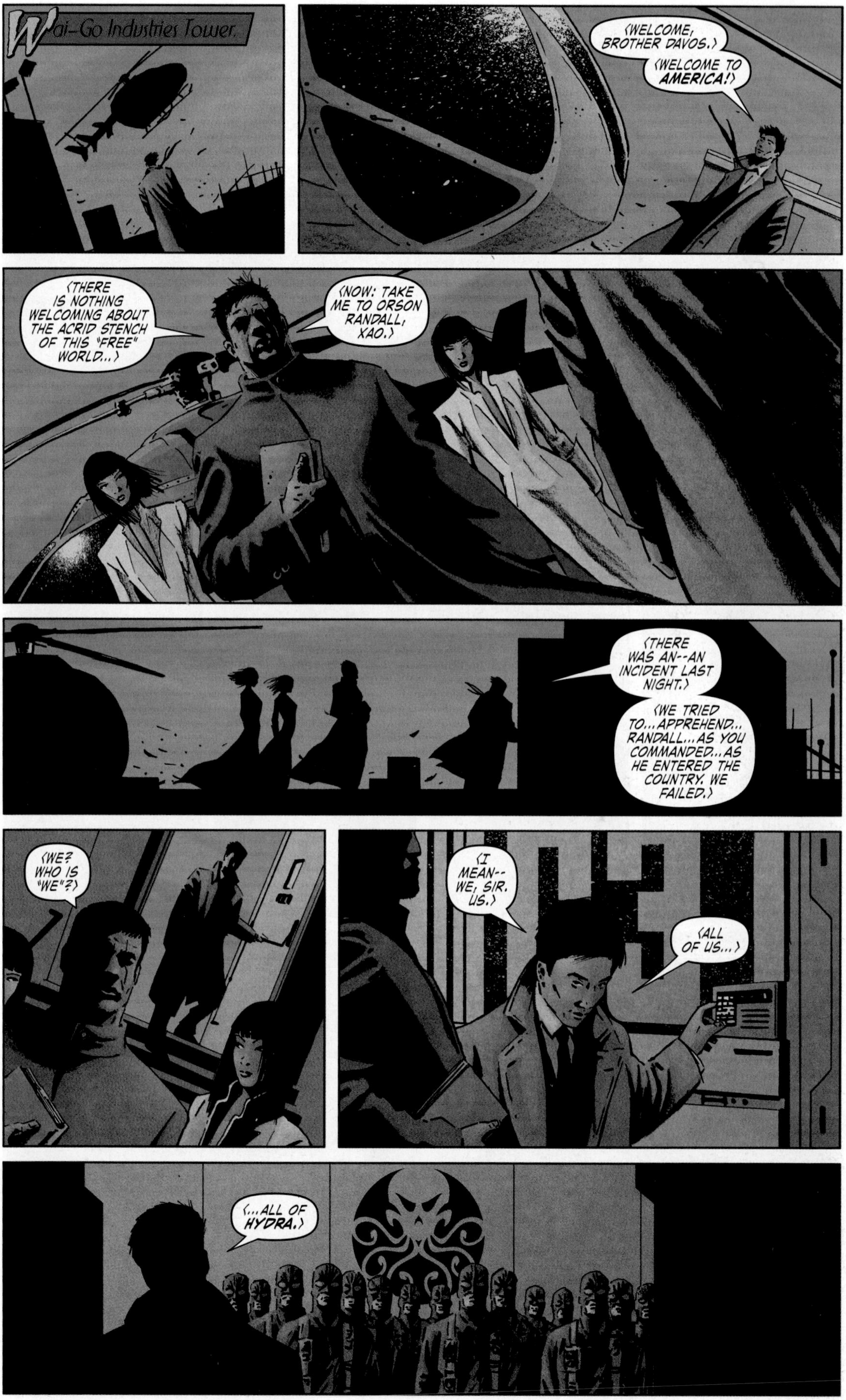
Wai-Go Industries Tower.
‹WELCOME, BROTHER DAVOS.›
‹WELCOME TO AMERICA!›
‹THERE IS NOTHING WELCOMING ABOUT THE ACRID STENCH OF THIS "FREE" WORLD...›
‹NOW: TAKE ME TO ORSON RANDALL, XAO.›
‹THERE WAS AN--AN INCIDENT LAST NIGHT.›
‹WE TRIED TO...APPREHEND... RANDALL...AS YOU COMMANDED...AS HE ENTERED THE COUNTRY. WE FAILED.›
‹WE? WHO IS "WE"?›
‹I MEAN-- WE, SIR. US.›
‹ALL OF US...›
‹...ALL OF HYDRA.›

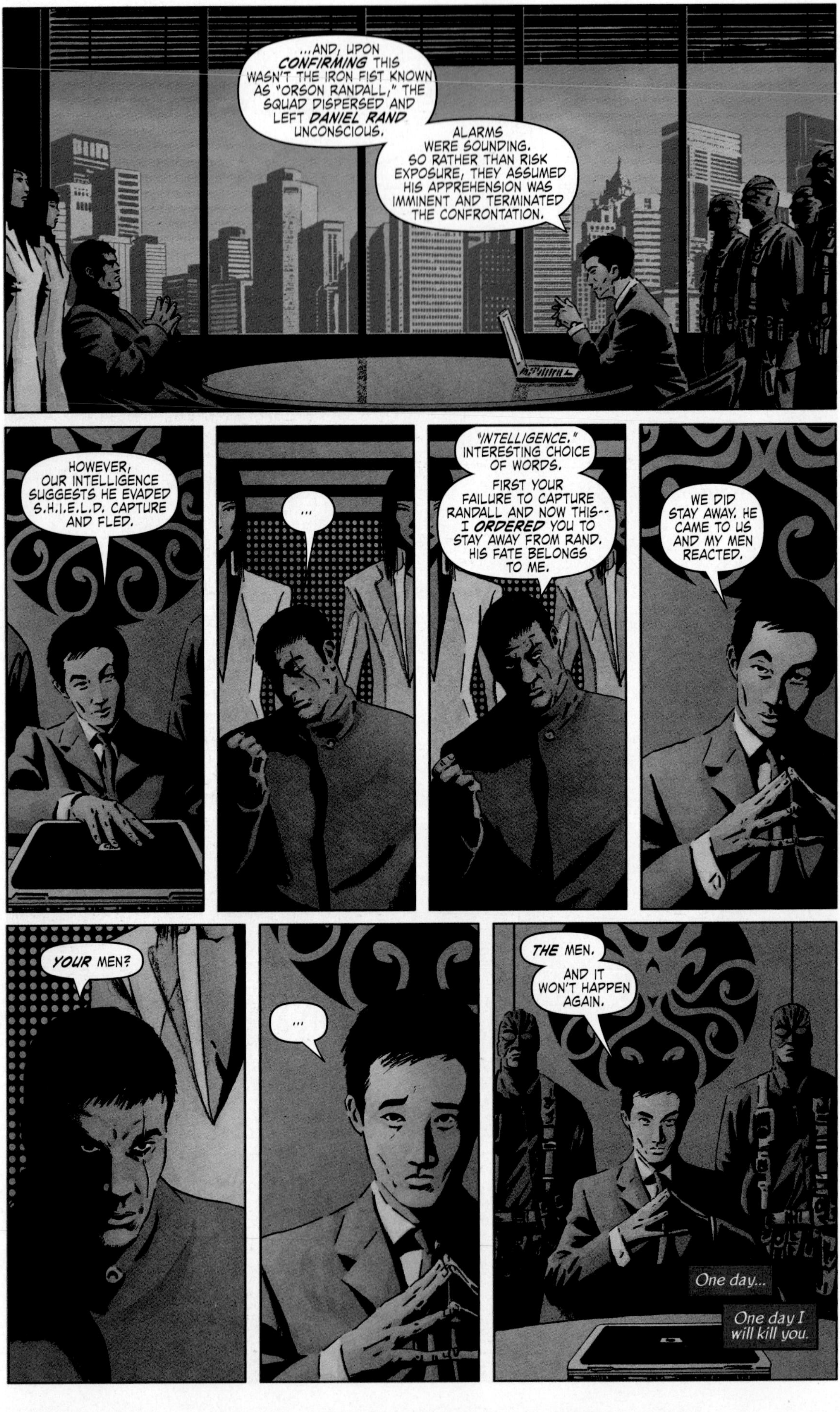
...AND, UPON CONFIRMING THIS WASN'T THE IRON FIST KNOWN AS "ORSON RANDALL," THE SQUAD DISPERSED AND LEFT DANIEL RAND UNCONSCIOUS.
ALARMS WERE SOUNDING. SO RATHER THAN RISK EXPOSURE, THEY ASSUMED HIS APPREHENSION WAS IMMINENT AND TERMINATED THE CONFRONTATION.
HOWEVER, OUR INTELLIGENCE SUGGESTS HE EVADED S.H.I.E.L.D. CAPTURE AND FLED.
...
"INTELLIGENCE." INTERESTING CHOICE OF WORDS.
FIRST YOUR FAILURE TO CAPTURE RANDALL AND NOW THIS-- I ORDERED YOU TO STAY AWAY FROM RAND. HIS FATE BELONGS TO ME.
WE DID STAY AWAY. HE CAME TO US AND MY MEN REACTED.
YOUR MEN?
...
THE MEN.
AND IT WON'T HAPPEN AGAIN.
One day...
One day I will kill you.

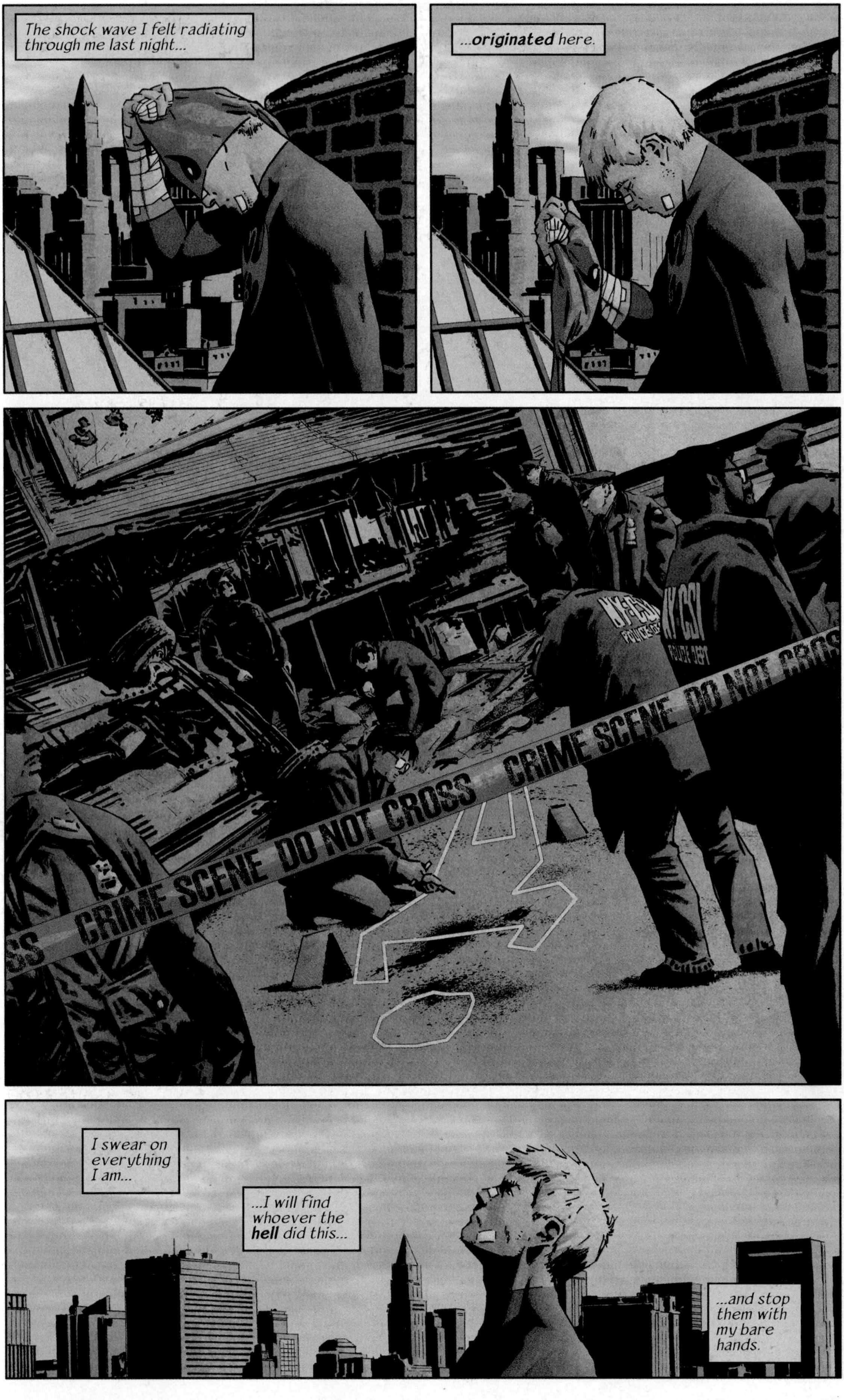
The shock wave I felt radiating through me last night...
...*originated* here.
SS CRIME SCENE DO NOT CROSS CRIME SCENE DO NOT CROSS
I swear on everything I am...
...I will find whoever the *hell* did this...
...and stop them with my bare hands.

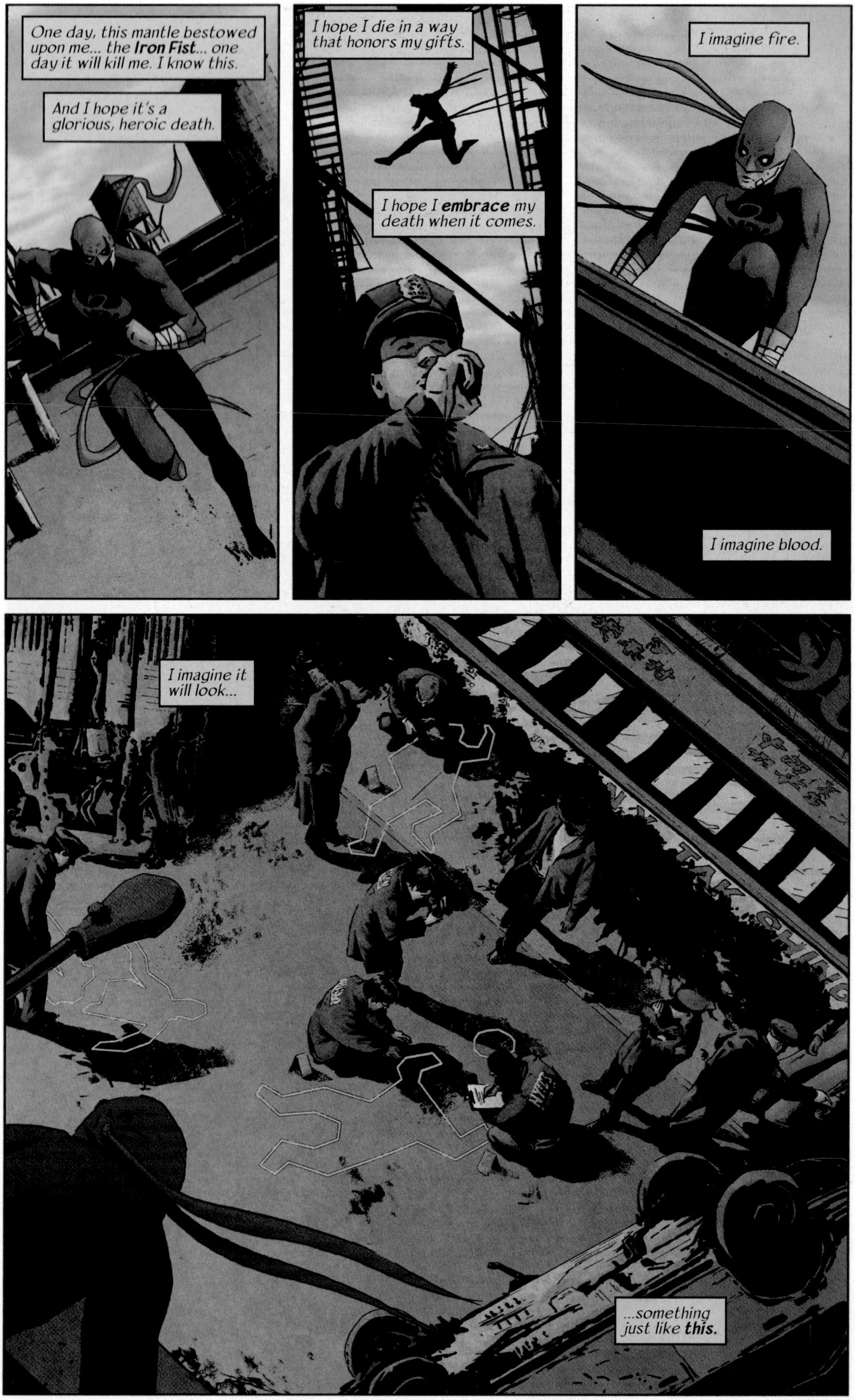
One day, this mantle bestowed upon me... the **Iron Fist**... one day it will kill me. I know this.
And I hope it's a glorious, heroic death.
I hope I die in a way that honors my gifts.
I hope I **embrace** my death when it comes.
I imagine fire.
I imagine blood.
I imagine it will look...
...something just like **this.**

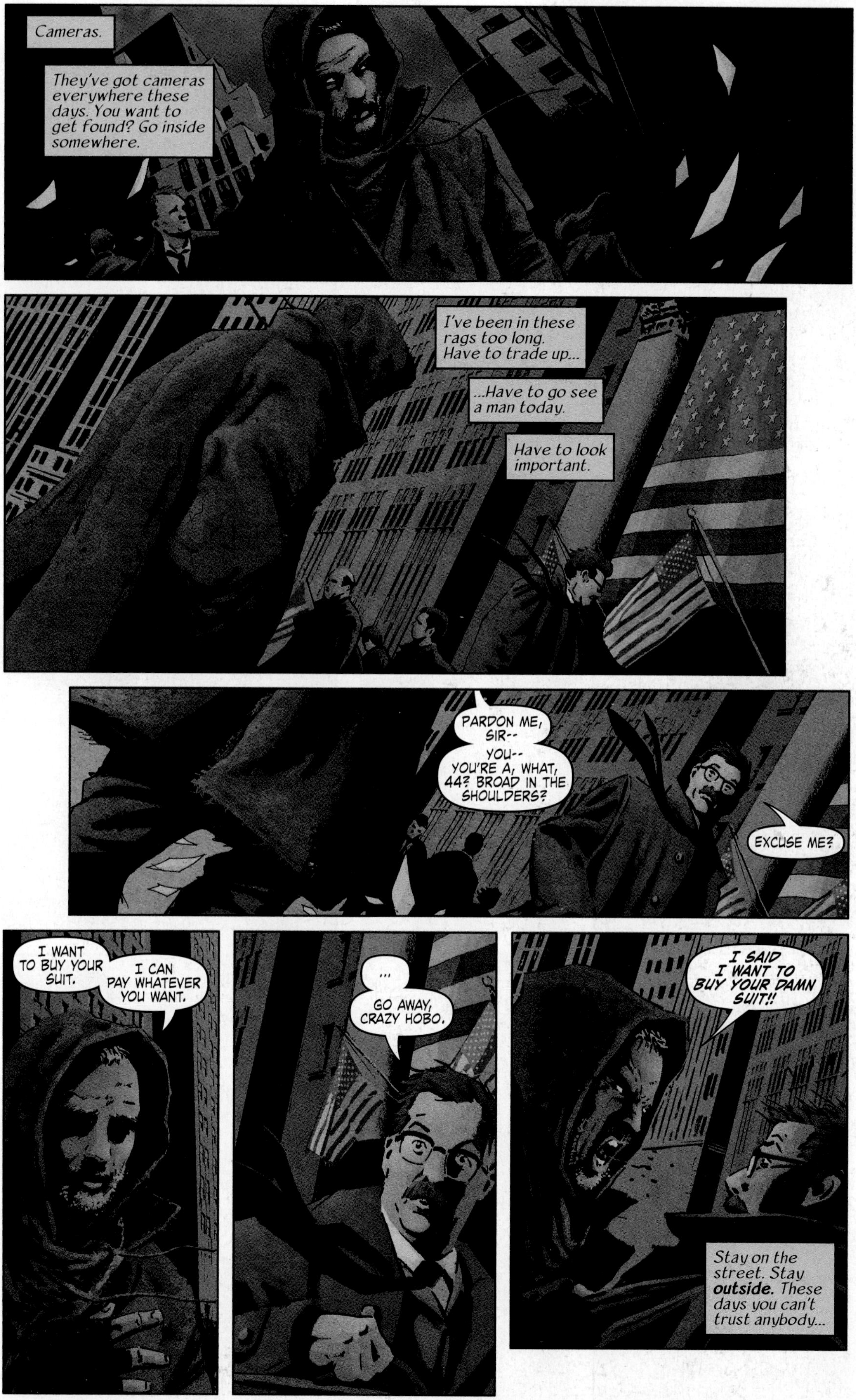
Cameras.
They've got cameras everywhere these days. You want to get found? Go inside somewhere.
I've been in these rags too long. Have to trade up...
...Have to go see a man today.
Have to look important.
PARDON ME, SIR-- YOU-- YOU'RE A, WHAT, 44? BROAD IN THE SHOULDERS?
EXCUSE ME?
I WANT TO BUY YOUR SUIT.
I CAN PAY WHATEVER YOU WANT.
... GO AWAY, CRAZY HOBO.
I SAID I WANT TO BUY YOUR DAMN SUIT!!
Stay on the street. Stay **outside.** These days you can't trust anybody...

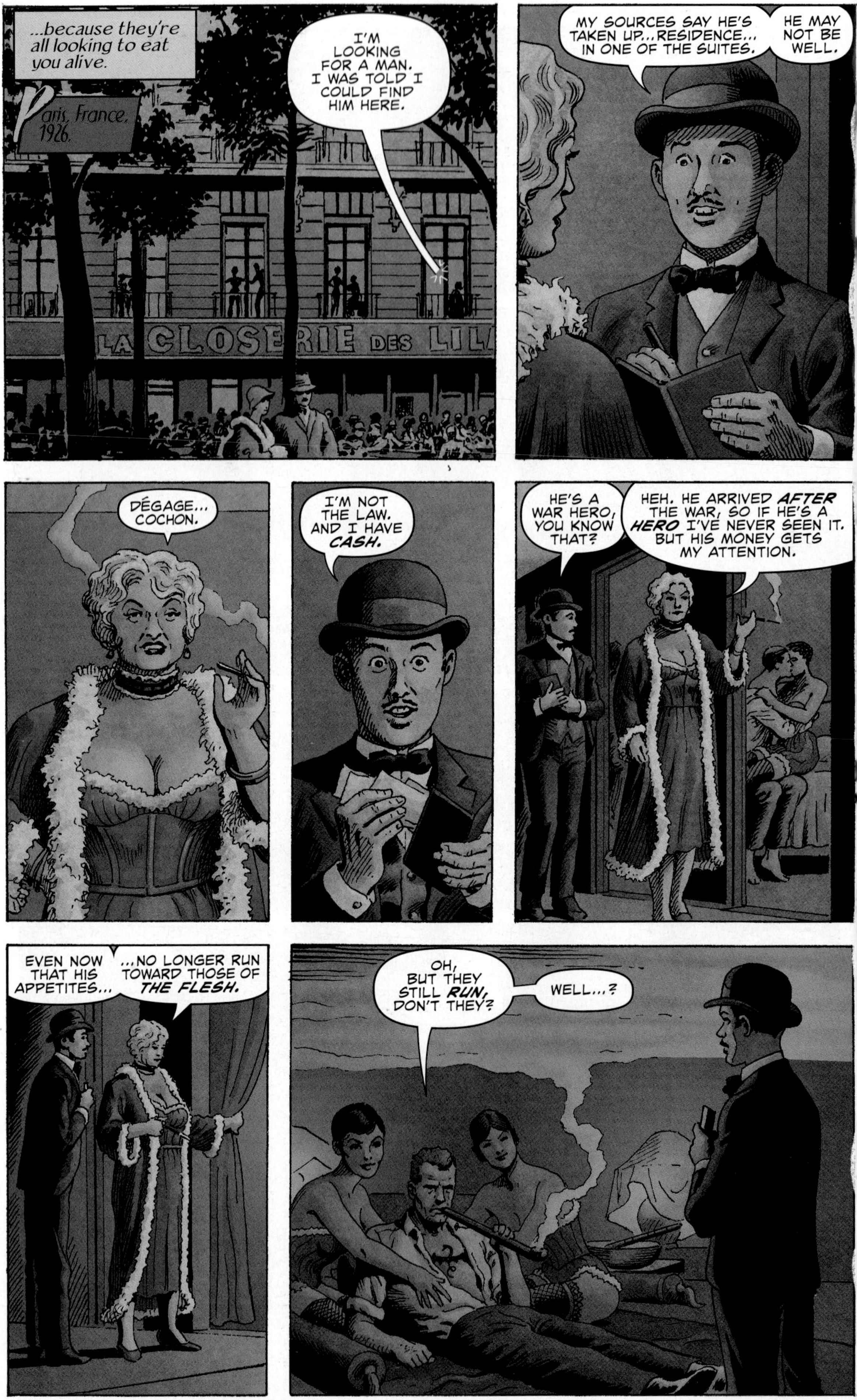
...because they're all looking to eat you alive.
Paris, France, 1926.
I'M LOOKING FOR A MAN. I WAS TOLD I COULD FIND HIM HERE.
LA CLOSERIE DES LIL
MY SOURCES SAY HE'S TAKEN UP...RESIDENCE... IN ONE OF THE SUITES.
HE MAY NOT BE WELL.
DÉGAGE... COCHON.
I'M NOT THE LAW. AND I HAVE **CASH.**
HE'S A WAR HERO, YOU KNOW THAT?
HEH. HE ARRIVED **AFTER** THE WAR, SO IF HE'S A **HERO** I'VE NEVER SEEN IT. BUT HIS MONEY GETS MY ATTENTION.
EVEN NOW THAT HIS APPETITES...
...NO LONGER RUN TOWARD THOSE OF **THE FLESH.**
OH, BUT THEY STILL **RUN,** DON'T THEY?
WELL...?

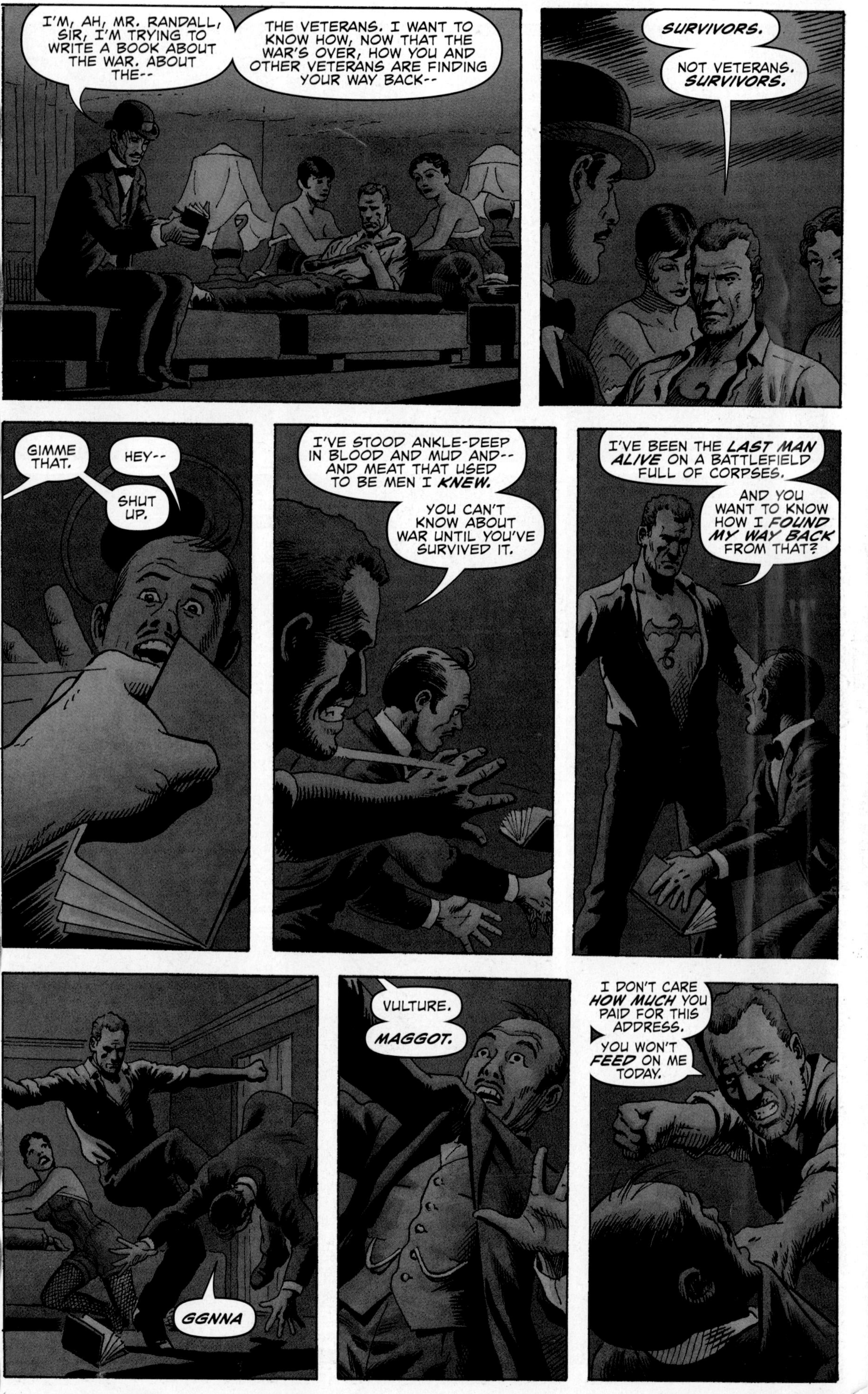
I'M, AH, MR. RANDALL, SIR, I'M TRYING TO WRITE A BOOK ABOUT THE WAR. ABOUT THE--
THE VETERANS. I WANT TO KNOW HOW, NOW THAT THE WAR'S OVER, HOW YOU AND OTHER VETERANS ARE FINDING YOUR WAY BACK--
SURVIVORS.
NOT VETERANS. SURVIVORS.
GIMME THAT.
HEY--
SHUT UP.
I'VE STOOD ANKLE-DEEP IN BLOOD AND MUD AND-- AND MEAT THAT USED TO BE MEN I KNEW.
YOU CAN'T KNOW ABOUT WAR UNTIL YOU'VE SURVIVED IT.
I'VE BEEN THE LAST MAN ALIVE ON A BATTLEFIELD FULL OF CORPSES.
AND YOU WANT TO KNOW HOW I FOUND MY WAY BACK FROM THAT?
GGNNA
VULTURE.
MAGGOT.
I DON'T CARE HOW MUCH YOU PAID FOR THIS ADDRESS.
YOU WON'T FEED ON ME TODAY.

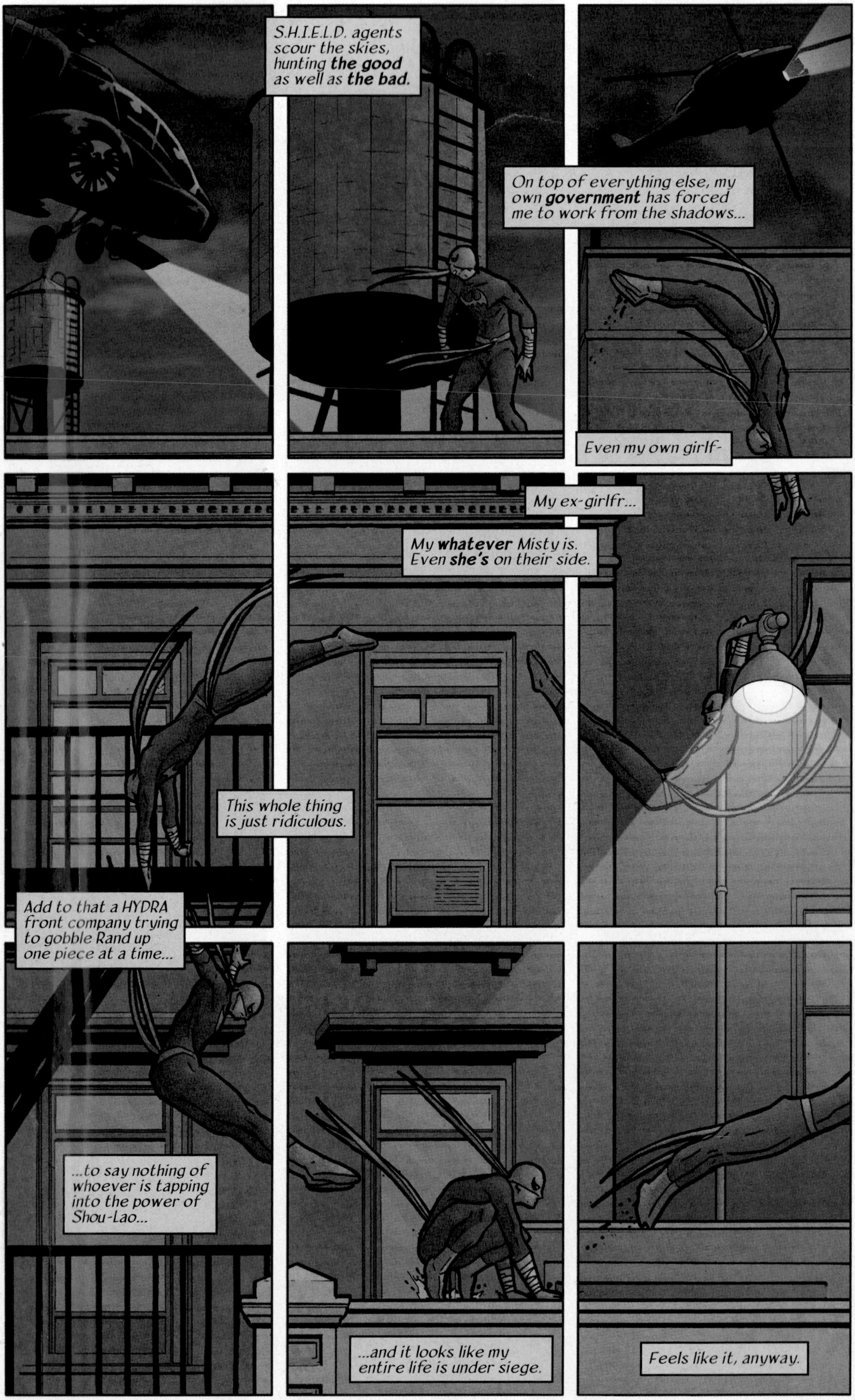
S.H.I.E.L.D. agents scour the skies, hunting **the good** as well as **the bad.**
On top of everything else, my own **government** has forced me to work from the shadows...
Even my own girlf-
My ex-girlfr...
My **whatever** Misty is. Even **she's** on their side.
This whole thing is just ridiculous.
Add to that a HYDRA front company trying to gobble Rand up one piece at a time...
...to say nothing of whoever is tapping into the power of Shou-Lao...
...and it looks like my entire life is under siege.
Feels like it, anyway.

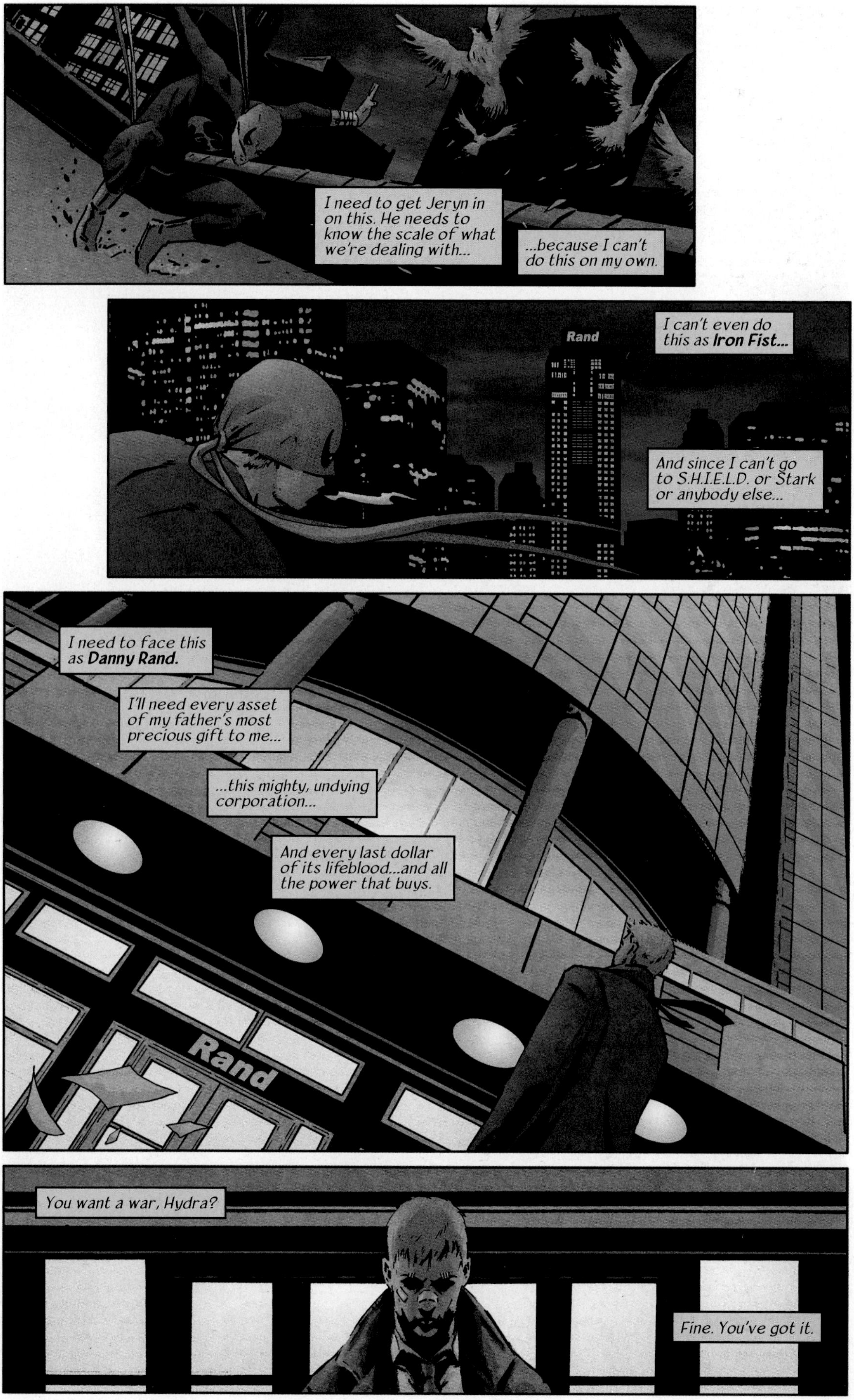
I need to get Jeryn in on this. He needs to know the scale of what we're dealing with...
...because I can't do this on my own.
I can't even do this as **Iron Fist...**
Rand
And since I can't go to S.H.I.E.L.D. or Stark or anybody else...
I need to face this as **Danny Rand.**
I'll need every asset of my father's most precious gift to me...
...this mighty, undying corporation...
And every last dollar of its lifeblood...and all the power that buys.
Rand
You want a war, Hydra?
Fine. You've got it.

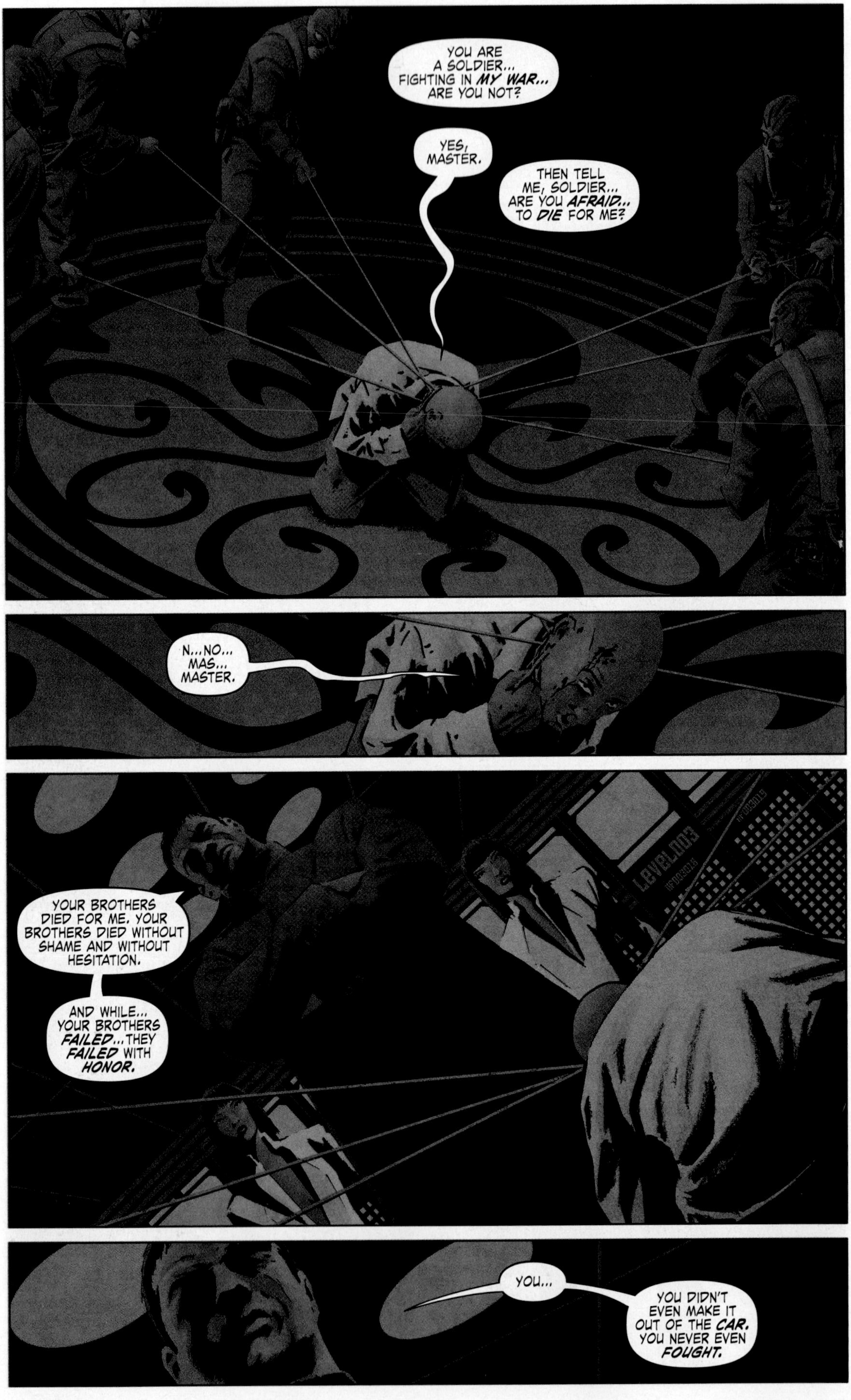
YOU ARE A SOLDIER... FIGHTING IN MY WAR... ARE YOU NOT?
YES, MASTER.
THEN TELL ME, SOLDIER... ARE YOU AFRAID... TO DIE FOR ME?
N...NO... MAS... MASTER.
YOUR BROTHERS DIED FOR ME. YOUR BROTHERS DIED WITHOUT SHAME AND WITHOUT HESITATION.
AND WHILE... YOUR BROTHERS FAILED... THEY FAILED WITH HONOR.
LEVEL 003
YOU...
YOU DIDN'T EVEN MAKE IT OUT OF THE CAR. YOU NEVER EVEN FOUGHT.

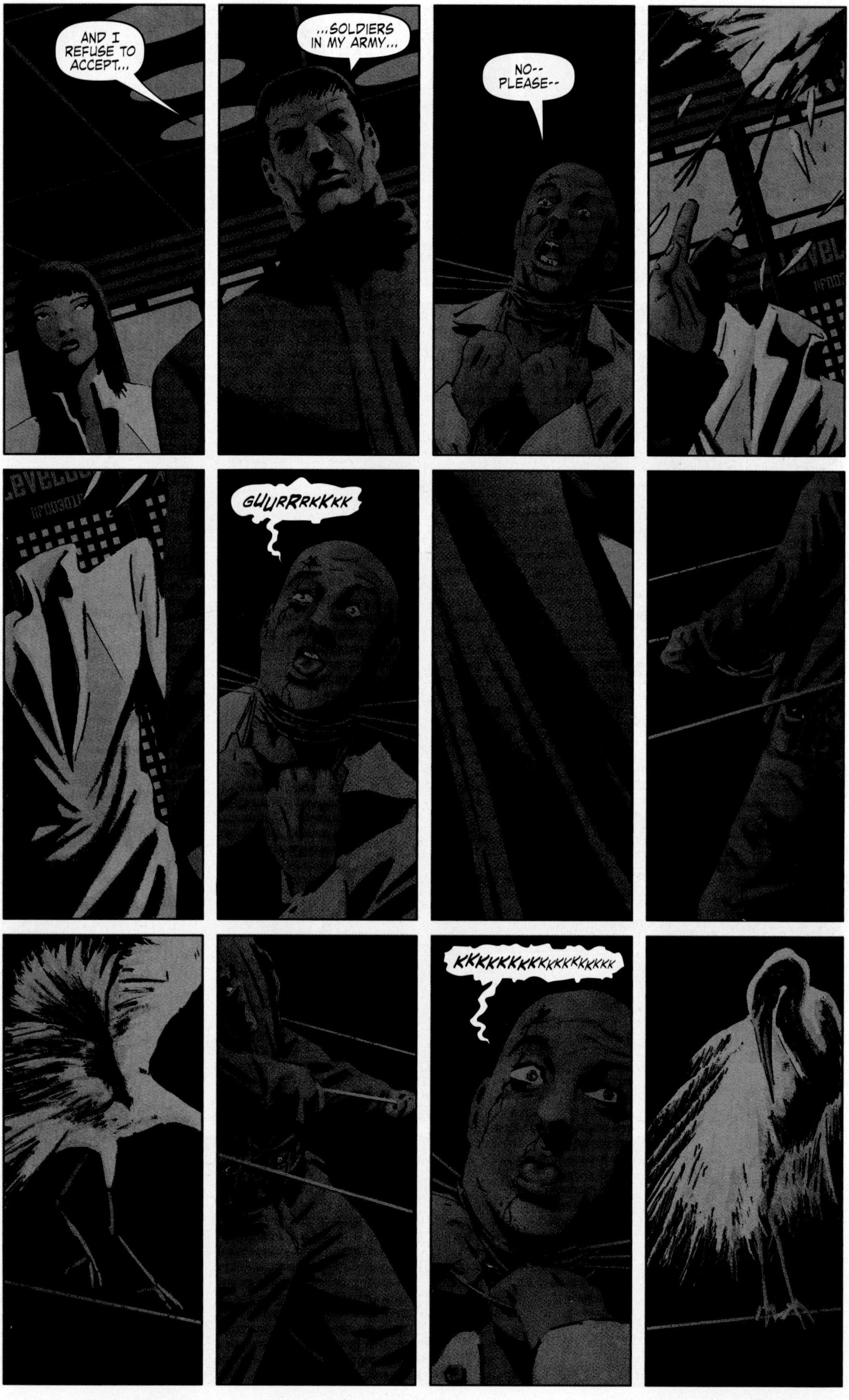
AND I REFUSE TO ACCEPT...
...SOLDIERS IN MY ARMY...
NO-- PLEASE--
GUURRRKKKK
KKKKKKKKKKKKKKKKKK

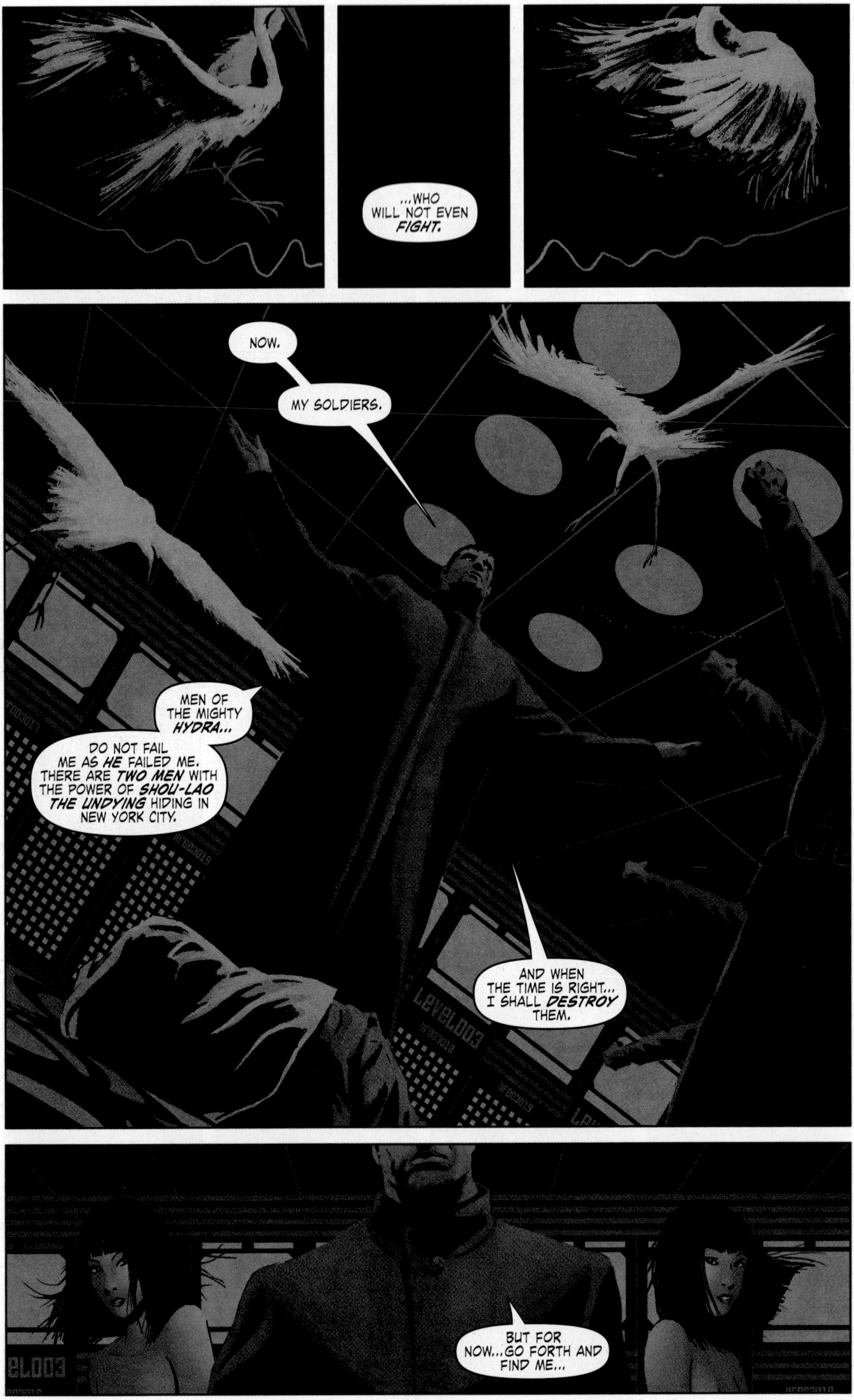
...WHO WILL NOT EVEN FIGHT.
NOW.
MY SOLDIERS.
MEN OF THE MIGHTY HYDRA...
DO NOT FAIL ME AS HE FAILED ME. THERE ARE TWO MEN WITH THE POWER OF SHOU-LAO THE UNDYING HIDING IN NEW YORK CITY.
AND WHEN THE TIME IS RIGHT... I SHALL DESTROY THEM.
BUT FOR NOW...GO FORTH AND FIND ME...

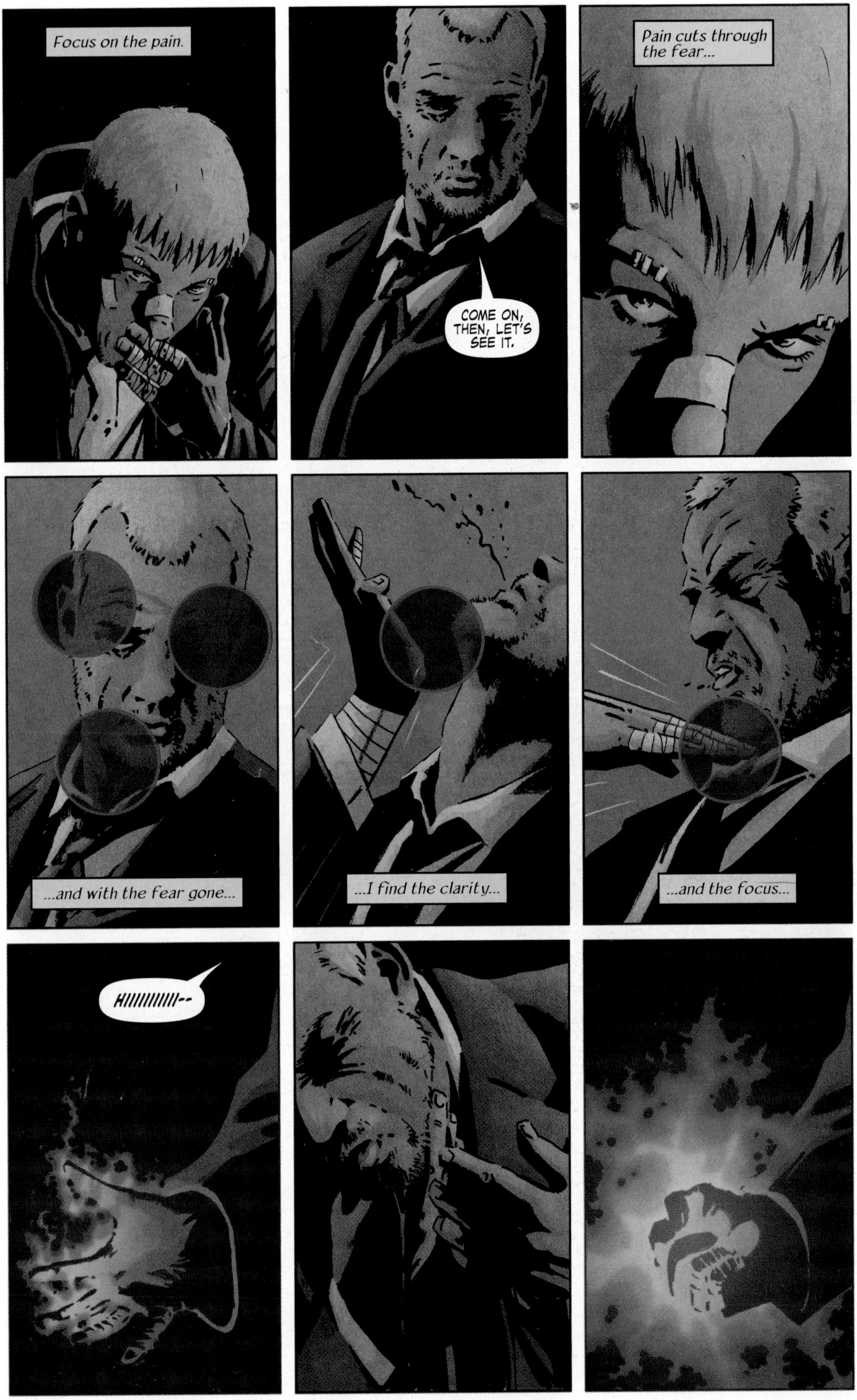
Focus on the pain.
COME ON, THEN, LET'S SEE IT.
Pain cuts through the fear...
...and with the fear gone...
...I find the clarity...
...and the focus...
HIIIIIIIIII--

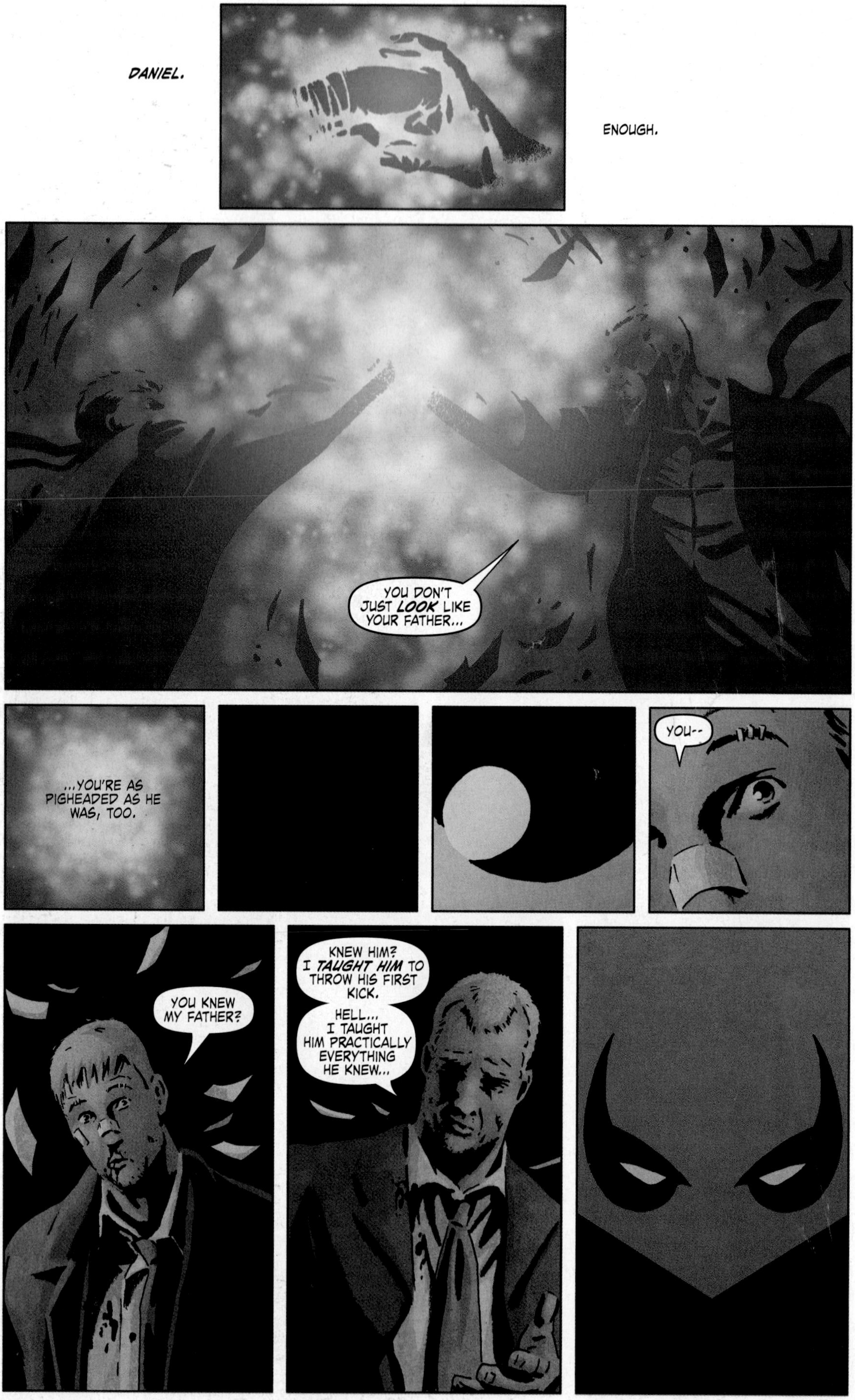
DANIEL.
ENOUGH.
YOU DON'T JUST LOOK LIKE YOUR FATHER...
...YOU'RE AS PIGHEADED AS HE WAS, TOO.
YOU--
YOU KNEW MY FATHER?
KNEW HIM? I TAUGHT HIM TO THROW HIS FIRST KICK.
HELL... I TAUGHT HIM PRACTICALLY EVERYTHING HE KNEW...

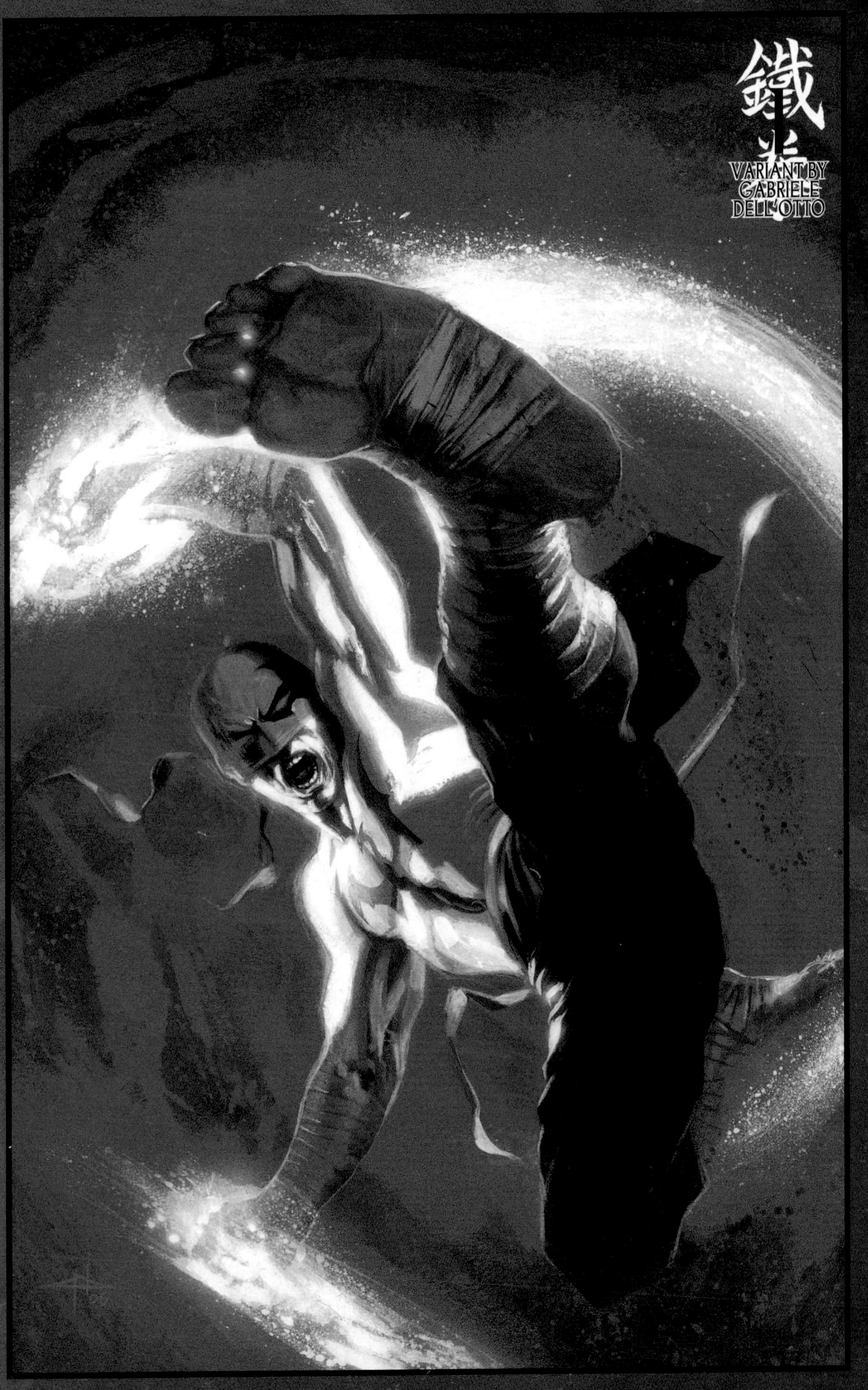

鐵拳
VARIANT BY
GABRIELE
DELL'OTTO

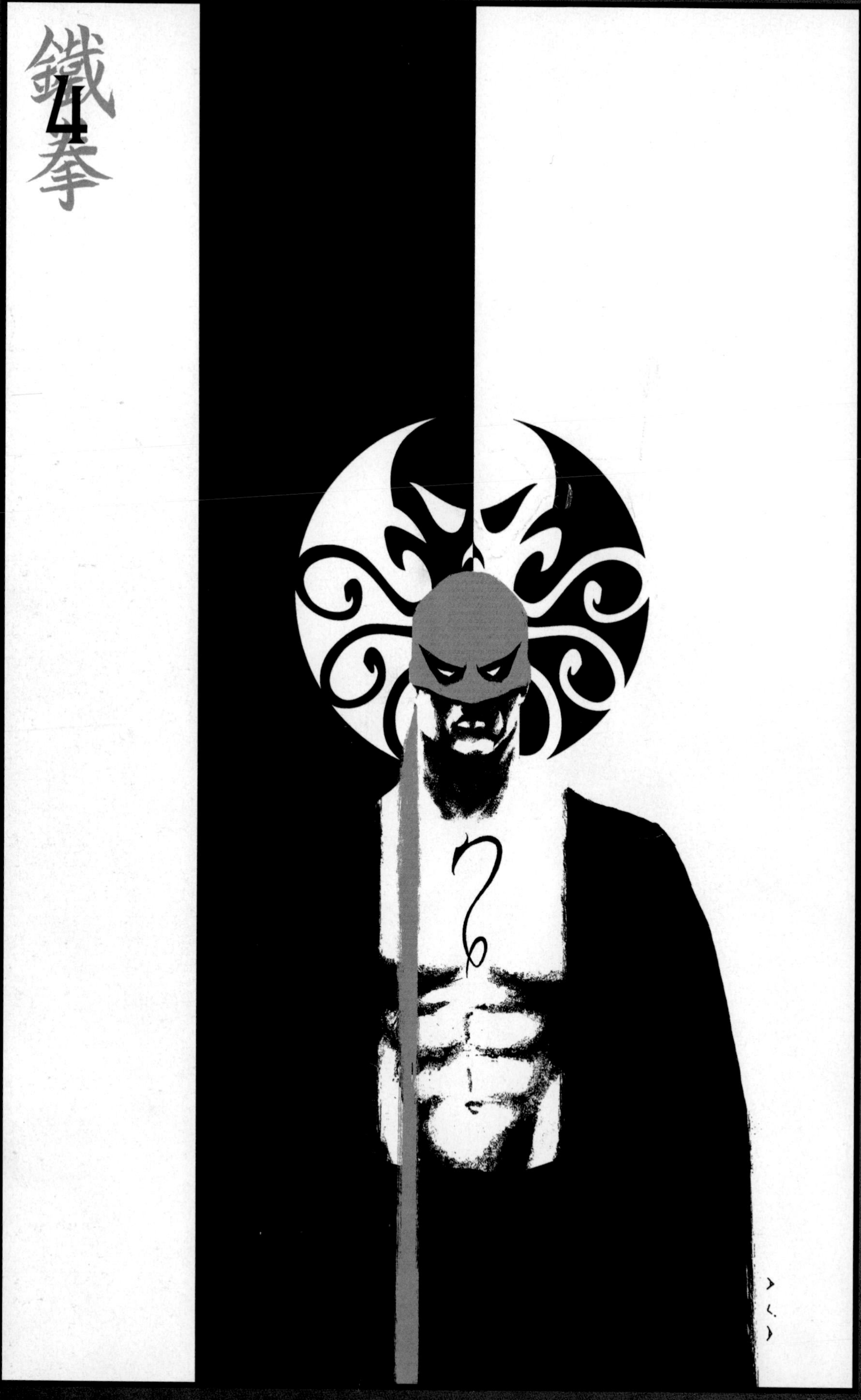
鐵拳
4

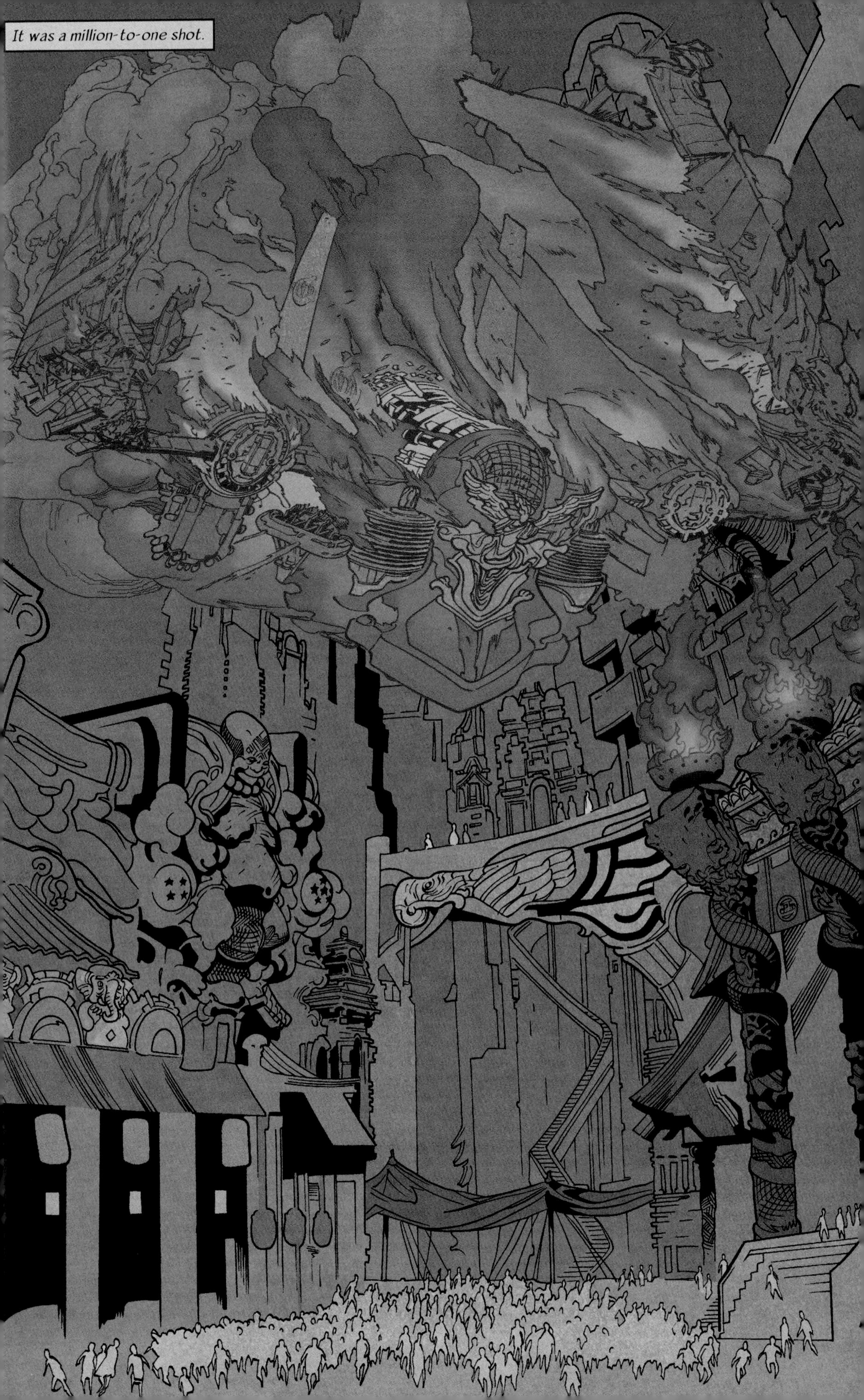
It was a million-to-one shot.

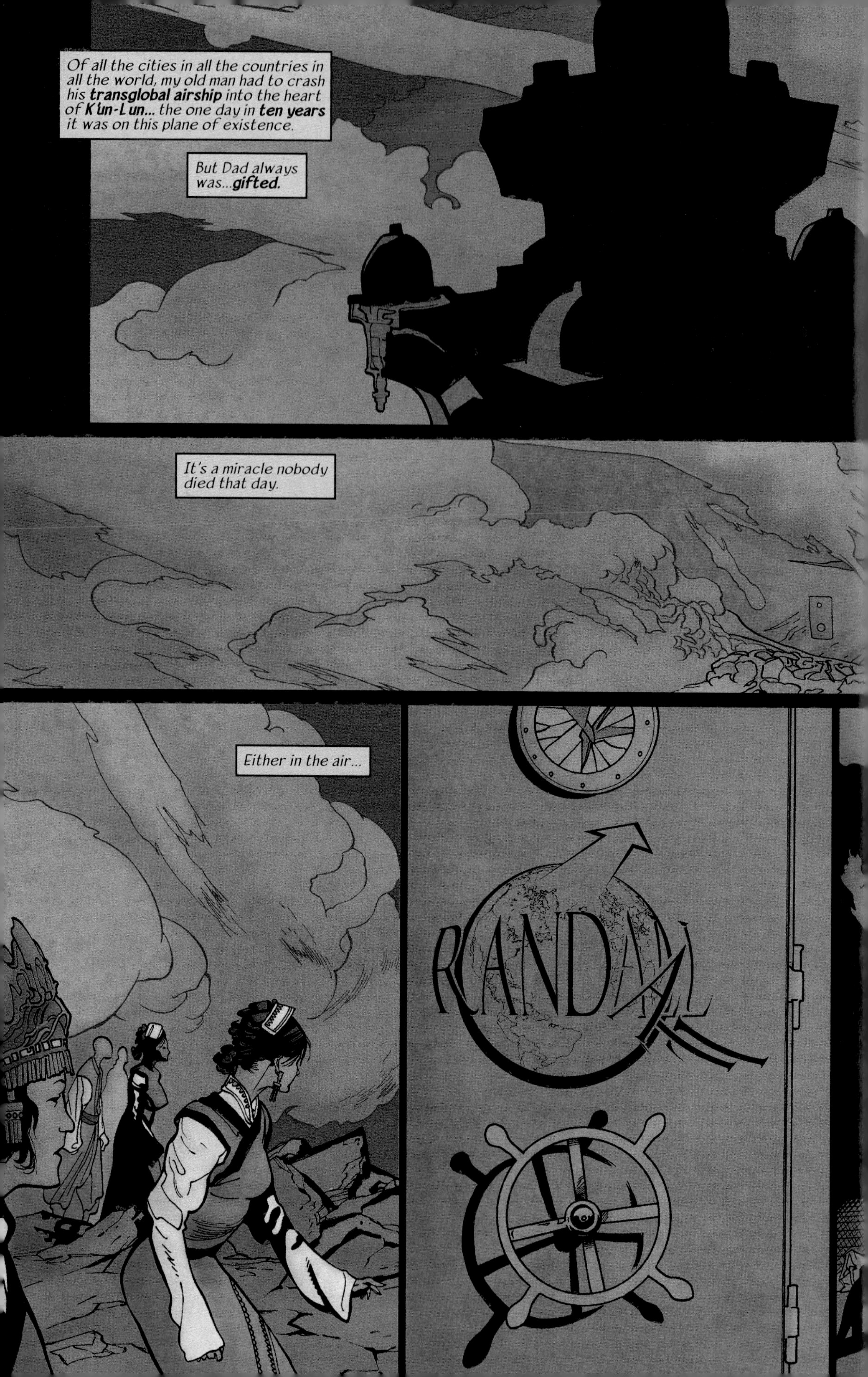
Of all the cities in all the countries in all the world, my old man had to crash his **transglobal airship** into the heart of **K'un-Lun...** the one day in **ten years** it was on this plane of existence.
But Dad always was...**gifted.**
It's a miracle nobody died that day.
Either in the air...
RANDALL

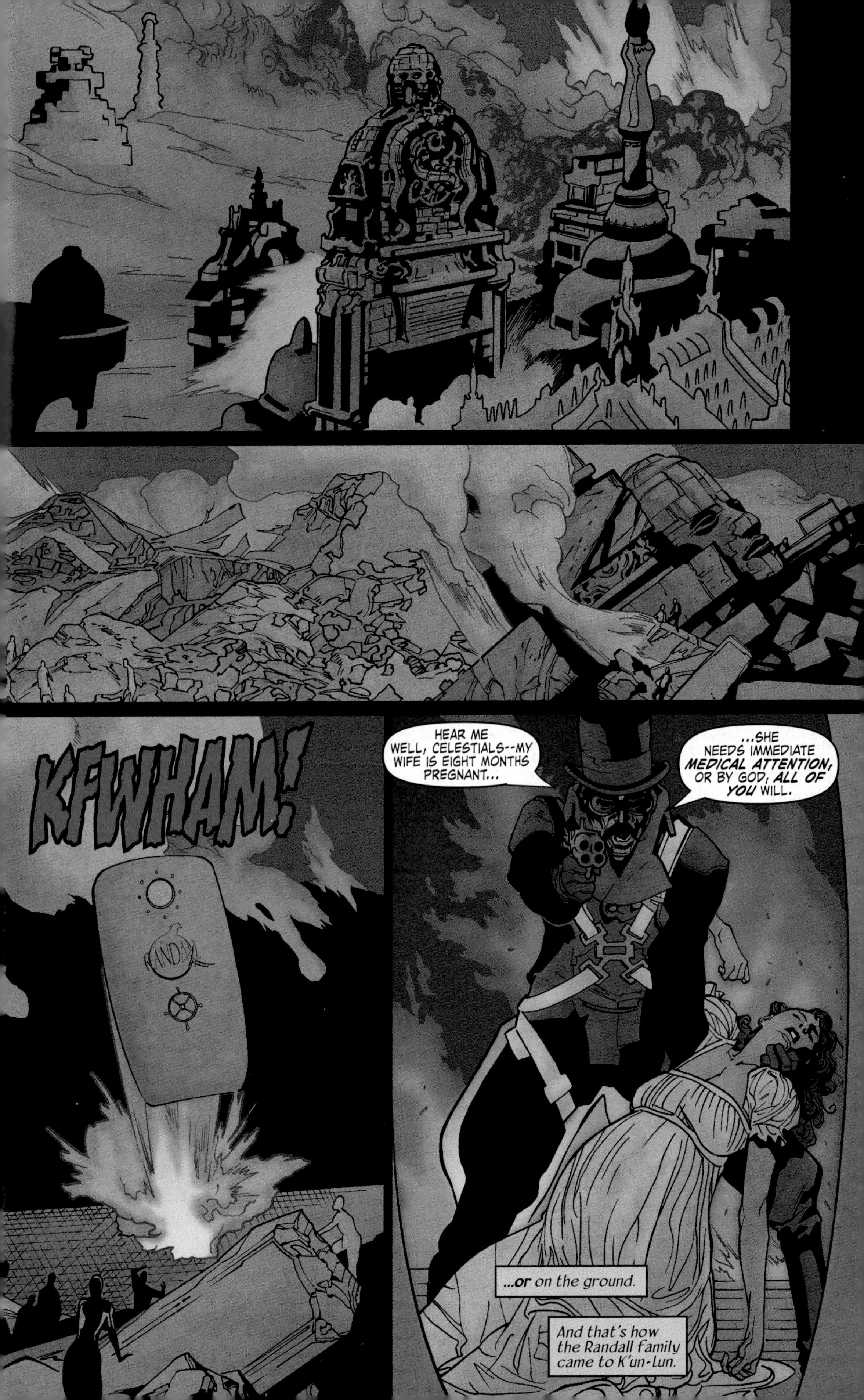
KFWHAM!
HEAR ME WELL, CELESTIALS--MY WIFE IS EIGHT MONTHS PREGNANT...
...SHE NEEDS IMMEDIATE MEDICAL ATTENTION, OR BY GOD, ALL OF YOU WILL.
...or on the ground.
And that's how the Randall family came to K'un-Lun.

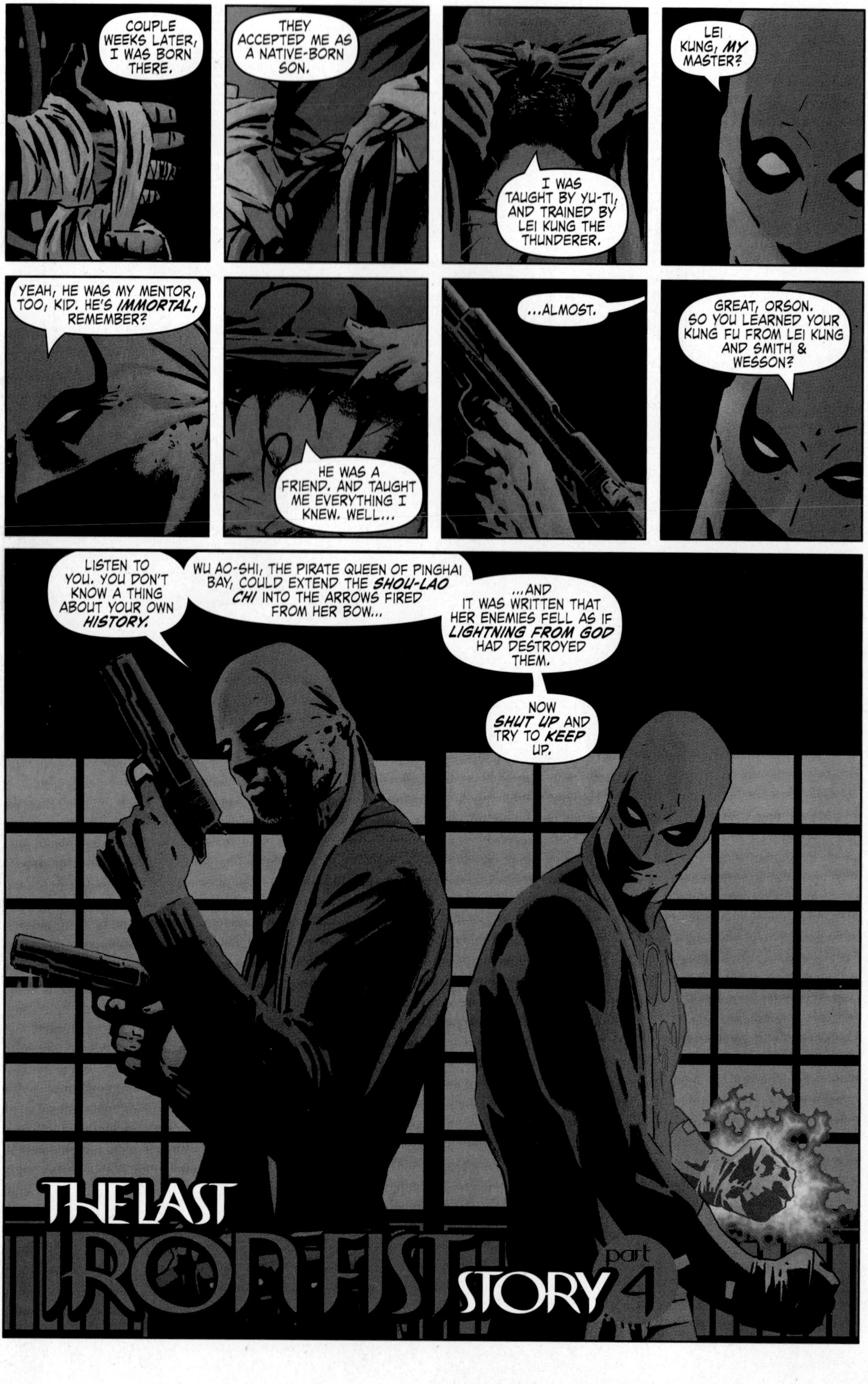
COUPLE WEEKS LATER, I WAS BORN THERE.
THEY ACCEPTED ME AS A NATIVE-BORN SON.
I WAS TAUGHT BY YU-TI, AND TRAINED BY LEI KUNG THE THUNDERER.
LEI KUNG, MY MASTER?
YEAH, HE WAS MY MENTOR, TOO, KID. HE'S IMMORTAL, REMEMBER?
HE WAS A FRIEND. AND TAUGHT ME EVERYTHING I KNEW. WELL...
...ALMOST.
GREAT, ORSON. SO YOU LEARNED YOUR KUNG FU FROM LEI KUNG AND SMITH & WESSON?
LISTEN TO YOU. YOU DON'T KNOW A THING ABOUT YOUR OWN HISTORY.
WU AO-SHI, THE PIRATE QUEEN OF PINGHAI BAY, COULD EXTEND THE SHOU-LAO CHI INTO THE ARROWS FIRED FROM HER BOW...
...AND IT WAS WRITTEN THAT HER ENEMIES FELL AS IF LIGHTNING FROM GOD HAD DESTROYED THEM.
NOW SHUT UP AND TRY TO KEEP UP.
THE LAST IRON FIST STORY part 4

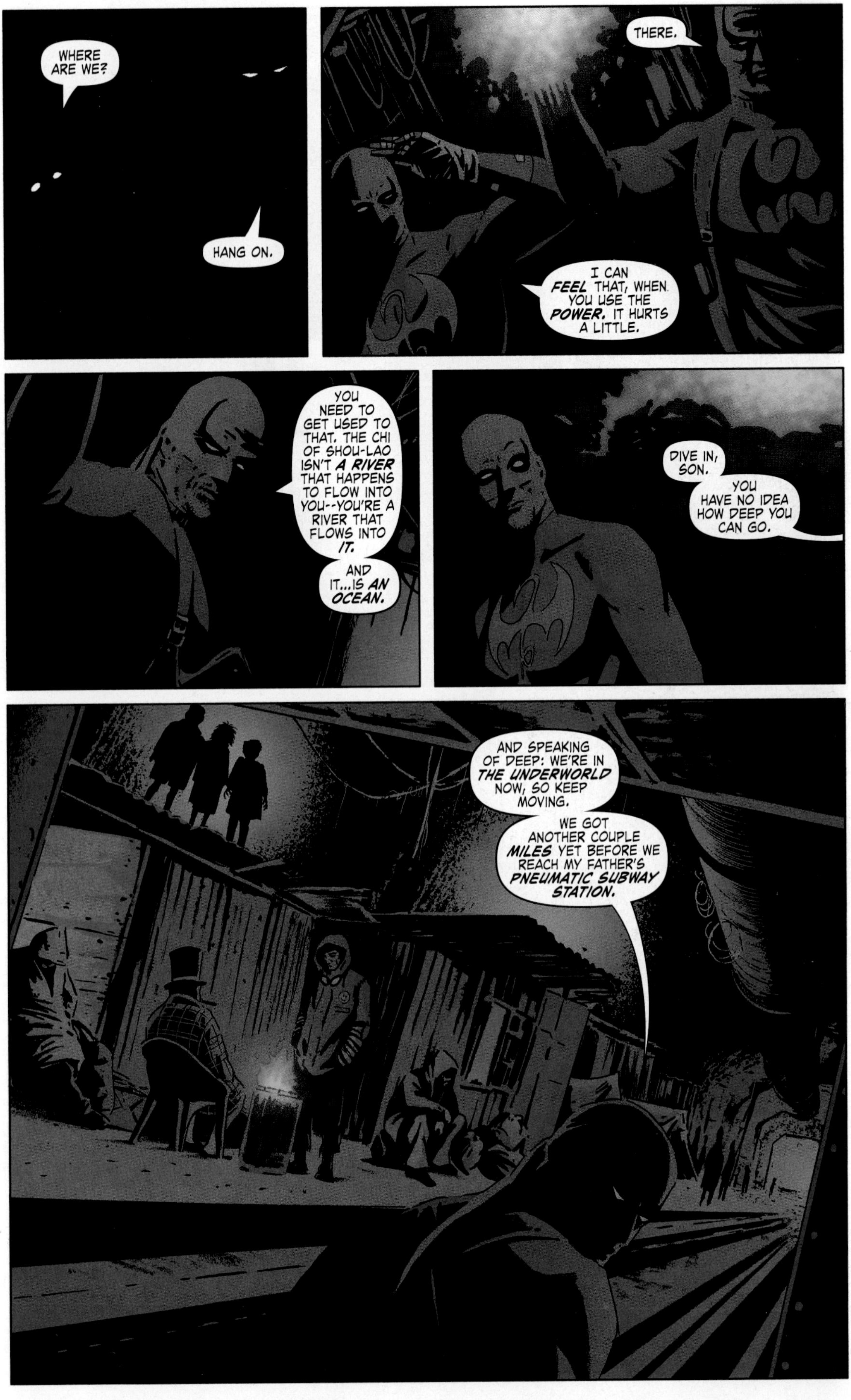
WHERE ARE WE?
HANG ON.
THERE.
I CAN FEEL THAT, WHEN YOU USE THE POWER. IT HURTS A LITTLE.
YOU NEED TO GET USED TO THAT. THE CHI OF SHOU-LAO ISN'T A RIVER THAT HAPPENS TO FLOW INTO YOU--YOU'RE A RIVER THAT FLOWS INTO IT.
AND IT...IS AN OCEAN.
DIVE IN, SON.
YOU HAVE NO IDEA HOW DEEP YOU CAN GO.
AND SPEAKING OF DEEP: WE'RE IN THE UNDERWORLD NOW, SO KEEP MOVING.
WE GOT ANOTHER COUPLE MILES YET BEFORE WE REACH MY FATHER'S PNEUMATIC SUBWAY STATION.

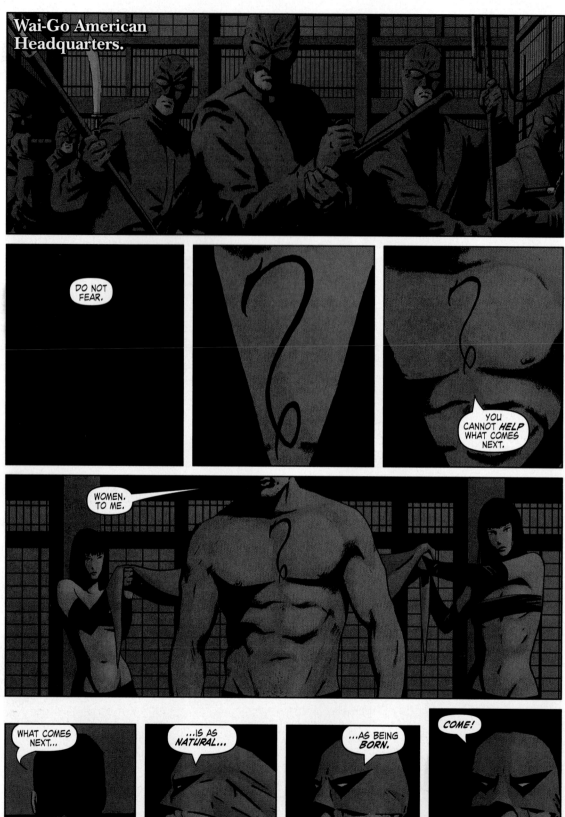

Wai-Go American Headquarters.

DO NOT FEAR.

YOU CANNOT *HELP* WHAT COMES NEXT.

WOMEN. TO ME.

WHAT COMES NEXT...

...IS AS *NATURAL*...

...AS BEING *BORN.*

COME!

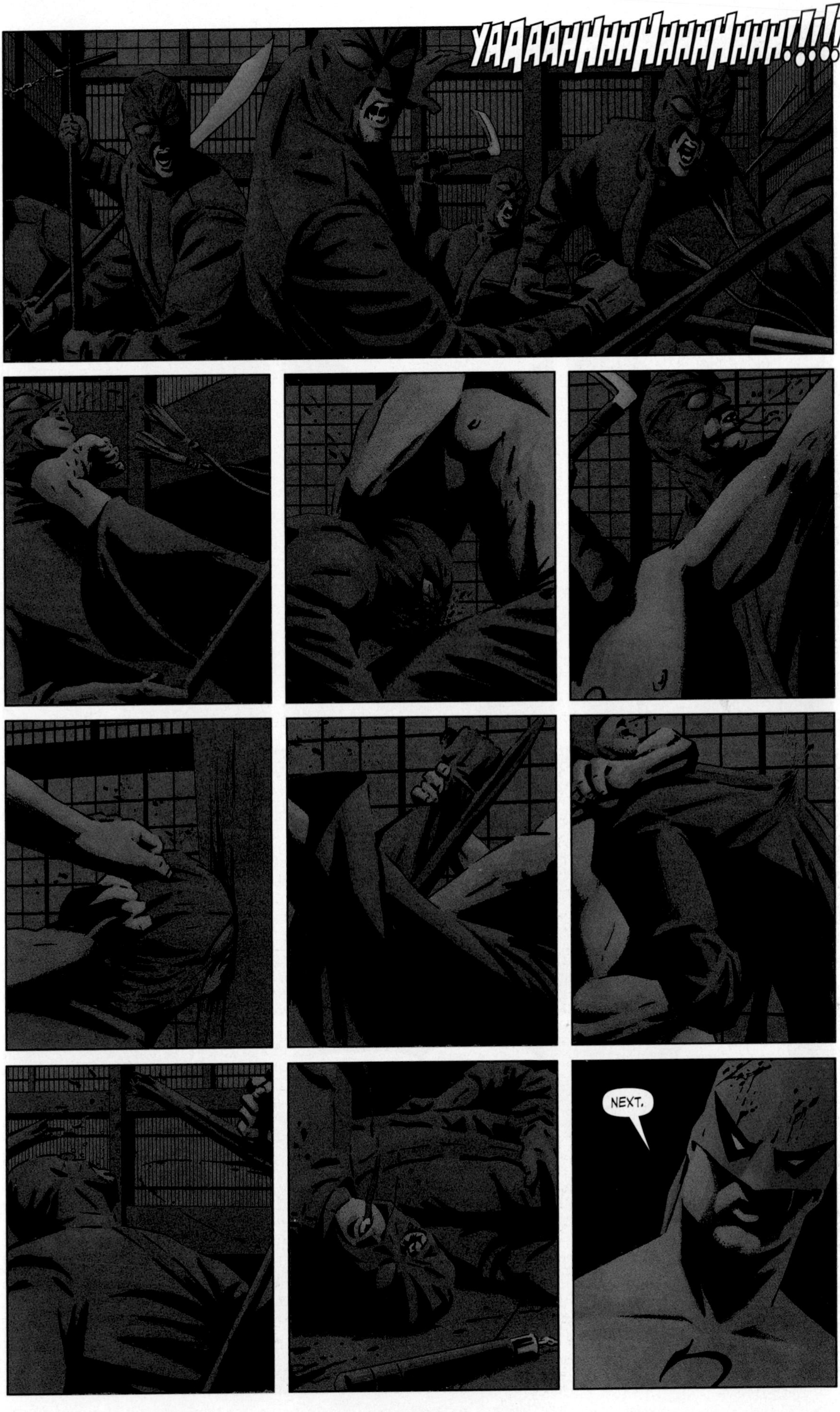
YAAAAHHHHHHHHHH!!!!
NEXT.

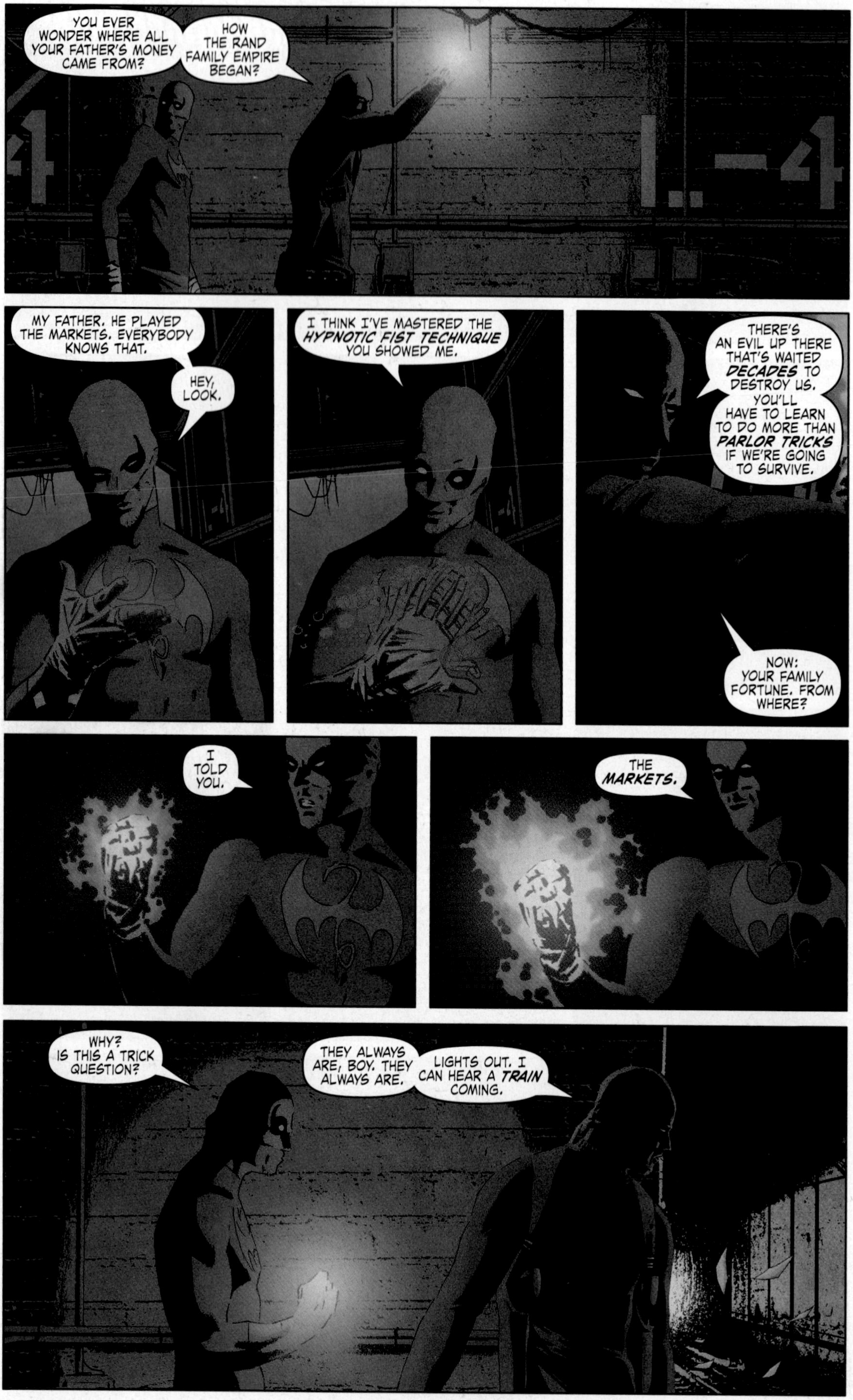
YOU EVER WONDER WHERE ALL YOUR FATHER'S MONEY CAME FROM?
HOW THE RAND FAMILY EMPIRE BEGAN?
MY FATHER. HE PLAYED THE MARKETS. EVERYBODY KNOWS THAT.
HEY, LOOK.
I THINK I'VE MASTERED THE HYPNOTIC FIST TECHNIQUE YOU SHOWED ME.
THERE'S AN EVIL UP THERE THAT'S WAITED DECADES TO DESTROY US. YOU'LL HAVE TO LEARN TO DO MORE THAN PARLOR TRICKS IF WE'RE GOING TO SURVIVE.
NOW: YOUR FAMILY FORTUNE. FROM WHERE?
I TOLD YOU.
THE MARKETS.
WHY? IS THIS A TRICK QUESTION?
THEY ALWAYS ARE, BOY. THEY ALWAYS ARE.
LIGHTS OUT. I CAN HEAR A TRAIN COMING.

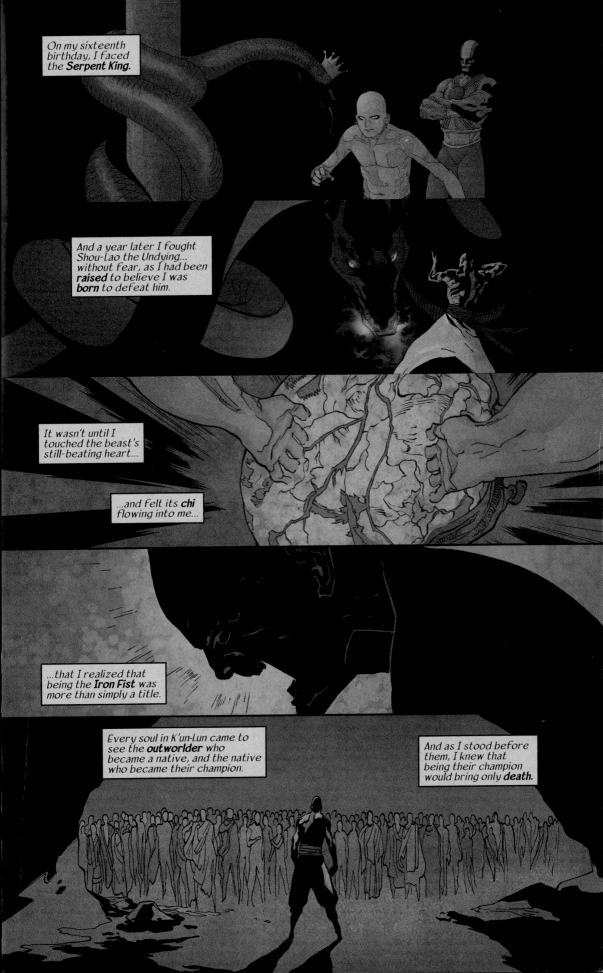

On my sixteenth birthday, I faced the **Serpent King.**

And a year later I fought Shou-Lao the Undying... without fear, as I had been **raised** to believe I was **born** to defeat him.

It wasn't until I touched the beast's still-beating heart...

...and felt its **chi** flowing into me...

...that I realized that being the **Iron Fist** was more than simply a title.

Every soul in K'un-Lun came to see the **outworlder** who became a native, and the native who became their champion.

And as I stood before them, I knew that being their champion would bring only **death.**

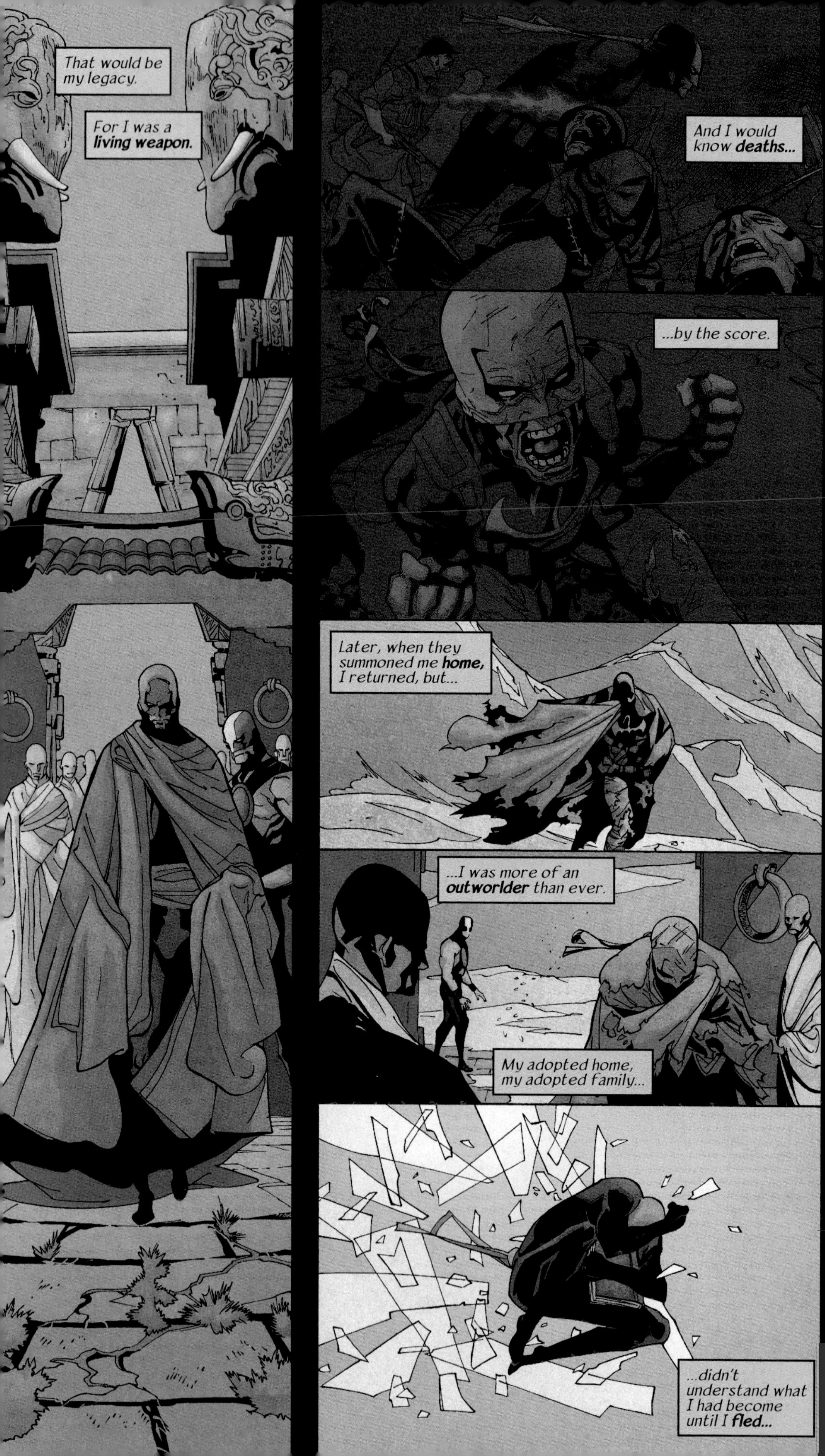
That would be my legacy.
For I was a **living weapon.**
And I would know **deaths...**
...by the score.
Later, when they summoned me **home,** I returned, but...
...I was more of an **outworlder** than ever.
My adopted home, my adopted family...
...didn't understand what I had become until I **fled...**

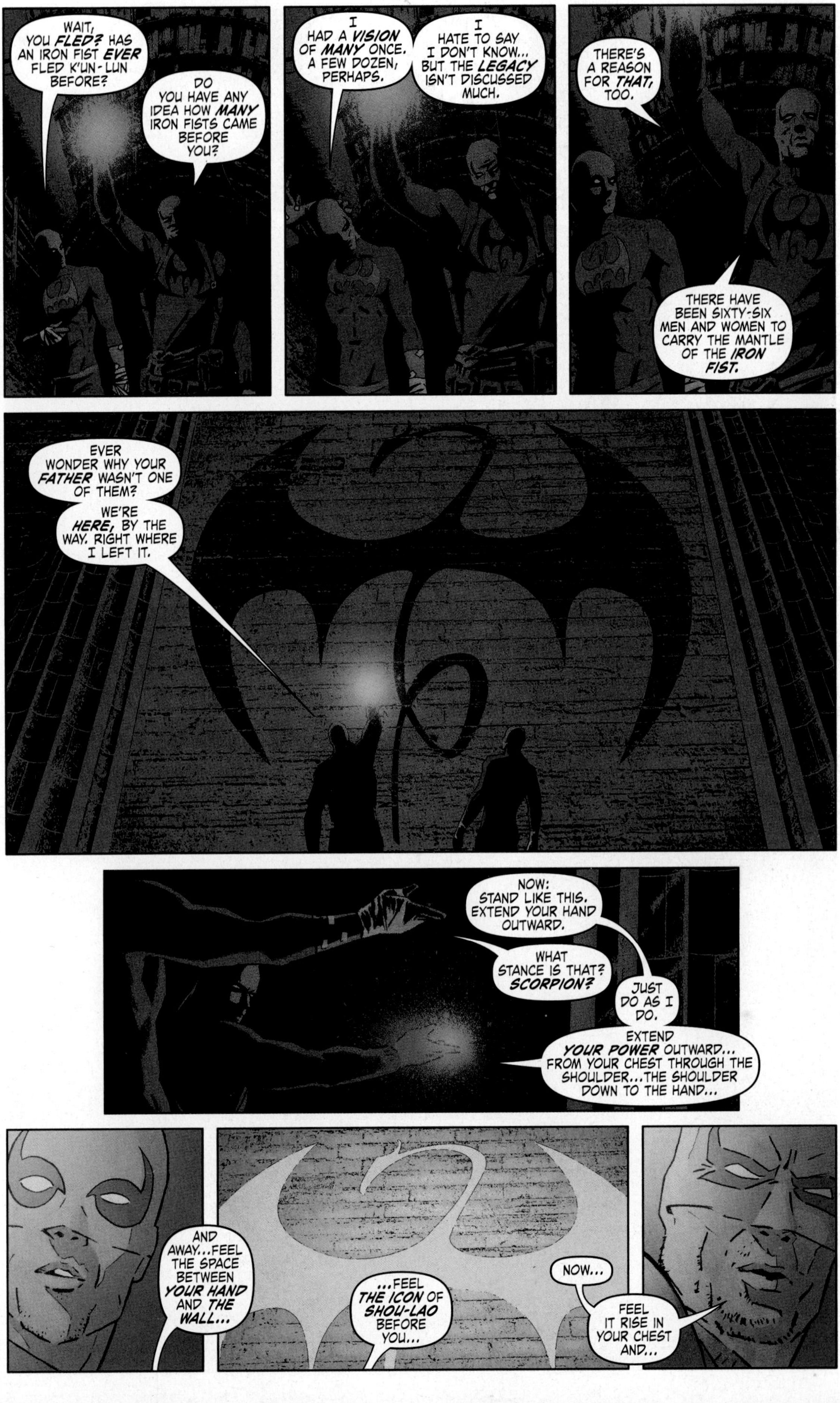
WAIT, YOU *FLED?* HAS AN IRON FIST *EVER* FLED K'UN-LUN BEFORE?
DO YOU HAVE ANY IDEA HOW *MANY* IRON FISTS CAME BEFORE YOU?
I HAD A *VISION* OF *MANY* ONCE. A FEW DOZEN, PERHAPS.
I HATE TO SAY I DON'T KNOW... BUT THE *LEGACY* ISN'T DISCUSSED MUCH.
THERE'S A REASON FOR *THAT,* TOO.
THERE HAVE BEEN SIXTY-SIX MEN AND WOMEN TO CARRY THE MANTLE OF THE *IRON FIST.*
EVER WONDER WHY YOUR *FATHER* WASN'T ONE OF THEM?
WE'RE *HERE,* BY THE WAY. RIGHT WHERE I LEFT IT.
NOW: STAND LIKE THIS. EXTEND YOUR HAND OUTWARD.
WHAT STANCE IS THAT? *SCORPION?*
JUST DO AS I DO.
EXTEND *YOUR POWER* OUTWARD... FROM YOUR CHEST THROUGH THE SHOULDER...THE SHOULDER DOWN TO THE HAND...
AND AWAY...FEEL THE SPACE BETWEEN *YOUR HAND* AND *THE WALL...*
...FEEL THE ICON OF SHOU-LAO BEFORE YOU...
NOW...
FEEL IT RISE IN YOUR CHEST AND...

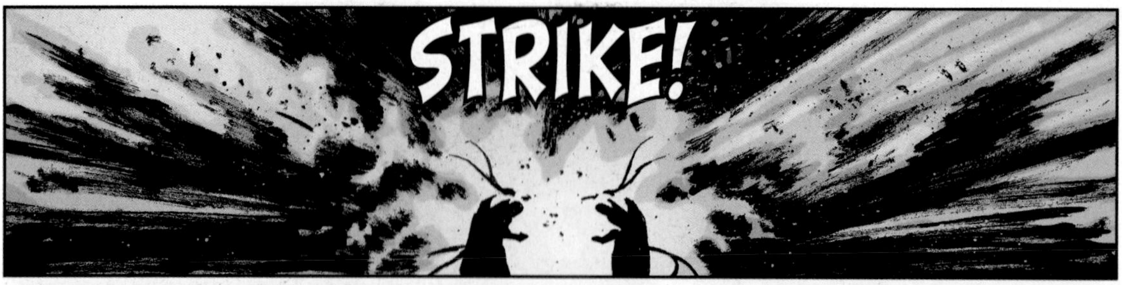
STRIKE!

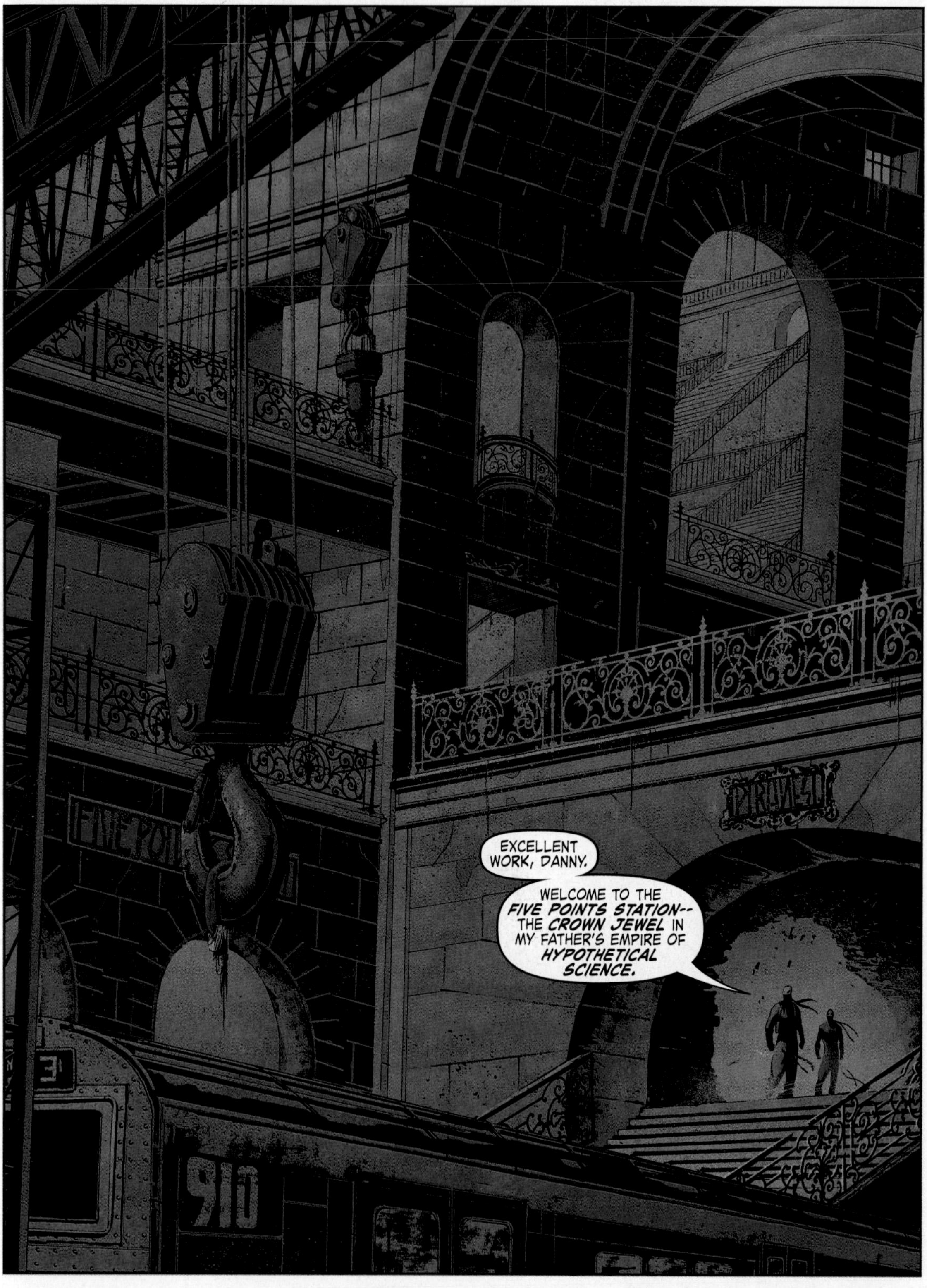
EXCELLENT WORK, DANNY.
WELCOME TO THE *FIVE POINTS STATION*-- THE *CROWN JEWEL* IN MY FATHER'S EMPIRE OF *HYPOTHETICAL SCIENCE.*
910

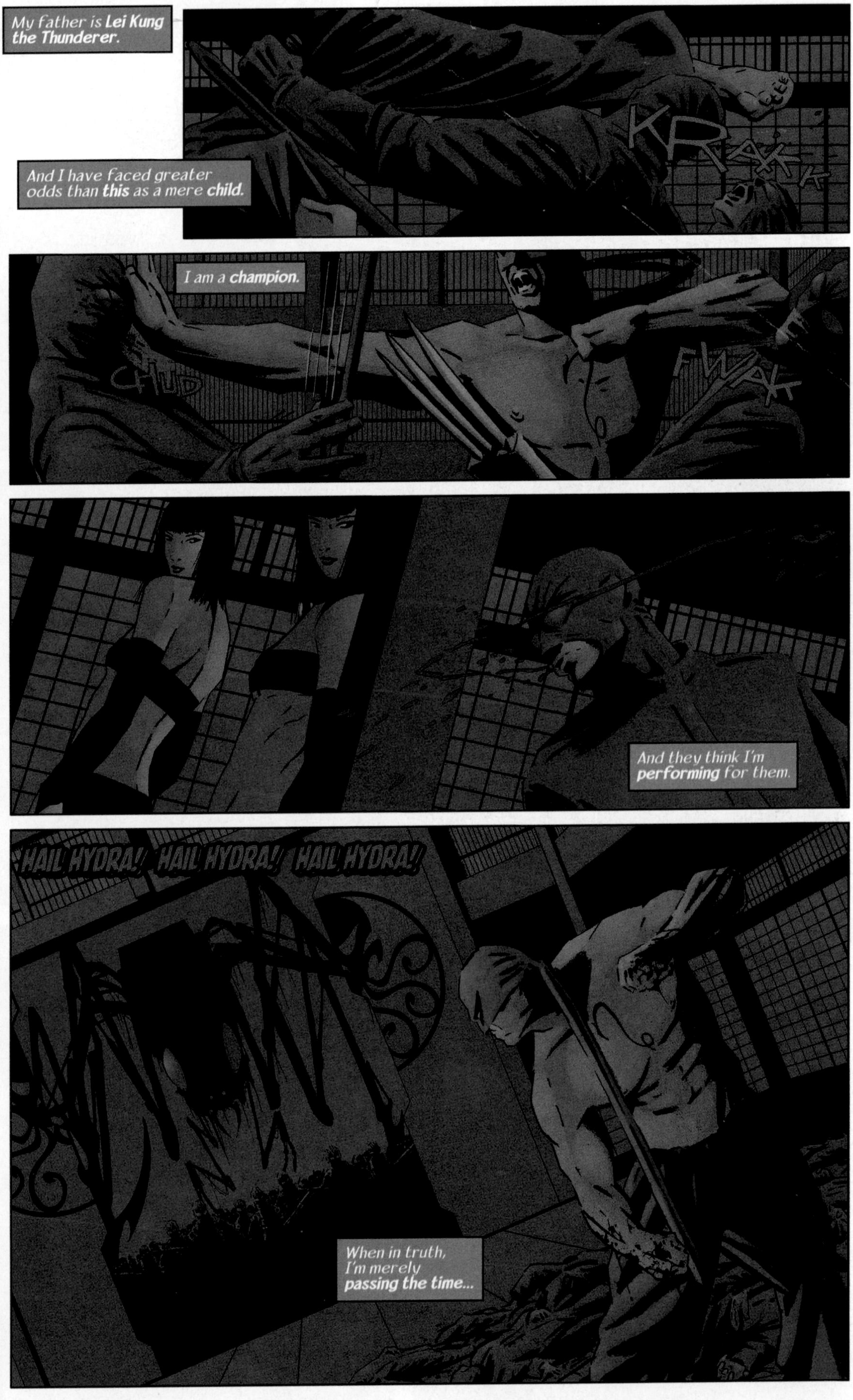
My father is **Lei Kung the Thunderer**.
KRAKK
And I have faced greater odds than **this** as a mere **child**.
I am a **champion**.
CHUD
FWAK
And they think I'm **performing** for them.
HAIL HYDRA! HAIL HYDRA! HAIL HYDRA!
When in truth, I'm merely **passing the time...**

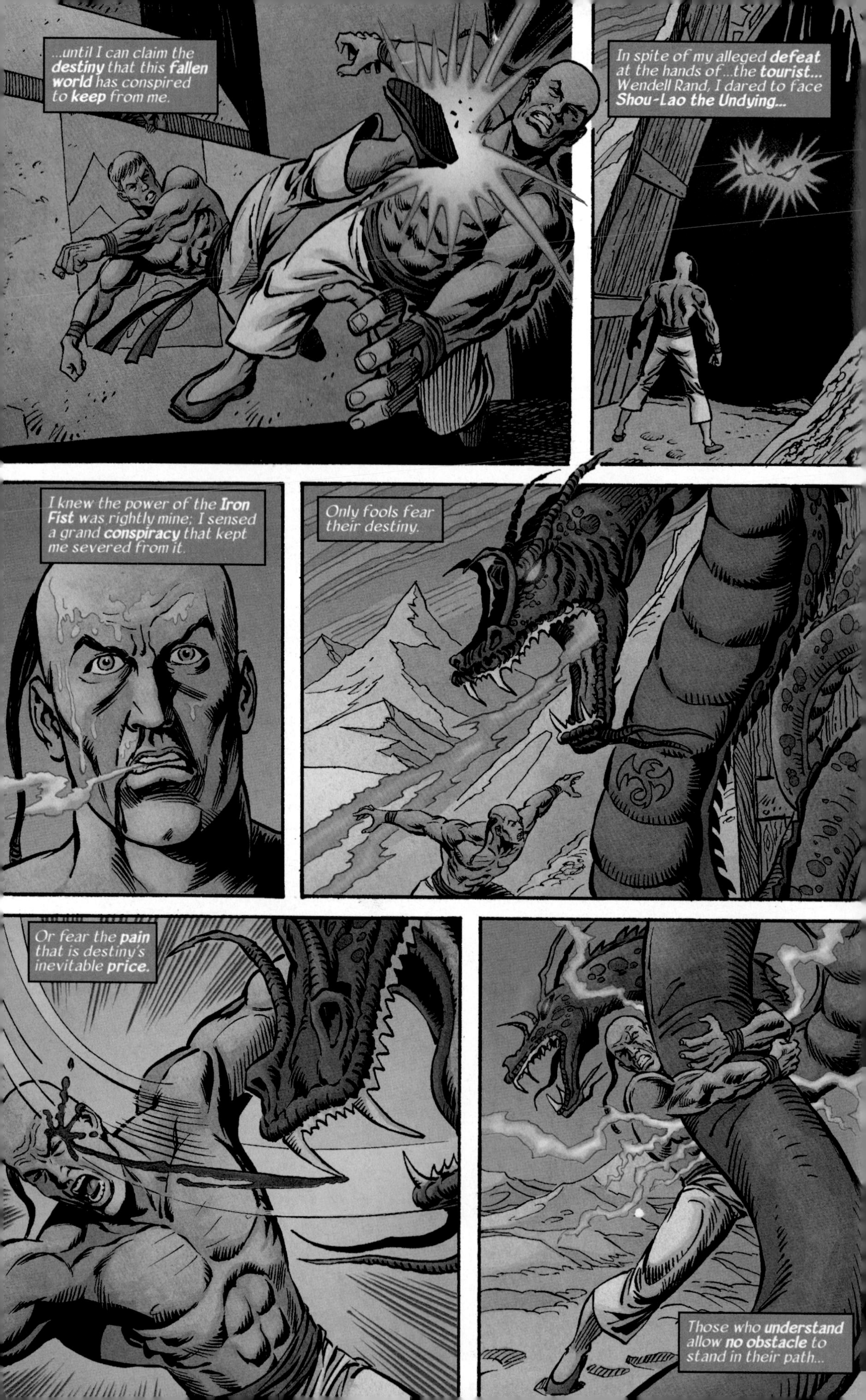

...until I can claim the destiny that this fallen world has conspired to keep from me.
In spite of my alleged defeat at the hands of...the tourist... Wendell Rand, I dared to face Shou-Lao the Undying...
I knew the power of the Iron Fist was rightly mine; I sensed a grand conspiracy that kept me severed from it.
Only fools fear their destiny.
Or fear the pain that is destiny's inevitable price.
Those who understand allow no obstacle to stand in their path...

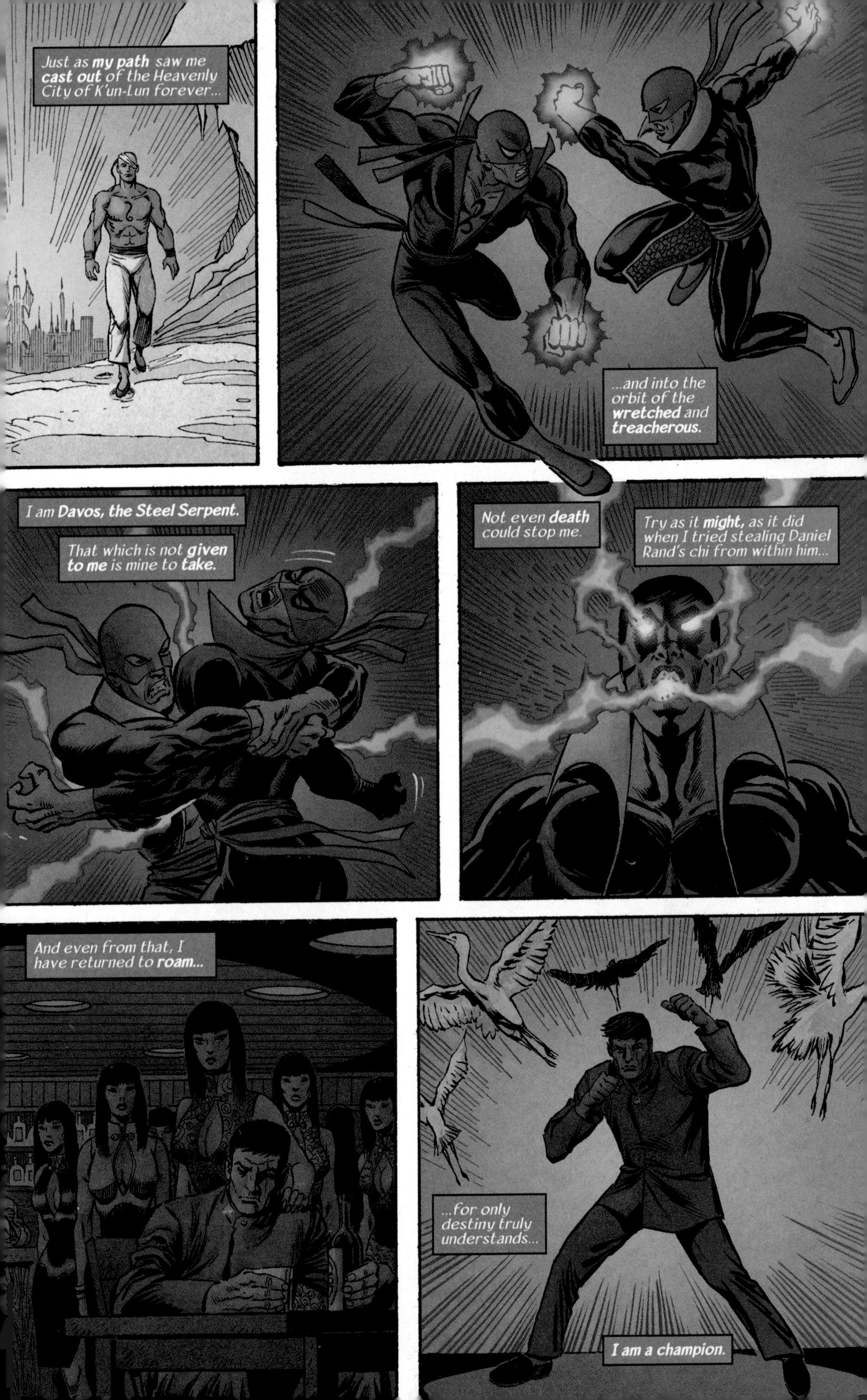
Just as **my path** saw me **cast out** of the Heavenly City of K'un-Lun forever...
...and into the orbit of the **wretched** and **treacherous.**
I am **Davos, the Steel Serpent.**
That which is not **given to me** is mine to **take.**
Not even **death** could stop me.
Try as it **might,** as it did when I tried stealing Daniel Rand's chi from within him...
And even from that, I have returned to **roam...**
...for only destiny truly understands...
I am a champion.

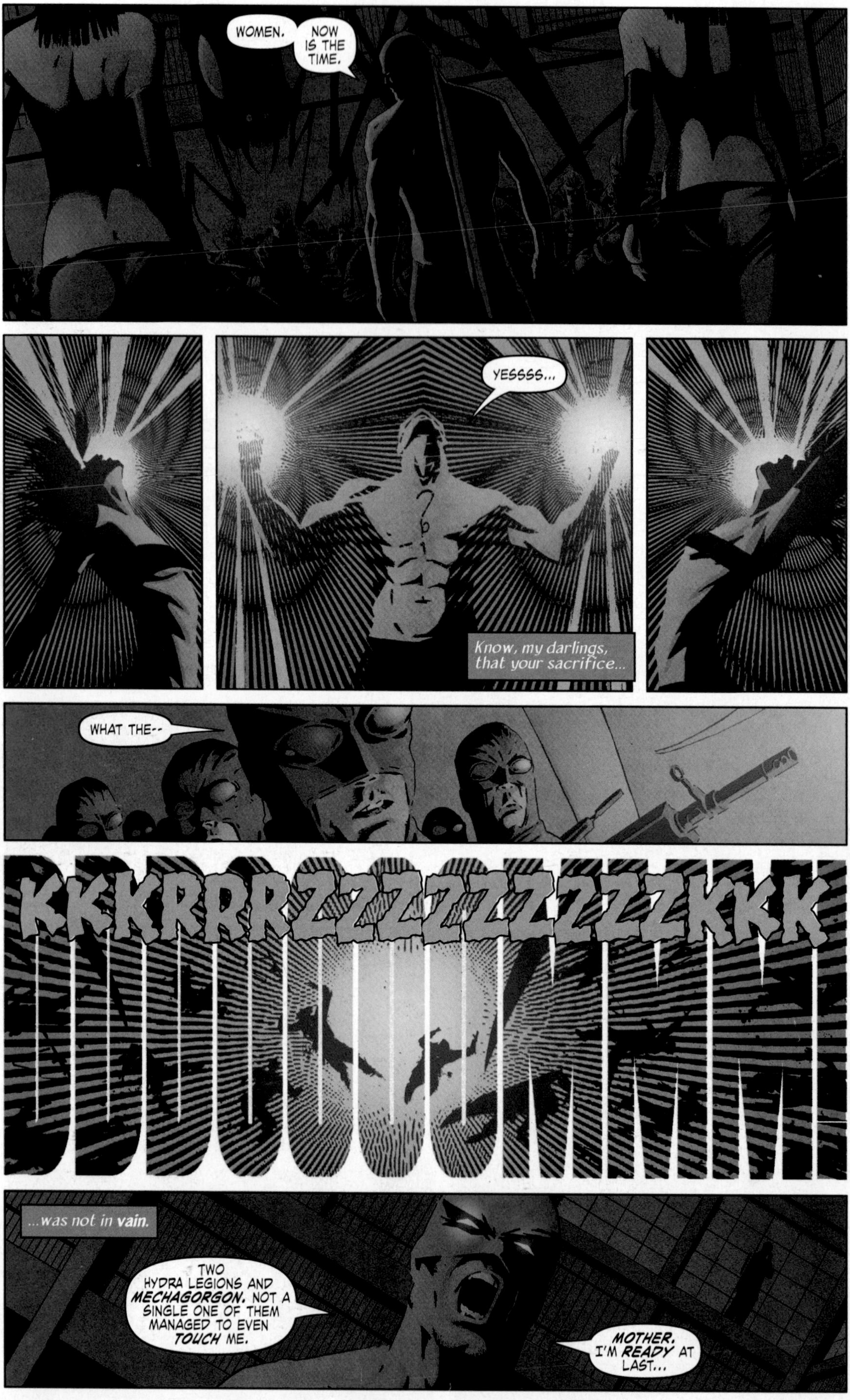
WOMEN.
NOW IS THE TIME.
YESSSS...
Know, my darlings, that your sacrifice...
WHAT THE--
KKKRRRZZZZZZZZZKKK
DDDOOOOOMMMM
...was not in vain.
TWO HYDRA LEGIONS AND MECHAGORGON. NOT A SINGLE ONE OF THEM MANAGED TO EVEN TOUCH ME.
MOTHER. I'M READY AT LAST...

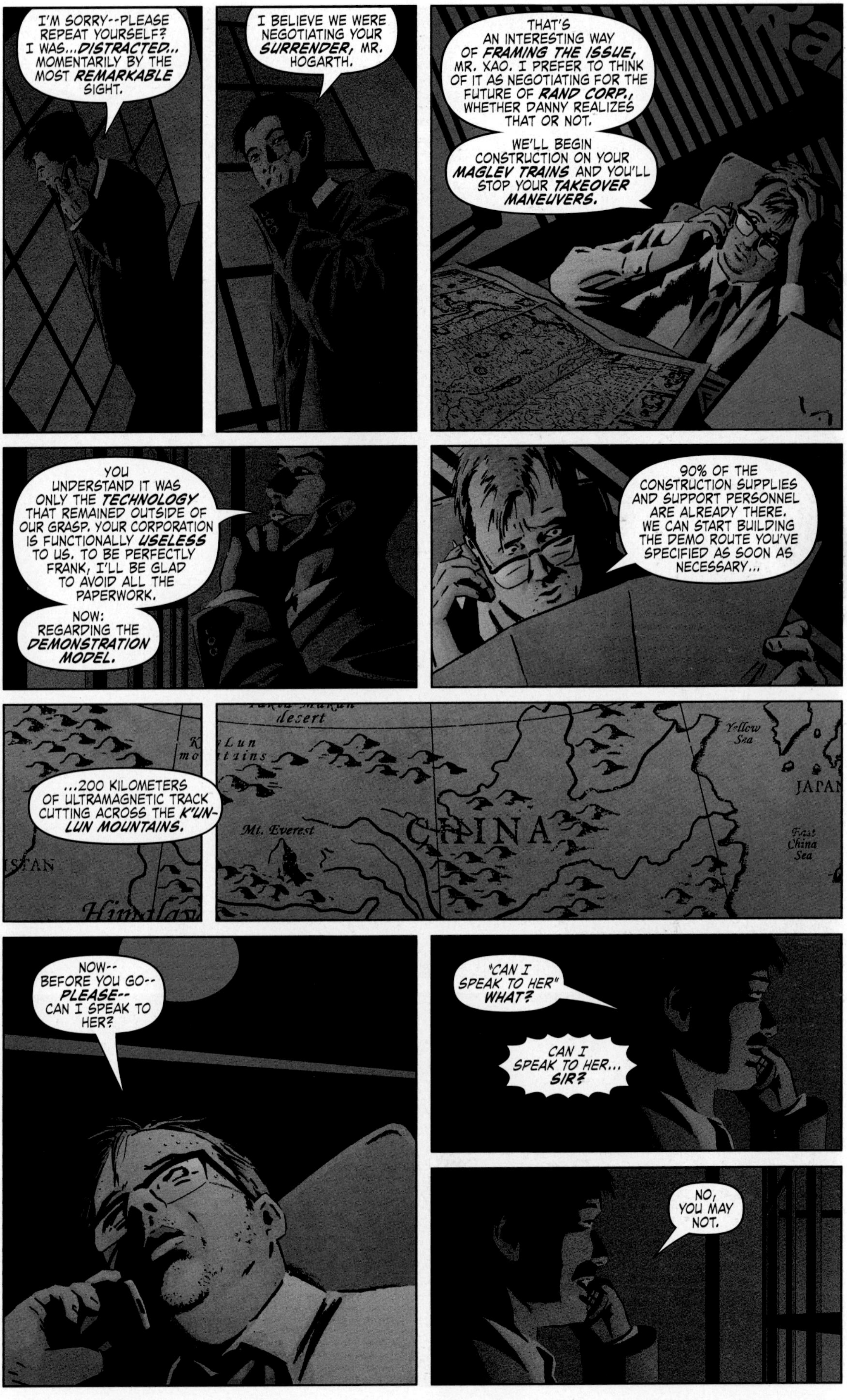
I'M SORRY--PLEASE REPEAT YOURSELF? I WAS...DISTRACTED... MOMENTARILY BY THE MOST REMARKABLE SIGHT.
I BELIEVE WE WERE NEGOTIATING YOUR SURRENDER, MR. HOGARTH.
THAT'S AN INTERESTING WAY OF FRAMING THE ISSUE, MR. XAO. I PREFER TO THINK OF IT AS NEGOTIATING FOR THE FUTURE OF RAND CORP., WHETHER DANNY REALIZES THAT OR NOT.
WE'LL BEGIN CONSTRUCTION ON YOUR MAGLEV TRAINS AND YOU'LL STOP YOUR TAKEOVER MANEUVERS.
YOU UNDERSTAND IT WAS ONLY THE TECHNOLOGY THAT REMAINED OUTSIDE OF OUR GRASP. YOUR CORPORATION IS FUNCTIONALLY USELESS TO US. TO BE PERFECTLY FRANK, I'LL BE GLAD TO AVOID ALL THE PAPERWORK.
NOW: REGARDING THE DEMONSTRATION MODEL.
90% OF THE CONSTRUCTION SUPPLIES AND SUPPORT PERSONNEL ARE ALREADY THERE. WE CAN START BUILDING THE DEMO ROUTE YOU'VE SPECIFIED AS SOON AS NECESSARY...
...200 KILOMETERS OF ULTRAMAGNETIC TRACK CUTTING ACROSS THE K'UN-LUN MOUNTAINS.
Mt. Everest
CHINA
Yellow Sea
JAPA
East China Sea
NOW--BEFORE YOU GO--PLEASE--CAN I SPEAK TO HER?
"CAN I SPEAK TO HER" WHAT?
CAN I SPEAK TO HER... SIR?
NO, YOU MAY NOT.

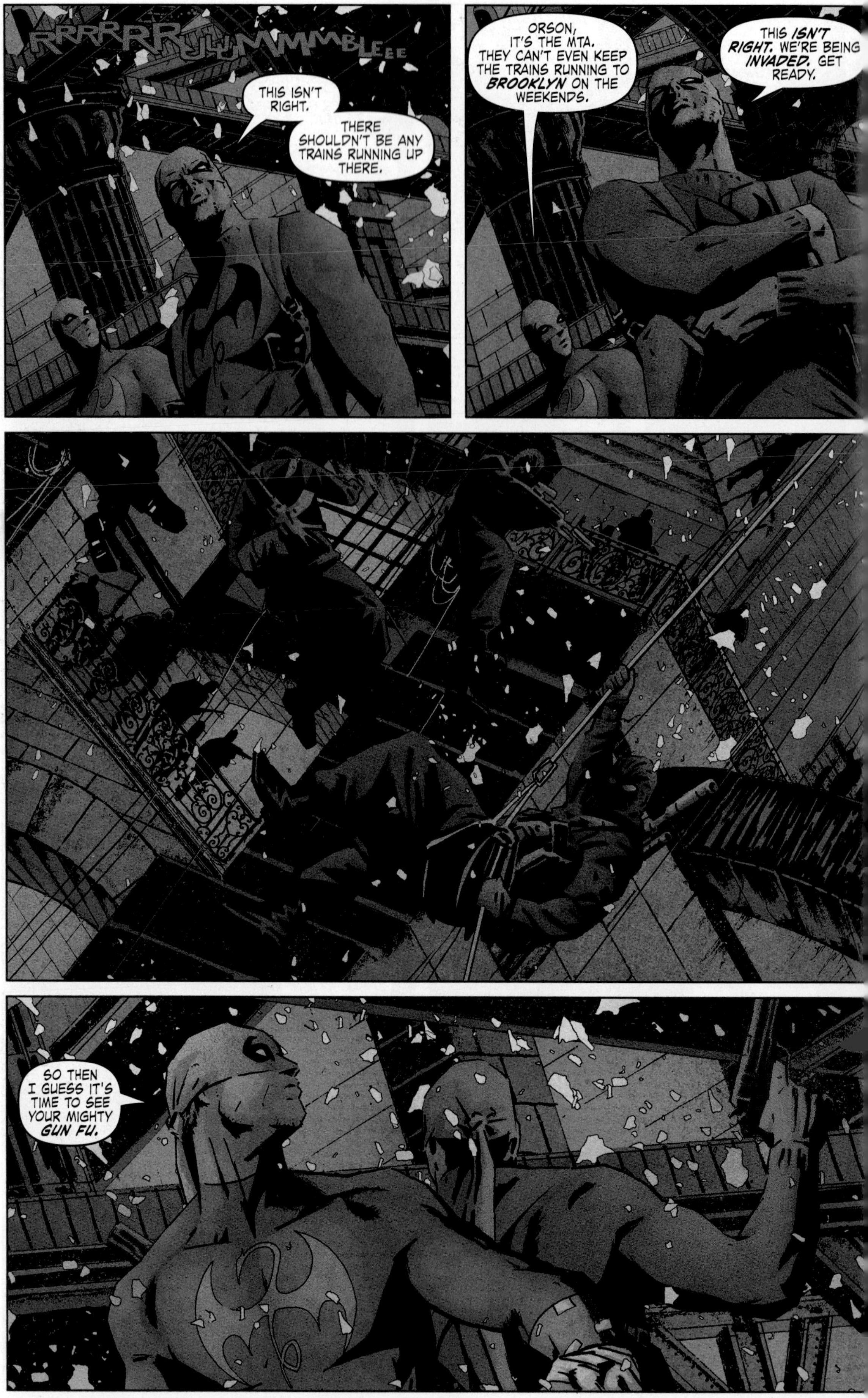
RRRRRRRUUUMMMMBLEEE
THIS ISN'T RIGHT.
THERE SHOULDN'T BE ANY TRAINS RUNNING UP THERE.
ORSON, IT'S THE MTA. THEY CAN'T EVEN KEEP THE TRAINS RUNNING TO *BROOKLYN* ON THE WEEKENDS.
THIS *ISN'T RIGHT.* WE'RE BEING *INVADED.* GET READY.
SO THEN I GUESS IT'S TIME TO SEE YOUR MIGHTY *GUN FU.*

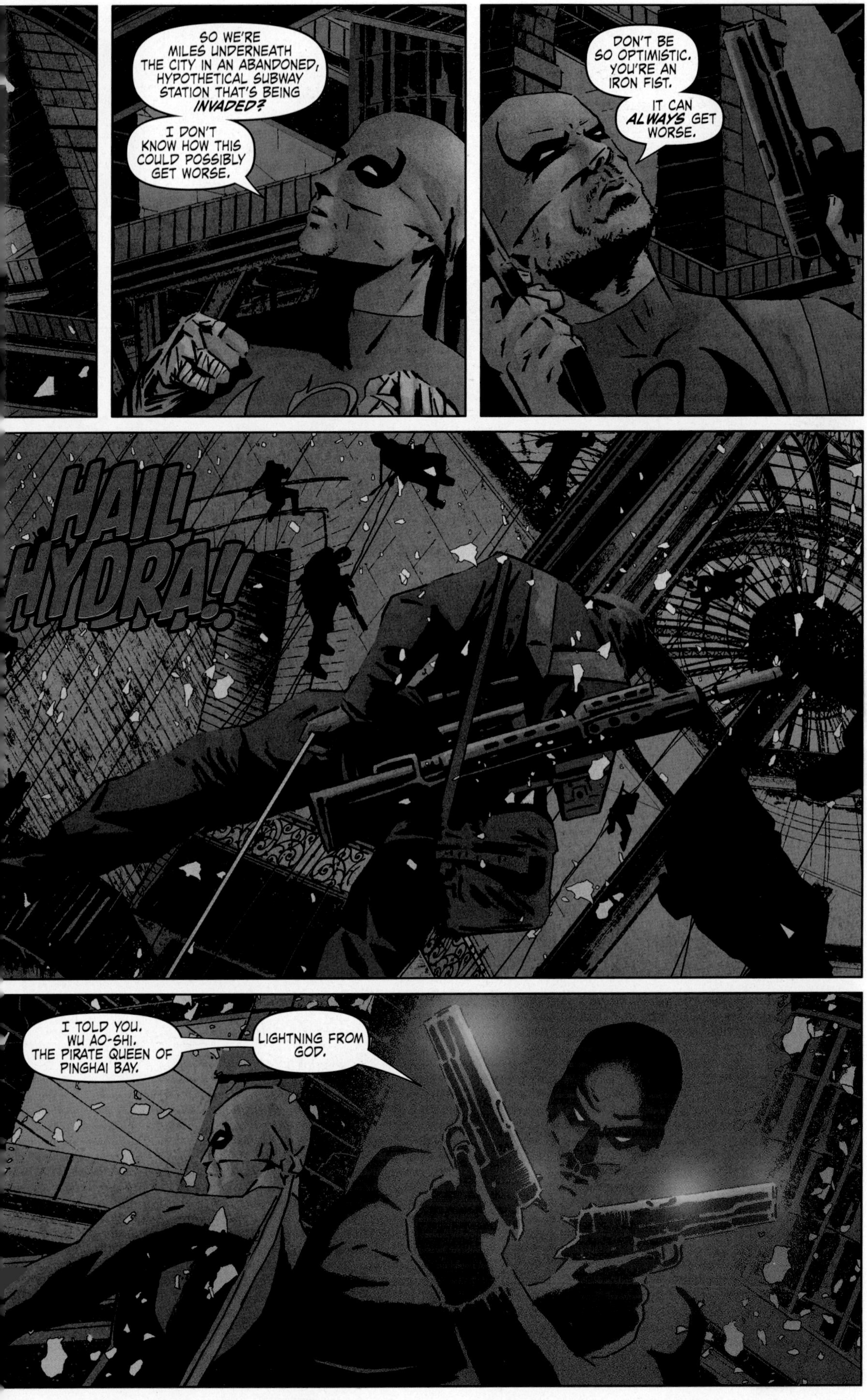
SO WE'RE MILES UNDERNEATH THE CITY IN AN ABANDONED, HYPOTHETICAL SUBWAY STATION THAT'S BEING *INVADED?*
I DON'T KNOW HOW THIS COULD POSSIBLY GET WORSE.
DON'T BE SO OPTIMISTIC. YOU'RE AN IRON FIST.
IT CAN *ALWAYS* GET WORSE.
HAIL HYDRA!!
I TOLD YOU. WU AO-SHI. THE PIRATE QUEEN OF PINGHAI BAY.
LIGHTNING FROM GOD.

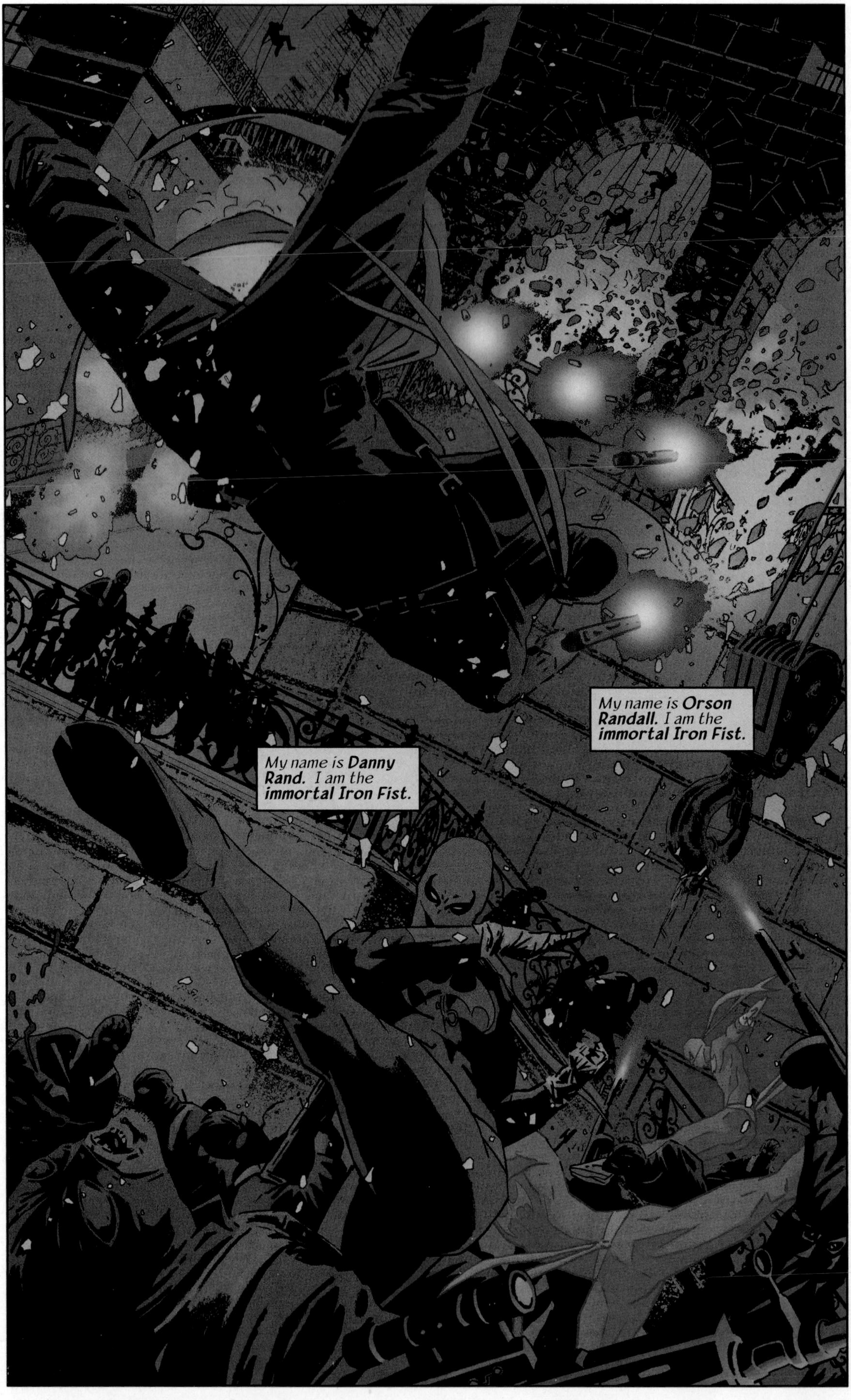
My name is Danny Rand. I am the immortal Iron Fist.
My name is Orson Randall. I am the immortal Iron Fist.

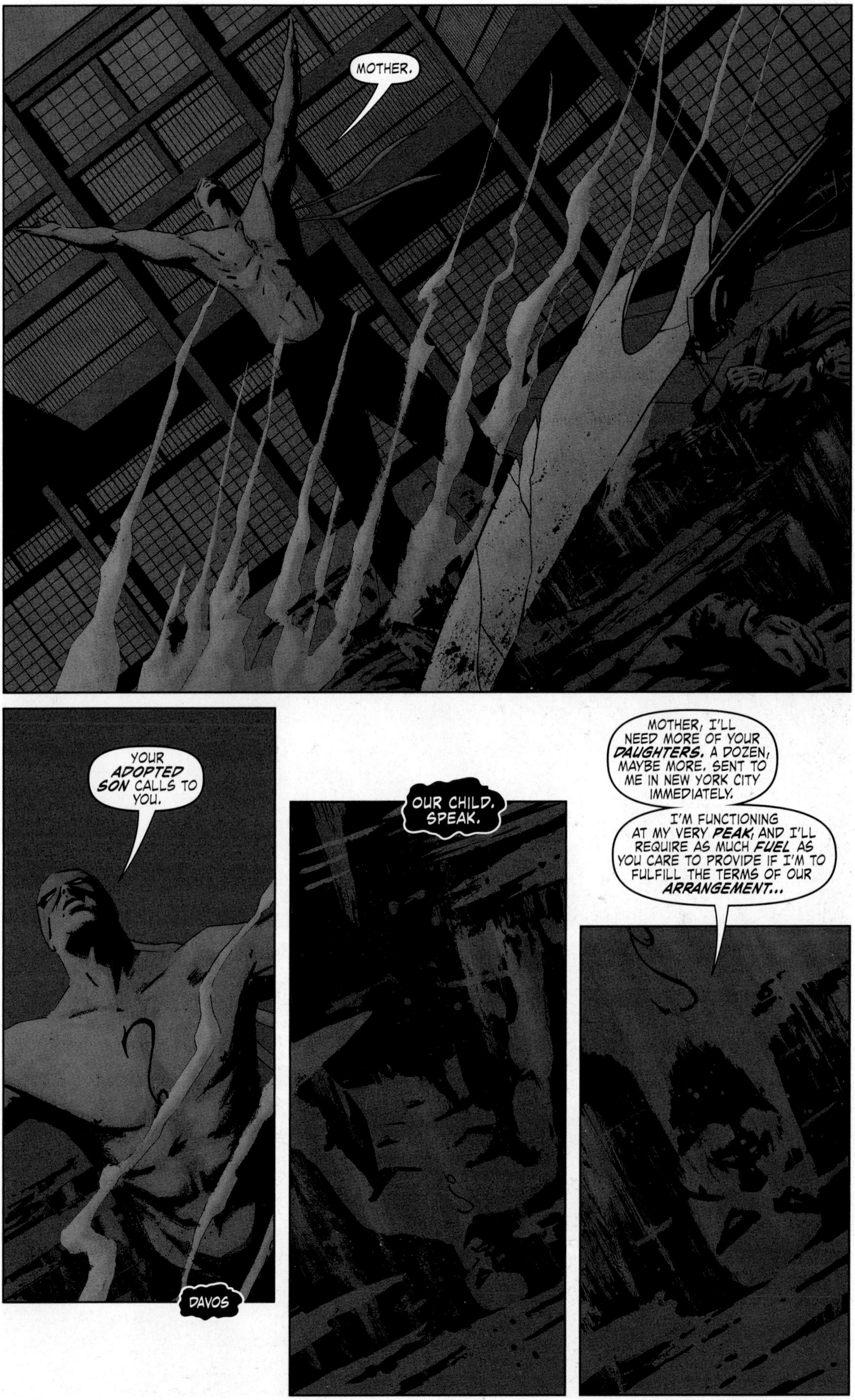
MOTHER.
YOUR ADOPTED SON CALLS TO YOU.
DAVOS
OUR CHILD. SPEAK.
MOTHER, I'LL NEED MORE OF YOUR DAUGHTERS. A DOZEN, MAYBE MORE. SENT TO ME IN NEW YORK CITY IMMEDIATELY.
I'M FUNCTIONING AT MY VERY PEAK, AND I'LL REQUIRE AS MUCH FUEL AS YOU CARE TO PROVIDE IF I'M TO FULFILL THE TERMS OF OUR ARRANGEMENT...

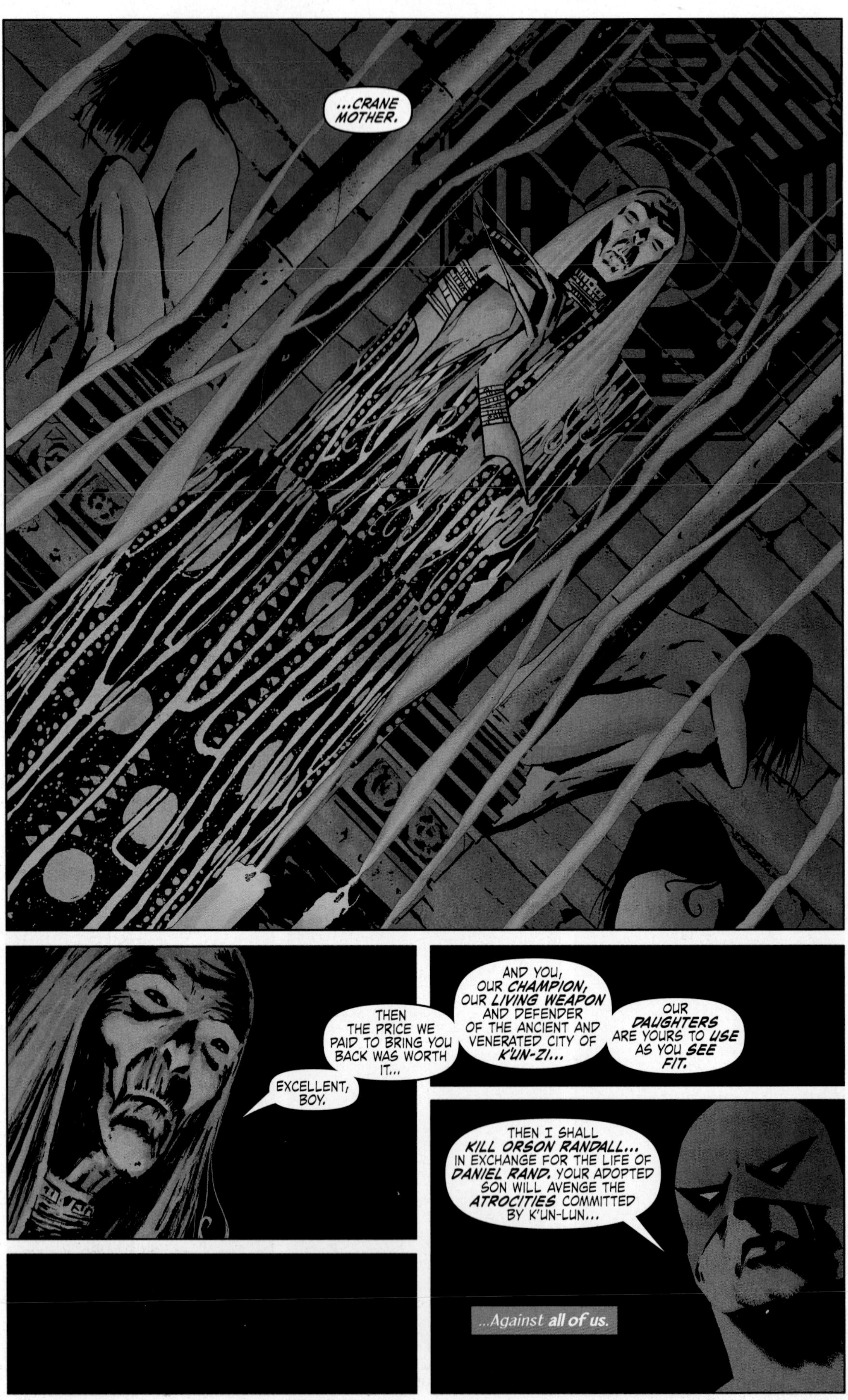
...CRANE MOTHER.
THEN THE PRICE WE PAID TO BRING YOU BACK WAS WORTH IT...
EXCELLENT, BOY.
AND YOU, OUR CHAMPION, OUR LIVING WEAPON AND DEFENDER OF THE ANCIENT AND VENERATED CITY OF K'UN-ZI...
OUR DAUGHTERS ARE YOURS TO USE AS YOU SEE FIT.
THEN I SHALL KILL ORSON RANDALL... IN EXCHANGE FOR THE LIFE OF DANIEL RAND. YOUR ADOPTED SON WILL AVENGE THE ATROCITIES COMMITTED BY K'UN-LUN...
...Against all of us.

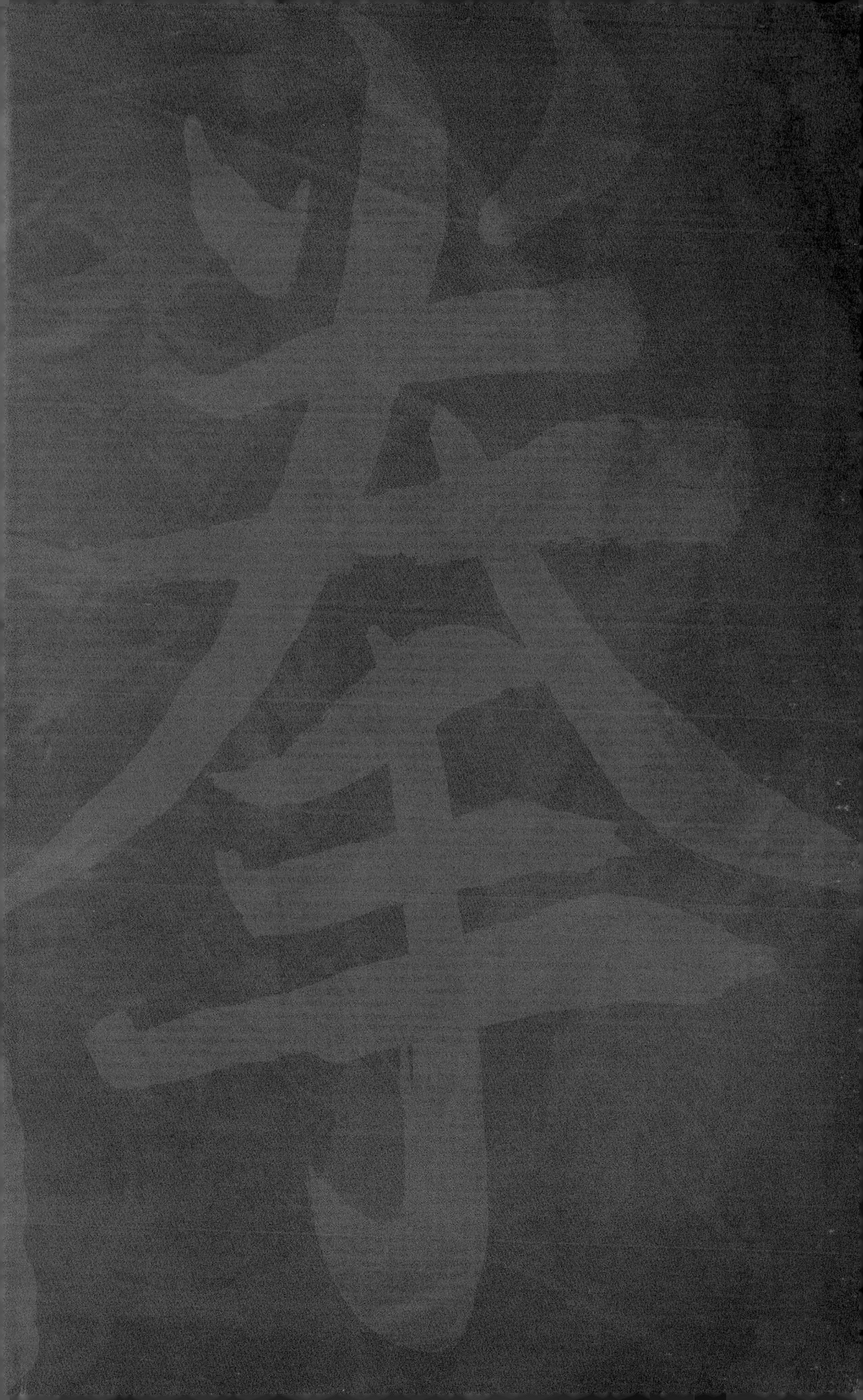
拳

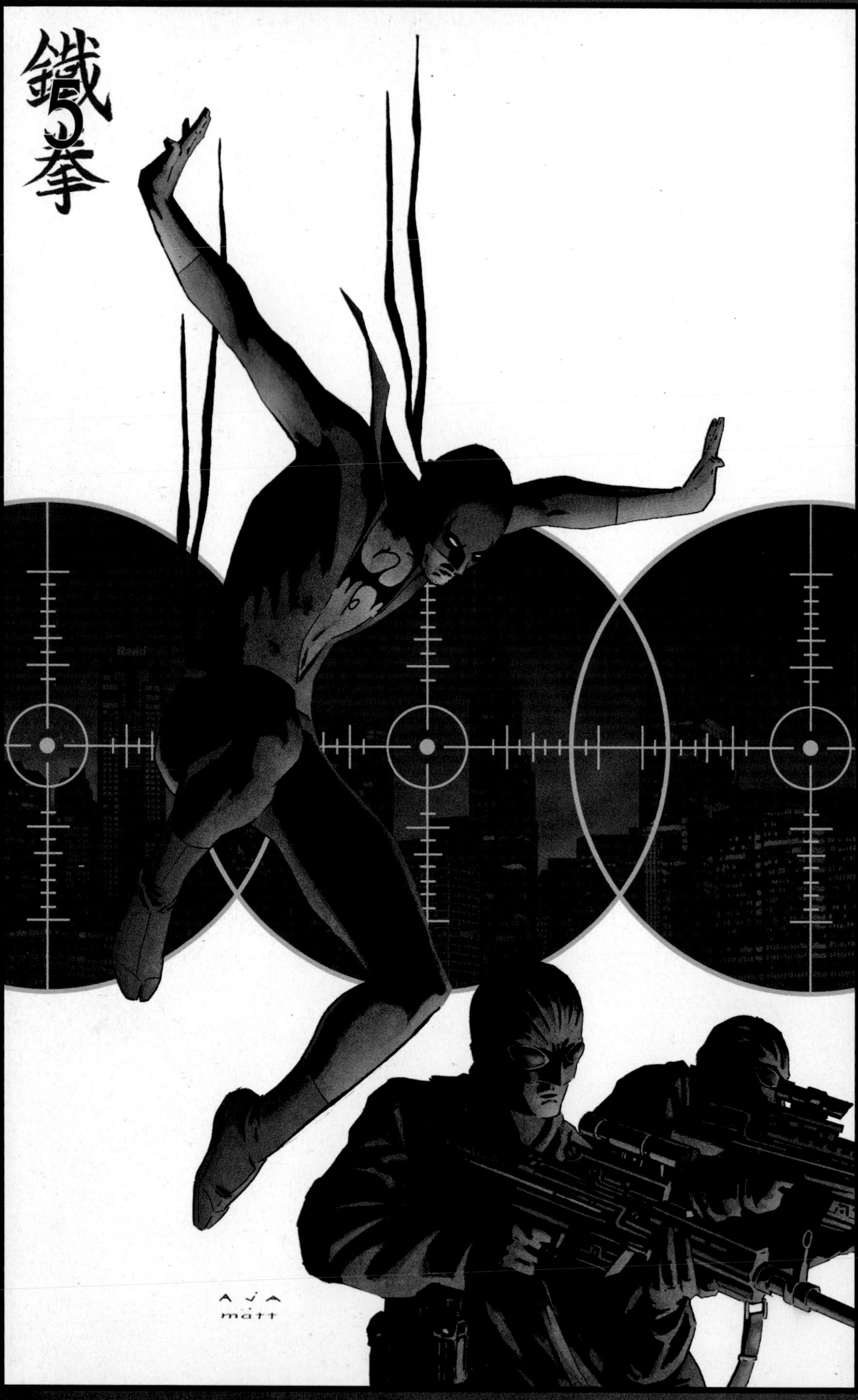
鐵
5
拳
AJA
matt

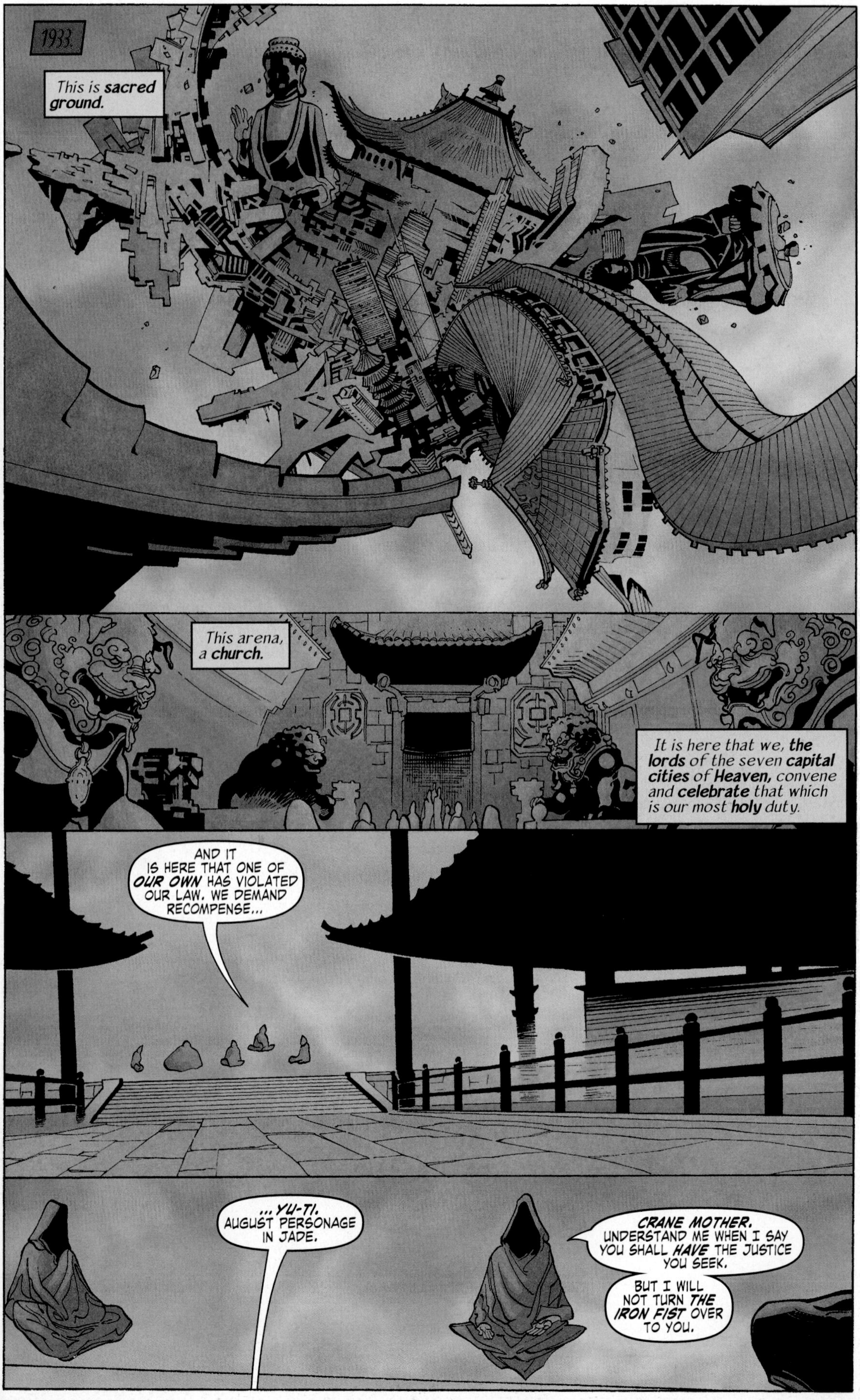
1933.
This is **sacred ground.**
This arena, a **church.**
It is here that we, **the lords** of the seven **capital cities** of **Heaven,** convene and **celebrate** that which is our most **holy** duty.
AND IT IS HERE THAT ONE OF ***OUR OWN*** HAS VIOLATED OUR LAW. WE DEMAND RECOMPENSE...
...YU-TI. AUGUST PERSONAGE IN JADE.
CRANE MOTHER. UNDERSTAND ME WHEN I SAY YOU SHALL ***HAVE*** THE JUSTICE YOU SEEK.
BUT I WILL NOT TURN ***THE IRON FIST*** OVER TO YOU.

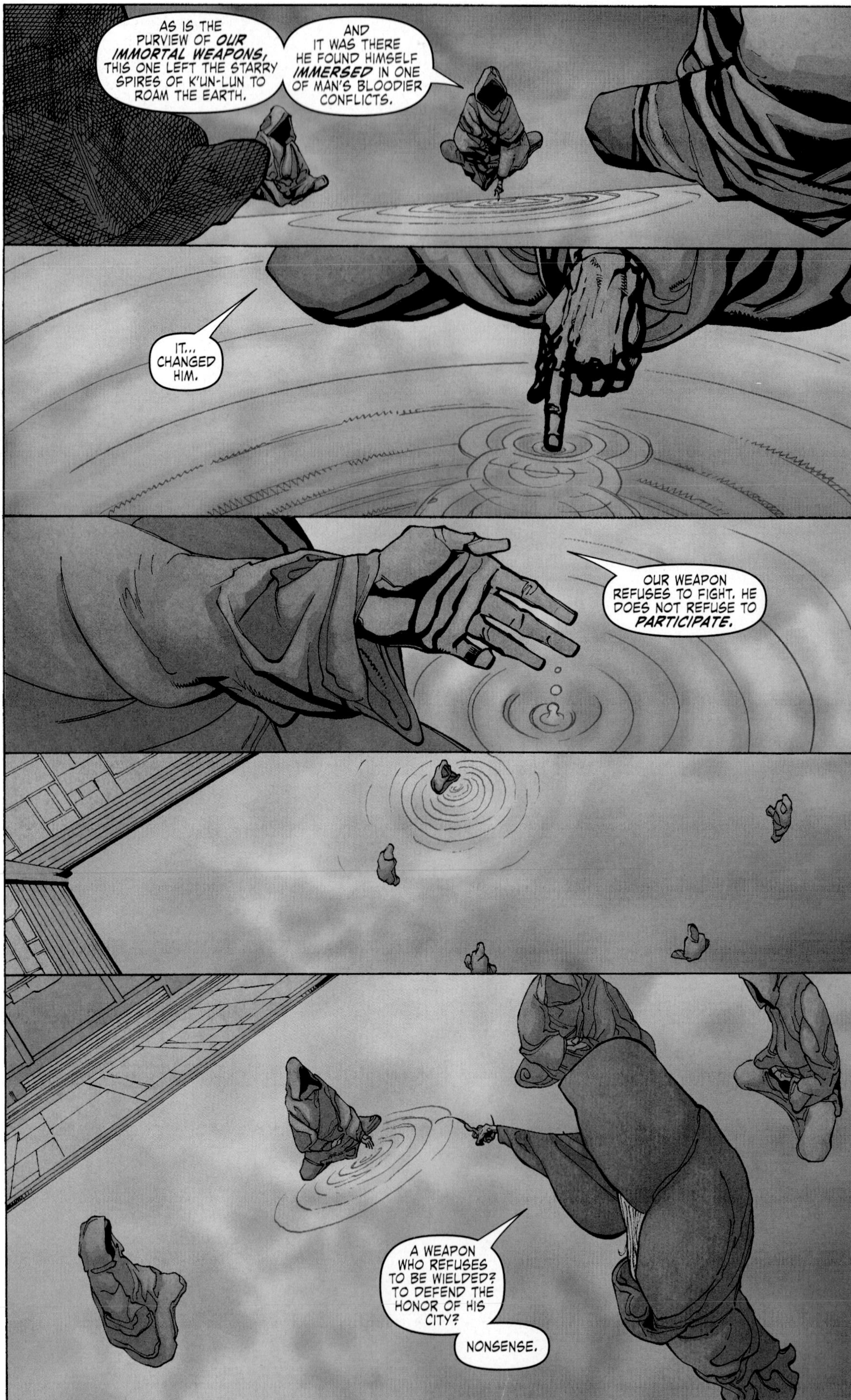
AS IS THE PURVIEW OF OUR IMMORTAL WEAPONS, THIS ONE LEFT THE STARRY SPIRES OF K'UN-LUN TO ROAM THE EARTH.
AND IT WAS THERE HE FOUND HIMSELF IMMERSED IN ONE OF MAN'S BLOODIER CONFLICTS.
IT... CHANGED HIM.
OUR WEAPON REFUSES TO FIGHT. HE DOES NOT REFUSE TO PARTICIPATE.
A WEAPON WHO REFUSES TO BE WIELDED? TO DEFEND THE HONOR OF HIS CITY?
NONSENSE.

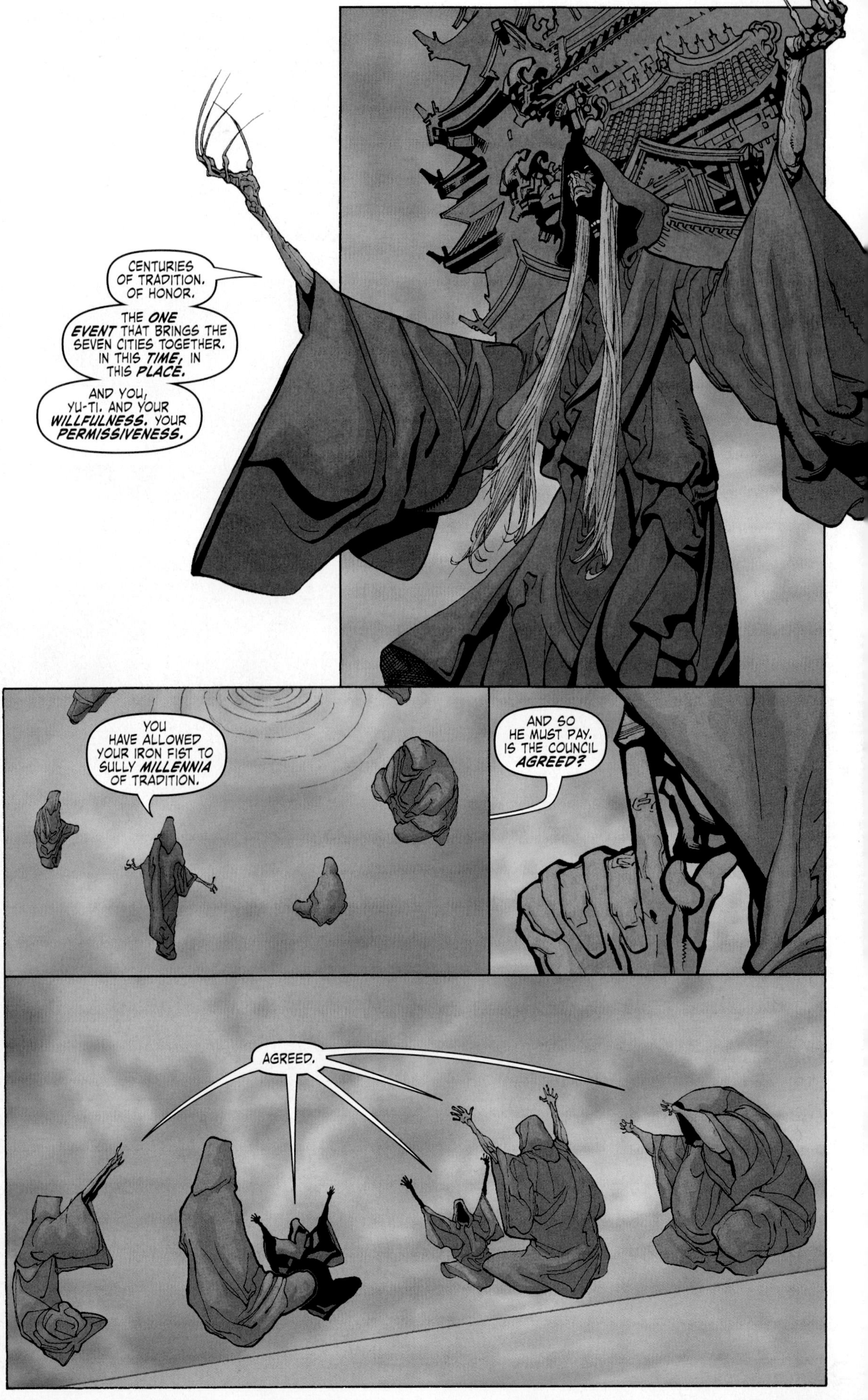
CENTURIES OF TRADITION. OF HONOR.
THE *ONE EVENT* THAT BRINGS THE SEVEN CITIES TOGETHER. IN THIS *TIME,* IN THIS *PLACE.*
AND YOU, YU-TI. AND YOUR *WILLFULNESS.* YOUR *PERMISSIVENESS.*
YOU HAVE ALLOWED YOUR IRON FIST TO SULLY *MILLENNIA* OF TRADITION.
AND SO HE MUST PAY. IS THE COUNCIL *AGREED?*
AGREED.

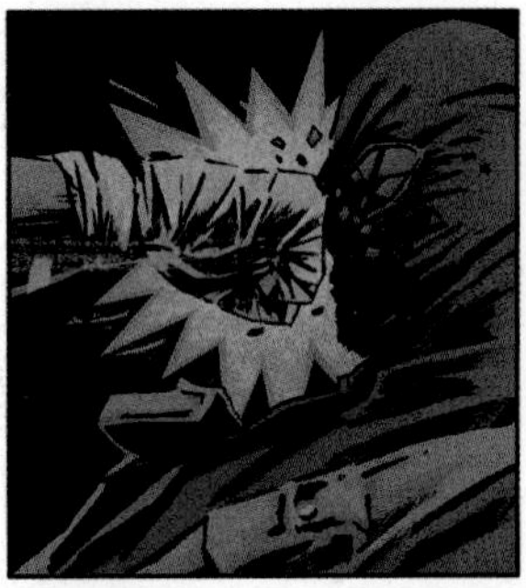
Golden star gouge.

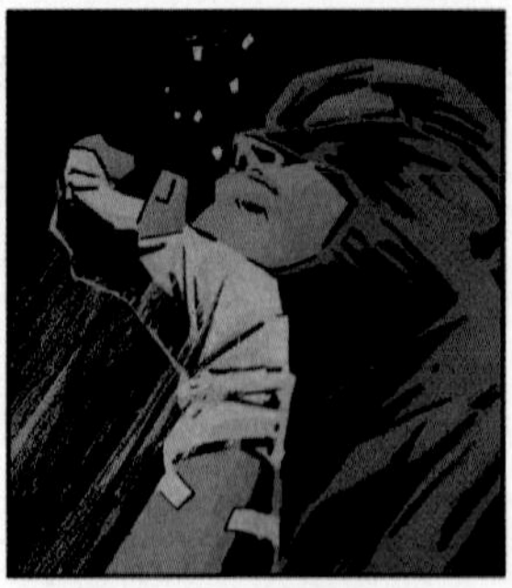
Strike of the silkworm's tooth.

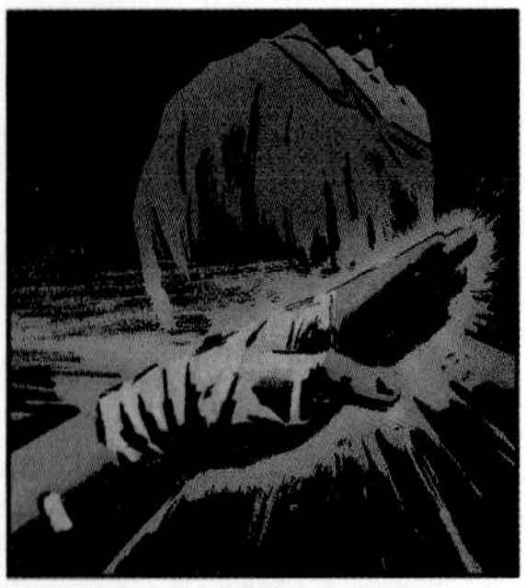
Burning dove chop.

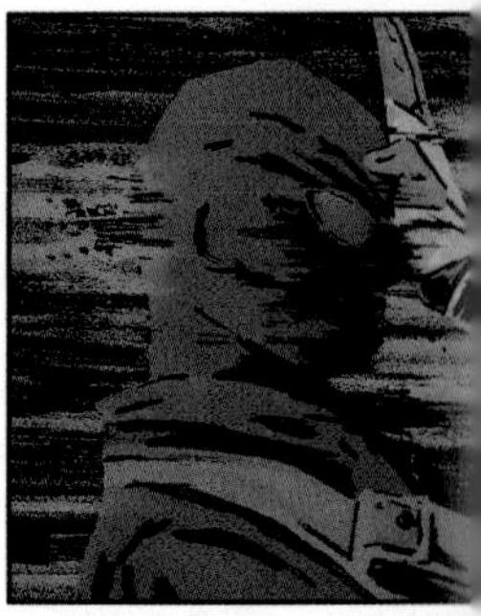
Palm of forty sorrows.

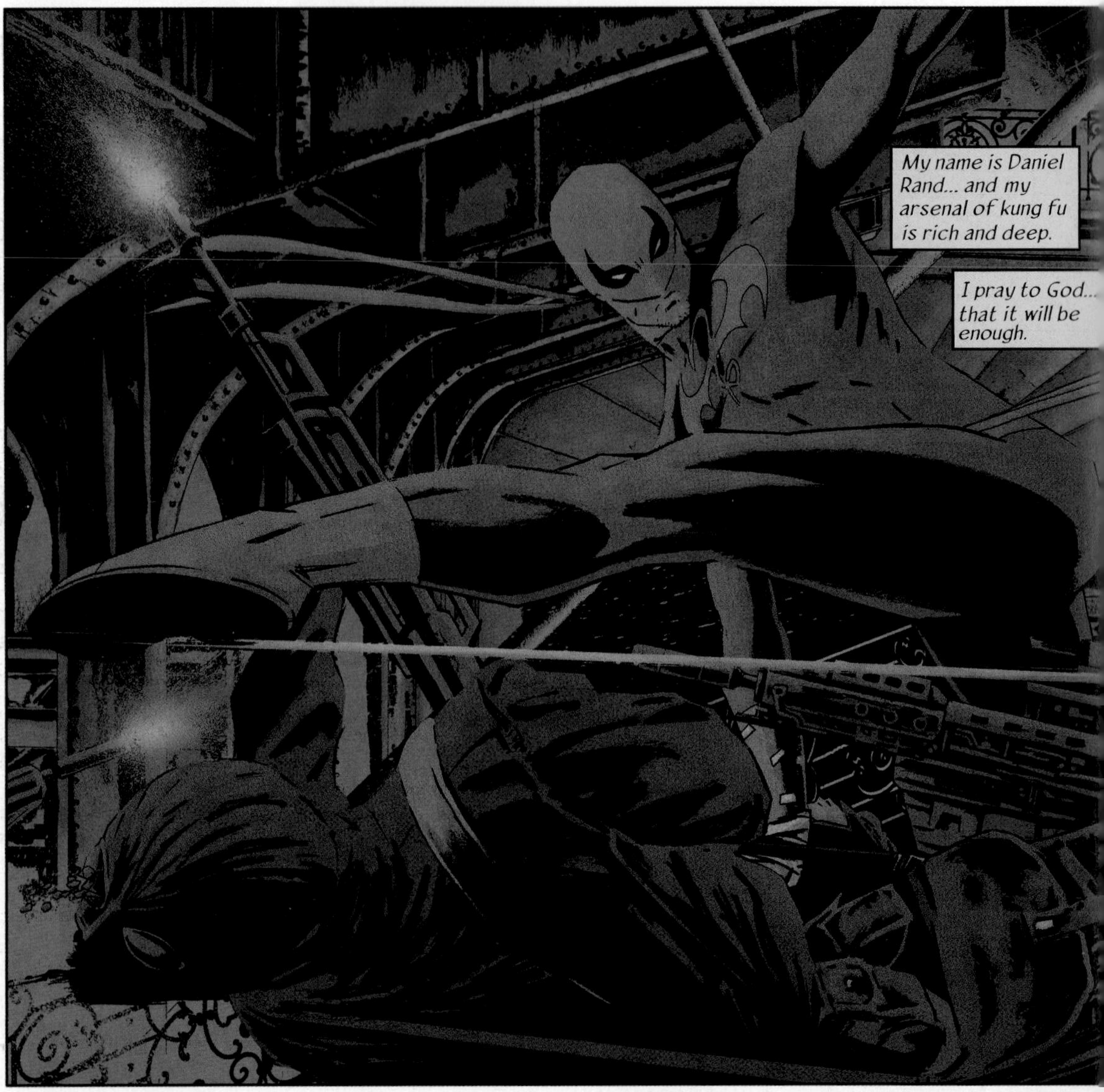
My name is Daniel Rand... and my arsenal of kung fu is rich and deep.
I pray to God... that it will be enough.

For Tony.

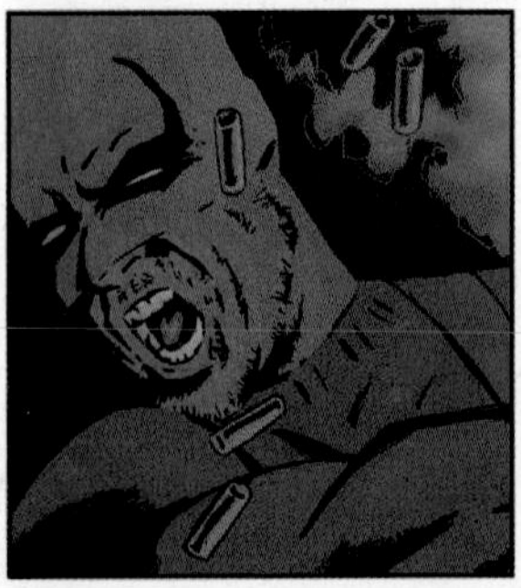

For Jean-Claude.

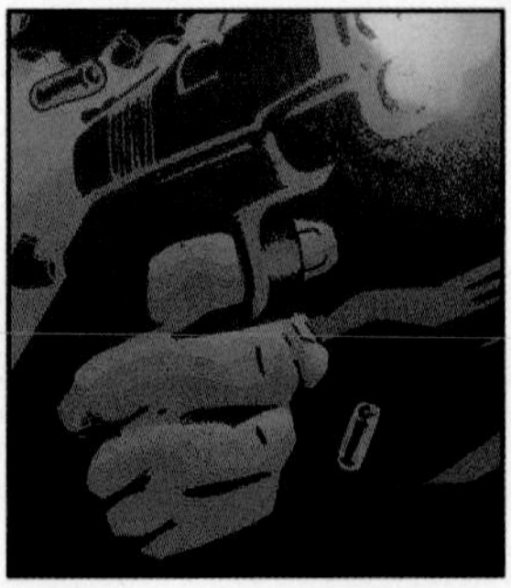

For Marie.

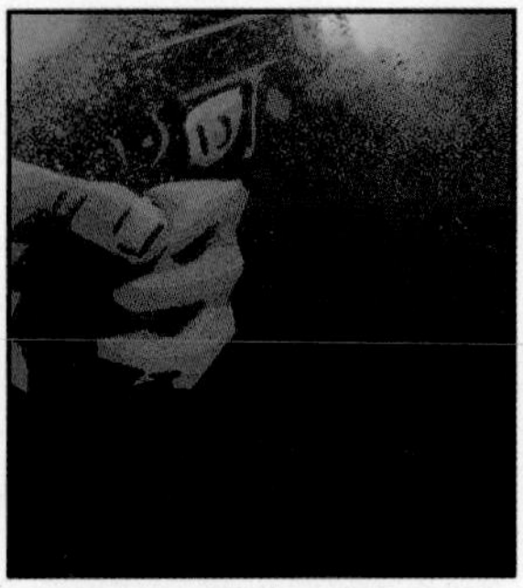

For Milo the cigarette dog

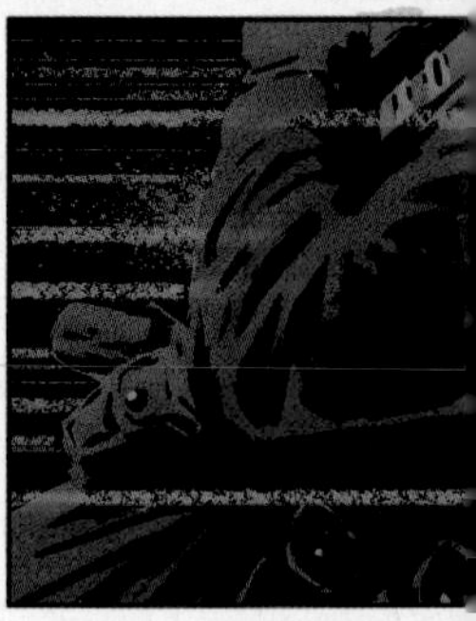

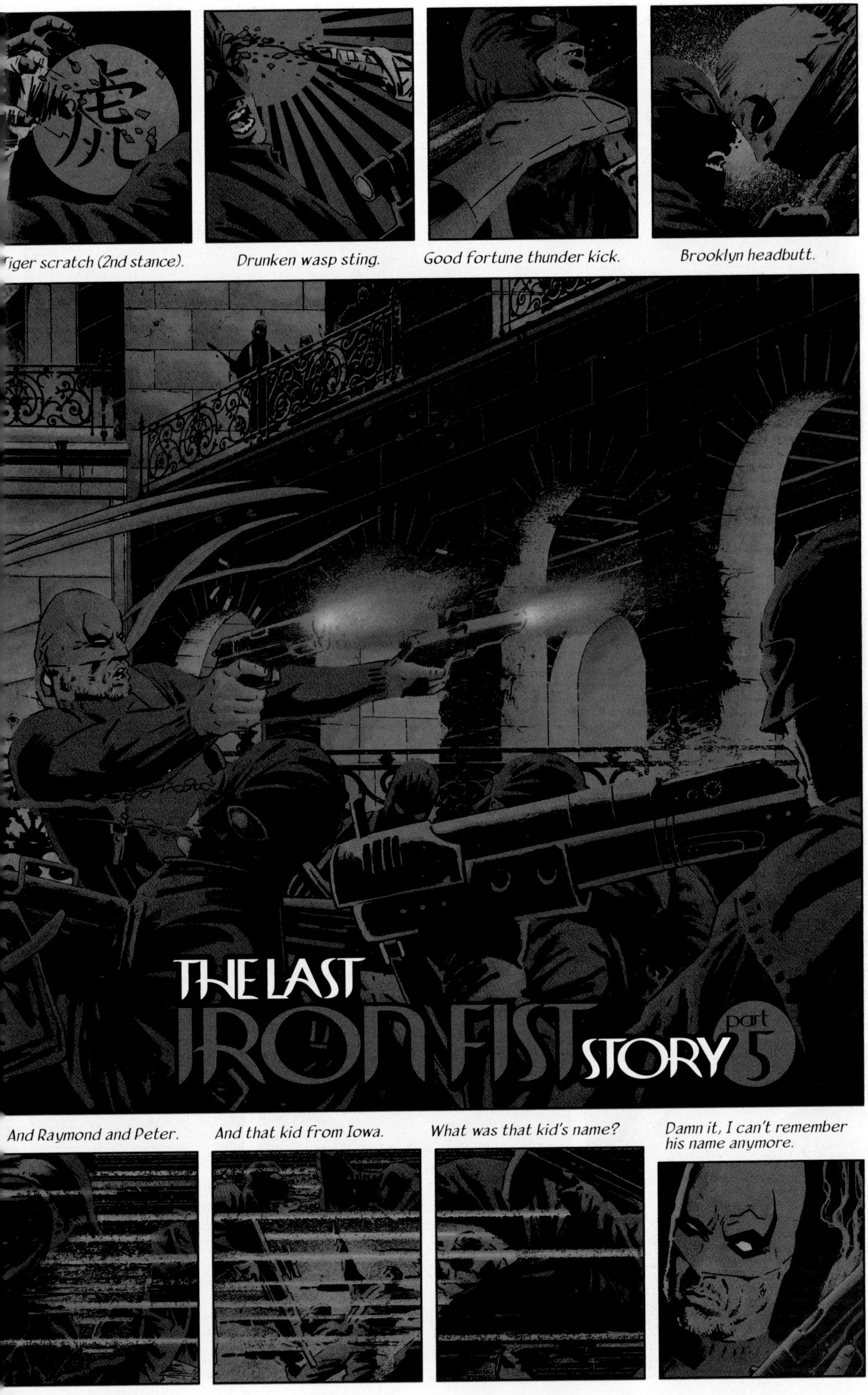
Tiger scratch (2nd stance).
Drunken wasp sting.
Good fortune thunder kick.
Brooklyn headbutt.
THE LAST IRON FIST STORY part 5
And Raymond and Peter.
And that kid from Iowa.
What was that kid's name?
Damn it, I can't remember his name anymore.

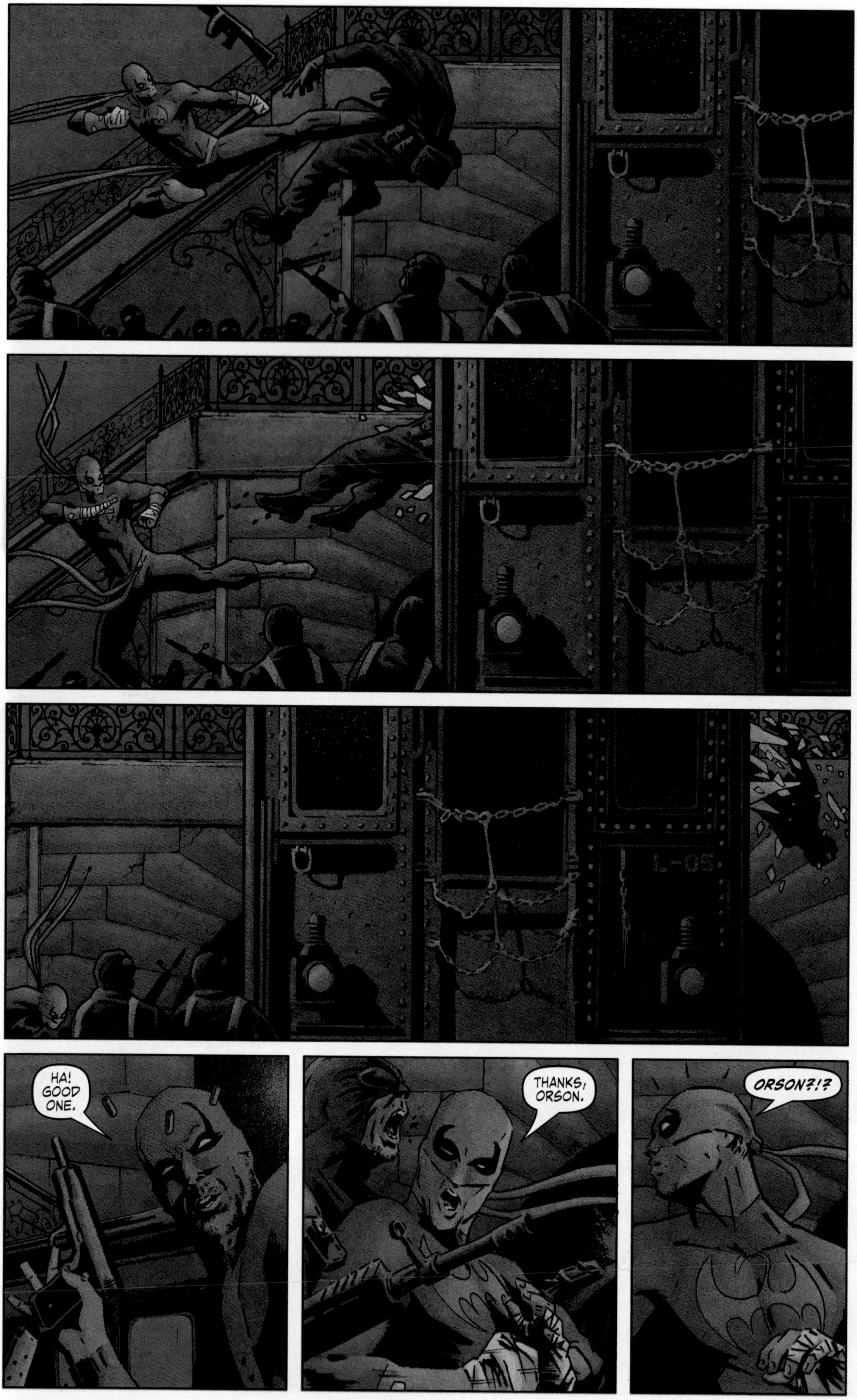
HA! GOOD ONE.
THANKS, ORSON.
ORSON?!?

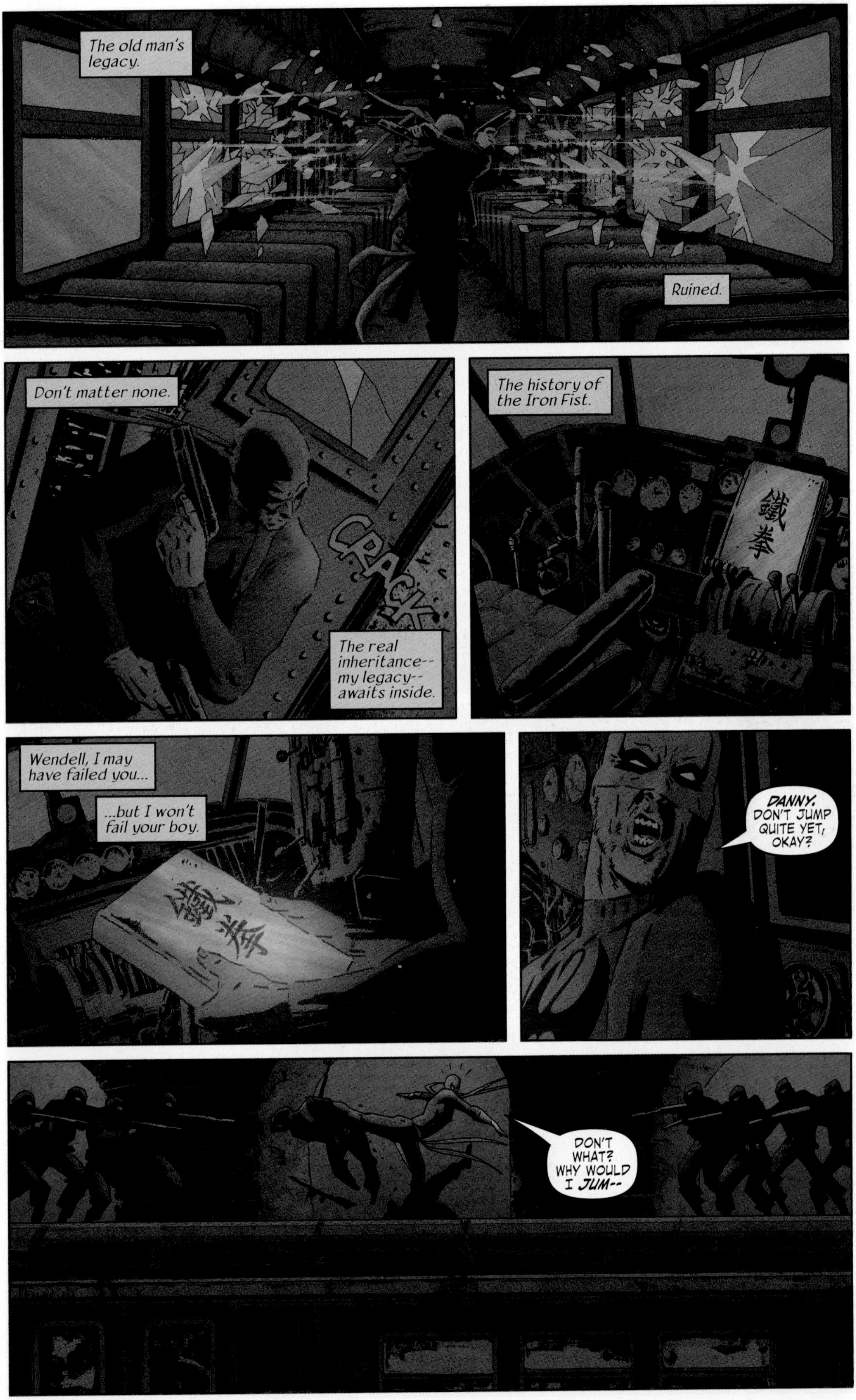
The old man's legacy.
Ruined.
Don't matter none.
CRACK
The real inheritance-- my legacy-- awaits inside.
The history of the Iron Fist.
鐵拳
Wendell, I may have failed you...
...but I won't fail your boy.
DANNY. DON'T JUMP QUITE YET, OKAY?
DON'T WHAT? WHY WOULD I JUM--

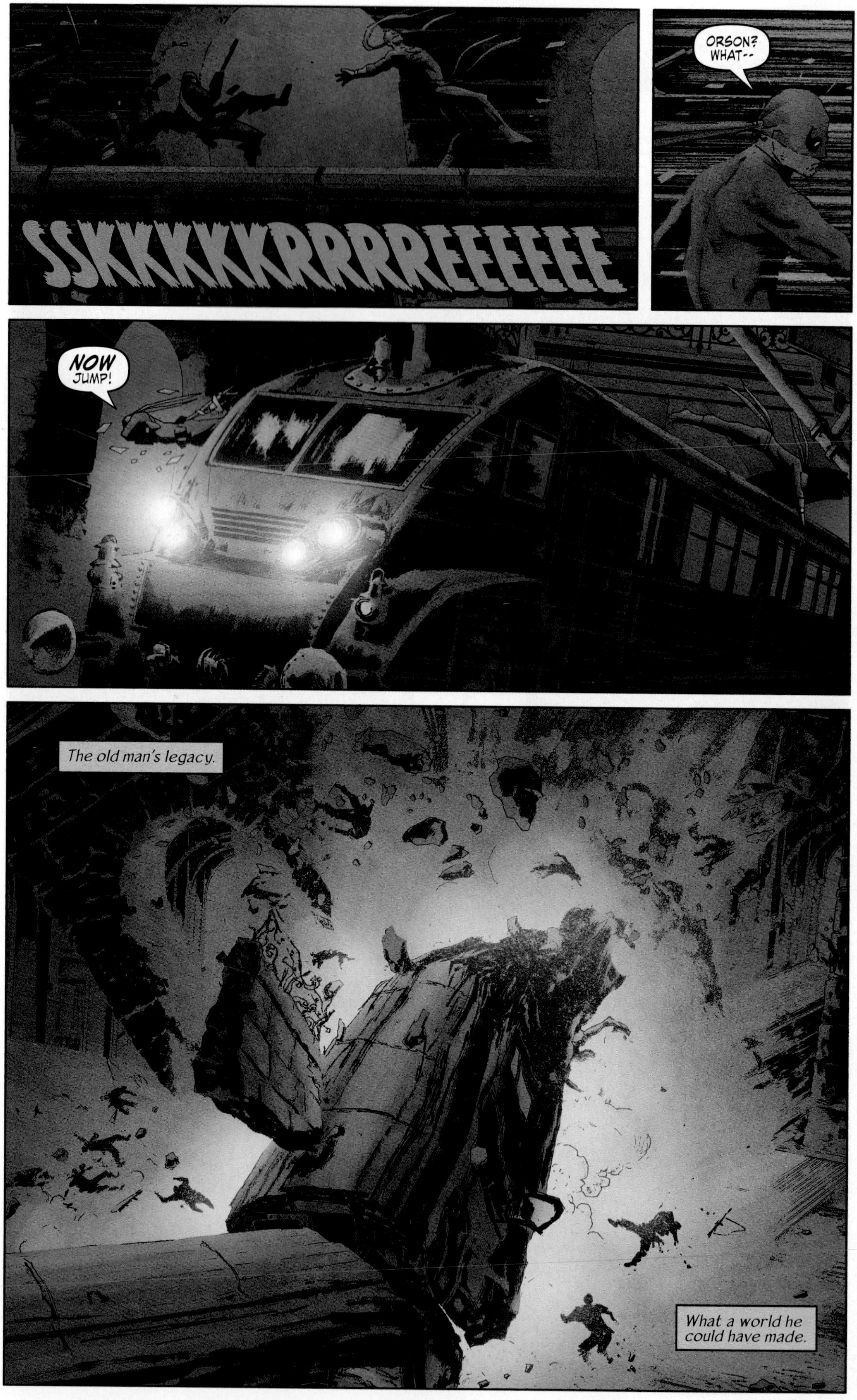
SSKKKKKRRRRREEEEEE
ORSON? WHAT--
NOW JUMP!
The old man's legacy.
What a world he could have made.

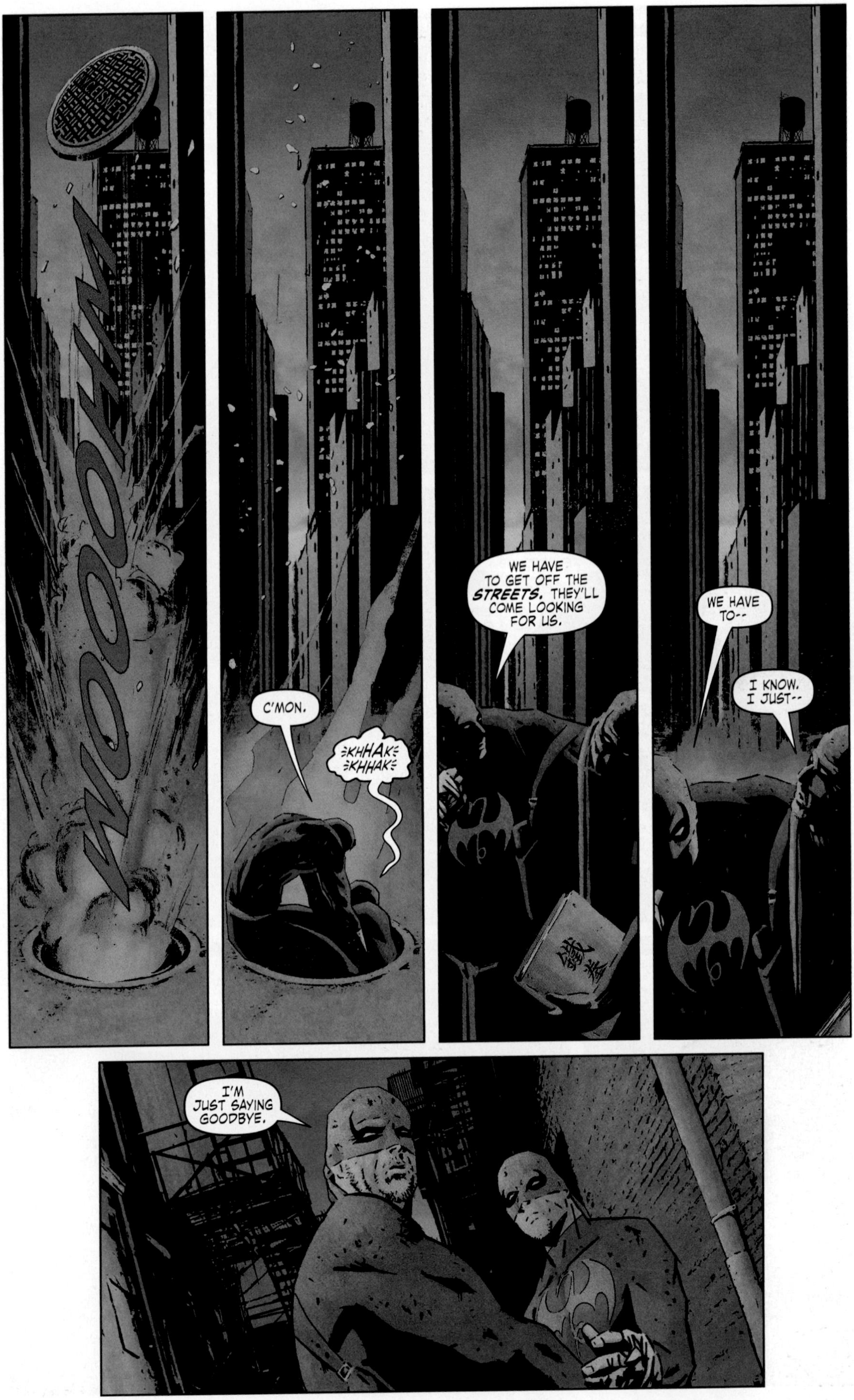
WHOOOOM
C'MON.
KHHAK KHHAK
WE HAVE TO GET OFF THE STREETS. THEY'LL COME LOOKING FOR US.
WE HAVE TO--
I KNOW. I JUST--
I'M JUST SAYING GOODBYE.

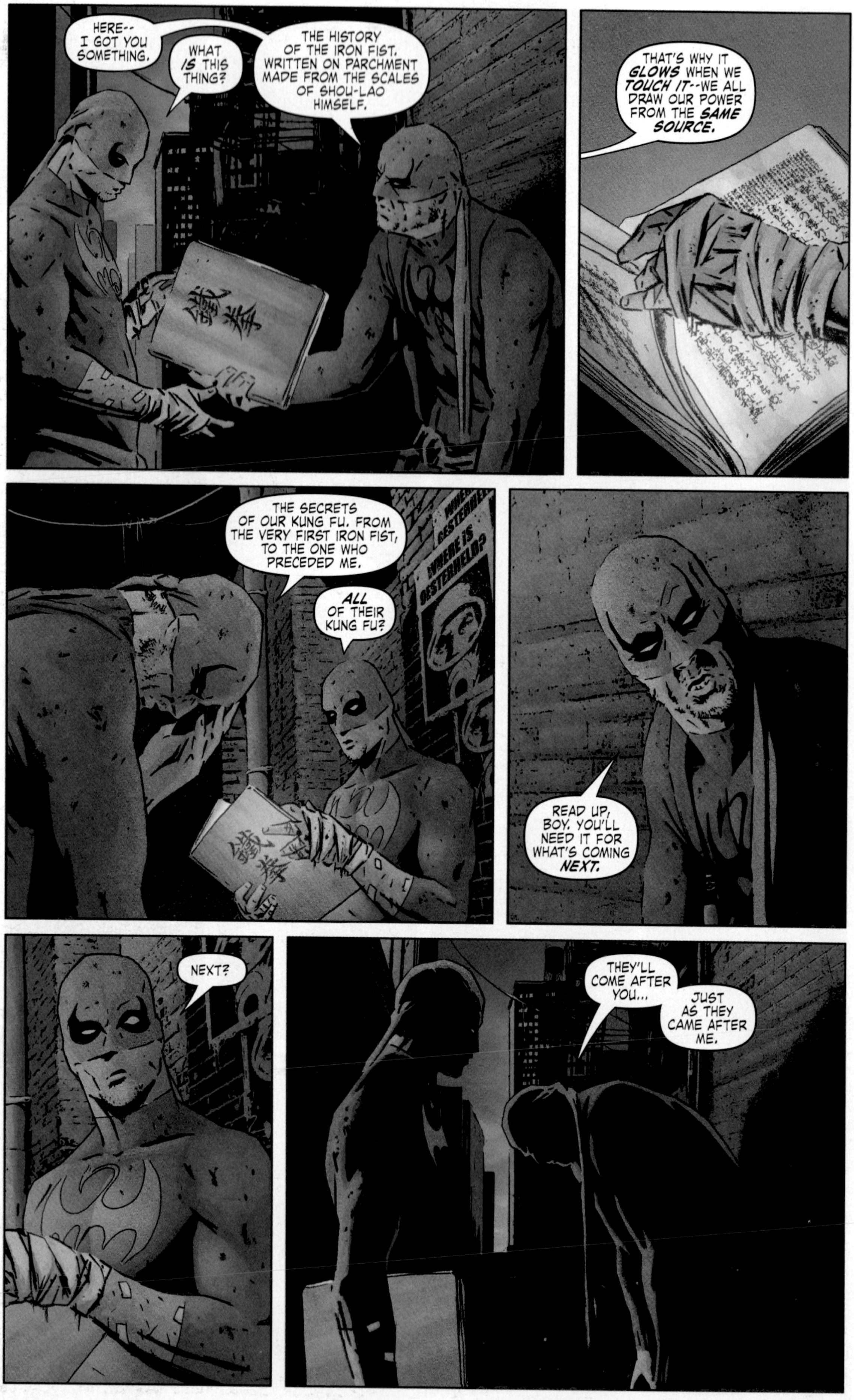
HERE--
I GOT YOU SOMETHING.
WHAT IS THIS THING?
THE HISTORY OF THE IRON FIST. WRITTEN ON PARCHMENT MADE FROM THE SCALES OF SHOU-LAO HIMSELF.
THAT'S WHY IT GLOWS WHEN WE TOUCH IT--WE ALL DRAW OUR POWER FROM THE SAME SOURCE.
THE SECRETS OF OUR KUNG FU. FROM THE VERY FIRST IRON FIST, TO THE ONE WHO PRECEDED ME.
ALL OF THEIR KUNG FU?
WHERE IS OESTERHELD?
READ UP, BOY. YOU'LL NEED IT FOR WHAT'S COMING NEXT.
NEXT?
THEY'LL COME AFTER YOU...
JUST AS THEY CAME AFTER ME.

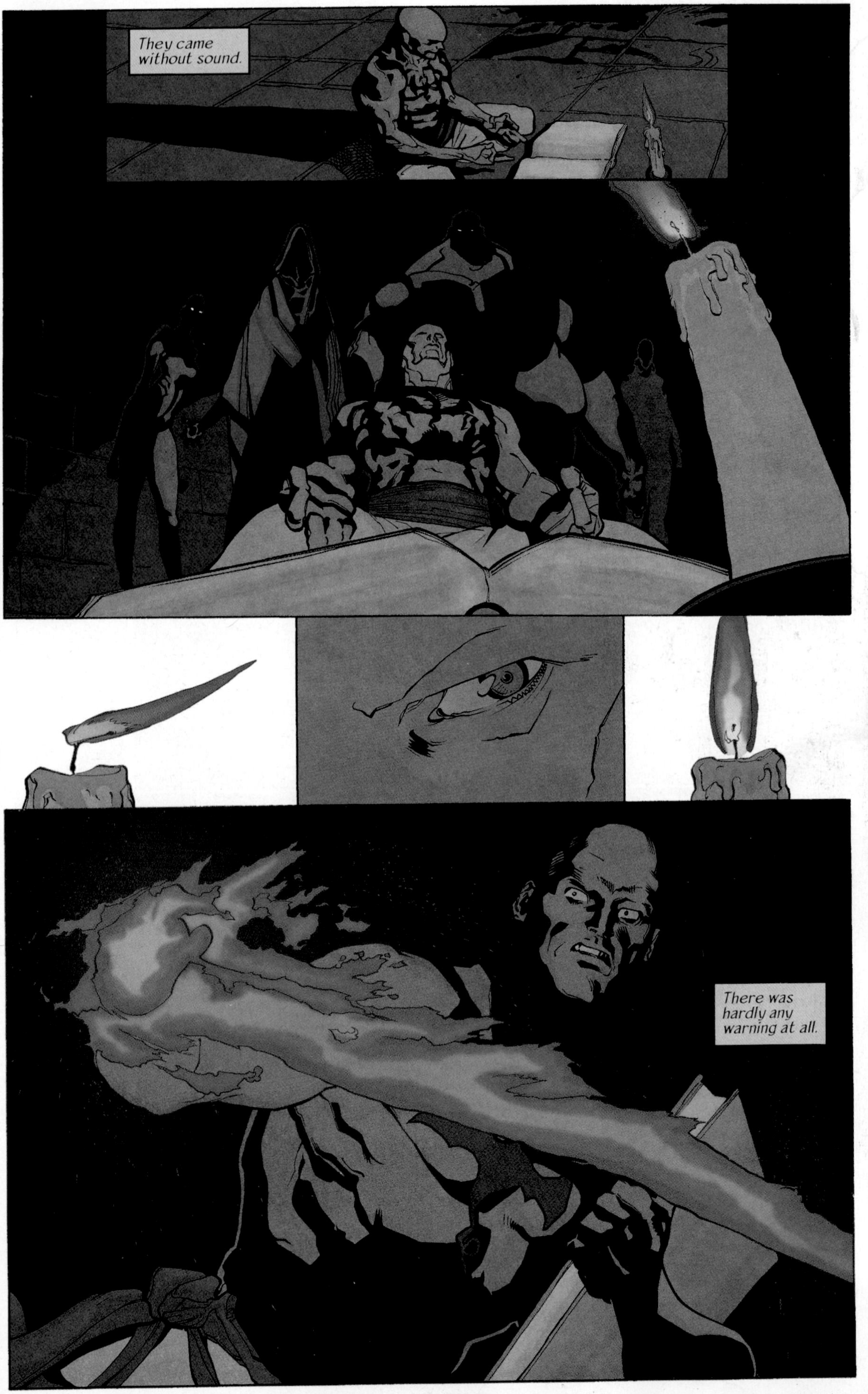
They came without sound.
There was hardly any warning at all.

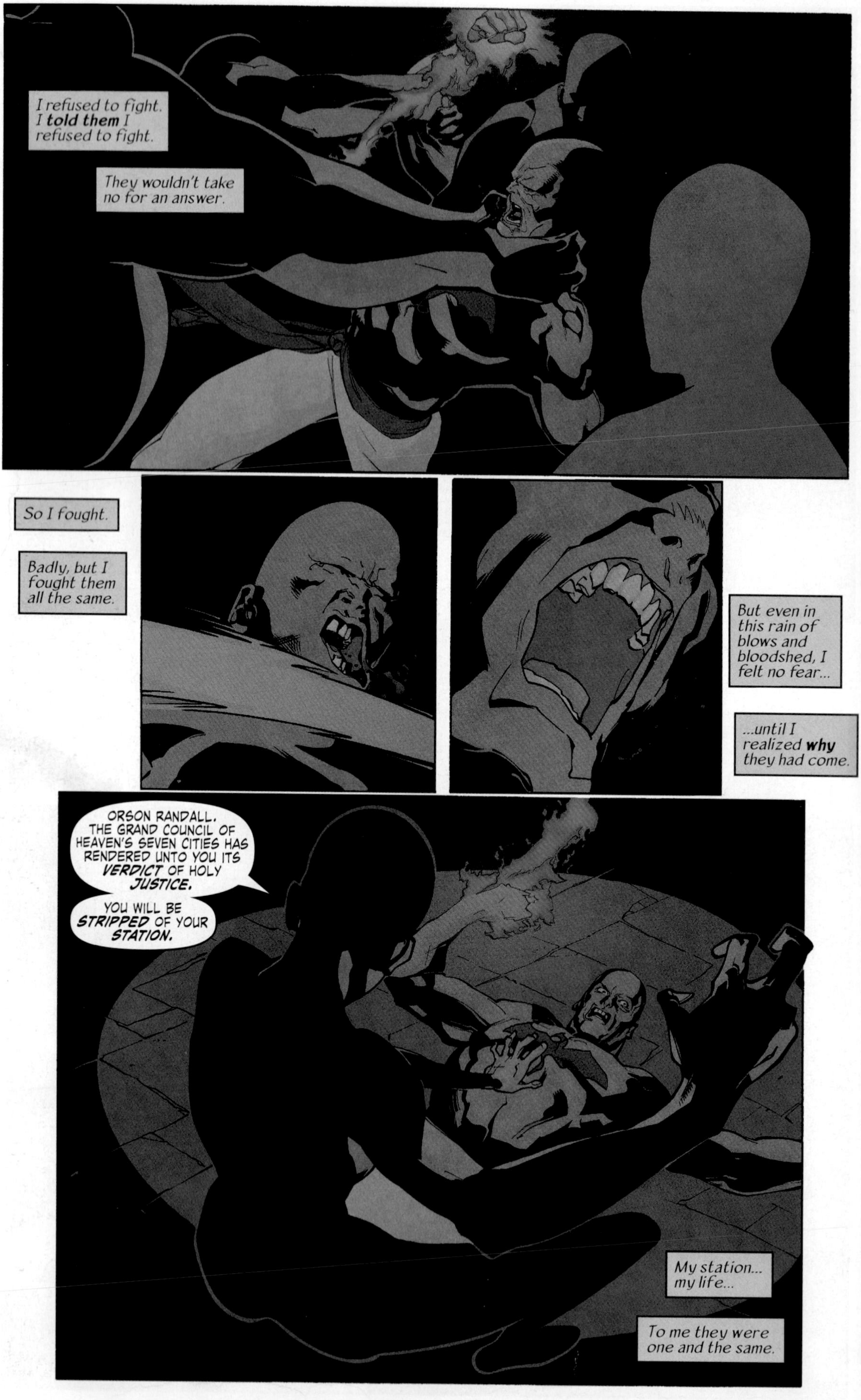
I refused to fight. I **told them** I refused to fight.
They wouldn't take no for an answer.
So I fought.
Badly, but I fought them all the same.
But even in this rain of blows and bloodshed, I felt no fear...
...until I realized **why** they had come.
ORSON RANDALL. THE GRAND COUNCIL OF HEAVEN'S SEVEN CITIES HAS RENDERED UNTO YOU ITS ***VERDICT*** OF HOLY ***JUSTICE.***
YOU WILL BE ***STRIPPED*** OF YOUR ***STATION.***
My station... my life...
To me they were one and the same.

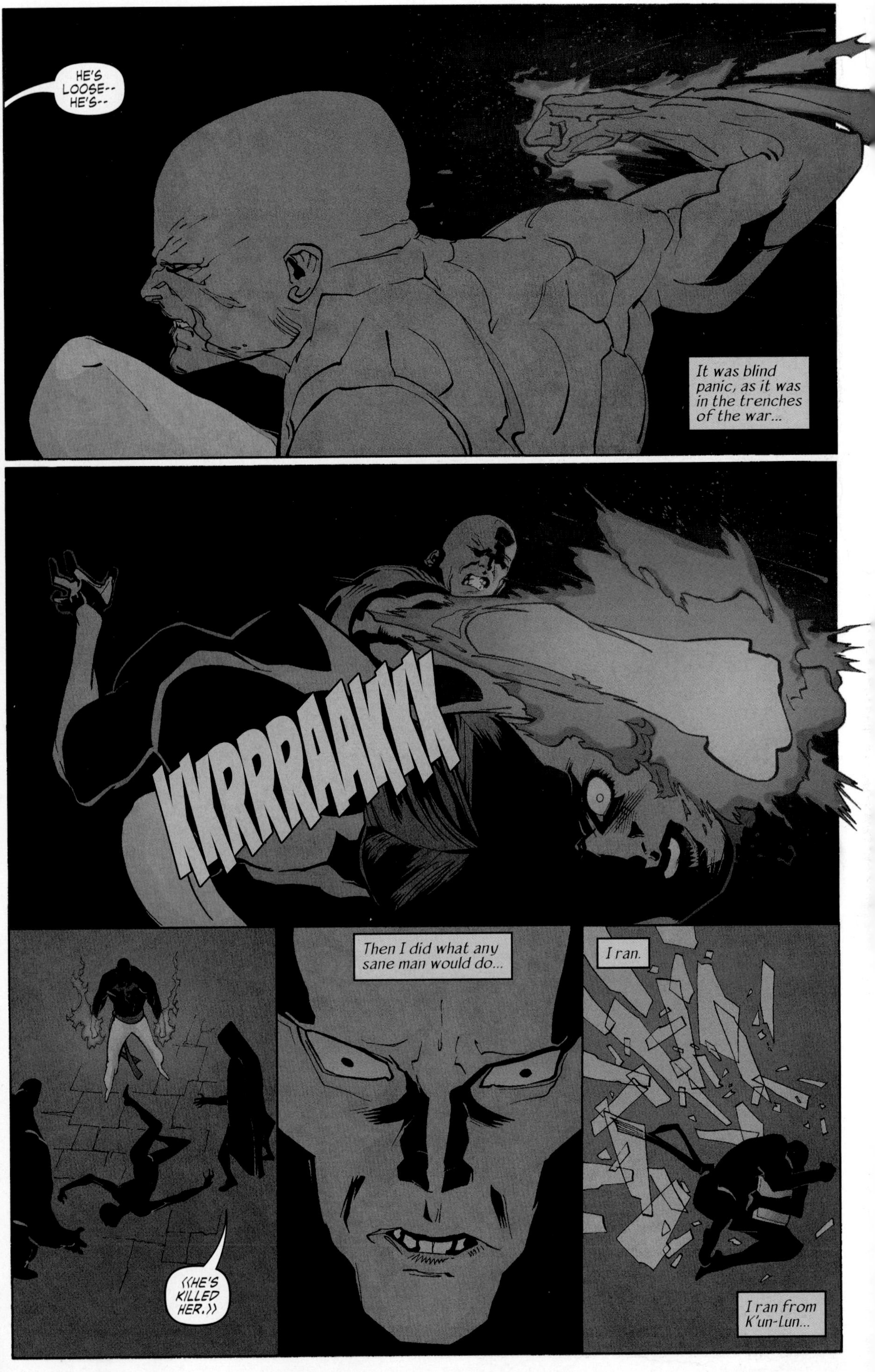
HE'S LOOSE-- HE'S--
It was blind panic, as it was in the trenches of the war...
KKRRRAAKKK
<<HE'S KILLED HER.>>
Then I did what any sane man would do...
I ran.
I ran from K'un-Lun...

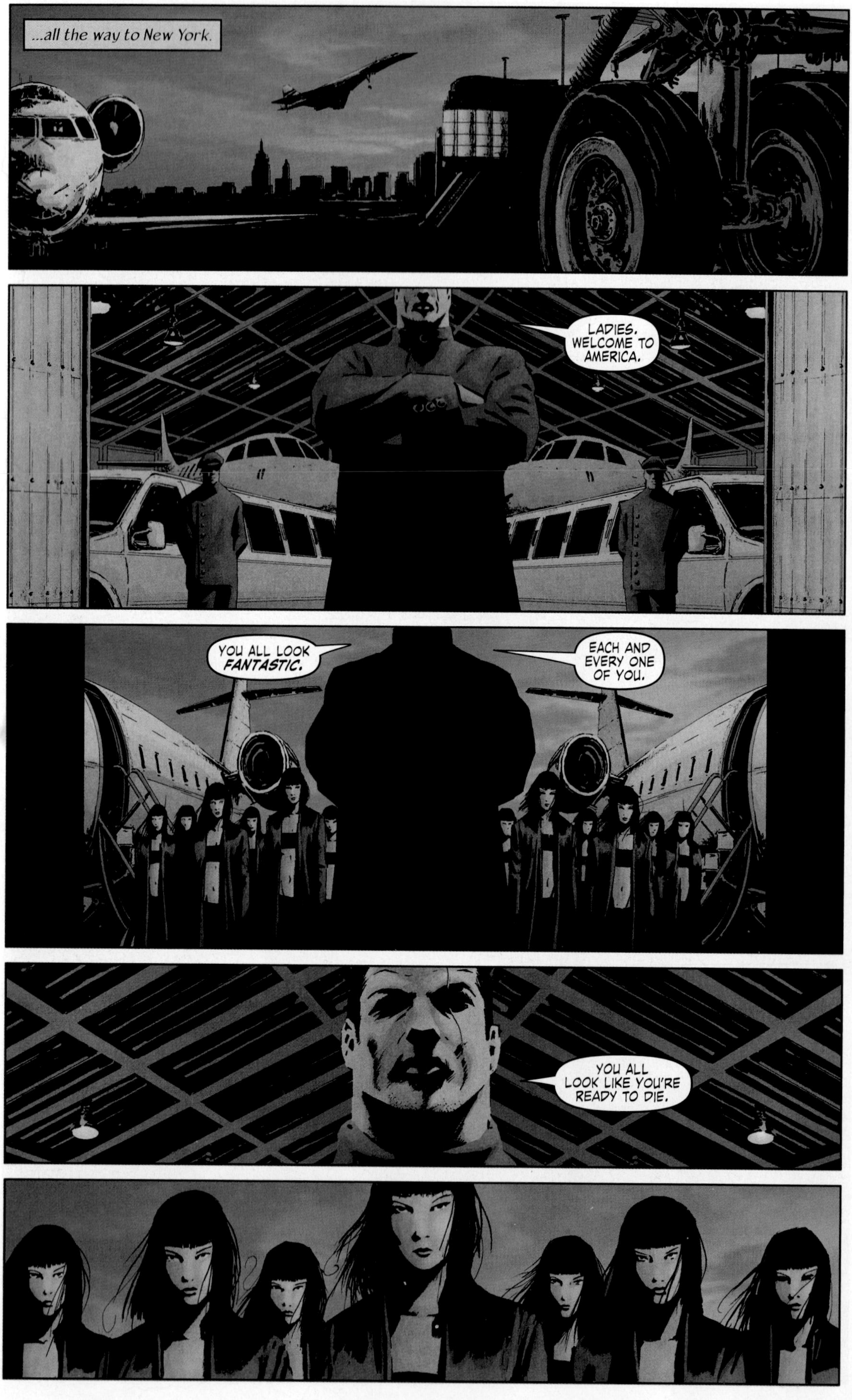
...all the way to New York.
LADIES. WELCOME TO AMERICA.
YOU ALL LOOK *FANTASTIC.*
EACH AND EVERY ONE OF YOU.
YOU ALL LOOK LIKE YOU'RE READY TO DIE.

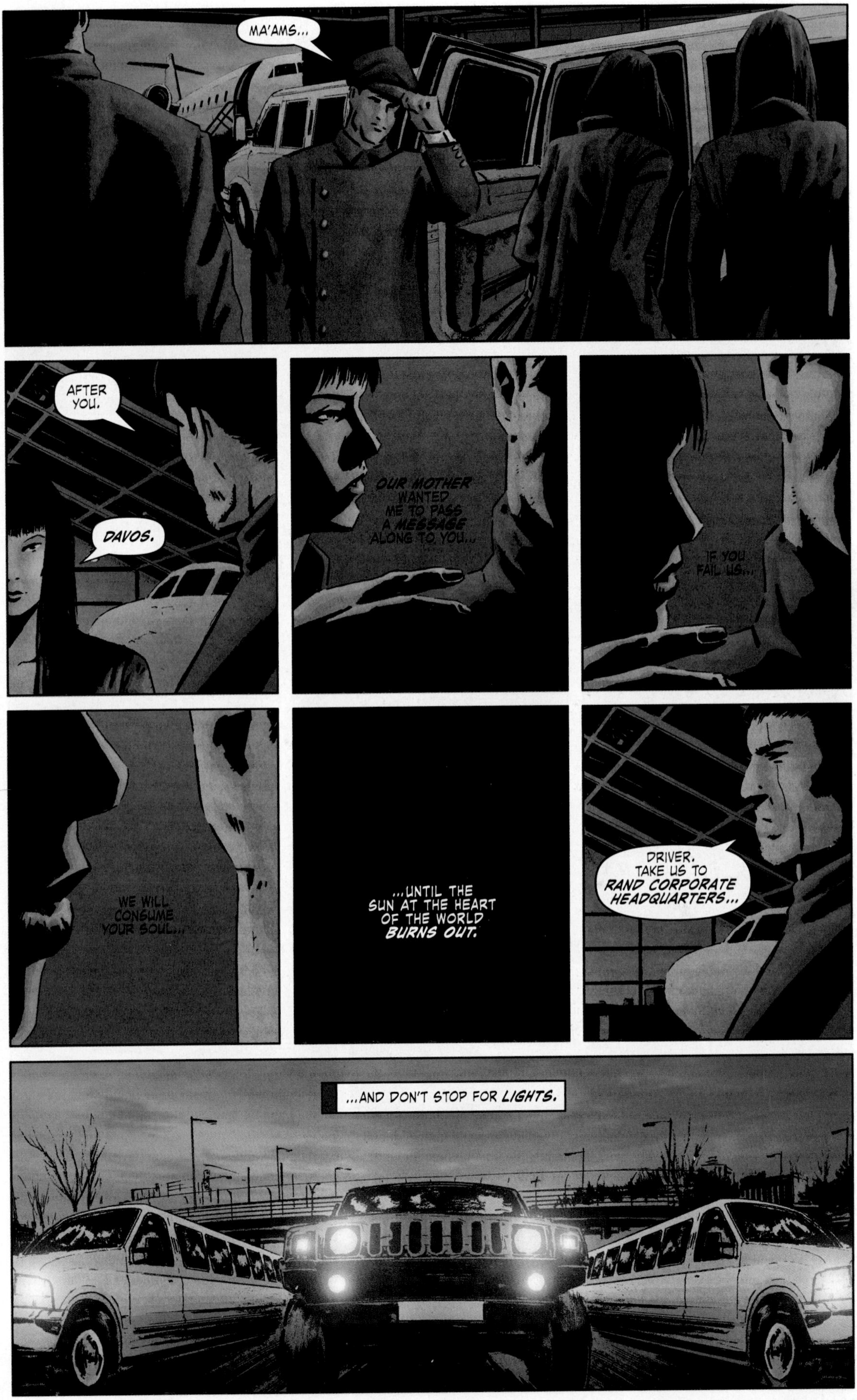
MA'AMS...
AFTER YOU.
DAVOS.
OUR MOTHER WANTED ME TO PASS A MESSAGE ALONG TO YOU...
IF YOU FAIL US...
WE WILL CONSUME YOUR SOUL...
...UNTIL THE SUN AT THE HEART OF THE WORLD BURNS OUT.
DRIVER. TAKE US TO RAND CORPORATE HEADQUARTERS...
...AND DON'T STOP FOR LIGHTS.

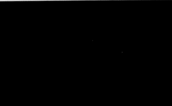

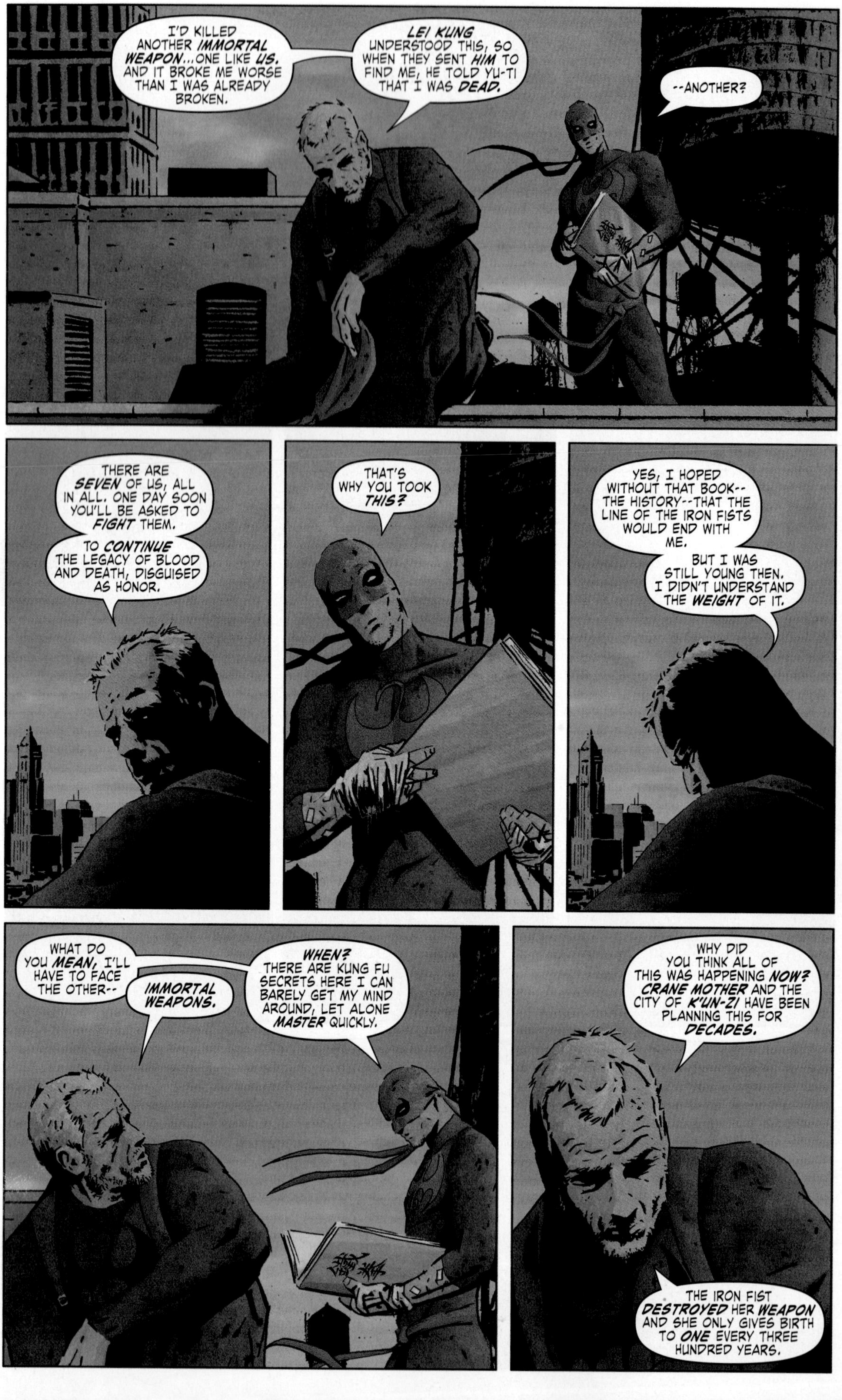
I'D KILLED ANOTHER IMMORTAL WEAPON...ONE LIKE US. AND IT BROKE ME WORSE THAN I WAS ALREADY BROKEN.
LEI KUNG UNDERSTOOD THIS, SO WHEN THEY SENT HIM TO FIND ME, HE TOLD YU-TI THAT I WAS DEAD.
--ANOTHER?
THERE ARE SEVEN OF US, ALL IN ALL. ONE DAY SOON YOU'LL BE ASKED TO FIGHT THEM.
TO CONTINUE THE LEGACY OF BLOOD AND DEATH, DISGUISED AS HONOR.
THAT'S WHY YOU TOOK THIS?
YES, I HOPED WITHOUT THAT BOOK--THE HISTORY--THAT THE LINE OF THE IRON FISTS WOULD END WITH ME.
BUT I WAS STILL YOUNG THEN. I DIDN'T UNDERSTAND THE WEIGHT OF IT.
WHAT DO YOU MEAN, I'LL HAVE TO FACE THE OTHER--
IMMORTAL WEAPONS.
WHEN? THERE ARE KUNG FU SECRETS HERE I CAN BARELY GET MY MIND AROUND, LET ALONE MASTER QUICKLY.
WHY DID YOU THINK ALL OF THIS WAS HAPPENING NOW? CRANE MOTHER AND THE CITY OF K'UN-ZI HAVE BEEN PLANNING THIS FOR DECADES.
THE IRON FIST DESTROYED HER WEAPON AND SHE ONLY GIVES BIRTH TO ONE EVERY THREE HUNDRED YEARS.

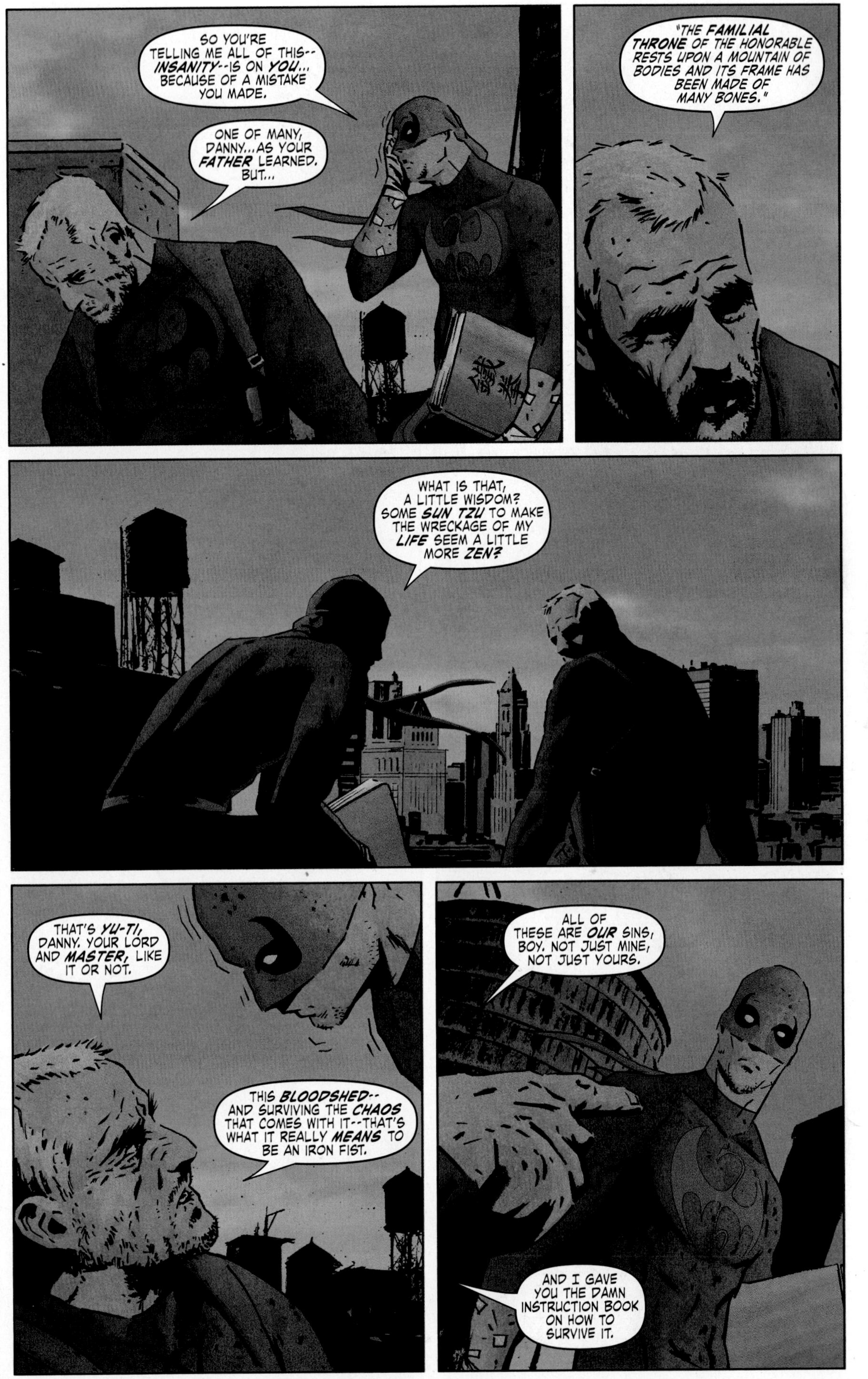
SO YOU'RE TELLING ME ALL OF THIS--INSANITY--IS ON YOU... BECAUSE OF A MISTAKE YOU MADE.
ONE OF MANY, DANNY...AS YOUR FATHER LEARNED. BUT...
"THE FAMILIAL THRONE OF THE HONORABLE RESTS UPON A MOUNTAIN OF BODIES AND ITS FRAME HAS BEEN MADE OF MANY BONES."
WHAT IS THAT, A LITTLE WISDOM? SOME SUN TZU TO MAKE THE WRECKAGE OF MY LIFE SEEM A LITTLE MORE ZEN?
THAT'S YU-TI, DANNY. YOUR LORD AND MASTER, LIKE IT OR NOT.
THIS BLOODSHED--AND SURVIVING THE CHAOS THAT COMES WITH IT--THAT'S WHAT IT REALLY MEANS TO BE AN IRON FIST.
ALL OF THESE ARE OUR SINS, BOY. NOT JUST MINE, NOT JUST YOURS.
AND I GAVE YOU THE DAMN INSTRUCTION BOOK ON HOW TO SURVIVE IT.

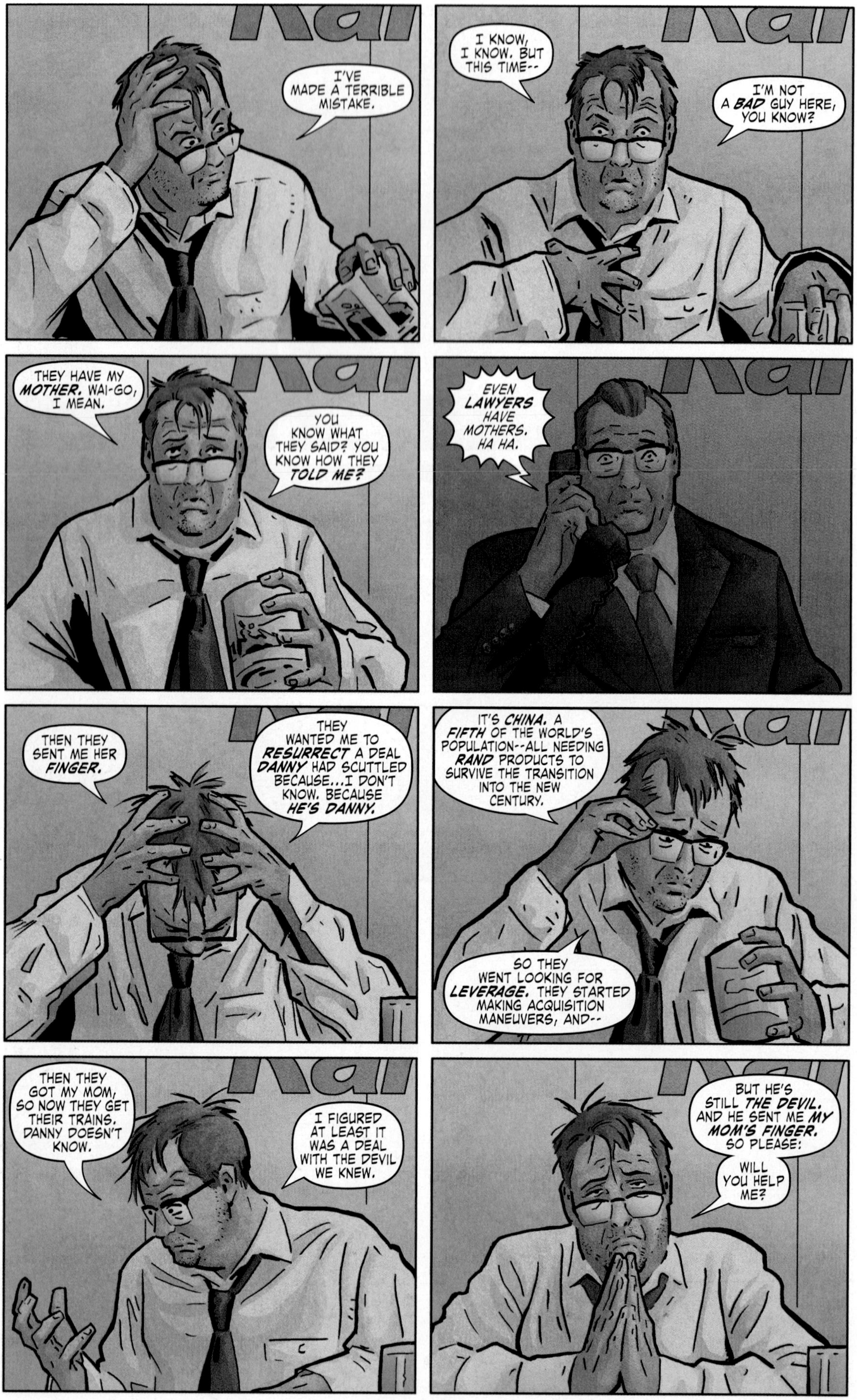
I'VE MADE A TERRIBLE MISTAKE.
I KNOW, I KNOW. BUT THIS TIME--
I'M NOT A *BAD* GUY HERE, YOU KNOW?
THEY HAVE MY *MOTHER.* WAI-GO, I MEAN.
YOU KNOW WHAT THEY SAID? YOU KNOW HOW THEY *TOLD ME?*
EVEN ***LAWYERS*** *HAVE MOTHERS. HA HA.*
THEN THEY SENT ME HER *FINGER.*
THEY WANTED ME TO *RESURRECT* A DEAL *DANNY* HAD SCUTTLED BECAUSE...I DON'T KNOW. BECAUSE *HE'S DANNY.*
IT'S *CHINA.* A *FIFTH* OF THE WORLD'S POPULATION--ALL NEEDING *RAND* PRODUCTS TO SURVIVE THE TRANSITION INTO THE NEW CENTURY.
SO THEY WENT LOOKING FOR *LEVERAGE.* THEY STARTED MAKING ACQUISITION MANEUVERS, AND--
THEN THEY GOT MY MOM, SO NOW THEY GET THEIR TRAINS. DANNY DOESN'T KNOW.
I FIGURED AT LEAST IT WAS A DEAL WITH THE DEVIL WE KNEW.
BUT HE'S STILL *THE DEVIL.* AND HE SENT ME *MY MOM'S FINGER.* SO PLEASE:
WILL YOU HELP ME?

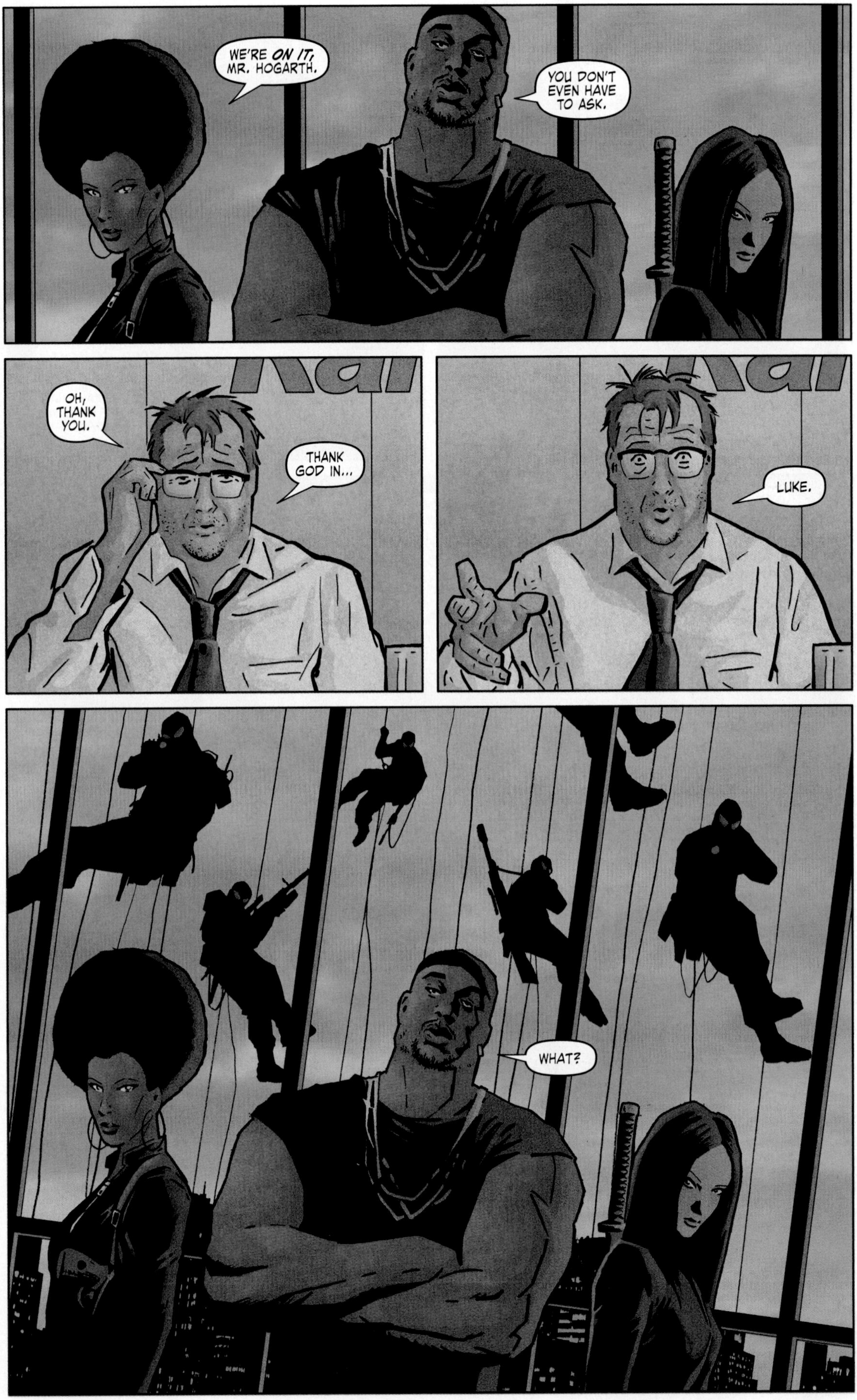
WE'RE ON IT, MR. HOGARTH.
YOU DON'T EVEN HAVE TO ASK.
OH, THANK YOU.
THANK GOD IN...
LUKE.
WHAT?

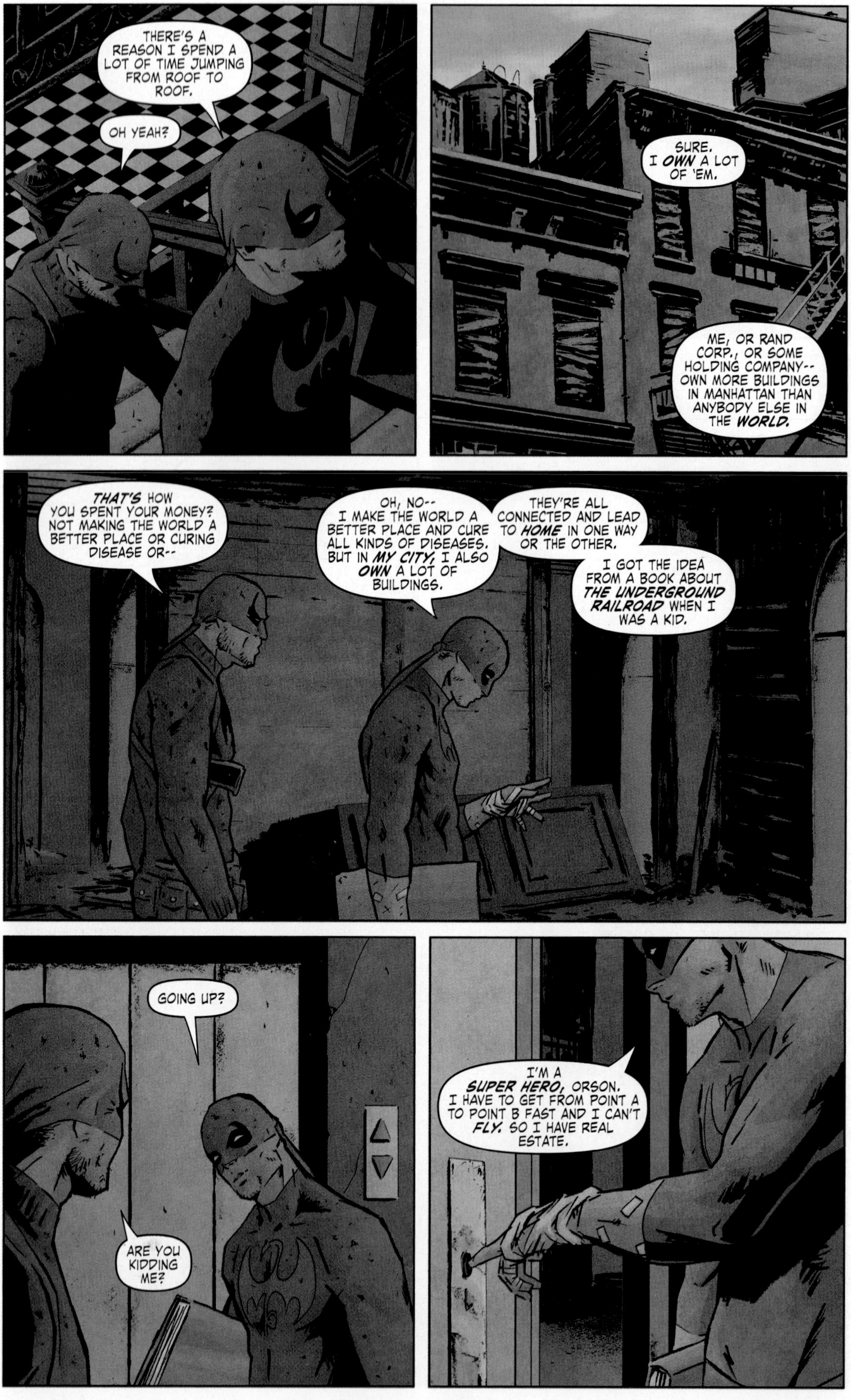
THERE'S A REASON I SPEND A LOT OF TIME JUMPING FROM ROOF TO ROOF.
OH YEAH?
SURE. I OWN A LOT OF 'EM.
ME, OR RAND CORP., OR SOME HOLDING COMPANY-- OWN MORE BUILDINGS IN MANHATTAN THAN ANYBODY ELSE IN THE WORLD.
THAT'S HOW YOU SPENT YOUR MONEY? NOT MAKING THE WORLD A BETTER PLACE OR CURING DISEASE OR--
OH, NO-- I MAKE THE WORLD A BETTER PLACE AND CURE ALL KINDS OF DISEASES. BUT IN MY CITY, I ALSO OWN A LOT OF BUILDINGS.
THEY'RE ALL CONNECTED AND LEAD TO HOME IN ONE WAY OR THE OTHER.
I GOT THE IDEA FROM A BOOK ABOUT THE UNDERGROUND RAILROAD WHEN I WAS A KID.
GOING UP?
ARE YOU KIDDING ME?
I'M A SUPER HERO, ORSON. I HAVE TO GET FROM POINT A TO POINT B FAST AND I CAN'T FLY. SO I HAVE REAL ESTATE.

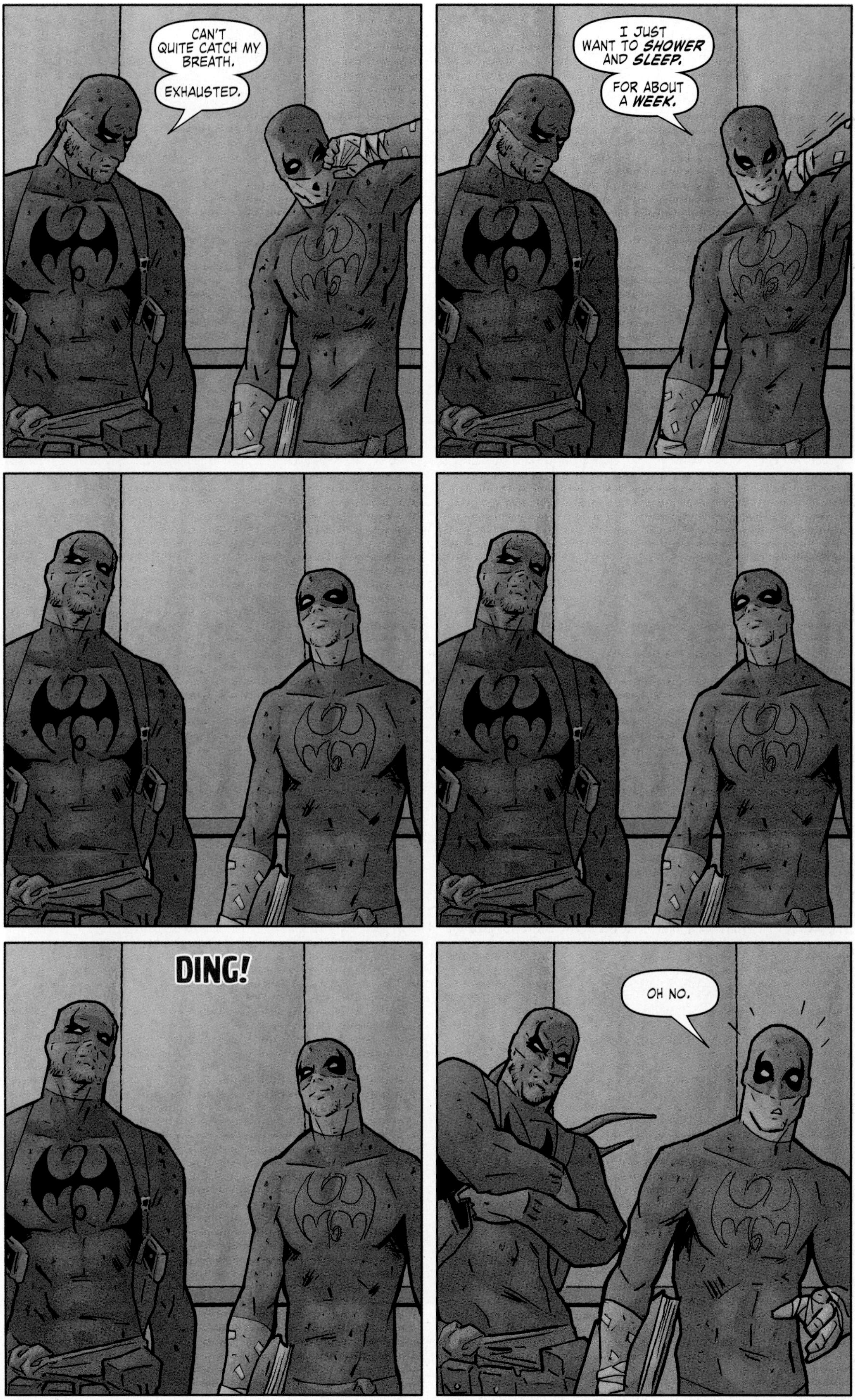
CAN'T QUITE CATCH MY BREATH.
EXHAUSTED.
I JUST WANT TO SHOWER AND SLEEP.
FOR ABOUT A WEEK.
DING!
OH NO.

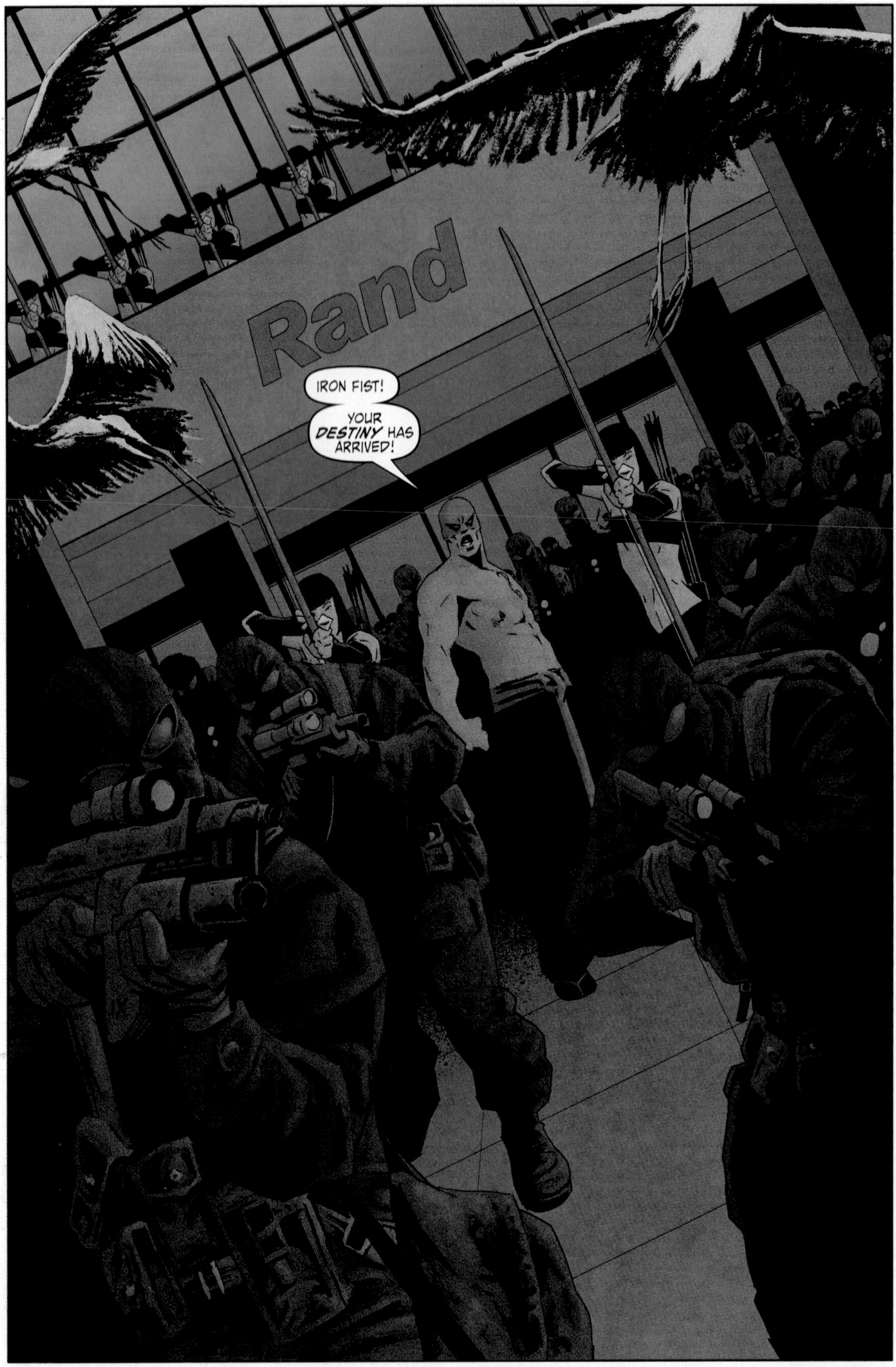
Rand
IRON FIST!
YOUR *DESTINY* HAS ARRIVED!

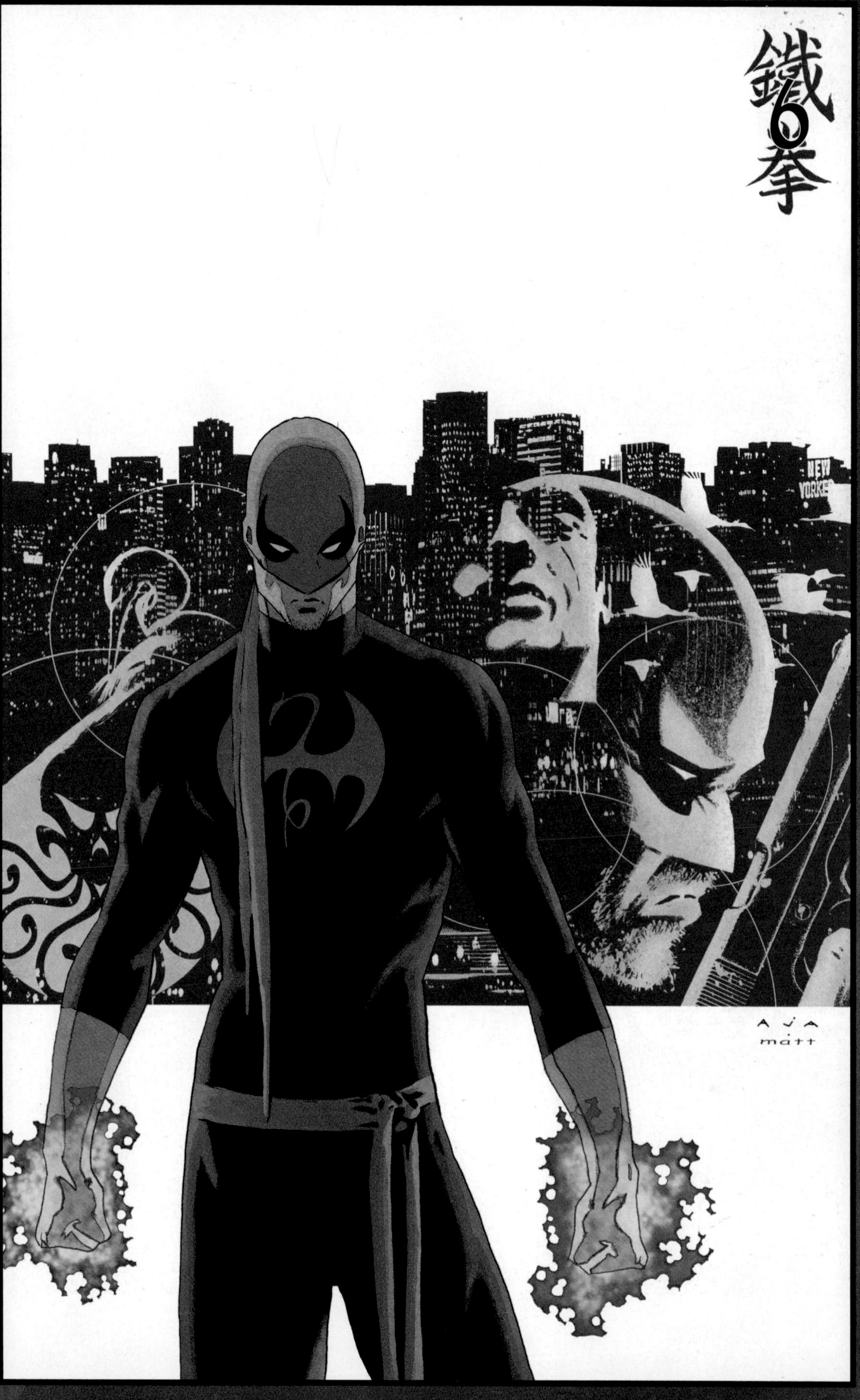
鐵
6
拳
NEW
YORKER
AJA
matt

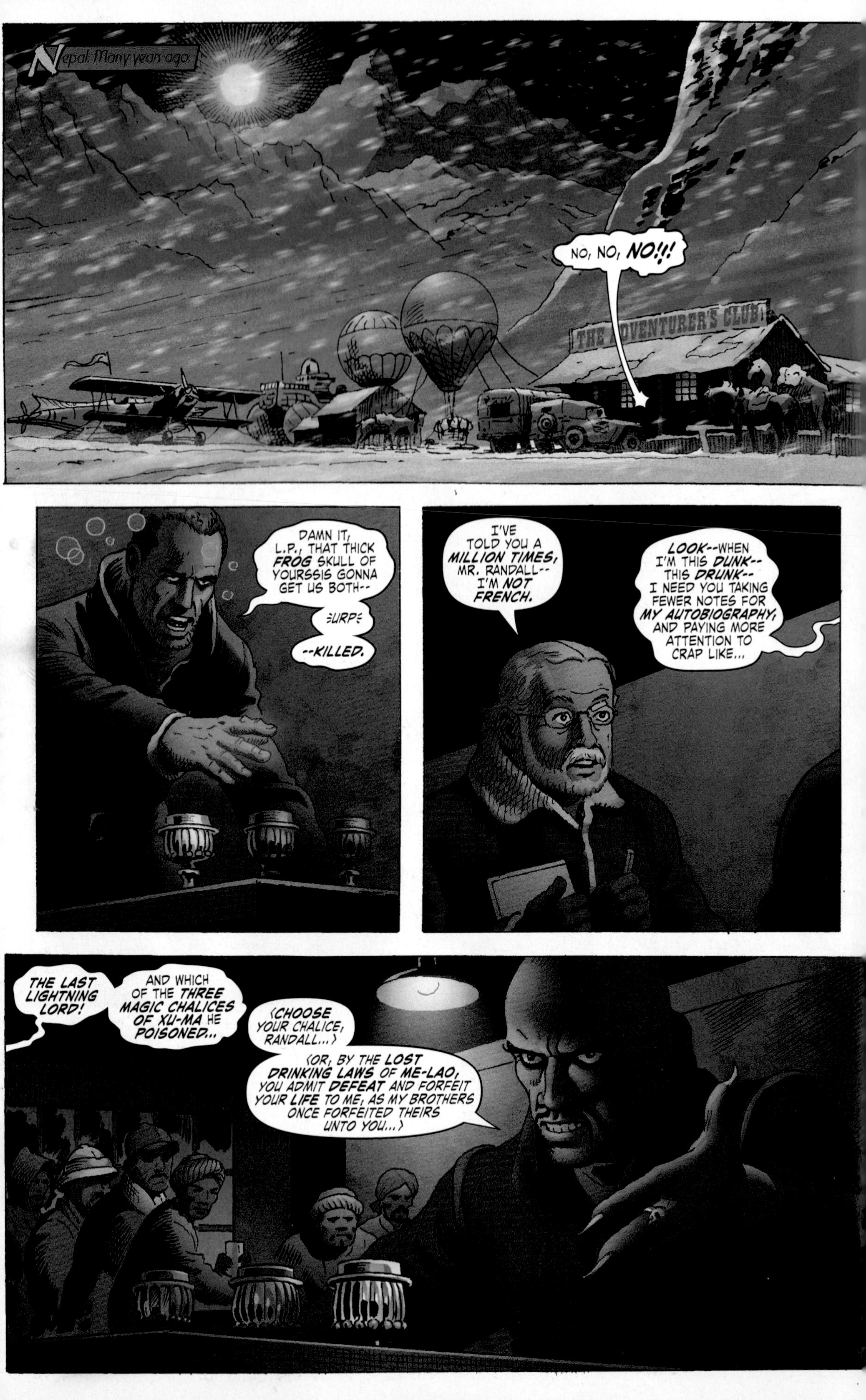
Nepal. Many years ago.
NO, NO, NO!!!
THE DVENTURER'S CLUB
DAMN IT, L.P., THAT THICK FROG SKULL OF YOURSSIS GONNA GET US BOTH--
URP
--KILLED.
I'VE TOLD YOU A MILLION TIMES, MR. RANDALL-- I'M NOT FRENCH.
LOOK--WHEN I'M THIS DUNK-- THIS DRUNK-- I NEED YOU TAKING FEWER NOTES FOR MY AUTOBIOGRAPHY, AND PAYING MORE ATTENTION TO CRAP LIKE...
THE LAST LIGHTNING LORD!
AND WHICH OF THE THREE MAGIC CHALICES OF XU-MA HE POISONED...
‹CHOOSE YOUR CHALICE, RANDALL...›
‹OR, BY THE LOST DRINKING LAWS OF ME-LAO, YOU ADMIT DEFEAT AND FORFEIT YOUR LIFE TO ME, AS MY BROTHERS ONCE FORFEITED THEIRS UNTO YOU...›

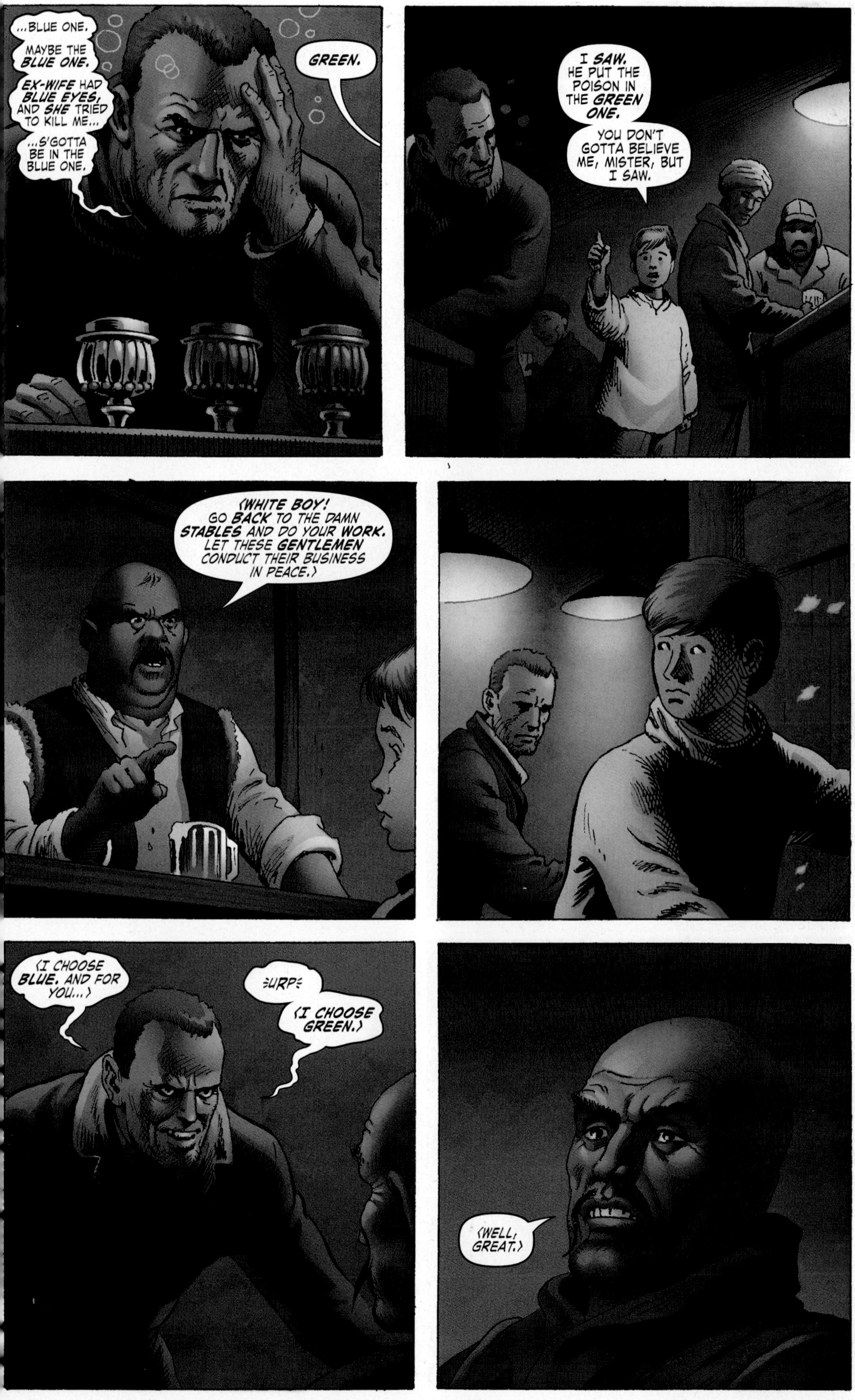
...BLUE ONE.
MAYBE THE BLUE ONE.
EX-WIFE HAD BLUE EYES, AND SHE TRIED TO KILL ME...
...S'GOTTA BE IN THE BLUE ONE.
GREEN.
I SAW. HE PUT THE POISON IN THE GREEN ONE.
YOU DON'T GOTTA BELIEVE ME, MISTER, BUT I SAW.
‹WHITE BOY! GO BACK TO THE DAMN STABLES AND DO YOUR WORK. LET THESE GENTLEMEN CONDUCT THEIR BUSINESS IN PEACE.›
‹I CHOOSE BLUE. AND FOR YOU...›
URP
‹I CHOOSE GREEN.›
‹WELL, GREAT.›

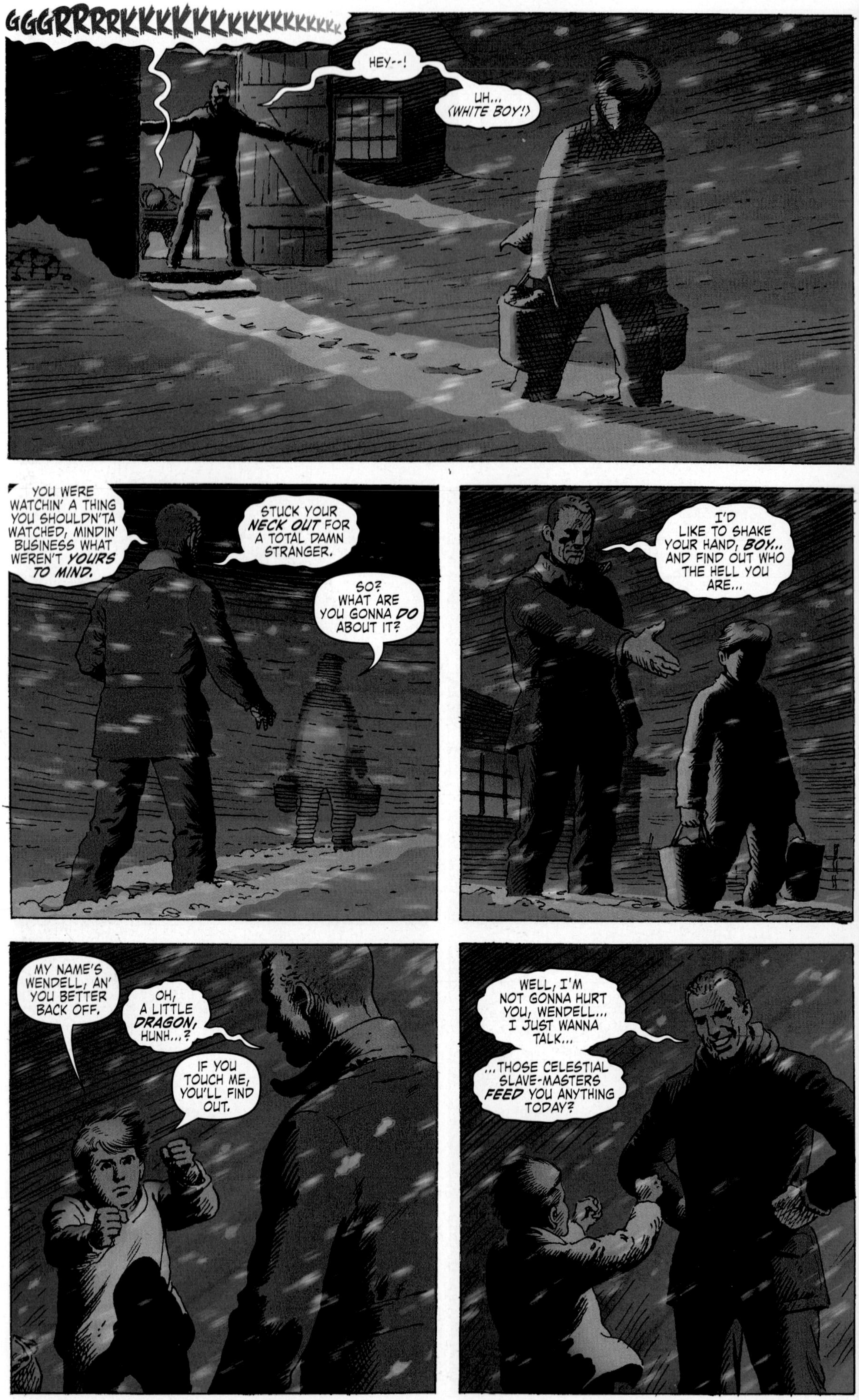
GGGRRRRKKKKKKKKKKKKKK
HEY--!
UH... ‹WHITE BOY!›
YOU WERE WATCHIN' A THING YOU SHOULDN'TA WATCHED, MINDIN' BUSINESS WHAT WEREN'T ***YOURS TO MIND.***
STUCK YOUR ***NECK OUT*** FOR A TOTAL DAMN STRANGER.
SO? WHAT ARE YOU GONNA ***DO*** ABOUT IT?
I'D LIKE TO SHAKE YOUR HAND, ***BOY...*** AND FIND OUT WHO THE HELL YOU ARE...
MY NAME'S WENDELL, AN' YOU BETTER BACK OFF.
OH, A LITTLE ***DRAGON,*** HUNH...?
IF YOU TOUCH ME, YOU'LL FIND OUT.
WELL, I'M NOT GONNA HURT YOU, WENDELL... I JUST WANNA TALK...
...THOSE CELESTIAL SLAVE-MASTERS ***FEED*** YOU ANYTHING TODAY?

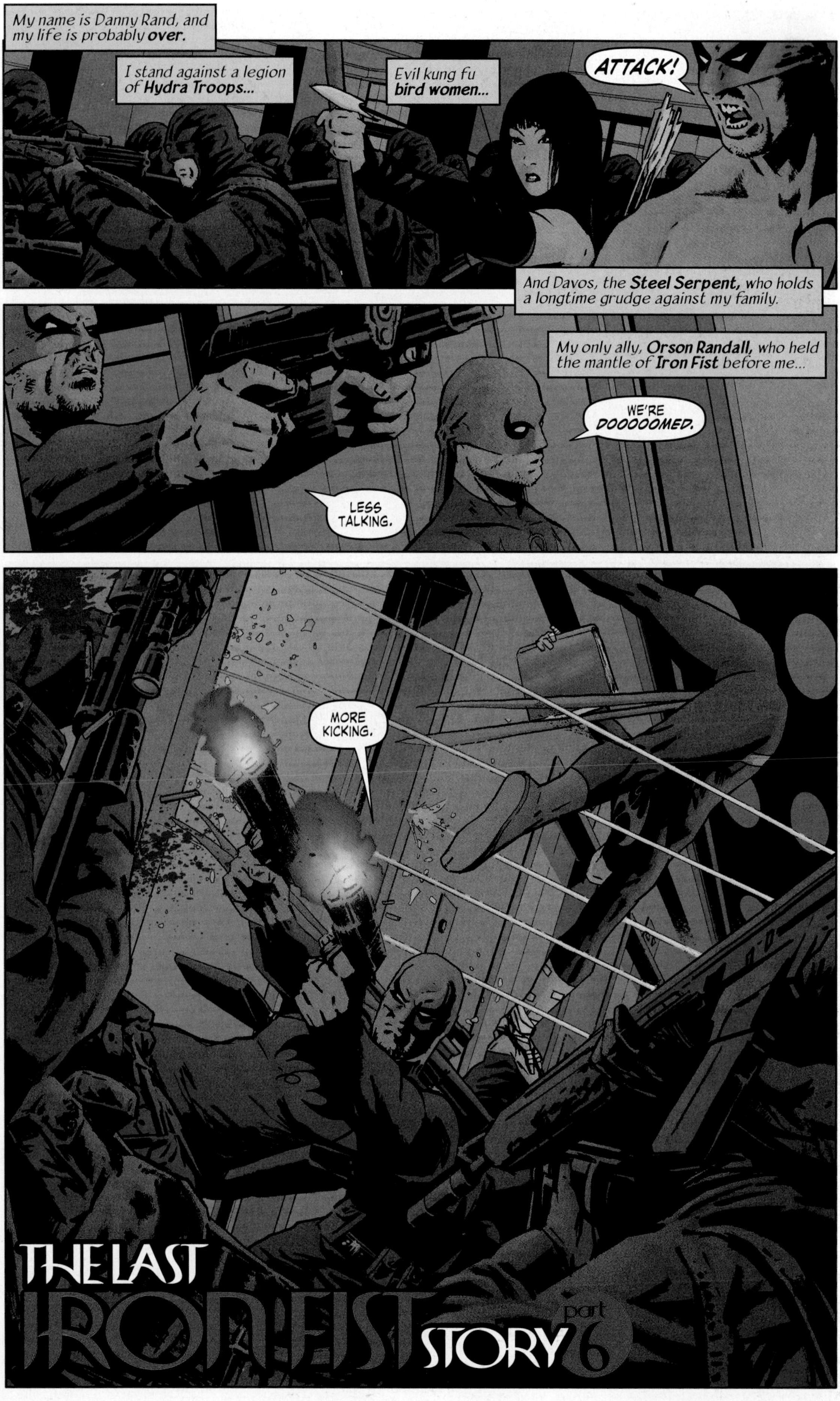
My name is Danny Rand, and my life is probably **over.**
I stand against a legion of **Hydra Troops...**
Evil kung fu **bird women...**
ATTACK!
And Davos, the **Steel Serpent,** who holds a longtime grudge against my family.
My only ally, **Orson Randall,** who held the mantle of **Iron Fist** before me...
LESS TALKING.
WE'RE *DOOOOOMED.*
MORE KICKING.
THE LAST IRON FIST STORY part 6

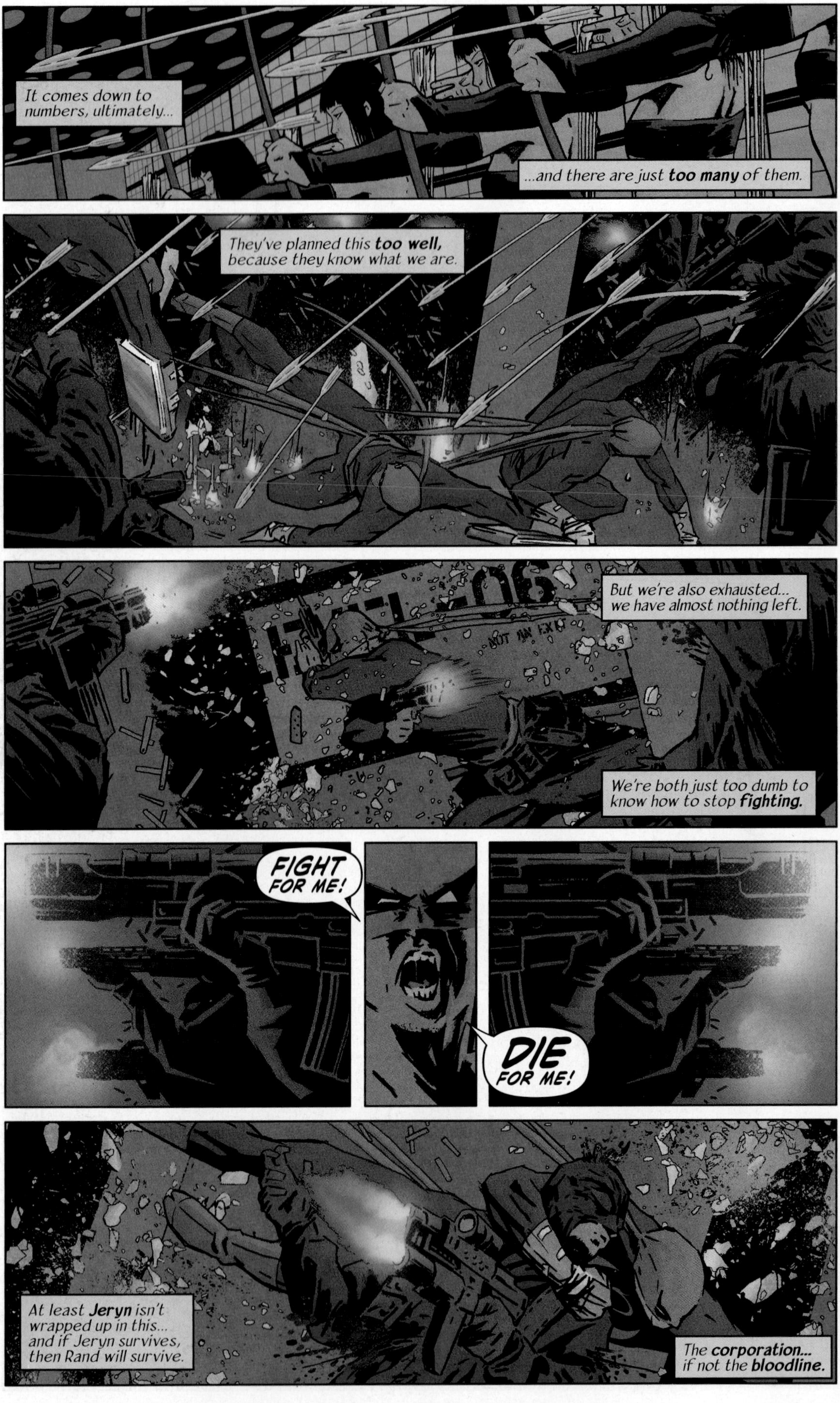

It comes down to numbers, ultimately...
...and there are just **too many** of them.
They've planned this **too well,** because they know what we are.
But we're also exhausted... we have almost nothing left.
NOT AN EXIT
We're both just too dumb to know how to stop **fighting.**
FIGHT FOR ME!
DIE FOR ME!
At least **Jeryn** isn't wrapped up in this... and if Jeryn survives, then Rand will survive.
The **corporation...** if not the **bloodline.**

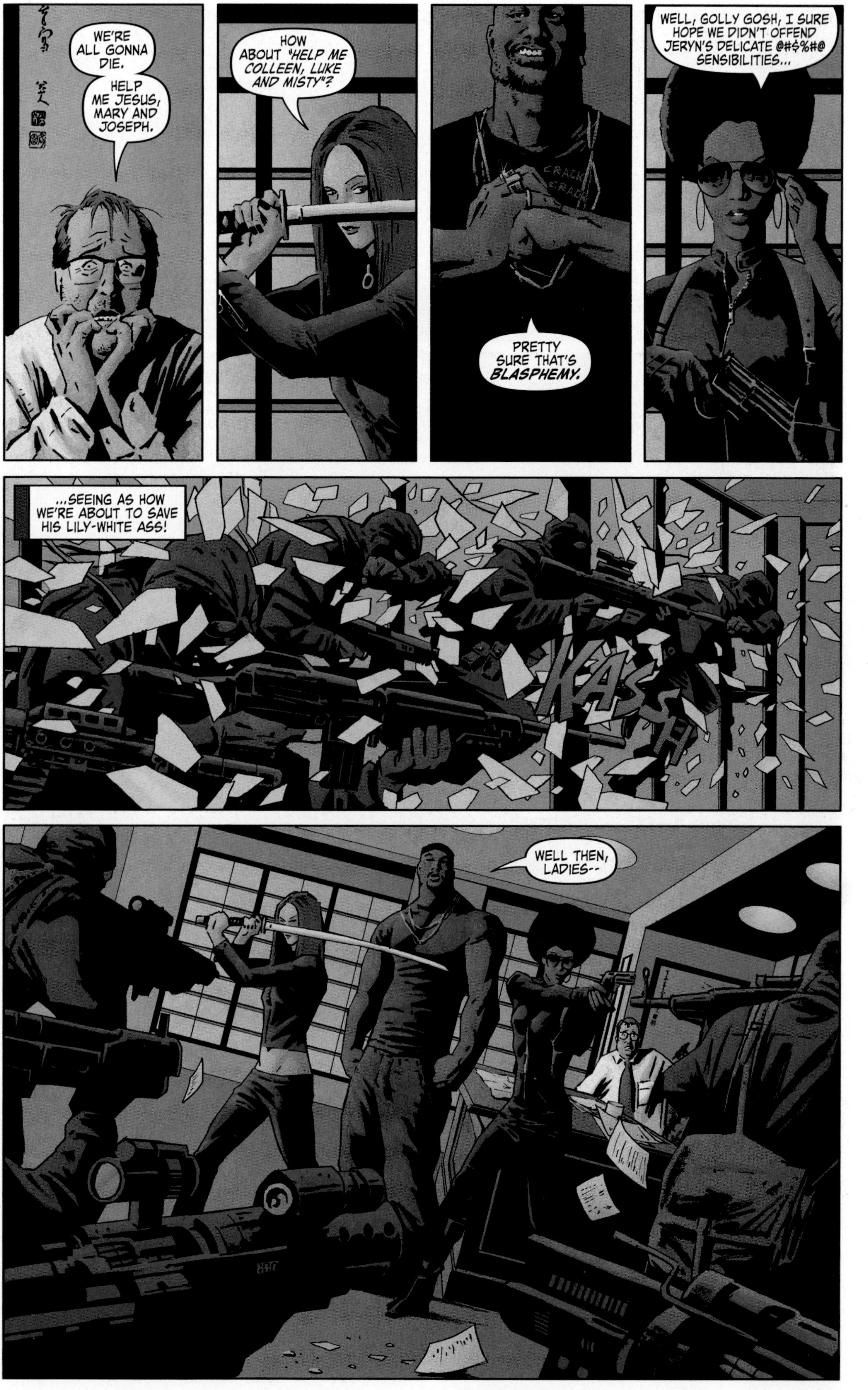
WE'RE ALL GONNA DIE.
HELP ME JESUS, MARY AND JOSEPH.
HOW ABOUT "HELP ME COLLEEN, LUKE AND MISTY"?
CRACK CRACK
PRETTY SURE THAT'S BLASPHEMY.
WELL, GOLLY GOSH, I SURE HOPE WE DIDN'T OFFEND JERYN'S DELICATE @#$%#@ SENSIBILITIES...
...SEEING AS HOW WE'RE ABOUT TO SAVE HIS LILY-WHITE ASS!
KASSH
WELL THEN, LADIES--

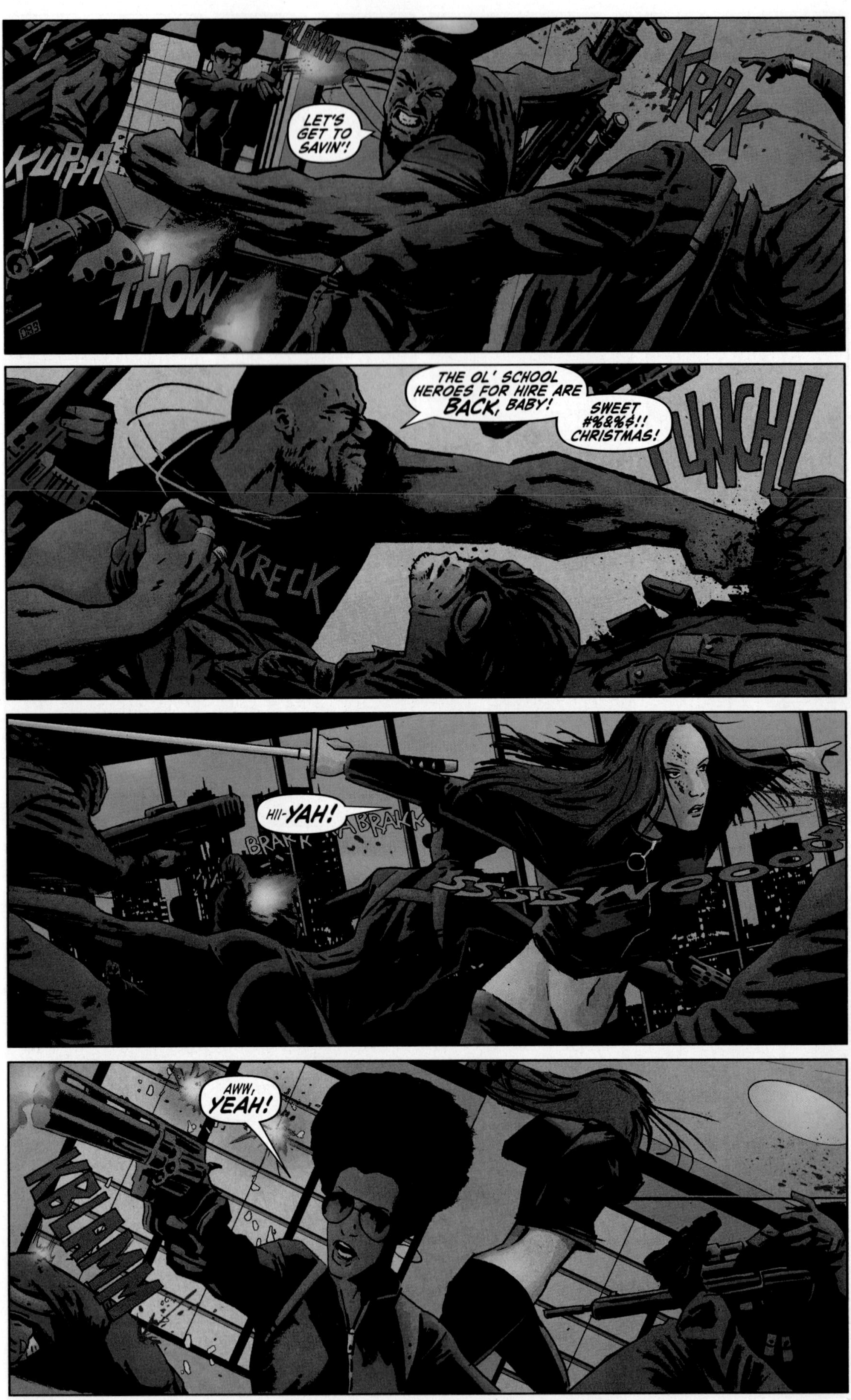
BLAMM
LET'S GET TO SAVIN'!
KRAK
KUPPA
THOW
THE OL' SCHOOL HEROES FOR HIRE ARE BACK, BABY!
SWEET #%&%$!! CHRISTMAS!
PUNCH!
KRECK
HII-YAH!
BRAKK
BRAKK
AWW, YEAH!
KBLAMM

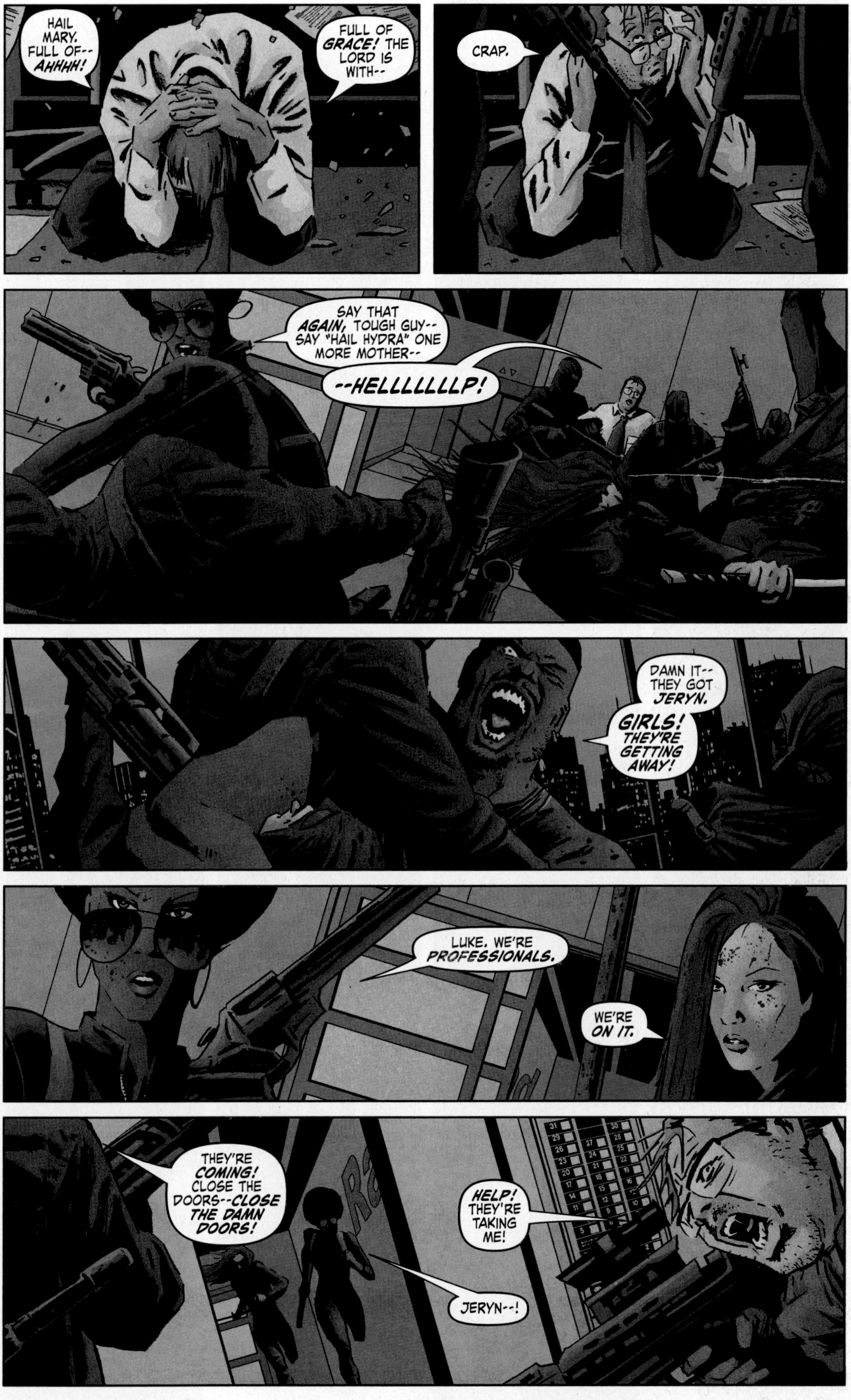
HAIL MARY. FULL OF-- AHHHH!
FULL OF GRACE! THE LORD IS WITH--
CRAP.
SAY THAT AGAIN, TOUGH GUY-- SAY "HAIL HYDRA" ONE MORE MOTHER--
--HELLLLLLLLP!
DAMN IT-- THEY GOT JERYN.
GIRLS! THEY'RE GETTING AWAY!
LUKE. WE'RE PROFESSIONALS.
WE'RE ON IT.
THEY'RE COMING! CLOSE THE DOORS--CLOSE THE DAMN DOORS!
HELP! THEY'RE TAKING ME!
JERYN--!

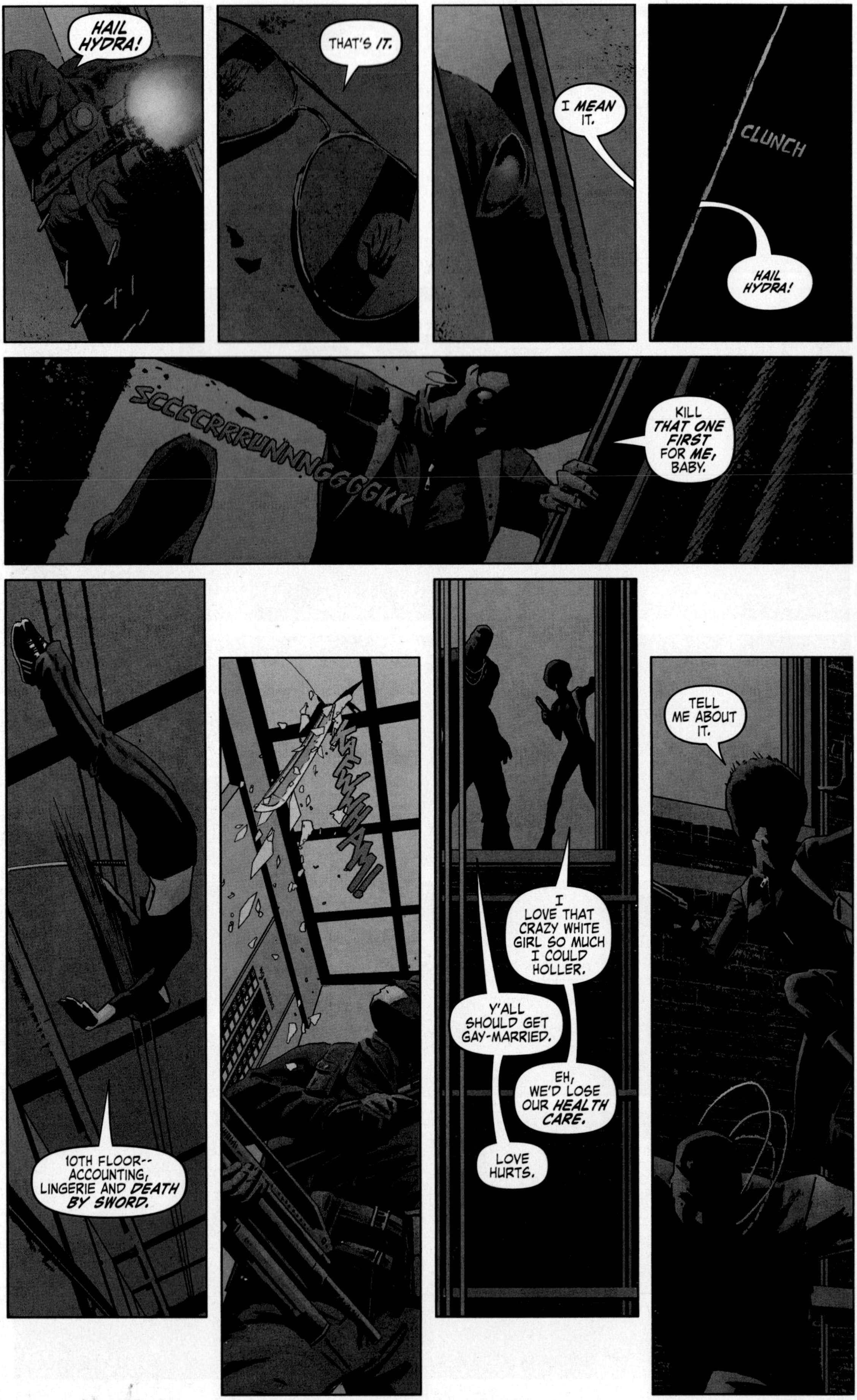
HAIL HYDRA!
THAT'S IT.
I MEAN IT.
CLUNCH
HAIL HYDRA!
SCCCCRRRRUNNNNGGGGKK
KILL THAT ONE FIRST FOR ME, BABY.
10TH FLOOR-- ACCOUNTING, LINGERIE AND DEATH BY SWORD.
KRAWHAM!
I LOVE THAT CRAZY WHITE GIRL SO MUCH I COULD HOLLER.
Y'ALL SHOULD GET GAY-MARRIED.
EH, WE'D LOSE OUR HEALTH CARE.
LOVE HURTS.
TELL ME ABOUT IT.

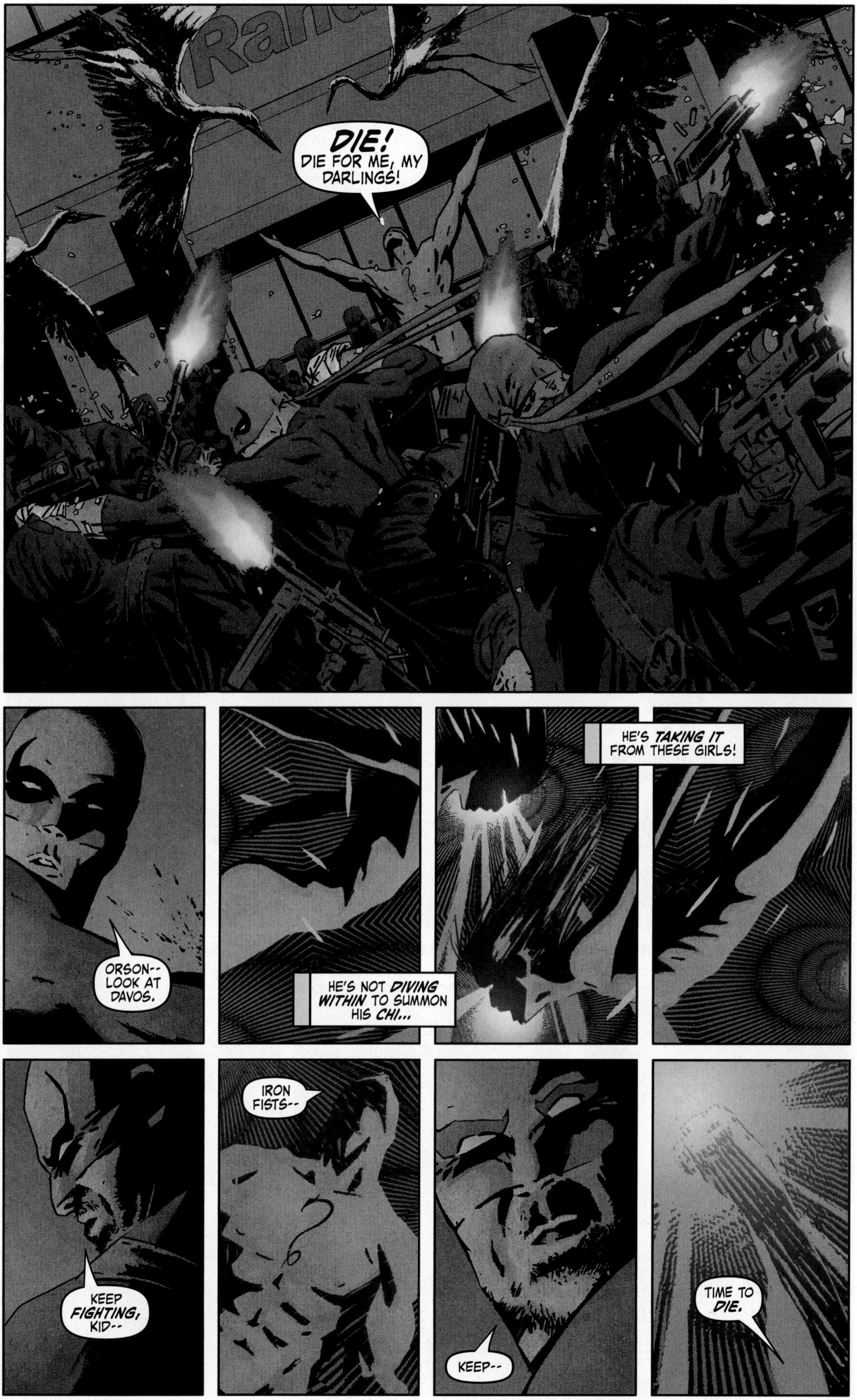
DIE!
DIE FOR ME, MY DARLINGS!
ORSON--
LOOK AT DAVOS.
HE'S NOT DIVING WITHIN TO SUMMON HIS CHI...
HE'S TAKING IT FROM THESE GIRLS!
KEEP FIGHTING, KID--
IRON FISTS--
KEEP--
TIME TO DIE.

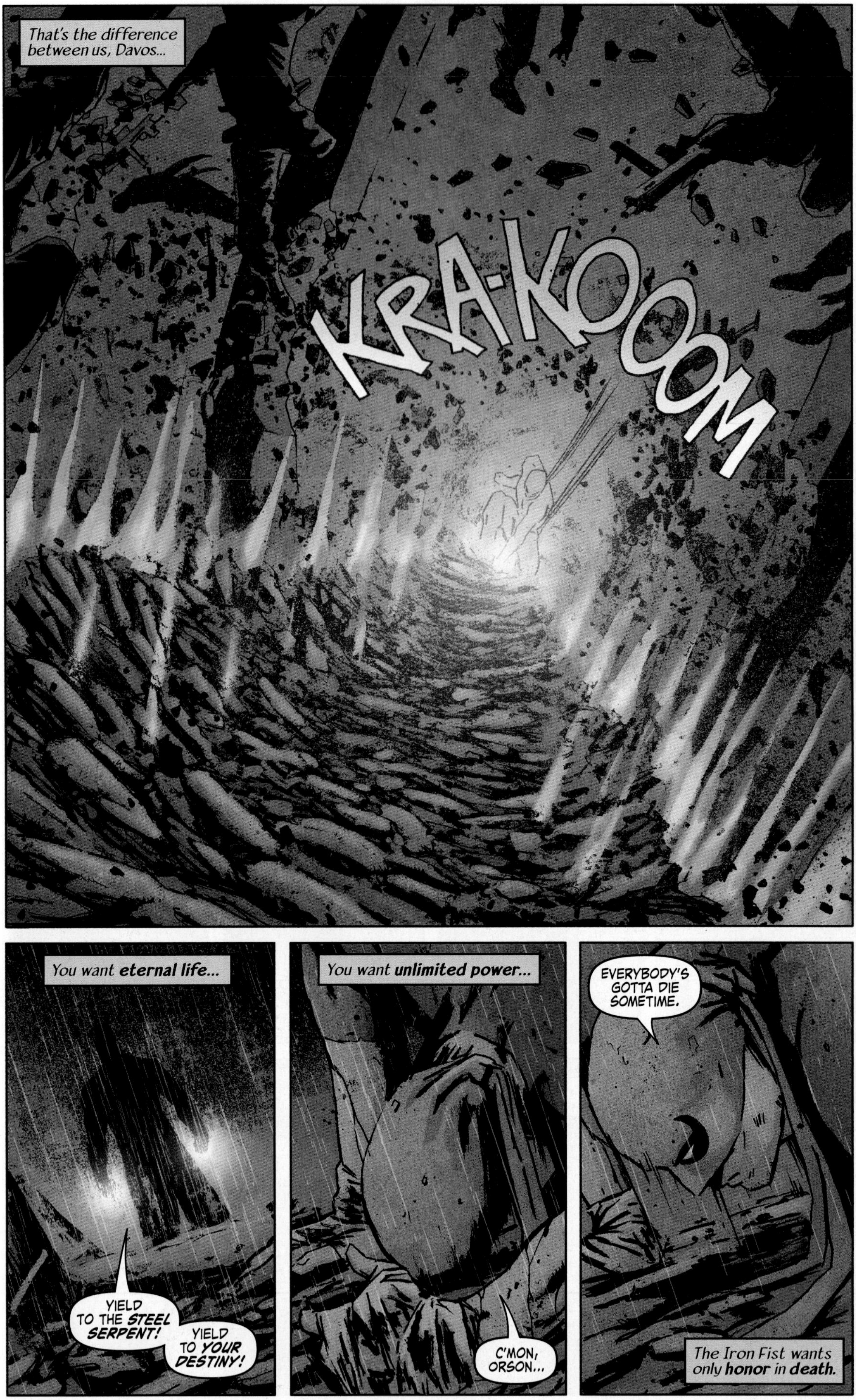
That's the difference between us, Davos...
KRA-KOOOM
You want eternal life...
YIELD TO THE STEEL SERPENT!
YIELD TO YOUR DESTINY!
You want unlimited power...
C'MON, ORSON...
EVERYBODY'S GOTTA DIE SOMETIME.
The Iron Fist wants only honor in death.

And in the time it takes me to...

DIE!

DIE!

blink

my

DIE!

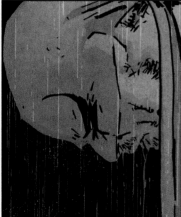

eyes...

...Orson decides that's **exactly** what he wants.

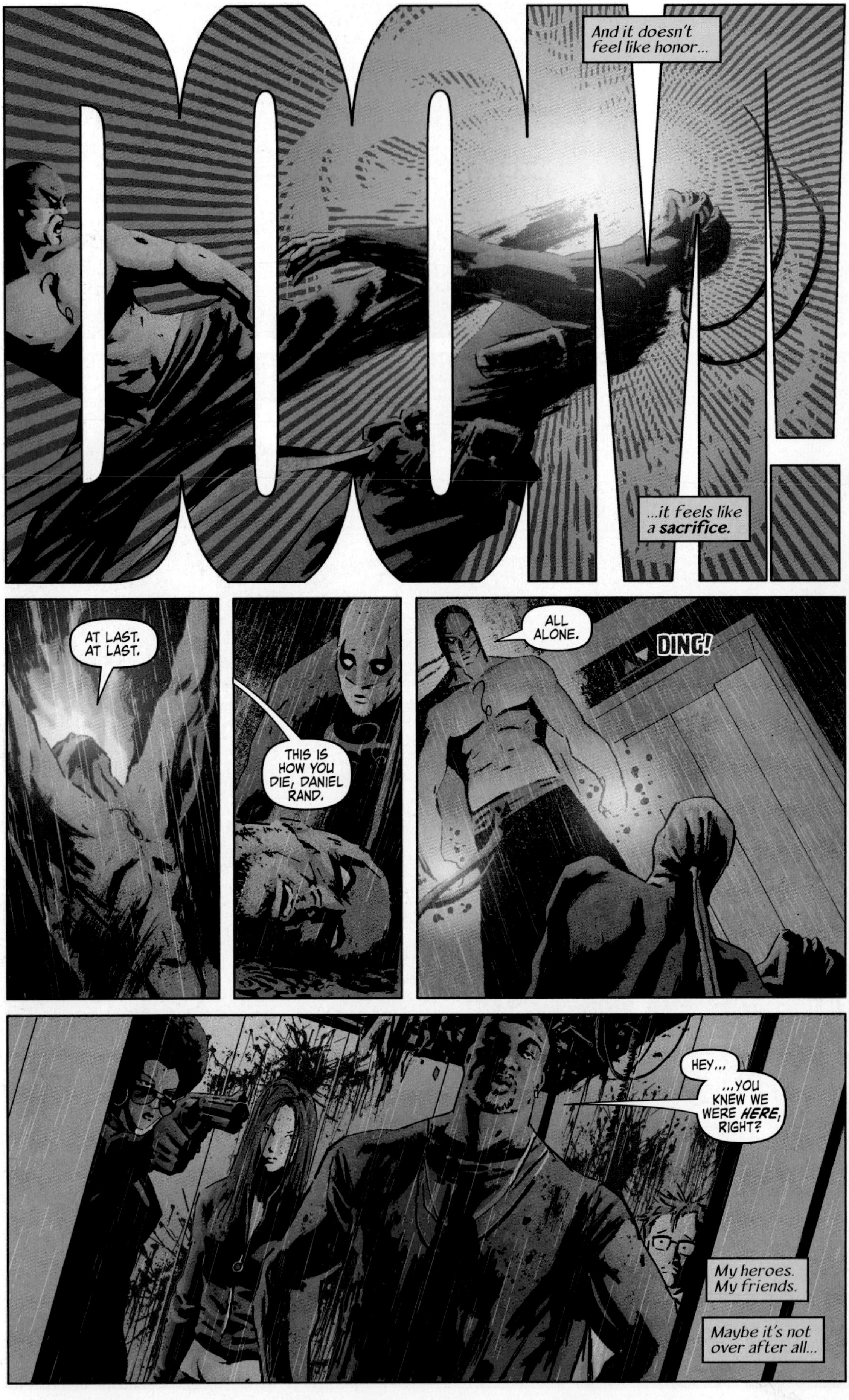

DOOM!
And it doesn't feel like honor...
...it feels like a *sacrifice.*
AT LAST. AT LAST.
THIS IS HOW YOU DIE, DANIEL RAND.
ALL ALONE.
DING!
HEY...
...YOU KNEW WE WERE *HERE*, RIGHT?
My heroes. My friends.
Maybe it's not over after all...

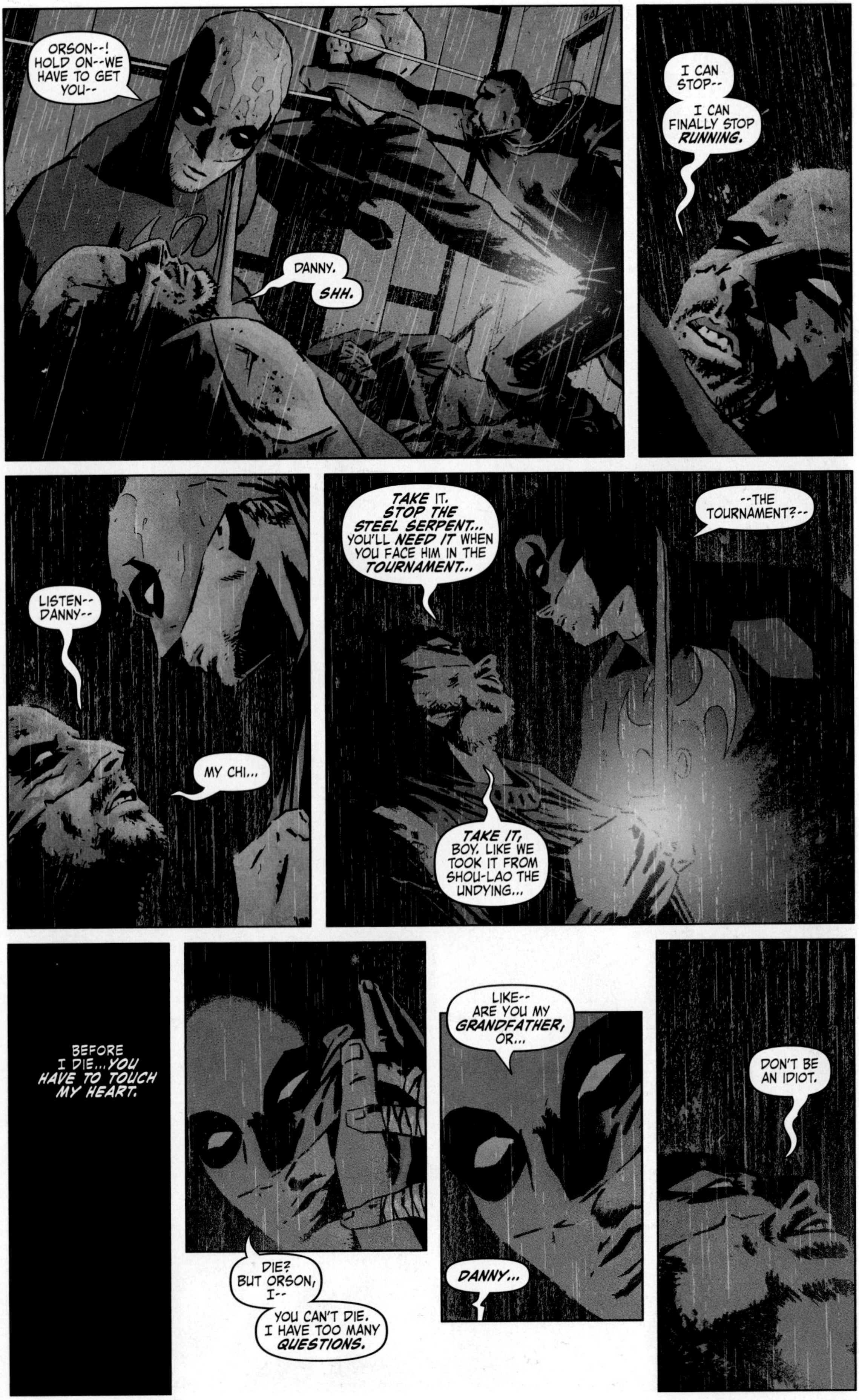
ORSON--! HOLD ON--WE HAVE TO GET YOU--
DANNY.
SHH.
I CAN STOP--
I CAN FINALLY STOP RUNNING.
LISTEN--DANNY--
MY CHI...
TAKE IT. STOP THE STEEL SERPENT... YOU'LL NEED IT WHEN YOU FACE HIM IN THE TOURNAMENT...
--THE TOURNAMENT?--
TAKE IT, BOY. LIKE WE TOOK IT FROM SHOU-LAO THE UNDYING...
BEFORE I DIE...YOU HAVE TO TOUCH MY HEART.
DIE? BUT ORSON, I--
YOU CAN'T DIE. I HAVE TOO MANY QUESTIONS.
LIKE--ARE YOU MY GRANDFATHER, OR...
DANNY...
DON'T BE AN IDIOT.

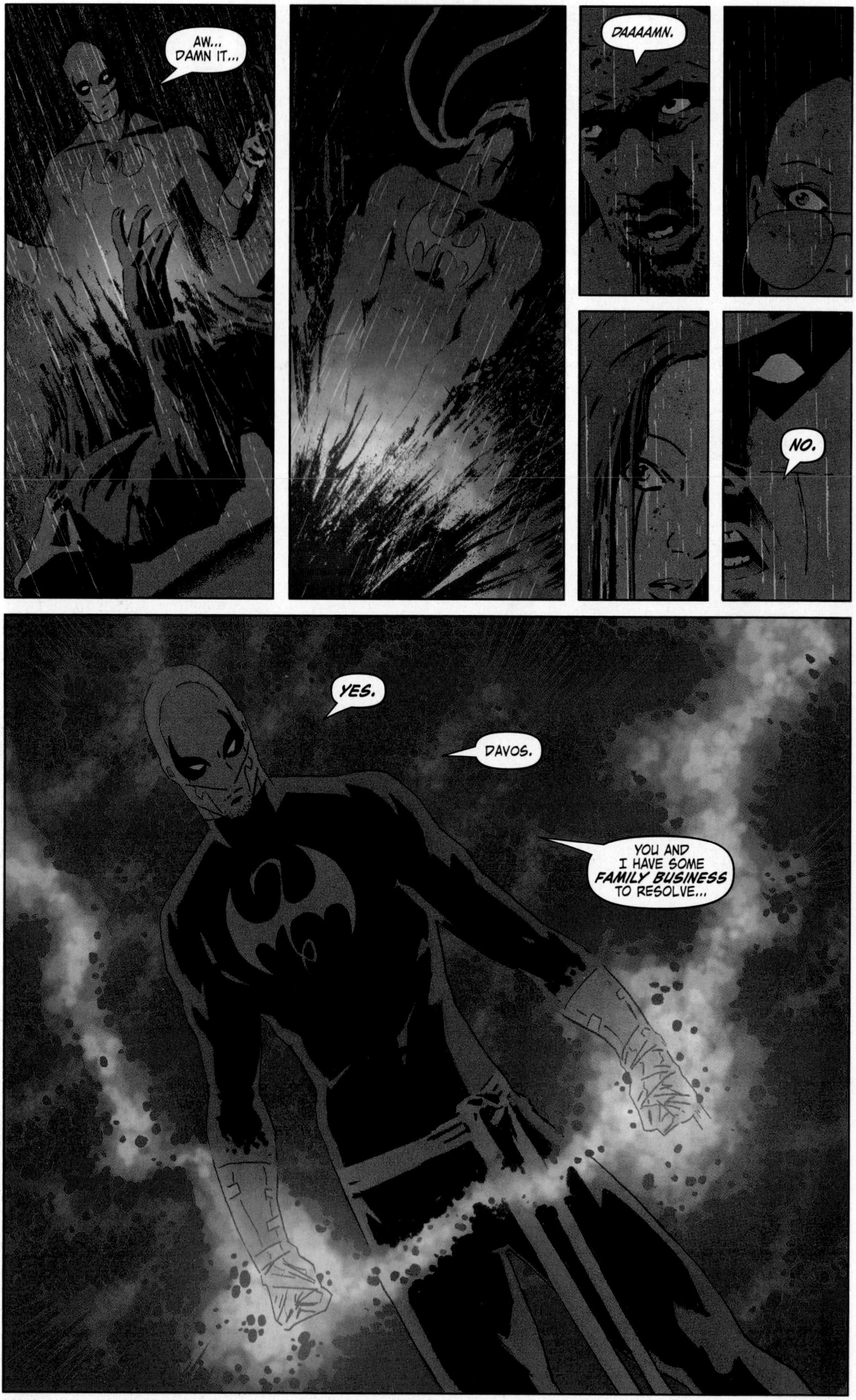
AW... DAMN IT...
DAAAAMN.
NO.
YES.
DAVOS.
YOU AND I HAVE SOME FAMILY BUSINESS TO RESOLVE...

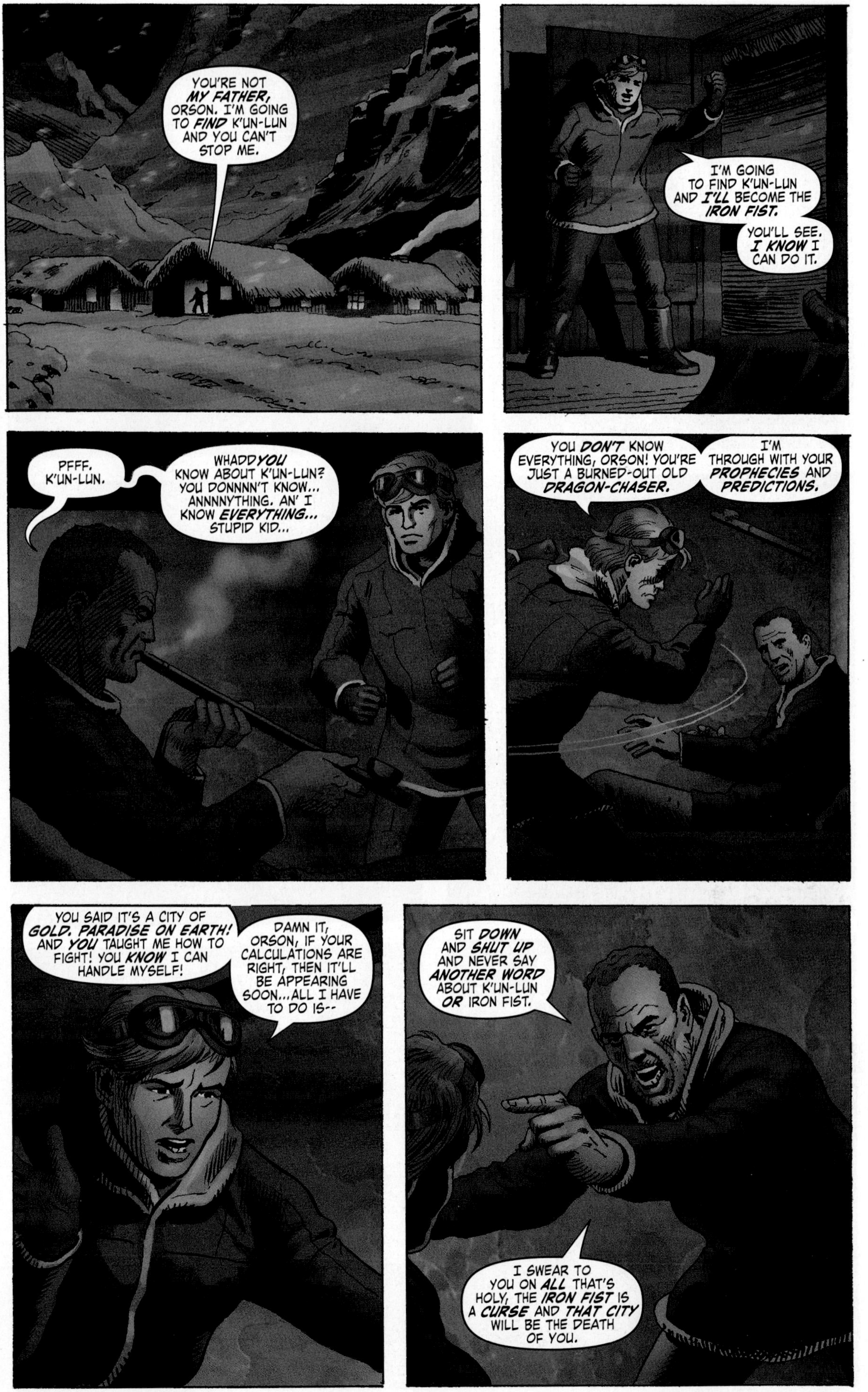
YOU'RE NOT MY FATHER, ORSON. I'M GOING TO FIND K'UN-LUN AND YOU CAN'T STOP ME.
I'M GOING TO FIND K'UN-LUN AND I'LL BECOME THE IRON FIST.
YOU'LL SEE. I KNOW I CAN DO IT.
PFFF. K'UN-LUN.
WHADDYOU KNOW ABOUT K'UN-LUN? YOU DONNNN'T KNOW... ANNNNYTHING. AN' I KNOW EVERYTHING... STUPID KID...
YOU DON'T KNOW EVERYTHING, ORSON! YOU'RE JUST A BURNED-OUT OLD DRAGON-CHASER.
I'M THROUGH WITH YOUR PROPHECIES AND PREDICTIONS.
YOU SAID IT'S A CITY OF GOLD. PARADISE ON EARTH! AND YOU TAUGHT ME HOW TO FIGHT! YOU KNOW I CAN HANDLE MYSELF!
DAMN IT, ORSON, IF YOUR CALCULATIONS ARE RIGHT, THEN IT'LL BE APPEARING SOON...ALL I HAVE TO DO IS--
SIT DOWN AND SHUT UP AND NEVER SAY ANOTHER WORD ABOUT K'UN-LUN OR IRON FIST.
I SWEAR TO YOU ON ALL THAT'S HOLY, THE IRON FIST IS A CURSE AND THAT CITY WILL BE THE DEATH OF YOU.

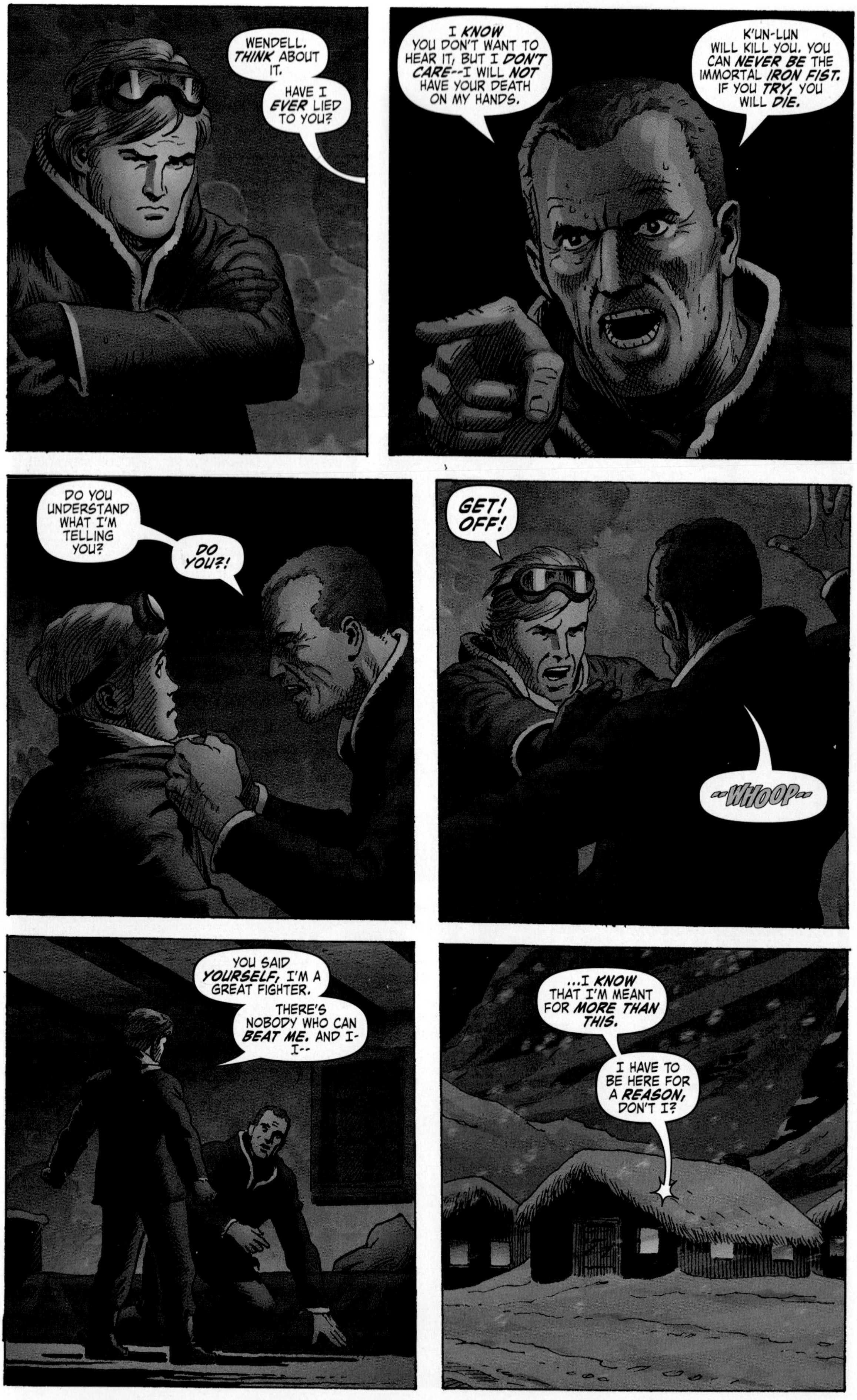
WENDELL. THINK ABOUT IT.
HAVE I EVER LIED TO YOU?
I KNOW YOU DON'T WANT TO HEAR IT, BUT I DON'T CARE--I WILL NOT HAVE YOUR DEATH ON MY HANDS.
K'UN-LUN WILL KILL YOU. YOU CAN NEVER BE THE IMMORTAL IRON FIST. IF YOU TRY, YOU WILL DIE.
DO YOU UNDERSTAND WHAT I'M TELLING YOU?
DO YOU?!
GET! OFF!
--WHOOP--
YOU SAID YOURSELF, I'M A GREAT FIGHTER.
THERE'S NOBODY WHO CAN BEAT ME. AND I-I--
...I KNOW THAT I'M MEANT FOR MORE THAN THIS.
I HAVE TO BE HERE FOR A REASON, DON'T I?

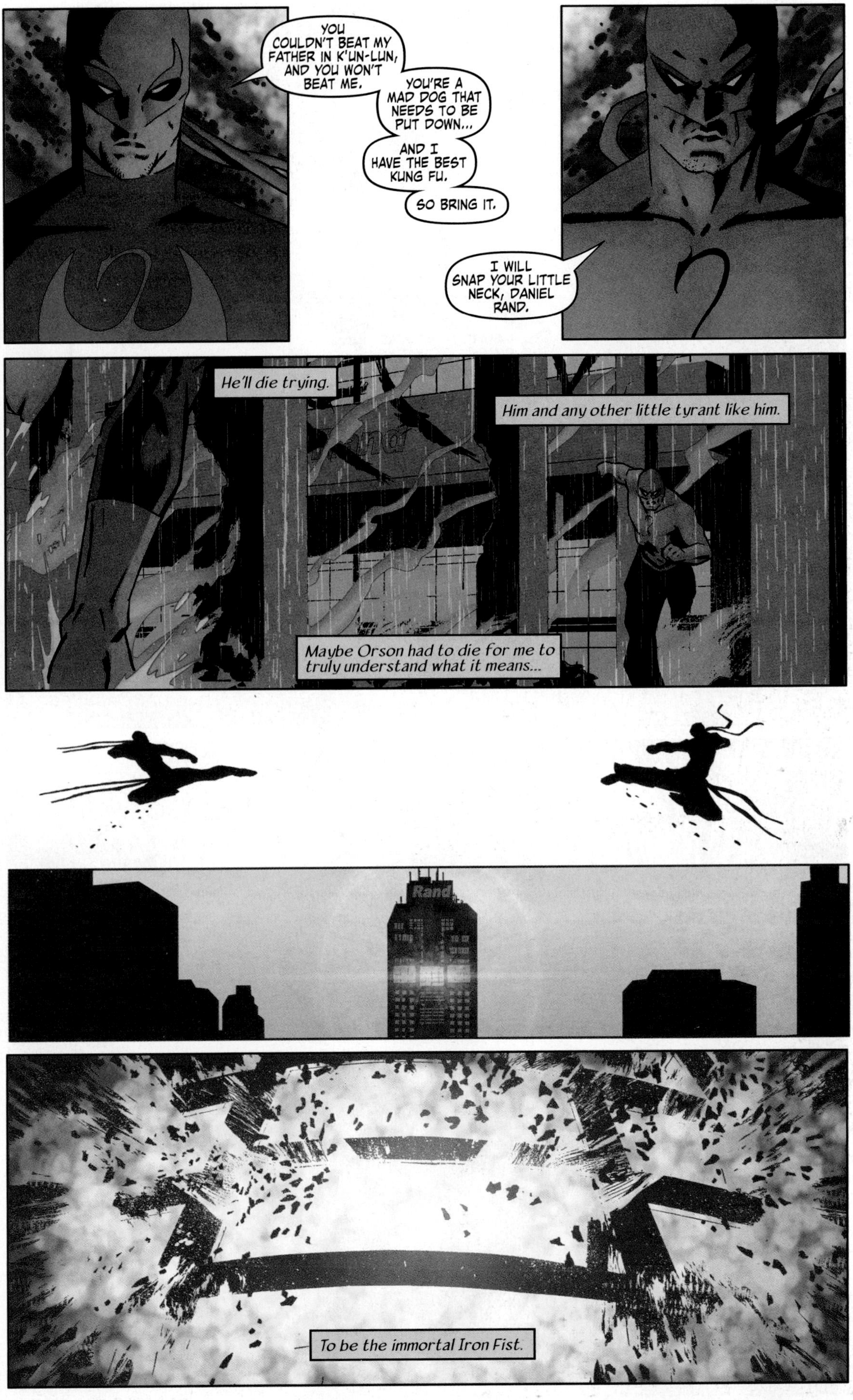
YOU COULDN'T BEAT MY FATHER IN K'UN-LUN, AND YOU WON'T BEAT ME.
YOU'RE A MAD DOG THAT NEEDS TO BE PUT DOWN...
AND I HAVE THE BEST KUNG FU.
SO BRING IT.
I WILL SNAP YOUR LITTLE NECK, DANIEL RAND.
He'll die trying.
Him and any other little tyrant like him.
Maybe Orson had to die for me to truly understand what it means...
Rand
To be the immortal Iron Fist.

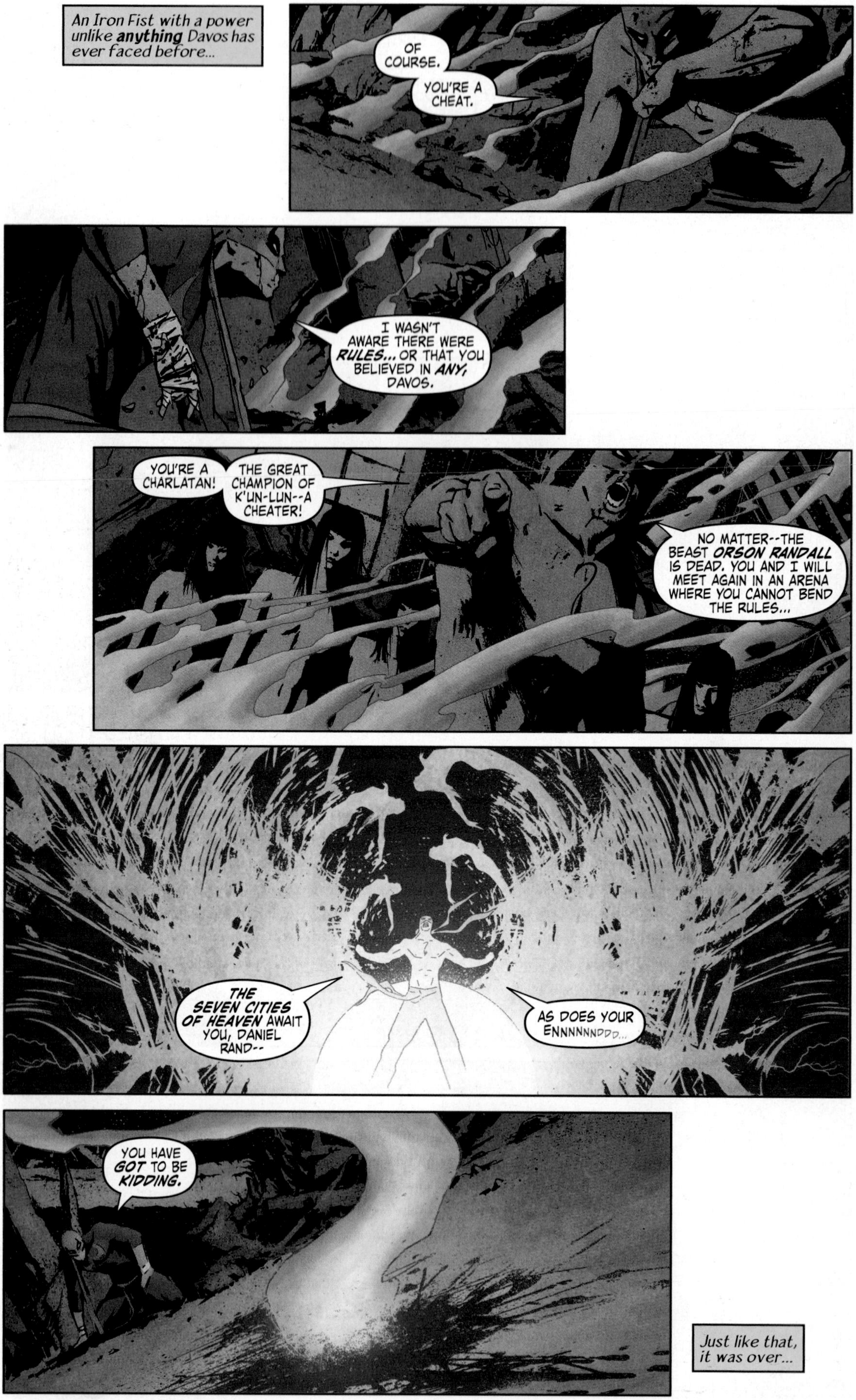
An Iron Fist with a power unlike **anything** Davos has ever faced before...
OF COURSE.
YOU'RE A CHEAT.
I WASN'T AWARE THERE WERE **RULES...** OR THAT YOU BELIEVED IN **ANY,** DAVOS.
YOU'RE A CHARLATAN!
THE GREAT CHAMPION OF K'UN-LUN--A CHEATER!
NO MATTER--THE BEAST **ORSON RANDALL** IS DEAD. YOU AND I WILL MEET AGAIN IN AN ARENA WHERE YOU CANNOT BEND THE RULES...
THE SEVEN CITIES OF HEAVEN AWAIT YOU, DANIEL RAND--
AS DOES YOUR ENNNNNNDDD...
YOU HAVE **GOT** TO BE **KIDDING.**
Just like that, it was over...

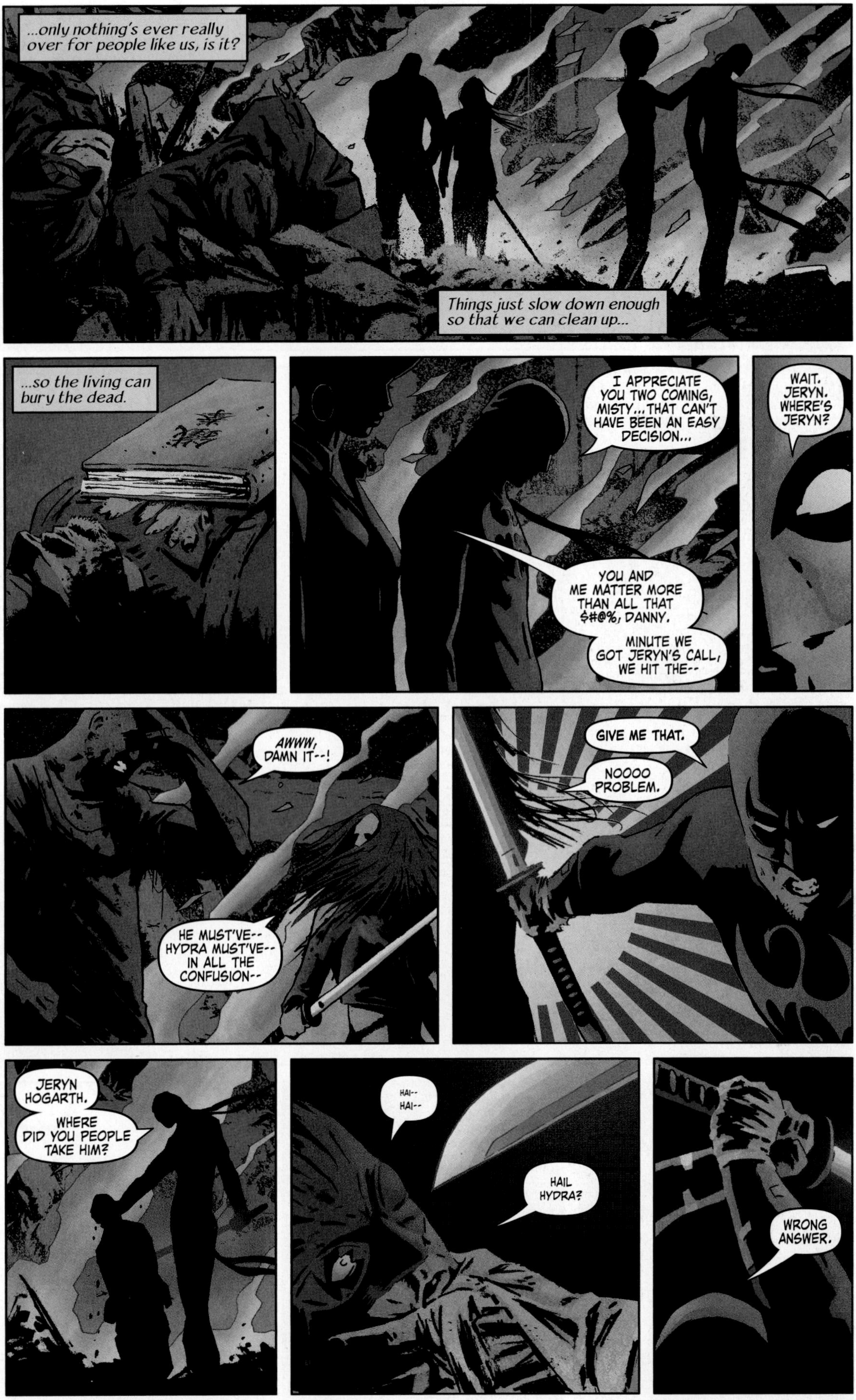
...only nothing's ever really over for people like us, is it?
Things just slow down enough so that we can clean up...
...so the living can bury the dead.
I APPRECIATE YOU TWO COMING, MISTY...THAT CAN'T HAVE BEEN AN EASY DECISION...
YOU AND ME MATTER MORE THAN ALL THAT $#@%, DANNY.
MINUTE WE GOT JERYN'S CALL, WE HIT THE--
WAIT. JERYN. WHERE'S JERYN?
AWWW, DAMN IT--!
HE MUST'VE-- HYDRA MUST'VE-- IN ALL THE CONFUSION--
GIVE ME THAT.
NOOOO PROBLEM.
JERYN HOGARTH.
WHERE DID YOU PEOPLE TAKE HIM?
HAI-- HAI--
HAIL HYDRA?
WRONG ANSWER.

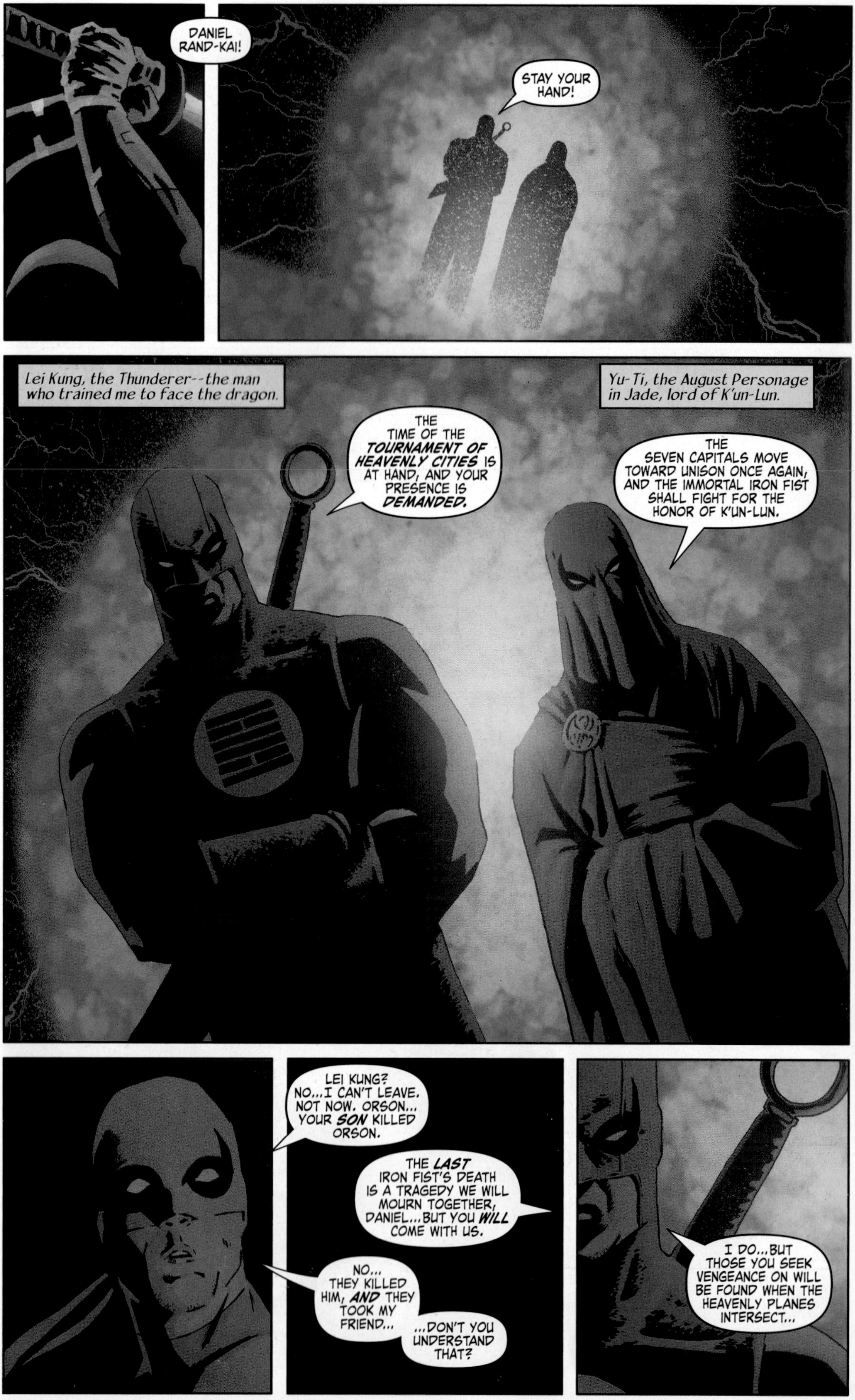
DANIEL RAND-KAI!
STAY YOUR HAND!
Lei Kung, the Thunderer--the man who trained me to face the dragon.
THE TIME OF THE TOURNAMENT OF HEAVENLY CITIES IS AT HAND, AND YOUR PRESENCE IS DEMANDED.
Yu-Ti, the August Personage in Jade, lord of K'un-Lun.
THE SEVEN CAPITALS MOVE TOWARD UNISON ONCE AGAIN, AND THE IMMORTAL IRON FIST SHALL FIGHT FOR THE HONOR OF K'UN-LUN.
LEI KUNG? NO...I CAN'T LEAVE. NOT NOW. ORSON... YOUR SON KILLED ORSON.
THE LAST IRON FIST'S DEATH IS A TRAGEDY WE WILL MOURN TOGETHER, DANIEL...BUT YOU WILL COME WITH US.
NO... THEY KILLED HIM, AND THEY TOOK MY FRIEND...
...DON'T YOU UNDERSTAND THAT?
I DO...BUT THOSE YOU SEEK VENGEANCE ON WILL BE FOUND WHEN THE HEAVENLY PLANES INTERSECT...

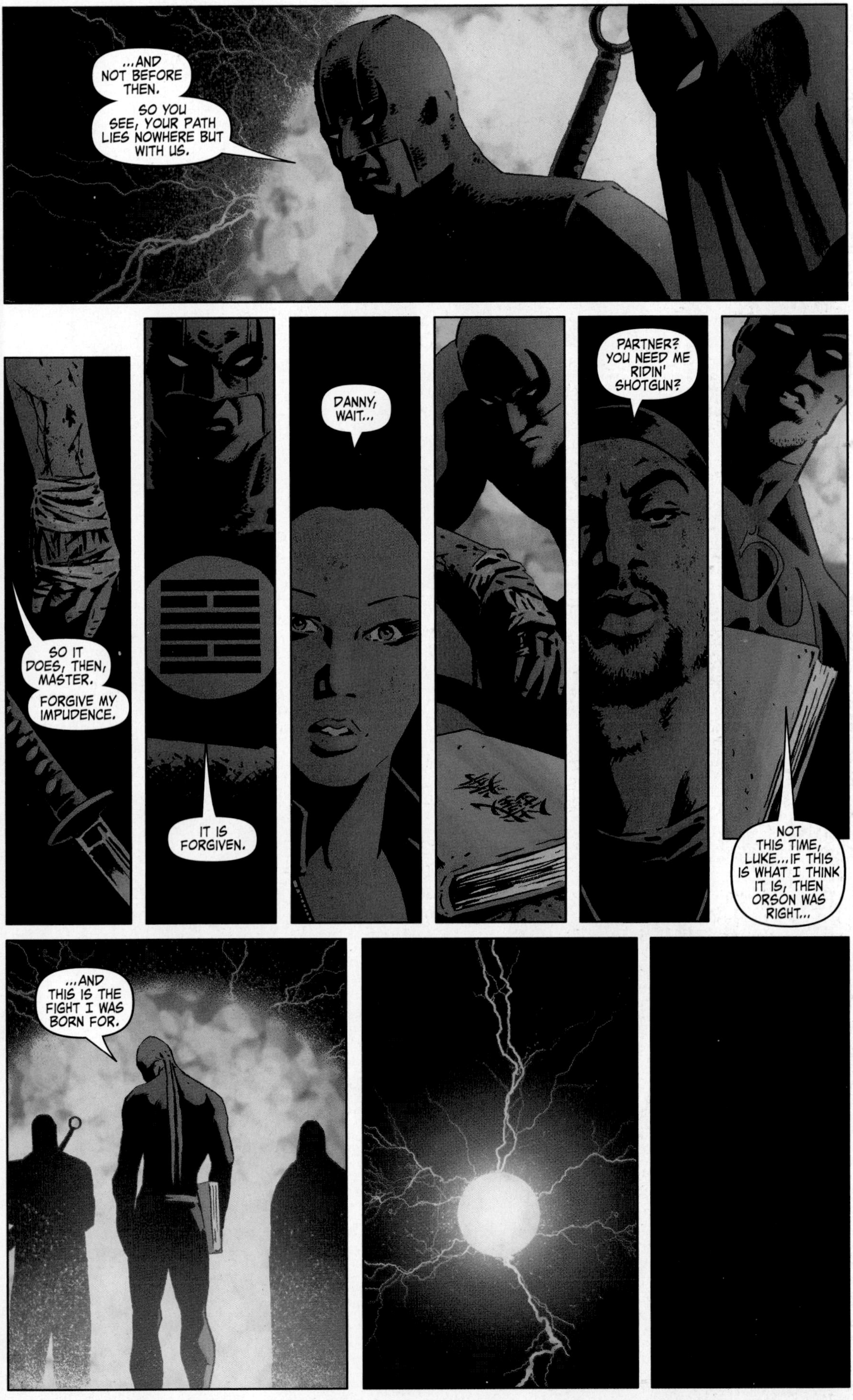
...AND NOT BEFORE THEN.
SO YOU SEE, YOUR PATH LIES NOWHERE BUT WITH US.
SO IT DOES, THEN, MASTER.
FORGIVE MY IMPUDENCE.
IT IS FORGIVEN.
DANNY, WAIT...
PARTNER? YOU NEED ME RIDIN' SHOTGUN?
NOT THIS TIME, LUKE...IF THIS IS WHAT I THINK IT IS, THEN ORSON WAS RIGHT...
...AND THIS IS THE FIGHT I WAS BORN FOR.

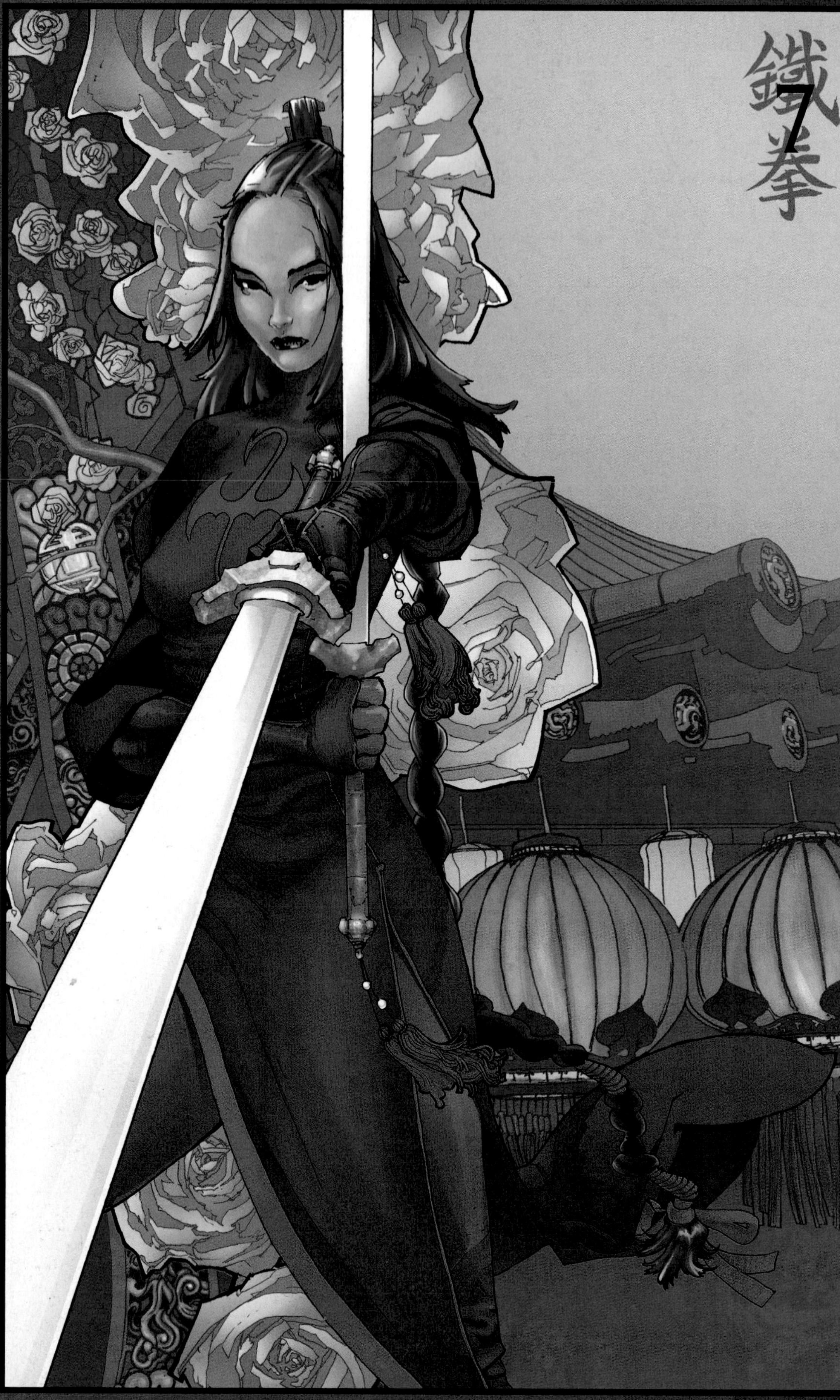
鐵拳
7

There have been sixty-six men and women to carry the mantle of THE IMMORTAL IRON FIST throughout the ages, men and women of great courage, valor, skill, and sacrifice. Sixty-six men and women have stood between man and the unstoppable forces of evil, willing to give all they have to hold back the hordes.

This is the story of one of them, as told in THE BOOK OF THE IRON FIST.

The Story of the Iron Fist Wu Ao-Shi

The Pirate Queen of Pinghai Bay

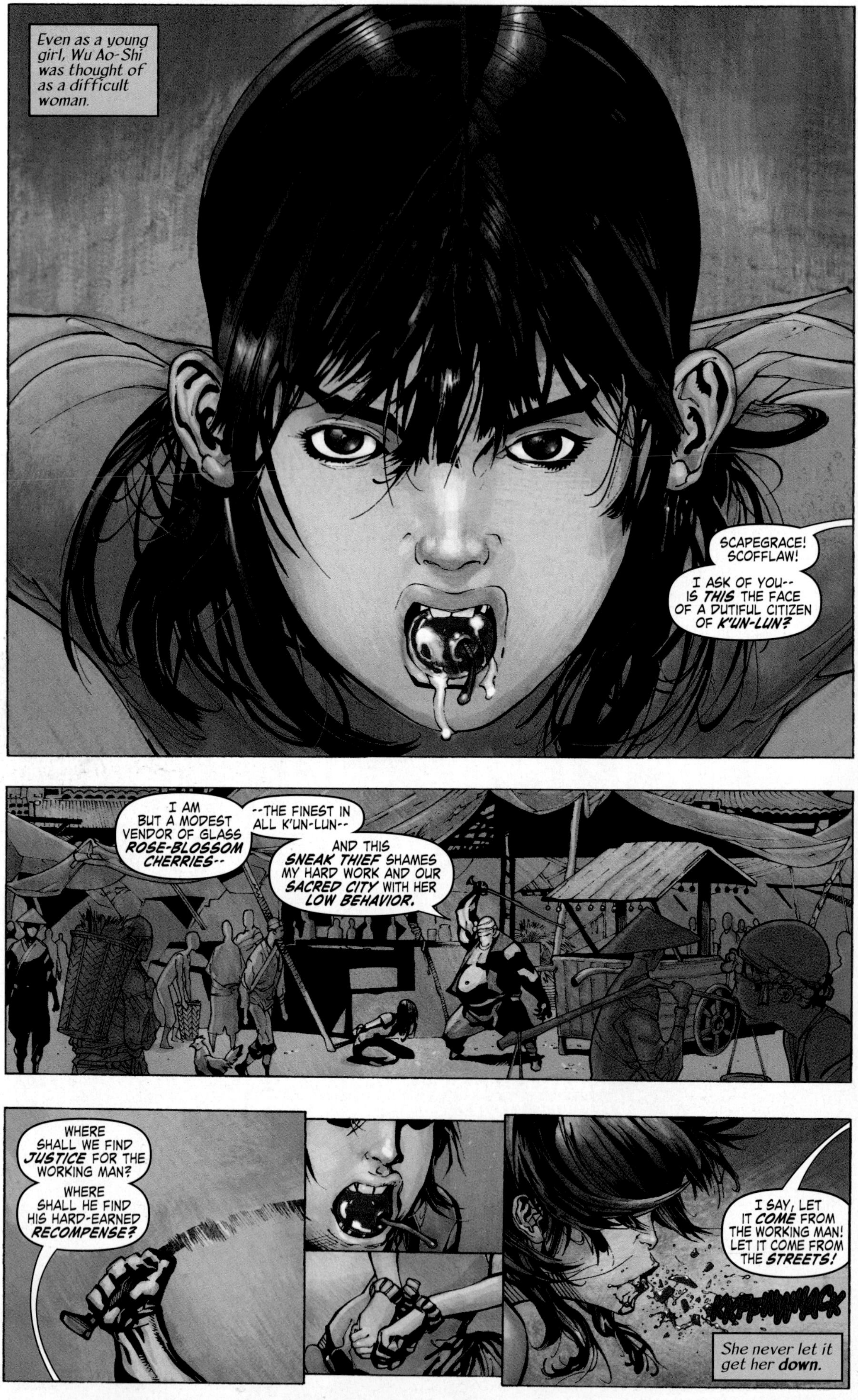
Even as a young girl, Wu Ao-Shi was thought of as a difficult woman.
SCAPEGRACE! SCOFFLAW!
I ASK OF YOU-- IS THIS THE FACE OF A DUTIFUL CITIZEN OF K'UN-LUN?
I AM BUT A MODEST VENDOR OF GLASS ROSE-BLOSSOM CHERRIES--
--THE FINEST IN ALL K'UN-LUN--
AND THIS SNEAK THIEF SHAMES MY HARD WORK AND OUR SACRED CITY WITH HER LOW BEHAVIOR.
WHERE SHALL WE FIND JUSTICE FOR THE WORKING MAN?
WHERE SHALL HE FIND HIS HARD-EARNED RECOMPENSE?
I SAY, LET IT COME FROM THE WORKING MAN! LET IT COME FROM THE STREETS!
She never let it get her down.

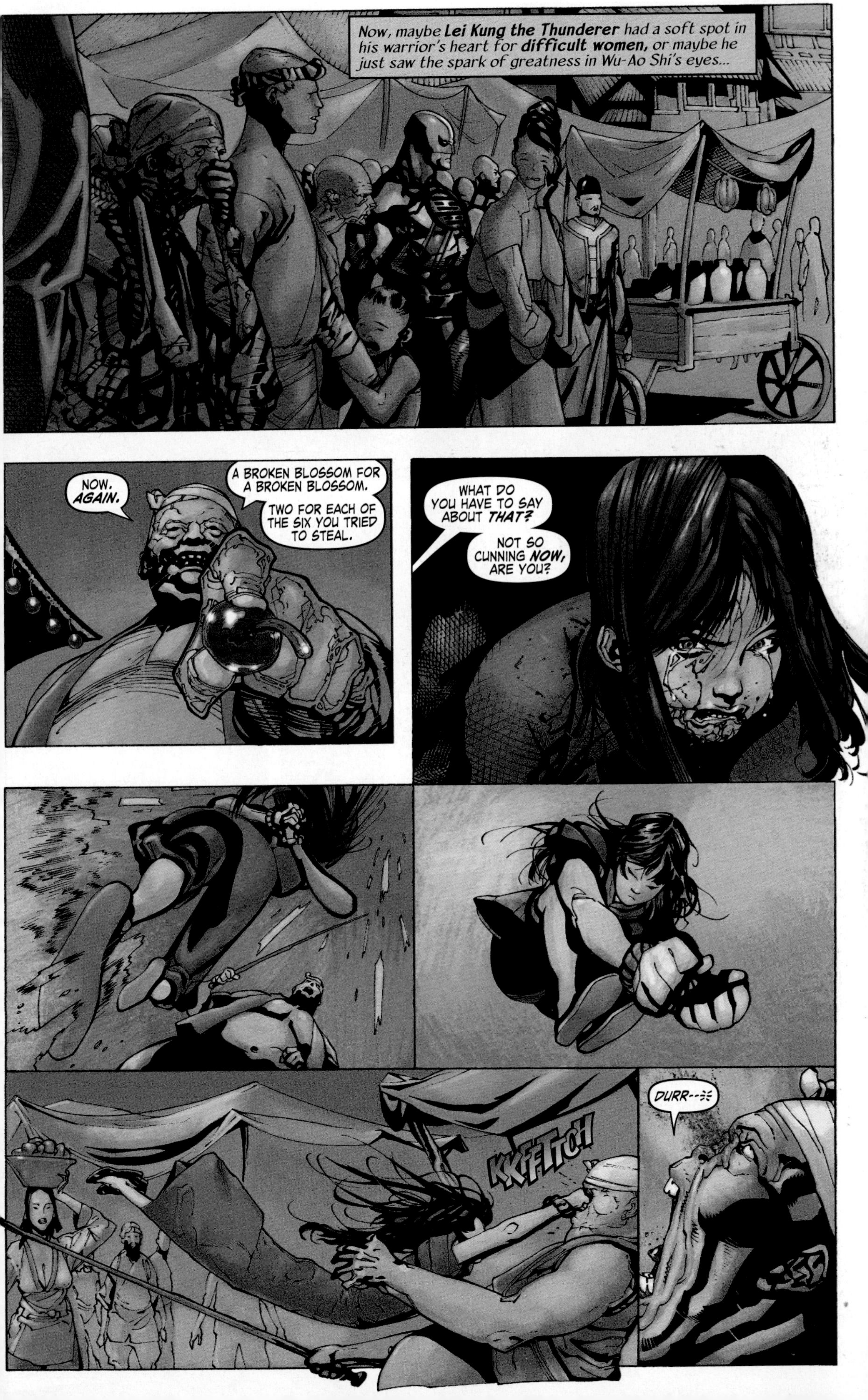
Now, maybe **Lei Kung the Thunderer** had a soft spot in his warrior's heart for **difficult women,** or maybe he just saw the spark of greatness in Wu-Ao Shi's eyes...
NOW. ***AGAIN.***
A BROKEN BLOSSOM FOR A BROKEN BLOSSOM.
TWO FOR EACH OF THE SIX YOU TRIED TO STEAL.
WHAT DO YOU HAVE TO SAY ABOUT ***THAT?***
NOT SO CUNNING ***NOW,*** ARE YOU?
KKFLTCH
DURR--

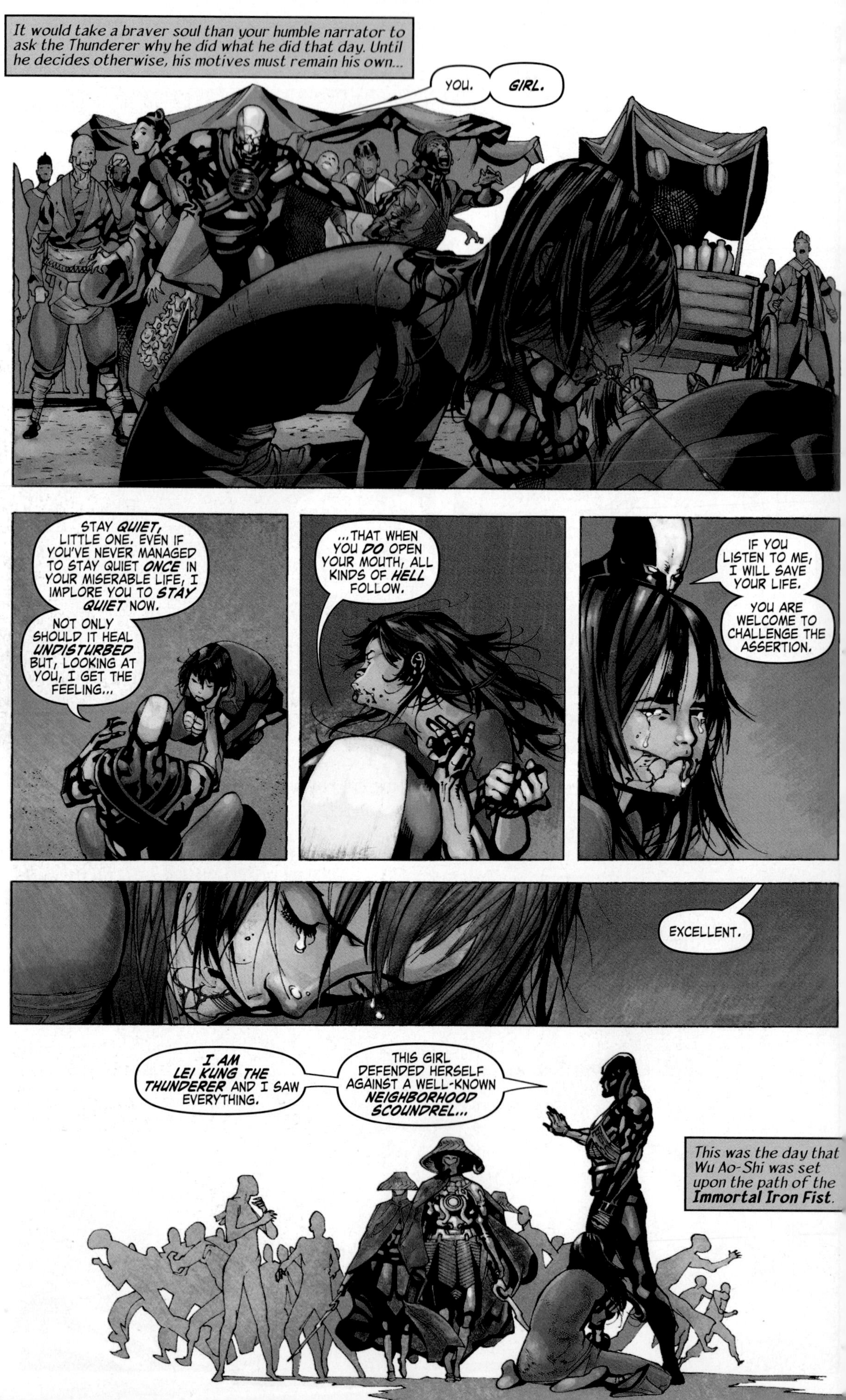
It would take a braver soul than your humble narrator to ask the Thunderer why he did what he did that day. Until he decides otherwise, his motives must remain his own...
YOU.
GIRL.
STAY QUIET, LITTLE ONE. EVEN IF YOU'VE NEVER MANAGED TO STAY QUIET ONCE IN YOUR MISERABLE LIFE, I IMPLORE YOU TO STAY QUIET NOW.
NOT ONLY SHOULD IT HEAL UNDISTURBED BUT, LOOKING AT YOU, I GET THE FEELING...
...THAT WHEN YOU DO OPEN YOUR MOUTH, ALL KINDS OF HELL FOLLOW.
IF YOU LISTEN TO ME, I WILL SAVE YOUR LIFE.
YOU ARE WELCOME TO CHALLENGE THE ASSERTION.
EXCELLENT.
I AM LEI KUNG THE THUNDERER AND I SAW EVERYTHING.
THIS GIRL DEFENDED HERSELF AGAINST A WELL-KNOWN NEIGHBORHOOD SCOUNDREL...
This was the day that Wu Ao-Shi was set upon the path of the Immortal Iron Fist.

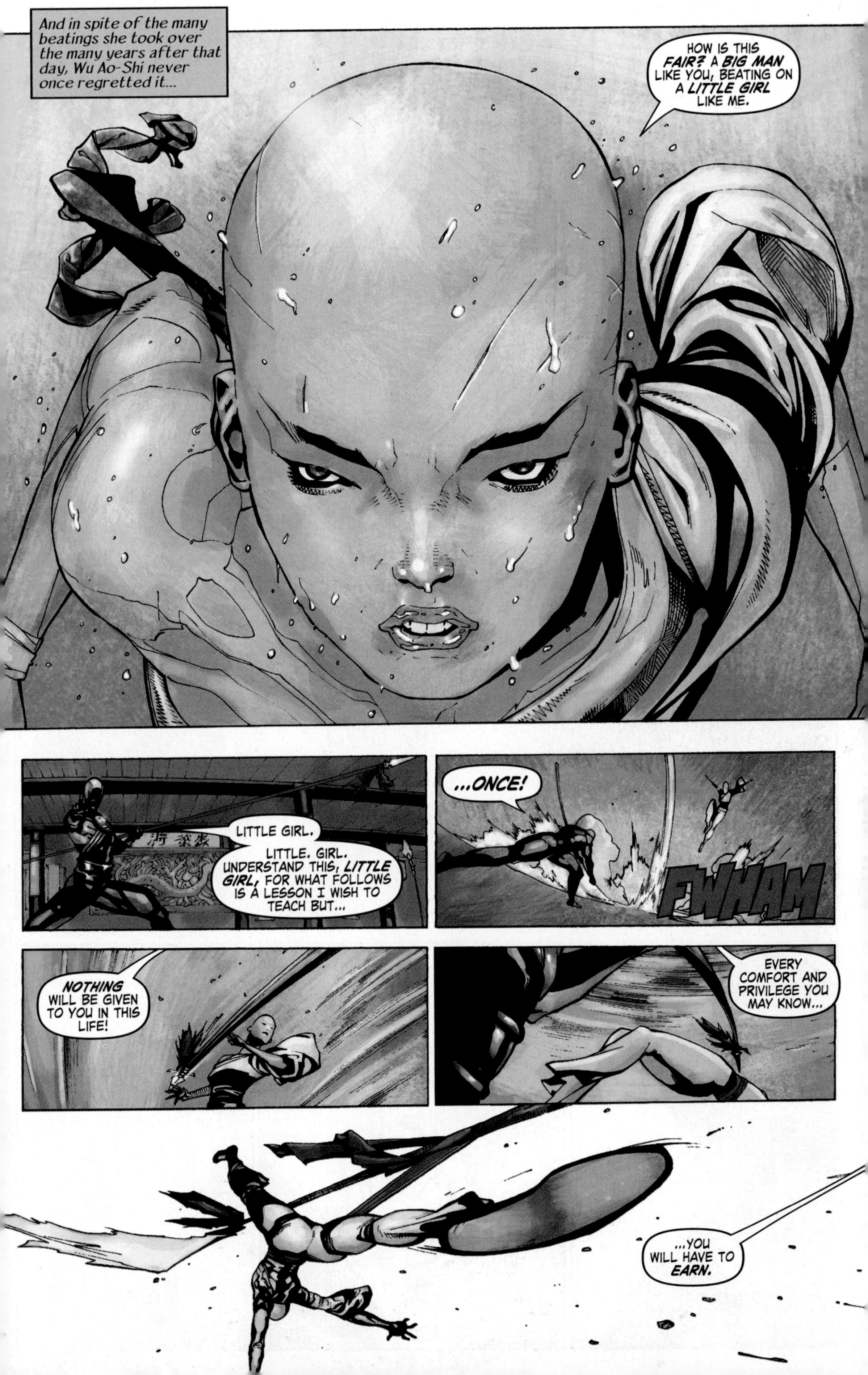

And in spite of the many beatings she took over the many years after that day, Wu Ao-Shi never once regretted it...
HOW IS THIS FAIR? A BIG MAN LIKE YOU, BEATING ON A LITTLE GIRL LIKE ME.
LITTLE GIRL.
LITTLE. GIRL. UNDERSTAND THIS, LITTLE GIRL, FOR WHAT FOLLOWS IS A LESSON I WISH TO TEACH BUT...
...ONCE!
FWHAM
NOTHING WILL BE GIVEN TO YOU IN THIS LIFE!
EVERY COMFORT AND PRIVILEGE YOU MAY KNOW...
...YOU WILL HAVE TO EARN.

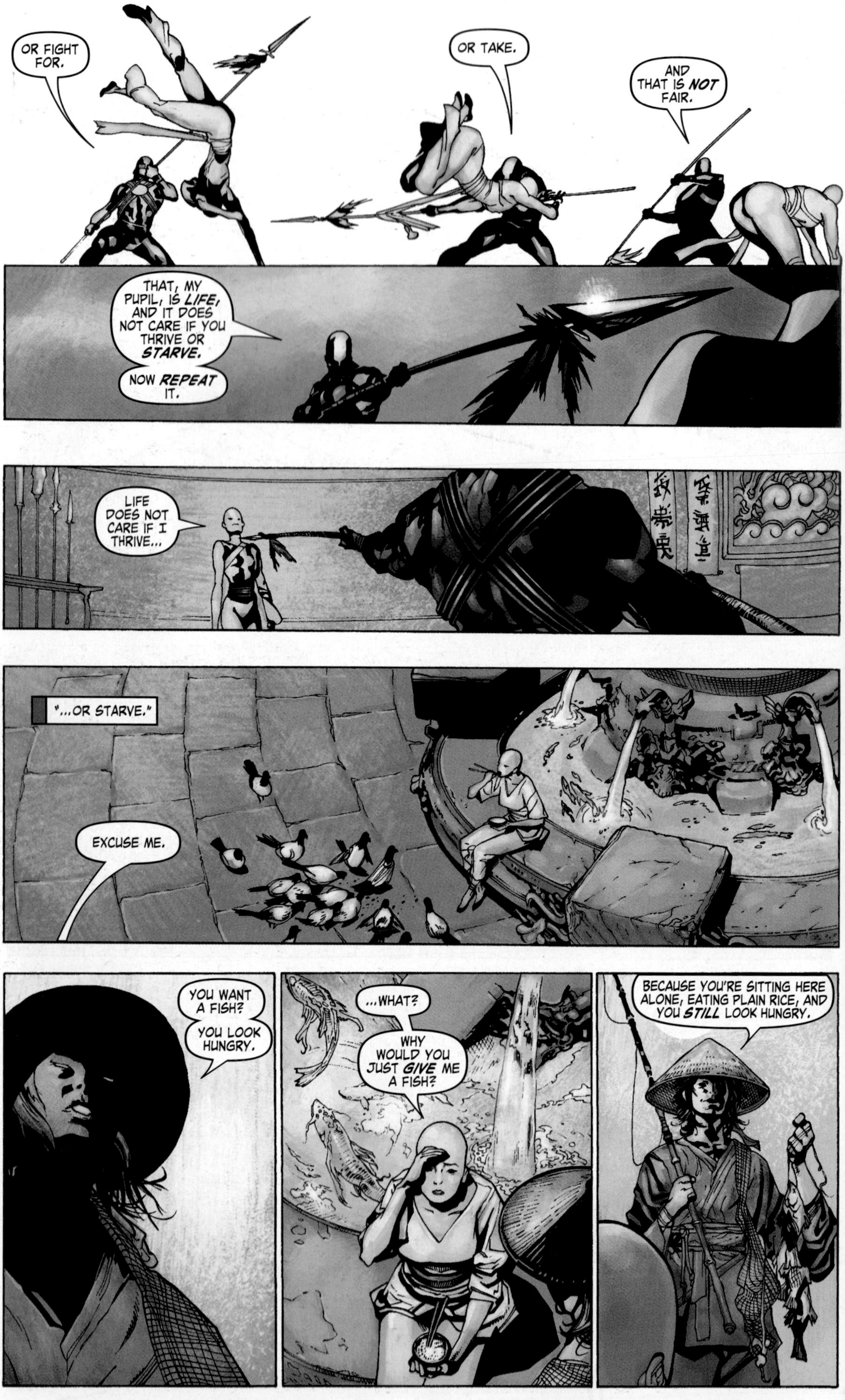

OR FIGHT FOR.
OR TAKE.
AND THAT IS NOT FAIR.
THAT, MY PUPIL, IS LIFE, AND IT DOES NOT CARE IF YOU THRIVE OR STARVE.
NOW REPEAT IT.
LIFE DOES NOT CARE IF I THRIVE...
"...OR STARVE."
EXCUSE ME.
YOU WANT A FISH?
YOU LOOK HUNGRY.
...WHAT?
WHY WOULD YOU JUST GIVE ME A FISH?
BECAUSE YOU'RE SITTING HERE ALONE, EATING PLAIN RICE, AND YOU STILL LOOK HUNGRY.

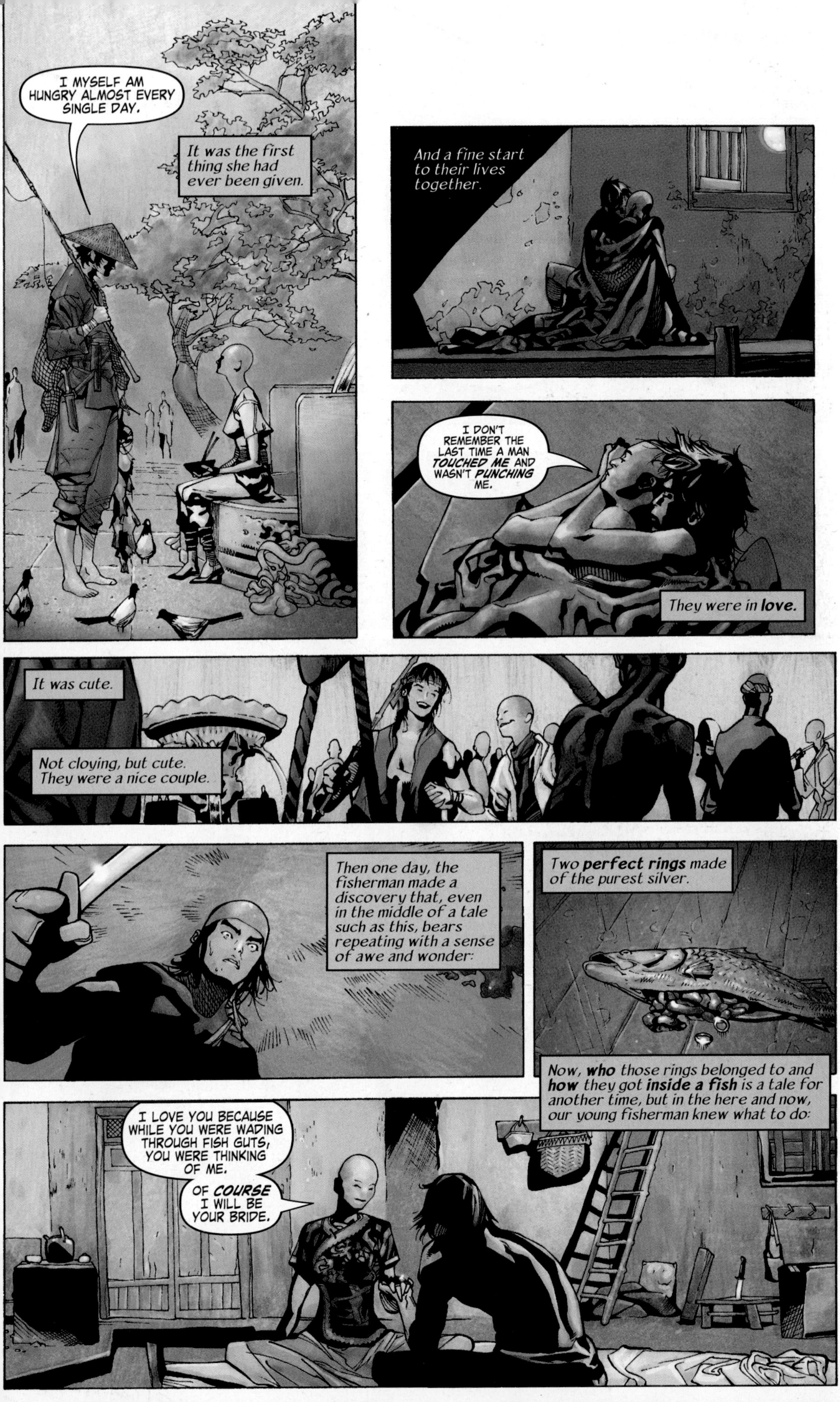

I MYSELF AM HUNGRY ALMOST EVERY SINGLE DAY.
It was the first thing she had ever been given.
And a fine start to their lives together.
I DON'T REMEMBER THE LAST TIME A MAN TOUCHED ME AND WASN'T PUNCHING ME.
They were in love.
It was cute.
Not cloying, but cute. They were a nice couple.
Then one day, the fisherman made a discovery that, even in the middle of a tale such as this, bears repeating with a sense of awe and wonder:
Two perfect rings made of the purest silver.
Now, who those rings belonged to and how they got inside a fish is a tale for another time, but in the here and now, our young fisherman knew what to do:
I LOVE YOU BECAUSE WHILE YOU WERE WADING THROUGH FISH GUTS, YOU WERE THINKING OF ME.
OF COURSE I WILL BE YOUR BRIDE.

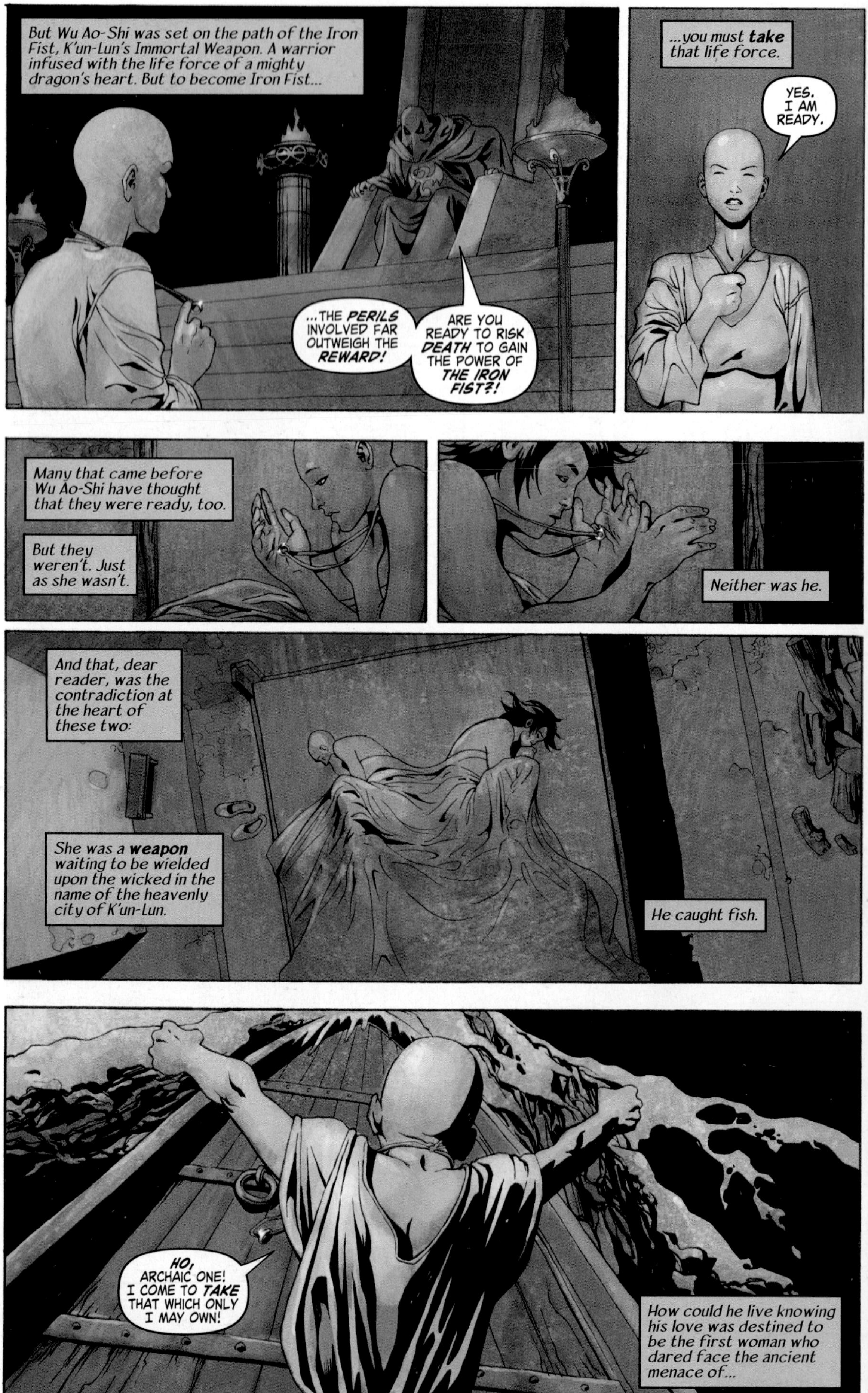
But Wu Ao-Shi was set on the path of the Iron Fist, K'un-Lun's Immortal Weapon. A warrior infused with the life force of a mighty dragon's heart. But to become Iron Fist...
ARE YOU READY TO RISK DEATH TO GAIN THE POWER OF THE IRON FIST?!
...THE PERILS INVOLVED FAR OUTWEIGH THE REWARD!
...you must take that life force.
YES. I AM READY.
Many that came before Wu Ao-Shi have thought that they were ready, too.
But they weren't. Just as she wasn't.
Neither was he.
And that, dear reader, was the contradiction at the heart of these two:
She was a weapon waiting to be wielded upon the wicked in the name of the heavenly city of K'un-Lun.
He caught fish.
HO, ARCHAIC ONE! I COME TO TAKE THAT WHICH ONLY I MAY OWN!
How could he live knowing his love was destined to be the first woman who dared face the ancient menace of...

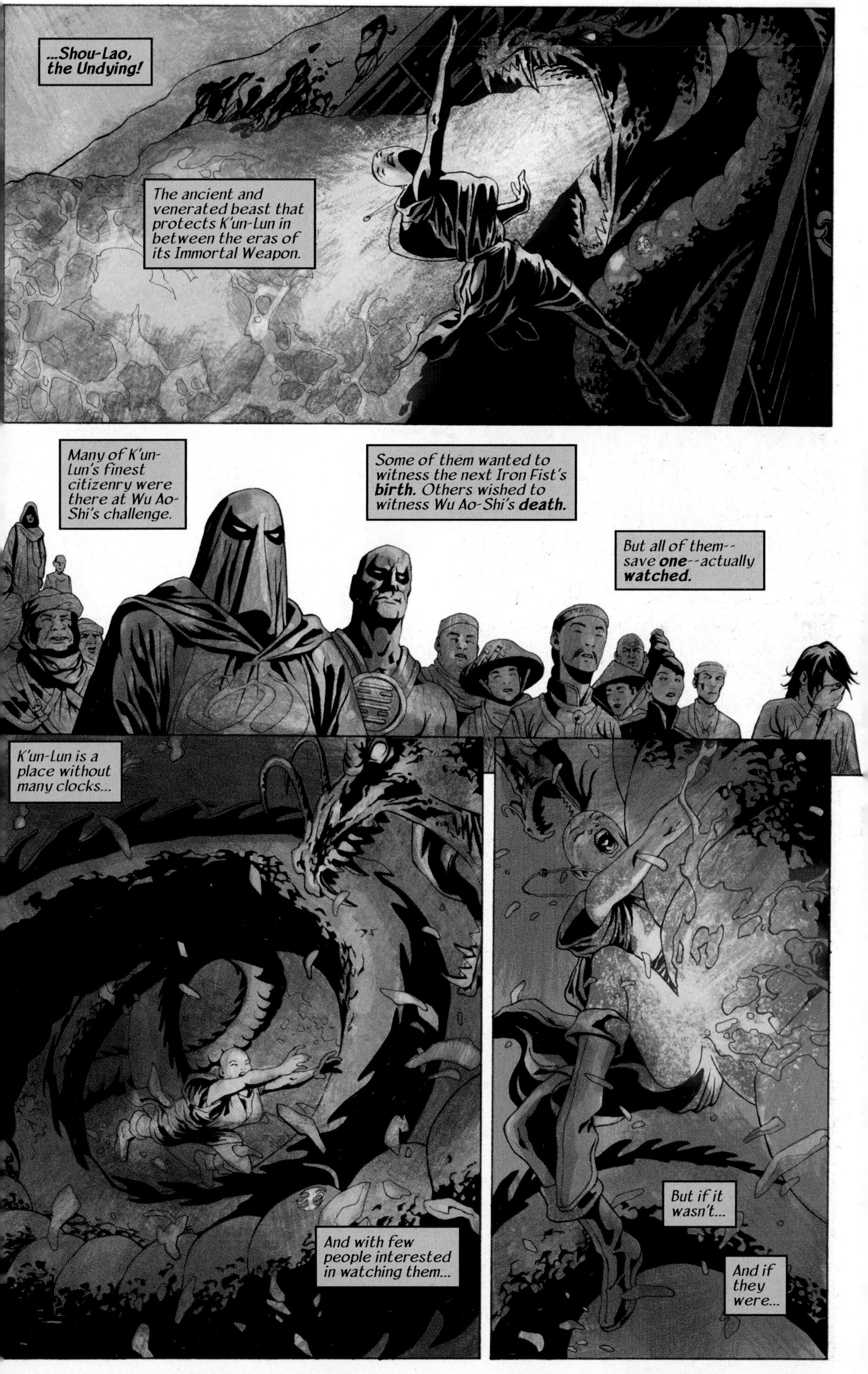
...Shou-Lao, the Undying!
The ancient and venerated beast that protects K'un-Lun in between the eras of its Immortal Weapon.
Many of K'un-Lun's finest citizenry were there at Wu Ao-Shi's challenge.
Some of them wanted to witness the next Iron Fist's **birth.** Others wished to witness Wu Ao-Shi's **death.**
But all of them--save **one**--actually **watched.**
K'un-Lun is a place without many clocks...
And with few people interested in watching them...
But if it wasn't...
And if they were...

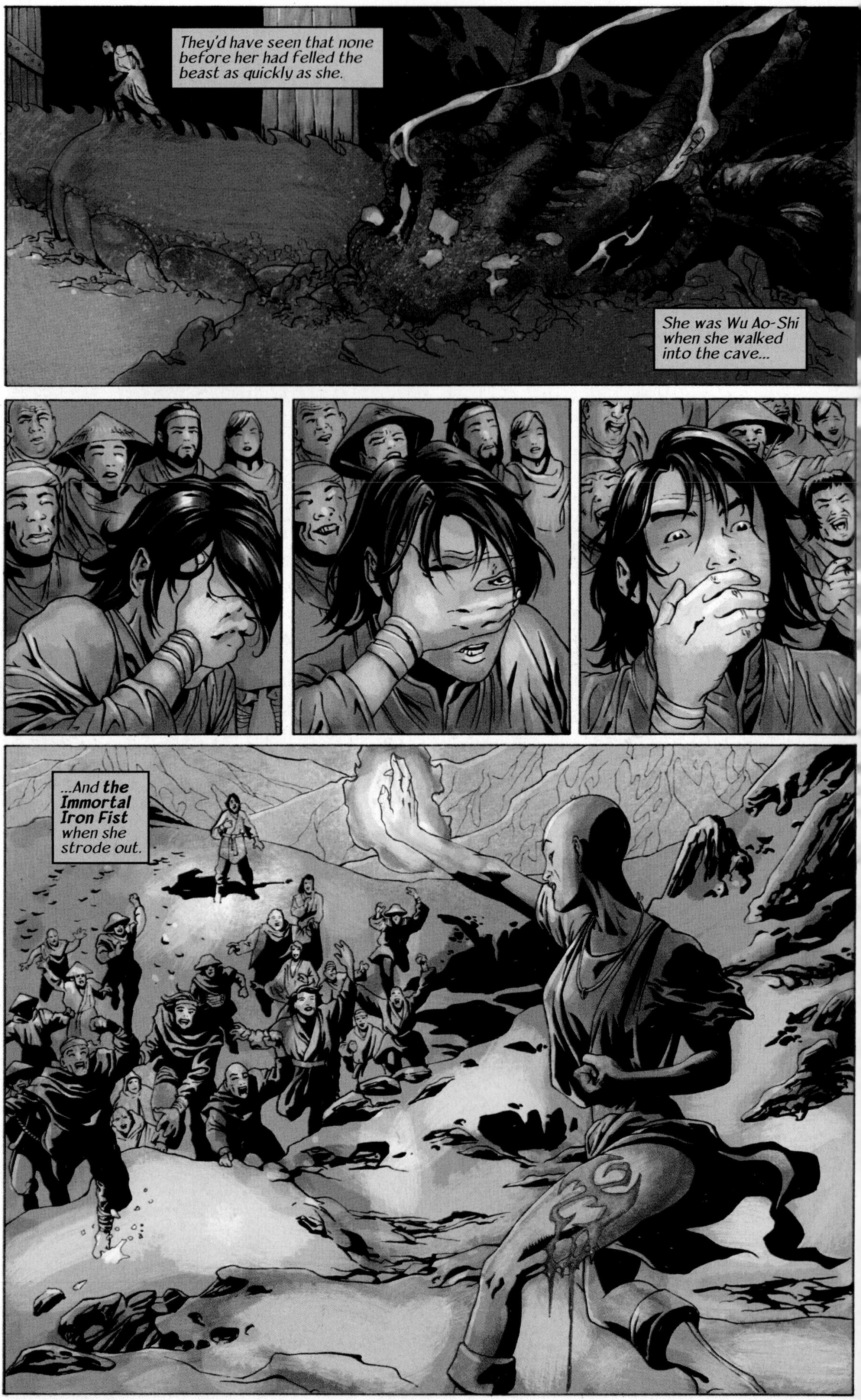
They'd have seen that none before her had felled the beast as quickly as she.
She was Wu Ao-Shi when she walked into the cave...
...And **the Immortal Iron Fist** when she strode out.

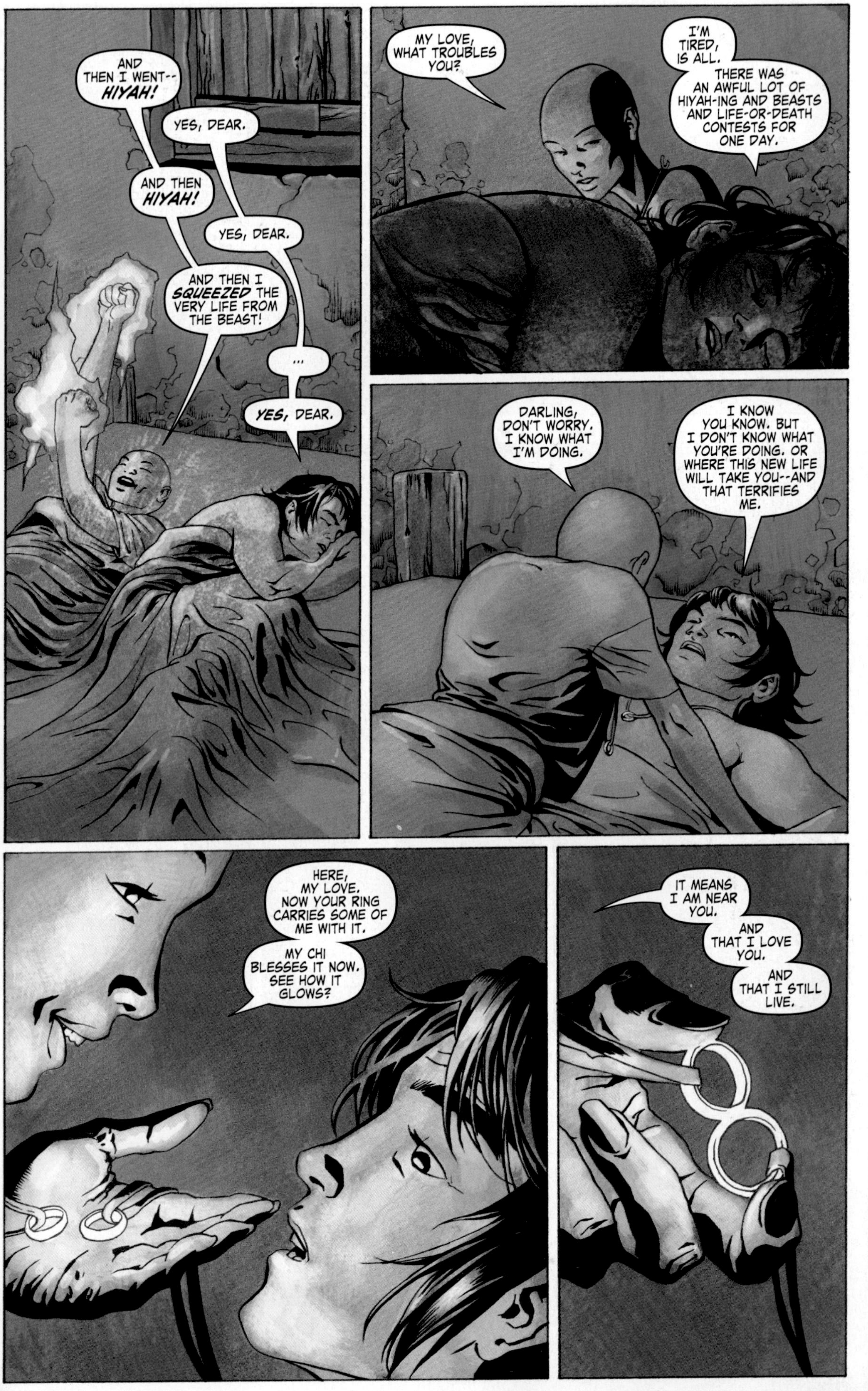
AND THEN I WENT-- HIYAH!
YES, DEAR.
AND THEN HIYAH!
YES, DEAR.
AND THEN I SQUEEZED THE VERY LIFE FROM THE BEAST!
...
YES, DEAR.
MY LOVE, WHAT TROUBLES YOU?
I'M TIRED, IS ALL.
THERE WAS AN AWFUL LOT OF HIYAH-ING AND BEASTS AND LIFE-OR-DEATH CONTESTS FOR ONE DAY.
DARLING, DON'T WORRY. I KNOW WHAT I'M DOING.
I KNOW YOU KNOW. BUT I DON'T KNOW WHAT YOU'RE DOING. OR WHERE THIS NEW LIFE WILL TAKE YOU--AND THAT TERRIFIES ME.
HERE, MY LOVE. NOW YOUR RING CARRIES SOME OF ME WITH IT.
MY CHI BLESSES IT NOW. SEE HOW IT GLOWS?
IT MEANS I AM NEAR YOU.
AND THAT I LOVE YOU.
AND THAT I STILL LIVE.

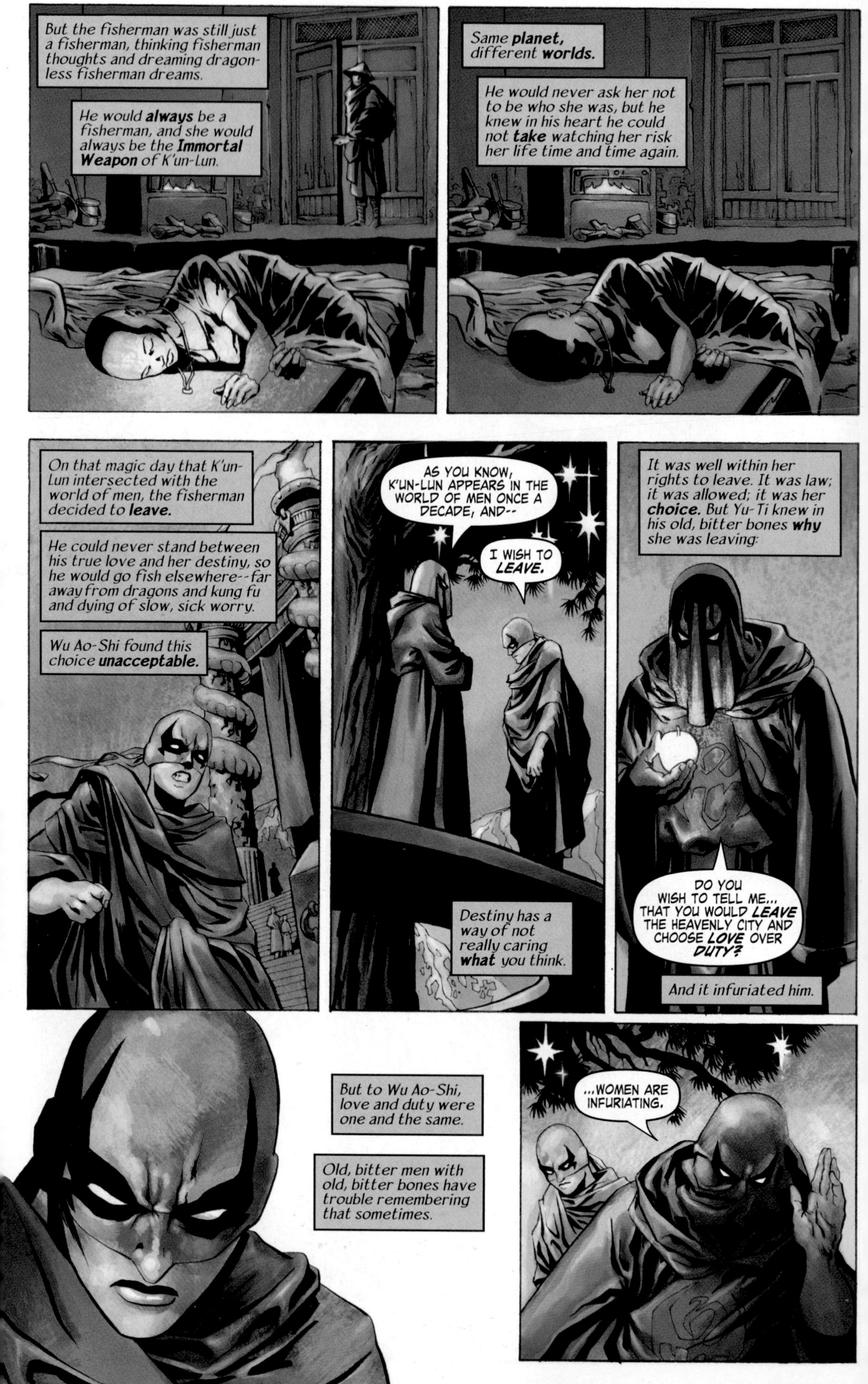

But the fisherman was still just a fisherman, thinking fisherman thoughts and dreaming dragonless fisherman dreams.
He would **always** be a fisherman, and she would always be the **Immortal Weapon** of K'un-Lun.
Same **planet**, different **worlds.**
He would never ask her not to be who she was, but he knew in his heart he could not **take** watching her risk her life time and time again.
On that magic day that K'un-Lun intersected with the world of men, the fisherman decided to **leave.**
He could never stand between his true love and her destiny, so he would go fish elsewhere--far away from dragons and kung fu and dying of slow, sick worry.
Wu Ao-Shi found this choice **unacceptable.**
AS YOU KNOW, K'UN-LUN APPEARS IN THE WORLD OF MEN ONCE A DECADE, AND--
I WISH TO ***LEAVE.***
Destiny has a way of not really caring **what** you think.
It was well within her rights to leave. It was law; it was allowed; it was her **choice.** But Yu-Ti knew in his old, bitter bones **why** she was leaving:
DO YOU WISH TO TELL ME... THAT YOU WOULD ***LEAVE*** THE HEAVENLY CITY AND CHOOSE ***LOVE*** OVER ***DUTY?***
And it infuriated him.
But to Wu Ao-Shi, love and duty were one and the same.
Old, bitter men with old, bitter bones have trouble remembering that sometimes.
...WOMEN ARE INFURIATING.

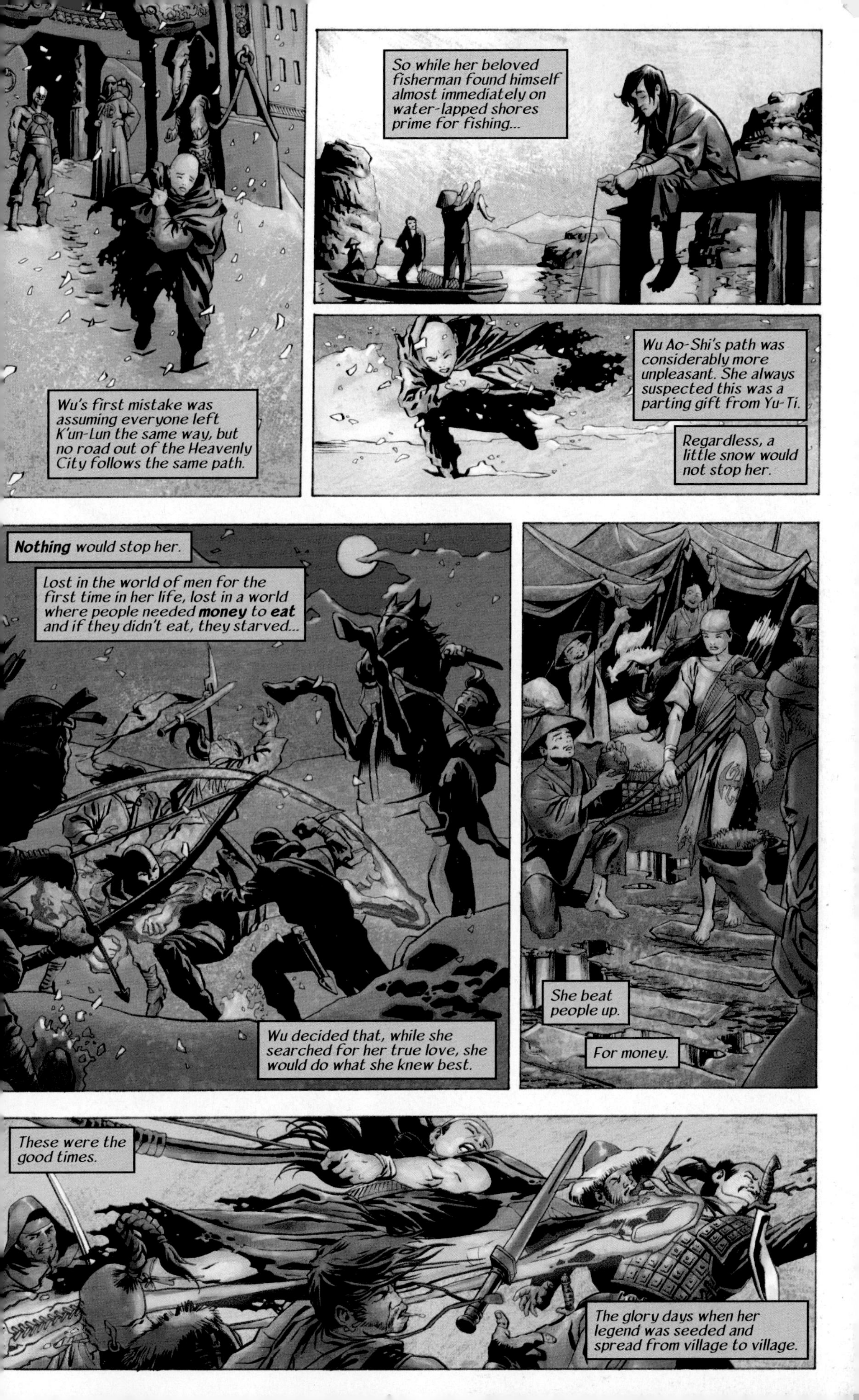
Wu's first mistake was assuming everyone left K'un-Lun the same way, but no road out of the Heavenly City follows the same path.
So while her beloved fisherman found himself almost immediately on water-lapped shores prime for fishing...
Wu Ao-Shi's path was considerably more unpleasant. She always suspected this was a parting gift from Yu-Ti.
Regardless, a little snow would not stop her.
Nothing would stop her.
Lost in the world of men for the first time in her life, lost in a world where people needed **money** to **eat** and if they didn't eat, they starved...
Wu decided that, while she searched for her true love, she would do what she knew best.
She beat people up.
For money.
These were the good times.
The glory days when her legend was seeded and spread from village to village.

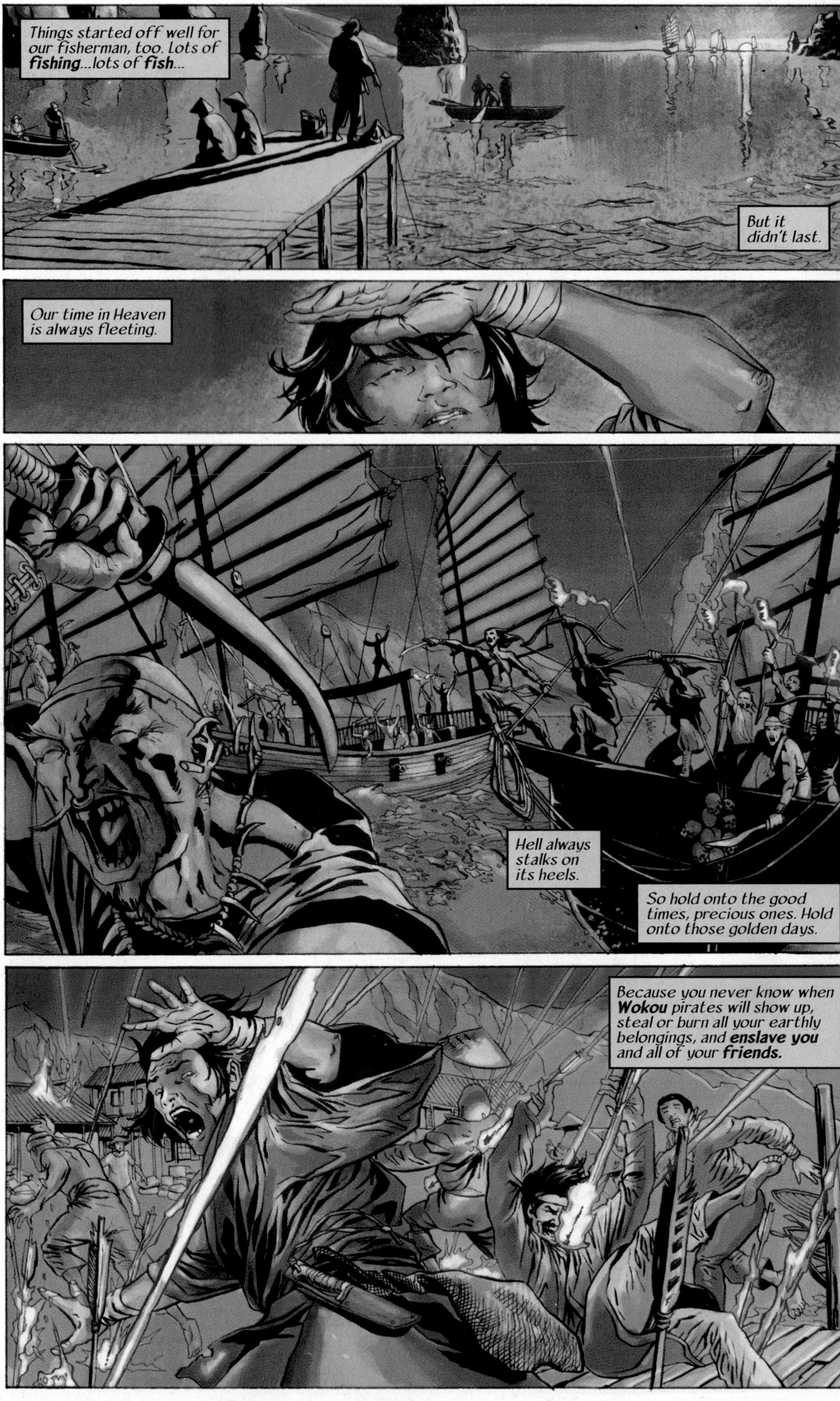
Things started off well for our fisherman, too. Lots of **fishing**...lots of **fish**...
But it didn't last.
Our time in Heaven is always fleeting.
Hell always stalks on its heels.
So hold onto the good times, precious ones. Hold onto those golden days.
Because you never know when **Wokou** pirates will show up, steal or burn all your earthly belongings, and **enslave you** and all of your **friends.**

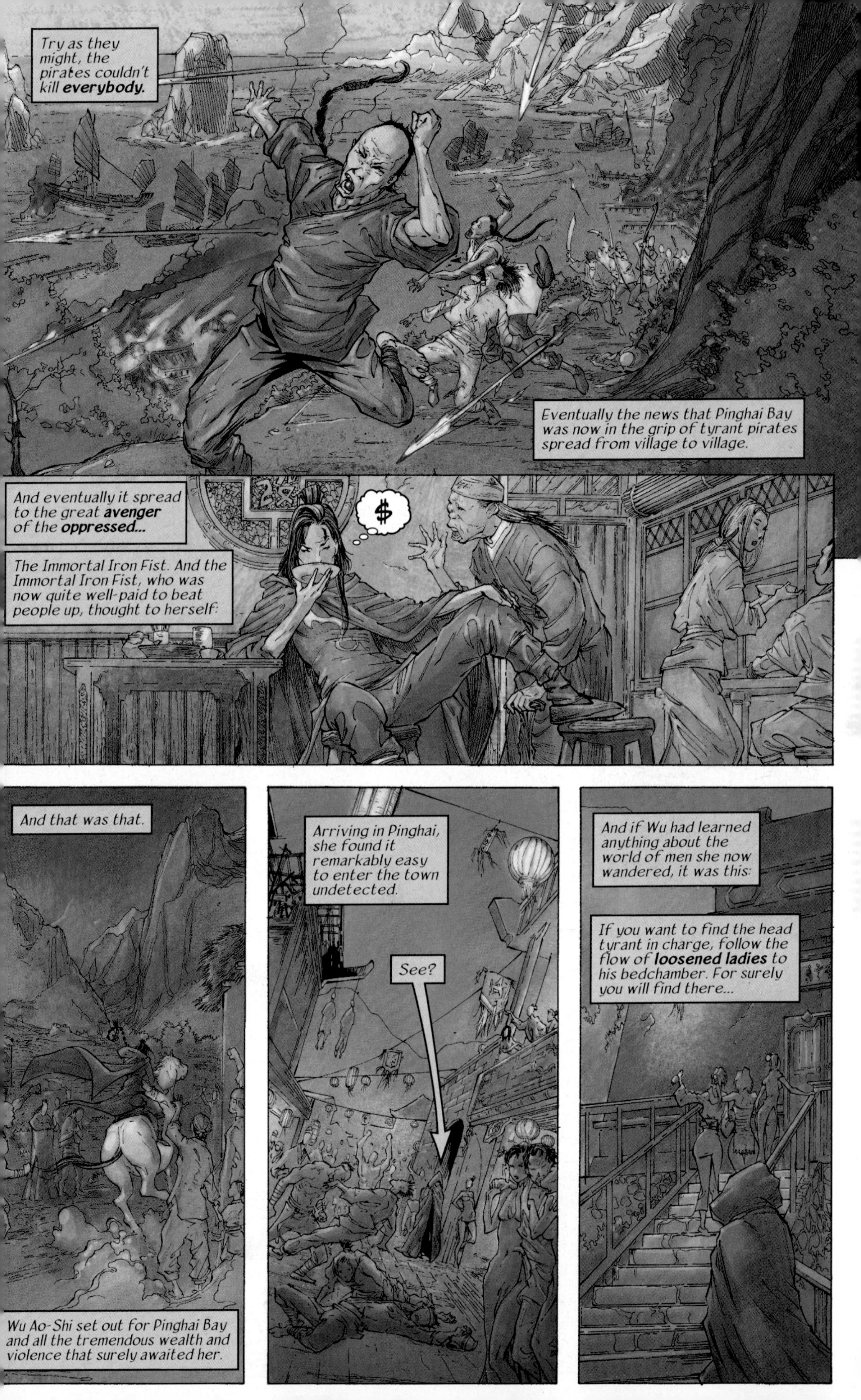

Try as they might, the pirates couldn't kill **everybody**.
Eventually the news that Pinghai Bay was now in the grip of tyrant pirates spread from village to village.
And eventually it spread to the great **avenger** of the **oppressed**...
The Immortal Iron Fist. And the Immortal Iron Fist, who was now quite well-paid to beat people up, thought to herself:
$
And that was that.
Wu Ao-Shi set out for Pinghai Bay and all the tremendous wealth and violence that surely awaited her.
Arriving in Pinghai, she found it remarkably easy to enter the town undetected.
See?
And if Wu had learned anything about the world of men she now wandered, it was this:
If you want to find the head tyrant in charge, follow the flow of **loosened ladies** to his bedchamber. For surely you will find there...

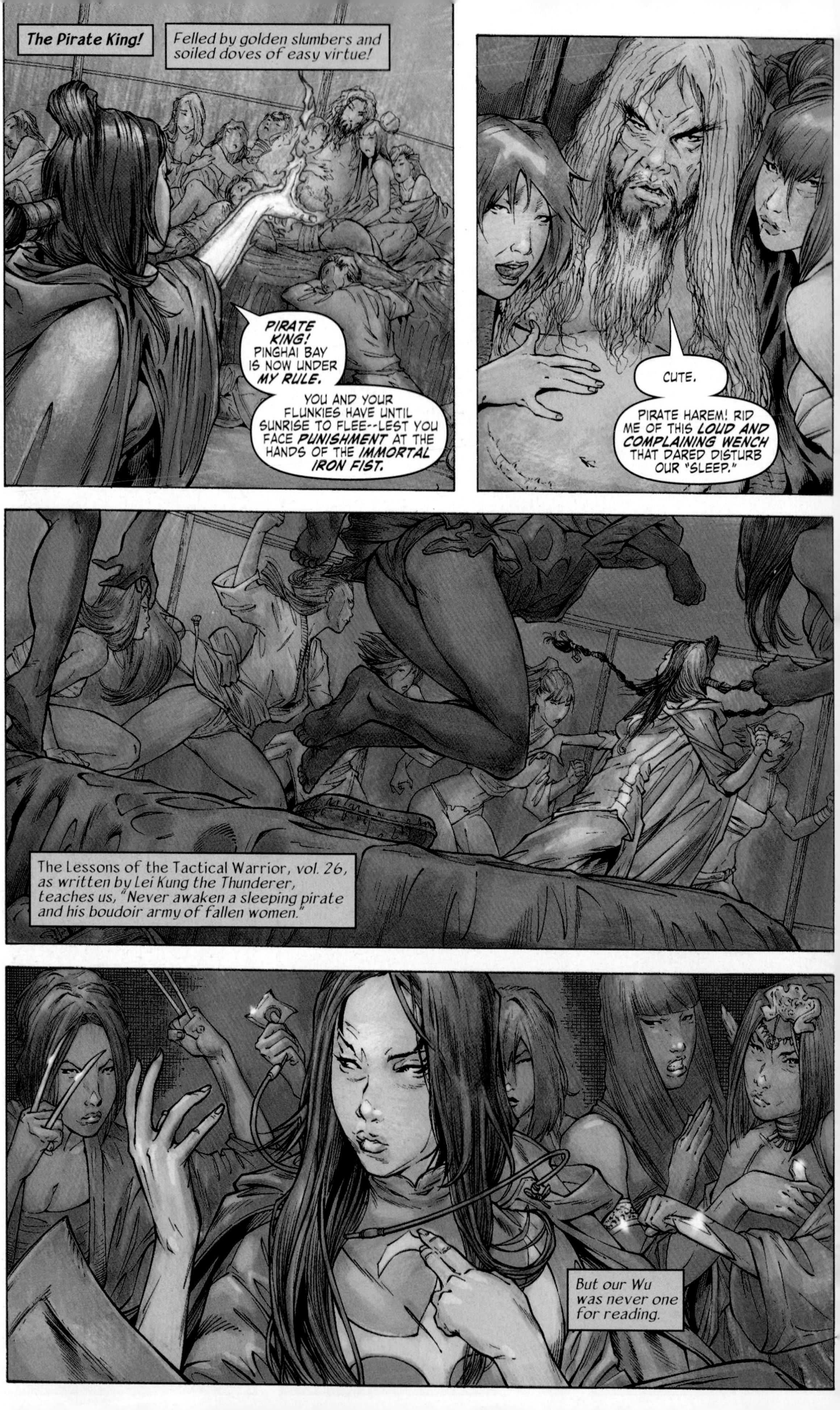
The Pirate King!
Felled by golden slumbers and soiled doves of easy virtue!
PIRATE KING! PINGHAI BAY IS NOW UNDER MY RULE.
YOU AND YOUR FLUNKIES HAVE UNTIL SUNRISE TO FLEE--LEST YOU FACE PUNISHMENT AT THE HANDS OF THE IMMORTAL IRON FIST.
CUTE.
PIRATE HAREM! RID ME OF THIS LOUD AND COMPLAINING WENCH THAT DARED DISTURB OUR "SLEEP."
The Lessons of the Tactical Warrior, vol. 26, as written by Lei Kung the Thunderer, teaches us, "Never awaken a sleeping pirate and his boudoir army of fallen women."
But our Wu was never one for reading.

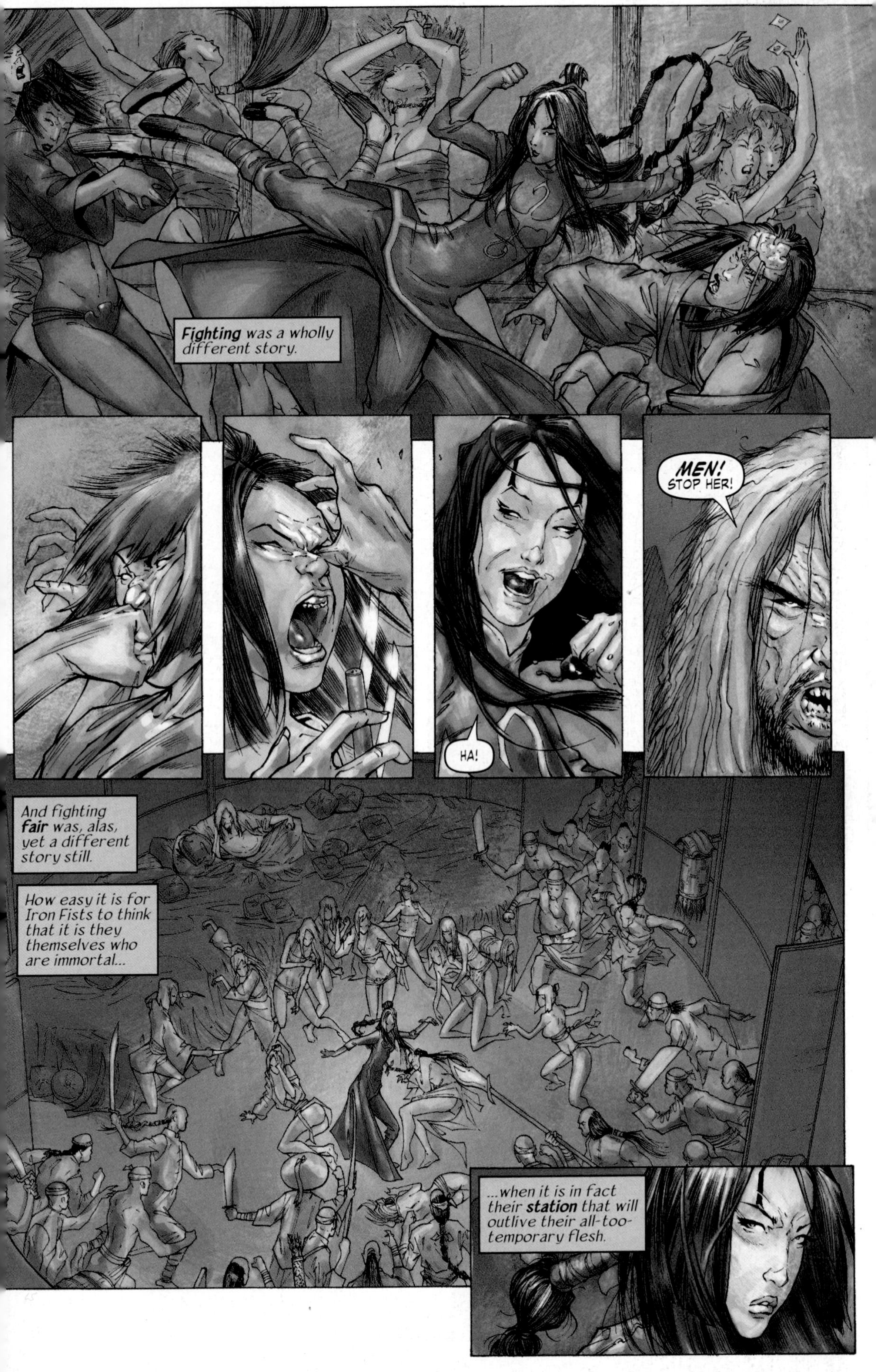
Fighting was a wholly different story.
MEN! STOP HER!
HA!
And fighting fair was, alas, yet a different story still.
How easy it is for Iron Fists to think that it is they themselves who are immortal...
...when it is in fact their station that will outlive their all-too-temporary flesh.

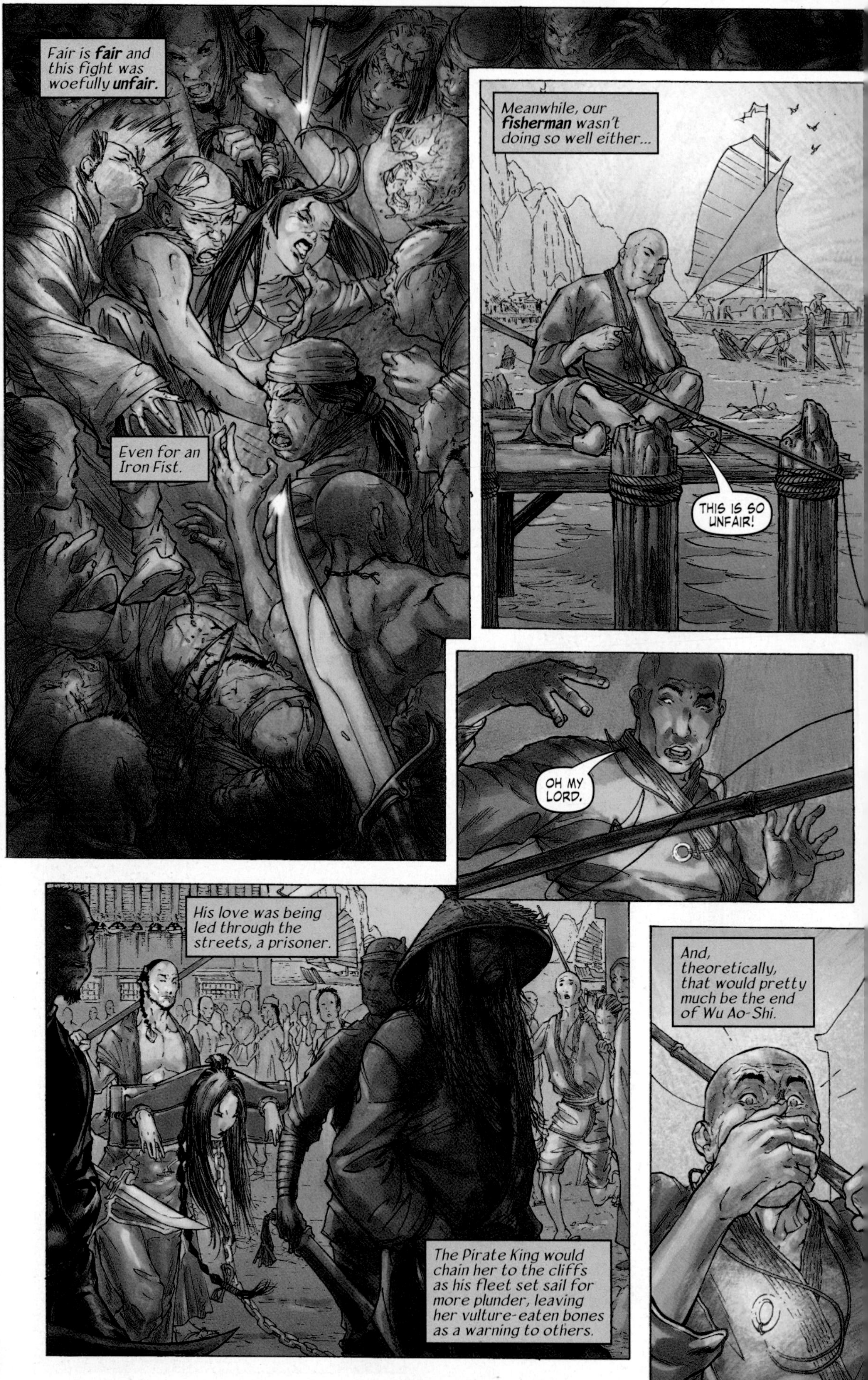
Fair is **fair** and this fight was woefully **unfair**.
Even for an Iron Fist.
Meanwhile, our **fisherman** wasn't doing so well either...
THIS IS SO UNFAIR!
OH MY LORD.
His love was being led through the streets, a prisoner.
The Pirate King would chain her to the cliffs as his fleet set sail for more plunder, leaving her vulture-eaten bones as a warning to others.
And, theoretically, that would pretty much be the end of Wu Ao-Shi.

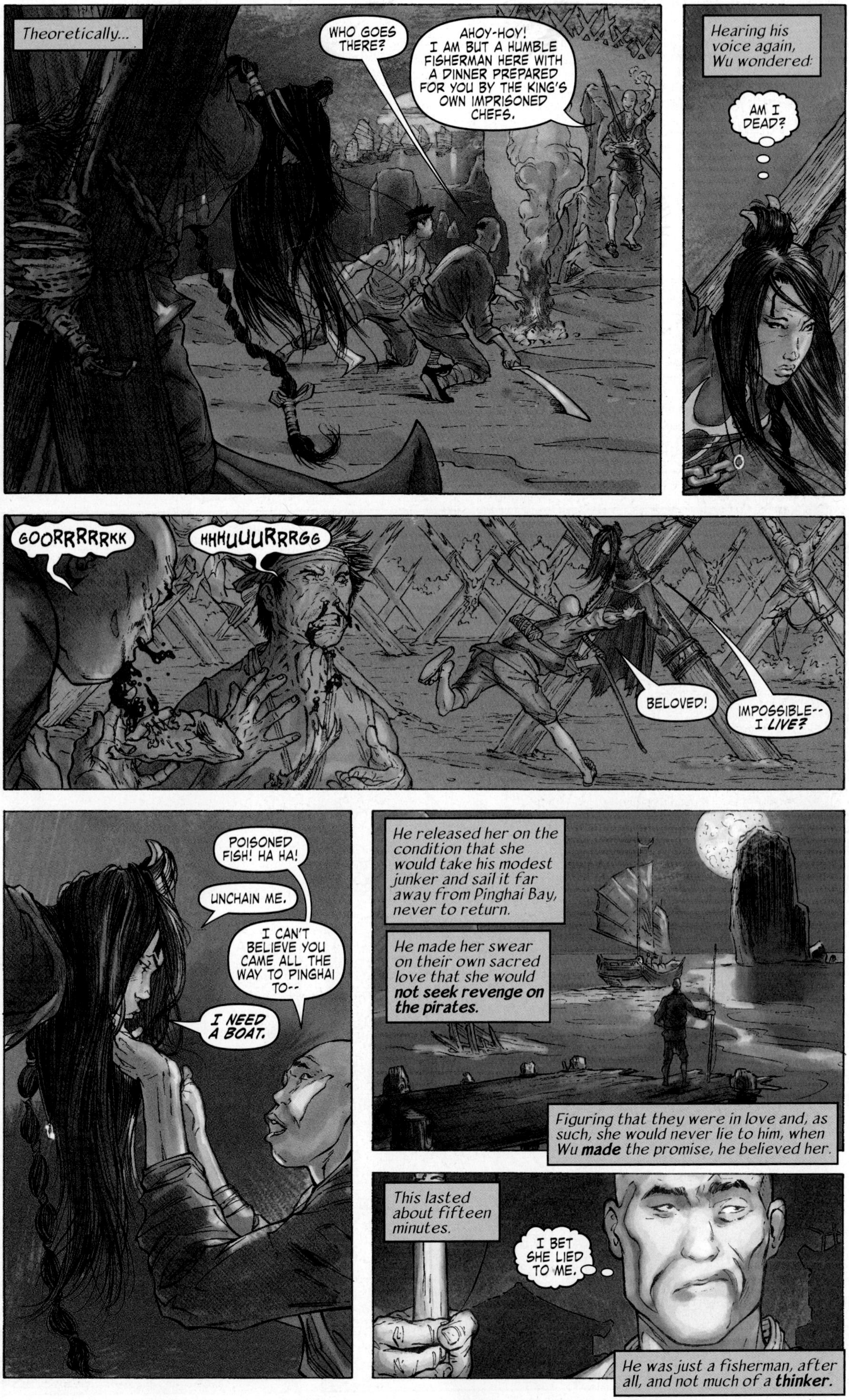
Theoretically...
WHO GOES THERE?
AHOY-HOY! I AM BUT A HUMBLE FISHERMAN HERE WITH A DINNER PREPARED FOR YOU BY THE KING'S OWN IMPRISONED CHEFS.
Hearing his voice again, Wu wondered:
AM I DEAD?
GOORRRRRKK
HHHUUURRRGG
BELOVED!
IMPOSSIBLE-- I LIVE?
POISONED FISH! HA HA!
UNCHAIN ME.
I CAN'T BELIEVE YOU CAME ALL THE WAY TO PINGHAI TO--
I NEED A BOAT.
He released her on the condition that she would take his modest junker and sail it far away from Pinghai Bay, never to return.
He made her swear on their own sacred love that she would not seek revenge on the pirates.
Figuring that they were in love and, as such, she would never lie to him, when Wu made the promise, he believed her.
This lasted about fifteen minutes.
I BET SHE LIED TO ME.
He was just a fisherman, after all, and not much of a thinker.

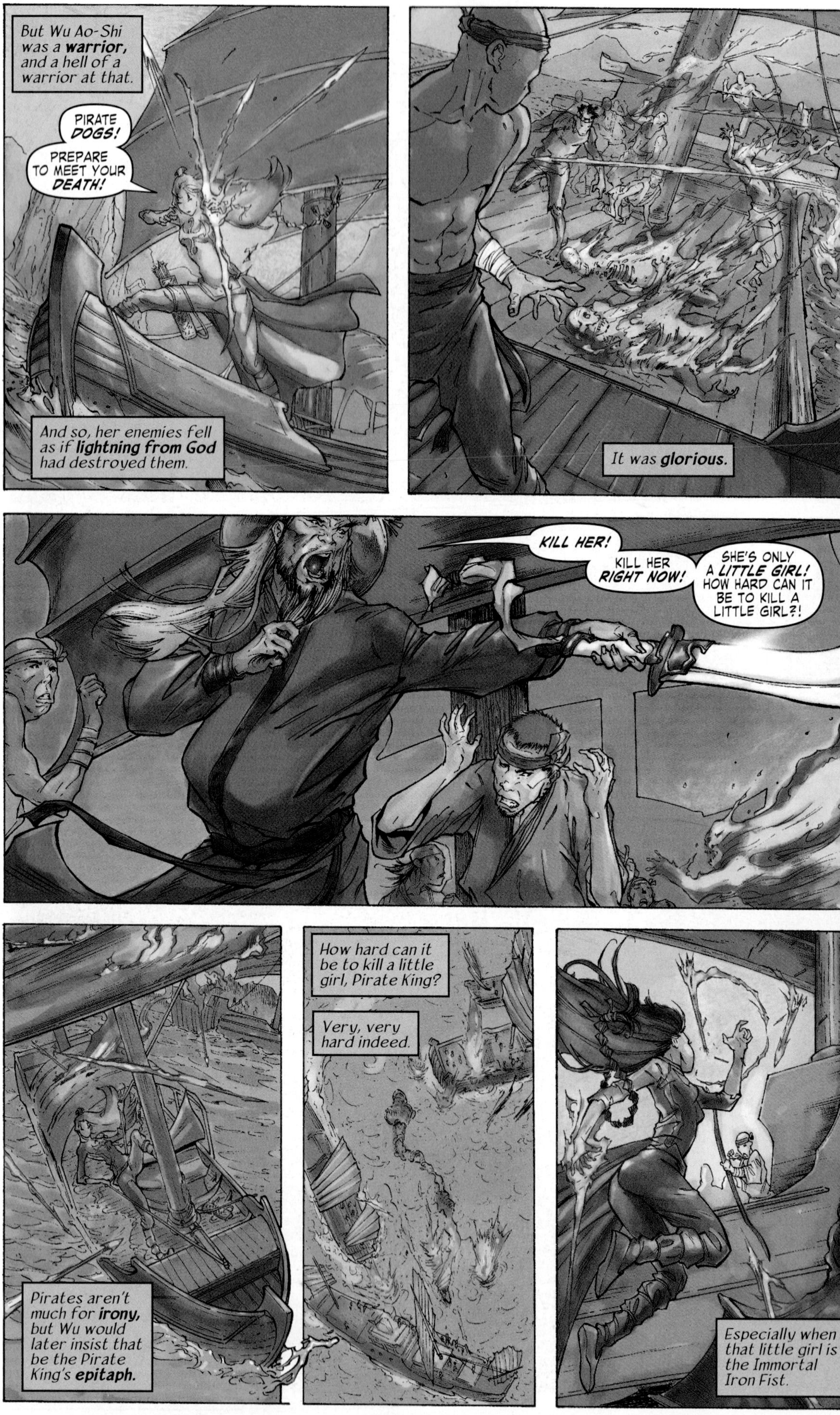
But Wu Ao-Shi was a **warrior,** and a hell of a warrior at that.
PIRATE *DOGS!*
PREPARE TO MEET YOUR *DEATH!*
And so, her enemies fell as if **lightning from God** had destroyed them.
It was **glorious.**
KILL HER!
KILL HER *RIGHT NOW!*
SHE'S ONLY A *LITTLE GIRL!* HOW HARD CAN IT BE TO KILL A LITTLE GIRL?!
Pirates aren't much for **irony,** but Wu would later insist that be the Pirate King's **epitaph.**
How hard can it be to kill a little girl, Pirate King?
Very, very hard indeed.
Especially when that little girl is the Immortal Iron Fist.

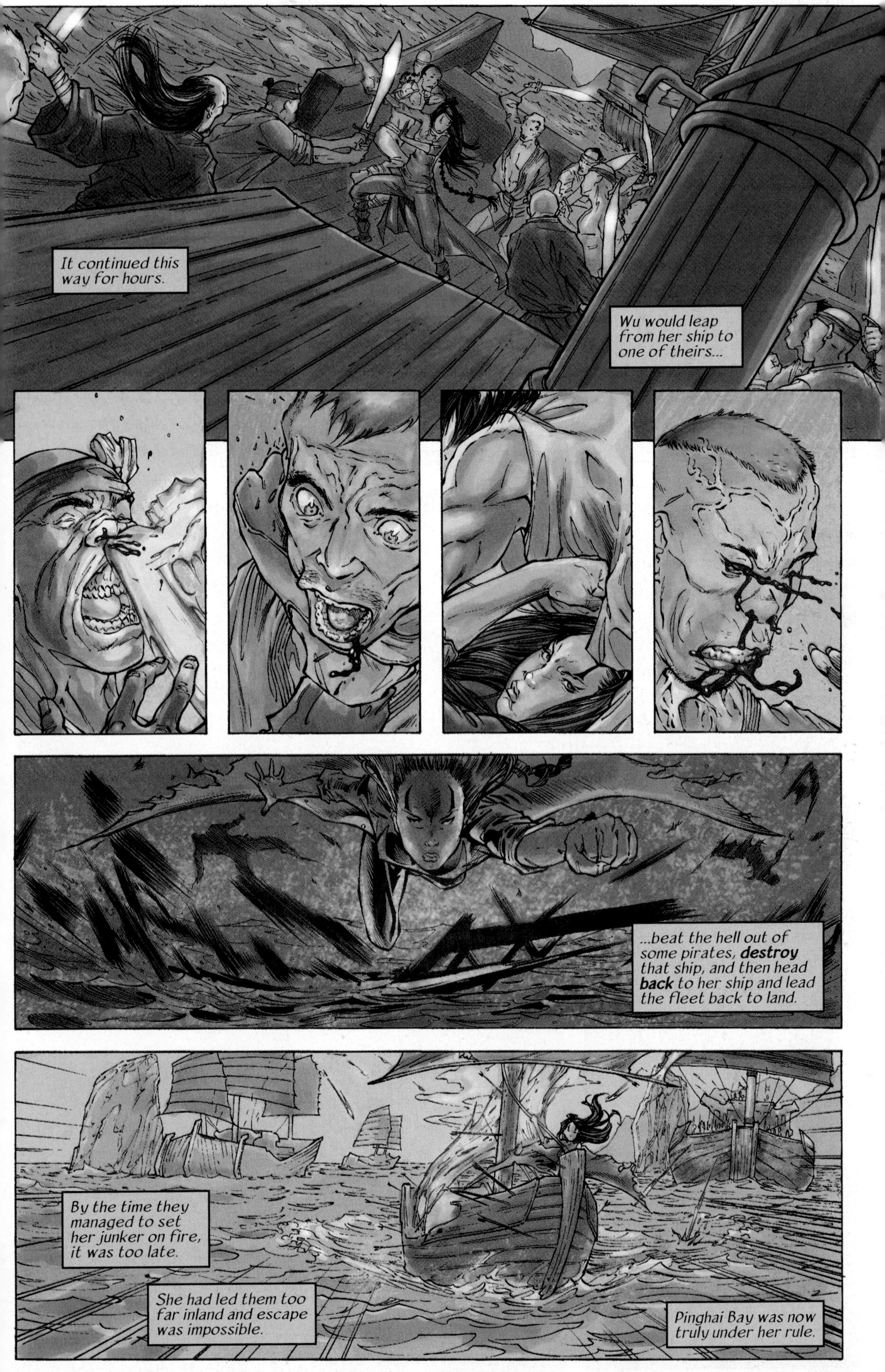
It continued this way for hours.
Wu would leap from her ship to one of theirs...
...beat the hell out of some pirates, **destroy** that ship, and then head **back** to her ship and lead the fleet back to land.
By the time they managed to set her junker on fire, it was too late.
She had led them too far inland and escape was impossible.
Pinghai Bay was now truly under her rule.

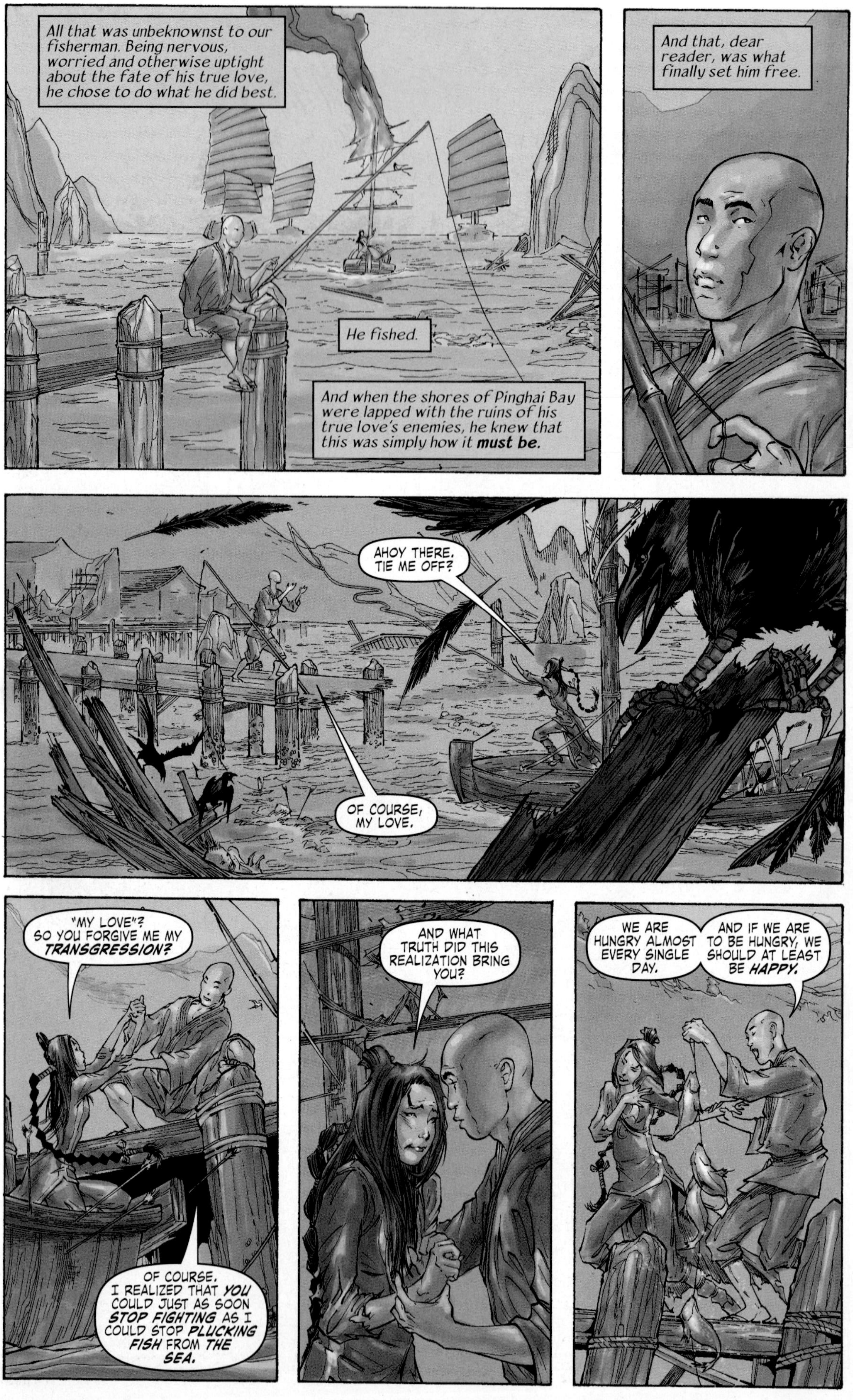
All that was unbeknownst to our fisherman. Being nervous, worried and otherwise uptight about the fate of his true love, he chose to do what he did best.
He fished.
And when the shores of Pinghai Bay were lapped with the ruins of his true love's enemies, he knew that this was simply how it must be.
And that, dear reader, was what finally set him free.
AHOY THERE. TIE ME OFF?
OF COURSE, MY LOVE.
"MY LOVE"? SO YOU FORGIVE ME MY TRANSGRESSION?
OF COURSE. I REALIZED THAT YOU COULD JUST AS SOON STOP FIGHTING AS I COULD STOP PLUCKING FISH FROM THE SEA.
AND WHAT TRUTH DID THIS REALIZATION BRING YOU?
WE ARE HUNGRY ALMOST EVERY SINGLE DAY.
AND IF WE ARE TO BE HUNGRY, WE SHOULD AT LEAST BE HAPPY.

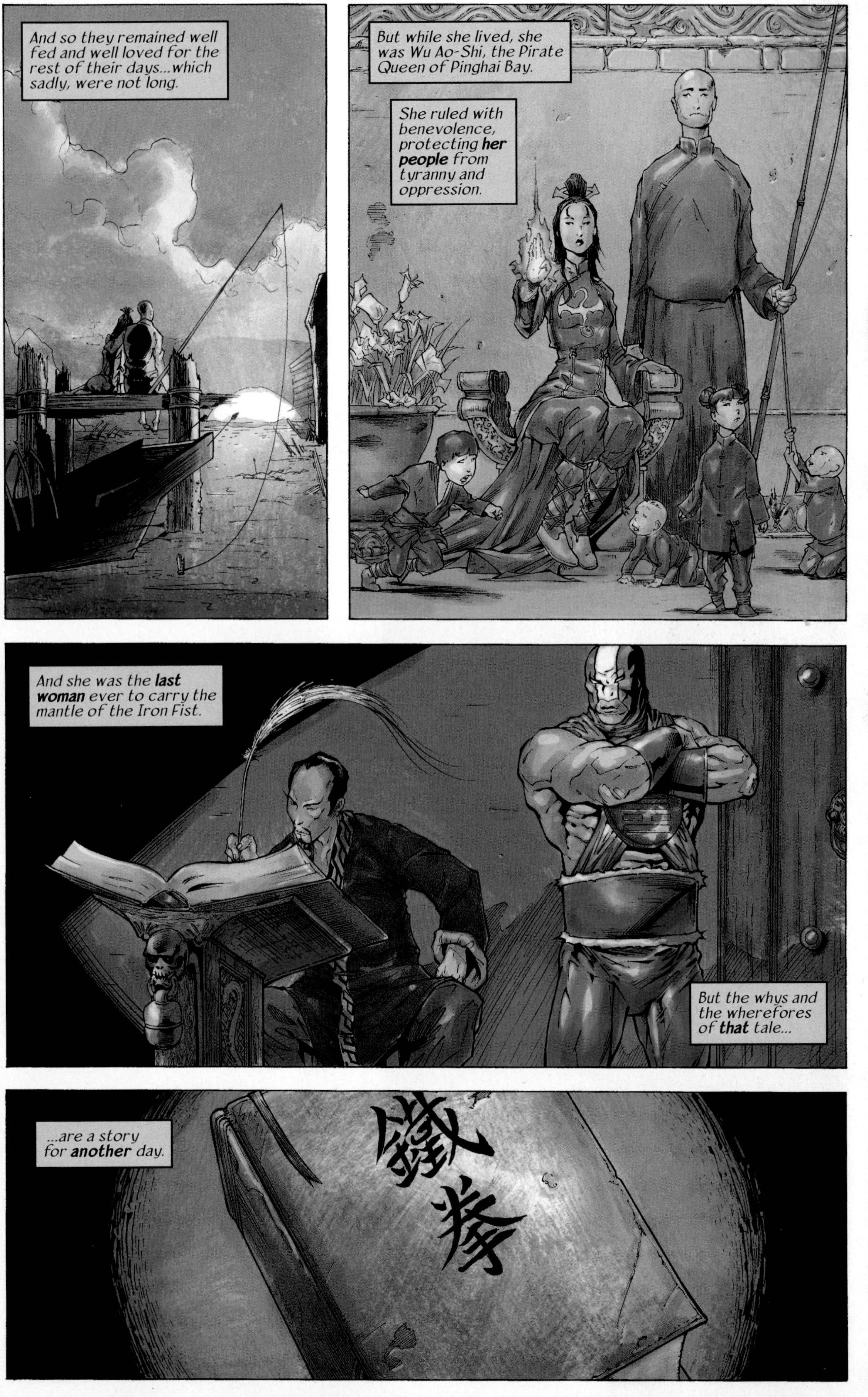
And so they remained well fed and well loved for the rest of their days...which sadly, were not long.
But while she lived, she was Wu Ao-Shi, the Pirate Queen of Pinghai Bay.
She ruled with benevolence, protecting **her people** from tyranny and oppression.
And she was the **last woman** ever to carry the mantle of the Iron Fist.
But the whys and the wherefores of **that** tale...
...are a story for **another** day.
鐵拳

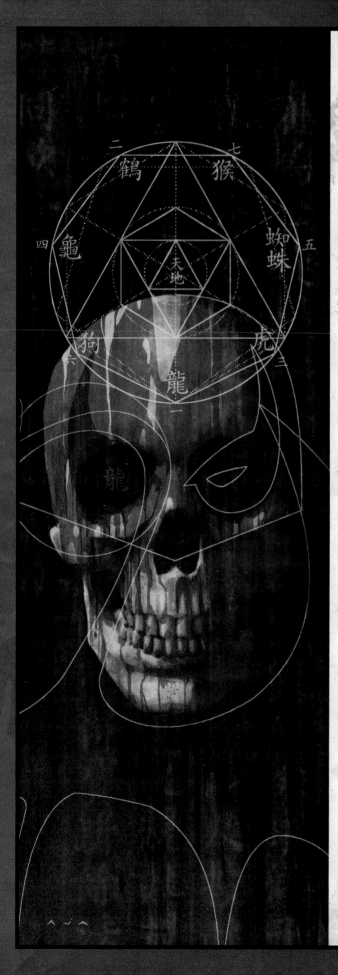

鐵拳

8

The  Capital
Cities
of Heaven

一

Round 1

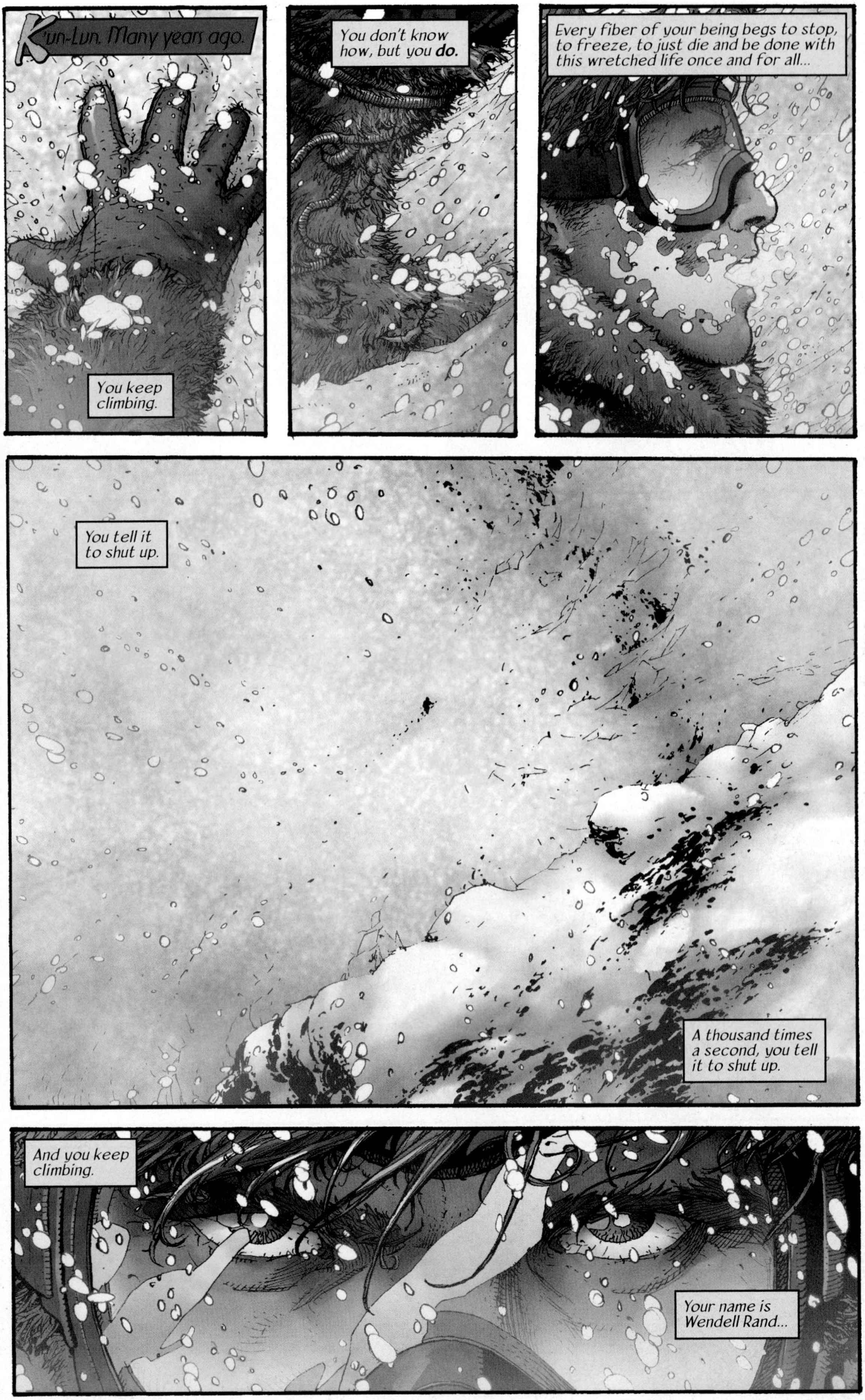
K'un-Lun. Many years ago.
You keep climbing.
You don't know how, but you **do.**
Every fiber of your being begs to stop, to freeze, to just die and be done with this wretched life once and for all...
You tell it to shut up.
A thousand times a second, you tell it to shut up.
And you keep climbing.
Your name is Wendell Rand...

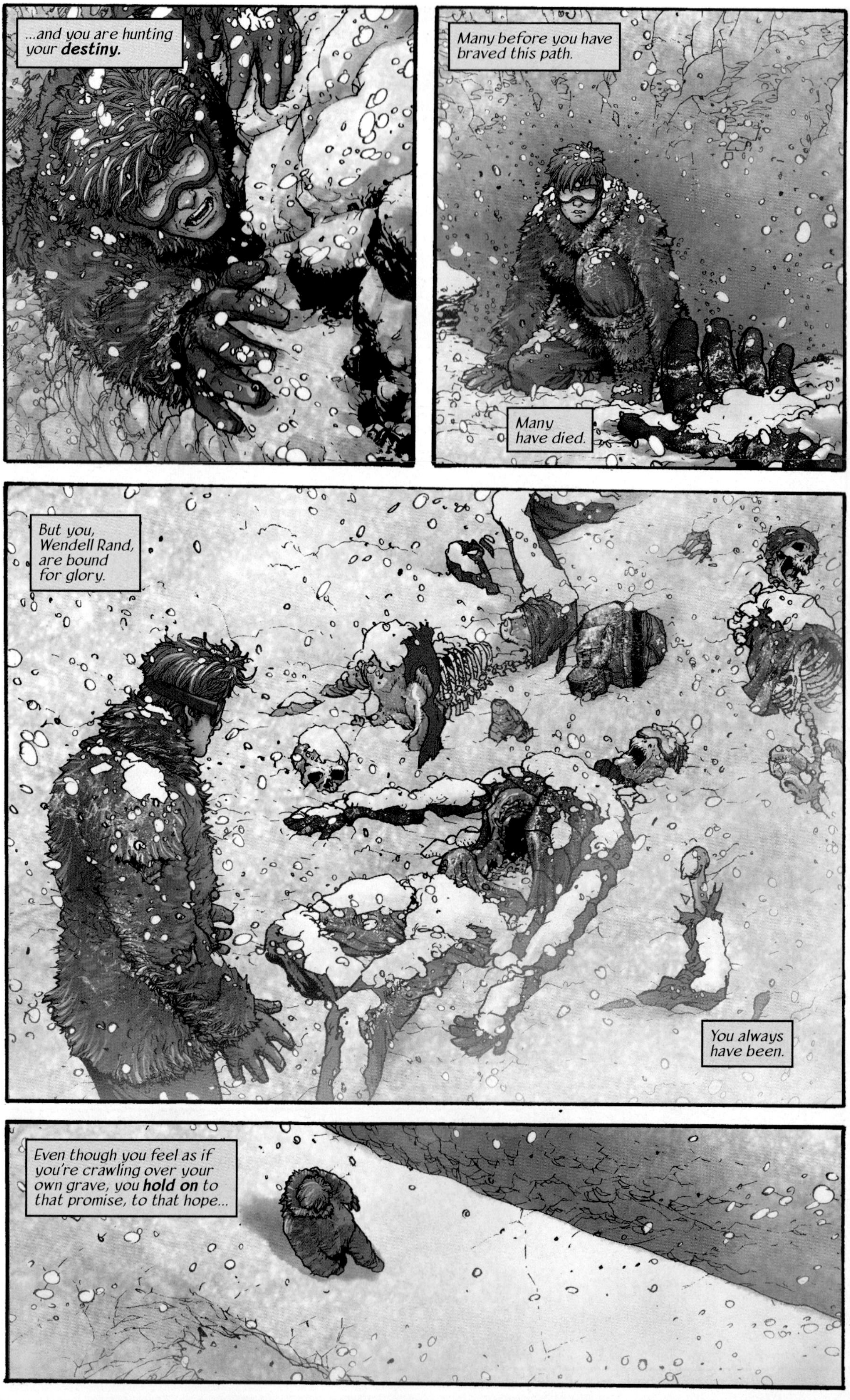
...and you are hunting your **destiny.**
Many before you have braved this path.
Many have died.
But you, Wendell Rand, are bound for glory.
You always have been.
Even though you feel as if you're crawling over your own grave, you **hold on** to that promise, to that hope...

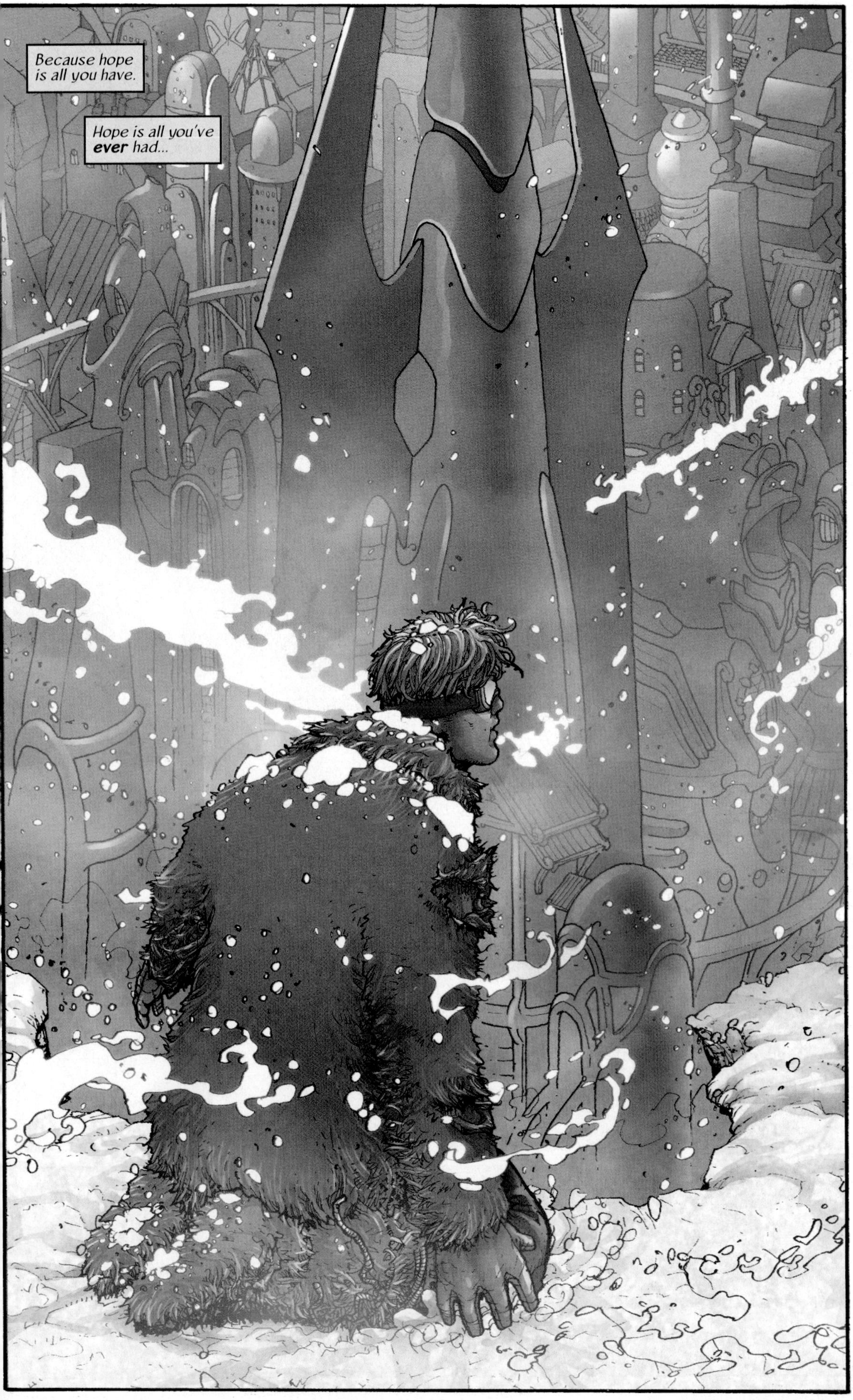
Because hope is all you have.
Hope is all you've **ever** had...

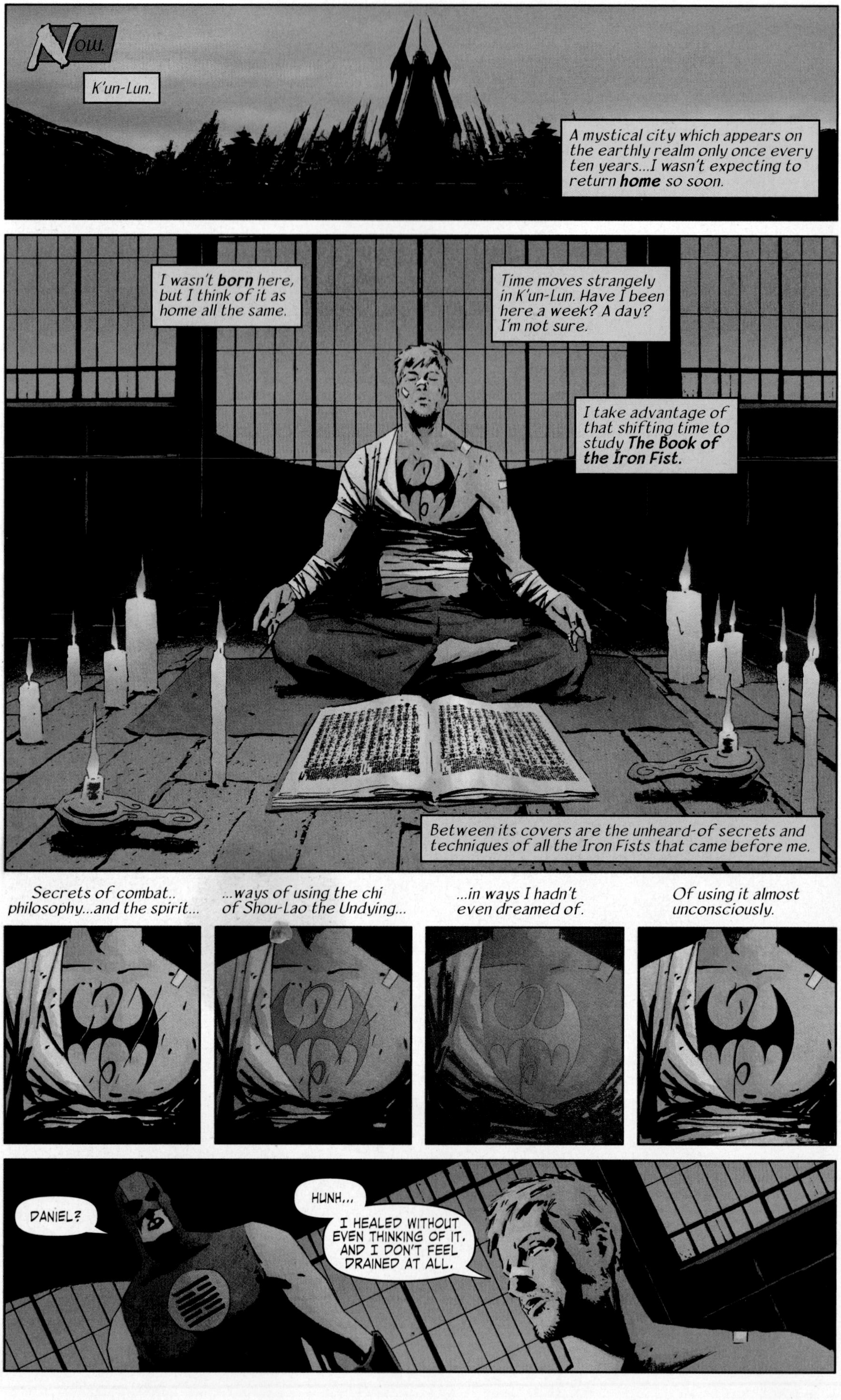
NOW.
K'un-Lun.
A mystical city which appears on the earthly realm only once every ten years...I wasn't expecting to return **home** so soon.
I wasn't **born** here, but I think of it as home all the same.
Time moves strangely in K'un-Lun. Have I been here a week? A day? I'm not sure.
I take advantage of that shifting time to study **The Book of the Iron Fist.**
Between its covers are the unheard-of secrets and techniques of all the Iron Fists that came before me.
Secrets of combat.. philosophy...and the spirit...
...ways of using the chi of Shou-Lao the Undying...
...in ways I hadn't even dreamed of.
Of using it almost unconsciously.
DANIEL?
HUNH...
I HEALED WITHOUT EVEN THINKING OF IT. AND I DON'T FEEL DRAINED AT ALL.

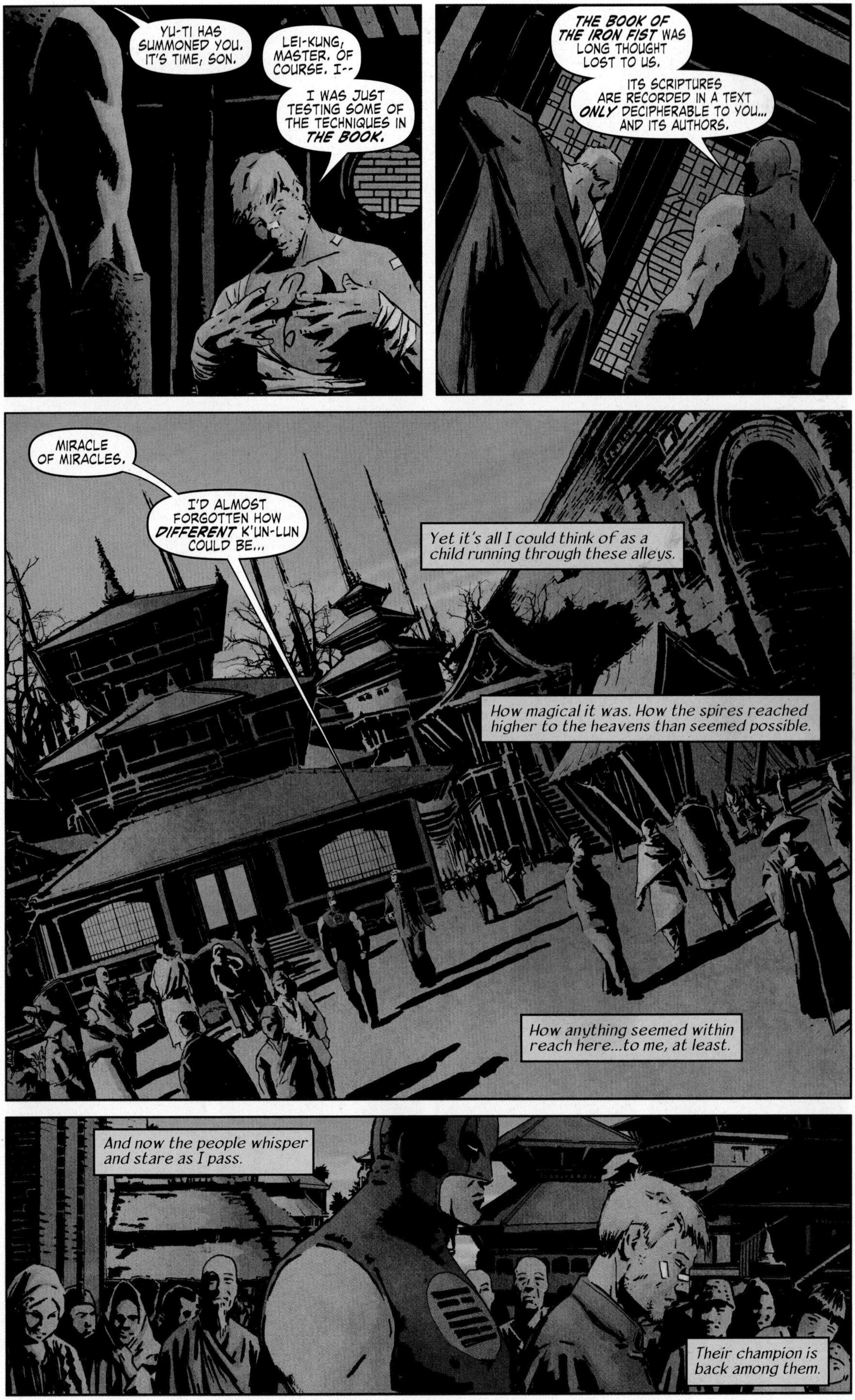
YU-TI HAS SUMMONED YOU. IT'S TIME, SON.
LEI-KUNG, MASTER. OF COURSE. I--
I WAS JUST TESTING SOME OF THE TECHNIQUES IN THE BOOK.
THE BOOK OF THE IRON FIST WAS LONG THOUGHT LOST TO US.
ITS SCRIPTURES ARE RECORDED IN A TEXT ONLY DECIPHERABLE TO YOU... AND ITS AUTHORS.
MIRACLE OF MIRACLES.
I'D ALMOST FORGOTTEN HOW DIFFERENT K'UN-LUN COULD BE...
Yet it's all I could think of as a child running through these alleys.
How magical it was. How the spires reached higher to the heavens than seemed possible.
How anything seemed within reach here...to me, at least.
And now the people whisper and stare as I pass.
Their champion is back among them.

K'UN-LUN IS ONE OF *SEVEN* CAPITAL CITIES OF HEAVEN. EACH APPEARING ON THE MORTAL PLANE ACCORDING TO TIMETABLES CHARTED AMONGST THE STARS.

BUT ONCE EVERY EIGHTY-EIGHT YEARS, THESE APPEARANCES ALIGN IN THE *HEAVENLY CONVERGENCE* AND WE CELEBRATE THIS WITH A *MIGHTY TOURNAMENT.*

SECTIONS OF EACH CITY JOIN TOGETHER, CREATING THE *HEART OF HEAVEN,* A PALACE WHERE OUR CONTESTS TAKE PLACE.

ASPECTS OF EACH CITY, AS WELL AS OF EARTH ITSELF, WILL BE FOUND HERE. IT IS UNLIKE ANYWHERE YOU HAVE BEEN, WITH RULES AND LAWS ONLY UNTO ITSELF.

IN EACH CITY RESIDES AN IMMORTAL WEAPON, LIKE YOURSELF, WITH THEIR OWN ICON AND FIGHTING STYLE.

EACH AS UNIQUE AS YOU, IRON FIST.

DURING THE LAST *CONVERGENCE,* YOUR PREDECESSOR REFUSED TO FIGHT. FOR THIS DISHONOR HE WAS TO BE *STRIPPED* OF HIS GIFTS.

HE RESISTED, AND ANOTHER CITY'S CHAMPION WAS *KILLED.* HE THEN FLED, AND THE CELEBRATION ENDED IN DISGRACE FOR US ALL.

THAT WILL *NOT* COME TO PASS THIS TIME.

NOW...DO YOU HAVE ANY QUESTIONS?

YES, MASTER.

WHY DIDN'T MY FATHER BECOME THE IRON FIST?

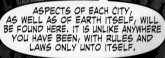

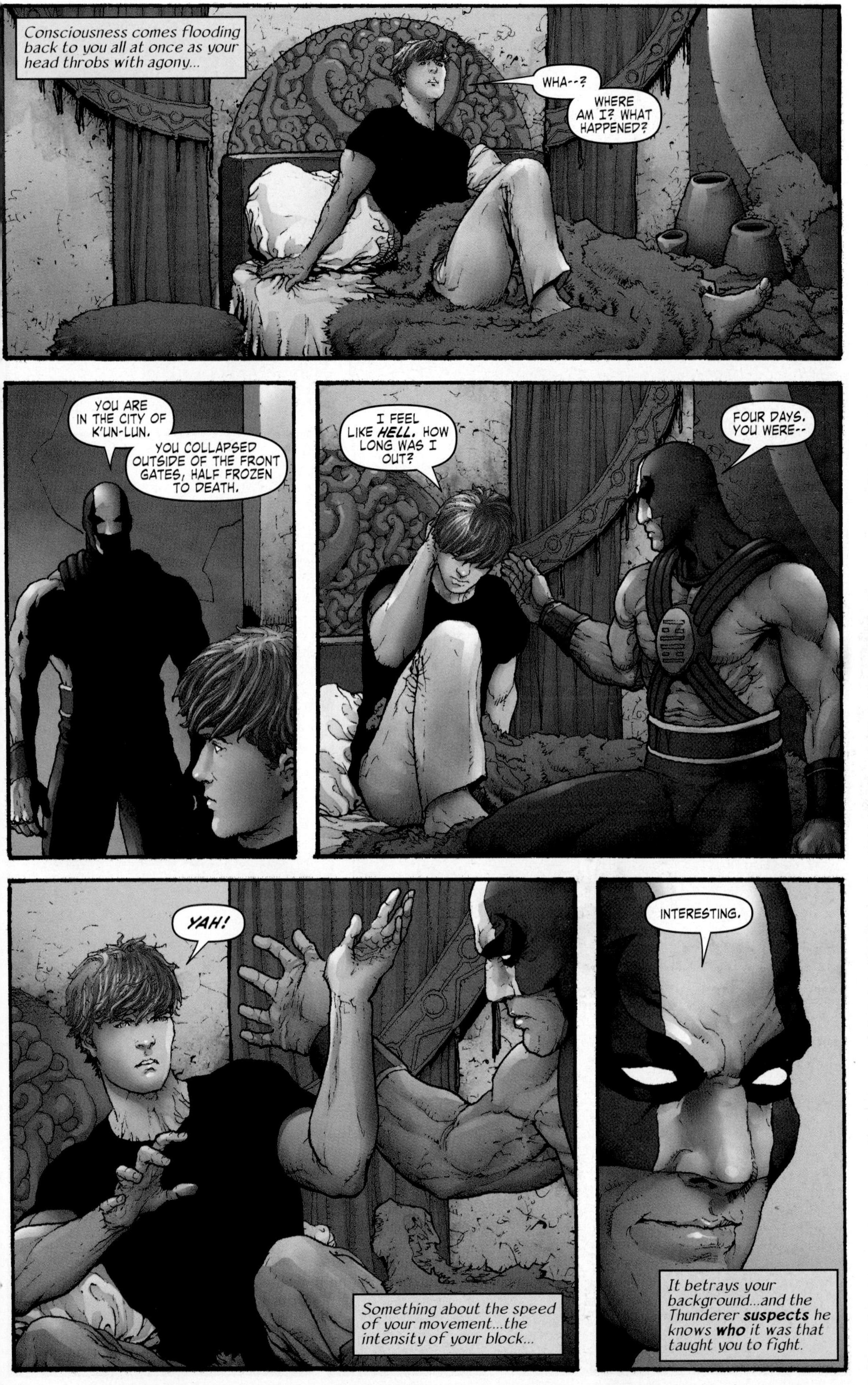

Consciousness comes flooding back to you all at once as your head throbs with agony...
WHA--?
WHERE AM I? WHAT HAPPENED?
YOU ARE IN THE CITY OF K'UN-LUN.
YOU COLLAPSED OUTSIDE OF THE FRONT GATES, HALF FROZEN TO DEATH.
I FEEL LIKE HELL. HOW LONG WAS I OUT?
FOUR DAYS. YOU WERE--
YAH!
Something about the speed of your movement...the intensity of your block...
INTERESTING.
It betrays your background...and the Thunderer suspects he knows who it was that taught you to fight.

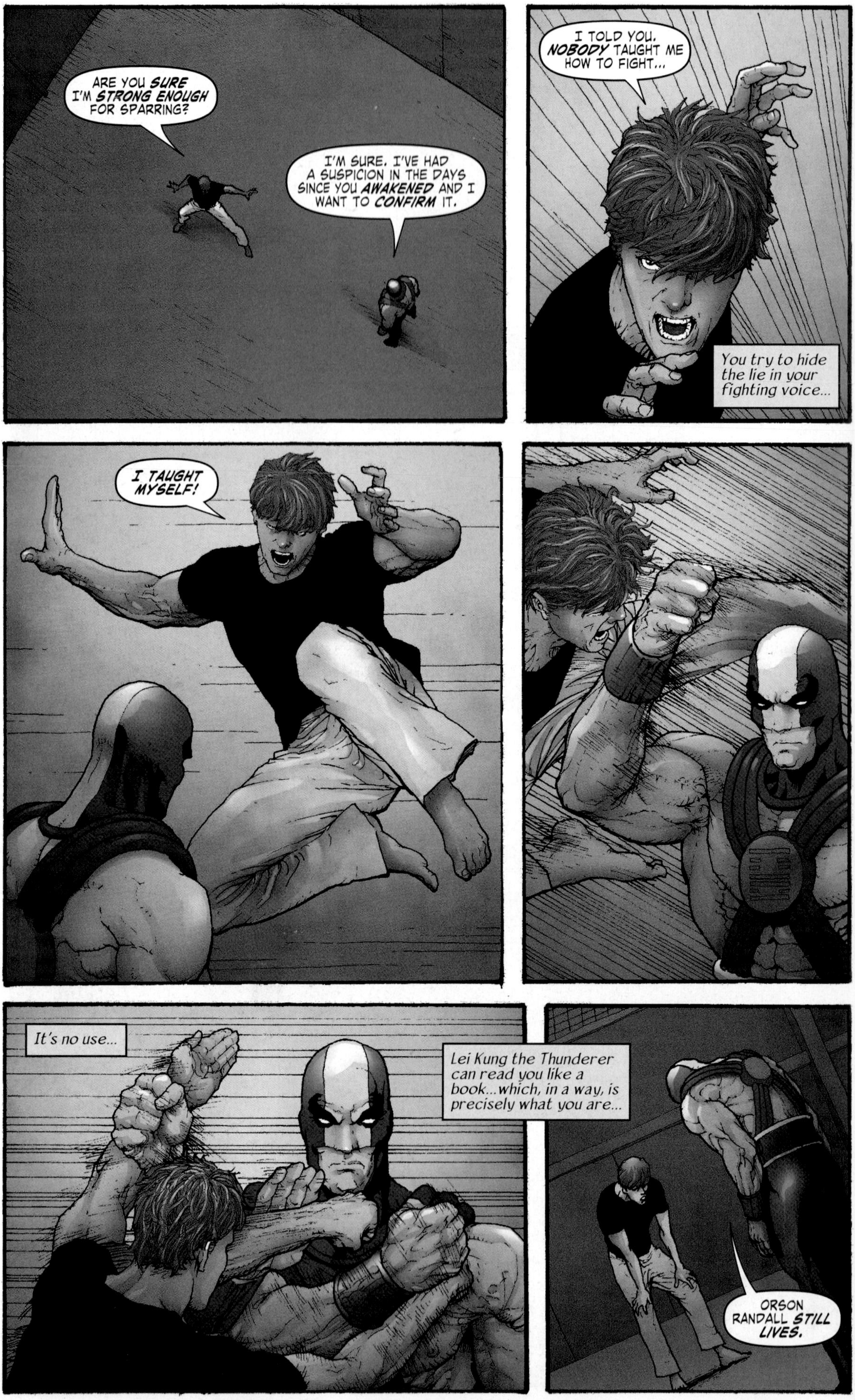
ARE YOU SURE I'M STRONG ENOUGH FOR SPARRING?
I'M SURE. I'VE HAD A SUSPICION IN THE DAYS SINCE YOU AWAKENED AND I WANT TO CONFIRM IT.
I TOLD YOU. NOBODY TAUGHT ME HOW TO FIGHT...
You try to hide the lie in your fighting voice...
I TAUGHT MYSELF!
It's no use...
Lei Kung the Thunderer can read you like a book...which, in a way, is precisely what you are...
ORSON RANDALL STILL LIVES.

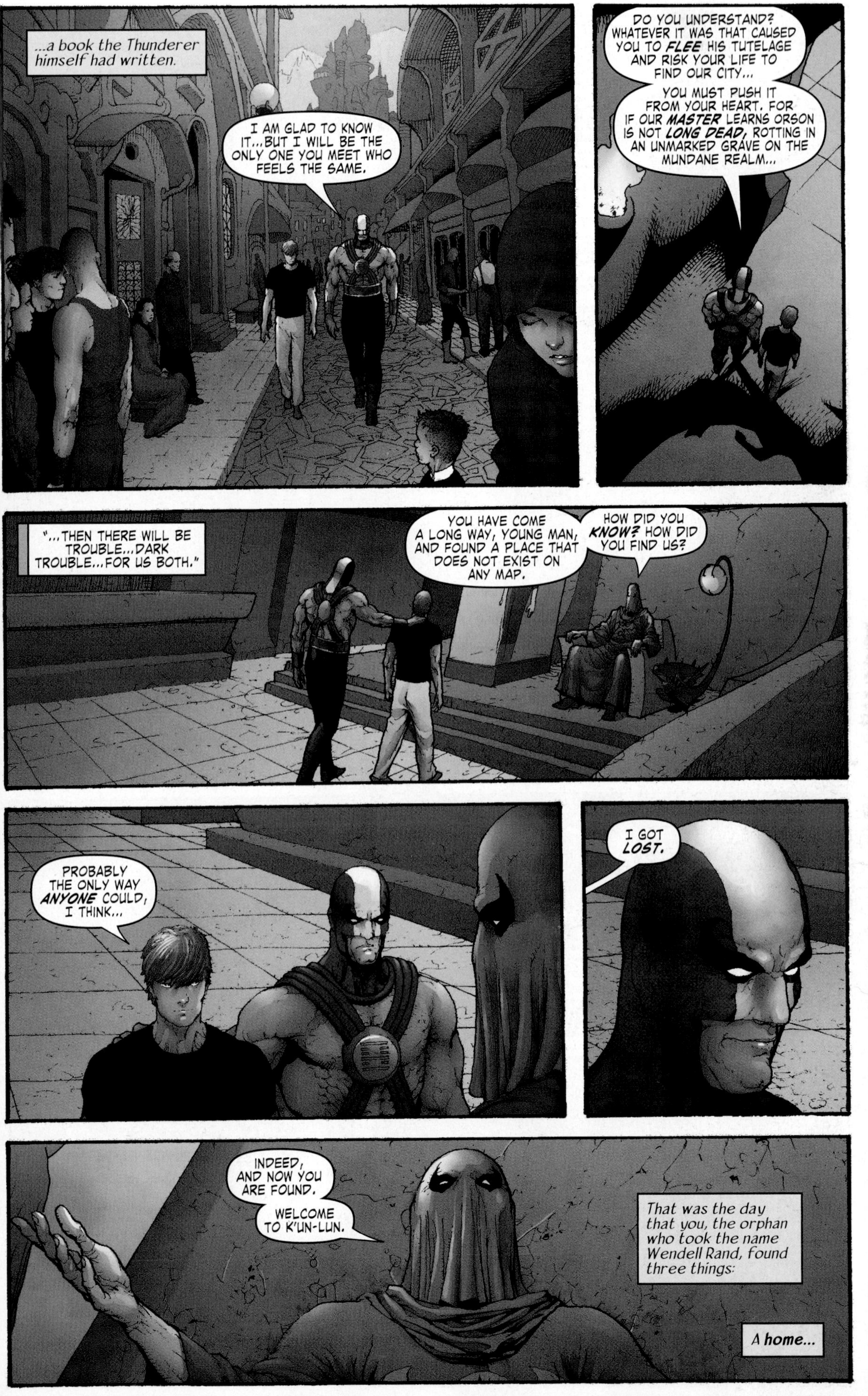
...a book the Thunderer himself had written.
I AM GLAD TO KNOW IT...BUT I WILL BE THE ONLY ONE YOU MEET WHO FEELS THE SAME.
DO YOU UNDERSTAND? WHATEVER IT WAS THAT CAUSED YOU TO FLEE HIS TUTELAGE AND RISK YOUR LIFE TO FIND OUR CITY...
YOU MUST PUSH IT FROM YOUR HEART. FOR IF OUR MASTER LEARNS ORSON IS NOT LONG DEAD, ROTTING IN AN UNMARKED GRAVE ON THE MUNDANE REALM...
"...THEN THERE WILL BE TROUBLE...DARK TROUBLE...FOR US BOTH."
YOU HAVE COME A LONG WAY, YOUNG MAN, AND FOUND A PLACE THAT DOES NOT EXIST ON ANY MAP.
HOW DID YOU KNOW? HOW DID YOU FIND US?
PROBABLY THE ONLY WAY ANYONE COULD, I THINK...
I GOT LOST.
INDEED, AND NOW YOU ARE FOUND.
WELCOME TO K'UN-LUN.
That was the day that you, the orphan who took the name Wendell Rand, found three things:
A home...

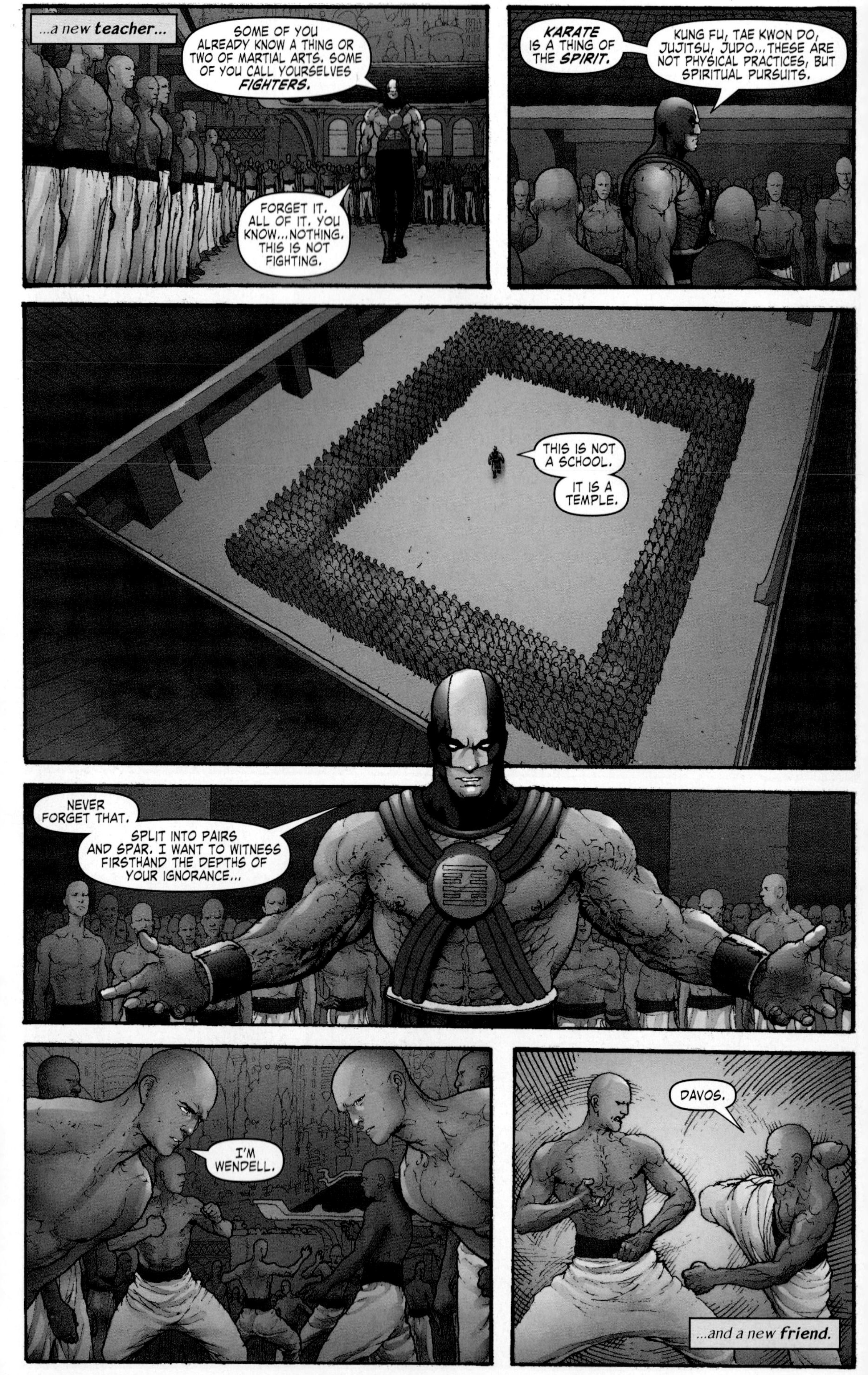
...a new teacher...
SOME OF YOU ALREADY KNOW A THING OR TWO OF MARTIAL ARTS. SOME OF YOU CALL YOURSELVES FIGHTERS.
FORGET IT. ALL OF IT. YOU KNOW...NOTHING. THIS IS NOT FIGHTING.
KARATE IS A THING OF THE SPIRIT.
KUNG FU, TAE KWON DO, JUJITSU, JUDO...THESE ARE NOT PHYSICAL PRACTICES, BUT SPIRITUAL PURSUITS.
THIS IS NOT A SCHOOL.
IT IS A TEMPLE.
NEVER FORGET THAT.
SPLIT INTO PAIRS AND SPAR. I WANT TO WITNESS FIRSTHAND THE DEPTHS OF YOUR IGNORANCE...
I'M WENDELL.
DAVOS.
...and a new friend.

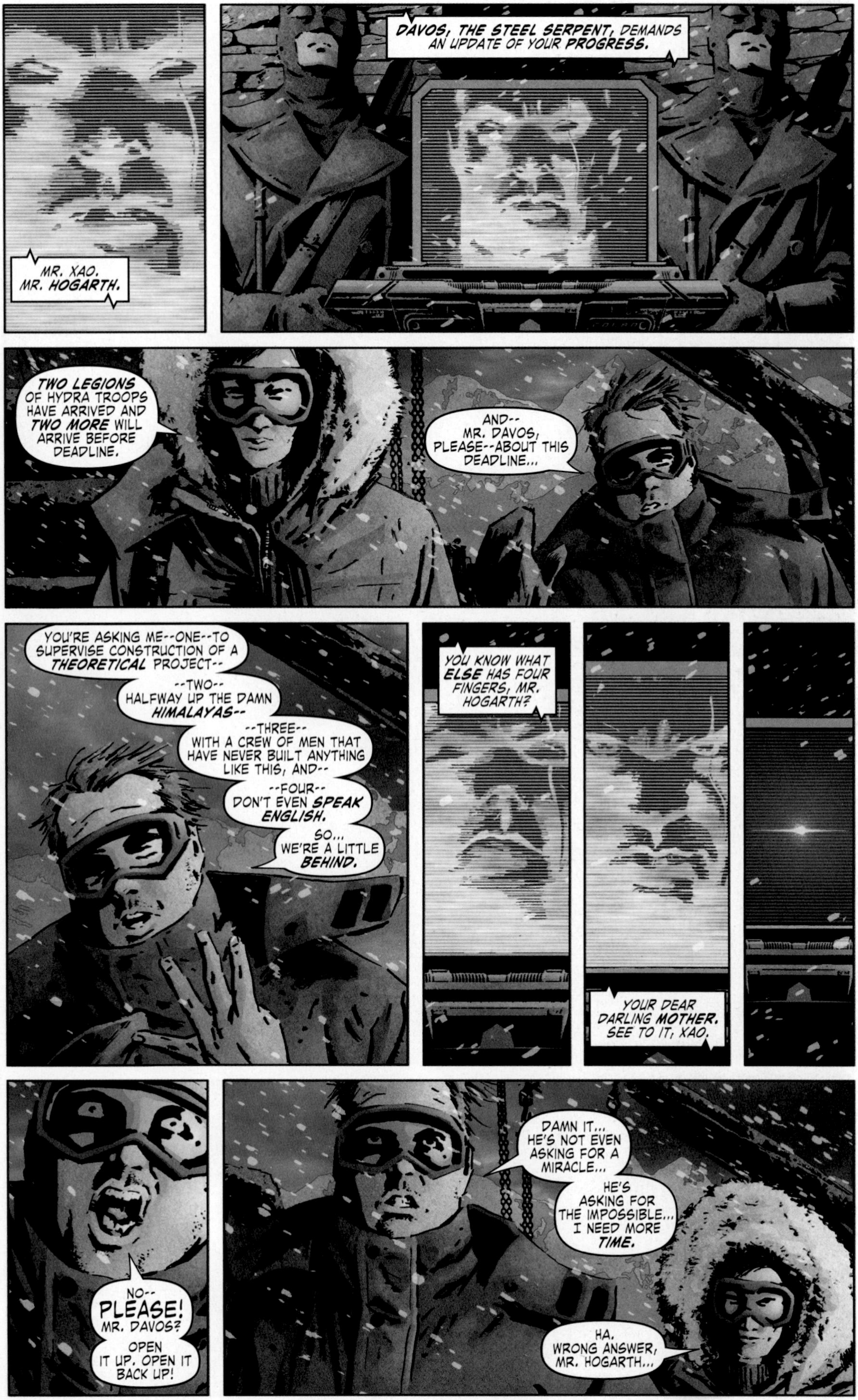
MR. XAO. MR. HOGARTH.
DAVOS, THE STEEL SERPENT, DEMANDS AN UPDATE OF YOUR PROGRESS.
TWO LEGIONS OF HYDRA TROOPS HAVE ARRIVED AND TWO MORE WILL ARRIVE BEFORE DEADLINE.
AND-- MR. DAVOS, PLEASE--ABOUT THIS DEADLINE...
YOU'RE ASKING ME--ONE--TO SUPERVISE CONSTRUCTION OF A THEORETICAL PROJECT--
--TWO-- HALFWAY UP THE DAMN HIMALAYAS--
--THREE-- WITH A CREW OF MEN THAT HAVE NEVER BUILT ANYTHING LIKE THIS, AND--
--FOUR-- DON'T EVEN SPEAK ENGLISH.
SO... WE'RE A LITTLE BEHIND.
YOU KNOW WHAT ELSE HAS FOUR FINGERS, MR. HOGARTH?
YOUR DEAR DARLING MOTHER. SEE TO IT, XAO.
NO-- PLEASE! MR. DAVOS?
OPEN IT UP. OPEN IT BACK UP!
DAMN IT... HE'S NOT EVEN ASKING FOR A MIRACLE...
HE'S ASKING FOR THE IMPOSSIBLE... I NEED MORE TIME.
HA. WRONG ANSWER, MR. HOGARTH...

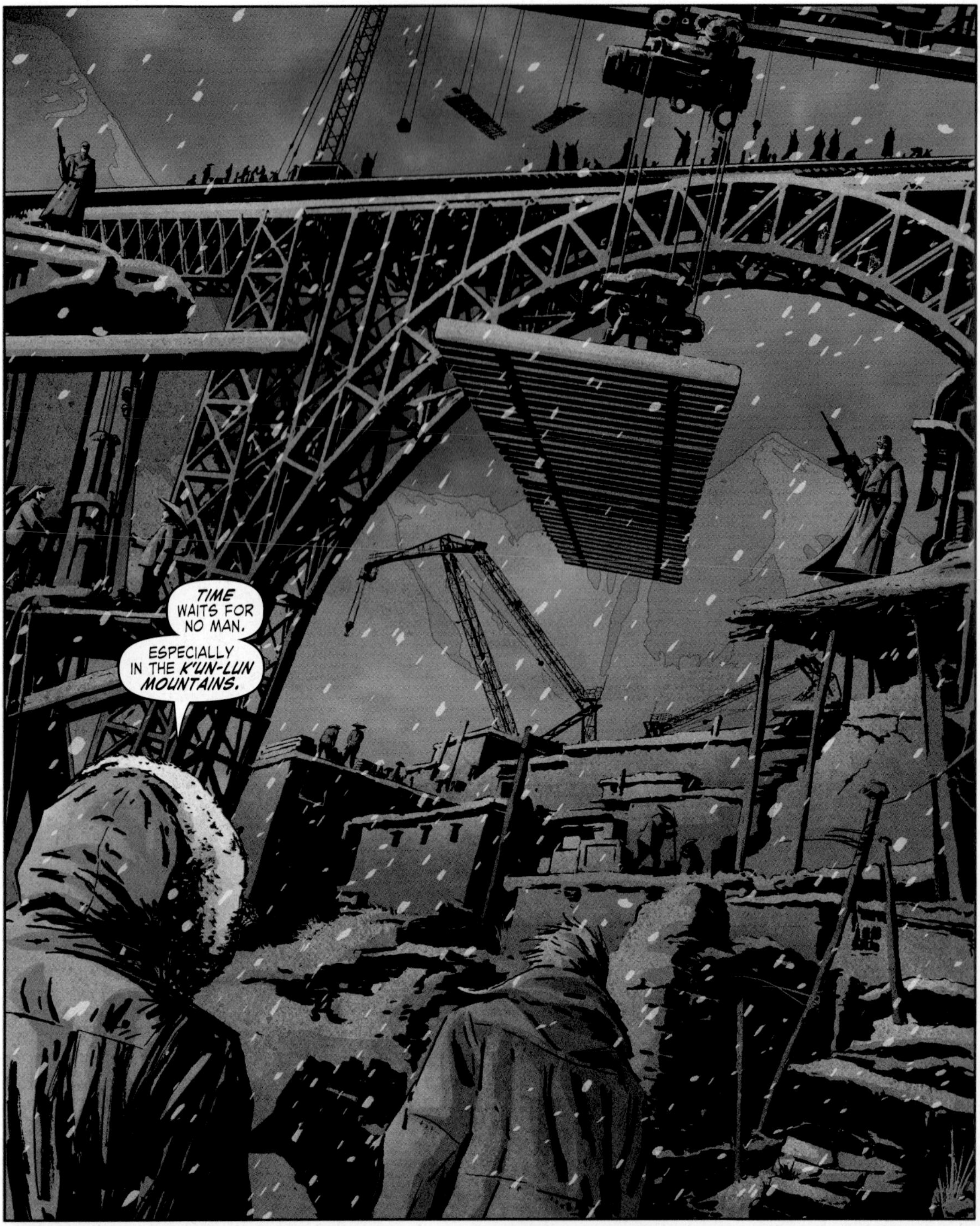
TIME WAITS FOR NO MAN.
ESPECIALLY IN THE K'UN-LUN MOUNTAINS.

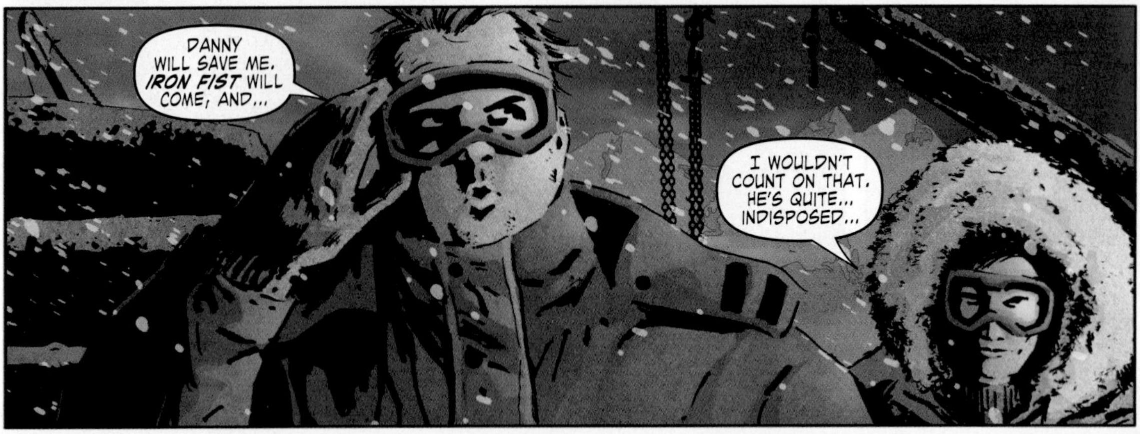
DANNY WILL SAVE ME. IRON FIST WILL COME, AND...
I WOULDN'T COUNT ON THAT. HE'S QUITE... INDISPOSED...

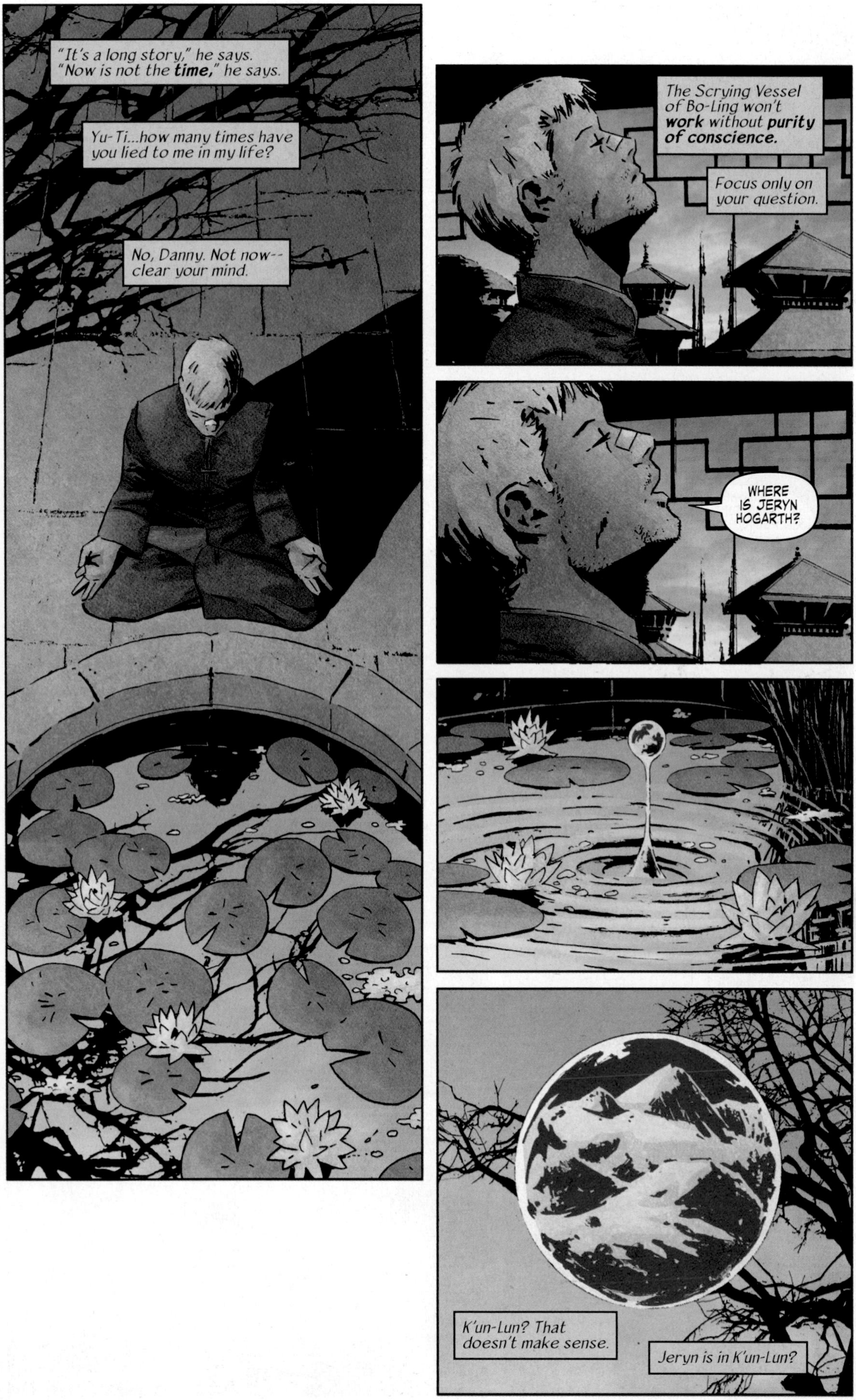
"It's a long story," he says.
"Now is not the **time,**" he says.
Yu-Ti...how many times have you lied to me in my life?
No, Danny. Not now--clear your mind.
The Scrying Vessel of Bo-Ling won't **work** without **purity of conscience.**
Focus only on your question.
WHERE IS JERYN HOGARTH?
K'un-Lun? That doesn't make sense.
Jeryn is in K'un-Lun?

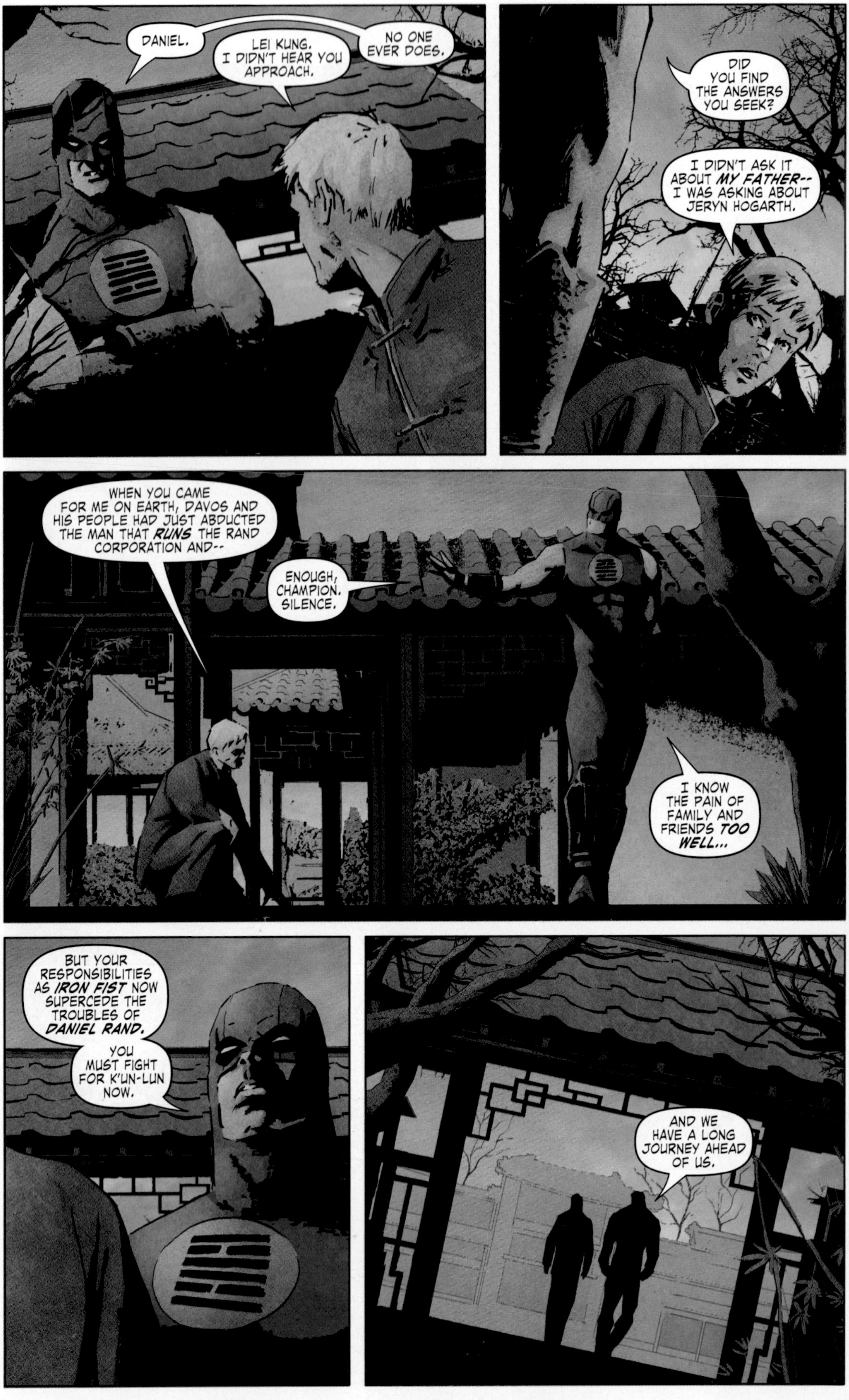
DANIEL.
LEI KUNG. I DIDN'T HEAR YOU APPROACH.
NO ONE EVER DOES.
DID YOU FIND THE ANSWERS YOU SEEK?
I DIDN'T ASK IT ABOUT MY FATHER-- I WAS ASKING ABOUT JERYN HOGARTH.
WHEN YOU CAME FOR ME ON EARTH, DAVOS AND HIS PEOPLE HAD JUST ABDUCTED THE MAN THAT RUNS THE RAND CORPORATION AND--
ENOUGH, CHAMPION. SILENCE.
I KNOW THE PAIN OF FAMILY AND FRIENDS TOO WELL...
BUT YOUR RESPONSIBILITIES AS IRON FIST NOW SUPERCEDE THE TROUBLES OF DANIEL RAND.
YOU MUST FIGHT FOR K'UN-LUN NOW.
AND WE HAVE A LONG JOURNEY AHEAD OF US.

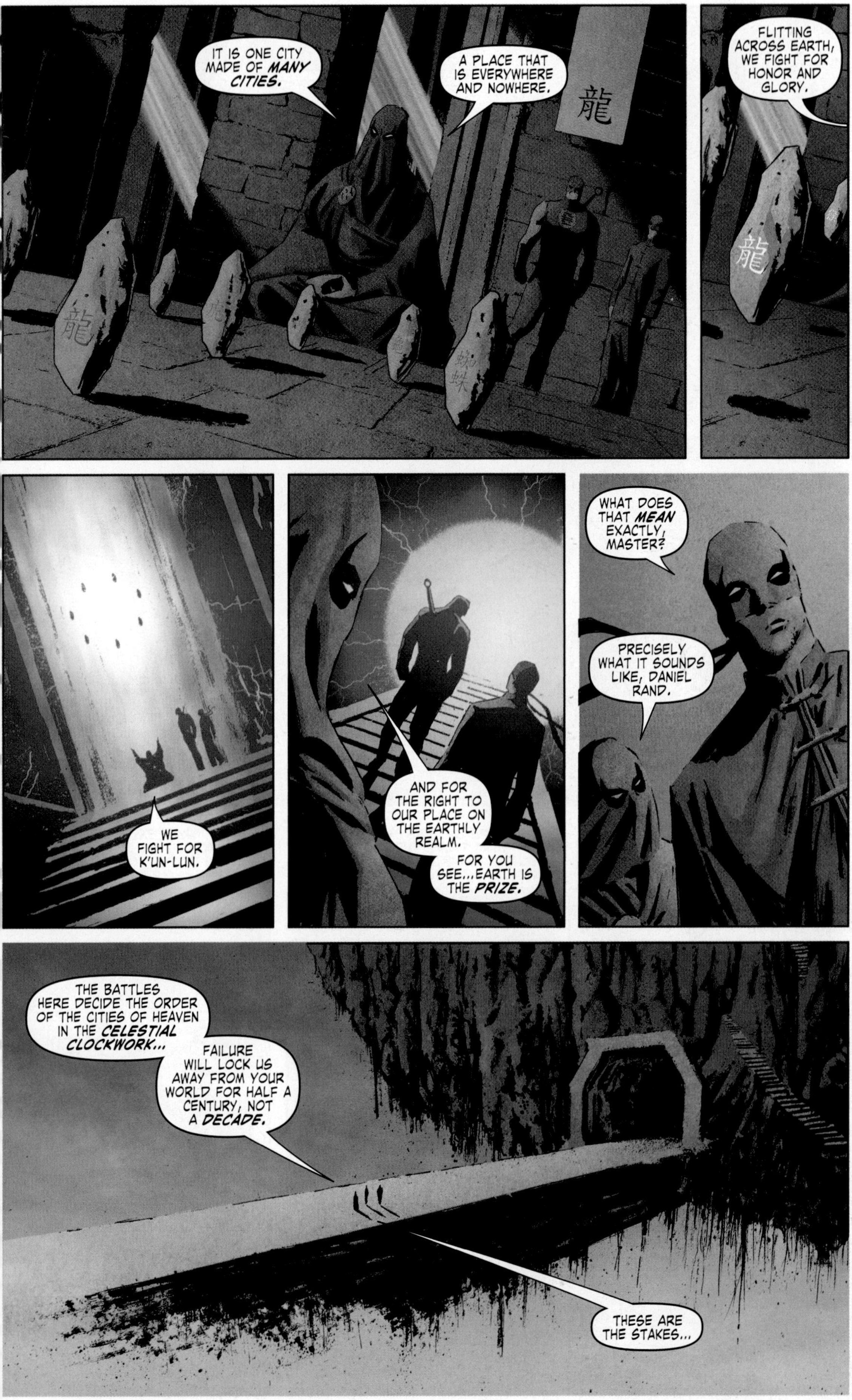
IT IS ONE CITY MADE OF **MANY CITIES.**
A PLACE THAT IS EVERYWHERE AND NOWHERE.
龍
FLITTING ACROSS EARTH, WE FIGHT FOR HONOR AND GLORY.
WE FIGHT FOR K'UN-LUN.
AND FOR THE RIGHT TO OUR PLACE ON THE EARTHLY REALM.
FOR YOU SEE...EARTH IS THE **PRIZE.**
WHAT DOES THAT **MEAN** EXACTLY, MASTER?
PRECISELY WHAT IT SOUNDS LIKE, DANIEL RAND.
THE BATTLES HERE DECIDE THE ORDER OF THE CITIES OF HEAVEN IN THE **CELESTIAL CLOCKWORK...**
FAILURE WILL LOCK US AWAY FROM YOUR WORLD FOR HALF A CENTURY, NOT A **DECADE.**
THESE ARE THE STAKES...

...NOW IT'S TIME TO MEET *YOUR OPPONENTS.*

"FAT COBRA...
HIS SIZE AND STRENGTH ARE ONLY OUTCLASSED BY HIS SPEED.

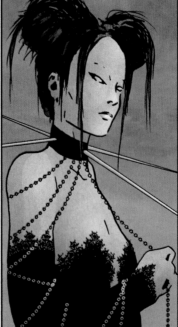

"THE BRIDE OF NINE SPIDERS...
HER HEART PUMPS THE COLDEST BLOOD IMAGINABLE...AND HORRORS INCONCEIVABLE TO MORTAL MEN.

"DOG BROTHER #1...
HERO TO ALL THE STRAYS ON ALL THE STREETS OF THE WORLD...A PRANKSTER ASSASSIN WHO RULES THE UNDER-CITY...

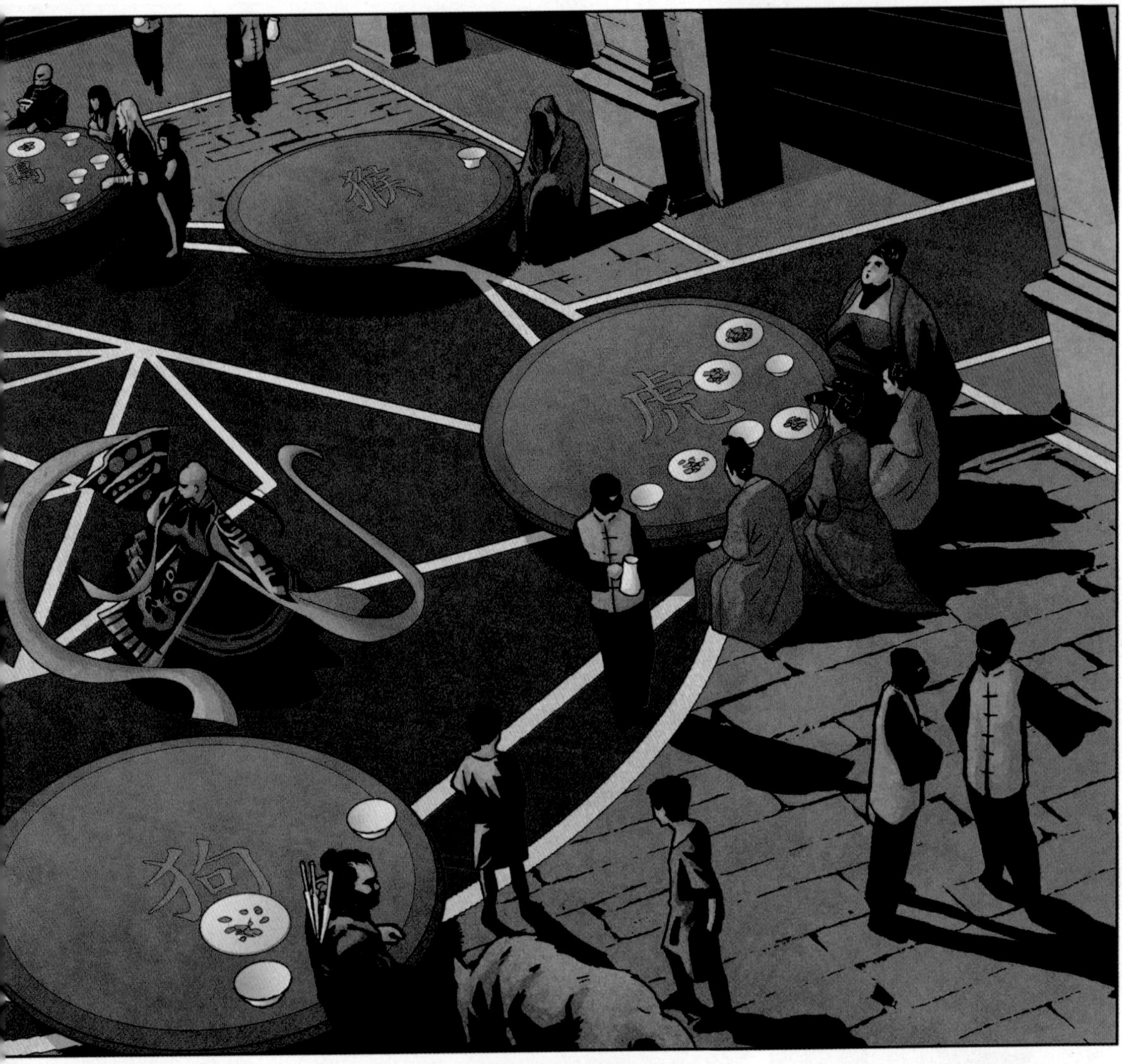
猴
虎
狗
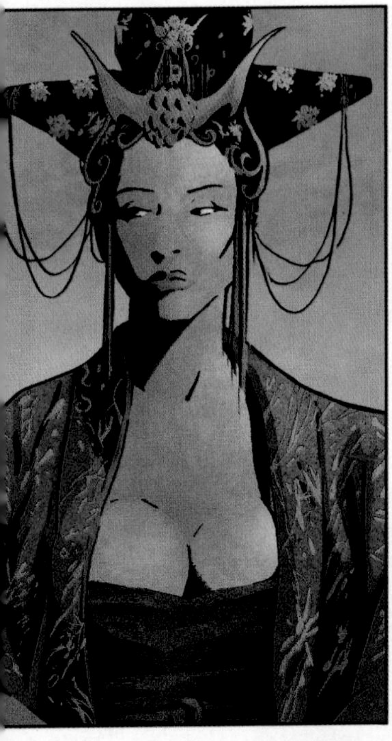
"TIGER'S BEAUTIFUL DAUGHTER... MANY A MAN HAS FOUND HIS DOOM AT HER HAND OR IN HER BED.
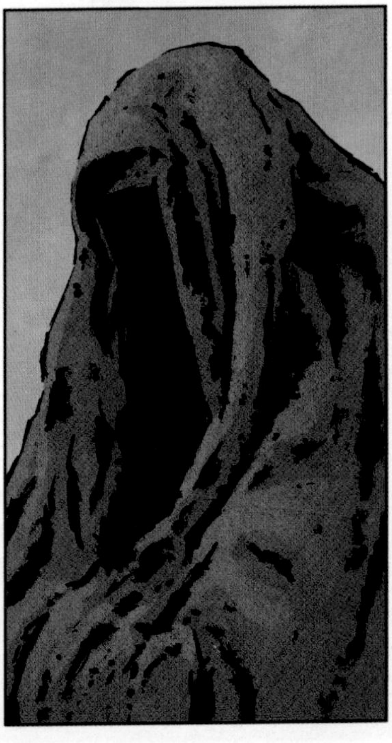
"THE PRINCE OF ORPHANS. MYSTERIOUS, EVEN TO WE WHO CULTIVATE UNENDING MYSTERY.
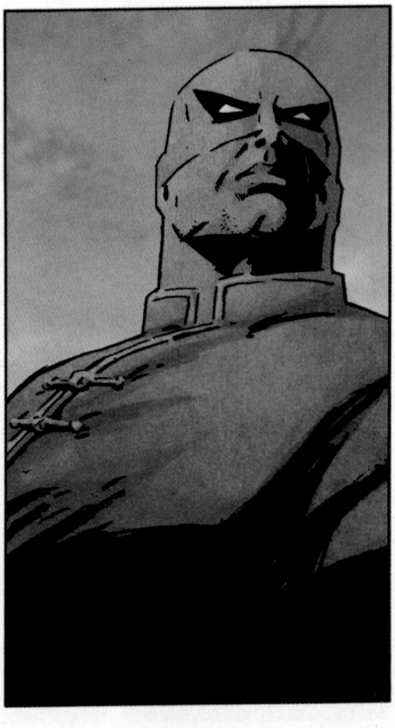
"AND THE NEW WEAPON OF K'UN-ZI...DAVOS. THE STEEL SERPENT... MASTER OF THE CRANES."

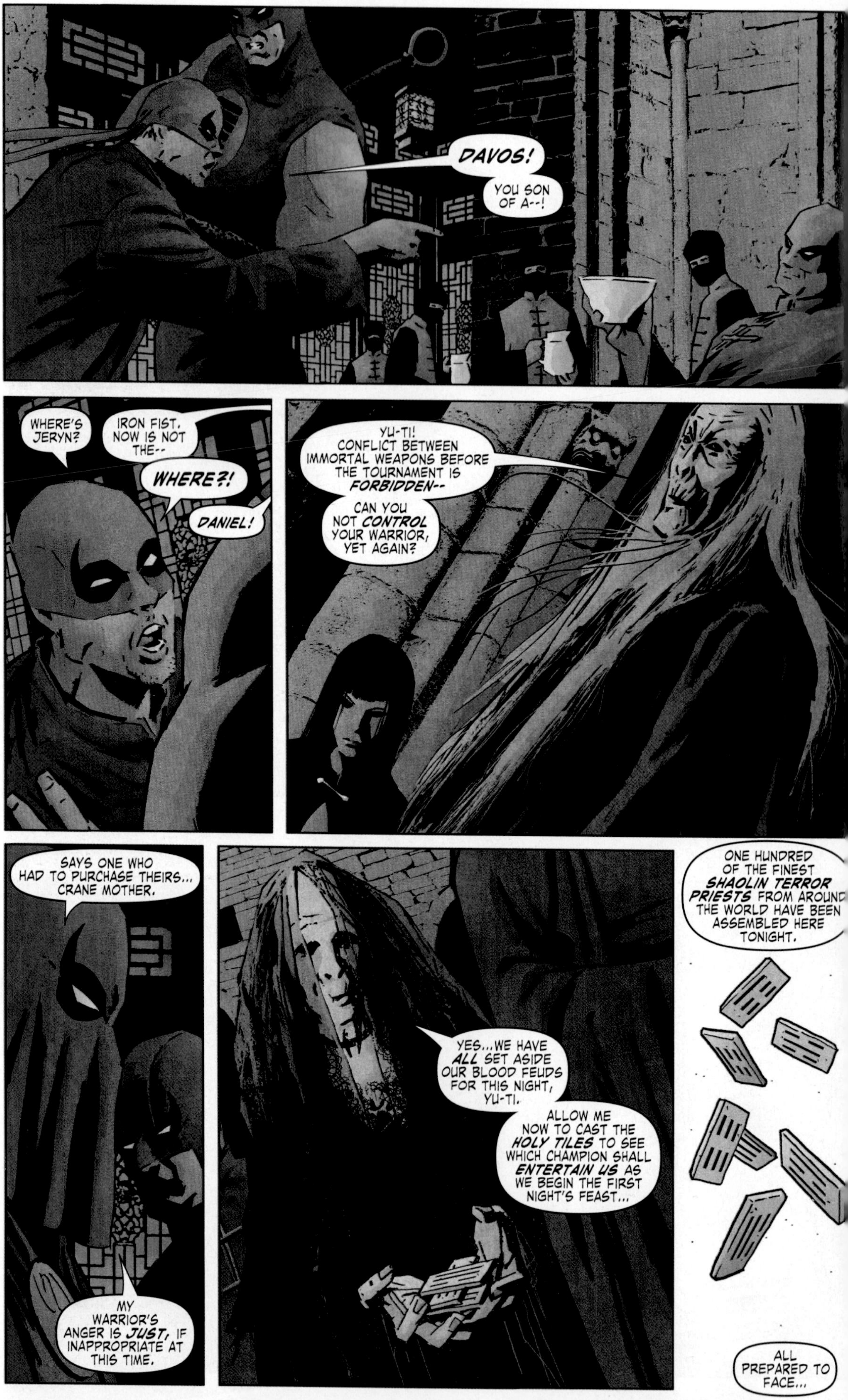
DAVOS!
YOU SON OF A--!
WHERE'S JERYN?
IRON FIST. NOW IS NOT THE--
WHERE?!
DANIEL!
YU-TI! CONFLICT BETWEEN IMMORTAL WEAPONS BEFORE THE TOURNAMENT IS FORBIDDEN--
CAN YOU NOT CONTROL YOUR WARRIOR, YET AGAIN?
SAYS ONE WHO HAD TO PURCHASE THEIRS... CRANE MOTHER.
MY WARRIOR'S ANGER IS JUST, IF INAPPROPRIATE AT THIS TIME.
YES...WE HAVE ALL SET ASIDE OUR BLOOD FEUDS FOR THIS NIGHT, YU-TI.
ALLOW ME NOW TO CAST THE HOLY TILES TO SEE WHICH CHAMPION SHALL ENTERTAIN US AS WE BEGIN THE FIRST NIGHT'S FEAST...
ONE HUNDRED OF THE FINEST SHAOLIN TERROR PRIESTS FROM AROUND THE WORLD HAVE BEEN ASSEMBLED HERE TONIGHT.
ALL PREPARED TO FACE...

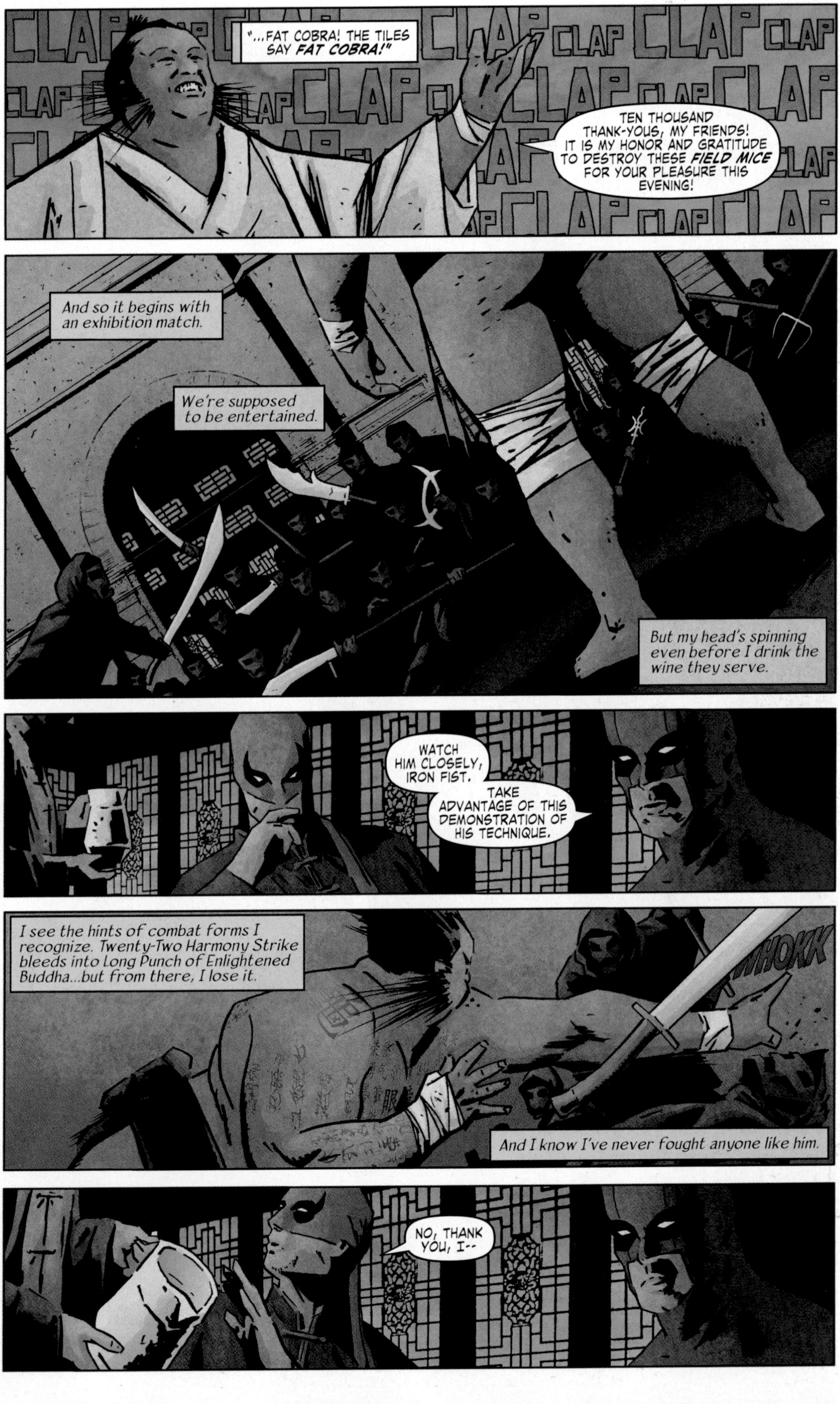
CLAP CLAP CLAP CLAP CLAP
"...FAT COBRA! THE TILES SAY *FAT COBRA!*"
TEN THOUSAND THANK-YOUS, MY FRIENDS! IT IS MY HONOR AND GRATITUDE TO DESTROY THESE *FIELD MICE* FOR YOUR PLEASURE THIS EVENING!
And so it begins with an exhibition match.
We're supposed to be entertained.
But my head's spinning even before I drink the wine they serve.
WATCH HIM CLOSELY, IRON FIST.
TAKE ADVANTAGE OF THIS DEMONSTRATION OF HIS TECHNIQUE.
I see the hints of combat forms I recognize. Twenty-Two Harmony Strike bleeds into Long Punch of Enlightened Buddha...but from there, I lose it.
WHOKK
And I know I've never fought anyone like him.
NO, THANK YOU, I--

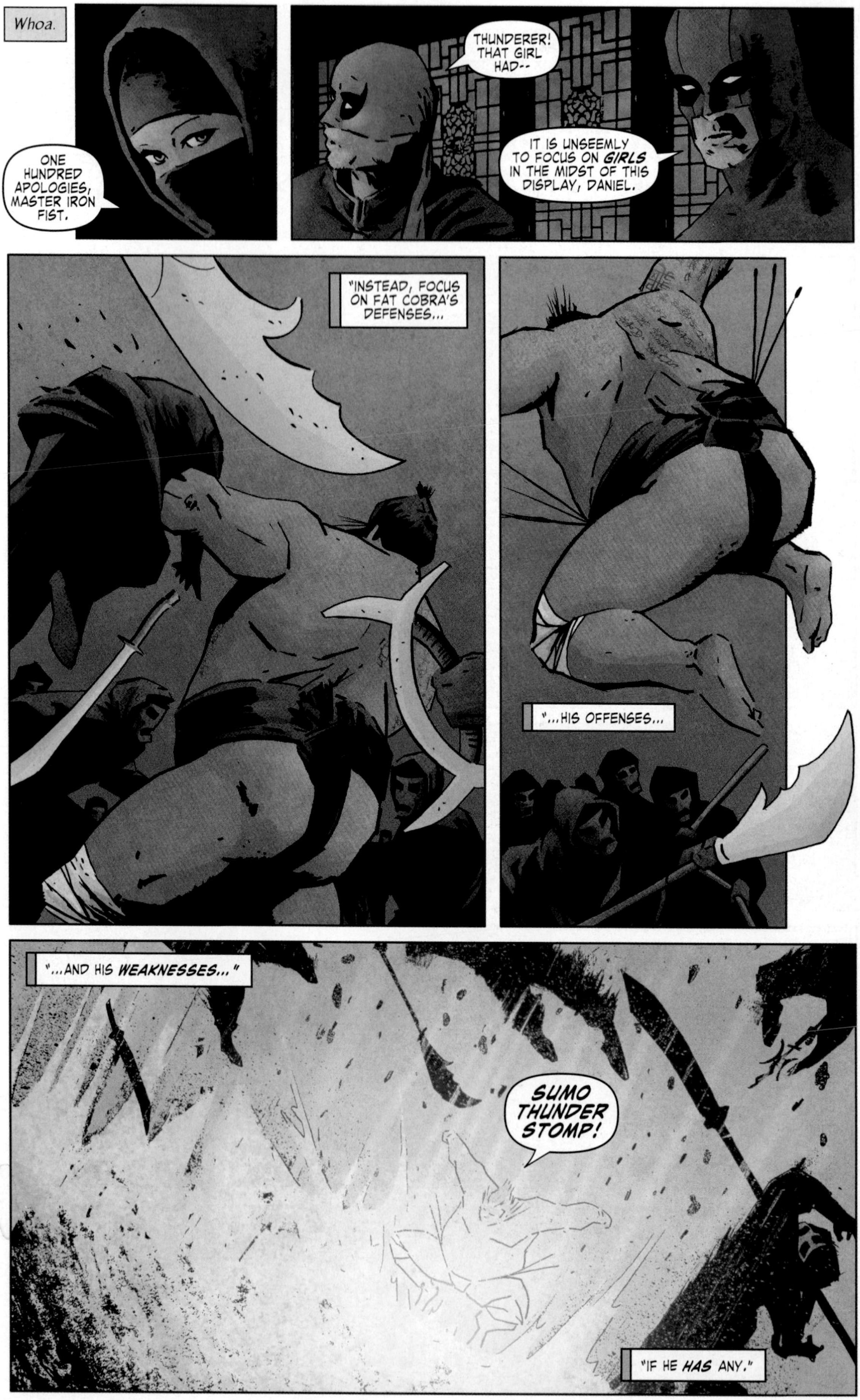
Whoa.
ONE HUNDRED APOLOGIES, MASTER IRON FIST.
THUNDERER! THAT GIRL HAD--
IT IS UNSEEMLY TO FOCUS ON *GIRLS* IN THE MIDST OF THIS DISPLAY, DANIEL.
"INSTEAD, FOCUS ON FAT COBRA'S DEFENSES...
"...HIS OFFENSES...
"...AND HIS *WEAKNESSES...*"
SUMO THUNDER STOMP!
"IF HE *HAS* ANY."

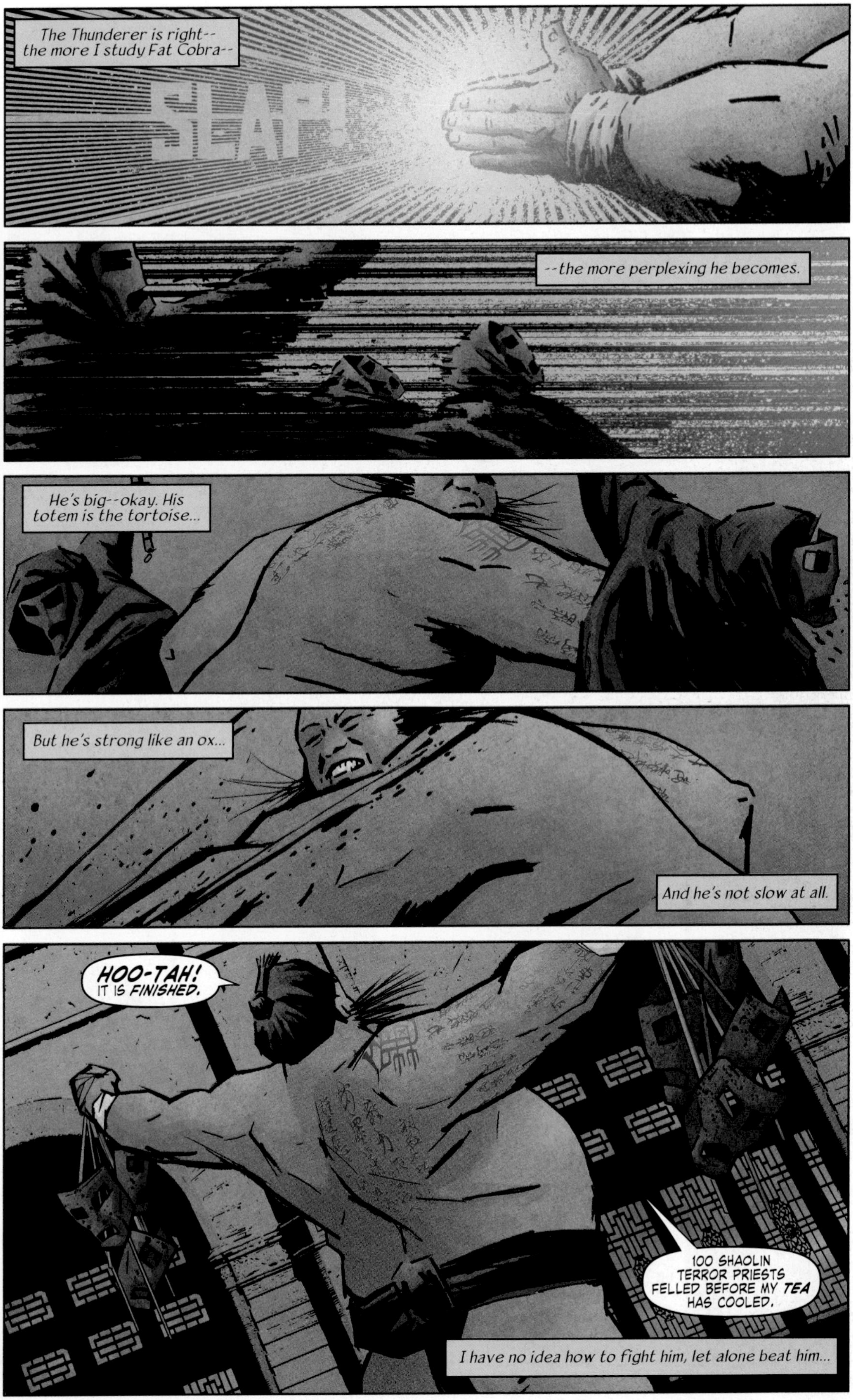
The Thunderer is right-- the more I study Fat Cobra--
SLAP!
--the more perplexing he becomes.
He's big--okay. His totem is the tortoise...
But he's strong like an ox...
And he's not slow at all.
HOO-TAH! IT IS FINISHED.
100 SHAOLIN TERROR PRIESTS FELLED BEFORE MY TEA HAS COOLED.
I have no idea how to fight him, let alone beat him...

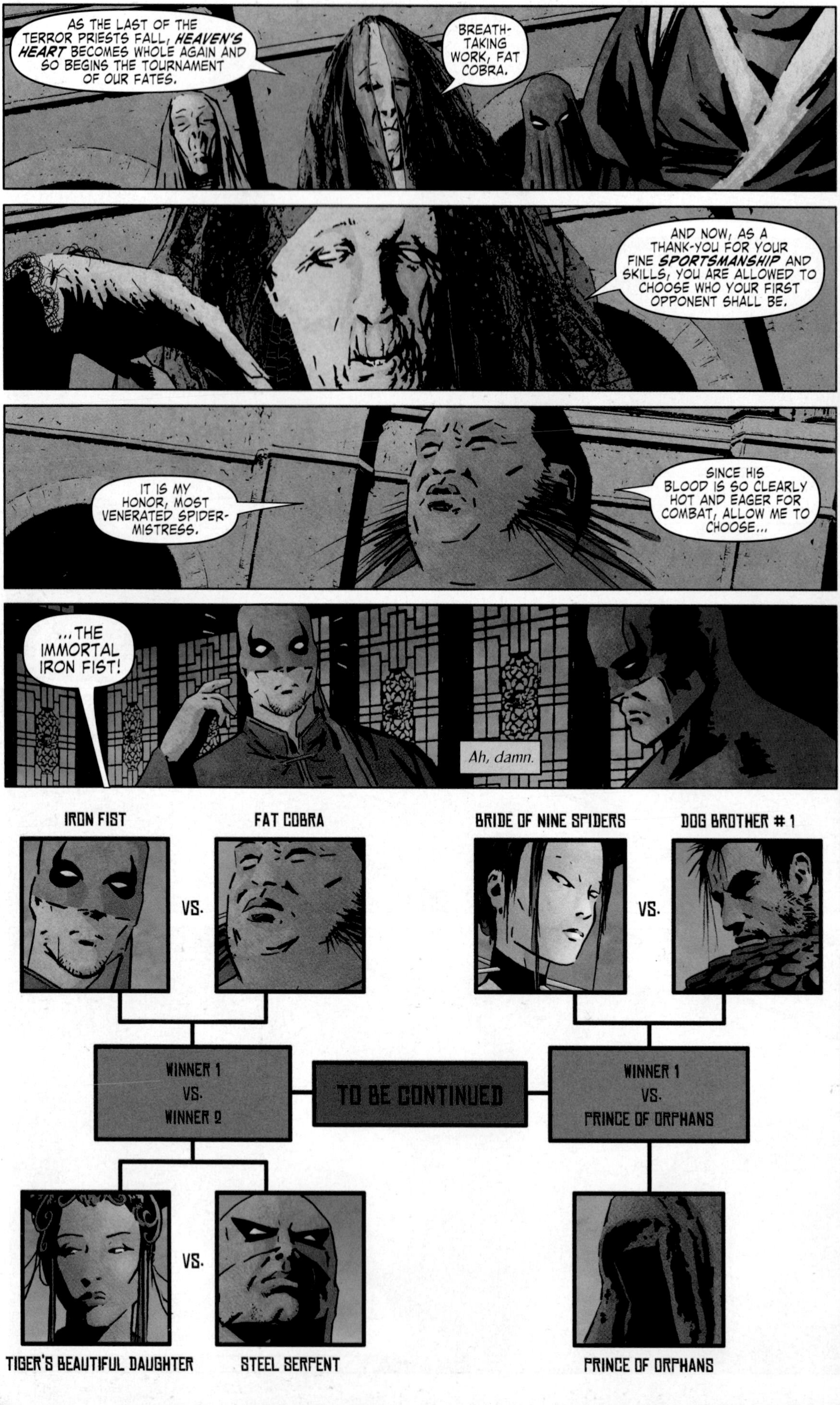
AS THE LAST OF THE TERROR PRIESTS FALL, HEAVEN'S HEART BECOMES WHOLE AGAIN AND SO BEGINS THE TOURNAMENT OF OUR FATES.
BREATH-TAKING WORK, FAT COBRA.
AND NOW, AS A THANK-YOU FOR YOUR FINE SPORTSMANSHIP AND SKILLS, YOU ARE ALLOWED TO CHOOSE WHO YOUR FIRST OPPONENT SHALL BE.
IT IS MY HONOR, MOST VENERATED SPIDER-MISTRESS.
SINCE HIS BLOOD IS SO CLEARLY HOT AND EAGER FOR COMBAT, ALLOW ME TO CHOOSE...
...THE IMMORTAL IRON FIST!
Ah, damn.
IRON FIST
VS.
FAT COBRA
BRIDE OF NINE SPIDERS
VS.
DOG BROTHER # 1
WINNER 1
VS.
WINNER 2
TO BE CONTINUED
WINNER 1
VS.
PRINCE OF ORPHANS
VS.
TIGER'S BEAUTIFUL DAUGHTER
STEEL SERPENT
PRINCE OF ORPHANS

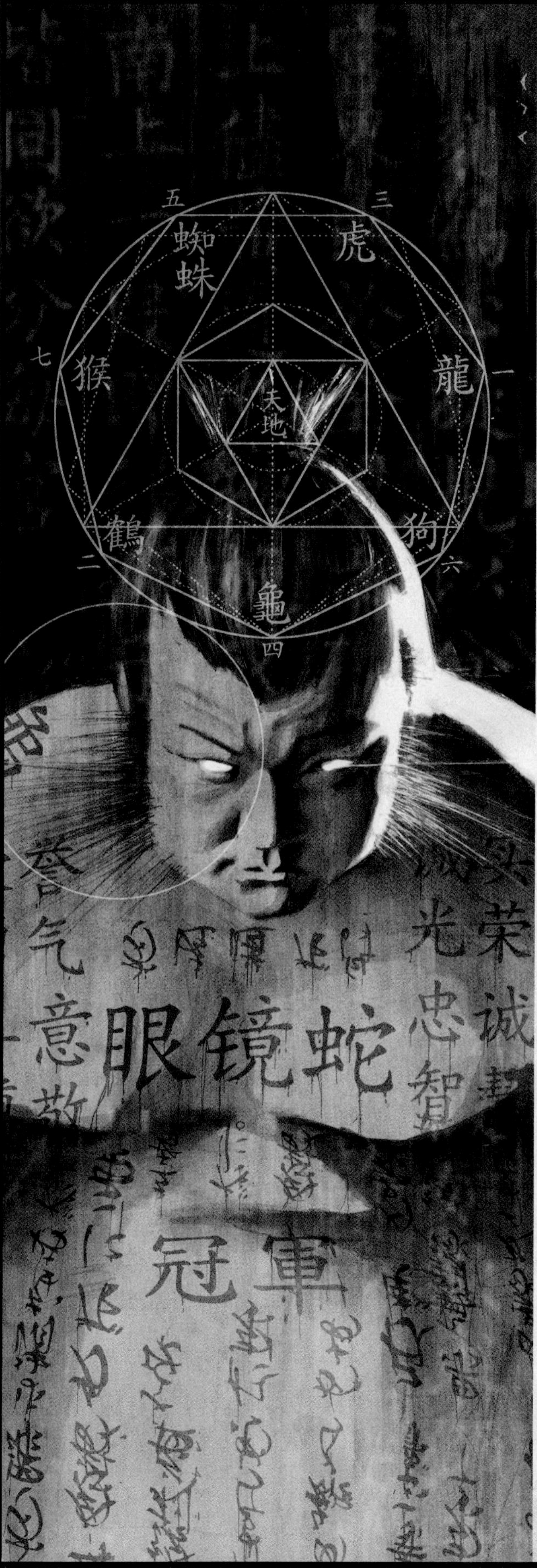
五
三
蜘蛛
虎
七
猴
龍
一
天地
鶴
狗
二
六
龜
四
栄
光
気
诚
忠
意
眼
镜
蛇
智
冠
軍

鐵拳 9

The 7 Capital Cities of Heaven

二

Round 2

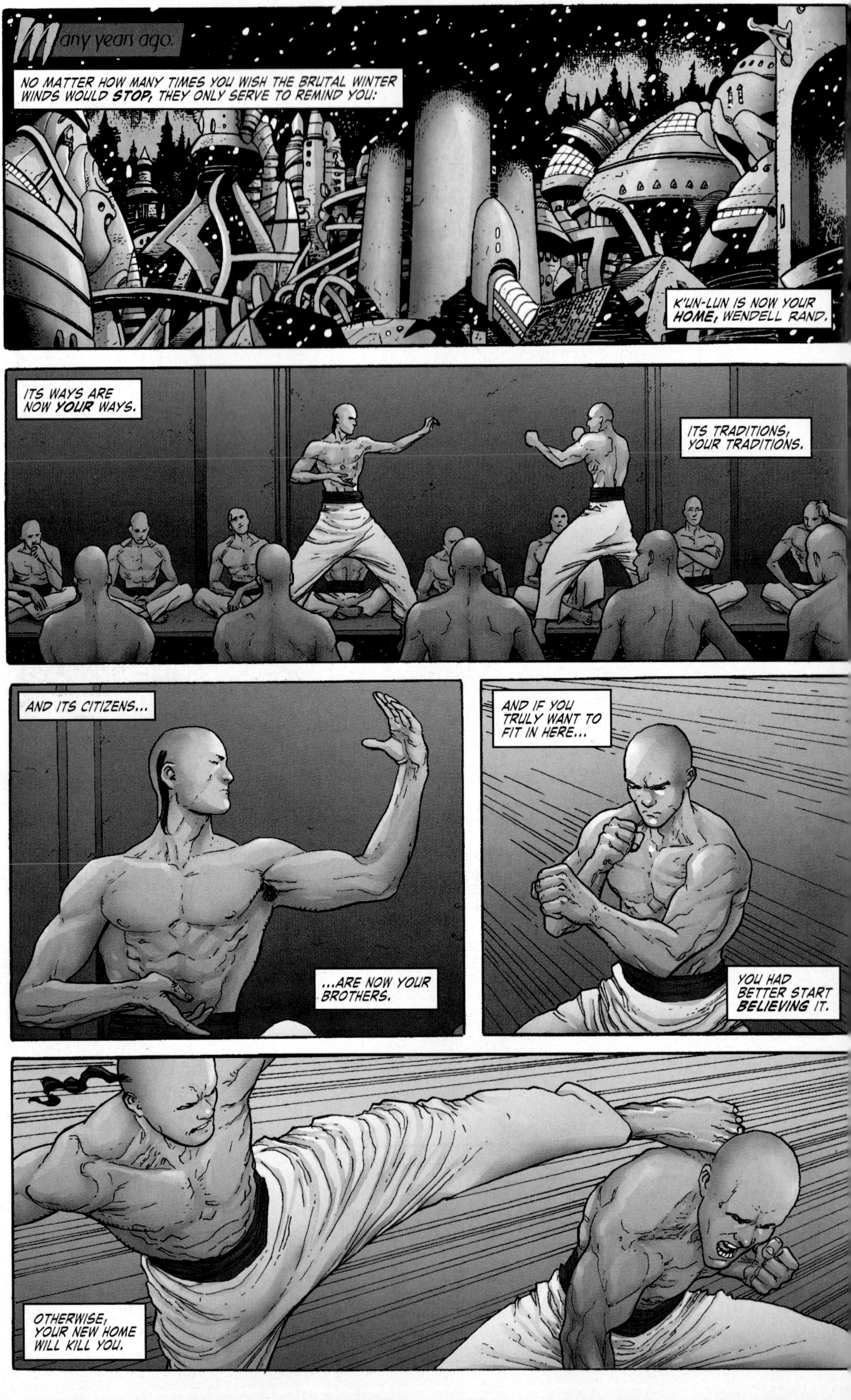
Many years ago.
NO MATTER HOW MANY TIMES YOU WISH THE BRUTAL WINTER WINDS WOULD STOP, THEY ONLY SERVE TO REMIND YOU:
K'UN-LUN IS NOW YOUR HOME, WENDELL RAND.
ITS WAYS ARE NOW YOUR WAYS.
ITS TRADITIONS, YOUR TRADITIONS.
AND ITS CITIZENS...
...ARE NOW YOUR BROTHERS.
AND IF YOU TRULY WANT TO FIT IN HERE...
YOU HAD BETTER START BELIEVING IT.
OTHERWISE, YOUR NEW HOME WILL KILL YOU.

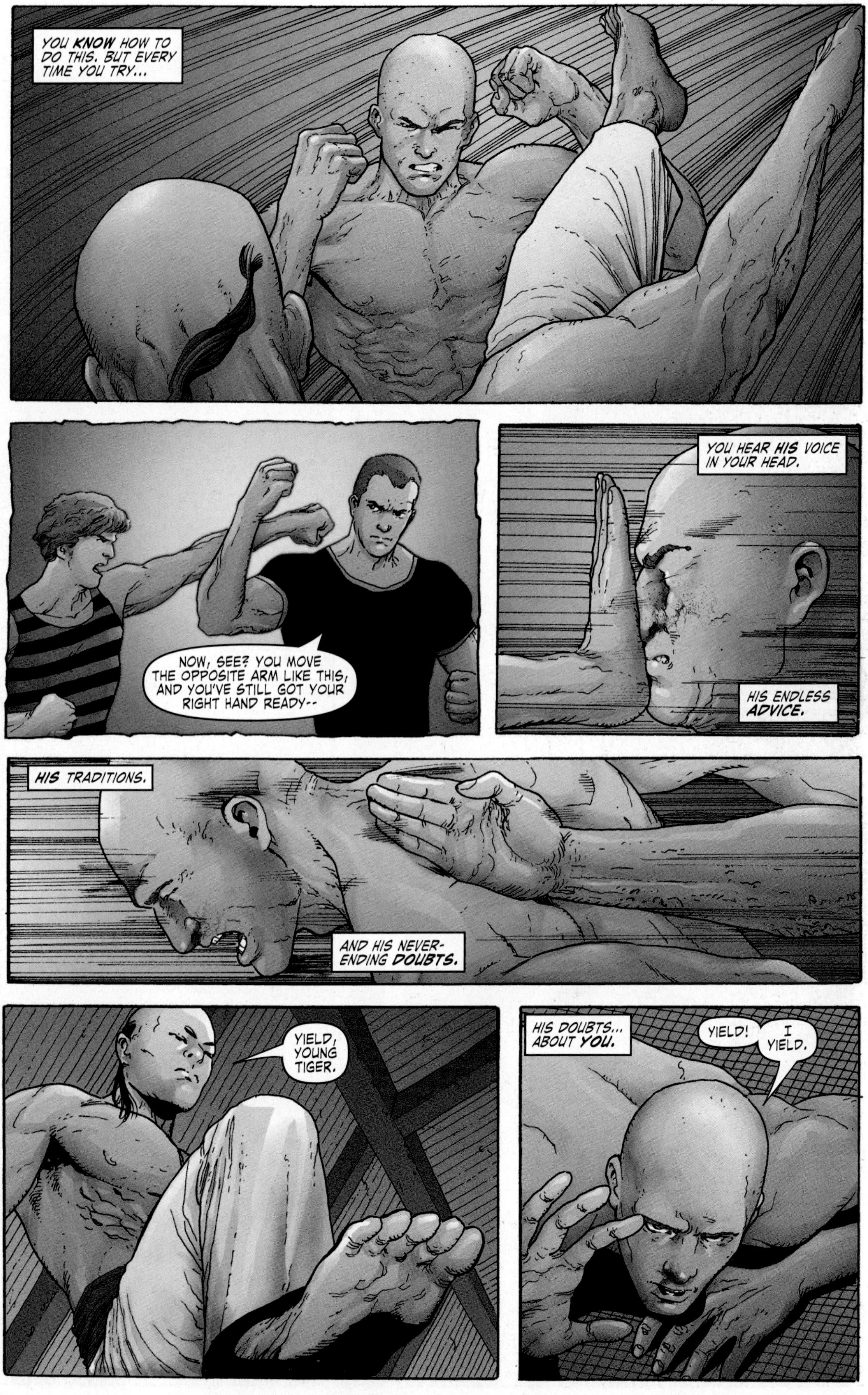
YOU KNOW HOW TO DO THIS. BUT EVERY TIME YOU TRY...
NOW, SEE? YOU MOVE THE OPPOSITE ARM LIKE THIS, AND YOU'VE STILL GOT YOUR RIGHT HAND READY--
YOU HEAR HIS VOICE IN YOUR HEAD.
HIS ENDLESS ADVICE.
HIS TRADITIONS.
AND HIS NEVER-ENDING DOUBTS.
YIELD, YOUNG TIGER.
HIS DOUBTS... ABOUT YOU.
YIELD!
I YIELD.

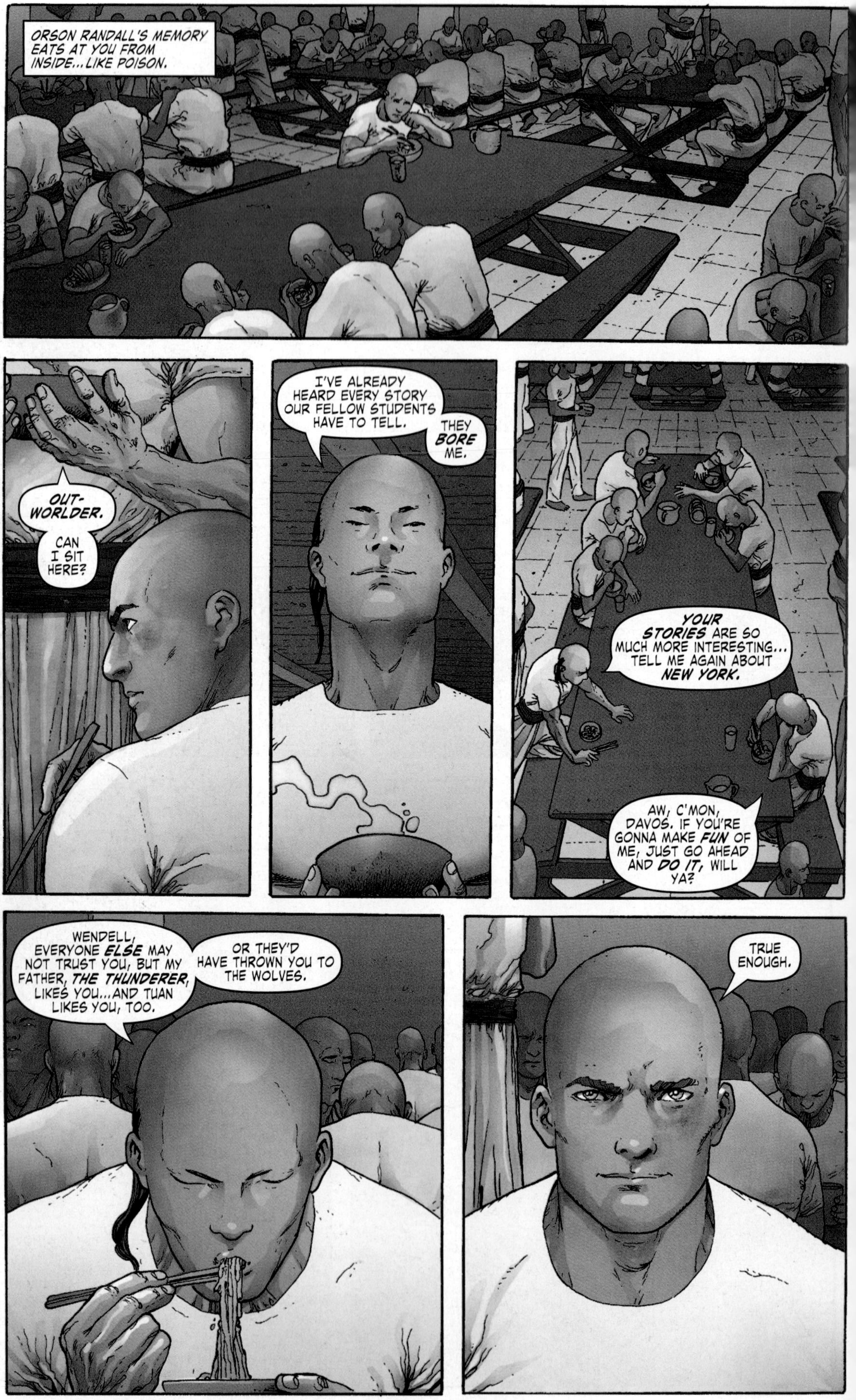
ORSON RANDALL'S MEMORY EATS AT YOU FROM INSIDE... LIKE POISON.
OUT-WORLDER.
CAN I SIT HERE?
I'VE ALREADY HEARD EVERY STORY OUR FELLOW STUDENTS HAVE TO TELL.
THEY BORE ME.
YOUR STORIES ARE SO MUCH MORE INTERESTING... TELL ME AGAIN ABOUT NEW YORK.
AW, C'MON, DAVOS. IF YOU'RE GONNA MAKE FUN OF ME, JUST GO AHEAD AND DO IT, WILL YA?
WENDELL, EVERYONE ELSE MAY NOT TRUST YOU, BUT MY FATHER, THE THUNDERER, LIKES YOU... AND TUAN LIKES YOU, TOO.
OR THEY'D HAVE THROWN YOU TO THE WOLVES.
TRUE ENOUGH.

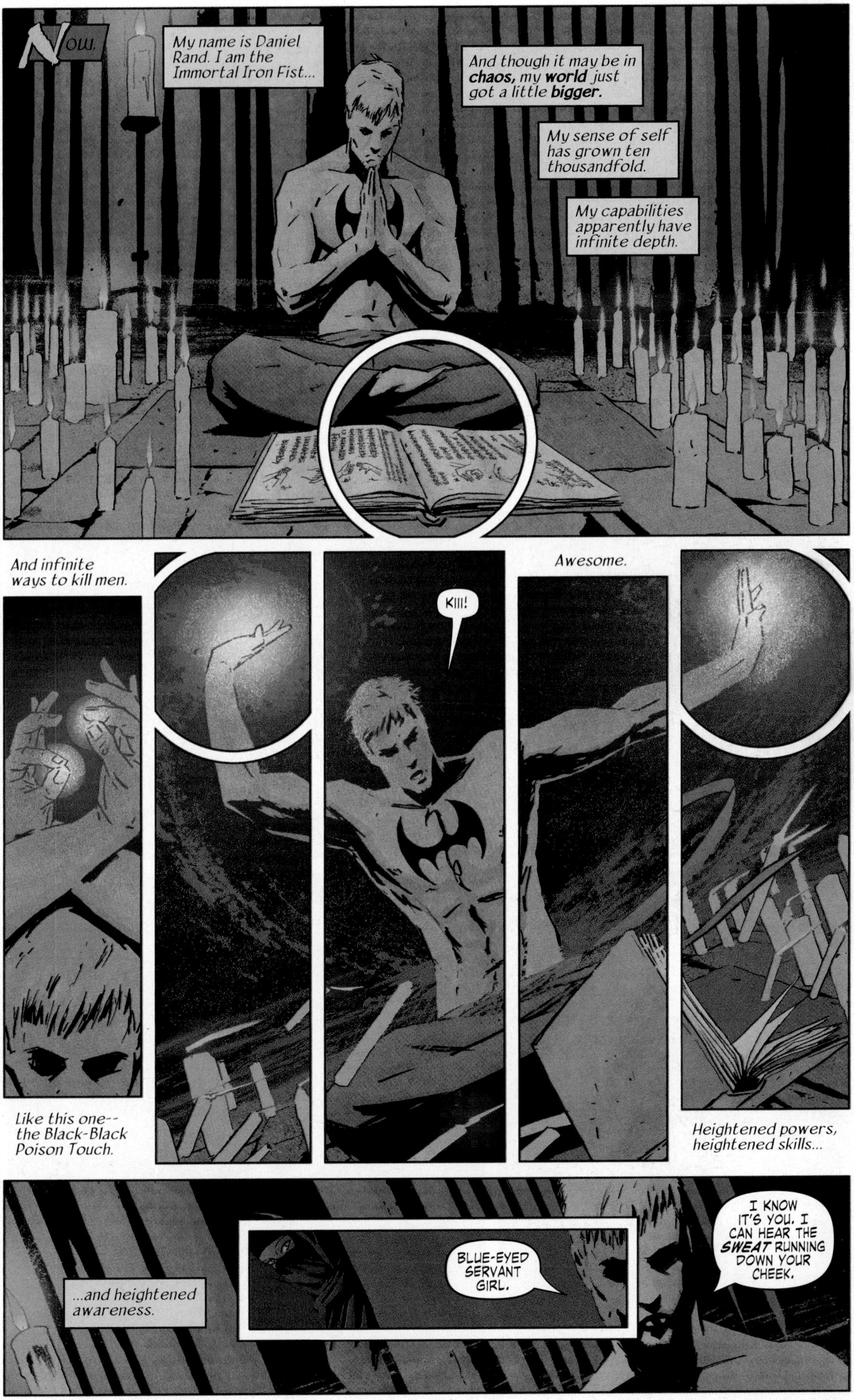
Now.
My name is Daniel Rand. I am the Immortal Iron Fist...
And though it may be in **chaos,** my **world** just got a little **bigger.**
My sense of self has grown ten thousandfold.
My capabilities apparently have infinite depth.
And infinite ways to kill men.
Like this one-- the Black-Black Poison Touch.
KIII!
Awesome.
Heightened powers, heightened skills...
...and heightened awareness.
BLUE-EYED SERVANT GIRL.
I KNOW IT'S YOU. I CAN HEAR THE **SWEAT** RUNNING DOWN YOUR CHEEK.

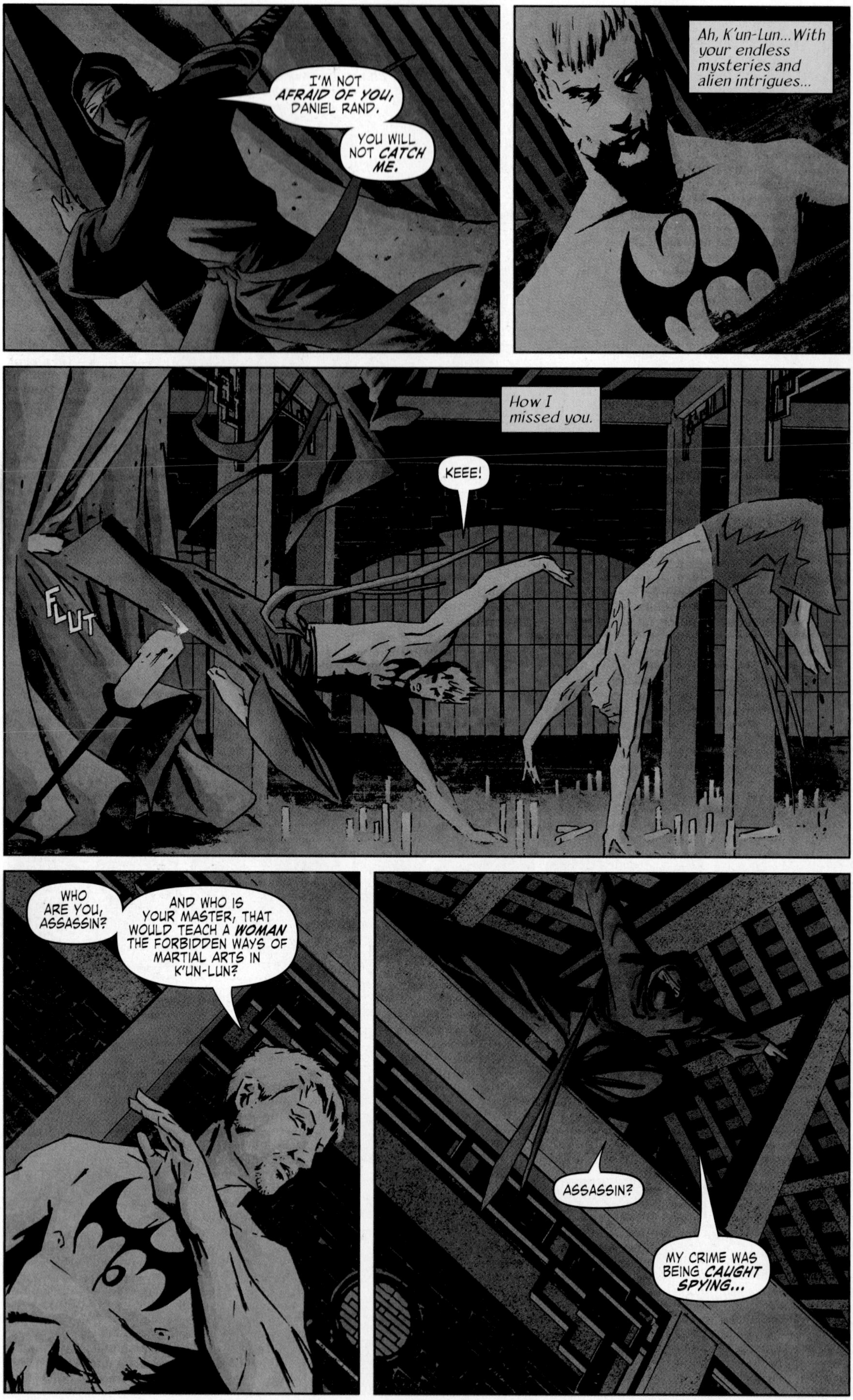
I'M NOT AFRAID OF YOU, DANIEL RAND.
YOU WILL NOT CATCH ME.
Ah, K'un-Lun... With your endless mysteries and alien intrigues...
How I missed you.
KEEE!
FLUT
WHO ARE YOU, ASSASSIN?
AND WHO IS YOUR MASTER, THAT WOULD TEACH A WOMAN THE FORBIDDEN WAYS OF MARTIAL ARTS IN K'UN-LUN?
ASSASSIN?
MY CRIME WAS BEING CAUGHT SPYING...

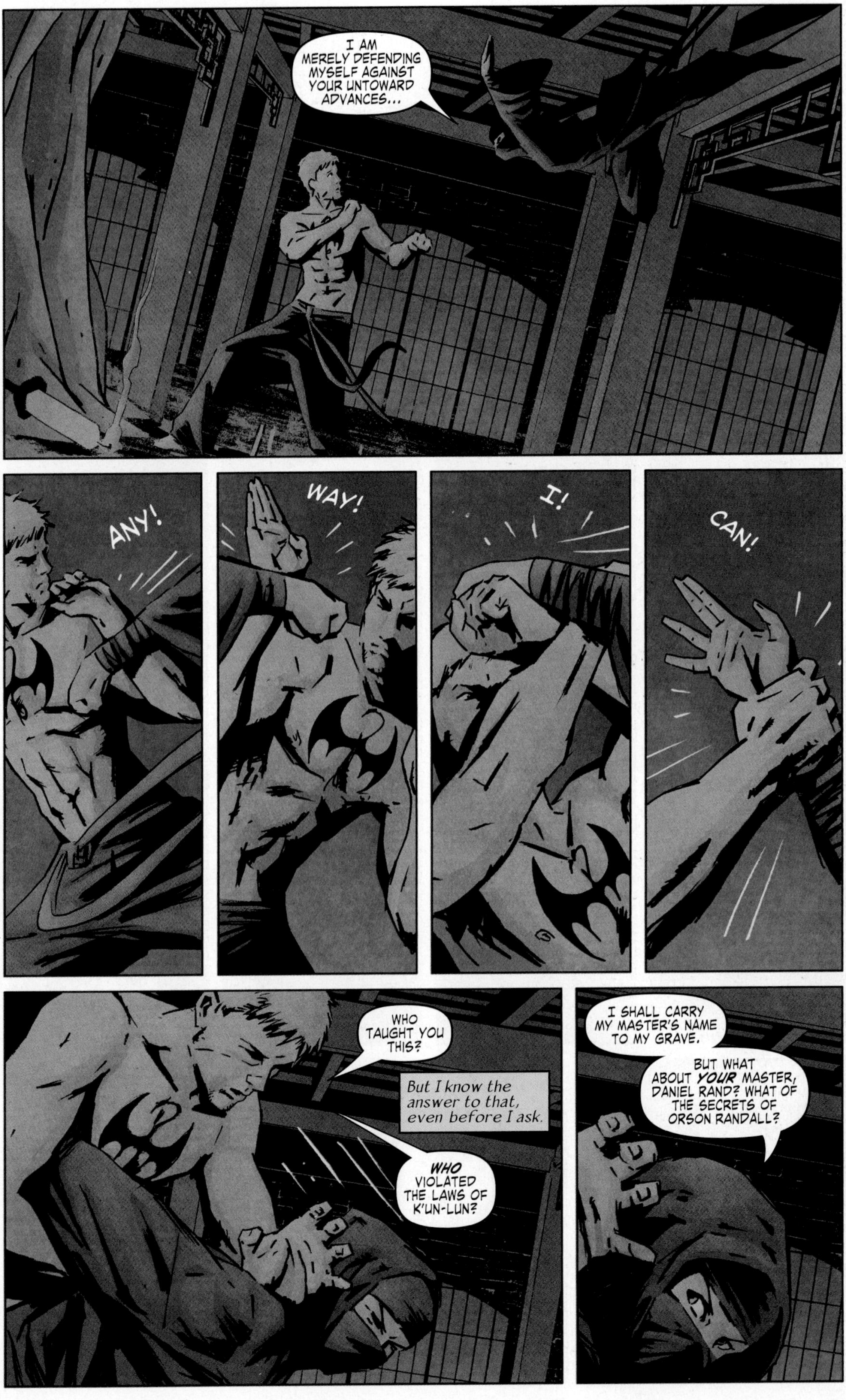
I AM MERELY DEFENDING MYSELF AGAINST YOUR UNTOWARD ADVANCES...
ANY!
WAY!
I!
CAN!
WHO TAUGHT YOU THIS?
But I know the answer to that, even before I ask.
WHO VIOLATED THE LAWS OF K'UN-LUN?
I SHALL CARRY MY MASTER'S NAME TO MY GRAVE.
BUT WHAT ABOUT YOUR MASTER, DANIEL RAND? WHAT OF THE SECRETS OF ORSON RANDALL?

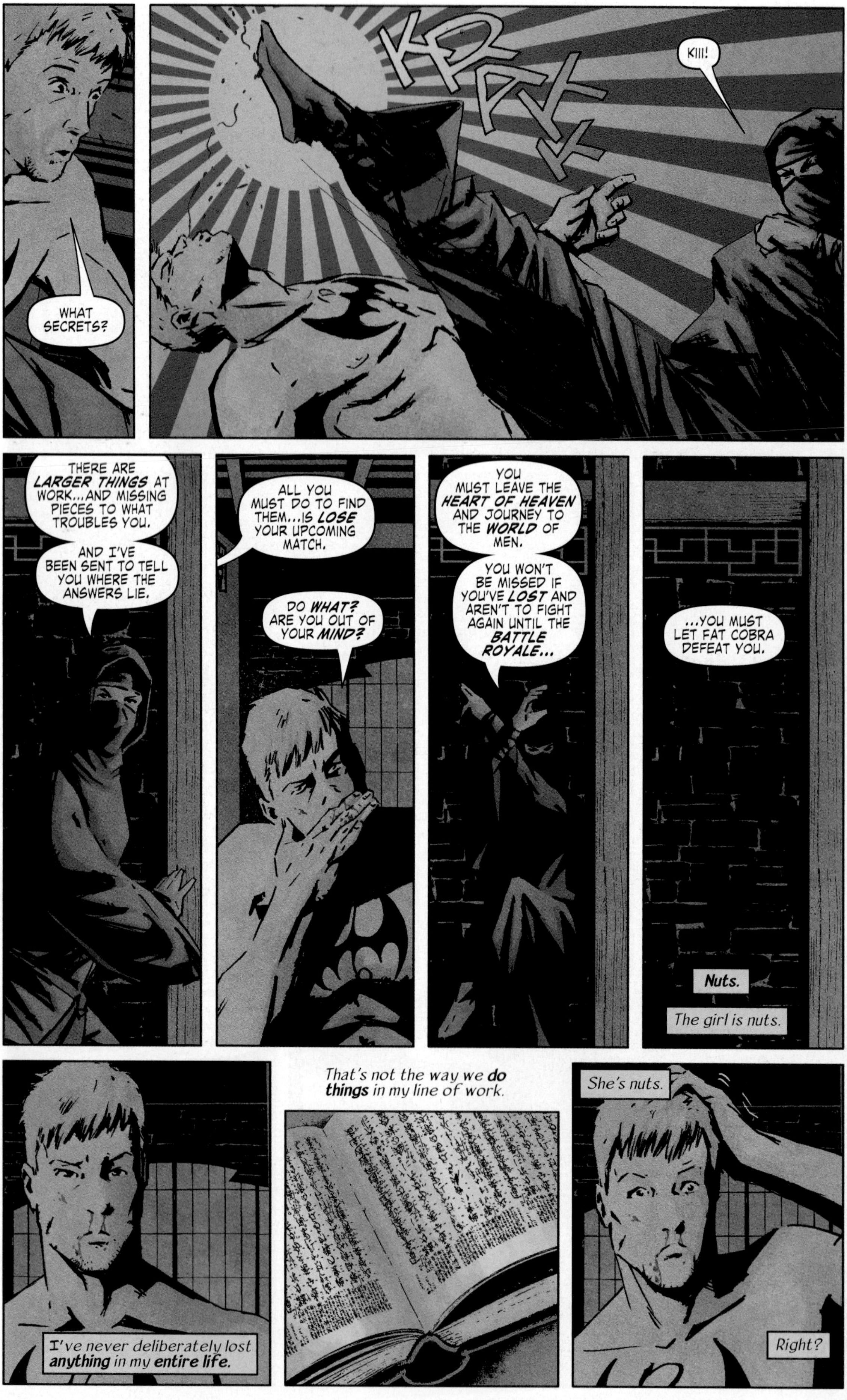
WHAT SECRETS?
KRAKK
KIII!
THERE ARE LARGER THINGS AT WORK...AND MISSING PIECES TO WHAT TROUBLES YOU.
AND I'VE BEEN SENT TO TELL YOU WHERE THE ANSWERS LIE.
ALL YOU MUST DO TO FIND THEM...IS LOSE YOUR UPCOMING MATCH.
DO WHAT? ARE YOU OUT OF YOUR MIND?
YOU MUST LEAVE THE HEART OF HEAVEN AND JOURNEY TO THE WORLD OF MEN.
YOU WON'T BE MISSED IF YOU'VE LOST AND AREN'T TO FIGHT AGAIN UNTIL THE BATTLE ROYALE...
...YOU MUST LET FAT COBRA DEFEAT YOU.
Nuts.
The girl is nuts.
I've never deliberately lost anything in my entire life.
That's not the way we do things in my line of work.
She's nuts.
Right?

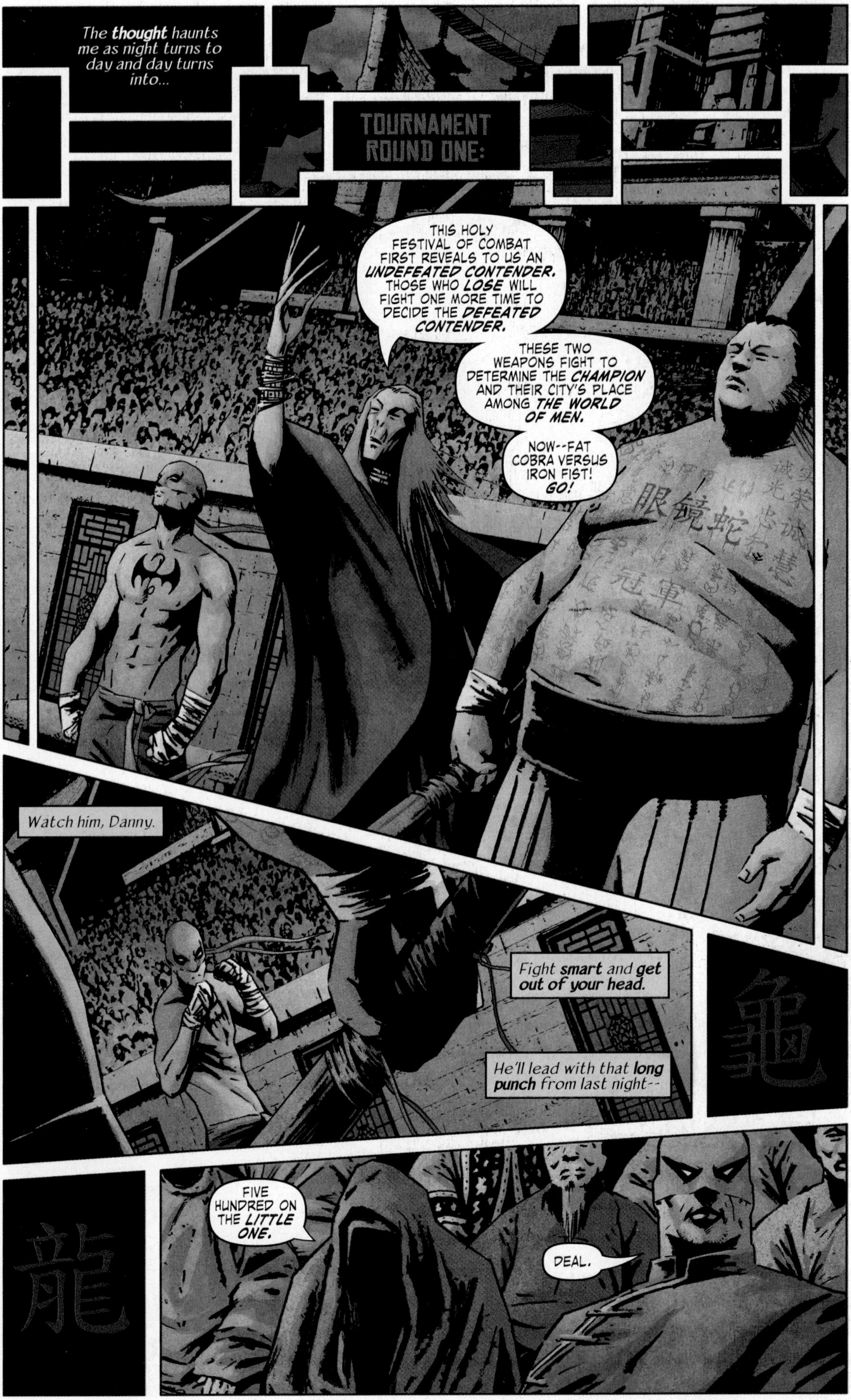

The thought haunts me as night turns to day and day turns into...
TOURNAMENT ROUND ONE:
THIS HOLY FESTIVAL OF COMBAT FIRST REVEALS TO US AN UNDEFEATED CONTENDER. THOSE WHO LOSE WILL FIGHT ONE MORE TIME TO DECIDE THE DEFEATED CONTENDER.
THESE TWO WEAPONS FIGHT TO DETERMINE THE CHAMPION AND THEIR CITY'S PLACE AMONG THE WORLD OF MEN.
NOW--FAT COBRA VERSUS IRON FIST! GO!
眼鏡蛇
冠軍
Watch him, Danny.
Fight smart and get out of your head.
He'll lead with that long punch from last night--
龜
龍
FIVE HUNDRED ON THE LITTLE ONE.
DEAL.

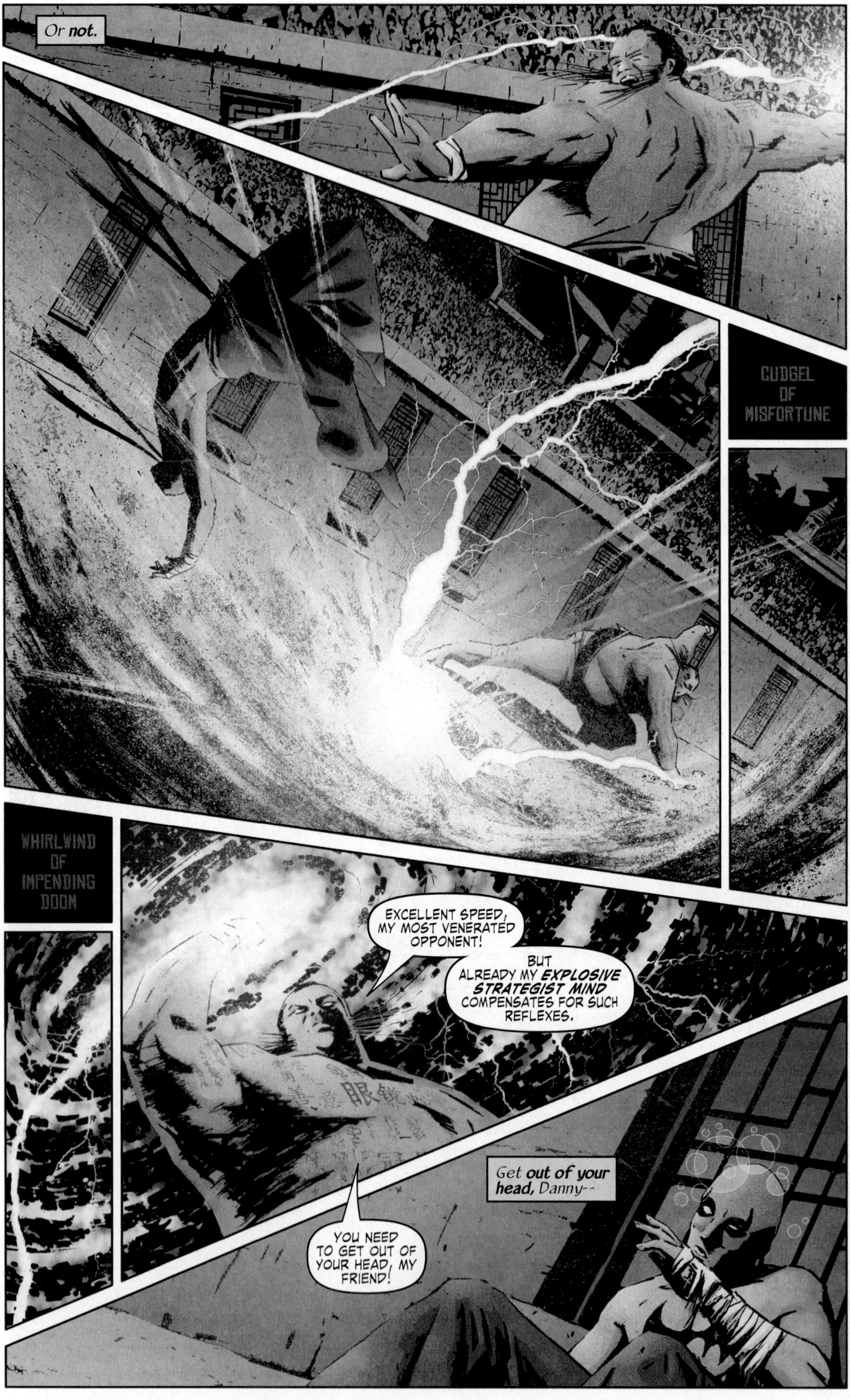
Or not.
CUDGEL OF MISFORTUNE
WHIRLWIND OF IMPENDING DOOM
EXCELLENT SPEED, MY MOST VENERATED OPPONENT!
BUT ALREADY MY EXPLOSIVE STRATEGIST MIND COMPENSATES FOR SUCH REFLEXES.
YOU NEED TO GET OUT OF YOUR HEAD, MY FRIEND!
Get out of your head, Danny--

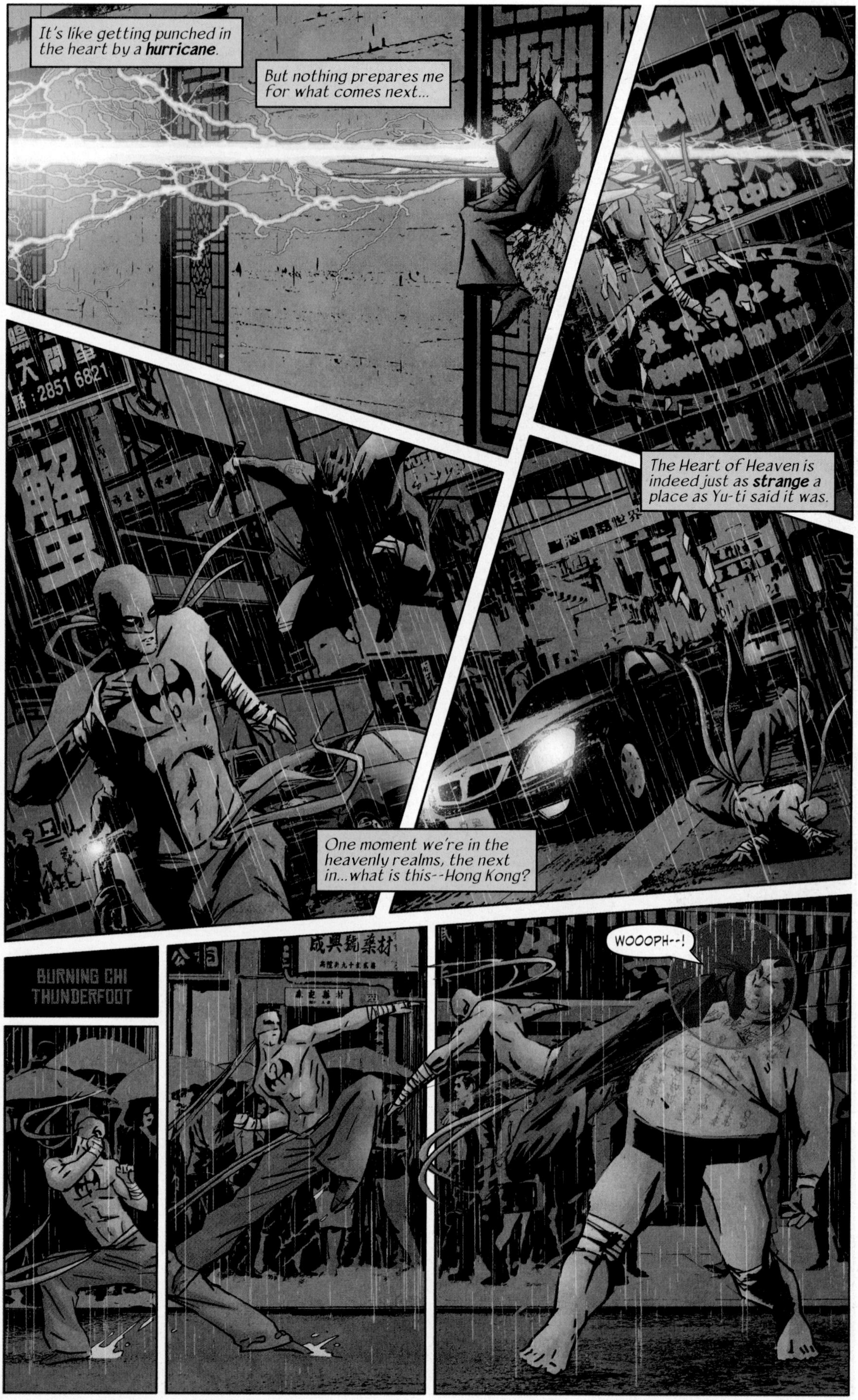

It's like getting punched in the heart by a **hurricane**.
But nothing prepares me for what comes next...
The Heart of Heaven is indeed just as **strange** a place as Yu-ti said it was.
One moment we're in the heavenly realms, the next in...what is this--Hong Kong?
BURNING CHI THUNDERFOOT
WOOOPH--!

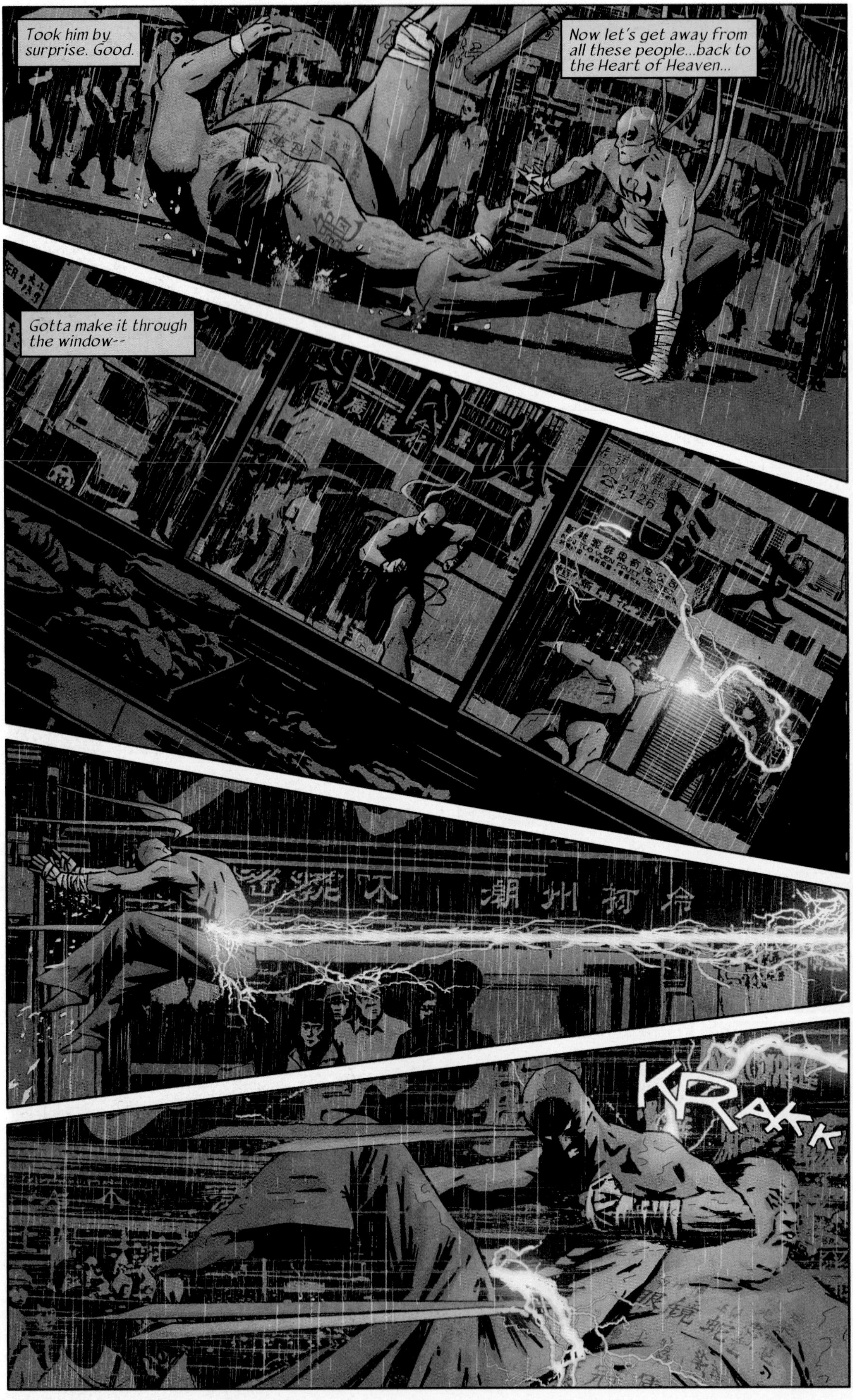
Took him by surprise. Good.
Now let's get away from all these people...back to the Heart of Heaven...
Gotta make it through the window--
KRAKK

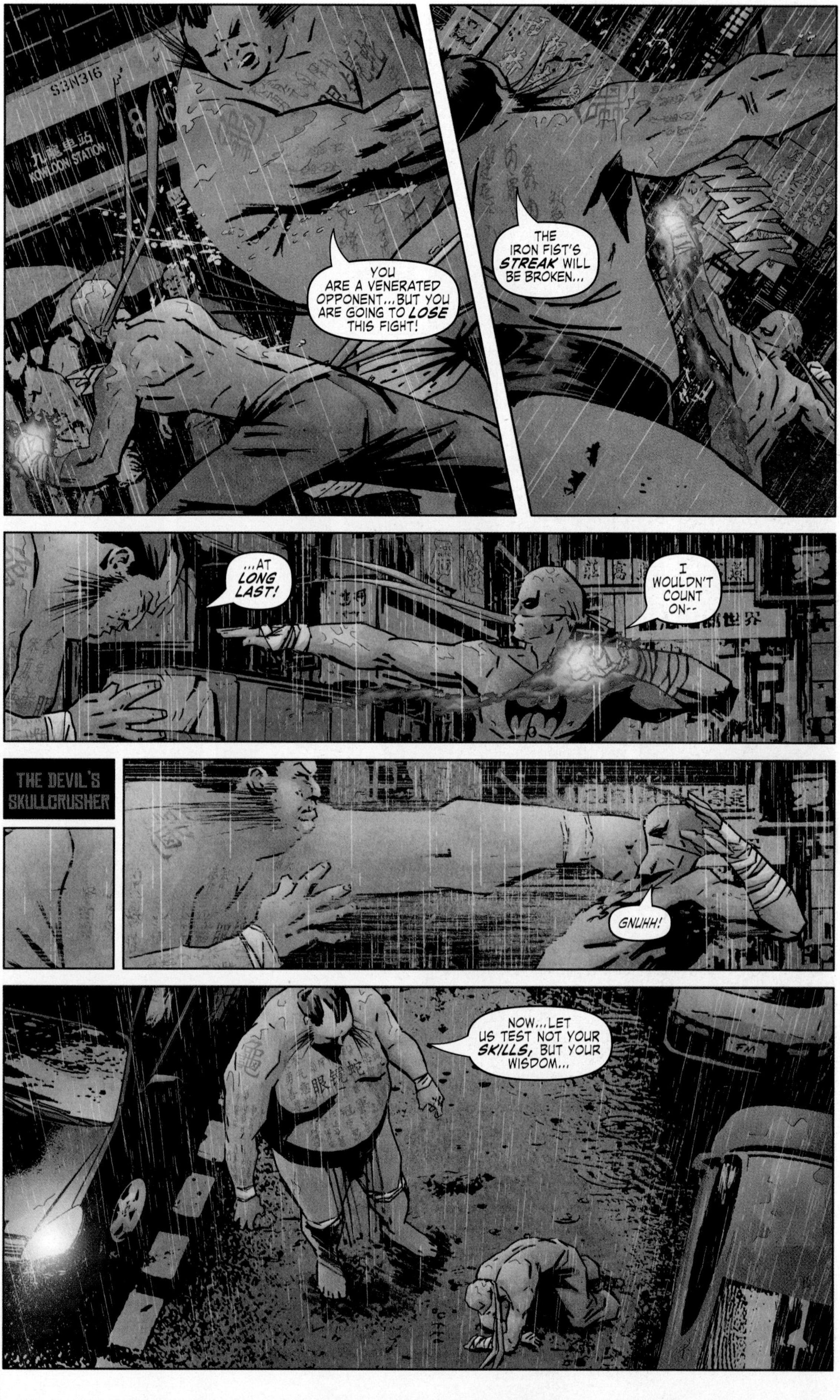
S3N316
九龍車站
KOWLOON STATION
YOU ARE A VENERATED OPPONENT...BUT YOU ARE GOING TO *LOSE* THIS FIGHT!
THE IRON FIST'S *STREAK* WILL BE BROKEN...
...AT *LONG LAST!*
I WOULDN'T COUNT ON--
世界
THE DEVIL'S SKULLCRUSHER
GNUHH!
NOW...LET US TEST NOT YOUR *SKILLS,* BUT YOUR WISDOM...
眼鏡蛇

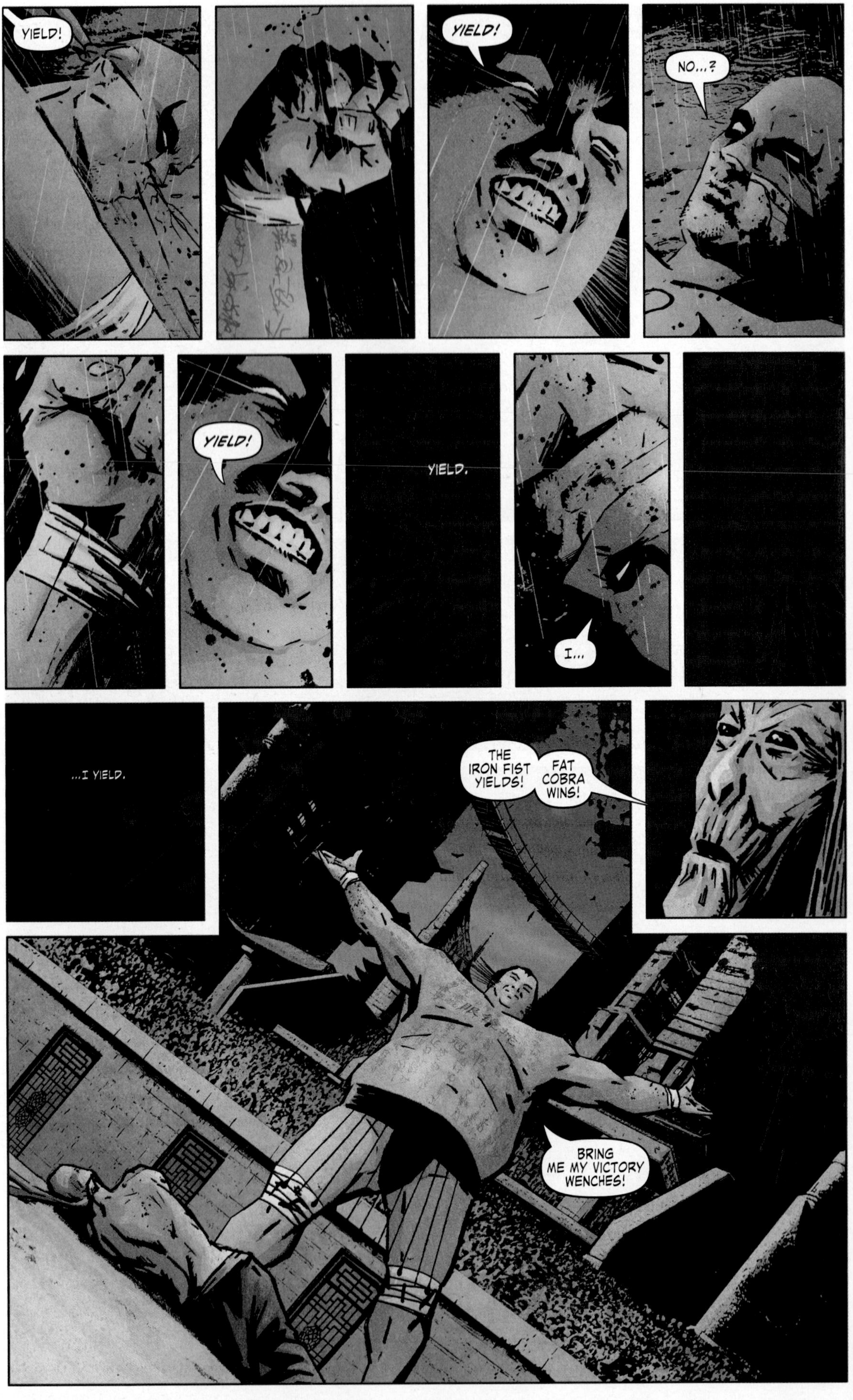
YIELD!
YIELD!
NO...?
YIELD!
YIELD.
I...
...I YIELD.
THE IRON FIST YIELDS!
FAT COBRA WINS!
BRING ME MY VICTORY WENCHES!

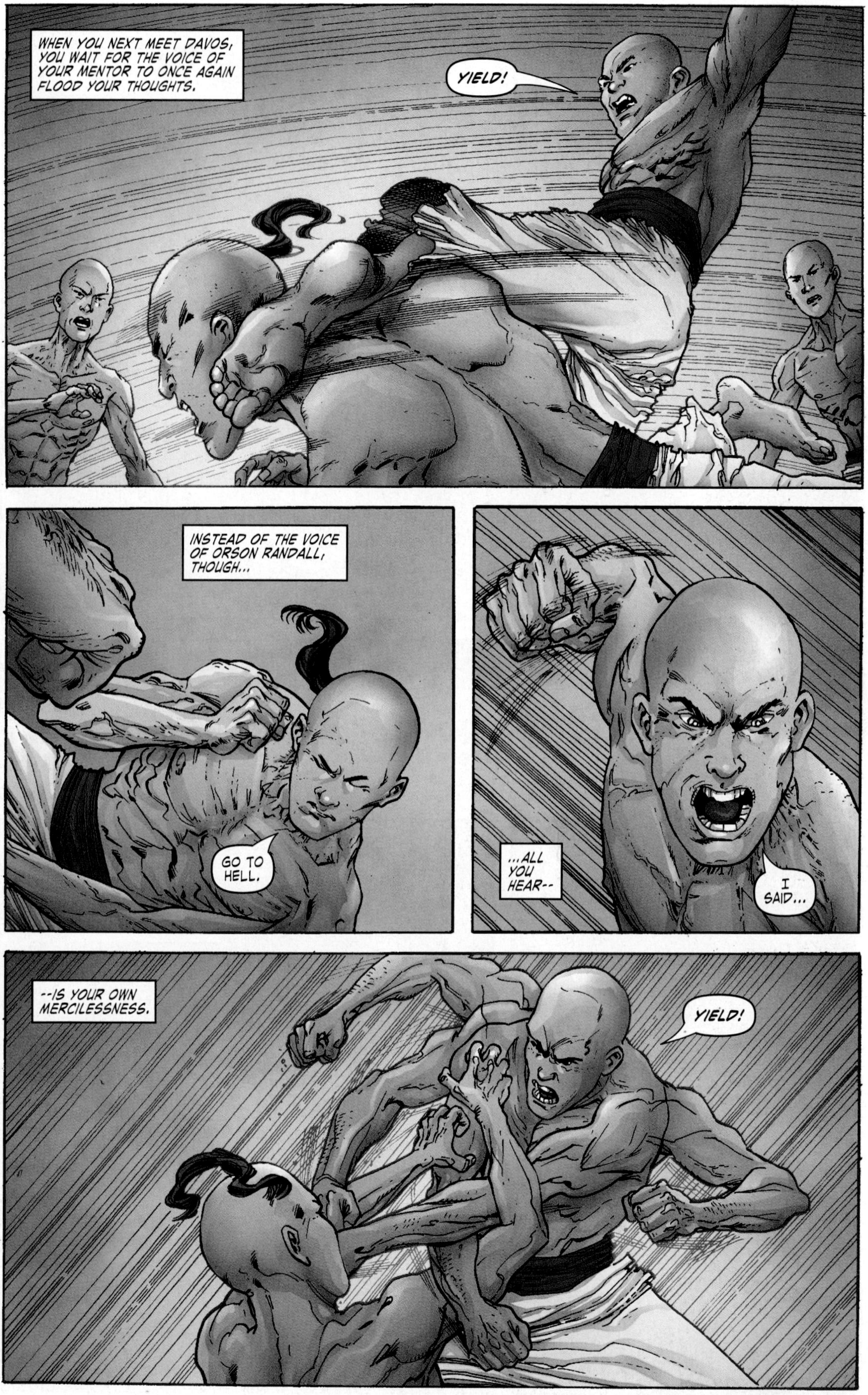
WHEN YOU NEXT MEET DAVOS, YOU WAIT FOR THE VOICE OF YOUR MENTOR TO ONCE AGAIN FLOOD YOUR THOUGHTS.
YIELD!
INSTEAD OF THE VOICE OF ORSON RANDALL, THOUGH...
GO TO HELL.
...ALL YOU HEAR--
I SAID...
--IS YOUR OWN MERCILESSNESS.
YIELD!

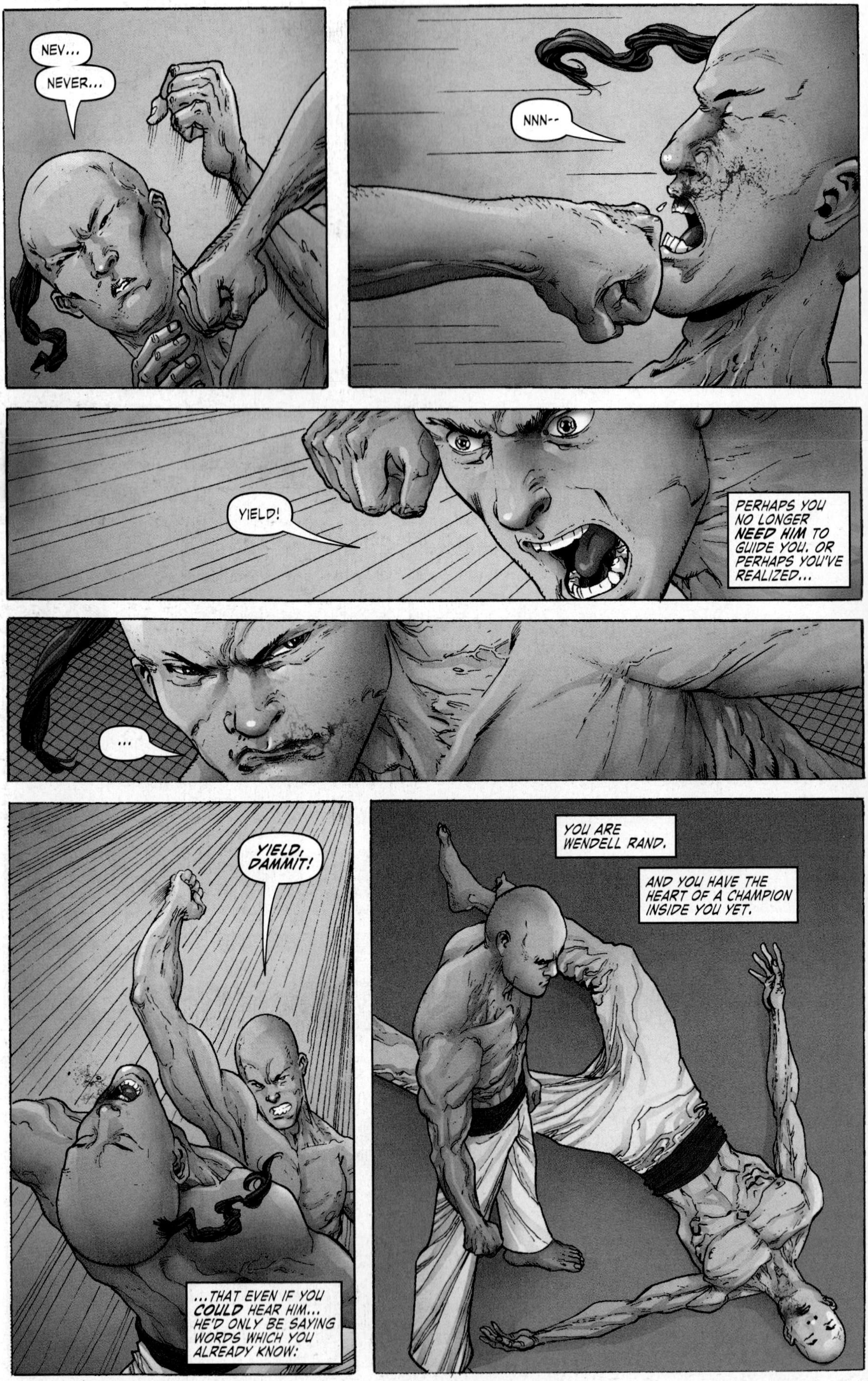
NEV...
NEVER...
NNN--
YIELD!
PERHAPS YOU NO LONGER NEED HIM TO GUIDE YOU. OR PERHAPS YOU'VE REALIZED...
...
YIELD, DAMMIT!
...THAT EVEN IF YOU COULD HEAR HIM... HE'D ONLY BE SAYING WORDS WHICH YOU ALREADY KNOW:
YOU ARE WENDELL RAND.
AND YOU HAVE THE HEART OF A CHAMPION INSIDE YOU YET.

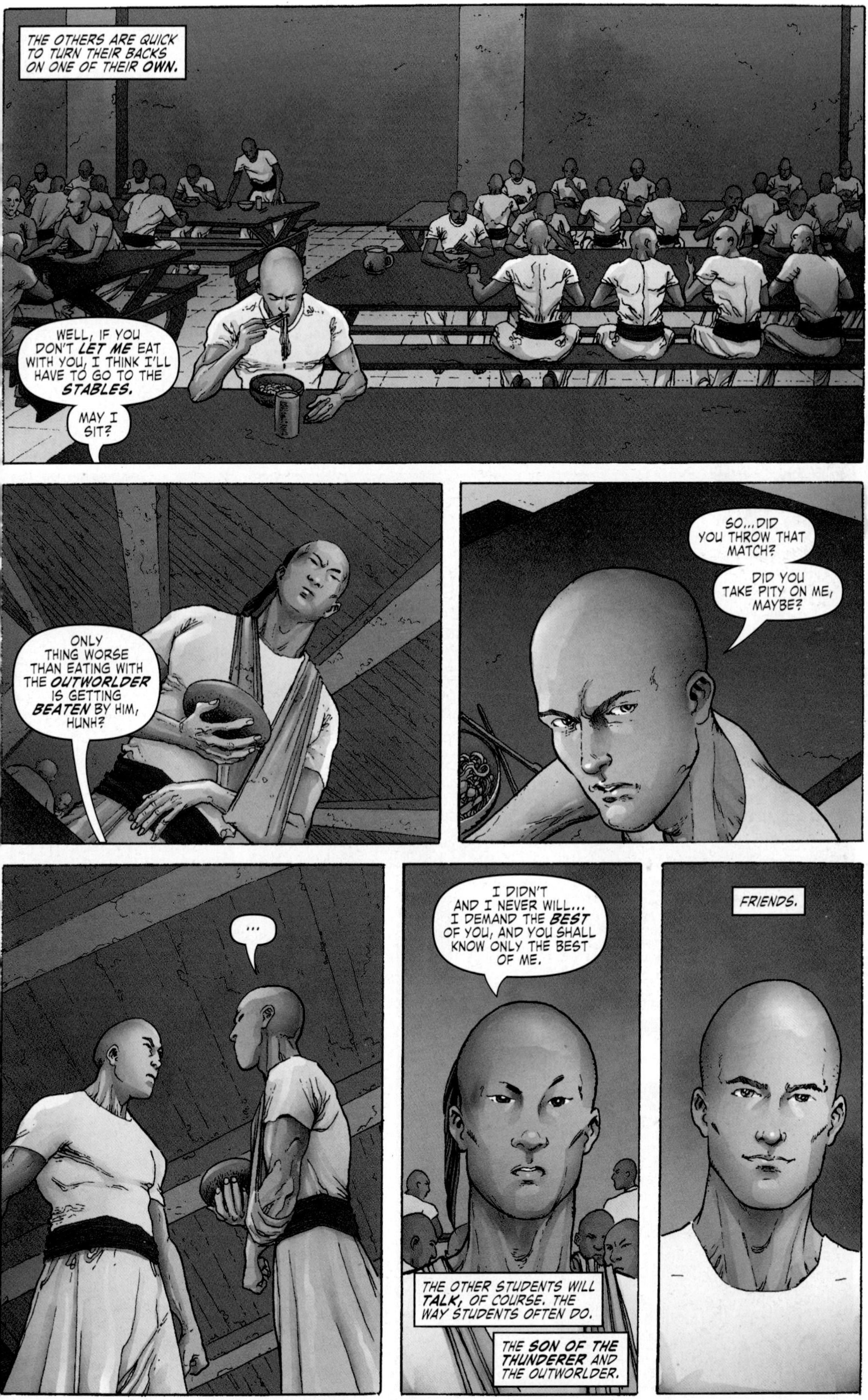
THE OTHERS ARE QUICK TO TURN THEIR BACKS ON ONE OF THEIR OWN.
WELL, IF YOU DON'T LET ME EAT WITH YOU, I THINK I'LL HAVE TO GO TO THE STABLES.
MAY I SIT?
ONLY THING WORSE THAN EATING WITH THE OUTWORLDER IS GETTING BEATEN BY HIM, HUNH?
SO...DID YOU THROW THAT MATCH?
DID YOU TAKE PITY ON ME, MAYBE?
...
I DIDN'T AND I NEVER WILL... I DEMAND THE BEST OF YOU, AND YOU SHALL KNOW ONLY THE BEST OF ME.
THE OTHER STUDENTS WILL TALK, OF COURSE. THE WAY STUDENTS OFTEN DO.
THE SON OF THE THUNDERER AND THE OUTWORLDER.
FRIENDS.

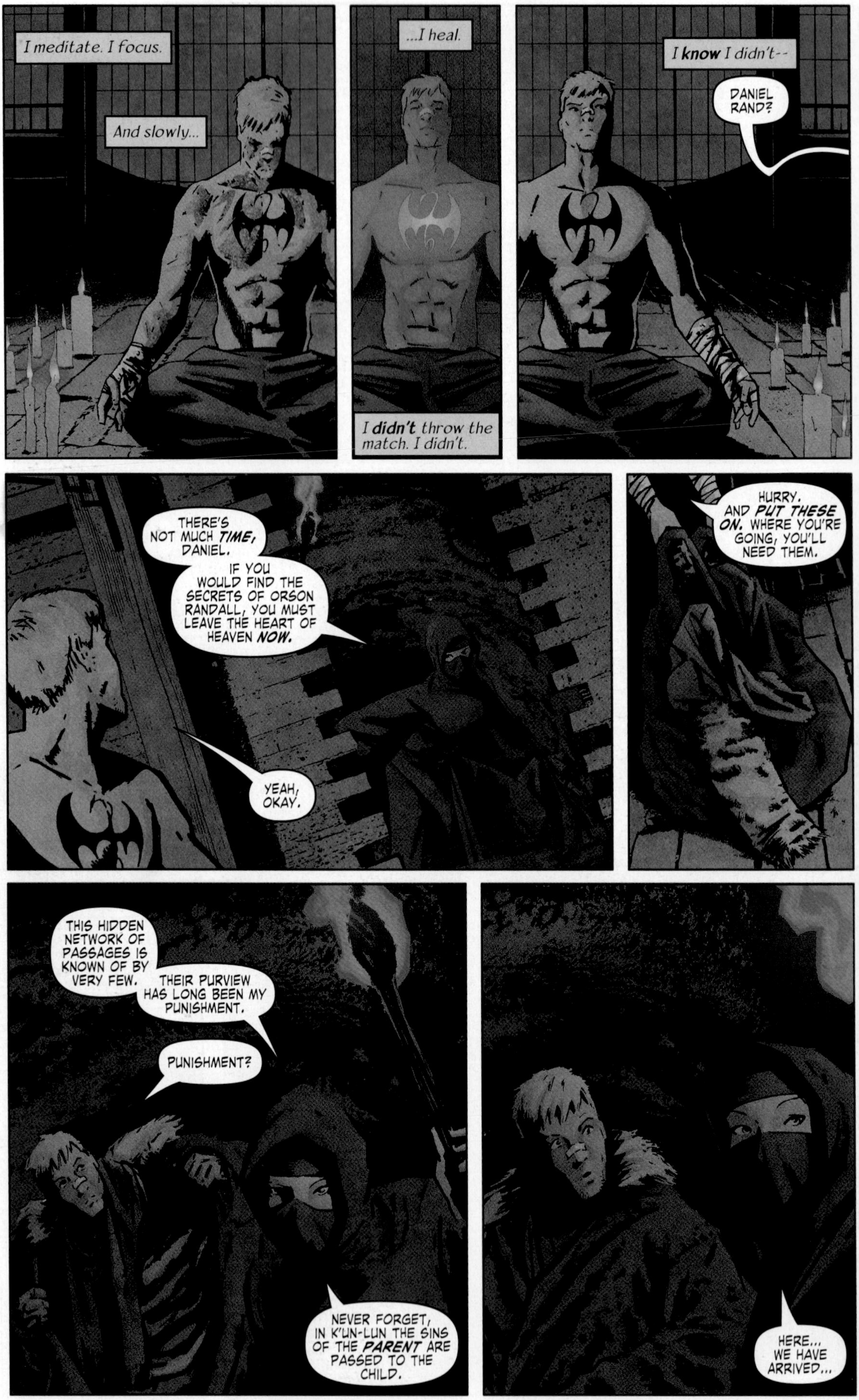
I meditate. I focus.
And slowly...
...I heal.
I didn't throw the match. I didn't.
I know I didn't--
DANIEL RAND?
THERE'S NOT MUCH TIME, DANIEL.
IF YOU WOULD FIND THE SECRETS OF ORSON RANDALL, YOU MUST LEAVE THE HEART OF HEAVEN NOW.
YEAH, OKAY.
HURRY. AND PUT THESE ON. WHERE YOU'RE GOING, YOU'LL NEED THEM.
THIS HIDDEN NETWORK OF PASSAGES IS KNOWN OF BY VERY FEW.
THEIR PURVIEW HAS LONG BEEN MY PUNISHMENT.
PUNISHMENT?
NEVER FORGET, IN K'UN-LUN THE SINS OF THE PARENT ARE PASSED TO THE CHILD.
HERE... WE HAVE ARRIVED...

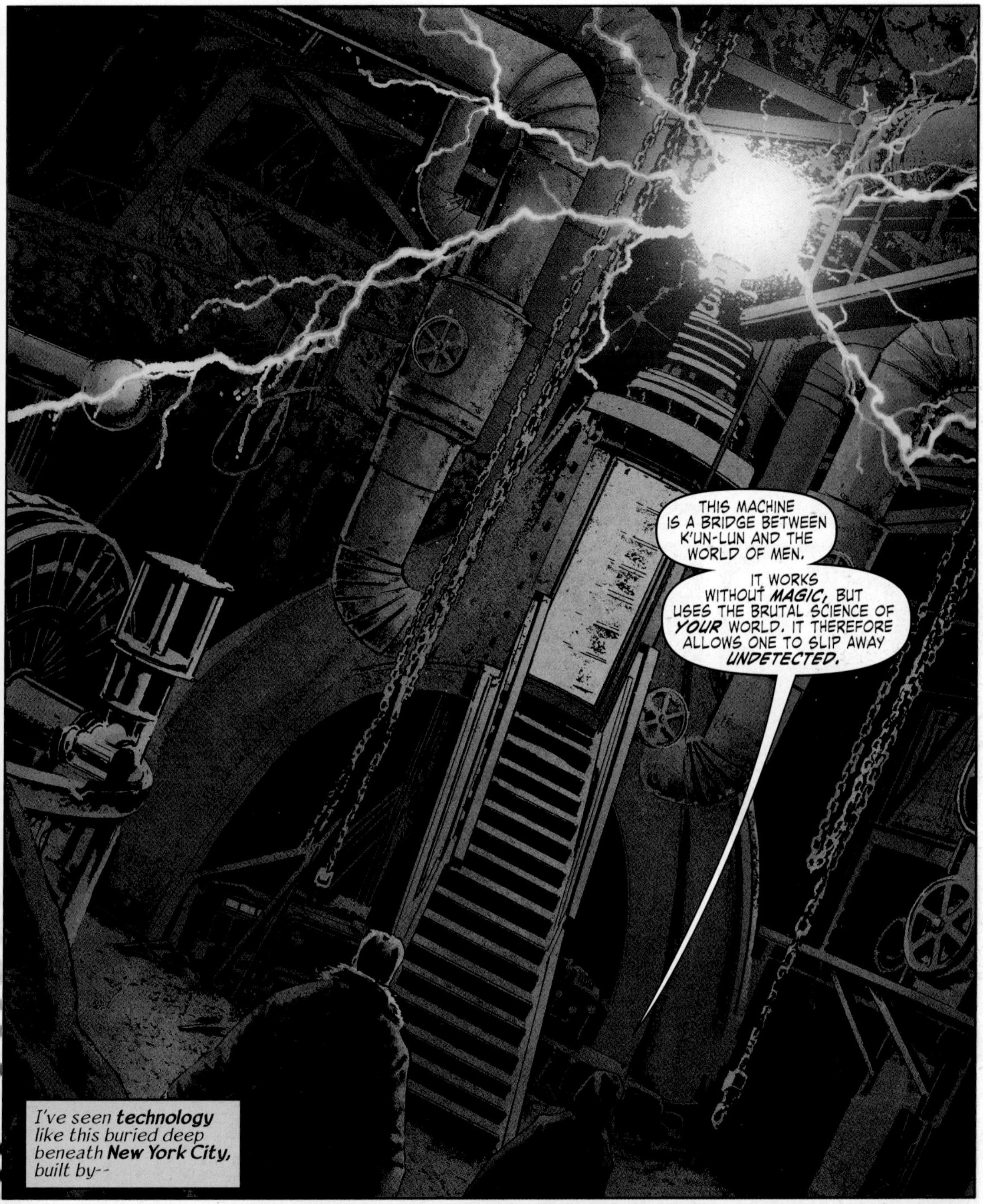
THIS MACHINE IS A BRIDGE BETWEEN K'UN-LUN AND THE WORLD OF MEN.
IT WORKS WITHOUT MAGIC, BUT USES THE BRUTAL SCIENCE OF YOUR WORLD. IT THEREFORE ALLOWS ONE TO SLIP AWAY UNDETECTED.
I've seen technology like this buried deep beneath New York City, built by--

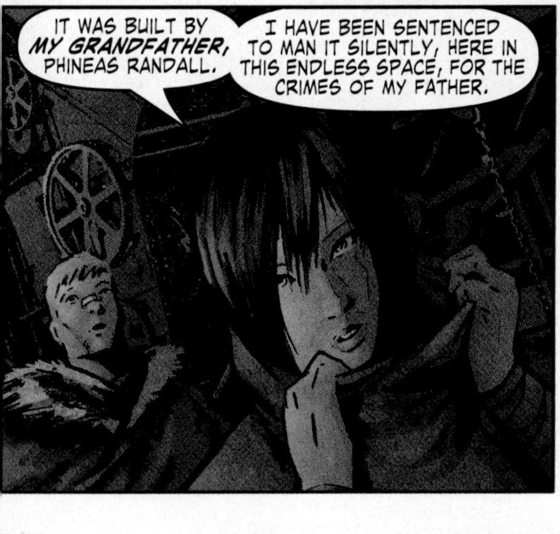
IT WAS BUILT BY MY GRANDFATHER, PHINEAS RANDALL.
I HAVE BEEN SENTENCED TO MAN IT SILENTLY, HERE IN THIS ENDLESS SPACE, FOR THE CRIMES OF MY FATHER.

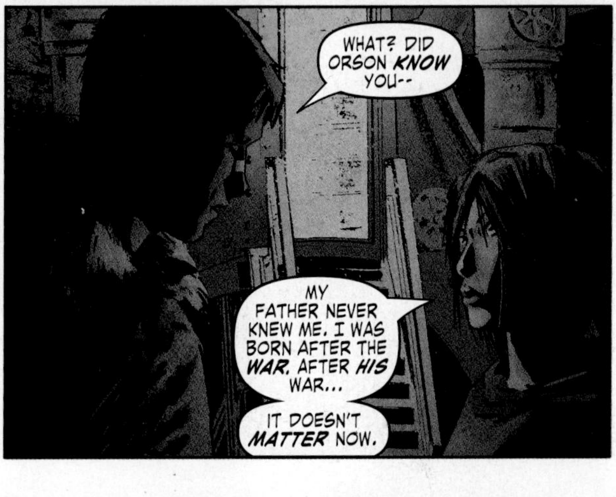
WHAT? DID ORSON KNOW YOU--
MY FATHER NEVER KNEW ME. I WAS BORN AFTER THE WAR, AFTER HIS WAR...
IT DOESN'T MATTER NOW.

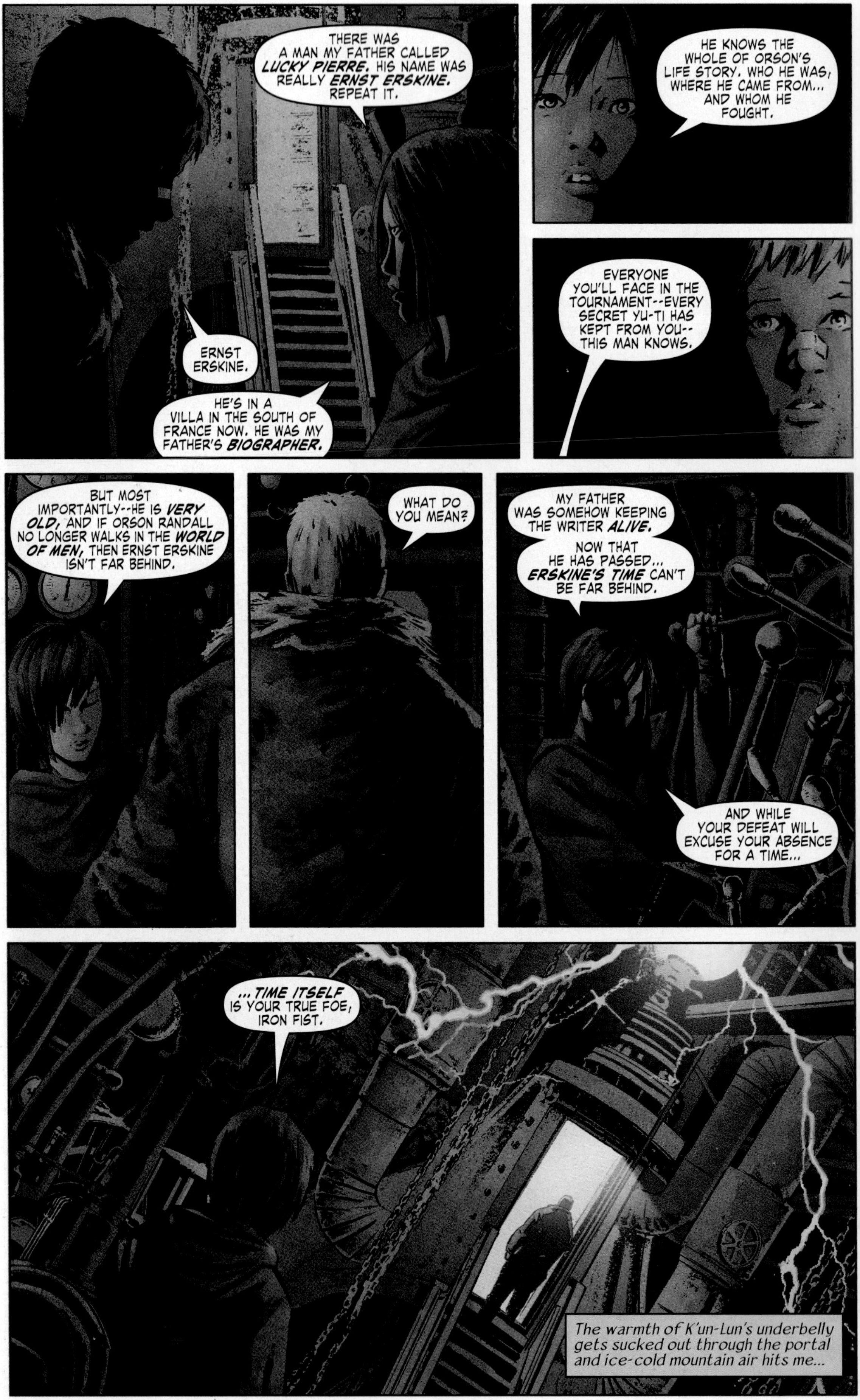
THERE WAS A MAN MY FATHER CALLED ***LUCKY PIERRE.*** HIS NAME WAS REALLY ***ERNST ERSKINE.*** REPEAT IT.
ERNST ERSKINE.
HE'S IN A VILLA IN THE SOUTH OF FRANCE NOW. HE WAS MY FATHER'S ***BIOGRAPHER.***
HE KNOWS THE WHOLE OF ORSON'S LIFE STORY. WHO HE WAS, WHERE HE CAME FROM... AND WHOM HE FOUGHT.
EVERYONE YOU'LL FACE IN THE TOURNAMENT--EVERY SECRET YU-TI HAS KEPT FROM YOU--THIS MAN KNOWS.
BUT MOST IMPORTANTLY--HE IS ***VERY OLD,*** AND IF ORSON RANDALL NO LONGER WALKS IN THE ***WORLD OF MEN,*** THEN ERNST ERSKINE ISN'T FAR BEHIND.
WHAT DO YOU MEAN?
MY FATHER WAS SOMEHOW KEEPING THE WRITER ***ALIVE.***
NOW THAT HE HAS PASSED... ***ERSKINE'S TIME*** CAN'T BE FAR BEHIND.
AND WHILE YOUR DEFEAT WILL EXCUSE YOUR ABSENCE FOR A TIME...
...TIME ITSELF IS YOUR TRUE FOE, IRON FIST.
The warmth of K'un-Lun's underbelly gets sucked out through the portal and ice-cold mountain air hits me...

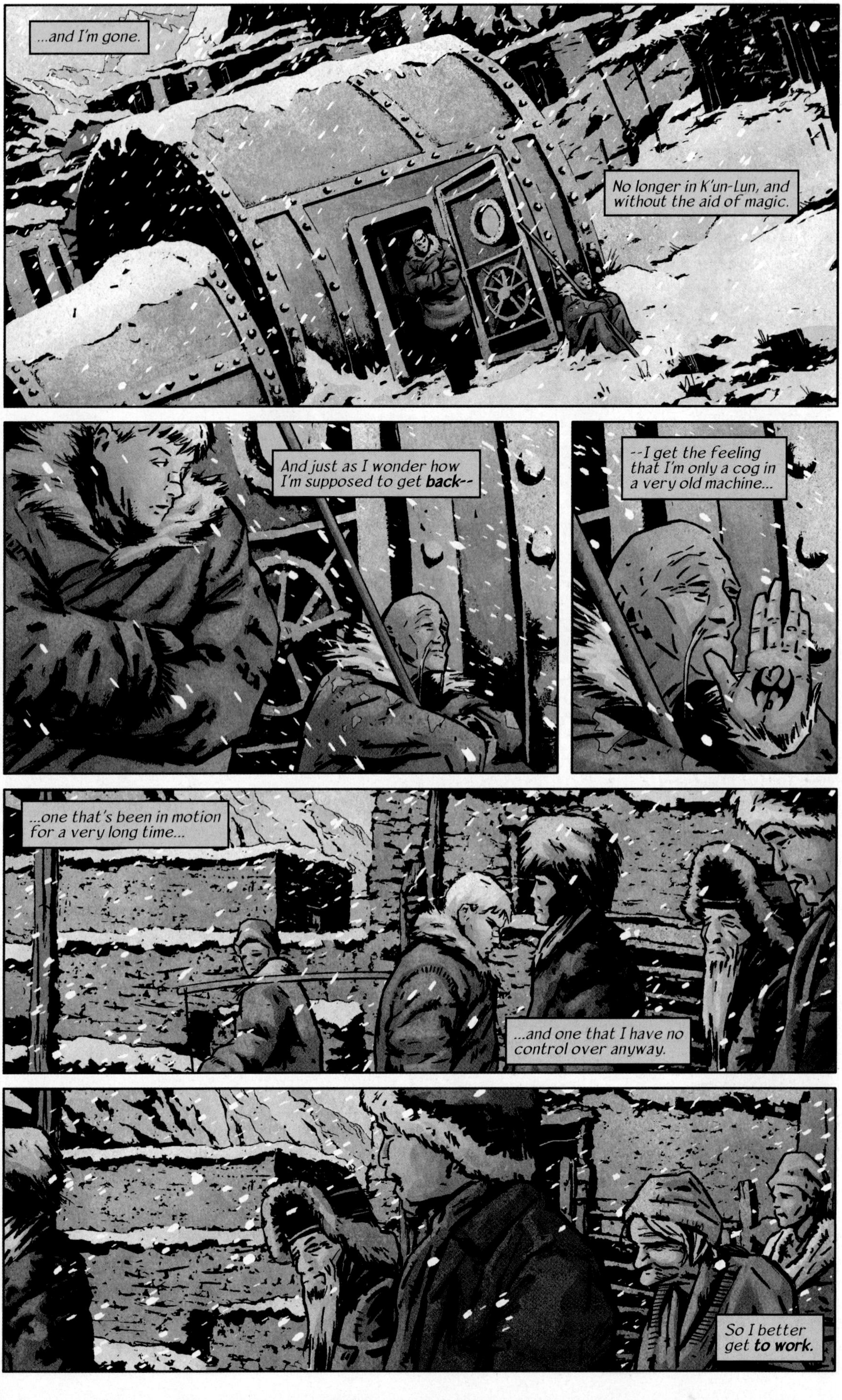
...and I'm gone.
No longer in K'un-Lun, and without the aid of magic.
And just as I wonder how I'm supposed to get **back**--
--I get the feeling that I'm only a cog in a very old machine...
...one that's been in motion for a very long time...
...and one that I have no control over anyway.
So I better get **to work.**

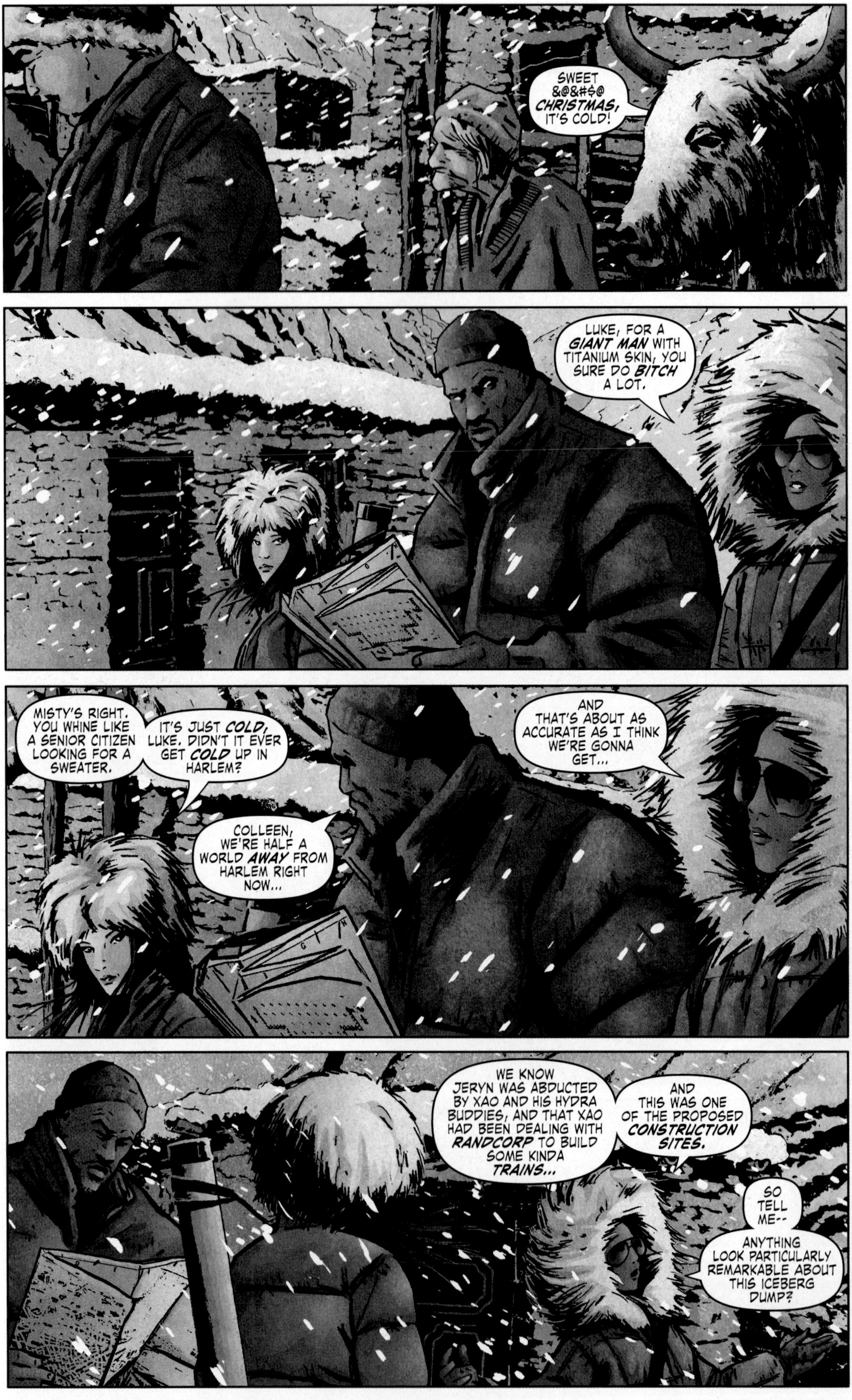
SWEET &@&#$@ CHRISTMAS, IT'S COLD!
LUKE, FOR A GIANT MAN WITH TITANIUM SKIN, YOU SURE DO BITCH A LOT.
MISTY'S RIGHT. YOU WHINE LIKE A SENIOR CITIZEN LOOKING FOR A SWEATER.
IT'S JUST COLD, LUKE. DIDN'T IT EVER GET COLD UP IN HARLEM?
COLLEEN, WE'RE HALF A WORLD AWAY FROM HARLEM RIGHT NOW...
AND THAT'S ABOUT AS ACCURATE AS I THINK WE'RE GONNA GET...
WE KNOW JERYN WAS ABDUCTED BY XAO AND HIS HYDRA BUDDIES, AND THAT XAO HAD BEEN DEALING WITH RANDCORP TO BUILD SOME KINDA TRAINS...
AND THIS WAS ONE OF THE PROPOSED CONSTRUCTION SITES.
SO TELL ME--
ANYTHING LOOK PARTICULARLY REMARKABLE ABOUT THIS ICEBERG DUMP?

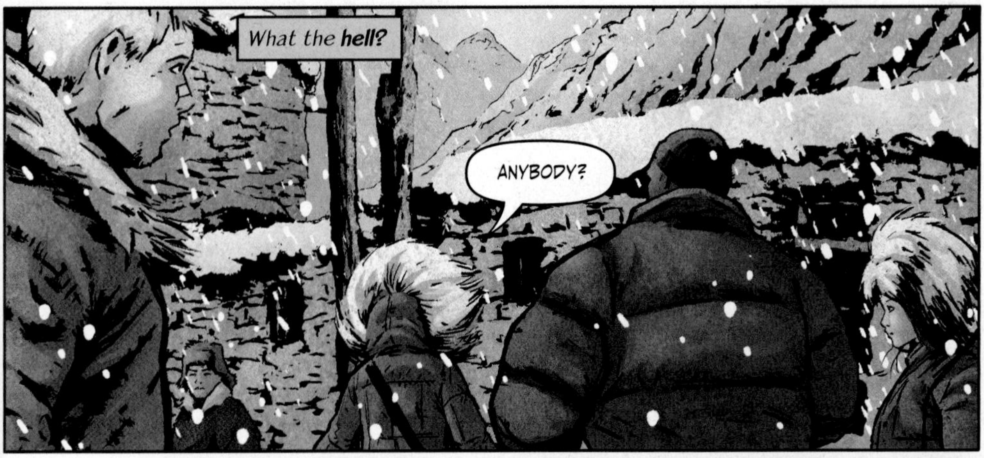
What the **hell?**
ANYBODY?

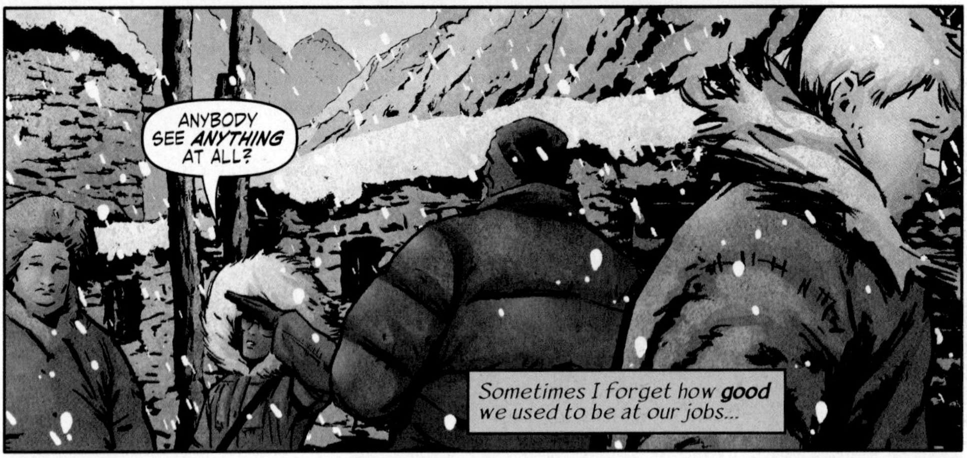
ANYBODY SEE ***ANYTHING*** AT ALL?
Sometimes I forget how **good** we used to be at our jobs...

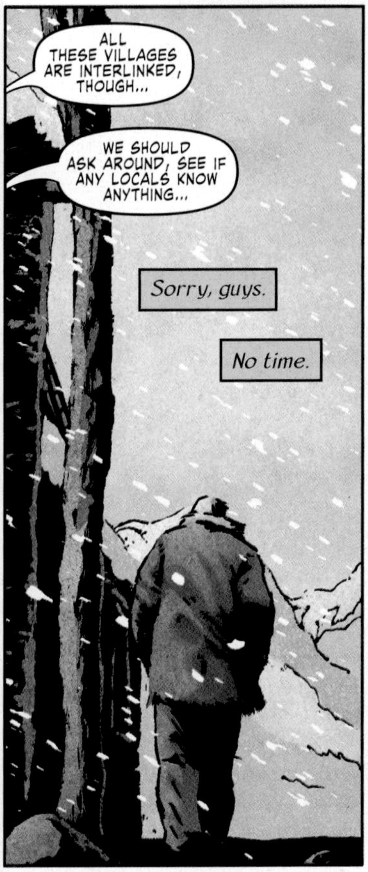
ALL THESE VILLAGES ARE INTERLINKED, THOUGH...
WE SHOULD ASK AROUND, SEE IF ANY LOCALS KNOW ANYTHING...
Sorry, guys.
No time.

*...I've got **two** worlds to save...*

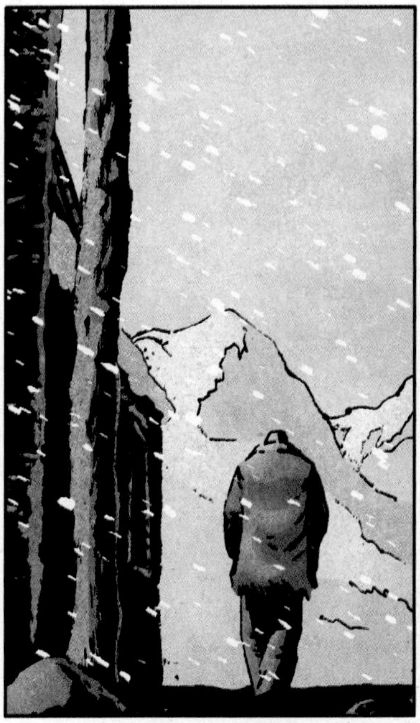

*And a dying old man to find...If I'm not too **late.***

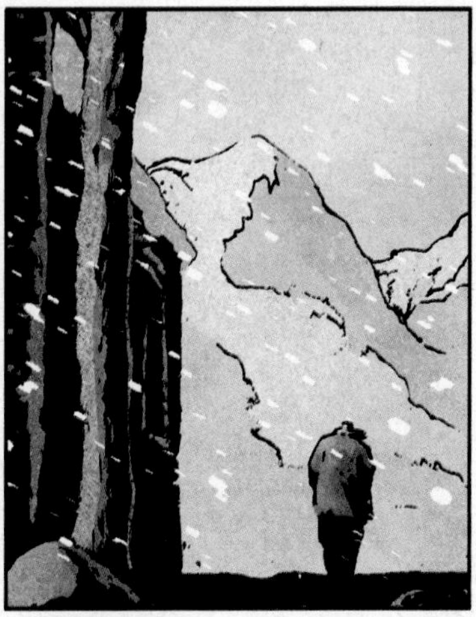

The 7 Capital
Cities
of Heaven

三

Round 3

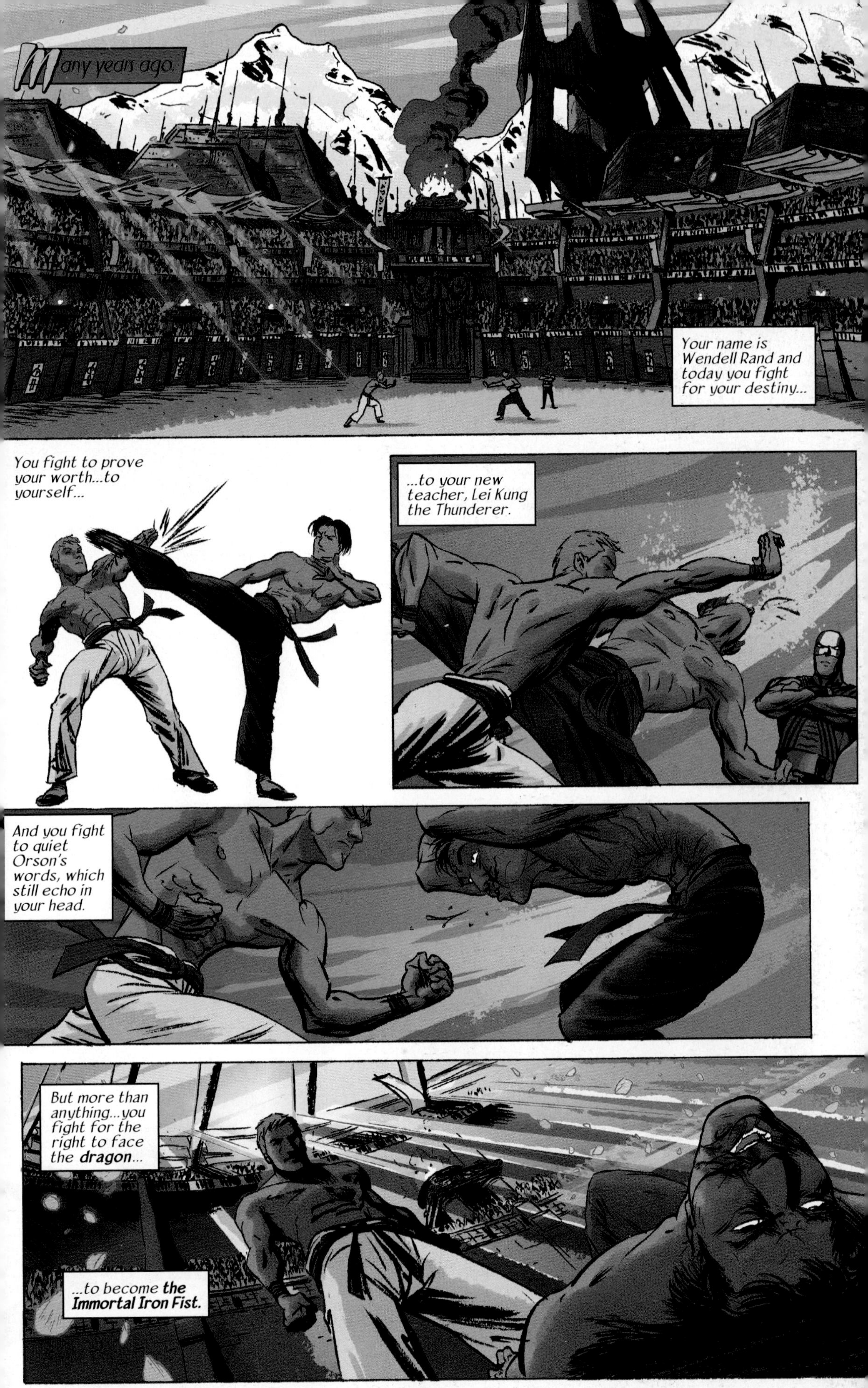
Many years ago.
Your name is Wendell Rand and today you fight for your destiny...
You fight to prove your worth...to yourself...
...to your new teacher, Lei Kung the Thunderer.
And you fight to quiet Orson's words, which still echo in your head.
But more than anything...you fight for the right to face the **dragon**...
...to become **the Immortal Iron Fist.**

Unfortunately, so does your best-- your only--friend...

...Davos, the son of the Thunderer.

A year ago you watched the previous class of fighters hold their elimination...

Until only one stood among them all...one man worthy of the challenge.

The dragon tore him to pieces.

That was the first time you felt **fear** about what lay ahead of you.

And when you realized it was possible you **both** could lose.

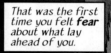

That even if either of you won victory over your opponents this day...

...The final words in this elimination would be spoken by **Shou-Lao the Undying.**

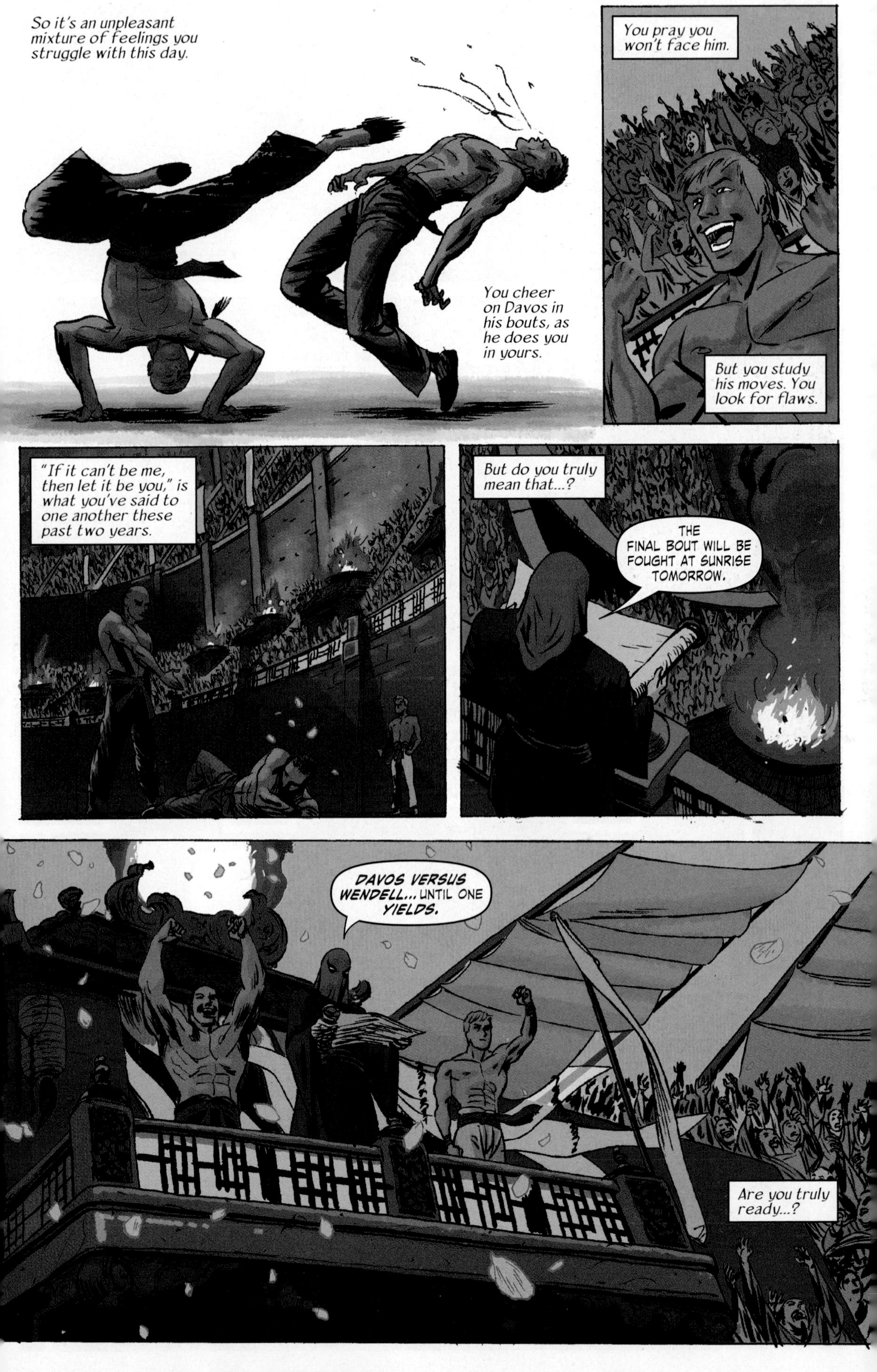
So it's an unpleasant mixture of feelings you struggle with this day.
You cheer on Davos in his bouts, as he does you in yours.
You pray you won't face him.
But you study his moves. You look for flaws.
"If it can't be me, then let it be you," is what you've said to one another these past two years.
But do you truly mean that...?
THE FINAL BOUT WILL BE FOUGHT AT SUNRISE TOMORROW.
DAVOS VERSUS WENDELL... UNTIL ONE YIELDS.
Are you truly ready...?

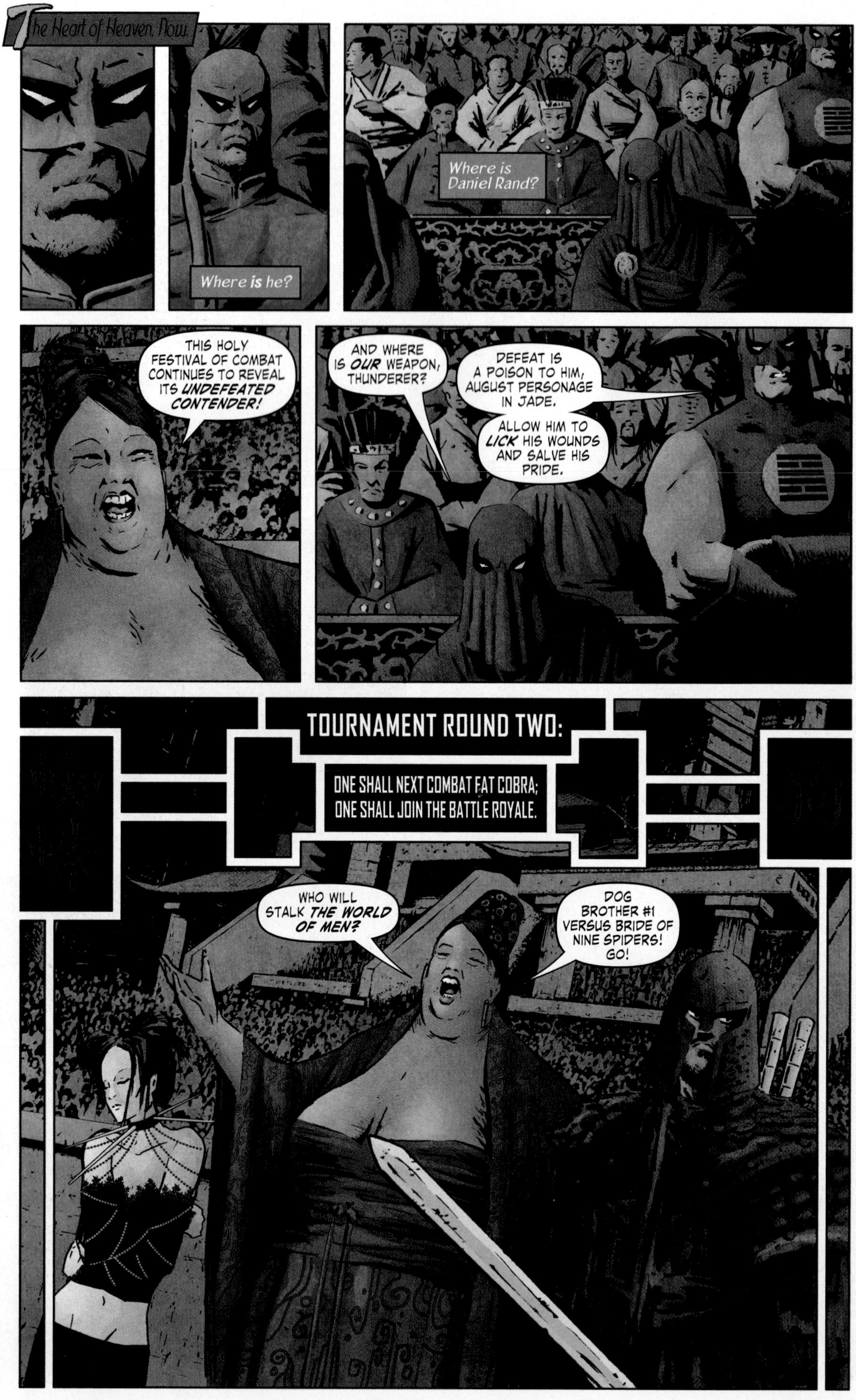
The Heart of Heaven. Now.
Where is he?
Where is Daniel Rand?
THIS HOLY FESTIVAL OF COMBAT CONTINUES TO REVEAL ITS UNDEFEATED CONTENDER!
AND WHERE IS OUR WEAPON, THUNDERER?
DEFEAT IS A POISON TO HIM, AUGUST PERSONAGE IN JADE.
ALLOW HIM TO LICK HIS WOUNDS AND SALVE HIS PRIDE.
TOURNAMENT ROUND TWO:
ONE SHALL NEXT COMBAT FAT COBRA;
ONE SHALL JOIN THE BATTLE ROYALE.
WHO WILL STALK THE WORLD OF MEN?
DOG BROTHER #1 VERSUS BRIDE OF NINE SPIDERS! GO!

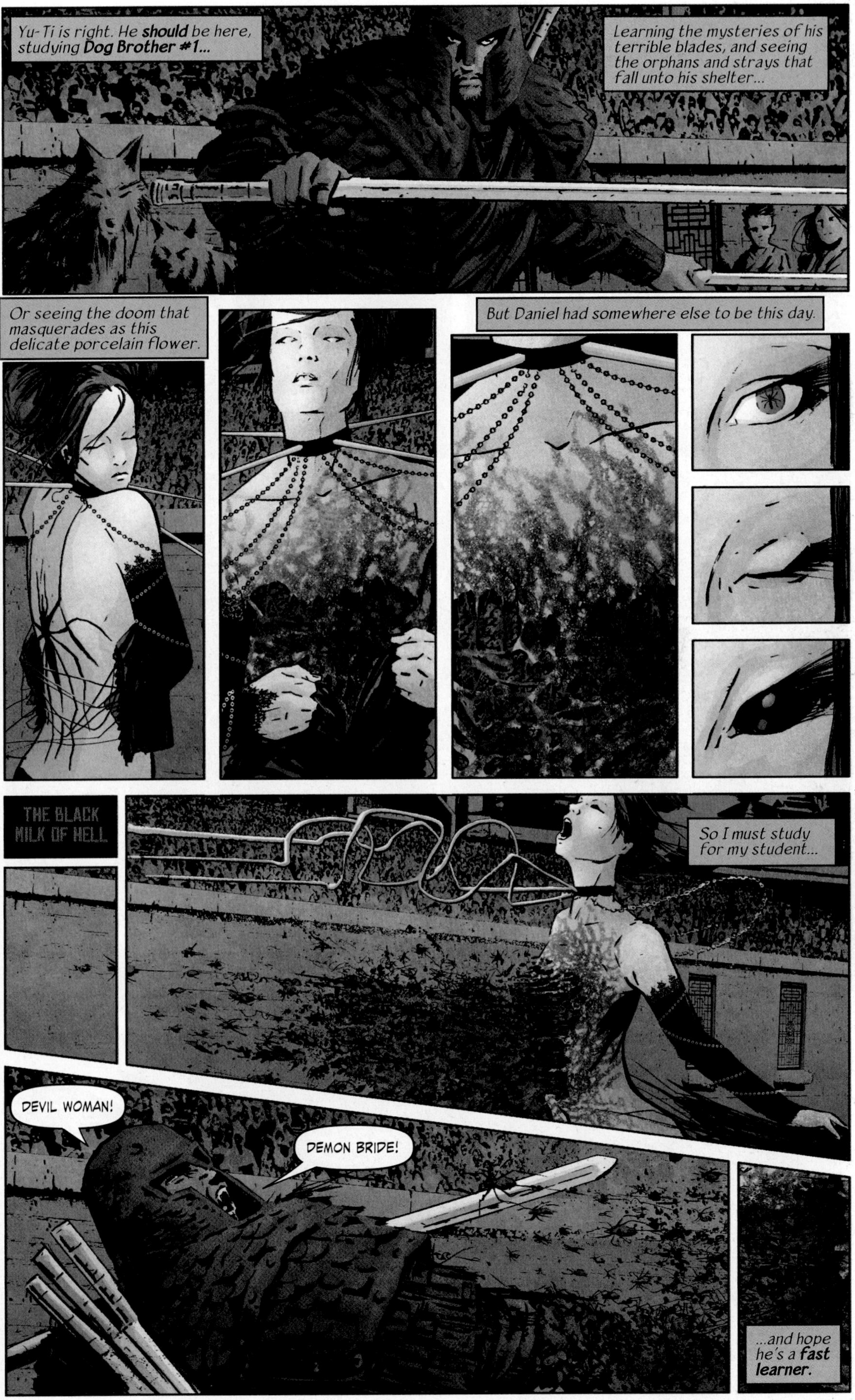
Yu-Ti is right. He should be here, studying Dog Brother #1...
Learning the mysteries of his terrible blades, and seeing the orphans and strays that fall unto his shelter...
Or seeing the doom that masquerades as this delicate porcelain flower.
But Daniel had somewhere else to be this day.
THE BLACK MILK OF HELL
So I must study for my student...
DEVIL WOMAN!
DEMON BRIDE!
...and hope he's a fast learner.

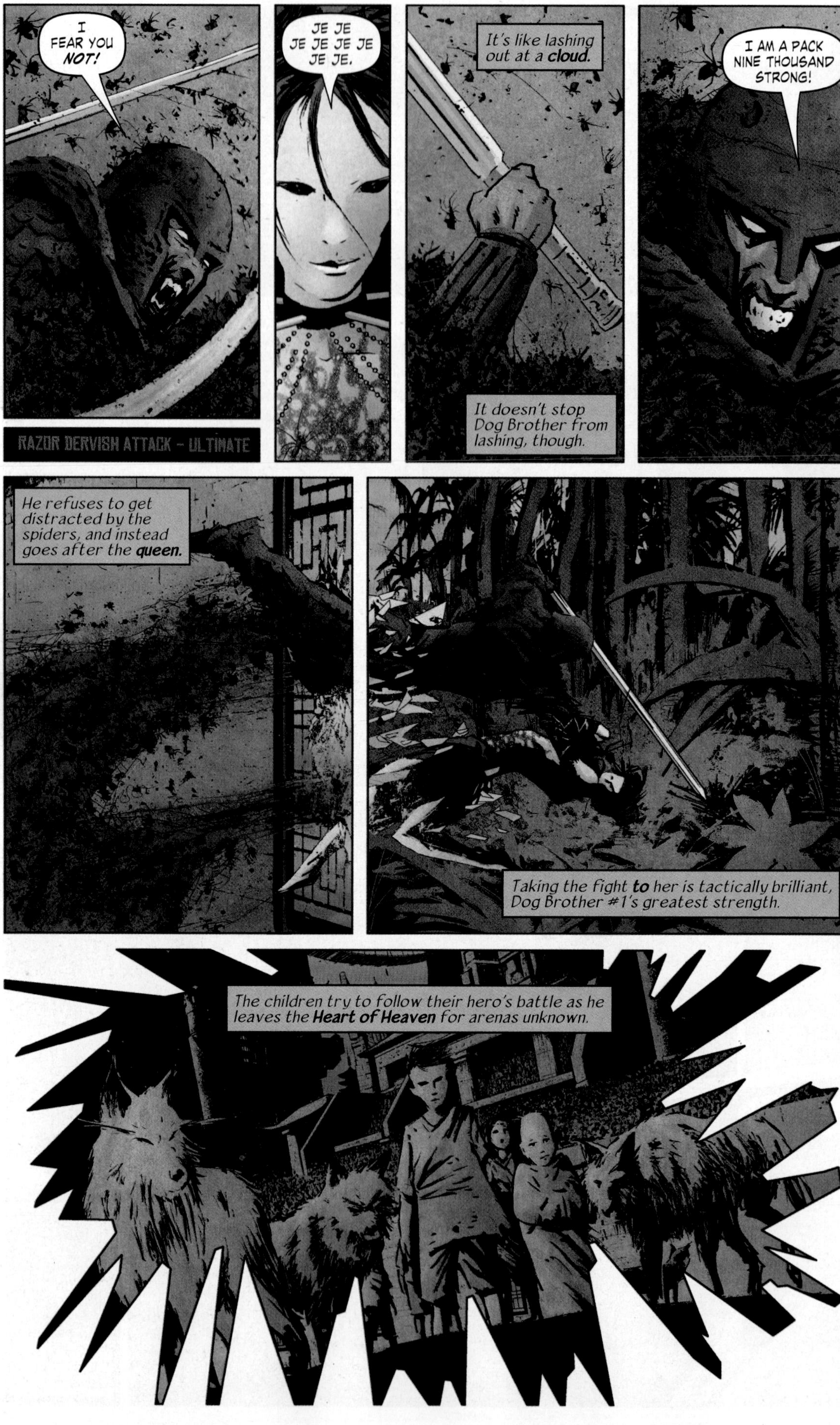
I FEAR YOU NOT!
RAZOR DERVISH ATTACK - ULTIMATE
JE JE JE JE JE JE JE JE.
It's like lashing out at a cloud.
It doesn't stop Dog Brother from lashing, though.
I AM A PACK NINE THOUSAND STRONG!
He refuses to get distracted by the spiders, and instead goes after the queen.
Taking the fight to her is tactically brilliant, Dog Brother #1's greatest strength.
The children try to follow their hero's battle as he leaves the Heart of Heaven for arenas unknown.

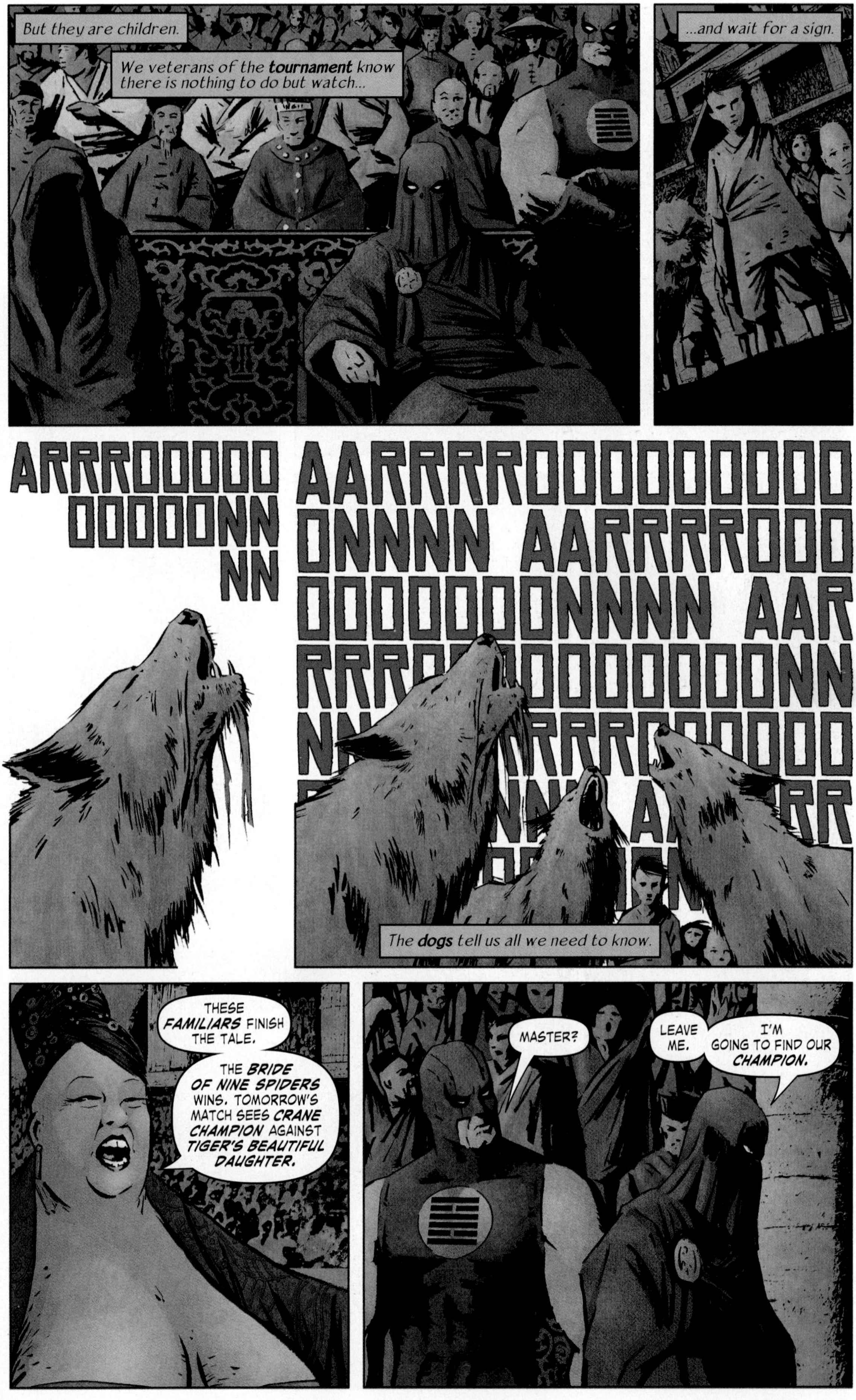
But they are children.
We veterans of the **tournament** know there is nothing to do but watch...
...and wait for a sign.
ARRROOOOO OOOOONN NN
AARRRROOOOOOOOO ONNNN AARRRROOO OOOOOOONNNN AAR
The **dogs** tell us all we need to know.
THESE ***FAMILIARS*** FINISH THE TALE.
THE ***BRIDE OF NINE SPIDERS*** WINS. TOMORROW'S MATCH SEES ***CRANE CHAMPION*** AGAINST ***TIGER'S BEAUTIFUL DAUGHTER.***
MASTER?
LEAVE ME.
I'M GOING TO FIND OUR ***CHAMPION.***

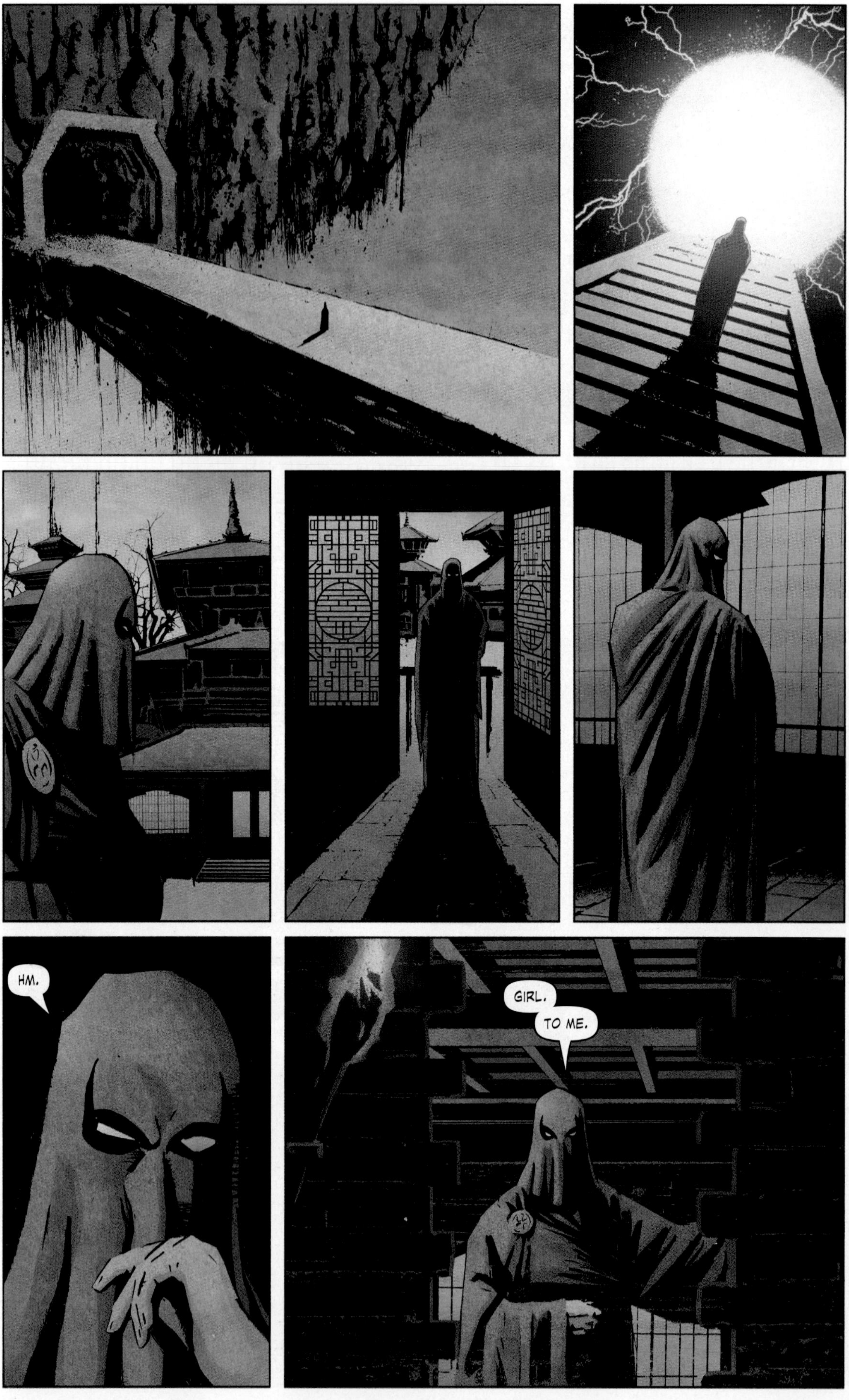
HM.
GIRL.
TO ME.

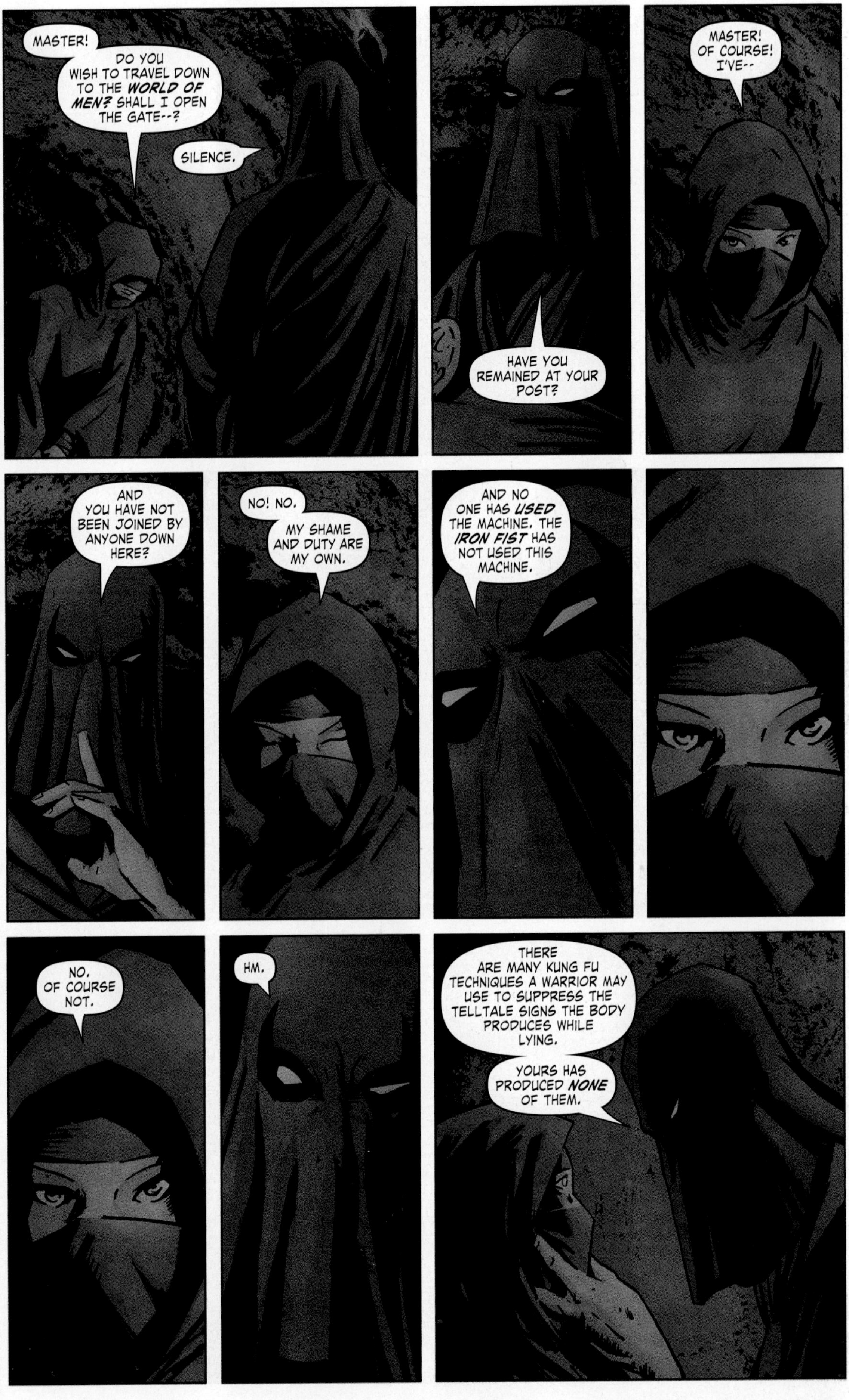
MASTER!
DO YOU WISH TO TRAVEL DOWN TO THE WORLD OF MEN? SHALL I OPEN THE GATE--?
SILENCE.
HAVE YOU REMAINED AT YOUR POST?
MASTER! OF COURSE! I'VE--
AND YOU HAVE NOT BEEN JOINED BY ANYONE DOWN HERE?
NO! NO.
MY SHAME AND DUTY ARE MY OWN.
AND NO ONE HAS USED THE MACHINE. THE IRON FIST HAS NOT USED THIS MACHINE.
NO. OF COURSE NOT.
HM.
THERE ARE MANY KUNG FU TECHNIQUES A WARRIOR MAY USE TO SUPPRESS THE TELLTALE SIGNS THE BODY PRODUCES WHILE LYING.
YOURS HAS PRODUCED NONE OF THEM.

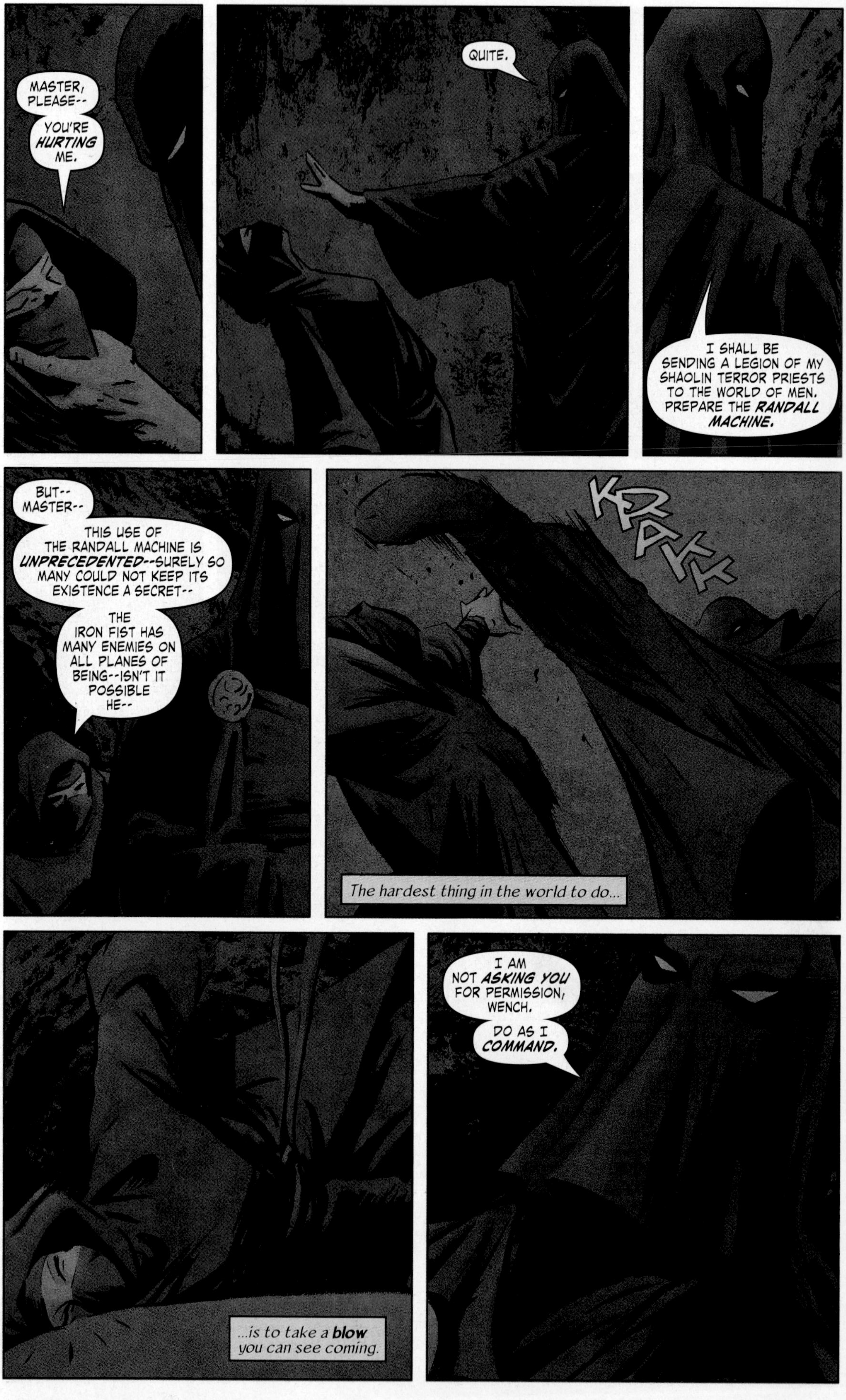

MASTER, PLEASE--
YOU'RE HURTING ME.
QUITE.
I SHALL BE SENDING A LEGION OF MY SHAOLIN TERROR PRIESTS TO THE WORLD OF MEN. PREPARE THE RANDALL MACHINE.
BUT--MASTER--
THIS USE OF THE RANDALL MACHINE IS UNPRECEDENTED--SURELY SO MANY COULD NOT KEEP ITS EXISTENCE A SECRET--
THE IRON FIST HAS MANY ENEMIES ON ALL PLANES OF BEING--ISN'T IT POSSIBLE HE--
KRAKK
The hardest thing in the world to do...
...is to take a blow you can see coming.
I AM NOT ASKING YOU FOR PERMISSION, WENCH.
DO AS I COMMAND.

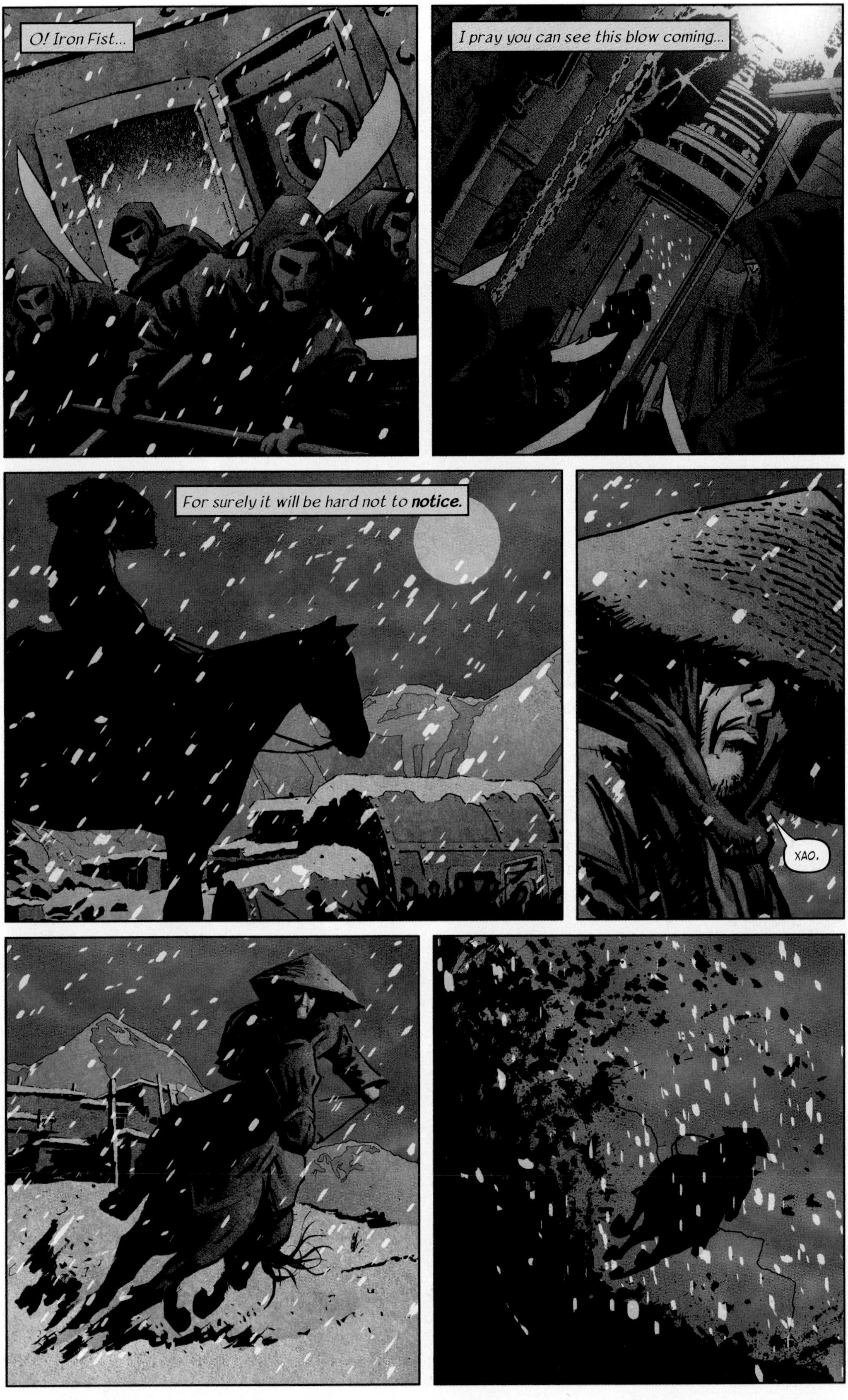
O! Iron Fist...
I pray you can see this blow coming...
For surely it will be hard not to **notice.**
XAO.

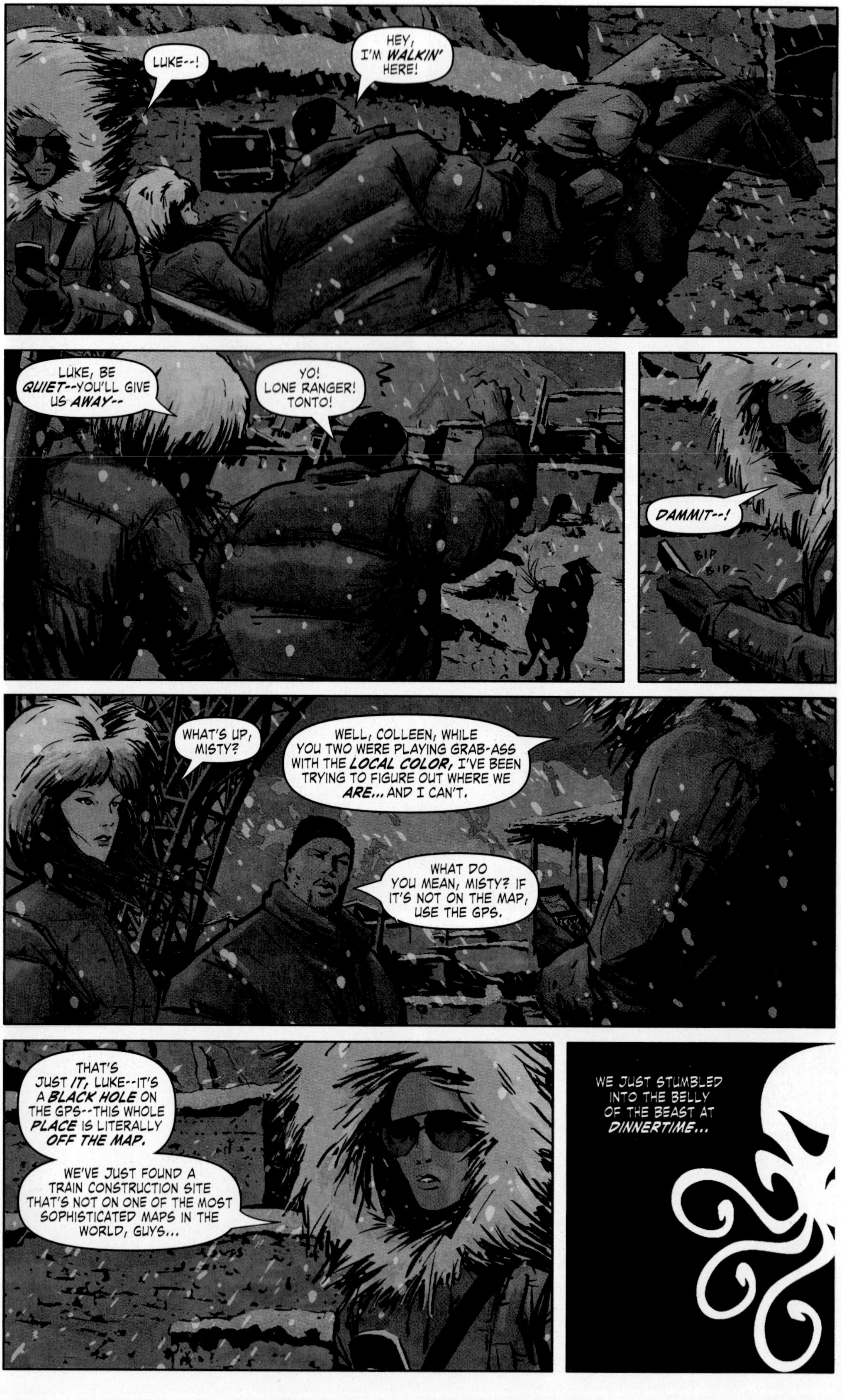
LUKE--!
HEY, I'M *WALKIN'* HERE!
LUKE, BE *QUIET*--YOU'LL GIVE US *AWAY*--
YO! LONE RANGER! TONTO!
DAMMIT--!
BIP BIP
WHAT'S UP, MISTY?
WELL, COLLEEN, WHILE YOU TWO WERE PLAYING GRAB-ASS WITH THE *LOCAL COLOR,* I'VE BEEN TRYING TO FIGURE OUT WHERE WE *ARE*... AND I CAN'T.
WHAT DO YOU MEAN, MISTY? IF IT'S NOT ON THE MAP, USE THE GPS.
THAT'S JUST *IT,* LUKE--IT'S A *BLACK HOLE* ON THE GPS--THIS WHOLE *PLACE* IS LITERALLY *OFF THE MAP.*
WE'VE JUST FOUND A TRAIN CONSTRUCTION SITE THAT'S NOT ON ONE OF THE MOST SOPHISTICATED MAPS IN THE WORLD, GUYS...
WE JUST STUMBLED INTO THE BELLY OF THE BEAST AT *DINNERTIME*...

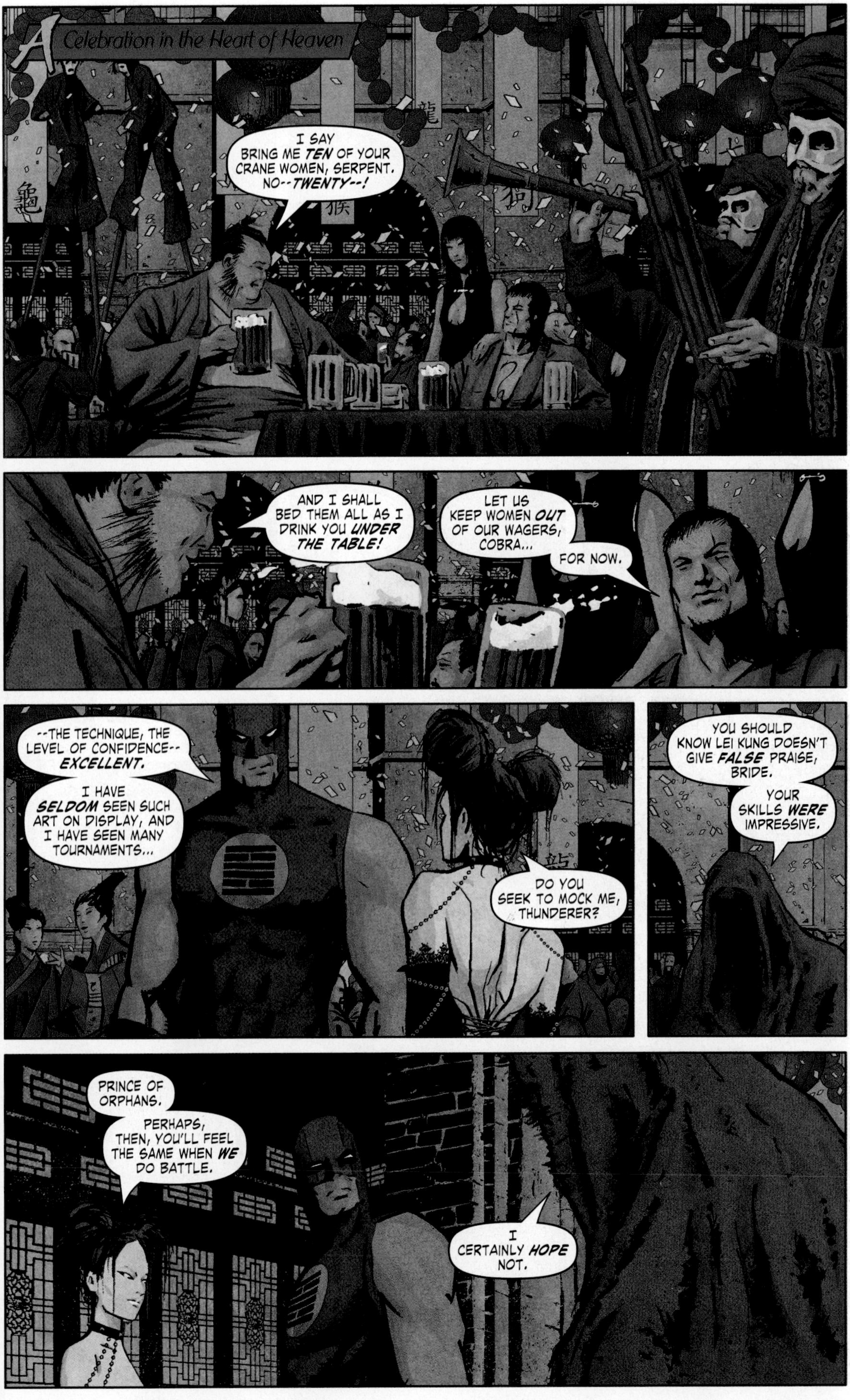
A Celebration in the Heart of Heaven
I SAY BRING ME TEN OF YOUR CRANE WOMEN, SERPENT. NO--TWENTY--!
AND I SHALL BED THEM ALL AS I DRINK YOU UNDER THE TABLE!
LET US KEEP WOMEN OUT OF OUR WAGERS, COBRA...
FOR NOW.
--THE TECHNIQUE, THE LEVEL OF CONFIDENCE-- EXCELLENT.
I HAVE SELDOM SEEN SUCH ART ON DISPLAY, AND I HAVE SEEN MANY TOURNAMENTS...
DO YOU SEEK TO MOCK ME, THUNDERER?
YOU SHOULD KNOW LEI KUNG DOESN'T GIVE FALSE PRAISE, BRIDE.
YOUR SKILLS WERE IMPRESSIVE.
PRINCE OF ORPHANS.
PERHAPS, THEN, YOU'LL FEEL THE SAME WHEN WE DO BATTLE.
I CERTAINLY HOPE NOT.

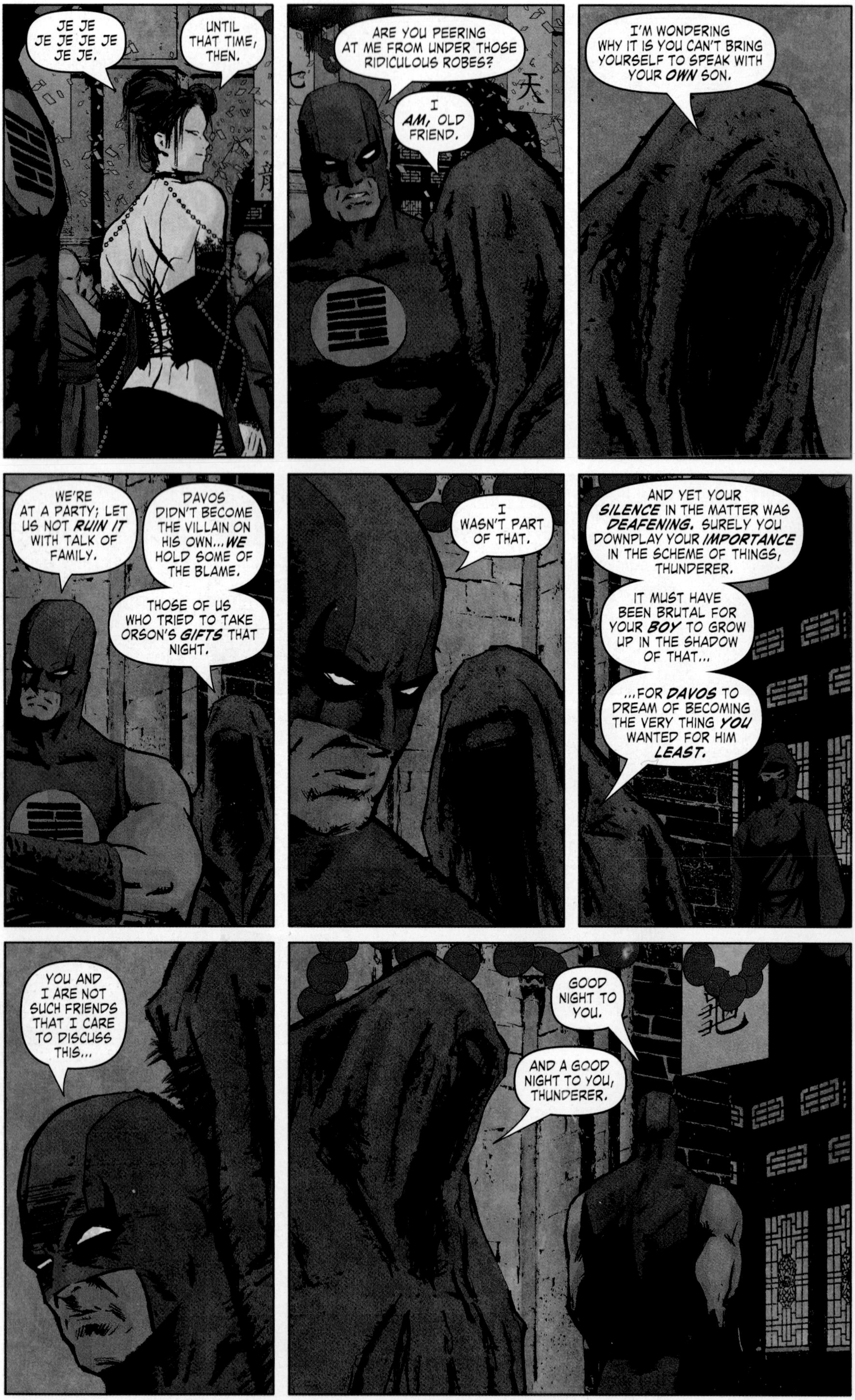
JE JE JE JE JE JE JE JE.
UNTIL THAT TIME, THEN.
ARE YOU PEERING AT ME FROM UNDER THOSE RIDICULOUS ROBES?
I AM, OLD FRIEND.
I'M WONDERING WHY IT IS YOU CAN'T BRING YOURSELF TO SPEAK WITH YOUR OWN SON.
WE'RE AT A PARTY; LET US NOT RUIN IT WITH TALK OF FAMILY.
DAVOS DIDN'T BECOME THE VILLAIN ON HIS OWN... WE HOLD SOME OF THE BLAME.
THOSE OF US WHO TRIED TO TAKE ORSON'S GIFTS THAT NIGHT.
I WASN'T PART OF THAT.
AND YET YOUR SILENCE IN THE MATTER WAS DEAFENING. SURELY YOU DOWNPLAY YOUR IMPORTANCE IN THE SCHEME OF THINGS, THUNDERER.
IT MUST HAVE BEEN BRUTAL FOR YOUR BOY TO GROW UP IN THE SHADOW OF THAT...
...FOR DAVOS TO DREAM OF BECOMING THE VERY THING YOU WANTED FOR HIM LEAST.
YOU AND I ARE NOT SUCH FRIENDS THAT I CARE TO DISCUSS THIS...
GOOD NIGHT TO YOU.
AND A GOOD NIGHT TO YOU, THUNDERER.

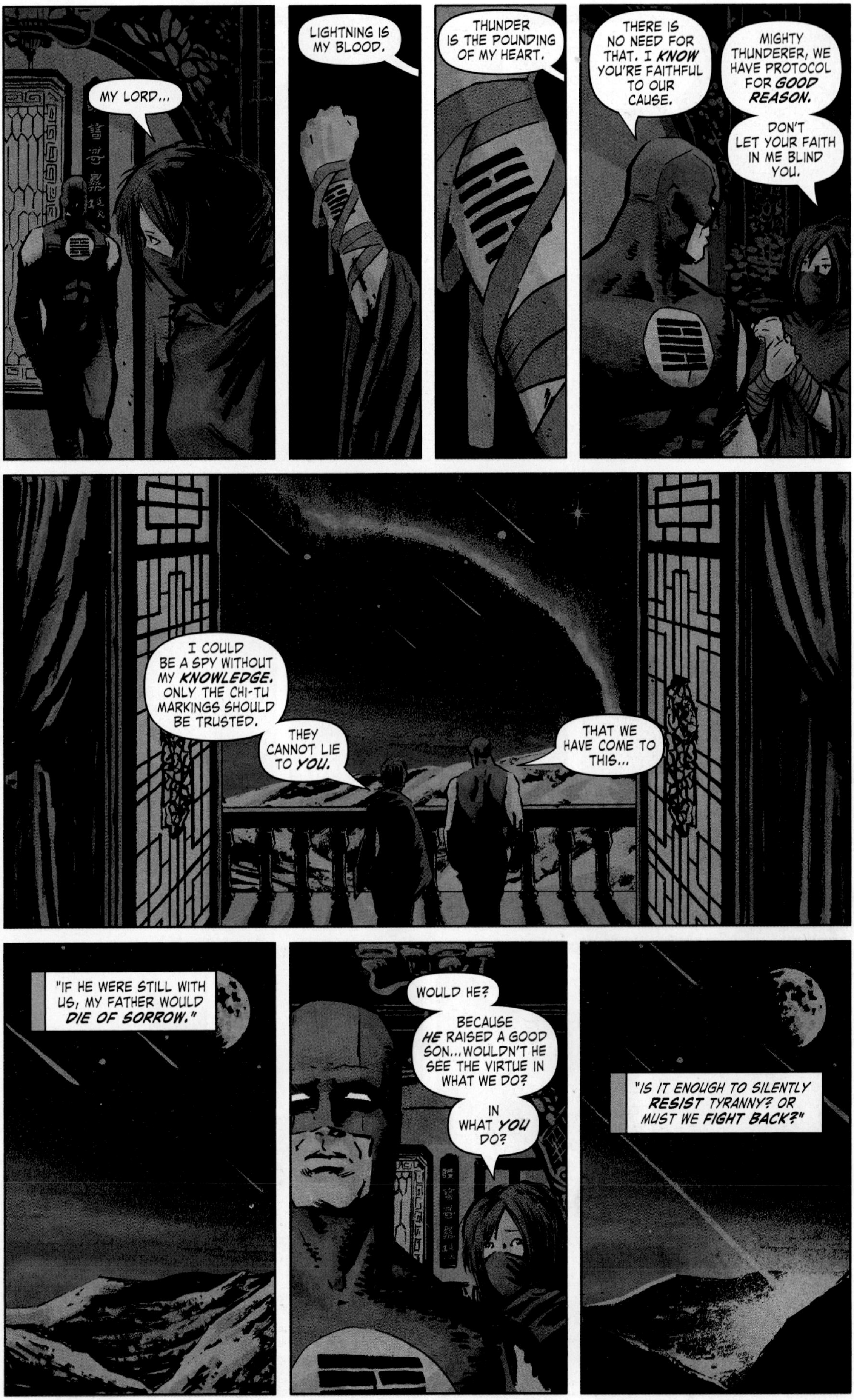
MY LORD...
LIGHTNING IS MY BLOOD.
THUNDER IS THE POUNDING OF MY HEART.
THERE IS NO NEED FOR THAT. I *KNOW* YOU'RE FAITHFUL TO OUR CAUSE.
MIGHTY THUNDERER, WE HAVE PROTOCOL FOR *GOOD REASON.*
DON'T LET YOUR FAITH IN ME BLIND YOU.
I COULD BE A SPY WITHOUT MY *KNOWLEDGE.* ONLY THE CHI-TU MARKINGS SHOULD BE TRUSTED.
THEY CANNOT LIE TO *YOU.*
THAT WE HAVE COME TO THIS...
"IF HE WERE STILL WITH US, MY FATHER WOULD *DIE OF SORROW.*"
WOULD HE?
BECAUSE *HE* RAISED A GOOD SON...WOULDN'T HE SEE THE VIRTUE IN WHAT WE DO?
IN WHAT *YOU* DO?
"IS IT ENOUGH TO SILENTLY *RESIST* TYRANNY? OR MUST WE *FIGHT BACK?*"

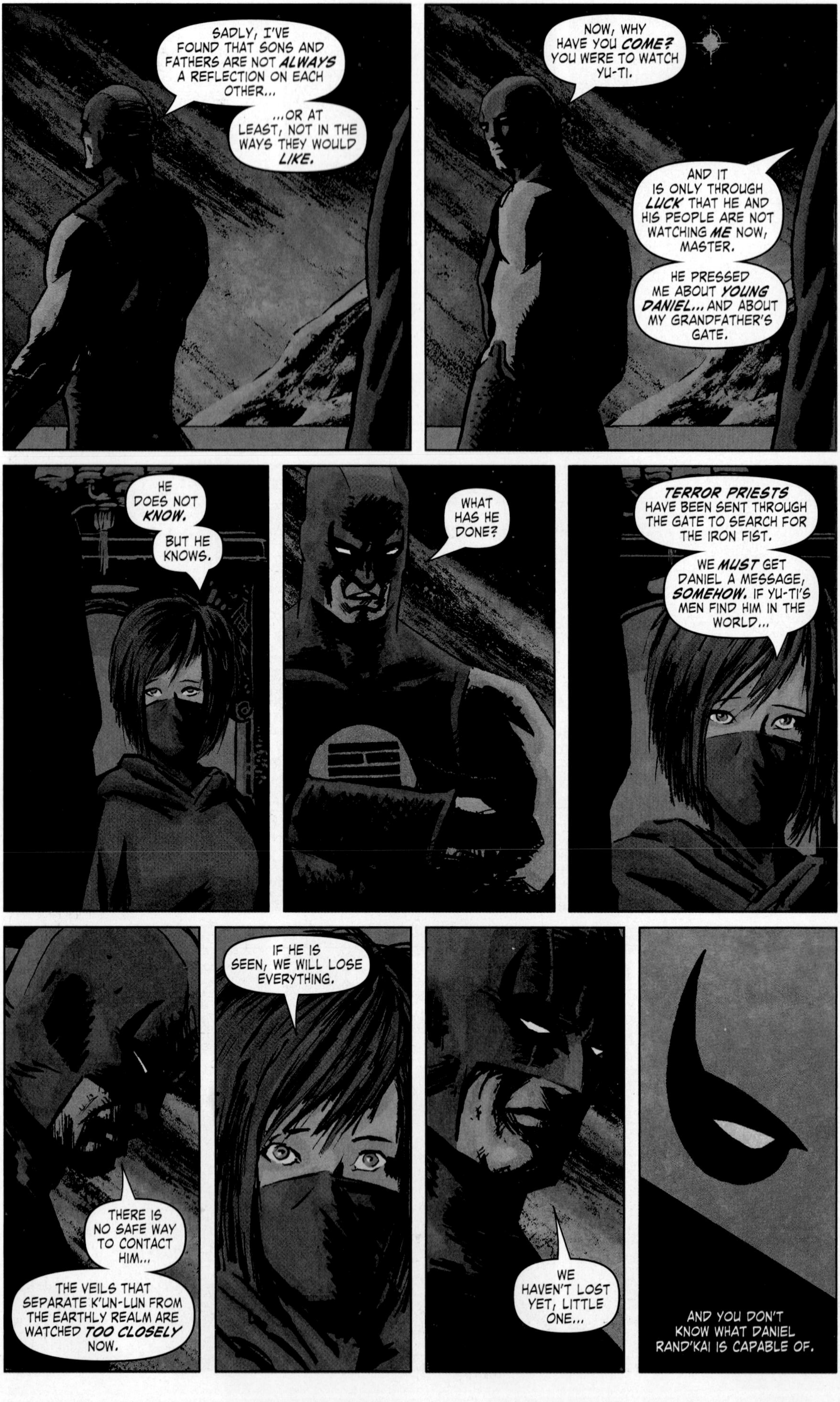
SADLY, I'VE FOUND THAT SONS AND FATHERS ARE NOT ALWAYS A REFLECTION ON EACH OTHER...
...OR AT LEAST, NOT IN THE WAYS THEY WOULD LIKE.
NOW, WHY HAVE YOU COME? YOU WERE TO WATCH YU-TI.
AND IT IS ONLY THROUGH LUCK THAT HE AND HIS PEOPLE ARE NOT WATCHING ME NOW, MASTER.
HE PRESSED ME ABOUT YOUNG DANIEL... AND ABOUT MY GRANDFATHER'S GATE.
HE DOES NOT KNOW.
BUT HE KNOWS.
WHAT HAS HE DONE?
TERROR PRIESTS HAVE BEEN SENT THROUGH THE GATE TO SEARCH FOR THE IRON FIST.
WE MUST GET DANIEL A MESSAGE, SOMEHOW. IF YU-TI'S MEN FIND HIM IN THE WORLD...
THERE IS NO SAFE WAY TO CONTACT HIM...
THE VEILS THAT SEPARATE K'UN-LUN FROM THE EARTHLY REALM ARE WATCHED TOO CLOSELY NOW.
IF HE IS SEEN, WE WILL LOSE EVERYTHING.
WE HAVEN'T LOST YET, LITTLE ONE...
AND YOU DON'T KNOW WHAT DANIEL RAND'KAI IS CAPABLE OF.

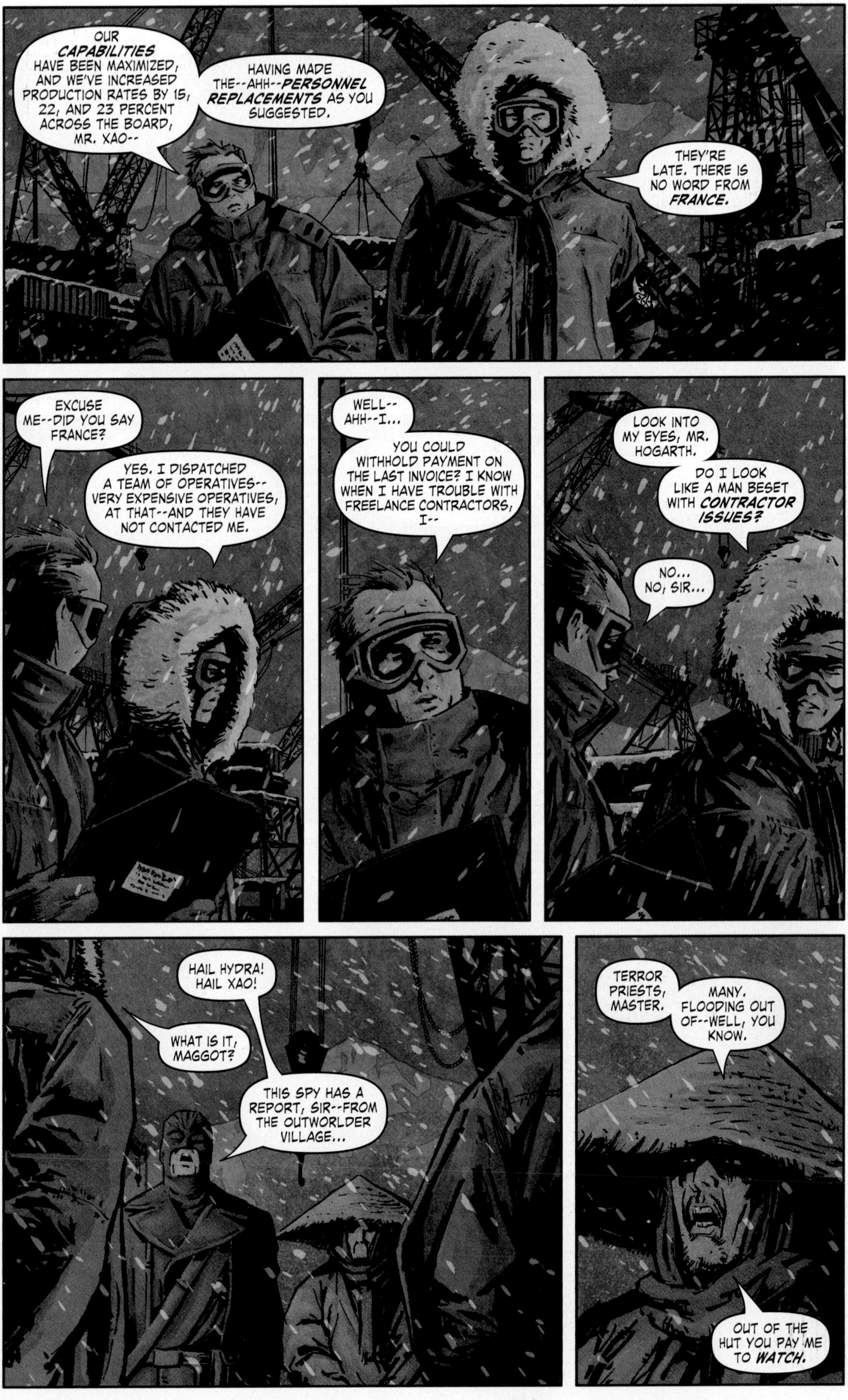
OUR CAPABILITIES HAVE BEEN MAXIMIZED, AND WE'VE INCREASED PRODUCTION RATES BY 15, 22, AND 23 PERCENT ACROSS THE BOARD, MR. XAO--
HAVING MADE THE--AHH--PERSONNEL REPLACEMENTS AS YOU SUGGESTED.
THEY'RE LATE. THERE IS NO WORD FROM FRANCE.
EXCUSE ME--DID YOU SAY FRANCE?
YES. I DISPATCHED A TEAM OF OPERATIVES--VERY EXPENSIVE OPERATIVES, AT THAT--AND THEY HAVE NOT CONTACTED ME.
WELL--AHH--I...
YOU COULD WITHHOLD PAYMENT ON THE LAST INVOICE? I KNOW WHEN I HAVE TROUBLE WITH FREELANCE CONTRACTORS, I--
LOOK INTO MY EYES, MR. HOGARTH.
DO I LOOK LIKE A MAN BESET WITH CONTRACTOR ISSUES?
NO... NO, SIR...
HAIL HYDRA! HAIL XAO!
WHAT IS IT, MAGGOT?
THIS SPY HAS A REPORT, SIR--FROM THE OUTWORLDER VILLAGE...
TERROR PRIESTS, MASTER.
MANY. FLOODING OUT OF--WELL, YOU KNOW.
OUT OF THE HUT YOU PAY ME TO WATCH.

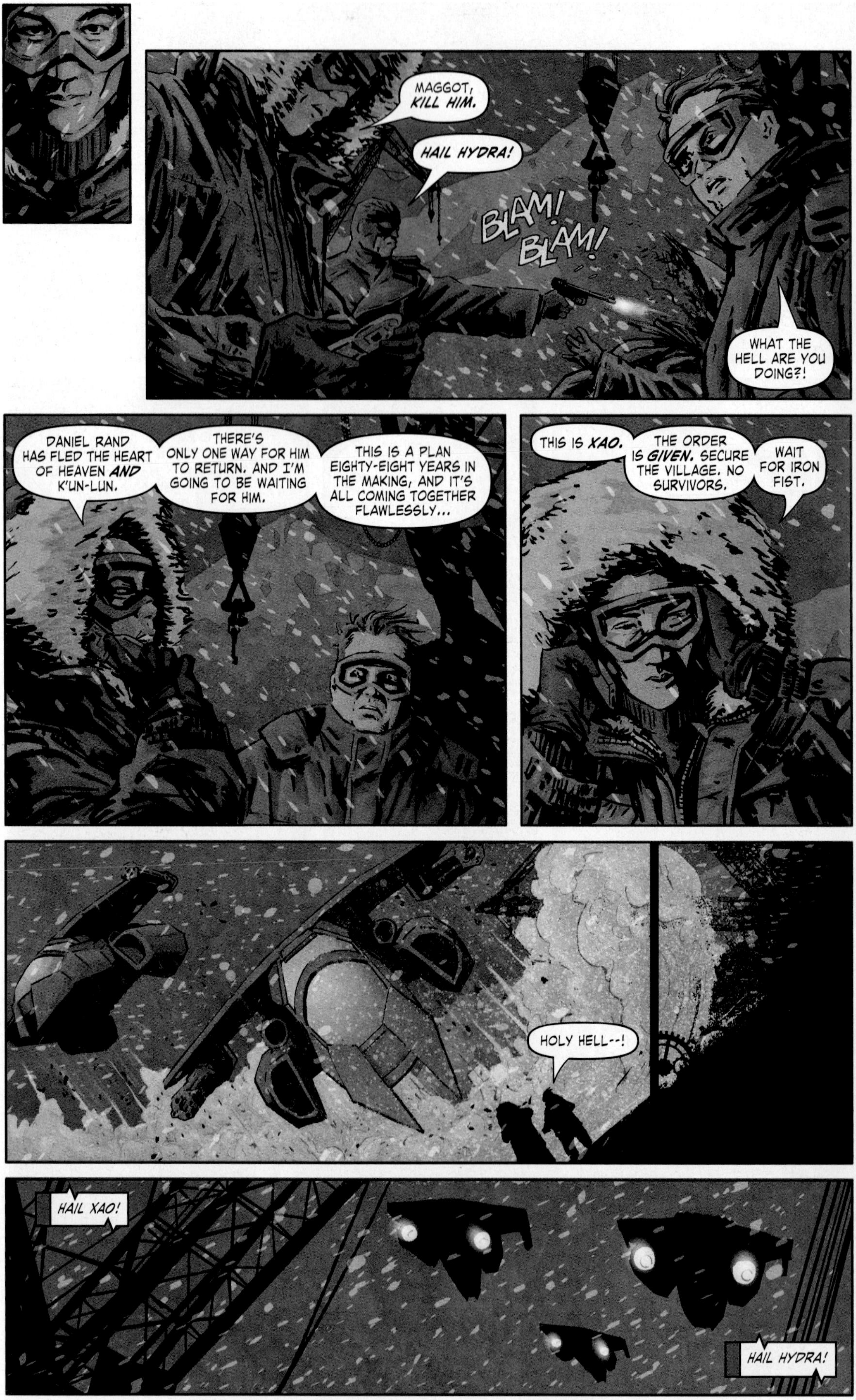
MAGGOT, KILL HIM.
HAIL HYDRA!
BLAM! BLAM!
WHAT THE HELL ARE YOU DOING?!
DANIEL RAND HAS FLED THE HEART OF HEAVEN AND K'UN-LUN.
THERE'S ONLY ONE WAY FOR HIM TO RETURN. AND I'M GOING TO BE WAITING FOR HIM.
THIS IS A PLAN EIGHTY-EIGHT YEARS IN THE MAKING, AND IT'S ALL COMING TOGETHER FLAWLESSLY...
THIS IS XAO.
THE ORDER IS GIVEN. SECURE THE VILLAGE. NO SURVIVORS.
WAIT FOR IRON FIST.
HOLY HELL--!
HAIL XAO!
HAIL HYDRA!

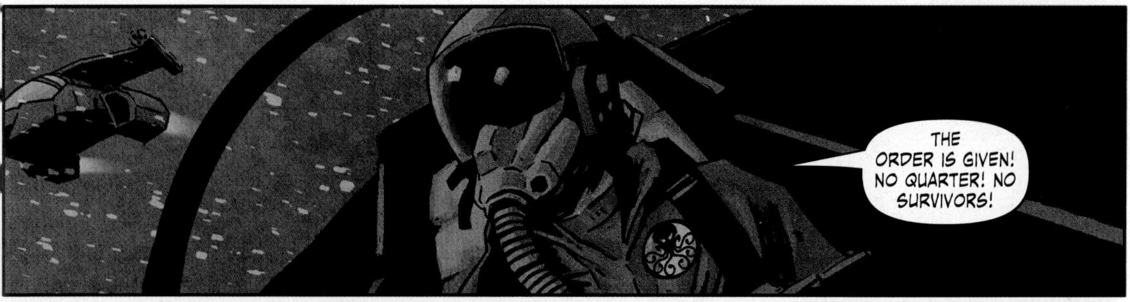
THE ORDER IS GIVEN! NO QUARTER! NO SURVIVORS!
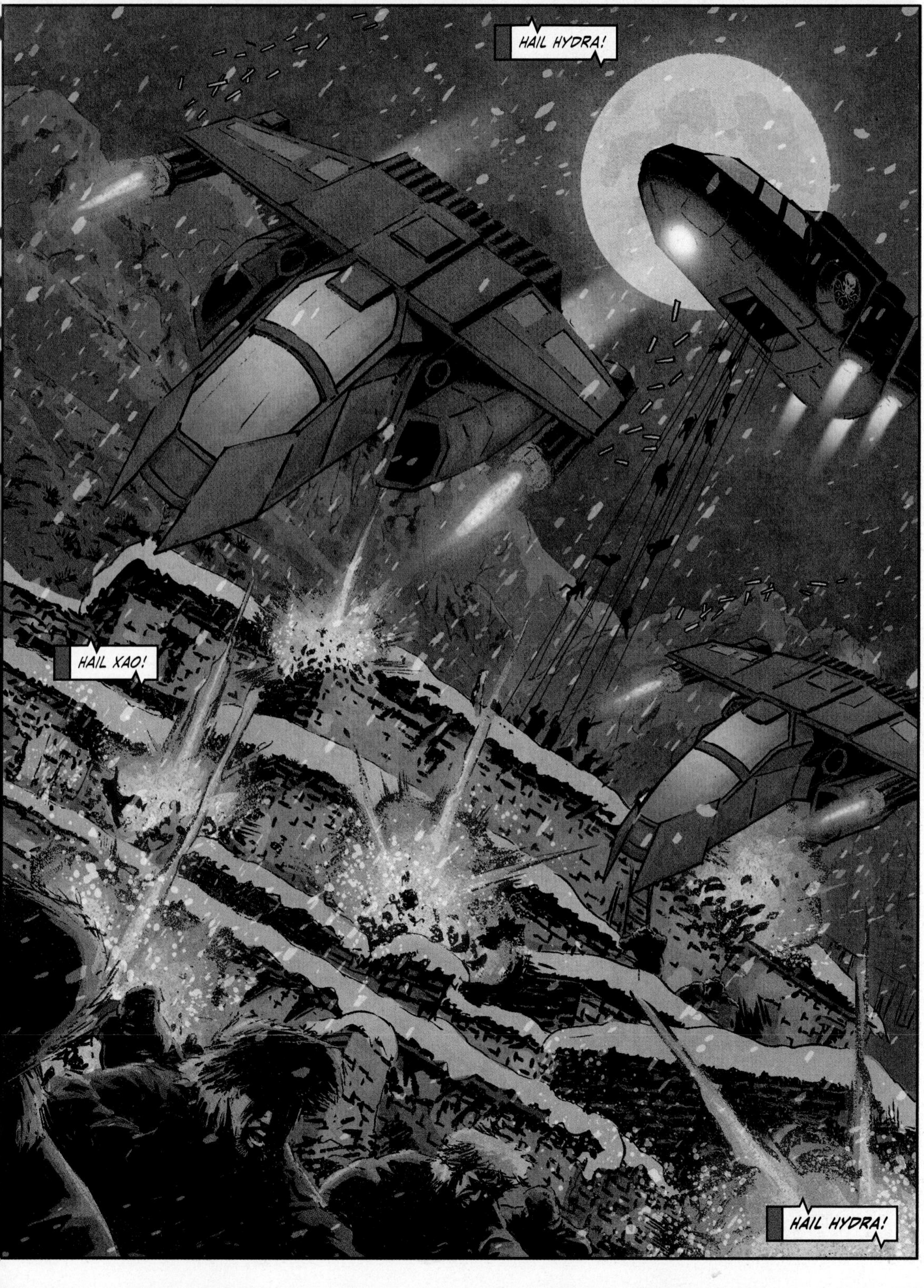
HAIL HYDRA!
HAIL XAO!
HAIL HYDRA!

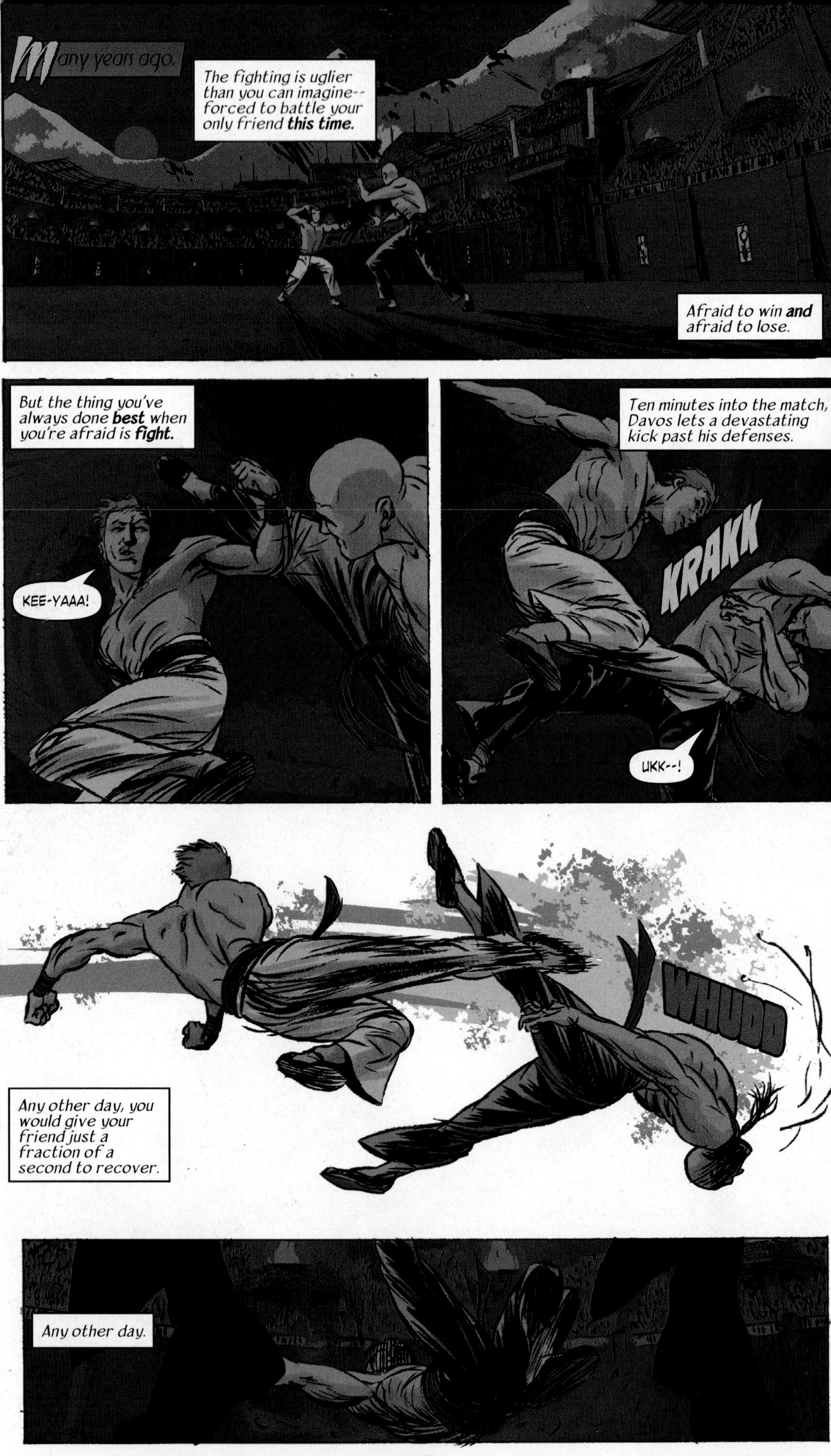
Many years ago.
The fighting is uglier than you can imagine-- forced to battle your only friend **this time.**
Afraid to win **and** afraid to lose.
But the thing you've always done **best** when you're afraid is **fight.**
KEE-YAAA!
Ten minutes into the match, Davos lets a devastating kick past his defenses.
KRAKK
UKK--!
WHUDD
Any other day, you would give your friend just a fraction of a second to recover.
Any other day.

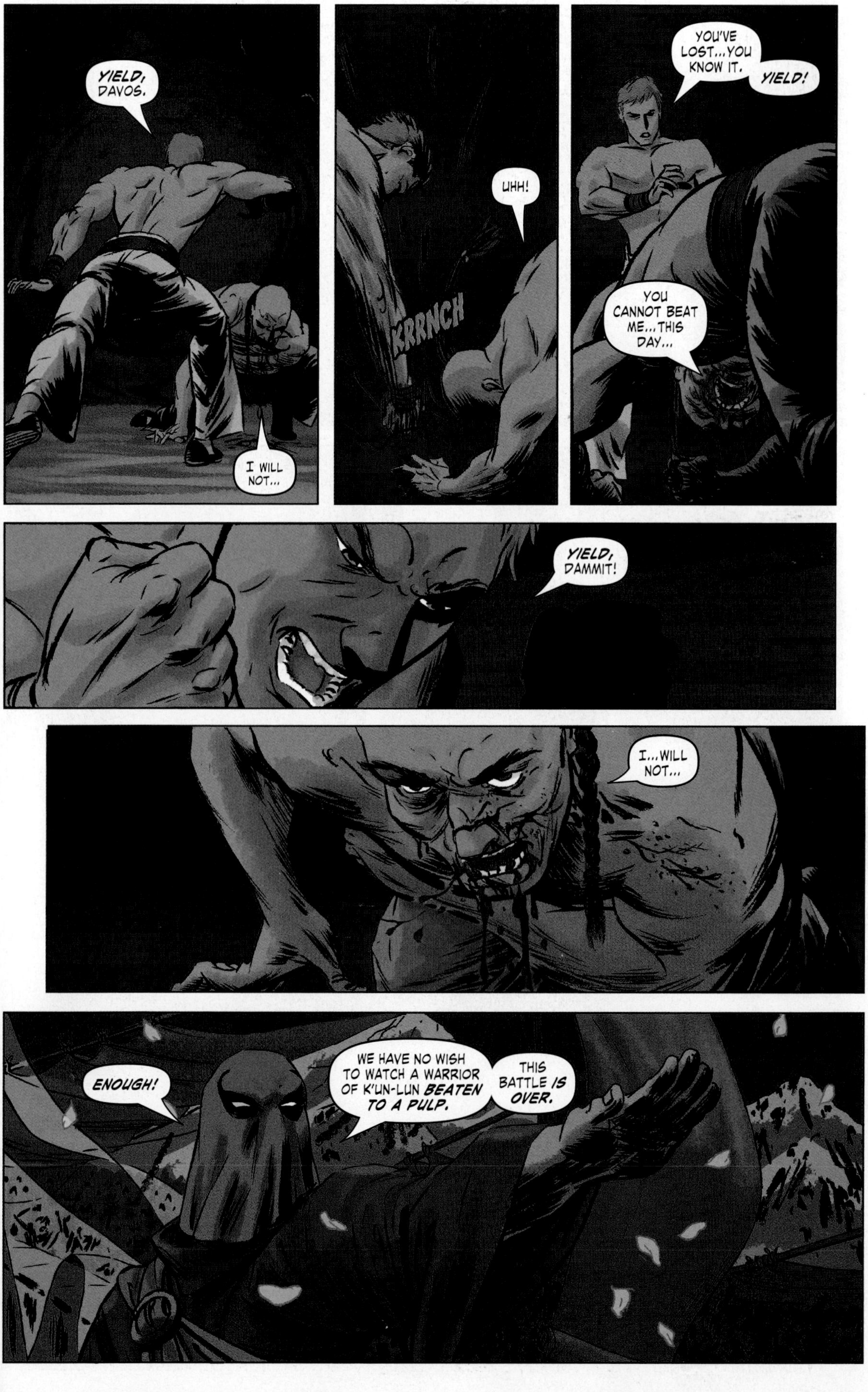
YIELD, DAVOS.
I WILL NOT...
UHH!
KRRNCH
YOU'VE LOST...YOU KNOW IT.
YIELD!
YOU CANNOT BEAT ME...THIS DAY...
YIELD, DAMMIT!
I...WILL NOT...
ENOUGH!
WE HAVE NO WISH TO WATCH A WARRIOR OF K'UN-LUN BEATEN TO A PULP.
THIS BATTLE IS OVER.

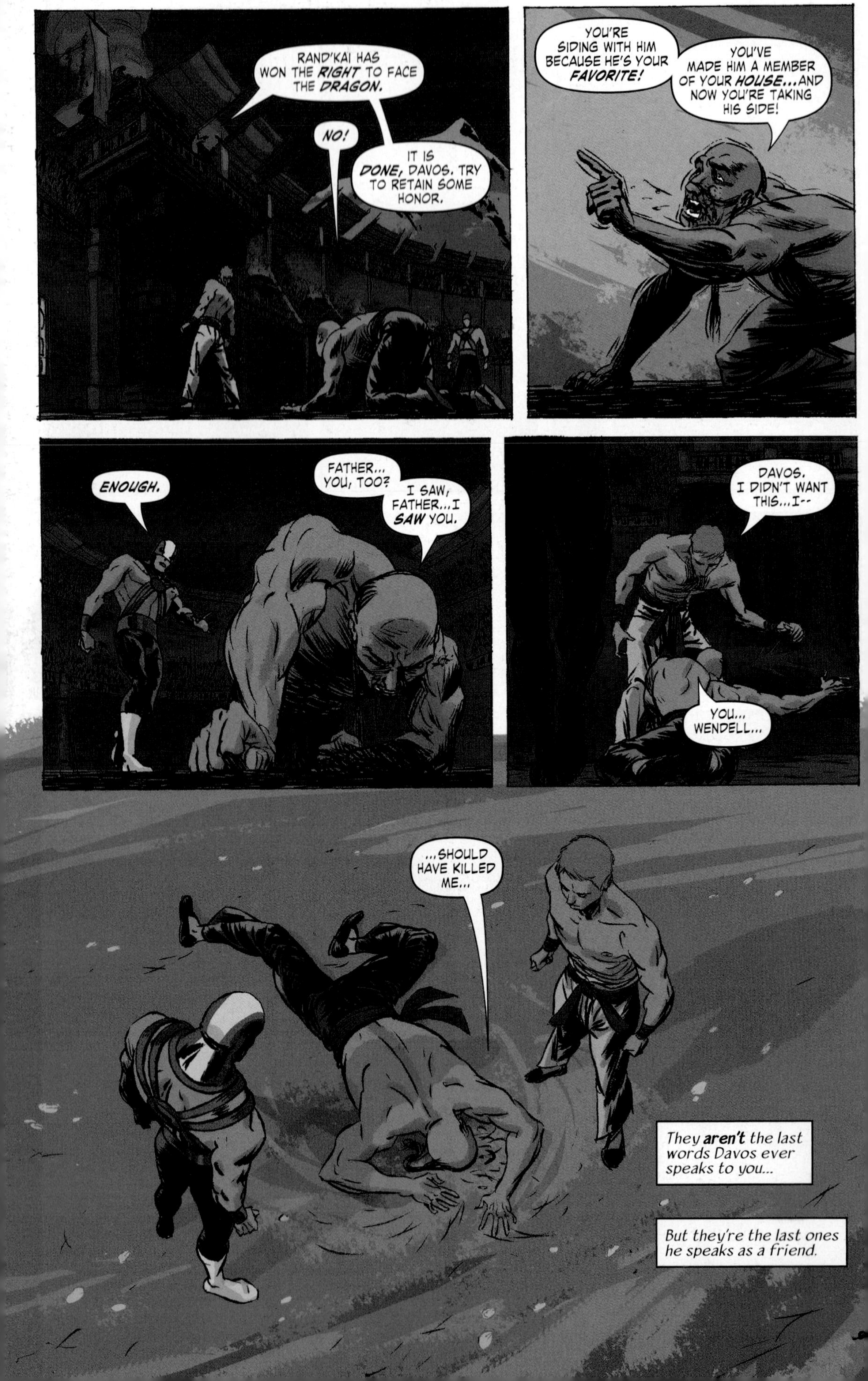
RAND'KAI HAS WON THE **RIGHT** TO FACE THE **DRAGON.**
NO!
IT IS **DONE,** DAVOS. TRY TO RETAIN SOME HONOR.
YOU'RE SIDING WITH HIM BECAUSE HE'S YOUR **FAVORITE!**
YOU'VE MADE HIM A MEMBER OF YOUR **HOUSE...** AND NOW YOU'RE TAKING HIS SIDE!
ENOUGH.
FATHER... YOU, TOO?
I SAW, FATHER... I **SAW** YOU.
DAVOS. I DIDN'T WANT THIS... I--
YOU... WENDELL...
...SHOULD HAVE KILLED ME...
*They **aren't** the last words Davos ever speaks to you...*
But they're the last ones he speaks as a friend.

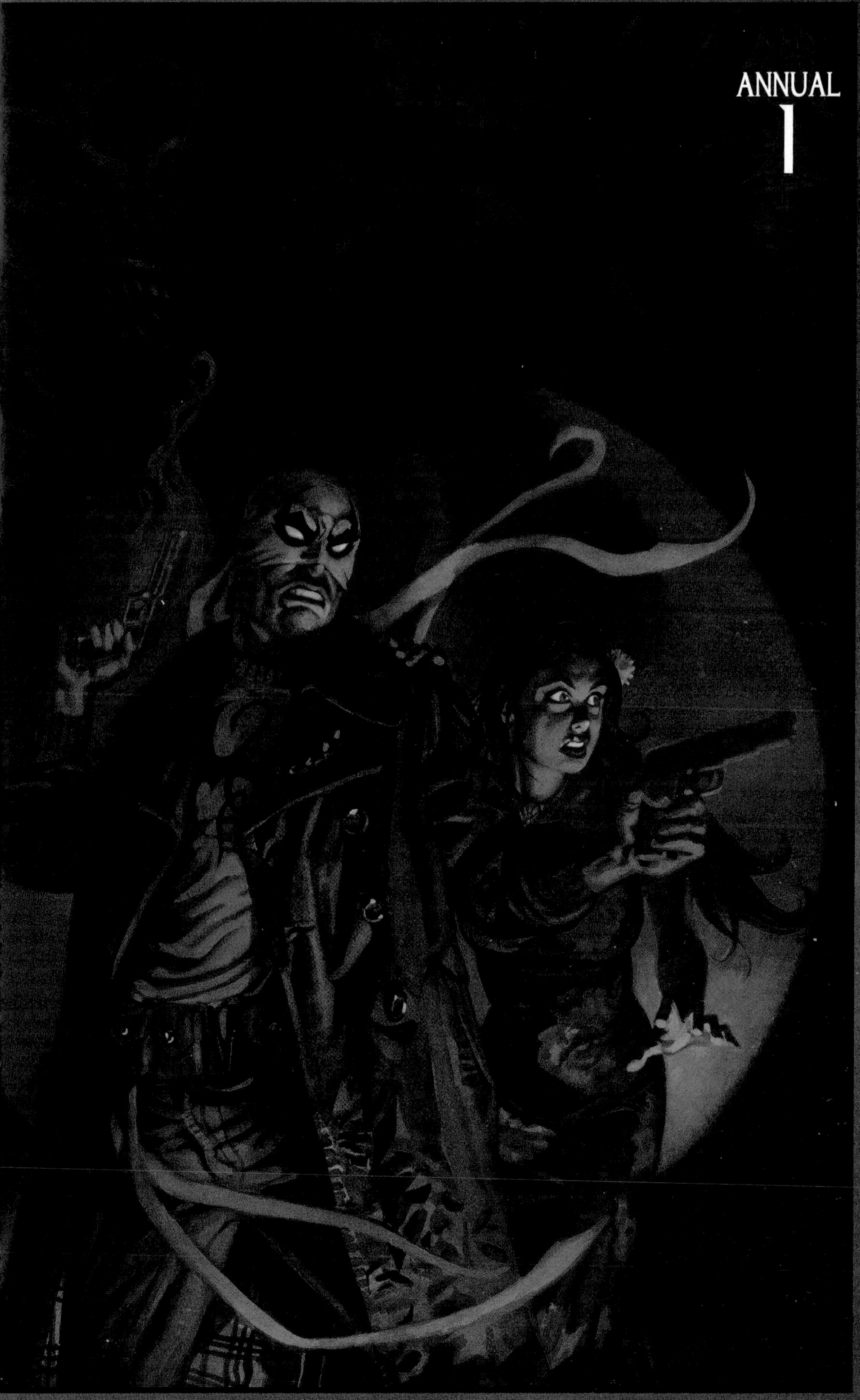
ANNUAL
1

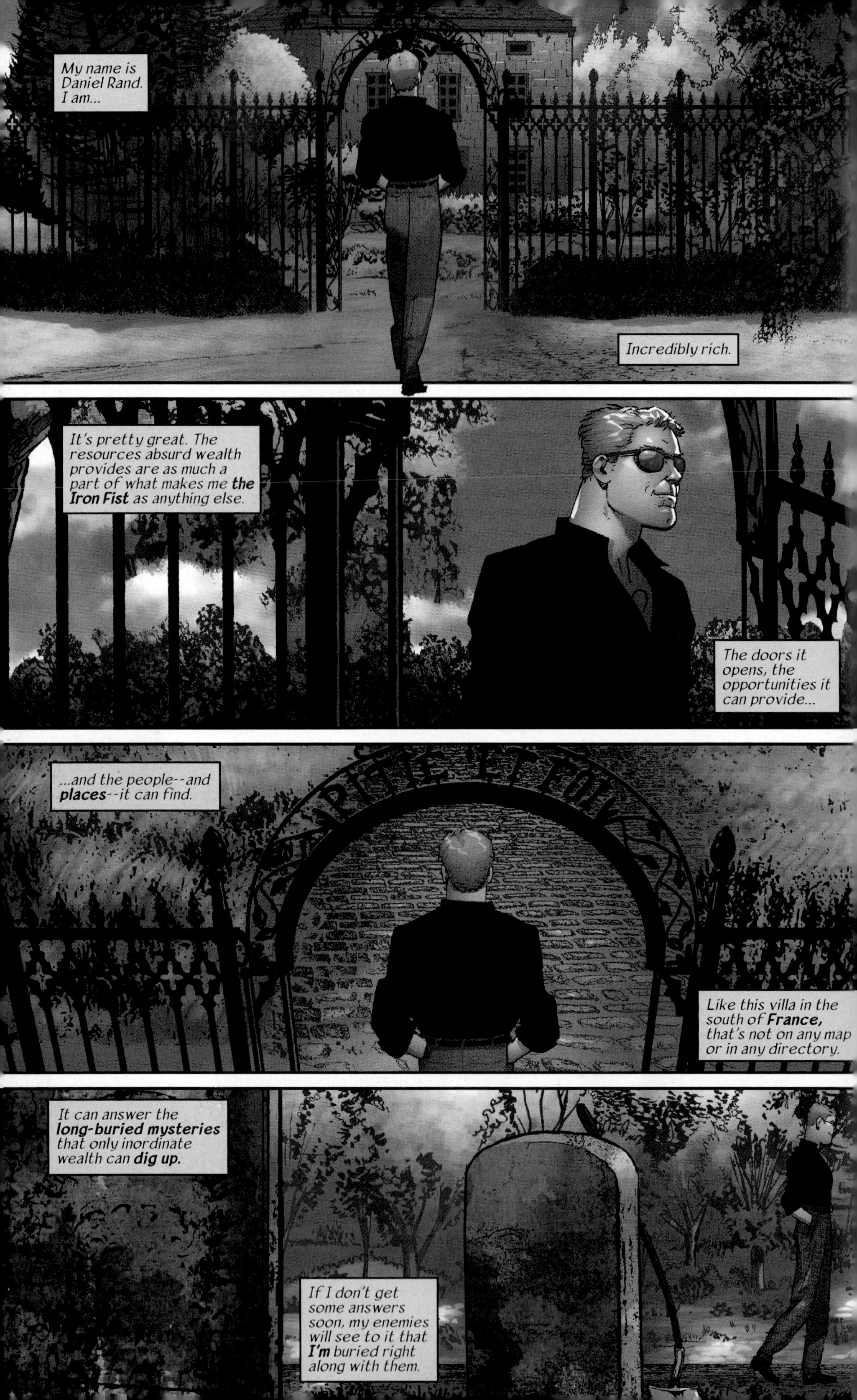
My name is Daniel Rand. I am...
Incredibly rich.
It's pretty great. The resources absurd wealth provides are as much a part of what makes me **the Iron Fist** as anything else.
The doors it opens, the opportunities it can provide...
...and the people--and **places**--it can find.
Like this villa in the south of **France,** that's not on any map or in any directory.
It can answer the **long-buried mysteries** that only inordinate wealth can **dig up.**
If I don't get some answers soon, my enemies will see to it that **I'm** buried right along with them.

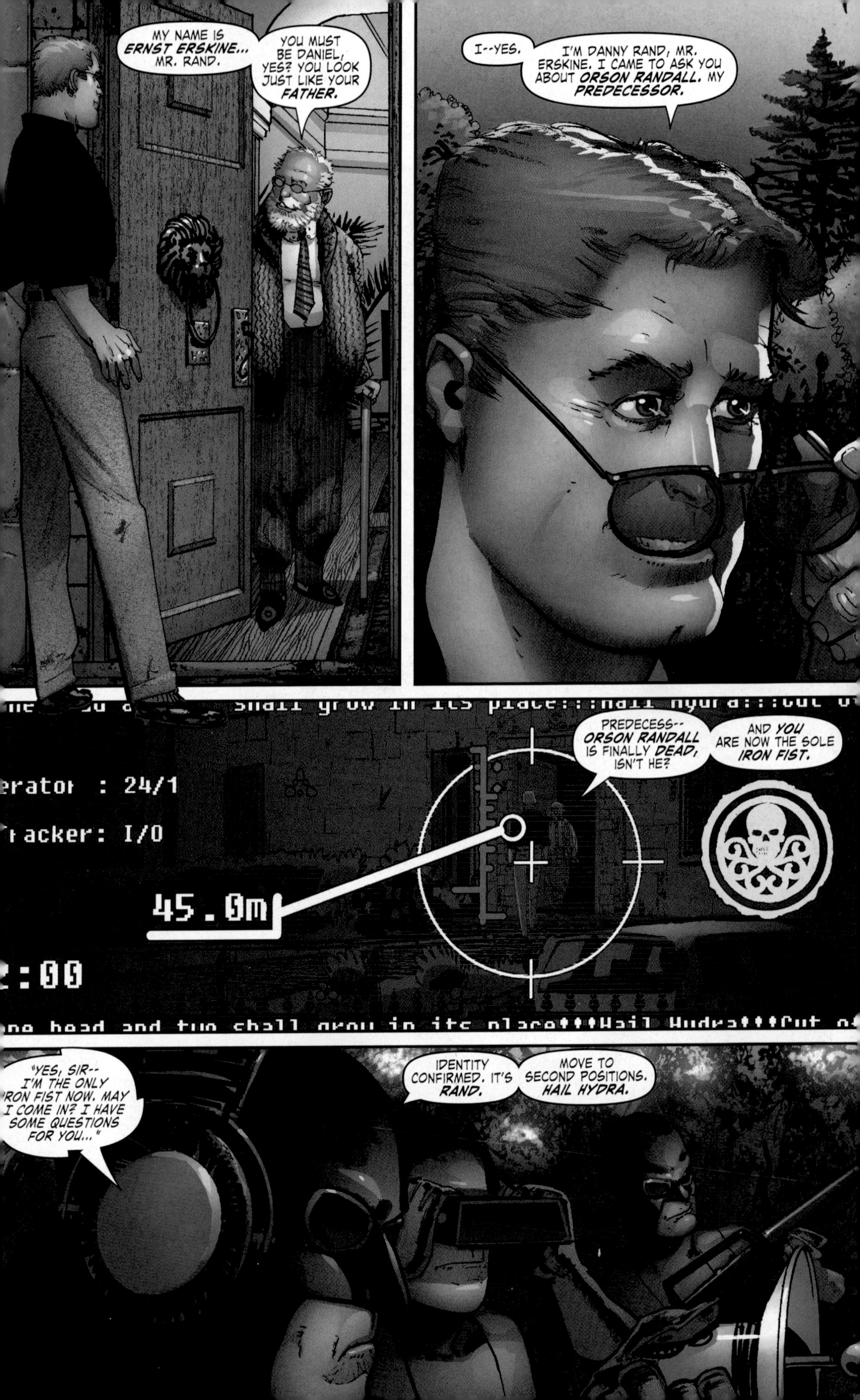
MY NAME IS ERNST ERSKINE... MR. RAND.
YOU MUST BE DANIEL, YES? YOU LOOK JUST LIKE YOUR FATHER.
I--YES.
I'M DANNY RAND, MR. ERSKINE. I CAME TO ASK YOU ABOUT ORSON RANDALL. MY PREDECESSOR.
erator : 24/1
racker: I/O
45.0m
:00
PREDECESS-- ORSON RANDALL IS FINALLY DEAD, ISN'T HE?
AND YOU ARE NOW THE SOLE IRON FIST.
"YES, SIR-- I'M THE ONLY IRON FIST NOW. MAY I COME IN? I HAVE SOME QUESTIONS FOR YOU..."
IDENTITY CONFIRMED. IT'S RAND.
MOVE TO SECOND POSITIONS. HAIL HYDRA.

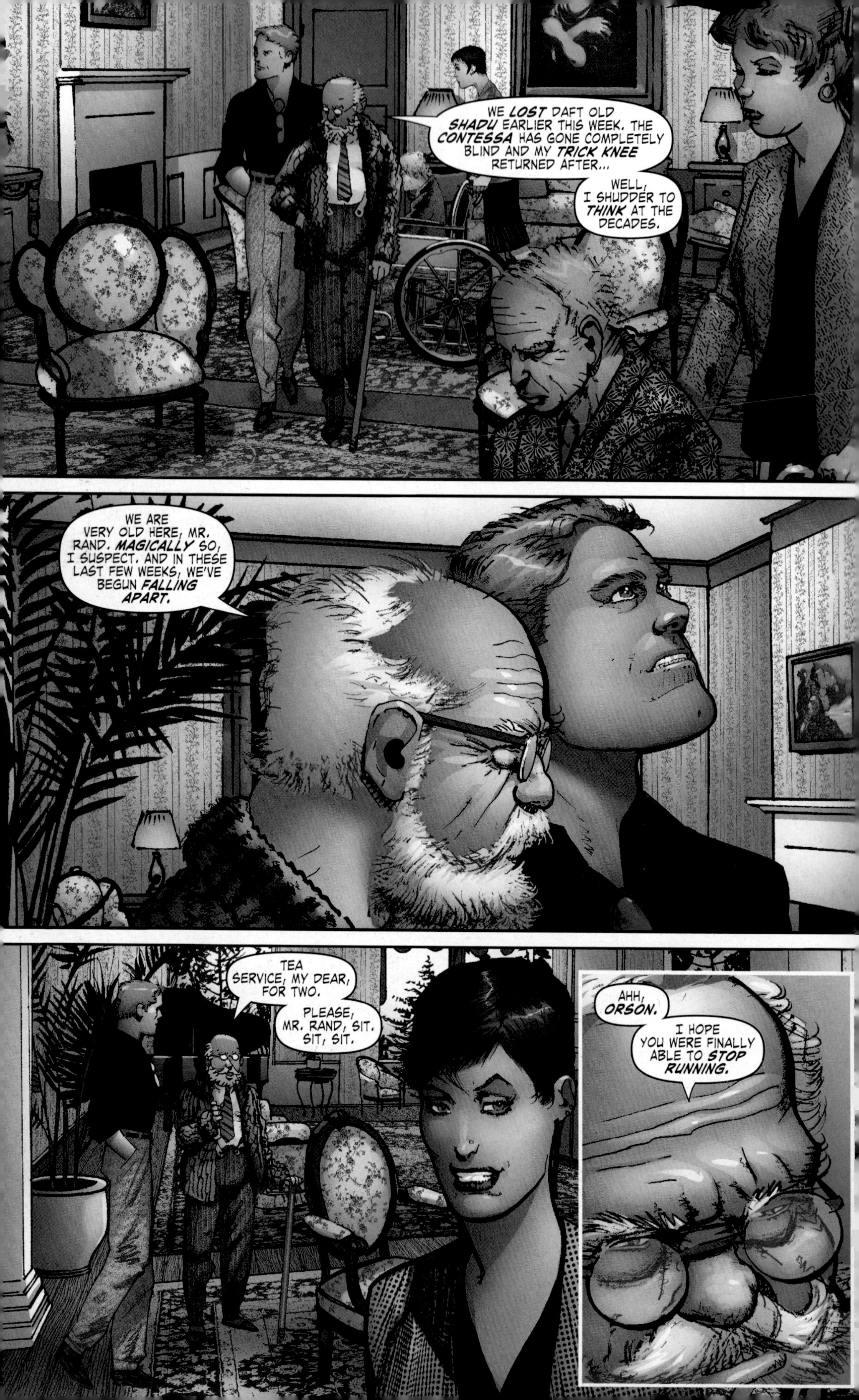
WE LOST DAFT OLD SHADU EARLIER THIS WEEK. THE CONTESSA HAS GONE COMPLETELY BLIND AND MY TRICK KNEE RETURNED AFTER...
WELL, I SHUDDER TO THINK AT THE DECADES.
WE ARE VERY OLD HERE, MR. RAND. MAGICALLY SO, I SUSPECT. AND IN THESE LAST FEW WEEKS, WE'VE BEGUN FALLING APART.
TEA SERVICE, MY DEAR, FOR TWO.
PLEASE, MR. RAND, SIT. SIT, SIT.
AHH, ORSON.
I HOPE YOU WERE FINALLY ABLE TO STOP RUNNING.

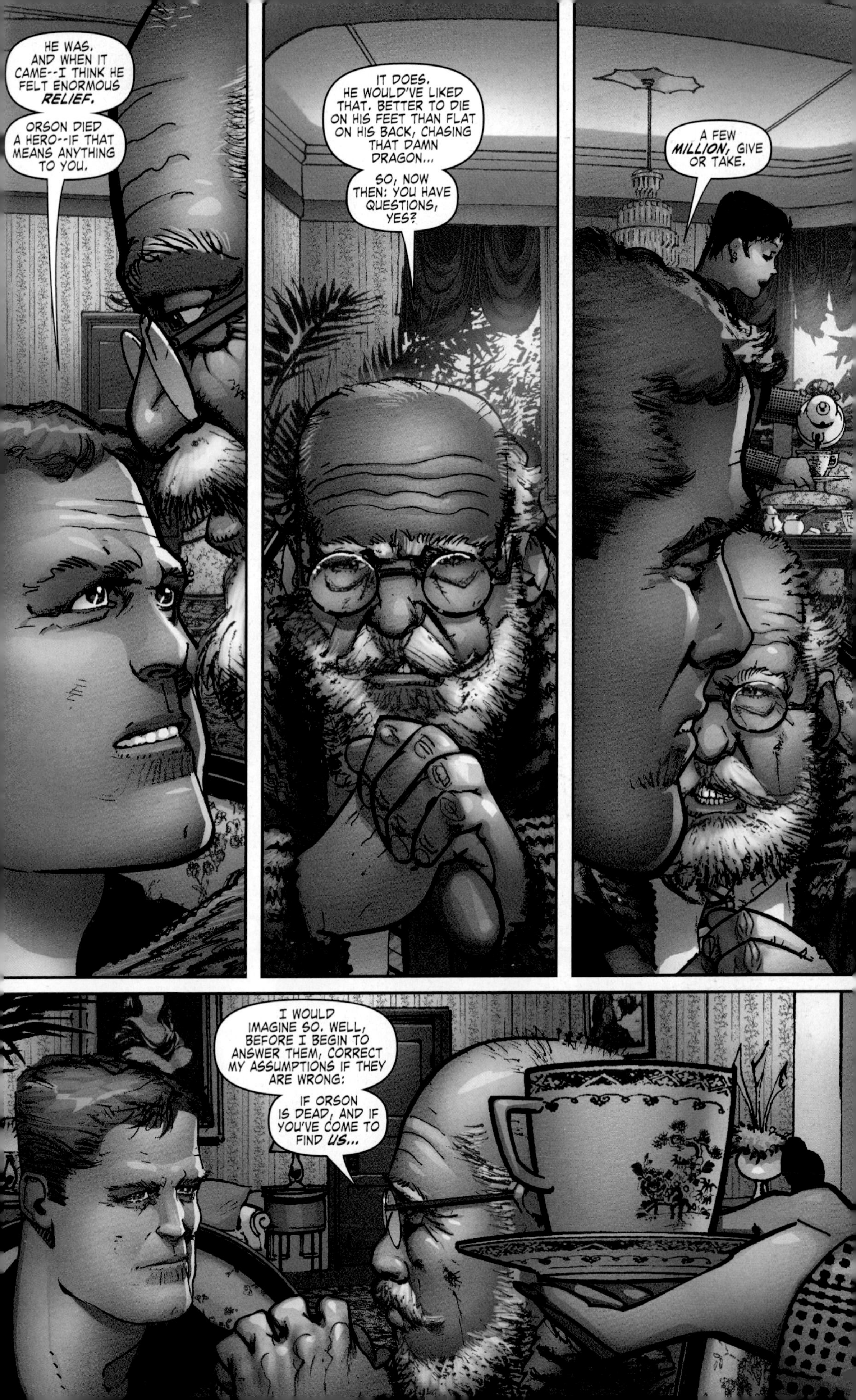
HE WAS. AND WHEN IT CAME--I THINK HE FELT ENORMOUS ***RELIEF.***
ORSON DIED A HERO--IF THAT MEANS ANYTHING TO YOU.
IT DOES. HE WOULD'VE LIKED THAT. BETTER TO DIE ON HIS FEET THAN FLAT ON HIS BACK, CHASING THAT DAMN DRAGON...
SO, NOW THEN: YOU HAVE QUESTIONS, YES?
A FEW ***MILLION***, GIVE OR TAKE.
I WOULD IMAGINE SO. WELL, BEFORE I BEGIN TO ANSWER THEM, CORRECT MY ASSUMPTIONS IF THEY ARE WRONG:
IF ORSON IS DEAD, AND IF YOU'VE COME TO FIND ***US...***

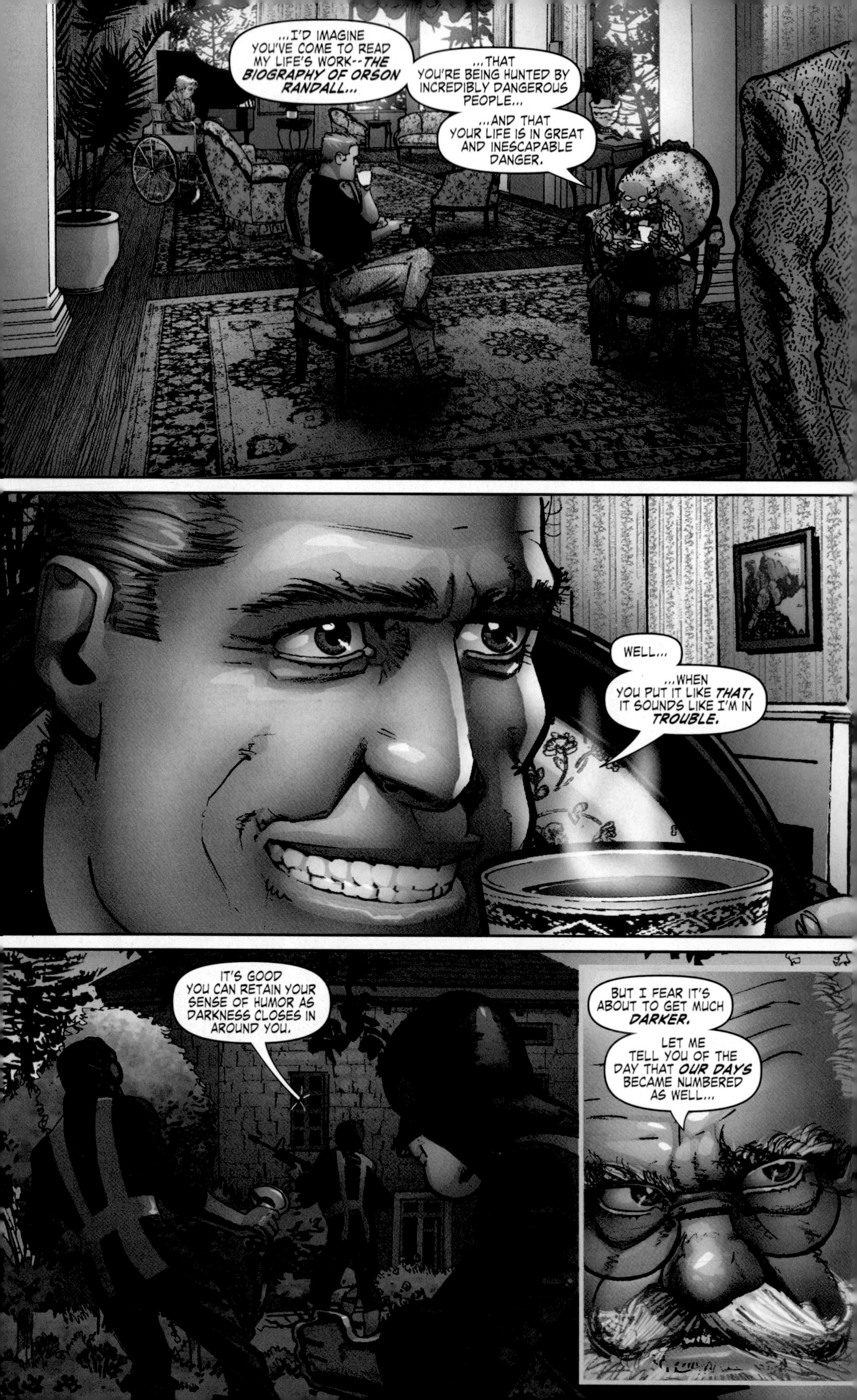
...I'D IMAGINE YOU'VE COME TO READ MY LIFE'S WORK--*THE BIOGRAPHY OF ORSON RANDALL...*
...THAT YOU'RE BEING HUNTED BY INCREDIBLY DANGEROUS PEOPLE...
...AND THAT YOUR LIFE IS IN GREAT AND INESCAPABLE DANGER.
WELL...
...WHEN YOU PUT IT LIKE *THAT,* IT SOUNDS LIKE I'M IN *TROUBLE.*
IT'S GOOD YOU CAN RETAIN YOUR SENSE OF HUMOR AS DARKNESS CLOSES IN AROUND YOU.
BUT I FEAR IT'S ABOUT TO GET MUCH *DARKER.*
LET ME TELL YOU OF THE DAY THAT *OUR DAYS* BECAME NUMBERED AS WELL...

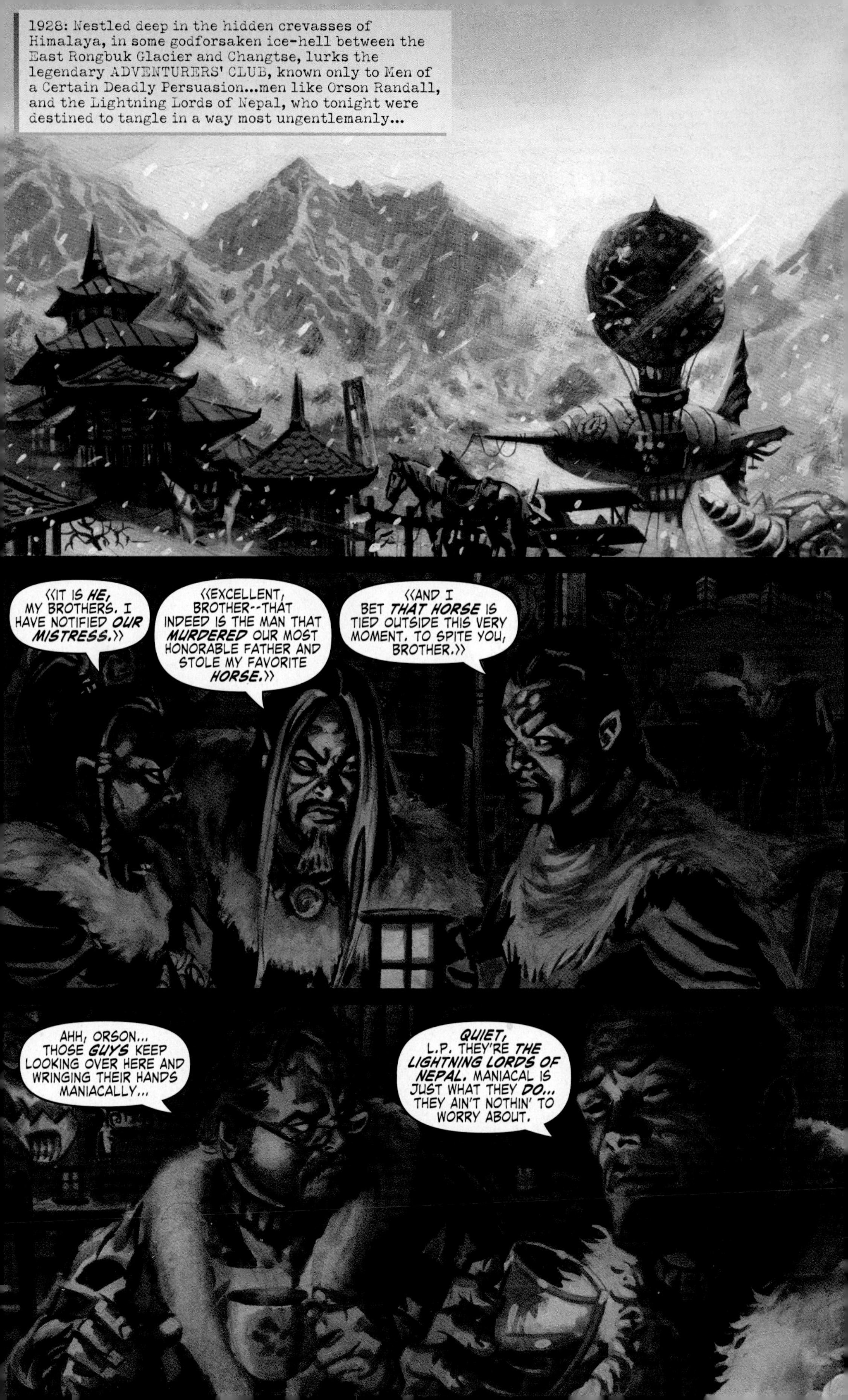
1928: Nestled deep in the hidden crevasses of Himalaya, in some godforsaken ice-hell between the East Rongbuk Glacier and Changtse, lurks the legendary ADVENTURERS' CLUB, known only to Men of a Certain Deadly Persuasion...men like Orson Randall, and the Lightning Lords of Nepal, who tonight were destined to tangle in a way most ungentlemanly...
<<IT IS *HE,* MY BROTHERS. I HAVE NOTIFIED ***OUR MISTRESS.***>>
<<EXCELLENT, BROTHER--THAT INDEED IS THE MAN THAT ***MURDERED*** OUR MOST HONORABLE FATHER AND STOLE MY FAVORITE ***HORSE.***>>
<<AND I BET ***THAT HORSE*** IS TIED OUTSIDE THIS VERY MOMENT. TO SPITE YOU, BROTHER.>>
AHH, ORSON... THOSE ***GUYS*** KEEP LOOKING OVER HERE AND WRINGING THEIR HANDS MANIACALLY...
QUIET, L.P. THEY'RE ***THE LIGHTNING LORDS OF NEPAL.*** MANIACAL IS JUST WHAT THEY ***DO...*** THEY AIN'T NOTHIN' TO WORRY ABOUT.

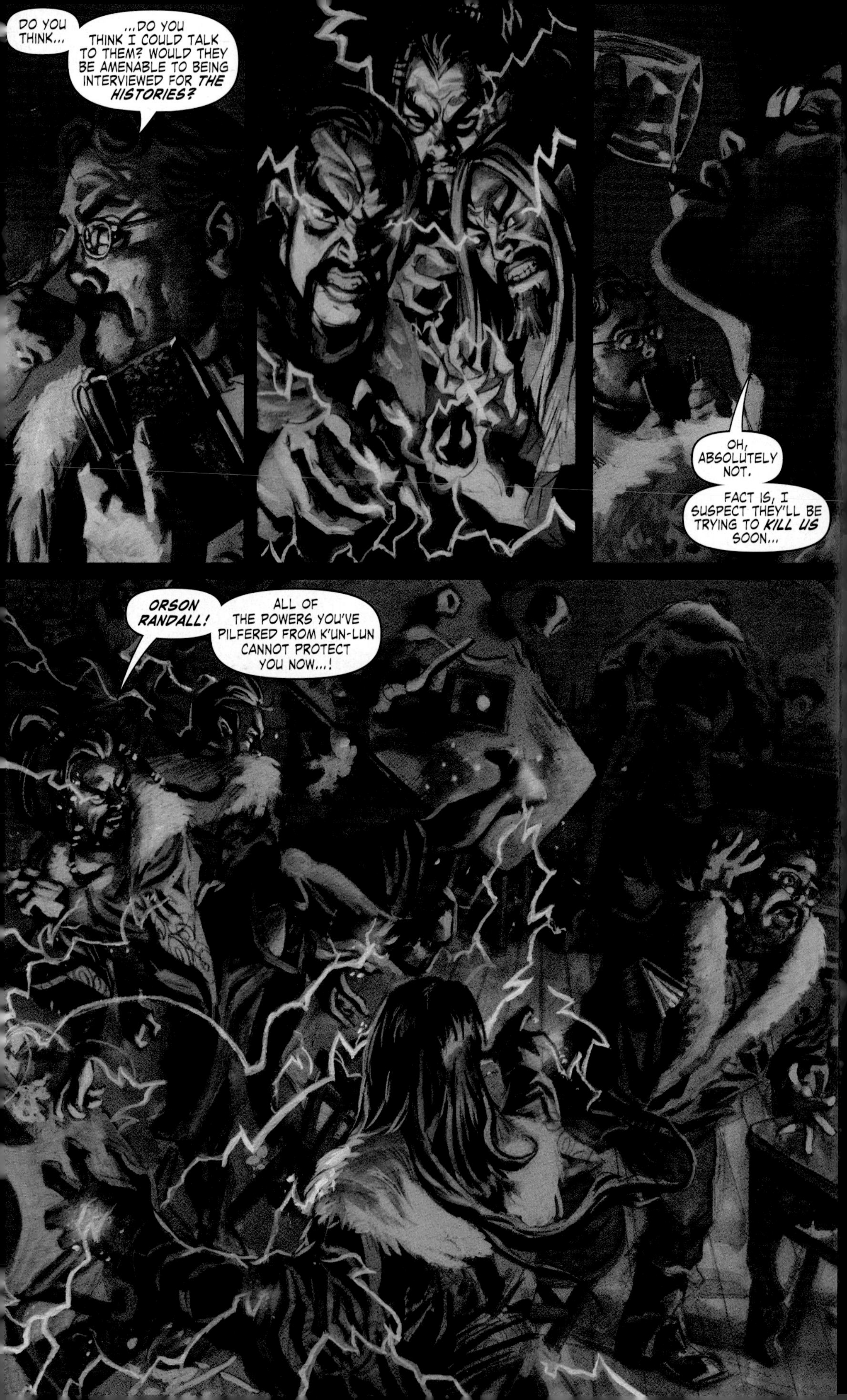
DO YOU THINK...
...DO YOU THINK I COULD TALK TO THEM? WOULD THEY BE AMENABLE TO BEING INTERVIEWED FOR *THE HISTORIES?*
OH, ABSOLUTELY NOT.
FACT IS, I SUSPECT THEY'LL BE TRYING TO *KILL US* SOON...
ORSON RANDALL!
ALL OF THE POWERS YOU'VE PILFERED FROM K'UN-LUN CANNOT PROTECT YOU NOW...!

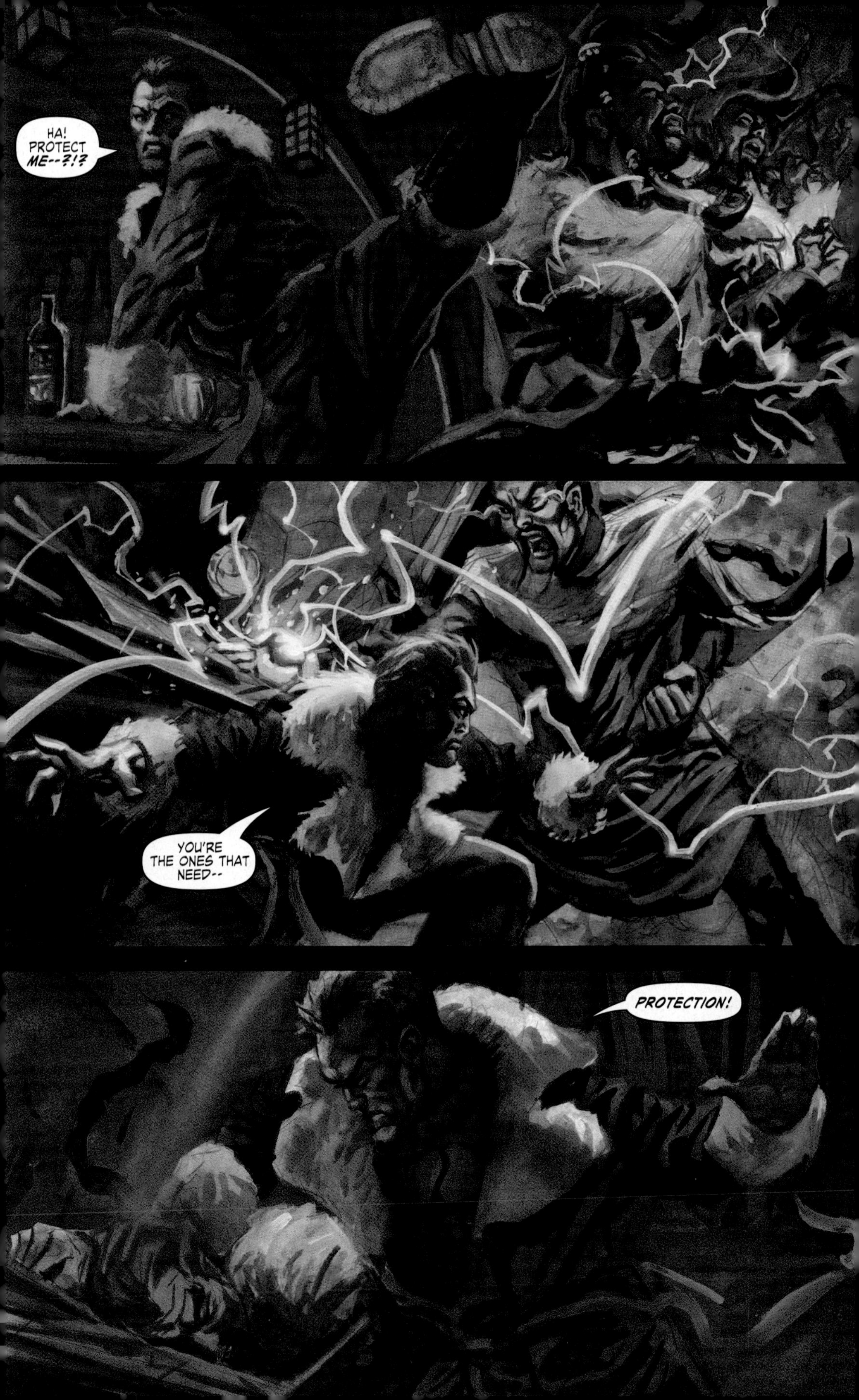
HA! PROTECT ME--?!?
YOU'RE THE ONES THAT NEED--
PROTECTION!

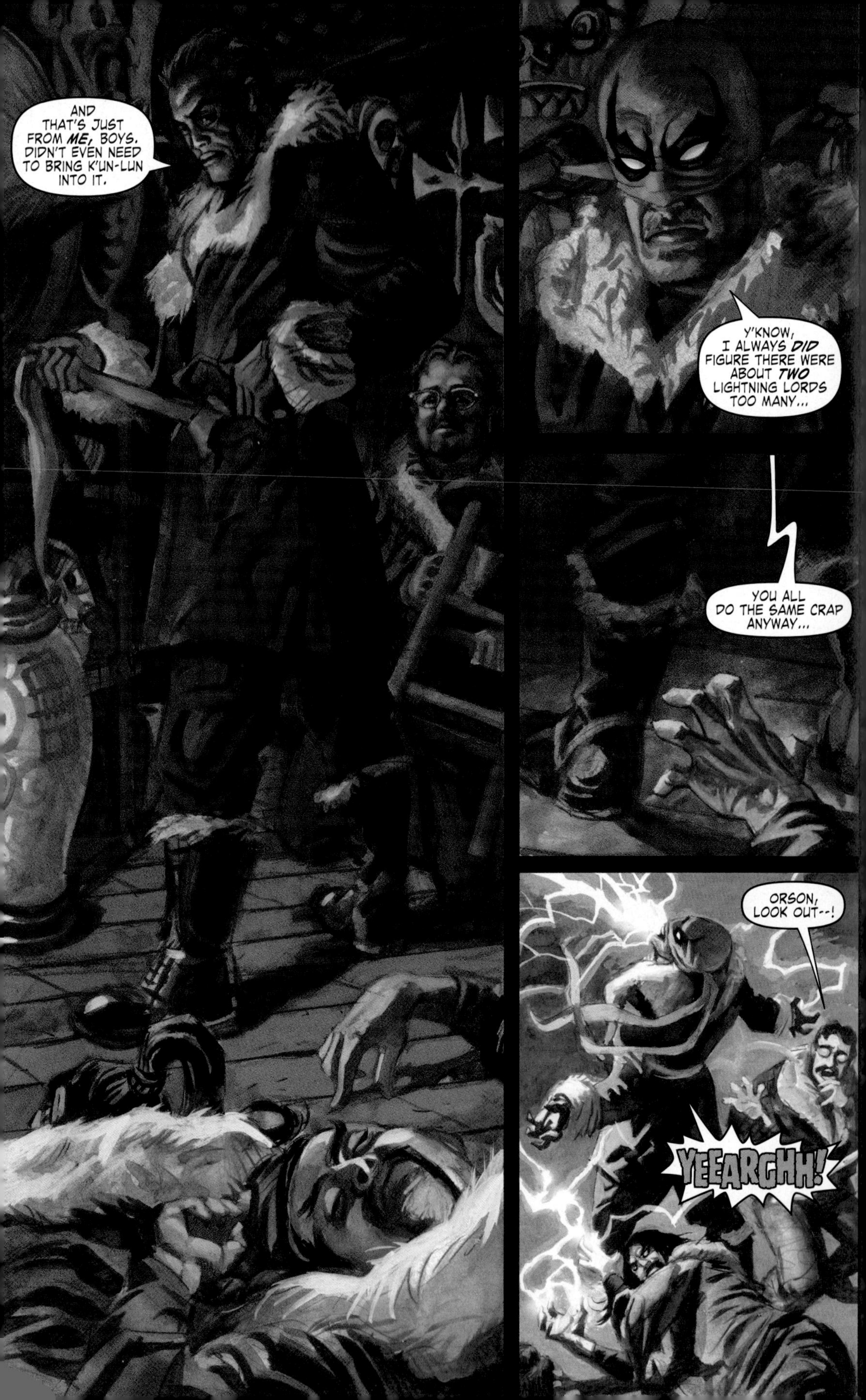
AND THAT'S JUST FROM *ME,* BOYS. DIDN'T EVEN NEED TO BRING K'UN-LUN INTO IT.
Y'KNOW, I ALWAYS *DID* FIGURE THERE WERE ABOUT *TWO* LIGHTNING LORDS TOO MANY...
YOU ALL DO THE SAME CRAP ANYWAY...
ORSON, LOOK OUT--!
YEEARGHH!

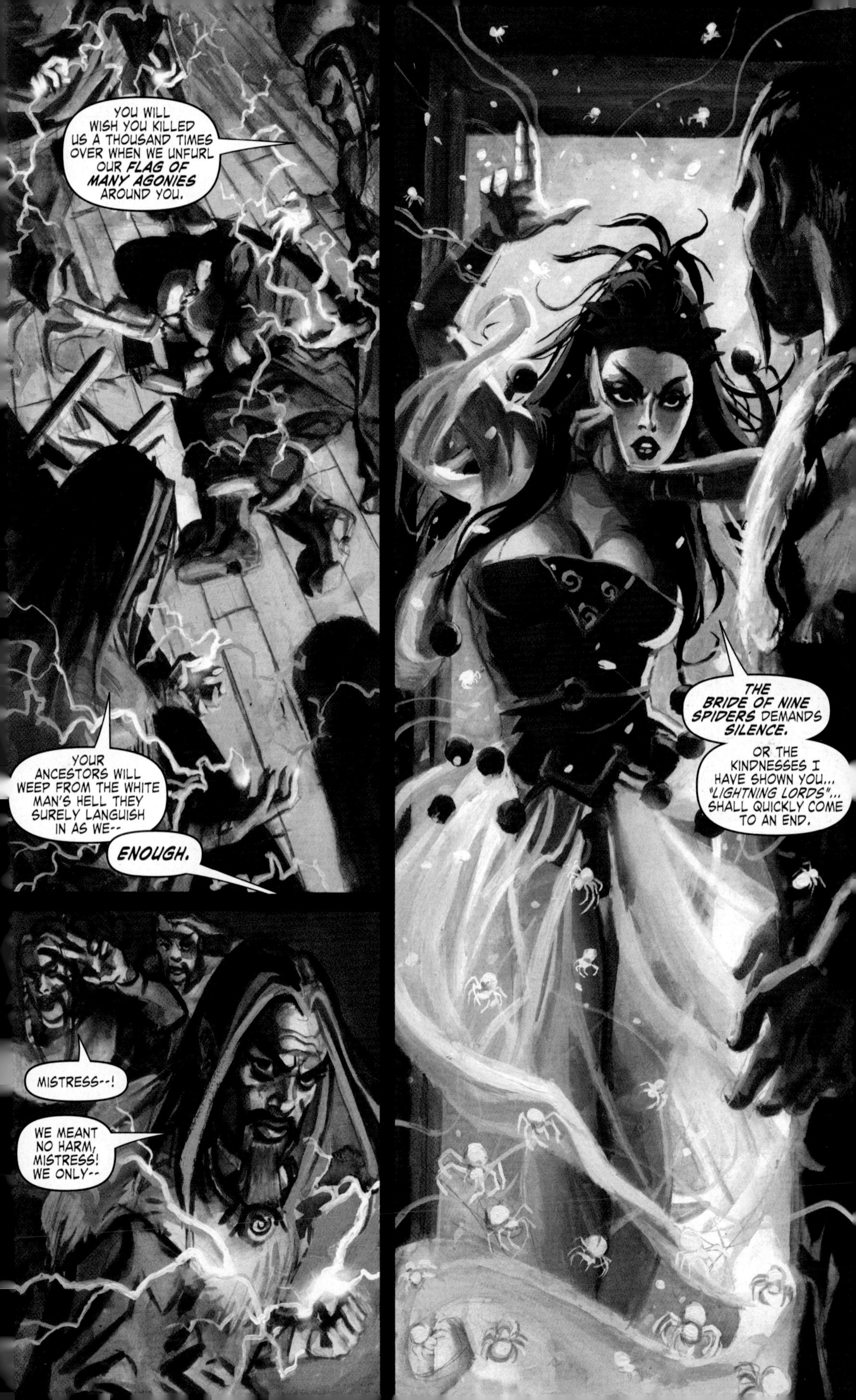
YOU WILL WISH YOU KILLED US A THOUSAND TIMES OVER WHEN WE UNFURL OUR *FLAG OF MANY AGONIES* AROUND YOU.
YOUR ANCESTORS WILL WEEP FROM THE WHITE MAN'S HELL THEY SURELY LANGUISH IN AS WE--
ENOUGH.
MISTRESS--!
WE MEANT NO HARM, MISTRESS! WE ONLY--
THE BRIDE OF NINE SPIDERS DEMANDS *SILENCE.*
OR THE KINDNESSES I HAVE SHOWN YOU... *"LIGHTNING LORDS"*... SHALL QUICKLY COME TO AN END.

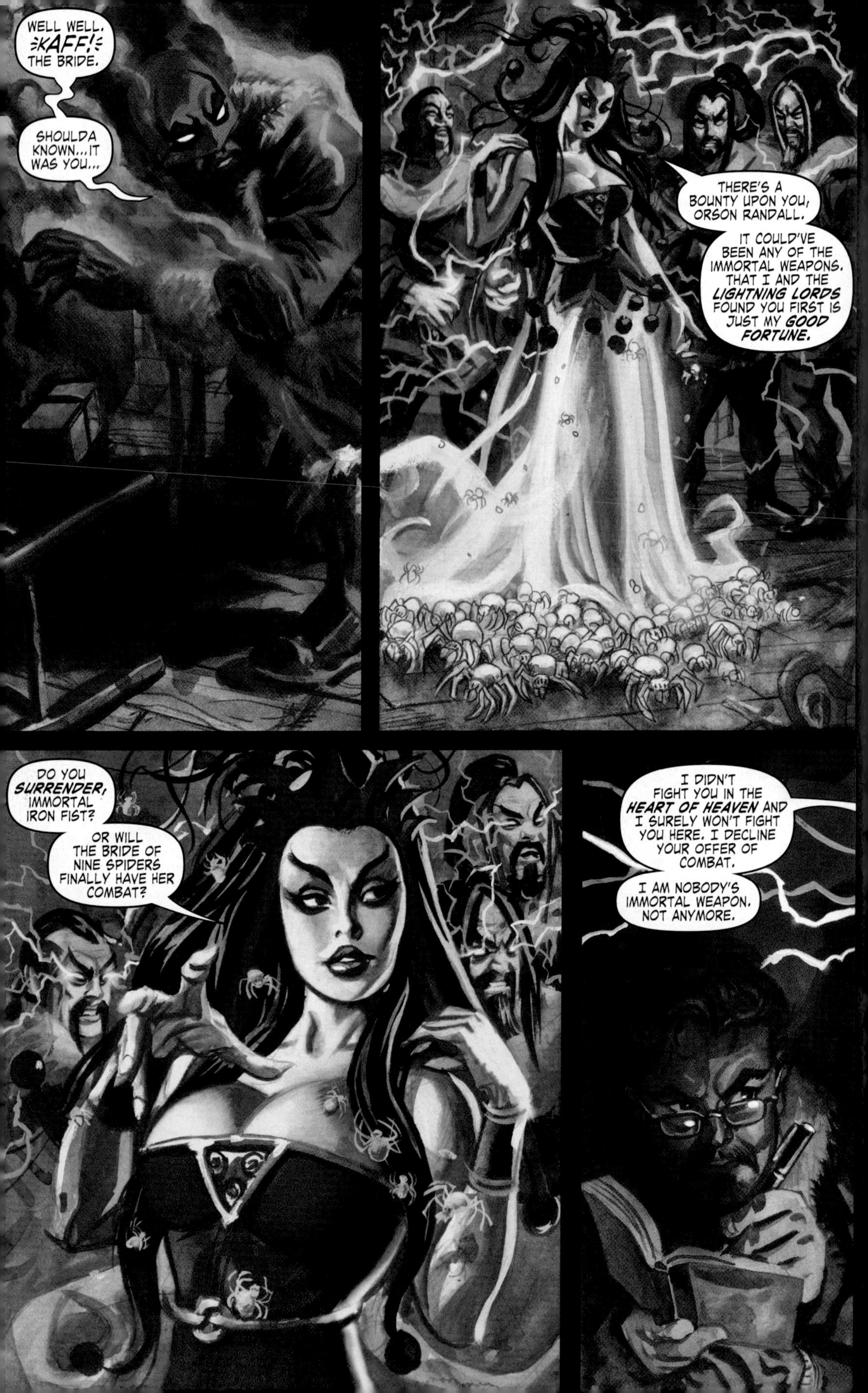
WELL WELL. *KAFF!* THE BRIDE.
SHOULDA KNOWN...IT WAS YOU...
THERE'S A BOUNTY UPON YOU, ORSON RANDALL.
IT COULD'VE BEEN ANY OF THE IMMORTAL WEAPONS. THAT I AND THE **LIGHTNING LORDS** FOUND YOU FIRST IS JUST MY **GOOD FORTUNE.**
DO YOU **SURRENDER,** IMMORTAL IRON FIST?
OR WILL THE BRIDE OF NINE SPIDERS FINALLY HAVE HER COMBAT?
I DIDN'T FIGHT YOU IN THE **HEART OF HEAVEN** AND I SURELY WON'T FIGHT YOU HERE. I DECLINE YOUR OFFER OF COMBAT.
I AM NOBODY'S IMMORTAL WEAPON. NOT ANYMORE.

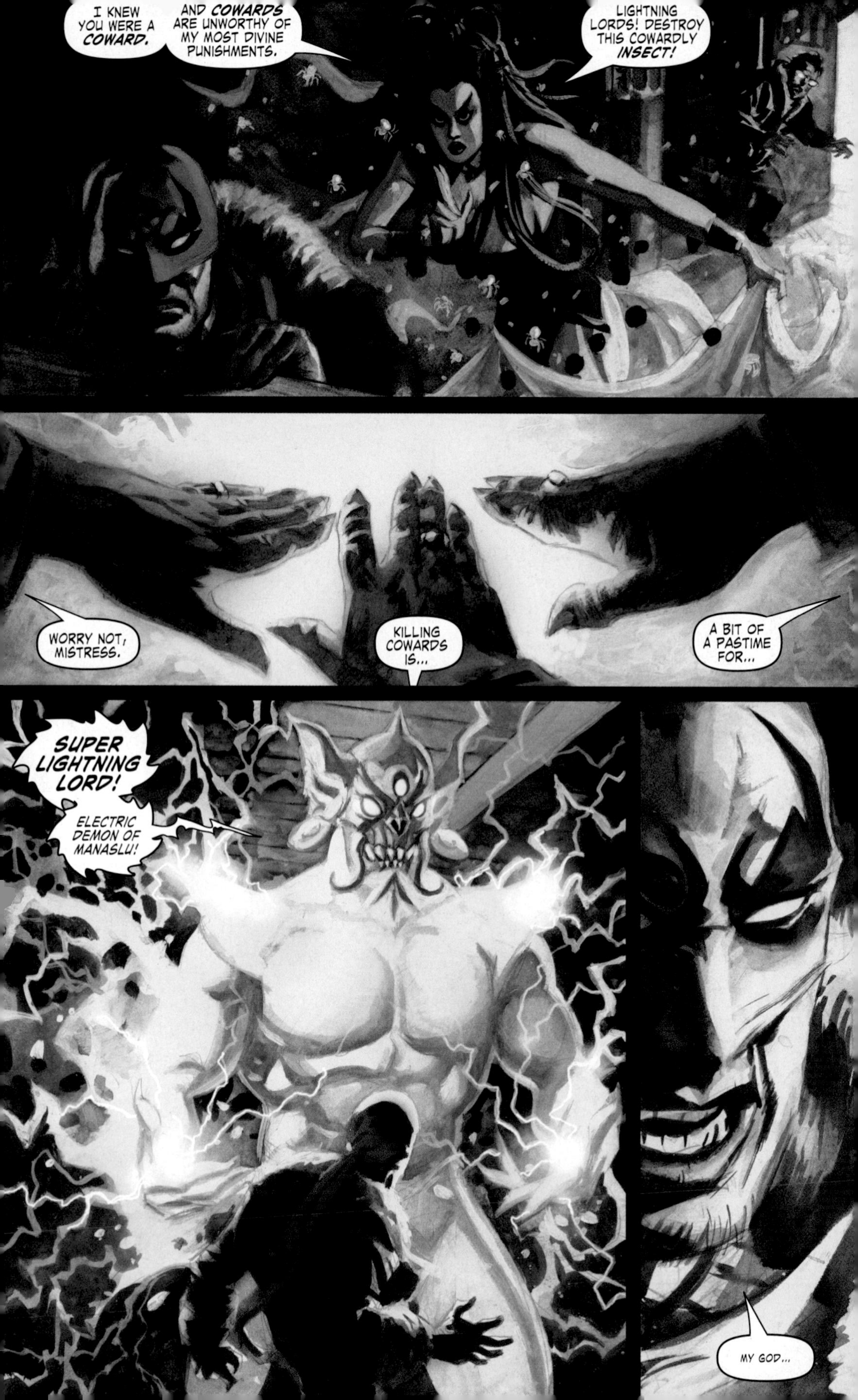
I KNEW YOU WERE A COWARD.
AND COWARDS ARE UNWORTHY OF MY MOST DIVINE PUNISHMENTS.
LIGHTNING LORDS! DESTROY THIS COWARDLY INSECT!
WORRY NOT, MISTRESS.
KILLING COWARDS IS...
A BIT OF A PASTIME FOR...
SUPER LIGHTNING LORD!
ELECTRIC DEMON OF MANASLU!
MY GOD...

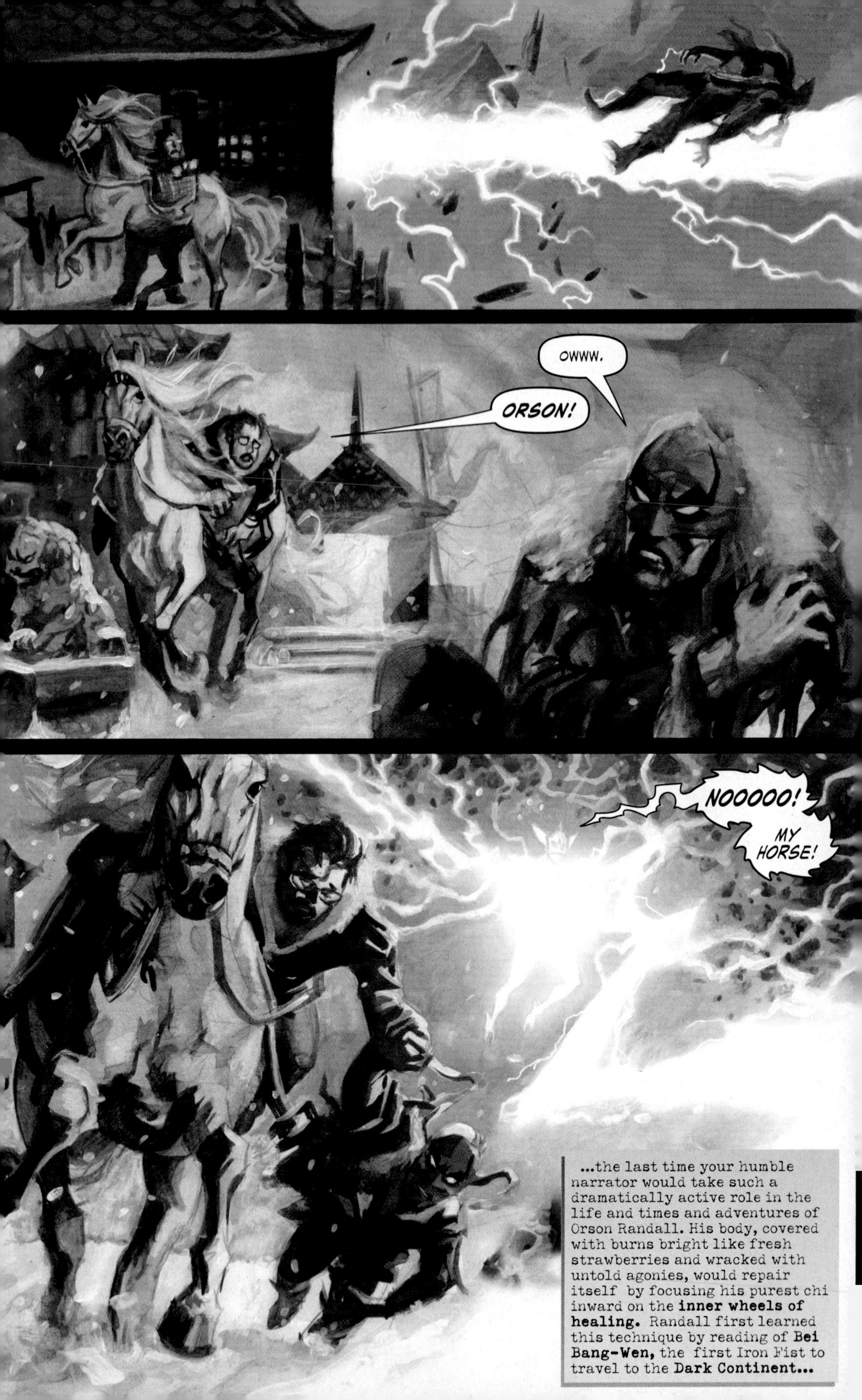
ORSON!
OWWW.
NOOOOO!
MY HORSE!
...the last time your humble narrator would take such a dramatically active role in the life and times and adventures of Orson Randall. His body, covered with burns bright like fresh strawberries and wracked with untold agonies, would repair itself by focusing his purest chi inward on the **inner wheels of healing.** Randall first learned this technique by reading of **Bei Bang-Wen,** the first Iron Fist to travel to the **Dark Continent...**

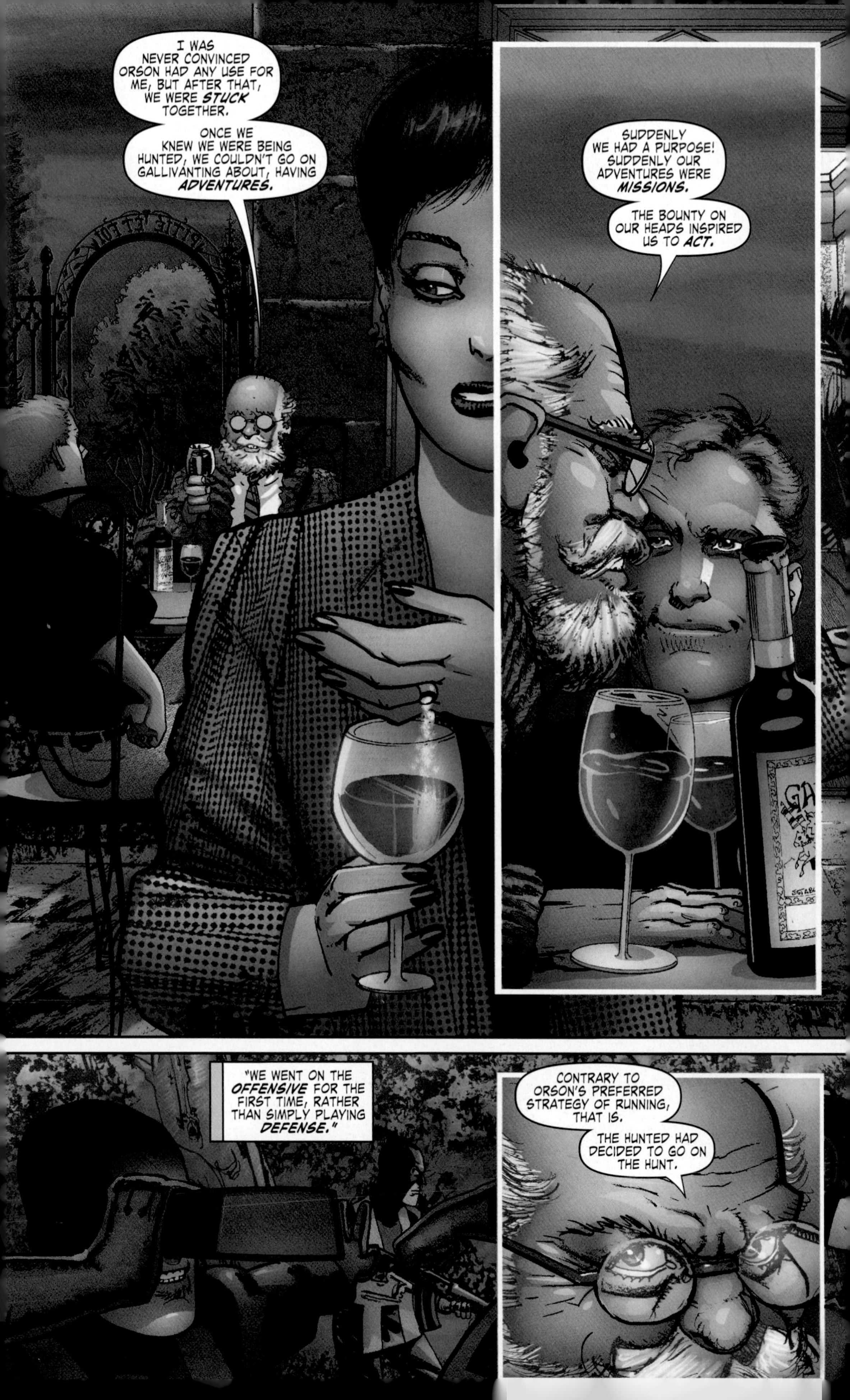
I WAS NEVER CONVINCED ORSON HAD ANY USE FOR ME, BUT AFTER THAT, WE WERE STUCK TOGETHER.
ONCE WE KNEW WE WERE BEING HUNTED, WE COULDN'T GO ON GALLIVANTING ABOUT, HAVING ADVENTURES.
SUDDENLY WE HAD A PURPOSE! SUDDENLY OUR ADVENTURES WERE MISSIONS.
THE BOUNTY ON OUR HEADS INSPIRED US TO ACT.
"WE WENT ON THE OFFENSIVE FOR THE FIRST TIME, RATHER THAN SIMPLY PLAYING DEFENSE."
CONTRARY TO ORSON'S PREFERRED STRATEGY OF RUNNING, THAT IS.
THE HUNTED HAD DECIDED TO GO ON THE HUNT.

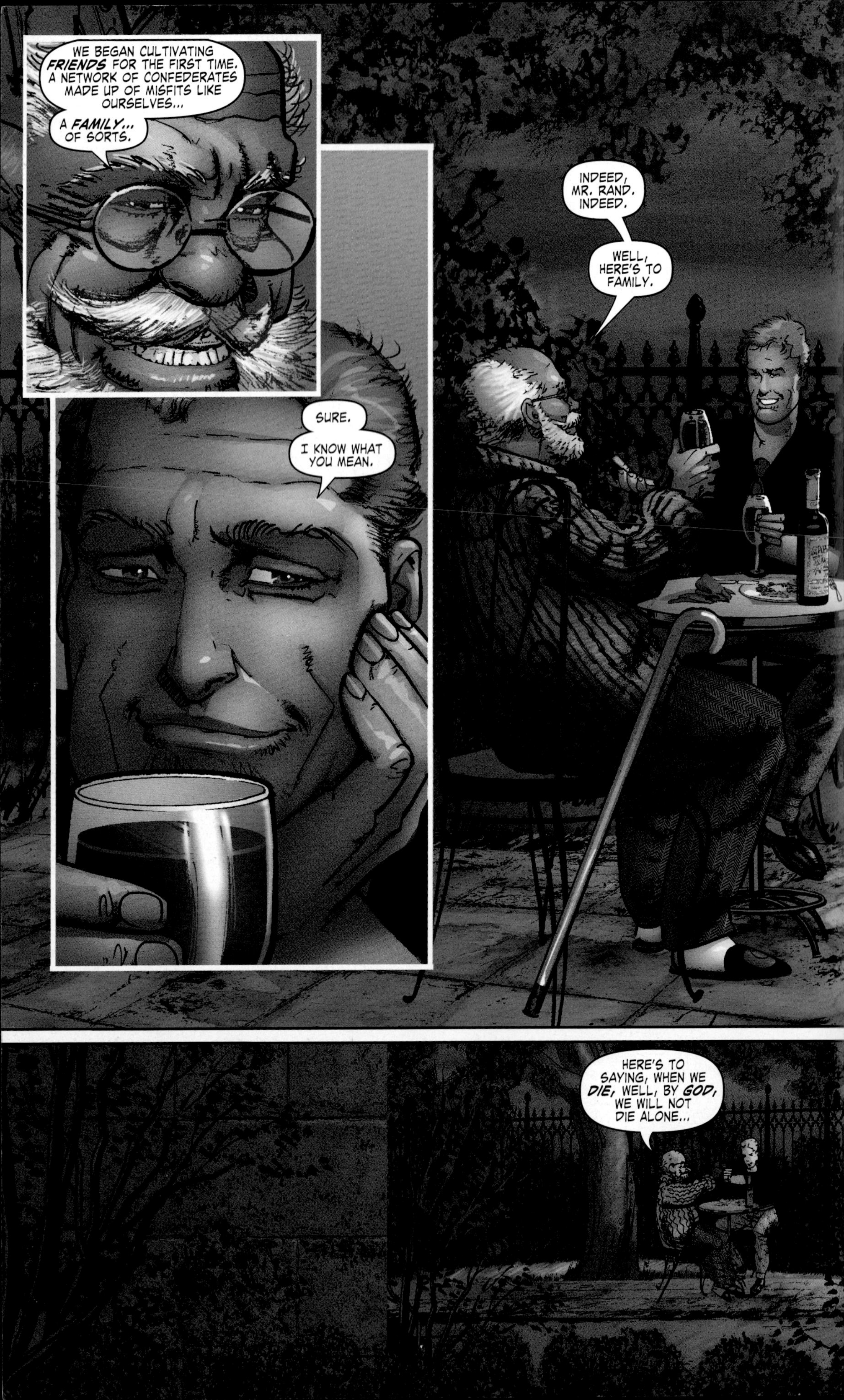
WE BEGAN CULTIVATING FRIENDS FOR THE FIRST TIME. A NETWORK OF CONFEDERATES MADE UP OF MISFITS LIKE OURSELVES...
A FAMILY... OF SORTS.
SURE.
I KNOW WHAT YOU MEAN.
INDEED, MR. RAND. INDEED.
WELL, HERE'S TO FAMILY.
HERE'S TO SAYING, WHEN WE DIE, WELL, BY GOD, WE WILL NOT DIE ALONE...

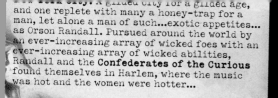 York City. A gilded city for a gilded age, and one replete with many a honey-trap for a man, let alone a man of such...exotic appetites... as Orson Randall. Pursued around the world by an ever-increasing array of wicked foes with an ever-increasing array of wicked abilities, Randall and the **Confederates of the Curious** found themselves in Harlem, where the music was hot and the women were hotter...

停止他！

杀害他！

--WHOOP--

ONCE AGAIN, IN *ENGLISH*, MR. RANDALL...

THE NINE-FOLD DAUGHTERS OF XAO SHALL HAVE THEIR *REVENGE*! AND ORSON RANDALL DIES ALONE.

I HAVE NO DOUBT I'M GONNA DIE SOMEDAY, SWEETHEART...

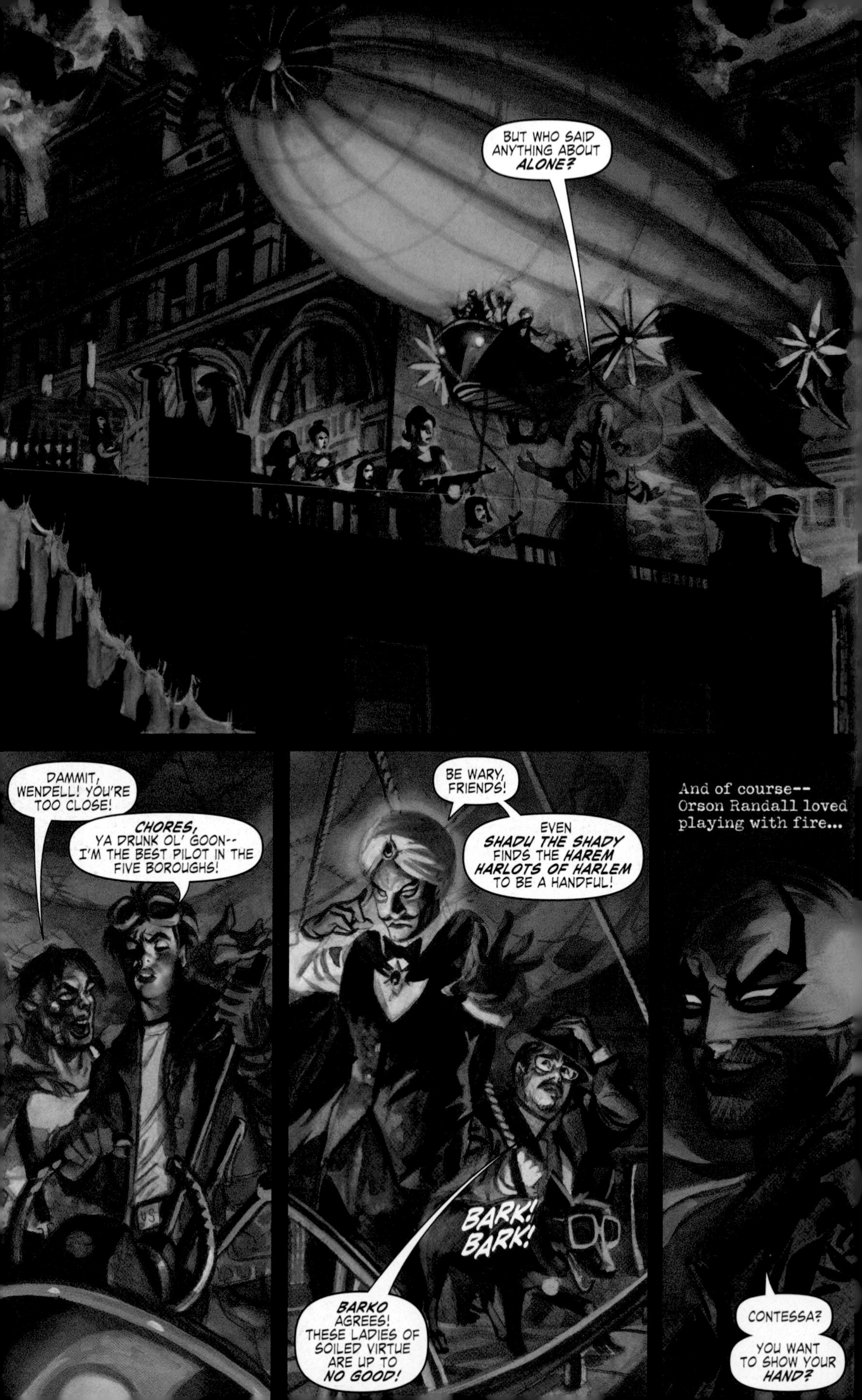
BUT WHO SAID ANYTHING ABOUT ALONE?
DAMMIT, WENDELL! YOU'RE TOO CLOSE!
CHORES, YA DRUNK OL' GOON-- I'M THE BEST PILOT IN THE FIVE BOROUGHS!
BE WARY, FRIENDS!
EVEN SHADU THE SHADY FINDS THE HAREM HARLOTS OF HARLEM TO BE A HANDFUL!
BARK! BARK!
BARKO AGREES! THESE LADIES OF SOILED VIRTUE ARE UP TO NO GOOD!
And of course-- Orson Randall loved playing with fire...
CONTESSA?
YOU WANT TO SHOW YOUR HAND?

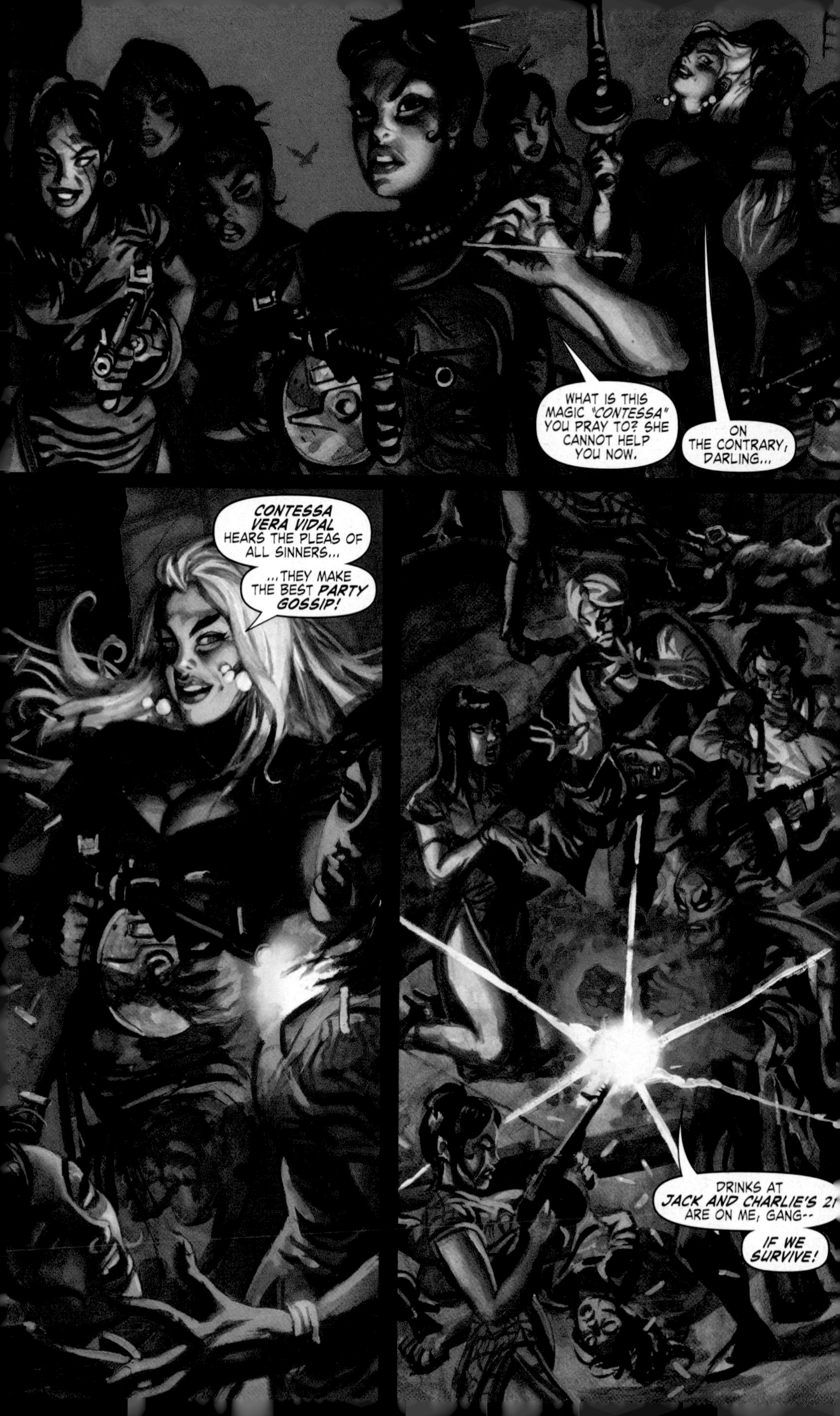
WHAT IS THIS MAGIC "CONTESSA" YOU PRAY TO? SHE CANNOT HELP YOU NOW.
ON THE CONTRARY, DARLING...
CONTESSA VERA VIDAL HEARS THE PLEAS OF ALL SINNERS...
...THEY MAKE THE BEST PARTY GOSSIP!
DRINKS AT JACK AND CHARLIE'S 21 ARE ON ME, GANG--
IF WE SURVIVE!

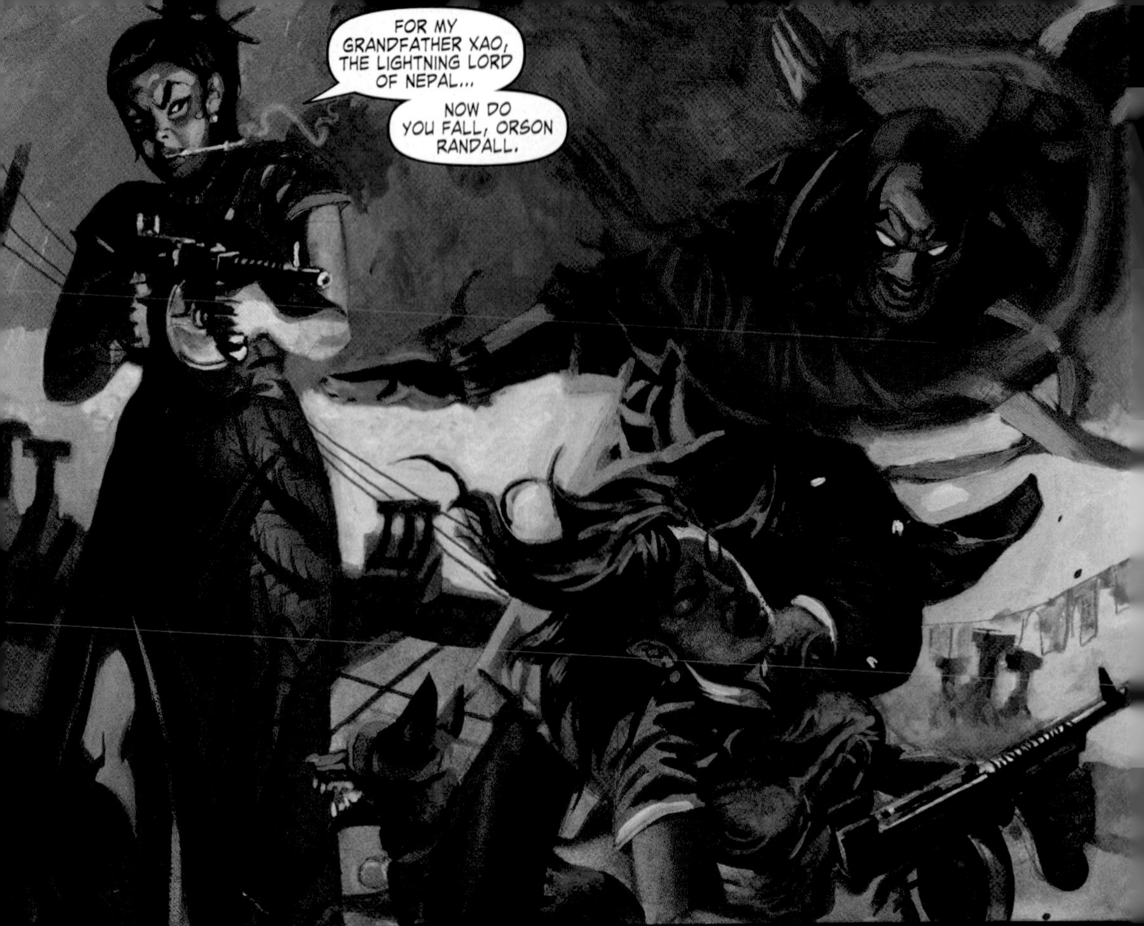
FOR MY GRANDFATHER XAO, THE LIGHTNING LORD OF NEPAL...
NOW DO YOU FALL, ORSON RANDALL.

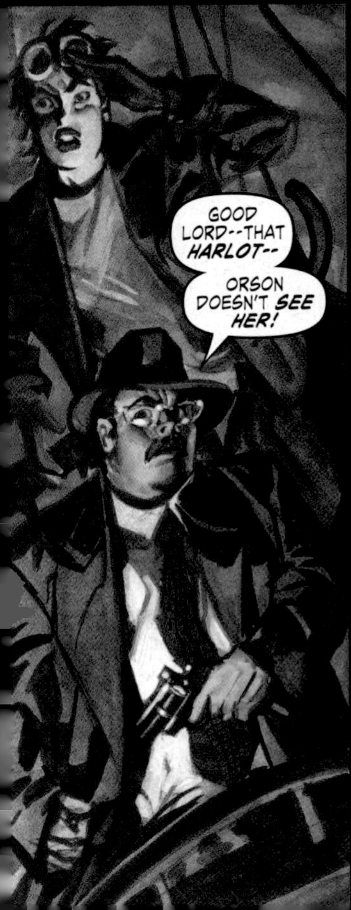
GOOD LORD--THAT *HARLOT*--
ORSON DOESN'T *SEE HER!*

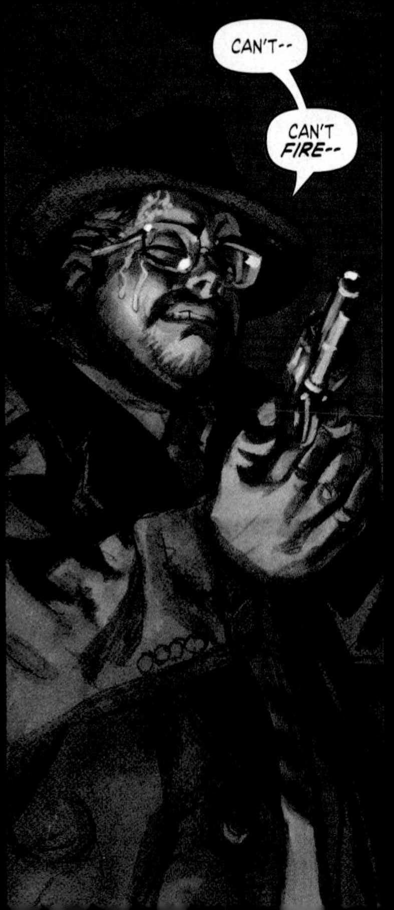
CAN'T--
CAN'T *FIRE*--

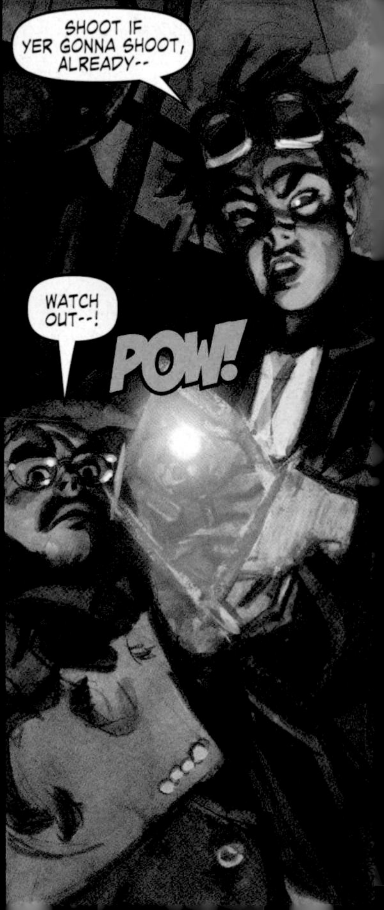
SHOOT IF YER GONNA SHOOT, ALREADY--
WATCH OUT--!
POW!

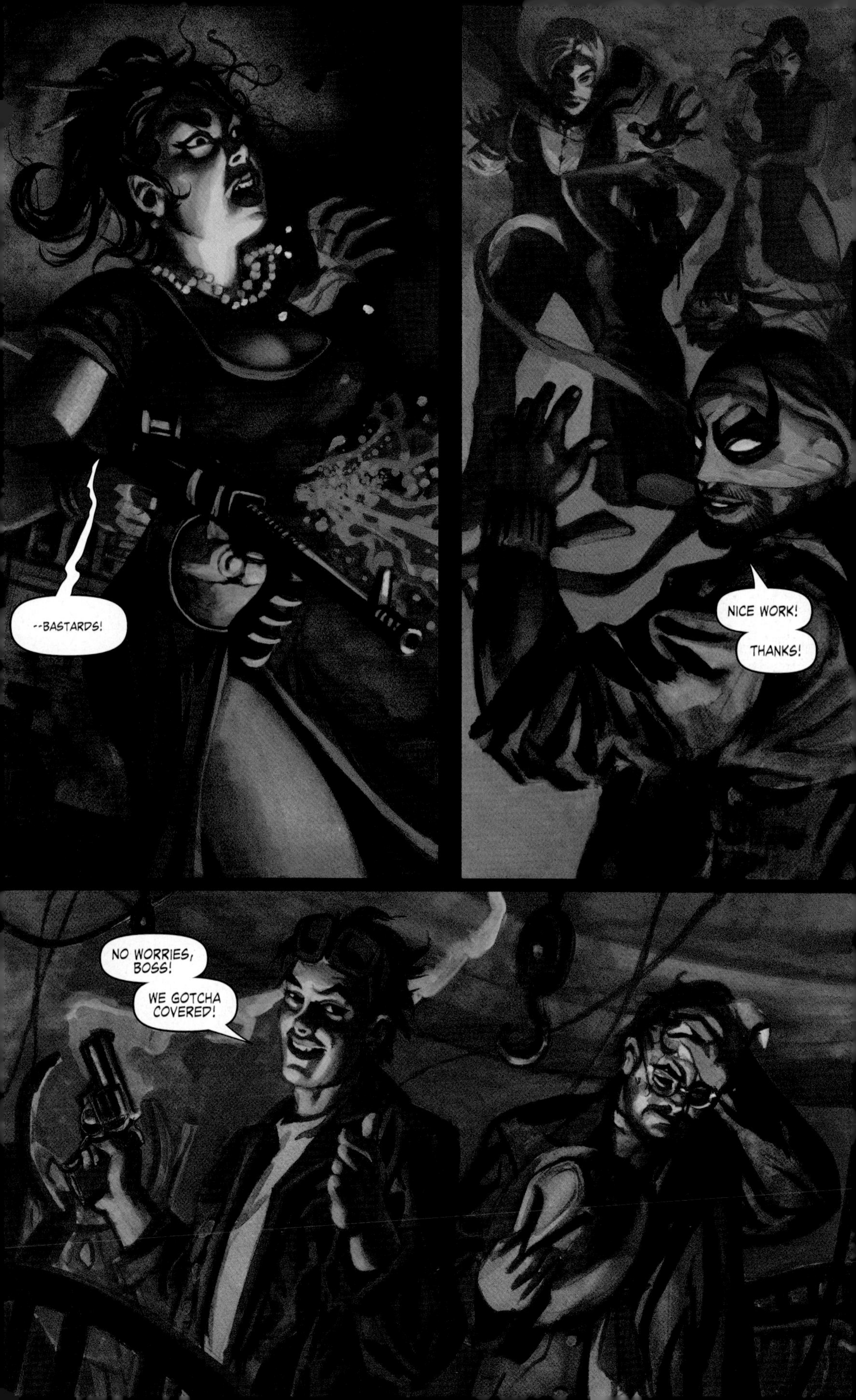
--BASTARDS!
NICE WORK!
THANKS!
NO WORRIES, BOSS!
WE GOTCHA COVERED!

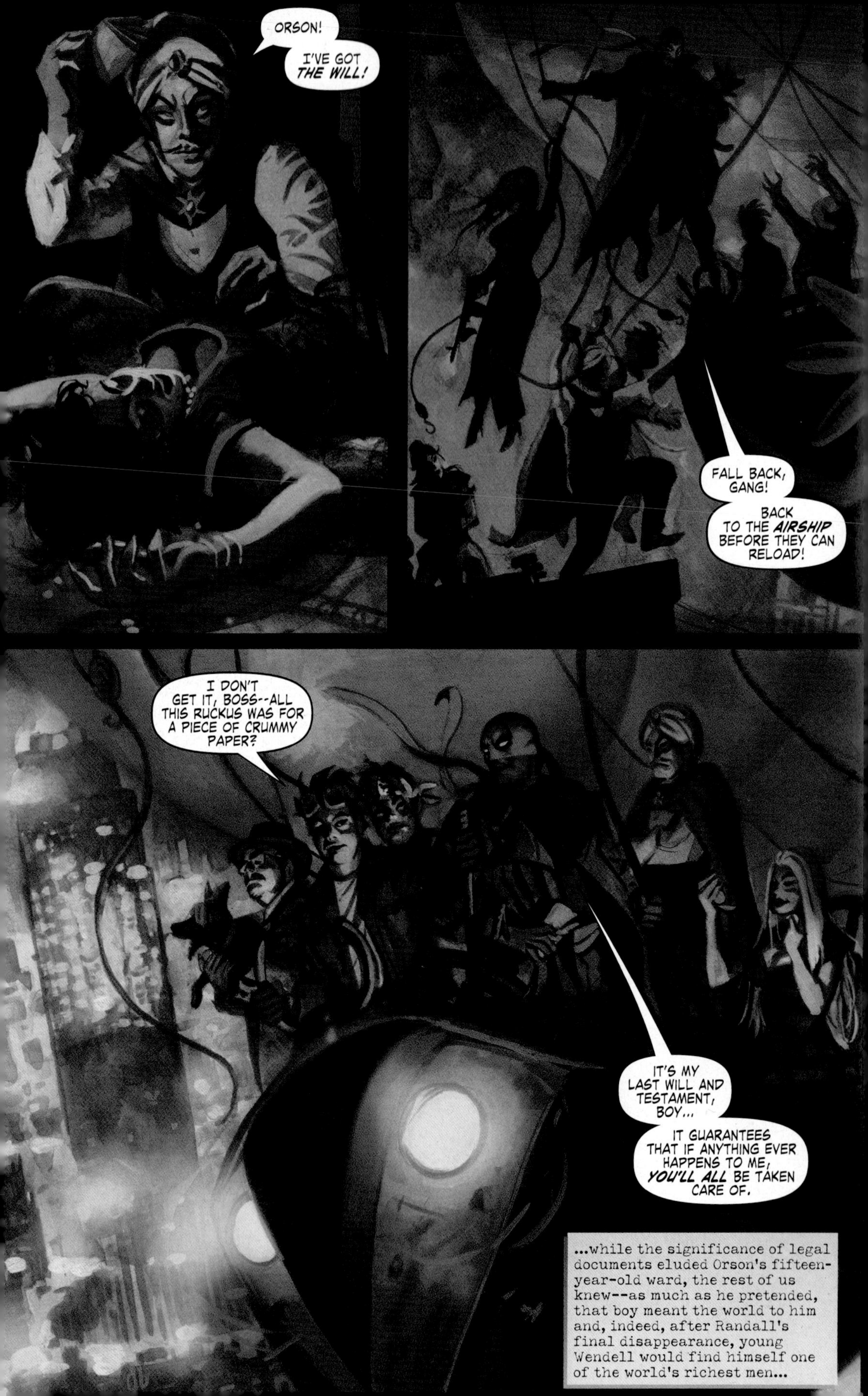
ORSON!
I'VE GOT *THE WILL!*
FALL BACK, GANG!
BACK TO THE *AIRSHIP* BEFORE THEY CAN RELOAD!
I DON'T GET IT, BOSS--ALL THIS RUCKUS WAS FOR A PIECE OF CRUMMY PAPER?
IT'S MY LAST WILL AND TESTAMENT, BOY...
IT GUARANTEES THAT IF ANYTHING EVER HAPPENS TO ME, *YOU'LL ALL* BE TAKEN CARE OF.
...while the significance of legal documents eluded Orson's fifteen-year-old ward, the rest of us knew--as much as he pretended, that boy meant the world to him and, indeed, after Randall's final disappearance, young Wendell would find himself one of the world's richest men...

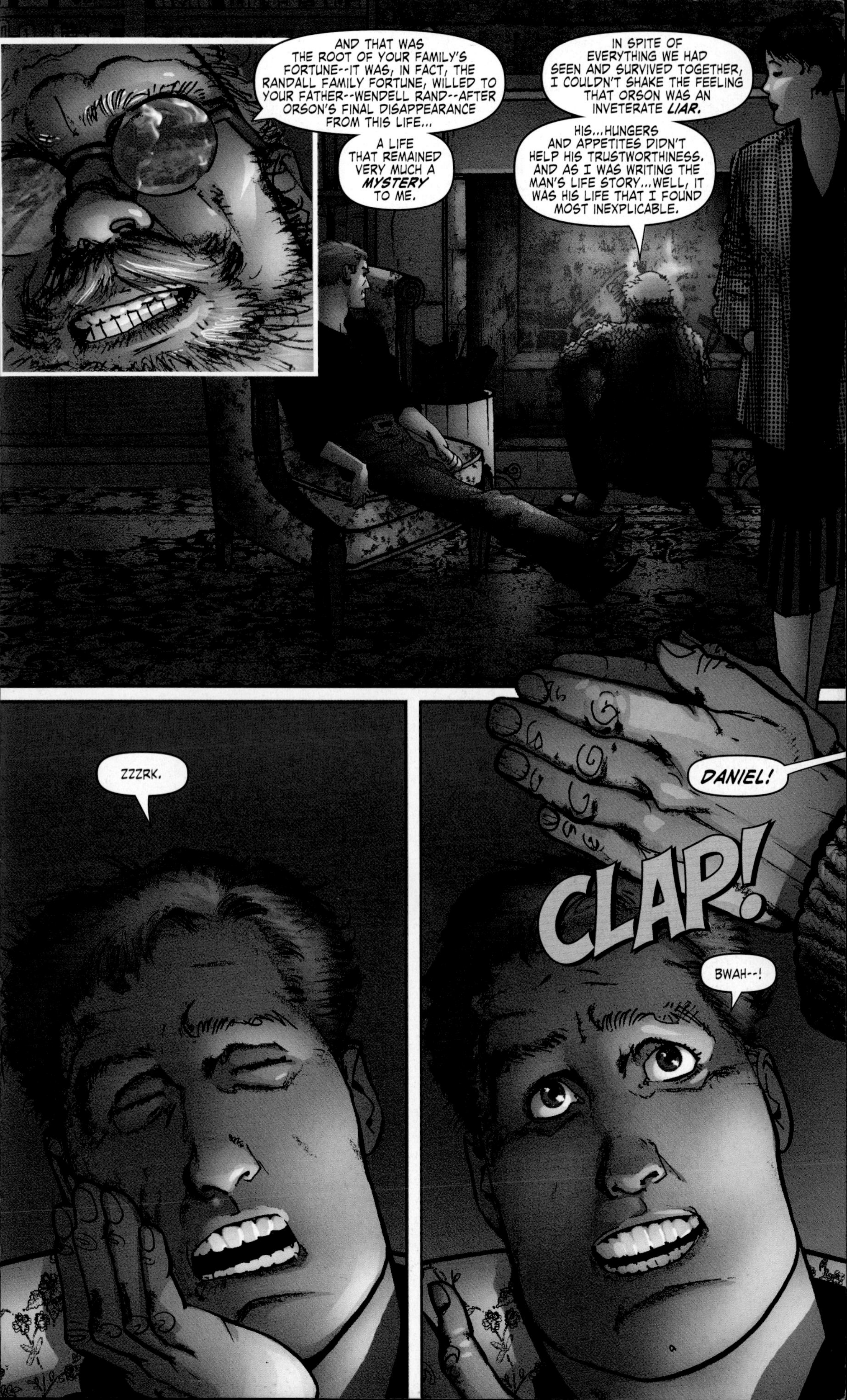
AND THAT WAS THE ROOT OF YOUR FAMILY'S FORTUNE--IT WAS, IN FACT, THE RANDALL FAMILY FORTUNE, WILLED TO YOUR FATHER--WENDELL RAND--AFTER ORSON'S FINAL DISAPPEARANCE FROM THIS LIFE...
A LIFE THAT REMAINED VERY MUCH A MYSTERY TO ME.
IN SPITE OF EVERYTHING WE HAD SEEN AND SURVIVED TOGETHER, I COULDN'T SHAKE THE FEELING THAT ORSON WAS AN INVETERATE LIAR.
HIS...HUNGERS AND APPETITES DIDN'T HELP HIS TRUSTWORTHINESS. AND AS I WAS WRITING THE MAN'S LIFE STORY...WELL, IT WAS HIS LIFE THAT I FOUND MOST INEXPLICABLE.
ZZZRK.
DANIEL!
CLAP!
BWAH--!

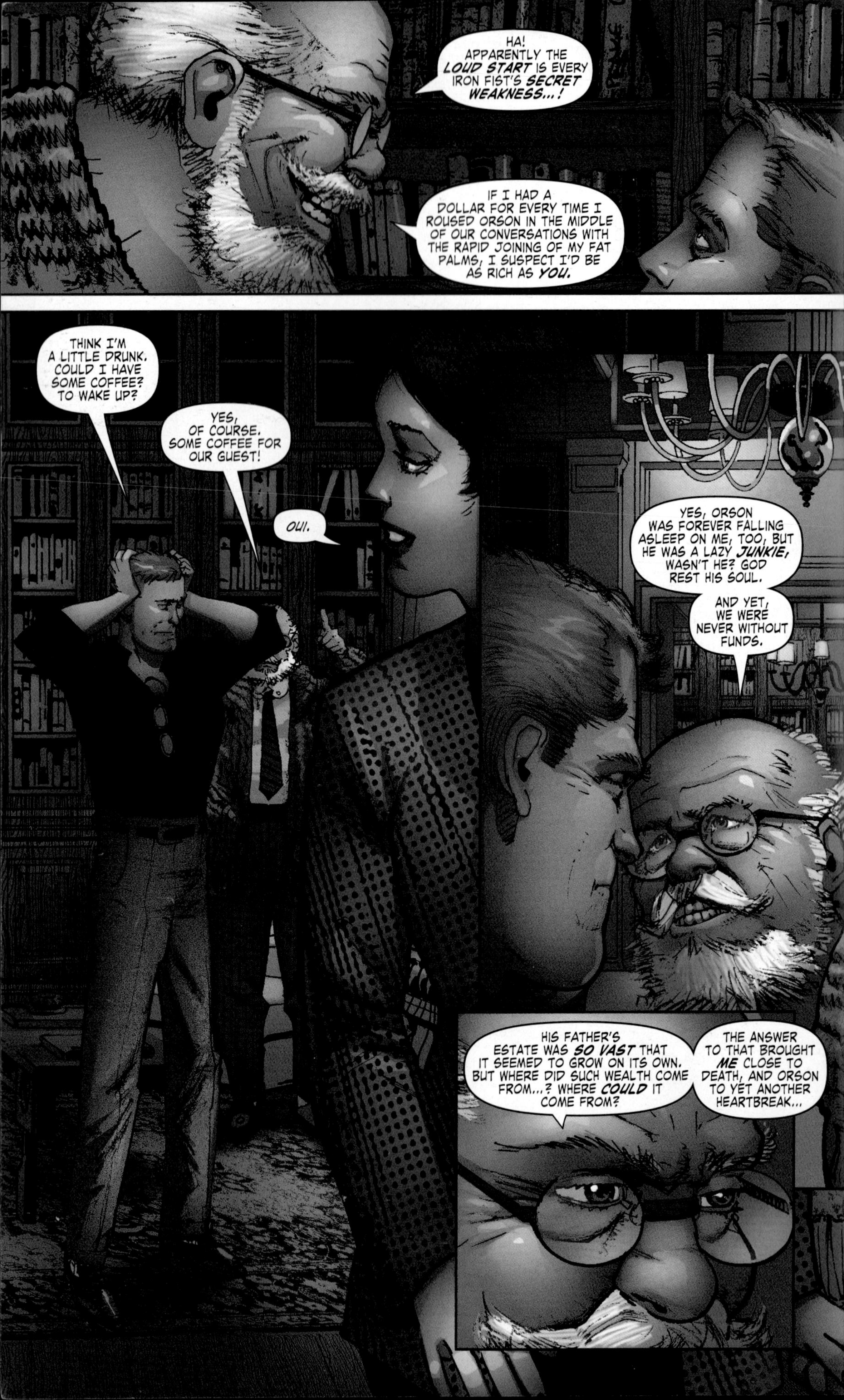
HA! APPARENTLY THE LOUD START IS EVERY IRON FIST'S SECRET WEAKNESS...!
IF I HAD A DOLLAR FOR EVERY TIME I ROUSED ORSON IN THE MIDDLE OF OUR CONVERSATIONS WITH THE RAPID JOINING OF MY FAT PALMS, I SUSPECT I'D BE AS RICH AS YOU.
THINK I'M A LITTLE DRUNK. COULD I HAVE SOME COFFEE? TO WAKE UP?
YES, OF COURSE. SOME COFFEE FOR OUR GUEST!
OUI.
YES, ORSON WAS FOREVER FALLING ASLEEP ON ME, TOO, BUT HE WAS A LAZY JUNKIE, WASN'T HE? GOD REST HIS SOUL.
AND YET, WE WERE NEVER WITHOUT FUNDS.
HIS FATHER'S ESTATE WAS SO VAST THAT IT SEEMED TO GROW ON ITS OWN. BUT WHERE DID SUCH WEALTH COME FROM...? WHERE COULD IT COME FROM?
THE ANSWER TO THAT BROUGHT ME CLOSE TO DEATH, AND ORSON TO YET ANOTHER HEARTBREAK...

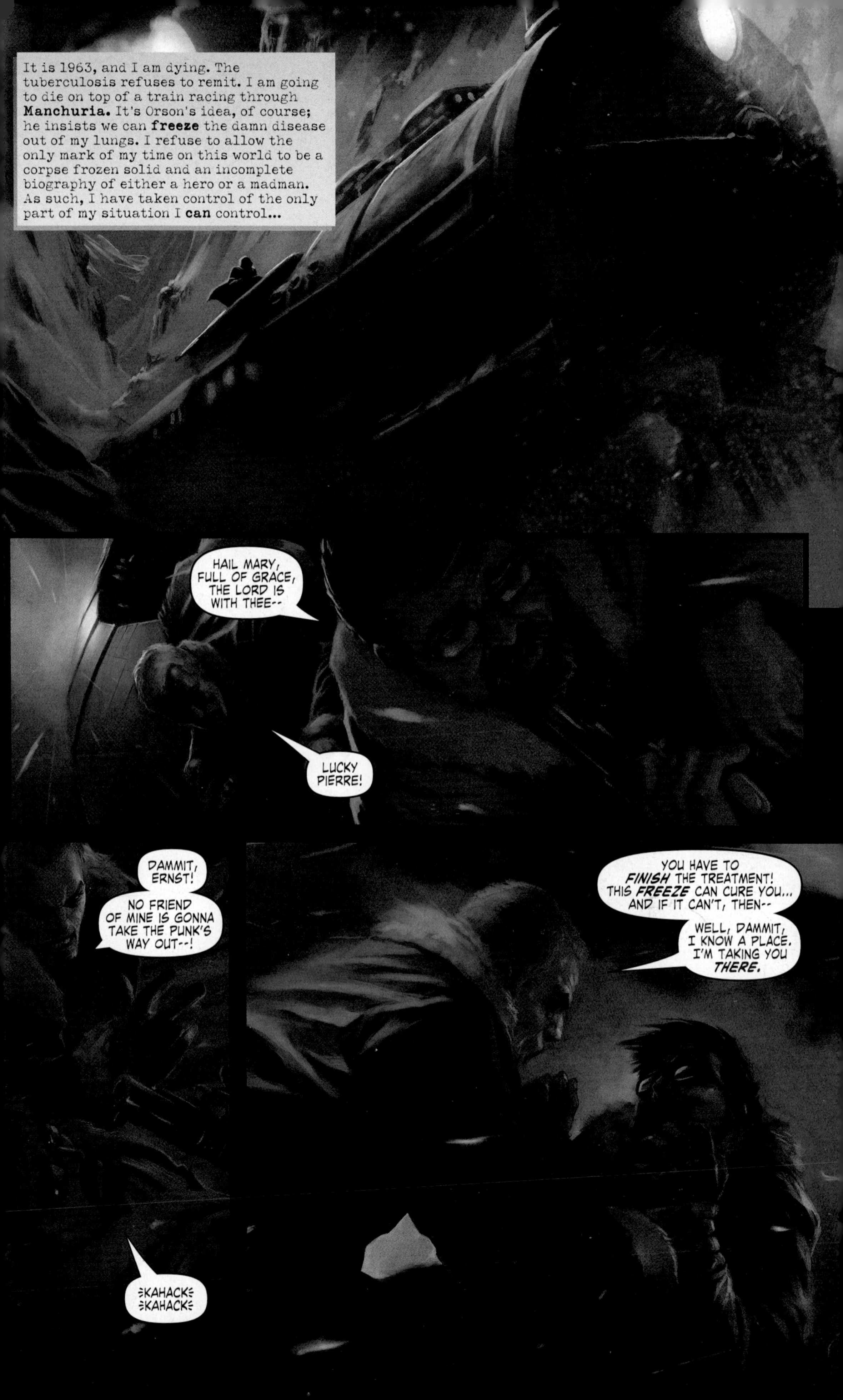
It is 1963, and I am dying. The tuberculosis refuses to remit. I am going to die on top of a train racing through **Manchuria.** It's Orson's idea, of course; he insists we can **freeze** the damn disease out of my lungs. I refuse to allow the only mark of my time on this world to be a corpse frozen solid and an incomplete biography of either a hero or a madman. As such, I have taken control of the only part of my situation I **can** control...
HAIL MARY, FULL OF GRACE, THE LORD IS WITH THEE--
LUCKY PIERRE!
DAMMIT, ERNST!
NO FRIEND OF MINE IS GONNA TAKE THE PUNK'S WAY OUT--!
YOU HAVE TO *FINISH* THE TREATMENT! THIS *FREEZE* CAN CURE YOU... AND IF IT CAN'T, THEN--
WELL, DAMMIT, I KNOW A PLACE. I'M TAKING YOU *THERE.*
KAHACK KAHACK

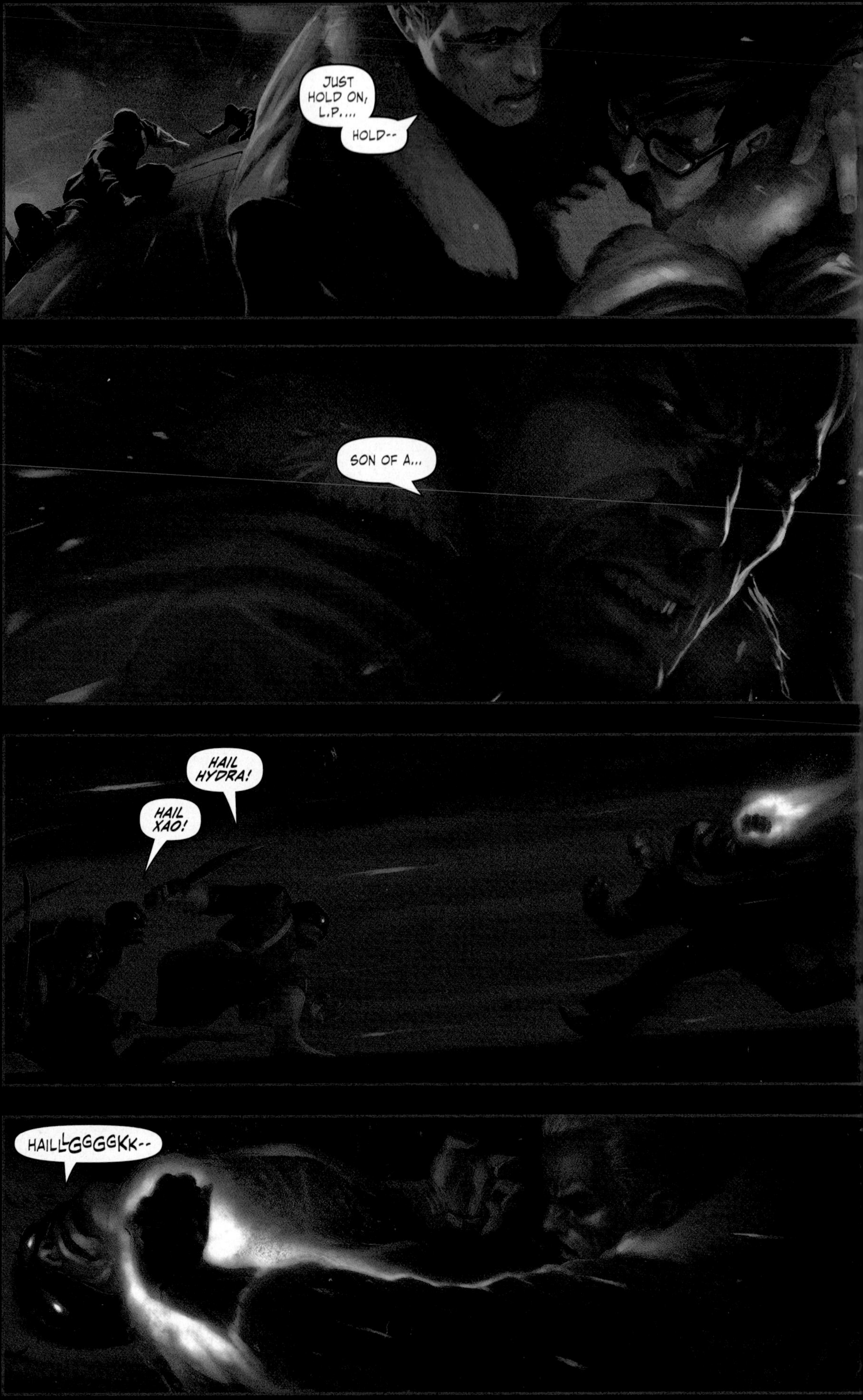
JUST HOLD ON, L.P.…
HOLD--
SON OF A…
HAIL HYDRA!
HAIL XAO!
HAILLGGGKK--

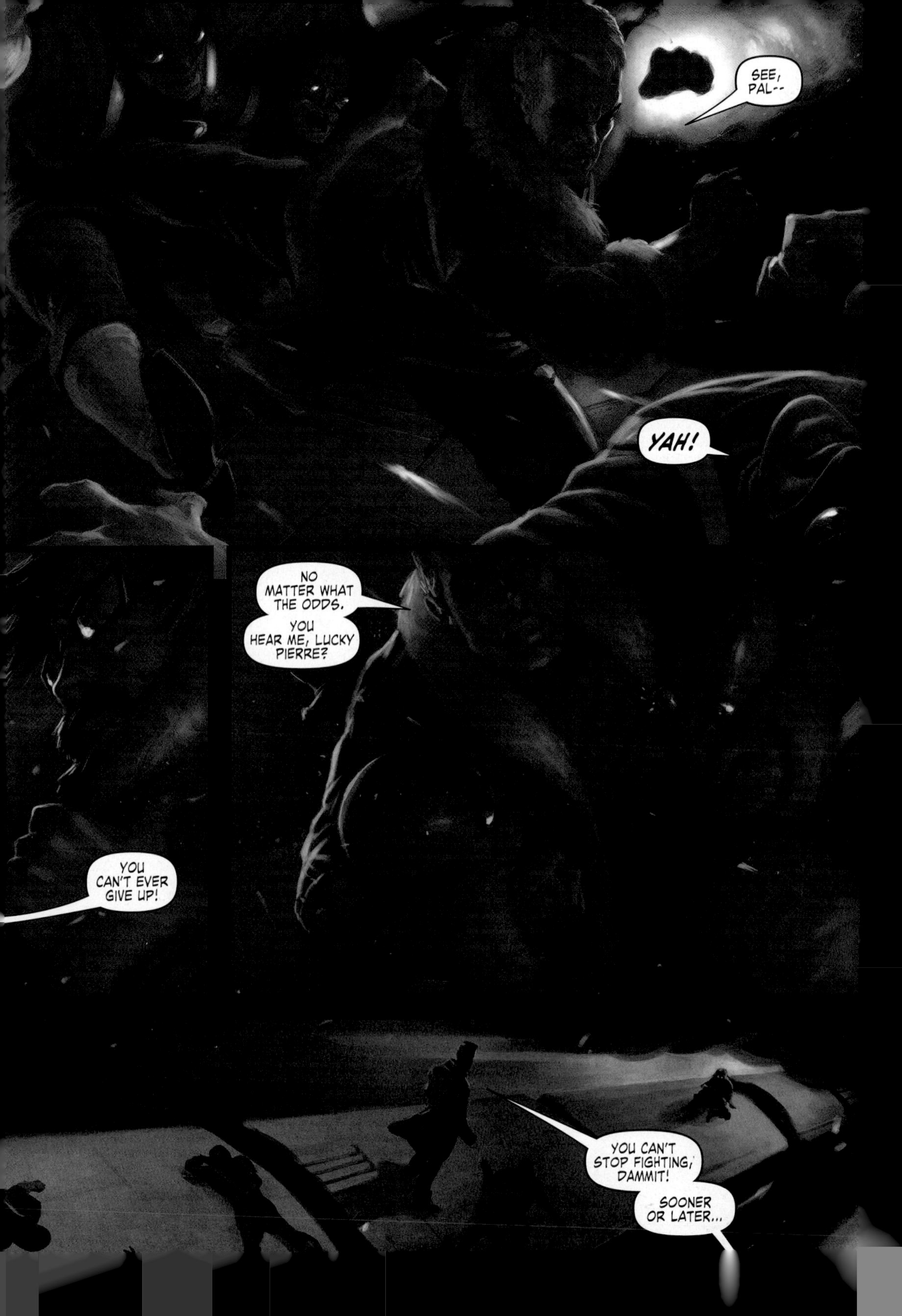
SEE, PAL--
YAH!
YOU CAN'T EVER GIVE UP!
NO MATTER WHAT THE ODDS.
YOU HEAR ME, LUCKY PIERRE?
YOU CAN'T STOP FIGHTING, DAMMIT!
SOONER OR LATER...

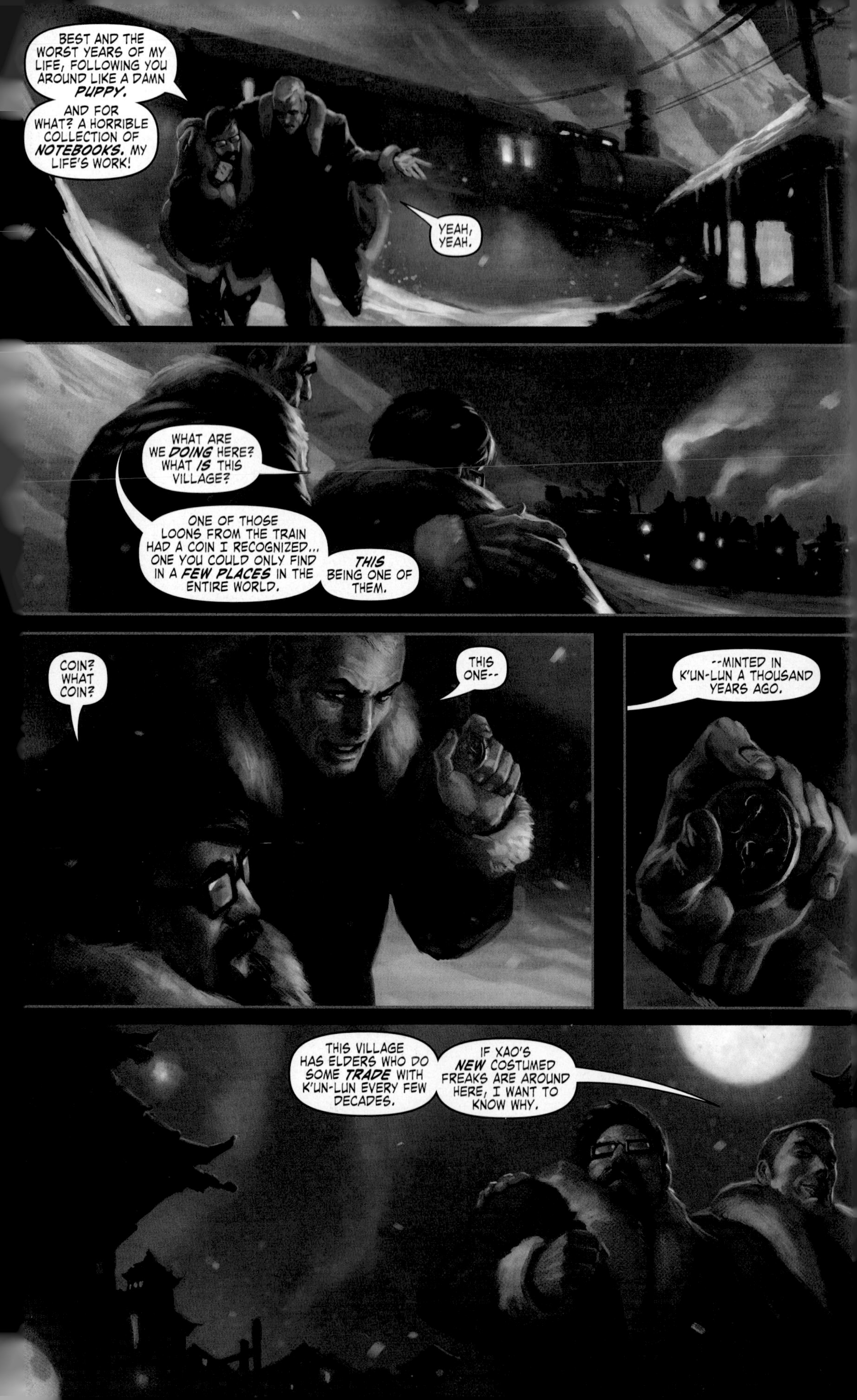
BEST AND THE WORST YEARS OF MY LIFE, FOLLOWING YOU AROUND LIKE A DAMN **PUPPY.**
AND FOR WHAT? A HORRIBLE COLLECTION OF **NOTEBOOKS.** MY LIFE'S WORK!
YEAH, YEAH.
WHAT ARE WE ***DOING*** HERE? WHAT ***IS*** THIS VILLAGE?
ONE OF THOSE LOONS FROM THE TRAIN HAD A COIN I RECOGNIZED... ONE YOU COULD ONLY FIND IN A ***FEW PLACES*** IN THE ENTIRE WORLD.
THIS BEING ONE OF THEM.
COIN? WHAT COIN?
THIS ONE--
--MINTED IN K'UN-LUN A THOUSAND YEARS AGO.
THIS VILLAGE HAS ELDERS WHO DO SOME ***TRADE*** WITH K'UN-LUN EVERY FEW DECADES.
IF XAO'S ***NEW*** COSTUMED FREAKS ARE AROUND HERE, I WANT TO KNOW WHY.

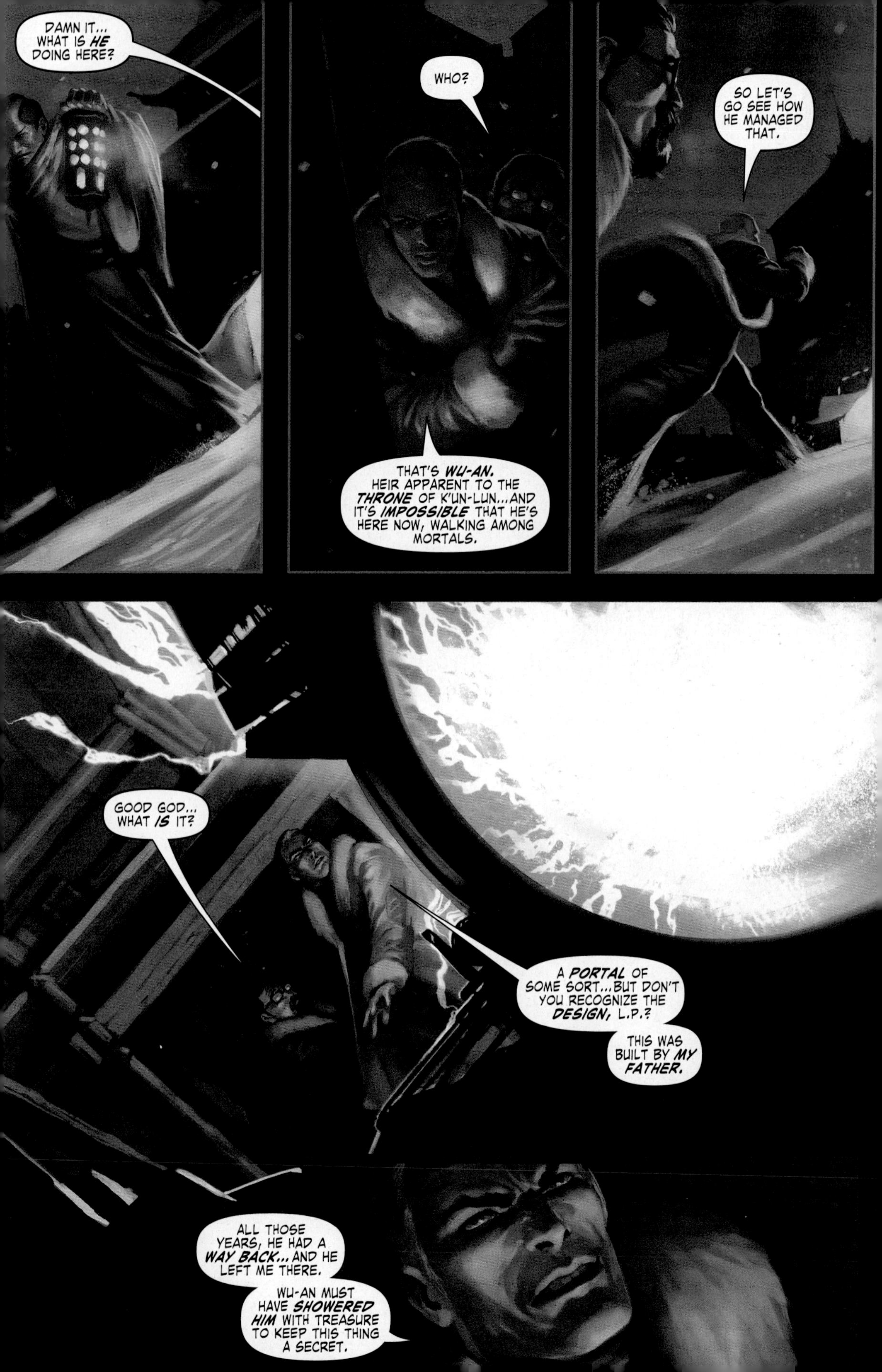

DAMN IT... WHAT IS *HE* DOING HERE?
WHO?
THAT'S ***WU-AN.*** HEIR APPARENT TO THE ***THRONE*** OF K'UN-LUN...AND IT'S ***IMPOSSIBLE*** THAT HE'S HERE NOW, WALKING AMONG MORTALS.
SO LET'S GO SEE HOW HE MANAGED THAT.
GOOD GOD... WHAT *IS* IT?
A ***PORTAL*** OF SOME SORT...BUT DON'T YOU RECOGNIZE THE ***DESIGN,*** L.P.?
THIS WAS BUILT BY ***MY FATHER.***
ALL THOSE YEARS, HE HAD A ***WAY BACK...*** AND HE LEFT ME THERE.
WU-AN MUST HAVE ***SHOWERED HIM*** WITH TREASURE TO KEEP THIS THING A SECRET.

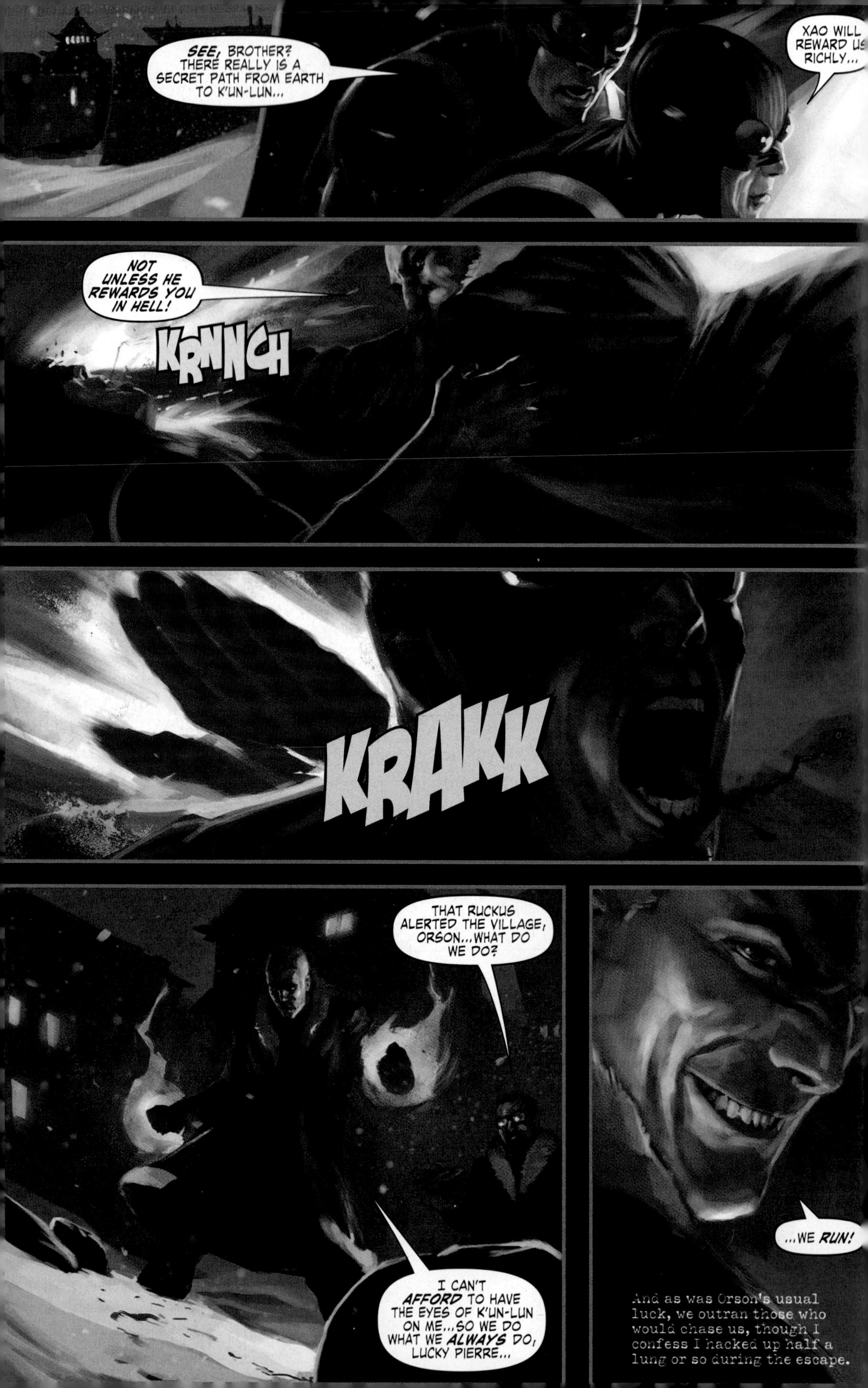

SEE, BROTHER? THERE REALLY IS A SECRET PATH FROM EARTH TO K'UN-LUN...
XAO WILL REWARD US RICHLY...
NOT UNLESS HE REWARDS YOU IN HELL!
KRNNCH
KRAKK
THAT RUCKUS ALERTED THE VILLAGE, ORSON...WHAT DO WE DO?
I CAN'T *AFFORD* TO HAVE THE EYES OF K'UN-LUN ON ME...SO WE DO WHAT WE *ALWAYS* DO, LUCKY PIERRE...
...WE *RUN!*
And as was Orson's usual luck, we outran those who would chase us, though I confess I hacked up half a lung or so during the escape.

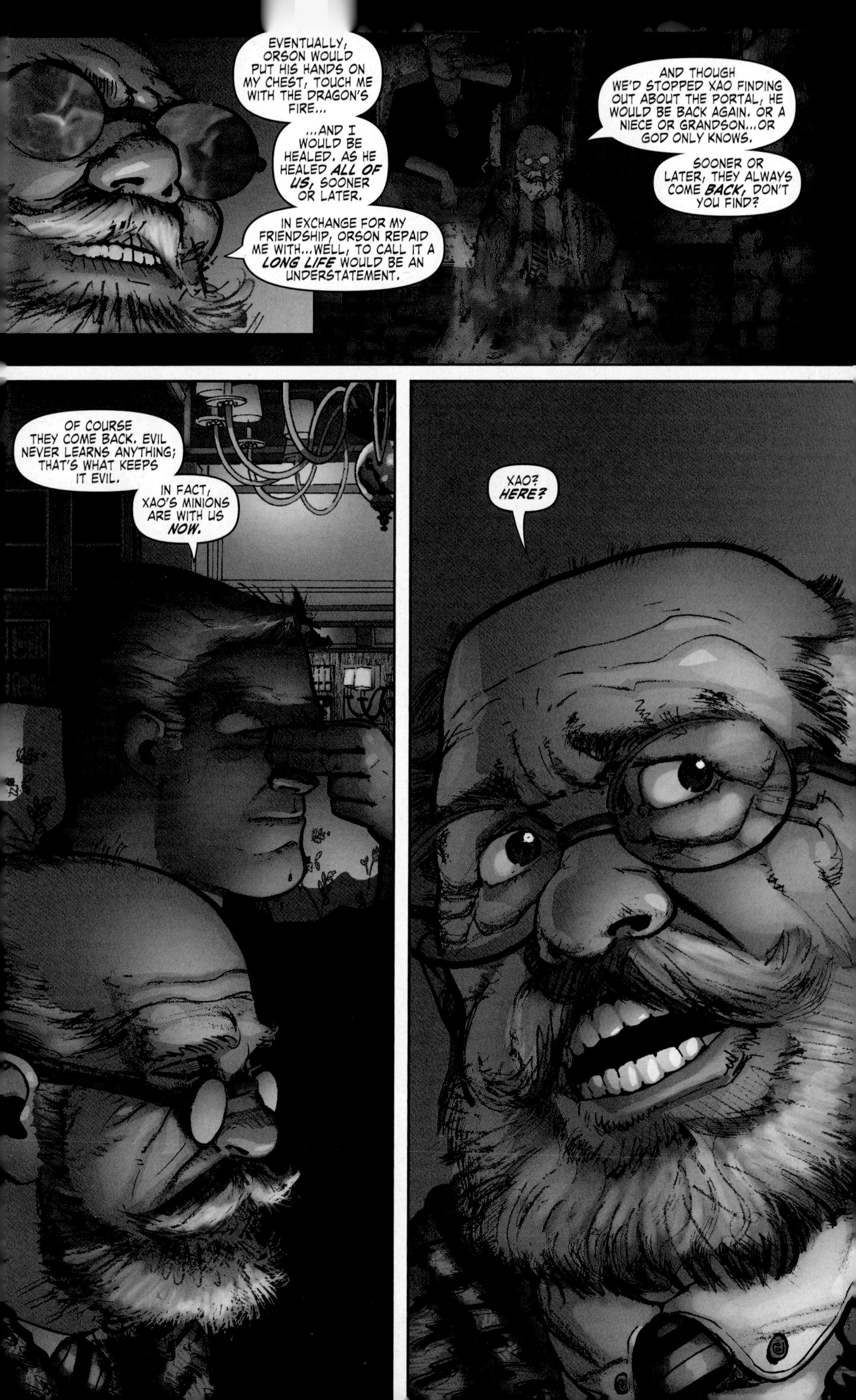
EVENTUALLY, ORSON WOULD PUT HIS HANDS ON MY CHEST, TOUCH ME WITH THE DRAGON'S FIRE...
...AND I WOULD BE HEALED. AS HE HEALED ***ALL OF US,*** SOONER OR LATER.
IN EXCHANGE FOR MY FRIENDSHIP, ORSON REPAID ME WITH...WELL, TO CALL IT A ***LONG LIFE*** WOULD BE AN UNDERSTATEMENT.
AND THOUGH WE'D STOPPED XAO FINDING OUT ABOUT THE PORTAL, HE WOULD BE BACK AGAIN. OR A NIECE OR GRANDSON...OR GOD ONLY KNOWS.
SOONER OR LATER, THEY ALWAYS COME ***BACK,*** DON'T YOU FIND?
OF COURSE THEY COME BACK. EVIL NEVER LEARNS ANYTHING; THAT'S WHAT KEEPS IT EVIL.
IN FACT, XAO'S MINIONS ARE WITH US ***NOW.***
XAO? ***HERE?***

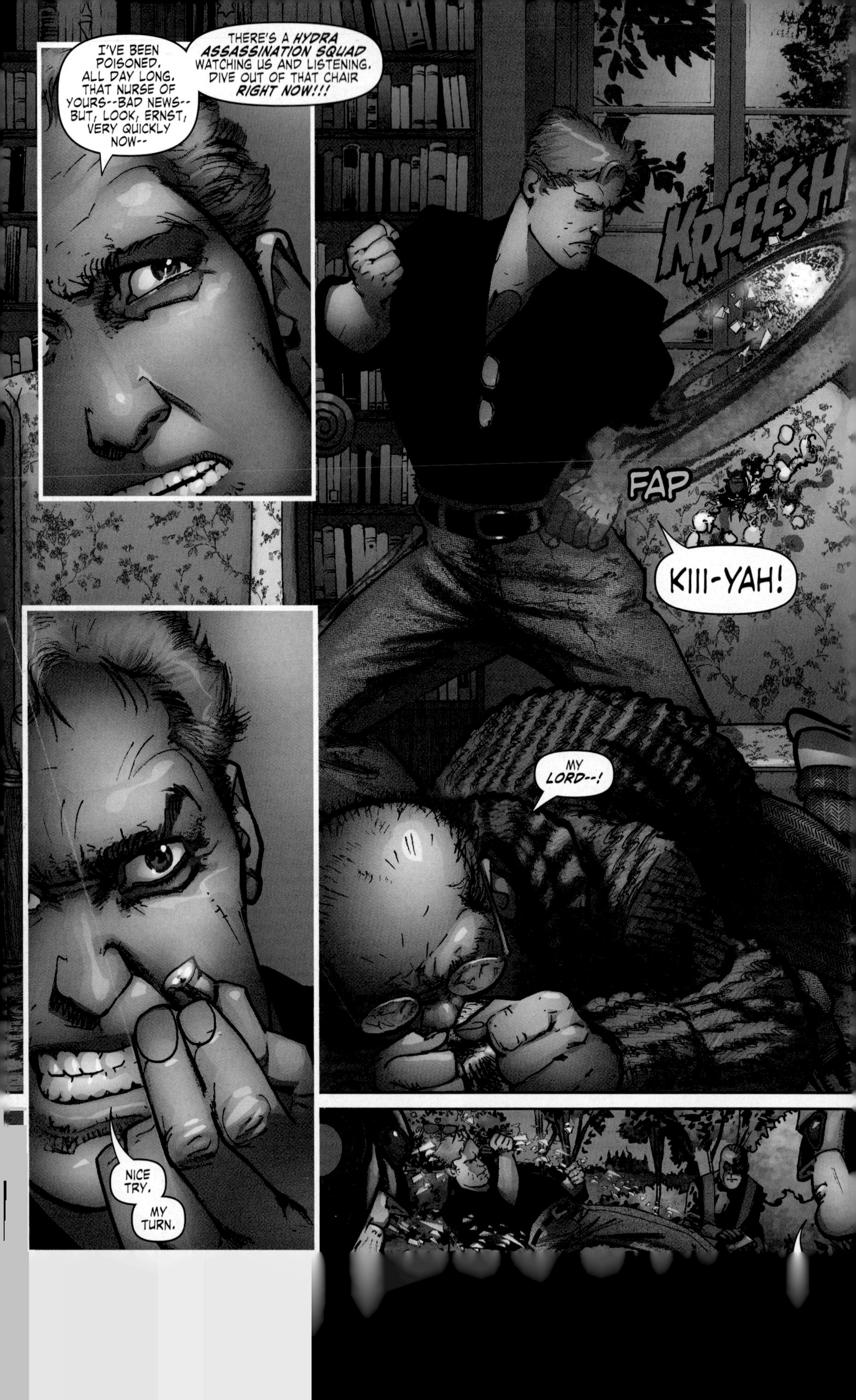
I'VE BEEN POISONED, ALL DAY LONG. THAT NURSE OF YOURS--BAD NEWS--BUT, LOOK, ERNST, VERY QUICKLY NOW--
THERE'S A HYDRA ASSASSINATION SQUAD WATCHING US AND LISTENING. DIVE OUT OF THAT CHAIR RIGHT NOW!!!
NICE TRY.
MY TURN.
KREEESH
FAP
KIII-YAH!
MY LORD--!

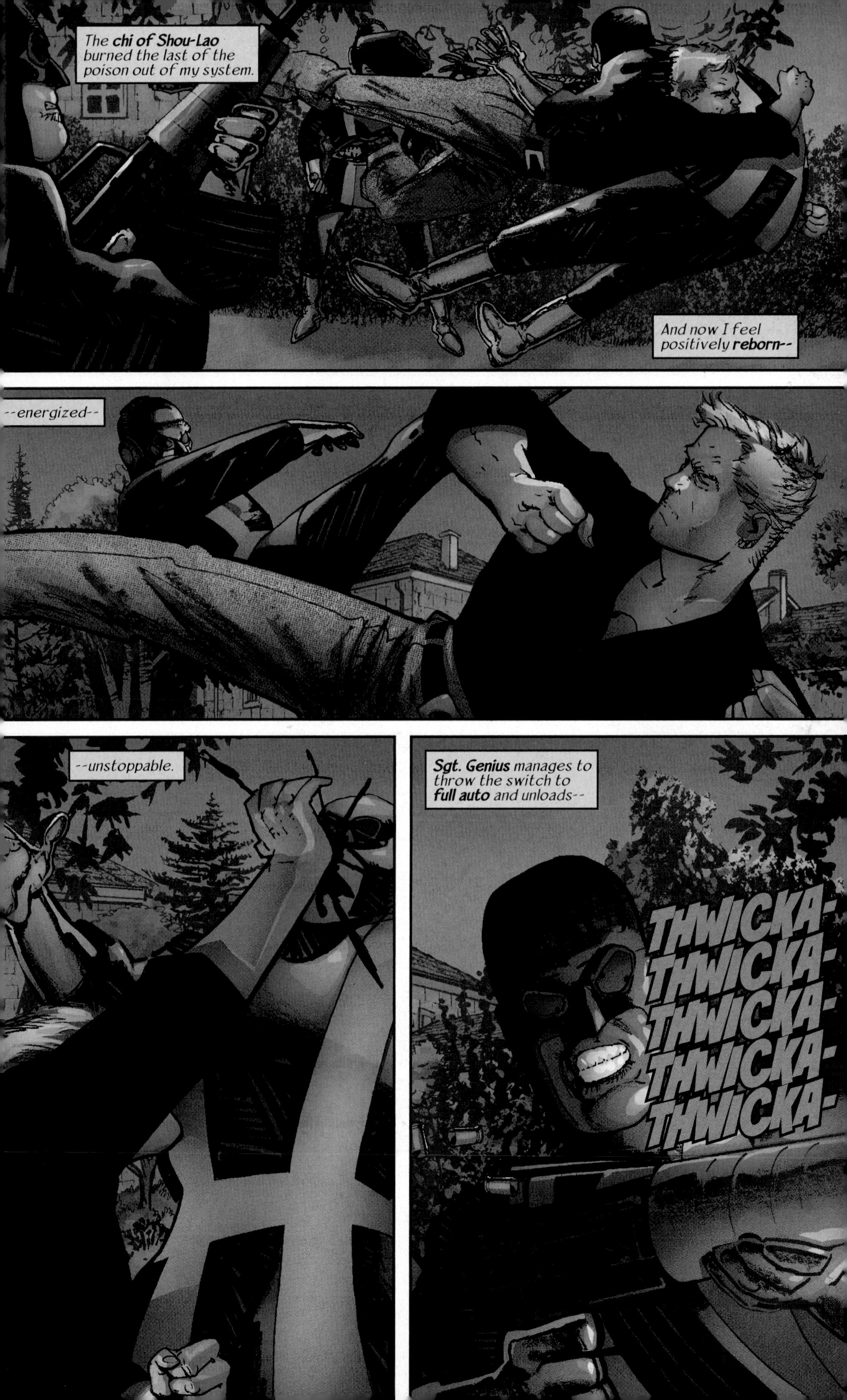
The **chi of Shou-Lao** burned the last of the poison out of my system.
And now I feel positively **reborn--**
--energized--
--unstoppable.
Sgt. Genius manages to throw the switch to **full auto** and unloads--
THWICKA-THWICKA-THWICKA-THWICKA-THWICKA-

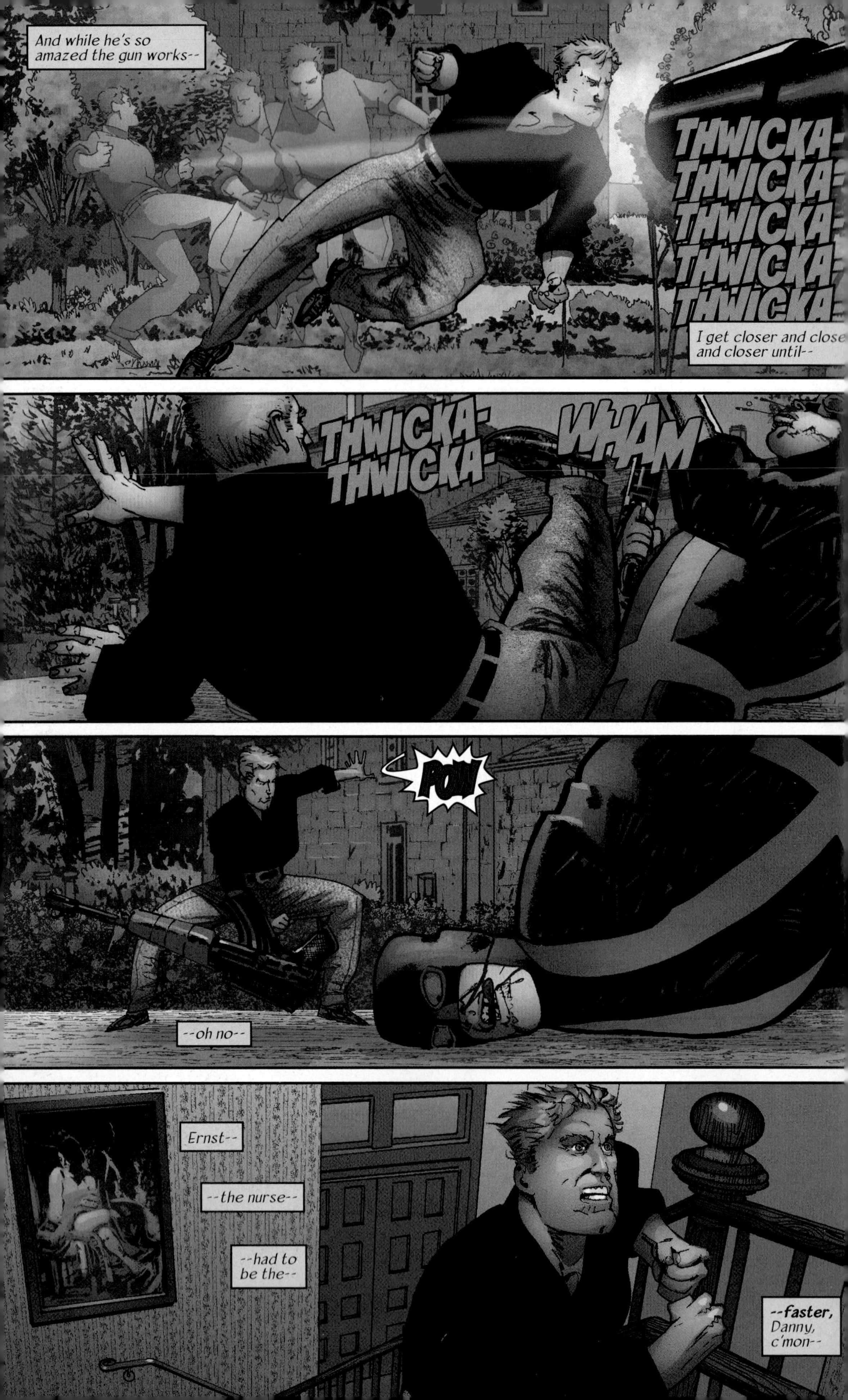

And while he's so amazed the gun works--
THWICKA-THWICKA-THWICKA-THWICKA-THWICKA
I get closer and close and closer until--
THWICKA-THWICKA-
WHAM
POW
--oh no--
Ernst--
--the nurse--
--had to be the--
--faster, Danny, c'mon--

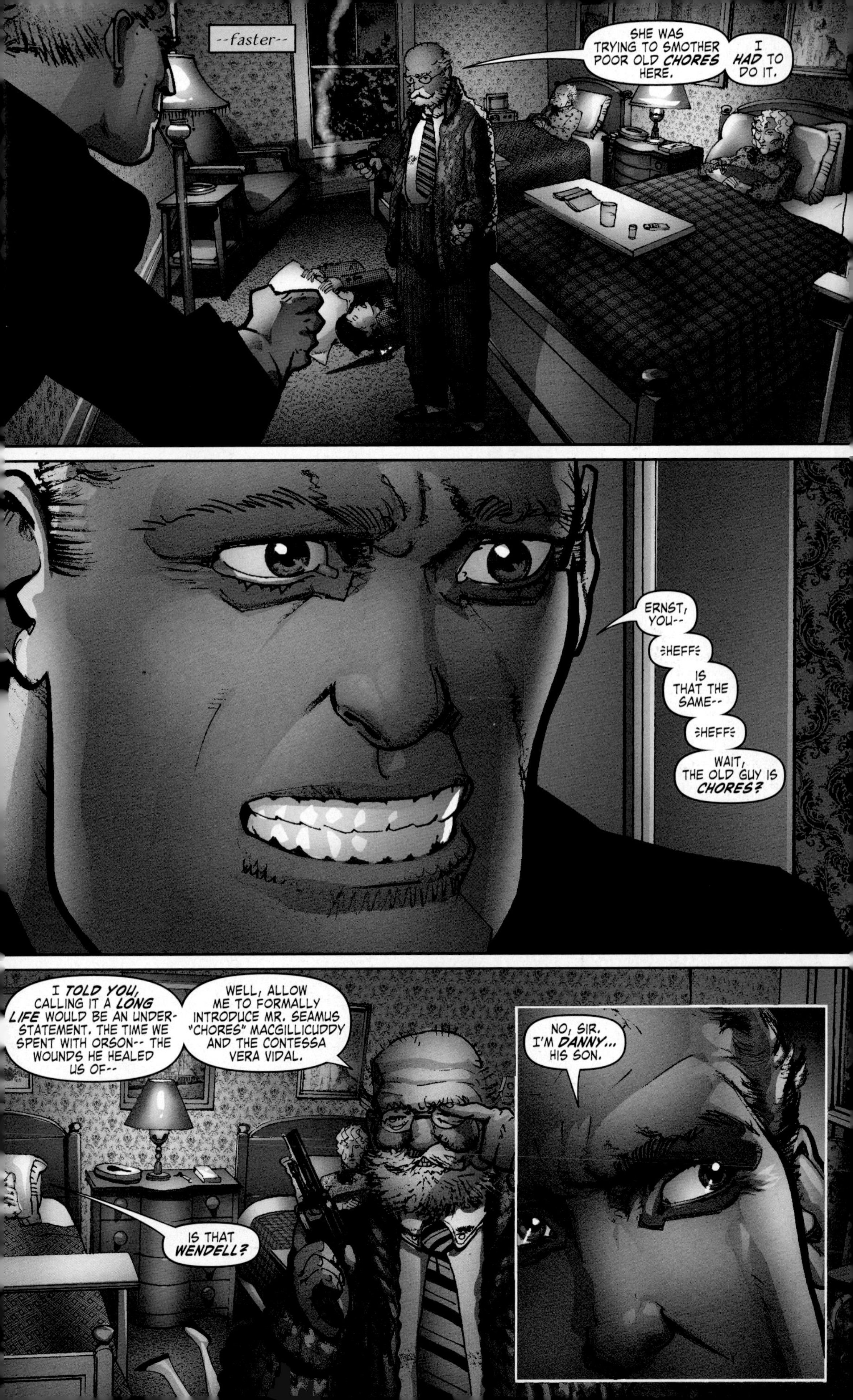
--faster--
SHE WAS TRYING TO SMOTHER POOR OLD CHORES HERE.
I HAD TO DO IT.
ERNST, YOU--
=HEFF=
IS THAT THE SAME--
=HEFF=
WAIT, THE OLD GUY IS CHORES?
I TOLD YOU, CALLING IT A LONG LIFE WOULD BE AN UNDER-STATEMENT. THE TIME WE SPENT WITH ORSON-- THE WOUNDS HE HEALED US OF--
WELL, ALLOW ME TO FORMALLY INTRODUCE MR. SEAMUS "CHORES" MACGILLICUDDY AND THE CONTESSA VERA VIDAL.
IS THAT WENDELL?
NO, SIR. I'M DANNY... HIS SON.

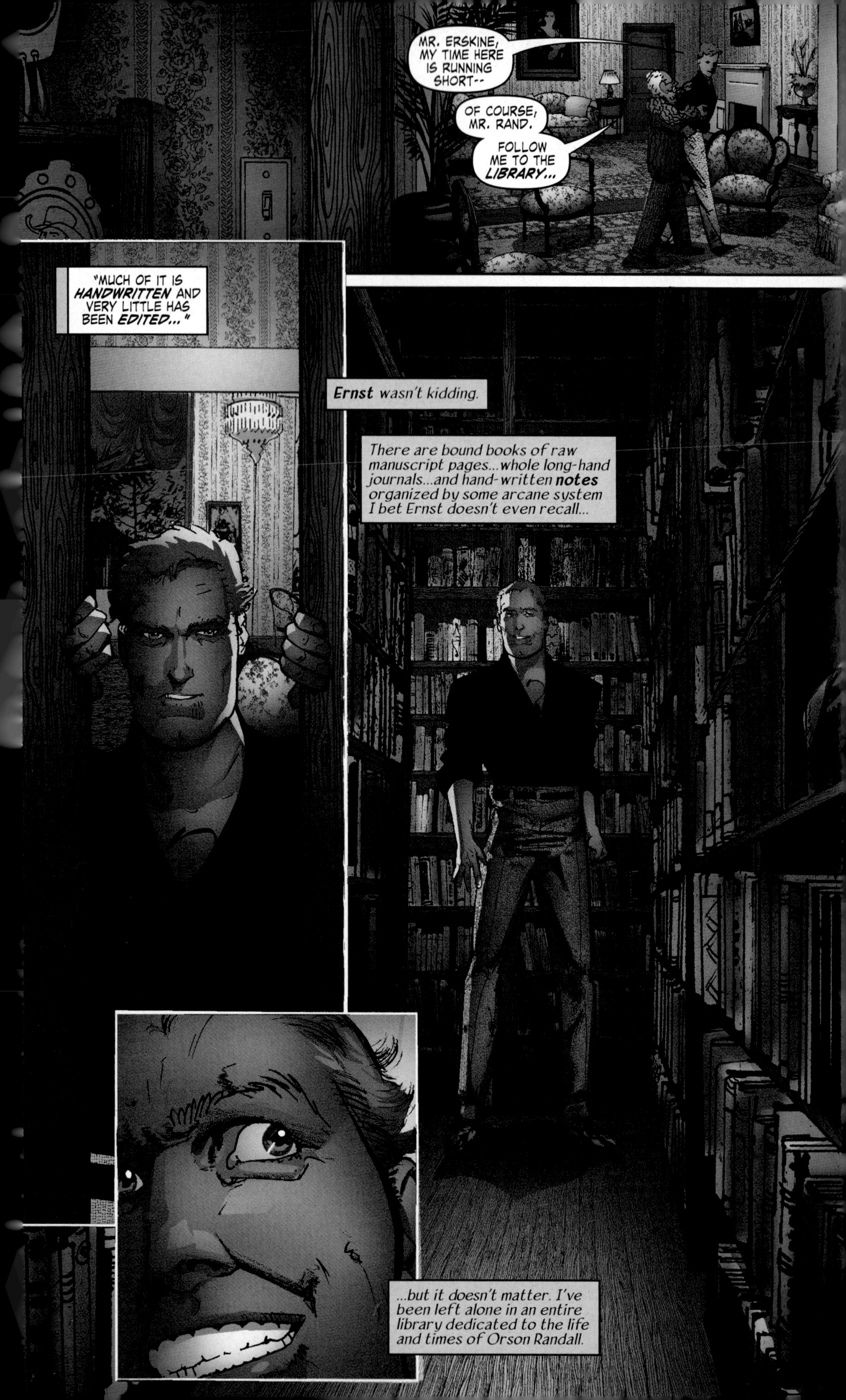
MR. ERSKINE, MY TIME HERE IS RUNNING SHORT--
OF COURSE, MR. RAND.
FOLLOW ME TO THE LIBRARY...
"MUCH OF IT IS HANDWRITTEN AND VERY LITTLE HAS BEEN EDITED..."
Ernst wasn't kidding.
There are bound books of raw manuscript pages...whole long-hand journals...and hand-written notes organized by some arcane system I bet Ernst doesn't even recall...
...but it doesn't matter. I've been left alone in an entire library dedicated to the life and times of Orson Randall.

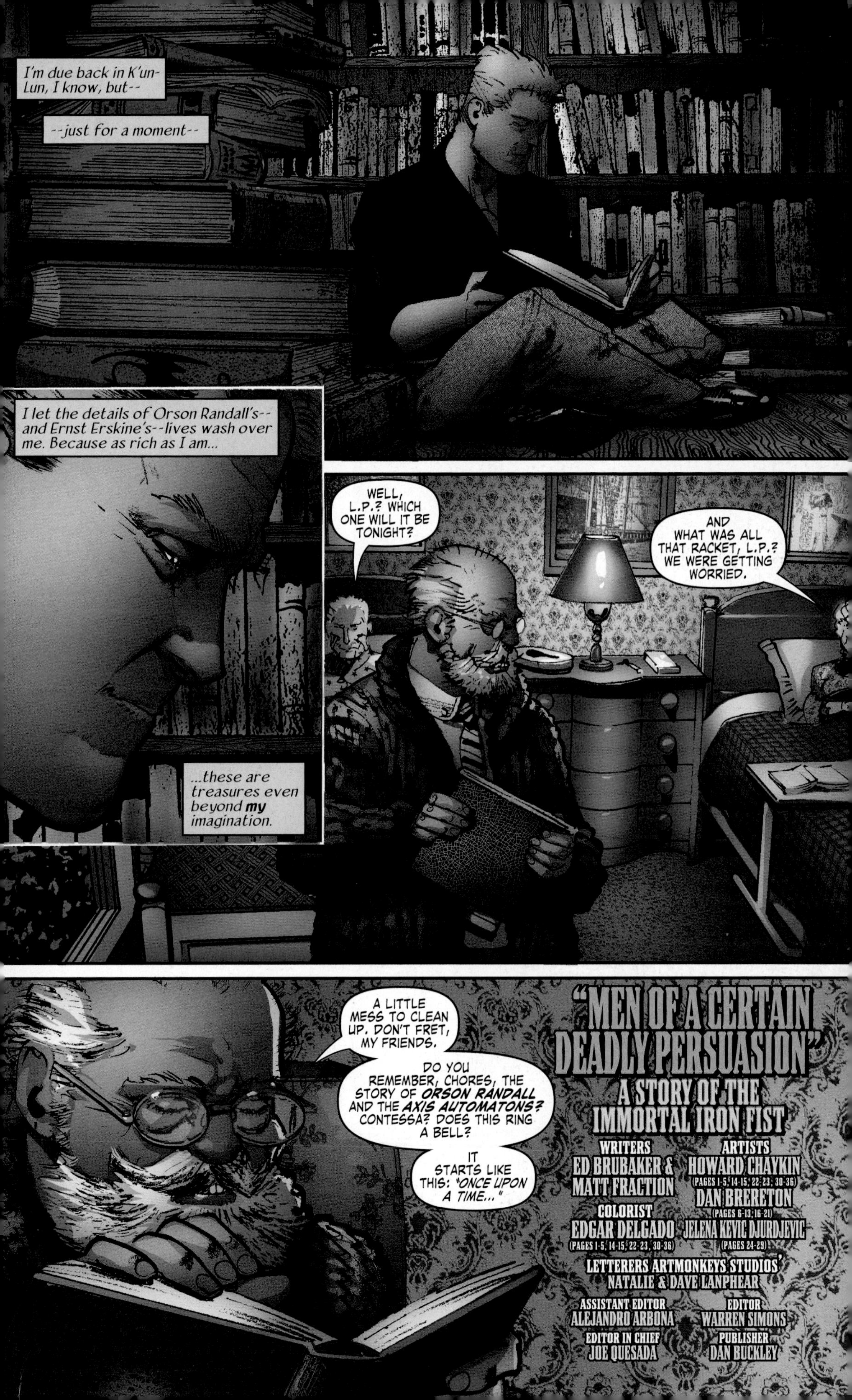
I'm due back in K'un-Lun, I know, but--
--just for a moment--
I let the details of Orson Randall's--and Ernst Erskine's--lives wash over me. Because as rich as I am...
...these are treasures even beyond **my** imagination.
WELL, L.P.? WHICH ONE WILL IT BE TONIGHT?
AND WHAT WAS ALL THAT RACKET, L.P.? WE WERE GETTING WORRIED.
A LITTLE MESS TO CLEAN UP. DON'T FRET, MY FRIENDS.
DO YOU REMEMBER, CHORES, THE STORY OF ***ORSON RANDALL*** AND THE ***AXIS AUTOMATONS?*** CONTESSA? DOES THIS RING A BELL?
IT STARTS LIKE THIS: *"ONCE UPON A TIME..."*
"MEN OF A CERTAIN DEADLY PERSUASION"
A STORY OF THE IMMORTAL IRON FIST
WRITERS ED BRUBAKER & MATT FRACTION
ARTISTS HOWARD CHAYKIN (PAGES 1-5, 14-15, 22-23, 30-36) DAN BRERETON (PAGES 6-13, 16-21) JELENA KEVIC DJURDJEVIC (PAGES 24-29)
COLORIST EDGAR DELGADO (PAGES 1-5, 14-15, 22-23, 30-36)
LETTERERS ARTMONKEYS STUDIOS' NATALIE & DAVE LANPHEAR
ASSISTANT EDITOR ALEJANDRO ARBONA
EDITOR WARREN SIMONS
EDITOR IN CHIEF JOE QUESADA
PUBLISHER DAN BUCKLEY

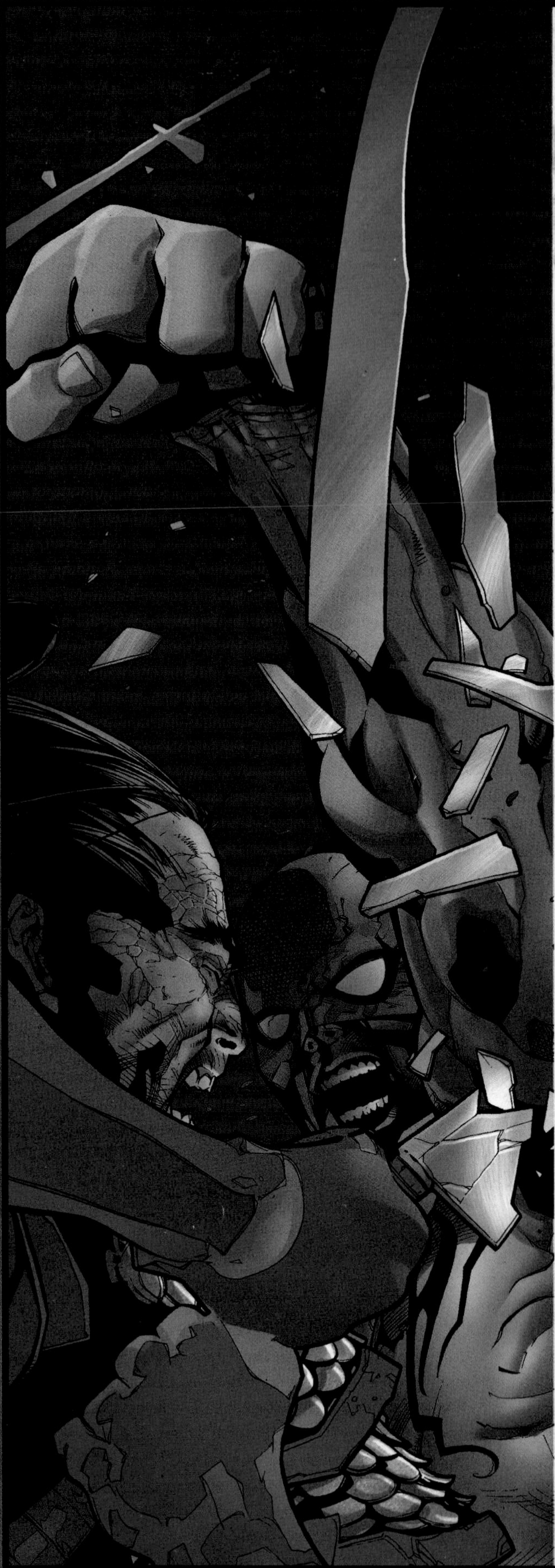

鐵拳 II

The 七 Capital Cities of Heaven

四 Round 4

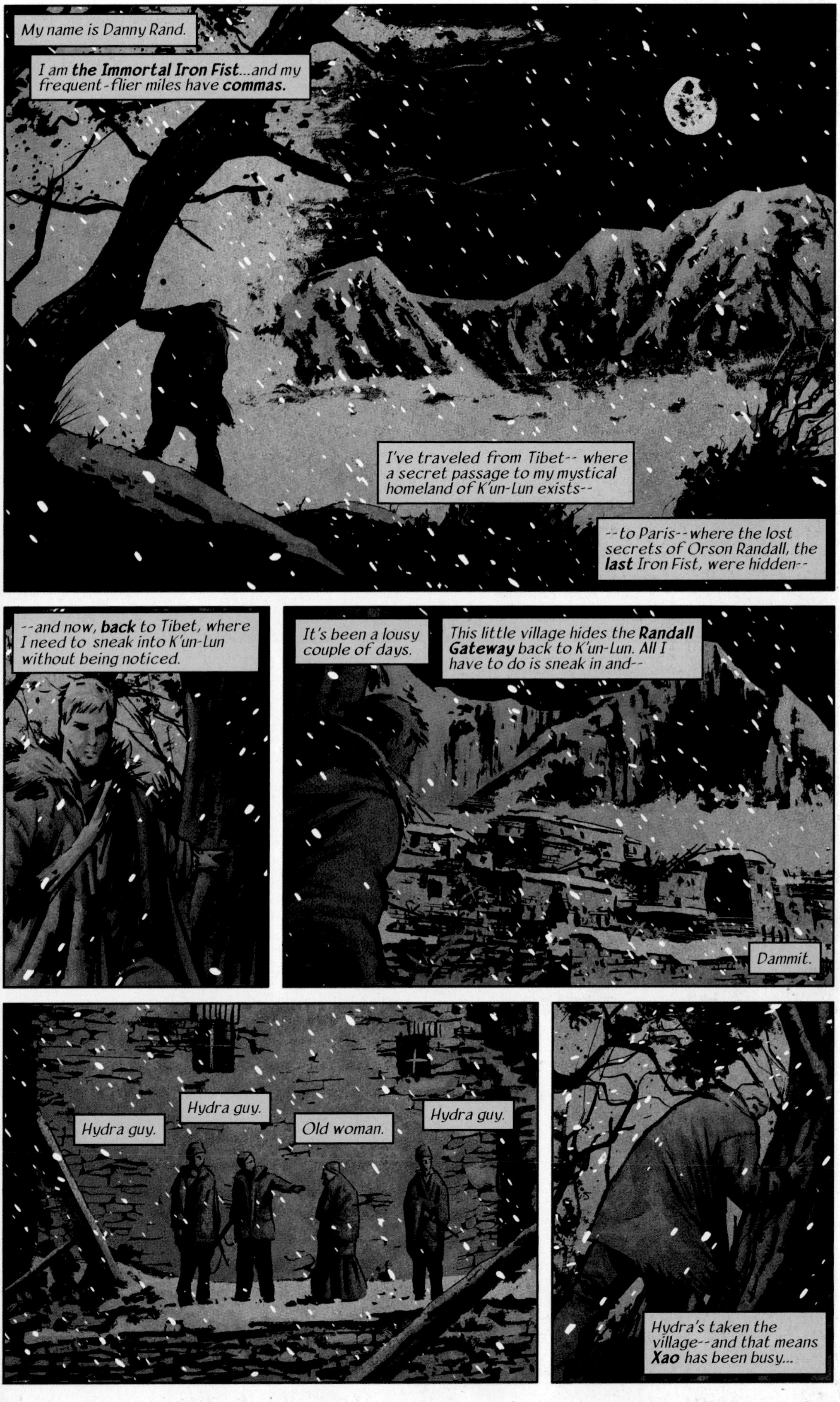
My name is Danny Rand.
I am **the Immortal Iron Fist**...and my frequent-flier miles have **commas.**
I've traveled from Tibet-- where a secret passage to my mystical homeland of K'un-Lun exists--
--to Paris--where the lost secrets of Orson Randall, the **last** Iron Fist, were hidden--
--and now, **back** to Tibet, where I need to sneak into K'un-Lun without being noticed.
It's been a lousy couple of days.
This little village hides the **Randall Gateway** back to K'un-Lun. All I have to do is sneak in and--
Dammit.
Hydra guy.
Hydra guy.
Old woman.
Hydra guy.
Hydra's taken the village--and that means **Xao** has been busy...

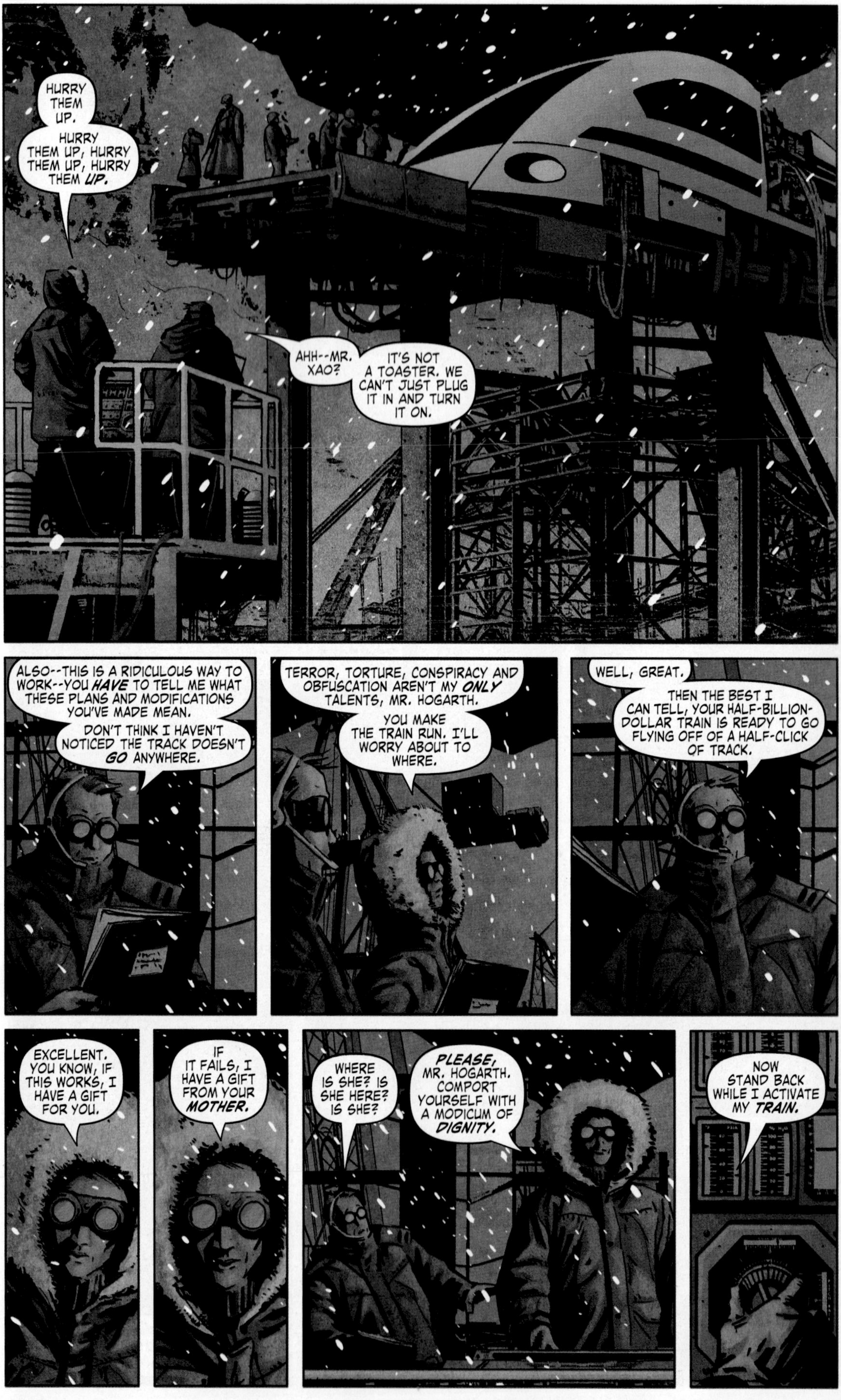
HURRY THEM UP.
HURRY THEM UP, HURRY THEM UP, HURRY THEM UP.
AHH--MR. XAO?
IT'S NOT A TOASTER. WE CAN'T JUST PLUG IT IN AND TURN IT ON.
ALSO--THIS IS A RIDICULOUS WAY TO WORK--YOU HAVE TO TELL ME WHAT THESE PLANS AND MODIFICATIONS YOU'VE MADE MEAN.
DON'T THINK I HAVEN'T NOTICED THE TRACK DOESN'T GO ANYWHERE.
TERROR, TORTURE, CONSPIRACY AND OBFUSCATION AREN'T MY ONLY TALENTS, MR. HOGARTH.
YOU MAKE THE TRAIN RUN. I'LL WORRY ABOUT TO WHERE.
WELL, GREAT.
THEN THE BEST I CAN TELL, YOUR HALF-BILLION-DOLLAR TRAIN IS READY TO GO FLYING OFF OF A HALF-CLICK OF TRACK.
EXCELLENT. YOU KNOW, IF THIS WORKS, I HAVE A GIFT FOR YOU.
IF IT FAILS, I HAVE A GIFT FROM YOUR MOTHER.
WHERE IS SHE? IS SHE HERE? IS SHE?
PLEASE, MR. HOGARTH. COMPORT YOURSELF WITH A MODICUM OF DIGNITY.
NOW STAND BACK WHILE I ACTIVATE MY TRAIN.

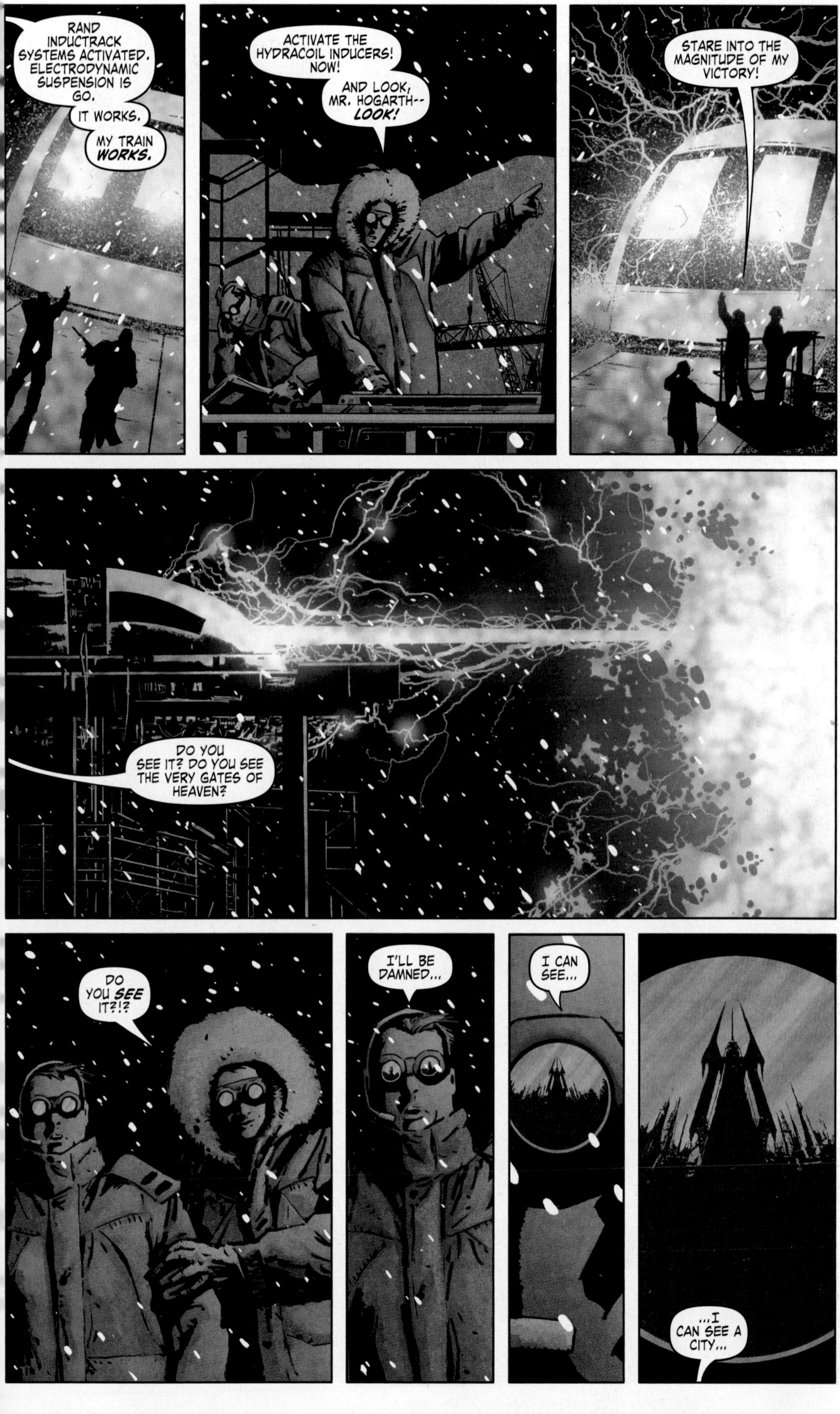
RAND INDUCTRACK SYSTEMS ACTIVATED. ELECTRODYNAMIC SUSPENSION IS GO.
IT WORKS.
MY TRAIN **WORKS.**
ACTIVATE THE HYDRACOIL INDUCERS! NOW!
AND LOOK, MR. HOGARTH-- **LOOK!**
STARE INTO THE MAGNITUDE OF MY VICTORY!
DO YOU SEE IT? DO YOU SEE THE VERY GATES OF HEAVEN?
DO YOU **SEE** IT?!?
I'LL BE DAMNED...
I CAN SEE...
...I CAN SEE A CITY...

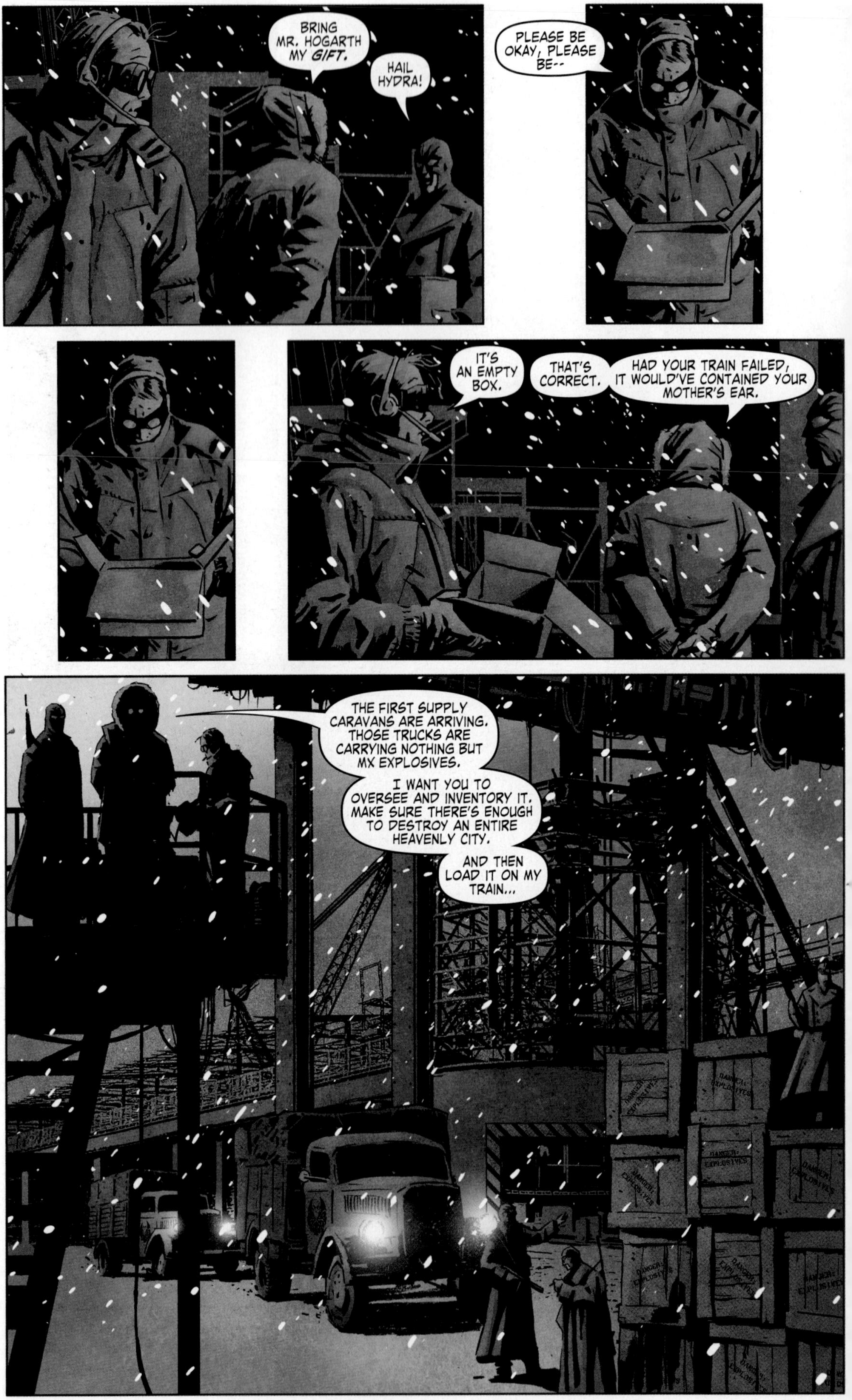
BRING MR. HOGARTH MY *GIFT*.
HAIL HYDRA!
PLEASE BE OKAY, PLEASE BE--
IT'S AN EMPTY BOX.
THAT'S CORRECT.
HAD YOUR TRAIN FAILED, IT WOULD'VE CONTAINED YOUR MOTHER'S EAR.
THE FIRST SUPPLY CARAVANS ARE ARRIVING. THOSE TRUCKS ARE CARRYING NOTHING BUT MX EXPLOSIVES.
I WANT YOU TO OVERSEE AND INVENTORY IT. MAKE SURE THERE'S ENOUGH TO DESTROY AN ENTIRE HEAVENLY CITY.
AND THEN LOAD IT ON MY TRAIN...

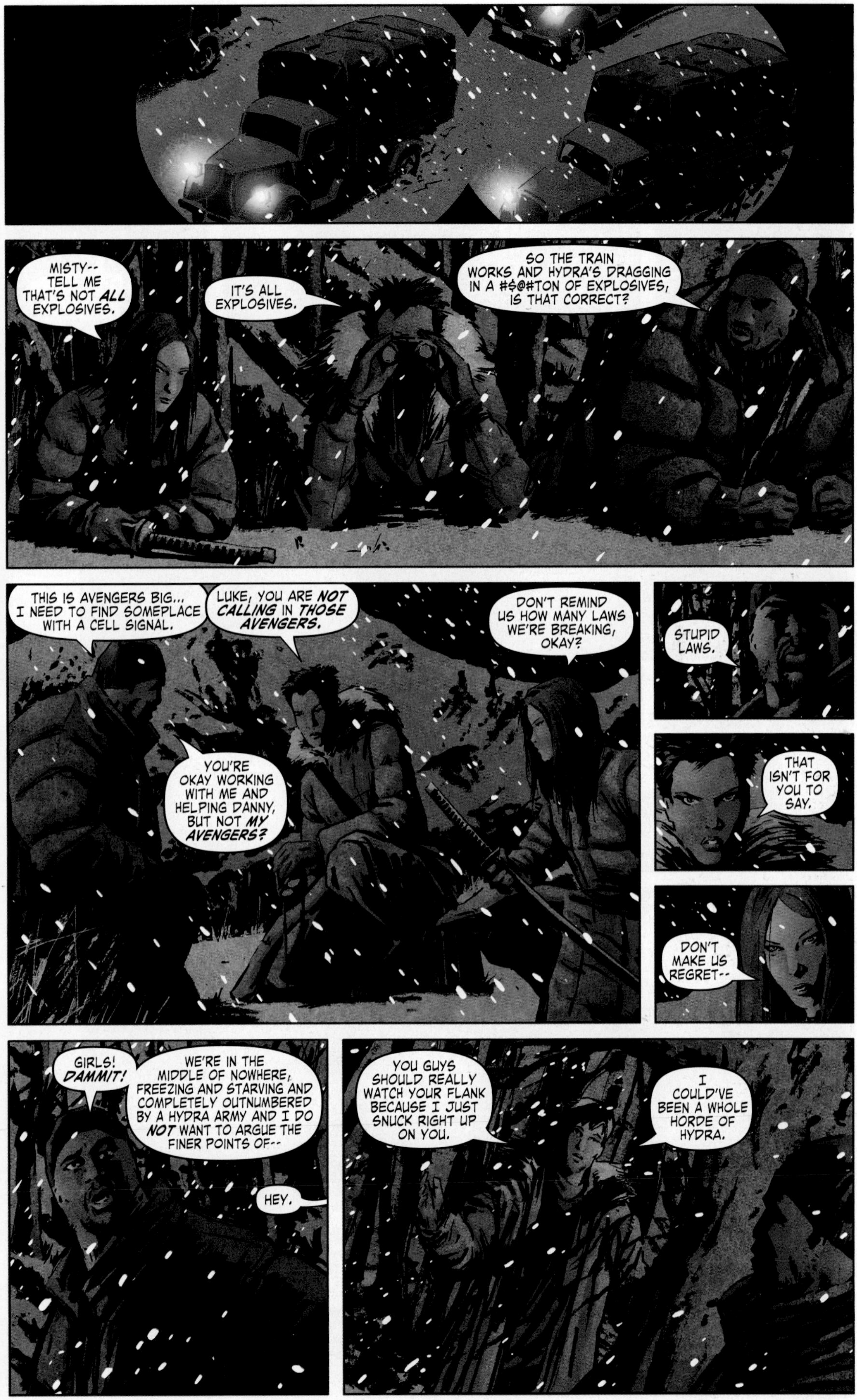
MISTY-- TELL ME THAT'S NOT *ALL* EXPLOSIVES.
IT'S ALL EXPLOSIVES.
SO THE TRAIN WORKS AND HYDRA'S DRAGGING IN A #$@#TON OF EXPLOSIVES, IS THAT CORRECT?
THIS IS AVENGERS BIG... I NEED TO FIND SOMEPLACE WITH A CELL SIGNAL.
LUKE, YOU ARE ***NOT CALLING*** IN ***THOSE AVENGERS.***
YOU'RE OKAY WORKING WITH ME AND HELPING DANNY, BUT NOT ***MY AVENGERS?***
DON'T REMIND US HOW MANY LAWS WE'RE BREAKING, OKAY?
STUPID LAWS.
THAT ISN'T FOR YOU TO SAY.
DON'T MAKE US REGRET--
GIRLS! ***DAMMIT!***
WE'RE IN THE MIDDLE OF NOWHERE, FREEZING AND STARVING AND COMPLETELY OUTNUMBERED BY A HYDRA ARMY AND I DO ***NOT*** WANT TO ARGUE THE FINER POINTS OF--
HEY.
YOU GUYS SHOULD REALLY WATCH YOUR FLANK BECAUSE I JUST SNUCK RIGHT UP ON YOU.
I COULD'VE BEEN A WHOLE HORDE OF HYDRA.

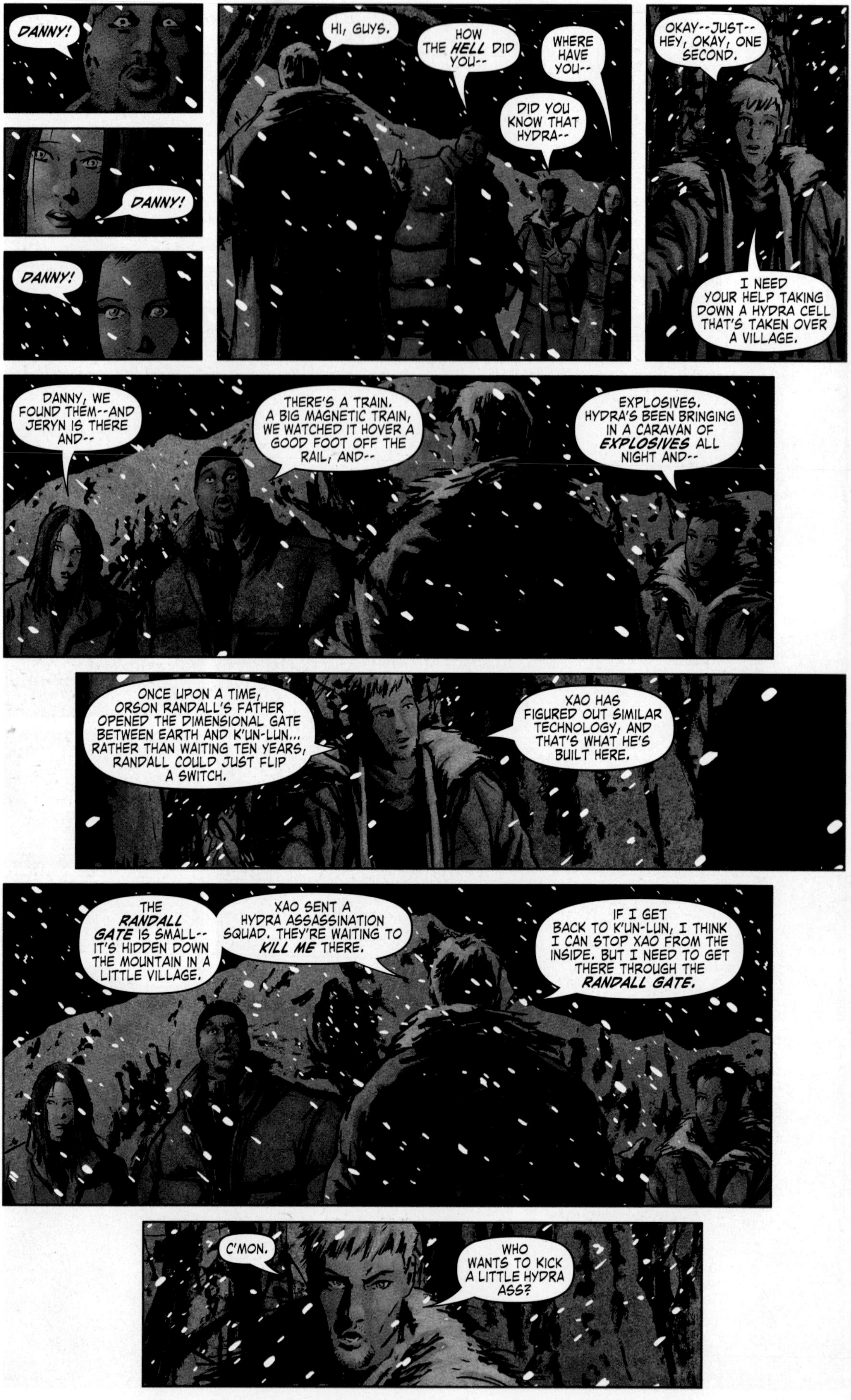
DANNY!
DANNY!
DANNY!
HI, GUYS.
HOW THE HELL DID YOU--
WHERE HAVE YOU--
DID YOU KNOW THAT HYDRA--
OKAY--JUST--HEY, OKAY, ONE SECOND.
I NEED YOUR HELP TAKING DOWN A HYDRA CELL THAT'S TAKEN OVER A VILLAGE.
DANNY, WE FOUND THEM--AND JERYN IS THERE AND--
THERE'S A TRAIN. A BIG MAGNETIC TRAIN, WE WATCHED IT HOVER A GOOD FOOT OFF THE RAIL, AND--
EXPLOSIVES. HYDRA'S BEEN BRINGING IN A CARAVAN OF EXPLOSIVES ALL NIGHT AND--
ONCE UPON A TIME, ORSON RANDALL'S FATHER OPENED THE DIMENSIONAL GATE BETWEEN EARTH AND K'UN-LUN... RATHER THAN WAITING TEN YEARS, RANDALL COULD JUST FLIP A SWITCH.
XAO HAS FIGURED OUT SIMILAR TECHNOLOGY, AND THAT'S WHAT HE'S BUILT HERE.
THE RANDALL GATE IS SMALL--IT'S HIDDEN DOWN THE MOUNTAIN IN A LITTLE VILLAGE.
XAO SENT A HYDRA ASSASSINATION SQUAD. THEY'RE WAITING TO KILL ME THERE.
IF I GET BACK TO K'UN-LUN, I THINK I CAN STOP XAO FROM THE INSIDE. BUT I NEED TO GET THERE THROUGH THE RANDALL GATE.
C'MON.
WHO WANTS TO KICK A LITTLE HYDRA ASS?

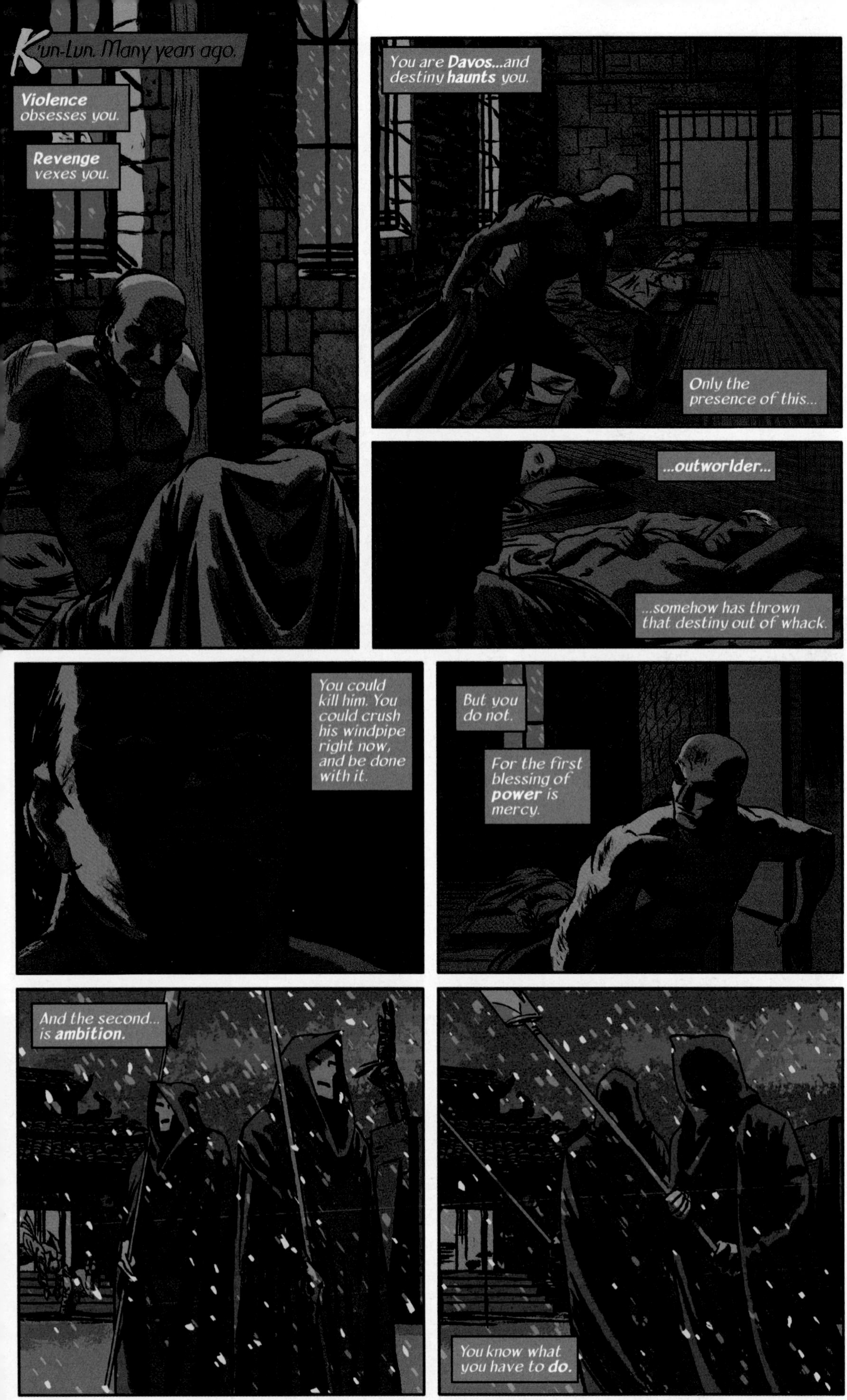
K'un-Lun. Many years ago.
Violence obsesses you.
Revenge vexes you.
You are Davos...and destiny haunts you.
Only the presence of this...
...outworlder...
...somehow has thrown that destiny out of whack.
You could kill him. You could crush his windpipe right now, and be done with it.
But you do not.
For the first blessing of power is mercy.
And the second... is ambition.
You know what you have to do.

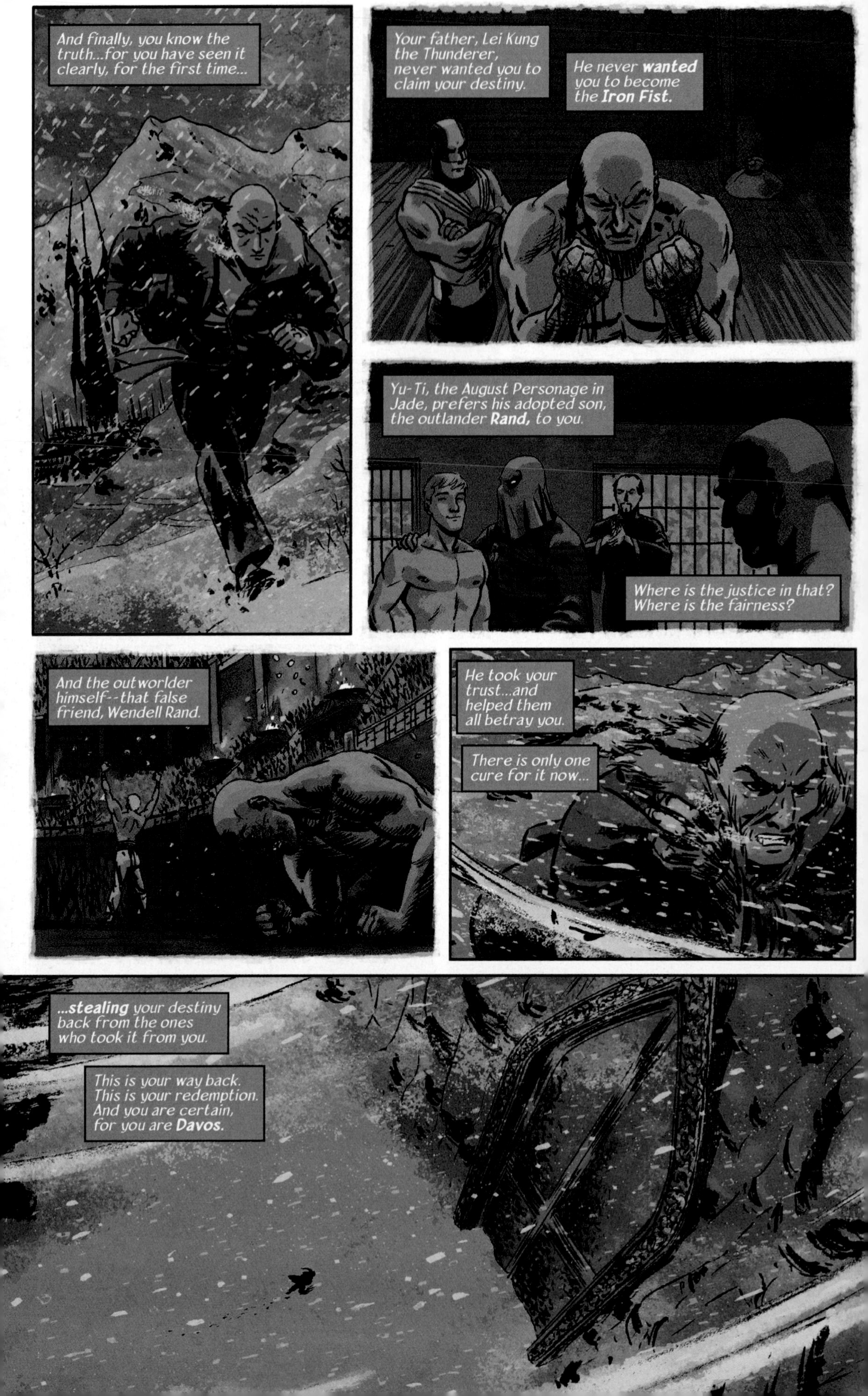
And finally, you know the truth...for you have seen it clearly, for the first time...
Your father, Lei Kung the Thunderer, never wanted you to claim your destiny.
He never **wanted** you to become the **Iron Fist.**
Yu-Ti, the August Personage in Jade, prefers his adopted son, the outlander **Rand,** to you.
Where is the justice in that? Where is the fairness?
And the outworlder himself--that false friend, Wendell Rand.
He took your trust...and helped them all betray you.
There is only one cure for it now...
...**stealing** your destiny back from the ones who took it from you.
This is your way back. This is your redemption. And you are certain, for you are **Davos.**

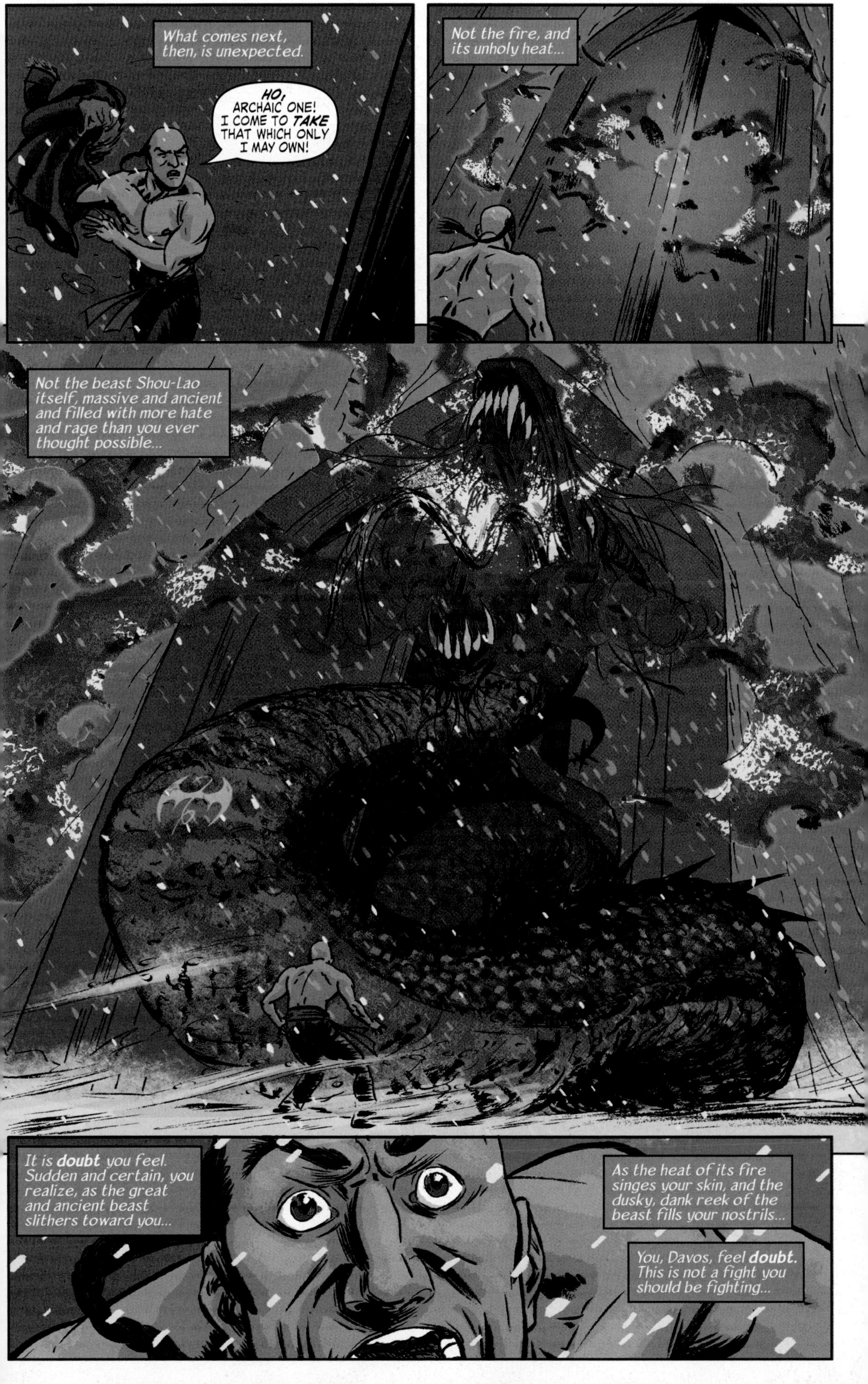
What comes next, then, is unexpected.
HO, ARCHAIC ONE! I COME TO TAKE THAT WHICH ONLY I MAY OWN!
Not the fire, and its unholy heat...
Not the beast Shou-Lao itself, massive and ancient and filled with more hate and rage than you ever thought possible...
It is doubt you feel. Sudden and certain, you realize, as the great and ancient beast slithers toward you...
As the heat of its fire singes your skin, and the dusky, dank reek of the beast fills your nostrils...
You, Davos, feel doubt. This is not a fight you should be fighting...

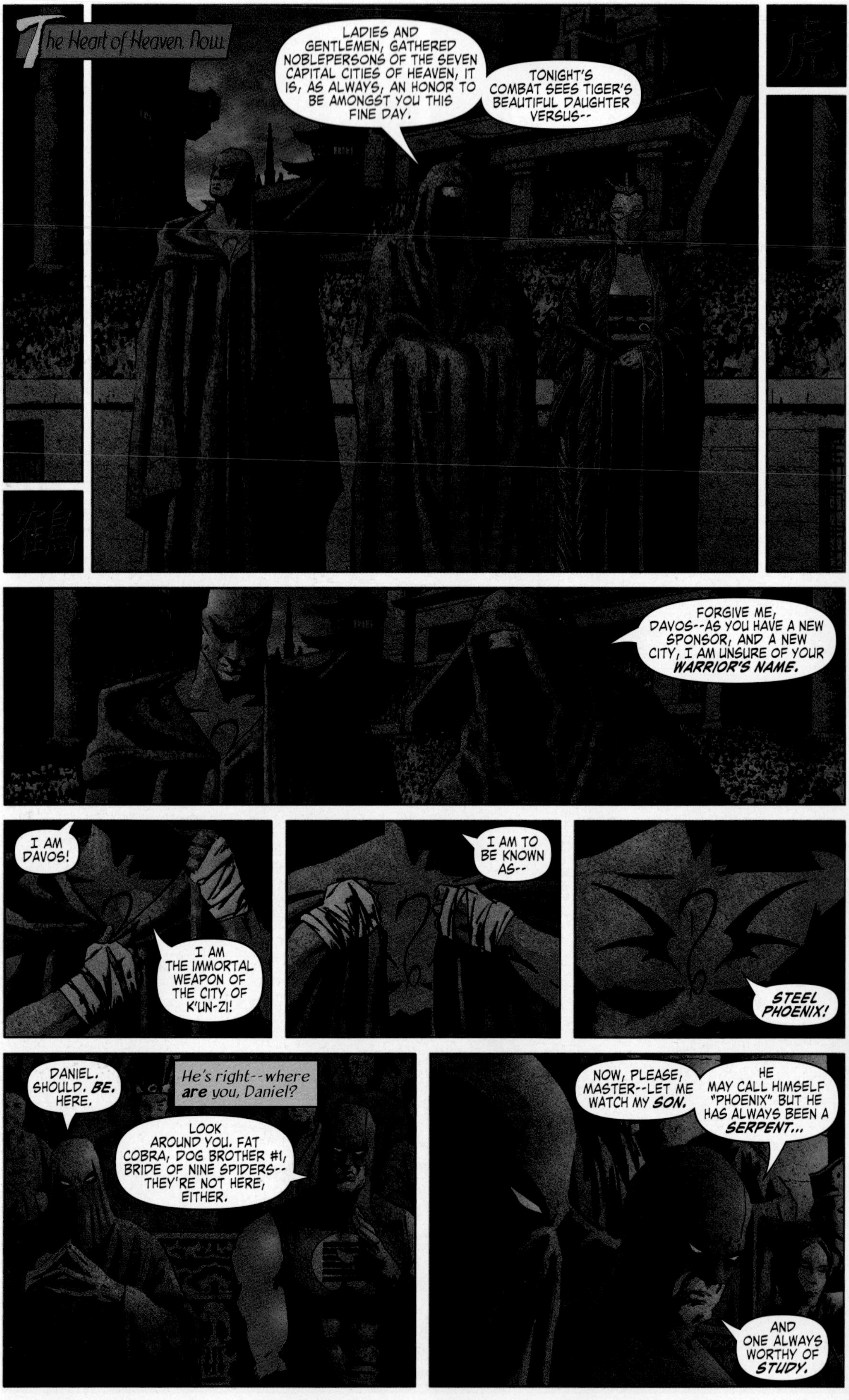
The Heart of Heaven. Now.
LADIES AND GENTLEMEN, GATHERED NOBLEPERSONS OF THE SEVEN CAPITAL CITIES OF HEAVEN, IT IS, AS ALWAYS, AN HONOR TO BE AMONGST YOU THIS FINE DAY.
TONIGHT'S COMBAT SEES TIGER'S BEAUTIFUL DAUGHTER VERSUS--
FORGIVE ME, DAVOS--AS YOU HAVE A NEW SPONSOR, AND A NEW CITY, I AM UNSURE OF YOUR WARRIOR'S NAME.
I AM DAVOS!
I AM THE IMMORTAL WEAPON OF THE CITY OF K'UN-ZI!
I AM TO BE KNOWN AS--
STEEL PHOENIX!
DANIEL. SHOULD. BE. HERE.
He's right--where are you, Daniel?
LOOK AROUND YOU. FAT COBRA, DOG BROTHER #1, BRIDE OF NINE SPIDERS--THEY'RE NOT HERE, EITHER.
NOW, PLEASE, MASTER--LET ME WATCH MY SON.
HE MAY CALL HIMSELF "PHOENIX" BUT HE HAS ALWAYS BEEN A SERPENT...
AND ONE ALWAYS WORTHY OF STUDY.

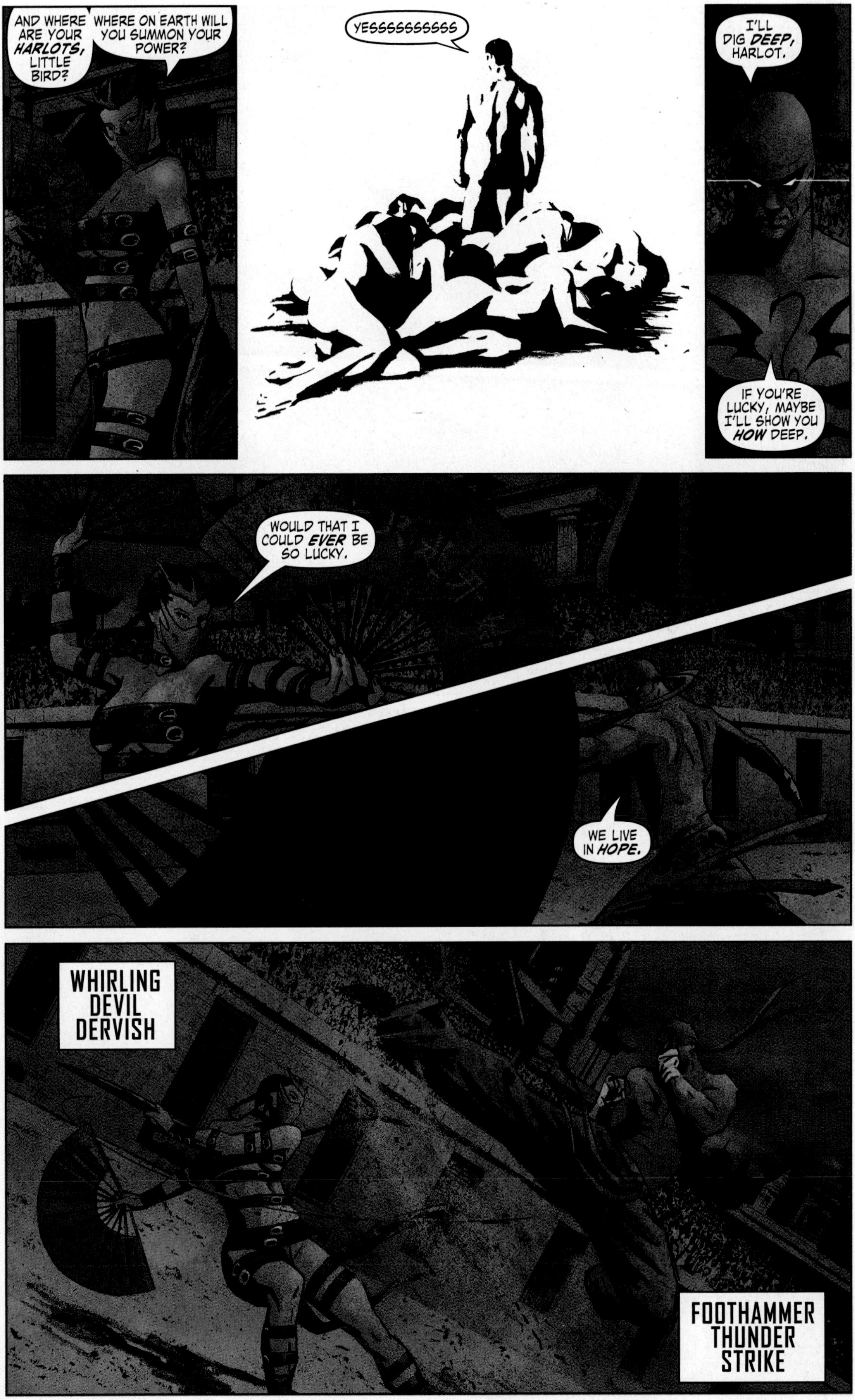
AND WHERE ARE YOUR HARLOTS, LITTLE BIRD?
WHERE ON EARTH WILL YOU SUMMON YOUR POWER?
YESSSSSSSSSSS
I'LL DIG DEEP, HARLOT.
IF YOU'RE LUCKY, MAYBE I'LL SHOW YOU HOW DEEP.
WOULD THAT I COULD EVER BE SO LUCKY.
WE LIVE IN HOPE.
WHIRLING DEVIL DERVISH
FOOTHAMMER THUNDER STRIKE

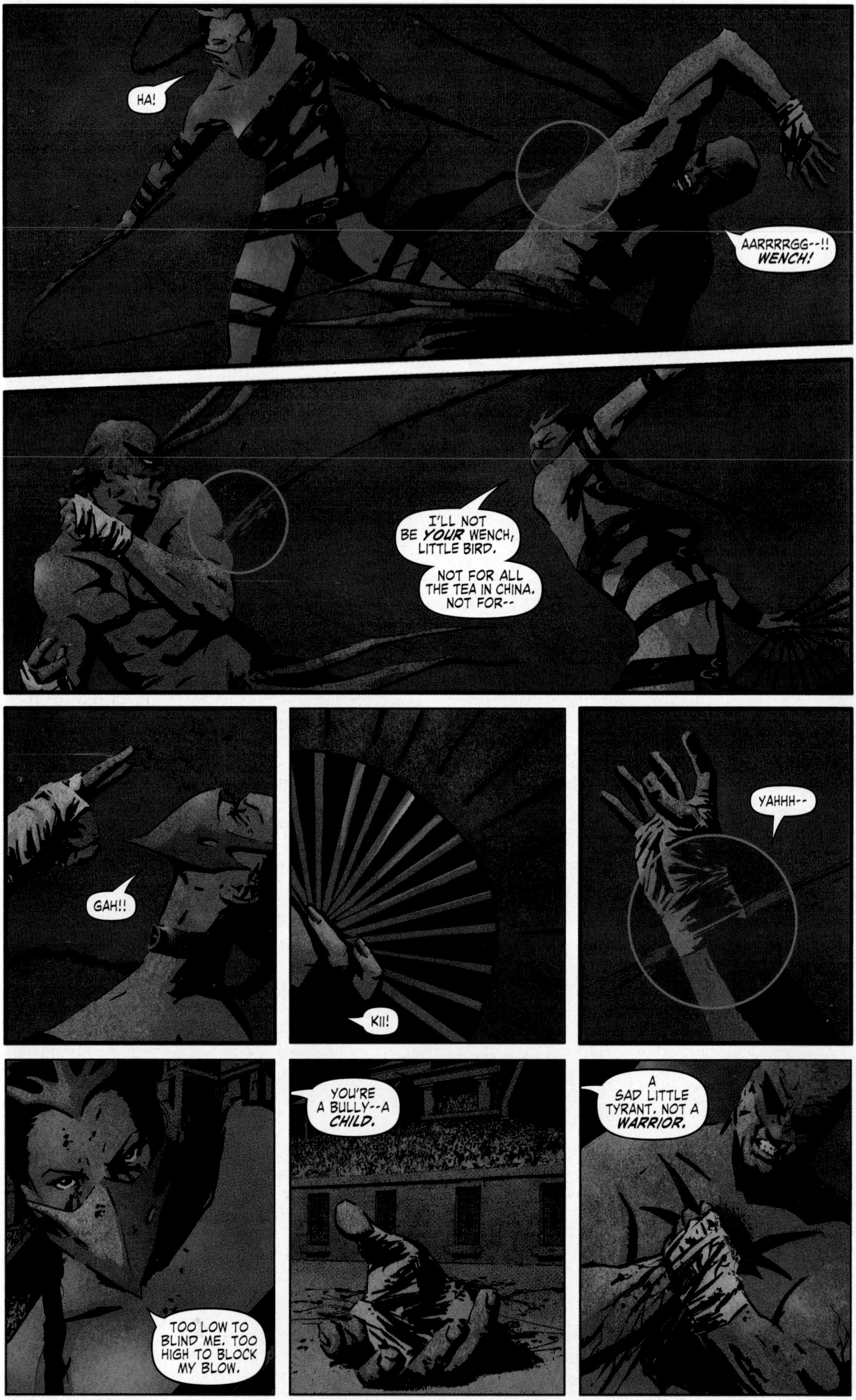
HA!
AARRRRGG--!! WENCH!
I'LL NOT BE YOUR WENCH, LITTLE BIRD.
NOT FOR ALL THE TEA IN CHINA. NOT FOR--
GAH!!
KII!
YAHHH--
TOO LOW TO BLIND ME. TOO HIGH TO BLOCK MY BLOW.
YOU'RE A BULLY--A CHILD.
A SAD LITTLE TYRANT. NOT A WARRIOR.

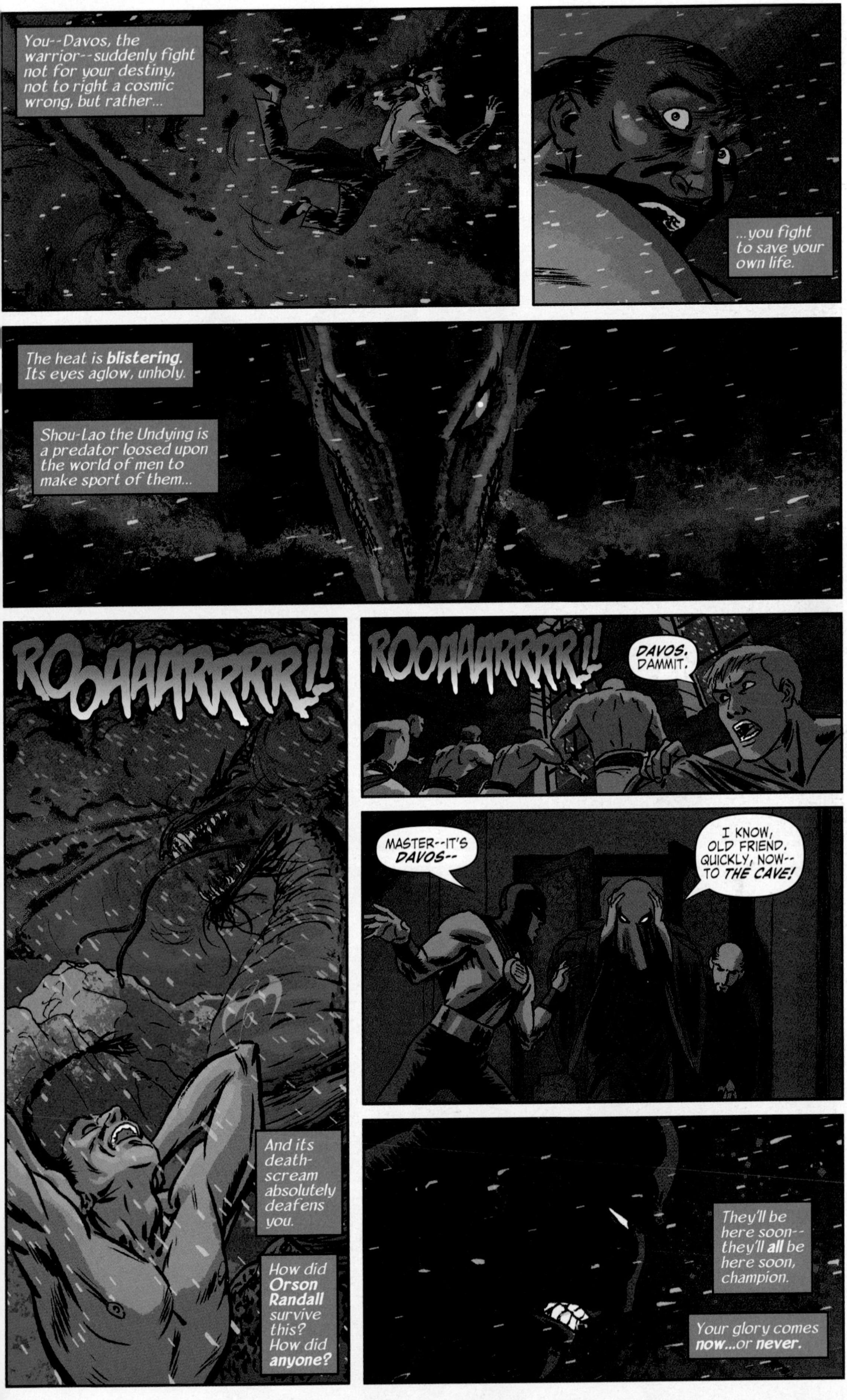
You--Davos, the warrior--suddenly fight not for your destiny, not to right a cosmic wrong, but rather...
...you fight to save your own life.
The heat is **blistering.** Its eyes aglow, unholy.
Shou-Lao the Undying is a predator loosed upon the world of men to make sport of them...
ROOAAARRRR!!
And its death-scream absolutely deafens you.
How did **Orson Randall** survive this? How did **anyone?**
ROOAAARRRR!!
DAVOS. DAMMIT.
MASTER--IT'S *DAVOS--*
I KNOW, OLD FRIEND. QUICKLY, NOW--TO *THE CAVE!*
They'll be here soon--they'll **all** be here soon, champion.
Your glory comes **now**...or **never.**

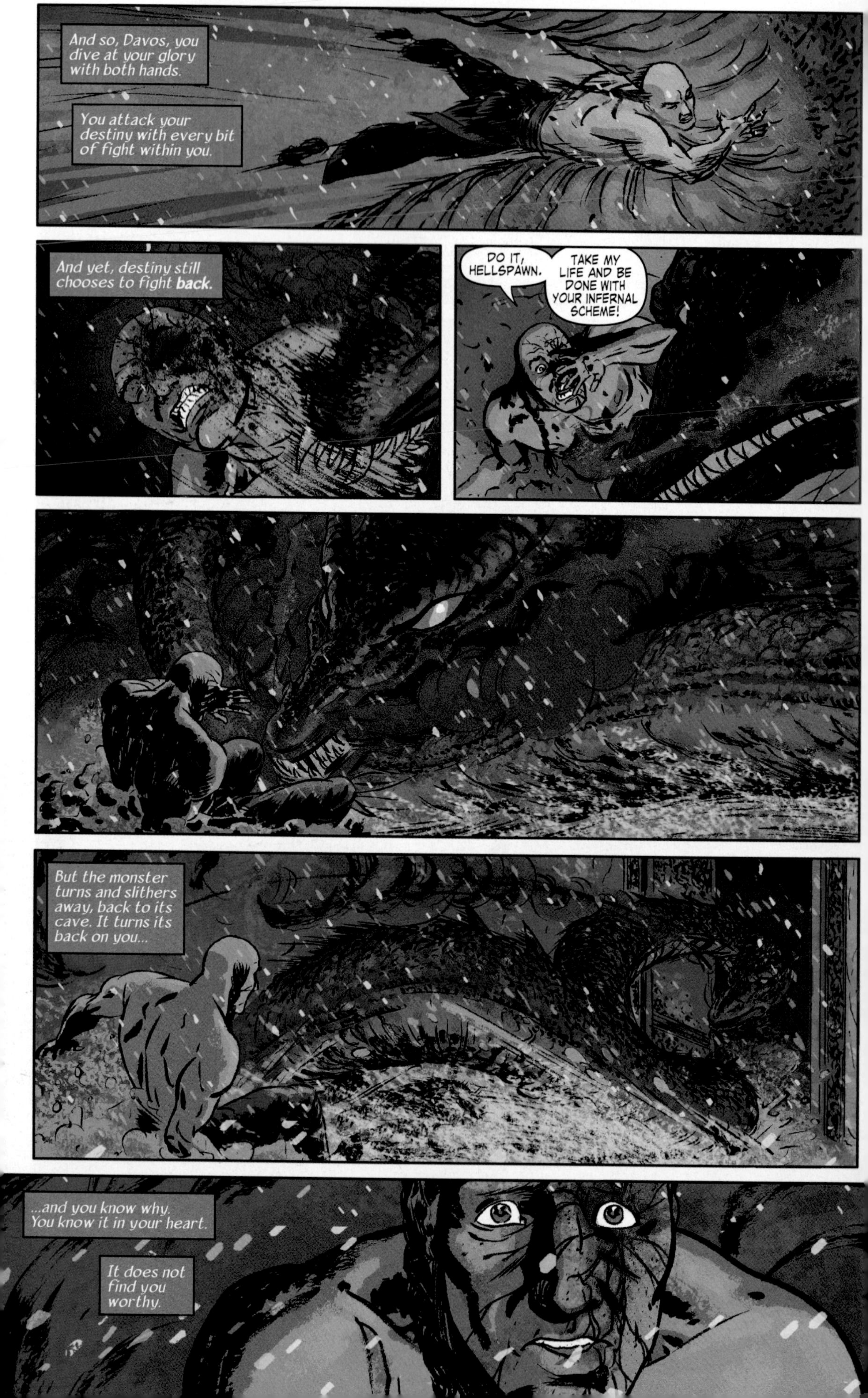
And so, Davos, you dive at your glory with both hands.
You attack your destiny with every bit of fight within you.
And yet, destiny still chooses to fight **back.**
DO IT, HELLSPAWN.
TAKE MY LIFE AND BE DONE WITH YOUR INFERNAL SCHEME!
But the monster turns and slithers away, back to its cave. It turns its back on you...
...and you know why. You know it in your heart.
It does not find you worthy.

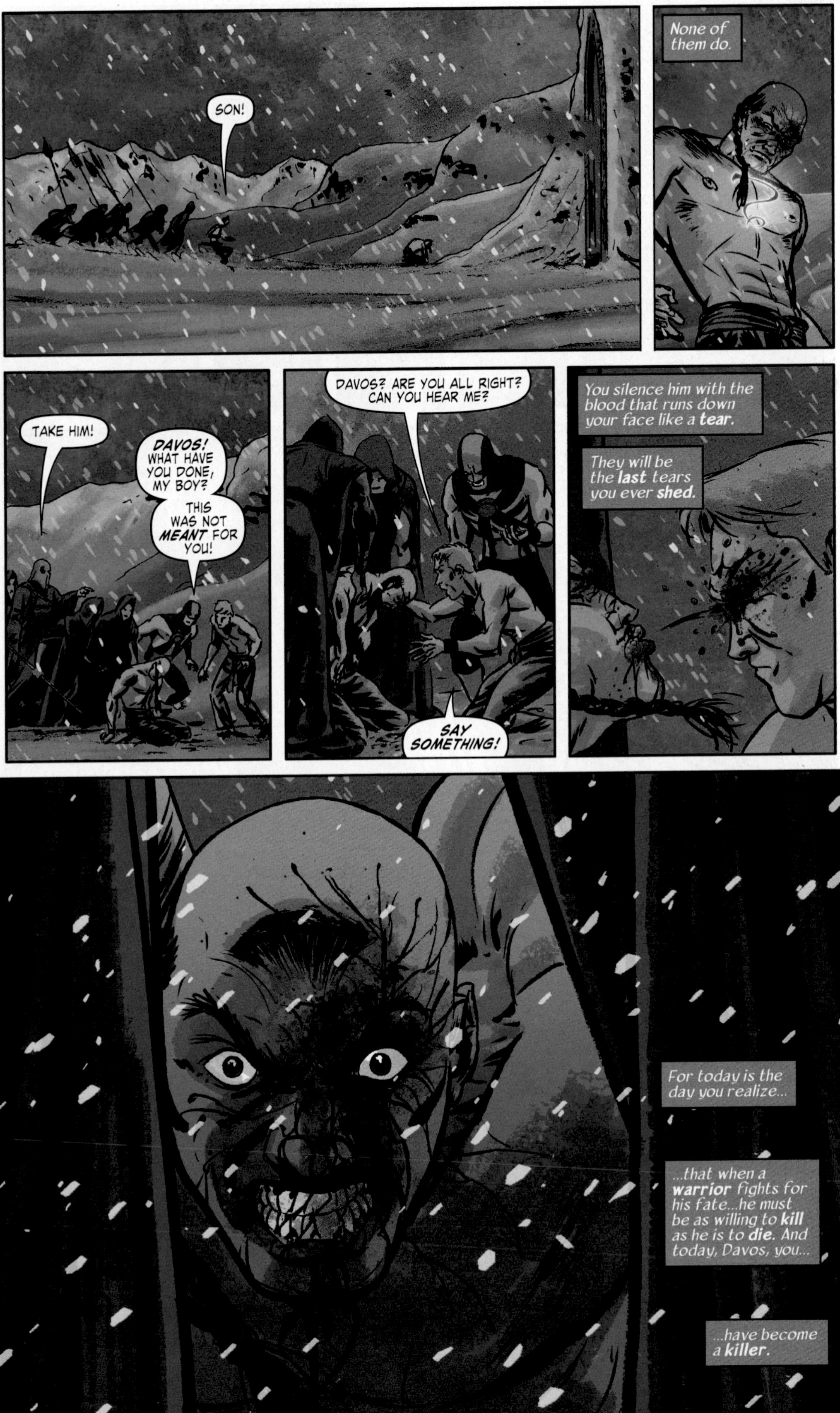

SON!
None of them do.
TAKE HIM!
DAVOS! WHAT HAVE YOU DONE, MY BOY?
THIS WAS NOT MEANT FOR YOU!
DAVOS? ARE YOU ALL RIGHT? CAN YOU HEAR ME?
SAY SOMETHING!
You silence him with the blood that runs down your face like a tear.
They will be the last tears you ever shed.
For today is the day you realize...
...that when a warrior fights for his fate...he must be as willing to kill as he is to die. And today, Davos, you...
...have become a killer.

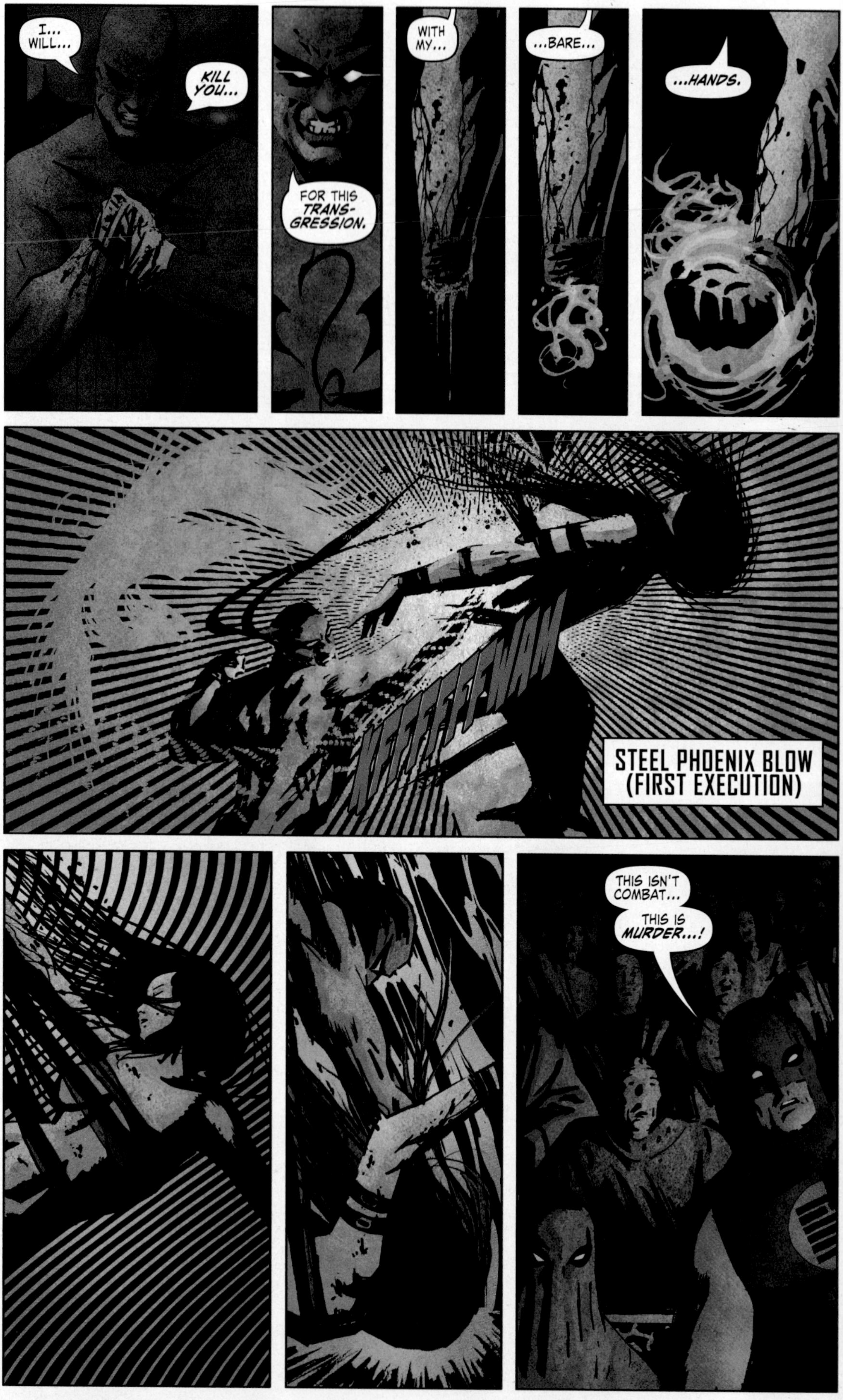
I... WILL...
KILL YOU...
FOR THIS TRANS-GRESSION.
WITH MY...
...BARE...
...HANDS.
KFFFFFFWAM
STEEL PHOENIX BLOW (FIRST EXECUTION)
THIS ISN'T COMBAT...
THIS IS MURDER...!

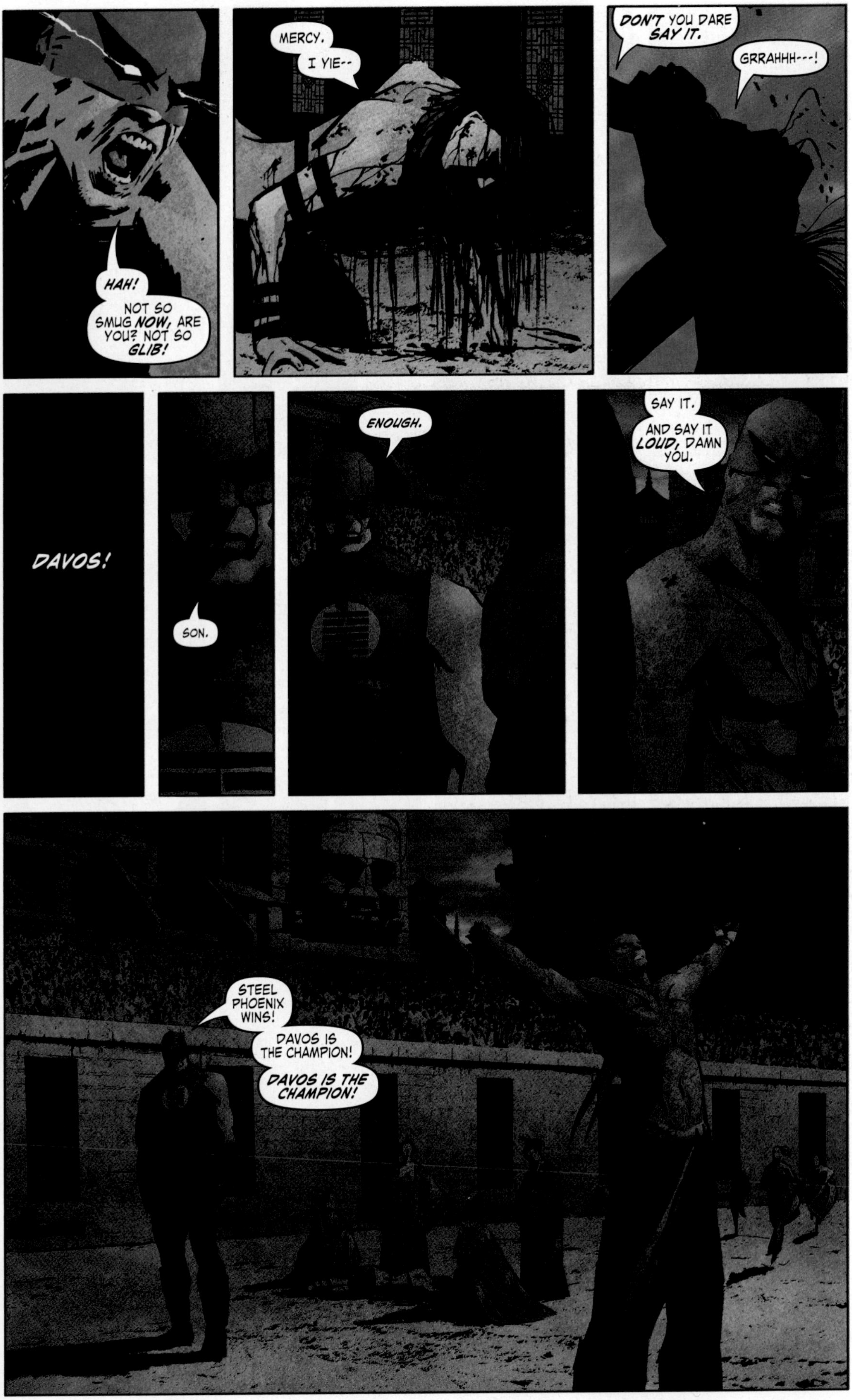
HAH!
NOT SO SMUG NOW, ARE YOU? NOT SO GLIB!
MERCY.
I YIE--
DON'T YOU DARE SAY IT.
GRRAHHH---!
DAVOS!
SON.
ENOUGH.
SAY IT.
AND SAY IT LOUD, DAMN YOU.
STEEL PHOENIX WINS!
DAVOS IS THE CHAMPION!
DAVOS IS THE CHAMPION!

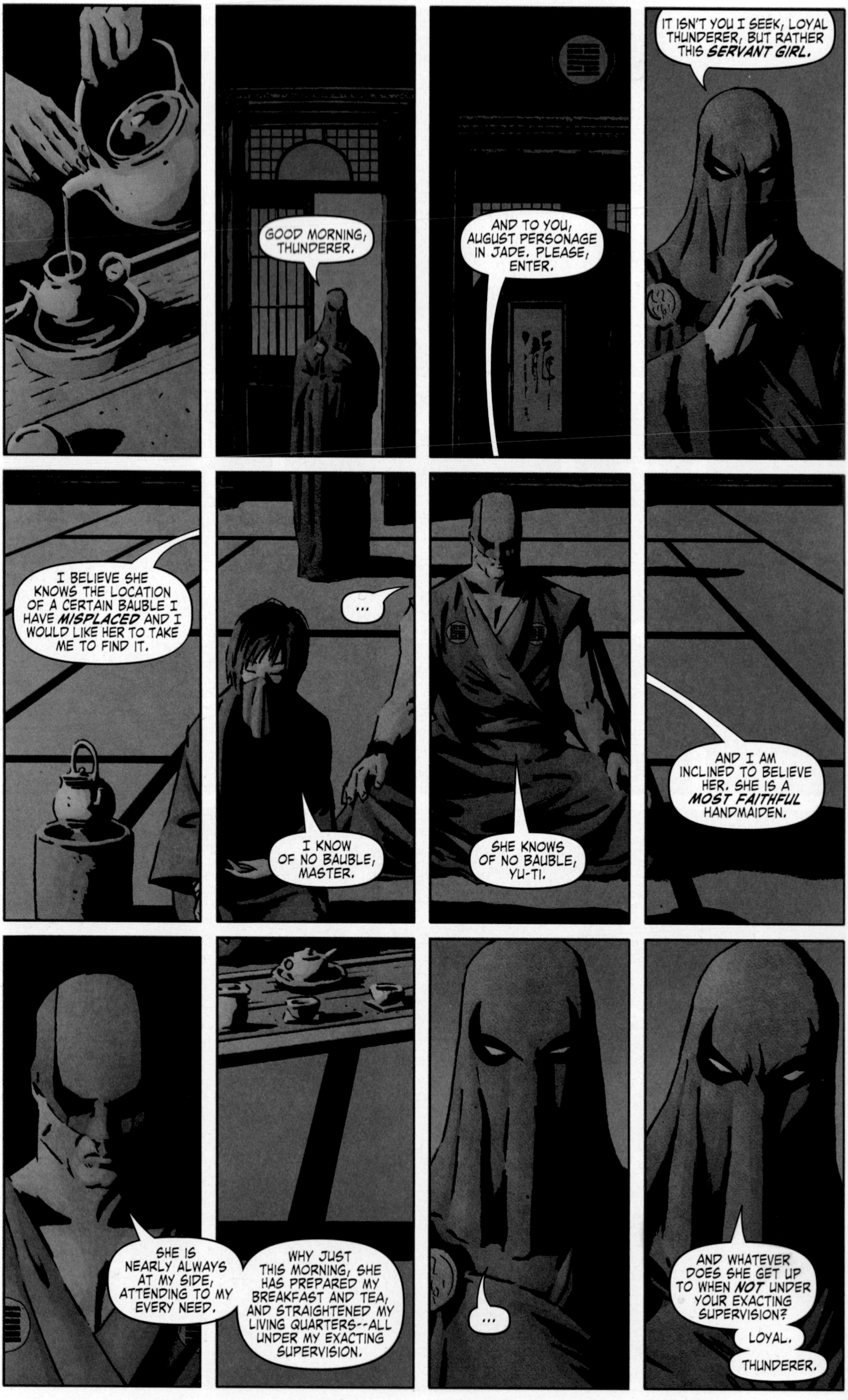
GOOD MORNING, THUNDERER.
AND TO YOU, AUGUST PERSONAGE IN JADE. PLEASE, ENTER.
IT ISN'T YOU I SEEK, LOYAL THUNDERER, BUT RATHER THIS *SERVANT GIRL.*
I BELIEVE SHE KNOWS THE LOCATION OF A CERTAIN BAUBLE I HAVE *MISPLACED* AND I WOULD LIKE HER TO TAKE ME TO FIND IT.
...
I KNOW OF NO BAUBLE, MASTER.
SHE KNOWS OF NO BAUBLE, YU-TI.
AND I AM INCLINED TO BELIEVE HER. SHE IS A *MOST FAITHFUL* HANDMAIDEN.
SHE IS NEARLY ALWAYS AT MY SIDE, ATTENDING TO MY EVERY NEED.
WHY JUST THIS MORNING, SHE HAS PREPARED MY BREAKFAST AND TEA, AND STRAIGHTENED MY LIVING QUARTERS--ALL UNDER MY EXACTING SUPERVISION.
...
AND WHATEVER DOES SHE GET UP TO WHEN *NOT* UNDER YOUR EXACTING SUPERVISION?
LOYAL.
THUNDERER.

...

WHATEVER DO YOU **MEAN**, AUGUST PERSONAGE IN JADE?

I HAVE INSTRUCTED HER ONLY AS THE LAWS OF K'UN-LUN--

--ONLY AS **YOUR LAWS**-- ALLOW.

FOOD PREPARATION, HOUSEKEEPING, WEAPONS UPKEEP, COMBAT MEDICINE, FISHING.

WHY DO YOU IMPLY OTHERWISE?

There is a **rift** in K'un-Lun that threatens to tear us all asunder.

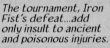

The tournament, Iron Fist's defeat....add only insult to ancient and poisonous injuries.

Long-seated tensions between the way **it always has been**...

...And the way my master thinks it **should** be.

Iron Fist...wherever you are...

Your home **needs you** to stop it from ripping itself apart.

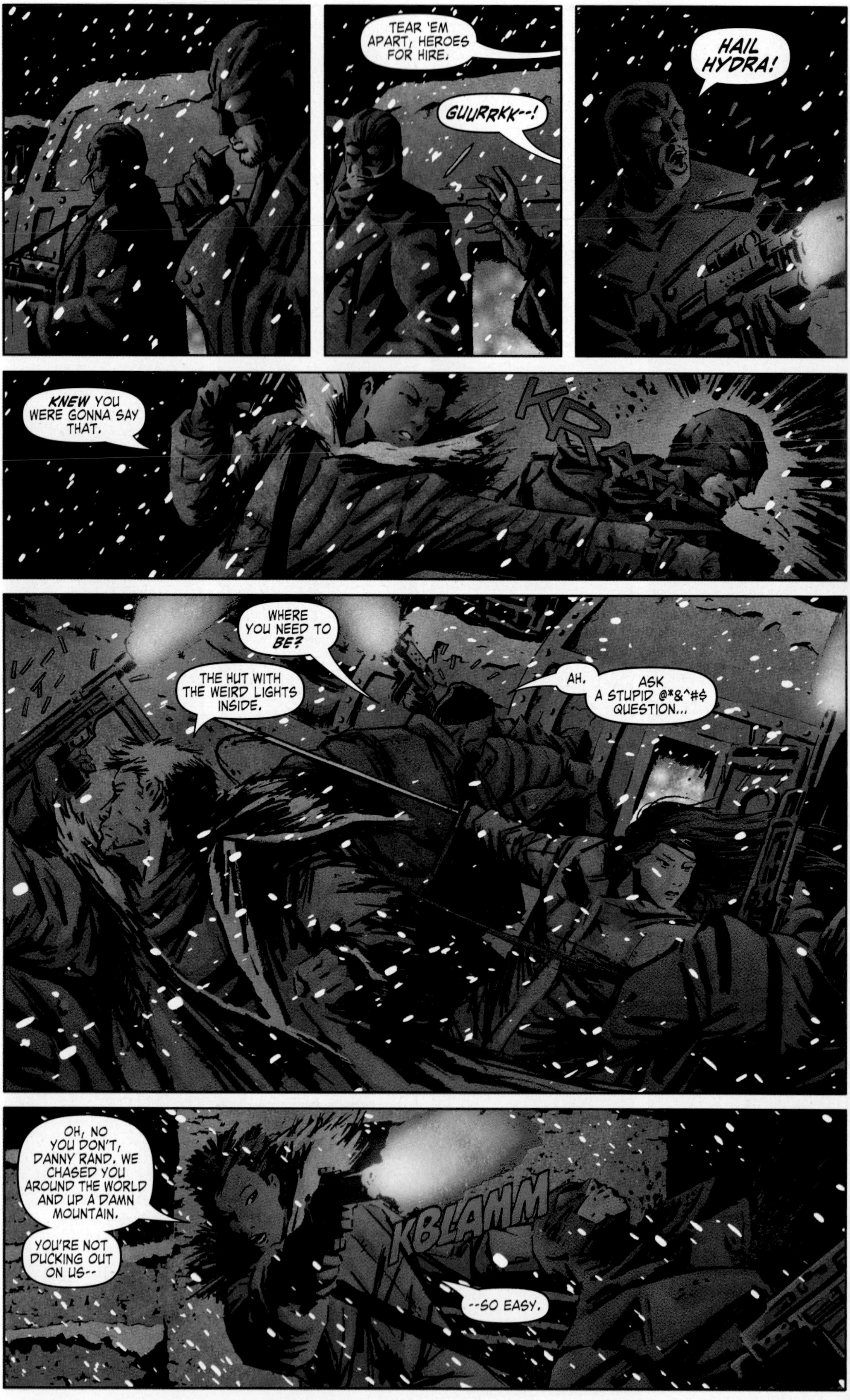
TEAR 'EM APART, HEROES FOR HIRE.
GUURRKK--!
HAIL HYDRA!
KNEW YOU WERE GONNA SAY THAT.
KRAKK
WHERE YOU NEED TO BE?
THE HUT WITH THE WEIRD LIGHTS INSIDE.
AH.
ASK A STUPID @*&^#$ QUESTION...
OH, NO YOU DON'T, DANNY RAND. WE CHASED YOU AROUND THE WORLD AND UP A DAMN MOUNTAIN.
YOU'RE NOT DUCKING OUT ON US--
KBLAMM
--SO EASY.

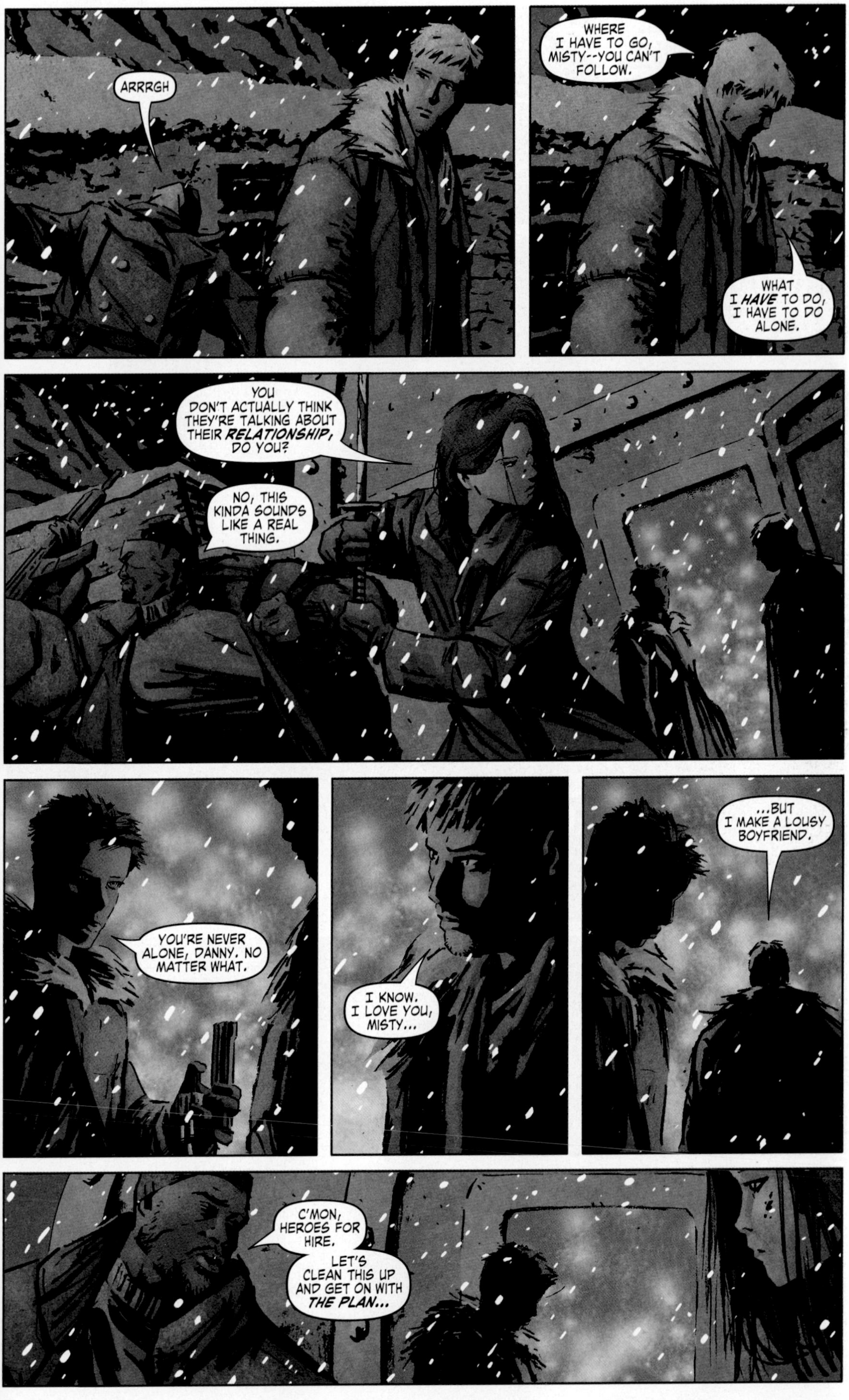
ARRRGH
WHERE I HAVE TO GO, MISTY--YOU CAN'T FOLLOW.
WHAT I HAVE TO DO, I HAVE TO DO ALONE.
YOU DON'T ACTUALLY THINK THEY'RE TALKING ABOUT THEIR RELATIONSHIP, DO YOU?
NO, THIS KINDA SOUNDS LIKE A REAL THING.
YOU'RE NEVER ALONE, DANNY. NO MATTER WHAT.
I KNOW. I LOVE YOU, MISTY...
...BUT I MAKE A LOUSY BOYFRIEND.
C'MON, HEROES FOR HIRE.
LET'S CLEAN THIS UP AND GET ON WITH THE PLAN...

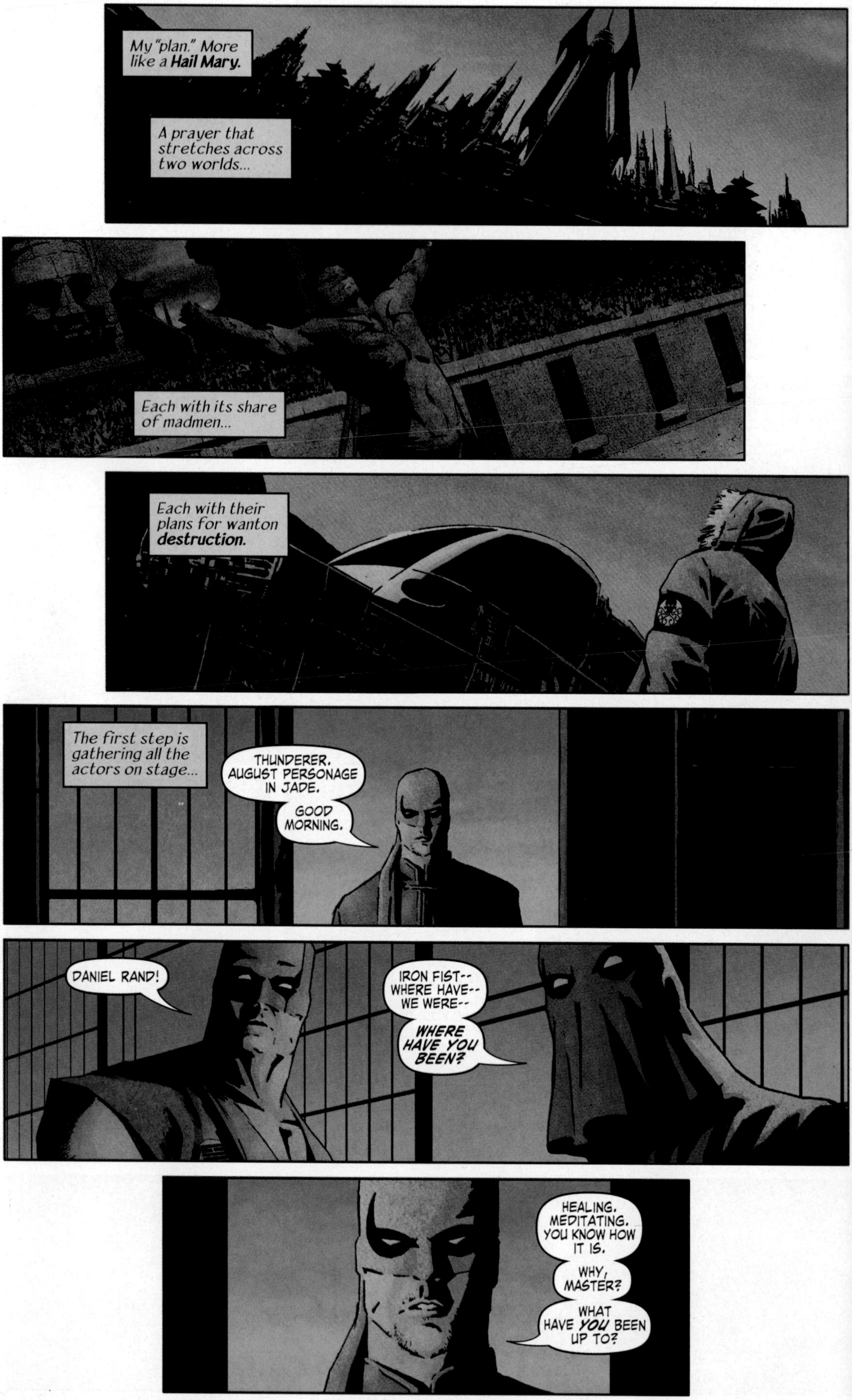
My "plan." More like a **Hail Mary.**
A prayer that stretches across two worlds...
Each with its share of madmen...
Each with their plans for wanton **destruction.**
The first step is gathering all the actors on stage...
THUNDERER. AUGUST PERSONAGE IN JADE.
GOOD MORNING.
DANIEL RAND!
IRON FIST-- WHERE HAVE-- WE WERE--
WHERE HAVE YOU BEEN?
HEALING. MEDITATING. YOU KNOW HOW IT IS.
WHY, MASTER?
WHAT HAVE ***YOU*** BEEN UP TO?

鐵 12 拳

The  Capital
Cities
of Heaven

五

Round 5

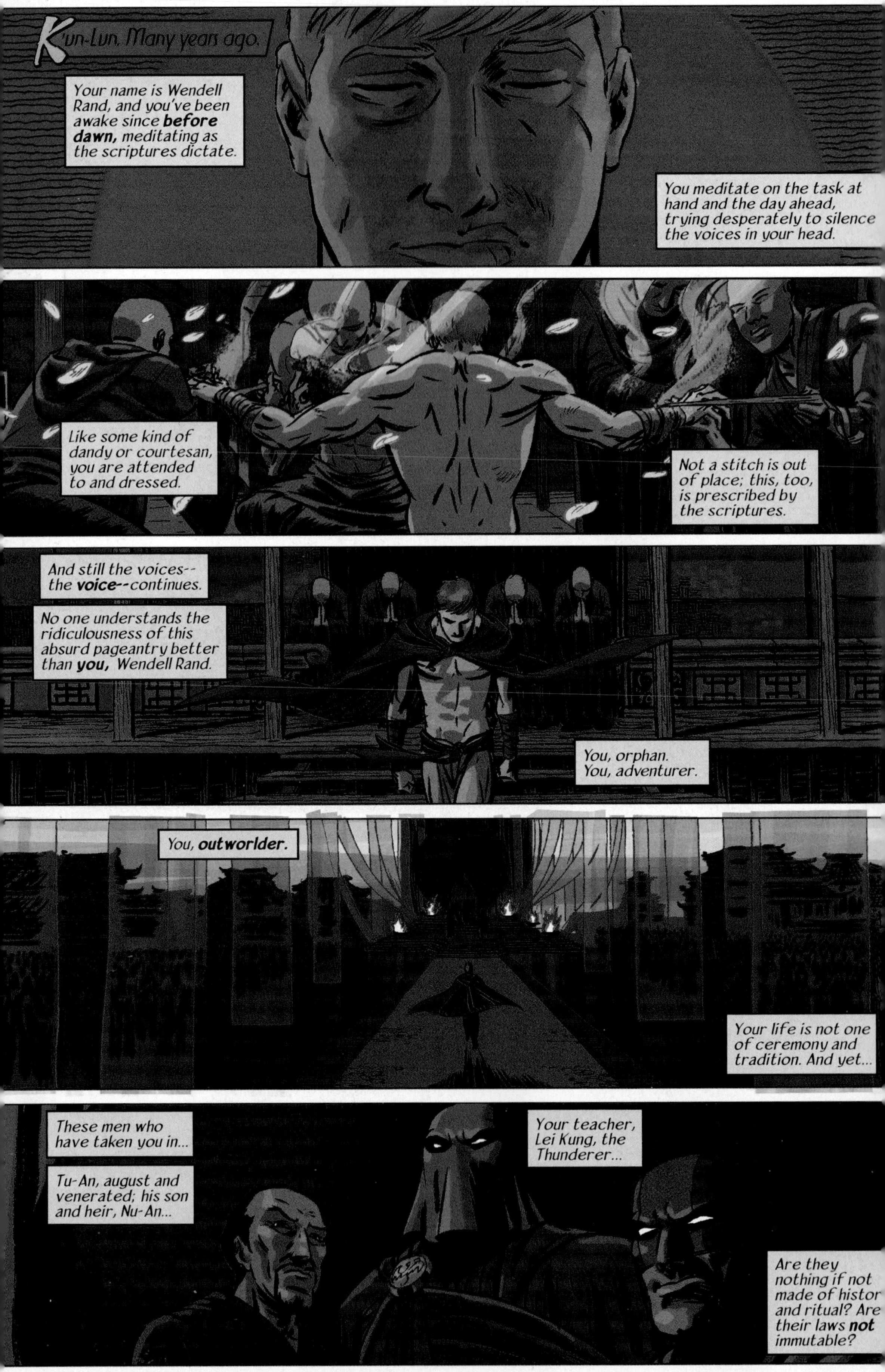
K'un-Lun. Many years ago.
Your name is Wendell Rand, and you've been awake since **before dawn,** meditating as the scriptures dictate.
You meditate on the task at hand and the day ahead, trying desperately to silence the voices in your head.
Like some kind of dandy or courtesan, you are attended to and dressed.
Not a stitch is out of place; this, too, is prescribed by the scriptures.
And still the voices-- the **voice**--continues.
No one understands the ridiculousness of this absurd pageantry better than **you,** Wendell Rand.
You, orphan. You, adventurer.
You, **outworlder.**
Your life is not one of ceremony and tradition. And yet...
These men who have taken you in...
Tu-An, august and venerated; his son and heir, Nu-An...
Your teacher, Lei Kung, the Thunderer...
Are they nothing if not made of histor and ritual? Are their laws **not** immutable?

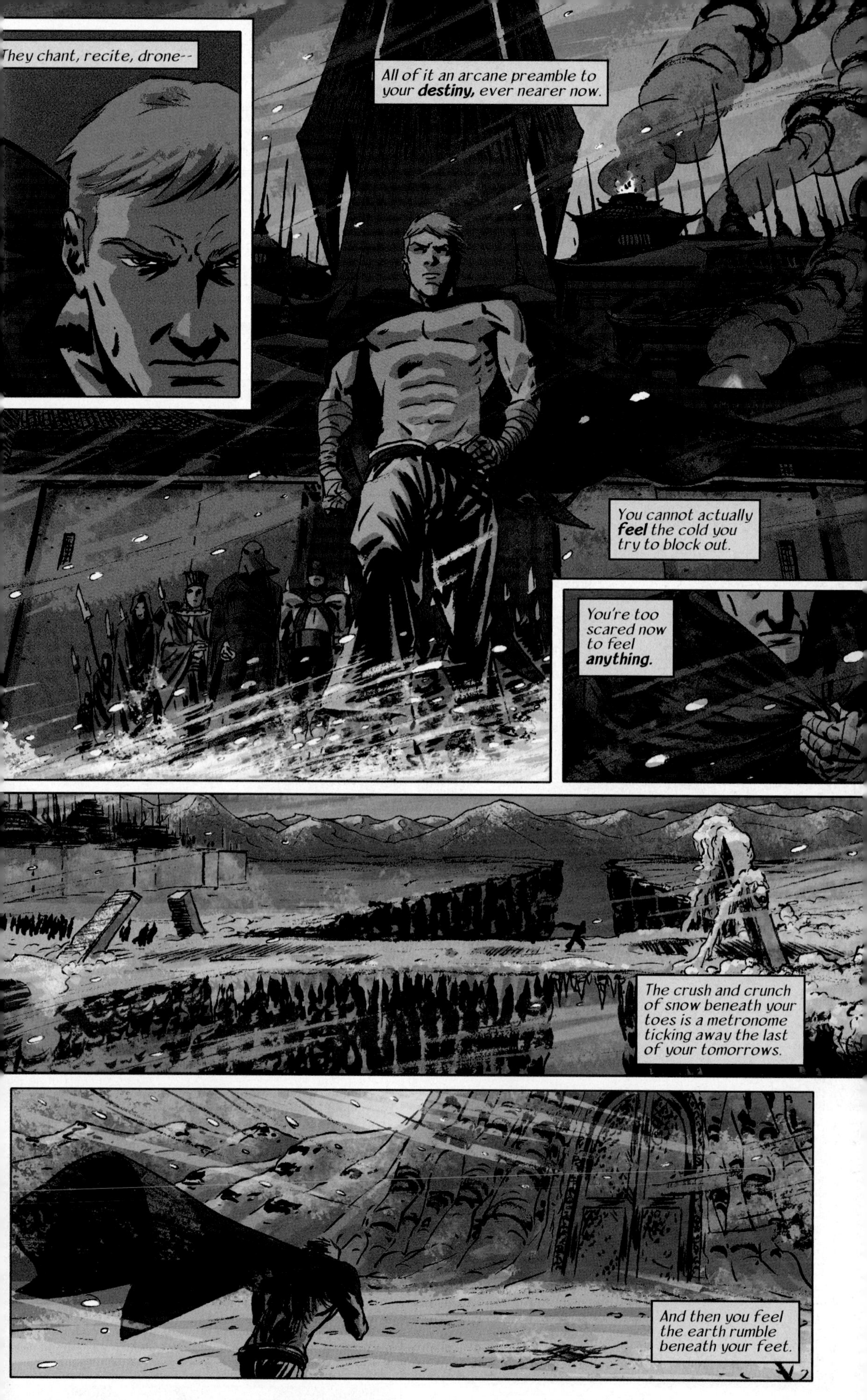
They chant, recite, drone--
All of it an arcane preamble to your **destiny,** ever nearer now.
You cannot actually **feel** the cold you try to block out.
You're too scared now to feel **anything.**
The crush and crunch of snow beneath your toes is a metronome ticking away the last of your tomorrows.
And then you feel the earth rumble beneath your feet.

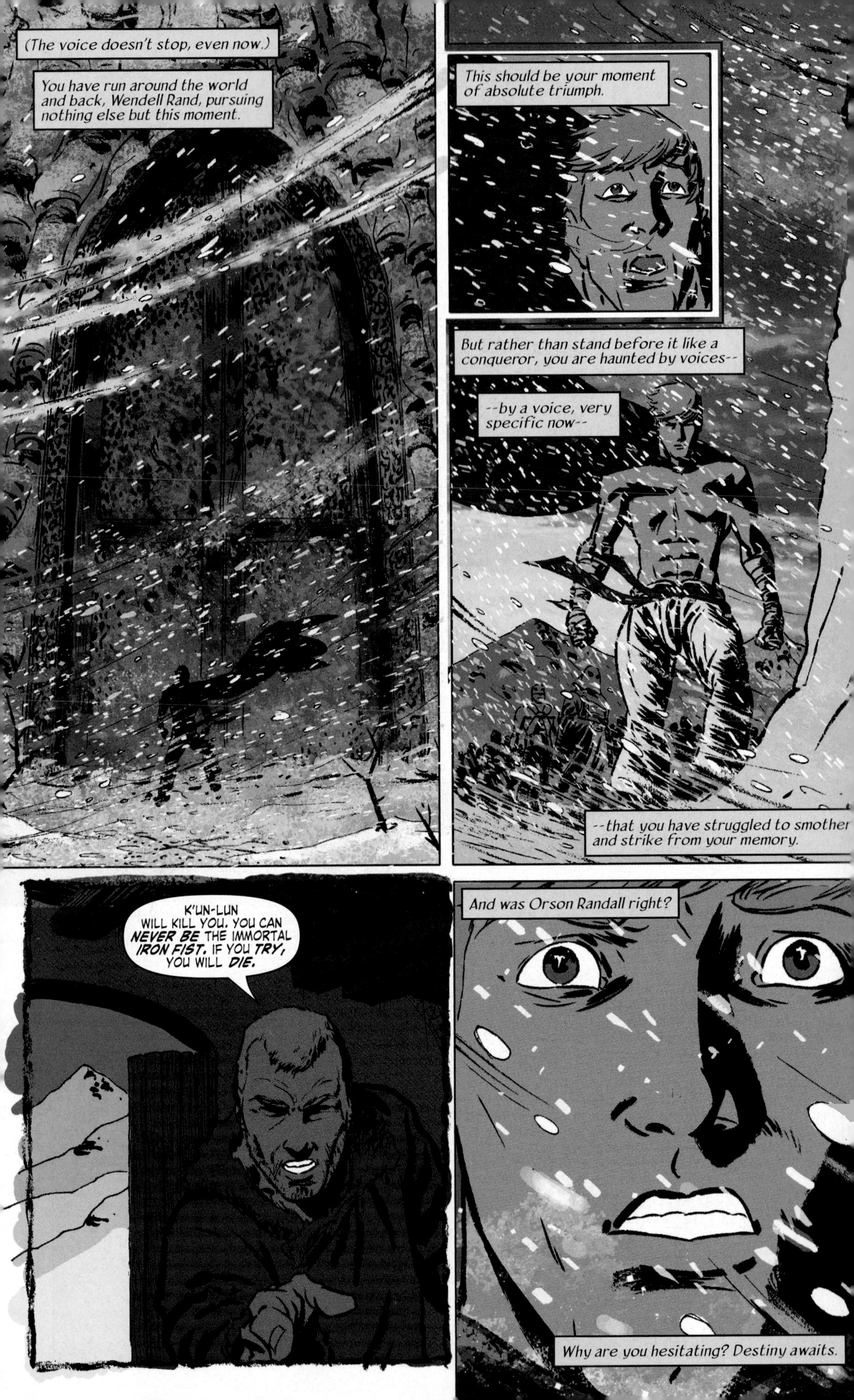
(The voice doesn't stop, even now.)
You have run around the world and back, Wendell Rand, pursuing nothing else but this moment.
This should be your moment of absolute triumph.
But rather than stand before it like a conqueror, you are haunted by voices--
--by a voice, very specific now--
--that you have struggled to smother and strike from your memory.
K'UN-LUN WILL KILL YOU. YOU CAN NEVER BE THE IMMORTAL IRON FIST. IF YOU TRY, YOU WILL DIE.
And was Orson Randall right?
Why are you hesitating? Destiny awaits.

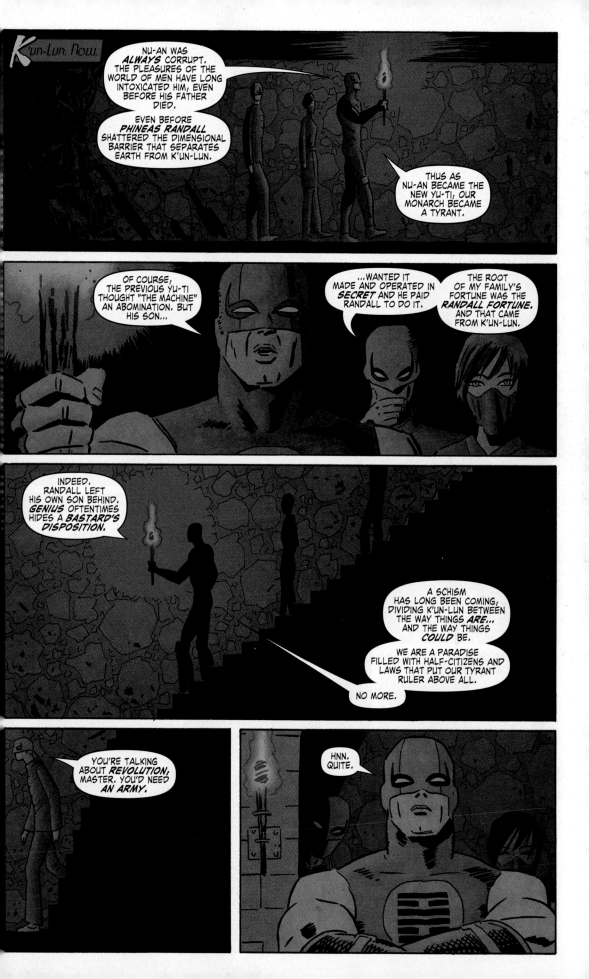

NU-AN WAS *ALWAYS* CORRUPT. THE PLEASURES OF THE WORLD OF MEN HAVE LONG INTOXICATED HIM, EVEN BEFORE HIS FATHER DIED.

EVEN BEFORE *PHINEAS RANDALL* SHATTERED THE DIMENSIONAL BARRIER THAT SEPARATES EARTH FROM K'UN-LUN.

THUS AS NU-AN BECAME THE NEW YU-TI, OUR MONARCH BECAME A TYRANT.

OF COURSE, THE PREVIOUS YU-TI THOUGHT "THE MACHINE" AN ABOMINATION. BUT HIS SON...

...WANTED IT MADE AND OPERATED IN *SECRET* AND HE PAID RANDALL TO DO IT.

THE ROOT OF MY FAMILY'S FORTUNE WAS THE *RANDALL FORTUNE.* AND THAT CAME FROM K'UN-LUN.

INDEED. RANDALL LEFT HIS OWN SON BEHIND. *GENIUS* OFTENTIMES HIDES A *BASTARD'S DISPOSITION.*

A SCHISM HAS LONG BEEN COMING, DIVIDING K'UN-LUN BETWEEN THE WAY THINGS *ARE*... AND THE WAY THINGS *COULD* BE.

WE ARE A PARADISE FILLED WITH HALF-CITIZENS AND LAWS THAT PUT OUR TYRANT RULER ABOVE ALL.

NO MORE.

YOU'RE TALKING ABOUT *REVOLUTION,* MASTER. YOU'D NEED *AN ARMY.*

HNN. QUITE.

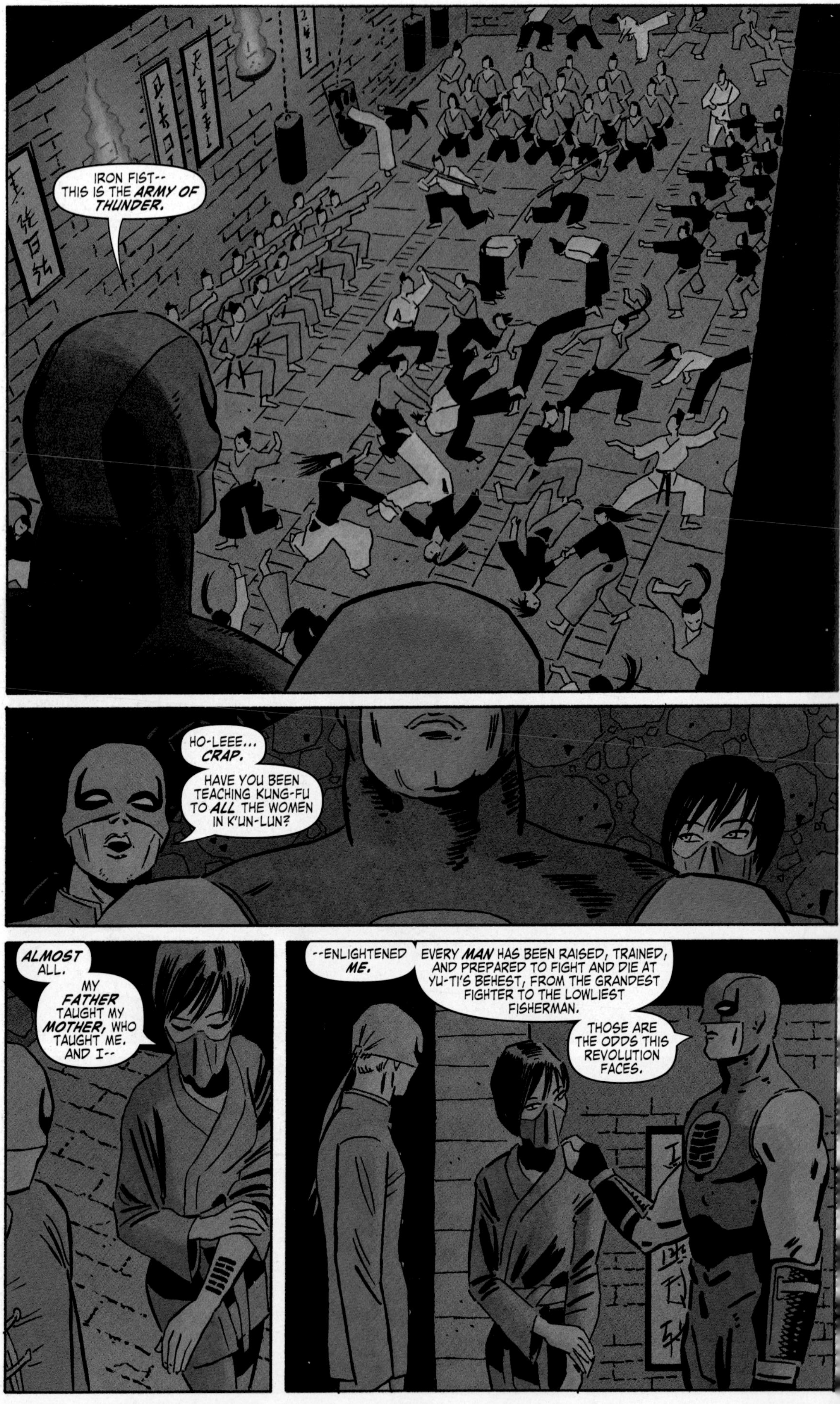
IRON FIST-- THIS IS THE **ARMY OF THUNDER.**
HO-LEEE... **CRAP.**
HAVE YOU BEEN TEACHING KUNG-FU TO **ALL** THE WOMEN IN K'UN-LUN?
ALMOST ALL.
MY **FATHER** TAUGHT MY **MOTHER,** WHO TAUGHT ME. AND I--
--ENLIGHTENED **ME.**
EVERY **MAN** HAS BEEN RAISED, TRAINED, AND PREPARED TO FIGHT AND DIE AT YU-TI'S BEHEST, FROM THE GRANDEST FIGHTER TO THE LOWLIEST FISHERMAN.
THOSE ARE THE ODDS THIS REVOLUTION FACES.

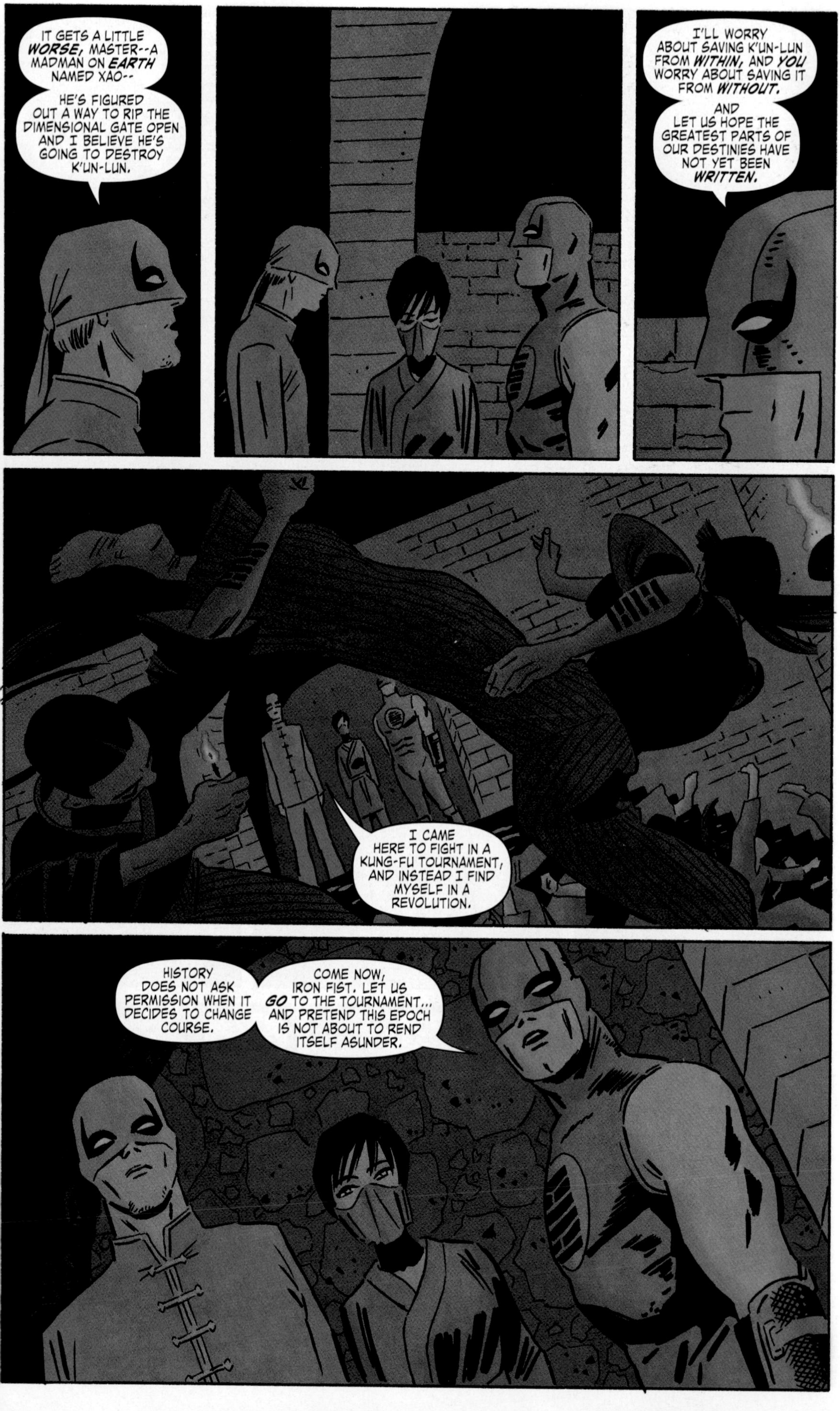
IT GETS A LITTLE *WORSE,* MASTER--A MADMAN ON *EARTH* NAMED XAO--
HE'S FIGURED OUT A WAY TO RIP THE DIMENSIONAL GATE OPEN AND I BELIEVE HE'S GOING TO DESTROY K'UN-LUN.
I'LL WORRY ABOUT SAVING K'UN-LUN FROM *WITHIN,* AND *YOU* WORRY ABOUT SAVING IT FROM *WITHOUT.*
AND LET US HOPE THE GREATEST PARTS OF OUR DESTINIES HAVE NOT YET BEEN *WRITTEN.*
I CAME HERE TO FIGHT IN A KUNG-FU TOURNAMENT, AND INSTEAD I FIND MYSELF IN A REVOLUTION.
HISTORY DOES NOT ASK PERMISSION WHEN IT DECIDES TO CHANGE COURSE.
COME NOW, IRON FIST. LET US *GO* TO THE TOURNAMENT... AND PRETEND THIS EPOCH IS NOT ABOUT TO REND ITSELF ASUNDER.

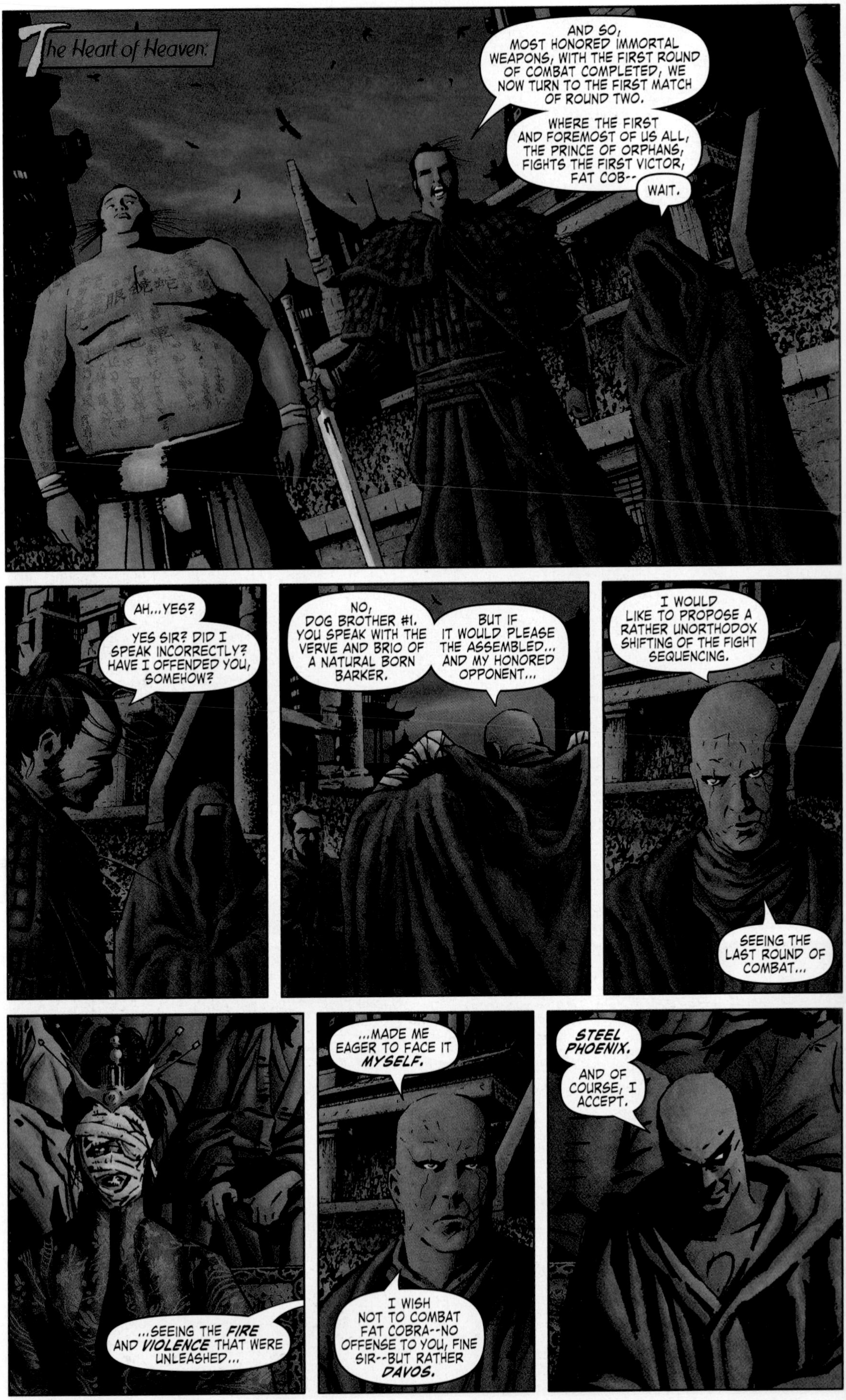
The Heart of Heaven.
AND SO, MOST HONORED IMMORTAL WEAPONS, WITH THE FIRST ROUND OF COMBAT COMPLETED, WE NOW TURN TO THE FIRST MATCH OF ROUND TWO.
WHERE THE FIRST AND FOREMOST OF US ALL, THE PRINCE OF ORPHANS, FIGHTS THE FIRST VICTOR, FAT COB--
WAIT.
AH...YES?
YES SIR? DID I SPEAK INCORRECTLY? HAVE I OFFENDED YOU, SOMEHOW?
NO, DOG BROTHER #1. YOU SPEAK WITH THE VERVE AND BRIO OF A NATURAL BORN BARKER.
BUT IF IT WOULD PLEASE THE ASSEMBLED... AND MY HONORED OPPONENT...
I WOULD LIKE TO PROPOSE A RATHER UNORTHODOX SHIFTING OF THE FIGHT SEQUENCING.
SEEING THE LAST ROUND OF COMBAT...
...SEEING THE FIRE AND VIOLENCE THAT WERE UNLEASHED...
...MADE ME EAGER TO FACE IT MYSELF.
I WISH NOT TO COMBAT FAT COBRA--NO OFFENSE TO YOU, FINE SIR--BUT RATHER DAVOS.
STEEL PHOENIX.
AND OF COURSE, I ACCEPT.

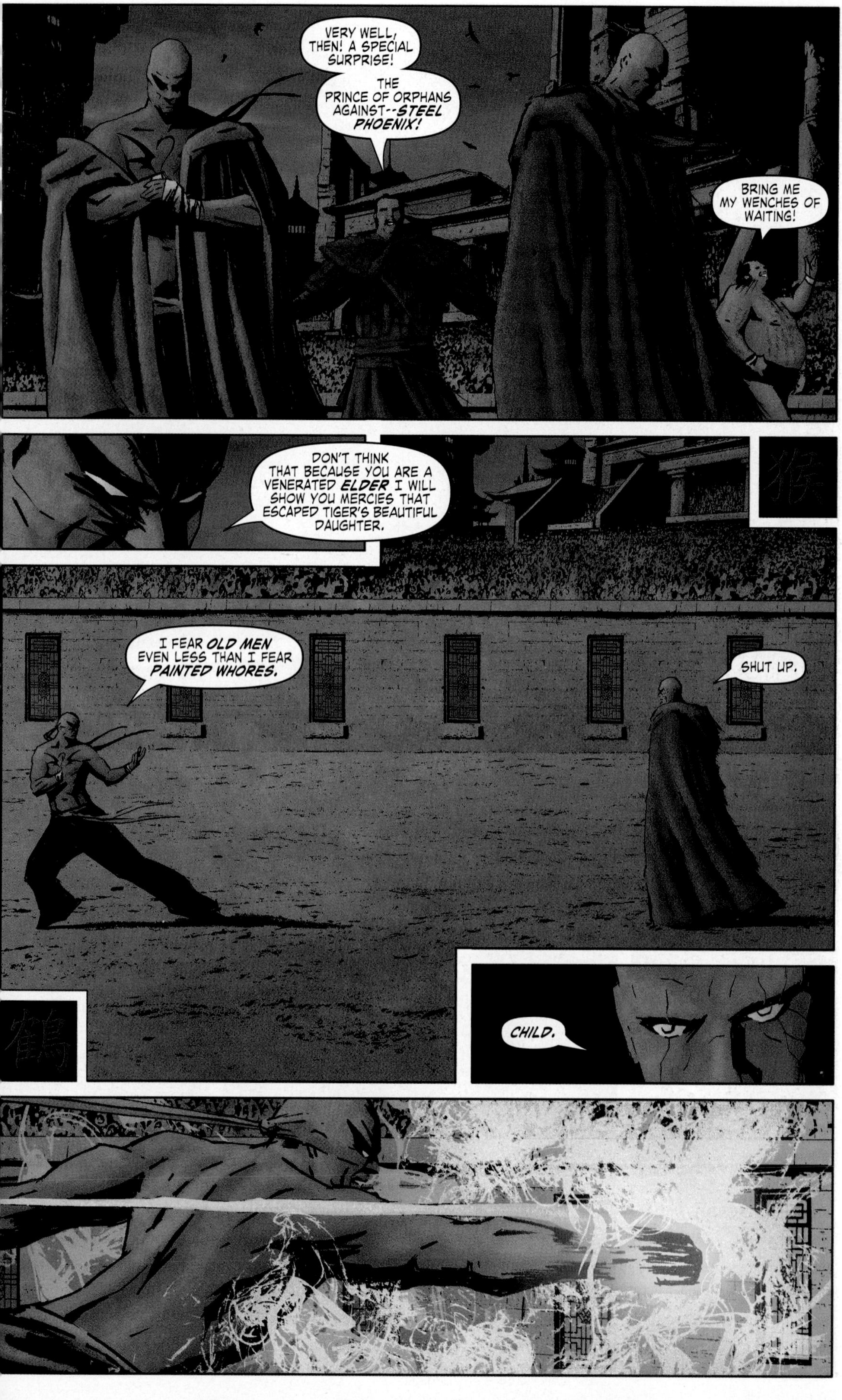
VERY WELL, THEN! A SPECIAL SURPRISE!
THE PRINCE OF ORPHANS AGAINST--STEEL PHOENIX!
BRING ME MY WENCHES OF WAITING!
DON'T THINK THAT BECAUSE YOU ARE A VENERATED ELDER I WILL SHOW YOU MERCIES THAT ESCAPED TIGER'S BEAUTIFUL DAUGHTER.
I FEAR OLD MEN EVEN LESS THAN I FEAR PAINTED WHORES.
SHUT UP.
CHILD.

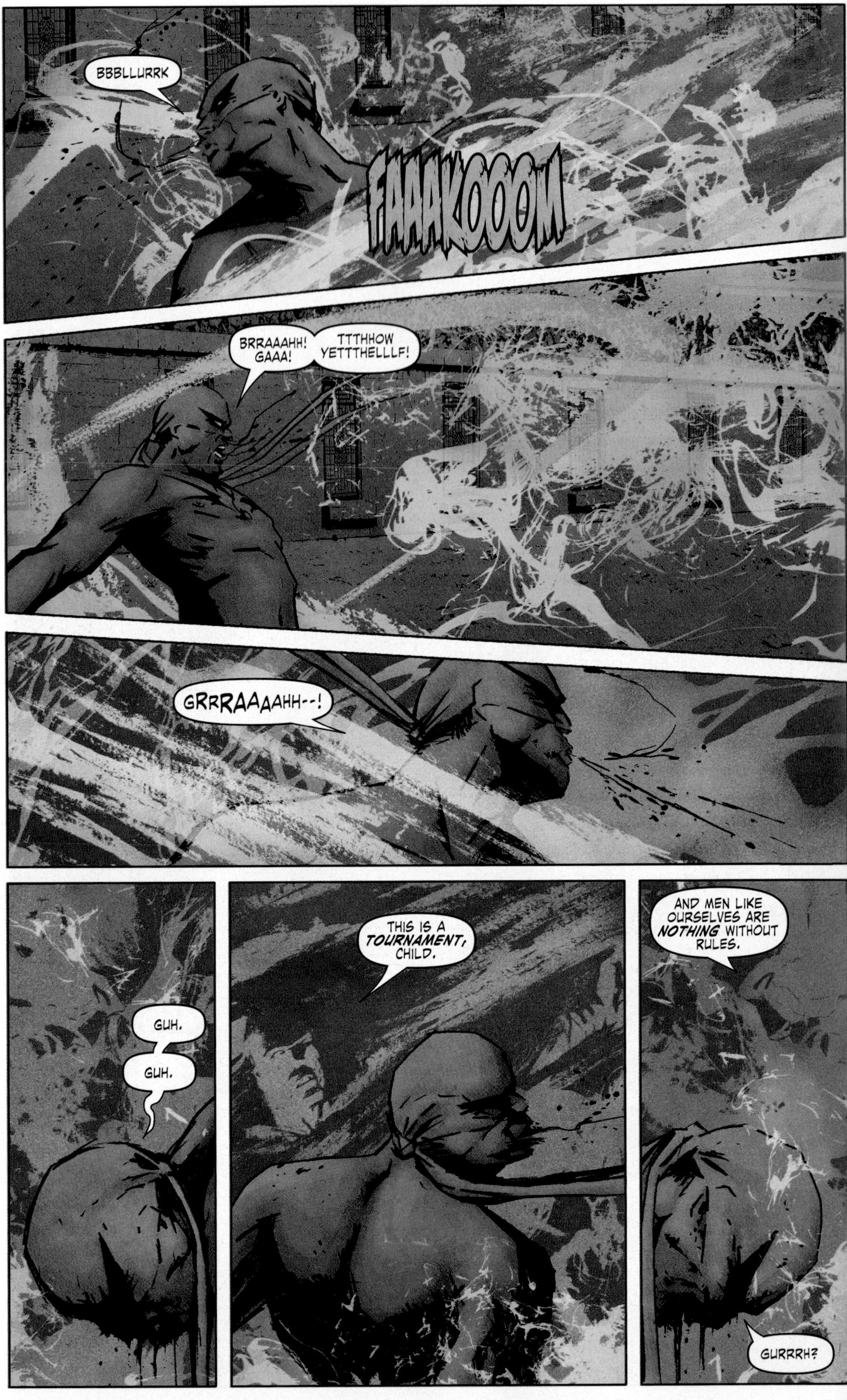
BBBLLURRK
FAAAKOOOM
BRRAAAHH! GAAA!
TTTHHOW YETTTHELLLF!
GRRRAAAAHH--!
GUH.
GUH.
THIS IS A *TOURNAMENT,* CHILD.
AND MEN LIKE OURSELVES ARE *NOTHING* WITHOUT RULES.
GURRRH?

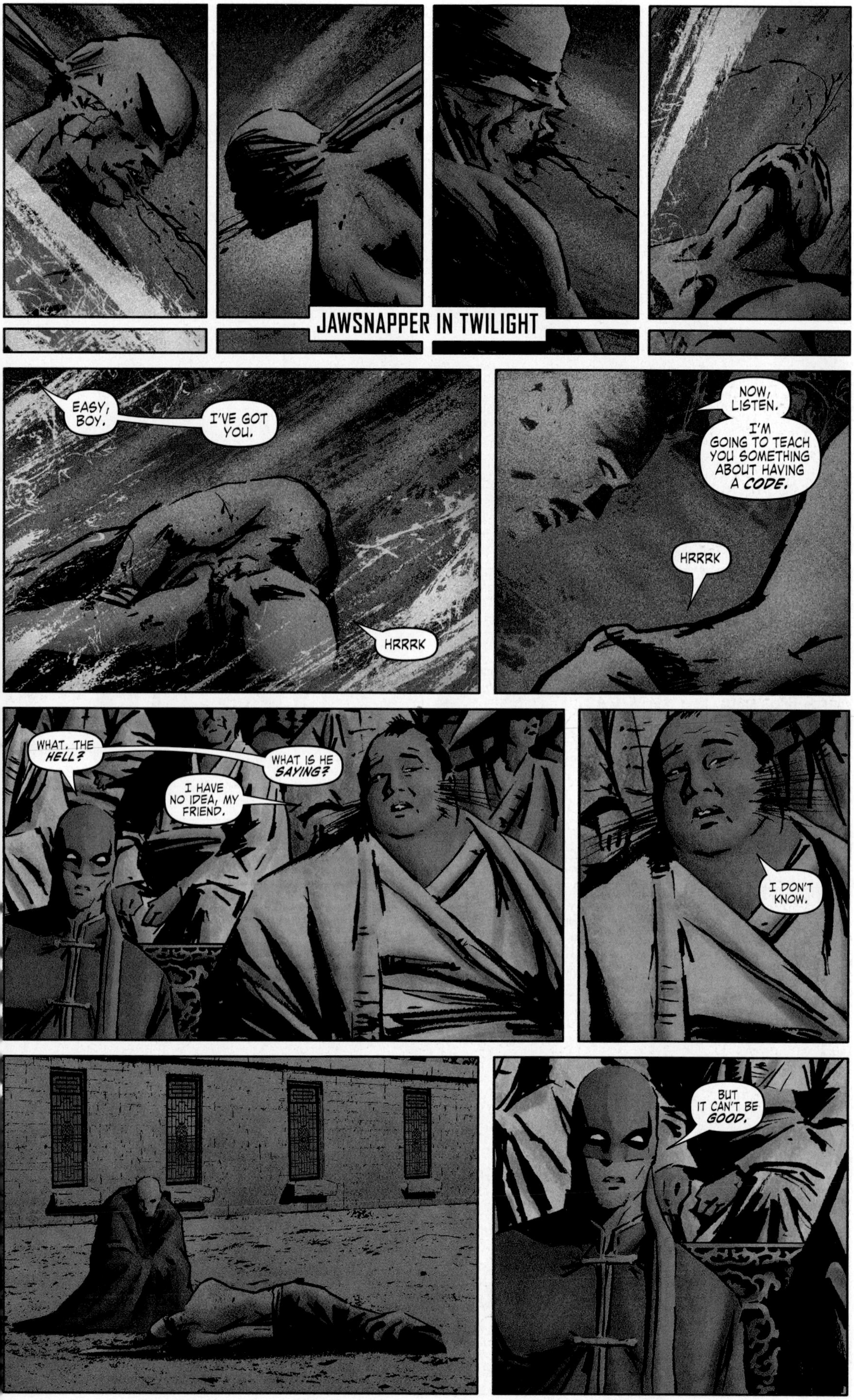
JAWSNAPPER IN TWILIGHT
EASY, BOY.
I'VE GOT YOU.
HRRRK
NOW, LISTEN.
I'M GOING TO TEACH YOU SOMETHING ABOUT HAVING A CODE.
HRRRK
WHAT. THE HELL?
WHAT IS HE SAYING?
I HAVE NO IDEA, MY FRIEND.
I DON'T KNOW.
BUT IT CAN'T BE GOOD.

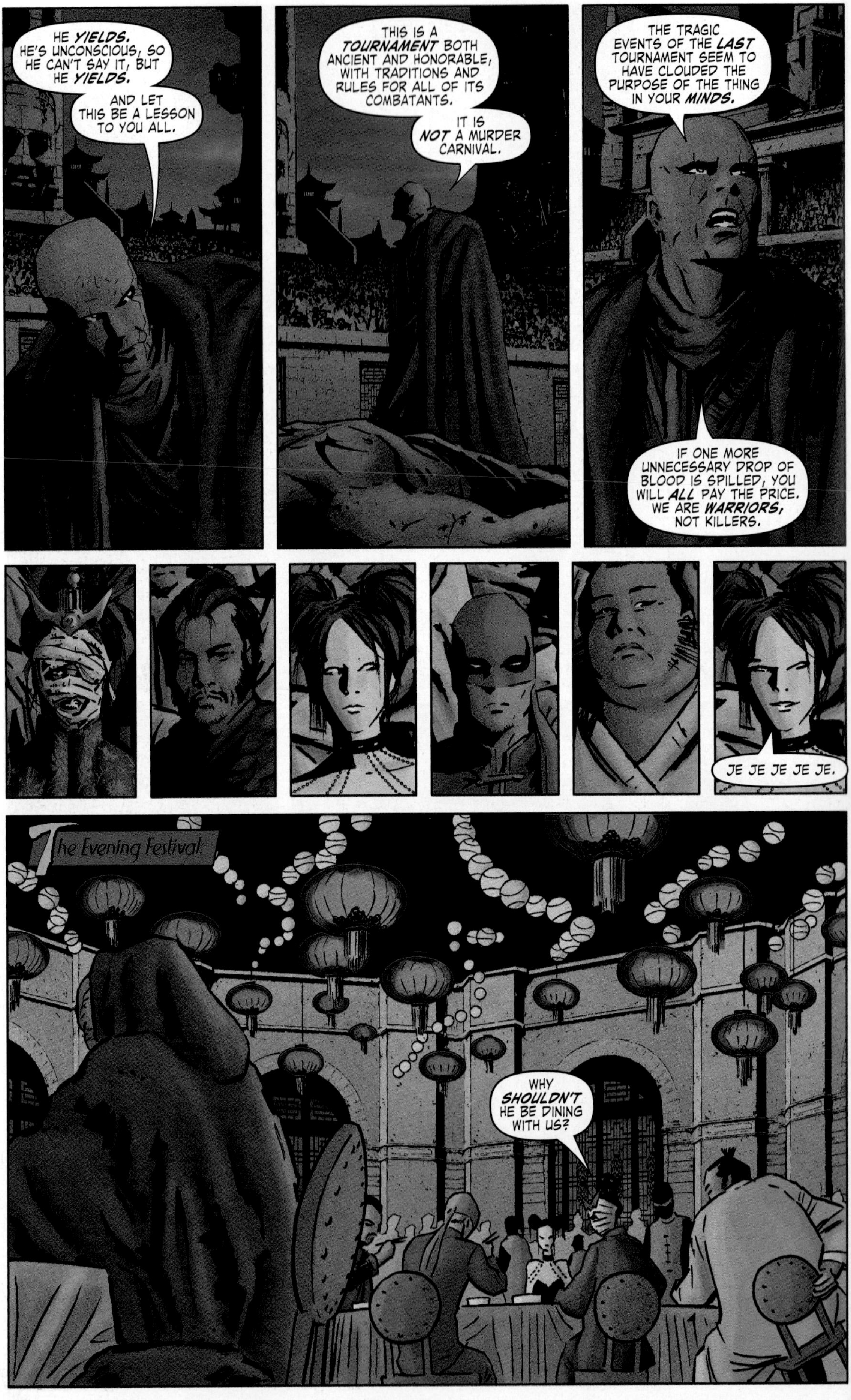
HE YIELDS. HE'S UNCONSCIOUS, SO HE CAN'T SAY IT, BUT HE YIELDS.
AND LET THIS BE A LESSON TO YOU ALL.
THIS IS A TOURNAMENT BOTH ANCIENT AND HONORABLE, WITH TRADITIONS AND RULES FOR ALL OF ITS COMBATANTS.
IT IS NOT A MURDER CARNIVAL.
THE TRAGIC EVENTS OF THE LAST TOURNAMENT SEEM TO HAVE CLOUDED THE PURPOSE OF THE THING IN YOUR MINDS.
IF ONE MORE UNNECESSARY DROP OF BLOOD IS SPILLED, YOU WILL ALL PAY THE PRICE. WE ARE WARRIORS, NOT KILLERS.
JE JE JE JE JE.
The Evening Festival
WHY SHOULDN'T HE BE DINING WITH US?

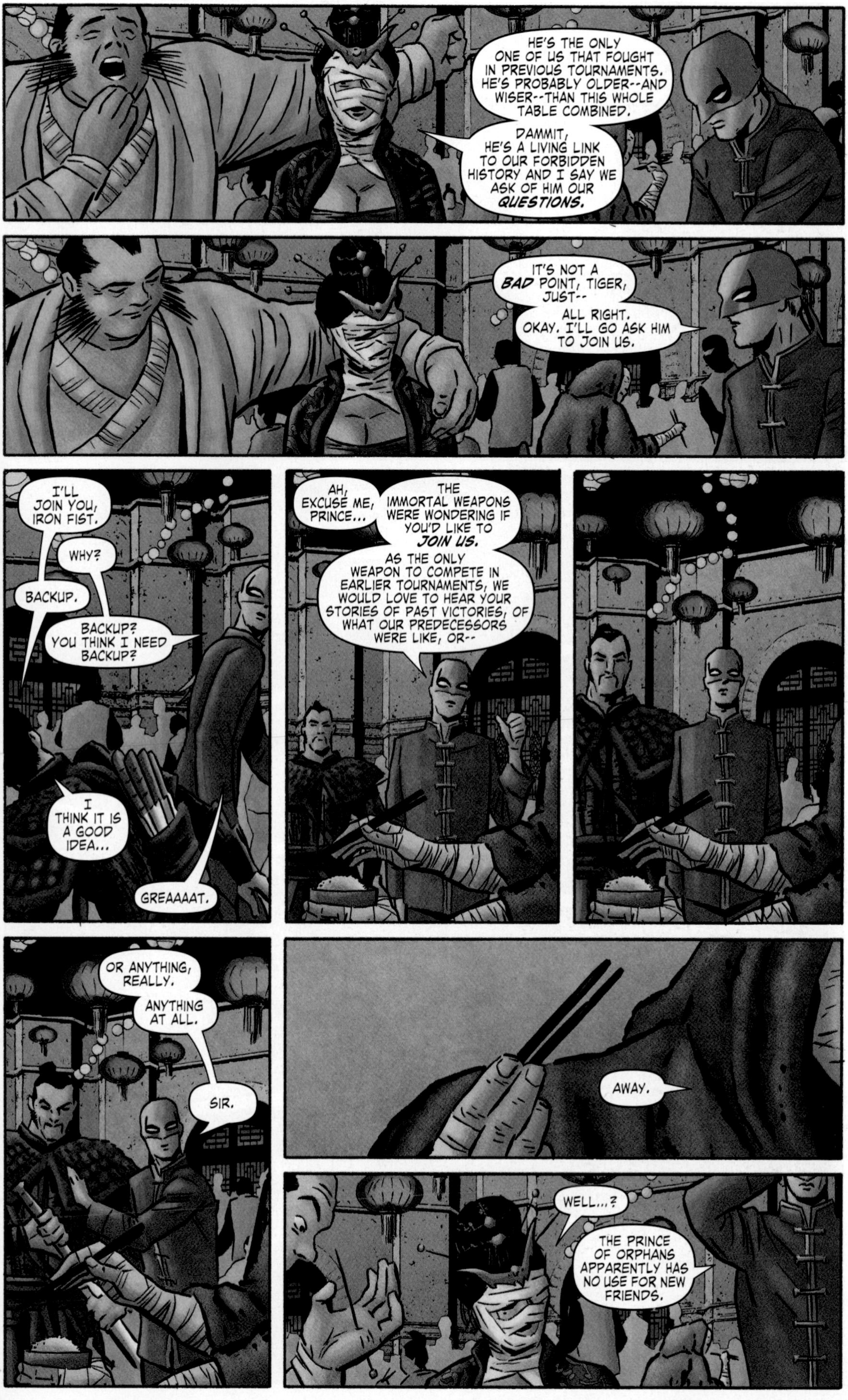
HE'S THE ONLY ONE OF US THAT FOUGHT IN PREVIOUS TOURNAMENTS. HE'S PROBABLY OLDER--AND WISER--THAN THIS WHOLE TABLE COMBINED.
DAMMIT, HE'S A LIVING LINK TO OUR FORBIDDEN HISTORY AND I SAY WE ASK OF HIM OUR QUESTIONS.
IT'S NOT A BAD POINT, TIGER, JUST--
ALL RIGHT. OKAY. I'LL GO ASK HIM TO JOIN US.
I'LL JOIN YOU, IRON FIST.
WHY?
BACKUP.
BACKUP? YOU THINK I NEED BACKUP?
I THINK IT IS A GOOD IDEA...
GREAAAAT.
AH, EXCUSE ME, PRINCE...
THE IMMORTAL WEAPONS WERE WONDERING IF YOU'D LIKE TO JOIN US.
AS THE ONLY WEAPON TO COMPETE IN EARLIER TOURNAMENTS, WE WOULD LOVE TO HEAR YOUR STORIES OF PAST VICTORIES, OF WHAT OUR PREDECESSORS WERE LIKE, OR--
OR ANYTHING, REALLY.
ANYTHING AT ALL.
SIR.
AWAY.
WELL...?
THE PRINCE OF ORPHANS APPARENTLY HAS NO USE FOR NEW FRIENDS.

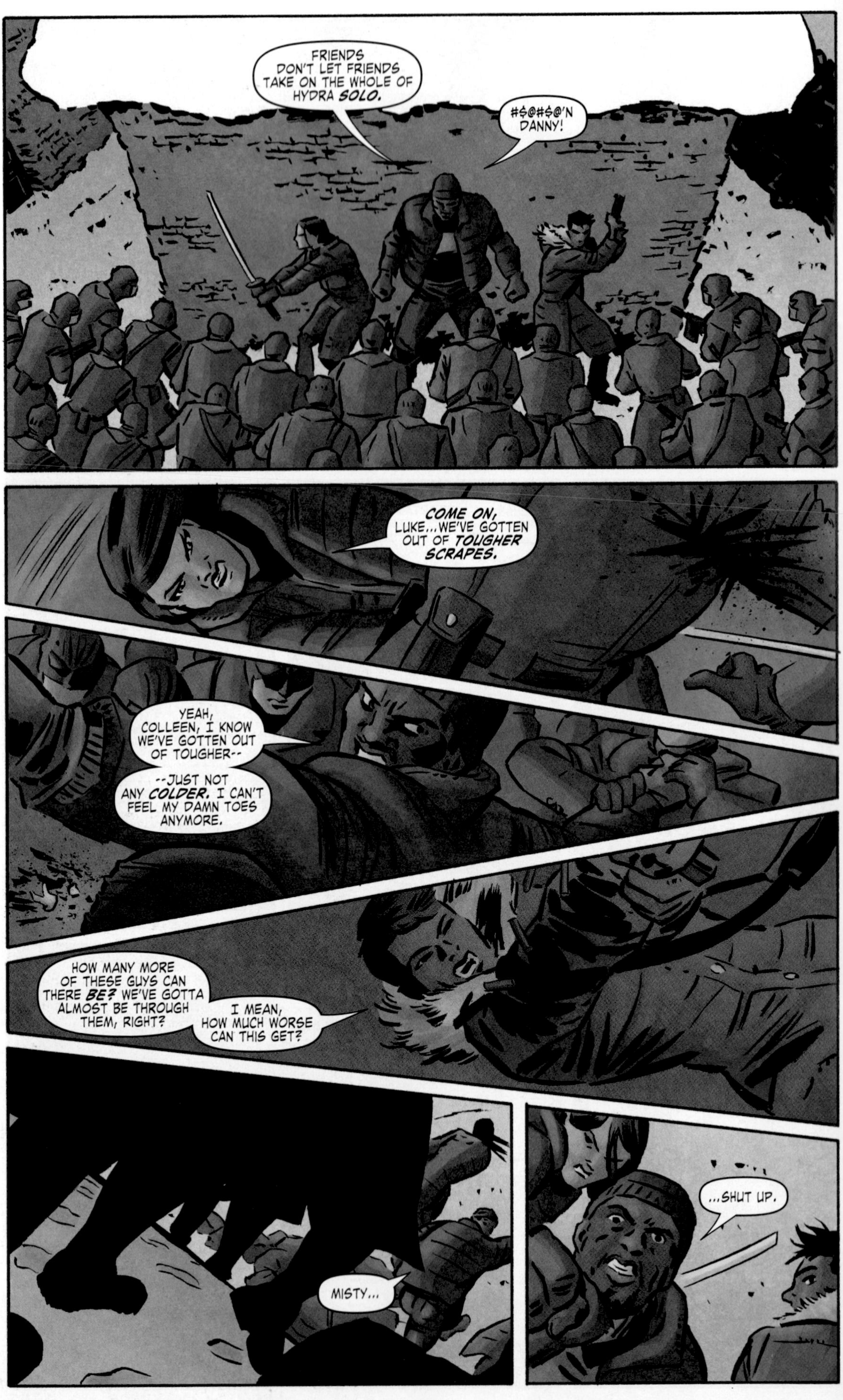
FRIENDS DON'T LET FRIENDS TAKE ON THE WHOLE OF HYDRA *SOLO.*
#$@#$@'N DANNY!
COME ON, LUKE...WE'VE GOTTEN OUT OF *TOUGHER SCRAPES.*
YEAH, COLLEEN, I KNOW WE'VE GOTTEN OUT OF TOUGHER--
--JUST NOT ANY *COLDER.* I CAN'T FEEL MY DAMN TOES ANYMORE.
HOW MANY MORE OF THESE GUYS CAN THERE *BE?* WE'VE GOTTA ALMOST BE THROUGH THEM, RIGHT?
I MEAN, HOW MUCH WORSE CAN THIS GET?
MISTY...
...SHUT UP.

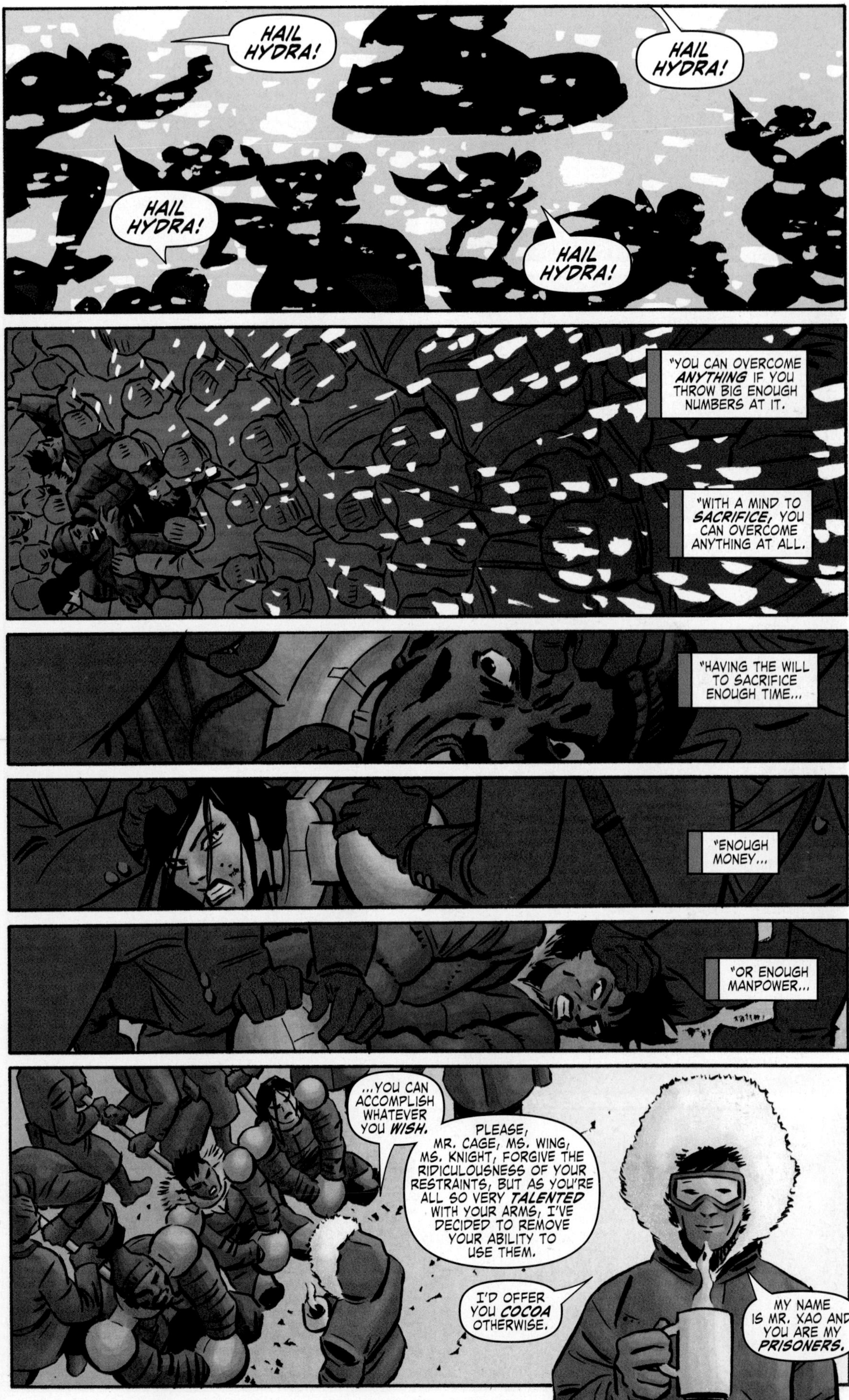
HAIL HYDRA!
HAIL HYDRA!
HAIL HYDRA!
HAIL HYDRA!
"YOU CAN OVERCOME ANYTHING IF YOU THROW BIG ENOUGH NUMBERS AT IT.
"WITH A MIND TO SACRIFICE, YOU CAN OVERCOME ANYTHING AT ALL.
"HAVING THE WILL TO SACRIFICE ENOUGH TIME...
"ENOUGH MONEY...
"OR ENOUGH MANPOWER...
...YOU CAN ACCOMPLISH WHATEVER YOU WISH.
PLEASE, MR. CAGE, MS. WING, MS. KNIGHT, FORGIVE THE RIDICULOUSNESS OF YOUR RESTRAINTS, BUT AS YOU'RE ALL SO VERY TALENTED WITH YOUR ARMS, I'VE DECIDED TO REMOVE YOUR ABILITY TO USE THEM.
I'D OFFER YOU COCOA OTHERWISE.
MY NAME IS MR. XAO AND YOU ARE MY PRISONERS.

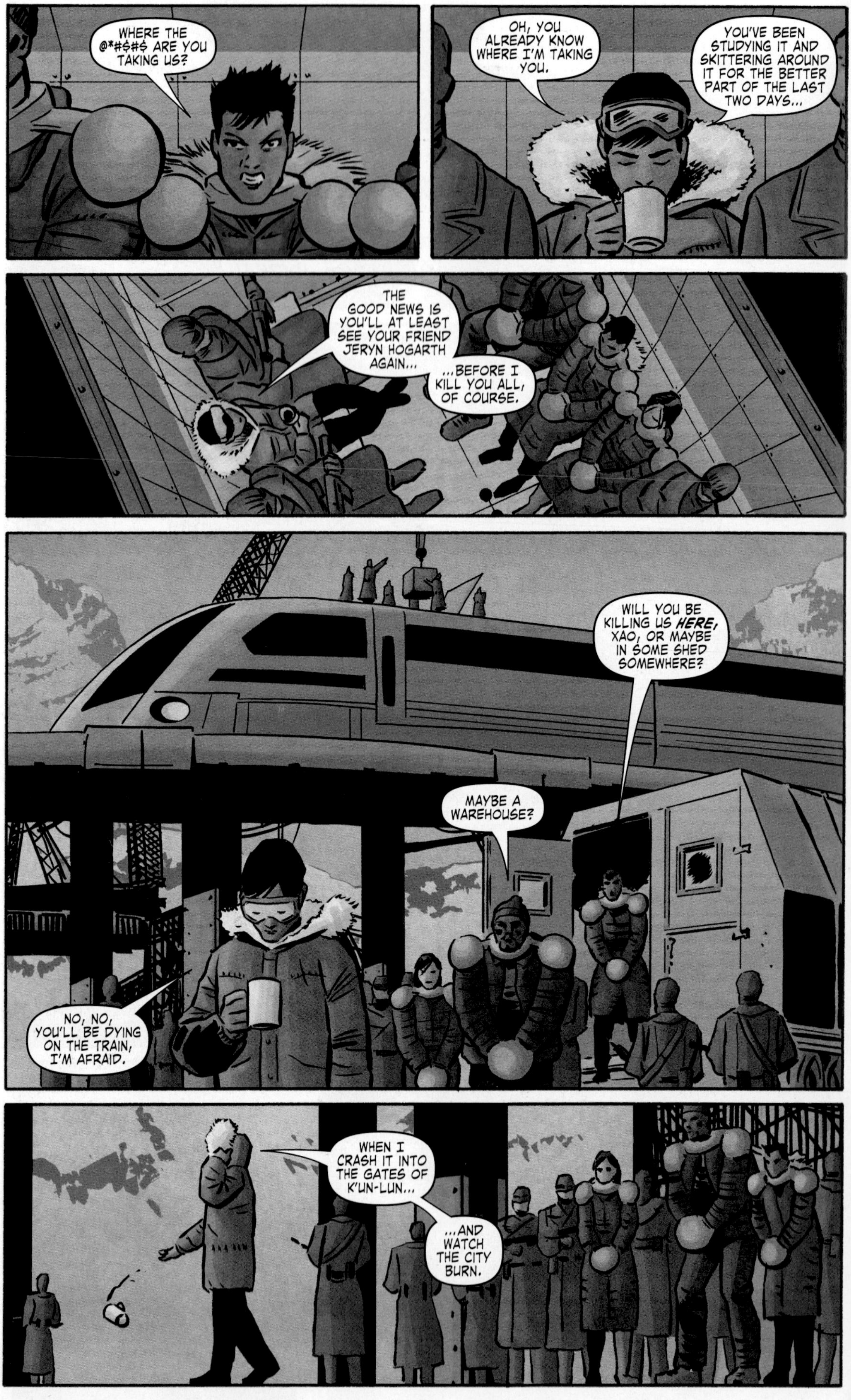
WHERE THE @*#$#$ ARE YOU TAKING US?
OH, YOU ALREADY KNOW WHERE I'M TAKING YOU.
YOU'VE BEEN STUDYING IT AND SKITTERING AROUND IT FOR THE BETTER PART OF THE LAST TWO DAYS...
THE GOOD NEWS IS YOU'LL AT LEAST SEE YOUR FRIEND JERYN HOGARTH AGAIN...
...BEFORE I KILL YOU ALL, OF COURSE.
WILL YOU BE KILLING US HERE, XAO, OR MAYBE IN SOME SHED SOMEWHERE?
MAYBE A WAREHOUSE?
NO, NO, YOU'LL BE DYING ON THE TRAIN, I'M AFRAID.
WHEN I CRASH IT INTO THE GATES OF K'UN-LUN...
...AND WATCH THE CITY BURN.

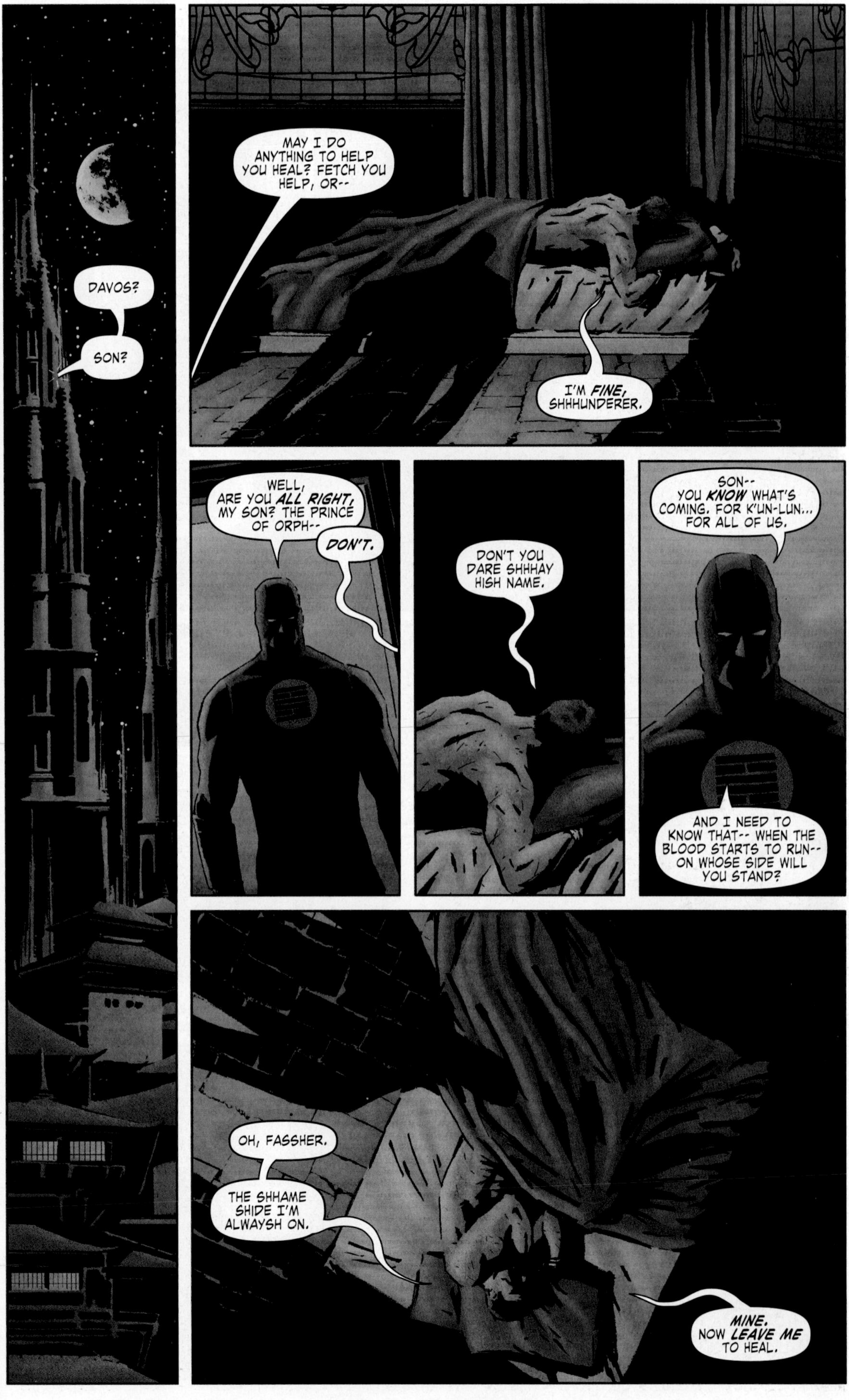
DAVOS?
SON?
MAY I DO ANYTHING TO HELP YOU HEAL? FETCH YOU HELP, OR--
I'M FINE, SHHHUNDERER.
WELL, ARE YOU ALL RIGHT, MY SON? THE PRINCE OF ORPH--
DON'T.
DON'T YOU DARE SHHHAY HISH NAME.
SON-- YOU KNOW WHAT'S COMING. FOR K'UN-LUN... FOR ALL OF US.
AND I NEED TO KNOW THAT-- WHEN THE BLOOD STARTS TO RUN-- ON WHOSE SIDE WILL YOU STAND?
OH, FASSHER.
THE SHHAME SHIDE I'M ALWAYSH ON.
MINE. NOW LEAVE ME TO HEAL.

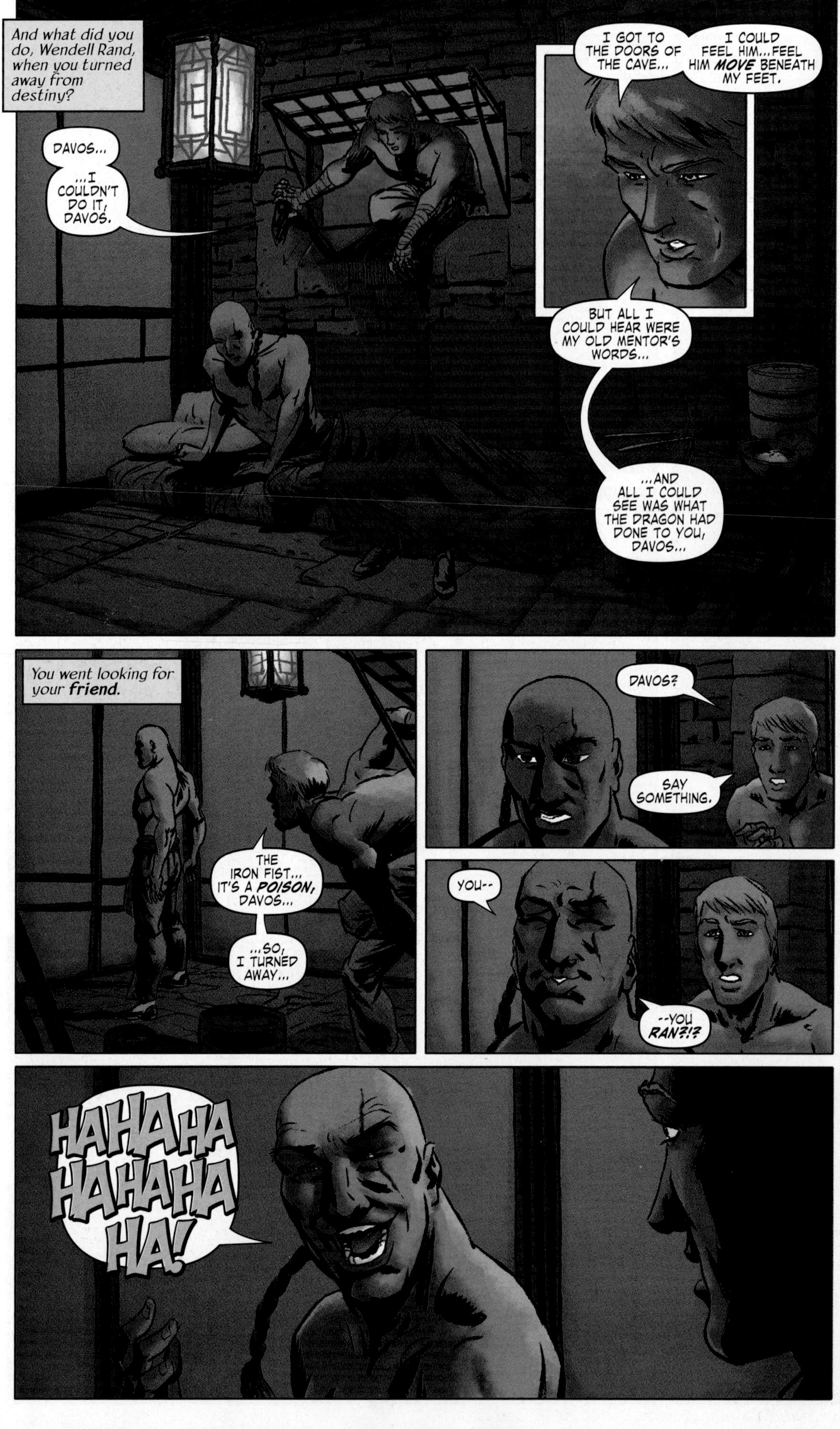
And what did you do, Wendell Rand, when you turned away from destiny?
DAVOS...
...I COULDN'T DO IT, DAVOS.
I GOT TO THE DOORS OF THE CAVE...
I COULD FEEL HIM...FEEL HIM MOVE BENEATH MY FEET.
BUT ALL I COULD HEAR WERE MY OLD MENTOR'S WORDS...
...AND ALL I COULD SEE WAS WHAT THE DRAGON HAD DONE TO YOU, DAVOS...
You went looking for your friend.
THE IRON FIST... IT'S A POISON, DAVOS...
...SO, I TURNED AWAY...
DAVOS?
SAY SOMETHING.
YOU--
--YOU RAN?!?
HAHAHA HAHAHA HA!

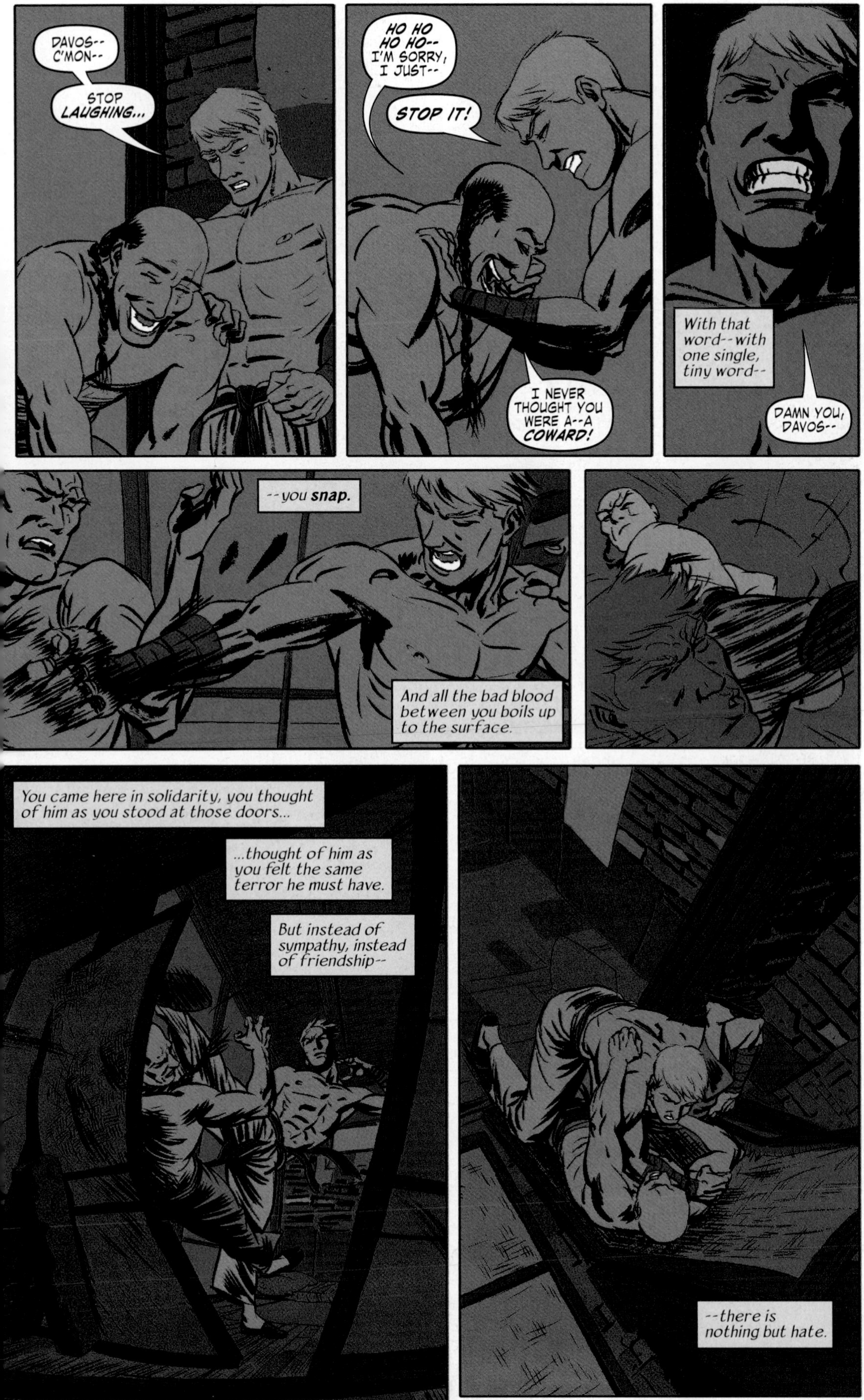
DAVOS-- C'MON--
STOP LAUGHING...
HO HO HO HO-- I'M SORRY, I JUST--
STOP IT!
I NEVER THOUGHT YOU WERE A--A COWARD!
With that word--with one single, tiny word--
DAMN YOU, DAVOS--
--you snap.
And all the bad blood between you boils up to the surface.
You came here in solidarity, you thought of him as you stood at those doors...
...thought of him as you felt the same terror he must have.
But instead of sympathy, instead of friendship--
--there is nothing but hate.

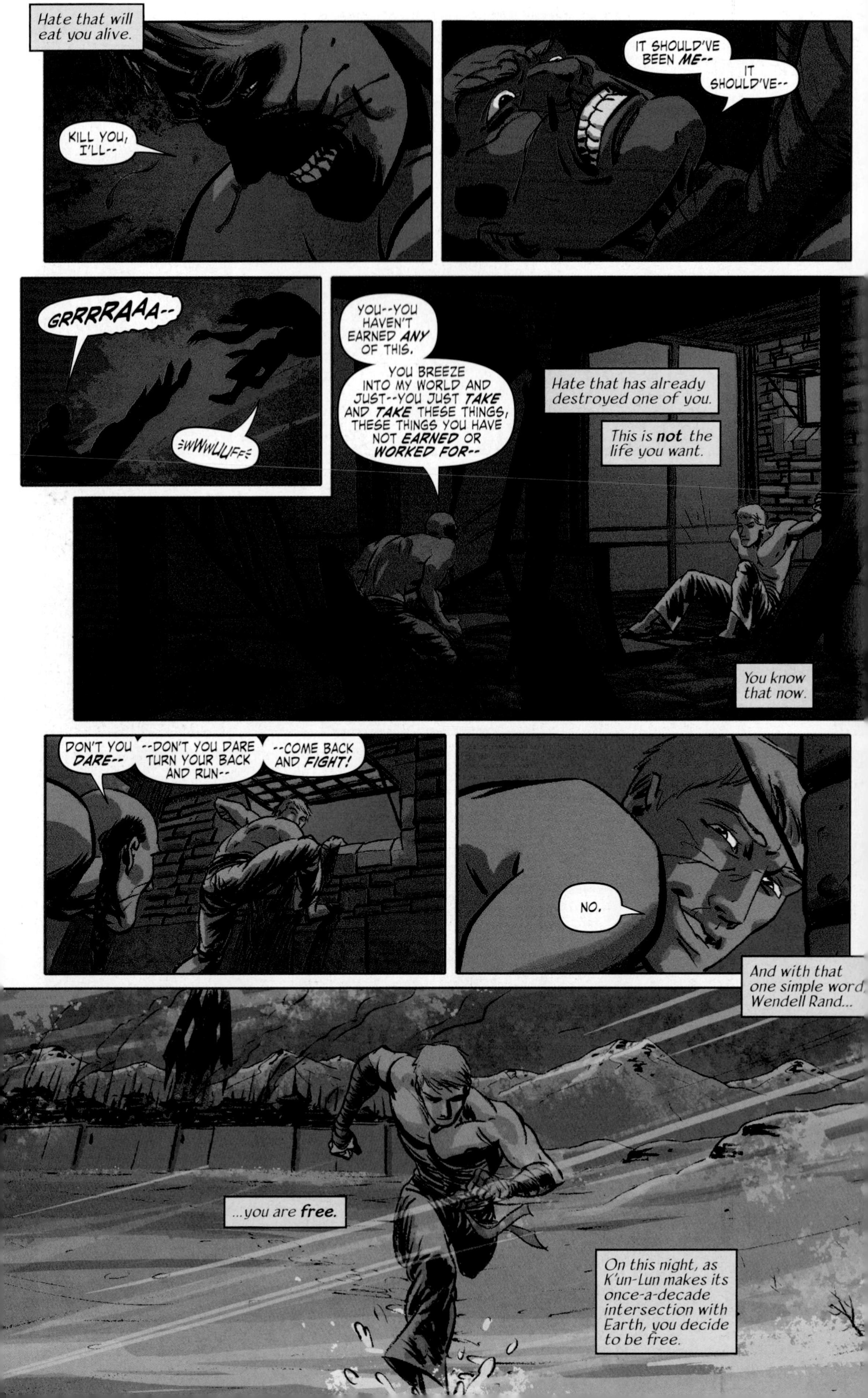
Hate that will eat you alive.
KILL YOU, I'LL--
IT SHOULD'VE BEEN ME--
IT SHOULD'VE--
GRRRRAAA--
WWWUUFF
YOU--YOU HAVEN'T EARNED ANY OF THIS.
YOU BREEZE INTO MY WORLD AND JUST--YOU JUST TAKE AND TAKE THESE THINGS, THESE THINGS YOU HAVE NOT EARNED OR WORKED FOR--
Hate that has already destroyed one of you.
This is not the life you want.
You know that now.
DON'T YOU DARE--
--DON'T YOU DARE TURN YOUR BACK AND RUN--
--COME BACK AND FIGHT!
NO.
And with that one simple word, Wendell Rand...
...you are free.
On this night, as K'un-Lun makes its once-a-decade intersection with Earth, you decide to be free.

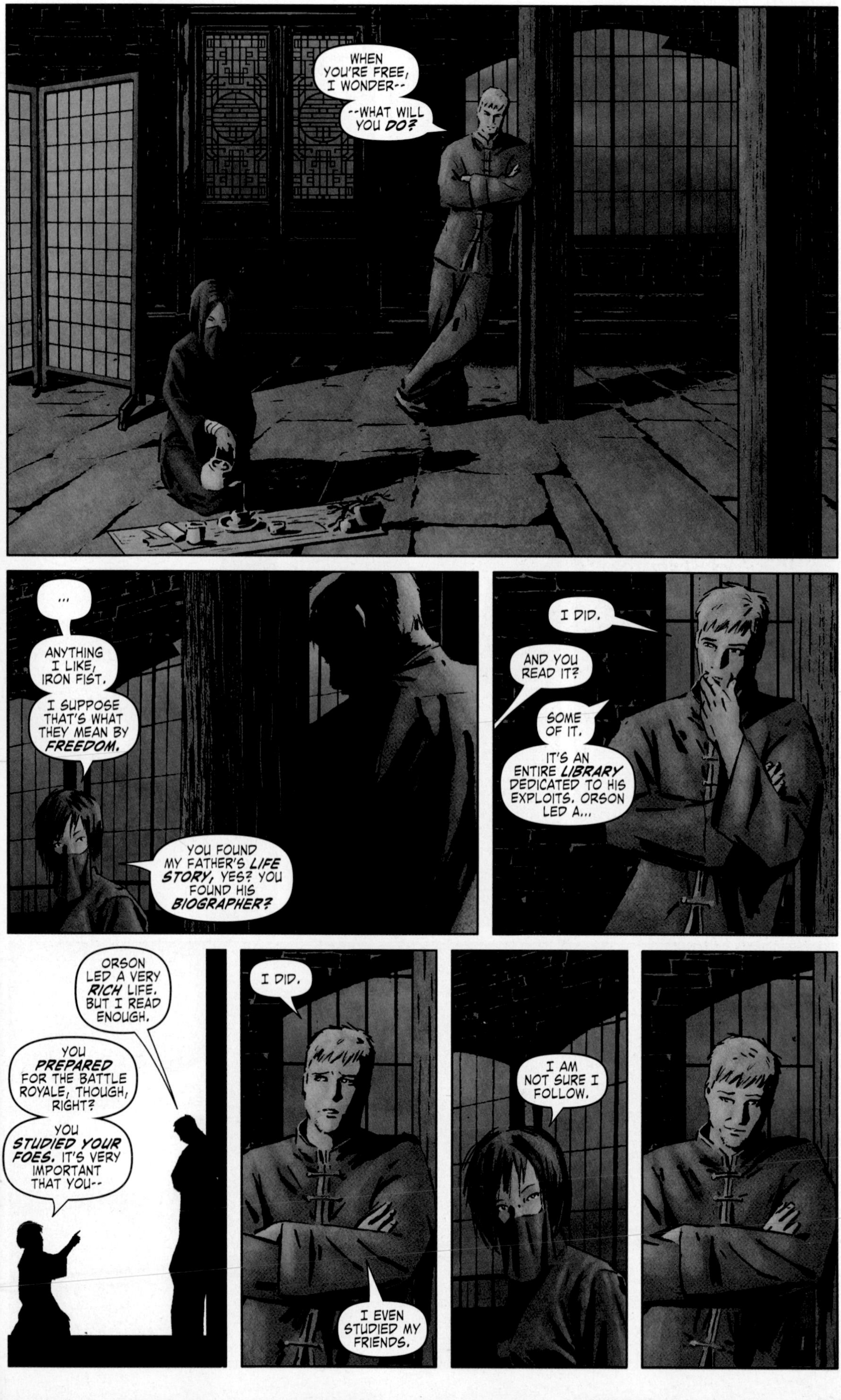
WHEN YOU'RE FREE, I WONDER--
--WHAT WILL YOU *DO?*
...
ANYTHING I LIKE, IRON FIST.
I SUPPOSE THAT'S WHAT THEY MEAN BY *FREEDOM.*
YOU FOUND MY FATHER'S *LIFE STORY,* YES? YOU FOUND HIS *BIOGRAPHER?*
I DID.
AND YOU READ IT?
SOME OF IT.
IT'S AN ENTIRE *LIBRARY* DEDICATED TO HIS EXPLOITS. ORSON LED A...
ORSON LED A VERY *RICH* LIFE. BUT I READ ENOUGH.
YOU *PREPARED* FOR THE BATTLE ROYALE, THOUGH, RIGHT?
YOU *STUDIED YOUR FOES.* IT'S VERY IMPORTANT THAT YOU--
I DID.
I EVEN STUDIED MY FRIENDS.
I AM NOT SURE I FOLLOW.

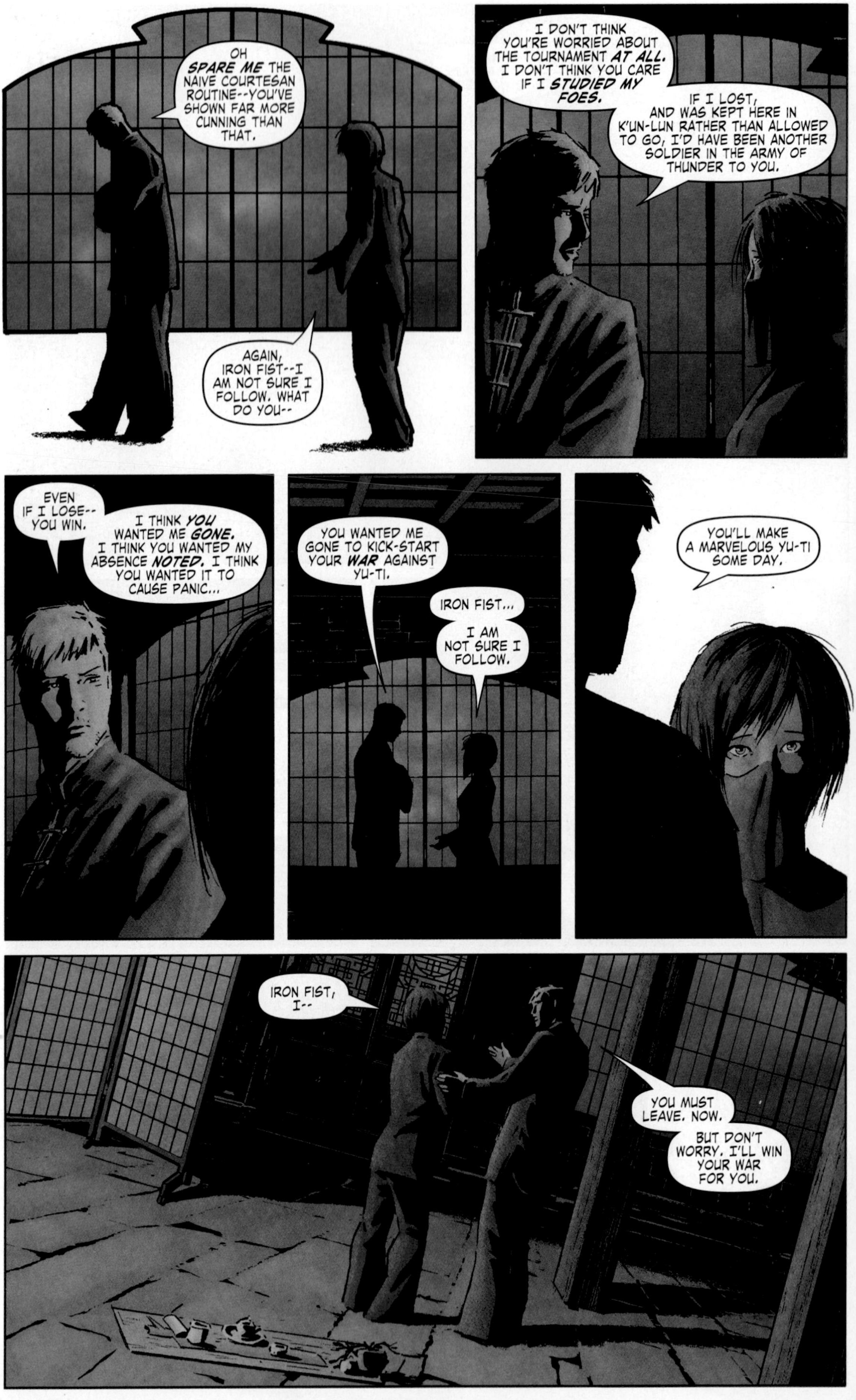
OH SPARE ME THE NAIVE COURTESAN ROUTINE--YOU'VE SHOWN FAR MORE CUNNING THAN THAT.
AGAIN, IRON FIST--I AM NOT SURE I FOLLOW. WHAT DO YOU--
I DON'T THINK YOU'RE WORRIED ABOUT THE TOURNAMENT AT ALL. I DON'T THINK YOU CARE IF I STUDIED MY FOES.
IF I LOST, AND WAS KEPT HERE IN K'UN-LUN RATHER THAN ALLOWED TO GO, I'D HAVE BEEN ANOTHER SOLDIER IN THE ARMY OF THUNDER TO YOU.
EVEN IF I LOSE--YOU WIN.
I THINK YOU WANTED ME GONE. I THINK YOU WANTED MY ABSENCE NOTED. I THINK YOU WANTED IT TO CAUSE PANIC...
YOU WANTED ME GONE TO KICK-START YOUR WAR AGAINST YU-TI.
IRON FIST...
I AM NOT SURE I FOLLOW.
YOU'LL MAKE A MARVELOUS YU-TI SOME DAY.
IRON FIST, I--
YOU MUST LEAVE. NOW.
BUT DON'T WORRY. I'LL WIN YOUR WAR FOR YOU.

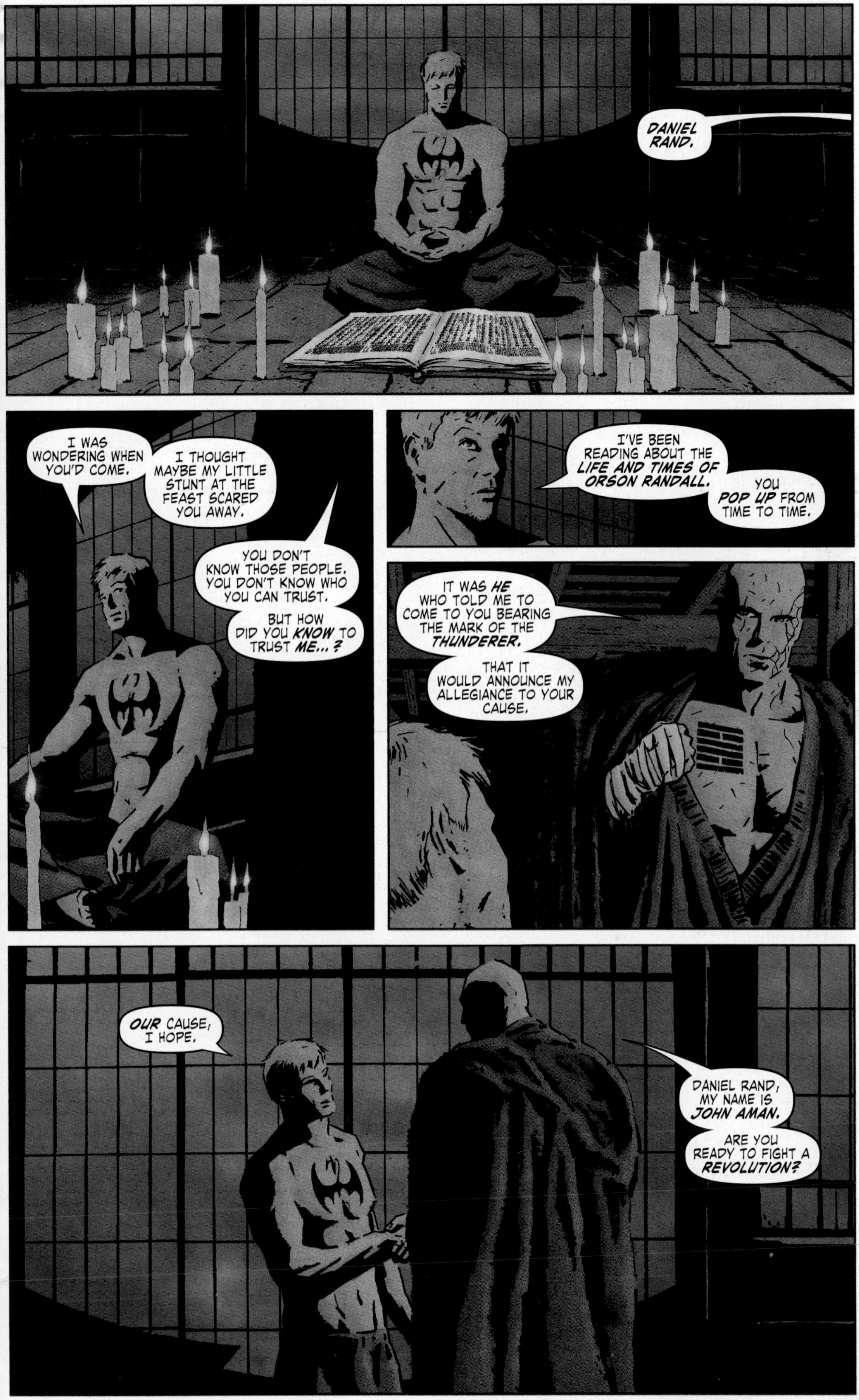
DANIEL RAND.
I WAS WONDERING WHEN YOU'D COME.
I THOUGHT MAYBE MY LITTLE STUNT AT THE FEAST SCARED YOU AWAY.
YOU DON'T KNOW THOSE PEOPLE. YOU DON'T KNOW WHO YOU CAN TRUST.
BUT HOW DID YOU KNOW TO TRUST ME...?
I'VE BEEN READING ABOUT THE LIFE AND TIMES OF ORSON RANDALL.
YOU POP UP FROM TIME TO TIME.
IT WAS HE WHO TOLD ME TO COME TO YOU BEARING THE MARK OF THE THUNDERER.
THAT IT WOULD ANNOUNCE MY ALLEGIANCE TO YOUR CAUSE.
OUR CAUSE, I HOPE.
DANIEL RAND, MY NAME IS JOHN AMAN.
ARE YOU READY TO FIGHT A REVOLUTION?

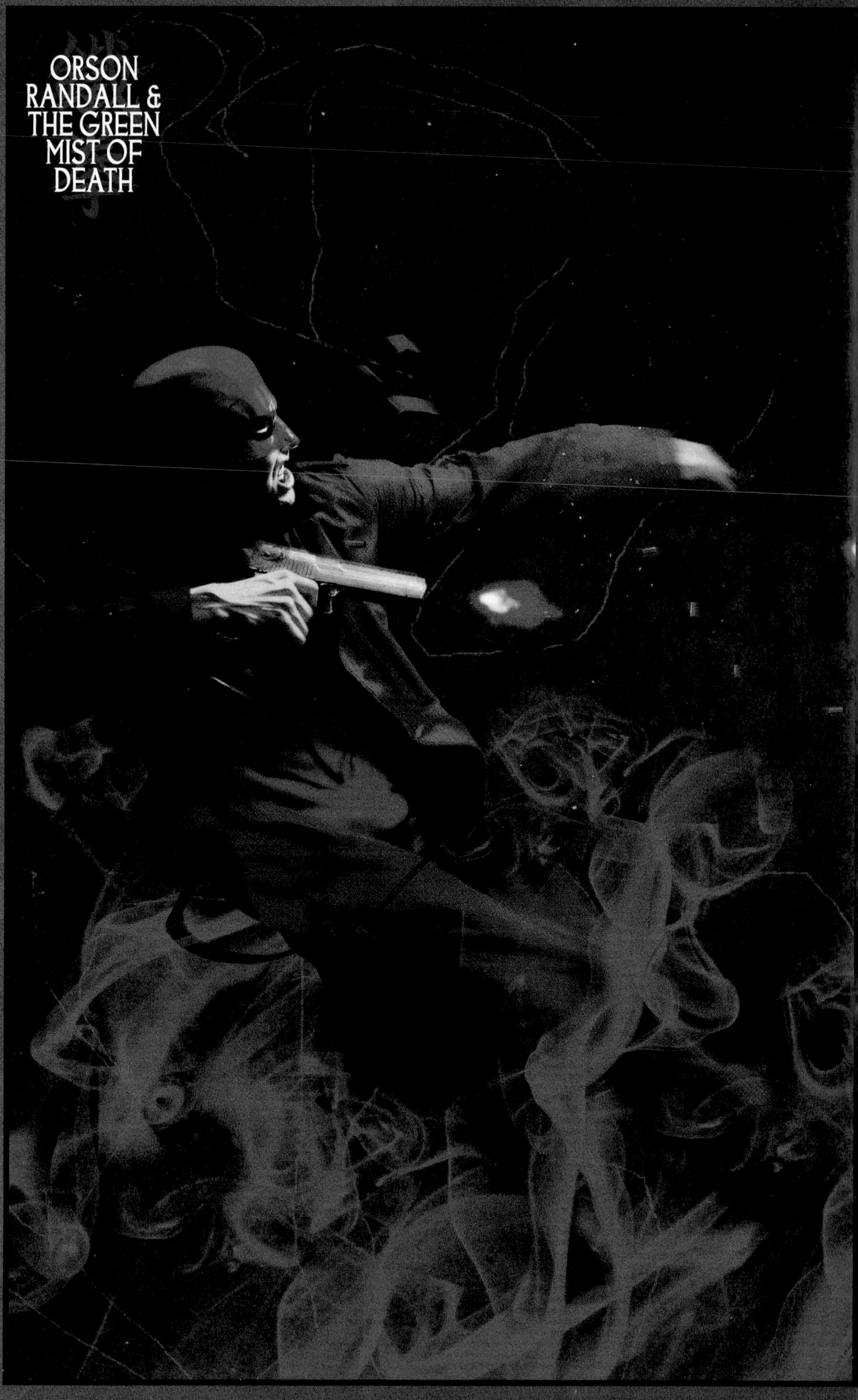
ORSON RANDALL & THE GREEN MIST OF DEATH

…son Randall! Hero, adventurer, dashing rogue! Born and raised in the mystical city of K'un-Lun, Orson defeated the dragon Shou-Lao the undying and gained extraordinary powers. With superhuman strength, speed, and fighting prowess, he became the city's Immortal Weapon! But after traveling to Earth and enduring the horrors of World War I, Orson refused to take part in the deadly tournament held every 88 years between K'un-Lun and the six other mystical cities. Resisting his fellow Immortal Weapons' use of force, Orson accidentally killed the Crane Champion of K'un-Zi, and fled.

For the next several decades — long before Danny Rand would travel to K'un-Lun and become successor to the title of the Immortal Iron Fist — Orson roamed the Earth, a bounty on his head. In the company of his makeshift family, the Confederates of the Curious — including Danny's father, Wendell Rand — Orson has evaded the pursuits of the Immortal Weapons and quested around the globe for justice and adventure as…

THE GOLDEN AGE IRON FIST!

Previously:

Danny Rand — the Iron Fist and present-day Immortal Weapon of K'un-Lun — fights a war on many fronts. As the Tournament of Heavenly Cities unfolds, Danny must secure victory for K'un-Lun in order to return to Earth…and he's already lost his first match. But while the round robin elimination moves on, Danny's trainer and master, Lei Kung the Thunderer, has enlisted his aid in revolution. Lei Kung is raising an army by training the women of K'un-Lun in the martial arts, and means to bring down the city's corrupt lord. They face overwhelming odds, and defeat is all but assured.

During the tournament, Danny attempted to befriend the Prince of Orphans — the oldest, most powerful and most venerated of the seven Immortal Weapons — and the least known and most mysterious. But Danny was rebuffed by the enigmatic warrior.

At first, anyway. As Lei Kung and Danny steeled themselves to launch their rebellion at dawn and rewrite the destiny of the Heavenly Cities, Danny was paid a private visit in his quarters. It was the Prince of Orphans — a.k.a. John Aman. He came to Danny bearing the mark of the Thunderer tattooed on his chest, announcing his allegiance to their cause…and asked how Danny knew to trust him. Danny revealed that he'd learned of Aman by reading of the life and adventures of the Iron Fist Orson Randall, where Aman made several appearances…

THE IMMORTAL IRON FIST: ORSON RANDALL AND THE GREEN MIST OF DEATH

Matt Fraction	Nick Dragotta, Mike Allred and Laura Allred	Russ Heath	Lewis LaRosa, Stefano Gaudiano and Matt Hollingsworth	Mitch Breitweiser and Matt Hollingsworth
Writer	Artists, Part One	Artist, Part Two	Artists, Part Three	Artists, Part Four

...rtmonkeys Studios	Paul Acerios	Alejandro Arbona	Warren Simons	Joe Quesada	Dan Buckley
Letterers	Production	Assistant Editor	Editor	Editor in Chief	Publisher

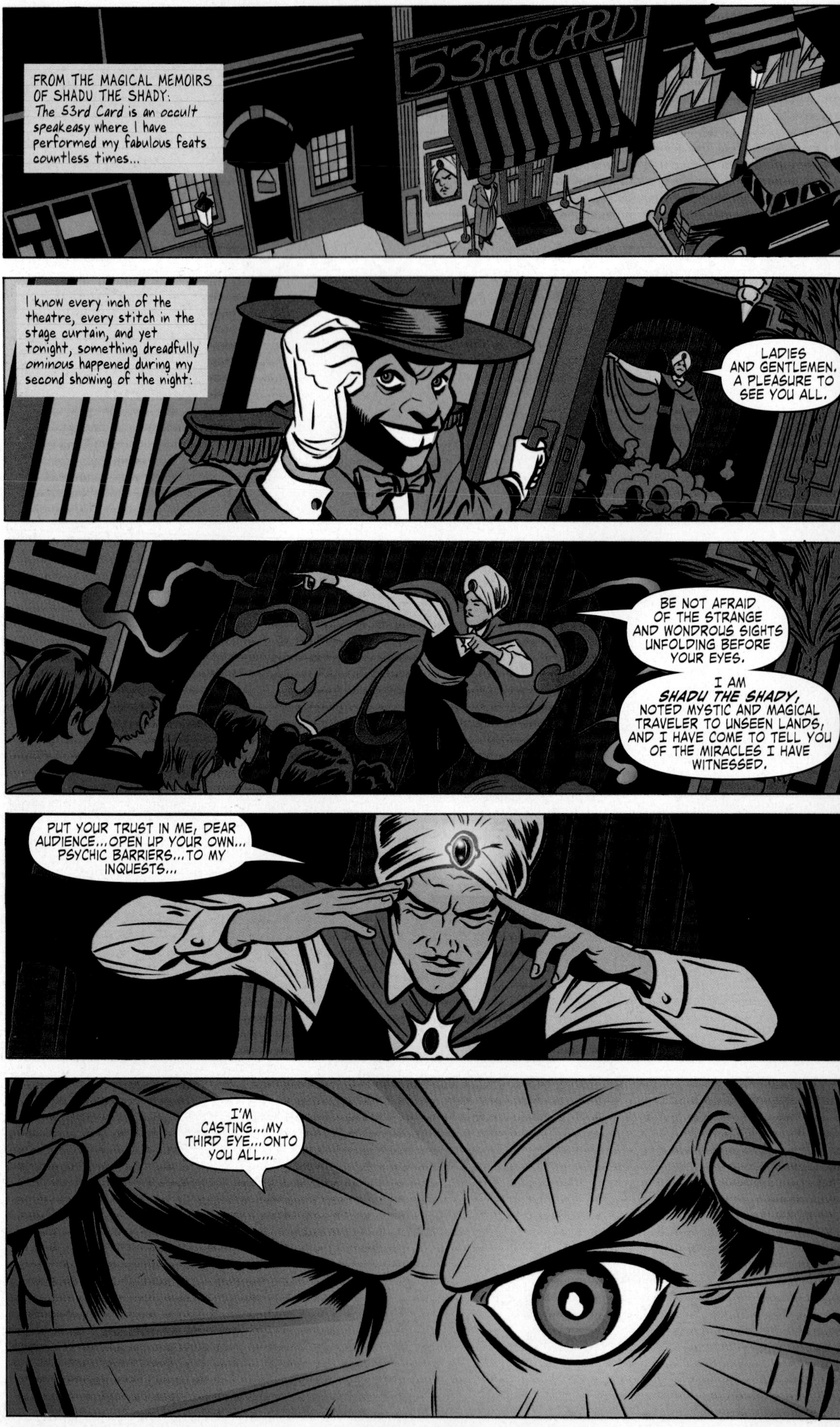
53rd CARD
FROM THE MAGICAL MEMOIRS OF SHADU THE SHADY: The 53rd Card is an occult speakeasy where I have performed my fabulous feats countless times...
I know every inch of the theatre, every stitch in the stage curtain, and yet tonight, something dreadfully ominous happened during my second showing of the night:
LADIES AND GENTLEMEN. A PLEASURE TO SEE YOU ALL.
BE NOT AFRAID OF THE STRANGE AND WONDROUS SIGHTS UNFOLDING BEFORE YOUR EYES.
I AM *SHADU THE SHADY,* NOTED MYSTIC AND MAGICAL TRAVELER TO UNSEEN LANDS, AND I HAVE COME TO TELL YOU OF THE MIRACLES I HAVE WITNESSED.
PUT YOUR TRUST IN ME, DEAR AUDIENCE...OPEN UP YOUR OWN... PSYCHIC BARRIERS...TO MY INQUESTS...
I'M CASTING...MY THIRD EYE...ONTO YOU ALL...

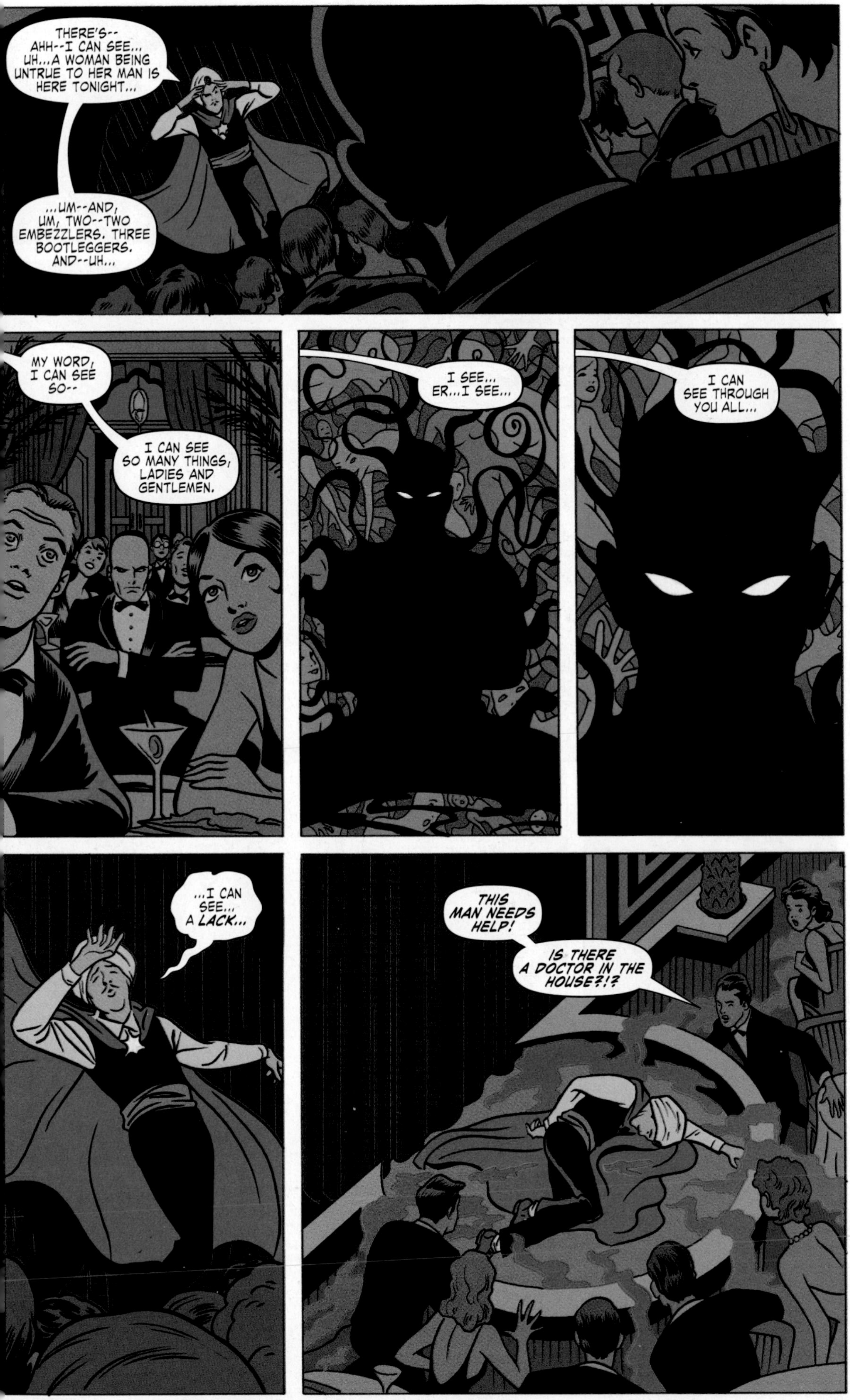
THERE'S-- AHH--I CAN SEE... UH...A WOMAN BEING UNTRUE TO HER MAN IS HERE TONIGHT...
...UM--AND, UM, TWO--TWO EMBEZZLERS. THREE BOOTLEGGERS. AND--UH...
MY WORD, I CAN SEE SO--
I CAN SEE SO MANY THINGS, LADIES AND GENTLEMEN.
I SEE... ER...I SEE...
I CAN SEE THROUGH YOU ALL...
...I CAN SEE... A *LACK*...
THIS MAN NEEDS HELP!
IS THERE A DOCTOR IN THE HOUSE?!?

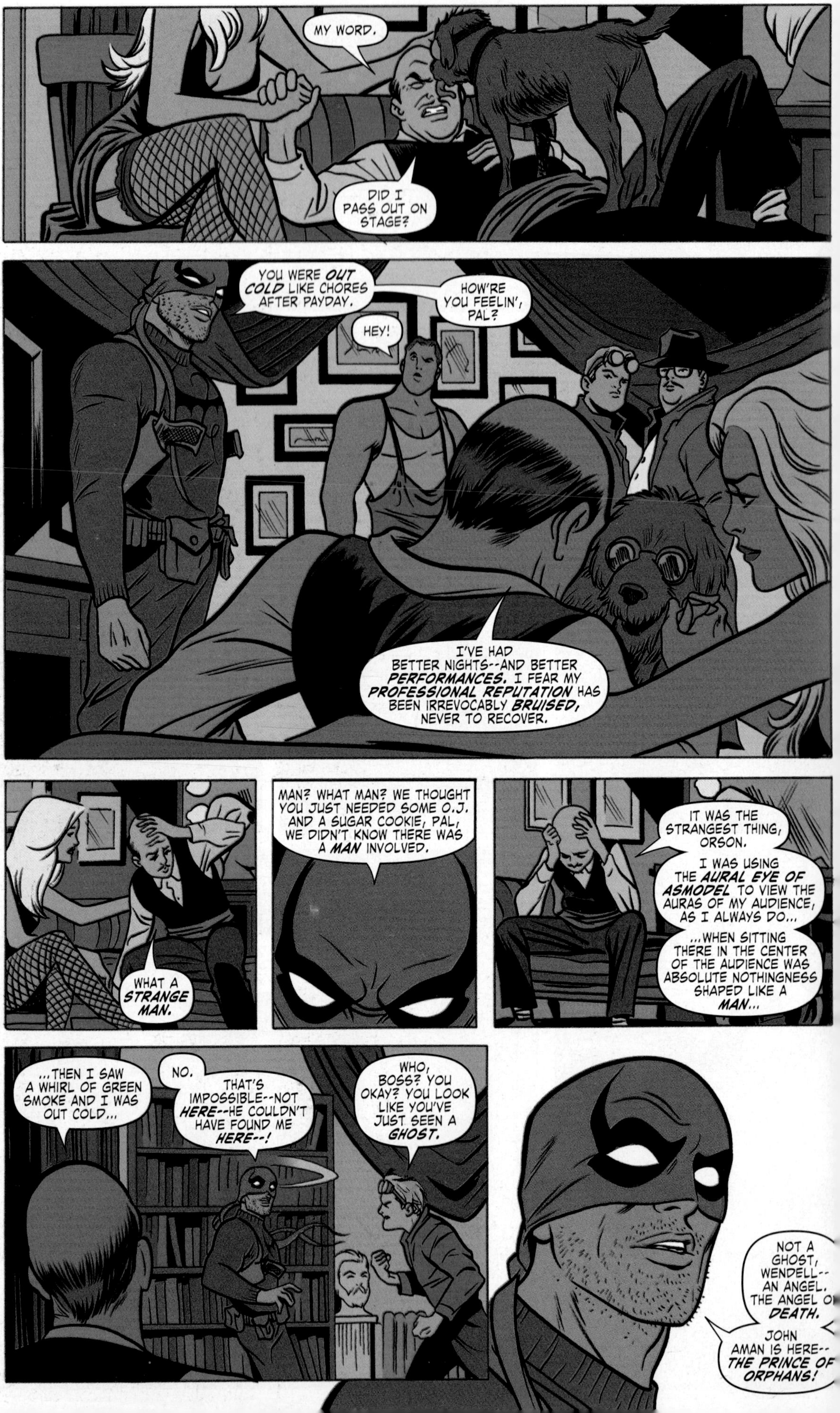

MY WORD.
DID I PASS OUT ON STAGE?
YOU WERE OUT COLD LIKE CHORES AFTER PAYDAY.
HEY!
HOW'RE YOU FEELIN', PAL?
I'VE HAD BETTER NIGHTS--AND BETTER PERFORMANCES. I FEAR MY PROFESSIONAL REPUTATION HAS BEEN IRREVOCABLY BRUISED, NEVER TO RECOVER.
WHAT A STRANGE MAN.
MAN? WHAT MAN? WE THOUGHT YOU JUST NEEDED SOME O.J. AND A SUGAR COOKIE, PAL, WE DIDN'T KNOW THERE WAS A MAN INVOLVED.
IT WAS THE STRANGEST THING, ORSON.
I WAS USING THE AURAL EYE OF ASMODEL TO VIEW THE AURAS OF MY AUDIENCE, AS I ALWAYS DO...
...WHEN SITTING THERE IN THE CENTER OF THE AUDIENCE WAS ABSOLUTE NOTHINGNESS SHAPED LIKE A MAN...
...THEN I SAW A WHIRL OF GREEN SMOKE AND I WAS OUT COLD...
NO.
THAT'S IMPOSSIBLE--NOT HERE--HE COULDN'T HAVE FOUND ME HERE--!
WHO, BOSS? YOU OKAY? YOU LOOK LIKE YOU'VE JUST SEEN A GHOST.
NOT A GHOST, WENDELL--AN ANGEL. THE ANGEL O DEATH.
JOHN AMAN IS HERE--THE PRINCE OF ORPHANS!

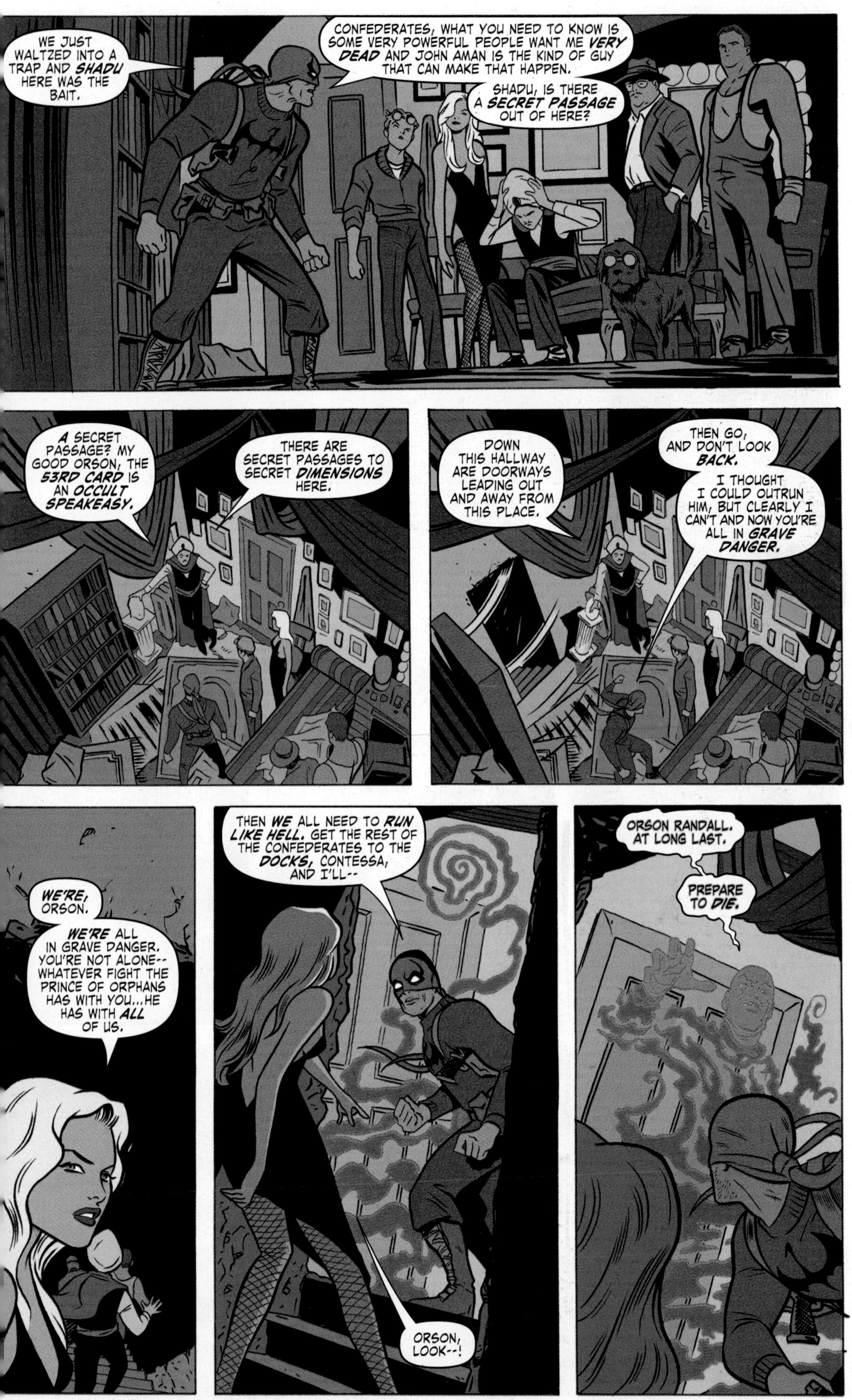
WE JUST WALTZED INTO A TRAP AND SHADU HERE WAS THE BAIT.
CONFEDERATES, WHAT YOU NEED TO KNOW IS SOME VERY POWERFUL PEOPLE WANT ME VERY DEAD AND JOHN AMAN IS THE KIND OF GUY THAT CAN MAKE THAT HAPPEN.
SHADU, IS THERE A SECRET PASSAGE OUT OF HERE?
A SECRET PASSAGE? MY GOOD ORSON, THE 53RD CARD IS AN OCCULT SPEAKEASY.
THERE ARE SECRET PASSAGES TO SECRET DIMENSIONS HERE.
DOWN THIS HALLWAY ARE DOORWAYS LEADING OUT AND AWAY FROM THIS PLACE.
THEN GO, AND DON'T LOOK BACK.
I THOUGHT I COULD OUTRUN HIM, BUT CLEARLY I CAN'T AND NOW YOU'RE ALL IN GRAVE DANGER.
WE'RE, ORSON.
WE'RE ALL IN GRAVE DANGER. YOU'RE NOT ALONE--WHATEVER FIGHT THE PRINCE OF ORPHANS HAS WITH YOU...HE HAS WITH ALL OF US.
THEN WE ALL NEED TO RUN LIKE HELL. GET THE REST OF THE CONFEDERATES TO THE DOCKS, CONTESSA, AND I'LL--
ORSON, LOOK--!
ORSON RANDALL. AT LONG LAST.
PREPARE TO DIE.

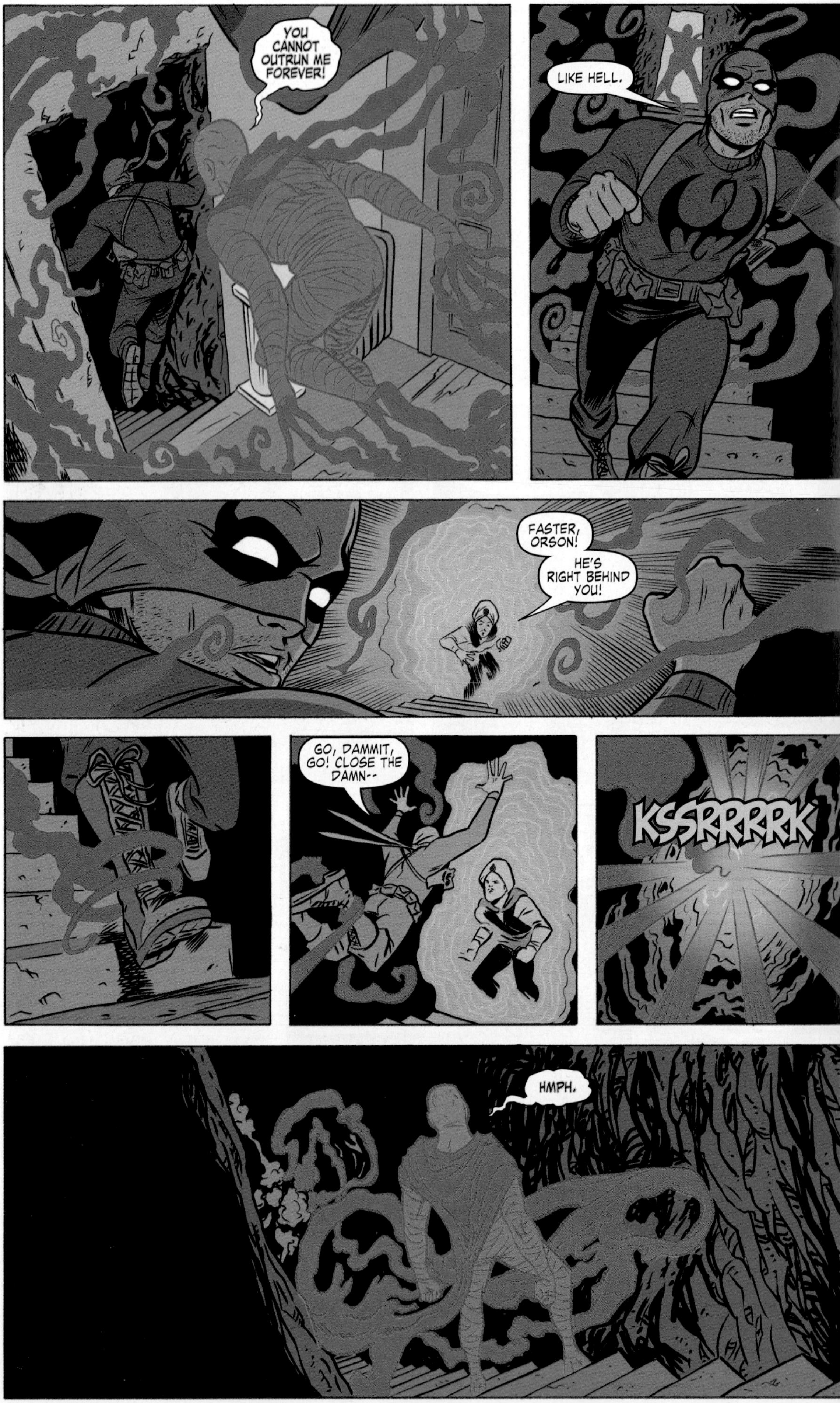
YOU CANNOT OUTRUN ME FOREVER!
LIKE HELL.
FASTER, ORSON!
HE'S RIGHT BEHIND YOU!
GO, DAMMIT, GO! CLOSE THE DAMN--
KSSRRRRK
HMPH.

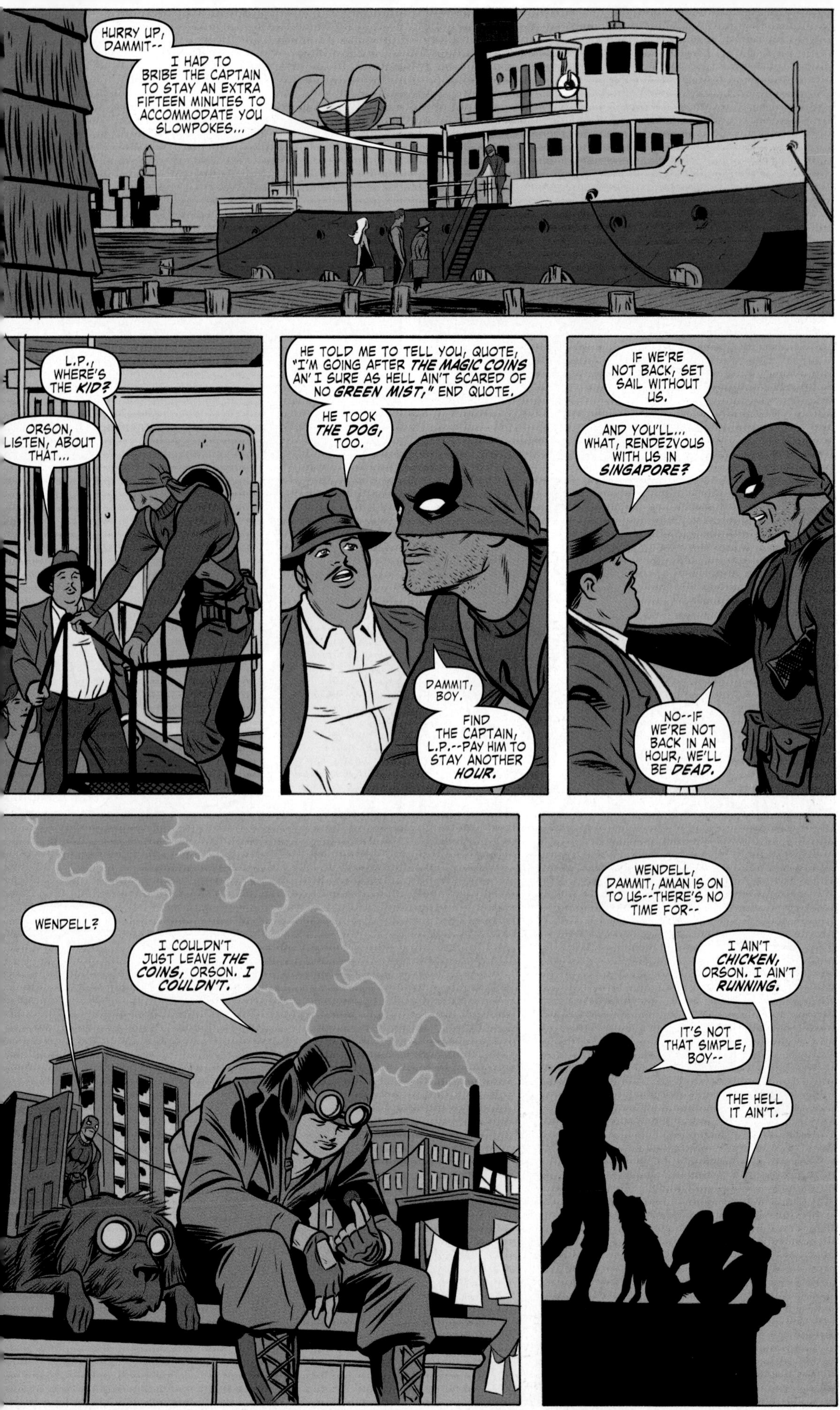
HURRY UP, DAMMIT--
I HAD TO BRIBE THE CAPTAIN TO STAY AN EXTRA FIFTEEN MINUTES TO ACCOMMODATE YOU SLOWPOKES...
L.P., WHERE'S THE KID?
ORSON, LISTEN, ABOUT THAT...
HE TOLD ME TO TELL YOU, QUOTE, "I'M GOING AFTER THE MAGIC COINS AN' I SURE AS HELL AIN'T SCARED OF NO GREEN MIST," END QUOTE.
HE TOOK THE DOG, TOO.
DAMMIT, BOY.
FIND THE CAPTAIN, L.P.--PAY HIM TO STAY ANOTHER HOUR.
IF WE'RE NOT BACK, SET SAIL WITHOUT US.
AND YOU'LL... WHAT, RENDEZVOUS WITH US IN SINGAPORE?
NO--IF WE'RE NOT BACK IN AN HOUR, WE'LL BE DEAD.
WENDELL?
I COULDN'T JUST LEAVE THE COINS, ORSON. I COULDN'T.
WENDELL, DAMMIT, AMAN IS ON TO US--THERE'S NO TIME FOR--
I AIN'T CHICKEN, ORSON. I AIN'T RUNNING.
IT'S NOT THAT SIMPLE, BOY--
THE HELL IT AIN'T.

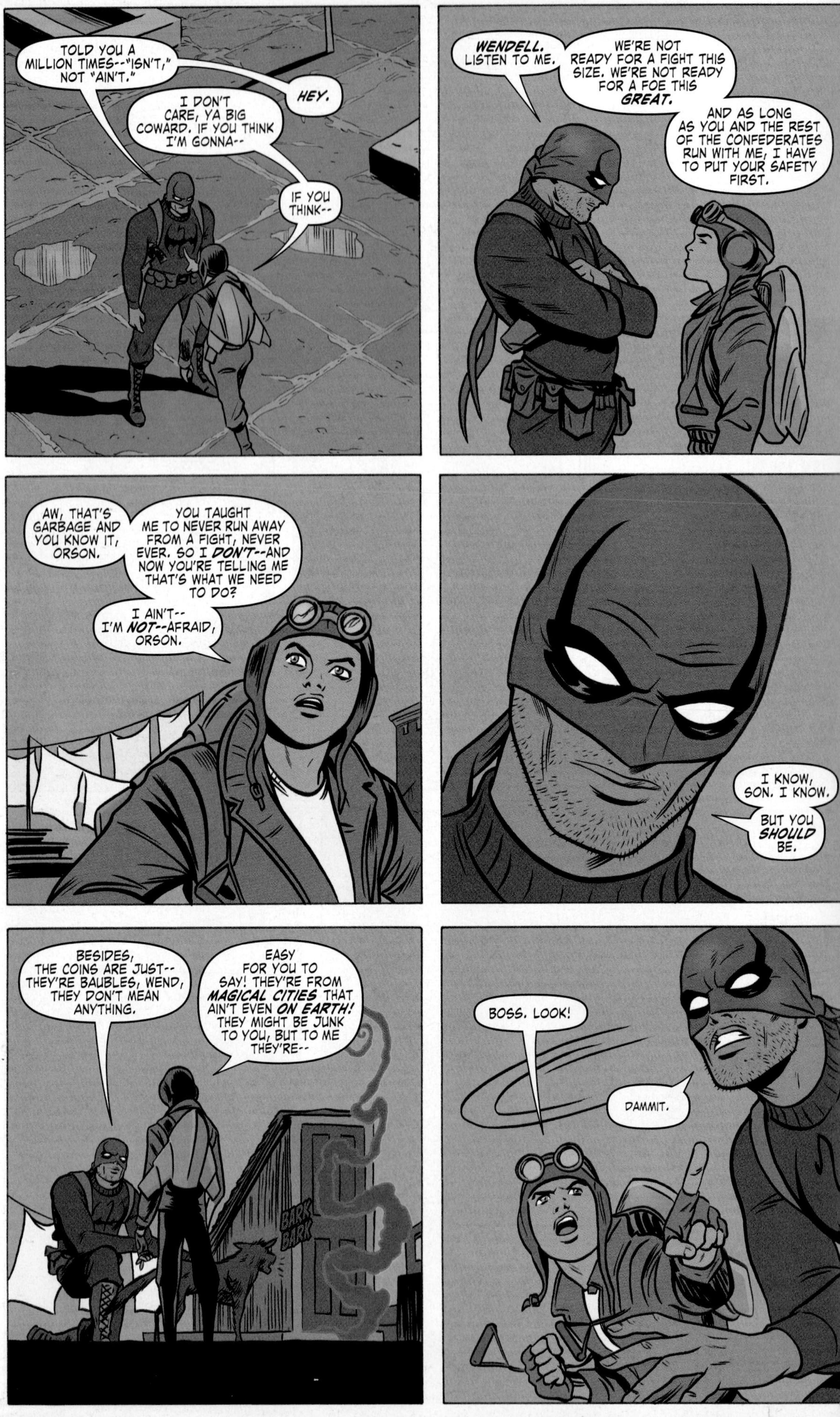
TOLD YOU A MILLION TIMES--"ISN'T," NOT "AIN'T."
HEY.
I DON'T CARE, YA BIG COWARD. IF YOU THINK I'M GONNA--
IF YOU THINK--
WENDELL. LISTEN TO ME.
WE'RE NOT READY FOR A FIGHT THIS SIZE. WE'RE NOT READY FOR A FOE THIS GREAT.
AND AS LONG AS YOU AND THE REST OF THE CONFEDERATES RUN WITH ME, I HAVE TO PUT YOUR SAFETY FIRST.
AW, THAT'S GARBAGE AND YOU KNOW IT, ORSON.
YOU TAUGHT ME TO NEVER RUN AWAY FROM A FIGHT, NEVER EVER. SO I DON'T--AND NOW YOU'RE TELLING ME THAT'S WHAT WE NEED TO DO?
I AIN'T-- I'M NOT--AFRAID, ORSON.
I KNOW, SON. I KNOW.
BUT YOU SHOULD BE.
BESIDES, THE COINS ARE JUST-- THEY'RE BAUBLES, WEND, THEY DON'T MEAN ANYTHING.
EASY FOR YOU TO SAY! THEY'RE FROM MAGICAL CITIES THAT AIN'T EVEN ON EARTH! THEY MIGHT BE JUNK TO YOU, BUT TO ME THEY'RE--
BARK BARK
BOSS. LOOK!
DAMMIT.

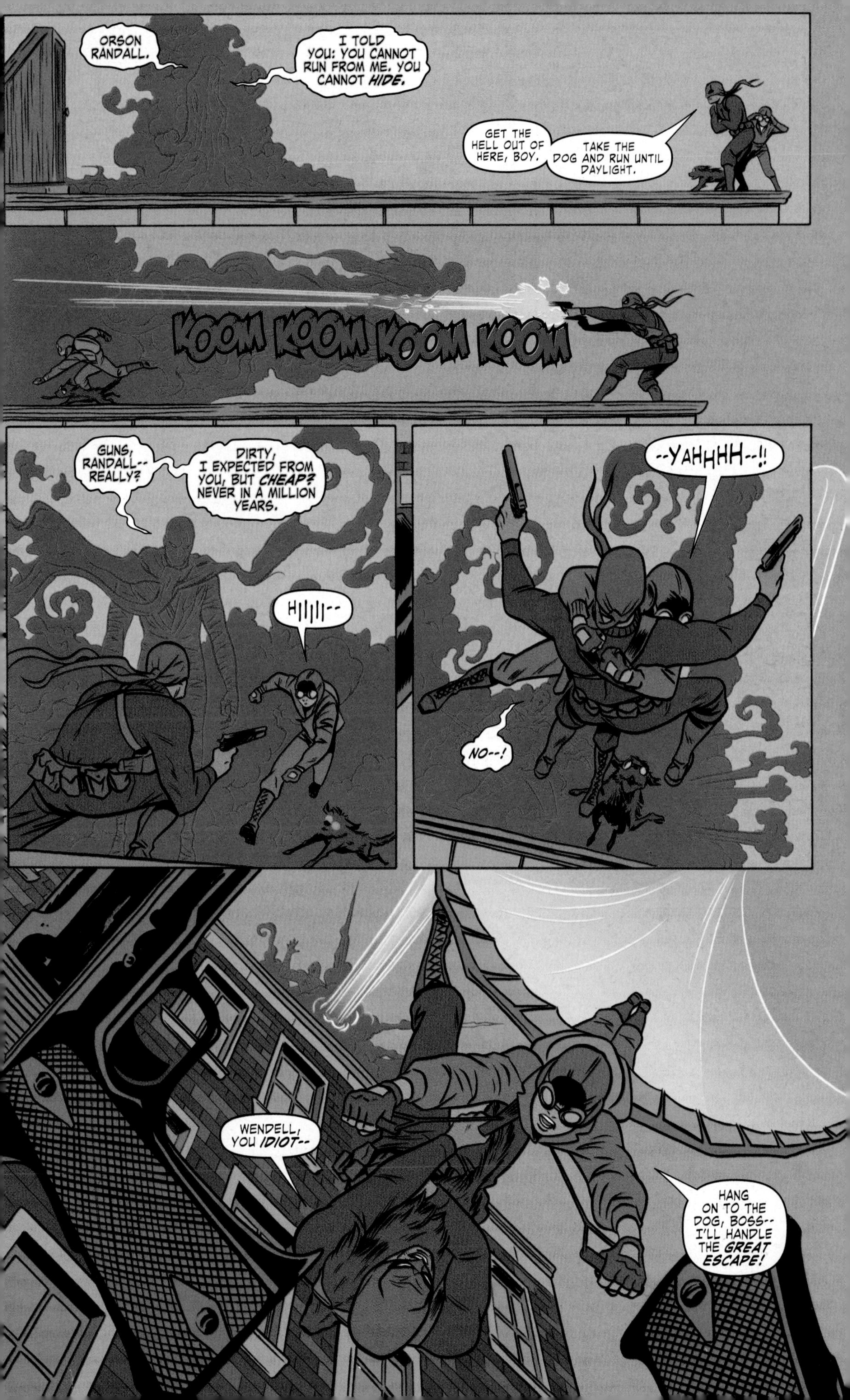
ORSON RANDALL.
I TOLD YOU: YOU CANNOT RUN FROM ME. YOU CANNOT HIDE.
GET THE HELL OUT OF HERE, BOY.
TAKE THE DOG AND RUN UNTIL DAYLIGHT.
KOOM KOOM KOOM KOOM
GUNS, RANDALL-- REALLY?
DIRTY, I EXPECTED FROM YOU, BUT CHEAP? NEVER IN A MILLION YEARS.
HIIIII--
--YAHHHH--!!
NO--!
WENDELL, YOU IDIOT--
HANG ON TO THE DOG, BOSS-- I'LL HANDLE THE GREAT ESCAPE!

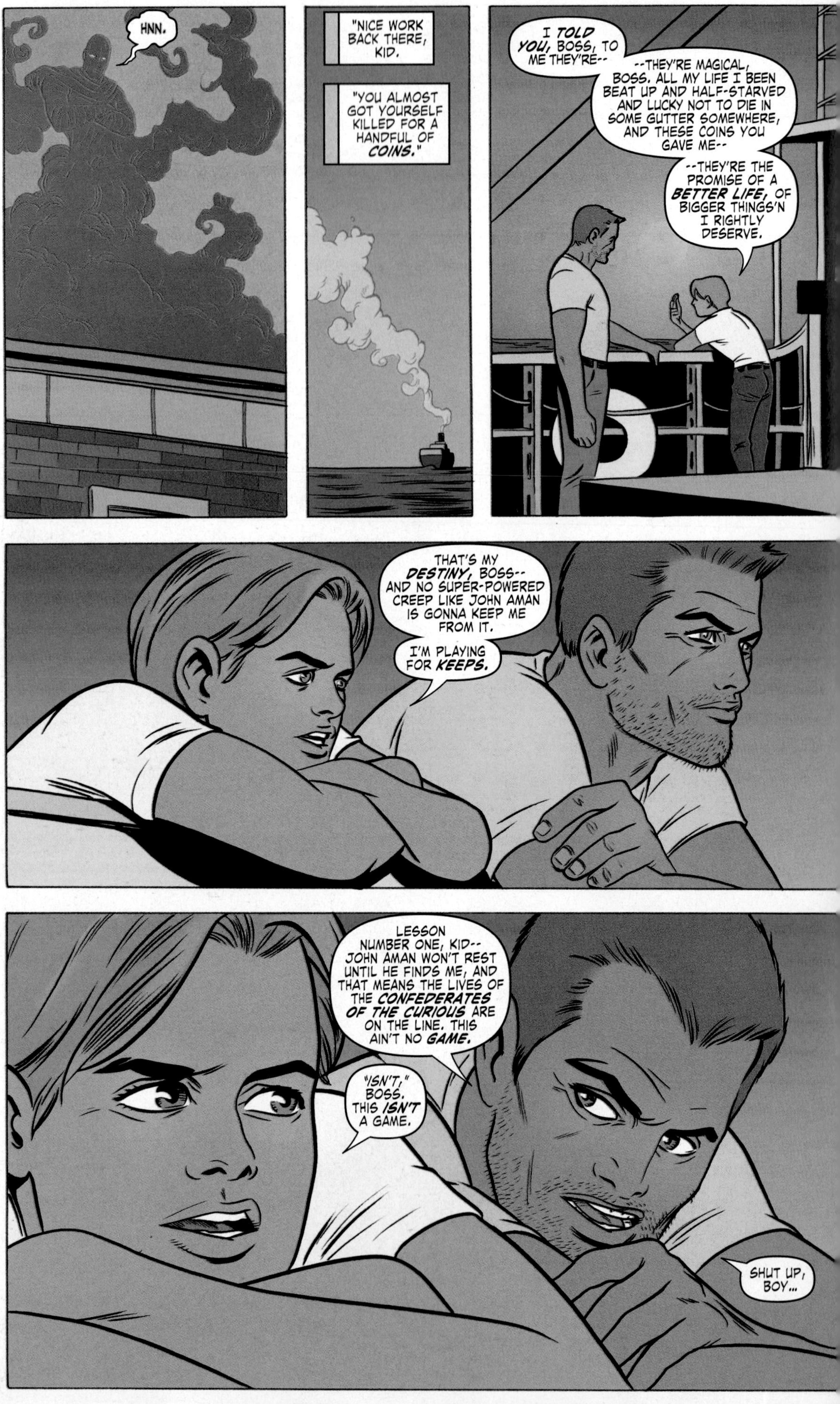
HNN.
"NICE WORK BACK THERE, KID.
"YOU ALMOST GOT YOURSELF KILLED FOR A HANDFUL OF COINS."
I TOLD YOU, BOSS, TO ME THEY'RE--
--THEY'RE MAGICAL, BOSS. ALL MY LIFE I BEEN BEAT UP AND HALF-STARVED AND LUCKY NOT TO DIE IN SOME GUTTER SOMEWHERE, AND THESE COINS YOU GAVE ME--
--THEY'RE THE PROMISE OF A BETTER LIFE, OF BIGGER THINGS'N I RIGHTLY DESERVE.
THAT'S MY DESTINY, BOSS--AND NO SUPER-POWERED CREEP LIKE JOHN AMAN IS GONNA KEEP ME FROM IT.
I'M PLAYING FOR KEEPS.
LESSON NUMBER ONE, KID--JOHN AMAN WON'T REST UNTIL HE FINDS ME, AND THAT MEANS THE LIVES OF THE CONFEDERATES OF THE CURIOUS ARE ON THE LINE. THIS AIN'T NO GAME.
"ISN'T," BOSS. THIS ISN'T A GAME.
SHUT UP, BOY...

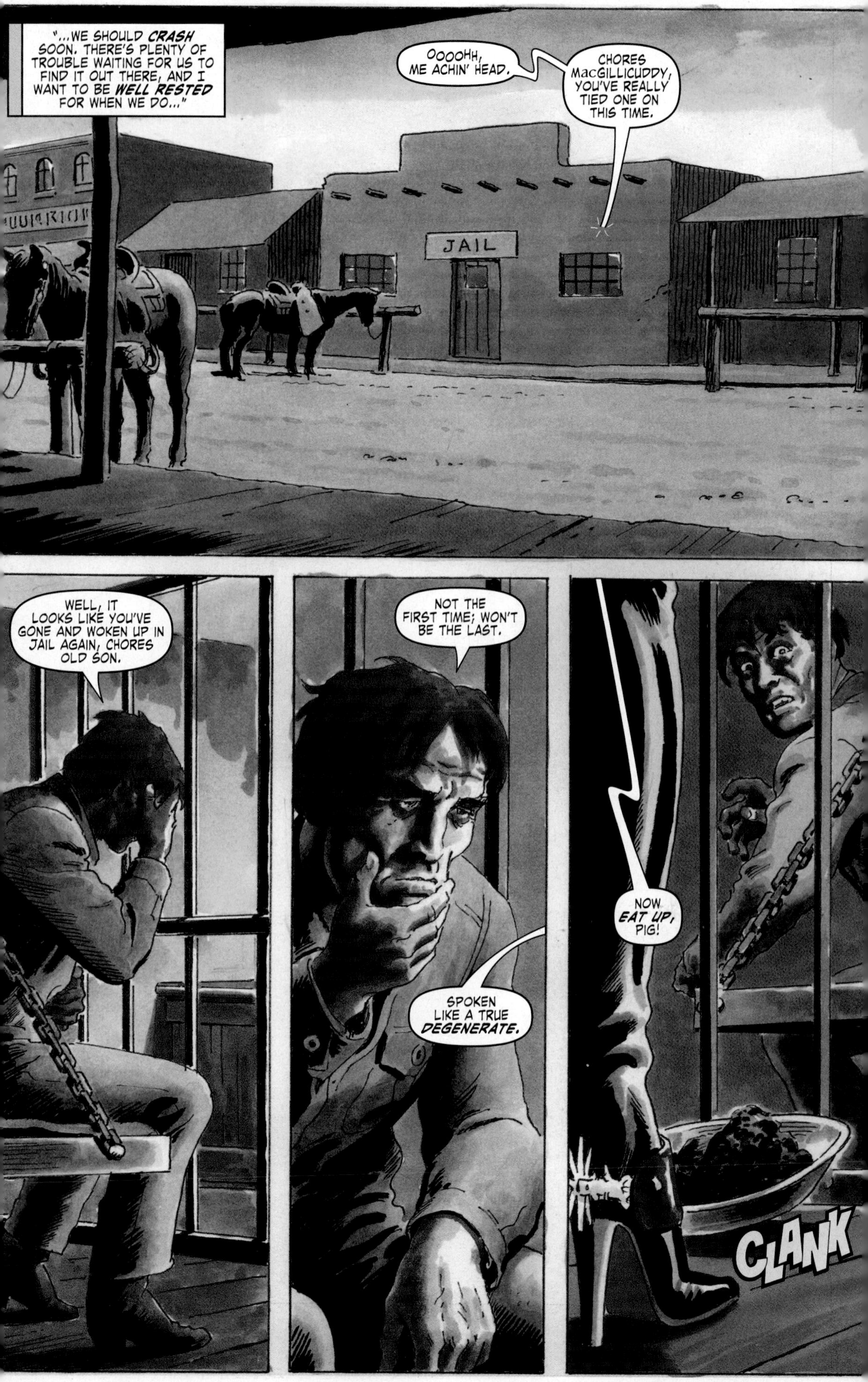
"...WE SHOULD CRASH SOON. THERE'S PLENTY OF TROUBLE WAITING FOR US TO FIND IT OUT THERE, AND I WANT TO BE WELL RESTED FOR WHEN WE DO..."
OOOOHH, ME ACHIN' HEAD.
CHORES MacGILLICUDDY, YOU'VE REALLY TIED ONE ON THIS TIME.
JAIL
WELL, IT LOOKS LIKE YOU'VE GONE AND WOKEN UP IN JAIL AGAIN, CHORES OLD SON.
NOT THE FIRST TIME; WON'T BE THE LAST.
SPOKEN LIKE A TRUE DEGENERATE.
NOW EAT UP, PIG!
CLANK

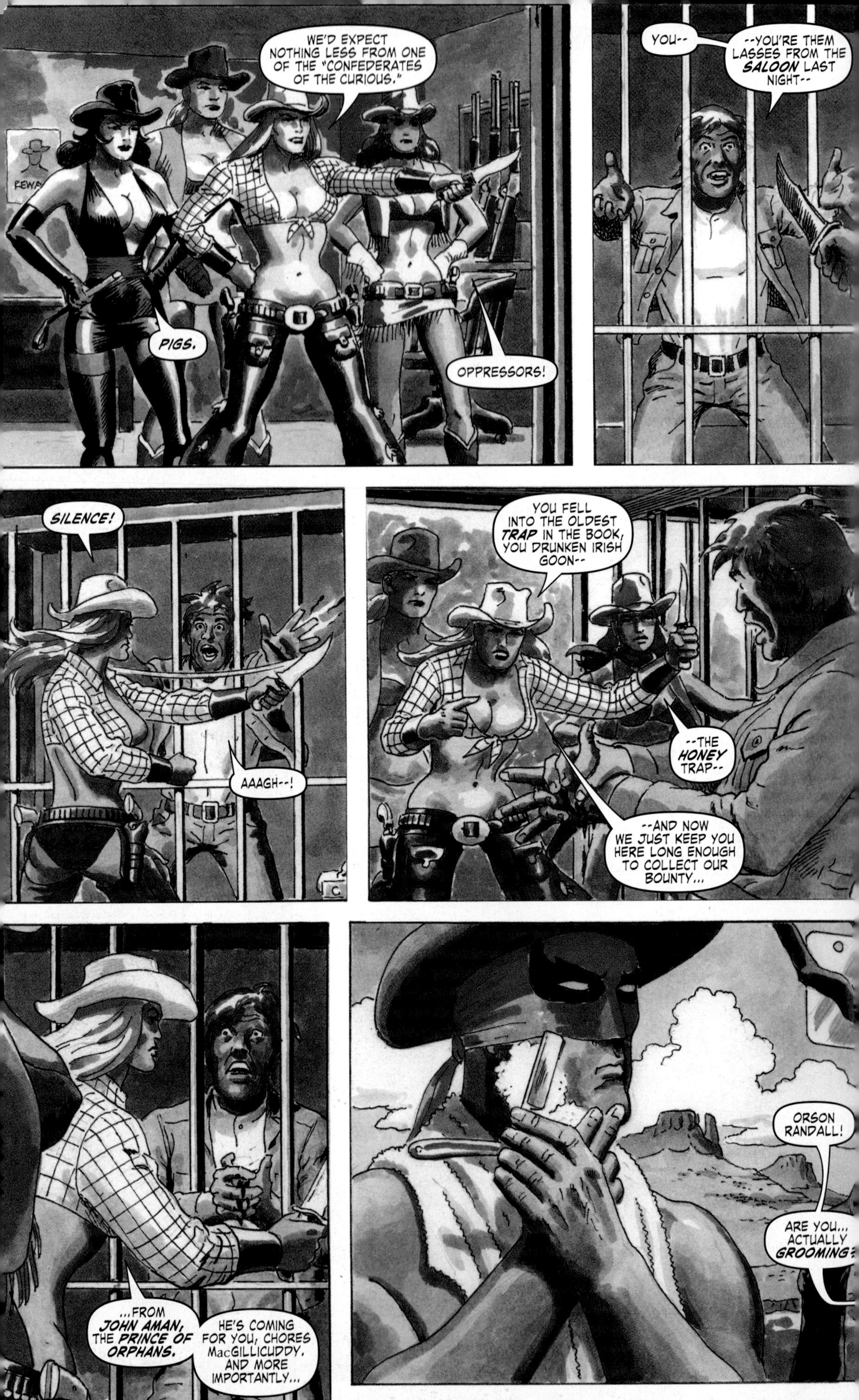
WE'D EXPECT NOTHING LESS FROM ONE OF THE "CONFEDERATES OF THE CURIOUS."
REWA
PIGS.
OPPRESSORS!
YOU--
--YOU'RE THEM LASSES FROM THE SALOON LAST NIGHT--
SILENCE!
AAAGH--!
YOU FELL INTO THE OLDEST TRAP IN THE BOOK, YOU DRUNKEN IRISH GOON--
--THE HONEY TRAP--
--AND NOW WE JUST KEEP YOU HERE LONG ENOUGH TO COLLECT OUR BOUNTY...
...FROM JOHN AMAN, THE PRINCE OF ORPHANS.
HE'S COMING FOR YOU, CHORES MacGILLICUDDY. AND MORE IMPORTANTLY...
ORSON RANDALL!
ARE YOU... ACTUALLY GROOMING

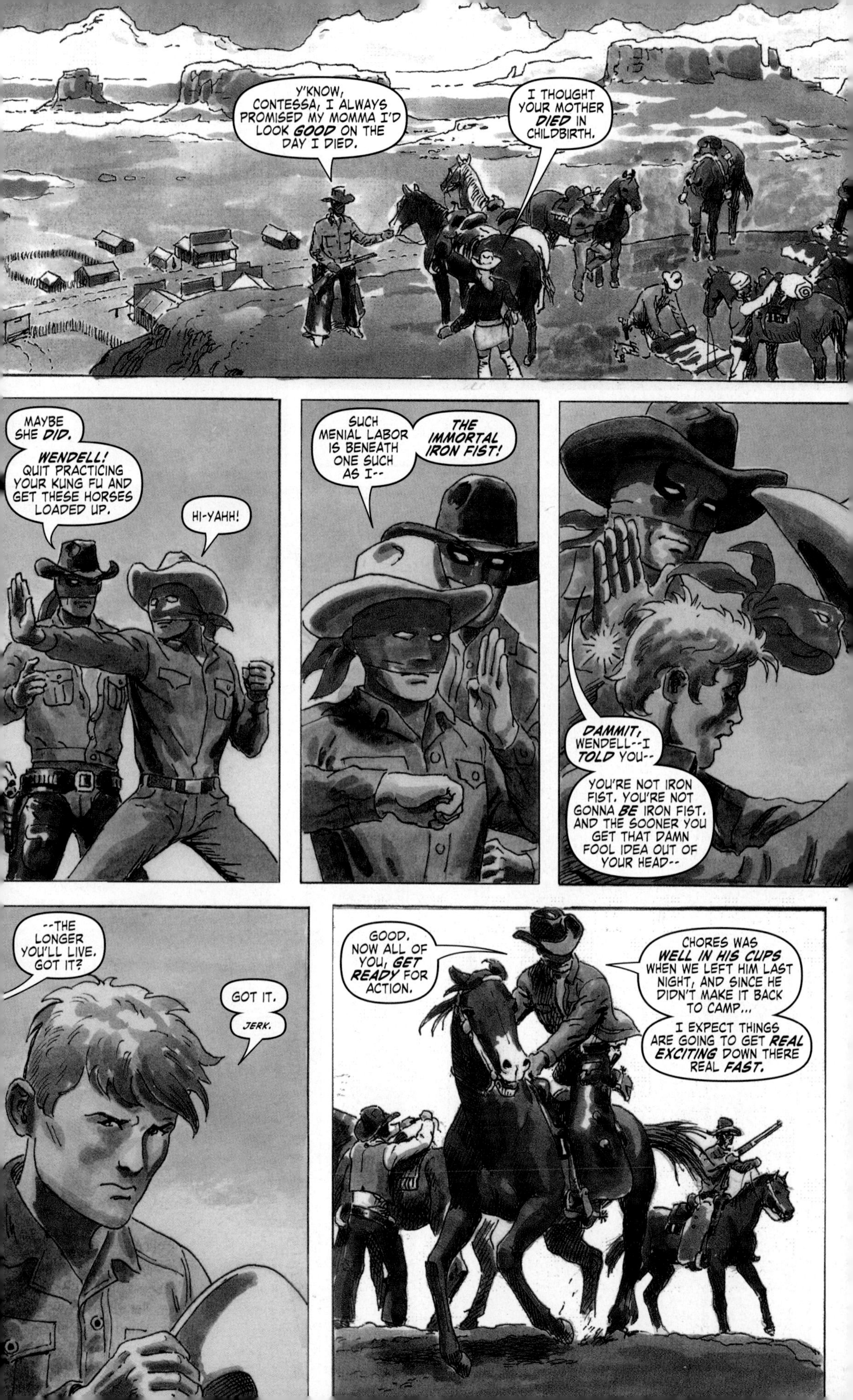
Y'KNOW, CONTESSA, I ALWAYS PROMISED MY MOMMA I'D LOOK GOOD ON THE DAY I DIED.
I THOUGHT YOUR MOTHER DIED IN CHILDBIRTH.
MAYBE SHE DID.
WENDELL! QUIT PRACTICING YOUR KUNG FU AND GET THESE HORSES LOADED UP.
HI-YAHH!
SUCH MENIAL LABOR IS BENEATH ONE SUCH AS I--
THE IMMORTAL IRON FIST!
DAMMIT, WENDELL--I TOLD YOU--
YOU'RE NOT IRON FIST. YOU'RE NOT GONNA BE IRON FIST. AND THE SOONER YOU GET THAT DAMN FOOL IDEA OUT OF YOUR HEAD--
--THE LONGER YOU'LL LIVE. GOT IT?
GOT IT.
JERK.
GOOD. NOW ALL OF YOU, GET READY FOR ACTION.
CHORES WAS WELL IN HIS CUPS WHEN WE LEFT HIM LAST NIGHT, AND SINCE HE DIDN'T MAKE IT BACK TO CAMP...
I EXPECT THINGS ARE GOING TO GET REAL EXCITING DOWN THERE REAL FAST.

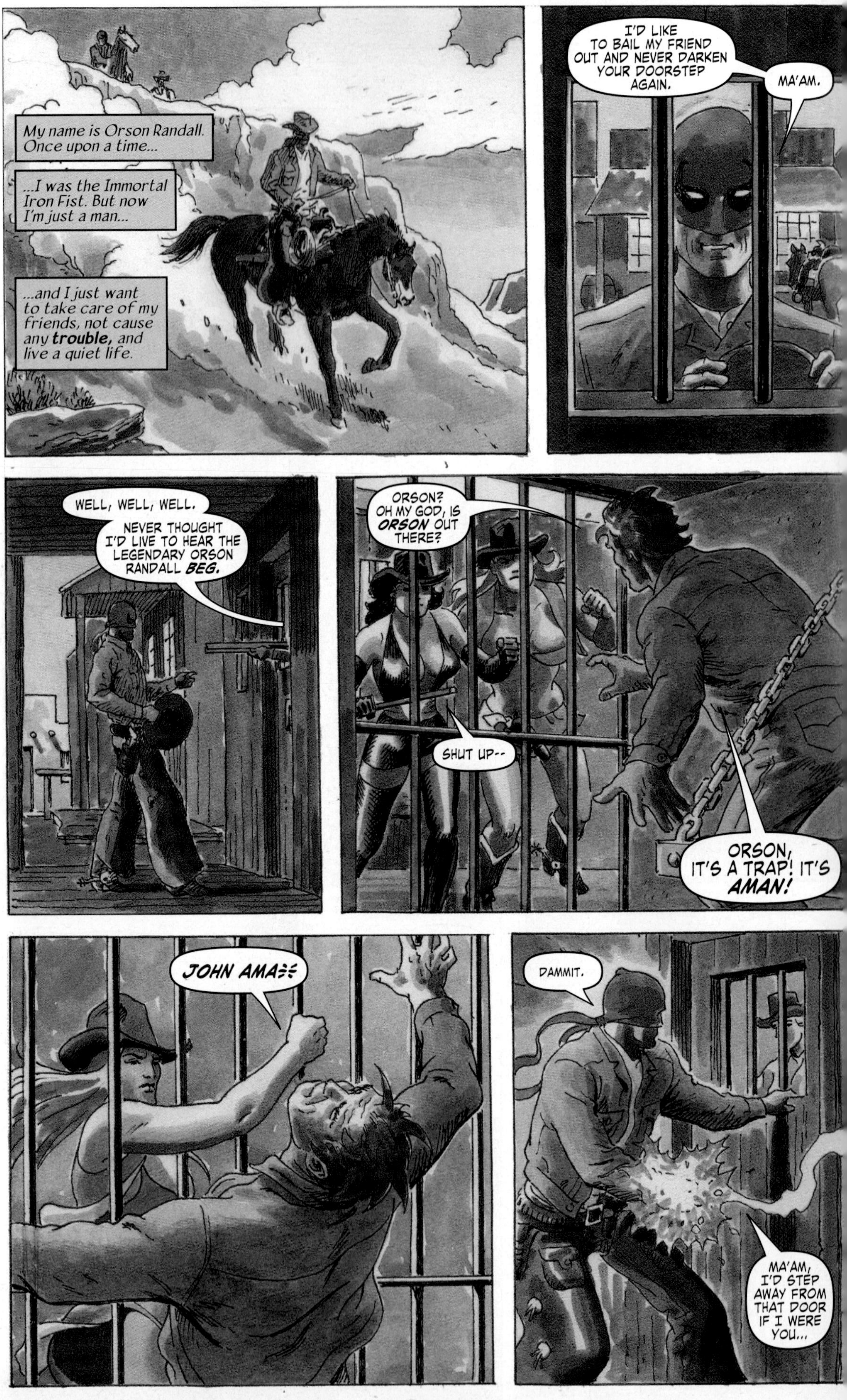
My name is Orson Randall. Once upon a time...
...I was the Immortal Iron Fist. But now I'm just a man...
...and I just want to take care of my friends, not cause any **trouble,** and live a quiet life.
I'D LIKE TO BAIL MY FRIEND OUT AND NEVER DARKEN YOUR DOORSTEP AGAIN.
MA'AM.
WELL, WELL, WELL.
NEVER THOUGHT I'D LIVE TO HEAR THE LEGENDARY ORSON RANDALL ***BEG.***
ORSON? OH MY GOD, IS ***ORSON*** OUT THERE?
SHUT UP--
ORSON, IT'S A TRAP! IT'S ***AMAN!***
JOHN AMA
DAMMIT.
MA'AM, I'D STEP AWAY FROM THAT DOOR IF I WERE YOU...

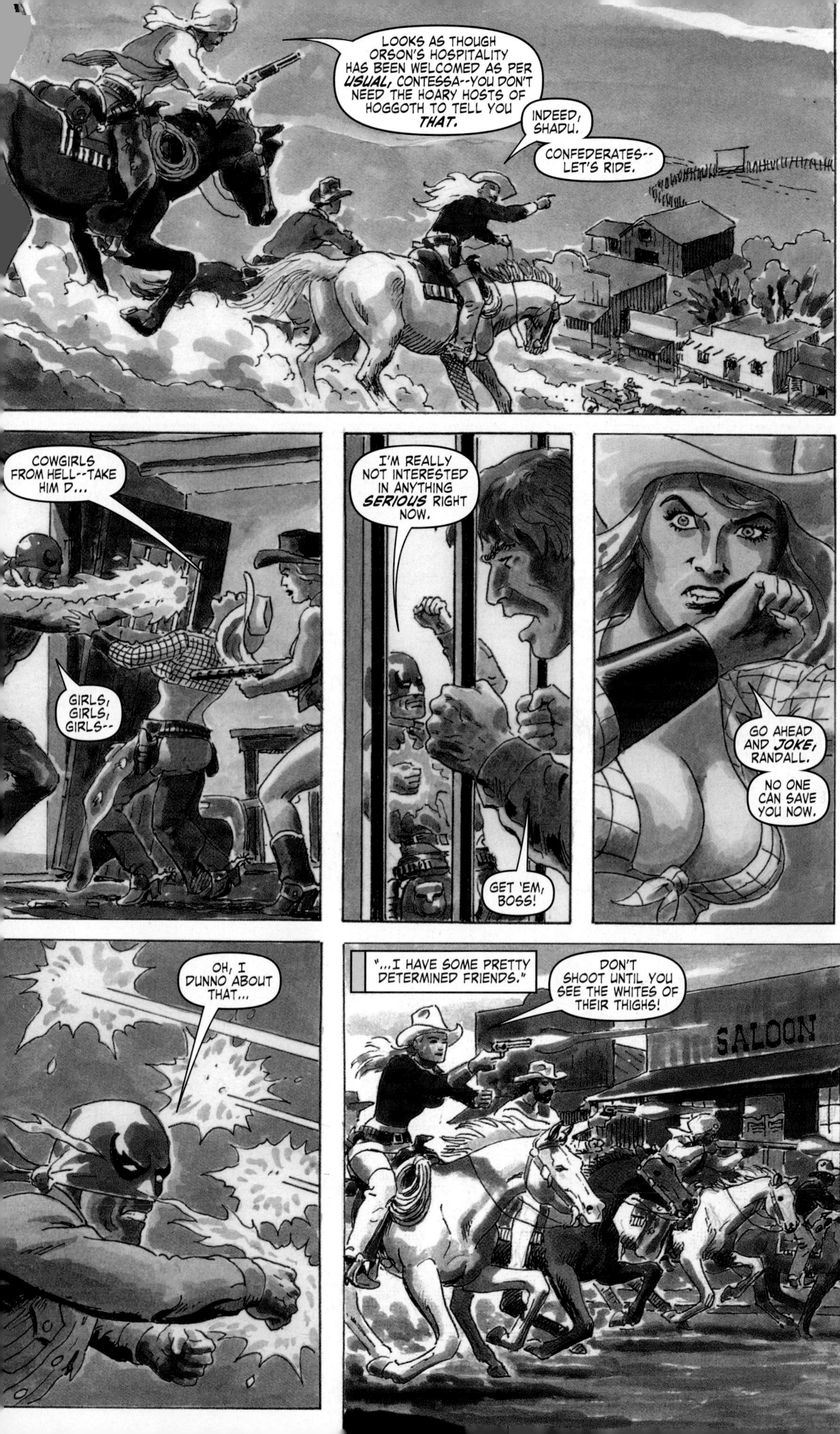
LOOKS AS THOUGH ORSON'S HOSPITALITY HAS BEEN WELCOMED AS PER USUAL, CONTESSA--YOU DON'T NEED THE HOARY HOSTS OF HOGGOTH TO TELL YOU THAT.
INDEED, SHADU.
CONFEDERATES--LET'S RIDE.
COWGIRLS FROM HELL--TAKE HIM D...
GIRLS, GIRLS, GIRLS--
I'M REALLY NOT INTERESTED IN ANYTHING SERIOUS RIGHT NOW.
GET 'EM, BOSS!
GO AHEAD AND JOKE, RANDALL.
NO ONE CAN SAVE YOU NOW.
OH, I DUNNO ABOUT THAT...
"...I HAVE SOME PRETTY DETERMINED FRIENDS."
DON'T SHOOT UNTIL YOU SEE THE WHITES OF THEIR THIGHS!
SALOON

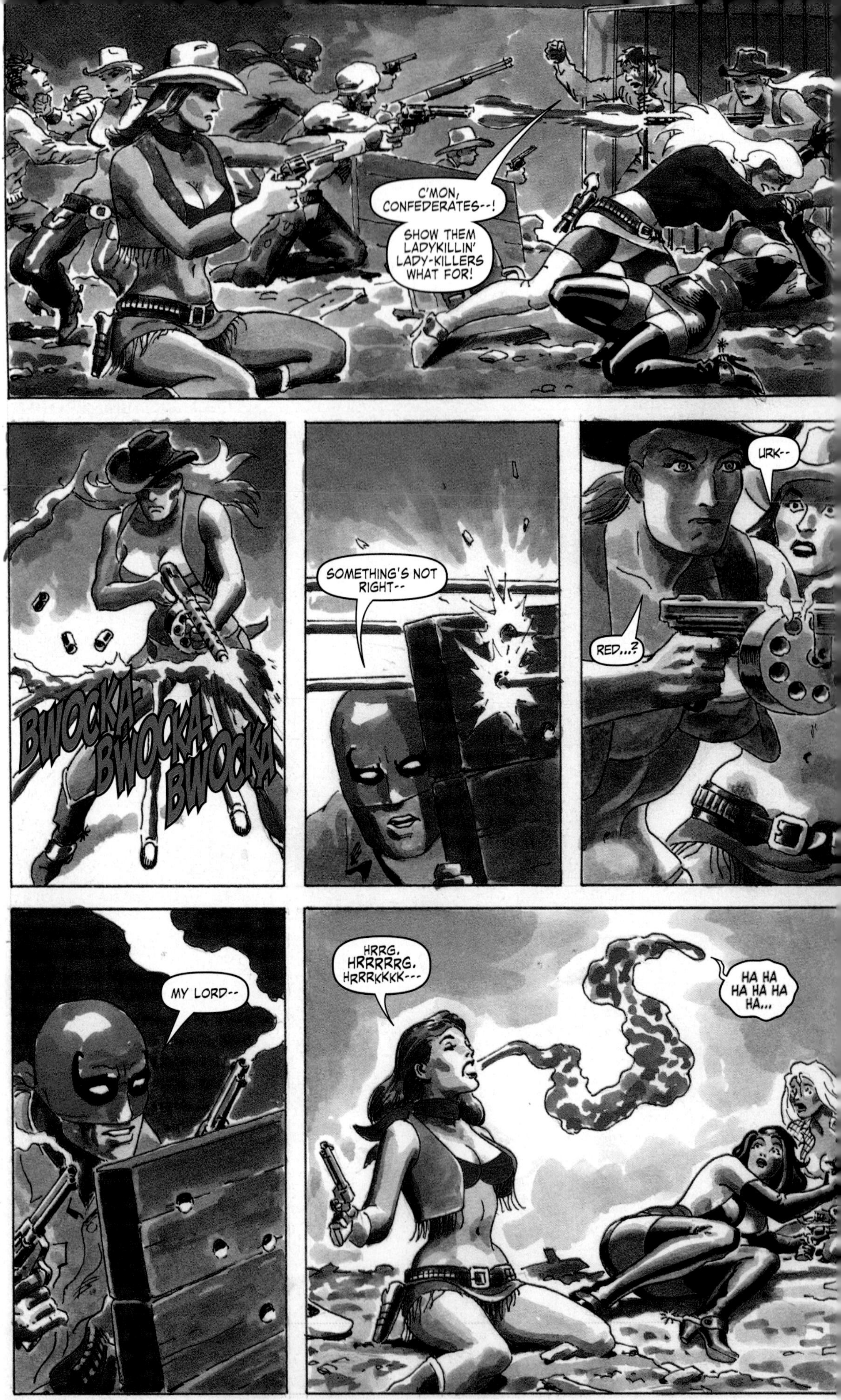
C'MON, CONFEDERATES--!
SHOW THEM LADYKILLIN' LADY-KILLERS WHAT FOR!
BWOCKA-BWOCKA-BWOCKA
SOMETHING'S NOT RIGHT--
URK--
RED...?
MY LORD--
HRRG. HRRRRRG. HRRRKKKK---
HA HA HA HA HA HA...

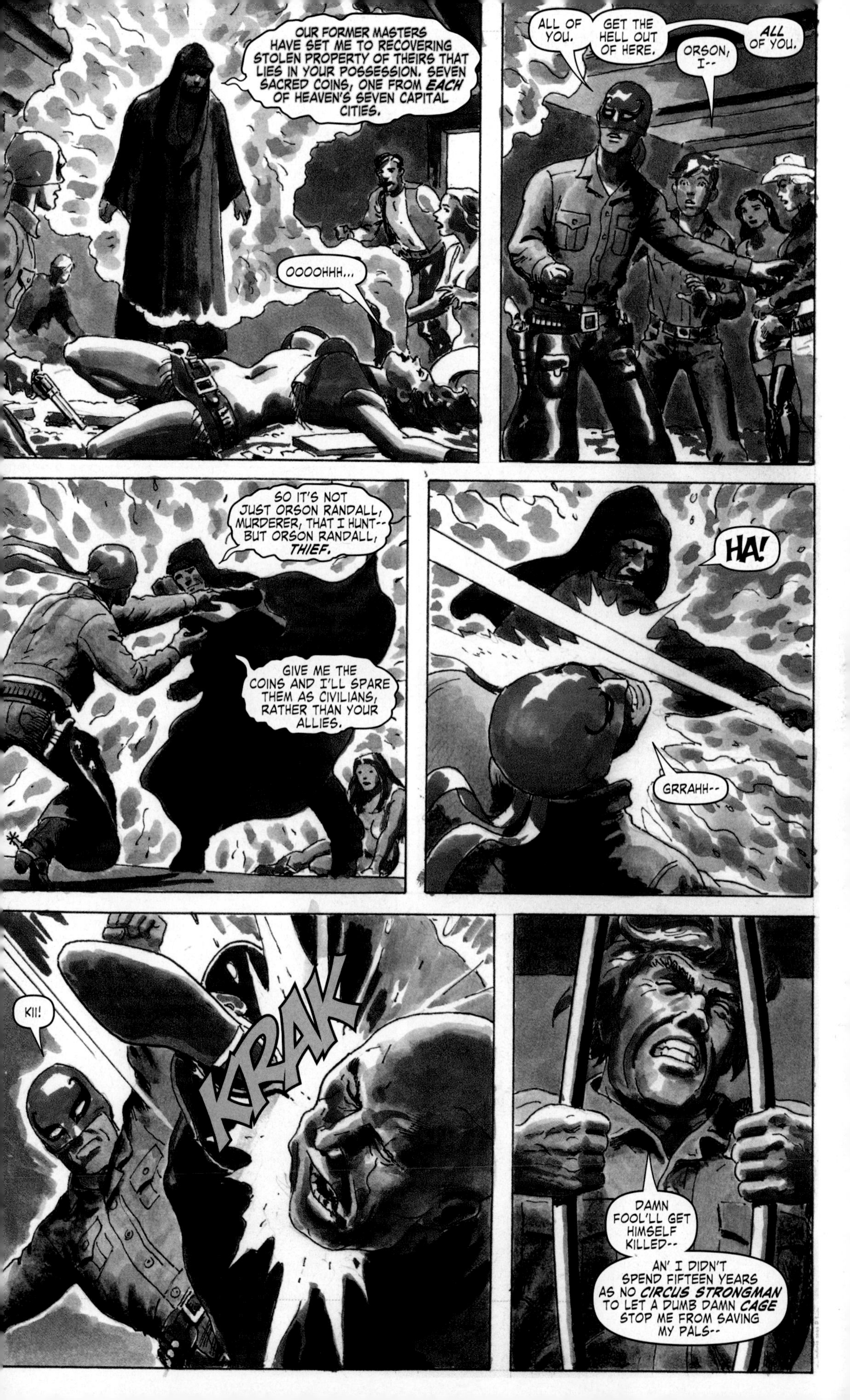
OUR FORMER MASTERS HAVE SET ME TO RECOVERING STOLEN PROPERTY OF THEIRS THAT LIES IN YOUR POSSESSION. SEVEN SACRED COINS, ONE FROM EACH OF HEAVEN'S SEVEN CAPITAL CITIES.
OOOOHHH...
ALL OF YOU.
GET THE HELL OUT OF HERE.
ORSON, I--
ALL OF YOU.
SO IT'S NOT JUST ORSON RANDALL, MURDERER, THAT I HUNT-- BUT ORSON RANDALL, THIEF.
GIVE ME THE COINS AND I'LL SPARE THEM AS CIVILIANS, RATHER THAN YOUR ALLIES.
HA!
GRRAHH--
KII!
KRAK
DAMN FOOL'LL GET HIMSELF KILLED--
AN' I DIDN'T SPEND FIFTEEN YEARS AS NO CIRCUS STRONGMAN TO LET A DUMB DAMN CAGE STOP ME FROM SAVING MY PALS--

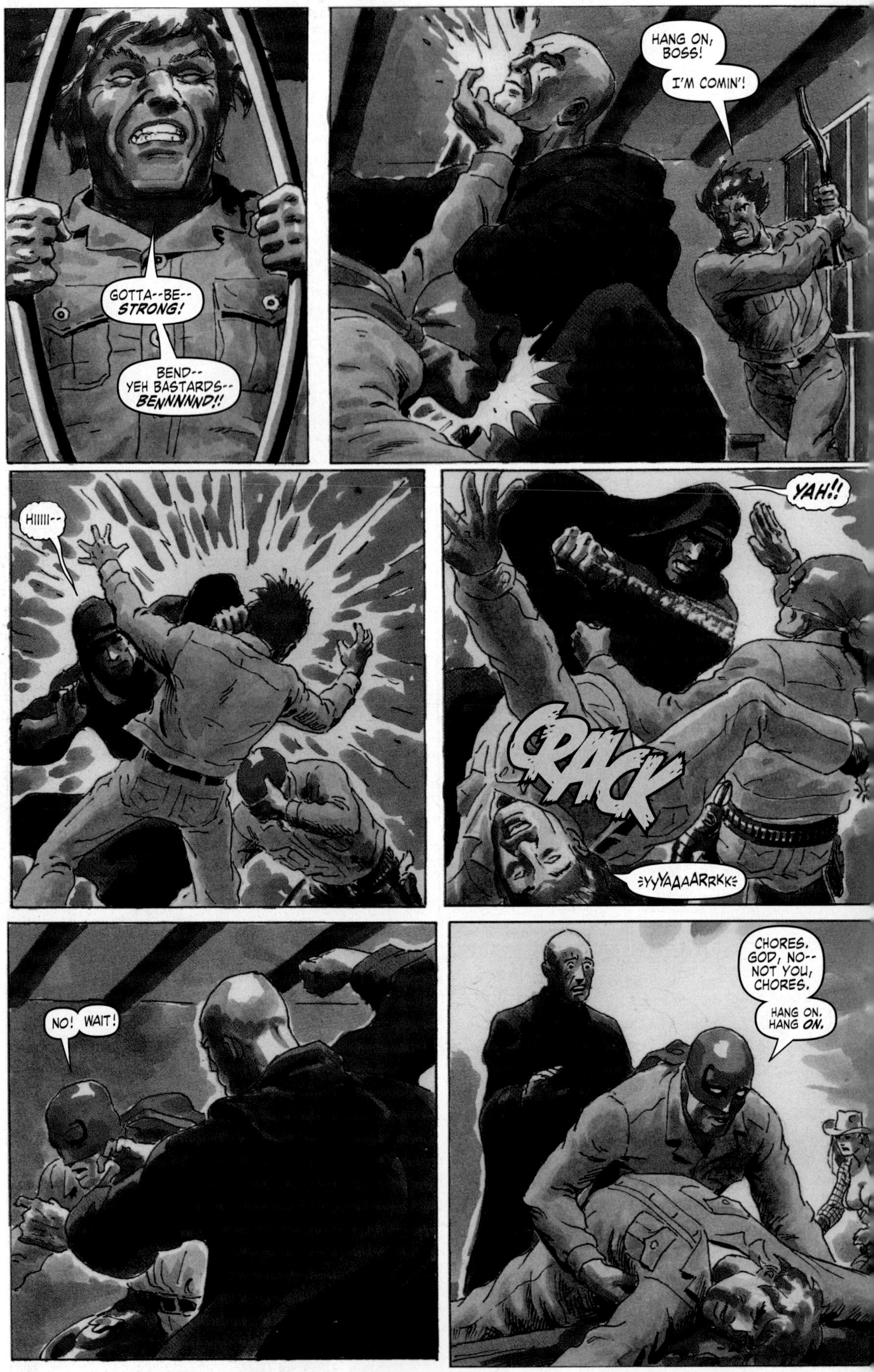
GOTTA--BE--
STRONG!
BEND--
YEH BASTARDS--
BENNNNND!!
HANG ON, BOSS!
I'M COMIN'!
HIIIII--
YAH!!
CRACK
YYYAAAARRKK
NO! WAIT!
CHORES. GOD, NO-- NOT YOU, CHORES.
HANG ON. HANG ON.

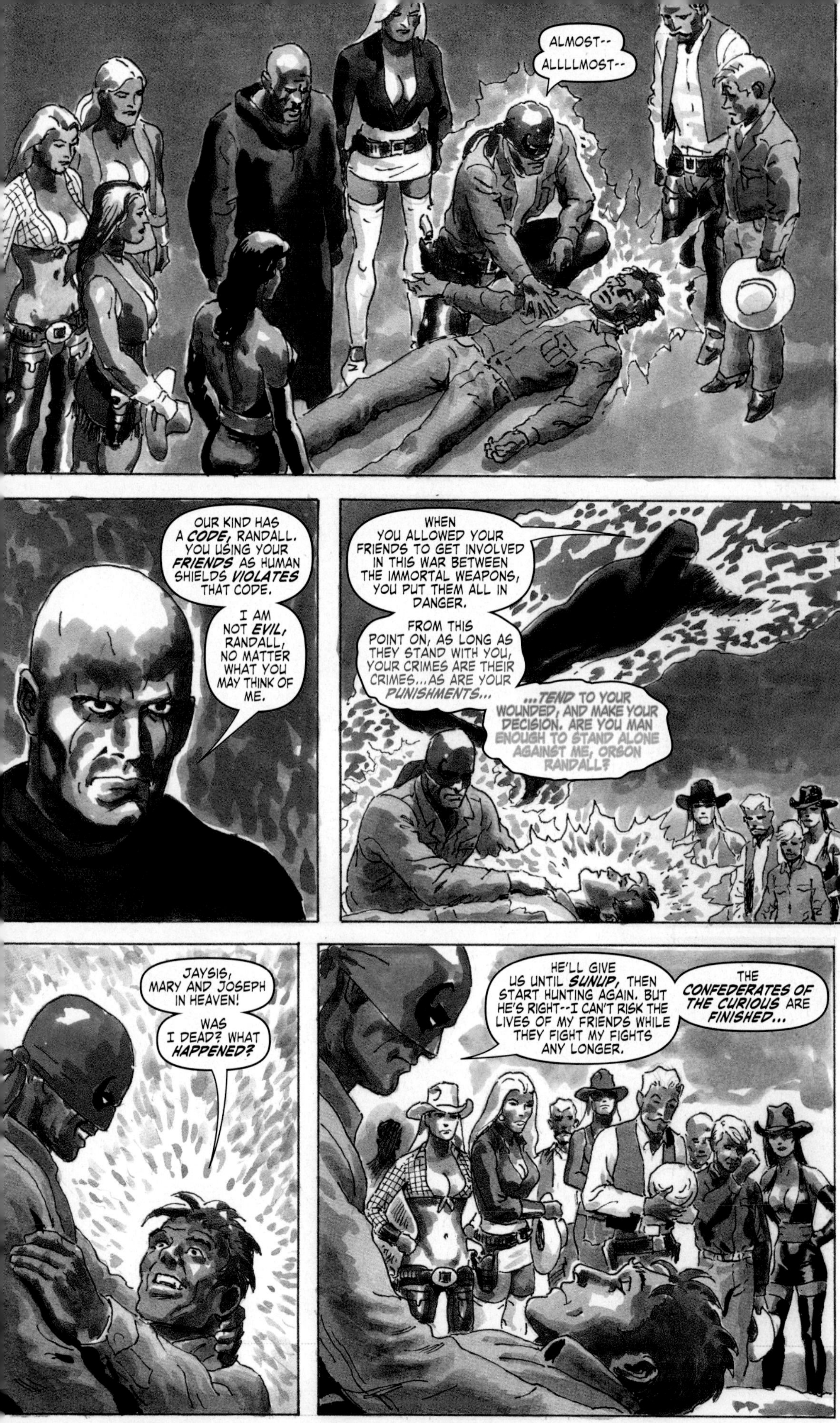
ALMOST-- ALLLLMOST--
OUR KIND HAS A *CODE,* RANDALL. YOU USING YOUR *FRIENDS* AS HUMAN SHIELDS *VIOLATES* THAT CODE.
I AM NOT *EVIL,* RANDALL, NO MATTER WHAT YOU MAY THINK OF ME.
WHEN YOU ALLOWED YOUR FRIENDS TO GET INVOLVED IN THIS WAR BETWEEN THE IMMORTAL WEAPONS, YOU PUT THEM ALL IN DANGER.
FROM THIS POINT ON, AS LONG AS THEY STAND WITH YOU, YOUR CRIMES ARE THEIR CRIMES...AS ARE YOUR *PUNISHMENTS...*
...*TEND* TO YOUR WOUNDED, AND MAKE YOUR DECISION. ARE YOU MAN ENOUGH TO STAND ALONE AGAINST ME, ORSON RANDALL?
JAYSIS, MARY AND JOSEPH IN HEAVEN!
WAS I DEAD? WHAT *HAPPENED?*
HE'LL GIVE US UNTIL *SUNUP,* THEN START HUNTING AGAIN. BUT HE'S RIGHT--I CAN'T RISK THE LIVES OF MY FRIENDS WHILE THEY FIGHT MY FIGHTS ANY LONGER.
THE *CONFEDERATES OF THE CURIOUS* ARE *FINISHED...*

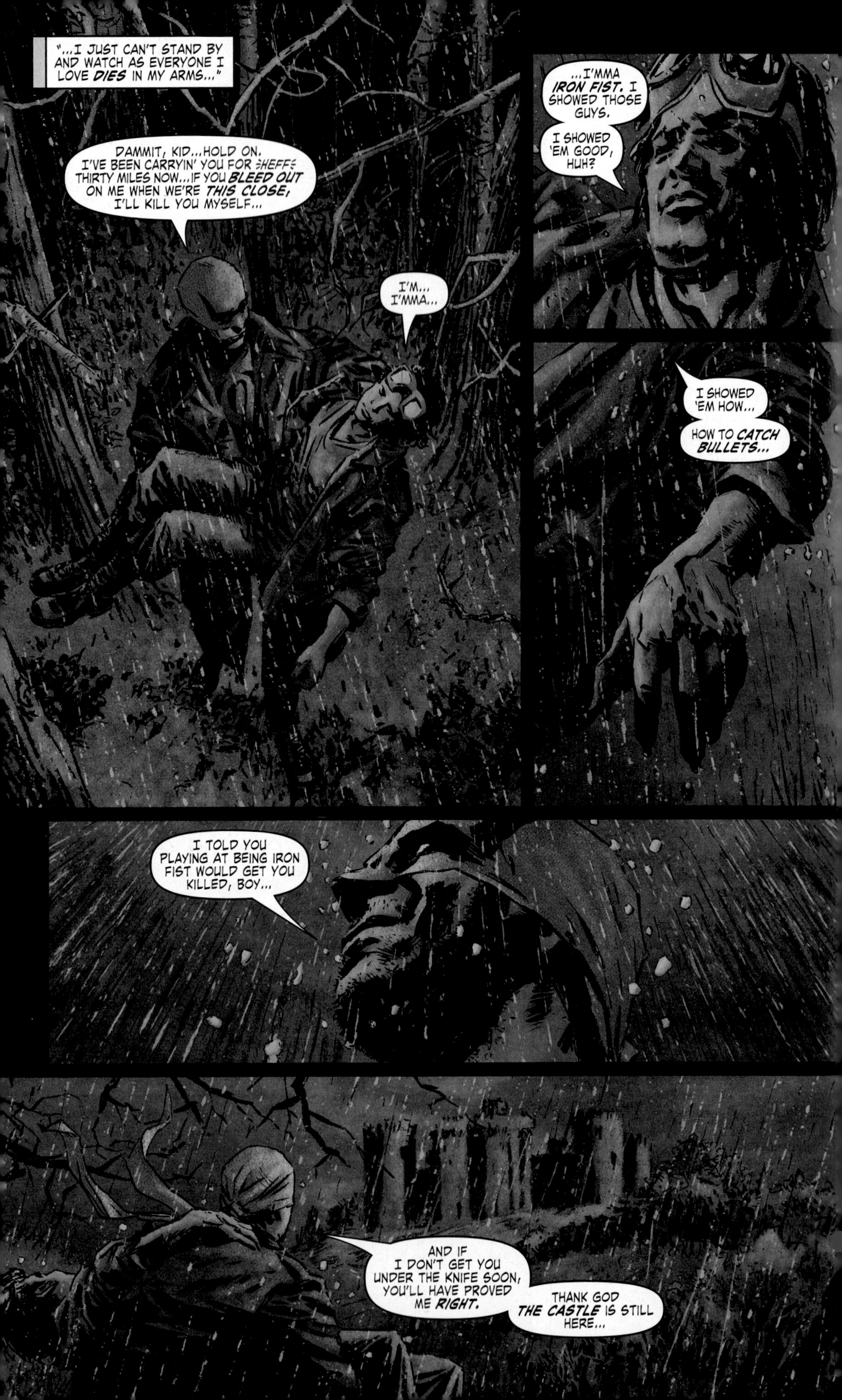

"...I JUST CAN'T STAND BY AND WATCH AS EVERYONE I LOVE *DIES* IN MY ARMS..."
DAMMIT, KID...HOLD ON. I'VE BEEN CARRYIN' YOU FOR =HEFF= THIRTY MILES NOW...IF YOU *BLEED OUT* ON ME WHEN WE'RE *THIS CLOSE,* I'LL KILL YOU MYSELF...
I'M... I'MMA...
...I'MMA *IRON FIST.* I SHOWED THOSE GUYS.
I SHOWED 'EM GOOD, HUH?
I SHOWED 'EM HOW...
HOW TO *CATCH BULLETS...*
I TOLD YOU PLAYING AT BEING IRON FIST WOULD GET YOU KILLED, BOY...
AND IF I DON'T GET YOU UNDER THE KNIFE SOON, YOU'LL HAVE PROVED ME *RIGHT.*
THANK GOD *THE CASTLE* IS STILL HERE...

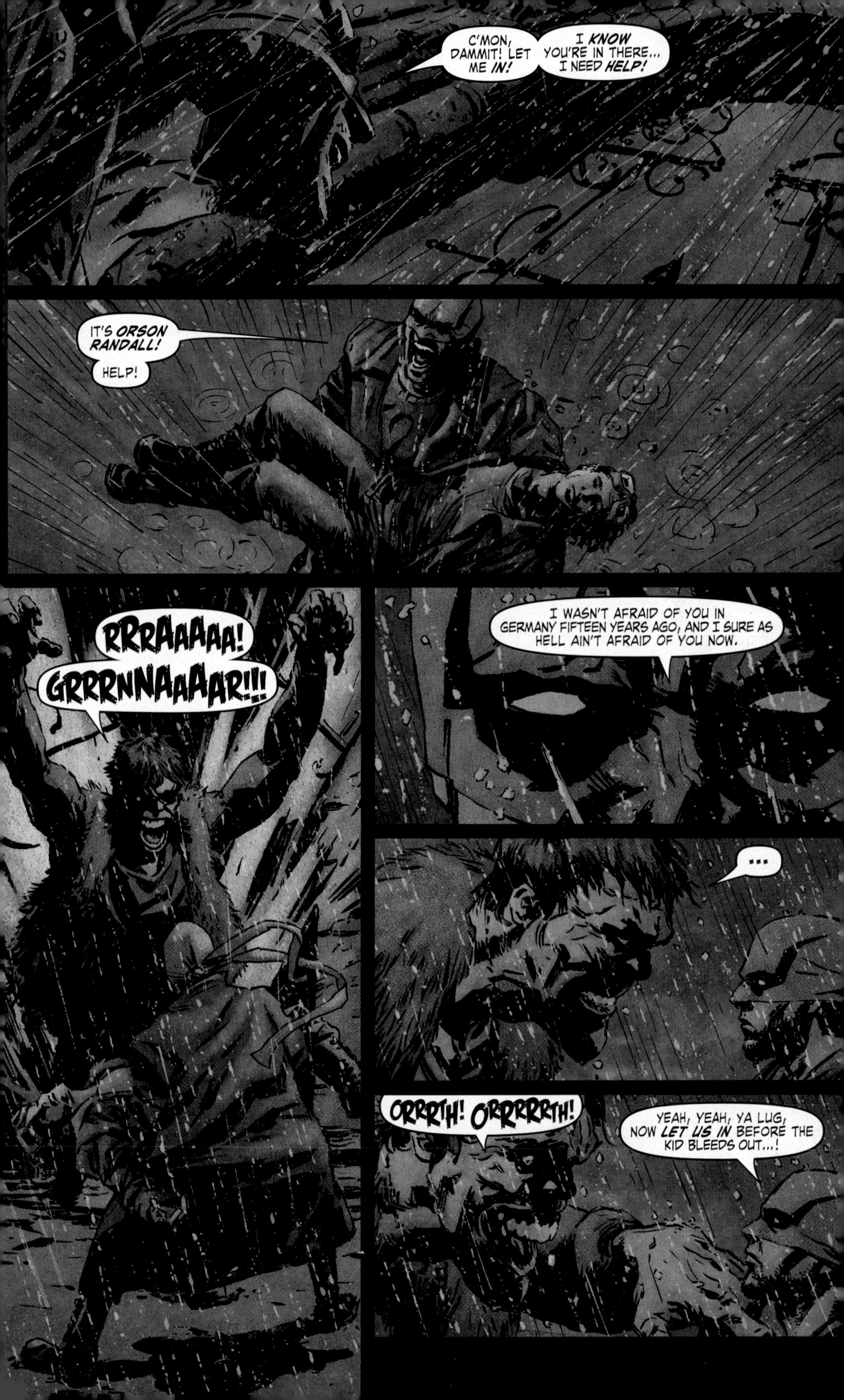
C'MON, DAMMIT! LET ME IN!
I KNOW YOU'RE IN THERE... I NEED HELP!
IT'S ORSON RANDALL!
HELP!
RRRAAAAA!
GRRRNNAAAAR!!!
I WASN'T AFRAID OF YOU IN GERMANY FIFTEEN YEARS AGO, AND I SURE AS HELL AIN'T AFRAID OF YOU NOW.
...
ORRRTH! ORRRRRTH!
YEAH, YEAH, YA LUG, NOW LET US IN BEFORE THE KID BLEEDS OUT...!

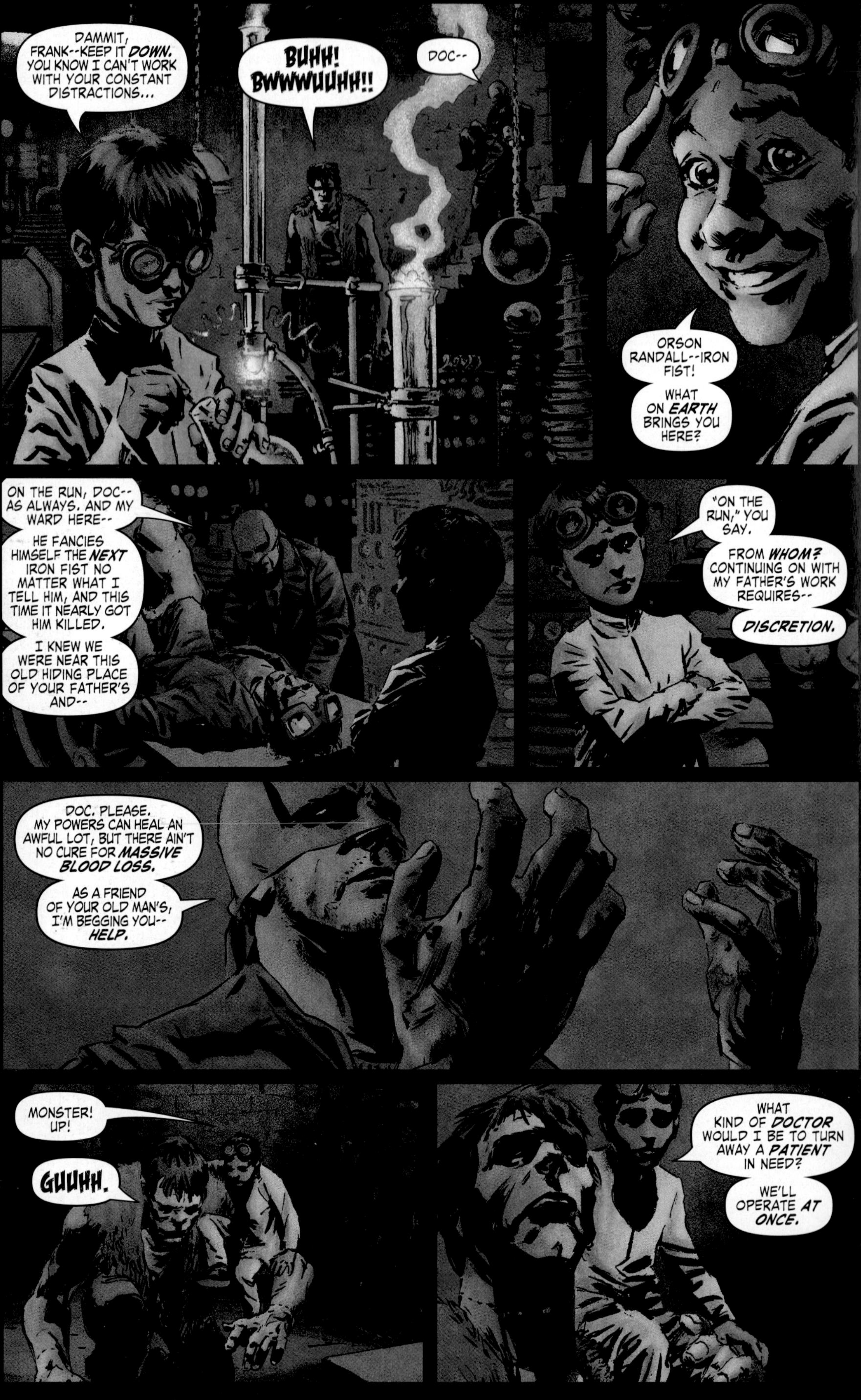
DAMMIT, FRANK--KEEP IT DOWN. YOU KNOW I CAN'T WORK WITH YOUR CONSTANT DISTRACTIONS...
BUHH! BWWWUUHH!!
DOC--
ORSON RANDALL--IRON FIST!
WHAT ON EARTH BRINGS YOU HERE?
ON THE RUN, DOC--AS ALWAYS. AND MY WARD HERE--
HE FANCIES HIMSELF THE NEXT IRON FIST NO MATTER WHAT I TELL HIM, AND THIS TIME IT NEARLY GOT HIM KILLED.
I KNEW WE WERE NEAR THIS OLD HIDING PLACE OF YOUR FATHER'S AND--
"ON THE RUN," YOU SAY.
FROM WHOM? CONTINUING ON WITH MY FATHER'S WORK REQUIRES--
DISCRETION.
DOC. PLEASE. MY POWERS CAN HEAL AN AWFUL LOT, BUT THERE AIN'T NO CURE FOR MASSIVE BLOOD LOSS.
AS A FRIEND OF YOUR OLD MAN'S, I'M BEGGING YOU--HELP.
MONSTER! UP!
GUUHH.
WHAT KIND OF DOCTOR WOULD I BE TO TURN AWAY A PATIENT IN NEED?
WE'LL OPERATE AT ONCE.

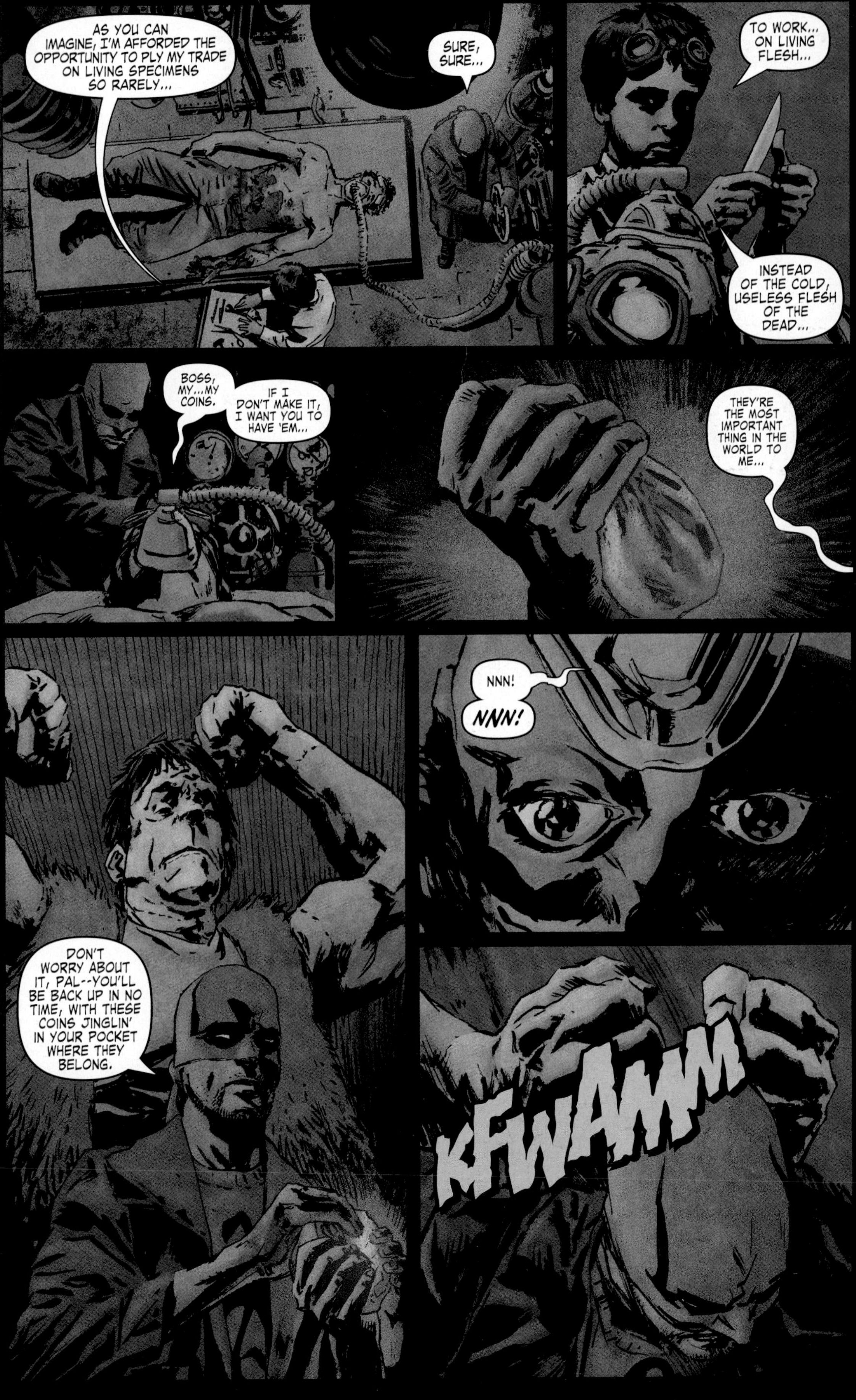
AS YOU CAN IMAGINE, I'M AFFORDED THE OPPORTUNITY TO PLY MY TRADE ON LIVING SPECIMENS SO RARELY...
SURE, SURE...
TO WORK... ON LIVING FLESH...
INSTEAD OF THE COLD, USELESS FLESH OF THE DEAD...
BOSS, MY...MY COINS.
IF I DON'T MAKE IT, I WANT YOU TO HAVE 'EM...
THEY'RE THE MOST IMPORTANT THING IN THE WORLD TO ME...
DON'T WORRY ABOUT IT, PAL--YOU'LL BE BACK UP IN NO TIME, WITH THESE COINS JINGLIN' IN YOUR POCKET WHERE THEY BELONG.
NNN!
NNN!
KFWAMM

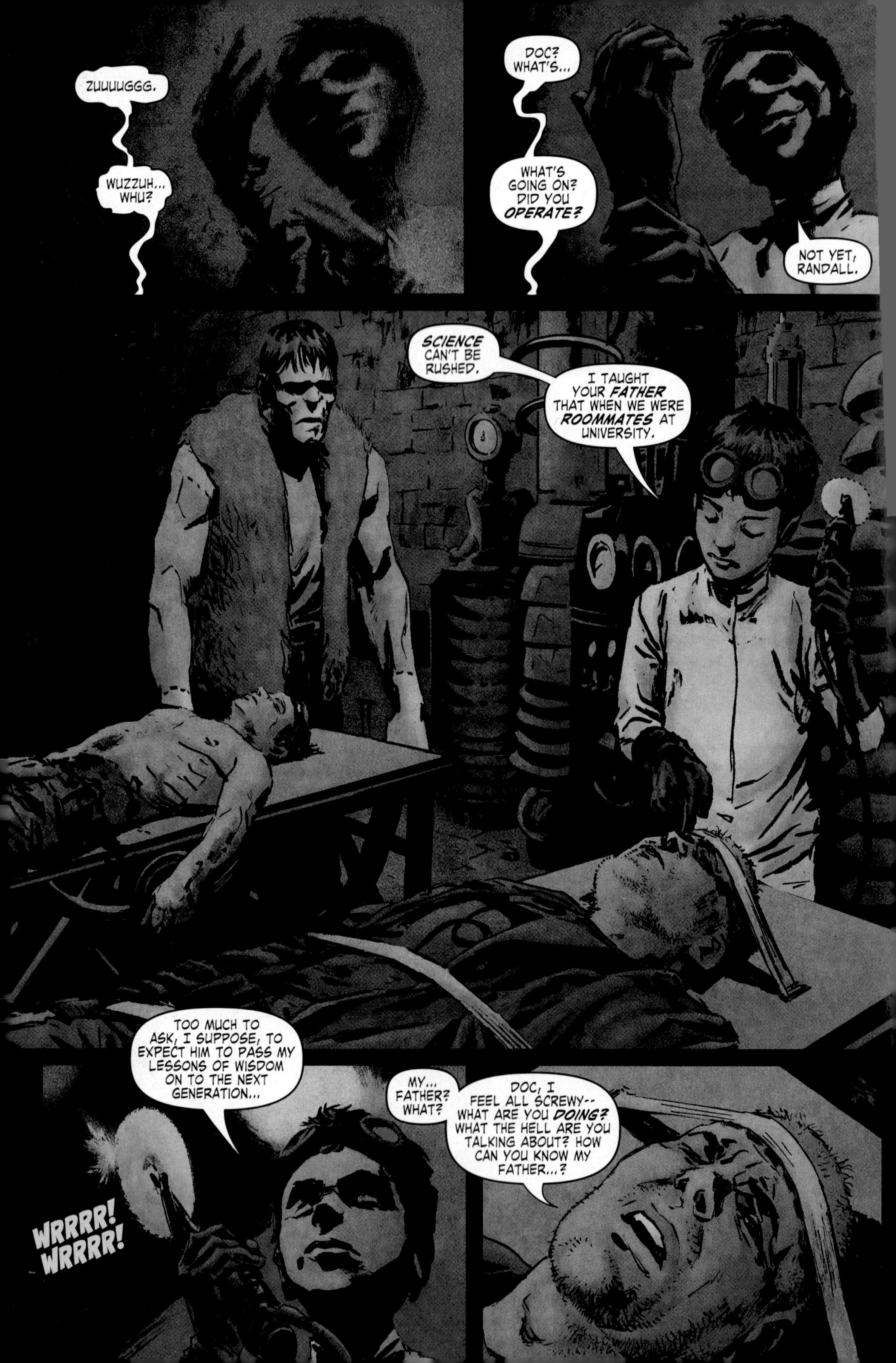
ZUUUUGGG.
WUZZUH... WHU?
DOC? WHAT'S...
WHAT'S GOING ON? DID YOU OPERATE?
NOT YET, RANDALL.
SCIENCE CAN'T BE RUSHED.
I TAUGHT YOUR FATHER THAT WHEN WE WERE ROOMMATES AT UNIVERSITY.
TOO MUCH TO ASK, I SUPPOSE, TO EXPECT HIM TO PASS MY LESSONS OF WISDOM ON TO THE NEXT GENERATION...
WRRRR! WRRRR!
MY... FATHER? WHAT?
DOC, I FEEL ALL SCREWY-- WHAT ARE YOU DOING? WHAT THE HELL ARE YOU TALKING ABOUT? HOW CAN YOU KNOW MY FATHER...?

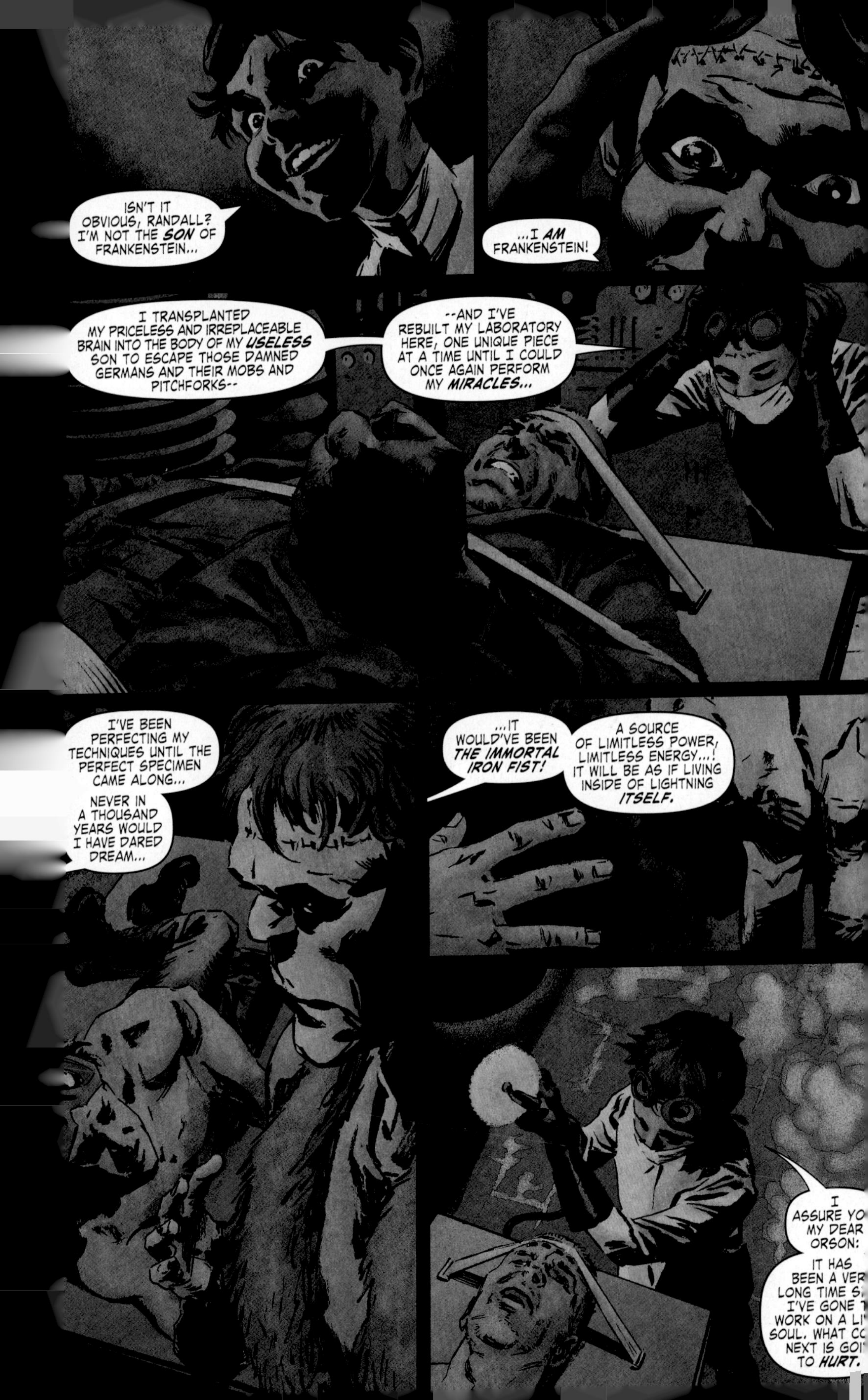
ISN'T IT OBVIOUS, RANDALL? I'M NOT THE SON OF FRANKENSTEIN...
...I AM FRANKENSTEIN!
I TRANSPLANTED MY PRICELESS AND IRREPLACEABLE BRAIN INTO THE BODY OF MY USELESS SON TO ESCAPE THOSE DAMNED GERMANS AND THEIR MOBS AND PITCHFORKS--
--AND I'VE REBUILT MY LABORATORY HERE, ONE UNIQUE PIECE AT A TIME UNTIL I COULD ONCE AGAIN PERFORM MY MIRACLES...
I'VE BEEN PERFECTING MY TECHNIQUES UNTIL THE PERFECT SPECIMEN CAME ALONG...
NEVER IN A THOUSAND YEARS WOULD I HAVE DARED DREAM...
...IT WOULD'VE BEEN THE IMMORTAL IRON FIST!
A SOURCE OF LIMITLESS POWER, LIMITLESS ENERGY...! IT WILL BE AS IF LIVING INSIDE OF LIGHTNING ITSELF.
I ASSURE YO MY DEAR ORSON:
IT HAS BEEN A VER LONG TIME S I'VE GONE WORK ON A LI SOUL. WHAT C NEXT IS GOI TO HURT.

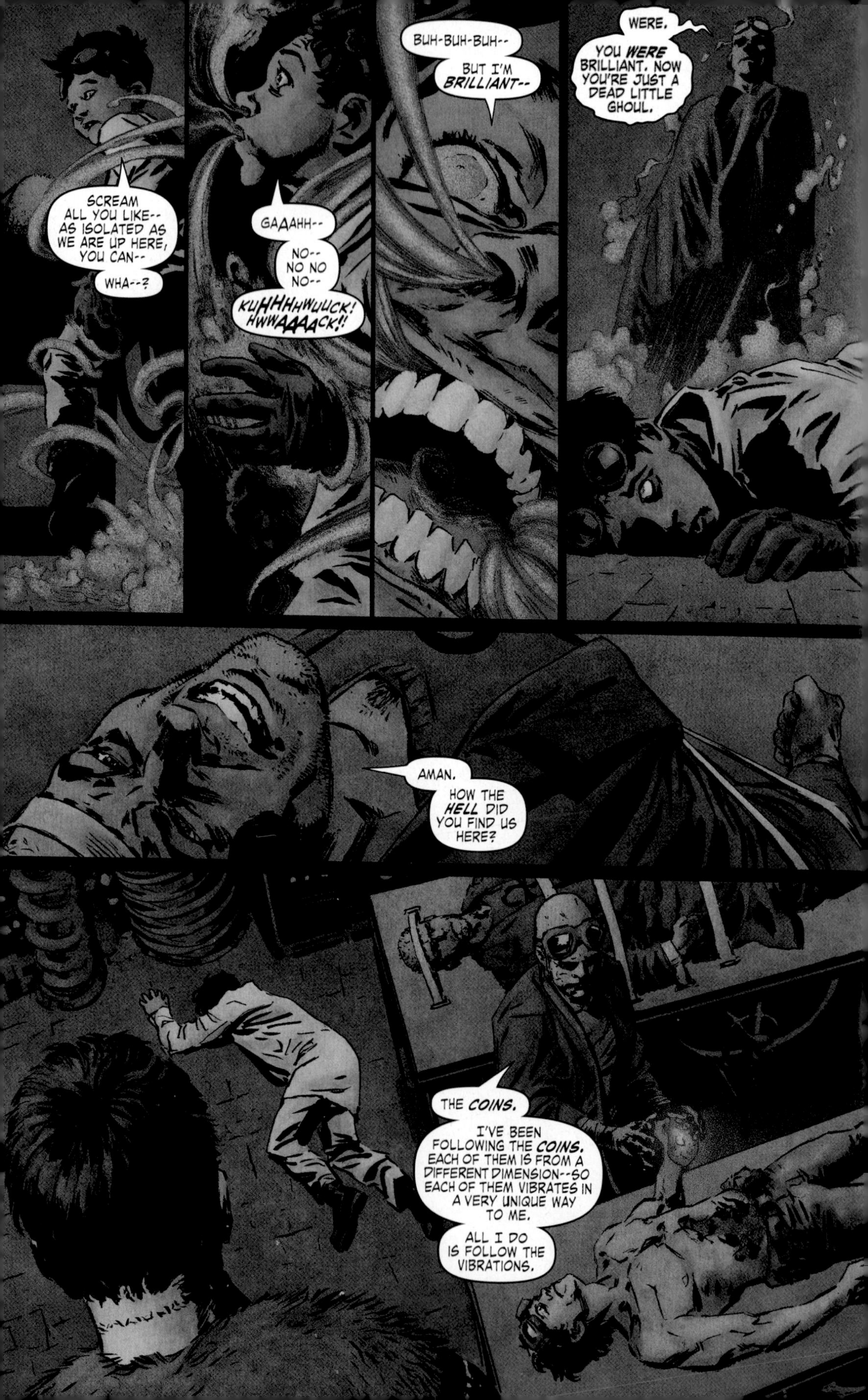
SCREAM ALL YOU LIKE-- AS ISOLATED AS WE ARE UP HERE, YOU CAN--
WHA--?
GAAAHH--
NO-- NO NO NO--
KUHHHHWUUCK! HWWAAAACK!!
BUH-BUH-BUH--
BUT I'M BRILLIANT--
WERE.
YOU WERE BRILLIANT. NOW YOU'RE JUST A DEAD LITTLE GHOUL.
AMAN.
HOW THE HELL DID YOU FIND US HERE?
THE COINS.
I'VE BEEN FOLLOWING THE COINS. EACH OF THEM IS FROM A DIFFERENT DIMENSION--SO EACH OF THEM VIBRATES IN A VERY UNIQUE WAY TO ME.
ALL I DO IS FOLLOW THE VIBRATIONS.

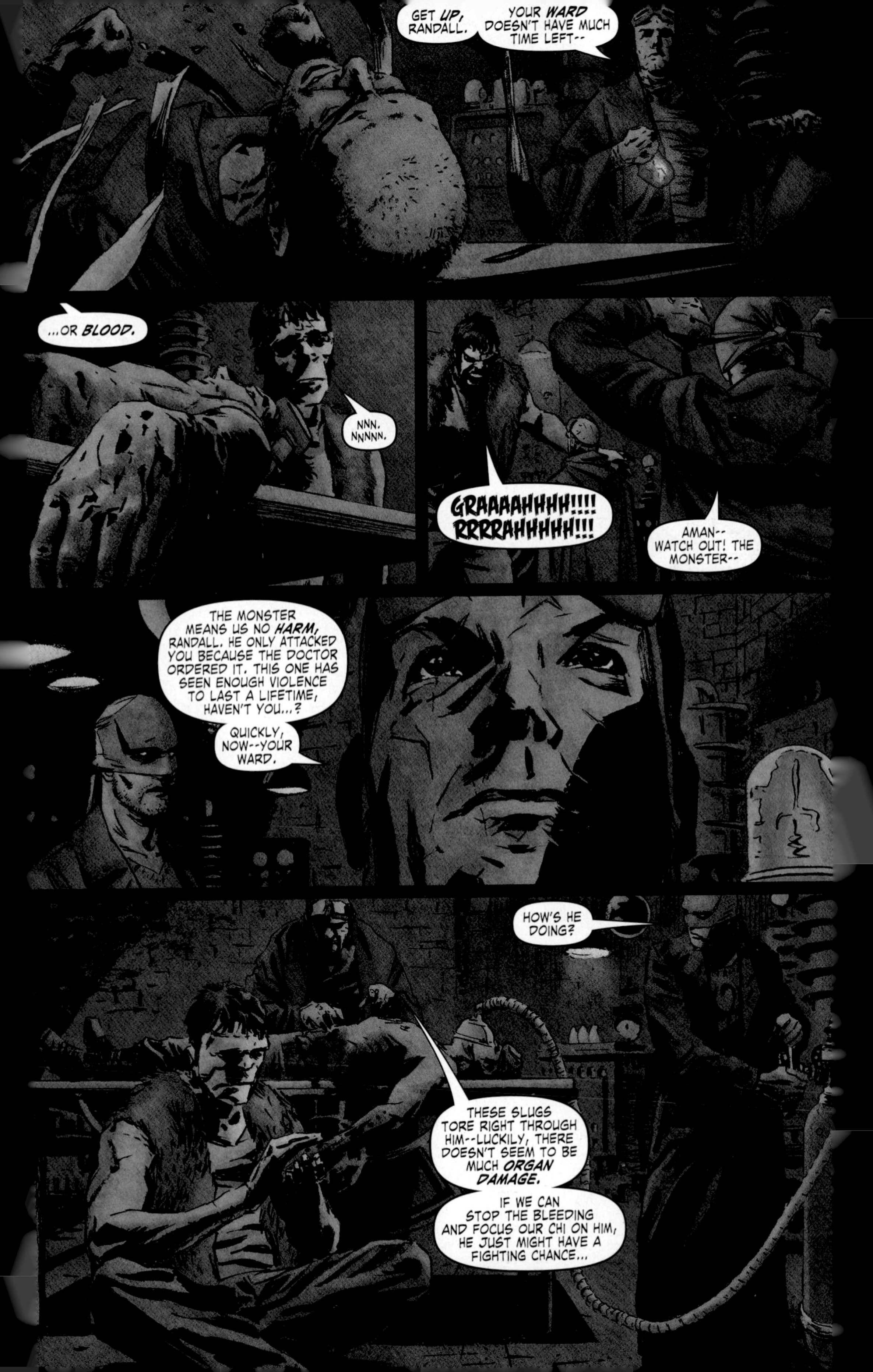
GET UP, RANDALL.
YOUR WARD DOESN'T HAVE MUCH TIME LEFT--
...OR BLOOD.
NNN. NNNNN.
GRAAAAHHHH!!!! RRRRAHHHHH!!!
AMAN-- WATCH OUT! THE MONSTER--
THE MONSTER MEANS US NO HARM, RANDALL. HE ONLY ATTACKED YOU BECAUSE THE DOCTOR ORDERED IT. THIS ONE HAS SEEN ENOUGH VIOLENCE TO LAST A LIFETIME, HAVEN'T YOU...?
QUICKLY, NOW--YOUR WARD.
HOW'S HE DOING?
THESE SLUGS TORE RIGHT THROUGH HIM--LUCKILY, THERE DOESN'T SEEM TO BE MUCH ORGAN DAMAGE.
IF WE CAN STOP THE BLEEDING AND FOCUS OUR CHI ON HIM, HE JUST MIGHT HAVE A FIGHTING CHANCE...

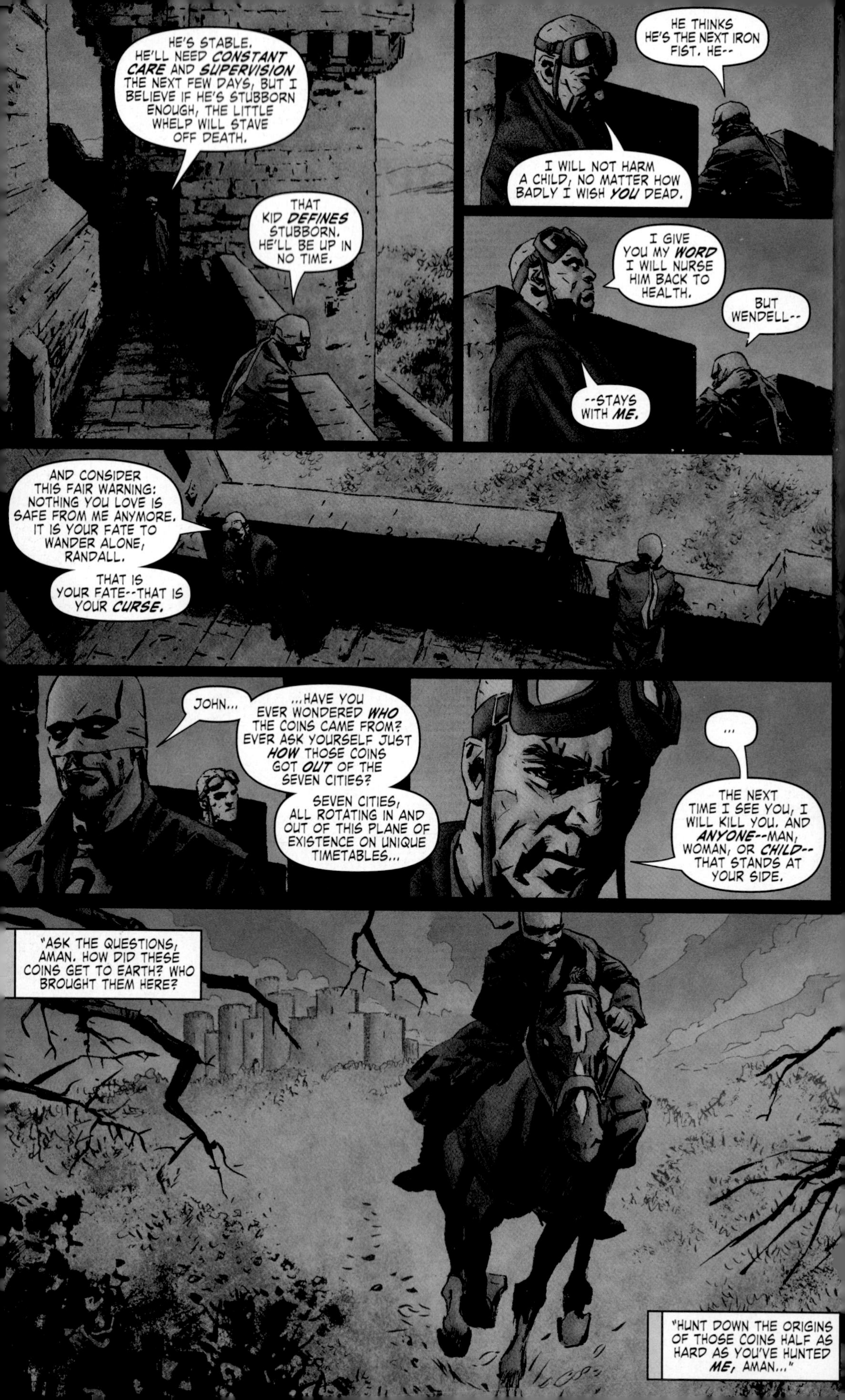
HE'S STABLE. HE'LL NEED CONSTANT CARE AND SUPERVISION THE NEXT FEW DAYS, BUT I BELIEVE IF HE'S STUBBORN ENOUGH, THE LITTLE WHELP WILL STAVE OFF DEATH.
THAT KID DEFINES STUBBORN. HE'LL BE UP IN NO TIME.
HE THINKS HE'S THE NEXT IRON FIST. HE--
I WILL NOT HARM A CHILD, NO MATTER HOW BADLY I WISH YOU DEAD.
I GIVE YOU MY WORD I WILL NURSE HIM BACK TO HEALTH.
BUT WENDELL--
--STAYS WITH ME.
AND CONSIDER THIS FAIR WARNING: NOTHING YOU LOVE IS SAFE FROM ME ANYMORE. IT IS YOUR FATE TO WANDER ALONE, RANDALL.
THAT IS YOUR FATE--THAT IS YOUR CURSE.
JOHN...
...HAVE YOU EVER WONDERED WHO THE COINS CAME FROM? EVER ASK YOURSELF JUST HOW THOSE COINS GOT OUT OF THE SEVEN CITIES?
SEVEN CITIES, ALL ROTATING IN AND OUT OF THIS PLANE OF EXISTENCE ON UNIQUE TIMETABLES...
...
THE NEXT TIME I SEE YOU, I WILL KILL YOU. AND ANYONE--MAN, WOMAN, OR CHILD--THAT STANDS AT YOUR SIDE.
"ASK THE QUESTIONS, AMAN. HOW DID THESE COINS GET TO EARTH? WHO BROUGHT THEM HERE?
"HUNT DOWN THE ORIGINS OF THOSE COINS HALF AS HARD AS YOU'VE HUNTED ME, AMAN..."

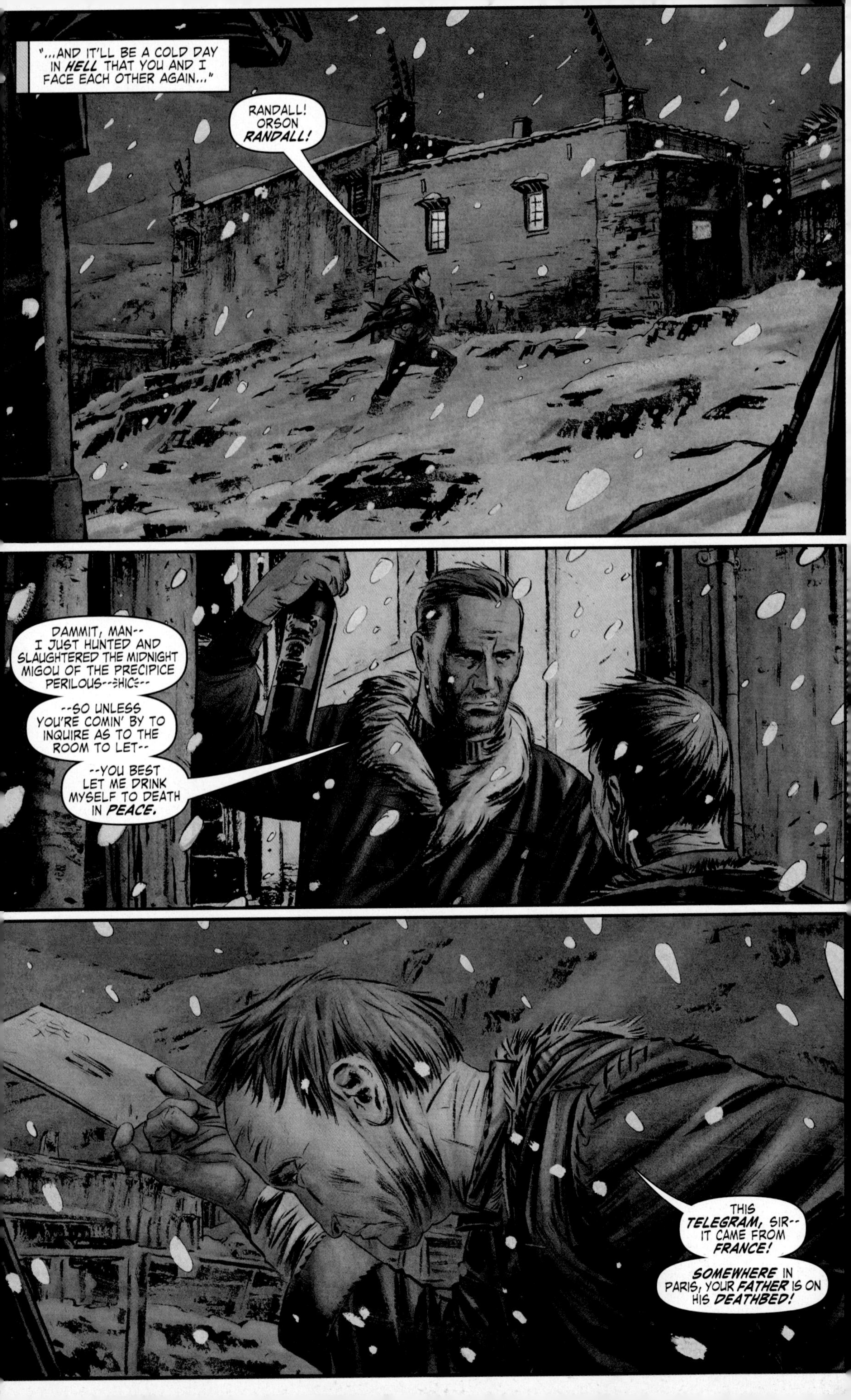
"...AND IT'LL BE A COLD DAY IN HELL THAT YOU AND I FACE EACH OTHER AGAIN..."
RANDALL! ORSON RANDALL!
DAMMIT, MAN-- I JUST HUNTED AND SLAUGHTERED THE MIDNIGHT MIGOU OF THE PRECIPICE PERILOUS--HIC--
--SO UNLESS YOU'RE COMIN' BY TO INQUIRE AS TO THE ROOM TO LET--
--YOU BEST LET ME DRINK MYSELF TO DEATH IN PEACE.
THIS TELEGRAM, SIR-- IT CAME FROM FRANCE!
SOMEWHERE IN PARIS, YOUR FATHER IS ON HIS DEATHBED!

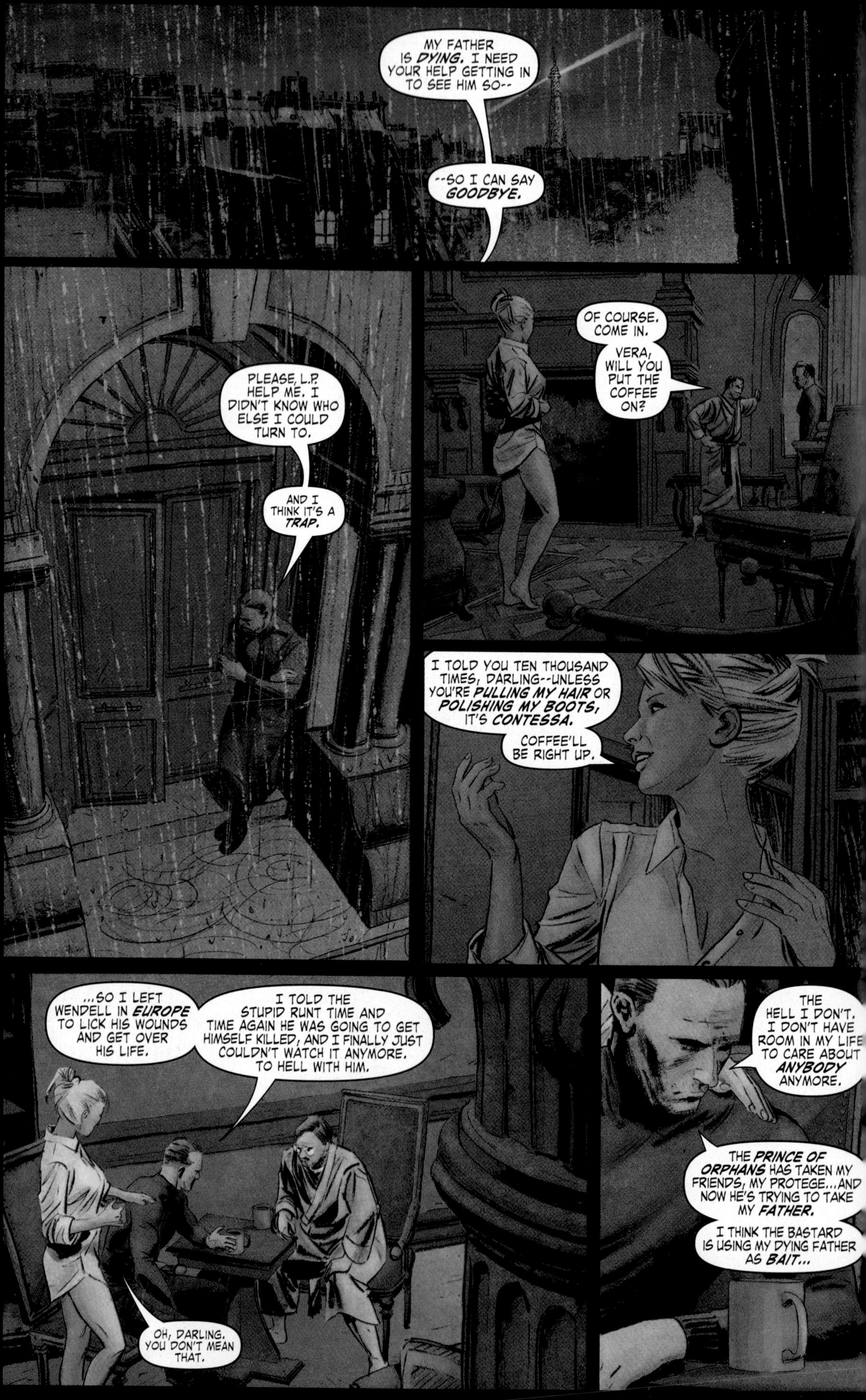

MY FATHER IS DYING. I NEED YOUR HELP GETTING IN TO SEE HIM SO--
--SO I CAN SAY GOODBYE.
PLEASE, L.P. HELP ME. I DIDN'T KNOW WHO ELSE I COULD TURN TO.
AND I THINK IT'S A TRAP.
OF COURSE. COME IN.
VERA, WILL YOU PUT THE COFFEE ON?
I TOLD YOU TEN THOUSAND TIMES, DARLING--UNLESS YOU'RE PULLING MY HAIR OR POLISHING MY BOOTS, IT'S CONTESSA.
COFFEE'LL BE RIGHT UP.
...SO I LEFT WENDELL IN EUROPE TO LICK HIS WOUNDS AND GET OVER HIS LIFE.
I TOLD THE STUPID RUNT TIME AND TIME AGAIN HE WAS GOING TO GET HIMSELF KILLED, AND I FINALLY JUST COULDN'T WATCH IT ANYMORE. TO HELL WITH HIM.
OH, DARLING. YOU DON'T MEAN THAT.
THE HELL I DON'T. I DON'T HAVE ROOM IN MY LIFE TO CARE ABOUT ANYBODY ANYMORE.
THE PRINCE OF ORPHANS HAS TAKEN MY FRIENDS, MY PROTEGE...AND NOW HE'S TRYING TO TAKE MY FATHER.
I THINK THE BASTARD IS USING MY DYING FATHER AS BAIT...

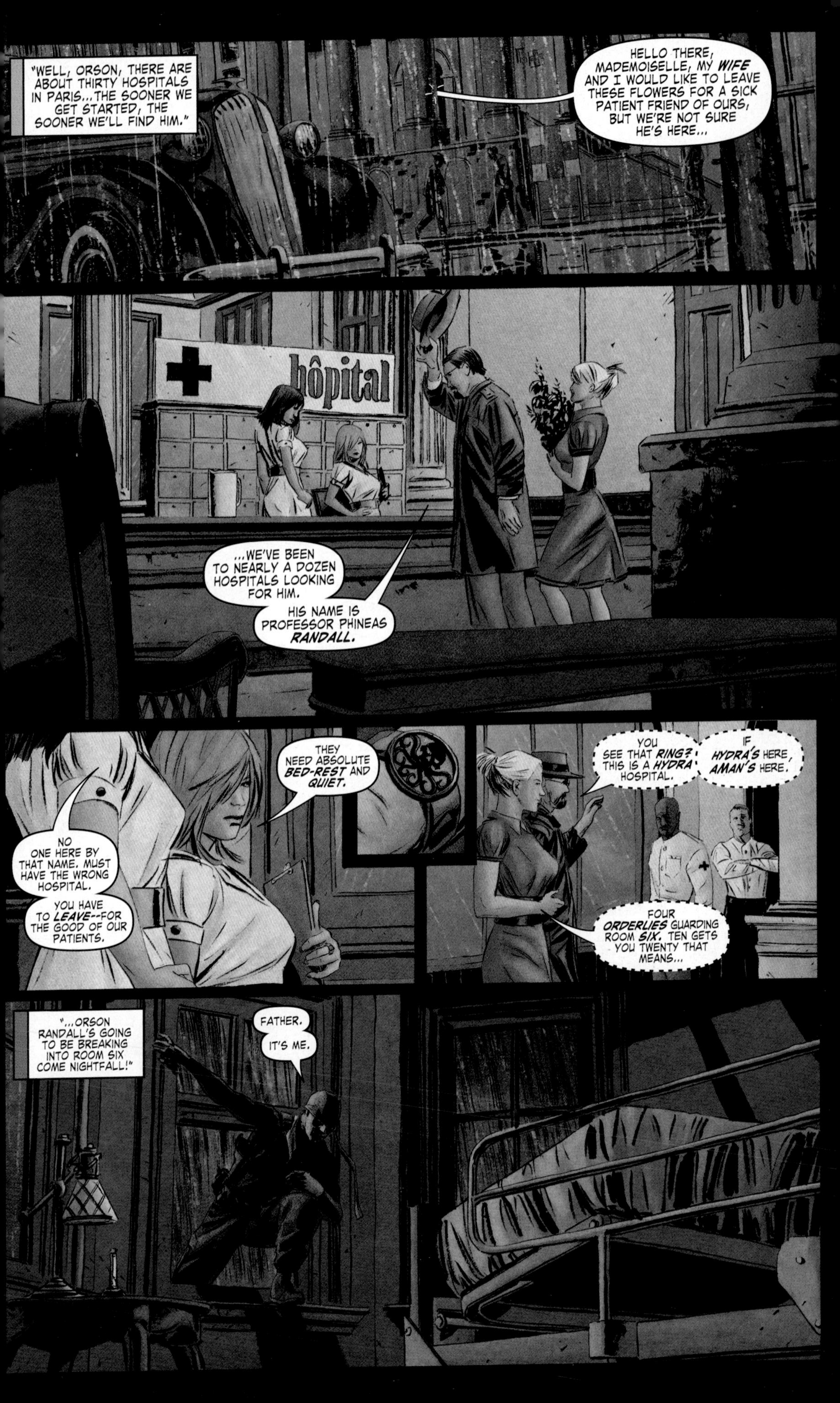
"WELL, ORSON, THERE ARE ABOUT THIRTY HOSPITALS IN PARIS...THE SOONER WE GET STARTED, THE SOONER WE'LL FIND HIM."
HELLO THERE, MADEMOISELLE, MY WIFE AND I WOULD LIKE TO LEAVE THESE FLOWERS FOR A SICK PATIENT FRIEND OF OURS, BUT WE'RE NOT SURE HE'S HERE...
hôpital
...WE'VE BEEN TO NEARLY A DOZEN HOSPITALS LOOKING FOR HIM.
HIS NAME IS PROFESSOR PHINEAS RANDALL.
NO ONE HERE BY THAT NAME. MUST HAVE THE WRONG HOSPITAL.
YOU HAVE TO LEAVE--FOR THE GOOD OF OUR PATIENTS.
THEY NEED ABSOLUTE BED-REST AND QUIET.
YOU SEE THAT RING? THIS IS A HYDRA HOSPITAL.
IF HYDRA'S HERE, AMAN'S HERE.
FOUR ORDERLIES GUARDING ROOM SIX. TEN GETS YOU TWENTY THAT MEANS...
"...ORSON RANDALL'S GOING TO BE BREAKING INTO ROOM SIX COME NIGHTFALL!"
FATHER.
IT'S ME.

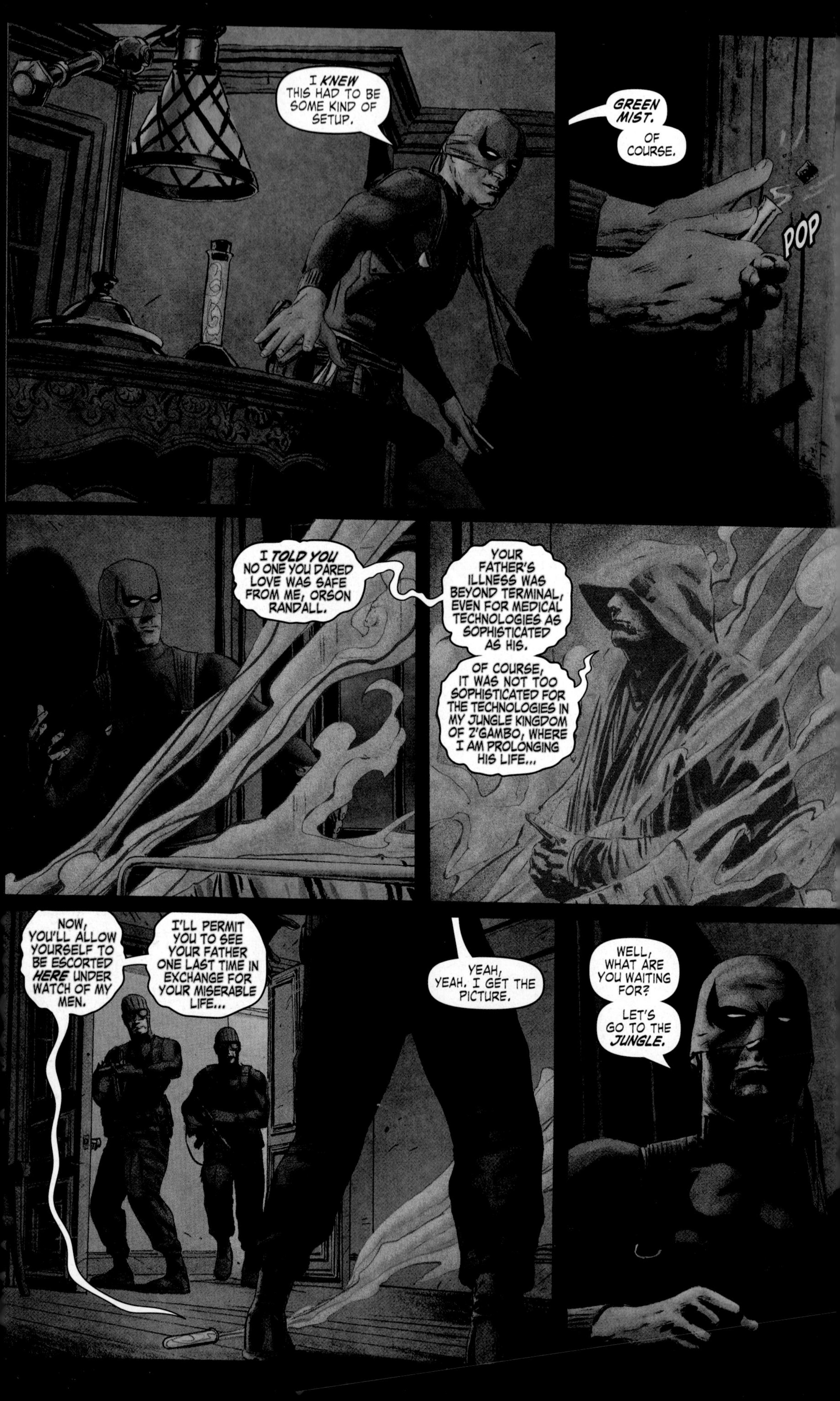
I KNEW THIS HAD TO BE SOME KIND OF SETUP.
GREEN MIST.
OF COURSE.
POP
I TOLD YOU NO ONE YOU DARED LOVE WAS SAFE FROM ME, ORSON RANDALL.
YOUR FATHER'S ILLNESS WAS BEYOND TERMINAL, EVEN FOR MEDICAL TECHNOLOGIES AS SOPHISTICATED AS HIS.
OF COURSE, IT WAS NOT TOO SOPHISTICATED FOR THE TECHNOLOGIES IN MY JUNGLE KINGDOM OF Z'GAMBO, WHERE I AM PROLONGING HIS LIFE...
NOW, YOU'LL ALLOW YOURSELF TO BE ESCORTED HERE UNDER WATCH OF MY MEN.
I'LL PERMIT YOU TO SEE YOUR FATHER ONE LAST TIME IN EXCHANGE FOR YOUR MISERABLE LIFE...
YEAH, YEAH. I GET THE PICTURE.
WELL, WHAT ARE YOU WAITING FOR?
LET'S GO TO THE JUNGLE.

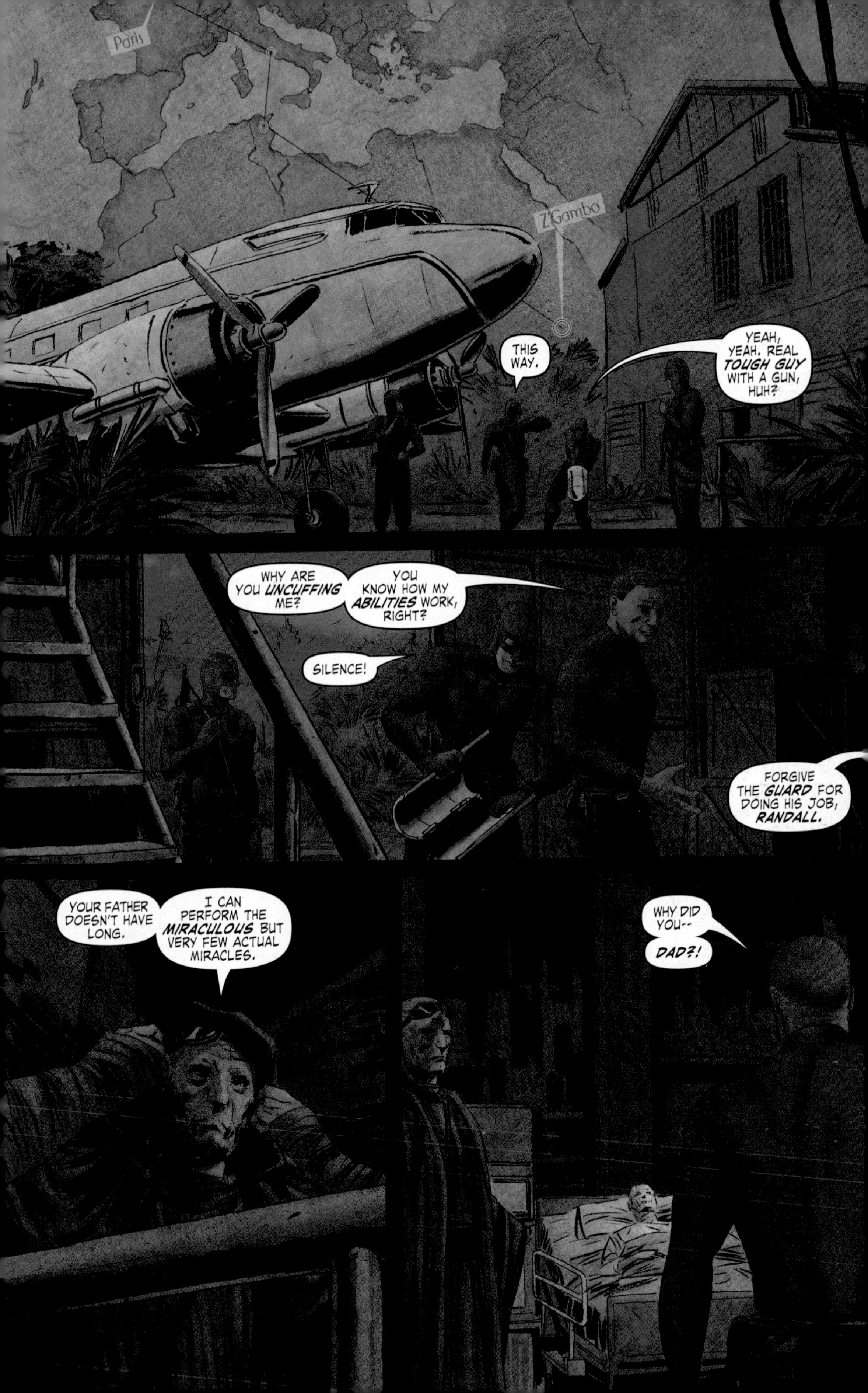
Paris
Z'Gambo
THIS WAY.
YEAH, YEAH. REAL TOUGH GUY WITH A GUN, HUH?
WHY ARE YOU UNCUFFING ME?
YOU KNOW HOW MY ABILITIES WORK, RIGHT?
SILENCE!
FORGIVE THE GUARD FOR DOING HIS JOB, RANDALL.
YOUR FATHER DOESN'T HAVE LONG.
I CAN PERFORM THE MIRACULOUS BUT VERY FEW ACTUAL MIRACLES.
WHY DID YOU--
DAD?!

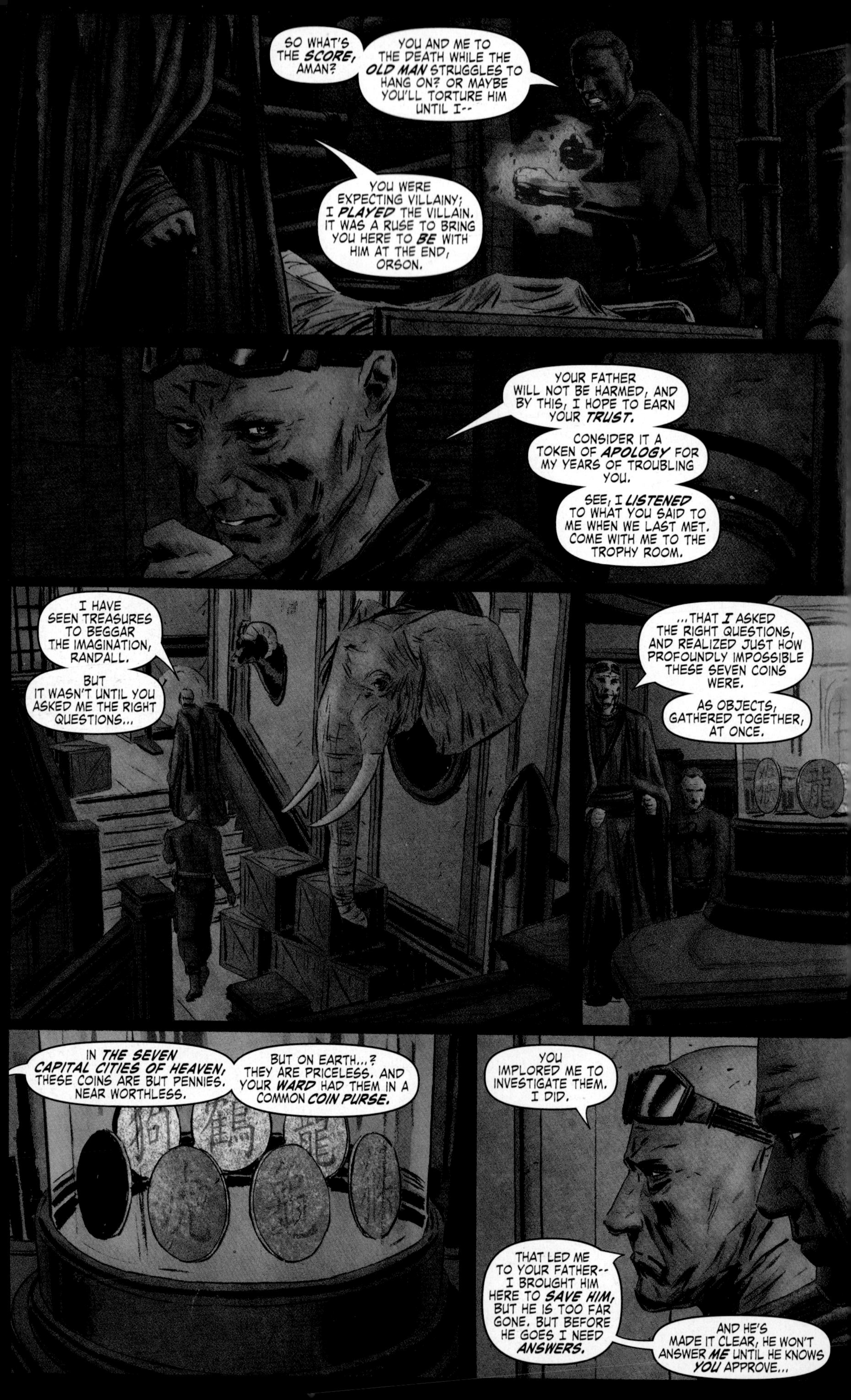
SO WHAT'S THE SCORE, AMAN?
YOU AND ME TO THE DEATH WHILE THE OLD MAN STRUGGLES TO HANG ON? OR MAYBE YOU'LL TORTURE HIM UNTIL I--
YOU WERE EXPECTING VILLAINY; I PLAYED THE VILLAIN. IT WAS A RUSE TO BRING YOU HERE TO BE WITH HIM AT THE END, ORSON.
YOUR FATHER WILL NOT BE HARMED, AND BY THIS, I HOPE TO EARN YOUR TRUST.
CONSIDER IT A TOKEN OF APOLOGY FOR MY YEARS OF TROUBLING YOU.
SEE, I LISTENED TO WHAT YOU SAID TO ME WHEN WE LAST MET. COME WITH ME TO THE TROPHY ROOM.
I HAVE SEEN TREASURES TO BEGGAR THE IMAGINATION, RANDALL.
BUT IT WASN'T UNTIL YOU ASKED ME THE RIGHT QUESTIONS...
...THAT I ASKED THE RIGHT QUESTIONS, AND REALIZED JUST HOW PROFOUNDLY IMPOSSIBLE THESE SEVEN COINS WERE.
AS OBJECTS, GATHERED TOGETHER, AT ONCE.
IN THE SEVEN CAPITAL CITIES OF HEAVEN, THESE COINS ARE BUT PENNIES. NEAR WORTHLESS.
BUT ON EARTH...? THEY ARE PRICELESS. AND YOUR WARD HAD THEM IN A COMMON COIN PURSE.
YOU IMPLORED ME TO INVESTIGATE THEM. I DID.
THAT LED ME TO YOUR FATHER-- I BROUGHT HIM HERE TO SAVE HIM, BUT HE IS TOO FAR GONE. BUT BEFORE HE GOES I NEED ANSWERS.
AND HE'S MADE IT CLEAR, HE WON'T ANSWER ME UNTIL HE KNOWS YOU APPROVE...

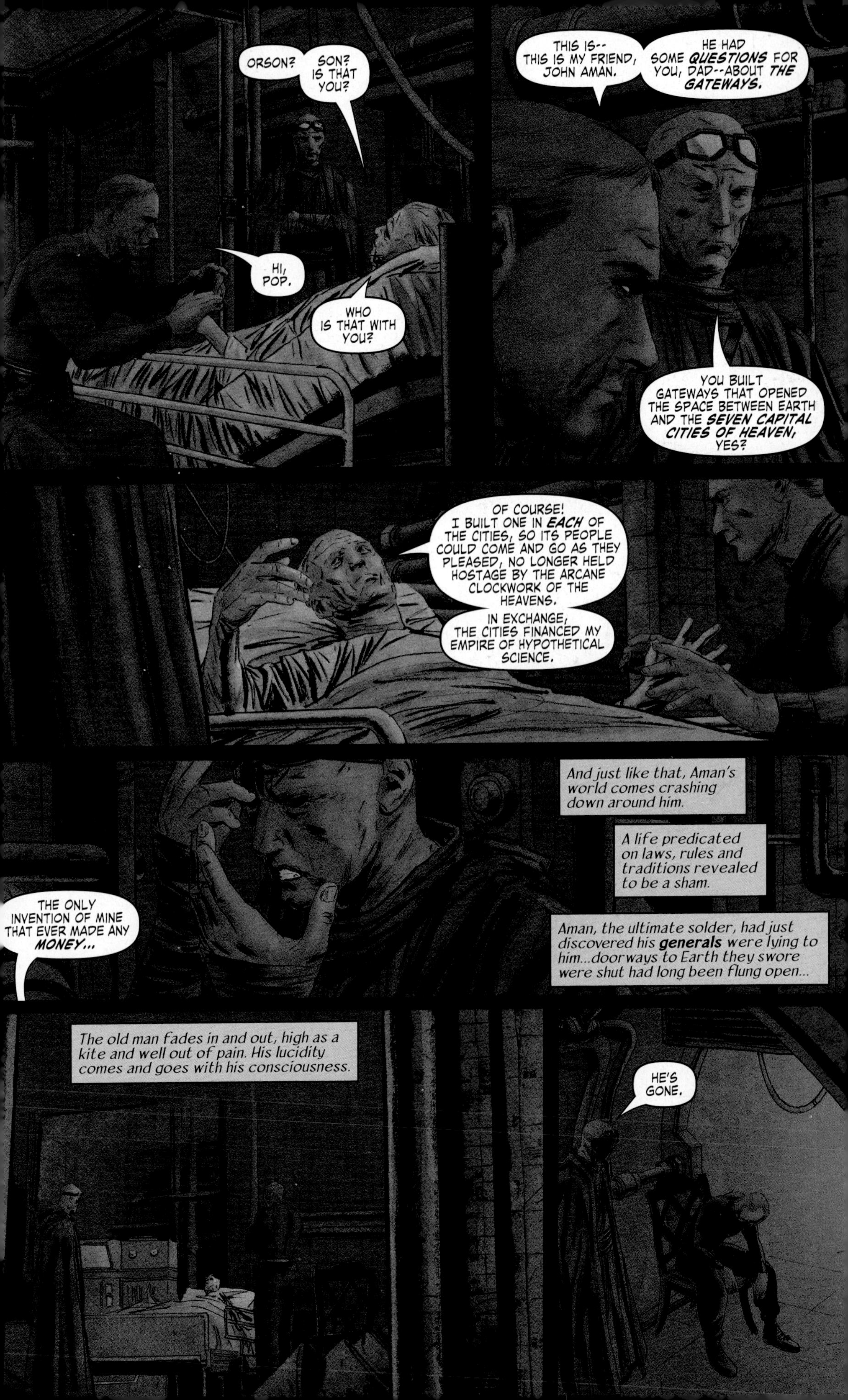
ORSON?
SON? IS THAT YOU?
HI, POP.
WHO IS THAT WITH YOU?
THIS IS-- THIS IS MY FRIEND, JOHN AMAN.
HE HAD SOME QUESTIONS FOR YOU, DAD--ABOUT THE GATEWAYS.
YOU BUILT GATEWAYS THAT OPENED THE SPACE BETWEEN EARTH AND THE SEVEN CAPITAL CITIES OF HEAVEN, YES?
OF COURSE! I BUILT ONE IN EACH OF THE CITIES, SO ITS PEOPLE COULD COME AND GO AS THEY PLEASED, NO LONGER HELD HOSTAGE BY THE ARCANE CLOCKWORK OF THE HEAVENS.
IN EXCHANGE, THE CITIES FINANCED MY EMPIRE OF HYPOTHETICAL SCIENCE.
THE ONLY INVENTION OF MINE THAT EVER MADE ANY MONEY...
And just like that, Aman's world comes crashing down around him.
A life predicated on laws, rules and traditions revealed to be a sham.
Aman, the ultimate solder, had just discovered his generals were lying to him...doorways to Earth they swore were shut had long been flung open...
The old man fades in and out, high as a kite and well out of pain. His lucidity comes and goes with his consciousness.
HE'S GONE.

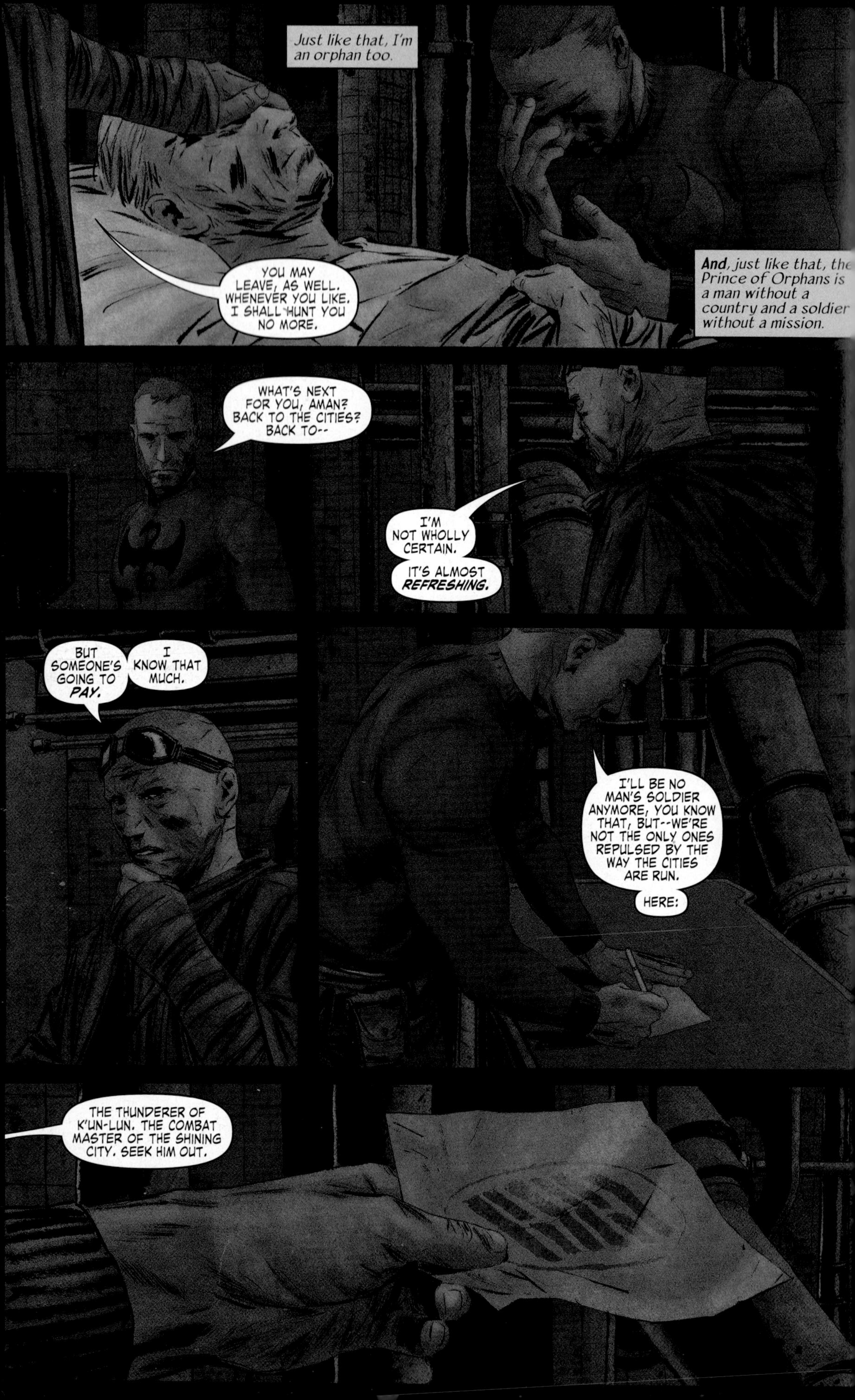

Just like that, I'm an orphan too.
YOU MAY LEAVE, AS WELL. WHENEVER YOU LIKE. I SHALL HUNT YOU NO MORE.
And, just like that, the Prince of Orphans is a man without a country and a soldier without a mission.
WHAT'S NEXT FOR YOU, AMAN? BACK TO THE CITIES? BACK TO--
I'M NOT WHOLLY CERTAIN.
IT'S ALMOST REFRESHING.
BUT SOMEONE'S GOING TO PAY.
I KNOW THAT MUCH.
I'LL BE NO MAN'S SOLDIER ANYMORE, YOU KNOW THAT, BUT--WE'RE NOT THE ONLY ONES REPULSED BY THE WAY THE CITIES ARE RUN.
HERE:
THE THUNDERER OF K'UN-LUN. THE COMBAT MASTER OF THE SHINING CITY. SEEK HIM OUT.

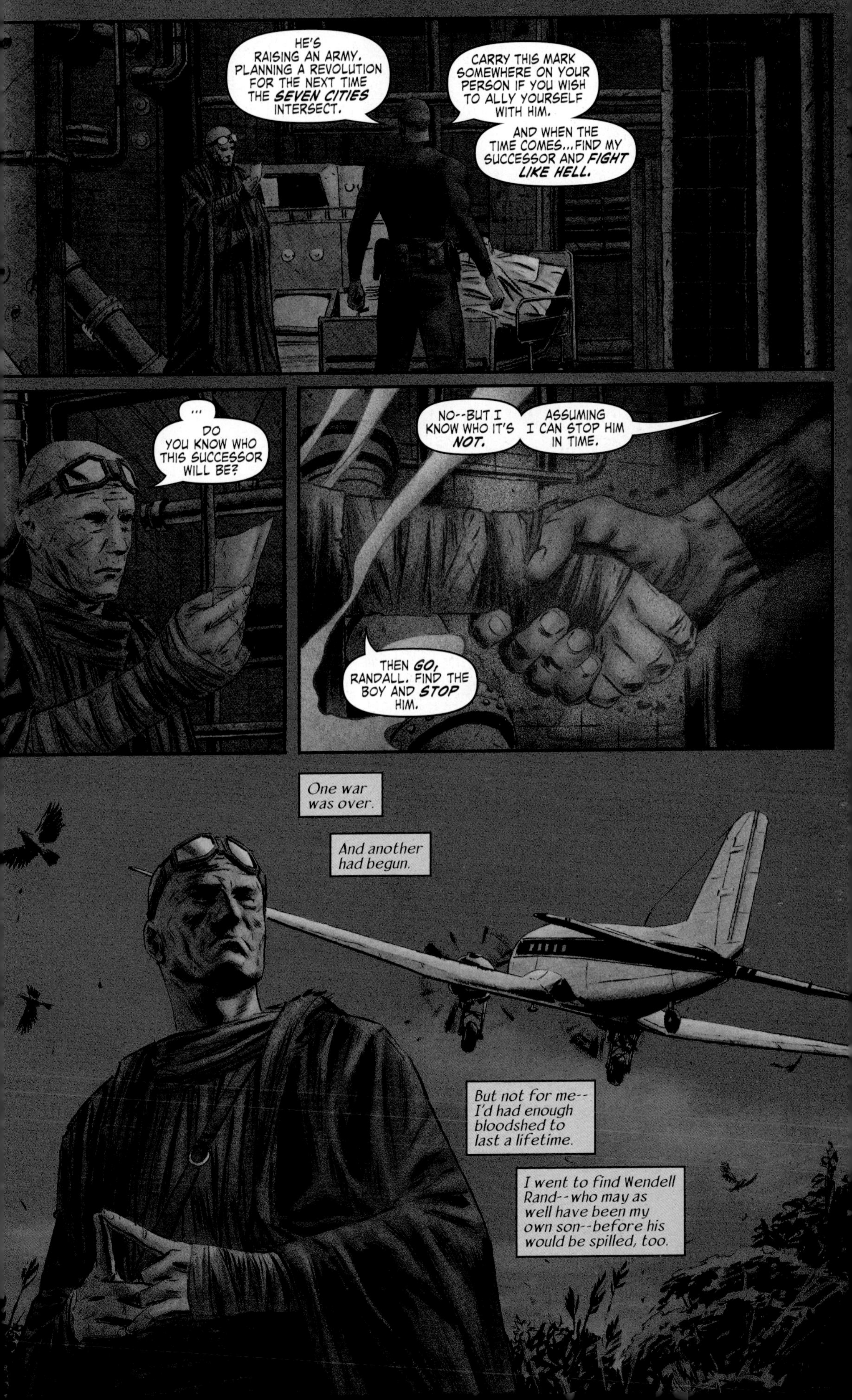
HE'S RAISING AN ARMY. PLANNING A REVOLUTION FOR THE NEXT TIME THE SEVEN CITIES INTERSECT.
CARRY THIS MARK SOMEWHERE ON YOUR PERSON IF YOU WISH TO ALLY YOURSELF WITH HIM.
AND WHEN THE TIME COMES...FIND MY SUCCESSOR AND FIGHT LIKE HELL.
... DO YOU KNOW WHO THIS SUCCESSOR WILL BE?
NO--BUT I KNOW WHO IT'S NOT.
ASSUMING I CAN STOP HIM IN TIME.
THEN GO, RANDALL. FIND THE BOY AND STOP HIM.
One war was over.
And another had begun.
But not for me--I'd had enough bloodshed to last a lifetime.
I went to find Wendell Rand--who may as well have been my own son--before his would be spilled, too.

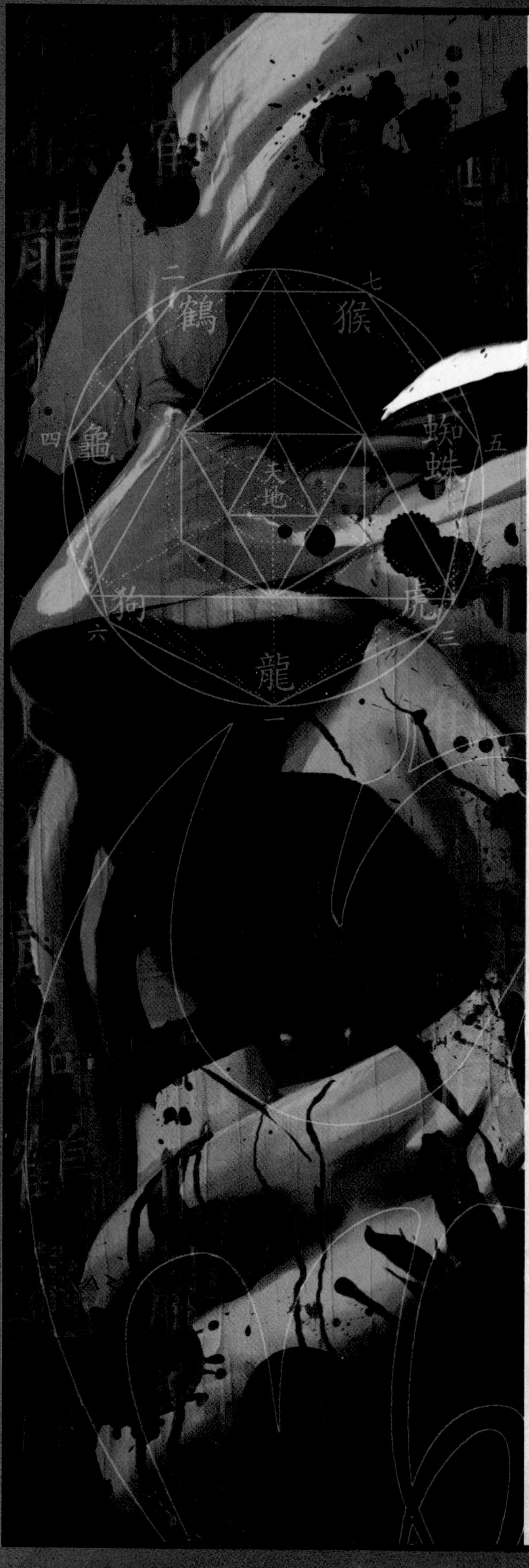

鶴
猴
龜
蜘蛛
狗
虎
龍

鐵拳 13

The 7 Capital Cities of Heaven

六

Round 6

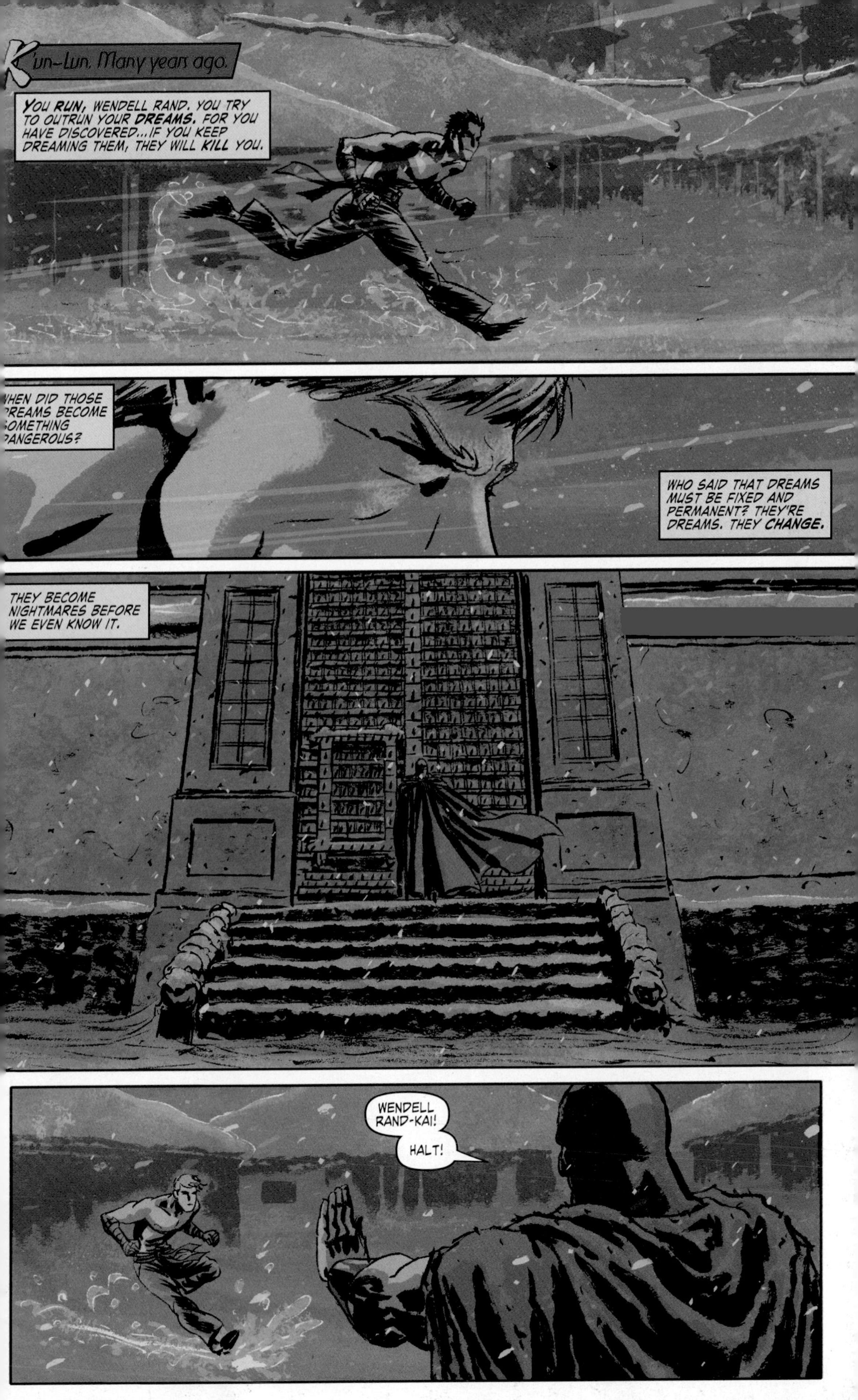
K'un-Lun, Many years ago.
YOU RUN, WENDELL RAND. YOU TRY TO OUTRUN YOUR DREAMS. FOR YOU HAVE DISCOVERED...IF YOU KEEP DREAMING THEM, THEY WILL KILL YOU.
WHEN DID THOSE DREAMS BECOME SOMETHING DANGEROUS?
WHO SAID THAT DREAMS MUST BE FIXED AND PERMANENT? THEY'RE DREAMS. THEY CHANGE.
THEY BECOME NIGHTMARES BEFORE WE EVEN KNOW IT.
WENDELL RAND-KAI!
HALT!

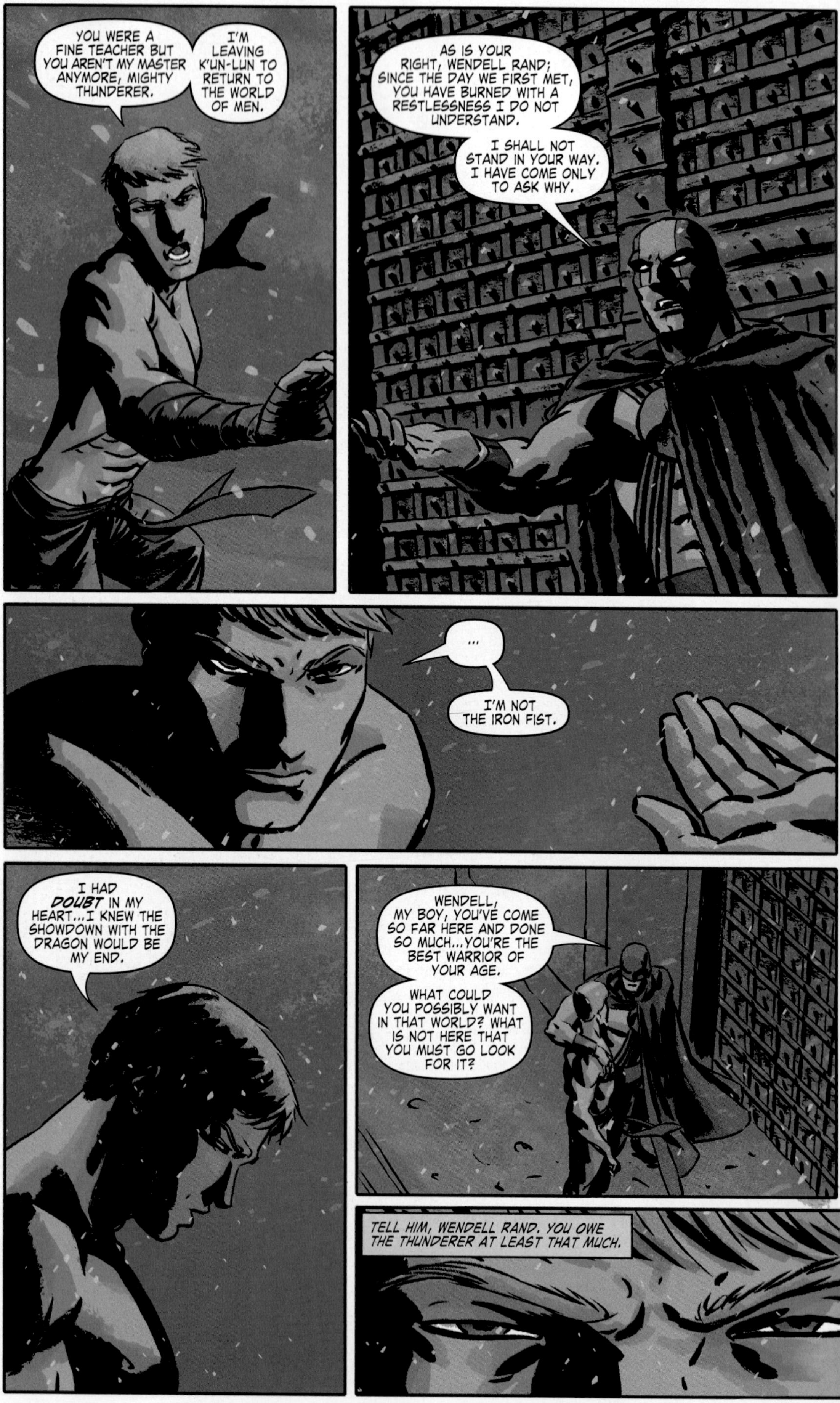
YOU WERE A FINE TEACHER BUT YOU AREN'T MY MASTER ANYMORE, MIGHTY THUNDERER.
I'M LEAVING K'UN-LUN TO RETURN TO THE WORLD OF MEN.
AS IS YOUR RIGHT, WENDELL RAND; SINCE THE DAY WE FIRST MET, YOU HAVE BURNED WITH A RESTLESSNESS I DO NOT UNDERSTAND.
I SHALL NOT STAND IN YOUR WAY. I HAVE COME ONLY TO ASK WHY.
...
I'M NOT THE IRON FIST.
I HAD *DOUBT* IN MY HEART...I KNEW THE SHOWDOWN WITH THE DRAGON WOULD BE MY END.
WENDELL, MY BOY, YOU'VE COME SO FAR HERE AND DONE SO MUCH...YOU'RE THE BEST WARRIOR OF YOUR AGE.
WHAT COULD YOU POSSIBLY WANT IN THAT WORLD? WHAT IS NOT HERE THAT YOU MUST GO LOOK FOR IT?
TELL HIM, WENDELL RAND. YOU OWE THE THUNDERER AT LEAST THAT MUCH.

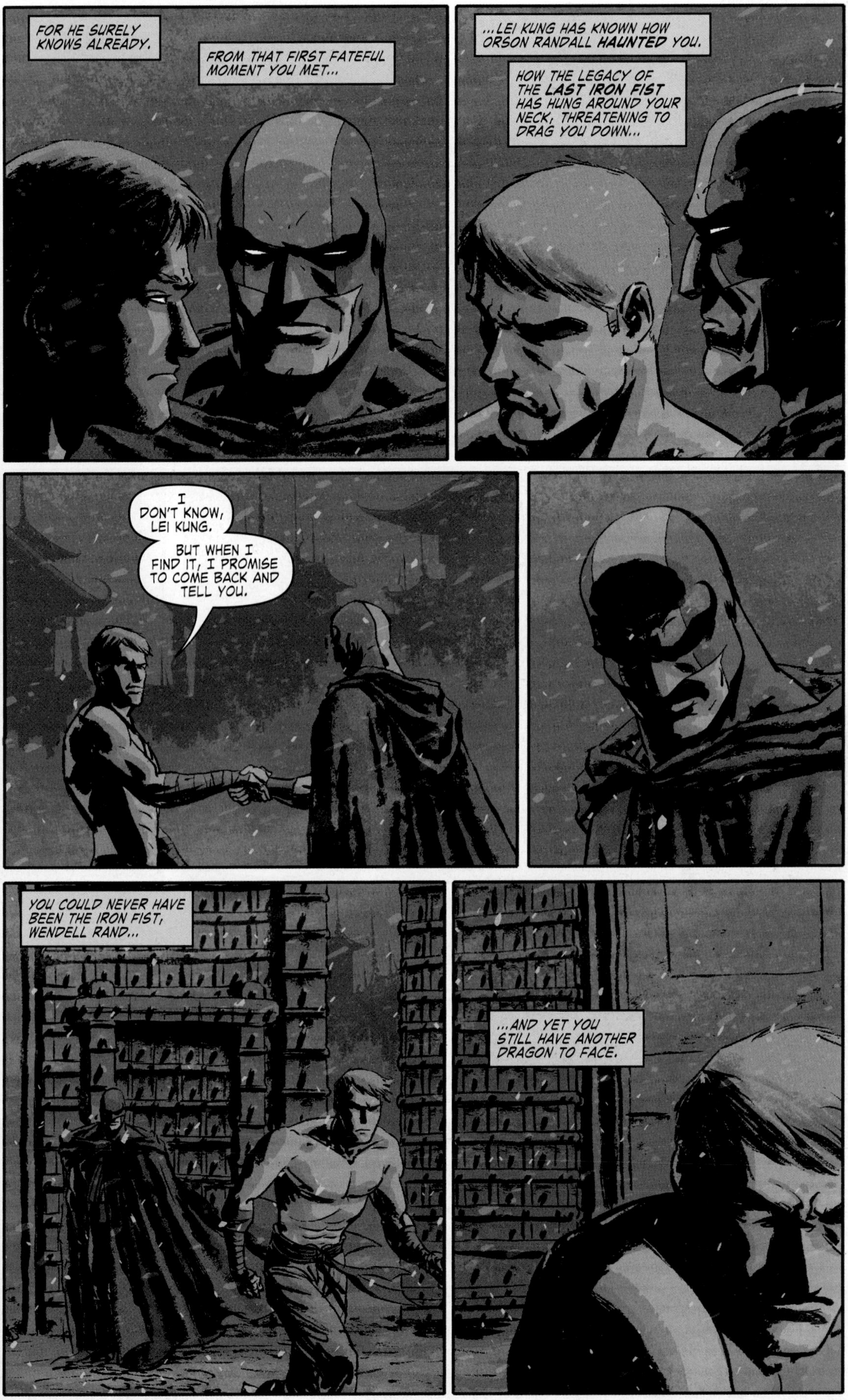
FOR HE SURELY KNOWS ALREADY.
FROM THAT FIRST FATEFUL MOMENT YOU MET...
...LEI KUNG HAS KNOWN HOW ORSON RANDALL HAUNTED YOU.
HOW THE LEGACY OF THE LAST IRON FIST HAS HUNG AROUND YOUR NECK, THREATENING TO DRAG YOU DOWN...
I DON'T KNOW, LEI KUNG.
BUT WHEN I FIND IT, I PROMISE TO COME BACK AND TELL YOU.
YOU COULD NEVER HAVE BEEN THE IRON FIST, WENDELL RAND...
...AND YET YOU STILL HAVE ANOTHER DRAGON TO FACE.

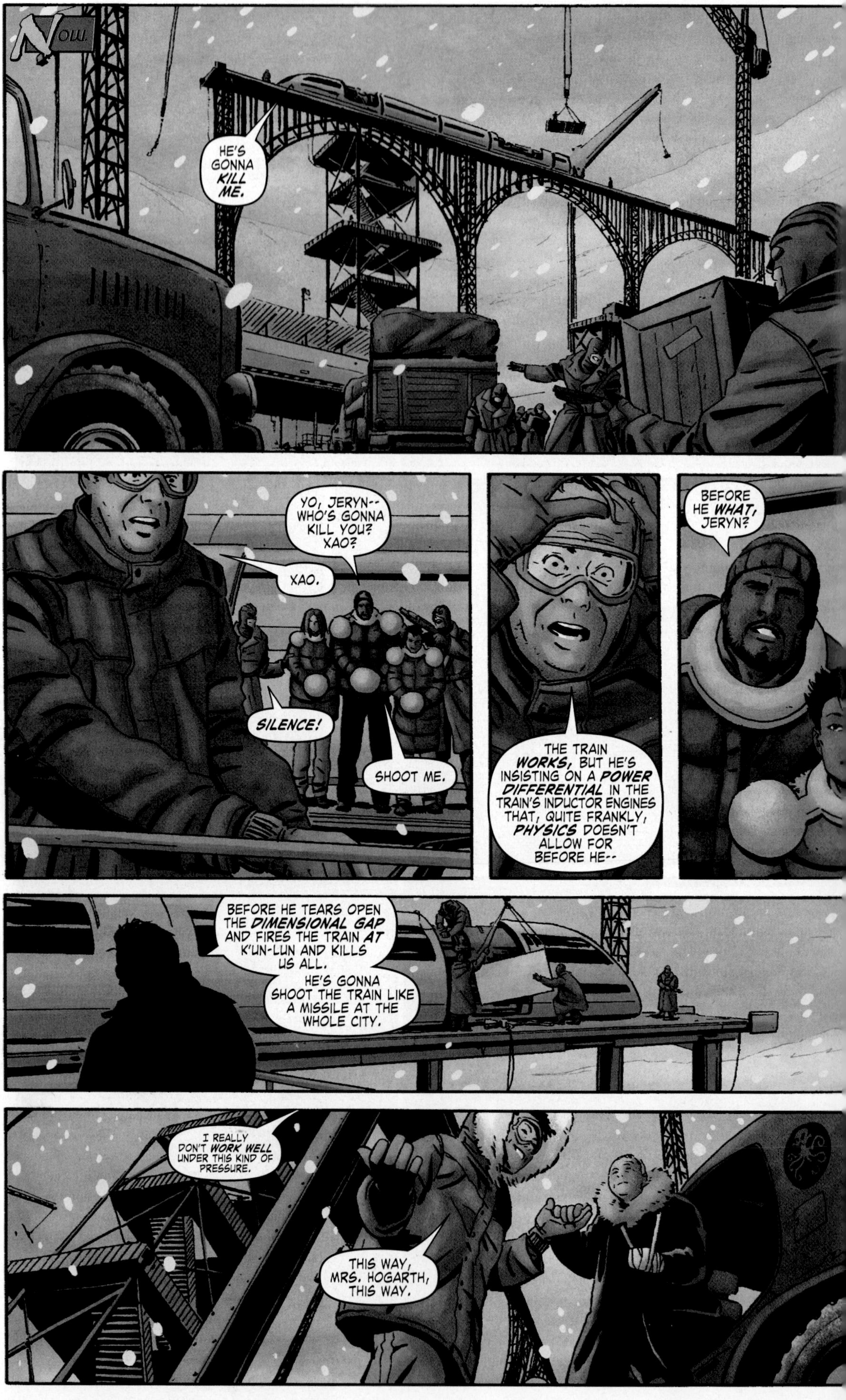
NOW.
HE'S GONNA KILL ME.
YO, JERYN-- WHO'S GONNA KILL YOU? XAO?
XAO.
SILENCE!
SHOOT ME.
THE TRAIN WORKS, BUT HE'S INSISTING ON A POWER DIFFERENTIAL IN THE TRAIN'S INDUCTOR ENGINES THAT, QUITE FRANKLY, PHYSICS DOESN'T ALLOW FOR BEFORE HE--
BEFORE HE WHAT, JERYN?
BEFORE HE TEARS OPEN THE DIMENSIONAL GAP AND FIRES THE TRAIN AT K'UN-LUN AND KILLS US ALL.
HE'S GONNA SHOOT THE TRAIN LIKE A MISSILE AT THE WHOLE CITY.
I REALLY DON'T WORK WELL UNDER THIS KIND OF PRESSURE.
THIS WAY, MRS. HOGARTH, THIS WAY.

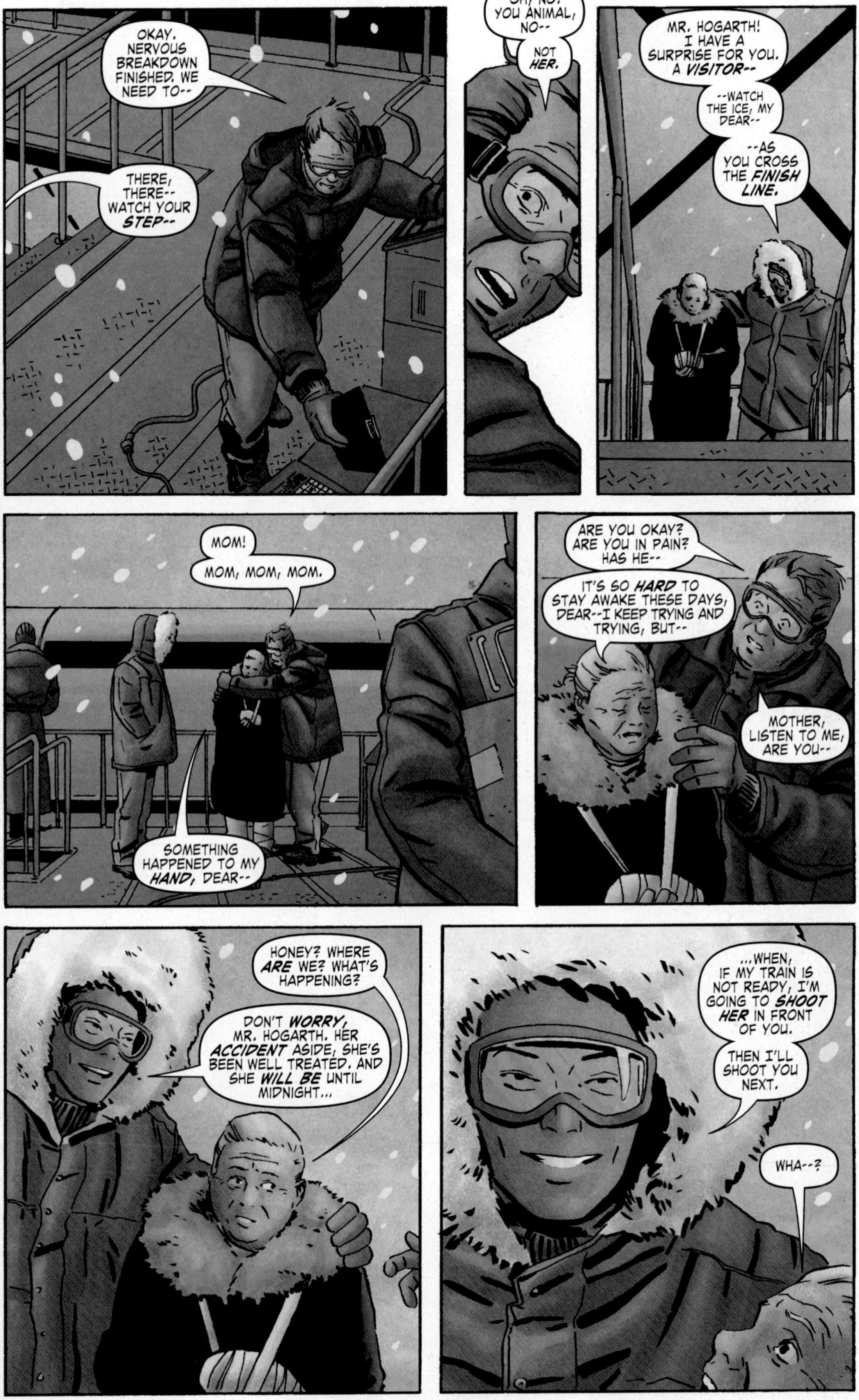
OKAY. NERVOUS BREAKDOWN FINISHED. WE NEED TO--
THERE, THERE--WATCH YOUR STEP--
OH, NO. YOU ANIMAL, NO--
NOT HER.
MR. HOGARTH! I HAVE A SURPRISE FOR YOU. A VISITOR--
--WATCH THE ICE, MY DEAR--
--AS YOU CROSS THE FINISH LINE.
MOM!
MOM, MOM, MOM.
SOMETHING HAPPENED TO MY HAND, DEAR--
ARE YOU OKAY? ARE YOU IN PAIN? HAS HE--
IT'S SO HARD TO STAY AWAKE THESE DAYS, DEAR--I KEEP TRYING AND TRYING, BUT--
MOTHER, LISTEN TO ME, ARE YOU--
HONEY? WHERE ARE WE? WHAT'S HAPPENING?
DON'T WORRY, MR. HOGARTH. HER ACCIDENT ASIDE, SHE'S BEEN WELL TREATED. AND SHE WILL BE UNTIL MIDNIGHT...
...WHEN, IF MY TRAIN IS NOT READY, I'M GOING TO SHOOT HER IN FRONT OF YOU.
THEN I'LL SHOOT YOU NEXT.
WHA--?

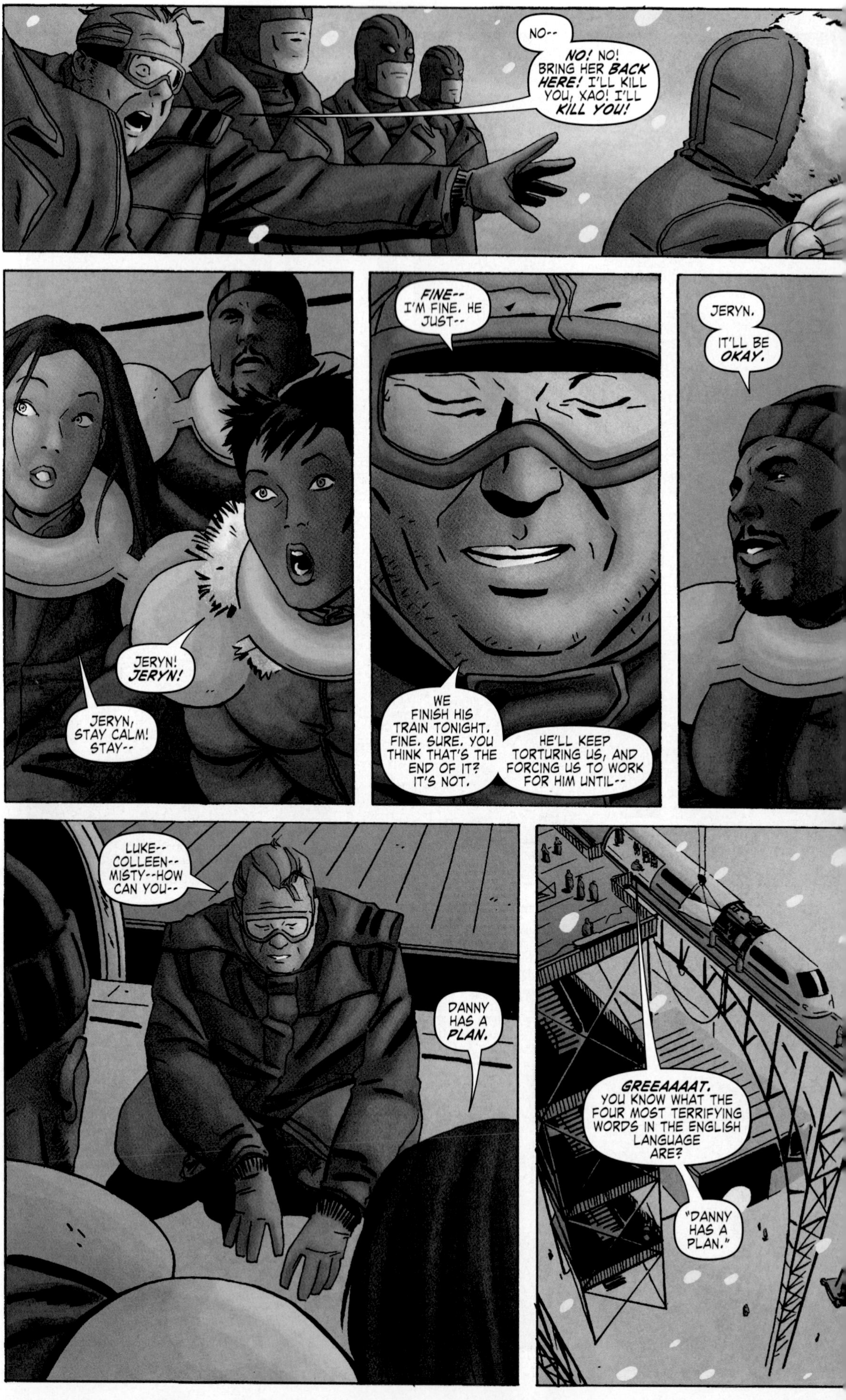
NO--
NO! NO! BRING HER BACK HERE! I'LL KILL YOU, XAO! I'LL KILL YOU!
JERYN! JERYN!
JERYN, STAY CALM! STAY--
FINE-- I'M FINE. HE JUST--
WE FINISH HIS TRAIN TONIGHT. FINE. SURE. YOU THINK THAT'S THE END OF IT? IT'S NOT.
HE'LL KEEP TORTURING US, AND FORCING US TO WORK FOR HIM UNTIL--
JERYN.
IT'LL BE OKAY.
LUKE-- COLLEEN-- MISTY--HOW CAN YOU--
DANNY HAS A PLAN.
GREEAAAAT. YOU KNOW WHAT THE FOUR MOST TERRIFYING WORDS IN THE ENGLISH LANGUAGE ARE?
"DANNY HAS A PLAN."

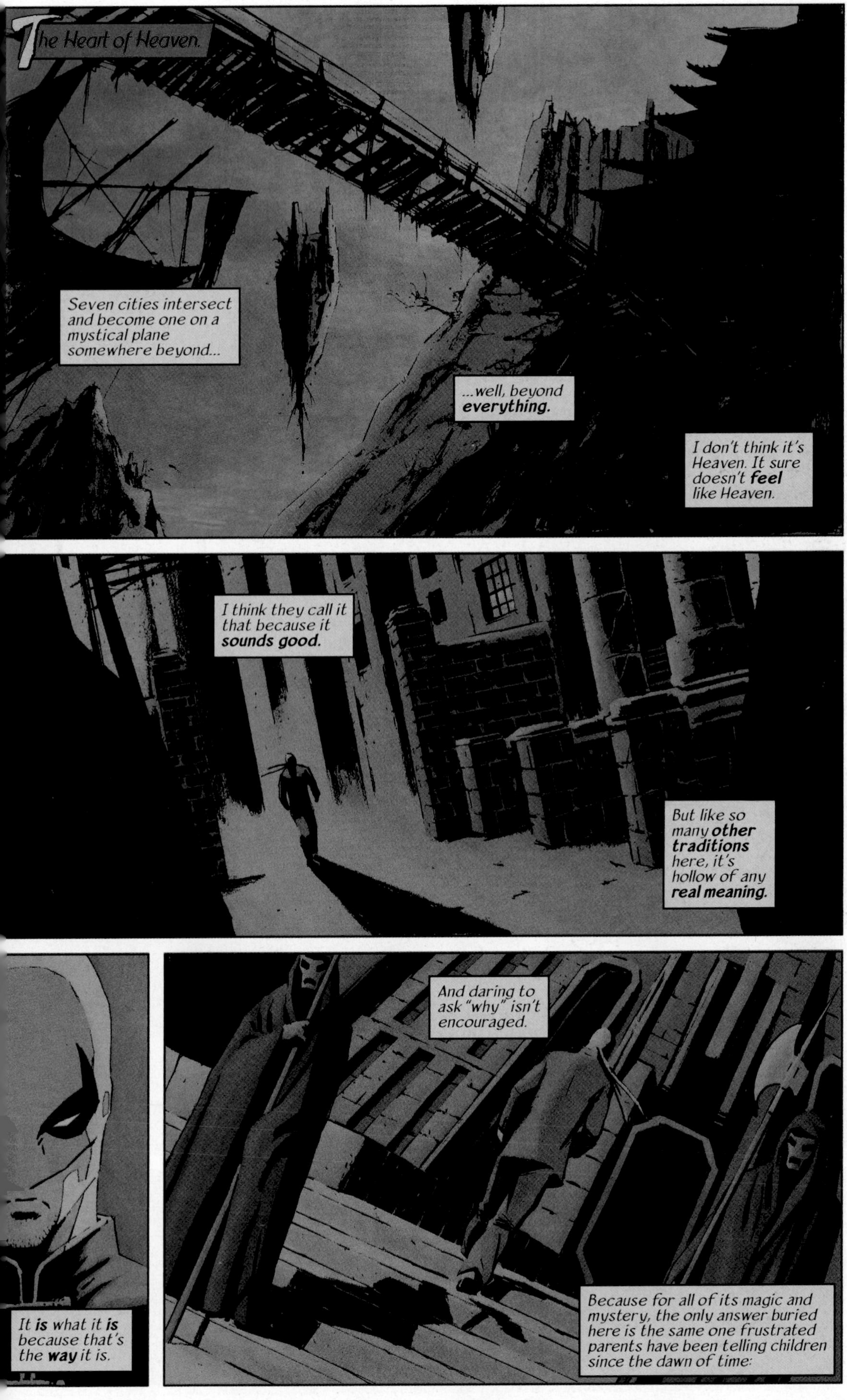
The Heart of Heaven.
Seven cities intersect and become one on a mystical plane somewhere beyond...
...well, beyond **everything.**
I don't think it's Heaven. It sure doesn't **feel** like Heaven.
I think they call it that because it **sounds good.**
But like so many **other traditions** here, it's hollow of any **real meaning.**
It **is** what it **is** because that's the **way** it is.
And daring to ask "why" isn't encouraged.
Because for all of its magic and mystery, the only answer buried here is the same one frustrated parents have been telling children since the dawn of time:

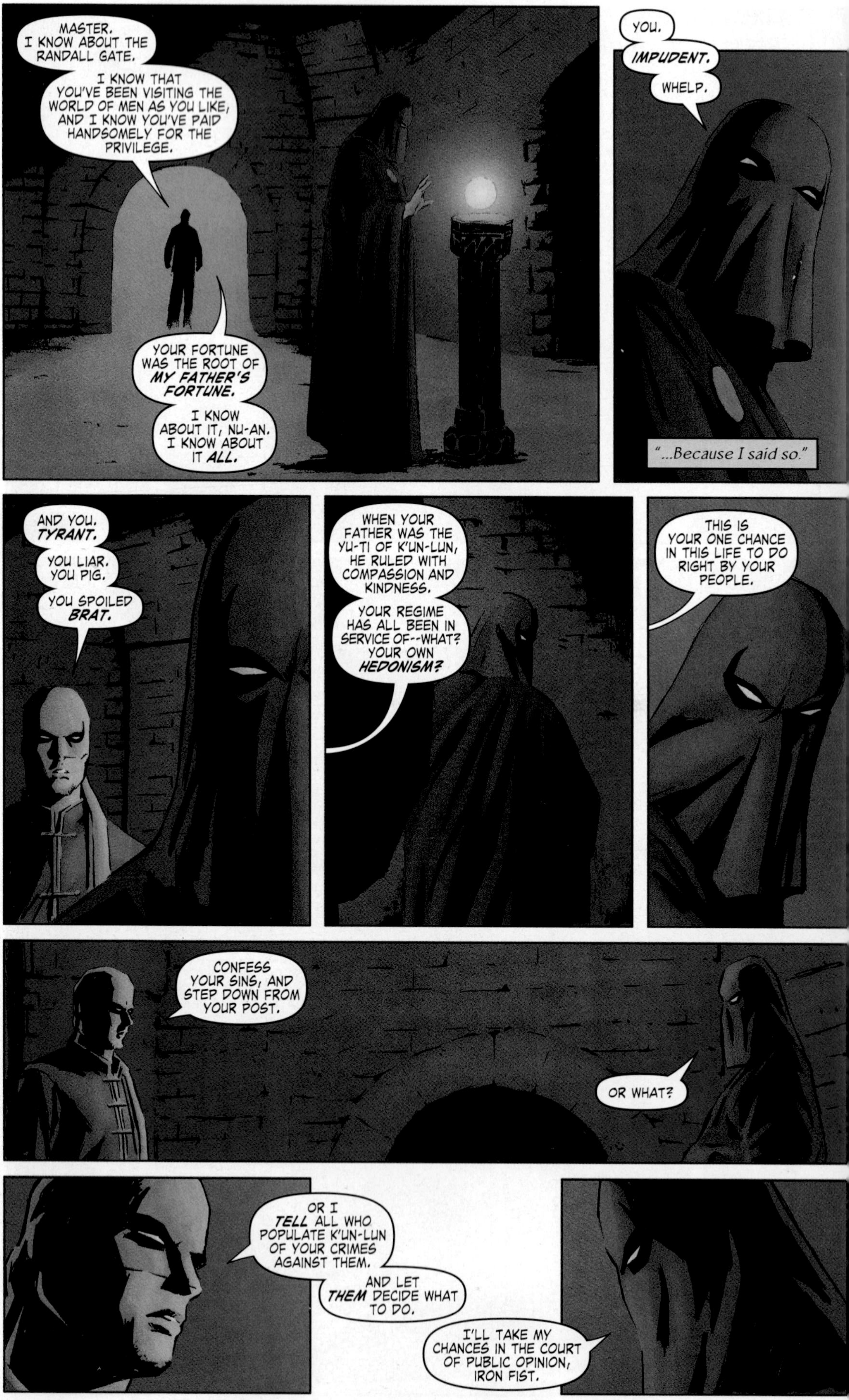
MASTER. I KNOW ABOUT THE RANDALL GATE.
I KNOW THAT YOU'VE BEEN VISITING THE WORLD OF MEN AS YOU LIKE, AND I KNOW YOU'VE PAID HANDSOMELY FOR THE PRIVILEGE.
YOUR FORTUNE WAS THE ROOT OF MY FATHER'S FORTUNE.
I KNOW ABOUT IT, NU-AN. I KNOW ABOUT IT ALL.
YOU.
IMPUDENT.
WHELP.
"...Because I said so."
AND YOU. TYRANT.
YOU LIAR. YOU PIG.
YOU SPOILED BRAT.
WHEN YOUR FATHER WAS THE YU-TI OF K'UN-LUN, HE RULED WITH COMPASSION AND KINDNESS.
YOUR REGIME HAS ALL BEEN IN SERVICE OF--WHAT? YOUR OWN HEDONISM?
THIS IS YOUR ONE CHANCE IN THIS LIFE TO DO RIGHT BY YOUR PEOPLE.
CONFESS YOUR SINS, AND STEP DOWN FROM YOUR POST.
OR WHAT?
OR I TELL ALL WHO POPULATE K'UN-LUN OF YOUR CRIMES AGAINST THEM.
AND LET THEM DECIDE WHAT TO DO.
I'LL TAKE MY CHANCES IN THE COURT OF PUBLIC OPINION, IRON FIST.

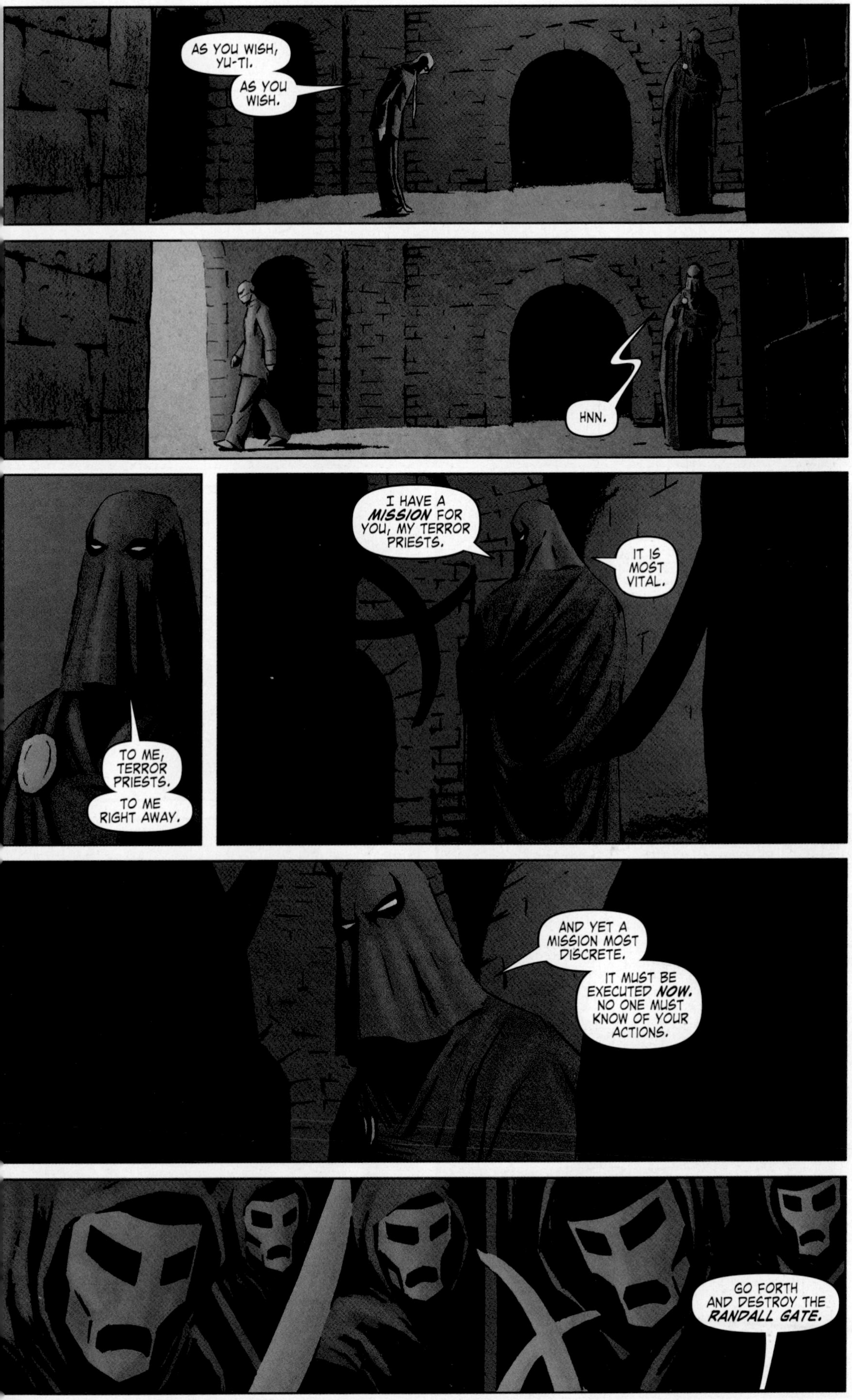
AS YOU WISH, YU-TI.
AS YOU WISH.
HNN.
TO ME, TERROR PRIESTS.
TO ME RIGHT AWAY.
I HAVE A MISSION FOR YOU, MY TERROR PRIESTS.
IT IS MOST VITAL.
AND YET A MISSION MOST DISCRETE.
IT MUST BE EXECUTED NOW. NO ONE MUST KNOW OF YOUR ACTIONS.
GO FORTH AND DESTROY THE RANDALL GATE.

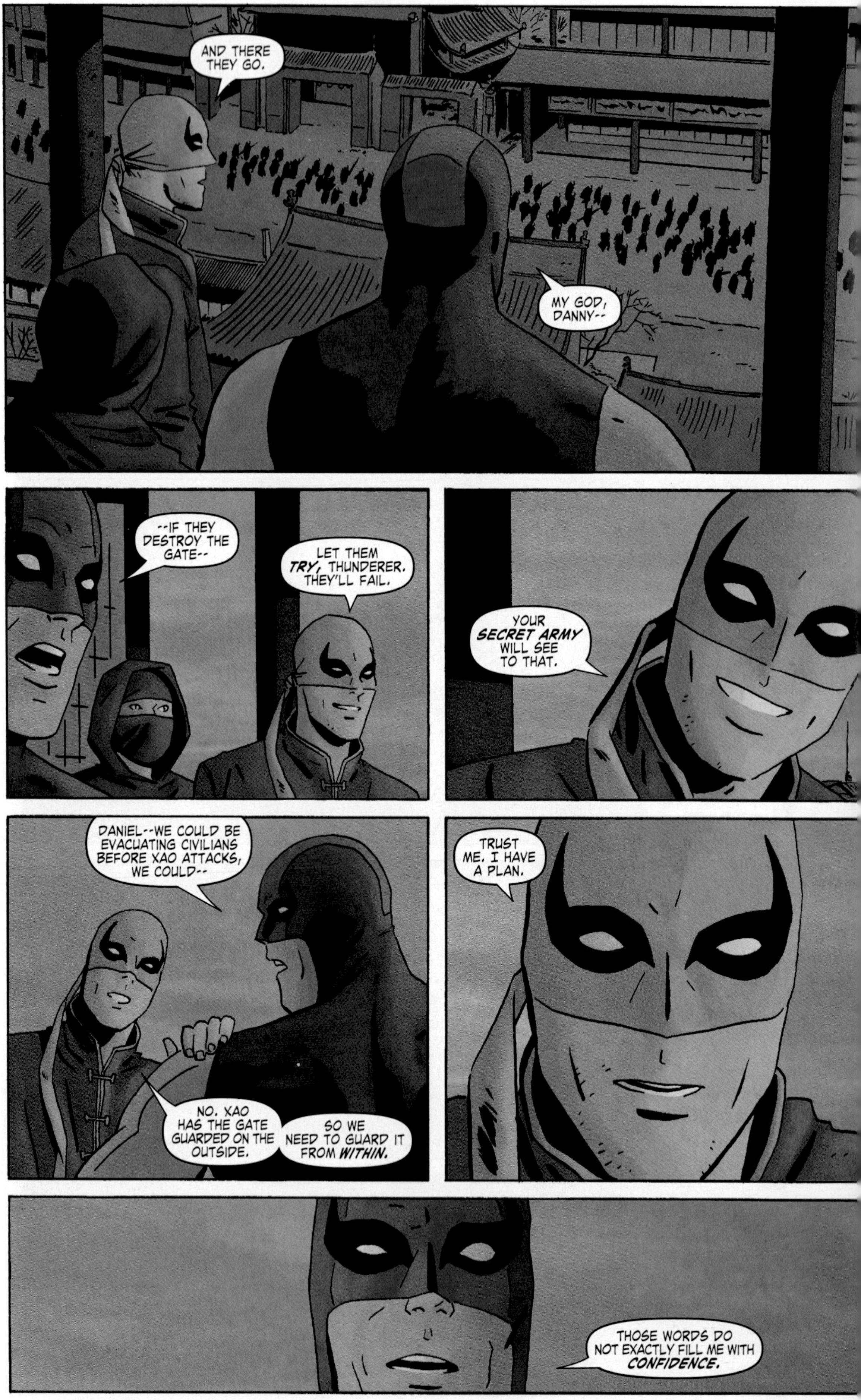
AND THERE THEY GO.
MY GOD, DANNY--
--IF THEY DESTROY THE GATE--
LET THEM *TRY*, THUNDERER. THEY'LL FAIL.
YOUR *SECRET ARMY* WILL SEE TO THAT.
DANIEL--WE COULD BE EVACUATING CIVILIANS BEFORE XAO ATTACKS, WE COULD--
NO. XAO HAS THE GATE GUARDED ON THE OUTSIDE.
SO WE NEED TO GUARD IT FROM *WITHIN.*
TRUST ME. I HAVE A PLAN.
THOSE WORDS DO NOT EXACTLY FILL ME WITH *CONFIDENCE.*

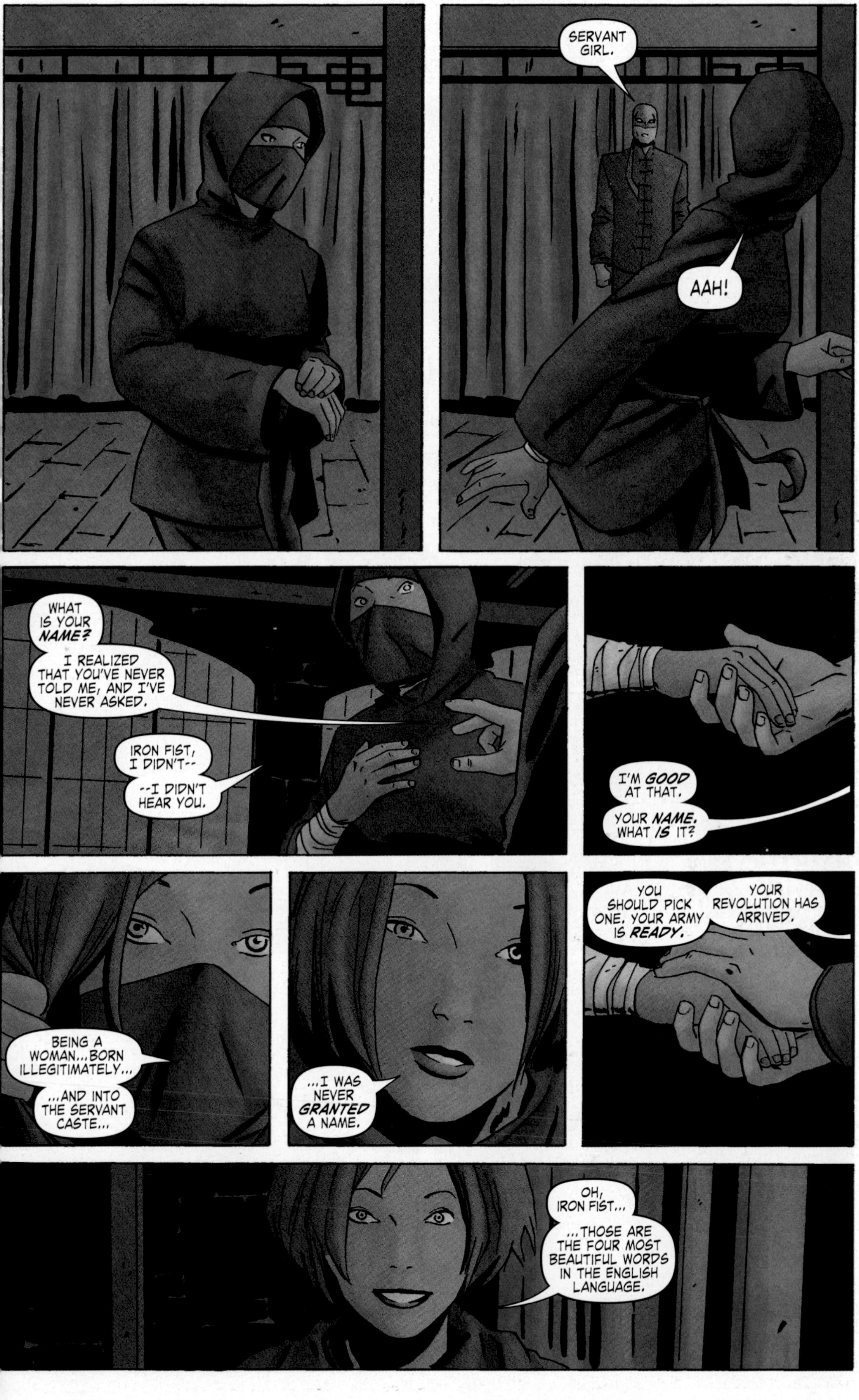

SERVANT GIRL.
AAH!
WHAT IS YOUR NAME?
I REALIZED THAT YOU'VE NEVER TOLD ME, AND I'VE NEVER ASKED.
IRON FIST, I DIDN'T--
--I DIDN'T HEAR YOU.
I'M GOOD AT THAT.
YOUR NAME. WHAT IS IT?
BEING A WOMAN...BORN ILLEGITIMATELY...
...AND INTO THE SERVANT CASTE...
...I WAS NEVER GRANTED A NAME.
YOU SHOULD PICK ONE. YOUR ARMY IS READY.
YOUR REVOLUTION HAS ARRIVED.
OH, IRON FIST...
...THOSE ARE THE FOUR MOST BEAUTIFUL WORDS IN THE ENGLISH LANGUAGE.

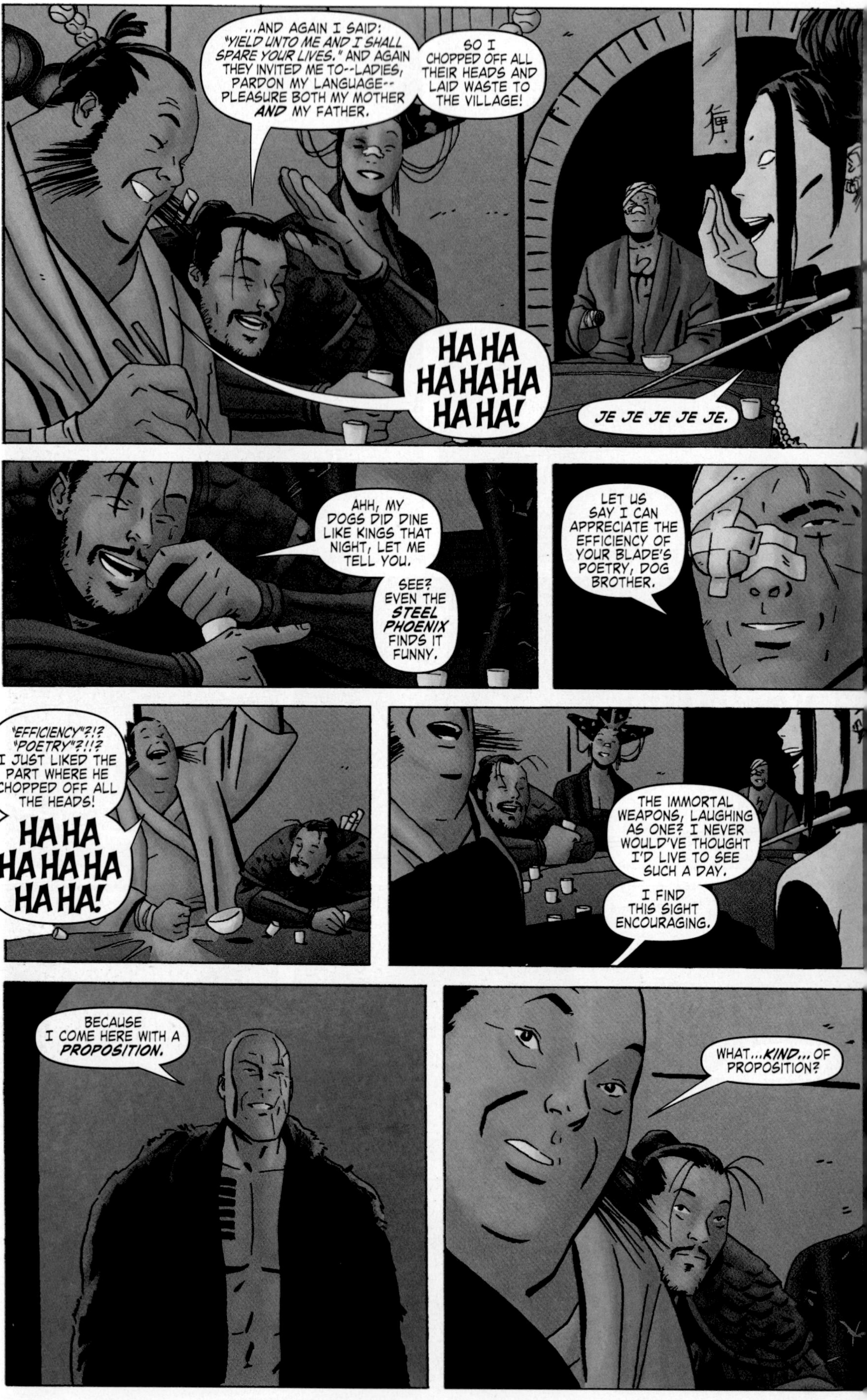
...AND AGAIN I SAID: "YIELD UNTO ME AND I SHALL SPARE YOUR LIVES." AND AGAIN THEY INVITED ME TO--LADIES, PARDON MY LANGUAGE--PLEASURE BOTH MY MOTHER AND MY FATHER.
SO I CHOPPED OFF ALL THEIR HEADS AND LAID WASTE TO THE VILLAGE!
HA HA HA HA HA HA HA!
JE JE JE JE JE.
AHH, MY DOGS DID DINE LIKE KINGS THAT NIGHT, LET ME TELL YOU.
SEE? EVEN THE STEEL PHOENIX FINDS IT FUNNY.
LET US SAY I CAN APPRECIATE THE EFFICIENCY OF YOUR BLADE'S POETRY, DOG BROTHER.
"EFFICIENCY"?!? "POETRY"?!!? I JUST LIKED THE PART WHERE HE CHOPPED OFF ALL THE HEADS!
HA HA HA HA HA HA HA!
THE IMMORTAL WEAPONS, LAUGHING AS ONE? I NEVER WOULD'VE THOUGHT I'D LIVE TO SEE SUCH A DAY.
I FIND THIS SIGHT ENCOURAGING.
BECAUSE I COME HERE WITH A PROPOSITION.
WHAT...KIND...OF PROPOSITION?

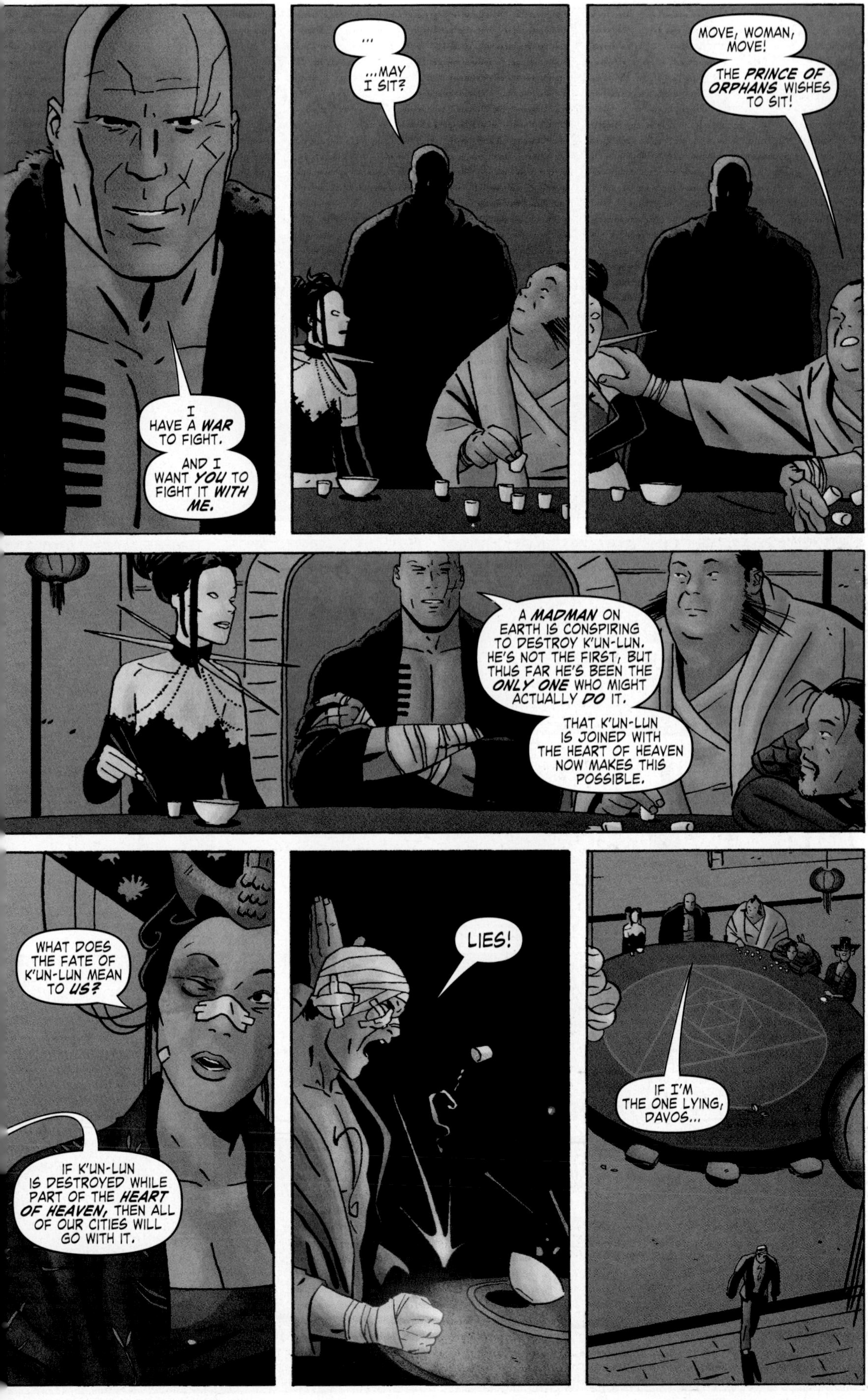
I HAVE A WAR TO FIGHT.
AND I WANT YOU TO FIGHT IT WITH ME.
...
...MAY I SIT?
MOVE, WOMAN, MOVE!
THE PRINCE OF ORPHANS WISHES TO SIT!
A MADMAN ON EARTH IS CONSPIRING TO DESTROY K'UN-LUN. HE'S NOT THE FIRST, BUT THUS FAR HE'S BEEN THE ONLY ONE WHO MIGHT ACTUALLY DO IT.
THAT K'UN-LUN IS JOINED WITH THE HEART OF HEAVEN NOW MAKES THIS POSSIBLE.
WHAT DOES THE FATE OF K'UN-LUN MEAN TO US?
IF K'UN-LUN IS DESTROYED WHILE PART OF THE HEART OF HEAVEN, THEN ALL OF OUR CITIES WILL GO WITH IT.
LIES!
IF I'M THE ONE LYING, DAVOS...

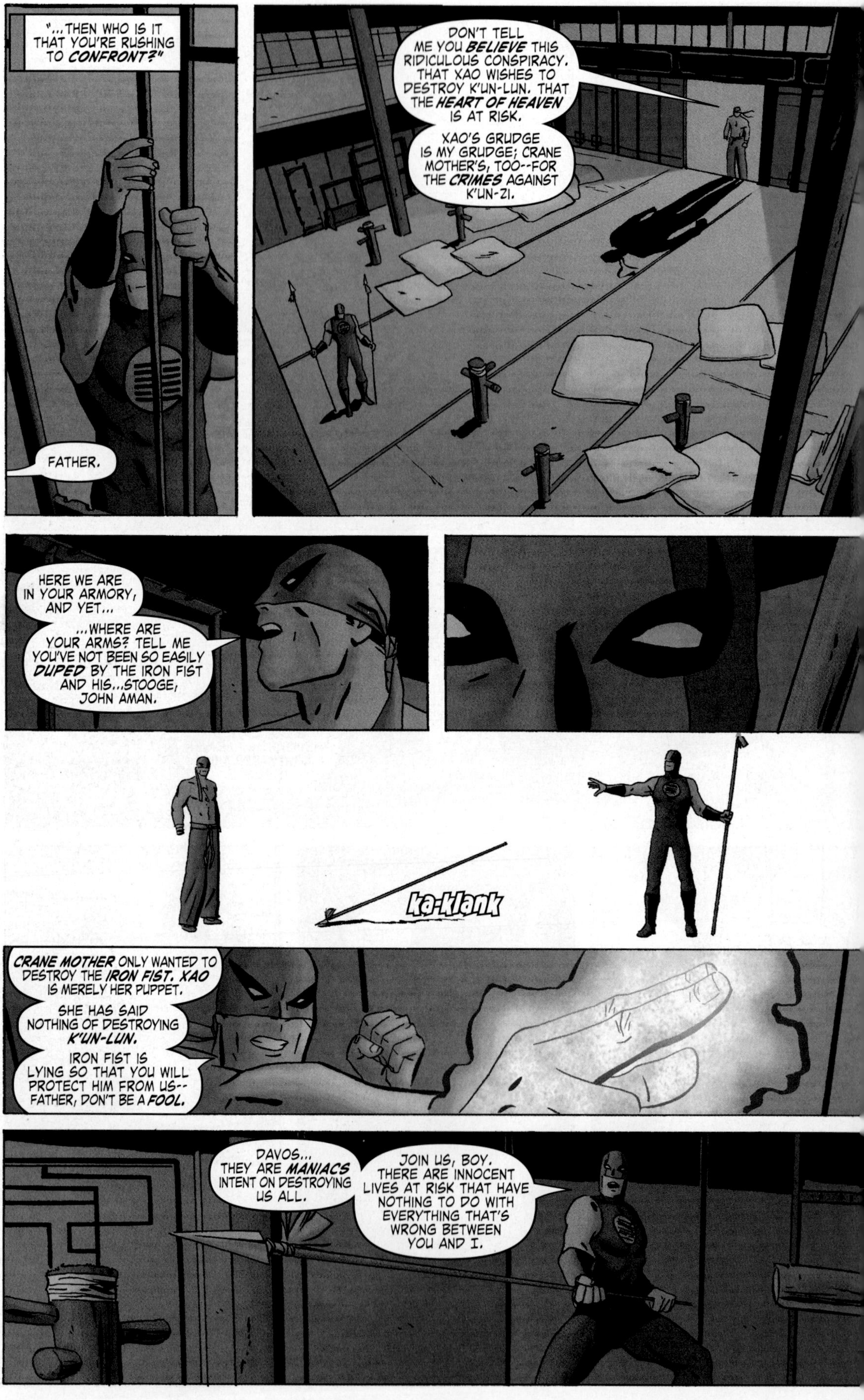
"...THEN WHO IS IT THAT YOU'RE RUSHING TO CONFRONT?"
FATHER.
DON'T TELL ME YOU BELIEVE THIS RIDICULOUS CONSPIRACY. THAT XAO WISHES TO DESTROY K'UN-LUN. THAT THE HEART OF HEAVEN IS AT RISK.
XAO'S GRUDGE IS MY GRUDGE; CRANE MOTHER'S, TOO--FOR THE CRIMES AGAINST K'UN-ZI.
HERE WE ARE IN YOUR ARMORY, AND YET...
...WHERE ARE YOUR ARMS? TELL ME YOU'VE NOT BEEN SO EASILY DUPED BY THE IRON FIST AND HIS...STOOGE, JOHN AMAN.
KA-KLANK
CRANE MOTHER ONLY WANTED TO DESTROY THE IRON FIST. XAO IS MERELY HER PUPPET.
SHE HAS SAID NOTHING OF DESTROYING K'UN-LUN.
IRON FIST IS LYING SO THAT YOU WILL PROTECT HIM FROM US-- FATHER, DON'T BE A FOOL.
DAVOS... THEY ARE MANIACS INTENT ON DESTROYING US ALL.
JOIN US, BOY. THERE ARE INNOCENT LIVES AT RISK THAT HAVE NOTHING TO DO WITH EVERYTHING THAT'S WRONG BETWEEN YOU AND I.

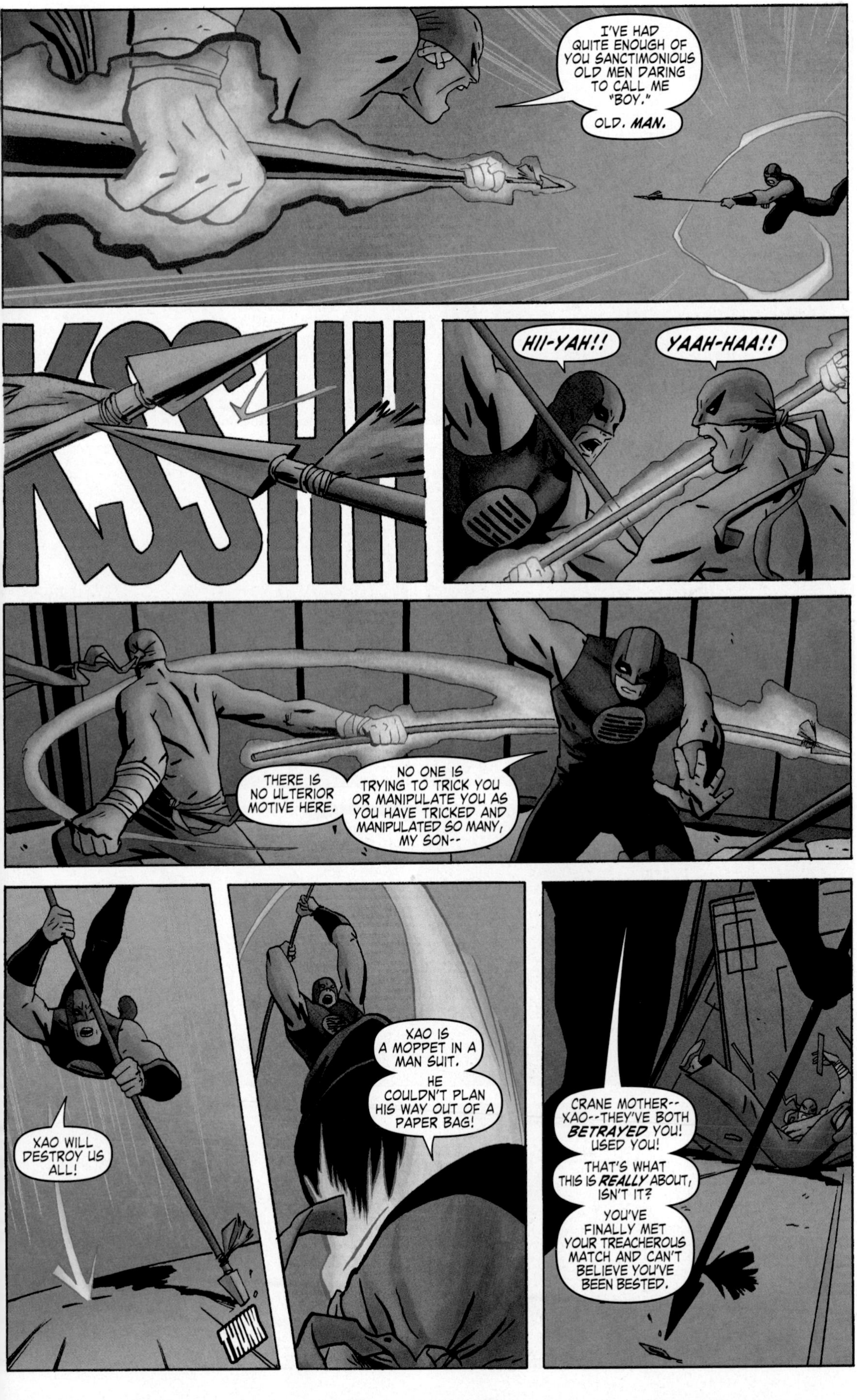
I'VE HAD QUITE ENOUGH OF YOU SANCTIMONIOUS OLD MEN DARING TO CALL ME "BOY."
OLD. *MAN.*
KSSHHH
HII-YAH!!
YAAH-HAA!!
THERE IS NO ULTERIOR MOTIVE HERE.
NO ONE IS TRYING TO TRICK YOU OR MANIPULATE YOU AS YOU HAVE TRICKED AND MANIPULATED SO MANY, MY SON--
XAO WILL DESTROY US ALL!
THUNK
XAO IS A MOPPET IN A MAN SUIT.
HE COULDN'T PLAN HIS WAY OUT OF A PAPER BAG!
CRANE MOTHER--XAO--THEY'VE BOTH *BETRAYED* YOU! USED YOU!
THAT'S WHAT THIS IS *REALLY* ABOUT, ISN'T IT?
YOU'VE FINALLY MET YOUR TREACHEROUS MATCH AND CAN'T BELIEVE YOU'VE BEEN BESTED.

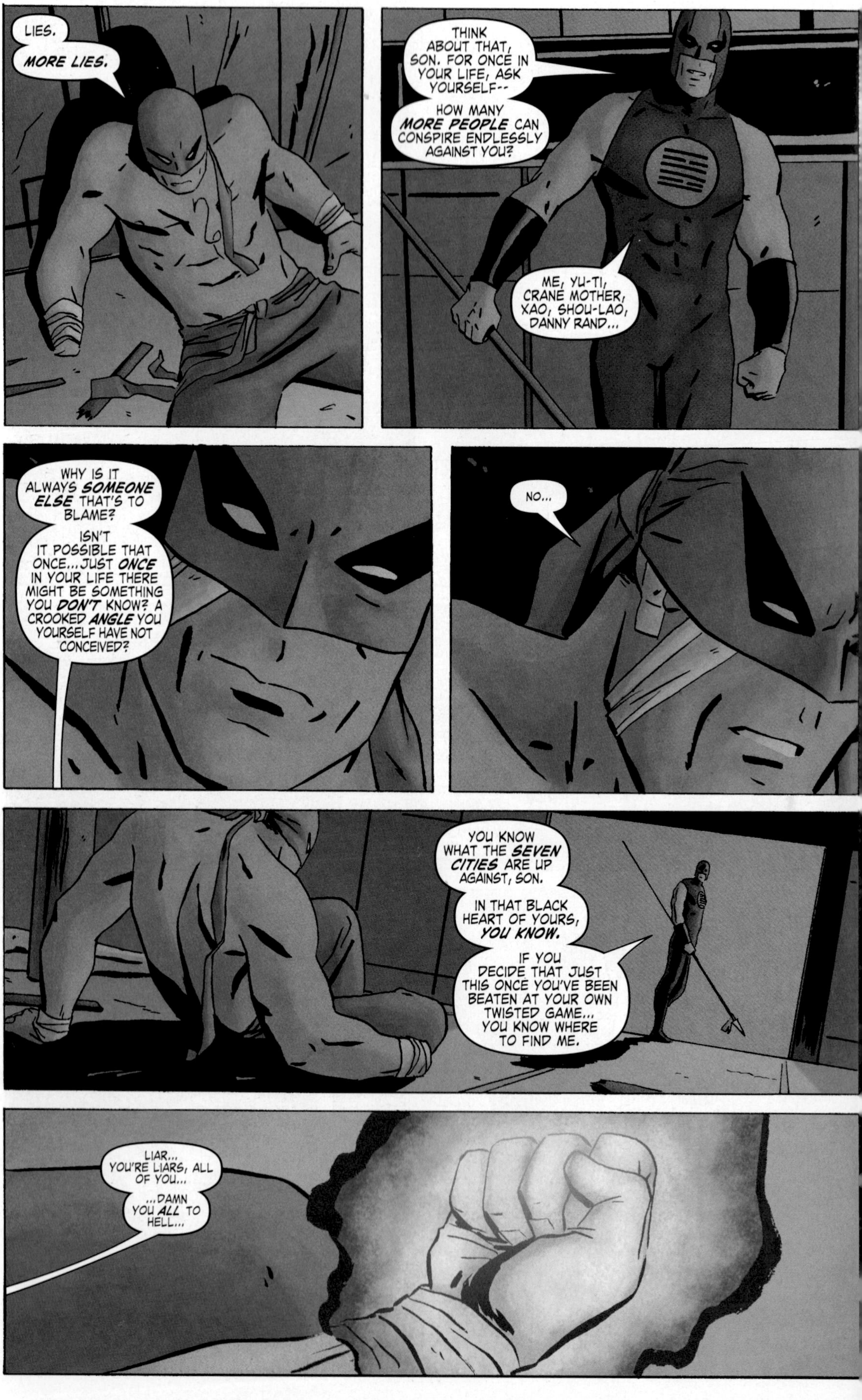
LIES.
MORE LIES.
THINK ABOUT THAT, SON. FOR ONCE IN YOUR LIFE, ASK YOURSELF--
HOW MANY MORE PEOPLE CAN CONSPIRE ENDLESSLY AGAINST YOU?
ME, YU-TI, CRANE MOTHER, XAO, SHOU-LAO, DANNY RAND...
WHY IS IT ALWAYS SOMEONE ELSE THAT'S TO BLAME?
ISN'T IT POSSIBLE THAT ONCE...JUST ONCE IN YOUR LIFE THERE MIGHT BE SOMETHING YOU DON'T KNOW? A CROOKED ANGLE YOU YOURSELF HAVE NOT CONCEIVED?
NO...
YOU KNOW WHAT THE SEVEN CITIES ARE UP AGAINST, SON.
IN THAT BLACK HEART OF YOURS, YOU KNOW.
IF YOU DECIDE THAT JUST THIS ONCE YOU'VE BEEN BEATEN AT YOUR OWN TWISTED GAME... YOU KNOW WHERE TO FIND ME.
LIAR... YOU'RE LIARS, ALL OF YOU...
...DAMN YOU ALL TO HELL...

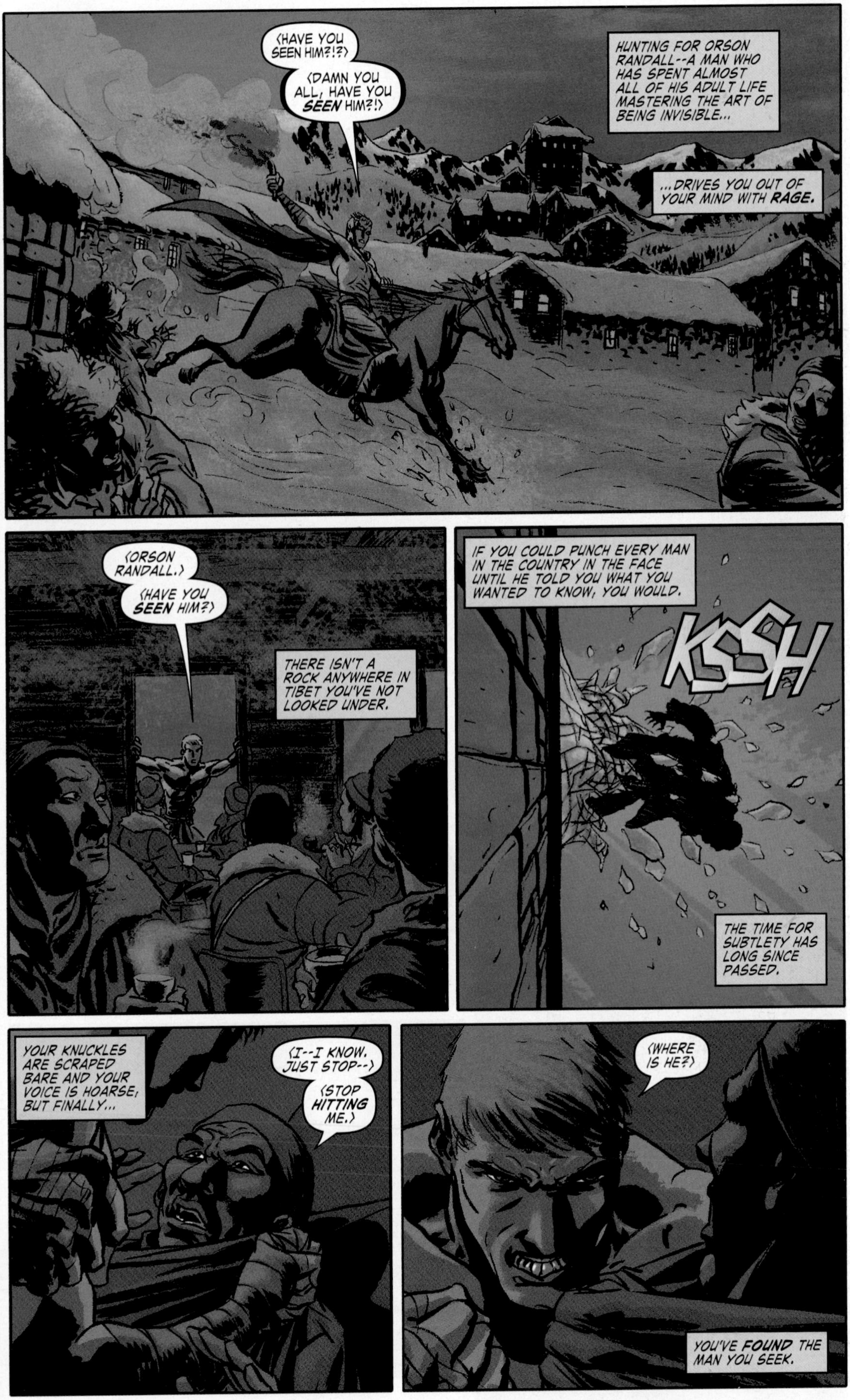
⟨HAVE YOU SEEN HIM?!?⟩
⟨DAMN YOU ALL, HAVE YOU SEEN HIM?!⟩
HUNTING FOR ORSON RANDALL--A MAN WHO HAS SPENT ALMOST ALL OF HIS ADULT LIFE MASTERING THE ART OF BEING INVISIBLE...
...DRIVES YOU OUT OF YOUR MIND WITH RAGE.
⟨ORSON RANDALL.⟩
⟨HAVE YOU SEEN HIM?⟩
THERE ISN'T A ROCK ANYWHERE IN TIBET YOU'VE NOT LOOKED UNDER.
IF YOU COULD PUNCH EVERY MAN IN THE COUNTRY IN THE FACE UNTIL HE TOLD YOU WHAT YOU WANTED TO KNOW, YOU WOULD.
KSSH
THE TIME FOR SUBTLETY HAS LONG SINCE PASSED.
YOUR KNUCKLES ARE SCRAPED BARE AND YOUR VOICE IS HOARSE, BUT FINALLY...
⟨I--I KNOW. JUST STOP--⟩
⟨STOP HITTING ME.⟩
⟨WHERE IS HE?⟩
YOU'VE FOUND THE MAN YOU SEEK.

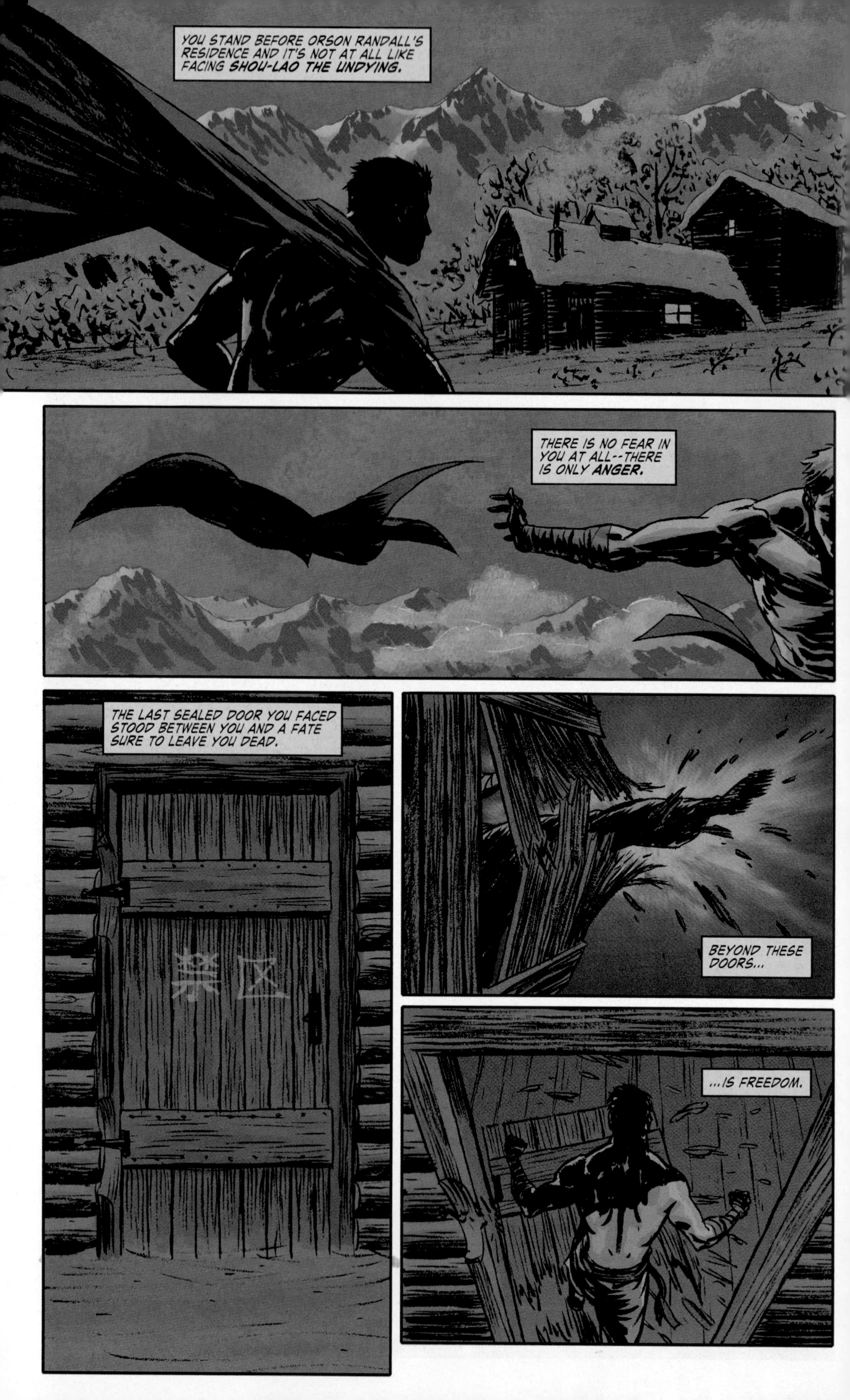
YOU STAND BEFORE ORSON RANDALL'S RESIDENCE AND IT'S NOT AT ALL LIKE FACING **SHOU-LAO THE UNDYING.**
THERE IS NO FEAR IN YOU AT ALL--THERE IS ONLY **ANGER.**
THE LAST SEALED DOOR YOU FACED STOOD BETWEEN YOU AND A FATE SURE TO LEAVE YOU DEAD.
禁区
BEYOND THESE DOORS...
...IS FREEDOM.

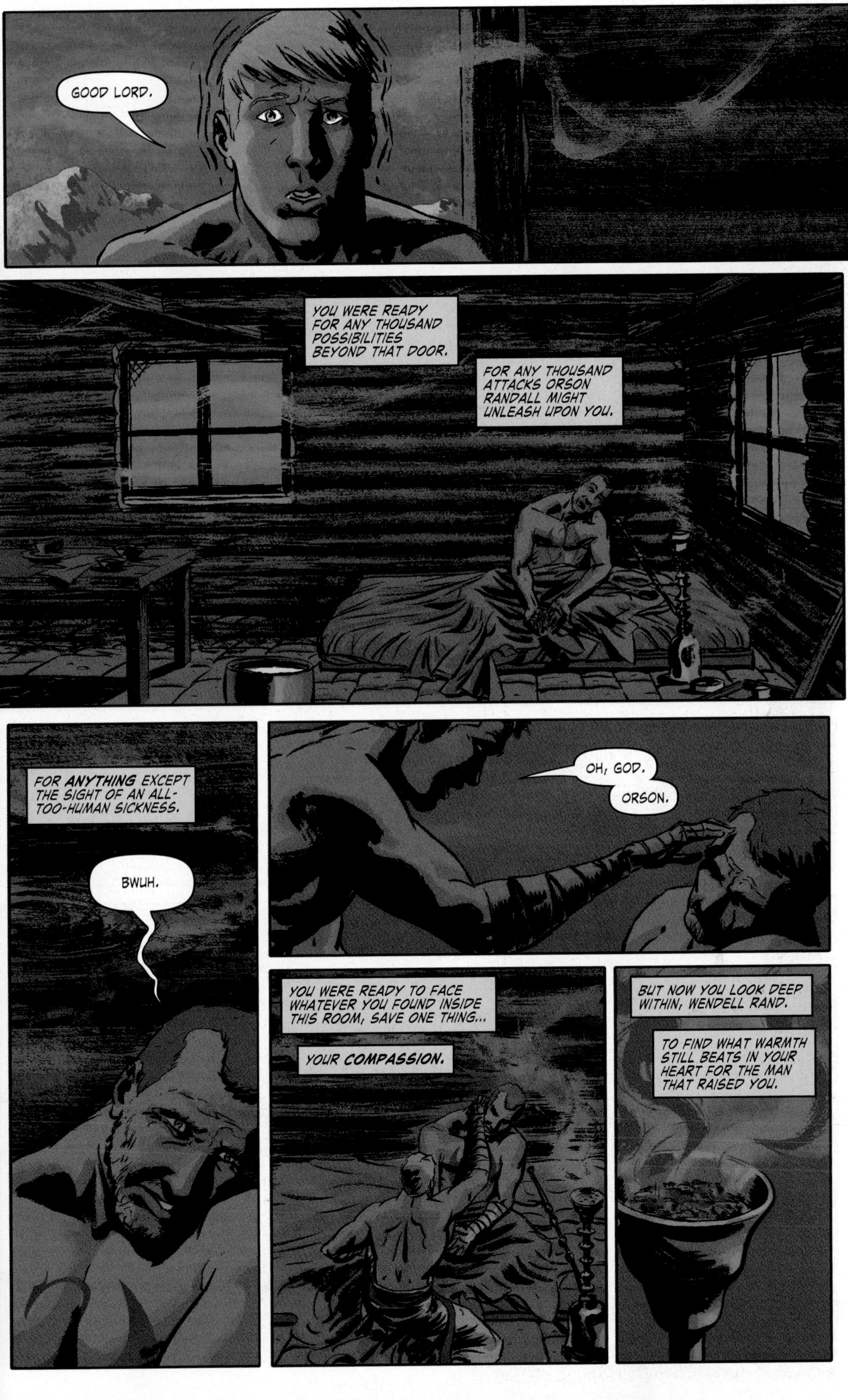
GOOD LORD.
YOU WERE READY FOR ANY THOUSAND POSSIBILITIES BEYOND THAT DOOR.
FOR ANY THOUSAND ATTACKS ORSON RANDALL MIGHT UNLEASH UPON YOU.
FOR **ANYTHING** EXCEPT THE SIGHT OF AN ALL-TOO-HUMAN SICKNESS.
BWUH.
OH, GOD.
ORSON.
YOU WERE READY TO FACE WHATEVER YOU FOUND INSIDE THIS ROOM, SAVE ONE THING...
YOUR **COMPASSION.**
BUT NOW YOU LOOK DEEP WITHIN, WENDELL RAND.
TO FIND WHAT WARMTH STILL BEATS IN YOUR HEART FOR THE MAN THAT RAISED YOU.

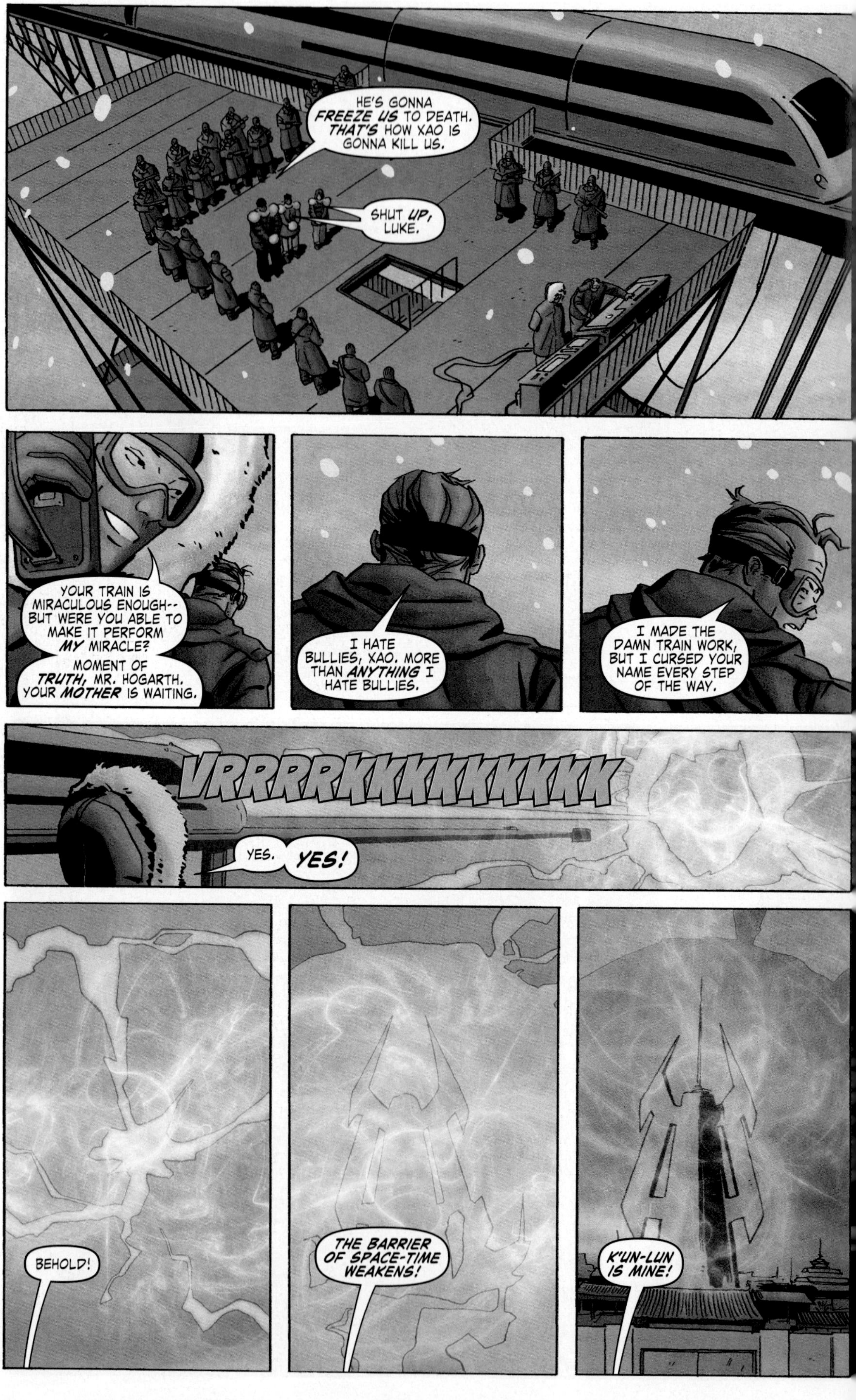
HE'S GONNA FREEZE US TO DEATH. THAT'S HOW XAO IS GONNA KILL US.
SHUT UP, LUKE.
YOUR TRAIN IS MIRACULOUS ENOUGH--BUT WERE YOU ABLE TO MAKE IT PERFORM MY MIRACLE?
MOMENT OF TRUTH, MR. HOGARTH. YOUR MOTHER IS WAITING.
I HATE BULLIES, XAO. MORE THAN ANYTHING I HATE BULLIES.
I MADE THE DAMN TRAIN WORK, BUT I CURSED YOUR NAME EVERY STEP OF THE WAY.
VRRRRKKKKKKKKKK
YES.
YES!
BEHOLD!
THE BARRIER OF SPACE-TIME WEAKENS!
K'UN-LUN IS MINE!

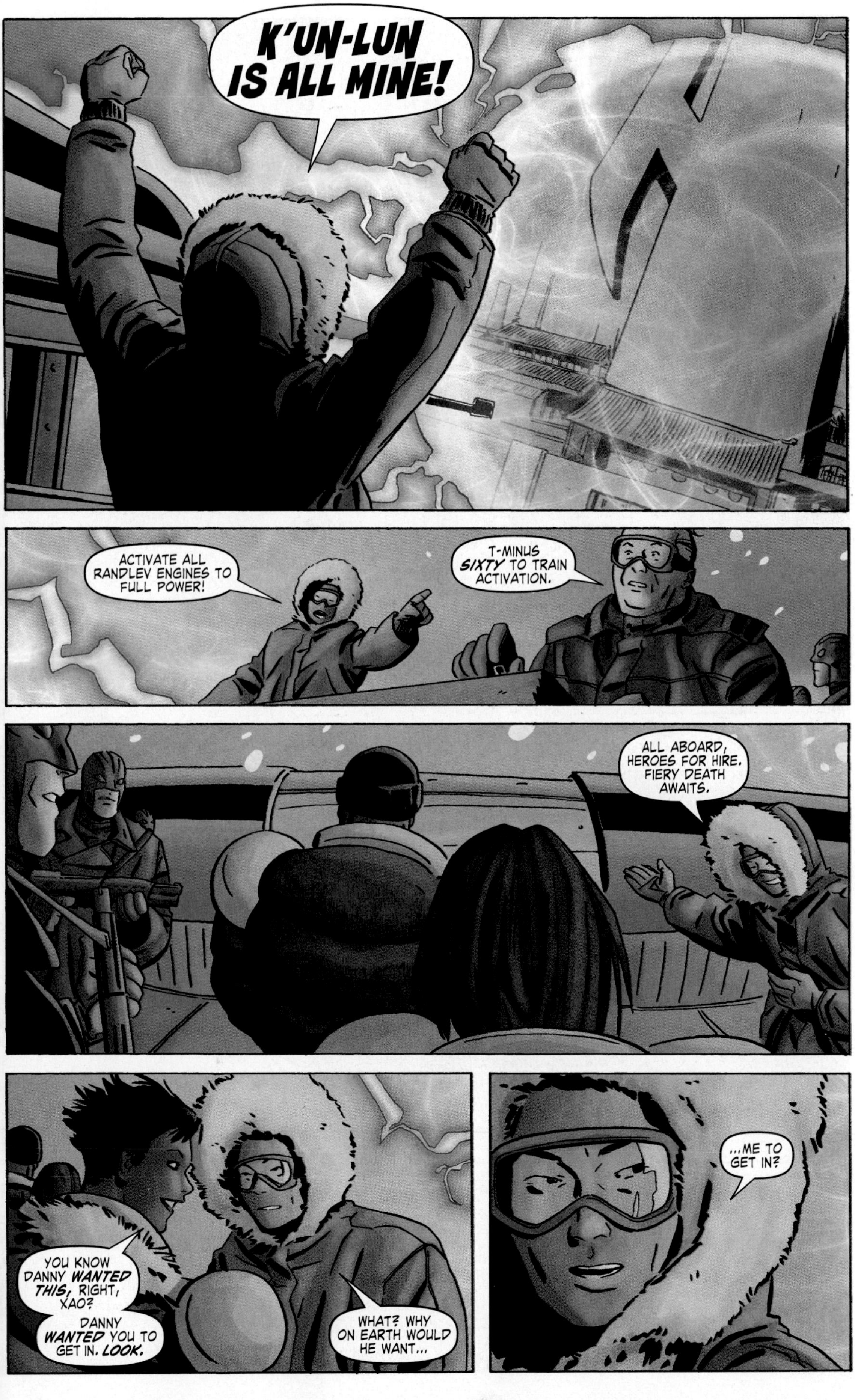
K'UN-LUN IS ALL MINE!
ACTIVATE ALL RANDLEV ENGINES TO FULL POWER!
T-MINUS SIXTY TO TRAIN ACTIVATION.
ALL ABOARD, HEROES FOR HIRE. FIERY DEATH AWAITS.
YOU KNOW DANNY WANTED THIS, RIGHT, XAO?
DANNY WANTED YOU TO GET IN. LOOK.
WHAT? WHY ON EARTH WOULD HE WANT...
...ME TO GET IN?

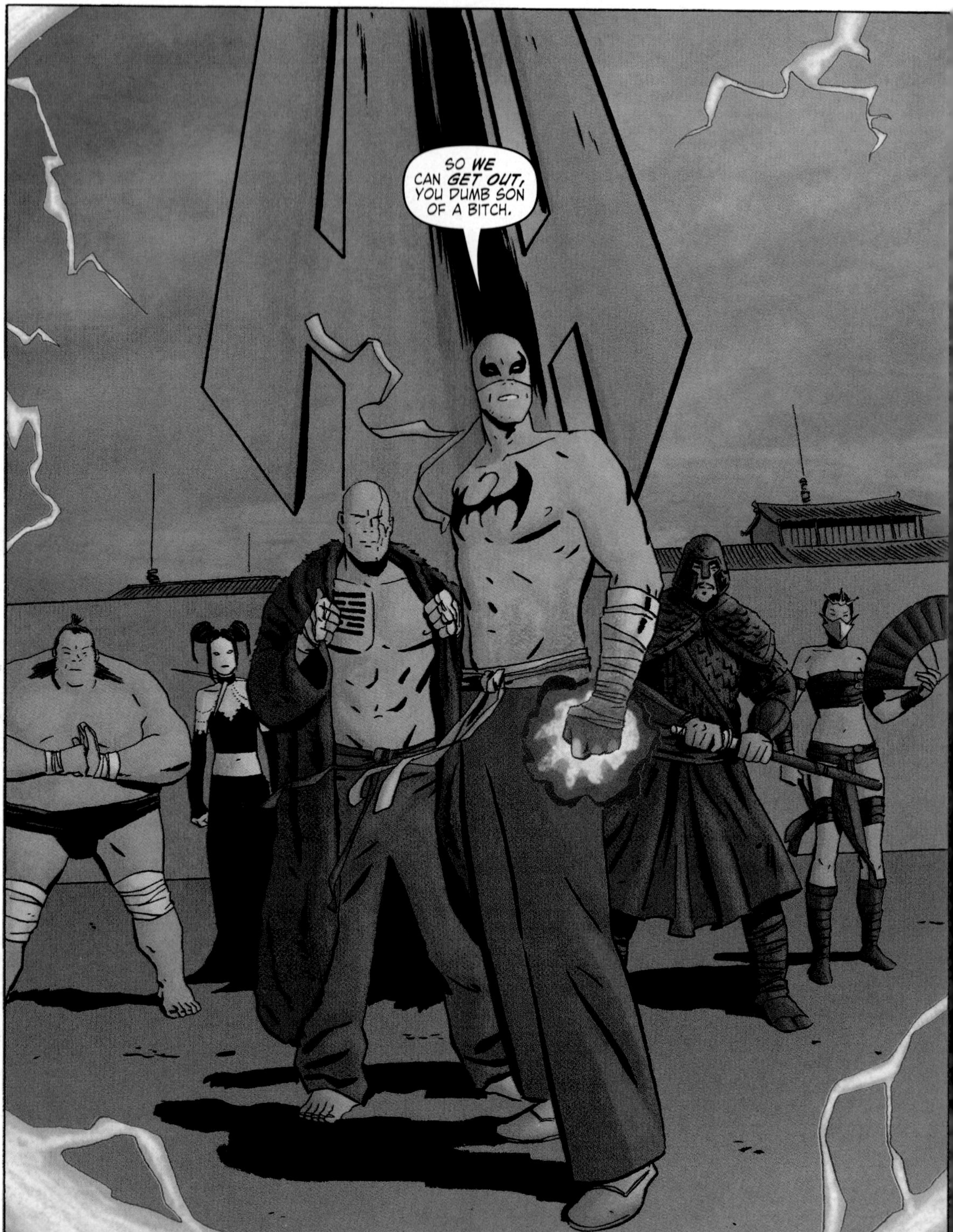
SO WE CAN GET OUT, YOU DUMB SON OF A BITCH.
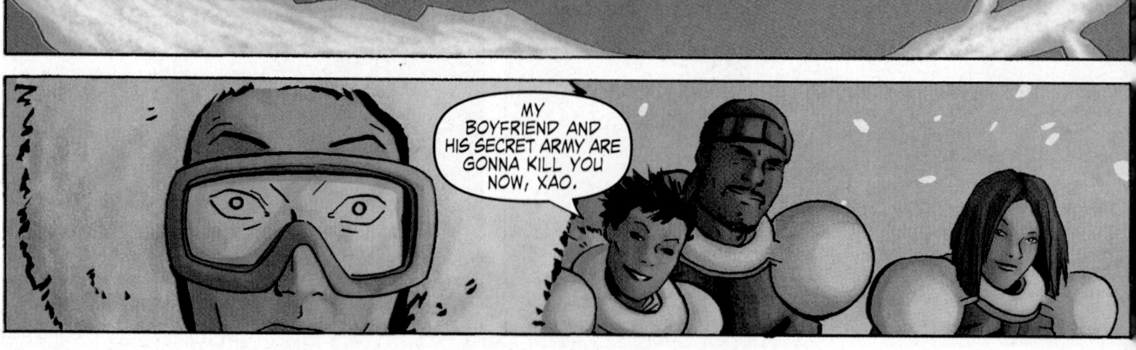
MY BOYFRIEND AND HIS SECRET ARMY ARE GONNA KILL YOU NOW, XAO.

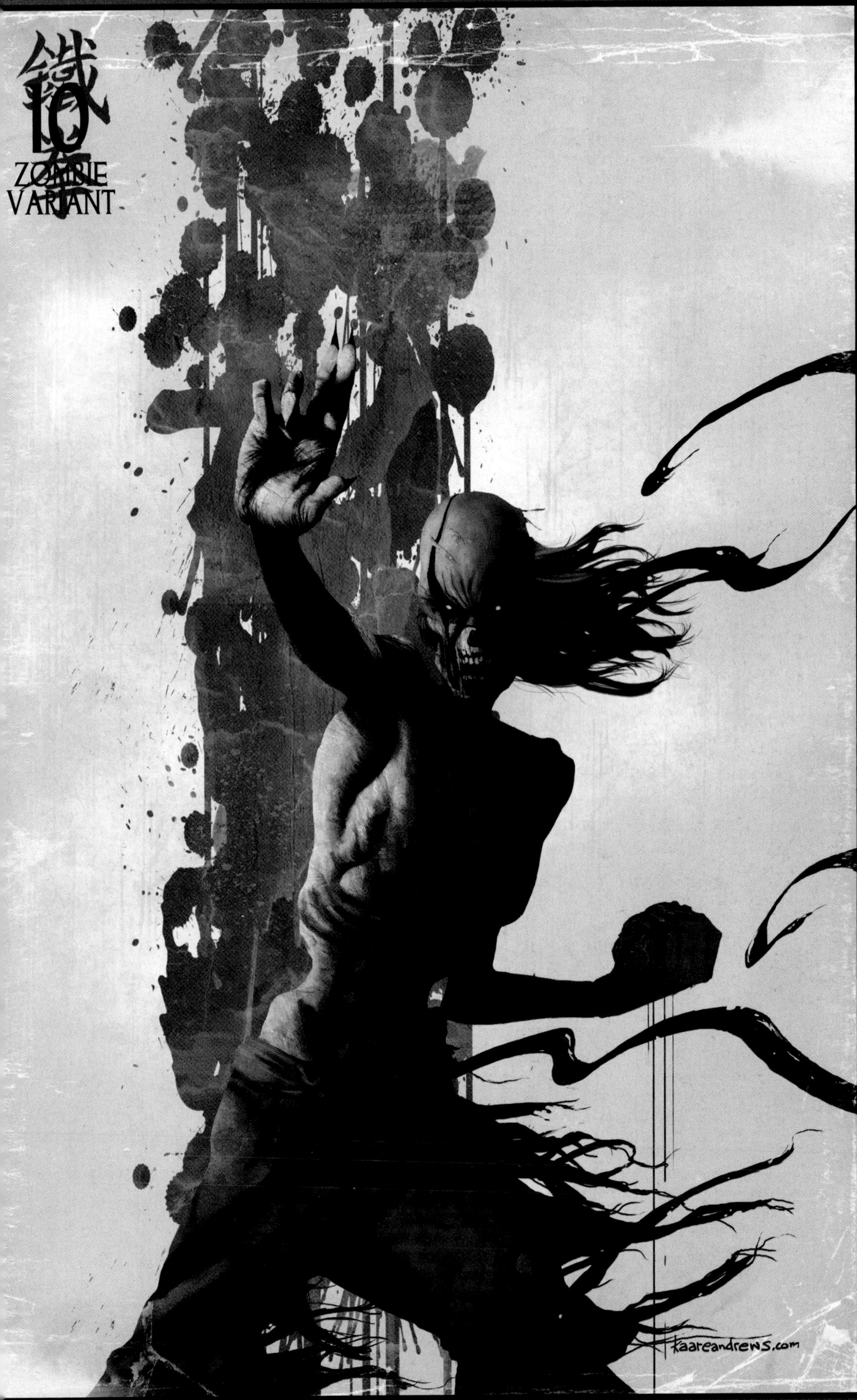

鐵拳
10
ZOMBIE
VARIANT
kaareandrews.com

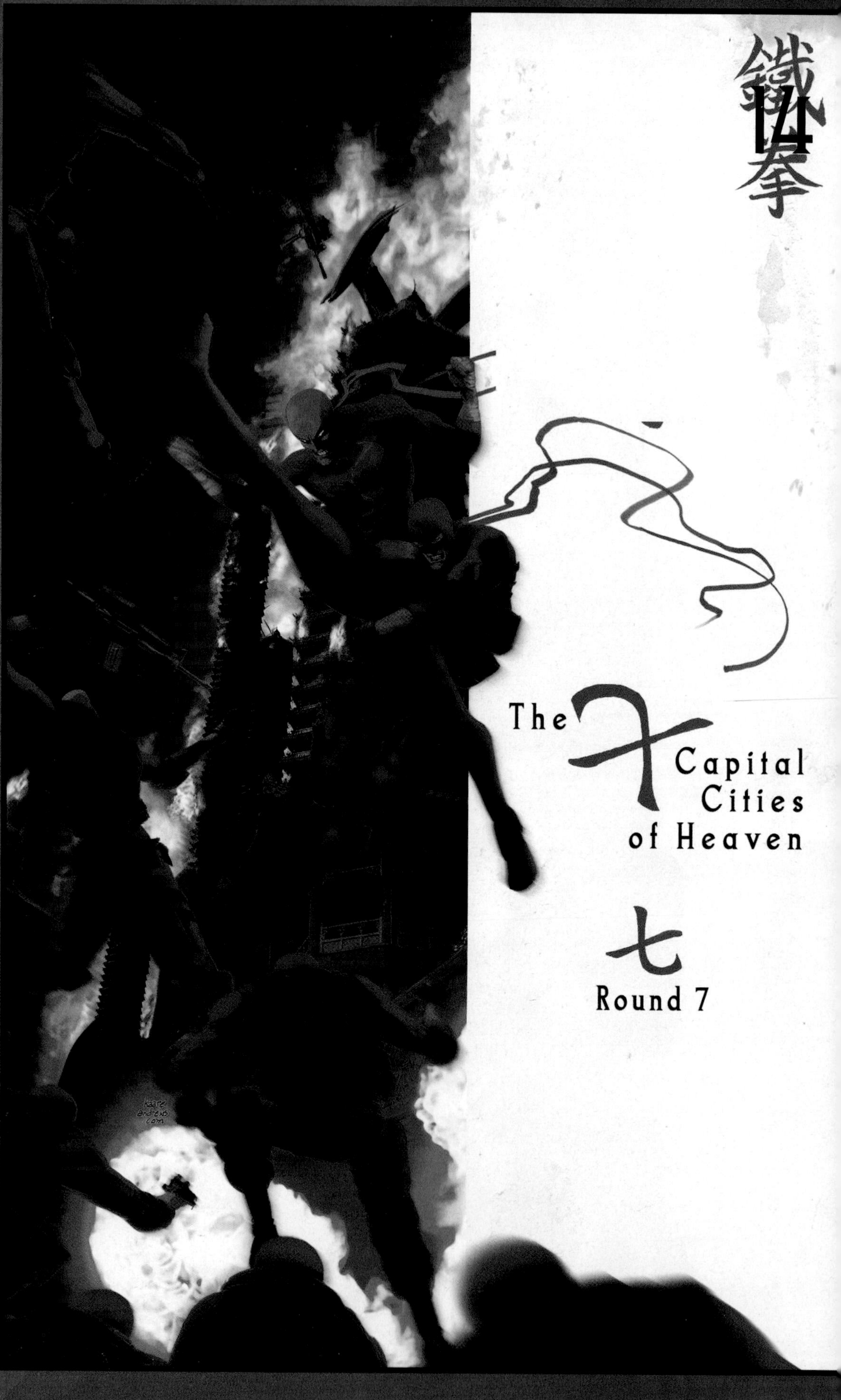
鐵拳
14
The 7 Capital Cities of Heaven
七
Round 7

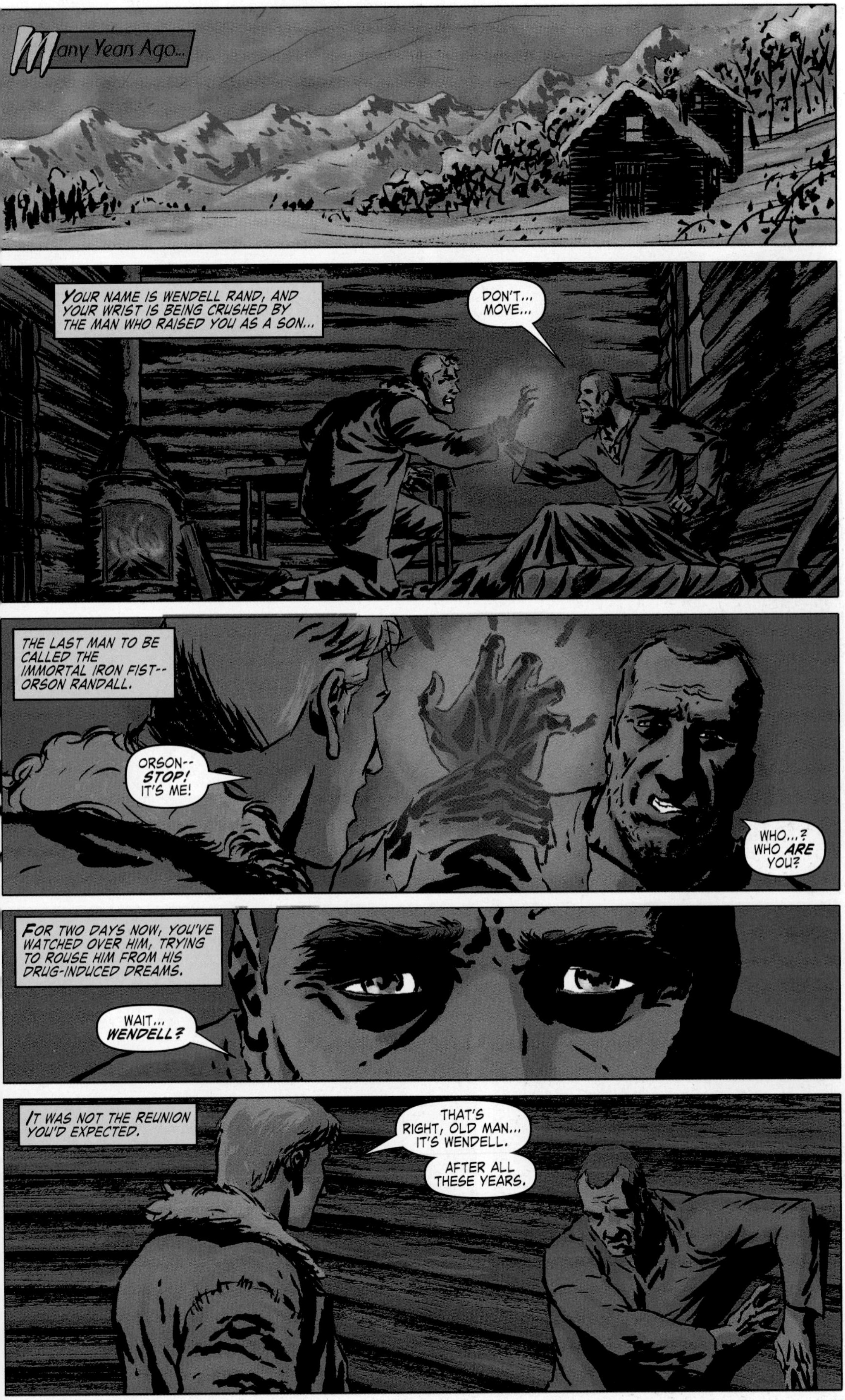
Many Years Ago...
YOUR NAME IS WENDELL RAND, AND YOUR WRIST IS BEING CRUSHED BY THE MAN WHO RAISED YOU AS A SON...
DON'T... MOVE...
THE LAST MAN TO BE CALLED THE IMMORTAL IRON FIST-- ORSON RANDALL.
ORSON-- STOP! IT'S ME!
WHO...? WHO ARE YOU?
FOR TWO DAYS NOW, YOU'VE WATCHED OVER HIM, TRYING TO ROUSE HIM FROM HIS DRUG-INDUCED DREAMS.
WAIT... WENDELL?
IT WAS NOT THE REUNION YOU'D EXPECTED.
THAT'S RIGHT, OLD MAN... IT'S WENDELL.
AFTER ALL THESE YEARS.

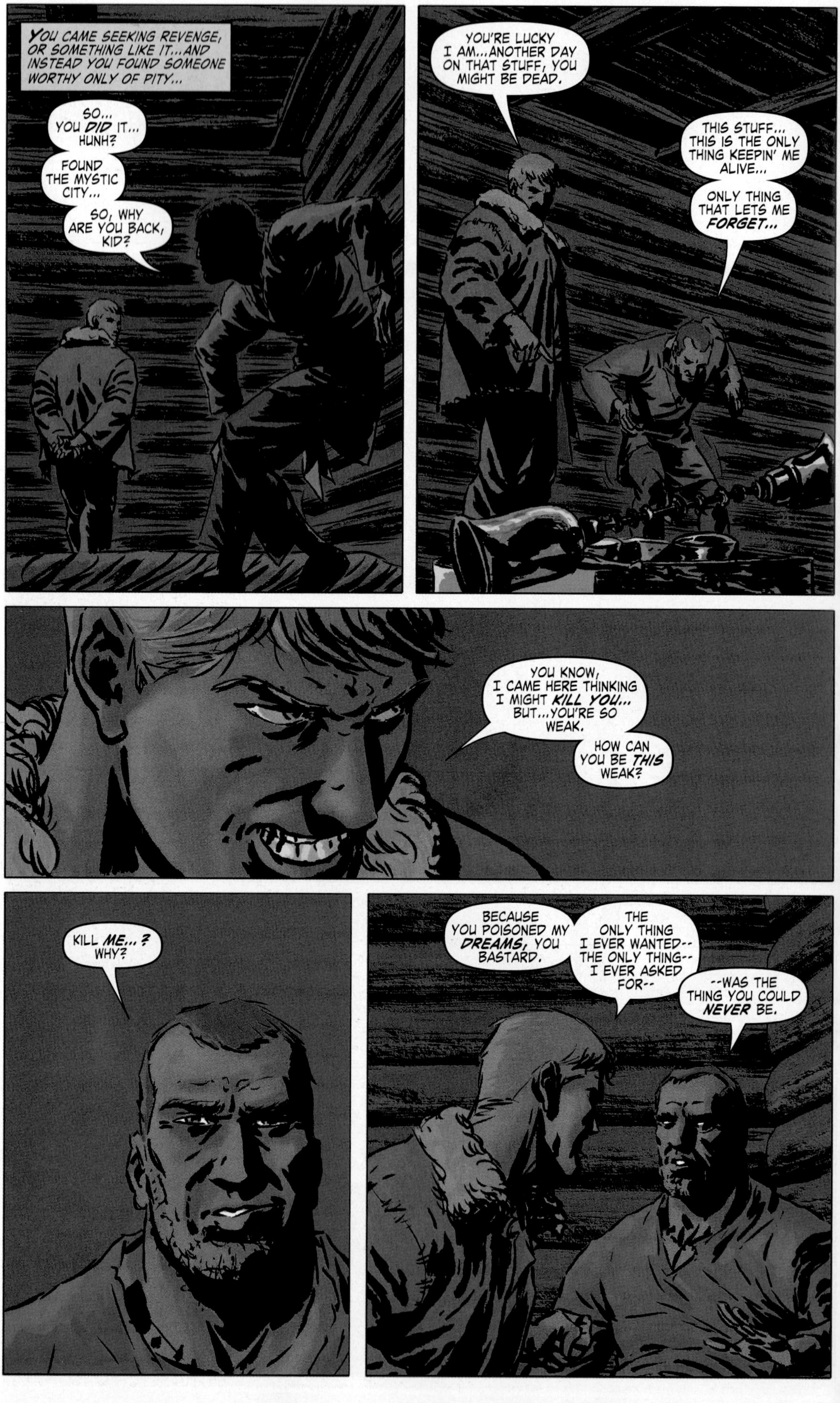
YOU CAME SEEKING REVENGE, OR SOMETHING LIKE IT...AND INSTEAD YOU FOUND SOMEONE WORTHY ONLY OF PITY...
SO... YOU DID IT... HUNH?
FOUND THE MYSTIC CITY...
SO, WHY ARE YOU BACK, KID?
YOU'RE LUCKY I AM...ANOTHER DAY ON THAT STUFF, YOU MIGHT BE DEAD.
THIS STUFF... THIS IS THE ONLY THING KEEPIN' ME ALIVE...
ONLY THING THAT LETS ME FORGET...
YOU KNOW, I CAME HERE THINKING I MIGHT KILL YOU... BUT...YOU'RE SO WEAK.
HOW CAN YOU BE THIS WEAK?
KILL ME...? WHY?
BECAUSE YOU POISONED MY DREAMS, YOU BASTARD.
THE ONLY THING I EVER WANTED-- THE ONLY THING-- I EVER ASKED FOR--
--WAS THE THING YOU COULD NEVER BE.

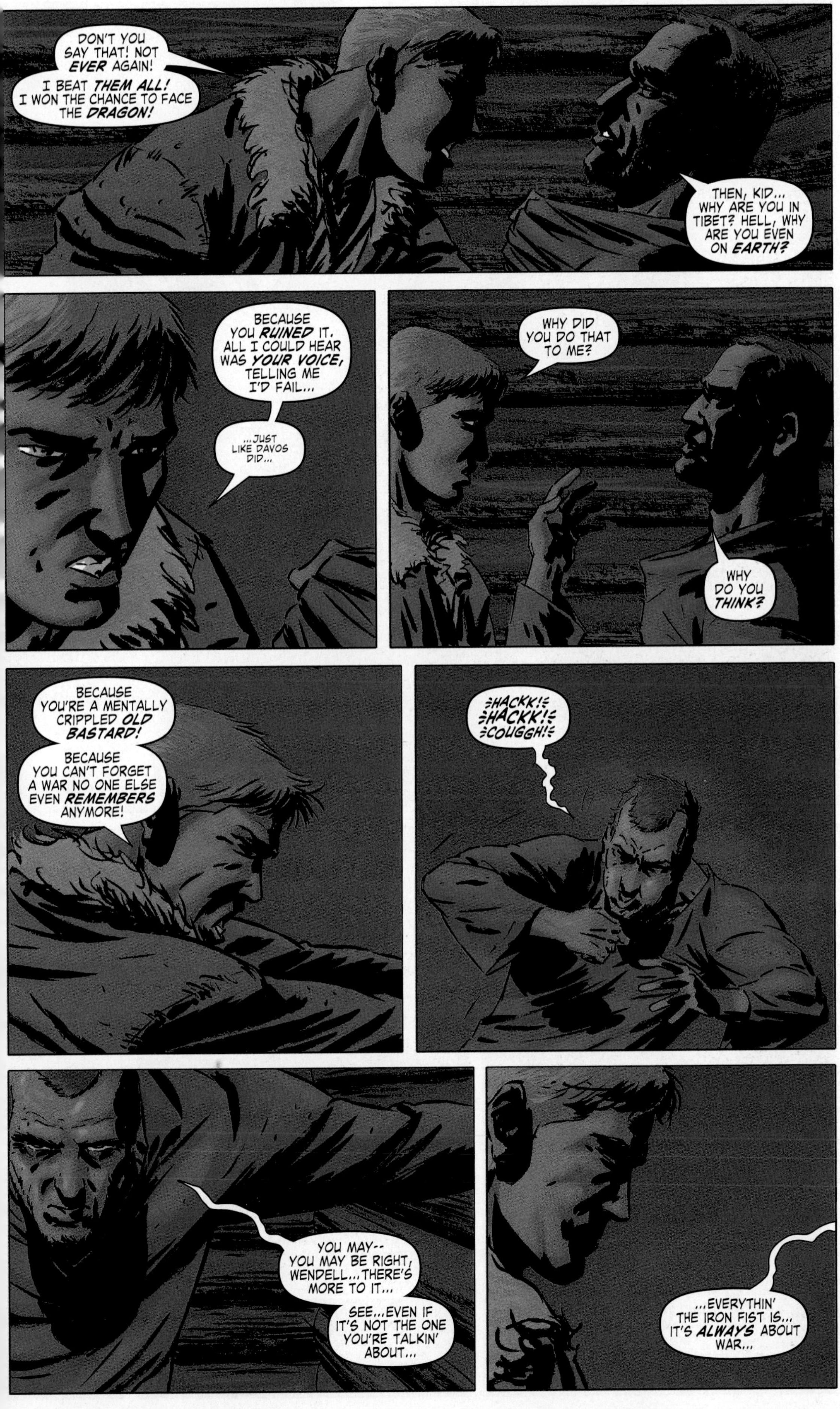
DON'T YOU SAY THAT! NOT EVER AGAIN!
I BEAT THEM ALL! I WON THE CHANCE TO FACE THE DRAGON!
THEN, KID... WHY ARE YOU IN TIBET? HELL, WHY ARE YOU EVEN ON EARTH?
BECAUSE YOU RUINED IT. ALL I COULD HEAR WAS YOUR VOICE, TELLING ME I'D FAIL...
...JUST LIKE DAVOS DID...
WHY DID YOU DO THAT TO ME?
WHY DO YOU THINK?
BECAUSE YOU'RE A MENTALLY CRIPPLED OLD BASTARD!
BECAUSE YOU CAN'T FORGET A WAR NO ONE ELSE EVEN REMEMBERS ANYMORE!
HACKK! HACKK! COUGGH!
YOU MAY-- YOU MAY BE RIGHT, WENDELL...THERE'S MORE TO IT...
SEE...EVEN IF IT'S NOT THE ONE YOU'RE TALKIN' ABOUT...
...EVERYTHIN' THE IRON FIST IS... IT'S ALWAYS ABOUT WAR...

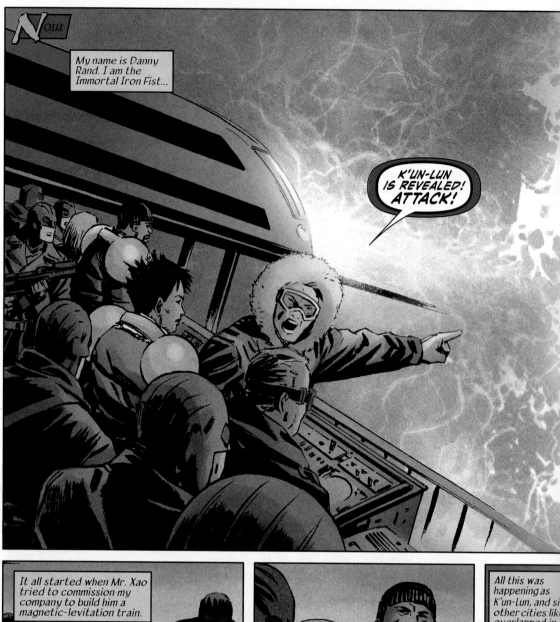

My name is Danny Rand. I am the Immortal Iron Fist...

K'UN-LUN IS REVEALED! ATTACK!

It all started when Mr. Xao tried to commission my company to build him a magnetic-levitation train.

PUT THE HOSTAGES IN! THE! TRAIN!

I said **no** because I didn't like him. I didn't know he wanted to destroy K'un-lun, but I suppose that level of **arrogance** shouldn't surprise me.

Xao kidnapped my right-hand man and his **mother** and forced him to build it **anyway.**

Then my best friends and my kind-of girlfriend (I guess) tried to save him, but they got captured, too.

All this was happening as K'un-Lun, and si other cities like overlapped in mystical dimen

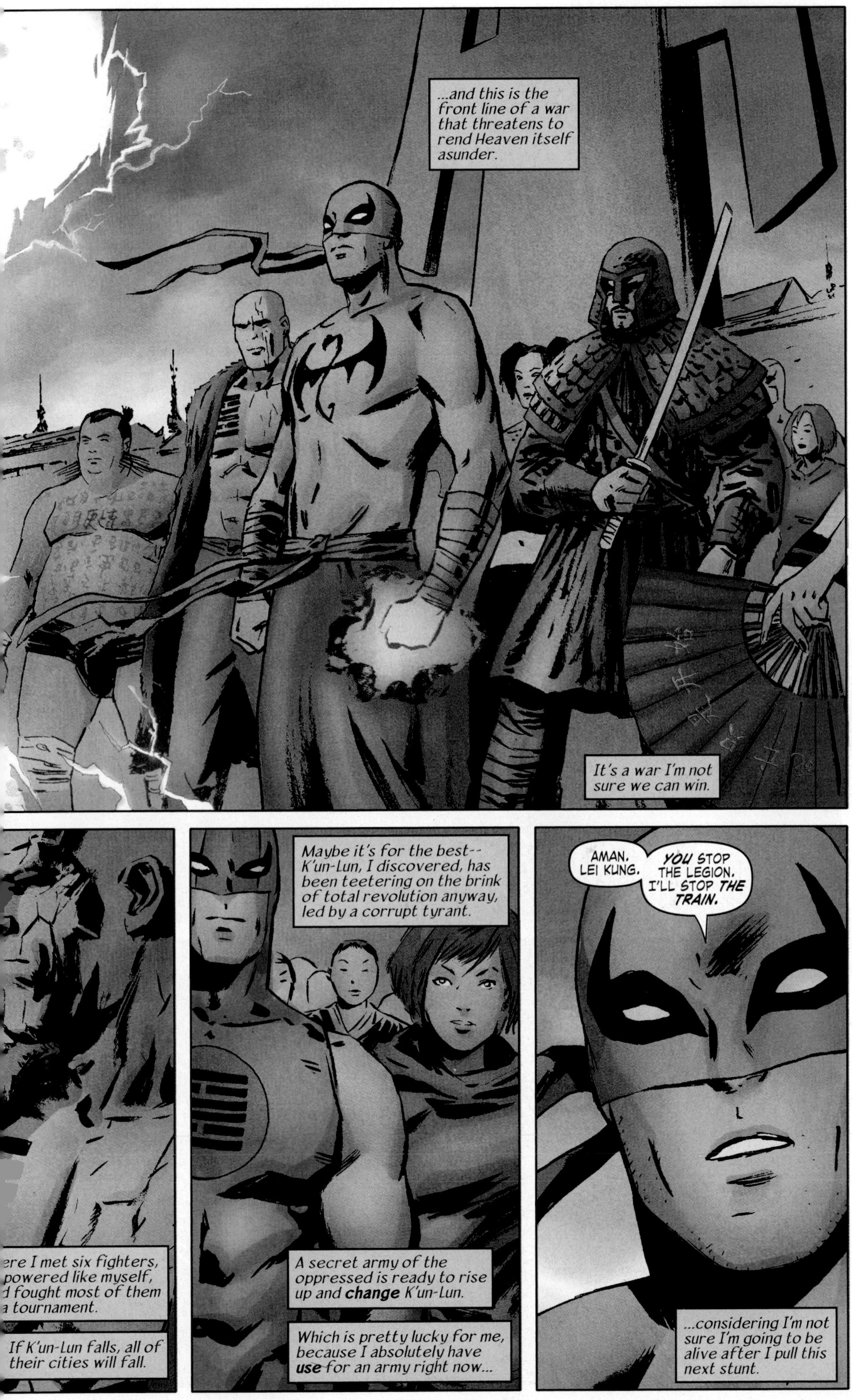
...and this is the front line of a war that threatens to rend Heaven itself asunder.
It's a war I'm not sure we can win.
ere I met six fighters, powered like myself, d fought most of them a tournament.
If K'un-Lun falls, all of their cities will fall.
Maybe it's for the best-- K'un-Lun, I discovered, has been teetering on the brink of total revolution anyway, led by a corrupt tyrant.
A secret army of the oppressed is ready to rise up and **change** K'un-Lun.
Which is pretty lucky for me, because I absolutely have **use** for an army right now...
AMAN. LEI KUNG.
YOU STOP THE LEGION. I'LL STOP **THE TRAIN.**
...considering I'm not sure I'm going to be alive after I pull this next stunt.

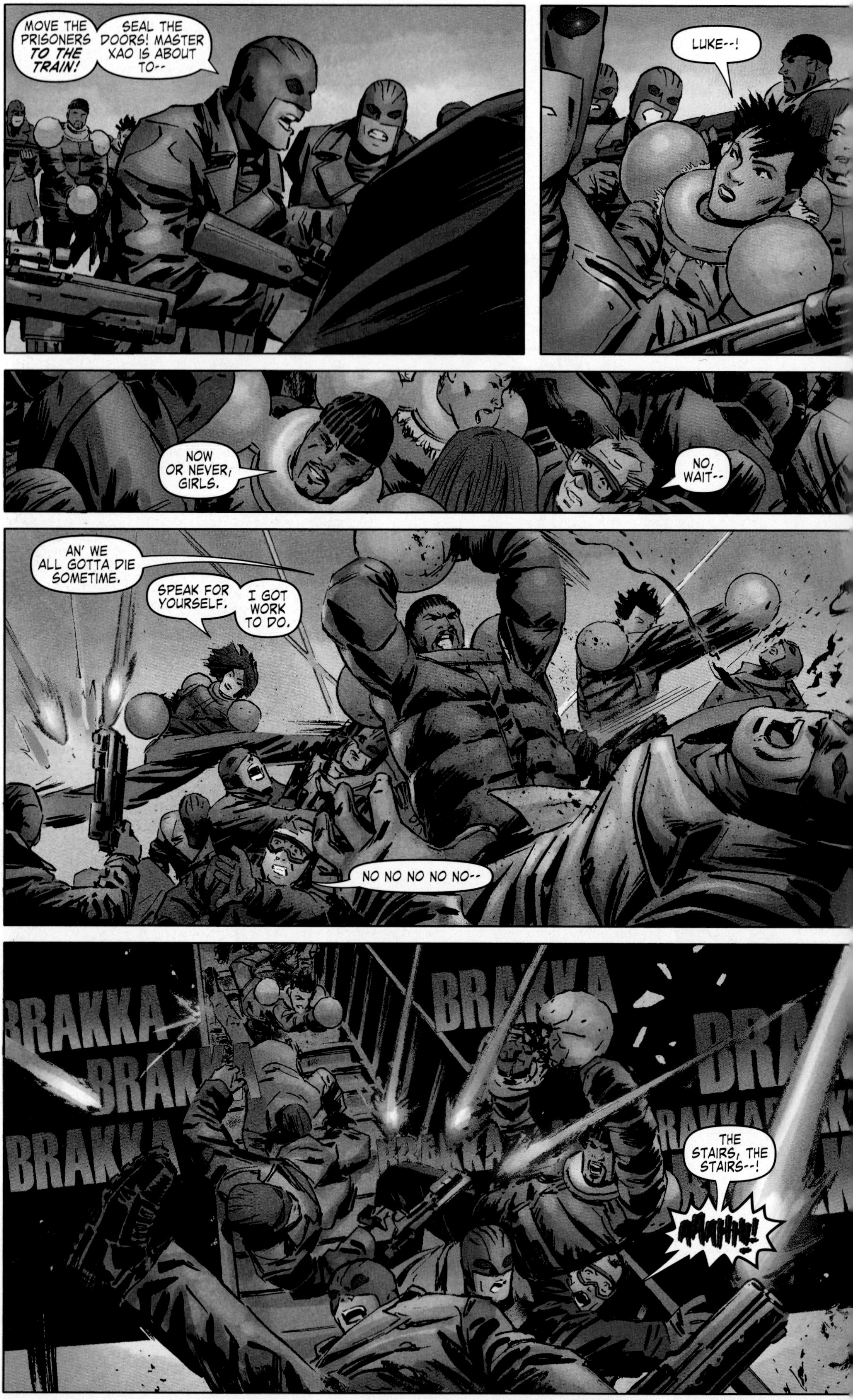
MOVE THE PRISONERS *TO THE TRAIN!*
SEAL THE DOORS! MASTER XAO IS ABOUT TO--
LUKE--!
NOW OR NEVER, GIRLS.
NO, WAIT--
AN' WE ALL GOTTA DIE SOMETIME.
SPEAK FOR YOURSELF.
I GOT WORK TO DO.
NO NO NO NO NO--
BRAKKA
BRAKKA
BRAKKA
BRAKKA
THE STAIRS, THE STAIRS--!

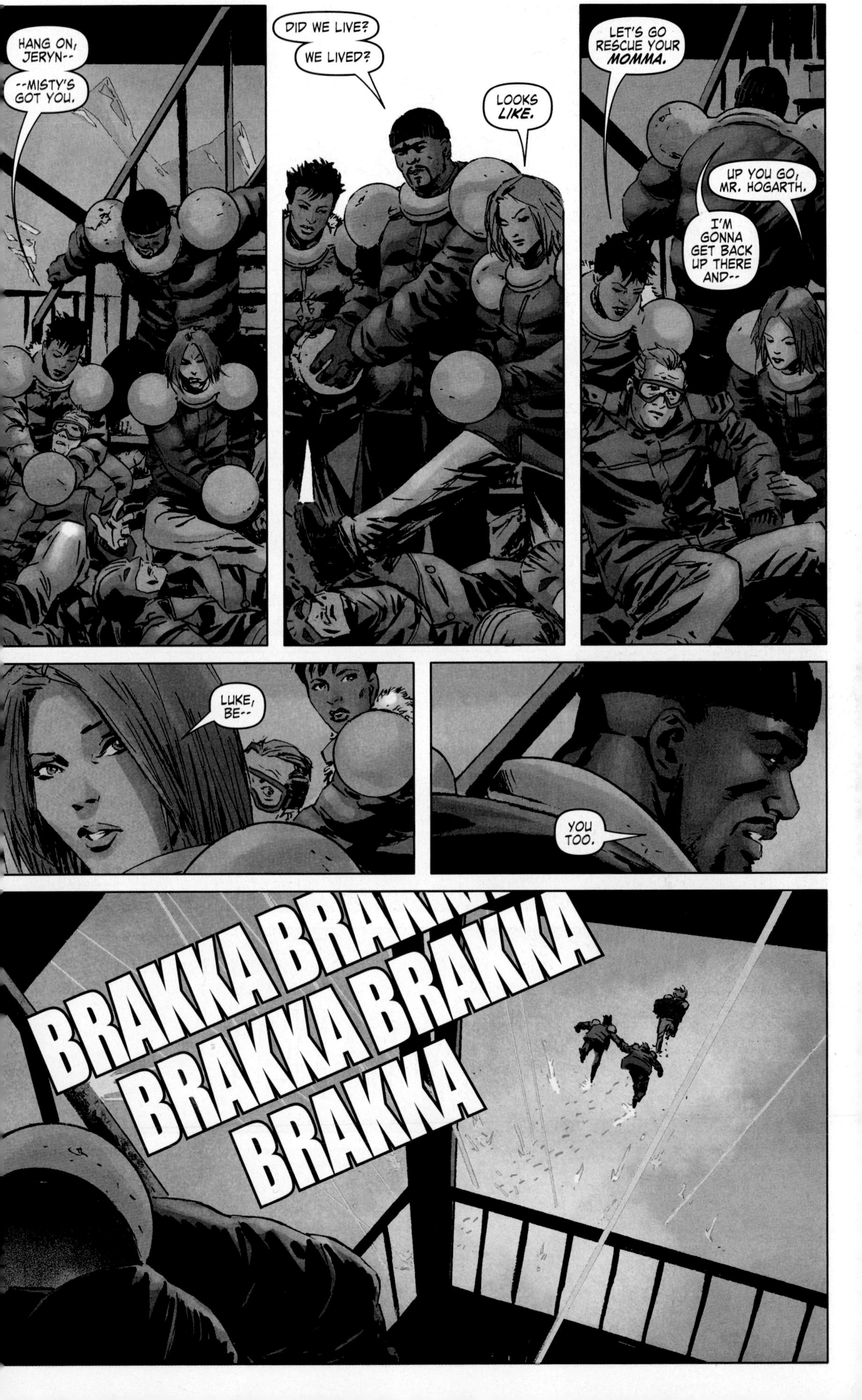
HANG ON, JERYN--
--MISTY'S GOT YOU.
DID WE LIVE?
WE LIVED?
LOOKS *LIKE.*
LET'S GO RESCUE YOUR *MOMMA.*
UP YOU GO, MR. HOGARTH.
I'M GONNA GET BACK UP THERE AND--
LUKE, BE--
YOU TOO.
BRAKKA BRAKKA BRAKKA BRAKKA BRAKKA

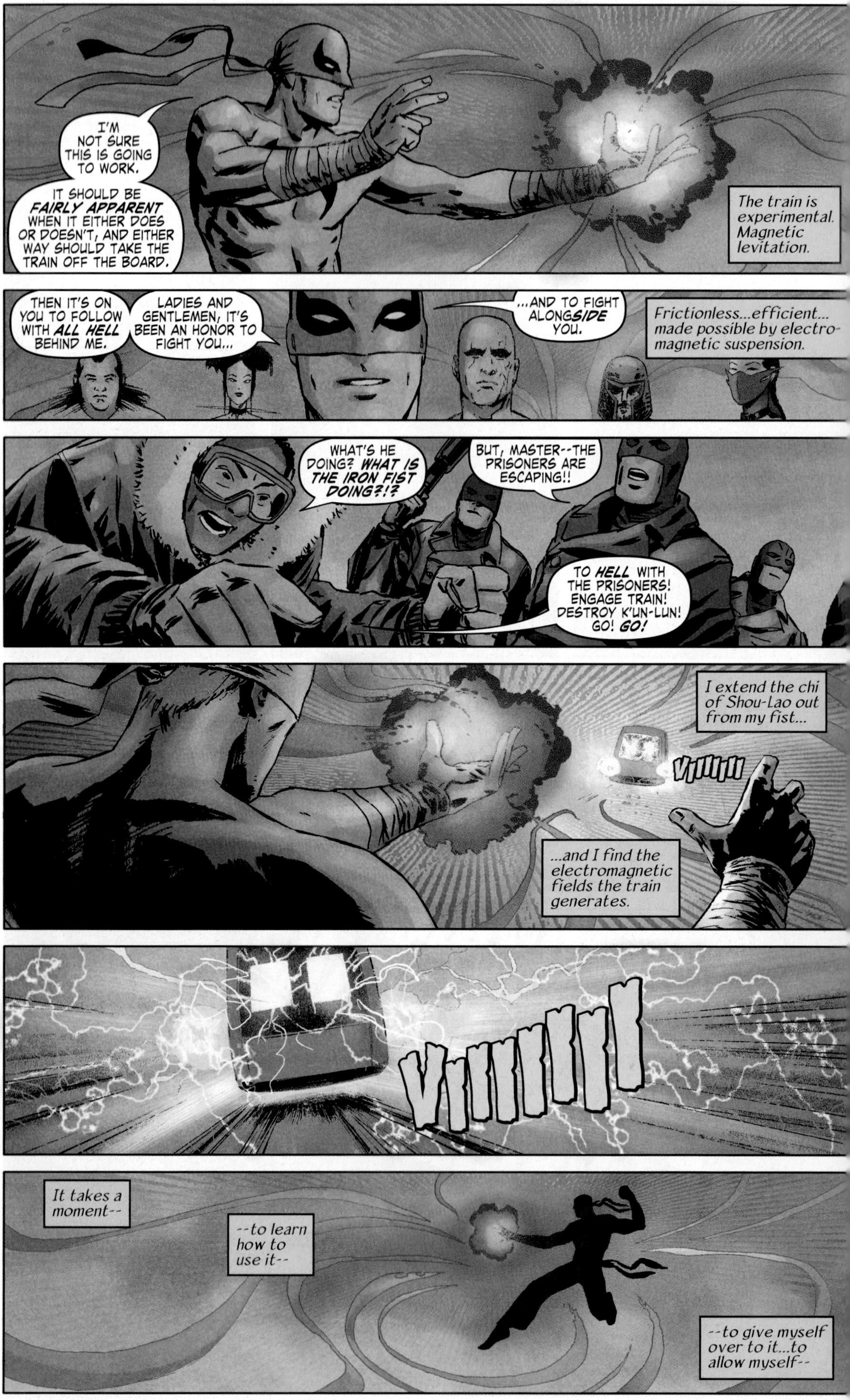
I'M NOT SURE THIS IS GOING TO WORK.
IT SHOULD BE **FAIRLY APPARENT** WHEN IT EITHER DOES OR DOESN'T, AND EITHER WAY SHOULD TAKE THE TRAIN OFF THE BOARD.
The train is experimental. Magnetic levitation.
THEN IT'S ON YOU TO FOLLOW WITH **ALL HELL** BEHIND ME.
LADIES AND GENTLEMEN, IT'S BEEN AN HONOR TO FIGHT YOU...
...AND TO FIGHT ALONG**SIDE** YOU.
Frictionless...efficient... made possible by electro-magnetic suspension.
WHAT'S HE DOING? **WHAT IS THE IRON FIST DOING?!?**
BUT, MASTER--THE PRISONERS ARE ESCAPING!!
TO **HELL** WITH THE PRISONERS! ENGAGE TRAIN! DESTROY K'UN-LUN! GO! **GO!**
I extend the chi of Shou-Lao out from my fist...
VRRRRRR
...and I find the electromagnetic fields the train generates.
VRRRRRRRR
It takes a moment--
--to learn how to use it--
--to give myself over to it...to allow myself--

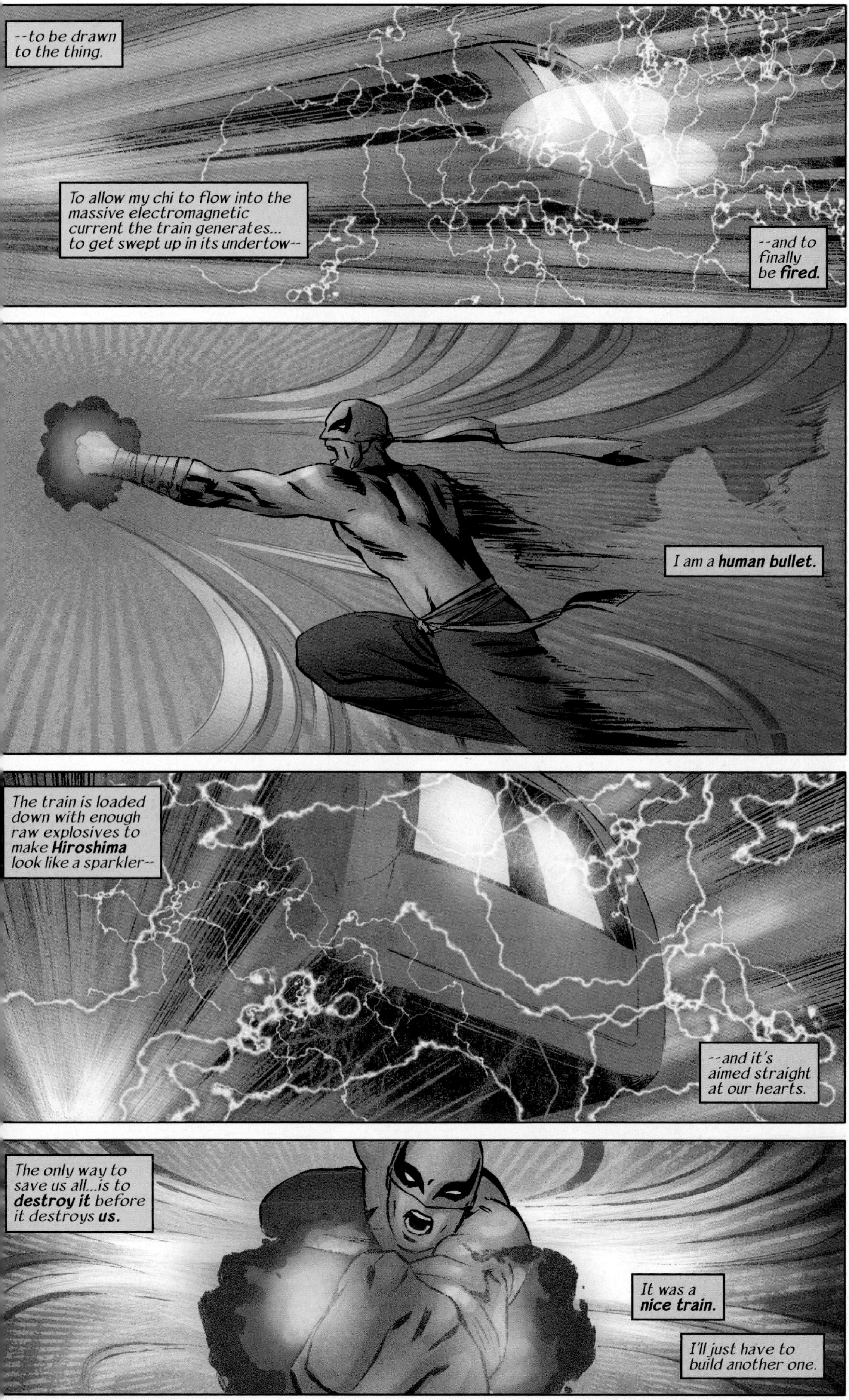
--to be drawn to the thing.
To allow my chi to flow into the massive electromagnetic current the train generates... to get swept up in its undertow--
--and to finally be **fired.**
I am a **human bullet.**
The train is loaded down with enough raw explosives to make **Hiroshima** look like a sparkler--
--and it's aimed straight at our hearts.
The only way to save us all...is to **destroy it** before it destroys **us.**
It was a **nice train.**
I'll just have to build another one.

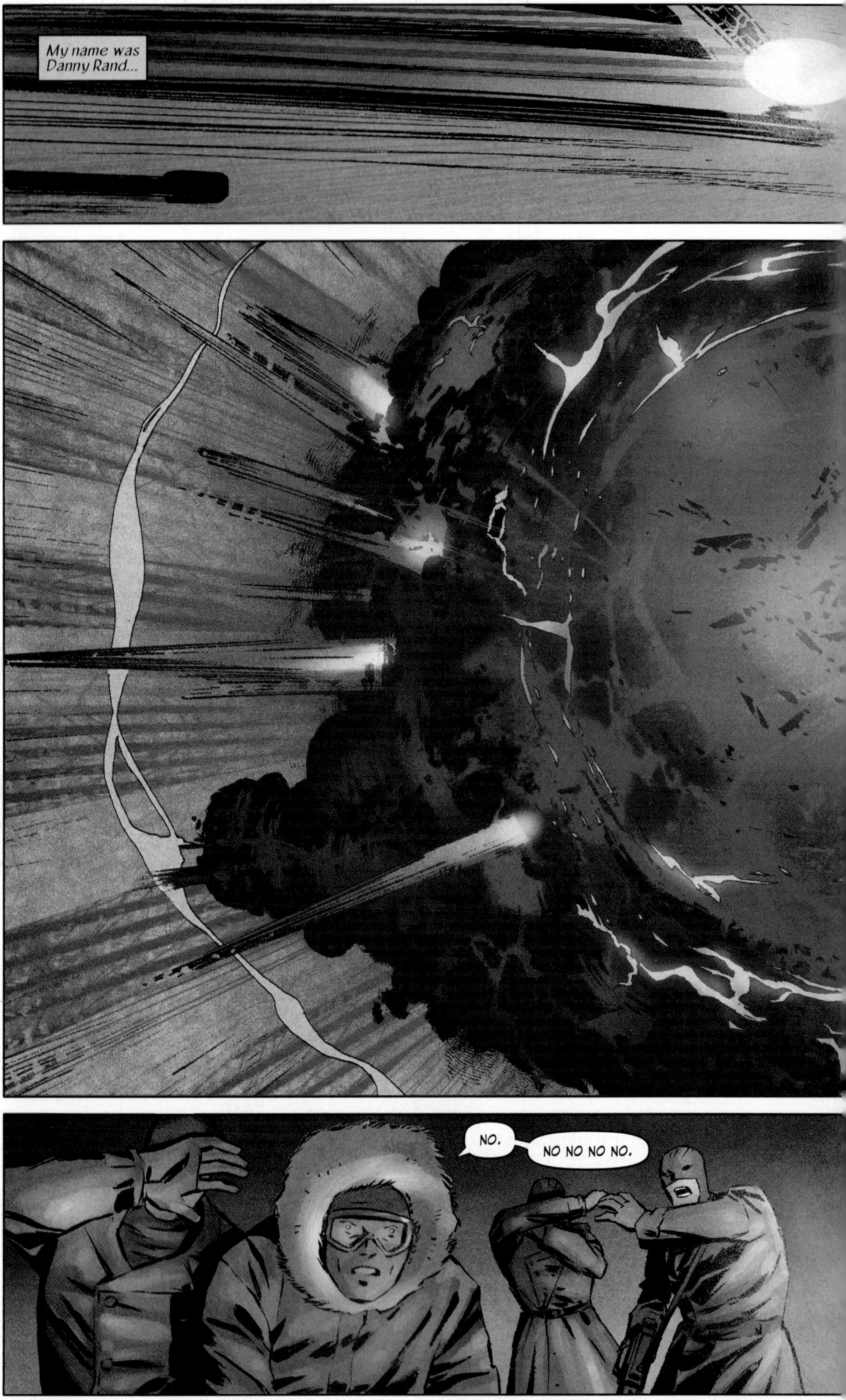
My name was Danny Rand...
NO.
NO NO NO NO.

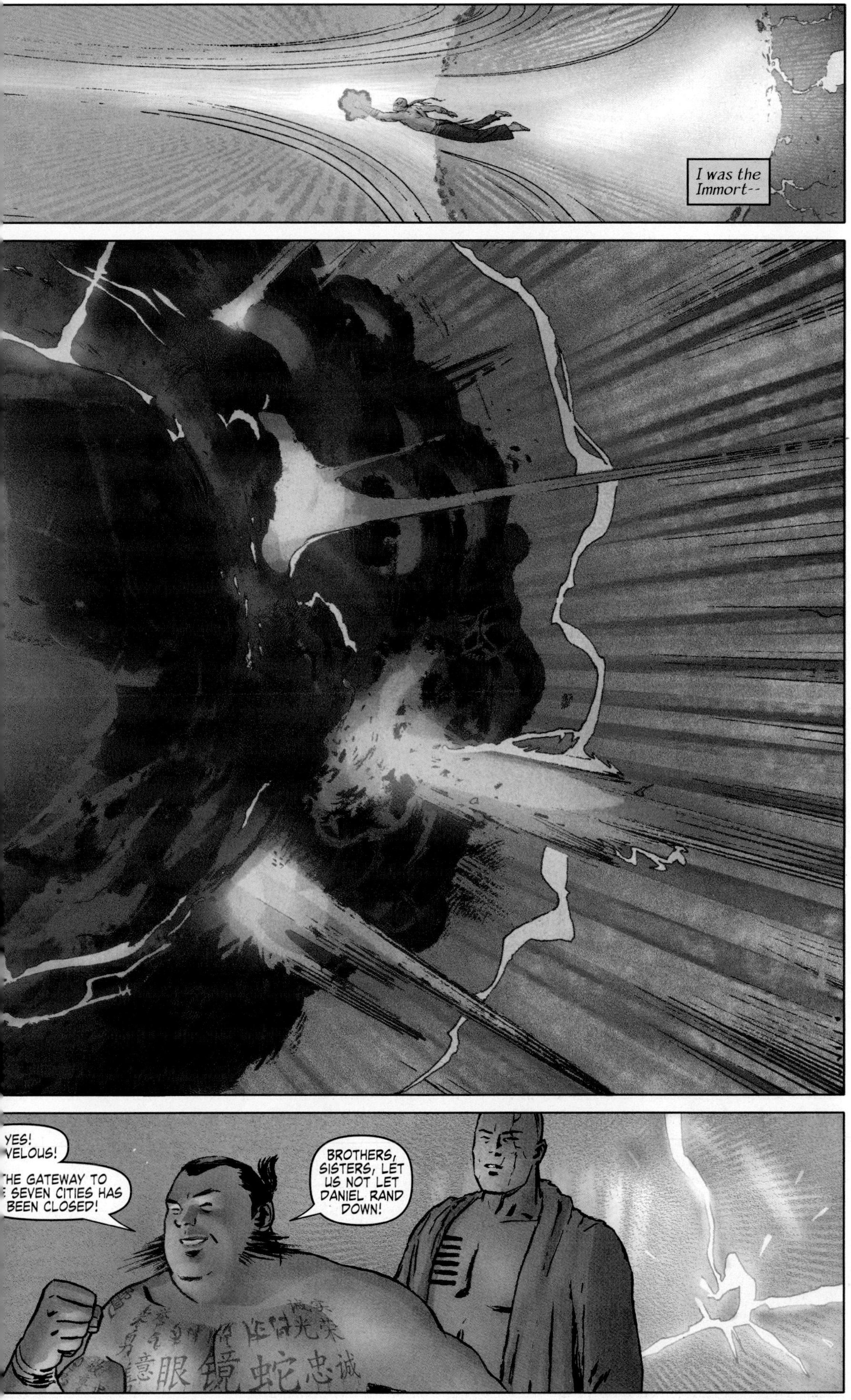
I was the Immort--
YES! VELOUS!
THE GATEWAY TO E SEVEN CITIES HAS BEEN CLOSED!
BROTHERS, SISTERS, LET US NOT LET DANIEL RAND DOWN!

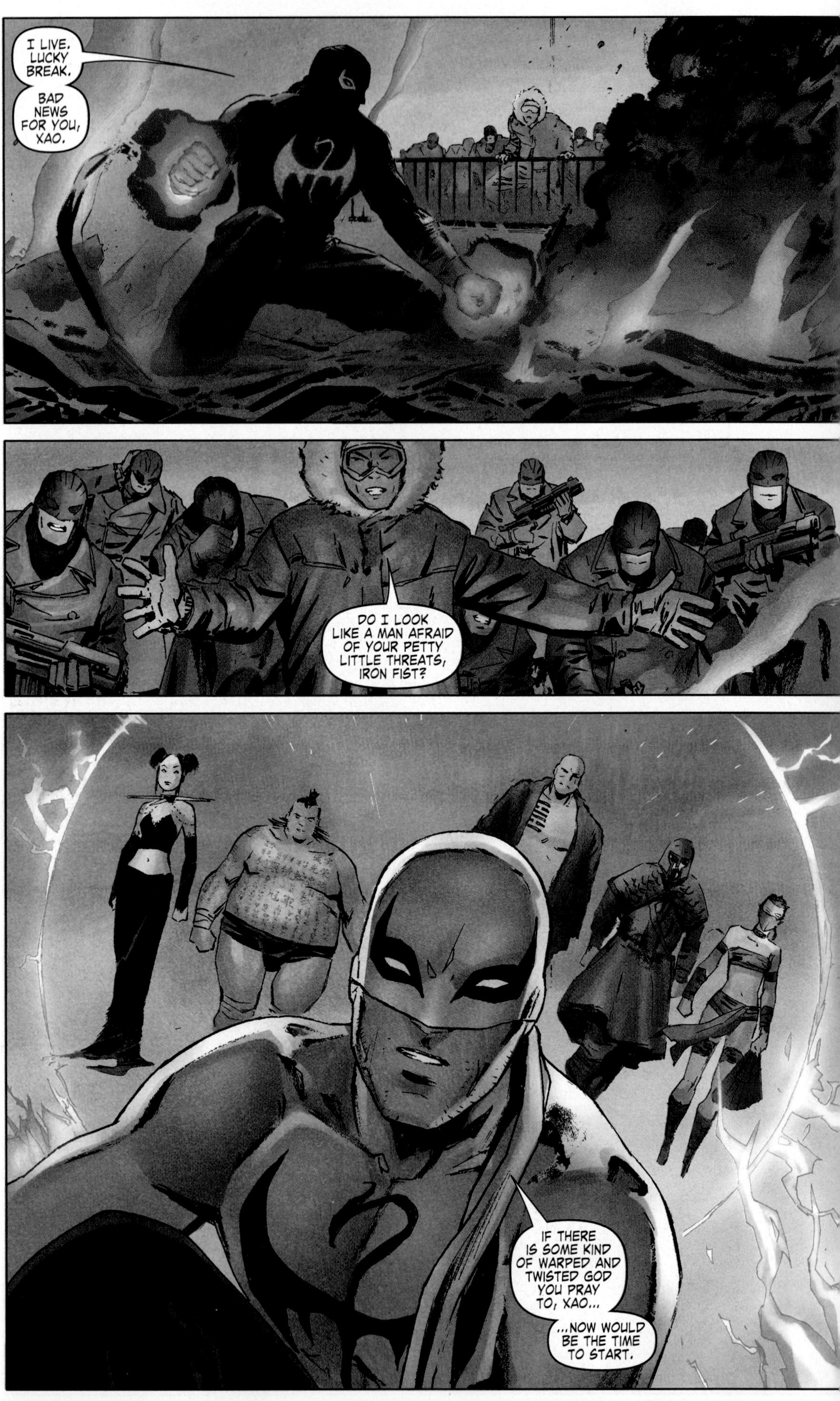
I LIVE. LUCKY BREAK.
BAD NEWS FOR YOU, XAO.
DO I LOOK LIKE A MAN AFRAID OF YOUR PETTY LITTLE THREATS, IRON FIST?
IF THERE IS SOME KIND OF WARPED AND TWISTED GOD YOU PRAY TO, XAO...
...NOW WOULD BE THE TIME TO START.

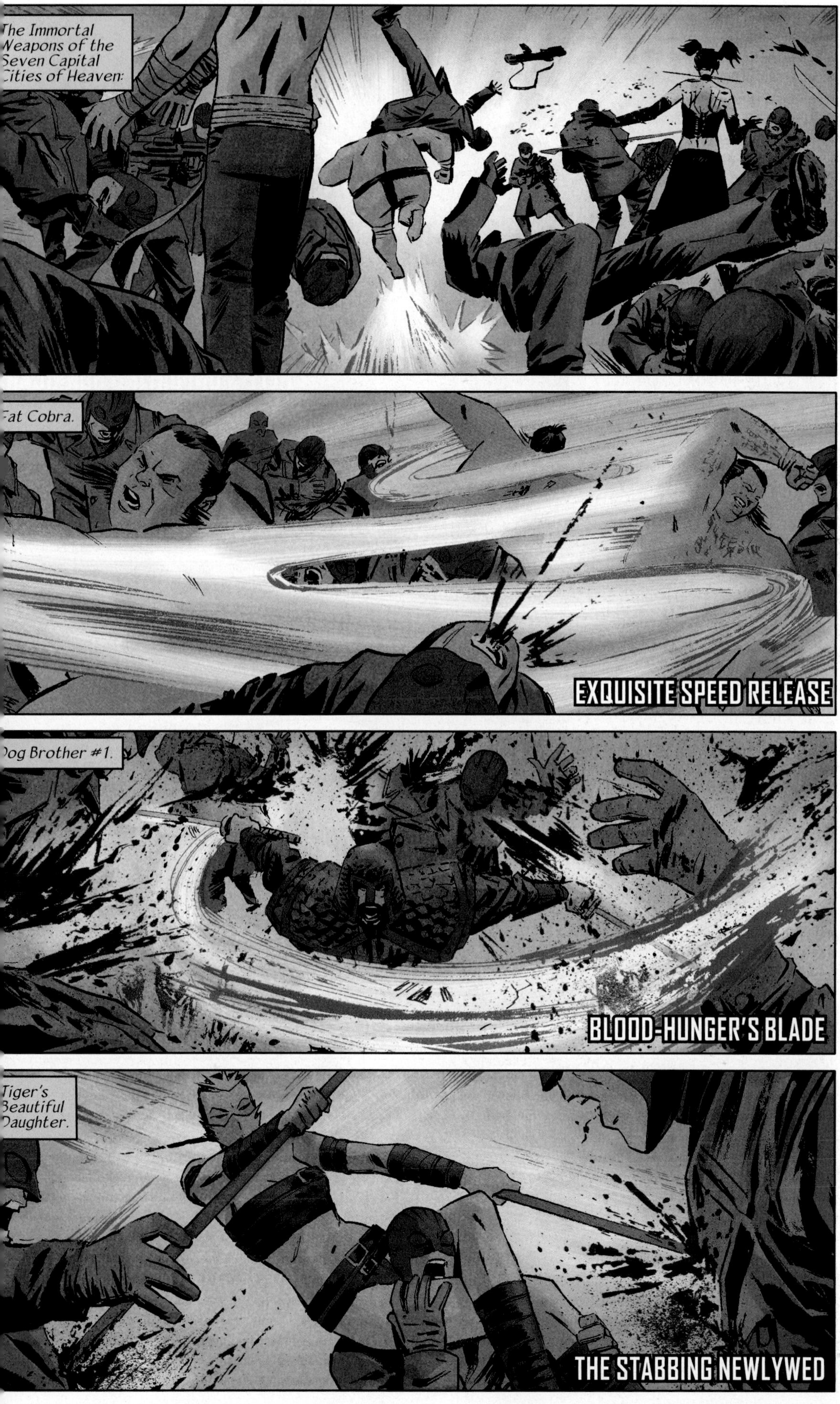
The Immortal Weapons of the Seven Capital Cities of Heaven:
Fat Cobra.
EXQUISITE SPEED RELEASE
Dog Brother #1.
BLOOD-HUNGER'S BLADE
Tiger's Beautiful Daughter.
THE STABBING NEWLYWED

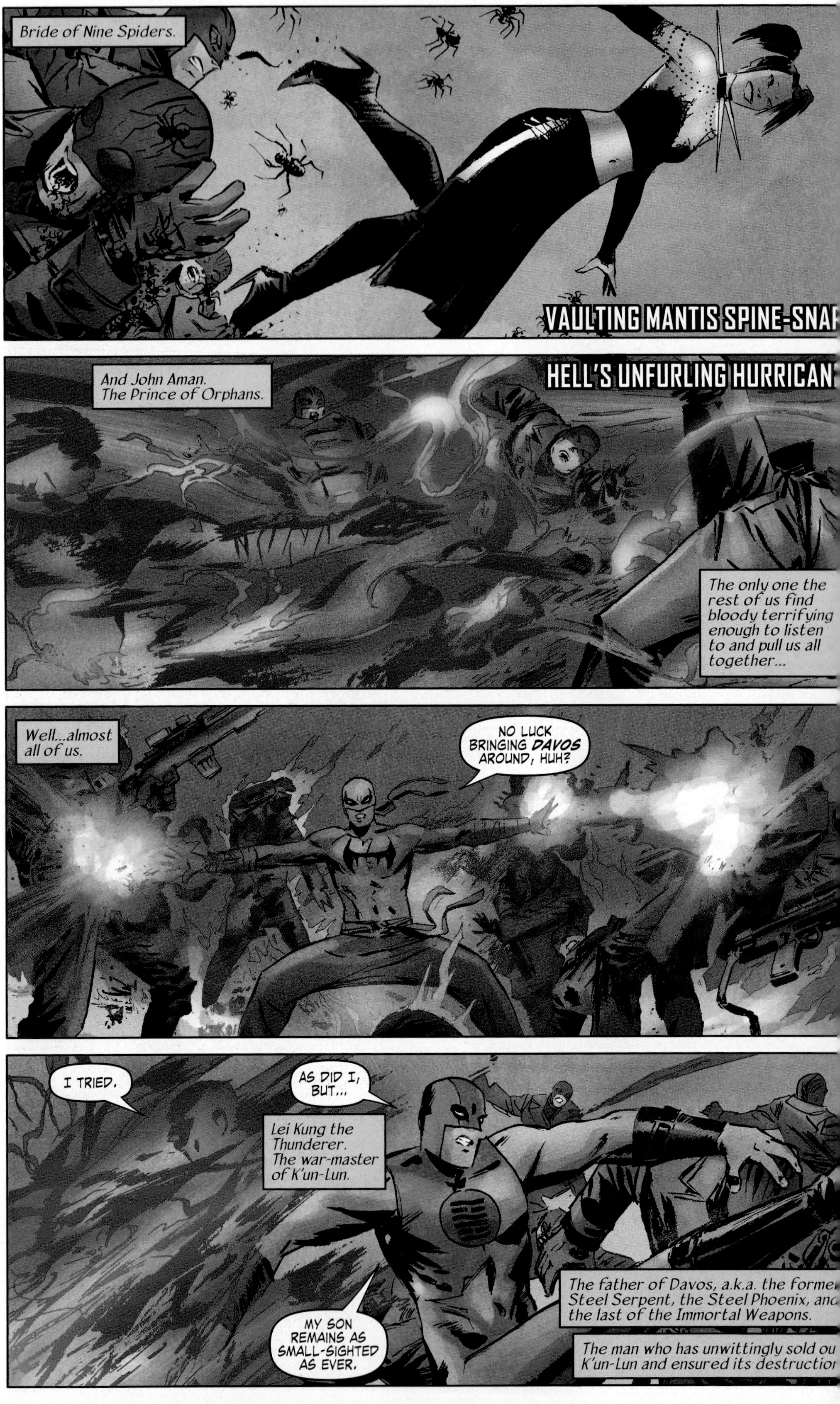

Bride of Nine Spiders.
VAULTING MANTIS SPINE-SNA
And John Aman.
The Prince of Orphans.
HELL'S UNFURLING HURRICAN
The only one the rest of us find bloody terrifying enough to listen to and pull us all together...
Well...almost all of us.
NO LUCK BRINGING *DAVOS* AROUND, HUH?
I TRIED.
AS DID I, BUT...
Lei Kung the Thunderer. The war-master of K'un-Lun.
The father of Davos, a.k.a. the forme Steel Serpent, the Steel Phoenix, and the last of the Immortal Weapons.
MY SON REMAINS AS SMALL-SIGHTED AS EVER.
The man who has unwittingly sold ou K'un-Lun and ensured its destructio

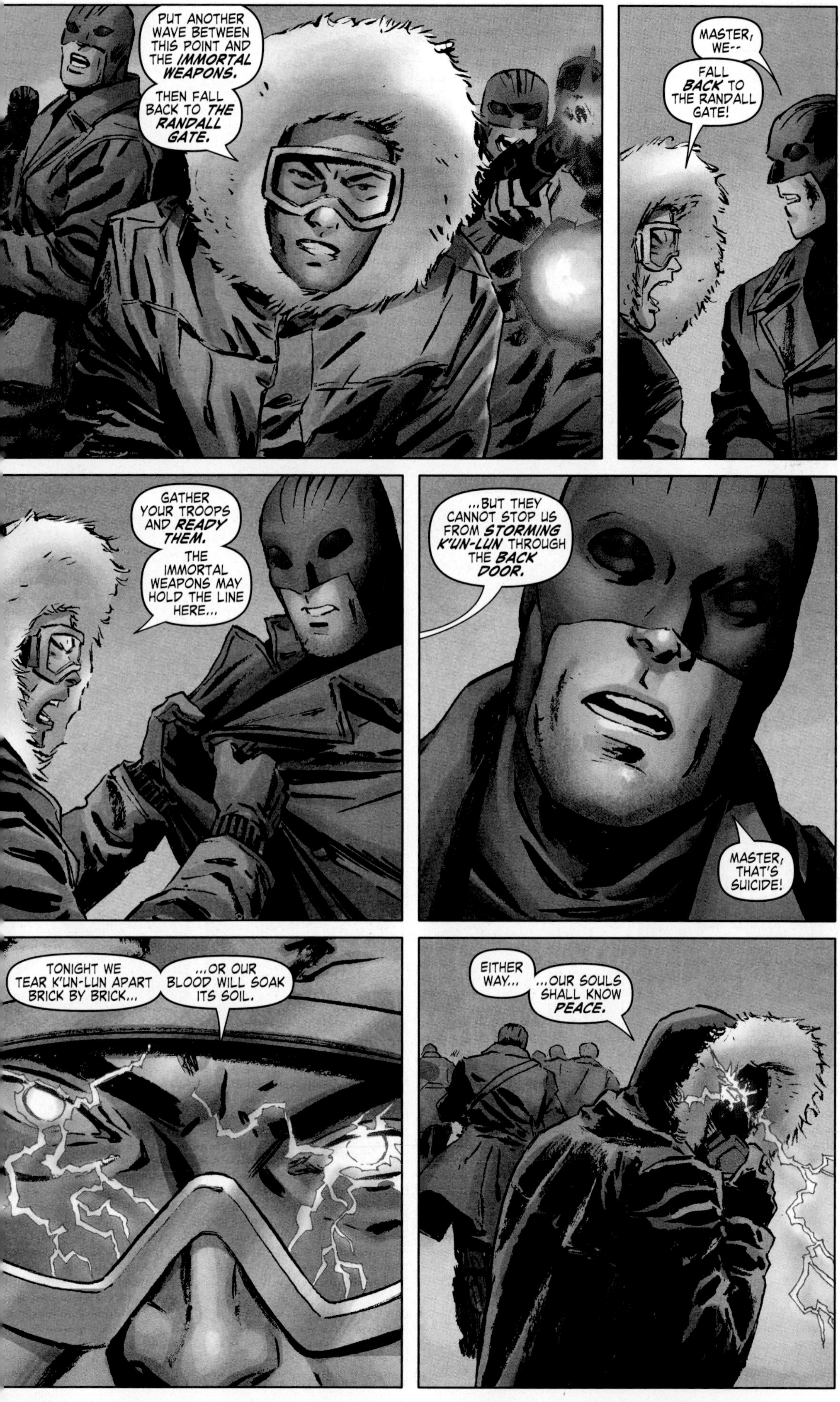
PUT ANOTHER WAVE BETWEEN THIS POINT AND THE IMMORTAL WEAPONS.
THEN FALL BACK TO THE RANDALL GATE.
MASTER, WE--
FALL BACK TO THE RANDALL GATE!
GATHER YOUR TROOPS AND READY THEM.
THE IMMORTAL WEAPONS MAY HOLD THE LINE HERE...
...BUT THEY CANNOT STOP US FROM STORMING K'UN-LUN THROUGH THE BACK DOOR.
MASTER, THAT'S SUICIDE!
TONIGHT WE TEAR K'UN-LUN APART BRICK BY BRICK...
...OR OUR BLOOD WILL SOAK ITS SOIL.
EITHER WAY...
...OUR SOULS SHALL KNOW PEACE.

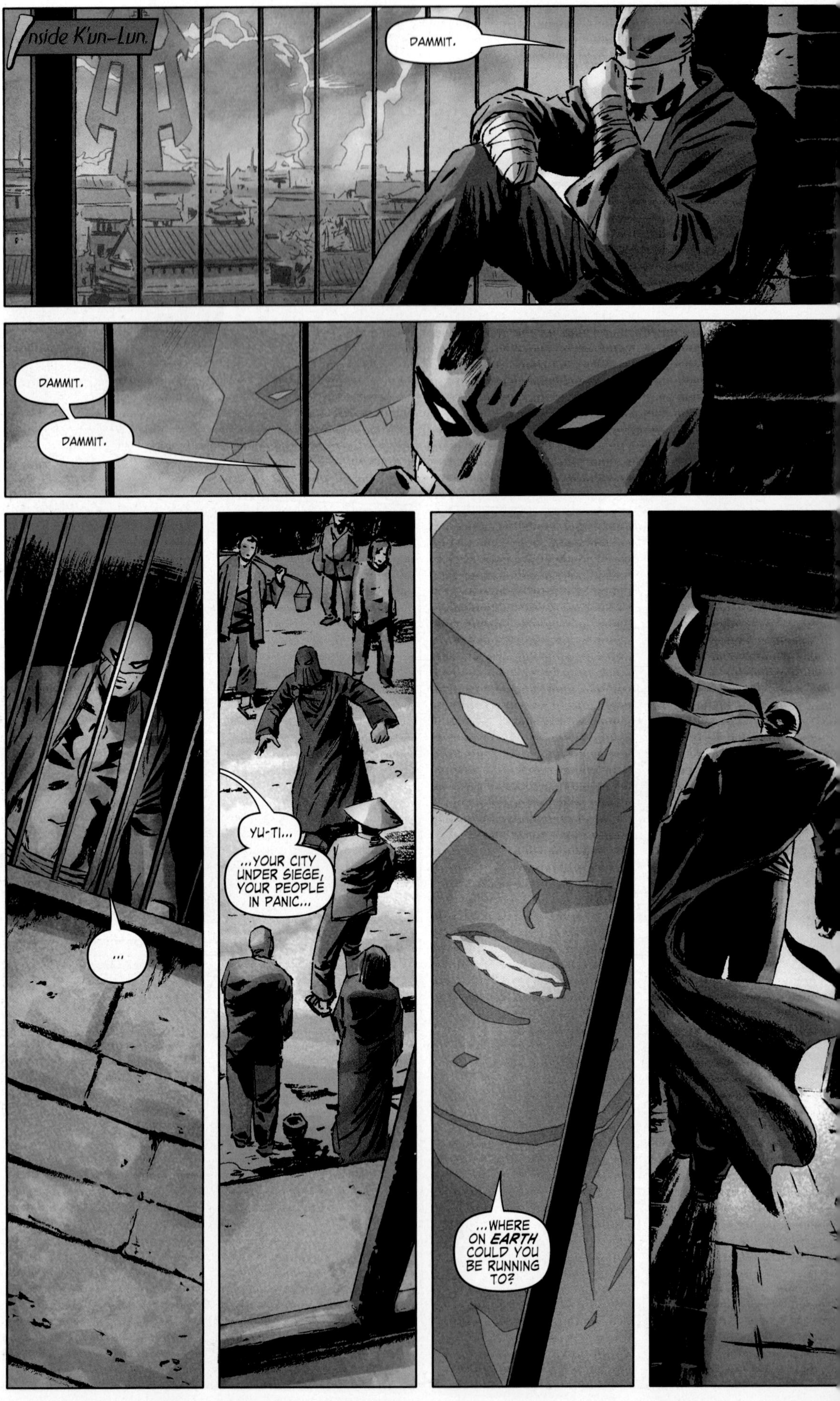
Inside K'un-Lun.
DAMMIT.
DAMMIT.
DAMMIT.
...
YU-TI...
...YOUR CITY UNDER SIEGE, YOUR PEOPLE IN PANIC...
...WHERE ON EARTH COULD YOU BE RUNNING TO?

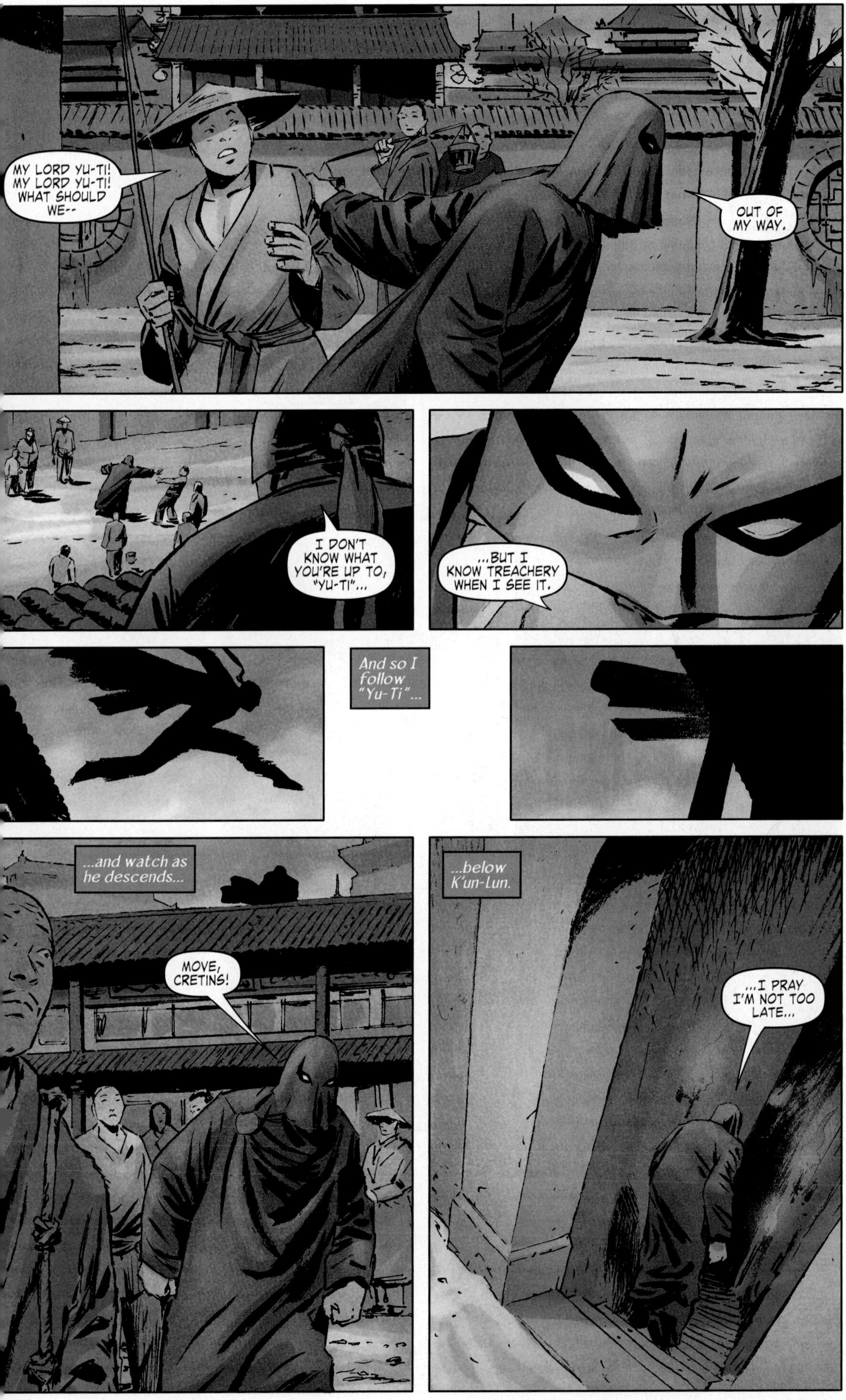
MY LORD YU-TI! MY LORD YU-TI! WHAT SHOULD WE--
OUT OF MY WAY.
I DON'T KNOW WHAT YOU'RE UP TO, "YU-TI"...
...BUT I KNOW TREACHERY WHEN I SEE IT.
And so I follow "Yu-Ti"...
...and watch as he descends...
MOVE, CRETINS!
...below K'un-Lun.
...I PRAY I'M NOT TOO LATE...

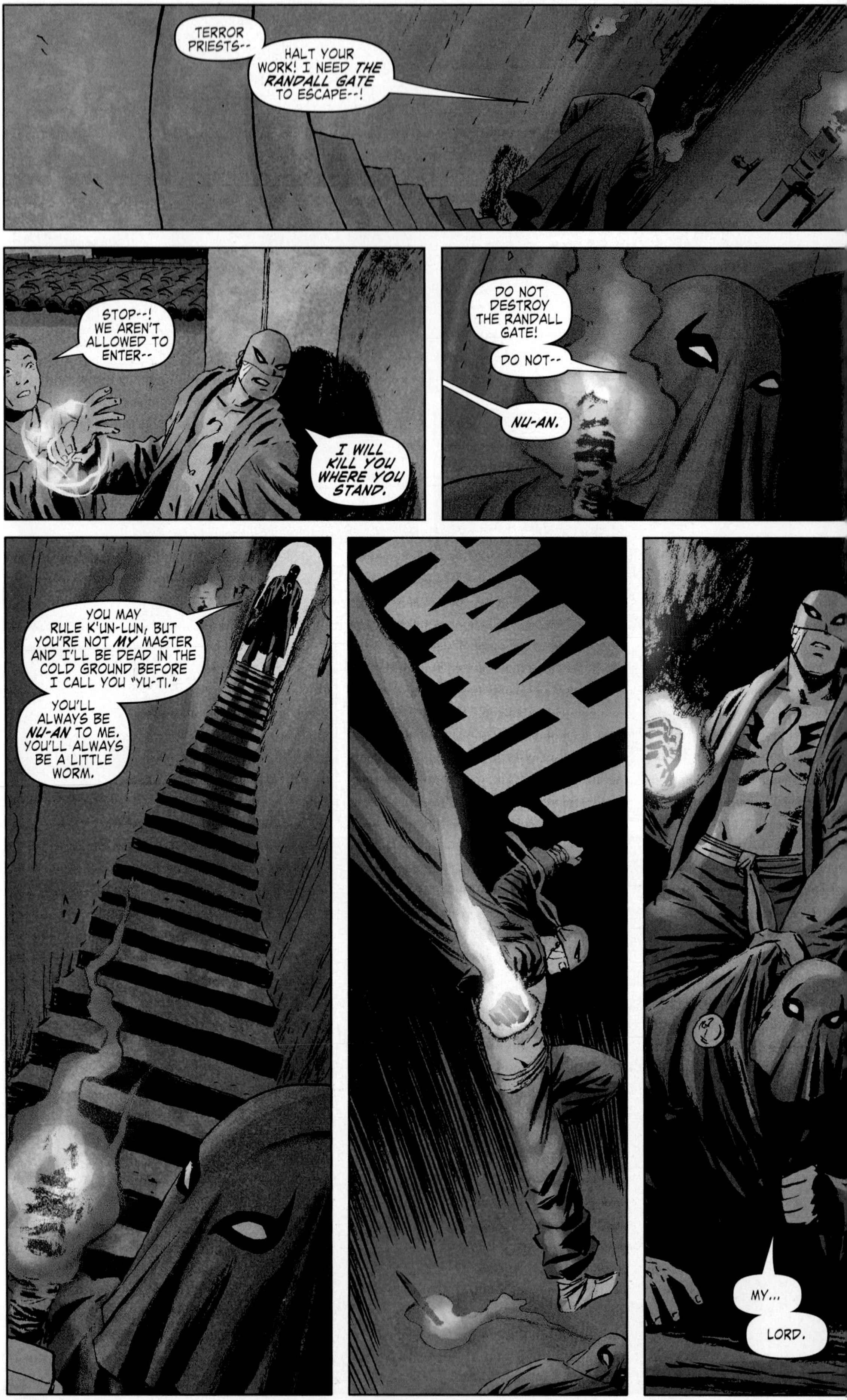
TERROR PRIESTS--
HALT YOUR WORK! I NEED THE RANDALL GATE TO ESCAPE--!
STOP--! WE AREN'T ALLOWED TO ENTER--
I WILL KILL YOU WHERE YOU STAND.
DO NOT DESTROY THE RANDALL GATE!
DO NOT--
NU-AN.
YOU MAY RULE K'UN-LUN, BUT YOU'RE NOT MY MASTER AND I'LL BE DEAD IN THE COLD GROUND BEFORE I CALL YOU "YU-TI."
YOU'LL ALWAYS BE NU-AN TO ME. YOU'LL ALWAYS BE A LITTLE WORM.
MY...
LORD.

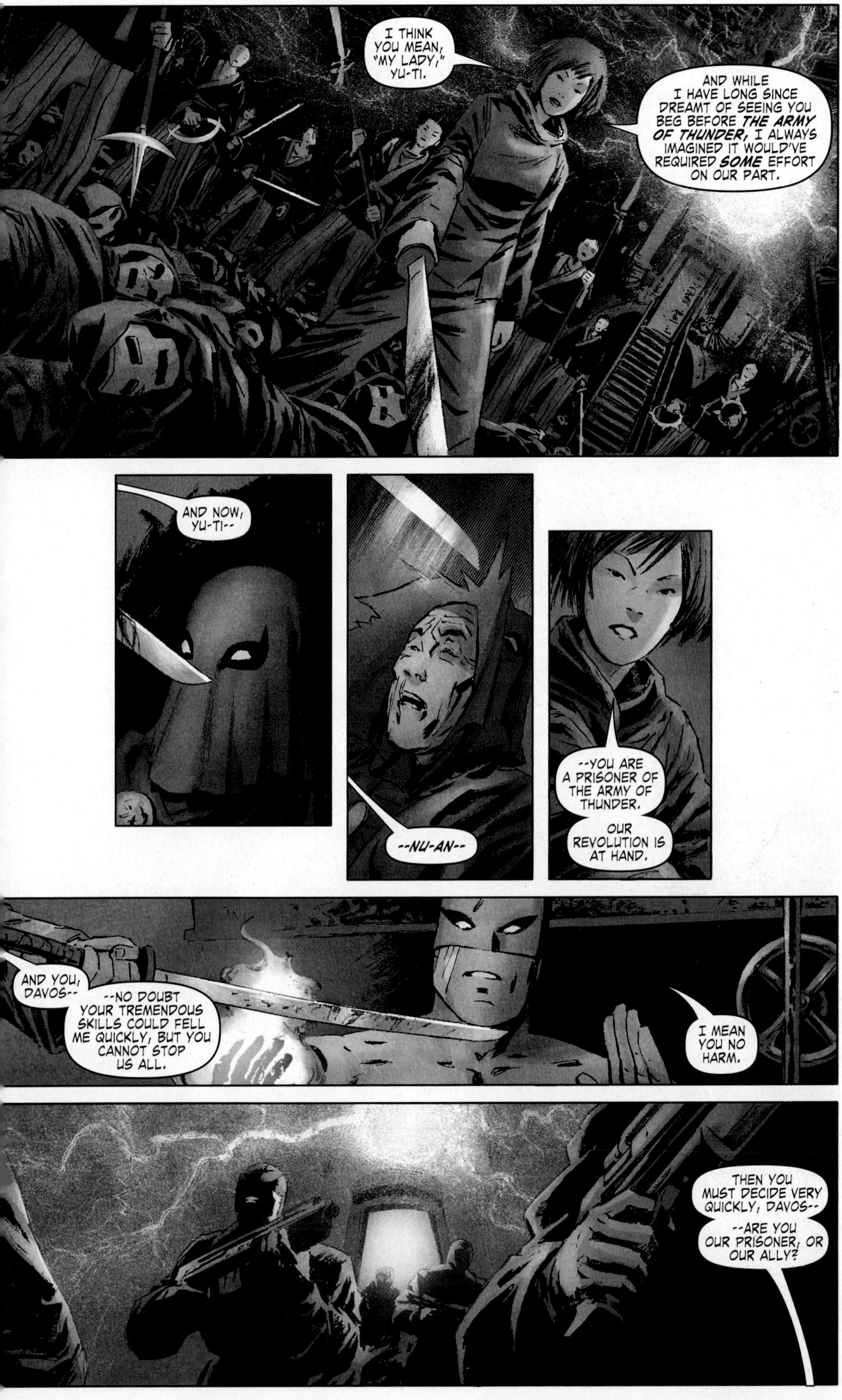
I THINK YOU MEAN, "MY LADY," YU-TI.
AND WHILE I HAVE LONG SINCE DREAMT OF SEEING YOU BEG BEFORE *THE ARMY OF THUNDER,* I ALWAYS IMAGINED IT WOULD'VE REQUIRED *SOME* EFFORT ON OUR PART.
AND NOW, YU-TI--
--NU-AN--
--YOU ARE A PRISONER OF THE ARMY OF THUNDER.
OUR REVOLUTION IS AT HAND.
AND YOU, DAVOS--
--NO DOUBT YOUR TREMENDOUS SKILLS COULD FELL ME QUICKLY, BUT YOU CANNOT STOP US ALL.
I MEAN YOU NO HARM.
THEN YOU MUST DECIDE VERY QUICKLY, DAVOS--
--ARE YOU OUR PRISONER, OR OUR ALLY?

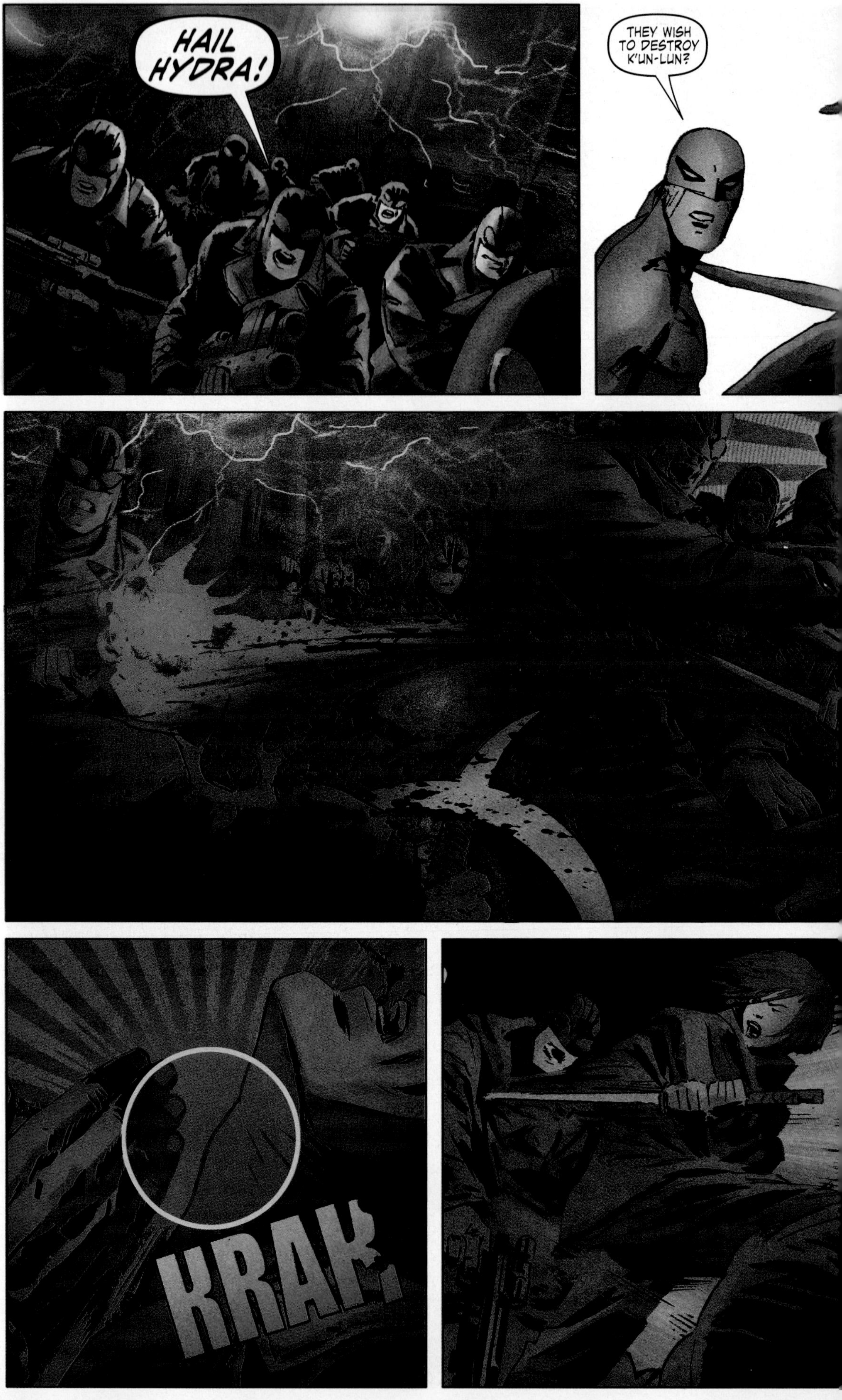
HAIL HYDRA!
THEY WISH TO DESTROY K'UN-LUN?
KRAK.

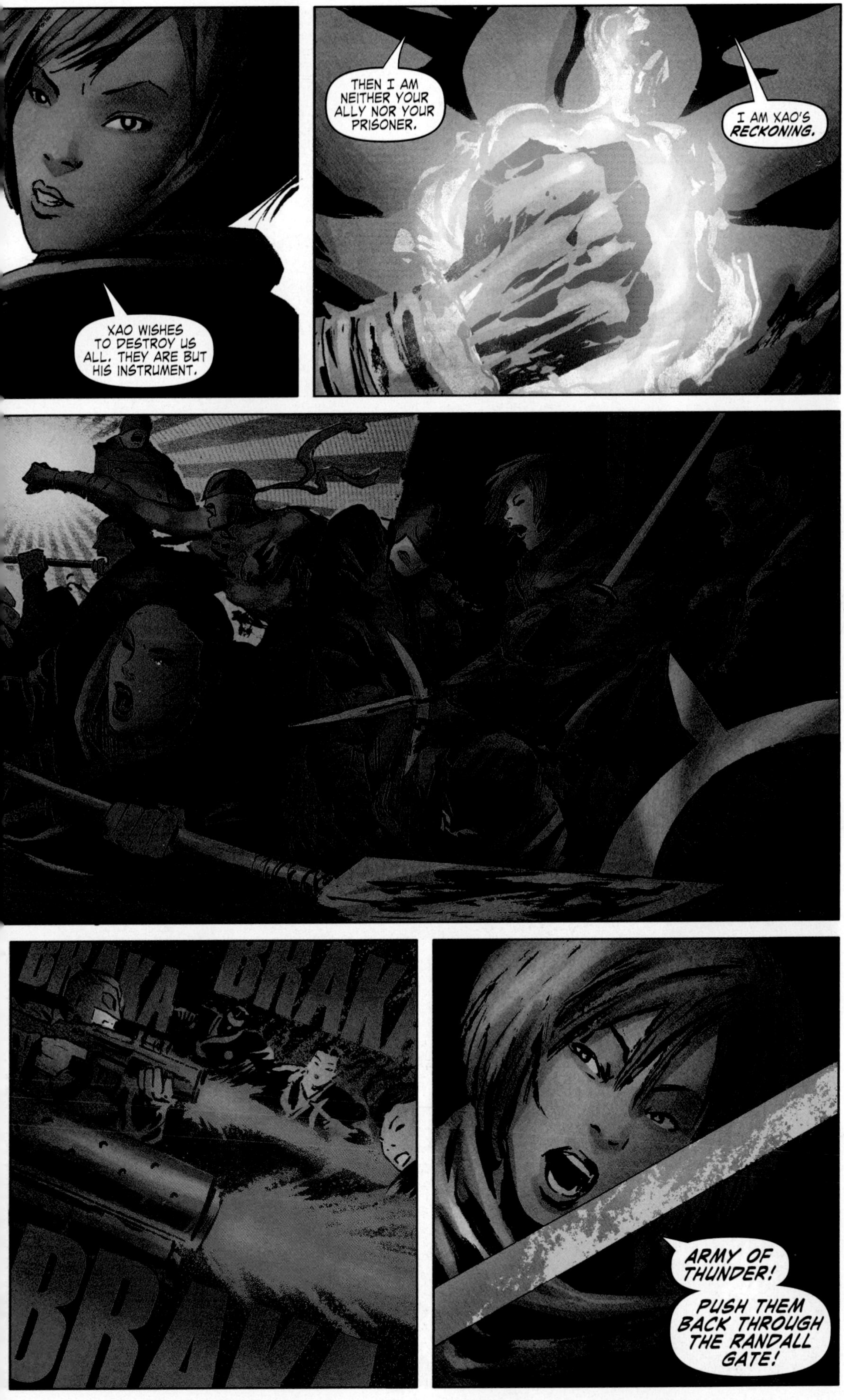
XAO WISHES TO DESTROY US ALL. THEY ARE BUT HIS INSTRUMENT.
THEN I AM NEITHER YOUR ALLY NOR YOUR PRISONER.
I AM XAO'S *RECKONING.*
ARMY OF THUNDER!
PUSH THEM BACK THROUGH THE RANDALL GATE!

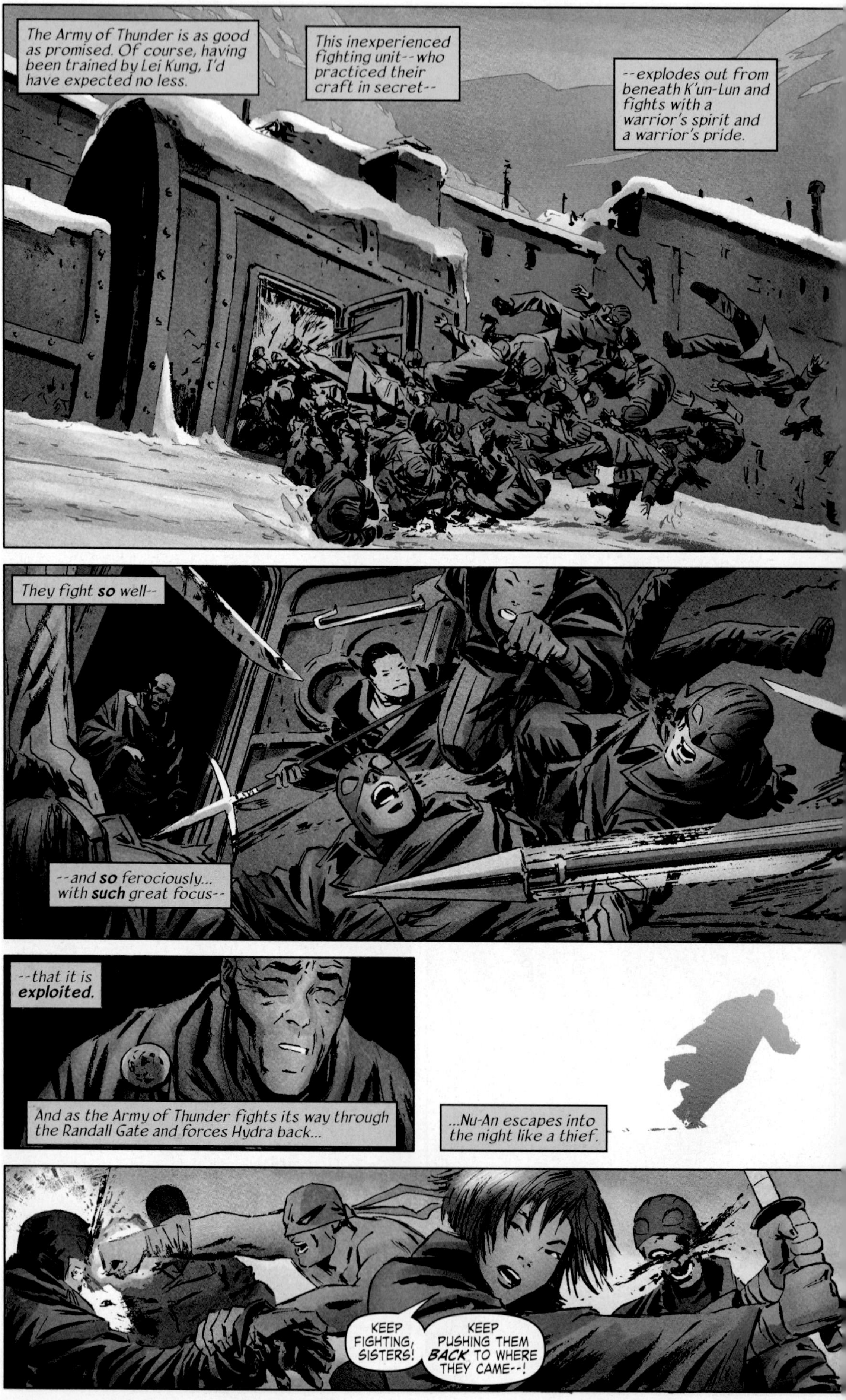
The Army of Thunder is as good as promised. Of course, having been trained by Lei Kung, I'd have expected no less.
This inexperienced fighting unit--who practiced their craft in secret--
--explodes out from beneath K'un-Lun and fights with a warrior's spirit and a warrior's pride.
They fight *so* well--
--and *so* ferociously... with *such* great focus--
--that it is *exploited.*
And as the Army of Thunder fights its way through the Randall Gate and forces Hydra back...
...Nu-An escapes into the night like a thief.
KEEP FIGHTING, SISTERS!
KEEP PUSHING THEM *BACK* TO WHERE THEY CAME--!

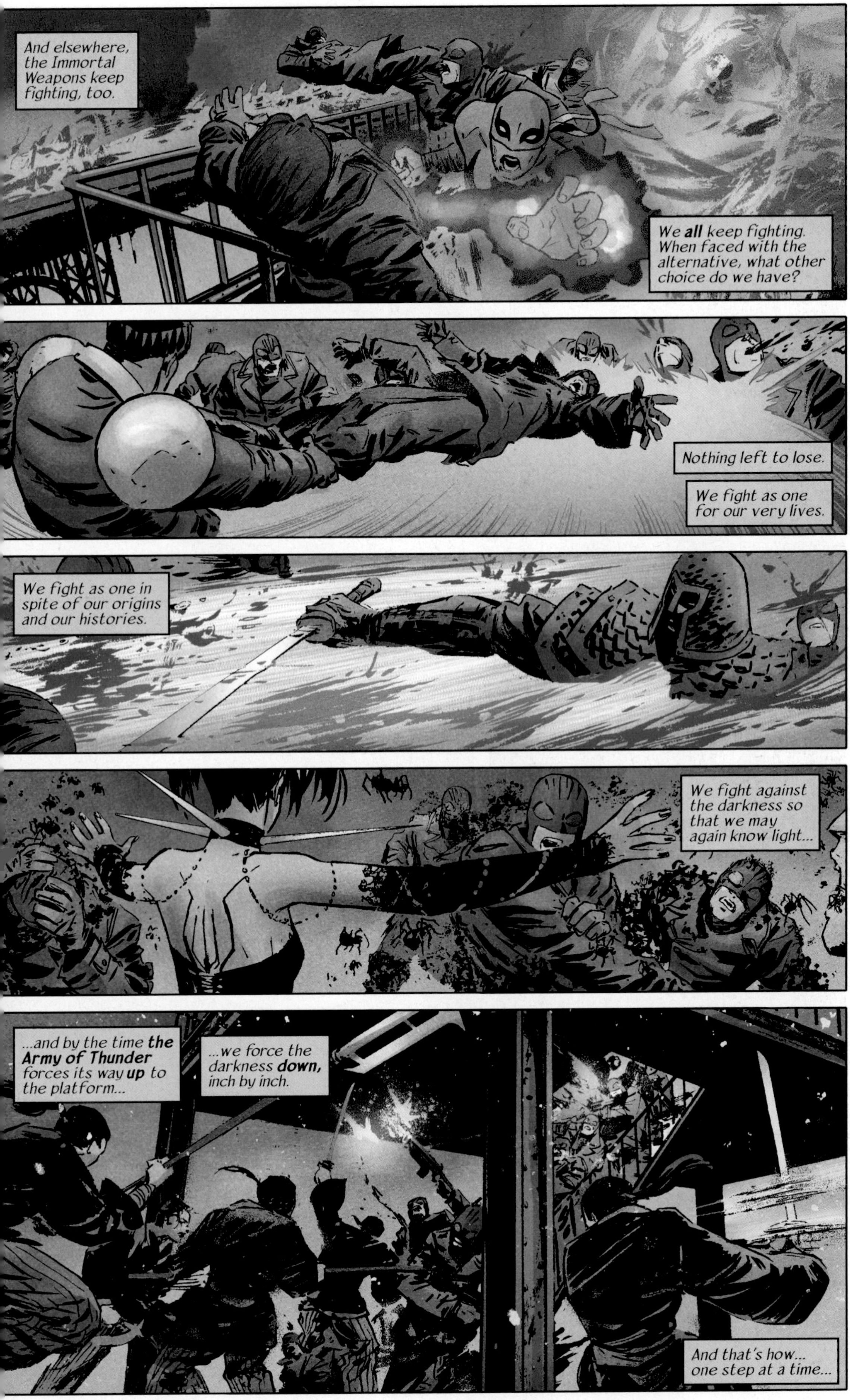
And elsewhere, the Immortal Weapons keep fighting, too.
We **all** keep fighting. When faced with the alternative, what other choice do we have?
Nothing left to lose.
We fight as one for our very lives.
We fight as one in spite of our origins and our histories.
We fight against the darkness so that we may again know light...
...and by the time **the Army of Thunder** forces its way **up** to the platform...
...we force the darkness **down,** inch by inch.
And that's how... one step at a time...

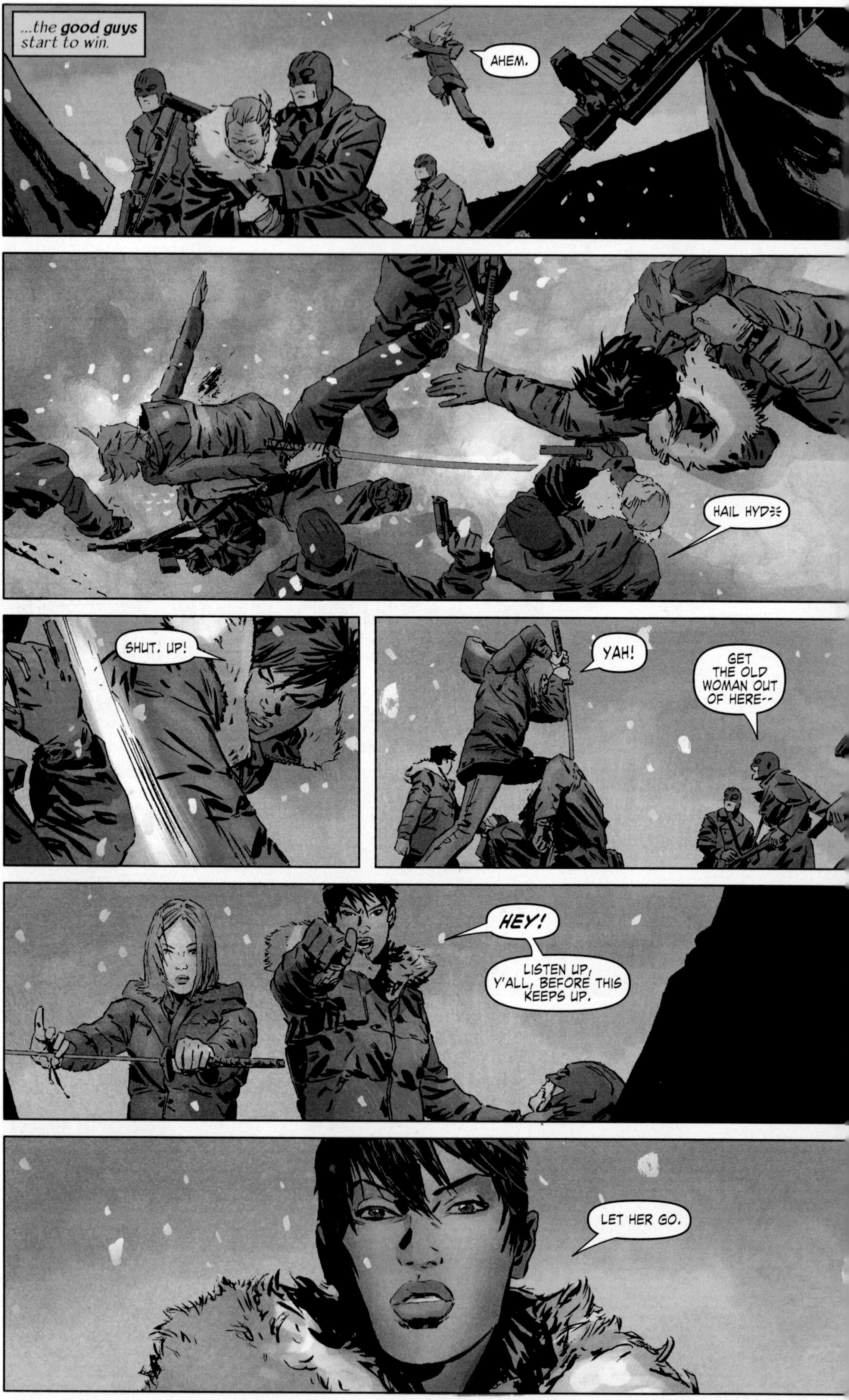
...the **good guys** start to win.
AHEM.
HAIL HYD≡≡
SHUT. UP!
YAH!
GET THE OLD WOMAN OUT OF HERE--
HEY!
LISTEN UP, Y'ALL, BEFORE THIS KEEPS UP.
LET HER GO.

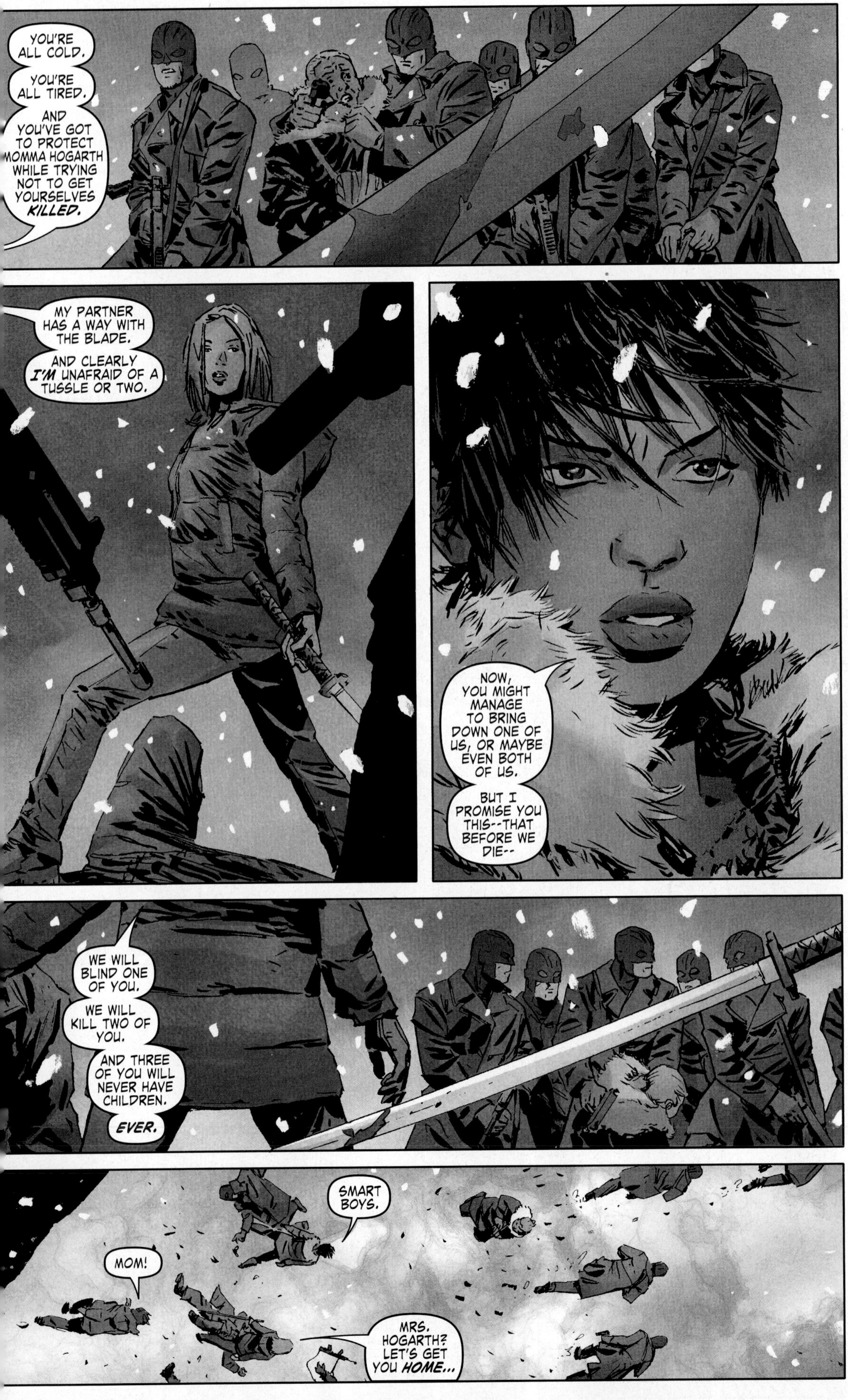
YOU'RE ALL COLD.
YOU'RE ALL TIRED.
AND YOU'VE GOT TO PROTECT MOMMA HOGARTH WHILE TRYING NOT TO GET YOURSELVES ***KILLED.***
MY PARTNER HAS A WAY WITH THE BLADE.
AND CLEARLY ***I'M*** UNAFRAID OF A TUSSLE OR TWO.
NOW, YOU MIGHT MANAGE TO BRING DOWN ONE OF US, OR MAYBE EVEN BOTH OF US.
BUT I PROMISE YOU THIS--THAT BEFORE WE DIE--
WE WILL BLIND ONE OF YOU.
WE WILL KILL TWO OF YOU.
AND THREE OF YOU WILL NEVER HAVE CHILDREN.
EVER.
MOM!
SMART BOYS.
MRS. HOGARTH? LET'S GET YOU ***HOME...***

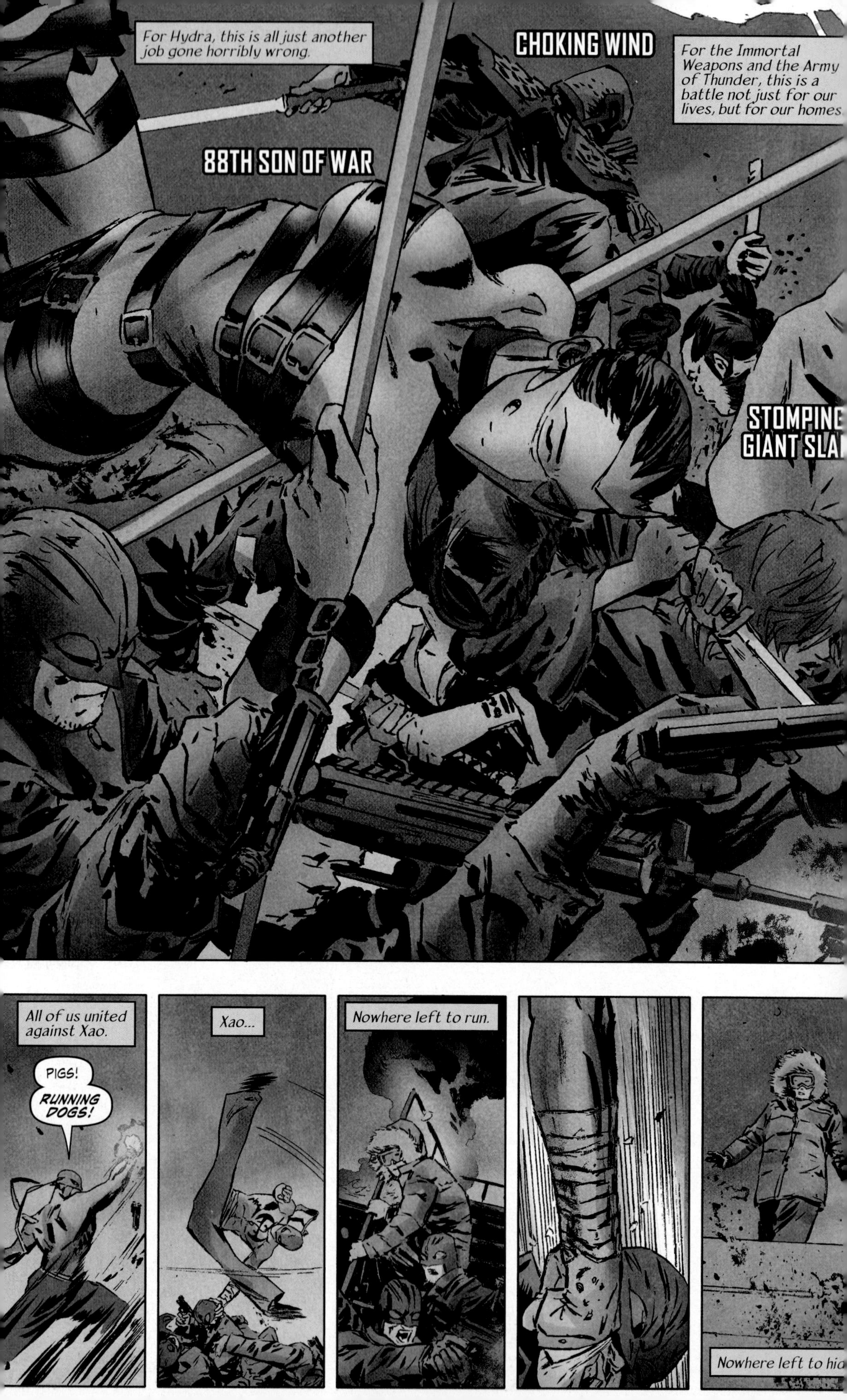
For Hydra, this is all just another job gone horribly wrong.
CHOKING WIND
For the Immortal Weapons and the Army of Thunder, this is a battle not just for our lives, but for our homes.
88TH SON OF WAR
STOMPING GIANT SLA
All of us united against Xao.
PIGS! RUNNING DOGS!
Xao...
Nowhere left to run.
Nowhere left to hi

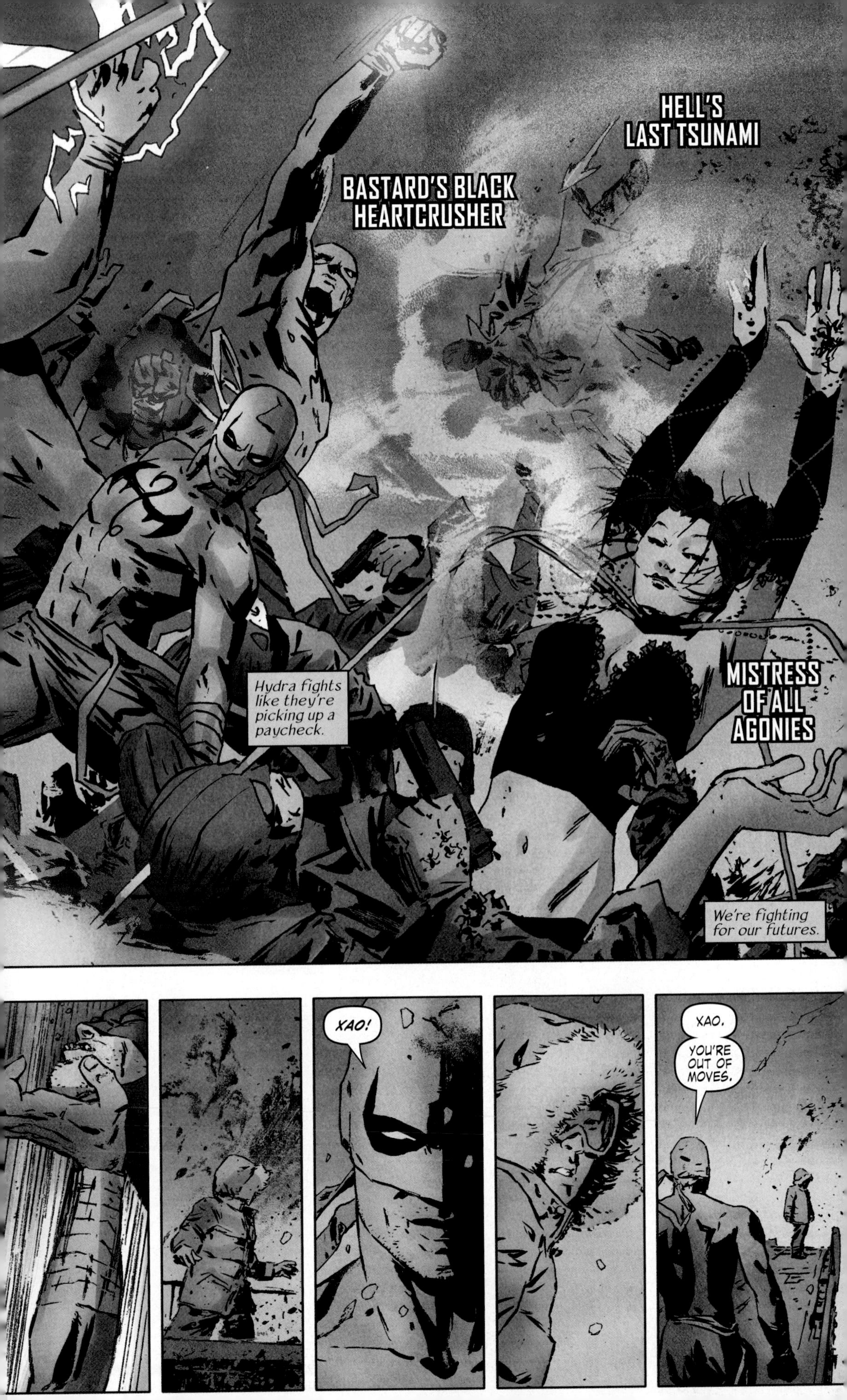
HELL'S LAST TSUNAMI
BASTARD'S BLACK HEARTCRUSHER
MISTRESS OF ALL AGONIES
Hydra fights like they're picking up a paycheck.
We're fighting for our futures.
XAO!
XAO.
YOU'RE OUT OF MOVES.

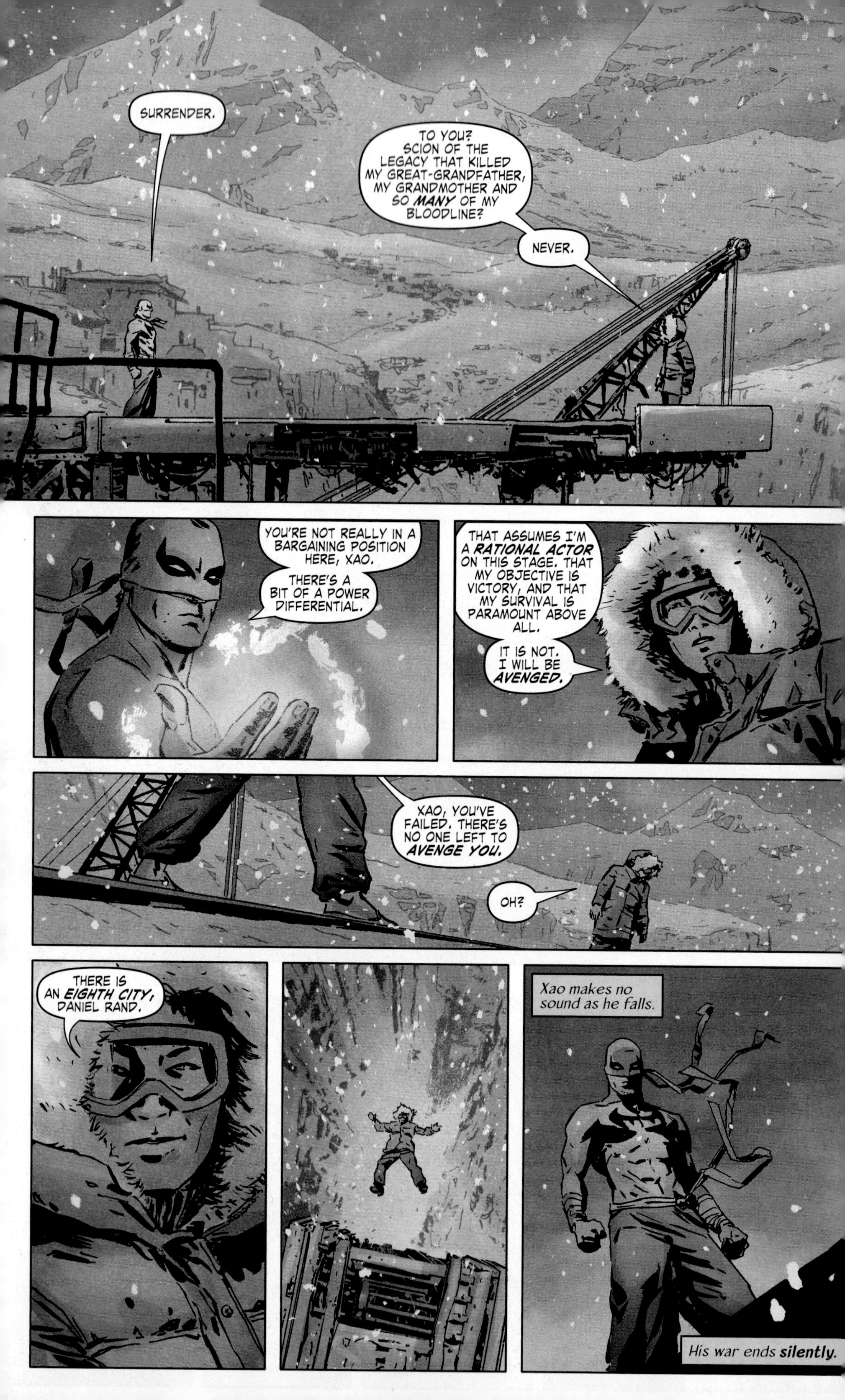
SURRENDER.
TO YOU? SCION OF THE LEGACY THAT KILLED MY GREAT-GRANDFATHER, MY GRANDMOTHER AND SO *MANY* OF MY BLOODLINE?
NEVER.
YOU'RE NOT REALLY IN A BARGAINING POSITION HERE, XAO.
THERE'S A BIT OF A POWER DIFFERENTIAL.
THAT ASSUMES I'M A *RATIONAL ACTOR* ON THIS STAGE. THAT MY OBJECTIVE IS VICTORY, AND THAT MY SURVIVAL IS PARAMOUNT ABOVE ALL.
IT IS NOT. I WILL BE *AVENGED.*
XAO, YOU'VE FAILED. THERE'S NO ONE LEFT TO *AVENGE YOU.*
OH?
THERE IS AN *EIGHTH CITY,* DANIEL RAND.
Xao makes no sound as he falls.
His war ends **silently.**

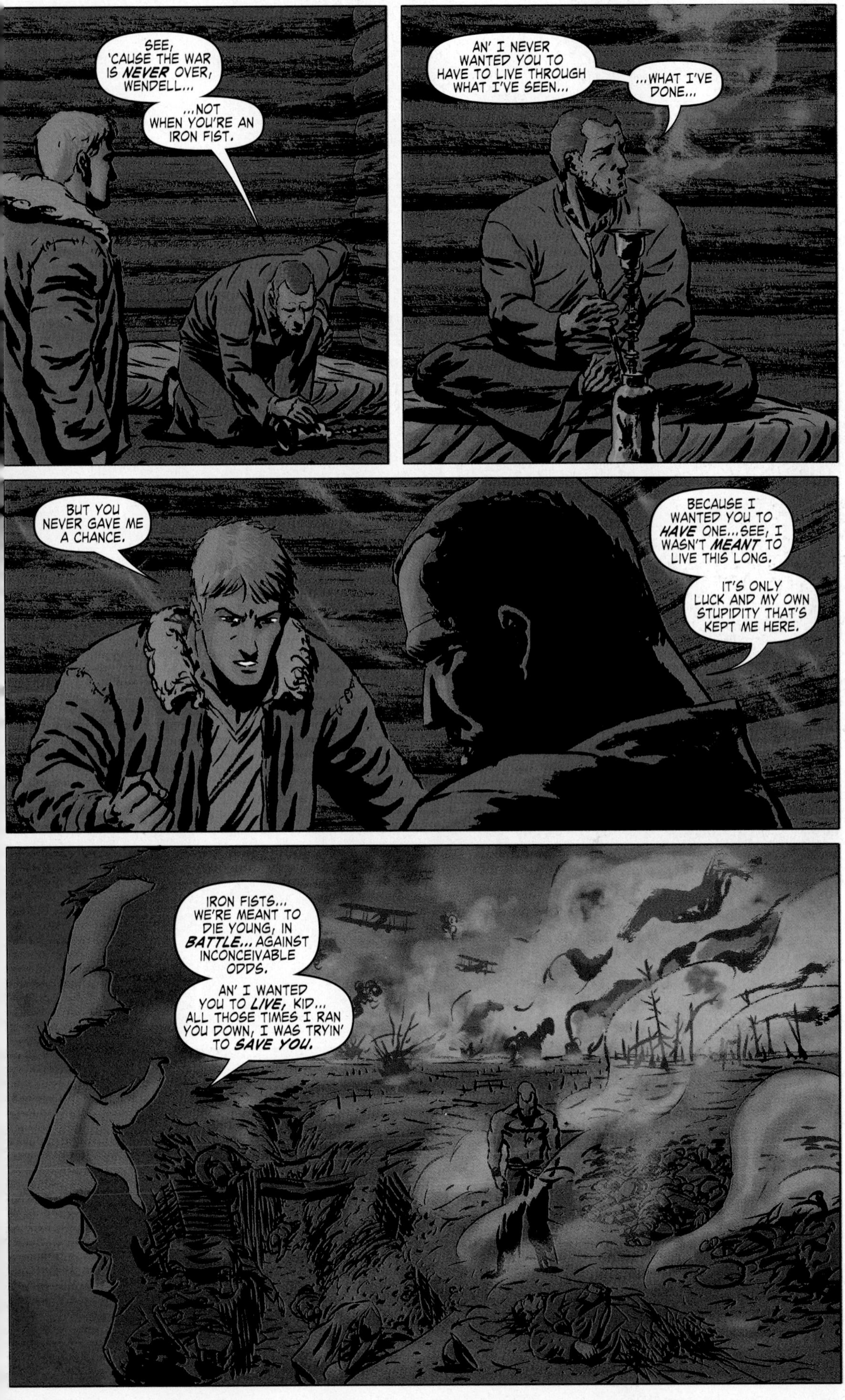
SEE, 'CAUSE THE WAR IS NEVER OVER, WENDELL...
...NOT WHEN YOU'RE AN IRON FIST.
AN' I NEVER WANTED YOU TO HAVE TO LIVE THROUGH WHAT I'VE SEEN...
...WHAT I'VE DONE...
BUT YOU NEVER GAVE ME A CHANCE.
BECAUSE I WANTED YOU TO HAVE ONE...SEE, I WASN'T MEANT TO LIVE THIS LONG.
IT'S ONLY LUCK AND MY OWN STUPIDITY THAT'S KEPT ME HERE.
IRON FISTS... WE'RE MEANT TO DIE YOUNG, IN BATTLE... AGAINST INCONCEIVABLE ODDS.
AN' I WANTED YOU TO LIVE, KID... ALL THOSE TIMES I RAN YOU DOWN, I WAS TRYIN' TO SAVE YOU.

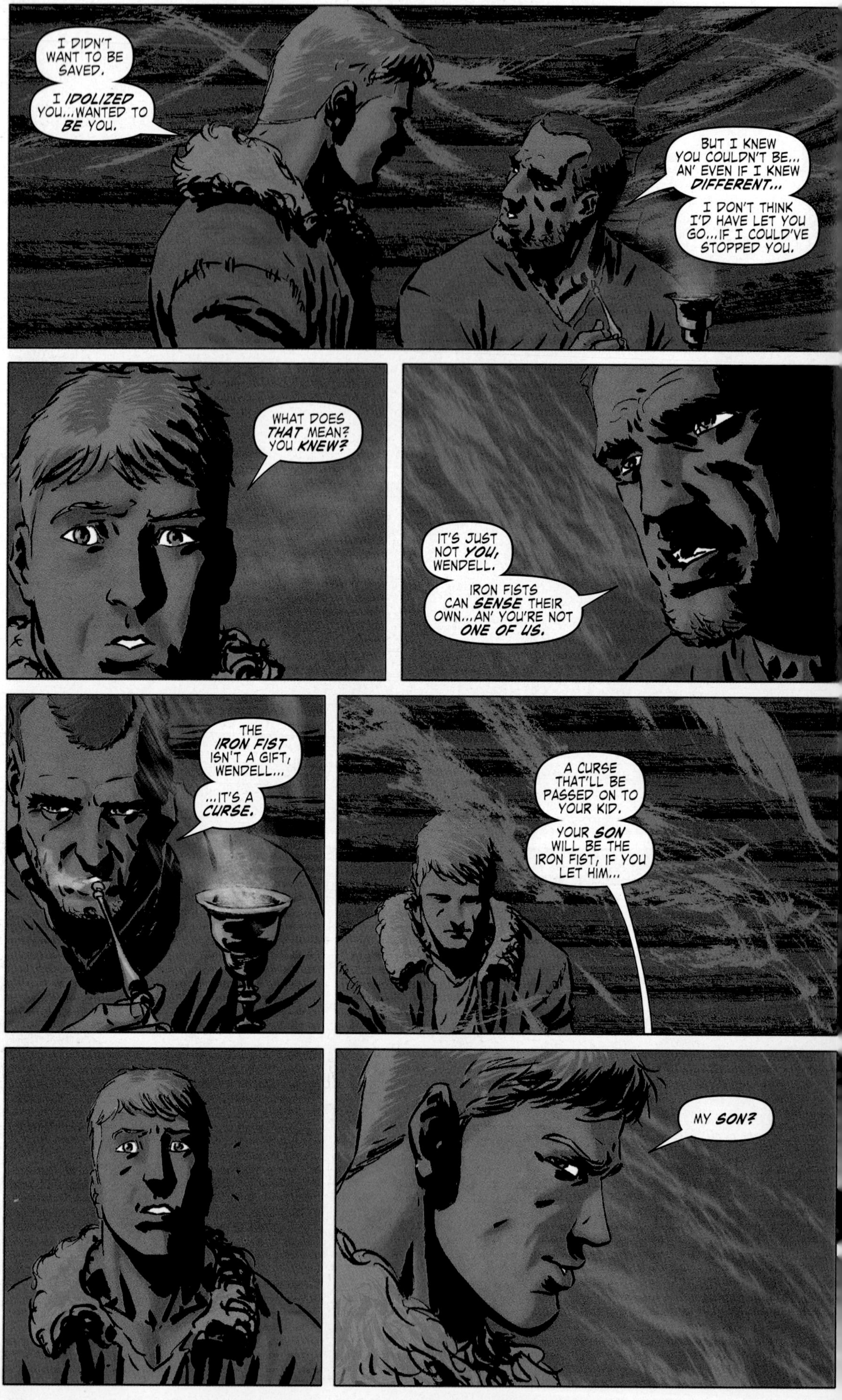
I DIDN'T WANT TO BE SAVED.
I *IDOLIZED* YOU...WANTED TO *BE* YOU.
BUT I KNEW YOU COULDN'T BE... AN' EVEN IF I KNEW *DIFFERENT...*
I DON'T THINK I'D HAVE LET YOU GO...IF I COULD'VE STOPPED YOU.
WHAT DOES *THAT* MEAN? YOU *KNEW?*
IT'S JUST NOT *YOU,* WENDELL.
IRON FISTS CAN *SENSE* THEIR OWN...AN' YOU'RE NOT *ONE OF US.*
THE *IRON FIST* ISN'T A GIFT, WENDELL...
...IT'S A *CURSE.*
A CURSE THAT'LL BE PASSED ON TO YOUR KID.
YOUR *SON* WILL BE THE IRON FIST, IF YOU LET HIM...
MY *SON?*

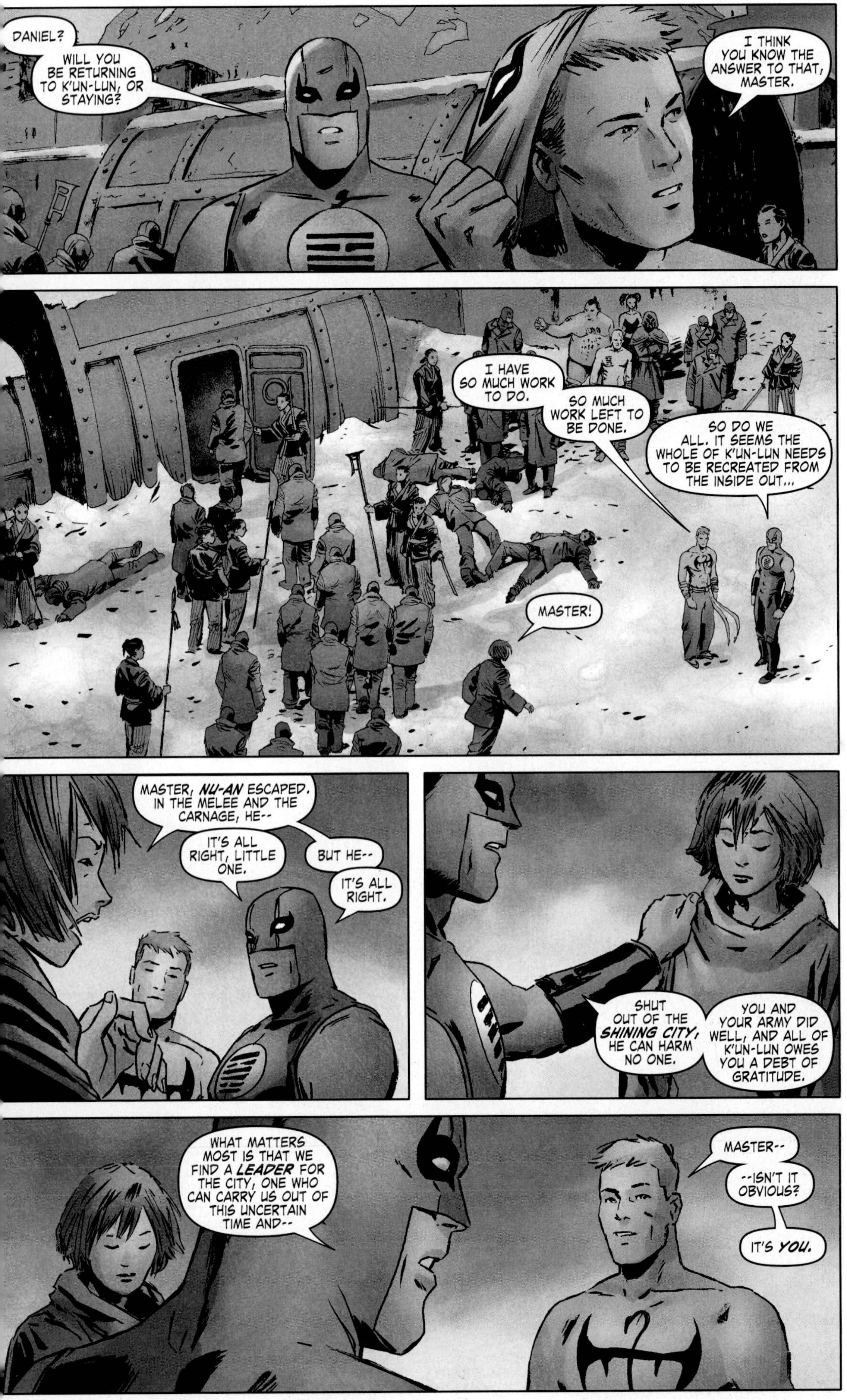
DANIEL?
WILL YOU BE RETURNING TO K'UN-LUN, OR STAYING?
I THINK YOU KNOW THE ANSWER TO THAT, MASTER.
I HAVE SO MUCH WORK TO DO.
SO MUCH WORK LEFT TO BE DONE.
SO DO WE ALL. IT SEEMS THE WHOLE OF K'UN-LUN NEEDS TO BE RECREATED FROM THE INSIDE OUT...
MASTER!
MASTER, NU-AN ESCAPED. IN THE MELEE AND THE CARNAGE, HE--
IT'S ALL RIGHT, LITTLE ONE.
BUT HE--
IT'S ALL RIGHT.
SHUT OUT OF THE SHINING CITY, HE CAN HARM NO ONE.
YOU AND YOUR ARMY DID WELL, AND ALL OF K'UN-LUN OWES YOU A DEBT OF GRATITUDE.
WHAT MATTERS MOST IS THAT WE FIND A LEADER FOR THE CITY, ONE WHO CAN CARRY US OUT OF THIS UNCERTAIN TIME AND--
MASTER--
--ISN'T IT OBVIOUS?
IT'S YOU.

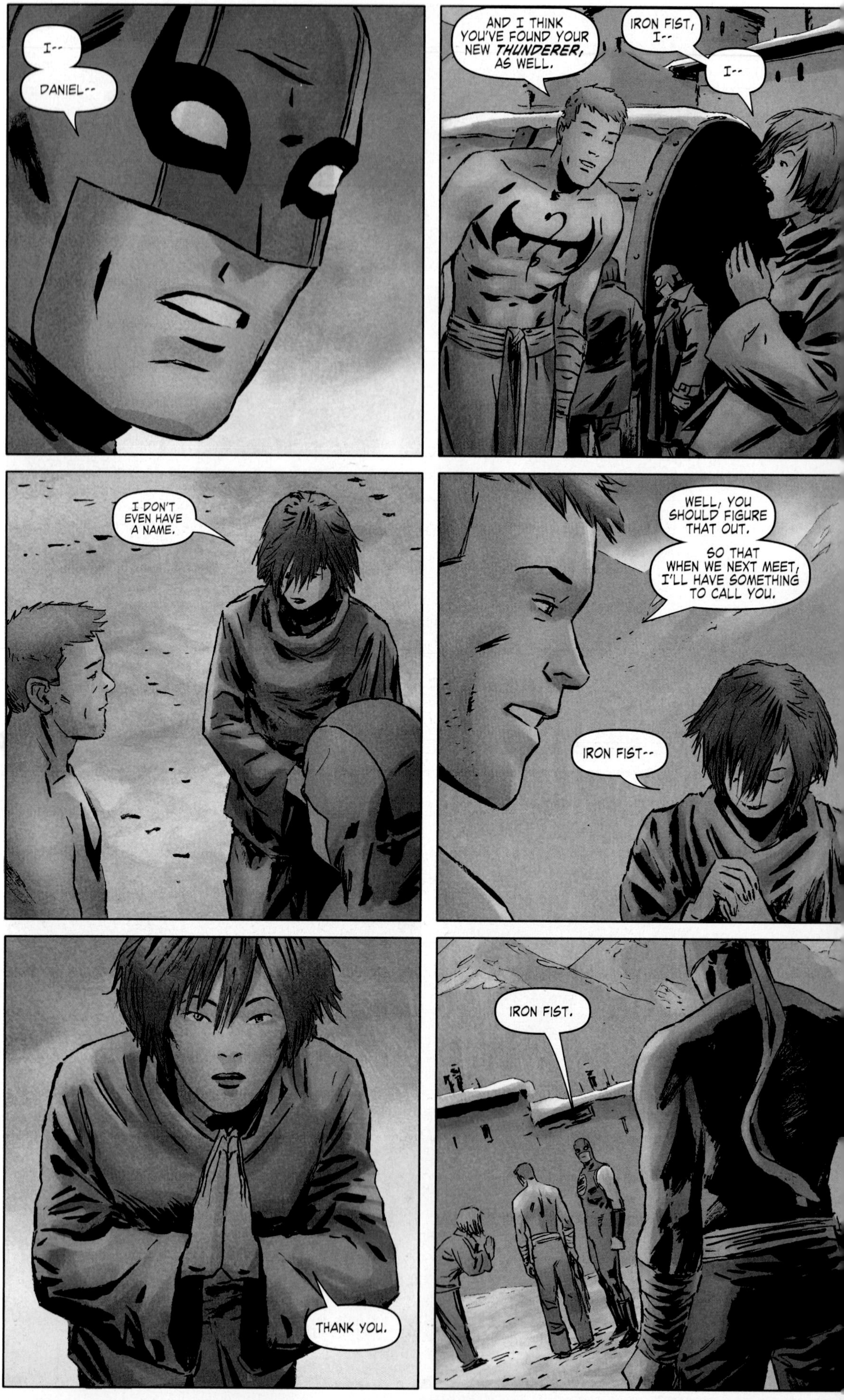
I--
DANIEL--
AND I THINK YOU'VE FOUND YOUR NEW *THUNDERER,* AS WELL.
IRON FIST, I--
I--
I DON'T EVEN HAVE A NAME.
WELL, YOU SHOULD FIGURE THAT OUT.
SO THAT WHEN WE NEXT MEET, I'LL HAVE SOMETHING TO CALL YOU.
IRON FIST--
THANK YOU.
IRON FIST.

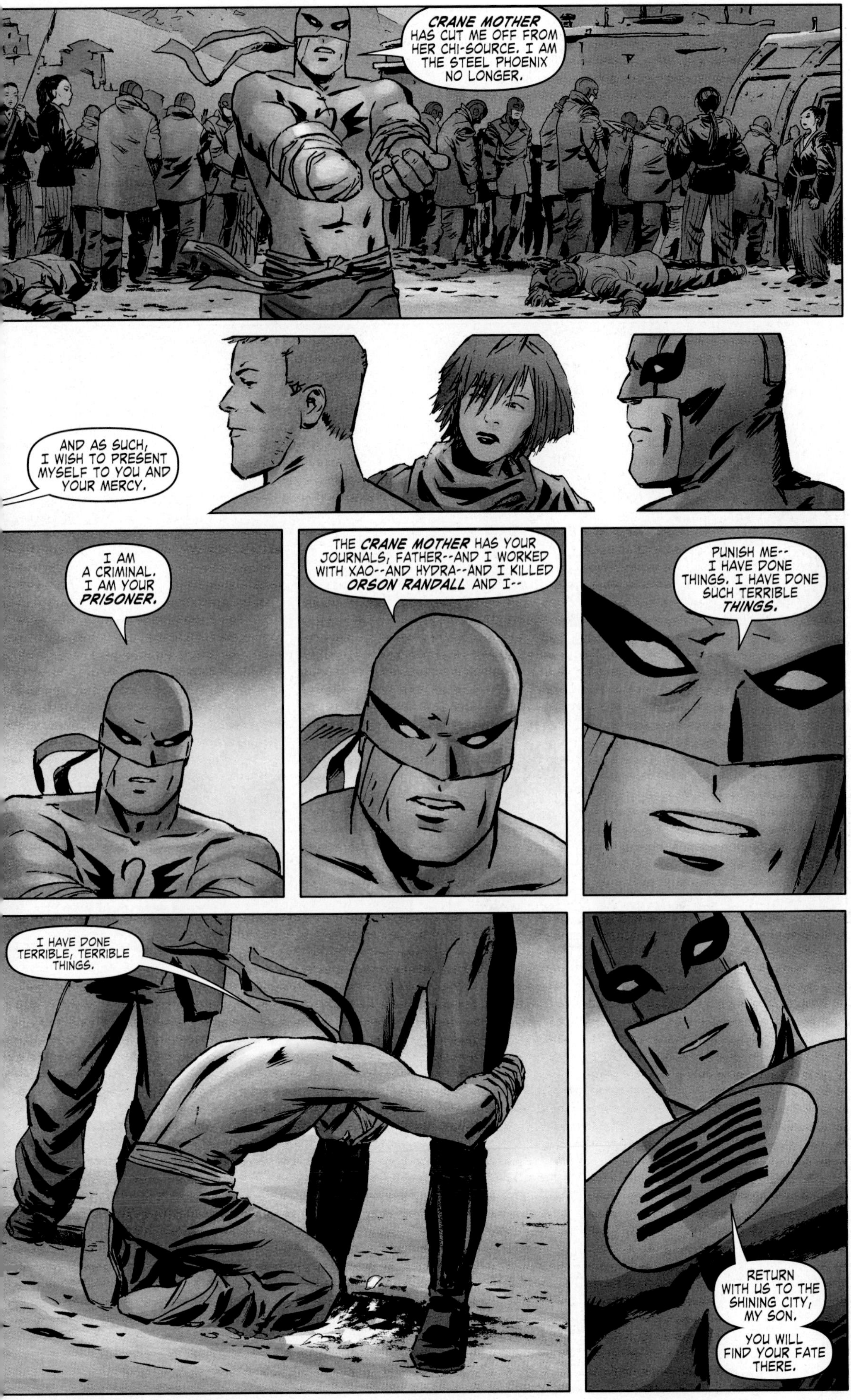
CRANE MOTHER HAS CUT ME OFF FROM HER CHI-SOURCE. I AM THE STEEL PHOENIX NO LONGER.
AND AS SUCH, I WISH TO PRESENT MYSELF TO YOU AND YOUR MERCY.
I AM A CRIMINAL. I AM YOUR PRISONER.
THE CRANE MOTHER HAS YOUR JOURNALS, FATHER--AND I WORKED WITH XAO--AND HYDRA--AND I KILLED ORSON RANDALL AND I--
PUNISH ME-- I HAVE DONE THINGS. I HAVE DONE SUCH TERRIBLE THINGS.
I HAVE DONE TERRIBLE, TERRIBLE THINGS.
RETURN WITH US TO THE SHINING CITY, MY SON.
YOU WILL FIND YOUR FATE THERE.

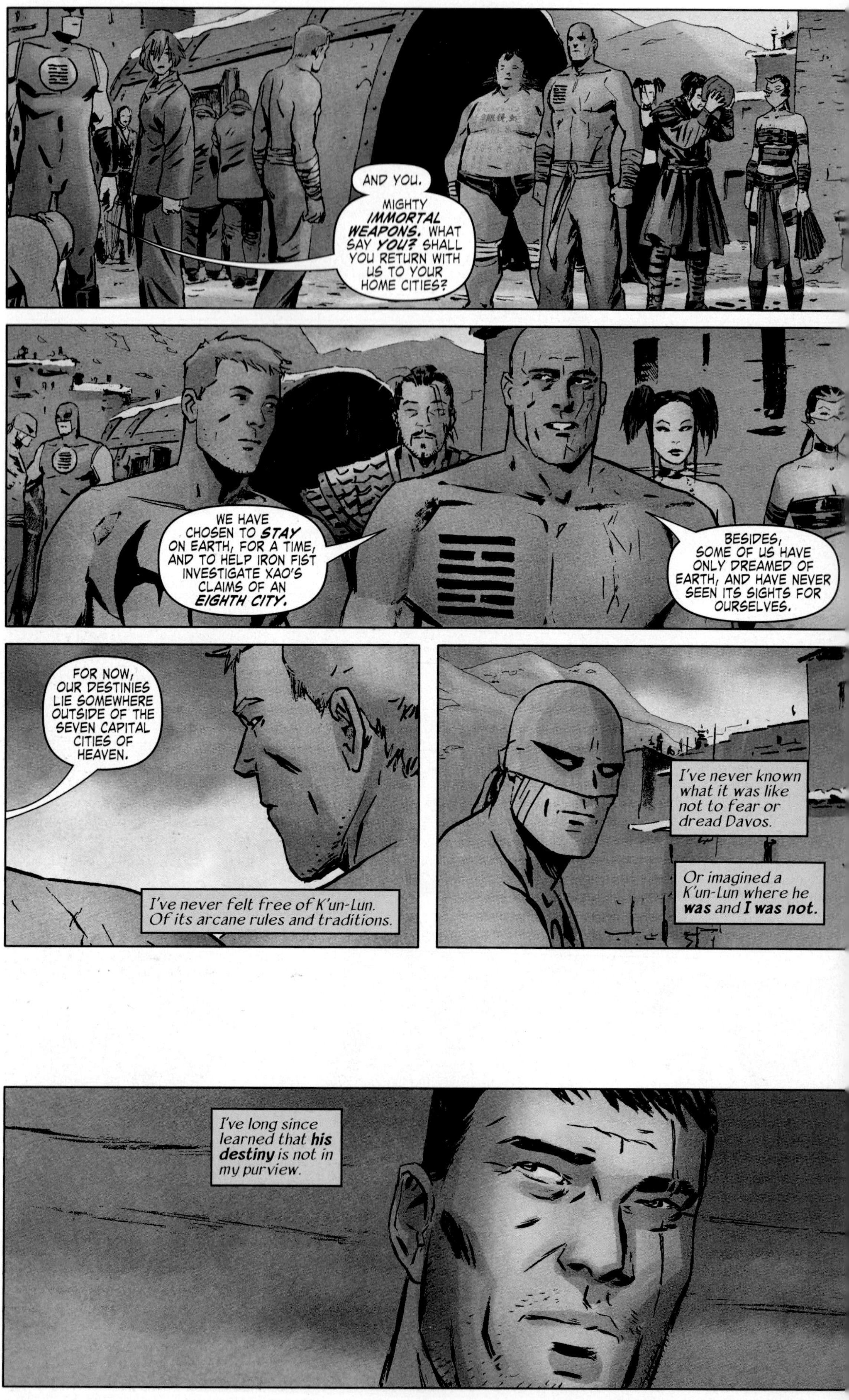
AND YOU.
MIGHTY IMMORTAL WEAPONS. WHAT SAY YOU? SHALL YOU RETURN WITH US TO YOUR HOME CITIES?
WE HAVE CHOSEN TO STAY ON EARTH, FOR A TIME, AND TO HELP IRON FIST INVESTIGATE XAO'S CLAIMS OF AN EIGHTH CITY.
BESIDES, SOME OF US HAVE ONLY DREAMED OF EARTH, AND HAVE NEVER SEEN ITS SIGHTS FOR OURSELVES.
FOR NOW, OUR DESTINIES LIE SOMEWHERE OUTSIDE OF THE SEVEN CAPITAL CITIES OF HEAVEN.
I've never felt free of K'un-Lun. Of its arcane rules and traditions.
I've never known what it was like not to fear or dread Davos.
Or imagined a K'un-Lun where he was and I was not.
I've long since learned that his destiny is not in my purview.

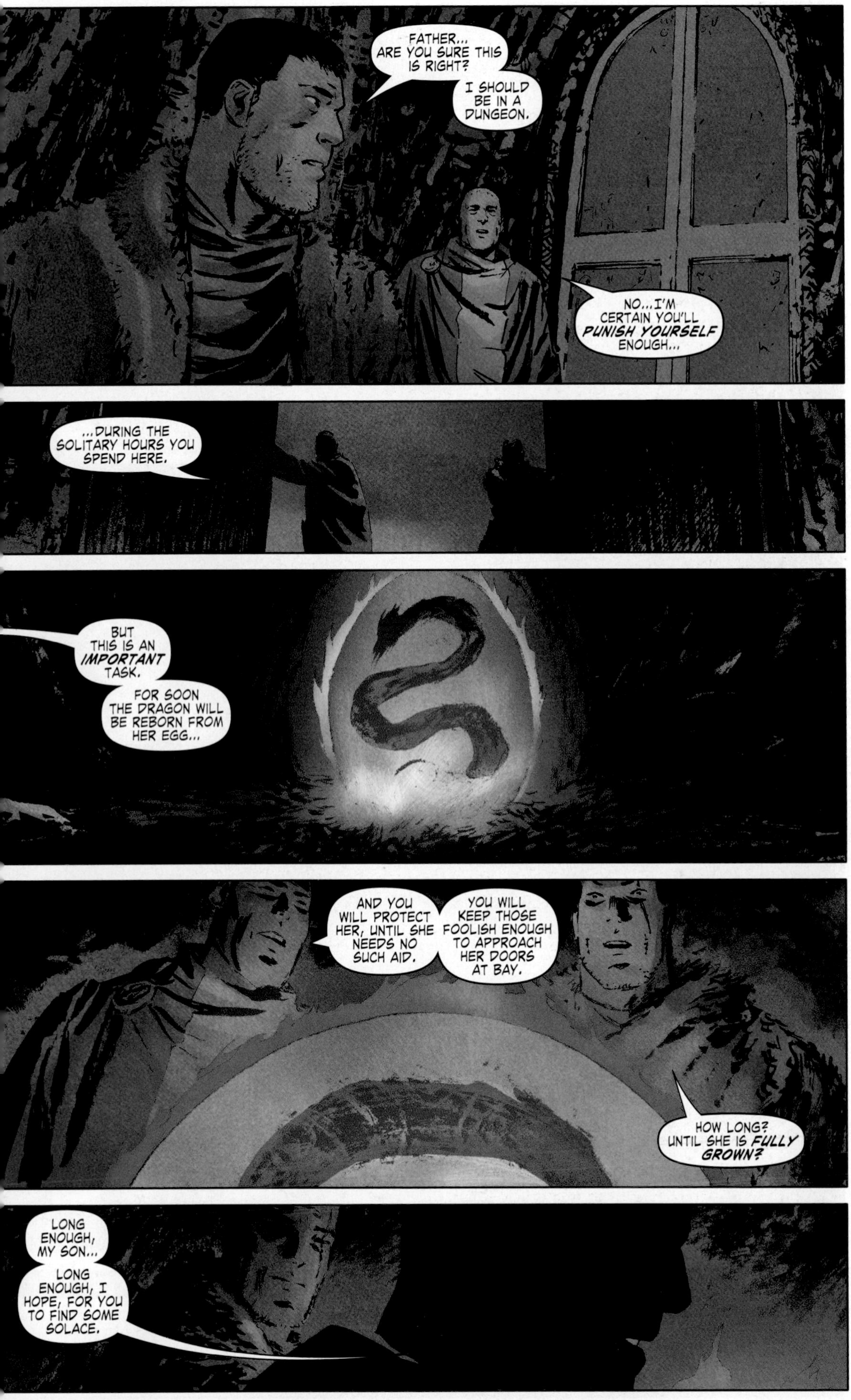
FATHER... ARE YOU SURE THIS IS RIGHT?
I SHOULD BE IN A DUNGEON.
NO...I'M CERTAIN YOU'LL **PUNISH YOURSELF** ENOUGH...
...DURING THE SOLITARY HOURS YOU SPEND HERE.
BUT THIS IS AN **IMPORTANT** TASK.
FOR SOON THE DRAGON WILL BE REBORN FROM HER EGG...
AND YOU WILL PROTECT HER, UNTIL SHE NEEDS NO SUCH AID.
YOU WILL KEEP THOSE FOOLISH ENOUGH TO APPROACH HER DOORS AT BAY.
HOW LONG? UNTIL SHE IS **FULLY GROWN?**
LONG ENOUGH, MY SON...
LONG ENOUGH, I HOPE, FOR YOU TO FIND SOME SOLACE.

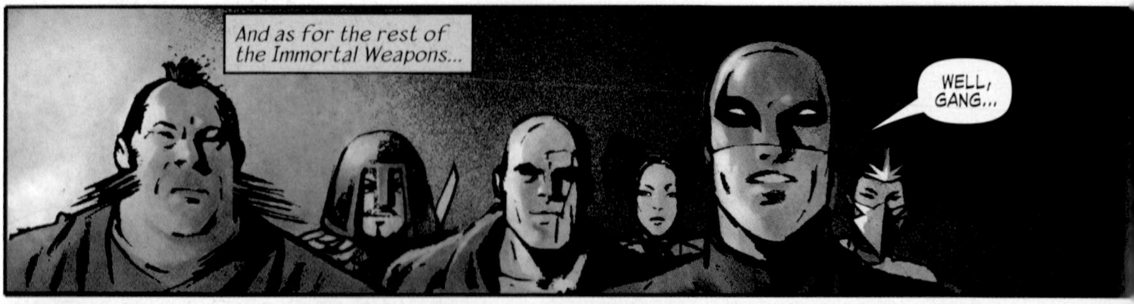
And as for the rest of the Immortal Weapons...
WELL, GANG...

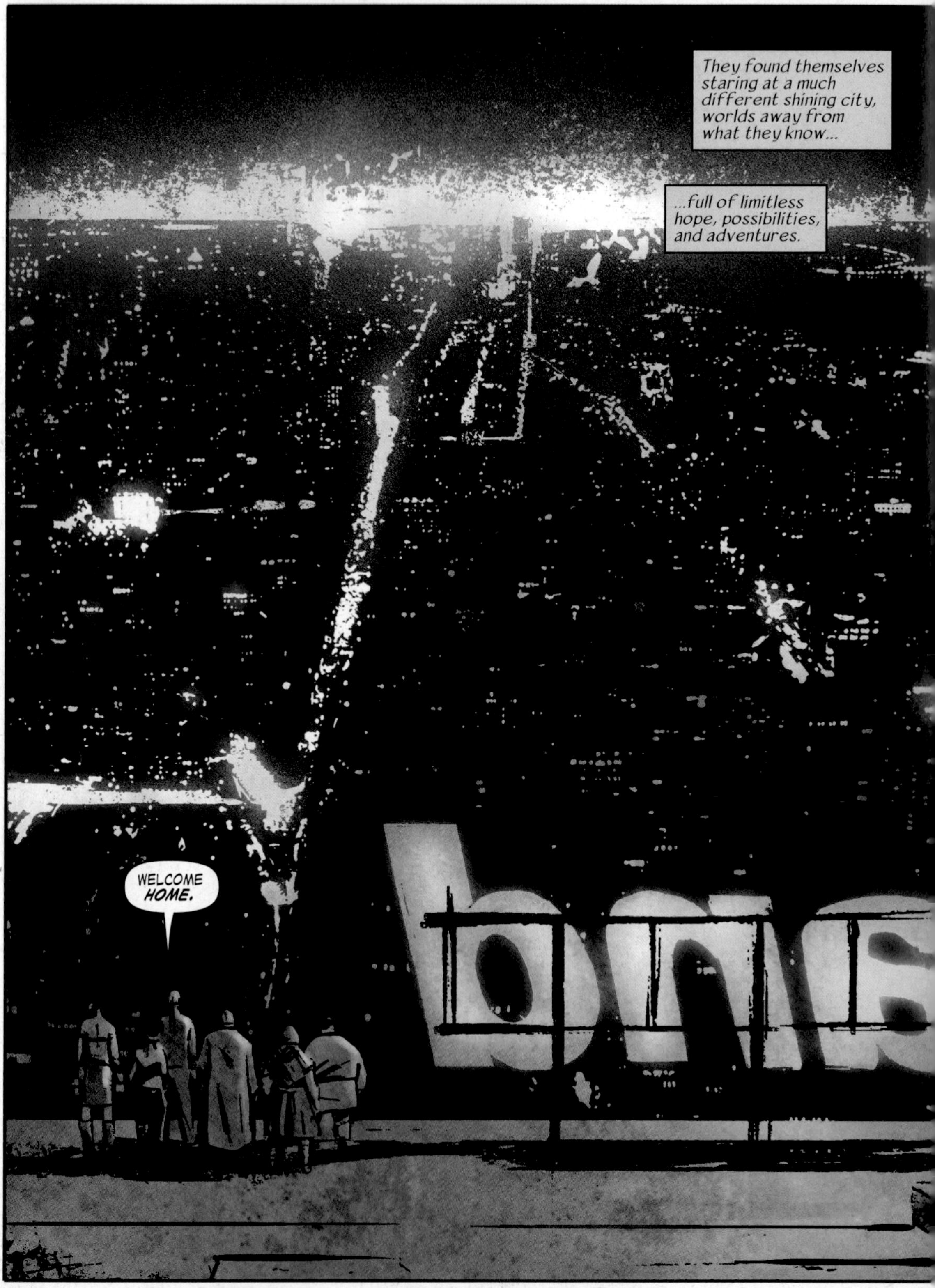
They found themselves staring at a much different shining city, worlds away from what they know...
...full of limitless hope, possibilities, and adventures.
WELCOME HOME.

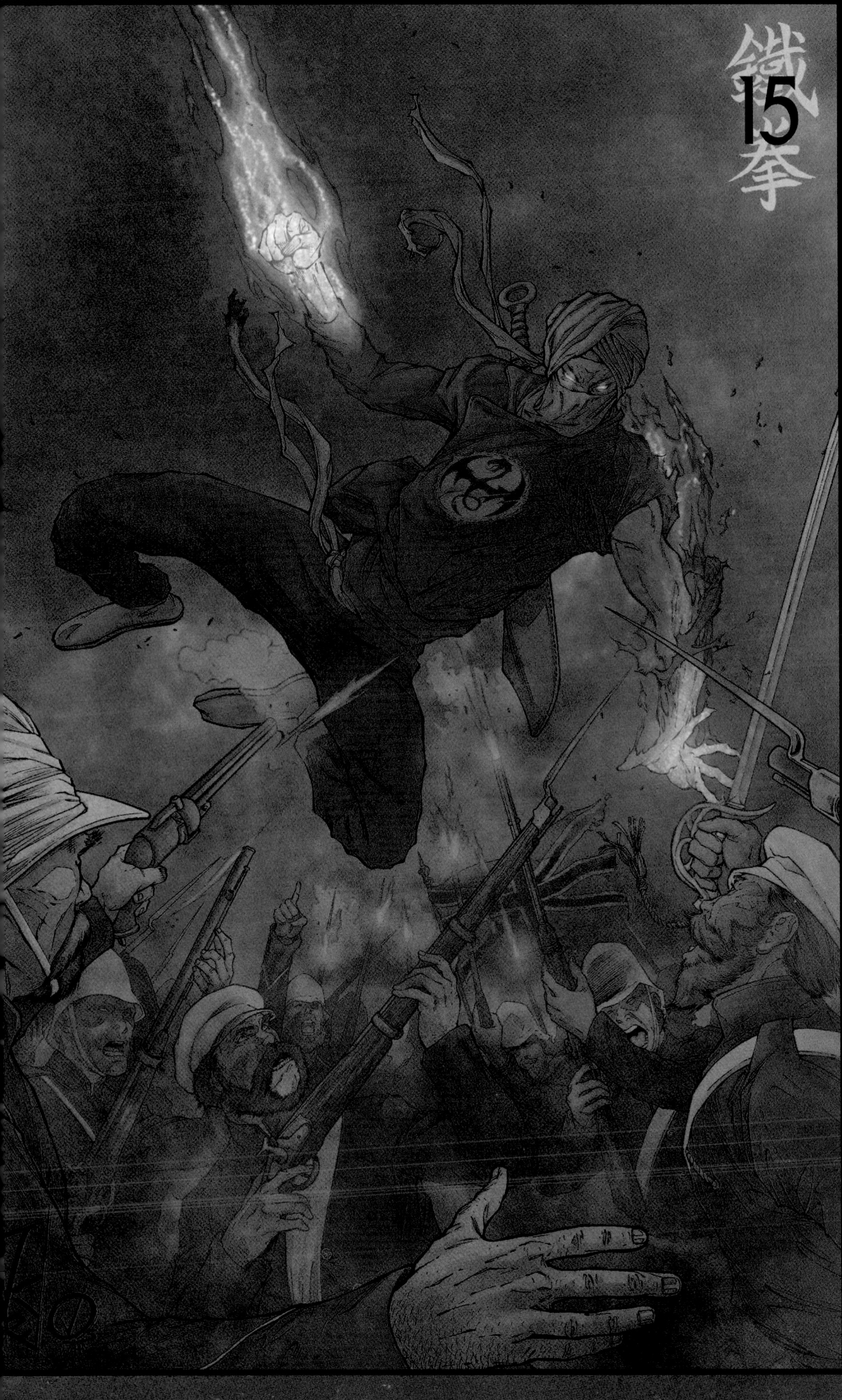
鐵拳
15

There have been sixty-six men and women to carry the mantle of THE IMMORTAL IRON FIST throughout the ages, men and women of great courage, valor, skill, and sacrifice. Sixty-six men and women have stood between man and the unstoppable forces of evil, willing to give all they have to hold back the hordes.

This is the story of one of them, as told in THE BOOK OF THE IRON FIST.

The Story of the Iron Fist Bei Bang-Wen
(1827-1860)

The Perfect Strategy Mind and his Miraculous Travels to the Dark Continent, and what Mysteries of the World and of the Self that He Learned There.

MATT FRACTION - WRITER
KHARI EVANS - PENCILER
VICTOR OLAZABA - INKER
JELENA KEVIC DJURDJEVIC &
PAUL MOUNTS - COLOR ART
DAVE LANPHEAR - LETTERER
IRENE LEE - PRODUCTION
ALEJANDRO ARBONA - ASSISTANT EDITOR
WARREN SIMONS - EDITOR
JOE QUESADA - EDITOR IN CHIEF
DAN BUCKLEY - PUBLISHER

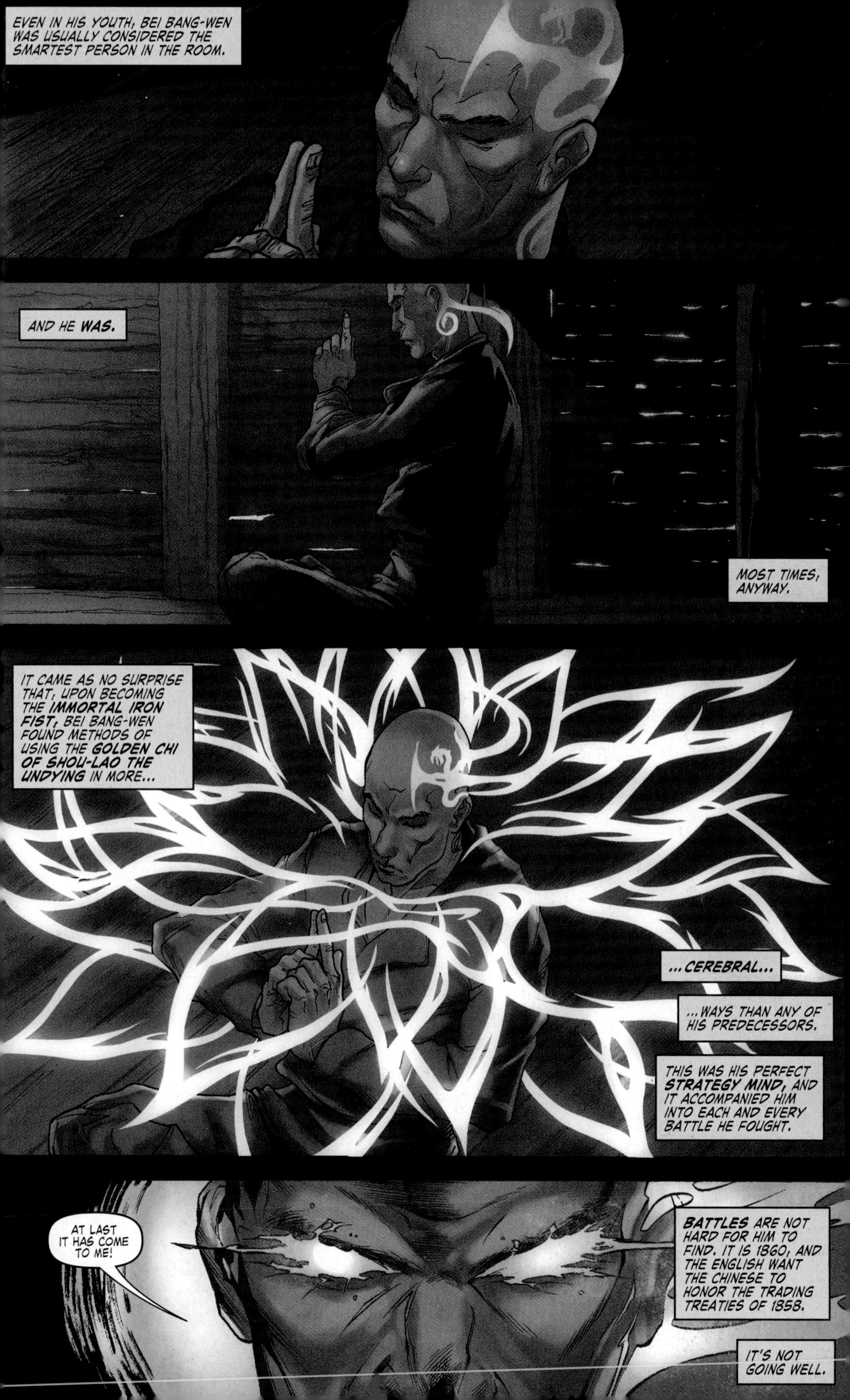
EVEN IN HIS YOUTH, BEI BANG-WEN WAS USUALLY CONSIDERED THE SMARTEST PERSON IN THE ROOM.
AND HE WAS.
MOST TIMES, ANYWAY.
IT CAME AS NO SURPRISE THAT, UPON BECOMING THE IMMORTAL IRON FIST, BEI BANG-WEN FOUND METHODS OF USING THE GOLDEN CHI OF SHOU-LAO THE UNDYING IN MORE...
...CEREBRAL...
...WAYS THAN ANY OF HIS PREDECESSORS.
THIS WAS HIS PERFECT STRATEGY MIND, AND IT ACCOMPANIED HIM INTO EACH AND EVERY BATTLE HE FOUGHT.
AT LAST IT HAS COME TO ME!
BATTLES ARE NOT HARD FOR HIM TO FIND. IT IS 1860, AND THE ENGLISH WANT THE CHINESE TO HONOR THE TRADING TREATIES OF 1858.
IT'S NOT GOING WELL.

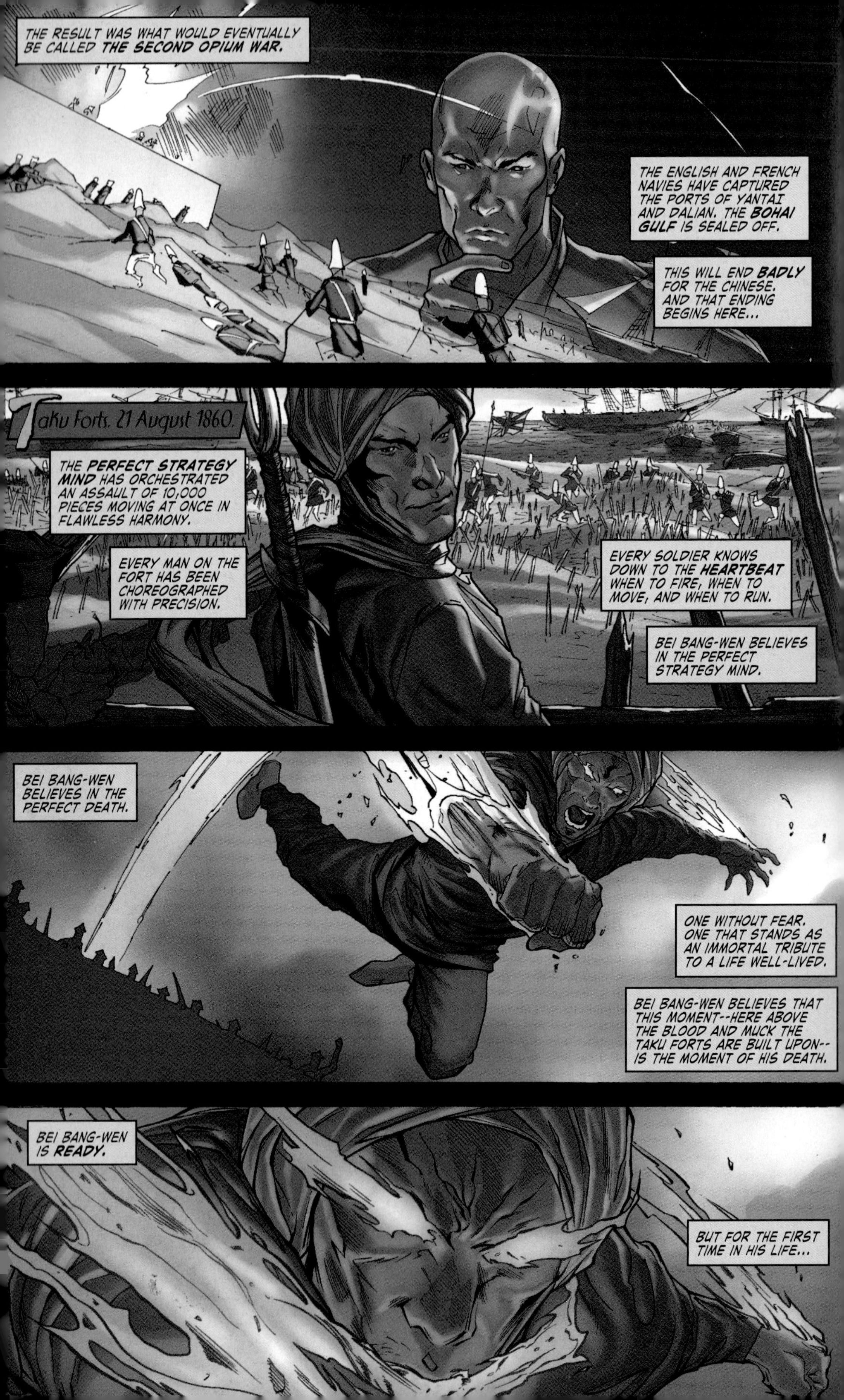
THE RESULT WAS WHAT WOULD EVENTUALLY BE CALLED THE SECOND OPIUM WAR.
THE ENGLISH AND FRENCH NAVIES HAVE CAPTURED THE PORTS OF YANTAI AND DALIAN. THE BOHAI GULF IS SEALED OFF.
THIS WILL END BADLY FOR THE CHINESE. AND THAT ENDING BEGINS HERE...
Taku Forts, 21 August 1860.
THE PERFECT STRATEGY MIND HAS ORCHESTRATED AN ASSAULT OF 10,000 PIECES MOVING AT ONCE IN FLAWLESS HARMONY.
EVERY MAN ON THE FORT HAS BEEN CHOREOGRAPHED WITH PRECISION.
EVERY SOLDIER KNOWS DOWN TO THE HEARTBEAT WHEN TO FIRE, WHEN TO MOVE, AND WHEN TO RUN.
BEI BANG-WEN BELIEVES IN THE PERFECT STRATEGY MIND.
BEI BANG-WEN BELIEVES IN THE PERFECT DEATH.
ONE WITHOUT FEAR. ONE THAT STANDS AS AN IMMORTAL TRIBUTE TO A LIFE WELL-LIVED.
BEI BANG-WEN BELIEVES THAT THIS MOMENT--HERE ABOVE THE BLOOD AND MUCK THE TAKU FORTS ARE BUILT UPON--IS THE MOMENT OF HIS DEATH.
BEI BANG-WEN IS READY.
BUT FOR THE FIRST TIME IN HIS LIFE...

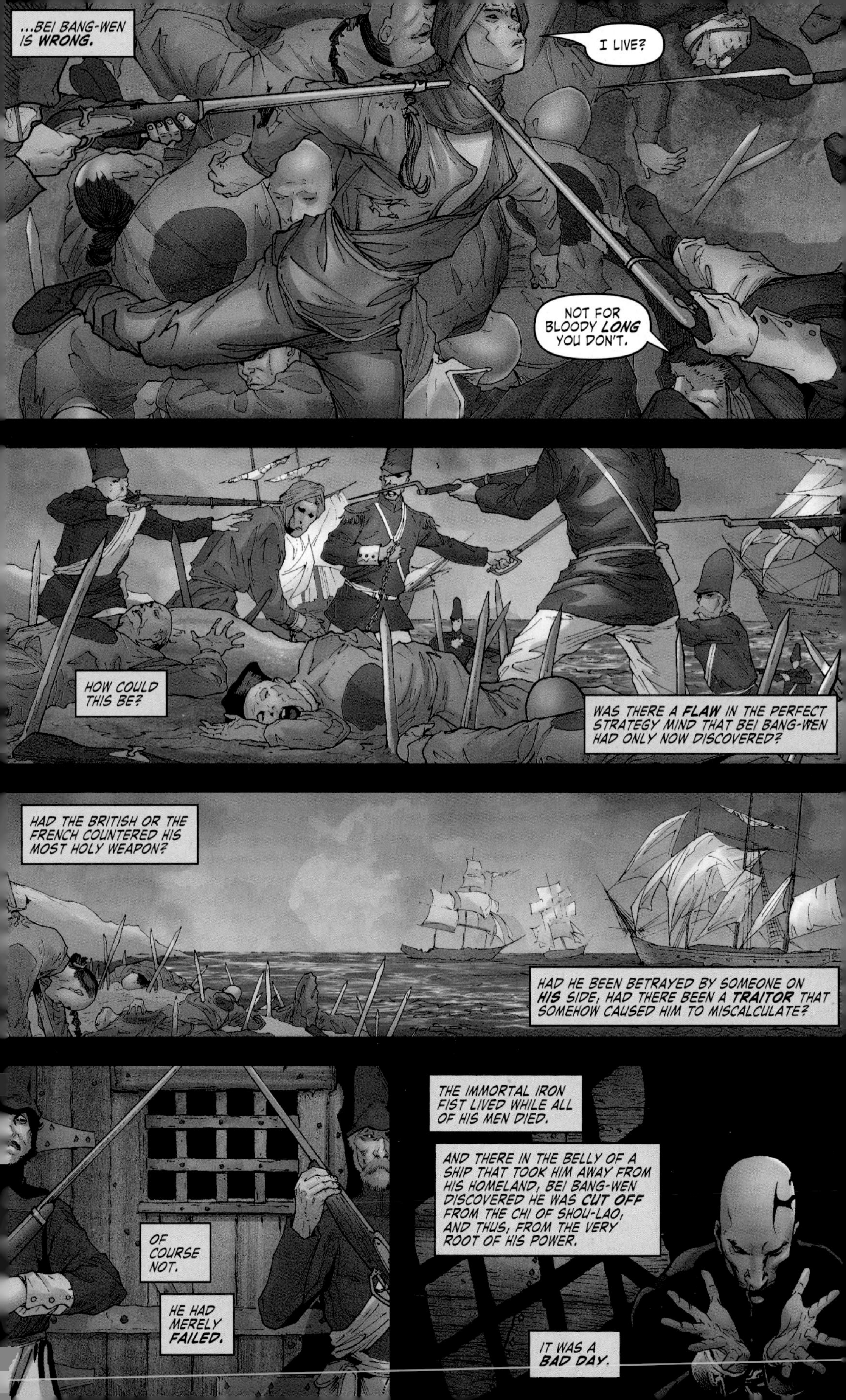
...BEI BANG-WEN IS WRONG.
I LIVE?
NOT FOR BLOODY LONG YOU DON'T.
HOW COULD THIS BE?
WAS THERE A FLAW IN THE PERFECT STRATEGY MIND THAT BEI BANG-WEN HAD ONLY NOW DISCOVERED?
HAD THE BRITISH OR THE FRENCH COUNTERED HIS MOST HOLY WEAPON?
HAD HE BEEN BETRAYED BY SOMEONE ON HIS SIDE, HAD THERE BEEN A TRAITOR THAT SOMEHOW CAUSED HIM TO MISCALCULATE?
OF COURSE NOT.
HE HAD MERELY FAILED.
THE IMMORTAL IRON FIST LIVED WHILE ALL OF HIS MEN DIED.
AND THERE IN THE BELLY OF A SHIP THAT TOOK HIM AWAY FROM HIS HOMELAND, BEI BANG-WEN DISCOVERED HE WAS CUT OFF FROM THE CHI OF SHOU-LAO, AND THUS, FROM THE VERY ROOT OF HIS POWER.
IT WAS A BAD DAY.

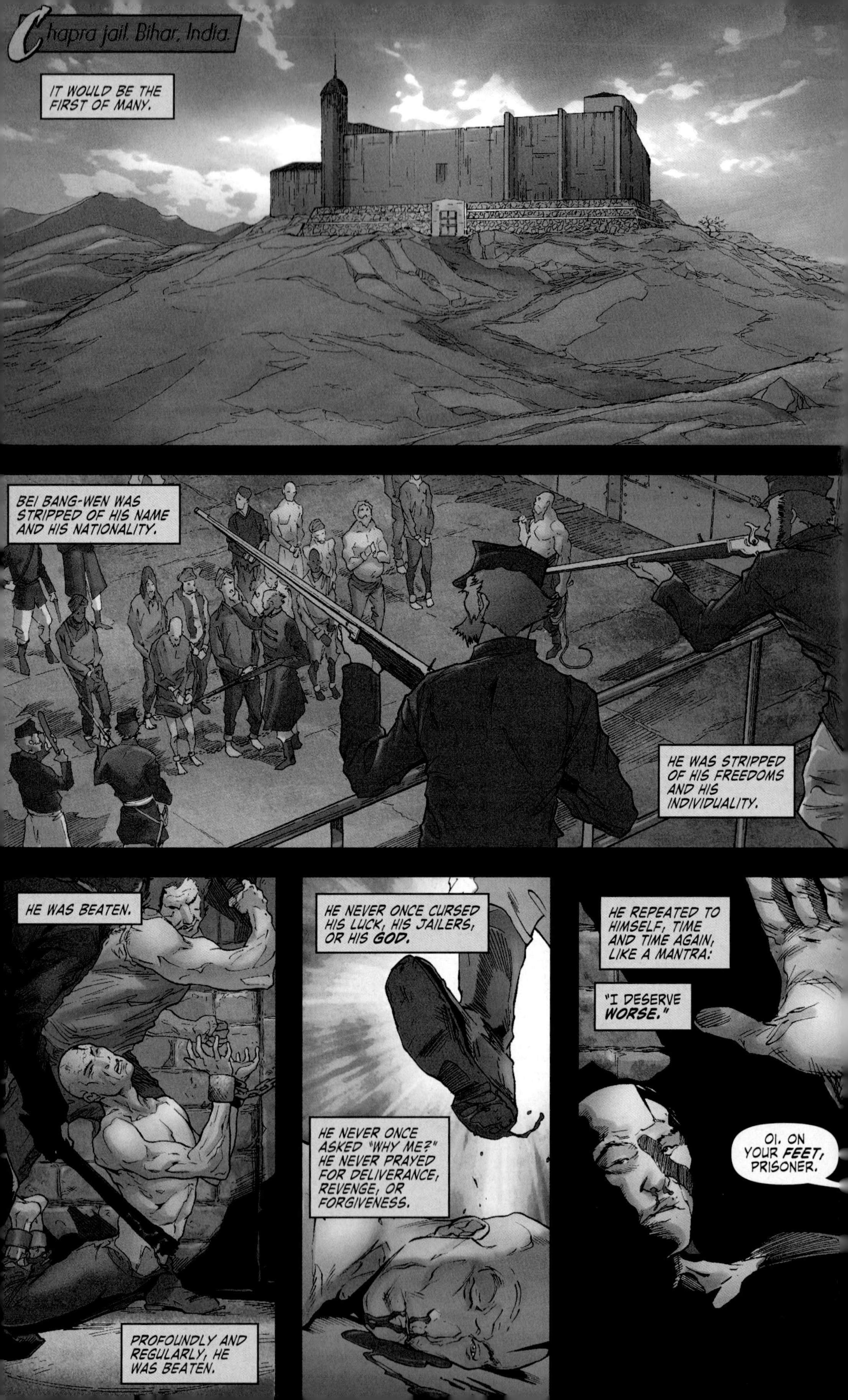
Chapra jail. Bihar, India.
IT WOULD BE THE FIRST OF MANY.
BEI BANG-WEN WAS STRIPPED OF HIS NAME AND HIS NATIONALITY.
HE WAS STRIPPED OF HIS FREEDOMS AND HIS INDIVIDUALITY.
HE WAS BEATEN.
PROFOUNDLY AND REGULARLY, HE WAS BEATEN.
HE NEVER ONCE CURSED HIS LUCK, HIS JAILERS, OR HIS GOD.
HE NEVER ONCE ASKED "WHY ME?" HE NEVER PRAYED FOR DELIVERANCE, REVENGE, OR FORGIVENESS.
HE REPEATED TO HIMSELF, TIME AND TIME AGAIN, LIKE A MANTRA:
"I DESERVE WORSE."
OI. ON YOUR FEET, PRISONER.

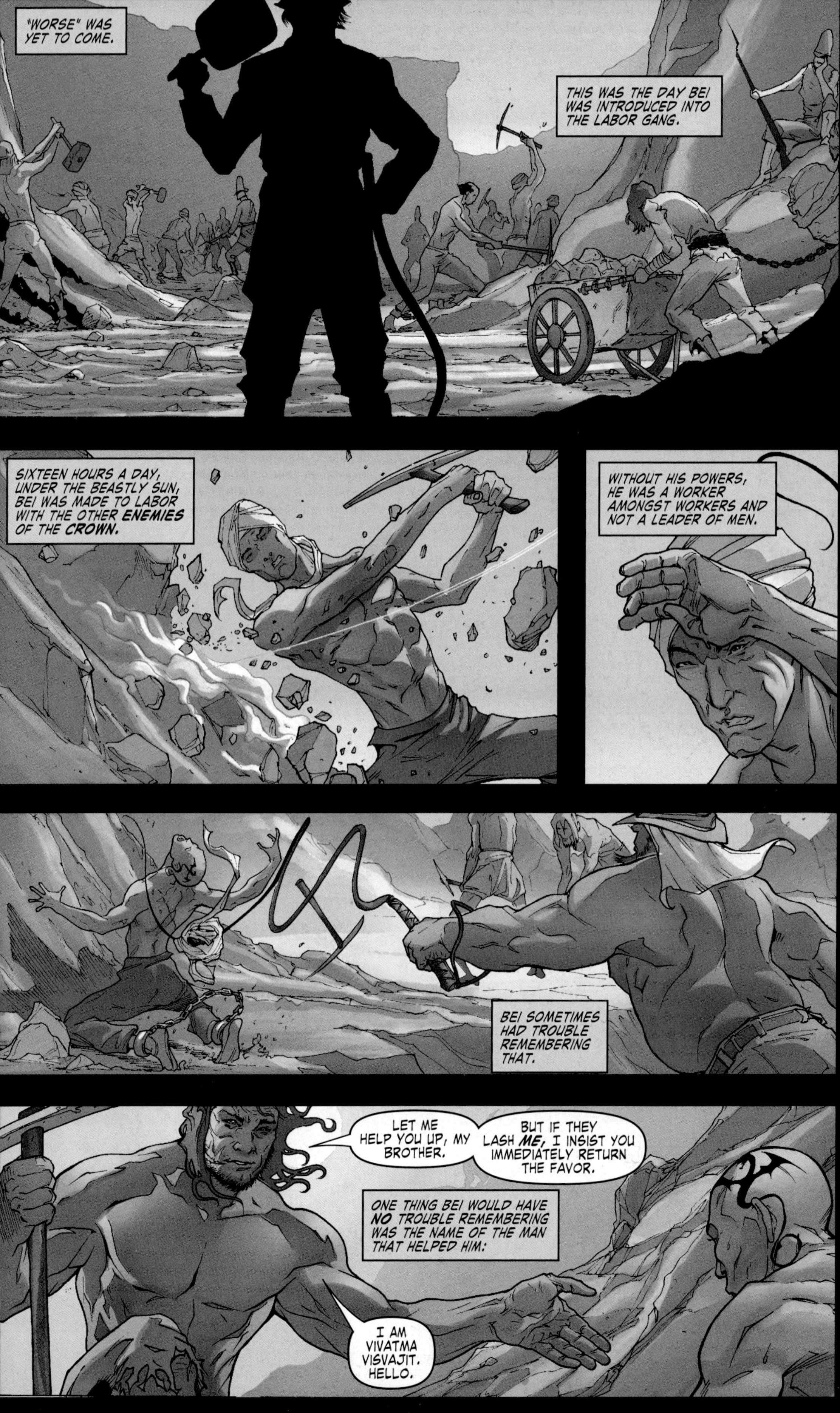
"WORSE" WAS YET TO COME.
THIS WAS THE DAY BEI WAS INTRODUCED INTO THE LABOR GANG.
SIXTEEN HOURS A DAY, UNDER THE BEASTLY SUN, BEI WAS MADE TO LABOR WITH THE OTHER **ENEMIES** OF THE **CROWN.**
WITHOUT HIS POWERS, HE WAS A WORKER AMONGST WORKERS AND NOT A LEADER OF MEN.
BEI SOMETIMES HAD TROUBLE REMEMBERING THAT.
LET ME HELP YOU UP, MY BROTHER.
BUT IF THEY LASH **ME,** I INSIST YOU IMMEDIATELY RETURN THE FAVOR.
ONE THING BEI WOULD HAVE **NO** TROUBLE REMEMBERING WAS THE NAME OF THE MAN THAT HELPED HIM:
I AM VIVATMA VISVAJIT. HELLO.

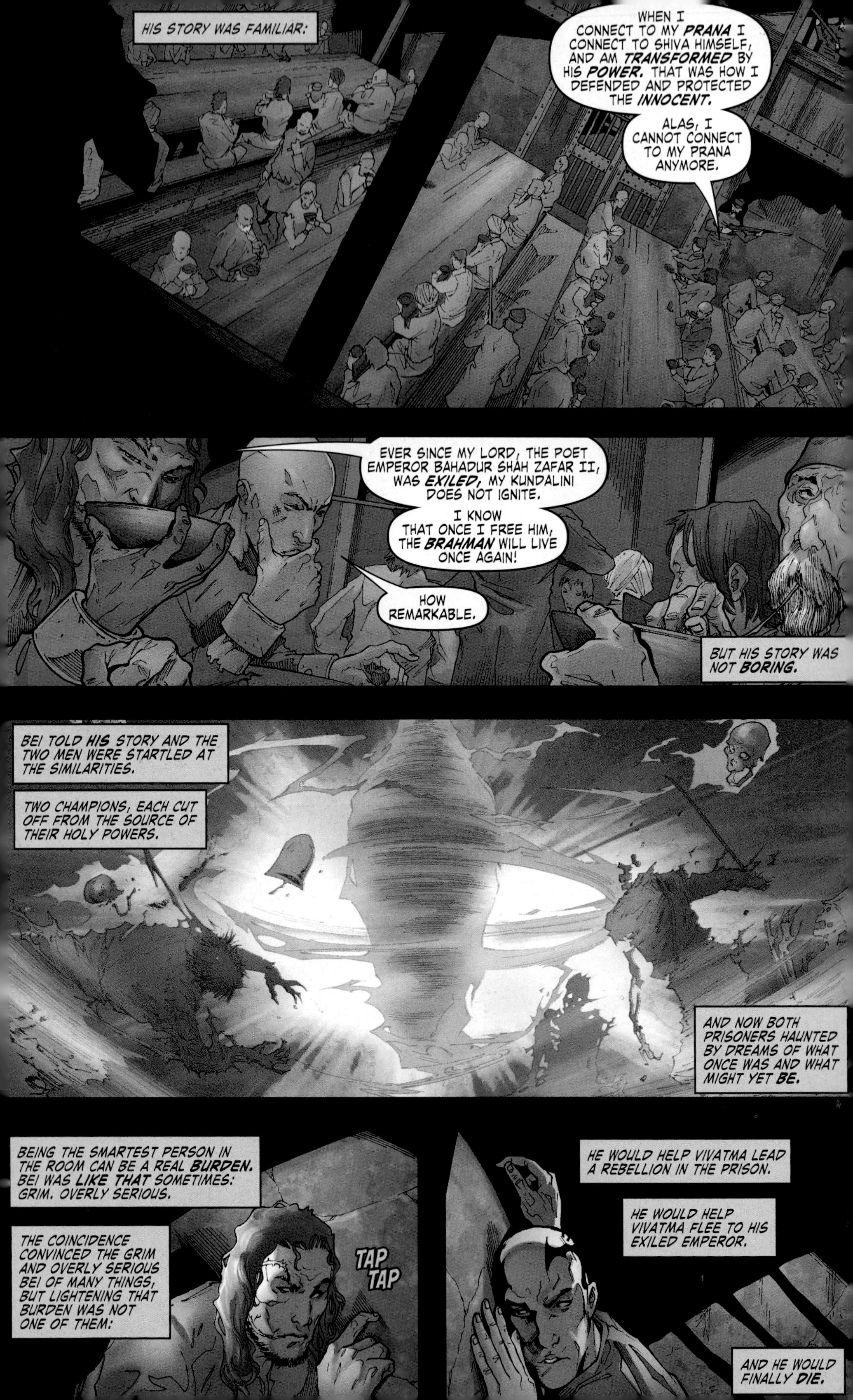
HIS STORY WAS FAMILIAR:
WHEN I CONNECT TO MY PRANA I CONNECT TO SHIVA HIMSELF, AND AM TRANSFORMED BY HIS POWER. THAT WAS HOW I DEFENDED AND PROTECTED THE INNOCENT.
ALAS, I CANNOT CONNECT TO MY PRANA ANYMORE.
EVER SINCE MY LORD, THE POET EMPEROR BAHADUR SHAH ZAFAR II, WAS EXILED, MY KUNDALINI DOES NOT IGNITE.
I KNOW THAT ONCE I FREE HIM, THE BRAHMAN WILL LIVE ONCE AGAIN!
HOW REMARKABLE.
BUT HIS STORY WAS NOT BORING.
BEI TOLD HIS STORY AND THE TWO MEN WERE STARTLED AT THE SIMILARITIES.
TWO CHAMPIONS, EACH CUT OFF FROM THE SOURCE OF THEIR HOLY POWERS.
AND NOW BOTH PRISONERS HAUNTED BY DREAMS OF WHAT ONCE WAS AND WHAT MIGHT YET BE.
BEING THE SMARTEST PERSON IN THE ROOM CAN BE A REAL BURDEN. BEI WAS LIKE THAT SOMETIMES: GRIM. OVERLY SERIOUS.
THE COINCIDENCE CONVINCED THE GRIM AND OVERLY SERIOUS BEI OF MANY THINGS, BUT LIGHTENING THAT BURDEN WAS NOT ONE OF THEM:
TAP TAP
HE WOULD HELP VIVATMA LEAD A REBELLION IN THE PRISON.
HE WOULD HELP VIVATMA FLEE TO HIS EXILED EMPEROR.
AND HE WOULD FINALLY DIE.

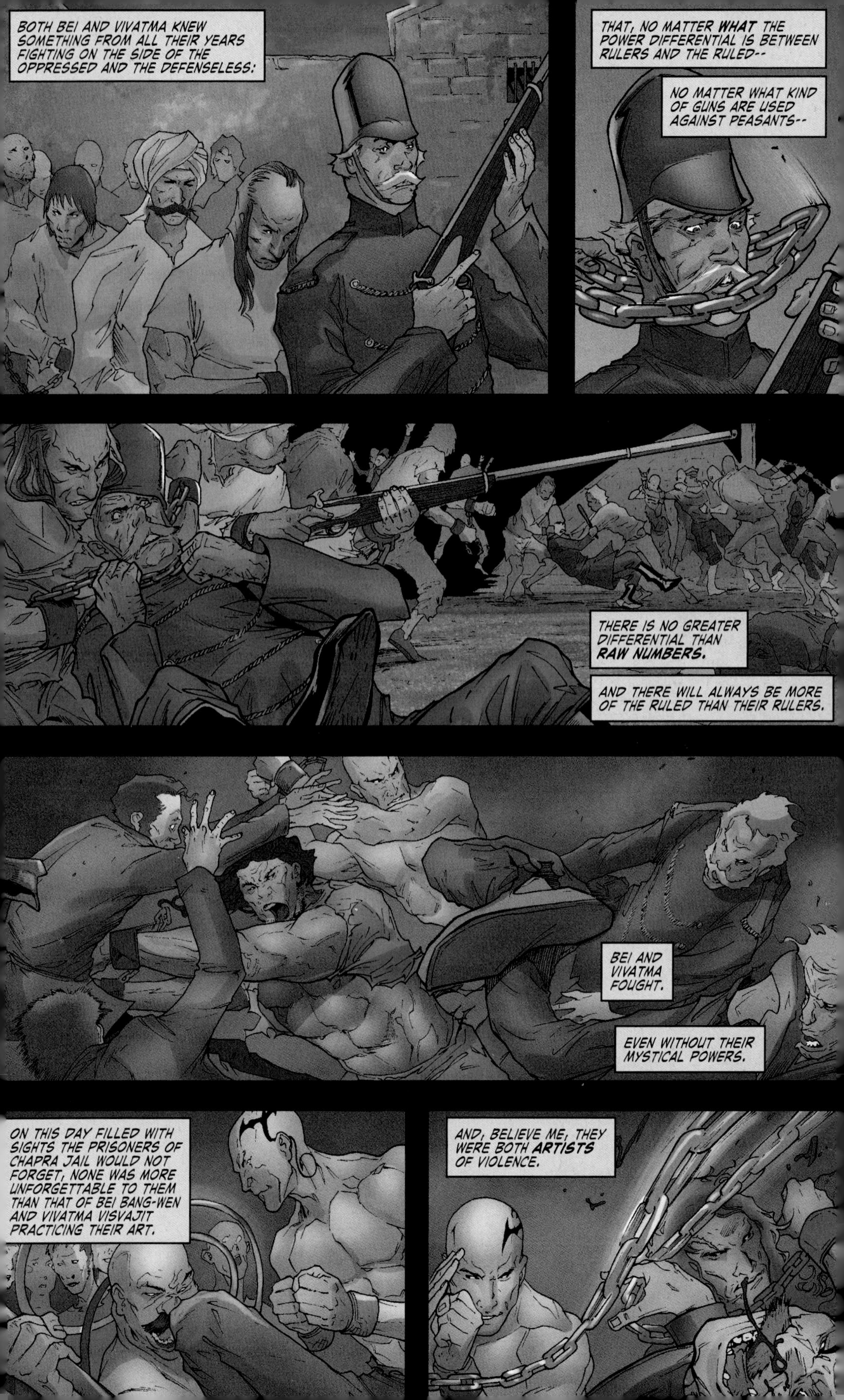
BOTH BEI AND VIVATMA KNEW SOMETHING FROM ALL THEIR YEARS FIGHTING ON THE SIDE OF THE OPPRESSED AND THE DEFENSELESS:
THAT, NO MATTER **WHAT** THE POWER DIFFERENTIAL IS BETWEEN RULERS AND THE RULED--
NO MATTER WHAT KIND OF GUNS ARE USED AGAINST PEASANTS--
THERE IS NO GREATER DIFFERENTIAL THAN **RAW NUMBERS.**
AND THERE WILL ALWAYS BE MORE OF THE RULED THAN THEIR RULERS.
BEI AND VIVATMA FOUGHT.
EVEN WITHOUT THEIR MYSTICAL POWERS.
ON THIS DAY FILLED WITH SIGHTS THE PRISONERS OF CHAPRA JAIL WOULD NOT FORGET, NONE WAS MORE UNFORGETTABLE TO THEM THAN THAT OF BEI BANG-WEN AND VIVATMA VISVAJIT PRACTICING THEIR ART.
AND, BELIEVE ME, THEY WERE BOTH **ARTISTS** OF VIOLENCE.

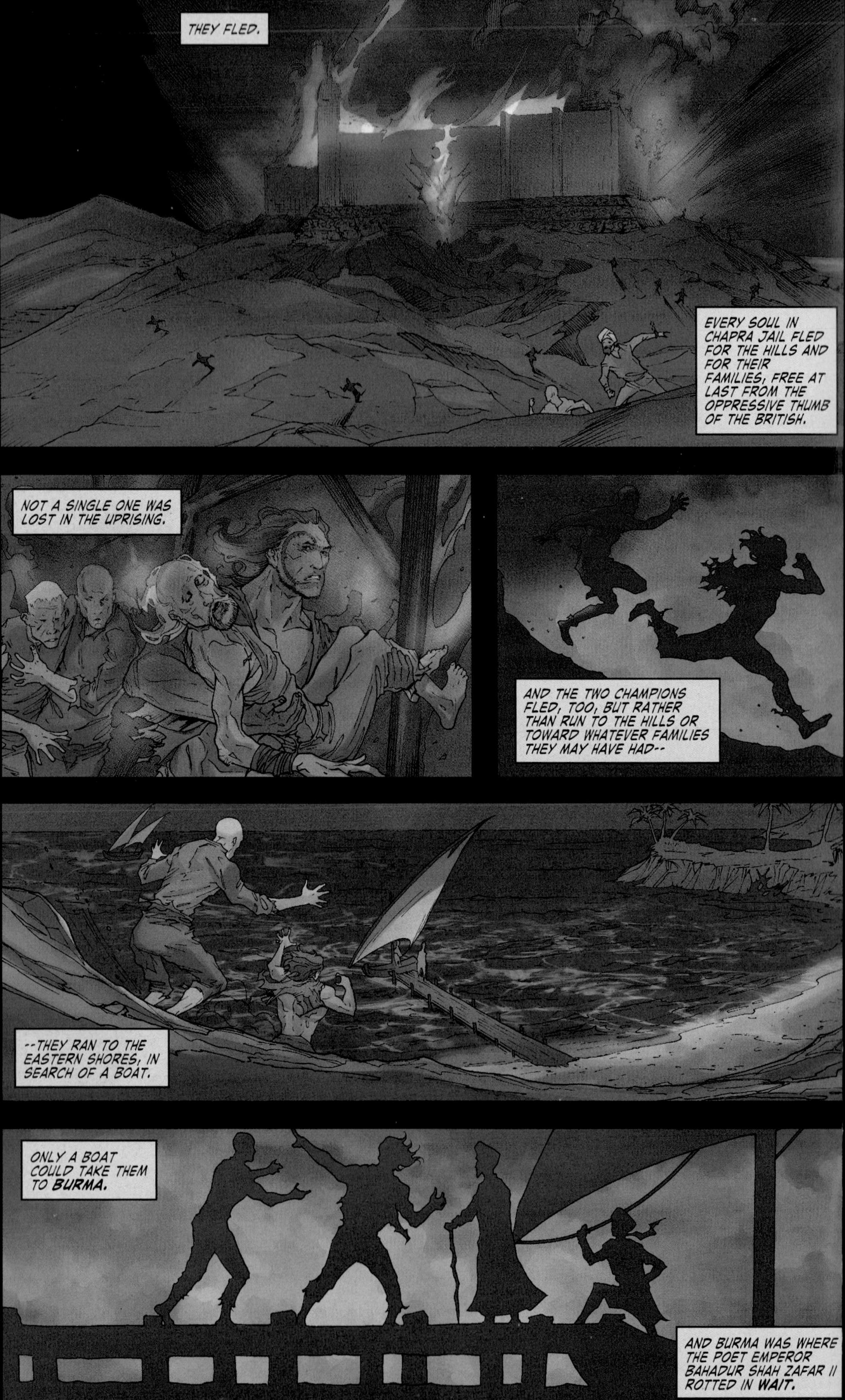
THEY FLED.
EVERY SOUL IN CHAPRA JAIL FLED FOR THE HILLS AND FOR THEIR FAMILIES, FREE AT LAST FROM THE OPPRESSIVE THUMB OF THE BRITISH.
NOT A SINGLE ONE WAS LOST IN THE UPRISING.
AND THE TWO CHAMPIONS FLED, TOO, BUT RATHER THAN RUN TO THE HILLS OR TOWARD WHATEVER FAMILIES THEY MAY HAVE HAD--
--THEY RAN TO THE EASTERN SHORES, IN SEARCH OF A BOAT.
ONLY A BOAT COULD TAKE THEM TO BURMA.
AND BURMA WAS WHERE THE POET EMPEROR BAHADUR SHAH ZAFAR II ROTTED IN WAIT.

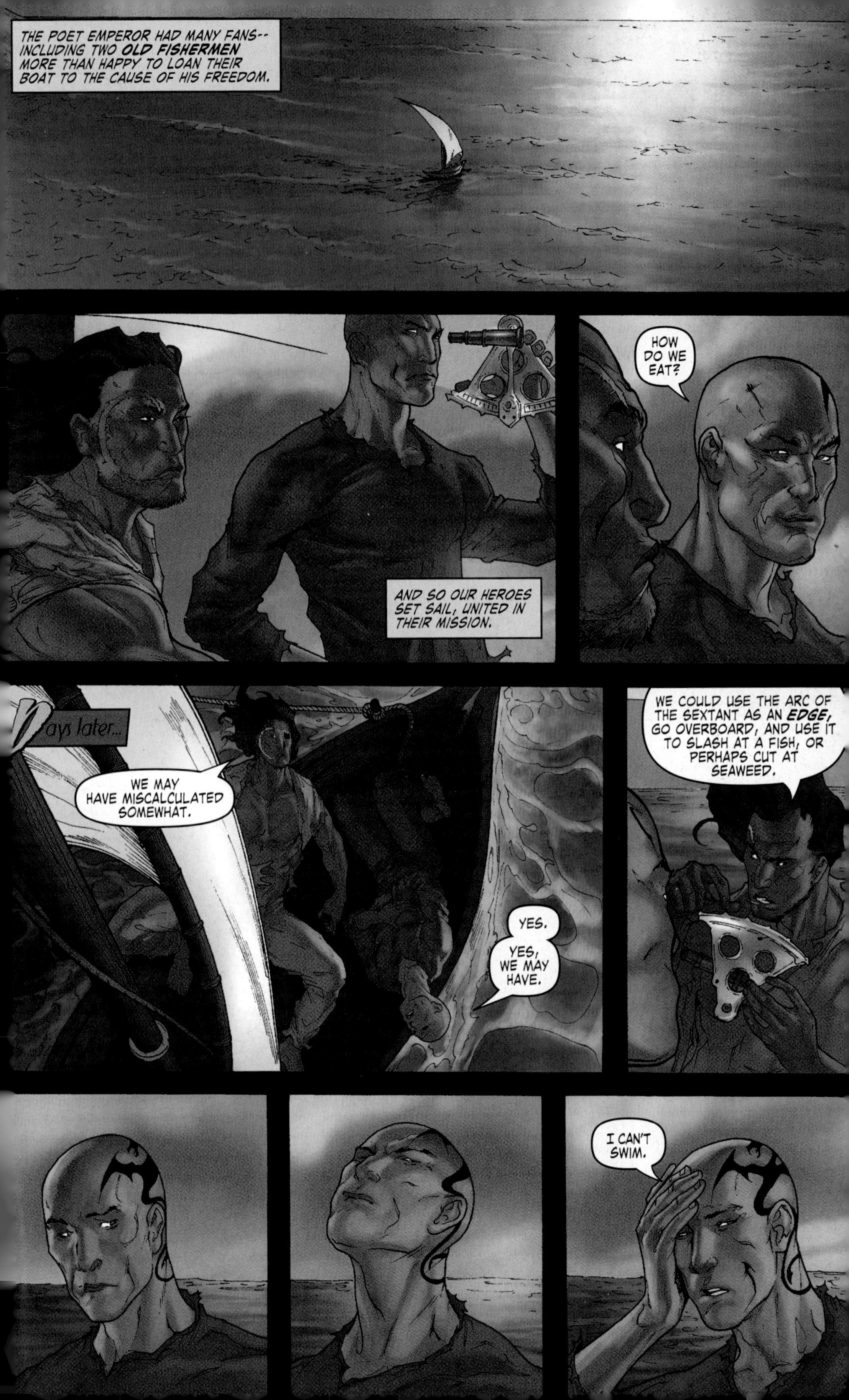
THE POET EMPEROR HAD MANY FANS-- INCLUDING TWO OLD FISHERMEN MORE THAN HAPPY TO LOAN THEIR BOAT TO THE CAUSE OF HIS FREEDOM.
AND SO OUR HEROES SET SAIL, UNITED IN THEIR MISSION.
HOW DO WE EAT?
Days later...
WE MAY HAVE MISCALCULATED SOMEWHAT.
YES.
YES, WE MAY HAVE.
WE COULD USE THE ARC OF THE SEXTANT AS AN EDGE, GO OVERBOARD, AND USE IT TO SLASH AT A FISH, OR PERHAPS CUT AT SEAWEED.
I CAN'T SWIM.

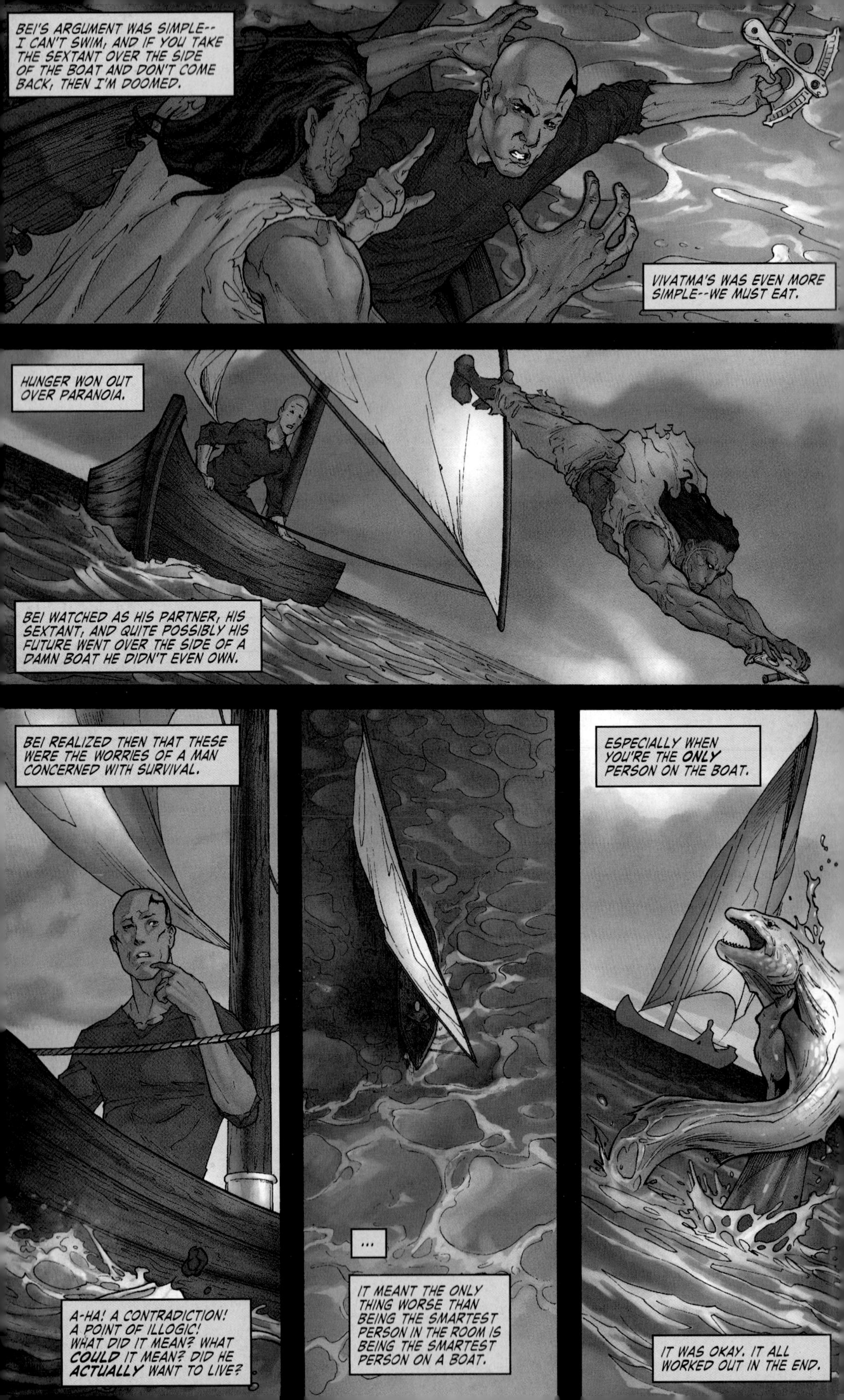

BEI'S ARGUMENT WAS SIMPLE-- I CAN'T SWIM, AND IF YOU TAKE THE SEXTANT OVER THE SIDE OF THE BOAT AND DON'T COME BACK, THEN I'M DOOMED.
VIVATMA'S WAS EVEN MORE SIMPLE--WE MUST EAT.
HUNGER WON OUT OVER PARANOIA.
BEI WATCHED AS HIS PARTNER, HIS SEXTANT, AND QUITE POSSIBLY HIS FUTURE WENT OVER THE SIDE OF A DAMN BOAT HE DIDN'T EVEN OWN.
BEI REALIZED THEN THAT THESE WERE THE WORRIES OF A MAN CONCERNED WITH SURVIVAL.
A-HA! A CONTRADICTION! A POINT OF ILLOGIC! WHAT DID IT MEAN? WHAT **COULD** IT MEAN? DID HE **ACTUALLY** WANT TO LIVE?
...
IT MEANT THE ONLY THING WORSE THAN BEING THE SMARTEST PERSON IN THE ROOM IS BEING THE SMARTEST PERSON ON A BOAT.
ESPECIALLY WHEN YOU'RE THE **ONLY** PERSON ON THE BOAT.
IT WAS OKAY. IT ALL WORKED OUT IN THE END.

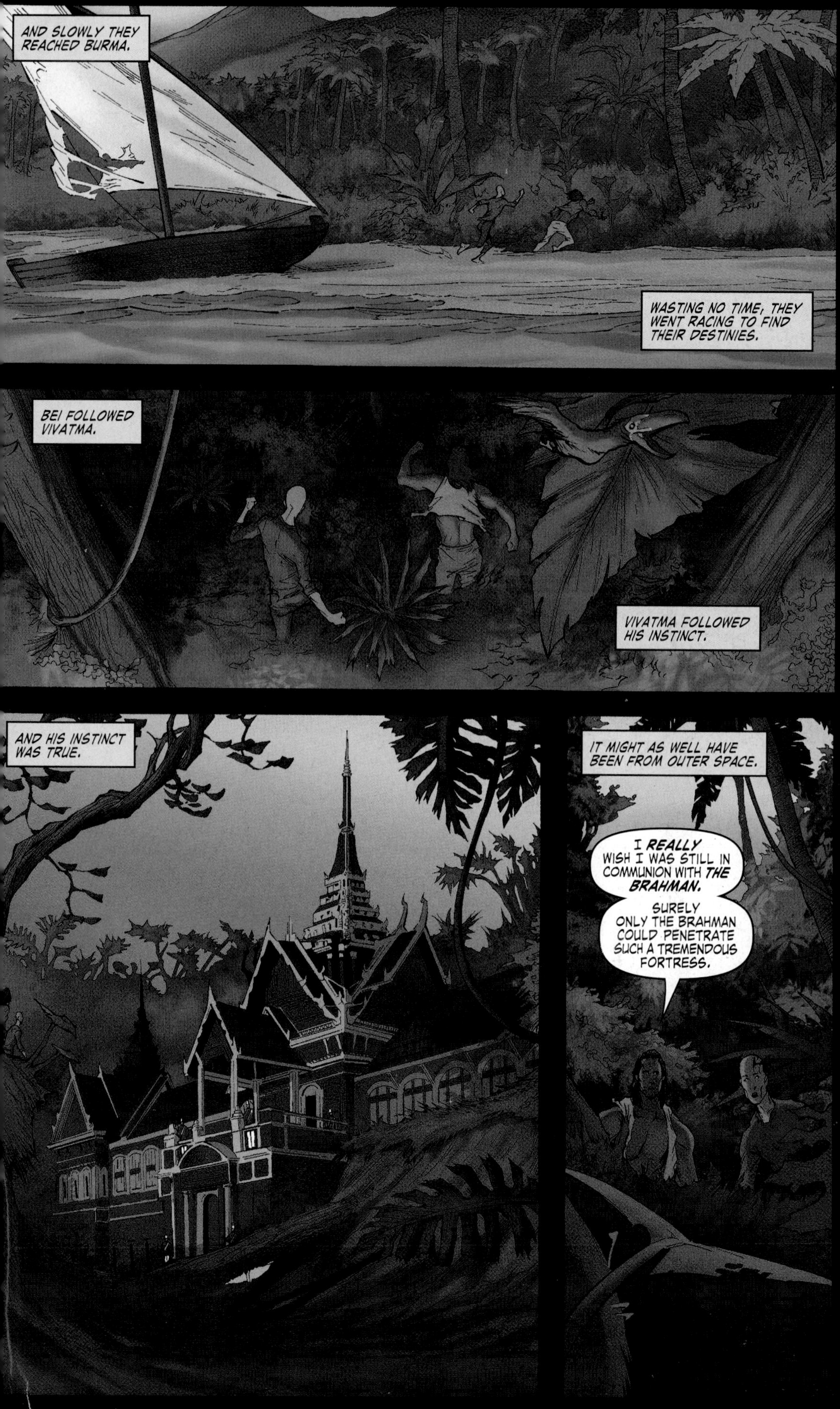

AND SLOWLY THEY REACHED BURMA.
WASTING NO TIME, THEY WENT RACING TO FIND THEIR DESTINIES.
BEI FOLLOWED VIVATMA.
VIVATMA FOLLOWED HIS INSTINCT.
AND HIS INSTINCT WAS TRUE.
IT MIGHT AS WELL HAVE BEEN FROM OUTER SPACE.
I **REALLY** WISH I WAS STILL IN COMMUNION WITH **THE BRAHMAN.**
SURELY ONLY THE BRAHMAN COULD PENETRATE SUCH A TREMENDOUS FORTRESS.

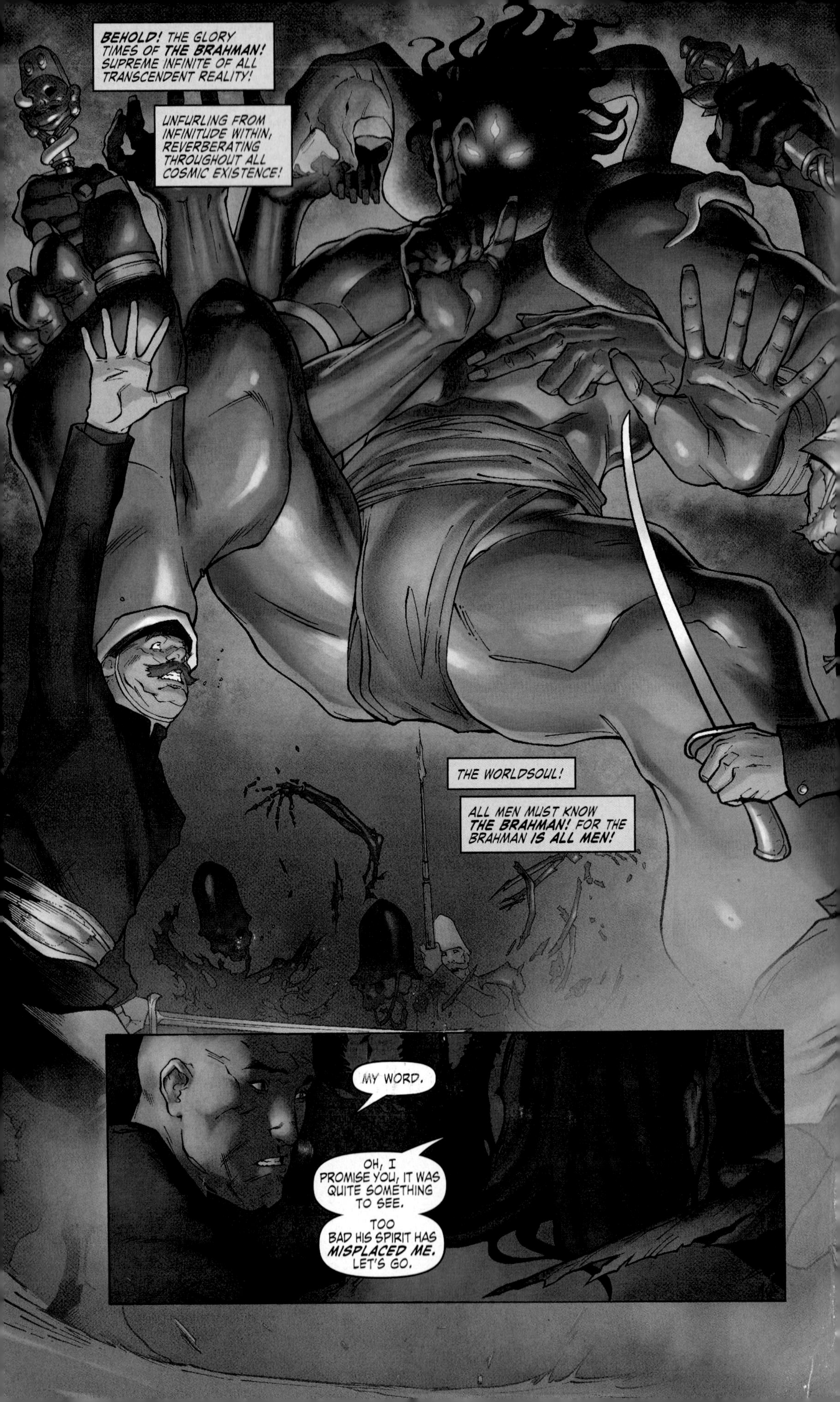
BEHOLD! THE GLORY TIMES OF THE BRAHMAN! SUPREME INFINITE OF ALL TRANSCENDENT REALITY!
UNFURLING FROM INFINITUDE WITHIN, REVERBERATING THROUGHOUT ALL COSMIC EXISTENCE!
THE WORLDSOUL!
ALL MEN MUST KNOW THE BRAHMAN! FOR THE BRAHMAN IS ALL MEN!
MY WORD.
OH, I PROMISE YOU, IT WAS QUITE SOMETHING TO SEE.
TOO BAD HIS SPIRIT HAS MISPLACED ME. LET'S GO.

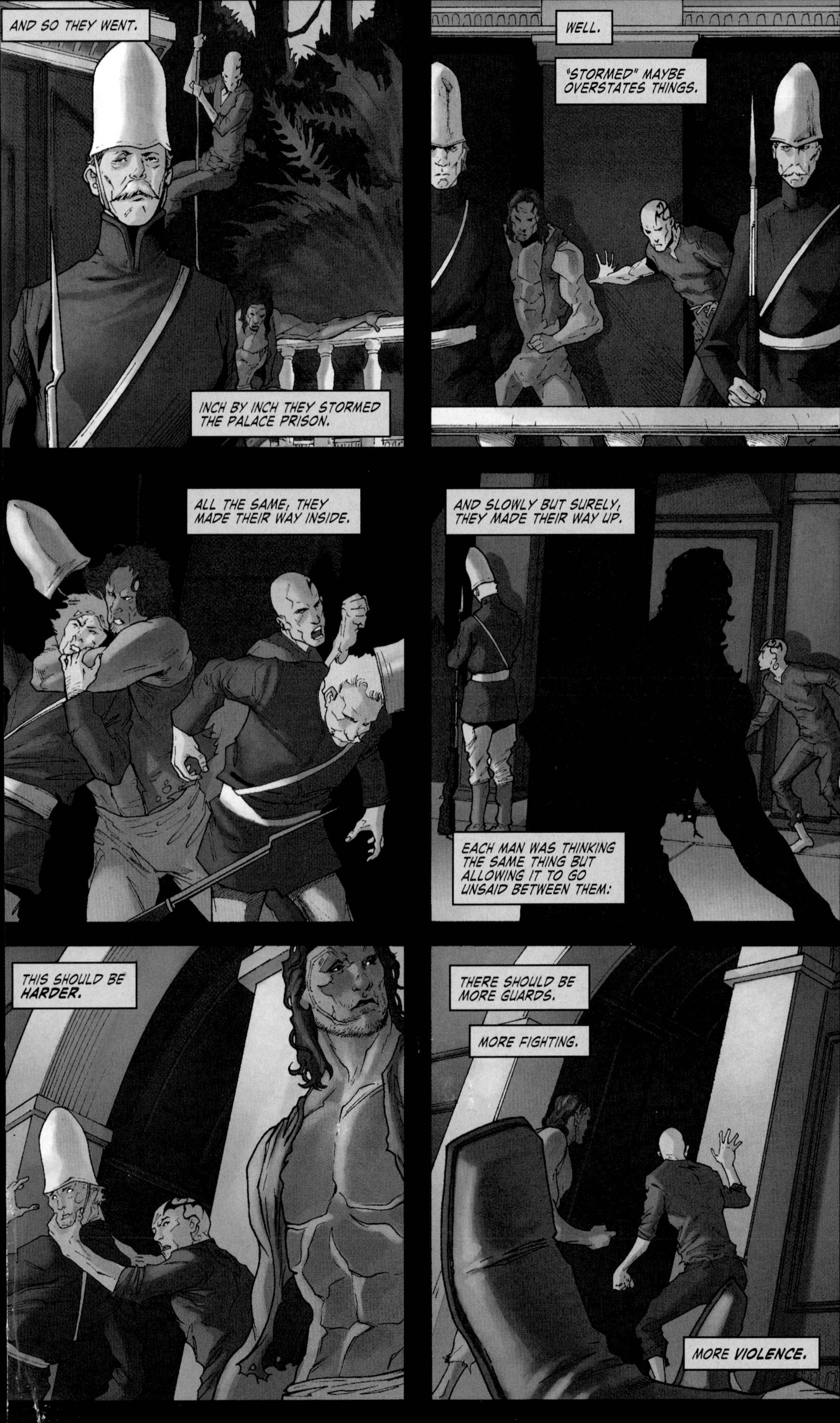
AND SO THEY WENT.
INCH BY INCH THEY STORMED THE PALACE PRISON.
WELL.
"STORMED" MAYBE OVERSTATES THINGS.
ALL THE SAME, THEY MADE THEIR WAY INSIDE.
AND SLOWLY BUT SURELY, THEY MADE THEIR WAY UP.
EACH MAN WAS THINKING THE SAME THING BUT ALLOWING IT TO GO UNSAID BETWEEN THEM:
THIS SHOULD BE **HARDER**.
THERE SHOULD BE MORE GUARDS.
MORE FIGHTING.
MORE **VIOLENCE**.

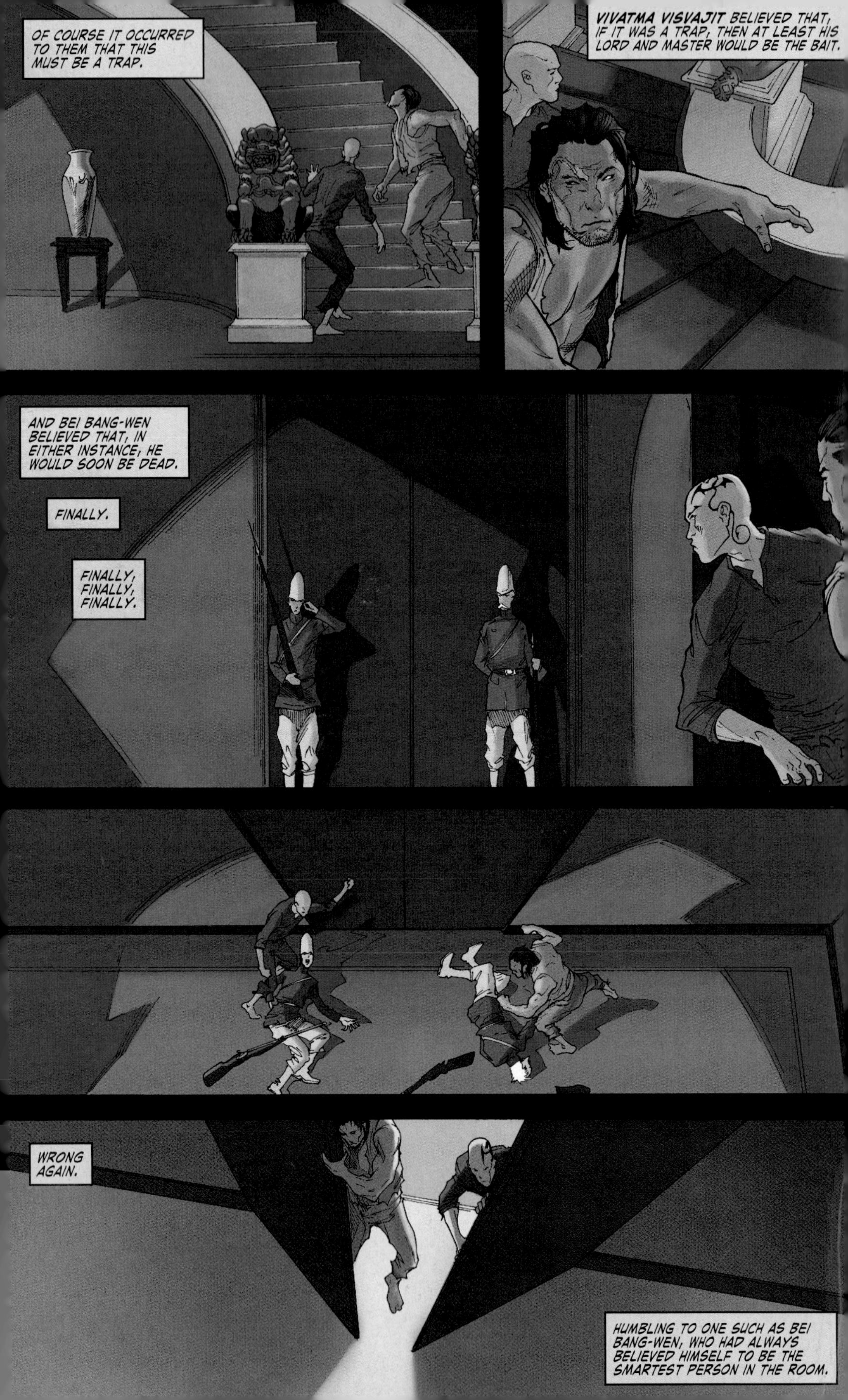
OF COURSE IT OCCURRED TO THEM THAT THIS MUST BE A TRAP.
VIVATMA VISVAJIT BELIEVED THAT, IF IT WAS A TRAP, THEN AT LEAST HIS LORD AND MASTER WOULD BE THE BAIT.
AND BEI BANG-WEN BELIEVED THAT, IN EITHER INSTANCE, HE WOULD SOON BE DEAD.
FINALLY.
FINALLY, FINALLY, FINALLY.
WRONG AGAIN.
HUMBLING TO ONE SUCH AS BEI BANG-WEN, WHO HAD ALWAYS BELIEVED HIMSELF TO BE THE SMARTEST PERSON IN THE ROOM.

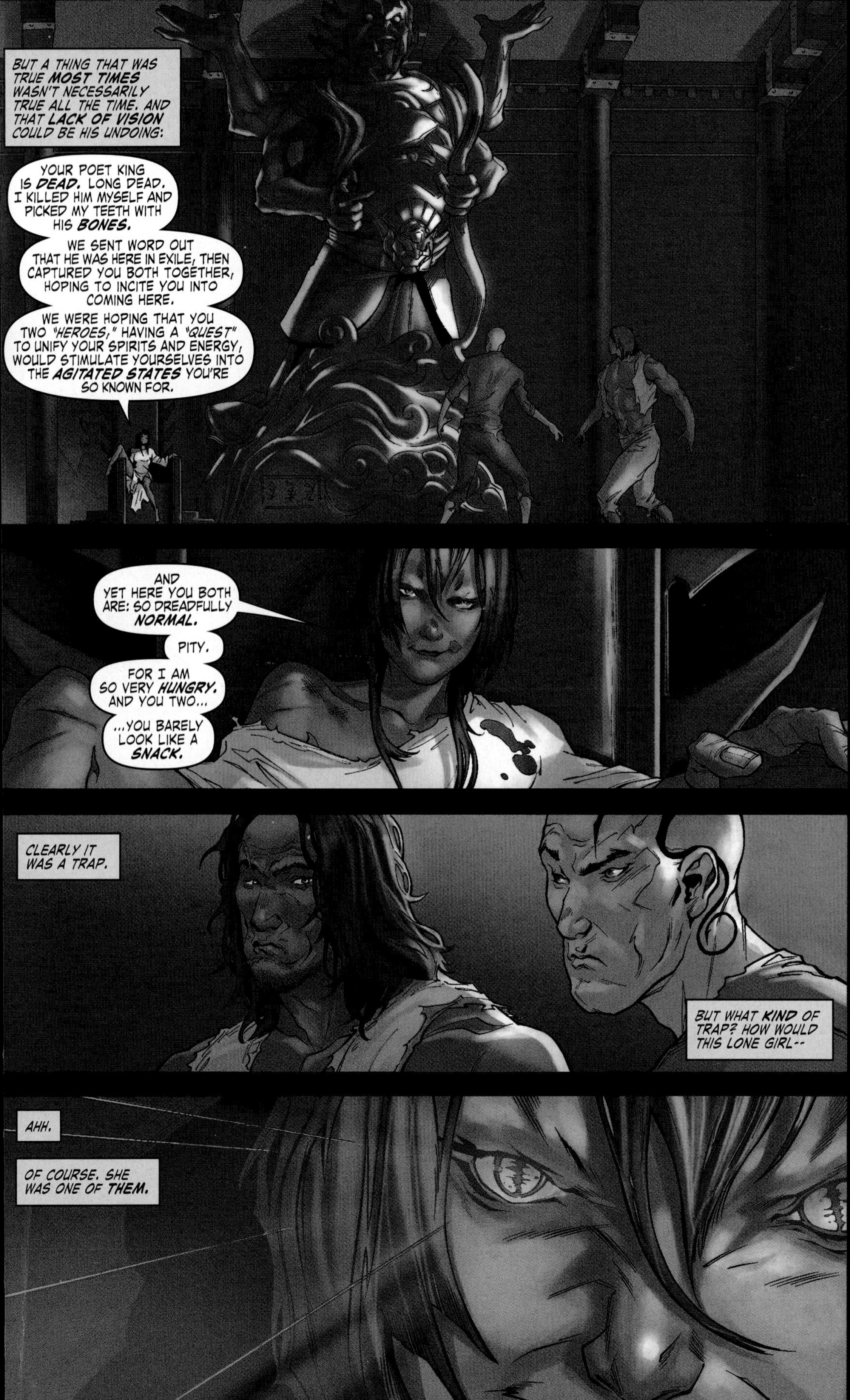
BUT A THING THAT WAS TRUE **MOST TIMES** WASN'T NECESSARILY TRUE ALL THE TIME. AND THAT **LACK OF VISION** COULD BE HIS UNDOING:
YOUR POET KING IS ***DEAD.*** LONG DEAD. I KILLED HIM MYSELF AND PICKED MY TEETH WITH HIS ***BONES.***
WE SENT WORD OUT THAT HE WAS HERE IN EXILE, THEN CAPTURED YOU BOTH TOGETHER, HOPING TO INCITE YOU INTO COMING HERE.
WE WERE HOPING THAT YOU TWO *"HEROES,"* HAVING A *"QUEST"* TO UNIFY YOUR SPIRITS AND ENERGY, WOULD STIMULATE YOURSELVES INTO THE ***AGITATED STATES*** YOU'RE SO KNOWN FOR.
AND YET HERE YOU BOTH ARE: SO DREADFULLY ***NORMAL.***
PITY.
FOR I AM SO VERY ***HUNGRY.*** AND YOU TWO...
...YOU BARELY LOOK LIKE A ***SNACK.***
CLEARLY IT WAS A TRAP.
BUT WHAT **KIND** OF TRAP? HOW WOULD THIS LONE GIRL--
AHH.
OF COURSE. SHE WAS ONE OF **THEM.**

TIGER JANI WAS LONG CONSIDERED TO BE A LOCAL GHOST STORY.

A FOLK LEGEND USED BY UGLY OLD WIDOWS TO FRIGHTEN OFF THE WET-EYED DRUNKS THAT INVARIABLY WOULD COME A'COURTIN' AFTER MIDNIGHT.

TIGER JANI IS REAL?

BEI HAD FORGOTTEN WHAT IT FELT LIKE TO **NOT** KNOW EVERYTHING ALL THE TIME.

THAT, AND THE SUDDEN BLOOD LOSS, CREATED IN HIM A FEELING LIKE UNTO EUPHORIA.

SUDDENLY DEATH DIDN'T SEEM LIKE SUCH A GREAT IDEA.

I SHALL FEAST UPON YOUR HOLY SOULS!

OH WELL.

VIVATMA WAS STUNNED. NOT BY THE GIRL'S TRANSFORMATION--

ALTHOUGH IT **WAS** STUNNING--

BUT BY FINDING HIMSELF QUITE SUDDENLY WITHOUT A DIRECTION.

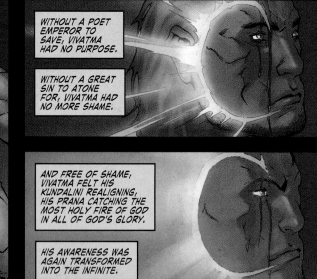

WITHOUT A POET EMPEROR TO SAVE, VIVATMA HAD NO PURPOSE.

WITHOUT A GREAT SIN TO ATONE FOR, VIVATMA HAD NO MORE SHAME.

AND FREE OF SHAME, VIVATMA FELT HIS KUNDALINI REALIGNING, HIS PRANA CATCHING THE MOST HOLY FIRE OF GOD IN ALL OF GOD'S GLORY.

HIS AWARENESS WAS AGAIN TRANSFORMED INTO THE INFINITE.

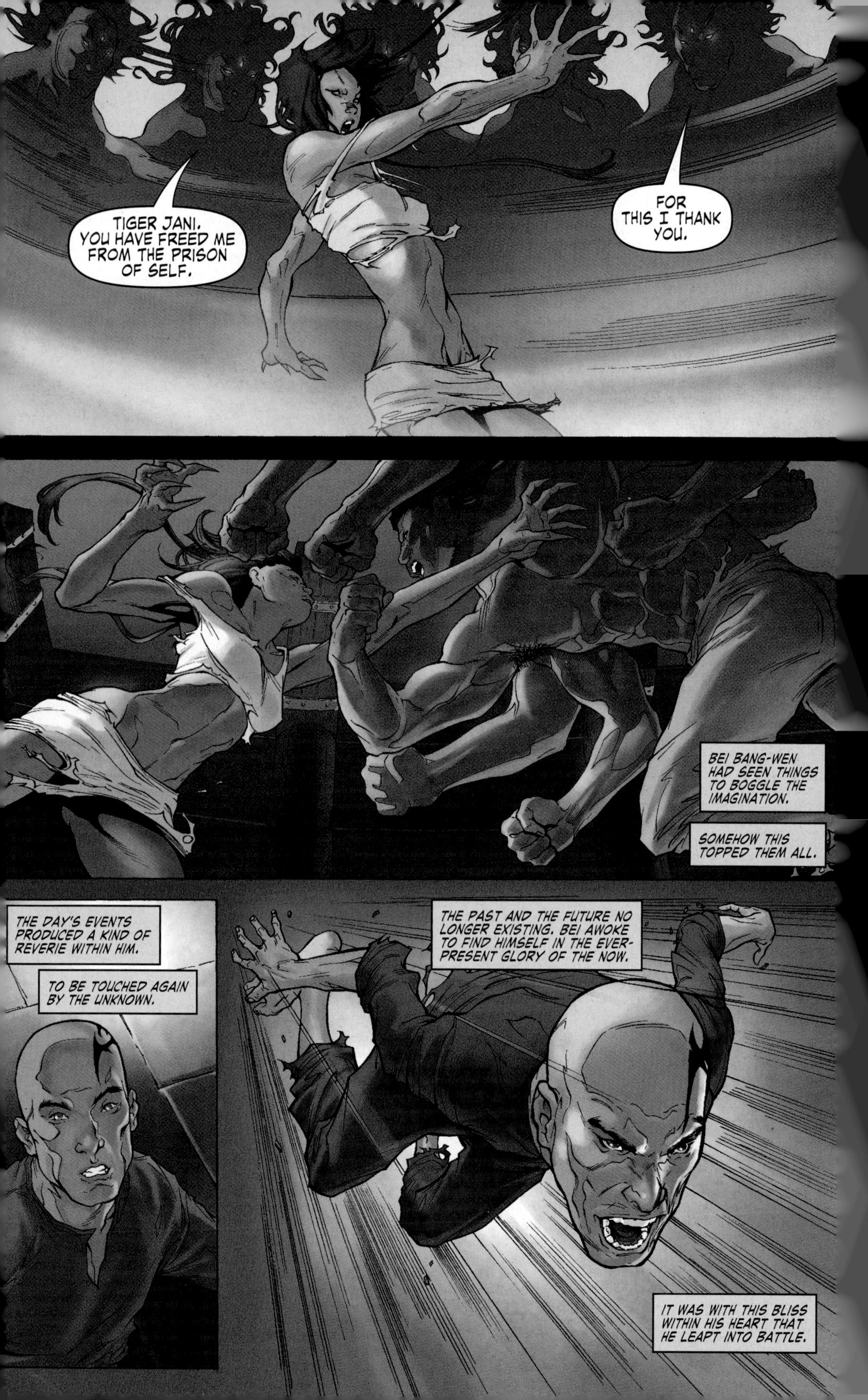
TIGER JANI. YOU HAVE FREED ME FROM THE PRISON OF SELF.
FOR THIS I THANK YOU.
BEI BANG-WEN HAD SEEN THINGS TO BOGGLE THE IMAGINATION.
SOMEHOW THIS TOPPED THEM ALL.
THE DAY'S EVENTS PRODUCED A KIND OF REVERIE WITHIN HIM.
TO BE TOUCHED AGAIN BY THE UNKNOWN.
THE PAST AND THE FUTURE NO LONGER EXISTING. BEI AWOKE TO FIND HIMSELF IN THE EVER-PRESENT GLORY OF THE NOW.
IT WAS WITH THIS BLISS WITHIN HIS HEART THAT HE LEAPT INTO BATTLE.

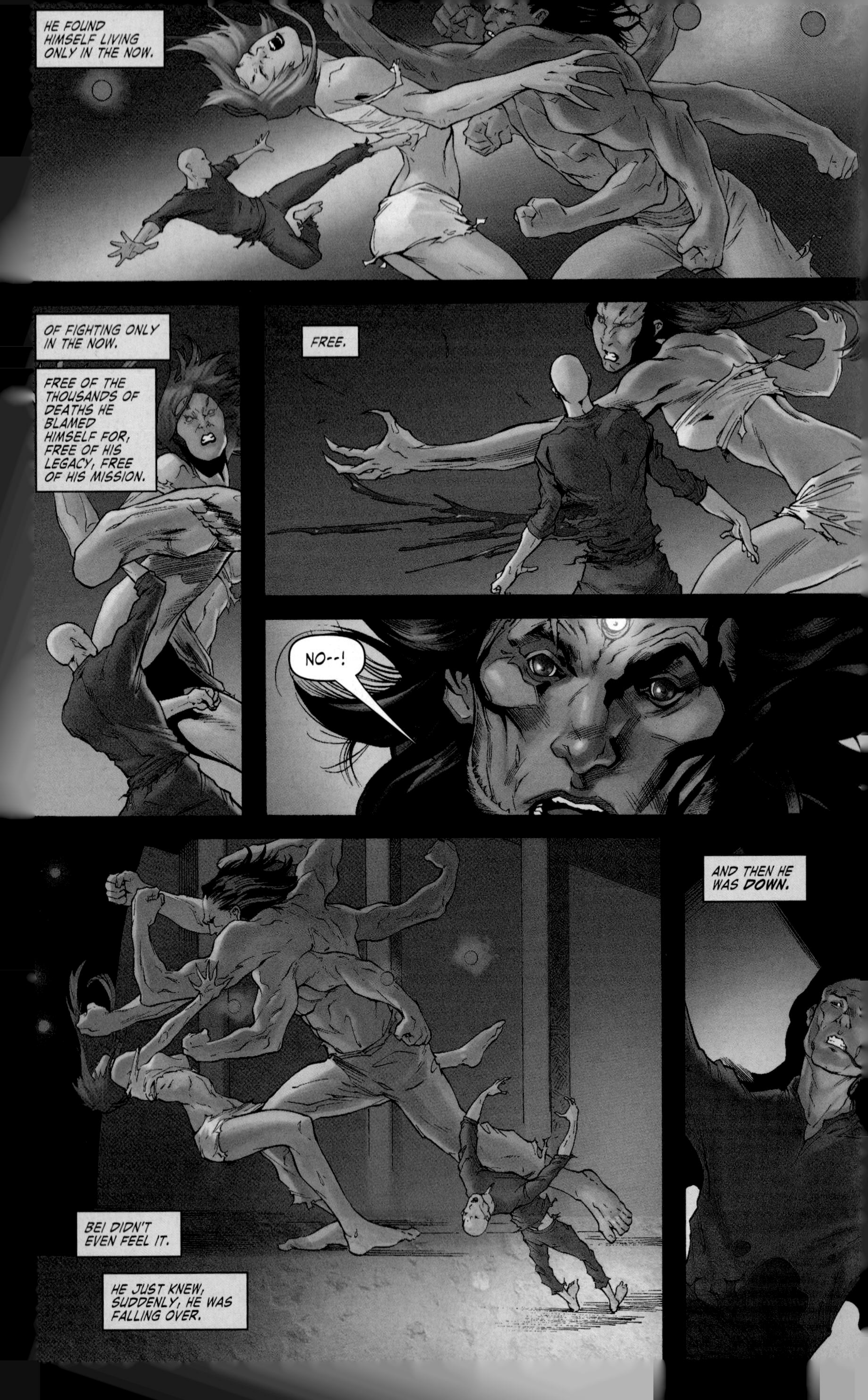
HE FOUND HIMSELF LIVING ONLY IN THE NOW.
OF FIGHTING ONLY IN THE NOW.
FREE OF THE THOUSANDS OF DEATHS HE BLAMED HIMSELF FOR, FREE OF HIS LEGACY, FREE OF HIS MISSION.
FREE.
NO--!
BEI DIDN'T EVEN FEEL IT.
HE JUST KNEW, SUDDENLY, HE WAS FALLING OVER.
AND THEN HE WAS **DOWN**.

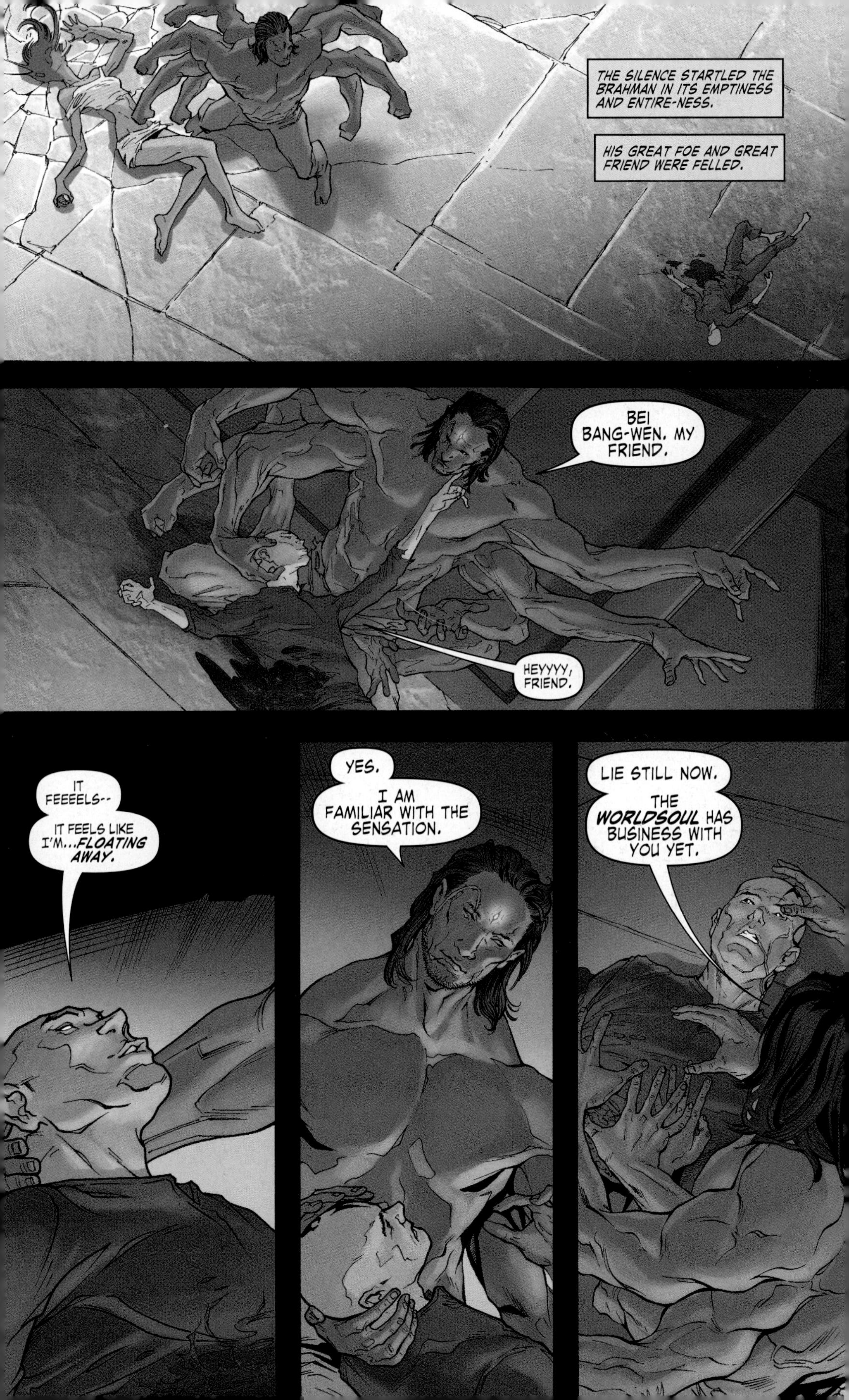
THE SILENCE STARTLED THE BRAHMAN IN ITS EMPTINESS AND ENTIRE-NESS.
HIS GREAT FOE AND GREAT FRIEND WERE FELLED.
BEI BANG-WEN. MY FRIEND.
HEYYYY, FRIEND.
IT FEEEELS--
IT FEELS LIKE I'M...FLOATING AWAY.
YES.
I AM FAMILIAR WITH THE SENSATION.
LIE STILL NOW.
THE WORLDSOUL HAS BUSINESS WITH YOU YET.

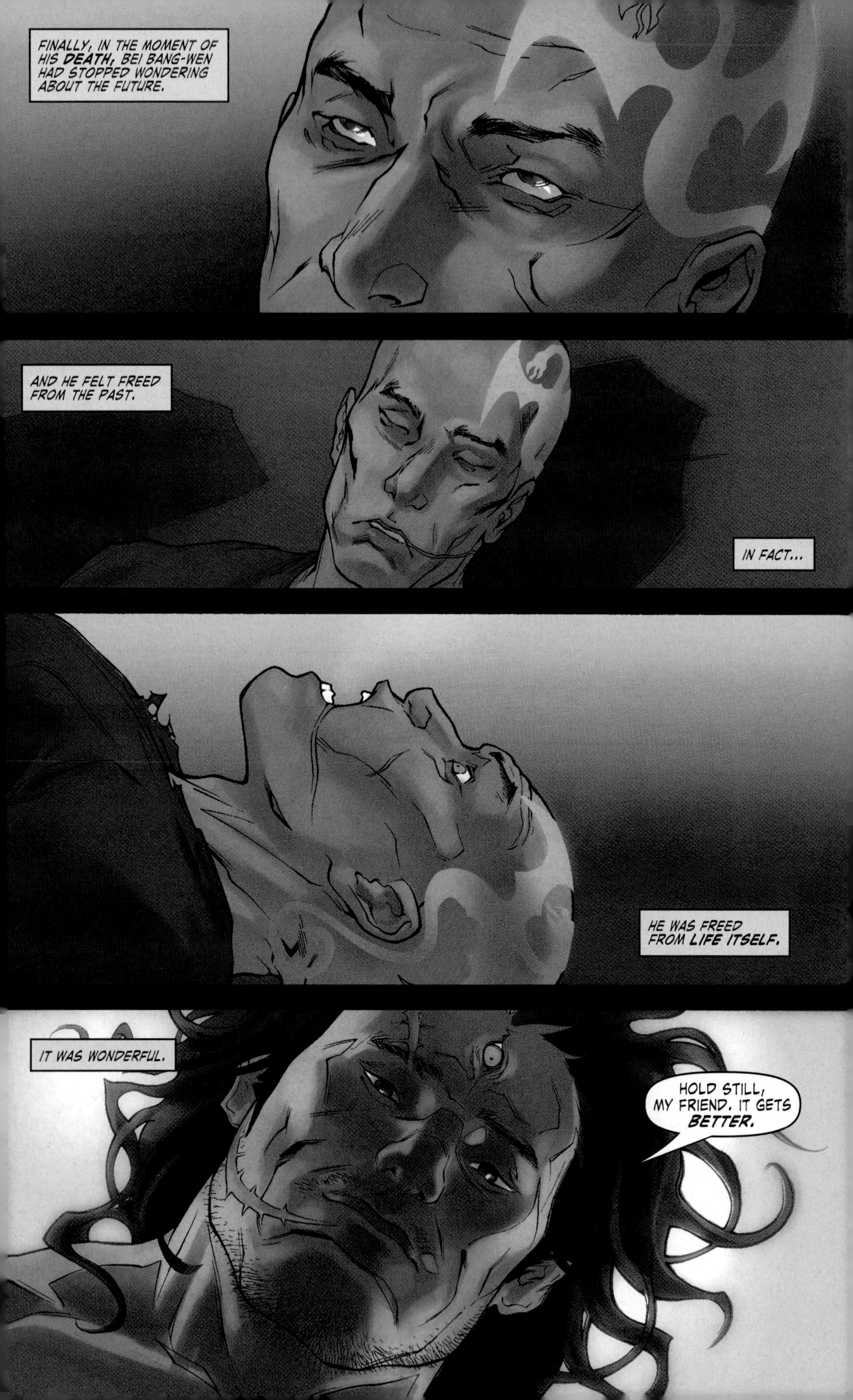
FINALLY, IN THE MOMENT OF HIS DEATH, BEI BANG-WEN HAD STOPPED WONDERING ABOUT THE FUTURE.
AND HE FELT FREED FROM THE PAST.
IN FACT...
HE WAS FREED FROM LIFE ITSELF.
IT WAS WONDERFUL.
HOLD STILL, MY FRIEND. IT GETS BETTER.

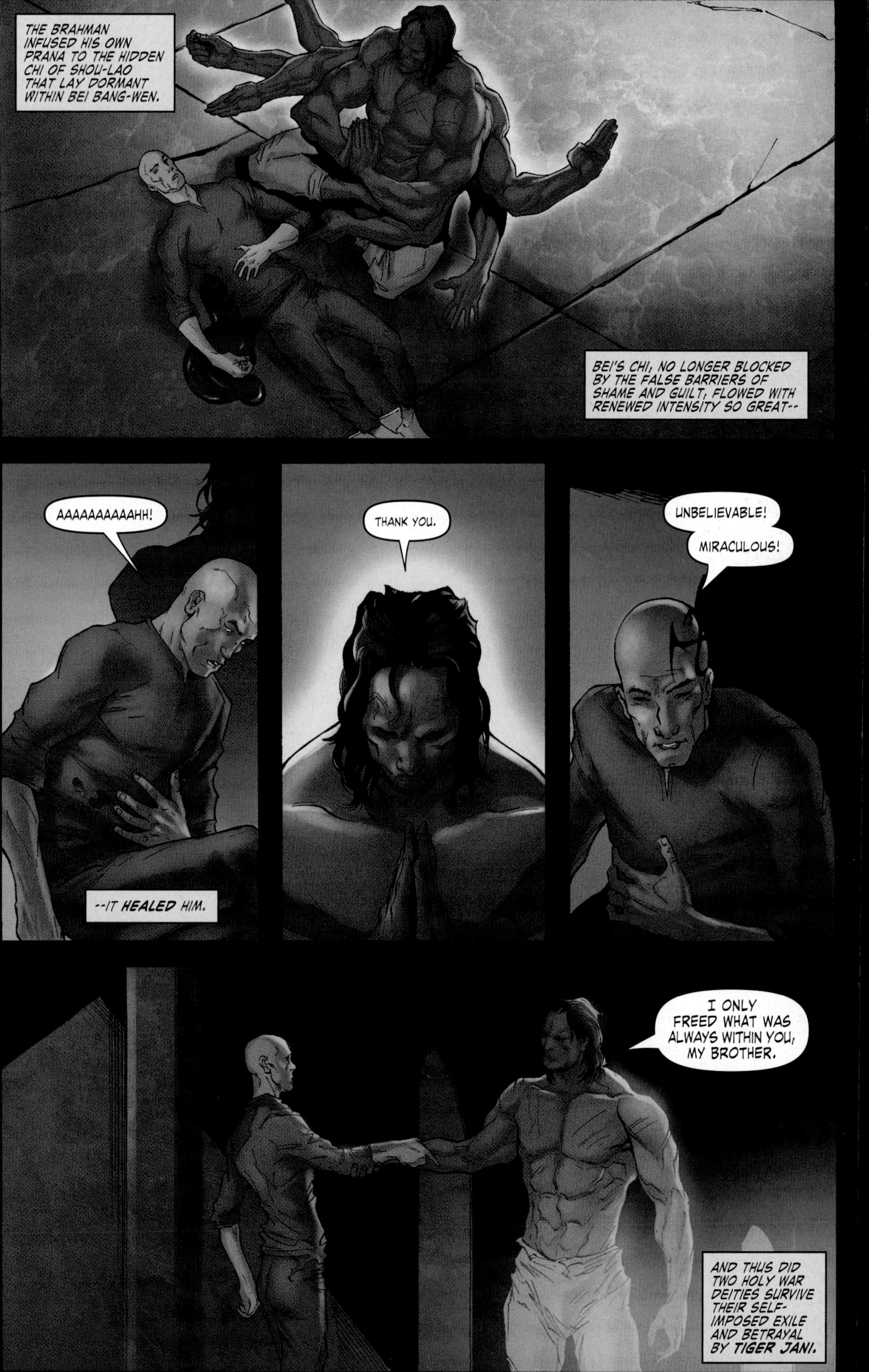
THE BRAHMAN INFUSED HIS OWN PRANA TO THE HIDDEN CHI OF SHOU-LAO THAT LAY DORMANT WITHIN BEI BANG-WEN.
BEI'S CHI, NO LONGER BLOCKED BY THE FALSE BARRIERS OF SHAME AND GUILT, FLOWED WITH RENEWED INTENSITY SO GREAT--
AAAAAAAAAAHH!
--IT HEALED HIM.
THANK YOU.
UNBELIEVABLE!
MIRACULOUS!
I ONLY FREED WHAT WAS ALWAYS WITHIN YOU, MY BROTHER.
AND THUS DID TWO HOLY WAR DEITIES SURVIVE THEIR SELF-IMPOSED EXILE AND BETRAYAL BY TIGER JANI.

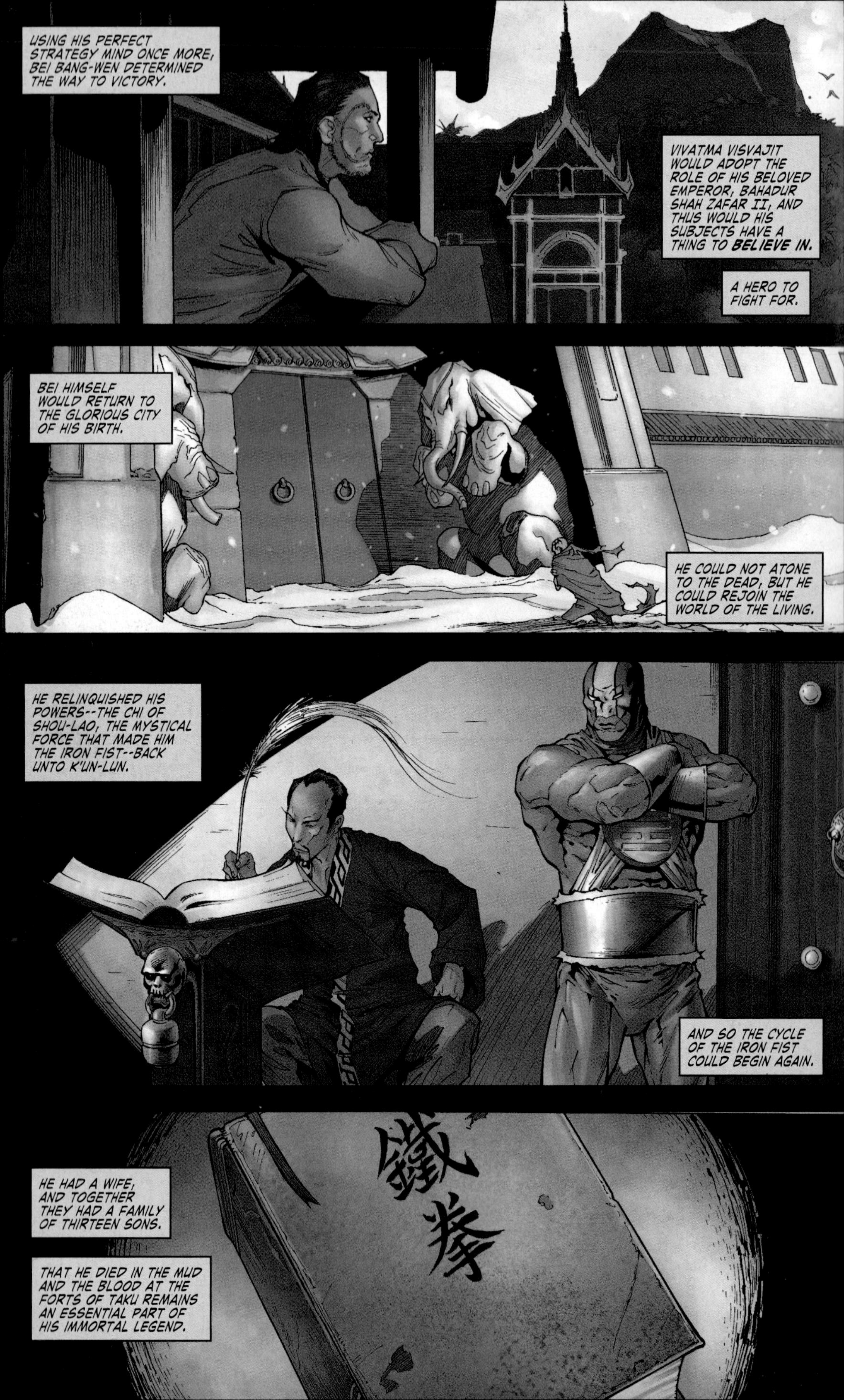
USING HIS PERFECT STRATEGY MIND ONCE MORE, BEI BANG-WEN DETERMINED THE WAY TO VICTORY.
VIVATMA VISVAJIT WOULD ADOPT THE ROLE OF HIS BELOVED EMPEROR, BAHADUR SHAH ZAFAR II, AND THUS WOULD HIS SUBJECTS HAVE A THING TO **BELIEVE IN.**
A HERO TO FIGHT FOR.
BEI HIMSELF WOULD RETURN TO THE GLORIOUS CITY OF HIS BIRTH.
HE COULD NOT ATONE TO THE DEAD, BUT HE COULD REJOIN THE WORLD OF THE LIVING.
HE RELINQUISHED HIS POWERS--THE CHI OF SHOU-LAO, THE MYSTICAL FORCE THAT MADE HIM THE IRON FIST--BACK UNTO K'UN-LUN.
AND SO THE CYCLE OF THE IRON FIST COULD BEGIN AGAIN.
HE HAD A WIFE, AND TOGETHER THEY HAD A FAMILY OF THIRTEEN SONS.
鐵拳
THAT HE DIED IN THE MUD AND THE BLOOD AT THE FORTS OF TAKU REMAINS AN ESSENTIAL PART OF HIS IMMORTAL LEGEND.

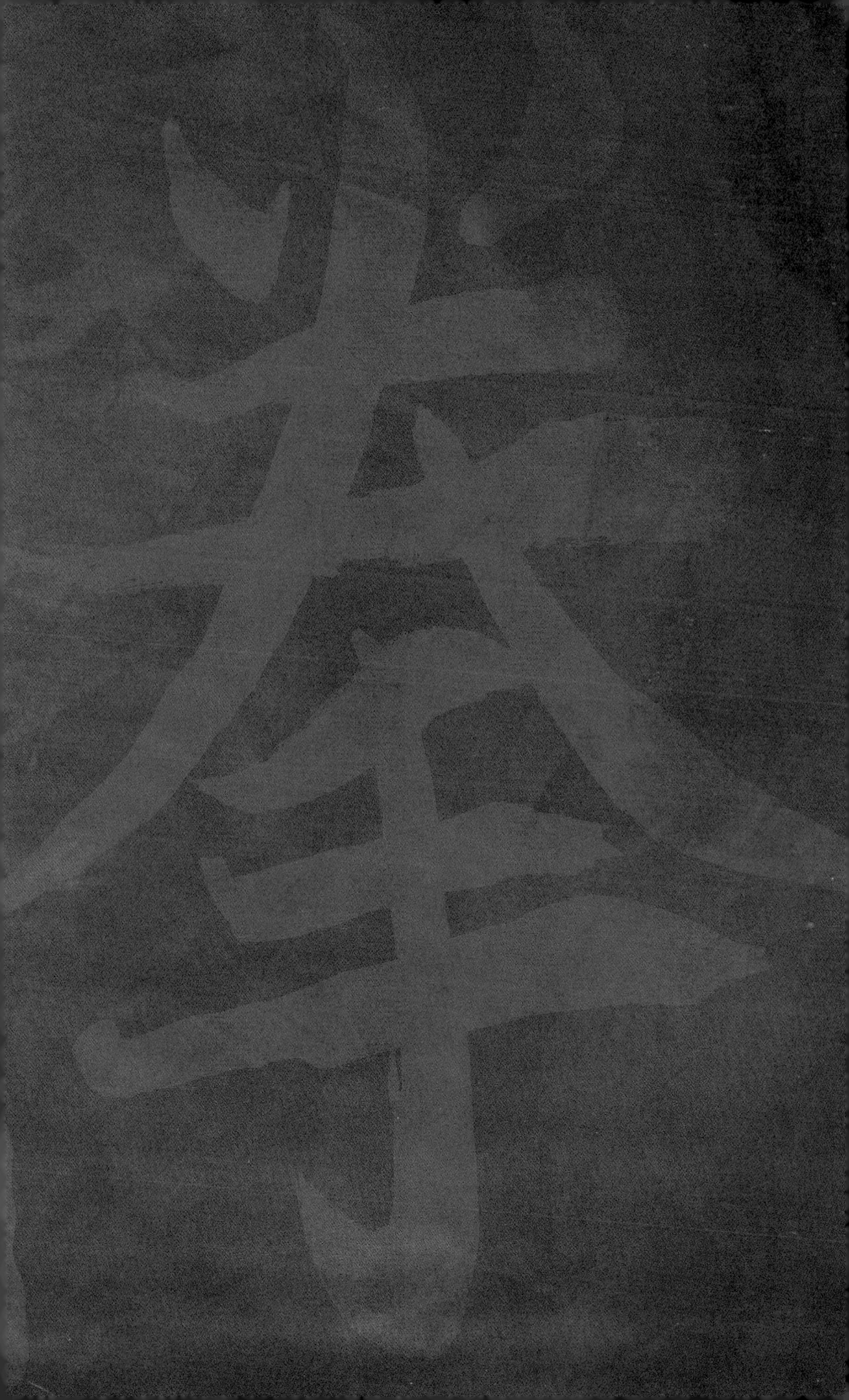
拳

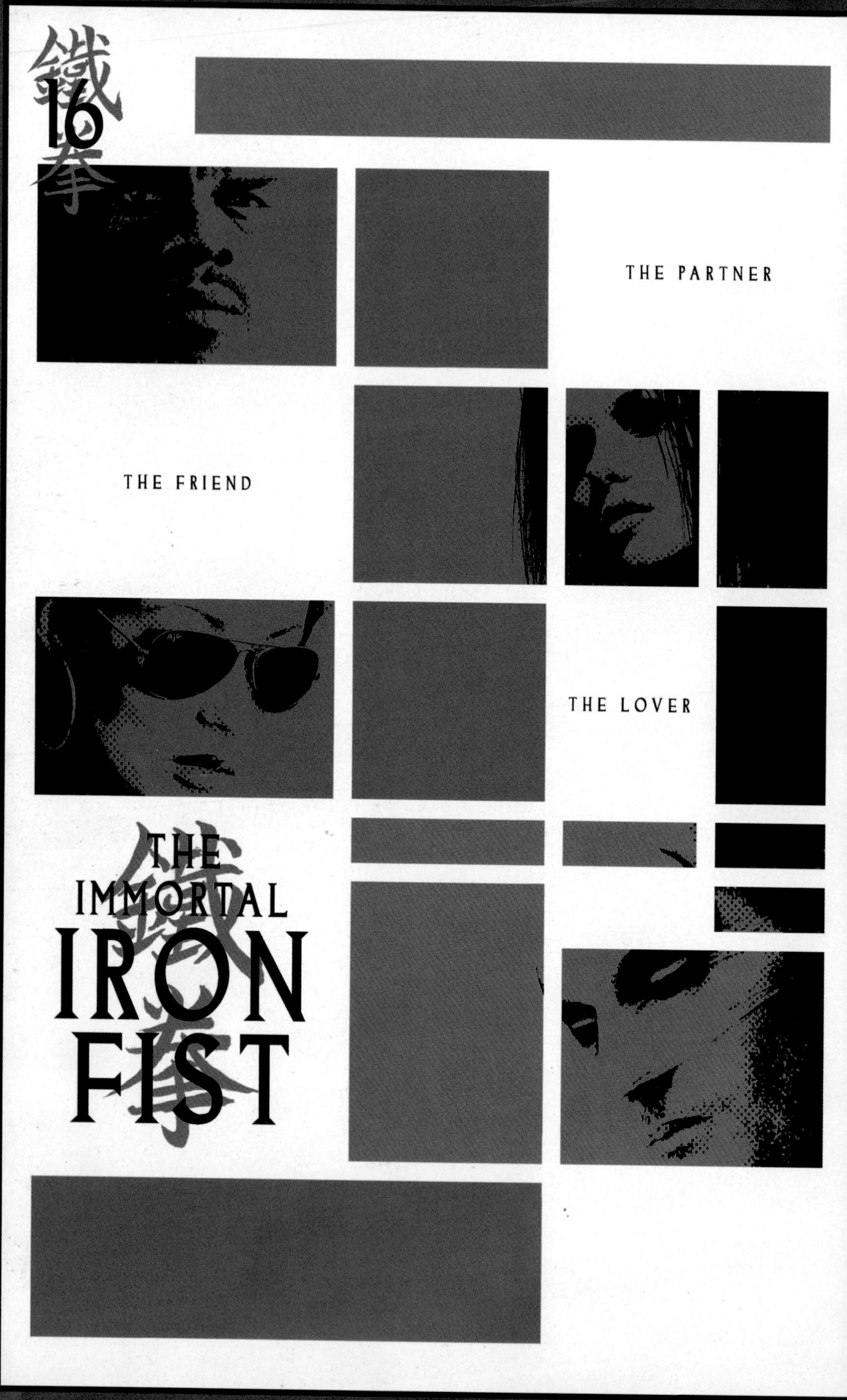
鐵拳
16
THE PARTNER
THE FRIEND
THE LOVER
THE IMMORTAL IRON FIST

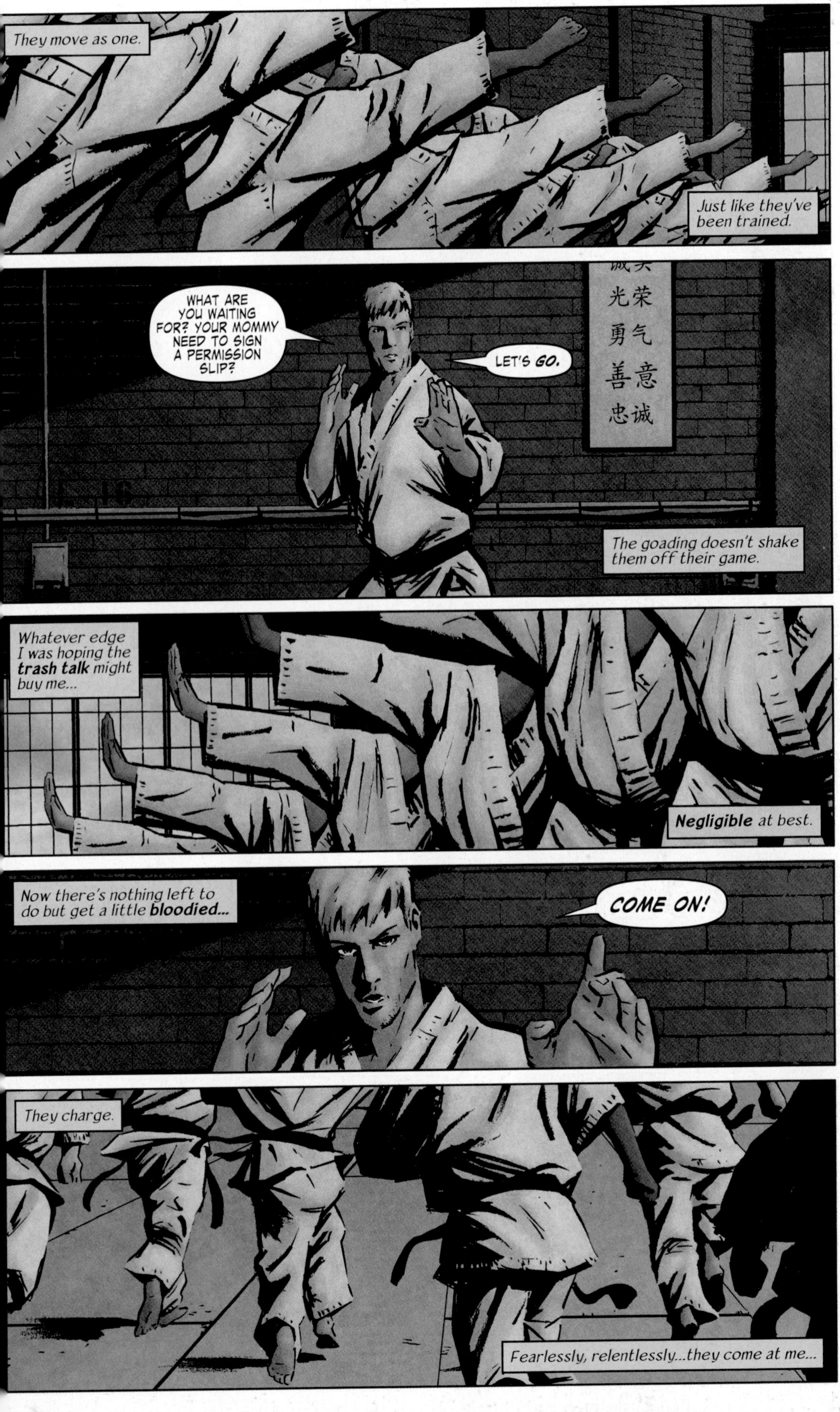
They move as one.
Just like they've been trained.
WHAT ARE YOU WAITING FOR? YOUR MOMMY NEED TO SIGN A PERMISSION SLIP?
LET'S GO.
荣气意诚
光勇善忠
The goading doesn't shake them off their game.
Whatever edge I was hoping the trash talk might buy me...
Negligible at best.
Now there's nothing left to do but get a little bloodied...
COME ON!
They charge.
Fearlessly, relentlessly...they come at me...

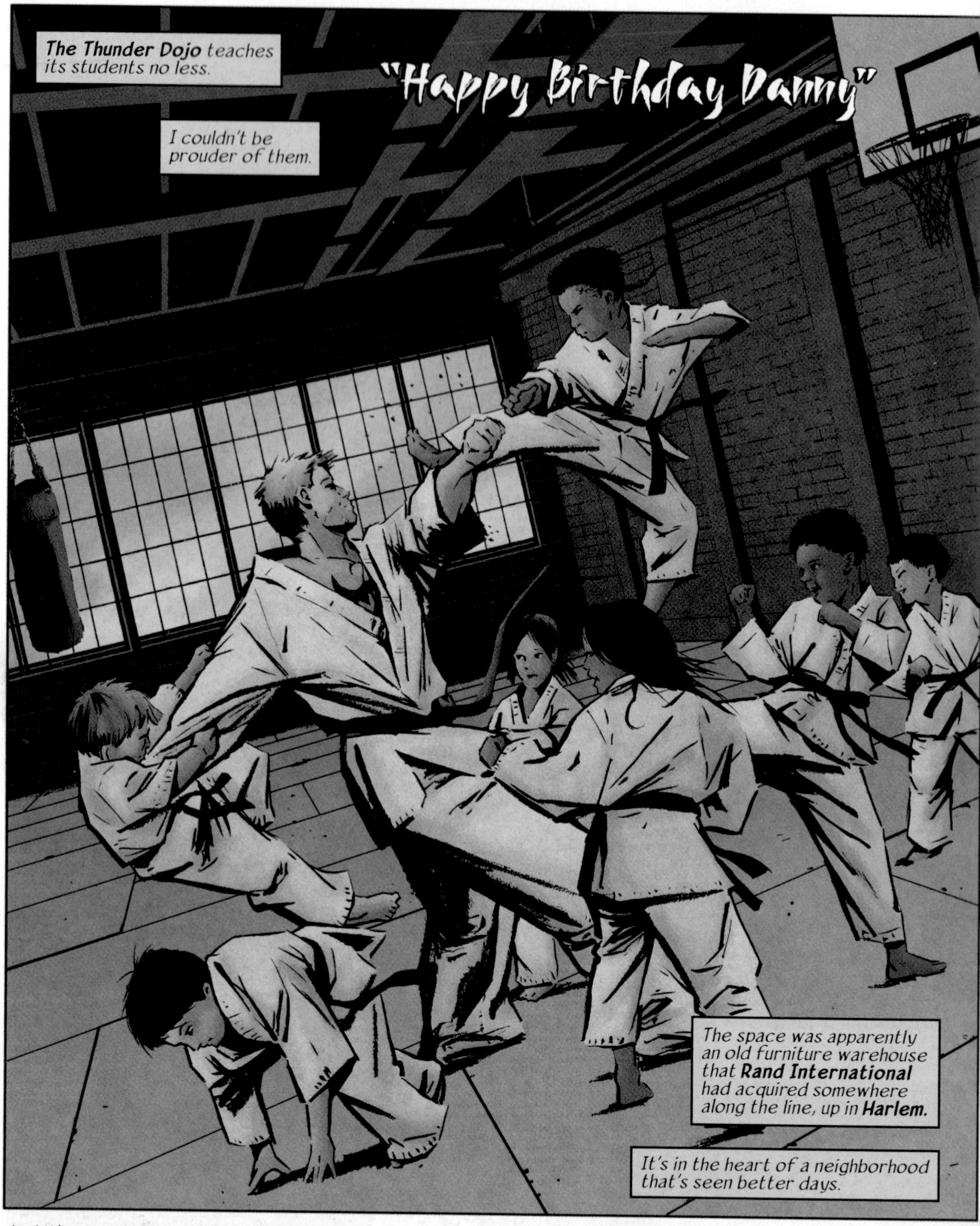

The Thunder Dojo teaches its students no less.
"Happy Birthday Danny"
I couldn't be prouder of them.
The space was apparently an old furniture warehouse that Rand International had acquired somewhere along the line, up in Harlem.
It's in the heart of a neighborhood that's seen better days.

And it's a neighborhood full of kids...

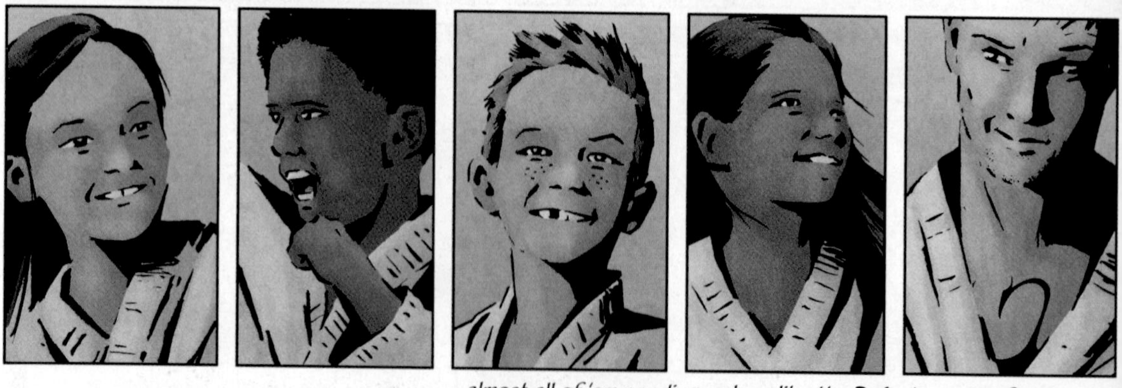

*...almost all of 'em needing a place like the **Dojo** to come after school.*

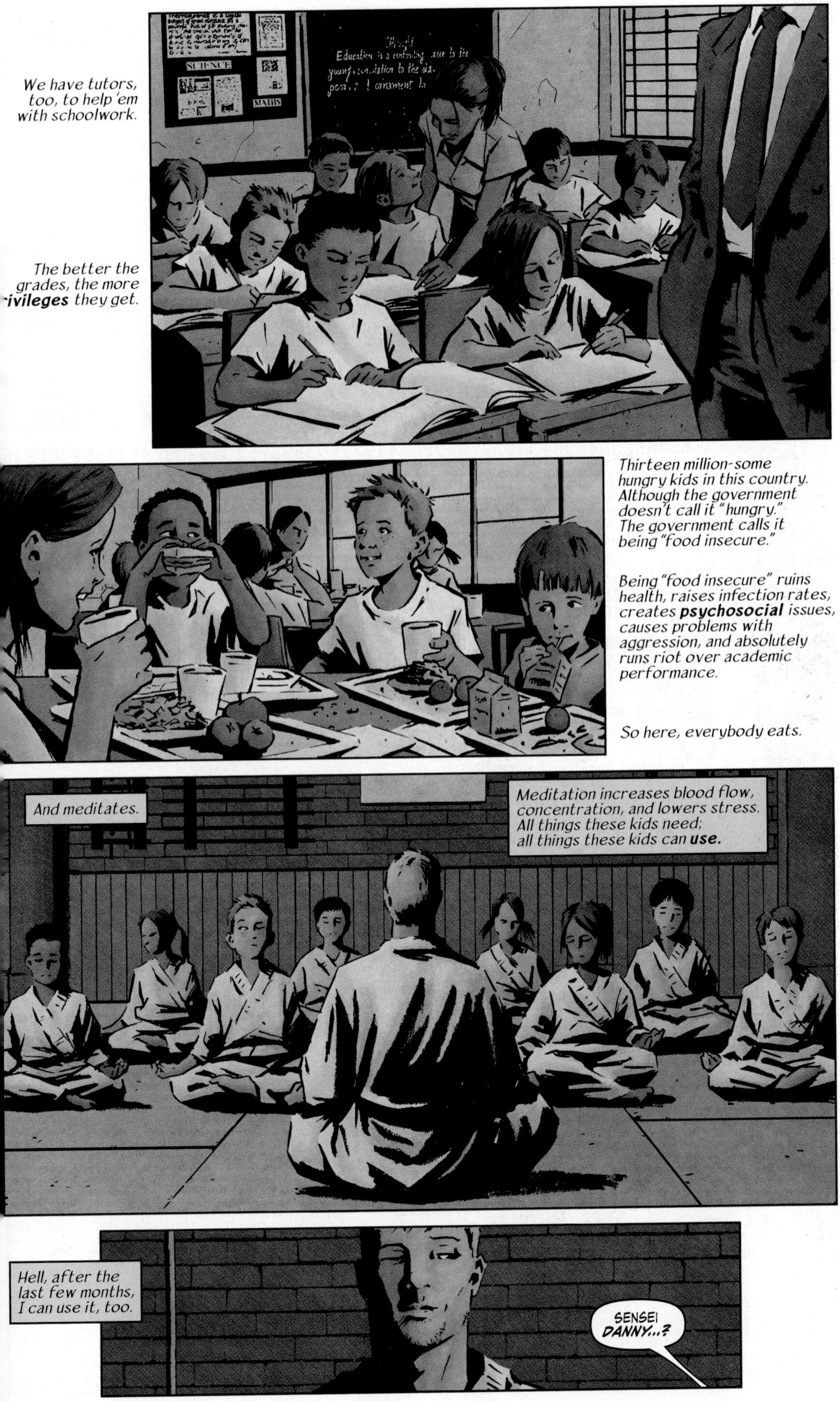

We have tutors, too, to help 'em with schoolwork.
SCIENCE
MATHS
The better the grades, the more **ivileges** they get.
Thirteen million-some hungry kids in this country. Although the government doesn't call it "hungry." The government calls it being "food insecure."
Being "food insecure" ruins health, raises infection rates, creates **psychosocial** issues, causes problems with aggression, and absolutely runs riot over academic performance.
So here, everybody eats.
And meditates.
Meditation increases blood flow, concentration, and lowers stress. All things these kids need; all things these kids can **use.**
Hell, after the last few months, I can use it, too.
SENSEI ***DANNY...?***

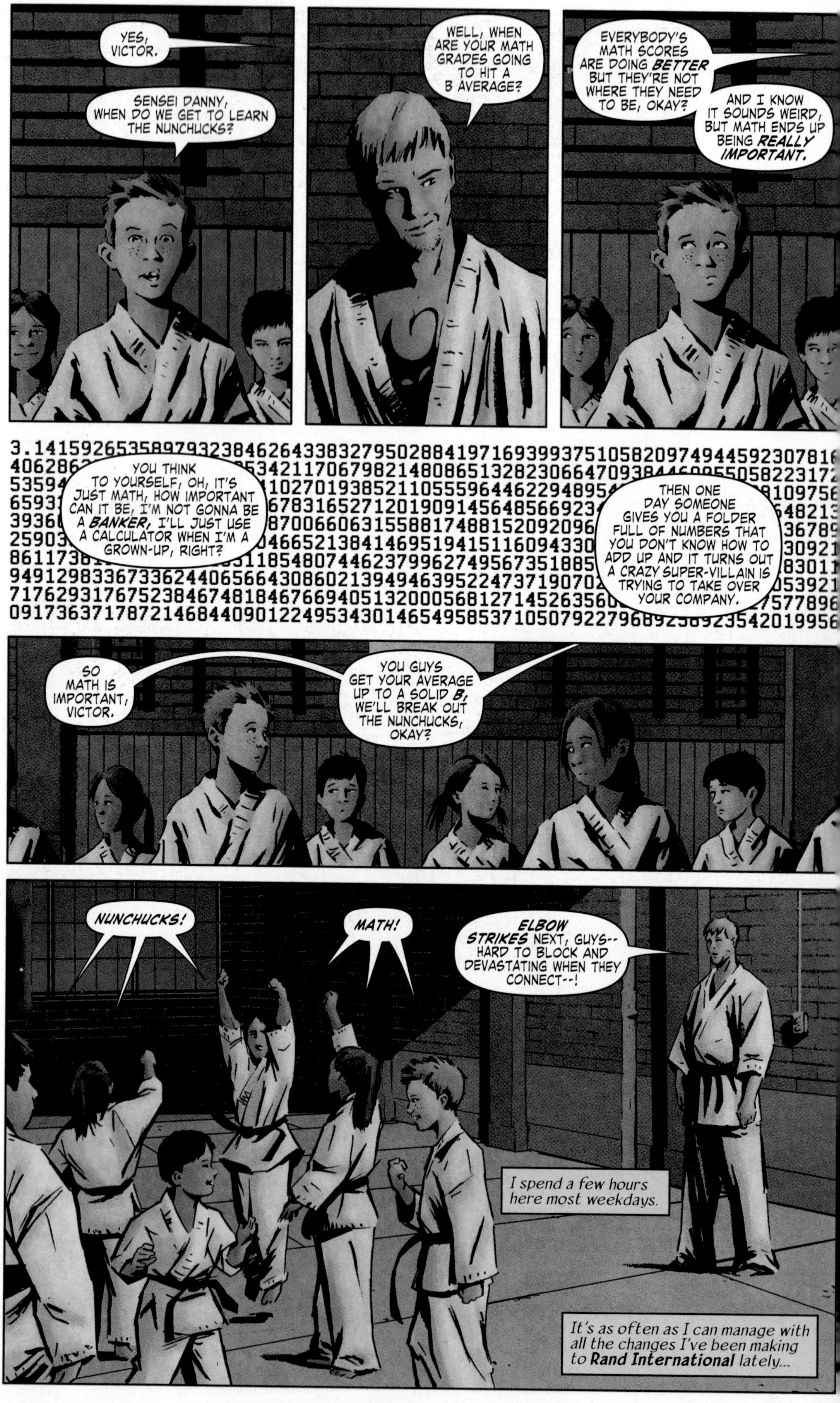

SENSEI DANNY, WHEN DO WE GET TO LEARN THE NUNCHUCKS?
YES, VICTOR.
WELL, WHEN ARE YOUR MATH GRADES GOING TO HIT A B AVERAGE?
EVERYBODY'S MATH SCORES ARE DOING BETTER BUT THEY'RE NOT WHERE THEY NEED TO BE, OKAY?
AND I KNOW IT SOUNDS WEIRD, BUT MATH ENDS UP BEING REALLY IMPORTANT.
3.141592653589793238462643383279502884197169399375105820974944592307816
YOU THINK TO YOURSELF, OH, IT'S JUST MATH, HOW IMPORTANT CAN IT BE, I'M NOT GONNA BE A BANKER, I'LL JUST USE A CALCULATOR WHEN I'M A GROWN-UP, RIGHT?
THEN ONE DAY SOMEONE GIVES YOU A FOLDER FULL OF NUMBERS THAT YOU DON'T KNOW HOW TO ADD UP AND IT TURNS OUT A CRAZY SUPER-VILLAIN IS TRYING TO TAKE OVER YOUR COMPANY.
SO MATH IS IMPORTANT, VICTOR.
YOU GUYS GET YOUR AVERAGE UP TO A SOLID B, WE'LL BREAK OUT THE NUNCHUCKS, OKAY?
NUNCHUCKS!
MATH!
ELBOW STRIKES NEXT, GUYS-- HARD TO BLOCK AND DEVASTATING WHEN THEY CONNECT--!
I spend a few hours here most weekdays.
It's as often as I can manage with all the changes I've been making to Rand International lately...

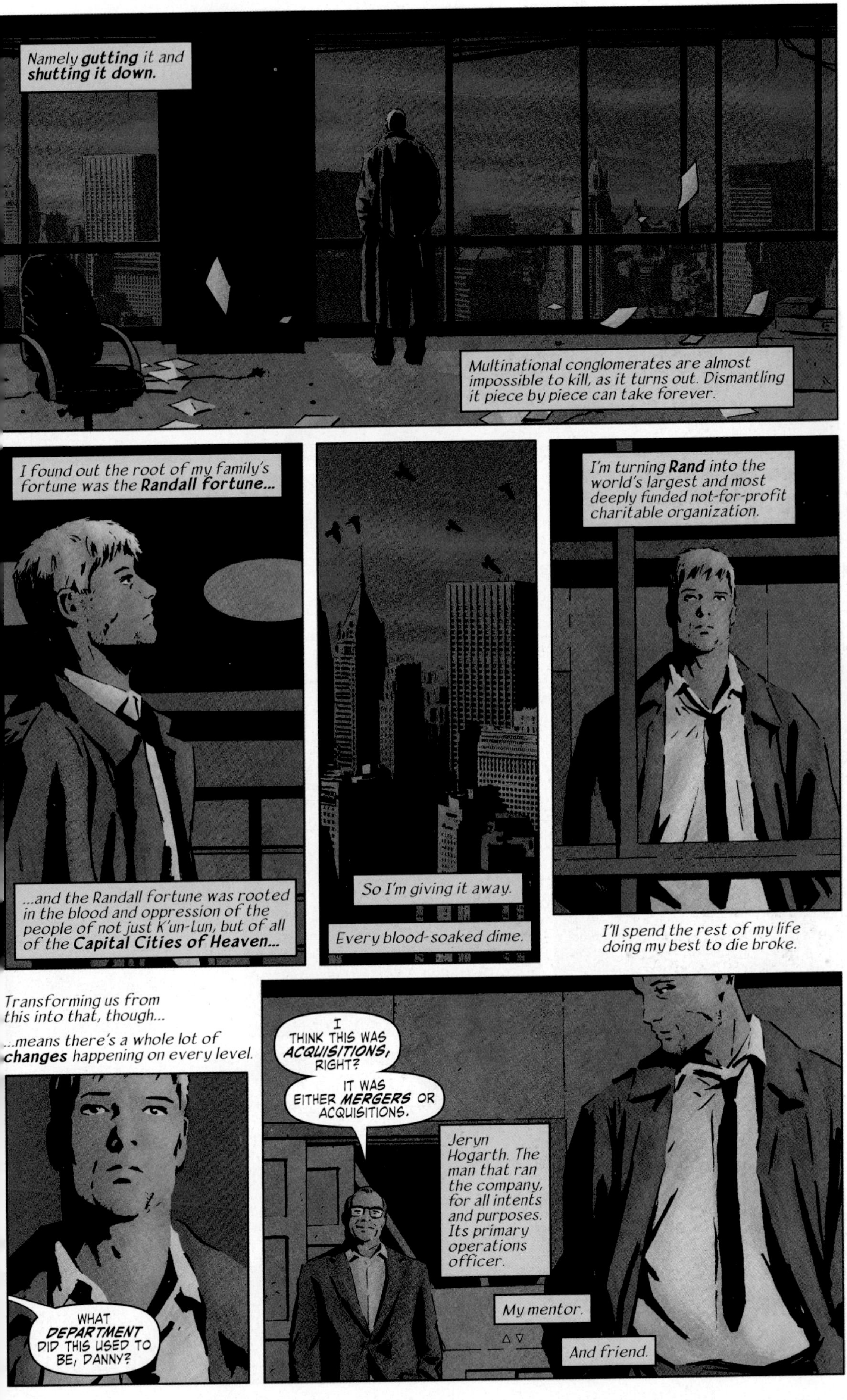
Namely **gutting** it and **shutting it down.**
Multinational conglomerates are almost impossible to kill, as it turns out. Dismantling it piece by piece can take forever.
I found out the root of my family's fortune was the **Randall fortune...**
...and the Randall fortune was rooted in the blood and oppression of the people of not just K'un-Lun, but of all of the **Capital Cities of Heaven...**
So I'm giving it away.
Every blood-soaked dime.
I'm turning **Rand** into the world's largest and most deeply funded not-for-profit charitable organization.
I'll spend the rest of my life doing my best to die broke.
Transforming us from this into that, though...
...means there's a whole lot of **changes** happening on every level.
WHAT ***DEPARTMENT*** DID THIS USED TO BE, DANNY?
I THINK THIS WAS ***ACQUISITIONS,*** RIGHT?
IT WAS EITHER ***MERGERS*** OR ACQUISITIONS.
Jeryn Hogarth. The man that ran the company, for all intents and purposes. Its primary operations officer.
My mentor.
And friend.

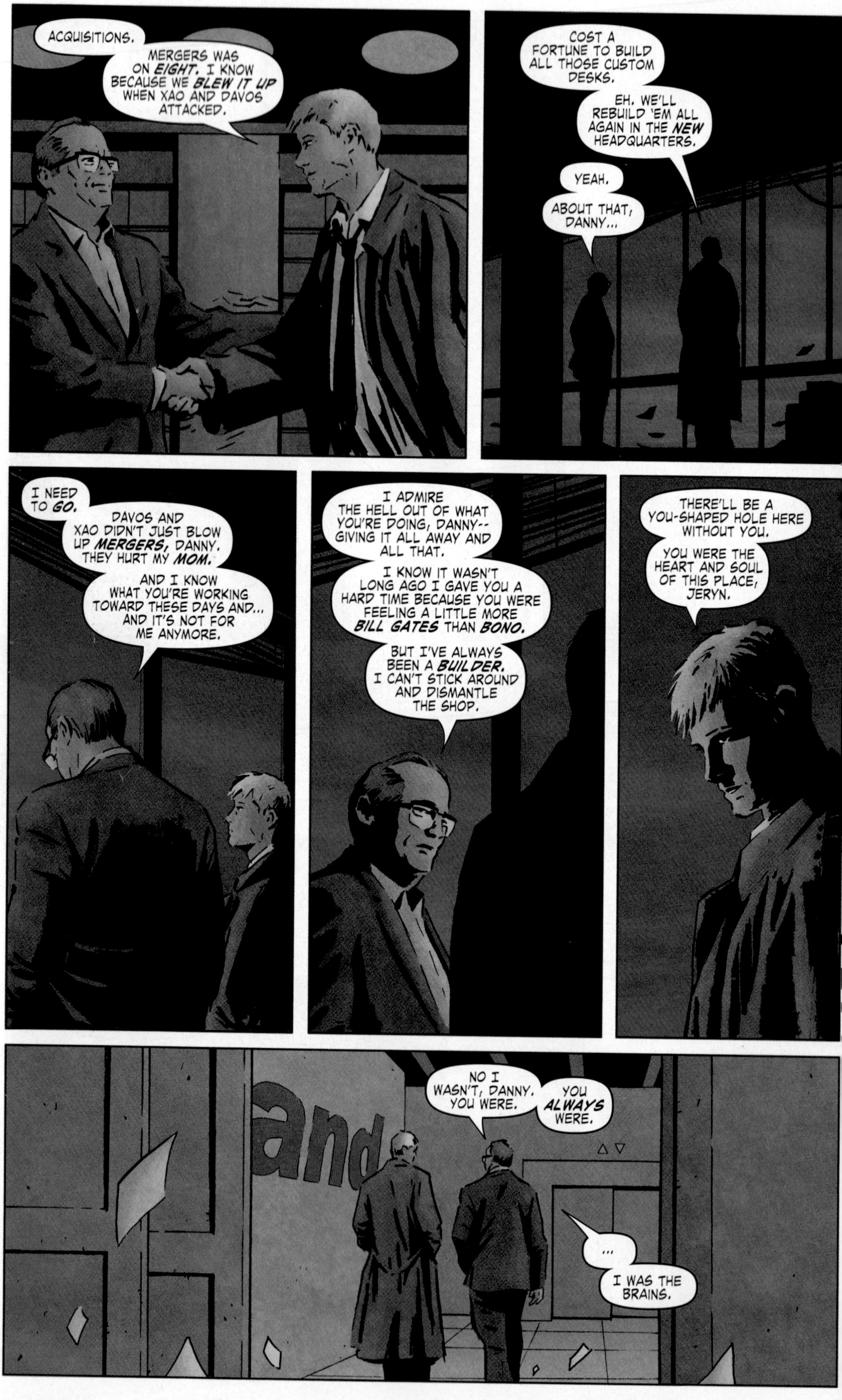
ACQUISITIONS.
MERGERS WAS ON *EIGHT.* I KNOW BECAUSE WE *BLEW IT UP* WHEN XAO AND DAVOS ATTACKED.
COST A FORTUNE TO BUILD ALL THOSE CUSTOM DESKS.
EH. WE'LL REBUILD 'EM ALL AGAIN IN THE *NEW* HEADQUARTERS.
YEAH.
ABOUT THAT, DANNY...
I NEED TO *GO.*
DAVOS AND XAO DIDN'T JUST BLOW UP *MERGERS,* DANNY. THEY HURT MY *MOM.*
AND I KNOW WHAT YOU'RE WORKING TOWARD THESE DAYS AND... AND IT'S NOT FOR ME ANYMORE.
I ADMIRE THE HELL OUT OF WHAT YOU'RE DOING, DANNY-- GIVING IT ALL AWAY AND ALL THAT.
I KNOW IT WASN'T LONG AGO I GAVE YOU A HARD TIME BECAUSE YOU WERE FEELING A LITTLE MORE *BILL GATES* THAN *BONO.*
BUT I'VE ALWAYS BEEN A *BUILDER.* I CAN'T STICK AROUND AND DISMANTLE THE SHOP.
THERE'LL BE A YOU-SHAPED HOLE HERE WITHOUT YOU.
YOU WERE THE HEART AND SOUL OF THIS PLACE, JERYN.
and
NO I WASN'T, DANNY. YOU WERE.
YOU *ALWAYS* WERE.
...
I WAS THE BRAINS.

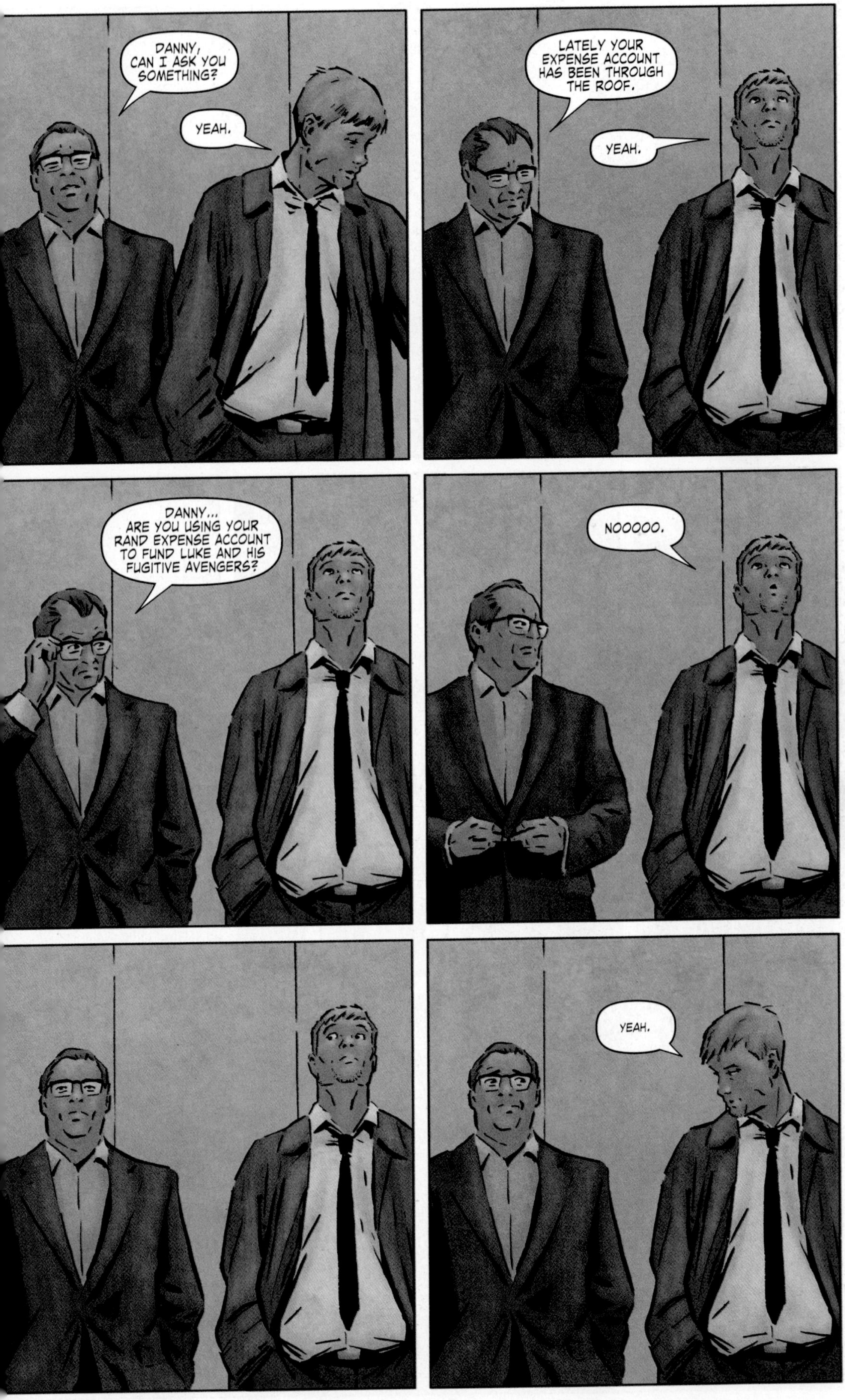
DANNY, CAN I ASK YOU SOMETHING?
YEAH.
LATELY YOUR EXPENSE ACCOUNT HAS BEEN THROUGH THE ROOF.
YEAH.
DANNY... ARE YOU USING YOUR RAND EXPENSE ACCOUNT TO FUND LUKE AND HIS FUGITIVE AVENGERS?
NOOOOO.
YEAH.

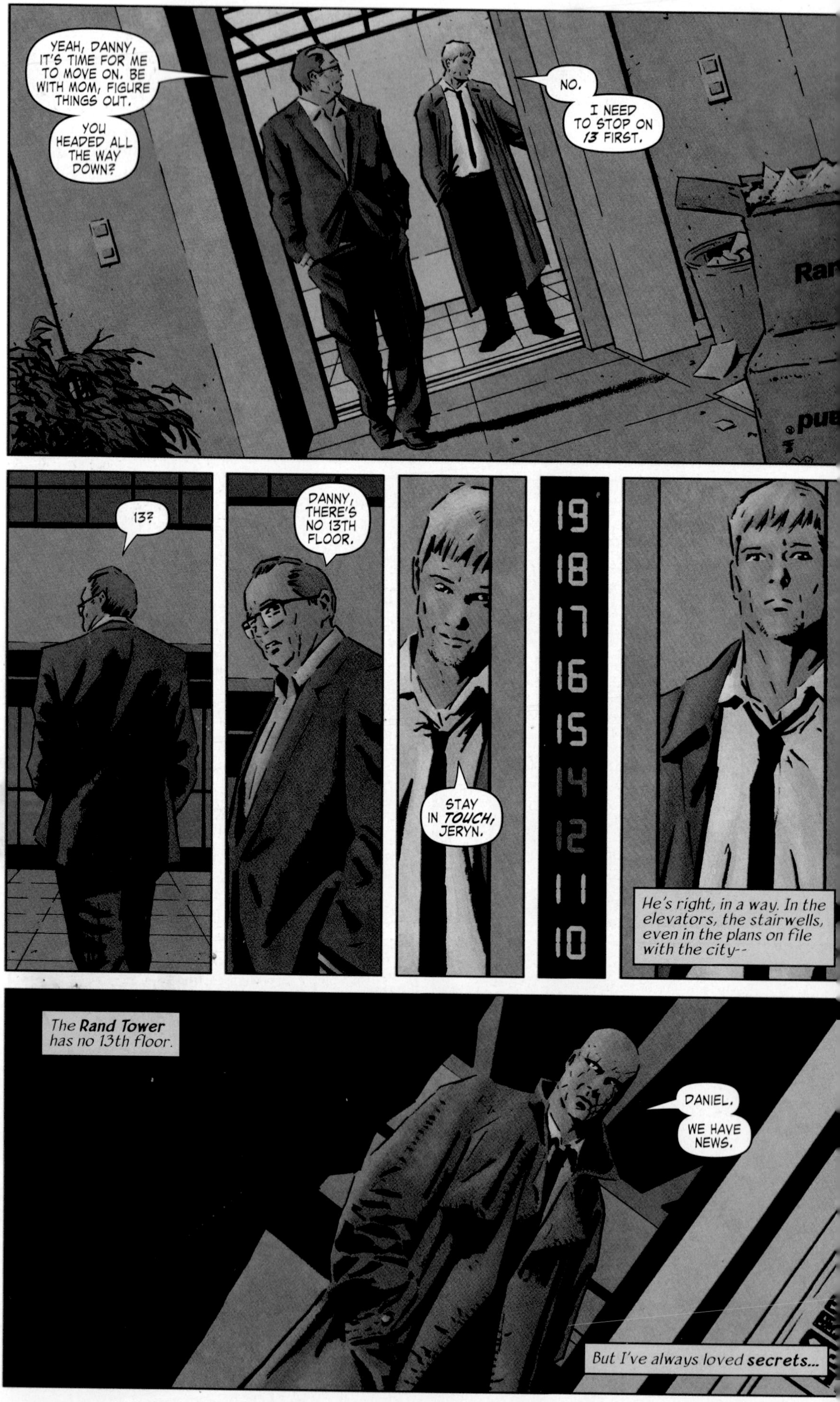
YEAH, DANNY, IT'S TIME FOR ME TO MOVE ON. BE WITH MOM, FIGURE THINGS OUT.
YOU HEADED ALL THE WAY DOWN?
NO.
I NEED TO STOP ON *13* FIRST.
13?
DANNY, THERE'S NO 13TH FLOOR.
STAY IN *TOUCH,* JERYN.
19
18
17
16
15
14
12
11
10
He's right, in a way. In the elevators, the stairwells, even in the plans on file with the city--
The **Rand Tower** has no 13th floor.
DANIEL.
WE HAVE NEWS.
But I've always loved **secrets...**

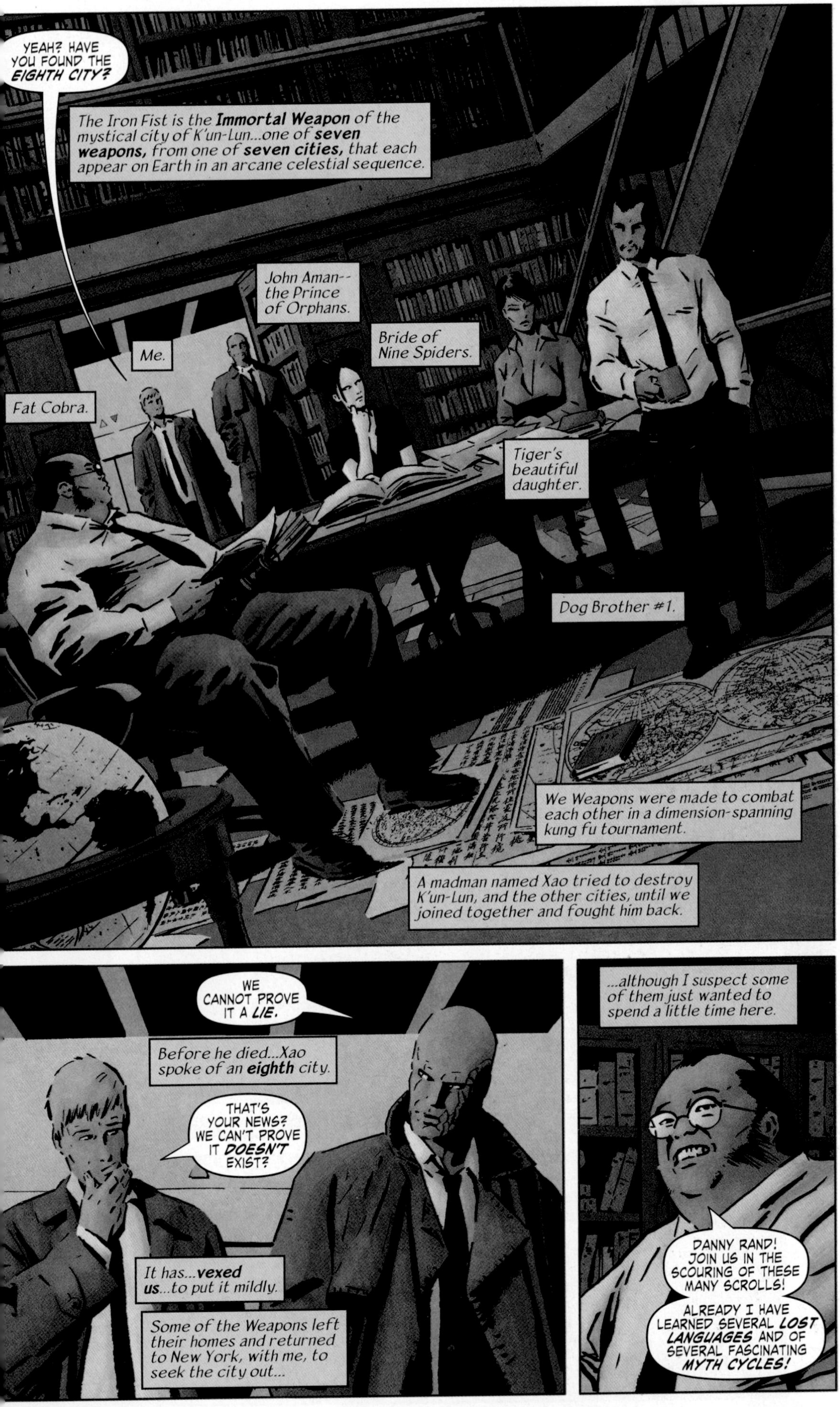
YEAH? HAVE YOU FOUND THE *EIGHTH CITY?*
The Iron Fist is the **Immortal Weapon** of the mystical city of K'un-Lun...one of **seven weapons,** from one of **seven cities,** that each appear on Earth in an arcane celestial sequence.
John Aman-- the Prince of Orphans.
Me.
Bride of Nine Spiders.
Fat Cobra.
Tiger's beautiful daughter.
Dog Brother #1.
We Weapons were made to combat each other in a dimension-spanning kung fu tournament.
A madman named Xao tried to destroy K'un-Lun, and the other cities, until we joined together and fought him back.
WE CANNOT PROVE IT A *LIE.*
Before he died...Xao spoke of an **eighth** city.
THAT'S YOUR NEWS? WE CAN'T PROVE IT *DOESN'T* EXIST?
It has...**vexed us**...to put it mildly.
Some of the Weapons left their homes and returned to New York, with me, to seek the city out...
...although I suspect some of them just wanted to spend a little time here.
DANNY RAND! JOIN US IN THE SCOURING OF THESE MANY SCROLLS!
ALREADY I HAVE LEARNED SEVERAL *LOST LANGUAGES* AND OF SEVERAL FASCINATING *MYTH CYCLES!*

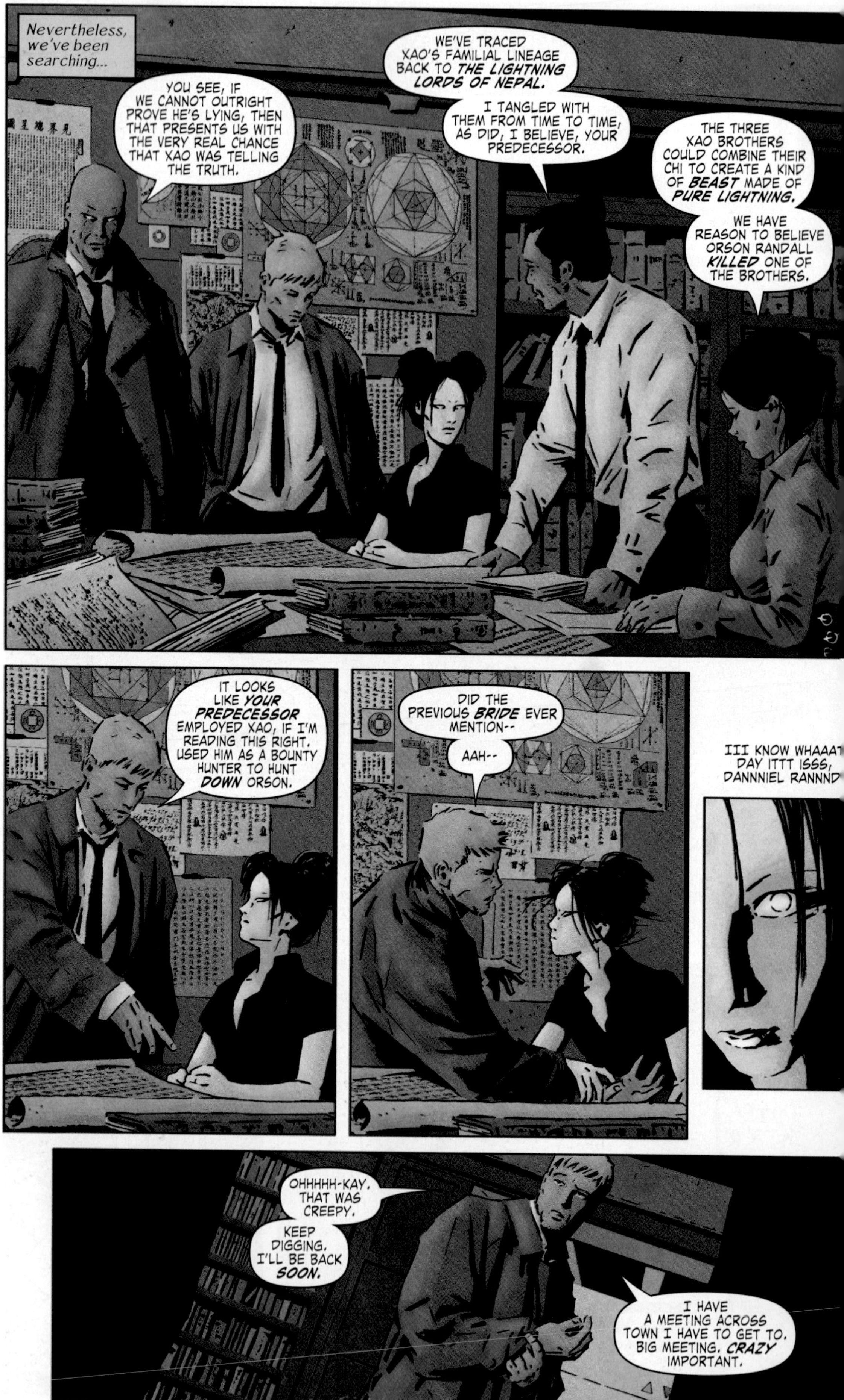
Nevertheless, we've been searching...
YOU SEE, IF WE CANNOT OUTRIGHT PROVE HE'S LYING, THEN THAT PRESENTS US WITH THE VERY REAL CHANCE THAT XAO WAS TELLING THE TRUTH.
WE'VE TRACED XAO'S FAMILIAL LINEAGE BACK TO THE LIGHTNING LORDS OF NEPAL.
I TANGLED WITH THEM FROM TIME TO TIME, AS DID, I BELIEVE, YOUR PREDECESSOR.
THE THREE XAO BROTHERS COULD COMBINE THEIR CHI TO CREATE A KIND OF BEAST MADE OF PURE LIGHTNING.
WE HAVE REASON TO BELIEVE ORSON RANDALL KILLED ONE OF THE BROTHERS.
IT LOOKS LIKE YOUR PREDECESSOR EMPLOYED XAO, IF I'M READING THIS RIGHT. USED HIM AS A BOUNTY HUNTER TO HUNT DOWN ORSON.
DID THE PREVIOUS BRIDE EVER MENTION--
AAH--
III KNOW WHAAAT DAY ITTT ISSS, DANNNIEL RANNND
OHHHHH-KAY. THAT WAS CREEPY.
KEEP DIGGING. I'LL BE BACK SOON.
I HAVE A MEETING ACROSS TOWN I HAVE TO GET TO. BIG MEETING. CRAZY IMPORTANT.

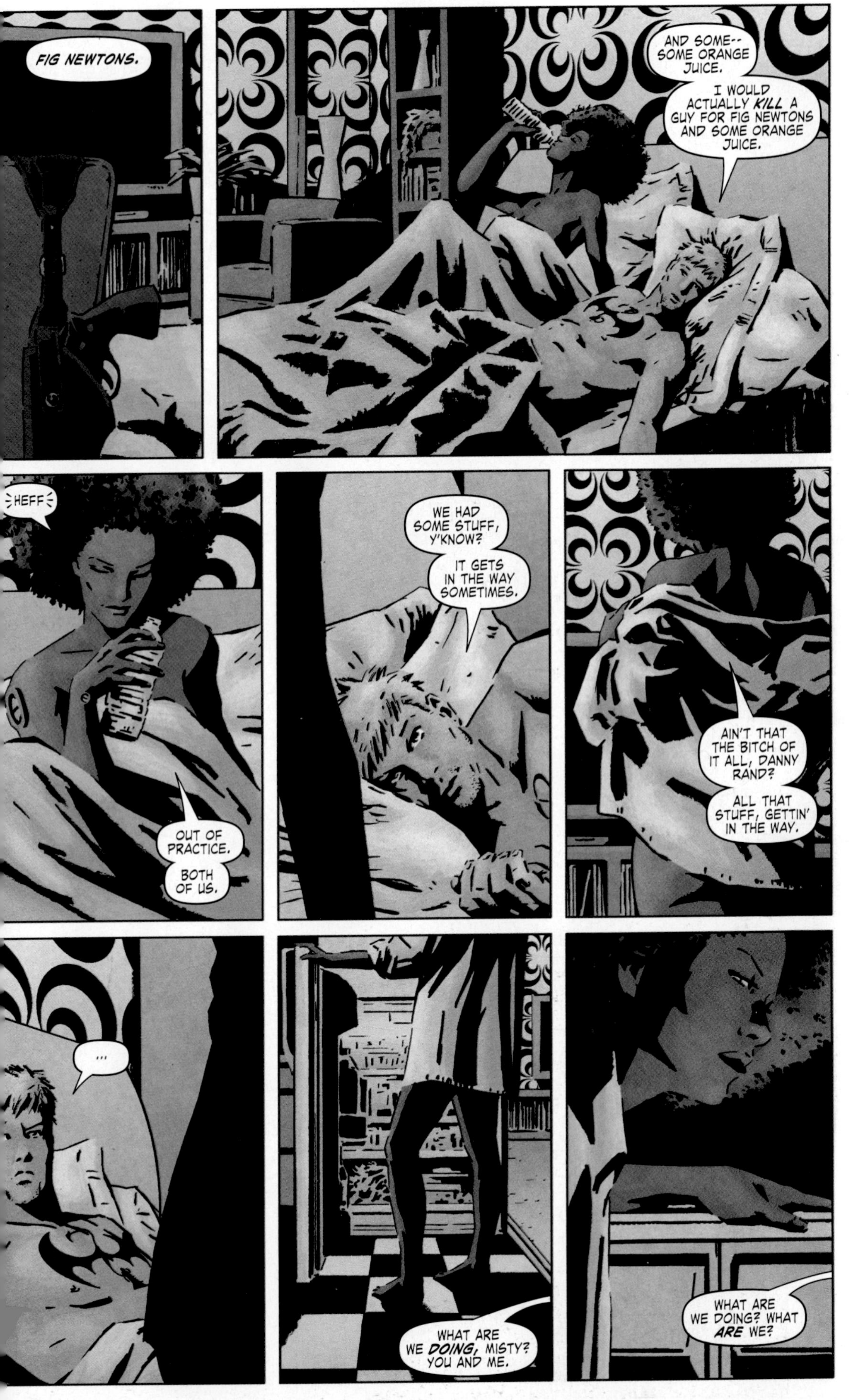
FIG NEWTONS.
AND SOME--SOME ORANGE JUICE.
I WOULD ACTUALLY KILL A GUY FOR FIG NEWTONS AND SOME ORANGE JUICE.
HEFF
OUT OF PRACTICE.
BOTH OF US.
WE HAD SOME STUFF, Y'KNOW?
IT GETS IN THE WAY SOMETIMES.
AIN'T THAT THE BITCH OF IT ALL, DANNY RAND?
ALL THAT STUFF, GETTIN' IN THE WAY.
...
WHAT ARE WE DOING, MISTY? YOU AND ME.
WHAT ARE WE DOING? WHAT ARE WE?

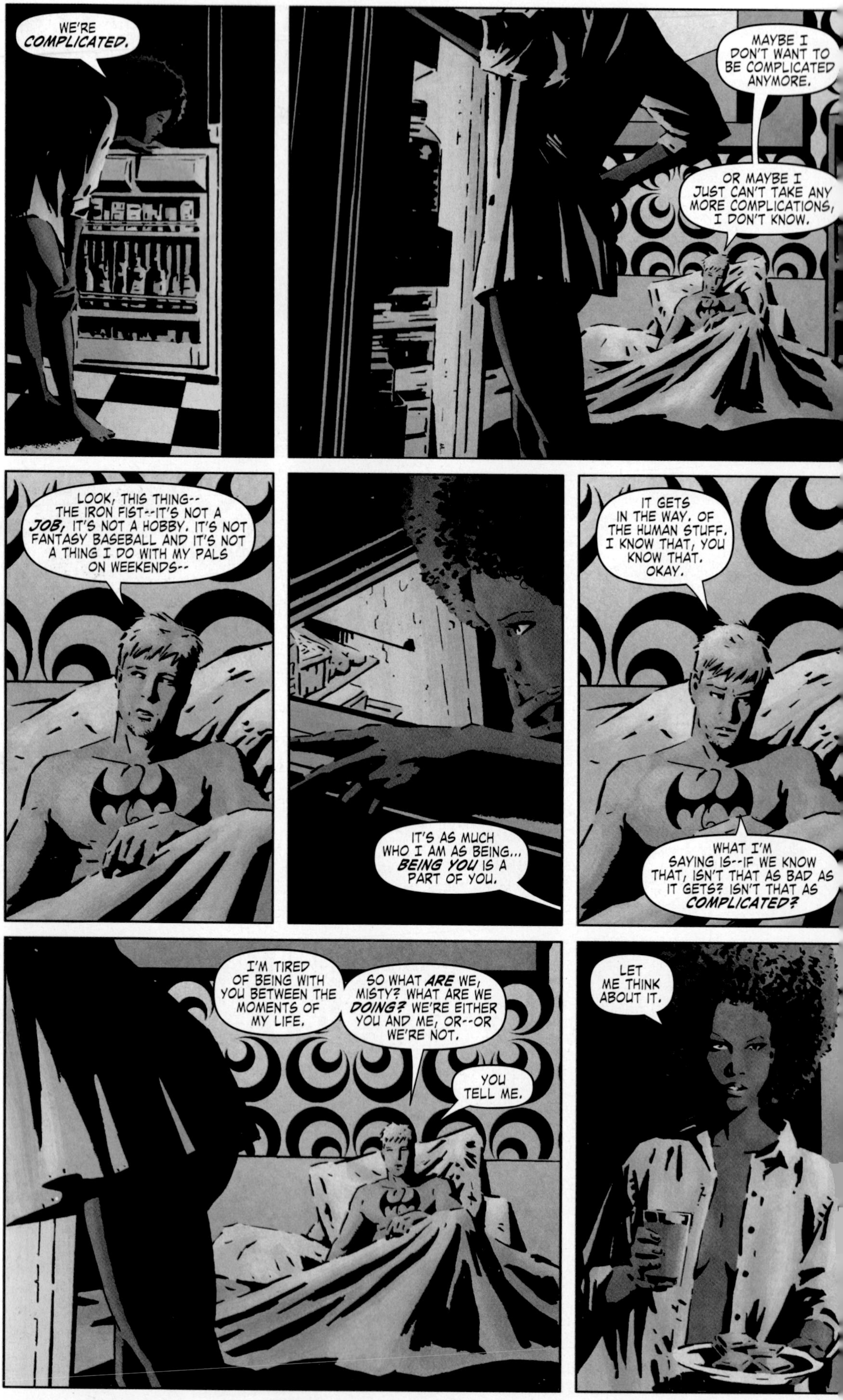
WE'RE *COMPLICATED.*
MAYBE I DON'T WANT TO BE COMPLICATED ANYMORE.
OR MAYBE I JUST CAN'T TAKE ANY MORE COMPLICATIONS, I DON'T KNOW.
LOOK, THIS THING--THE IRON FIST--IT'S NOT A *JOB*, IT'S NOT A HOBBY. IT'S NOT FANTASY BASEBALL AND IT'S NOT A THING I DO WITH MY PALS ON WEEKENDS--
IT'S AS MUCH WHO I AM AS BEING... *BEING YOU* IS A PART OF YOU.
IT GETS IN THE WAY. OF THE HUMAN STUFF. I KNOW THAT, YOU KNOW THAT. OKAY.
WHAT I'M SAYING IS--IF WE KNOW THAT, ISN'T THAT AS BAD AS IT GETS? ISN'T THAT AS *COMPLICATED?*
I'M TIRED OF BEING WITH YOU BETWEEN THE MOMENTS OF MY LIFE.
SO WHAT *ARE* WE, MISTY? WHAT ARE WE *DOING?* WE'RE EITHER YOU AND ME, OR--OR WE'RE NOT.
YOU TELL ME.
LET ME THINK ABOUT IT.

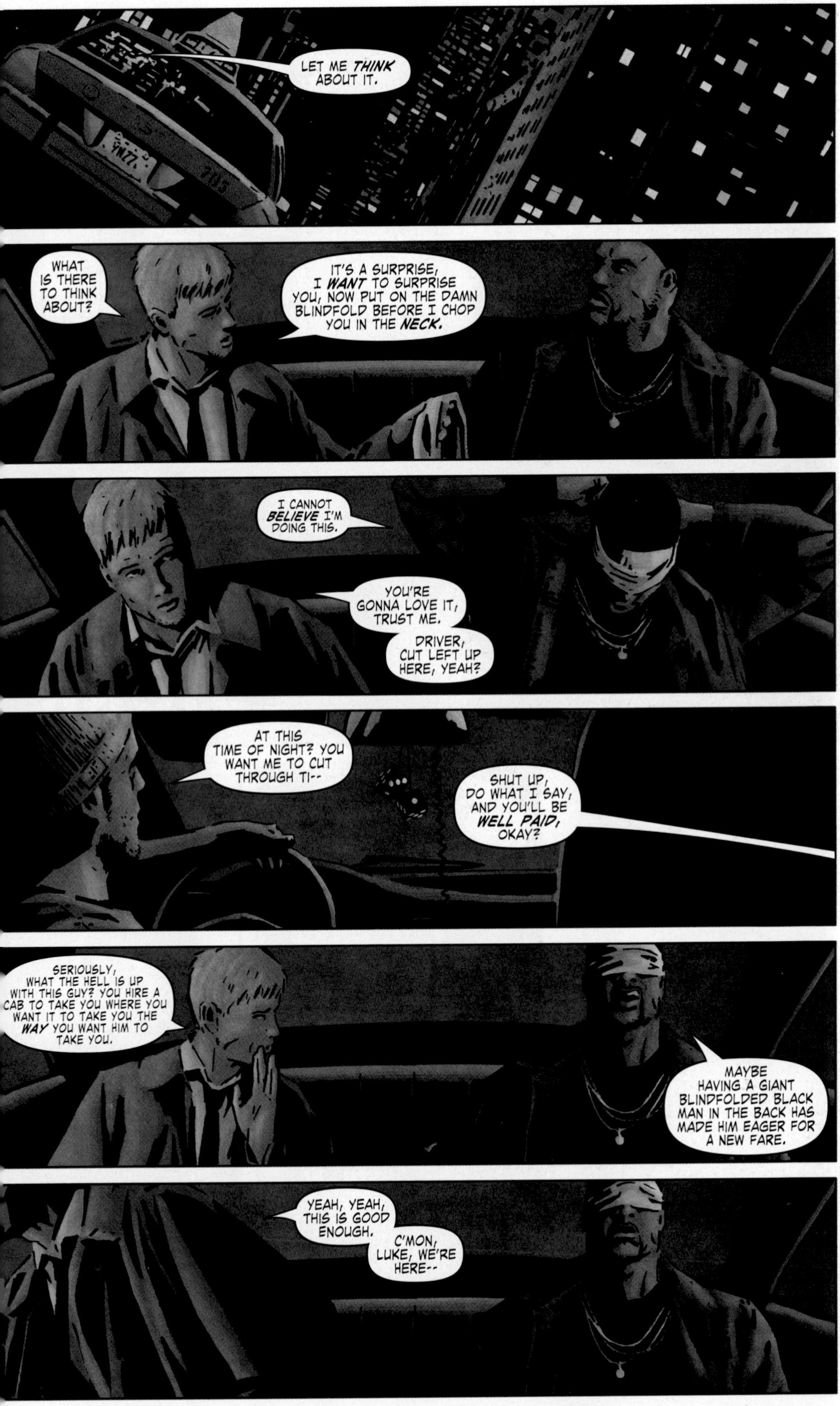
LET ME THINK ABOUT IT.
WHAT IS THERE TO THINK ABOUT?
IT'S A SURPRISE, I WANT TO SURPRISE YOU, NOW PUT ON THE DAMN BLINDFOLD BEFORE I CHOP YOU IN THE NECK.
I CANNOT BELIEVE I'M DOING THIS.
YOU'RE GONNA LOVE IT, TRUST ME.
DRIVER, CUT LEFT UP HERE, YEAH?
AT THIS TIME OF NIGHT? YOU WANT ME TO CUT THROUGH TI--
SHUT UP, DO WHAT I SAY, AND YOU'LL BE WELL PAID, OKAY?
SERIOUSLY, WHAT THE HELL IS UP WITH THIS GUY? YOU HIRE A CAB TO TAKE YOU WHERE YOU WANT IT TO TAKE YOU THE WAY YOU WANT HIM TO TAKE YOU.
MAYBE HAVING A GIANT BLINDFOLDED BLACK MAN IN THE BACK HAS MADE HIM EAGER FOR A NEW FARE.
YEAH, YEAH, THIS IS GOOD ENOUGH.
C'MON, LUKE, WE'RE HERE--

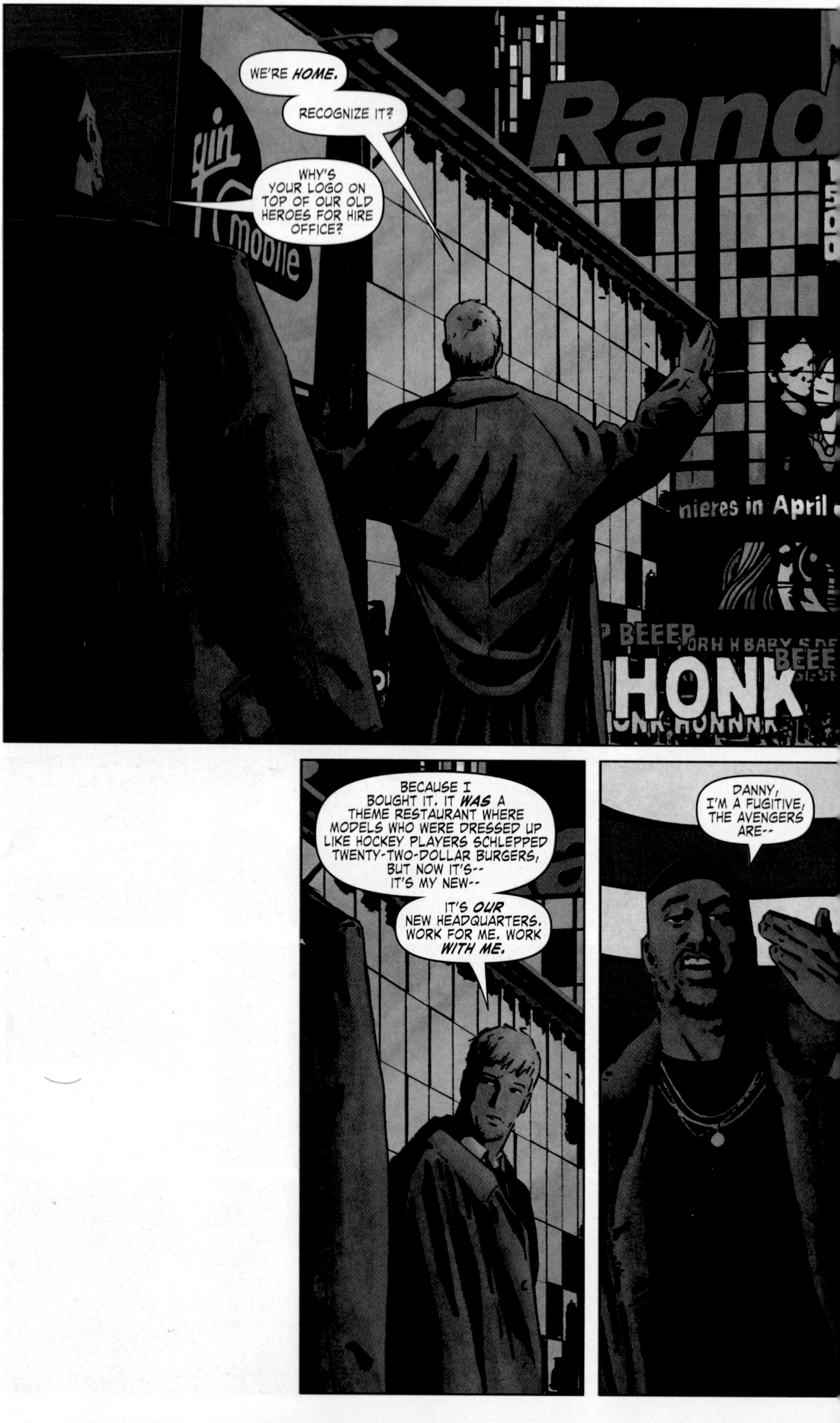
WE'RE *HOME.*
RECOGNIZE IT?
WHY'S YOUR LOGO ON TOP OF OUR OLD HEROES FOR HIRE OFFICE?
Rand
nieres in April
BEEEP
BEEE
HONK
BECAUSE I BOUGHT IT. IT *WAS* A THEME RESTAURANT WHERE MODELS WHO WERE DRESSED UP LIKE HOCKEY PLAYERS SCHLEPPED TWENTY-TWO-DOLLAR BURGERS, BUT NOW IT'S-- IT'S MY NEW--
IT'S *OUR* NEW HEADQUARTERS. WORK FOR ME. WORK *WITH ME.*
DANNY, I'M A FUGITIVE, THE AVENGERS ARE--

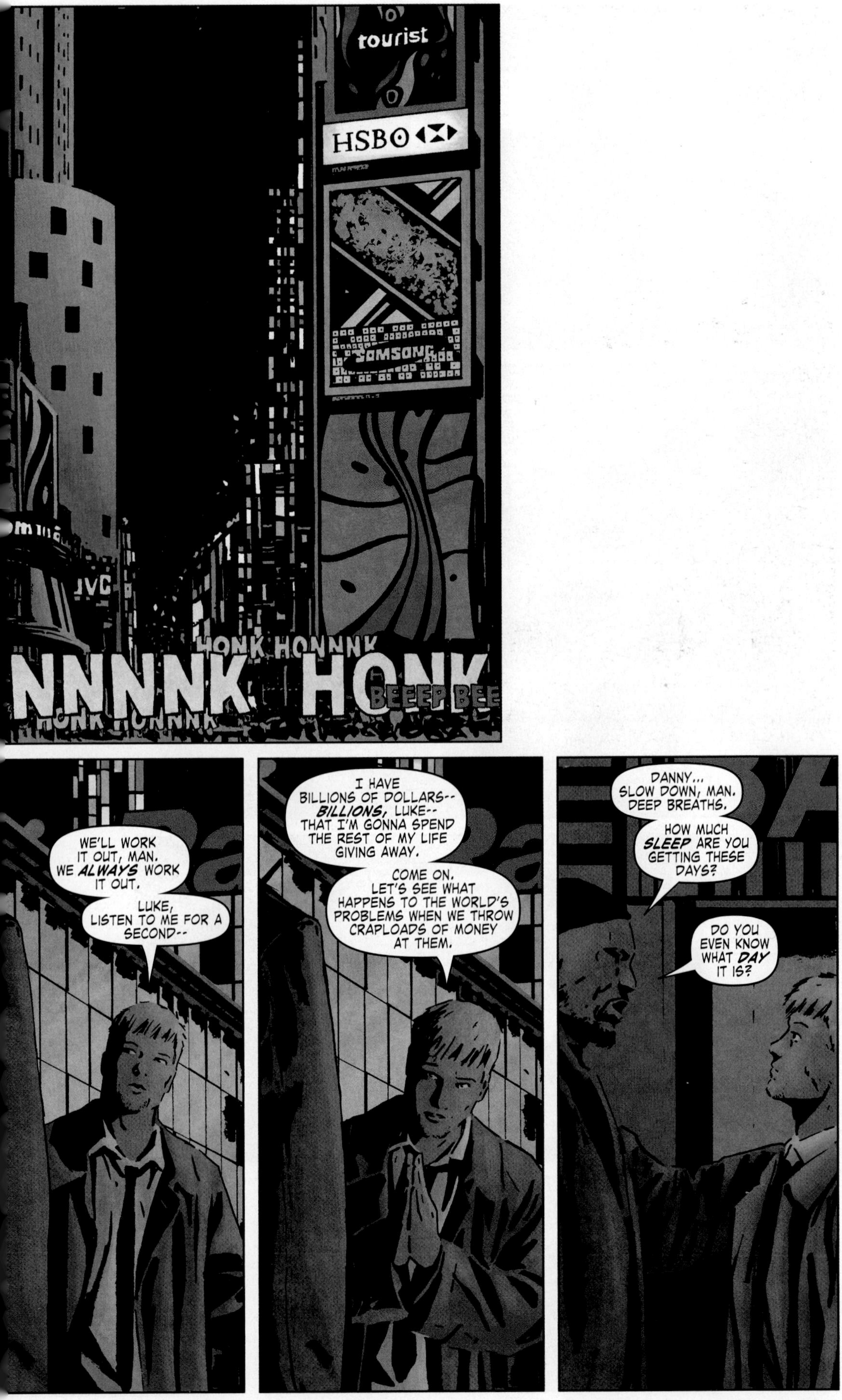

tourist
HSBO
SOMSONG
JVC
HONK HONNNK
NNNNK. HONK
BEEEP BEE
WE'LL WORK IT OUT, MAN. WE ALWAYS WORK IT OUT.
LUKE, LISTEN TO ME FOR A SECOND--
I HAVE BILLIONS OF DOLLARS-- BILLIONS, LUKE-- THAT I'M GONNA SPEND THE REST OF MY LIFE GIVING AWAY.
COME ON. LET'S SEE WHAT HAPPENS TO THE WORLD'S PROBLEMS WHEN WE THROW CRAPLOADS OF MONEY AT THEM.
DANNY... SLOW DOWN, MAN. DEEP BREATHS.
HOW MUCH SLEEP ARE YOU GETTING THESE DAYS?
DO YOU EVEN KNOW WHAT DAY IT IS?

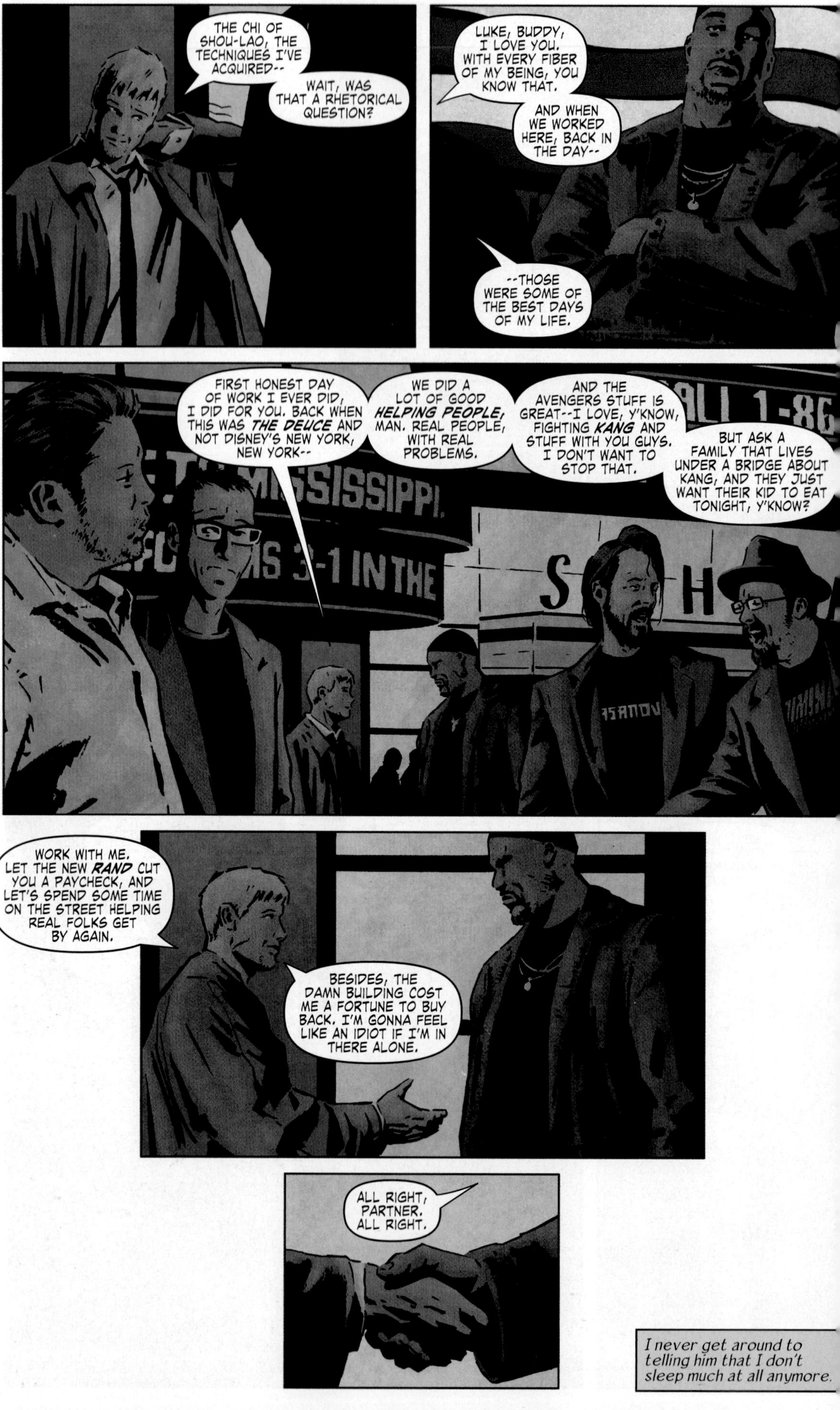
THE CHI OF SHOU-LAO, THE TECHNIQUES I'VE ACQUIRED--
WAIT, WAS THAT A RHETORICAL QUESTION?
LUKE, BUDDY, I LOVE YOU. WITH EVERY FIBER OF MY BEING, YOU KNOW THAT.
AND WHEN WE WORKED HERE, BACK IN THE DAY--
--THOSE WERE SOME OF THE BEST DAYS OF MY LIFE.
FIRST HONEST DAY OF WORK I EVER DID, I DID FOR YOU. BACK WHEN THIS WAS *THE DEUCE* AND NOT DISNEY'S NEW YORK, NEW YORK--
WE DID A LOT OF GOOD *HELPING PEOPLE,* MAN. REAL PEOPLE, WITH REAL PROBLEMS.
AND THE AVENGERS STUFF IS GREAT--I LOVE, Y'KNOW, FIGHTING *KANG* AND STUFF WITH YOU GUYS. I DON'T WANT TO STOP THAT.
BUT ASK A FAMILY THAT LIVES UNDER A BRIDGE ABOUT KANG, AND THEY JUST WANT THEIR KID TO EAT TONIGHT, Y'KNOW?
WORK WITH ME. LET THE NEW *RAND* CUT YOU A PAYCHECK, AND LET'S SPEND SOME TIME ON THE STREET HELPING REAL FOLKS GET BY AGAIN.
BESIDES, THE DAMN BUILDING COST ME A FORTUNE TO BUY BACK. I'M GONNA FEEL LIKE AN IDIOT IF I'M IN THERE ALONE.
ALL RIGHT, PARTNER. ALL RIGHT.
I never get around to telling him that I don't sleep much at all anymore.

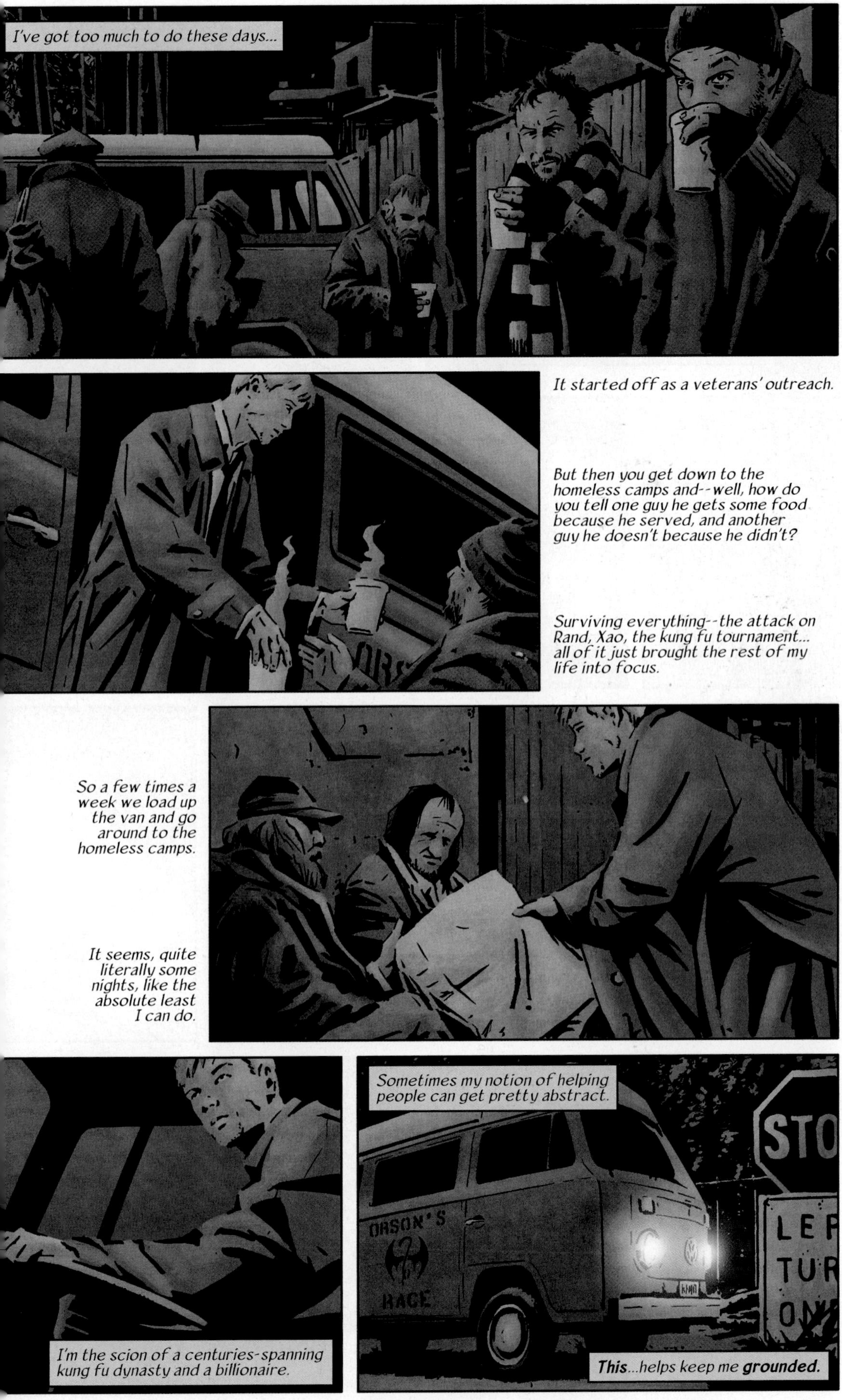
I've got too much to do these days...
It started off as a veterans' outreach.
But then you get down to the homeless camps and--well, how do you tell one guy he gets some food because he served, and another guy he doesn't because he didn't?
Surviving everything--the attack on Rand, Xao, the kung fu tournament... all of it just brought the rest of my life into focus.
So a few times a week we load up the van and go around to the homeless camps.
It seems, quite literally some nights, like the absolute least I can do.
I'm the scion of a centuries-spanning kung fu dynasty and a billionaire.
Sometimes my notion of helping people can get pretty abstract.
ORSON'S
This...helps keep me **grounded.**

And I dive within to stay centered.

To stay sane, to stay focused...

...I dive into the chi of Shou-Lao...

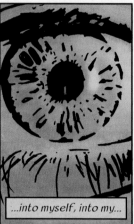

...into myself, into my...

...into my soul.

And for the first time in my life...

...I'm not alone.

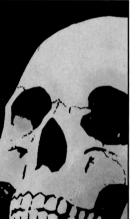

The legacy I am a part of is no longer a secret kept from me by the mysterious and powerful...

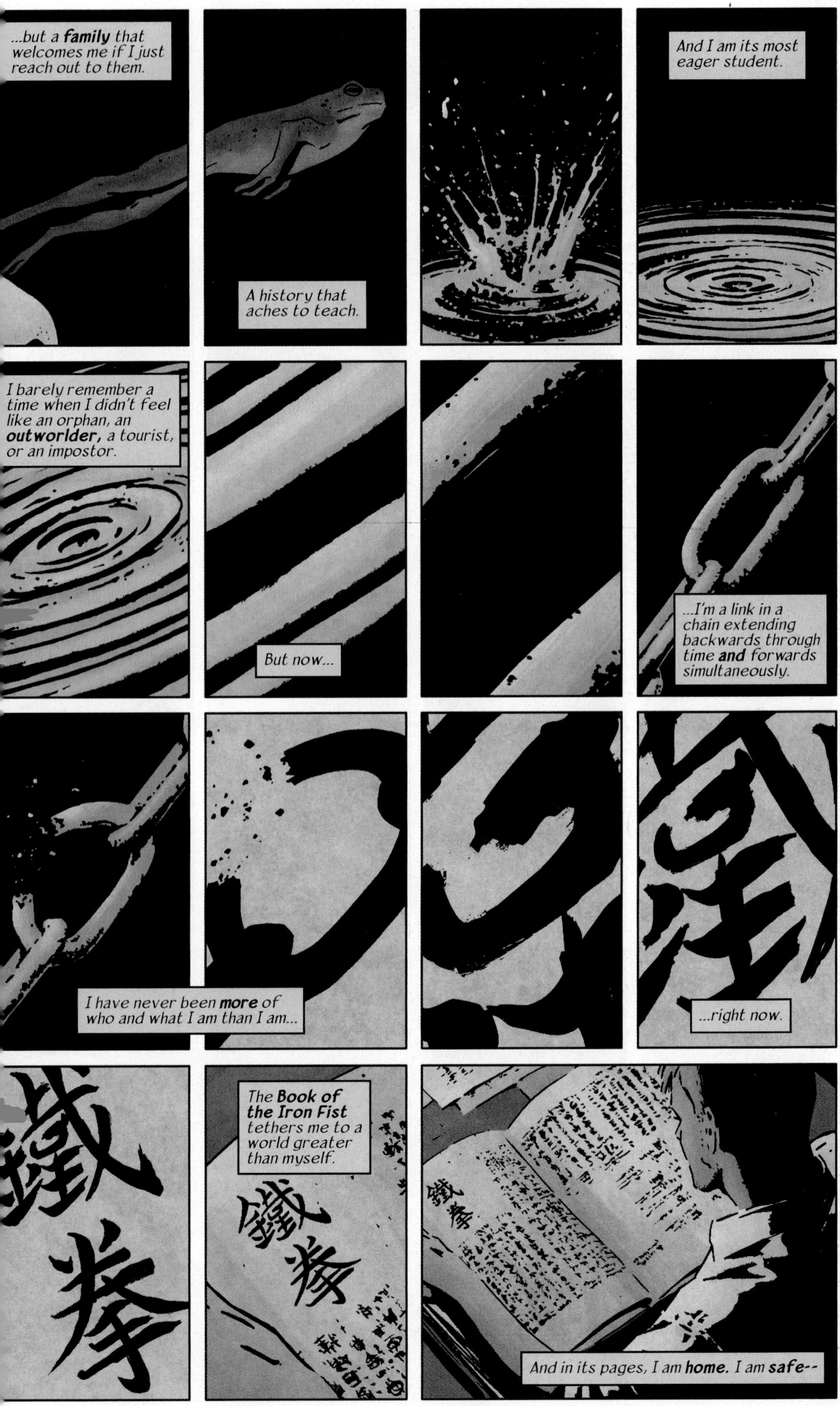
...but a **family** that welcomes me if I just reach out to them.
A history that aches to teach.
And I am its most eager student.
I barely remember a time when I didn't feel like an orphan, an **outworlder,** a tourist, or an impostor.
But now...
...I'm a link in a chain extending backwards through time **and** forwards simultaneously.
I have never been **more** of who and what I am than I am...
...right now.
The **Book of the Iron Fist** tethers me to a world greater than myself.
And in its pages, I am **home.** I am **safe--**

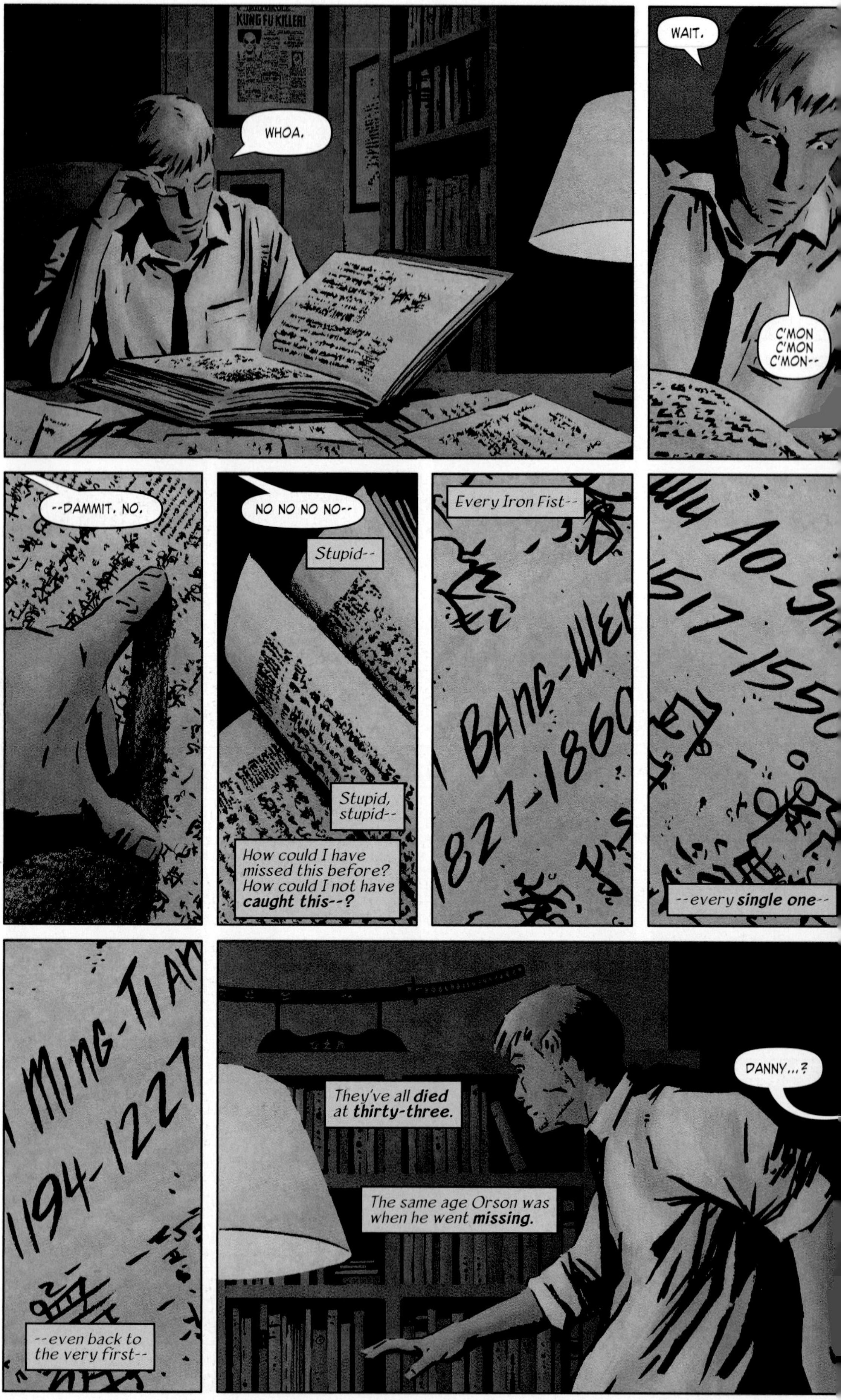
KUNG FU KILLER!
WHOA.
WAIT.
C'MON
C'MON
C'MON--
--DAMMIT. NO.
NO NO NO NO--
Stupid--
Stupid,
stupid--
How could I have
missed this before?
How could I not have
caught this--?
Every Iron Fist--
BANG-WE
1827-1860
AO-SH
1517-1550
--every **single one**--
MING-TIA
1194-1227
--even back to
the very first--
They've all **died**
at **thirty-three.**
The same age Orson was
when he went **missing.**
DANNY...?

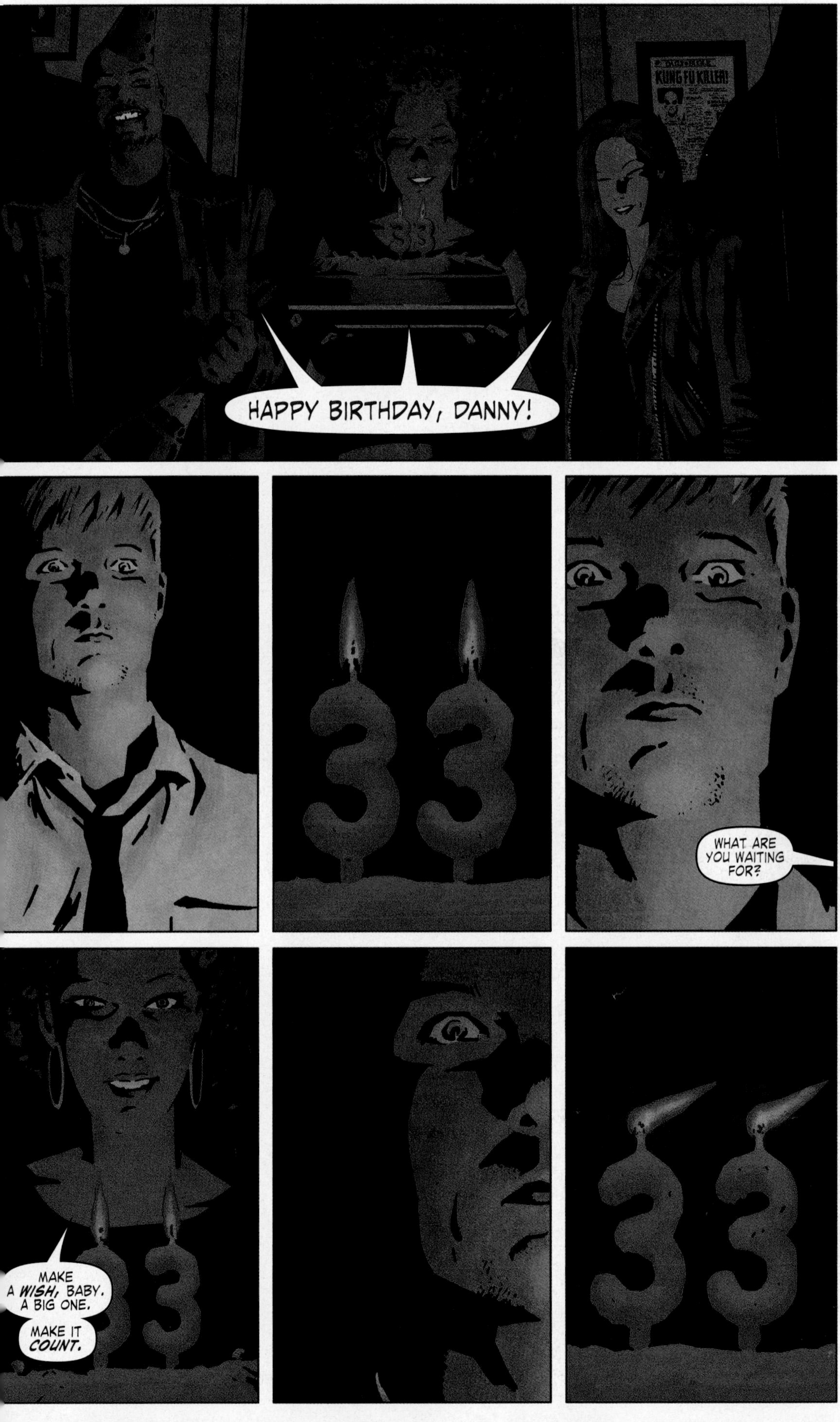
KUNG FU KILLER!
HAPPY BIRTHDAY, DANNY!
WHAT ARE YOU WAITING FOR?
MAKE A *WISH,* BABY. A BIG ONE.
MAKE IT *COUNT.*

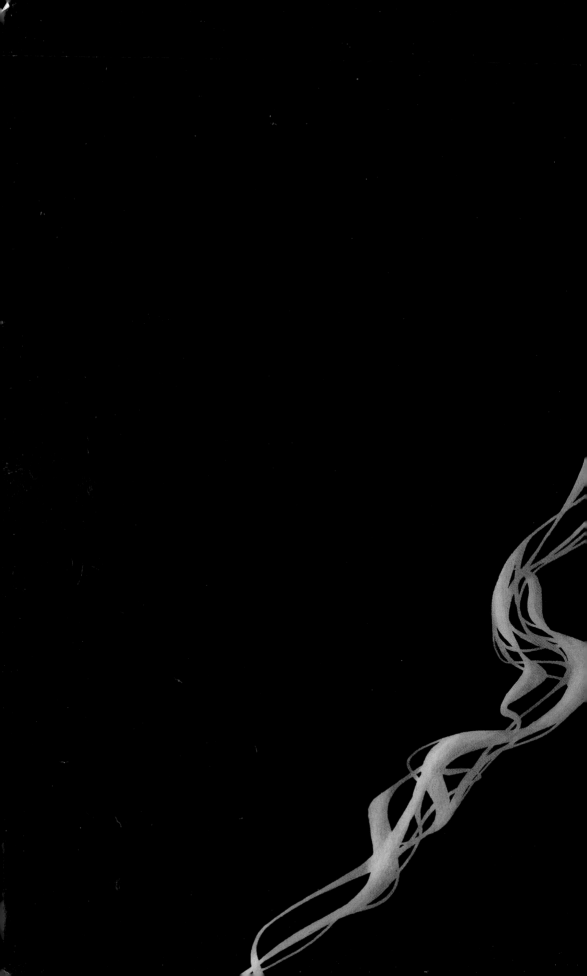

The following 8-page story was first printed in the one-shot *Civil War: Choosing Sides*. Tying into *Civil War*, this "issue #0" story bridges the gap between the pages of *Daredevil* — where Danny Rand masqueraded as the Man Without Fear to cover for his imprisoned friend Matt Murdock — and *Iron Fist #1.*

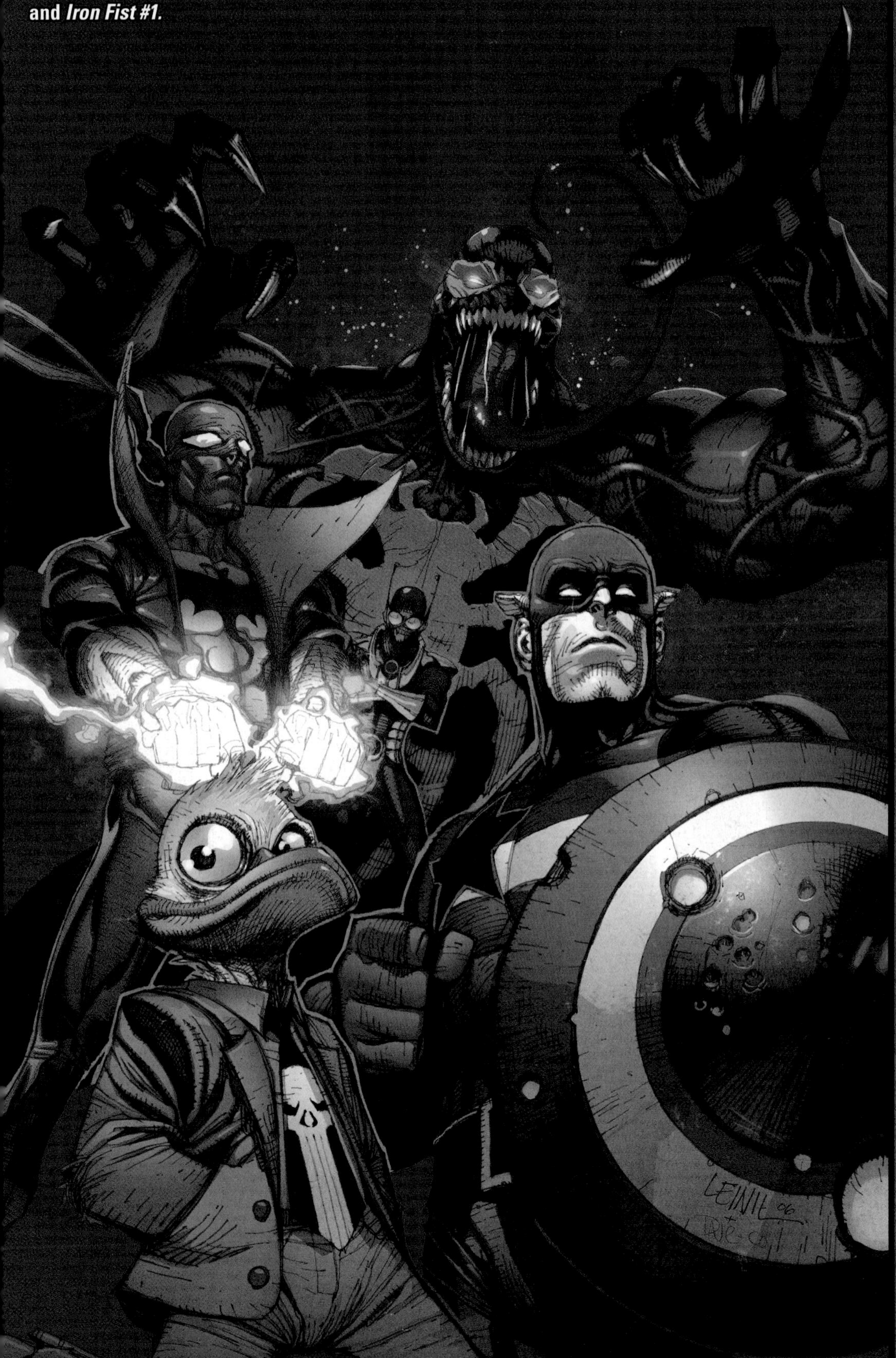

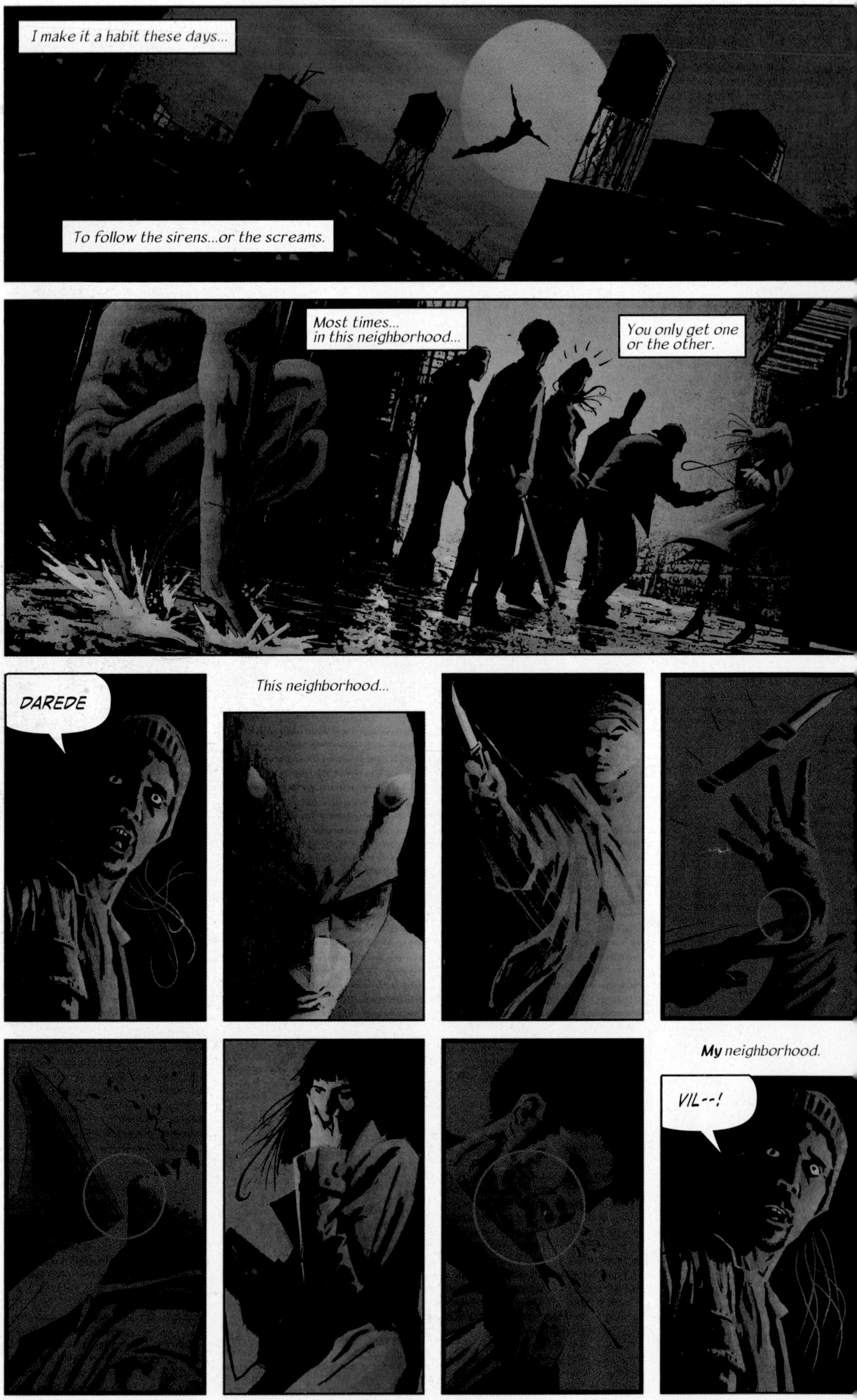
I make it a habit these days...
To follow the sirens...or the screams.
Most times... in this neighborhood...
You only get one or the other.
DAREDE
This neighborhood...
My neighborhood.
VIL--!

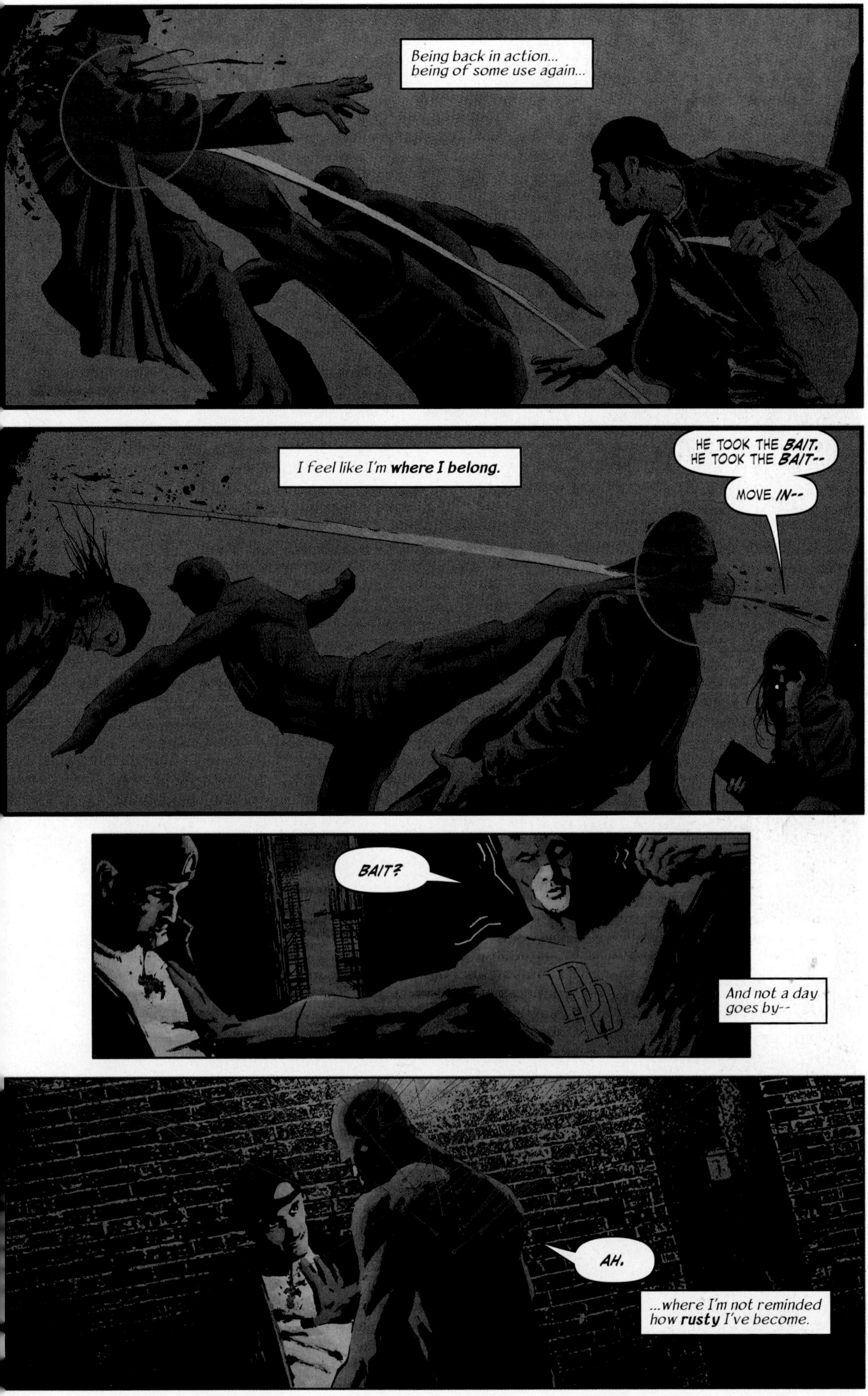
Being back in action... being of some use again...
I feel like I'm **where I belong.**
HE TOOK THE ***BAIT.*** HE TOOK THE ***BAIT--***
MOVE ***IN--***
BAIT?
And not a day goes by--
AH.
...where I'm not reminded how **rusty** I've become.

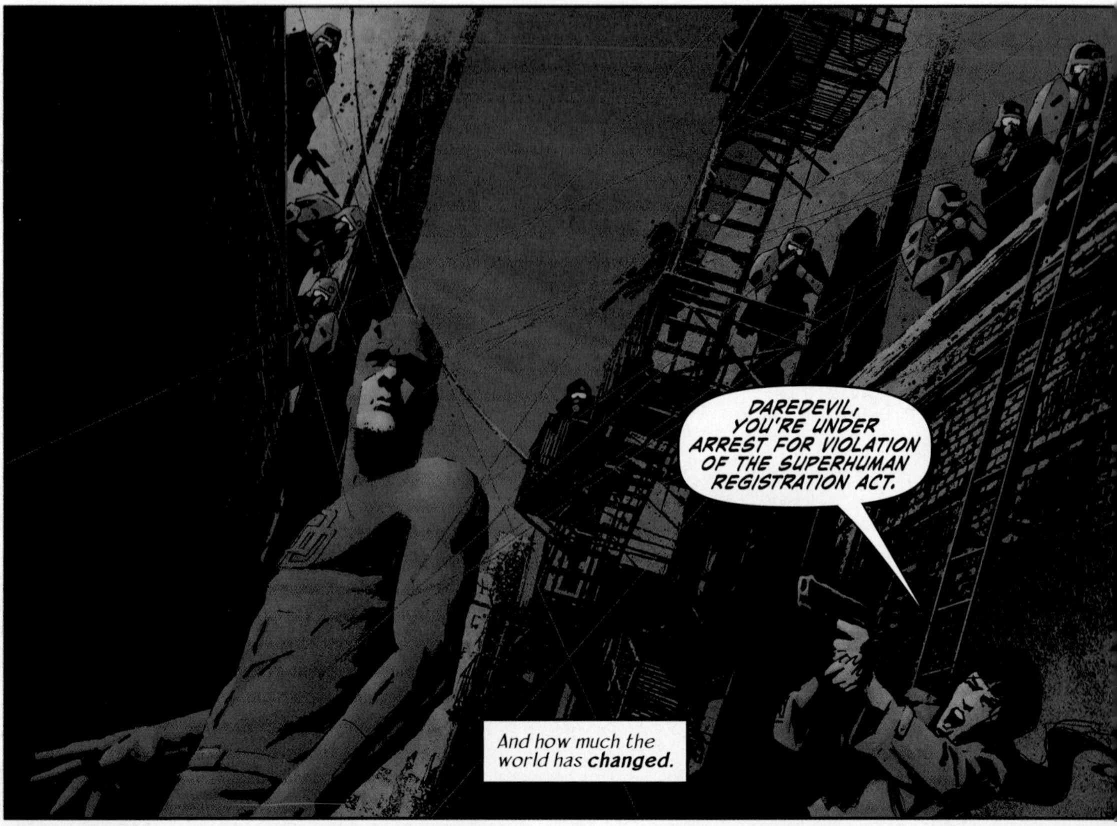
DAREDEVIL, YOU'RE UNDER ARREST FOR VIOLATION OF THE SUPERHUMAN REGISTRATION ACT.
And how much the world has **changed**.

THE IMMORTAL IRON FIST
"CHOOSING SIDES"

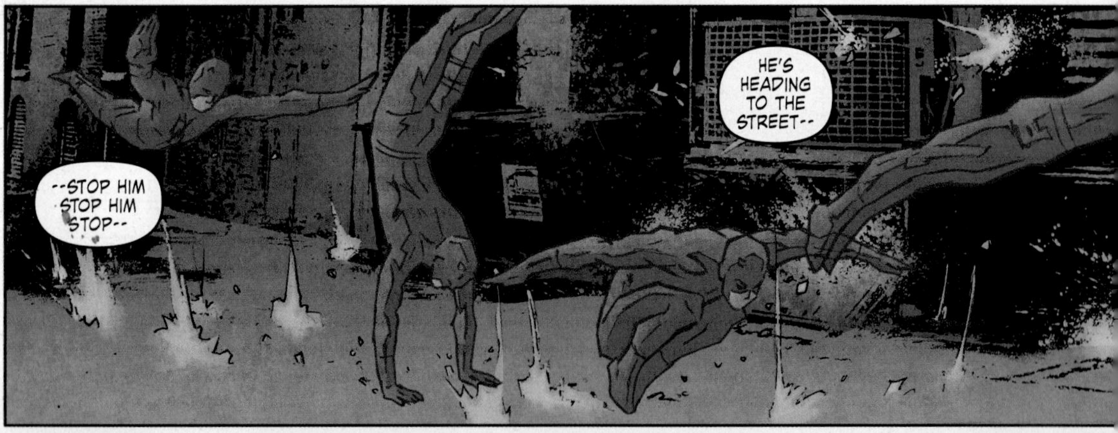
--STOP HIM STOP HIM STOP--
HE'S HEADING TO THE STREET--

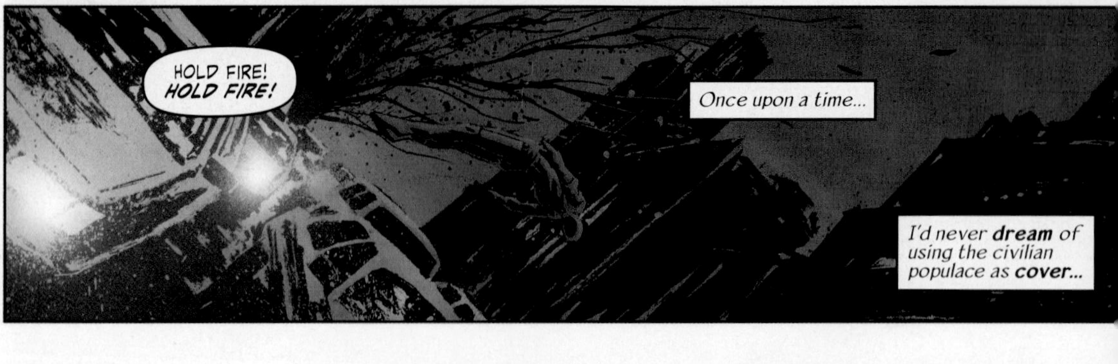
HOLD FIRE! **HOLD FIRE!**
Once upon a time...
I'd never **dream** of using the civilian populace as **cover**...

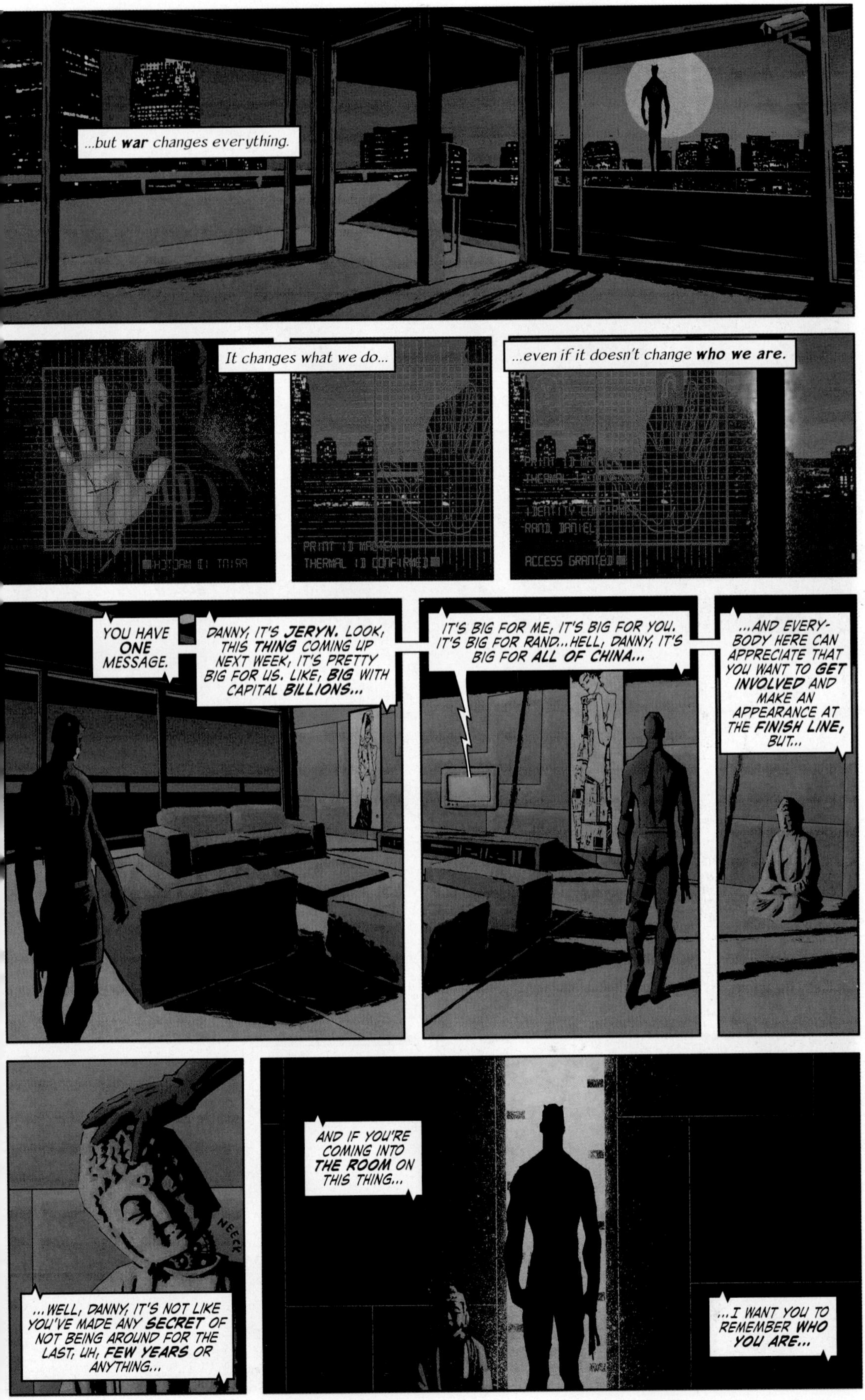
...but **war** changes everything.
It changes what we do...
...even if it doesn't change **who we are.**
THERMAL ID CONFIRMED
RAND, DANIEL
ACCESS GRANTED
YOU HAVE **ONE** MESSAGE.
DANNY, IT'S **JERYN.** LOOK, THIS **THING** COMING UP NEXT WEEK, IT'S PRETTY BIG FOR US. LIKE, **BIG** WITH CAPITAL **BILLIONS...**
IT'S BIG FOR ME, IT'S BIG FOR YOU. IT'S BIG FOR RAND...HELL, DANNY, IT'S BIG FOR **ALL OF CHINA...**
...AND EVERY-BODY HERE CAN APPRECIATE THAT YOU WANT TO **GET INVOLVED** AND MAKE AN APPEARANCE AT THE **FINISH LINE,** BUT...
NEECK
...WELL, DANNY, IT'S NOT LIKE YOU'VE MADE ANY **SECRET** OF NOT BEING AROUND FOR THE LAST, UH, **FEW YEARS** OR ANYTHING...
AND IF YOU'RE COMING INTO **THE ROOM** ON THIS THING...
...I WANT YOU TO REMEMBER **WHO YOU ARE...**

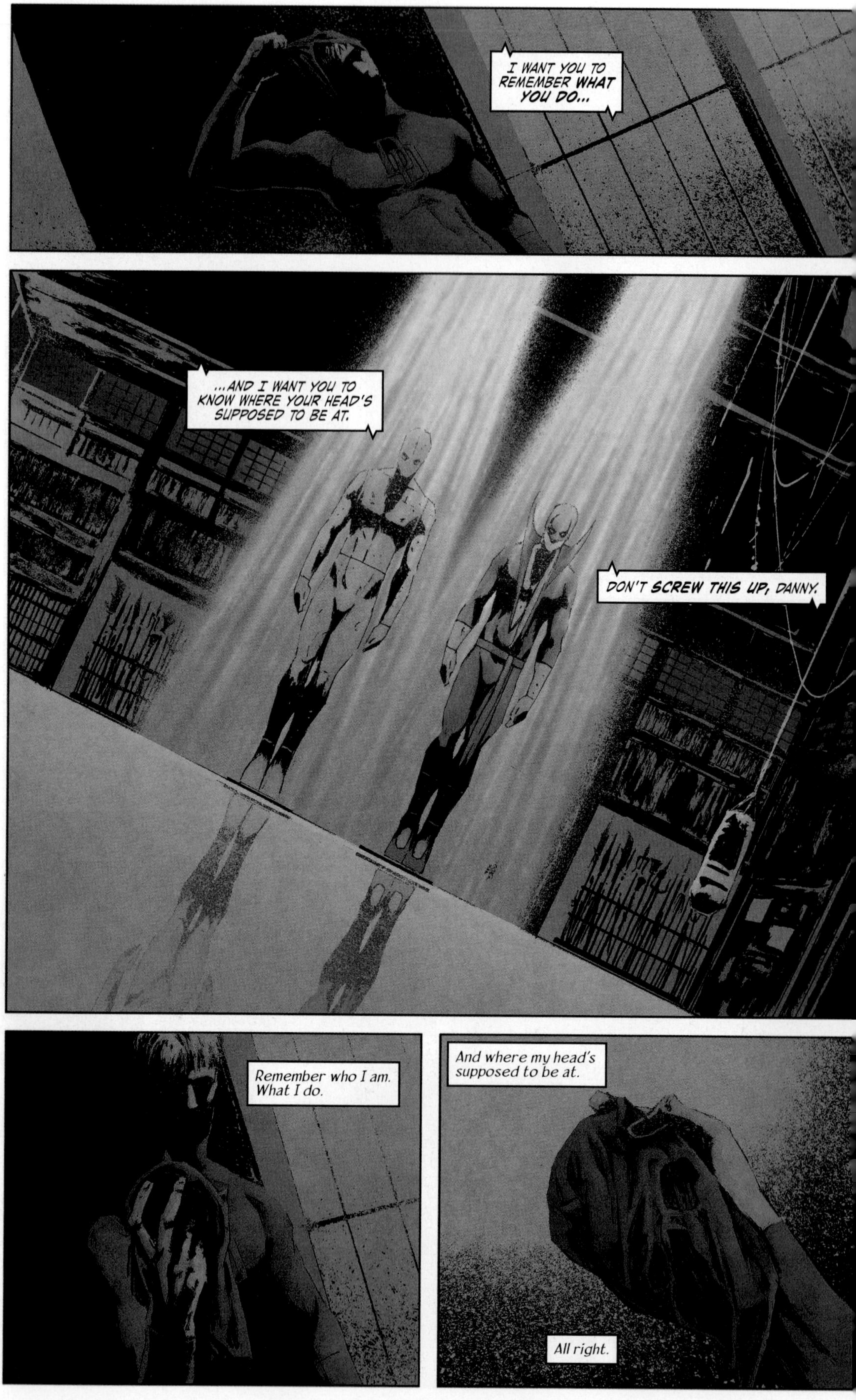
I WANT YOU TO REMEMBER WHAT YOU DO...
...AND I WANT YOU TO KNOW WHERE YOUR HEAD'S SUPPOSED TO BE AT.
DON'T SCREW THIS UP, DANNY.
Remember who I am. What I do.
And where my head's supposed to be at.
All right.

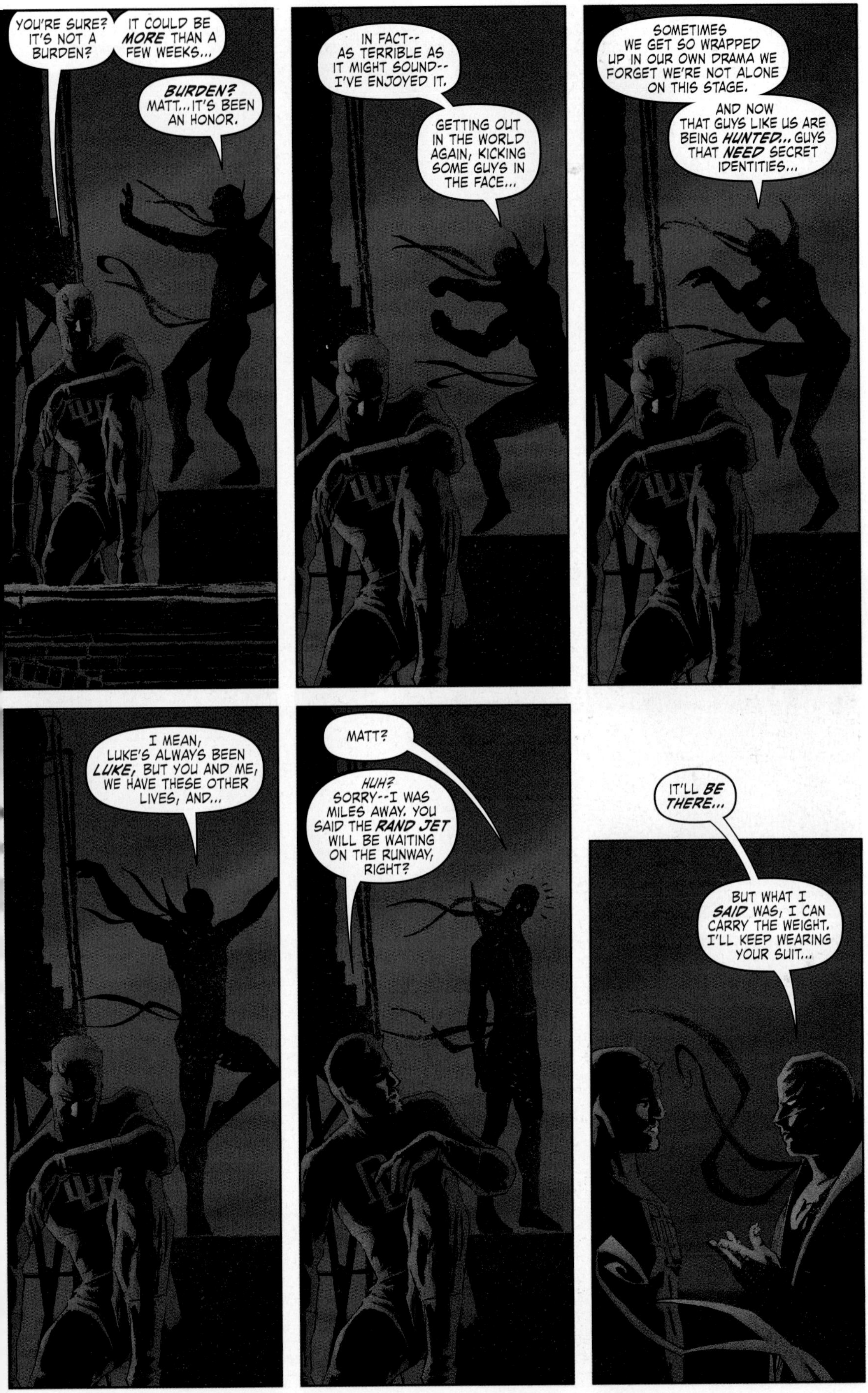
YOU'RE SURE? IT'S NOT A BURDEN?
IT COULD BE MORE THAN A FEW WEEKS...
BURDEN? MATT...IT'S BEEN AN HONOR.
IN FACT-- AS TERRIBLE AS IT MIGHT SOUND-- I'VE ENJOYED IT.
GETTING OUT IN THE WORLD AGAIN, KICKING SOME GUYS IN THE FACE...
SOMETIMES WE GET SO WRAPPED UP IN OUR OWN DRAMA WE FORGET WE'RE NOT ALONE ON THIS STAGE.
AND NOW THAT GUYS LIKE US ARE BEING HUNTED... GUYS THAT NEED SECRET IDENTITIES...
I MEAN, LUKE'S ALWAYS BEEN LUKE, BUT YOU AND ME, WE HAVE THESE OTHER LIVES, AND...
MATT?
HUH? SORRY--I WAS MILES AWAY. YOU SAID THE RAND JET WILL BE WAITING ON THE RUNWAY, RIGHT?
IT'LL BE THERE...
BUT WHAT I SAID WAS, I CAN CARRY THE WEIGHT. I'LL KEEP WEARING YOUR SUIT...

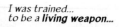

"...UNTIL YOU DON'T NEED ME TO ANYMORE."

*I was trained... to be a **living weapon**...*

*Before me, the beast called **Shou-Lao, the Undying,** lay slain...my flesh **marked** as his own...*

*And I plunged my hands into his burning and unholy **heart**...*

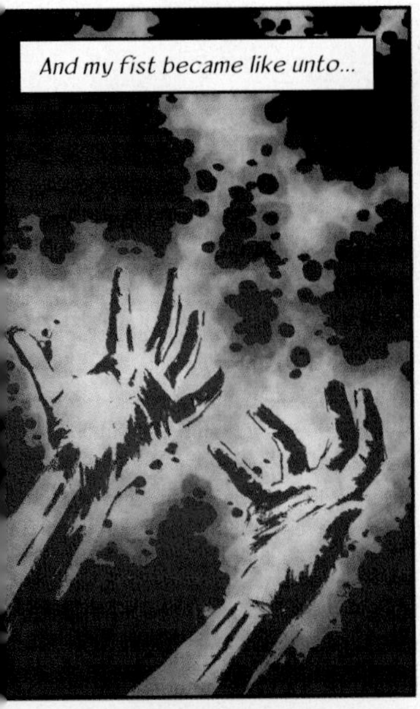
And my fist became like unto...

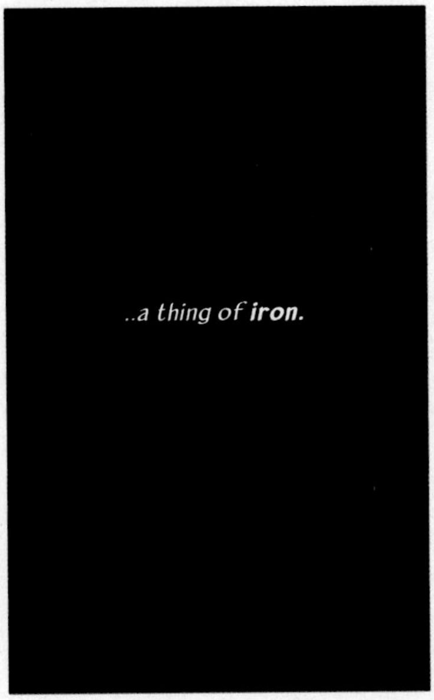
..a thing of **iron.**

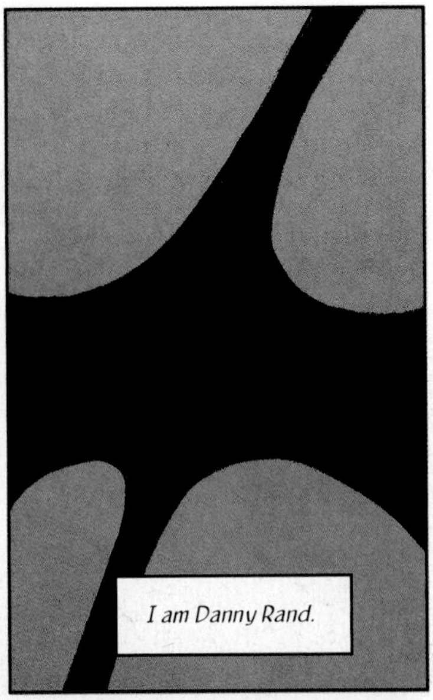
I am Danny Rand.

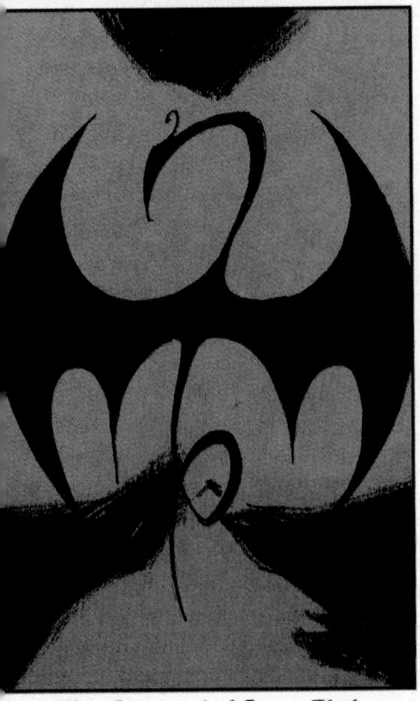

The Immortal Iron Fist.

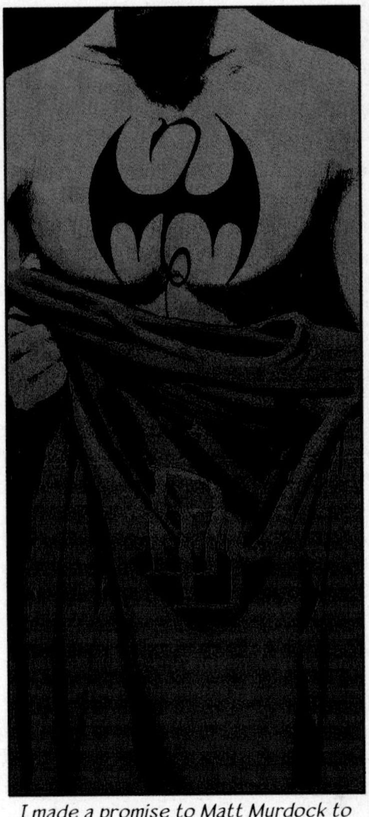

I made a promise to Matt Murdock to wear his mask...I've fought this war in his place... And I'll continue to.

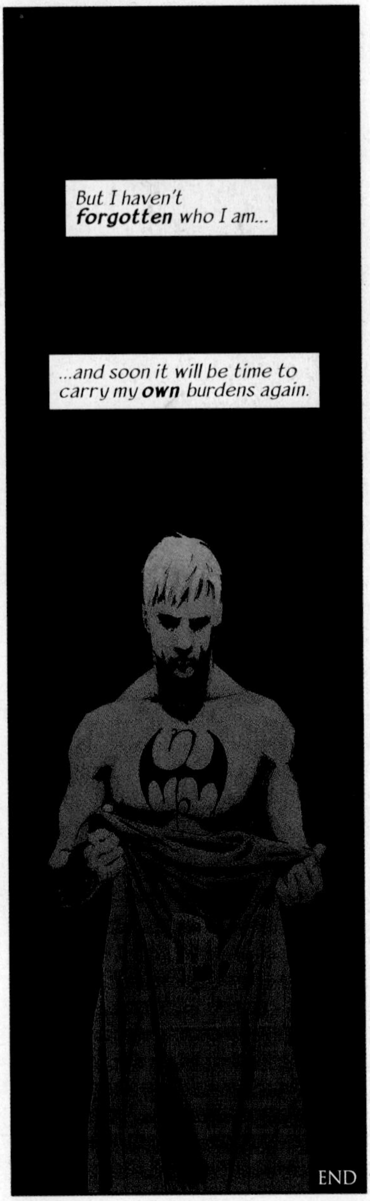
But I haven't **forgotten** who I am...
...and soon it will be time to carry my **own** burdens again.
END

THE ORIGIN OF DANNY RAND

Immortal Iron Fist: The Origin of Danny Rand #1 **reprinted Rand's first appearance from** ***Marvel Premiere #15-16*** **with a new framing sequence by Matt Fraction and Kano, presented here.**

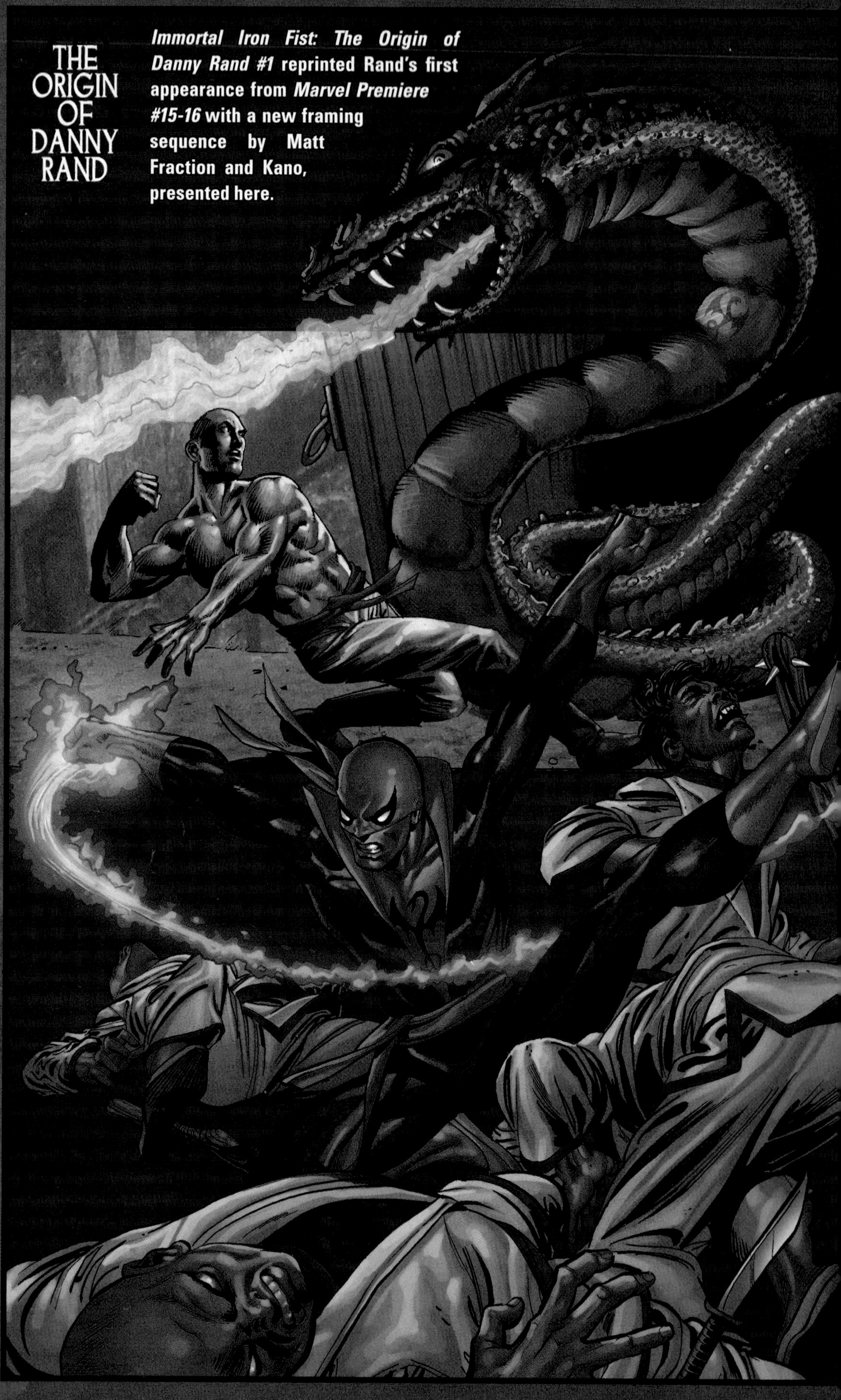

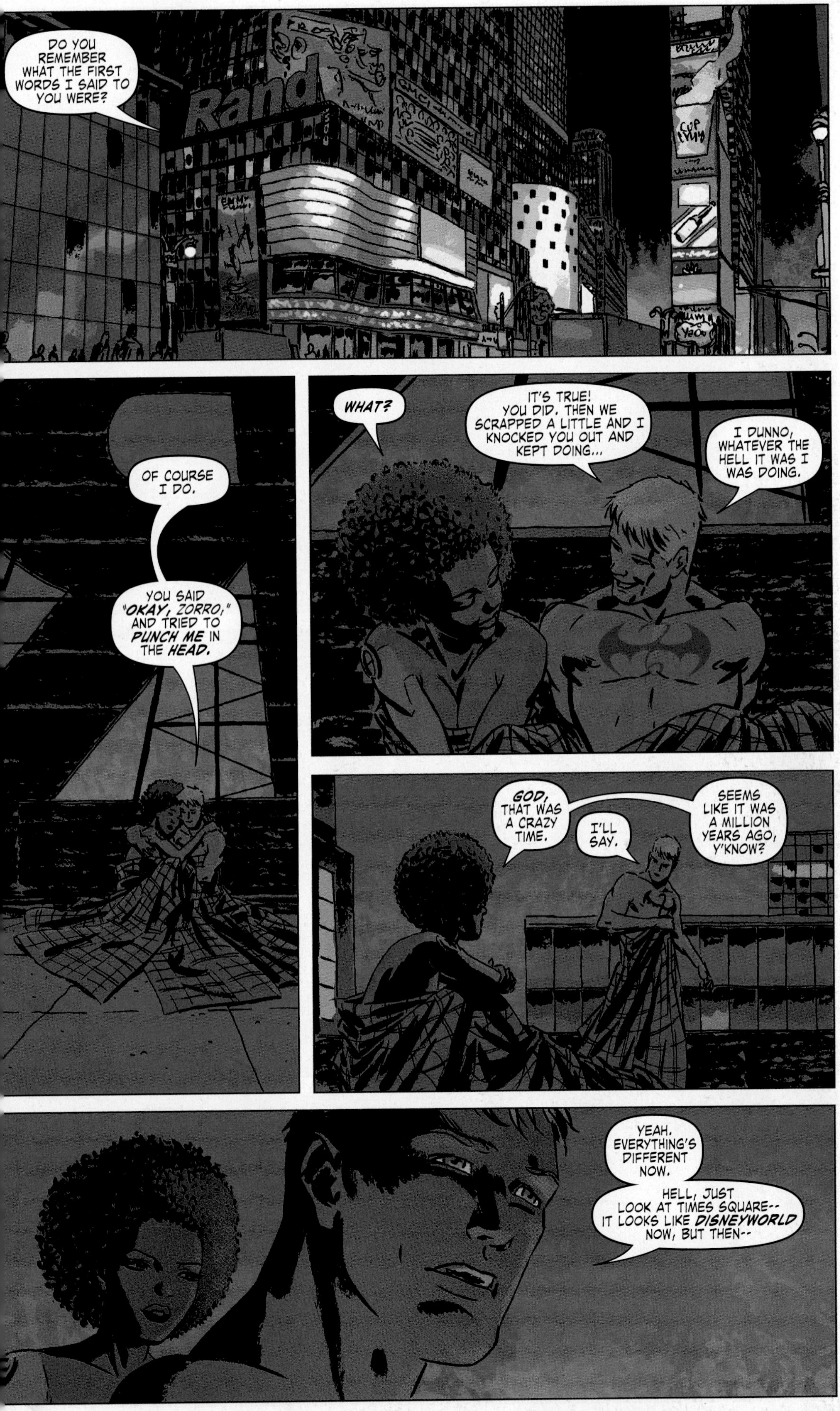

DO YOU REMEMBER WHAT THE FIRST WORDS I SAID TO YOU WERE?
OF COURSE I DO.
YOU SAID "*OKAY, ZORRO,*" AND TRIED TO ***PUNCH ME*** IN THE ***HEAD.***
WHAT?
IT'S TRUE! YOU DID. THEN WE SCRAPPED A LITTLE AND I KNOCKED YOU OUT AND KEPT DOING...
I DUNNO, WHATEVER THE HELL IT WAS I WAS DOING.
GOD, THAT WAS A CRAZY TIME.
I'LL SAY.
SEEMS LIKE IT WAS A MILLION YEARS AGO, Y'KNOW?
YEAH. EVERYTHING'S DIFFERENT NOW.
HELL, JUST LOOK AT TIMES SQUARE-- IT LOOKS LIKE ***DISNEYWORLD*** NOW, BUT THEN--

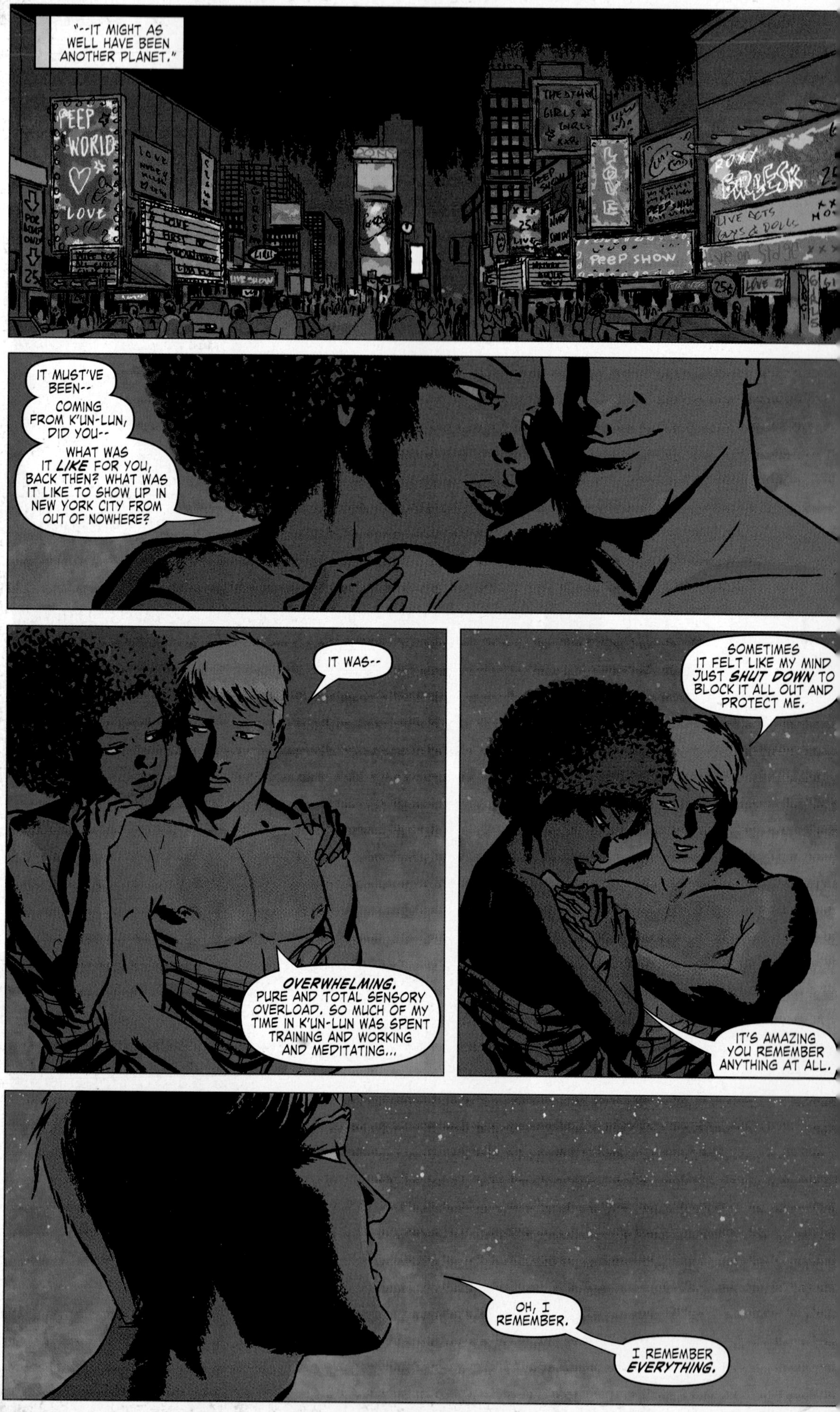
"--IT MIGHT AS WELL HAVE BEEN ANOTHER PLANET."
PEEP WORLD
LOVE
PEEP SHOW
LIVE SHOW
IT MUST'VE BEEN--
COMING FROM K'UN-LUN, DID YOU--
WHAT WAS IT *LIKE* FOR YOU, BACK THEN? WHAT WAS IT LIKE TO SHOW UP IN NEW YORK CITY FROM OUT OF NOWHERE?
IT WAS--
OVERWHELMING. PURE AND TOTAL SENSORY OVERLOAD. SO MUCH OF MY TIME IN K'UN-LUN WAS SPENT TRAINING AND WORKING AND MEDITATING...
SOMETIMES IT FELT LIKE MY MIND JUST ***SHUT DOWN*** TO BLOCK IT ALL OUT AND PROTECT ME.
IT'S AMAZING YOU REMEMBER ANYTHING AT ALL.
OH, I REMEMBER.
I REMEMBER ***EVERYTHING.***

THE IMMORTAL IRON FIST

WRITTEN BY *ED BRUBAKER* & *MATT FRACTION*
ART BY *DAVID AJA* WITH *TRAVEL FOREMAN*
EDITED BY *WARREN SIMONS*

OVERVIEW

In the early adventures of Iron Fist some 30 years ago, we saw a costume behind a glass case in the Mystical City of K'un-Lun, described to young Danny as the garb of the hero of K'un-Lun, "the Immortal Iron Fist." Where did this costume come from? Why did it wait for Danny under glass? And why was it just sitting there all those years? Doesn't this imply that, as long as K'un-Lun exists and has existed, an Iron Fist protected and will protect it? And what does it mean to be the Immortal Iron Fist? As the once-in-a-decade return of the Mystical City of K'un-Lun approaches, lately Danny Rand spends his nights wondering what it means to be Iron Fist and why he even bothers.

STORY

We open in a small village on the Chinese hillside in 1200 A.D. The hordes of Ghengis Khan ride with abandon toward this peaceful village of farmers and miners. Their hoofs raise a terrifying cloud of smoke, and the villagers see it coming, stunned with fear. This is the end for them. Murder, rape, slavery. The end.

Except a man in a greenish robe stands on the road before the town, his wicker hat pulled low over his head, waiting to greet the oncoming horde. As the horde gets closer, he looks up and raises one fist — it burns and sparkles with energy. He smiles. This is what it means to be an Iron Fist.

But DANNY RAND doesn't know anything about that.

Not yet, anyway.

For him, the path of Iron Fist started as one of revenge for his parents' murder, and since then he's wandered adrift, aware only of his squandered talents and gifts. Following the events of Daredevil and Civil War, Danny needs to find himself, and maybe that means finding his way back to the path of the Iron Fist. After months of masquerading as DD, Danny's refreshed perspective on the role of a hero has him looking differently at his entire life. And in the midst of this, a strange but familiar man enters his life... The man who was Iron Fist before Danny! We'll learn that this man gave up the Iron Fist mantle and wandered the world in the aftermath of World War I, his greatest failure robbing him of both his life's goal and the will to fight on. He holds the dubious honor of being one of the few Iron Fists to ever just quit — most Iron Fists die during combat.

This is their story: how the final fight of the Pulp Era Iron Fist intertwines with the rebirth of the modern one. This old hero will teach Danny Rand that being an Iron Fist means more than just putting on a costume and fighting super-villains. It's about standing up against oppressors, even with million-to-one odds, and not giving up until you succeed, or you're dead.

And through this meeting, Danny and his new mentor end up on the trail of a newly reincarnated MANDARIN, who has evil plans that will end with him leading an army to take over K'un-Lun when it reappears. The Mandarin, cast out of K'un-Lun as a child, has long-savored the day when he would destroy it — and that day, finally, has arrived.

The climax of our story features Danny and the Pulp Era Iron Fist holding off the Mandarin's forces in the snowy mountains where K'un-Lun will soon reappear. As they turn back the Mandarin's relentless hordes of Shao-Lin terror priests, the mystical city appears as the older Iron Fist breathes his last breath, gazing at his beloved home. After nearly 100 years, the prodigal son has returned, and the monks carry his body to rest. LEI KUNG THE THUNDERER (Danny's teacher) offers to let Danny return to the city, but Danny says no: his place is in the world, where he's needed… And a new era dawns for Iron Fist!

That's the broadest brush-strokes of the story, obviously, and we've got some cool ideas about opening each issue with a scene of one of the previous Iron Fists, throughout history, really fleshing out the Legend of the Immortal Iron Fist as we go along. We think it's going to be a fun and intriguing mini, and might even spawn a sequel or two, and certainly reposition Iron Fist as more than just a kung fu riff from the Seventies.

THE IMMORTAL IRON FIST #0
"CHOOSING SIDES"
ORIGINAL SCRIPT EXCERPT
WRITTEN BY *ED BRUBAKER* & *MATT FRACTION*
ART BY *DAVID AJA*

SCENE ONE:
PAGE ONE

David — This is a four-tiered page. It opens with full panel running the width of the page; the second tier is the same way; then we close with our last two tiers being made up of four panels each.

1 — A full tier ESTABLISHING SHOT on the rooftops of Hell's Kitchen at night. Throw in some of those Frank Miller watertowers. DAREDEVIL is leaping from one side to the next, illuminated against a big full moon.

    CAP (DANNY): I make it a habit these days…

    CAP (DANNY): To follow the sirens… or the screams.

2 — A full tier shot as DAREDEVIL lands crouched at the mouth of a dead-end alley where a group of FIVE THUGS have a WOMAN cornered…she's backed up against the wall and holds her purse out as an offering; these guys have knives out and ain't lookin' for cash.

    CAP (DANNY): Most times…in this neighborhood…

    CAP (DANNY): You only get one or the other.

3 — This is the start of the third tier and the fast, staccato little panels. In this case, it's a shot of a THUG, in awe, looking to his RIGHT.

    THUG: Darede—

4 — ON DAREDEVIL, grinning.

    CAP (DANNY): This neighborhood…

5 — ON A THUG'S HAND, knife gripped firmly.

6 — A gloved red hand smashes into that hand's wrist, loosening the knife.

7 — Fourth tier. DAREDEVIL'S FOOT connects with a THUG'S NECK, just below the chin.

8 — From behind a THUG as two gloved red hands CHOP DOWN on either side of the neck.

9 — On the WOMAN, frozen with fear.

10 — ON THE THUG FROM PANEL 3, now looking to his left.

    THUG: vil—!

    CAP (DANNY): My neighborhood.

PAGE TWO

1 — FULL TIER PANEL: DD unleashes a tremendous kick straight back, his leg moving with the velocity of a freight train. His foot connects with the chest of a THUG and sends him backwards into the wall behind him, bits of bricks exploding with his impact.

    CAP (DANNY): Being back in action...being of some use again...

2 — FULL TIER PANEL: DD swings that leg around and connects with ANOTHER THUG, sending him backwards. It's not as powerful a kick— he'll have to move in to finish the job. The WOMAN is speaking into her cuff like a Secret Service agent...

    CAP (DANNY): ...I feel like I'm where I belong.

    WOMAN: He took the bait, he took the bait—

    WOMAN: Move in—

3 — FULL TIER PANEL: DD, in profile, has jammed that last THUG back into the alley wall, pinning him by smashing his flattened palm into the guy's chest with his LEFT HAND, and drawing his RIGHT back into a fist, ready to strike. DD cocks his head a little, his finishing blow delayed by the woman's odd statement.

    DAREDEVIL: Bait?

    CAP (DANNY): And not a day goes by...

4 — FULL TIER PANEL: From BEHIND DD, hand still flattend onto the THUG'S chest, as he looks back over his shoulder and up—his hand, his head, the wall all around him, even the THUG, are all lit up with RED TRACER DOTS, the tell-tale sign of laser-sights being aimed at you... DD's just stumbled into a trap and he's just realized it.

    DAREDEVIL: Ah.

    CAP (DANNY): ...Where I'm not reminded how

THE IMMORTAL IRON FIST #1
ORIGINAL SCRIPT EXCERPT
WRITTEN BY *ED BRUBAKER* & *MATT FRACTION*

Note on the lettering — Make the captions and the narrative two different fonts, please.

PAGE ONE

1—A long shot- establishing. A peaceful farming village in Medieval Asia, at the base of a wide mountain range.

    LOCATION CAPS: A very long time ago...

2—Closer on the village and its farmers, working in the rice paddies and grain fields, as they look up. In the foreground of the panel, a man in green and yellow robes, is walking past them. But they aren't looking at him, they're looking away, into the distance.

    CAPTION: The village is insignificant...300 lives more or less.

3—And now we see what they're looking at. An army of horsemen, with swords and spears ready, the horde of Ghengis Khan, rides toward us from across the valley, dust billowing up behind them as they gallop, hungry for pillage.

    CAPTION: The armies of the Khan...

    CAPTION: ...No man dares stand in their way.

4—Back with the farmers, as they start to flee toward their hovel-like homes. One kid, being dragged along by his father, points off-panel, to where the man in green robes was heading.

    BOY: <Father... who – who is that man?>

PAGES TWO & THREE

1—Across the top third of both pages—a big shot of the army approaching. It's horrifying, these men are pure savages, smiling as they ride to deliver death to destruction. Their swords held high, ready for action, screaming and hooting, like animals.

> NARR: Who am I?

2—Another full tier across both pages. Now we see the man in the green robes more clearly. He stands before the village, which we see behind him, the farmers and peasants rushing to their homes in the background. The man in green and yellow is wearing a wicker hat that covers the top half of his face, and he's in a kung fu pose of some kind, ready, his right hand not yet a fist, though.

> NARR: I am the Iron Fist.

These last three are on one tier across the bottom of the page.

3—Back with the army approaching, closer on their faces, their swords raised high, ready to strike.

> NARR: I stand before the unstoppable hordes...

4—Closer on the man in green robes, as he raises his right hand, now a fist, and smiles.

> NARR: ...And I hold them back.

5—Same, as the fist begins to glow with energy. He's going to kick their asses.

> NARR: That's what I do.

> NARR: What I've always done.

PAGES FOUR & FIVE

1—Double-page spread. Bam, we're in the present day, and our Iron Fist is on the rooftops of New York, in the middle of a HUGE hand-to-hand fight with so many agents of Hydra that we can't count them. Just a sheer mass of people. Some are shooting at him with crazy Hydra guns, some are just trying to fight him. It's the middle of the night. Danny's hand is glowing as he does a kung fu move and sends three of them flying backwards. But it's clear he's overwhelmed by their numbers, or soon will be.

NARR: I am the Iron Fist.

NARR: I hold back the storm...

NARR: ...When nothing else can.

Title and credits go here

TITLE: THE LAST IRON FIST STORY – One of Six

CREDITS: Brubaker and Fraction – Writers / David Aja – Art / Matt Hollingsworth – Color Art / Dave Lanphear – Lettering / Warren Simons – Editor

PAGES SIX & SEVEN

1—Another long panel stretching across the top tier of both panels. Iron Fist, across the top of whatever building we're on, leads with his glowing fist streaking through the HYDRA agents like a shooting star, sending NINE HYDRA GUYS sprawling like bowling pins. Through the windows nearest the rooftop, we can see throngs of MORE HYDRA GUYS, all rushing to climb out of the windows, or up the fire escape, or otherwise looking upwards. And if Danny's worried about any of them, nothing about his posture suggests it. He's got a big grin on his face.

LETTERING NOTE: next to each falling HYDRA AGENT, put one of these captions.

> NARR: It should have been you, Father.

> NARR: You were meant to carry on this legacy, long before I was born...

NARR: But you chose to return to the world, instead...

NARR: To build the company I now run...

NARR: To fall in love and make a family...

NARR: And now everything I am...

NARR: ...I am because of you...

NARR: I'm what you would have been...

NARR: ...If tragedy hadn't knocked you from the path.

2—Panels 2-5 make up our next tier, each one a FLASHBACK PANEL: We're in the Himlayas, hunting for K'un-Lun Mountain. What looks like a solid mile of footprints in the snow are being made by four bodies—three ADULTS (two MEN and a WOMAN) and a CHILD. The two men are arguing over a map, one pointing in a different direction than where they're heading. (See MARVEL PREMIERE #15 for any reference you might need.)

NARR: Lost...

3—FLASHBACK PANEL: On a snow-covered bridge of ice we see HAROLD MEECHUM, raising a boot up, preparing to crush the hand of WENDELL RAND, dangling off of the bridge for dear life. Meechum holds a rope in one hand that's wrapped around Wendell's waist.

NARR: Betrayed...

4—DANNY and his MOTHER make their way through the frozen wasteland as a pack of ravenous WOLVES swarm around them in a pack.

NARR: Hunted...

5—FLASHBACK PANEL: High overhead a fragile, dangling rope bridge, little DANNY runs for his life as his Mother stays her ground at the bridge's mouth, the only thing between her son and the wolfpack.

NARR: Orphaned...

6—FLASHBACK PANEL: BIG PANEL, huge reveal, eating up the rest of PAGE SIX. We're behind YOUNG DANNY as he first sees the mystical, magical, awesomenical city of K'un-Lun. He and an ARCTIC HUNTER with a crossbow (see MARVEL PREMIERE #16 for ref) are at the end of a long procession of HUNTERS entering the city. It is epic, strange, and otherworldly, glowing and warm in the heart of the tundra.

NARR: But finally, miraculously... Saved.

7—Annnnnd we're back in the modern day. BIG PANEL, eating up what's left of PAGE SEVEN. Like our last panel, we're behind DANNY/IRON FIST, and we're angling up on a glorious metropolis—Manhattan. Nearest we can see the RAND logo burning in the night atop a magnificent skyscraper. There's now an array of HYDRA GUYS surrounding Danny in a crescent formation. They're hesitating. They know Danny's about to strike.

NARR: Some legacies are our birthright...

NARR: And others we simply fall into...

CHARACTER DESIGNS

with commentary by artist David Aja

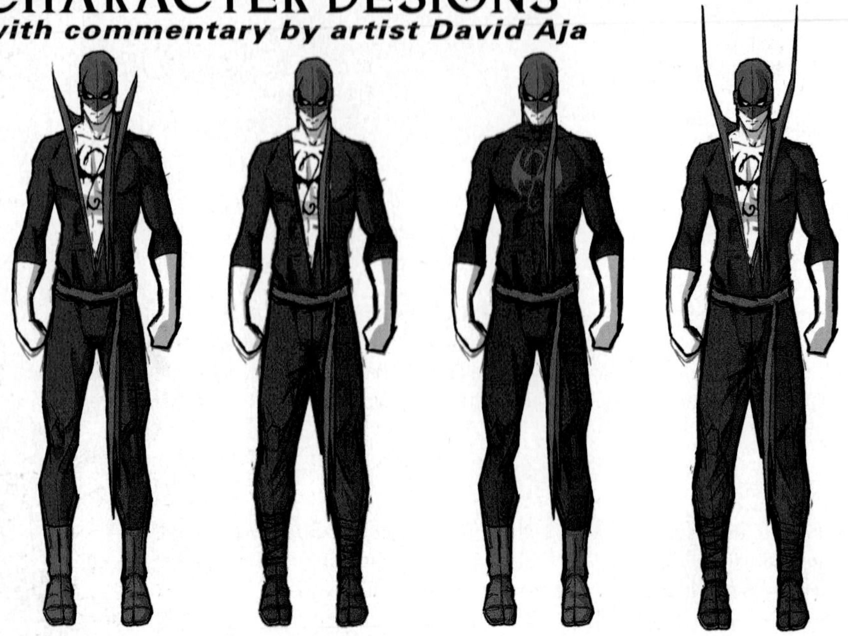

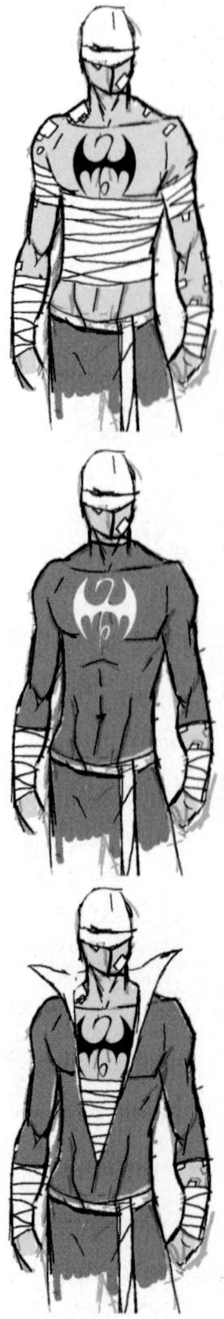

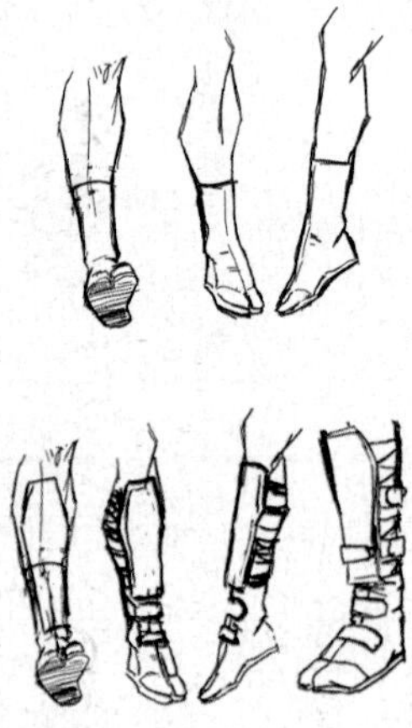

We all agreed the costume needed a minor update, and the first thing Ed suggested was changing his ankle slippers for 'ninja'-type boots. After that, we started working out the details: wide pants, cinched pants; collar, no collar; combinations of colors...but always keeping the spirit of the original costume.

Changing the suit was always part of my plan. I think the collar takes away some of the dynamic impact, and the open chest could work in the '70s...but today, not really. I intended to visualize the new costume design [at right] side by side with the current Luke Cage and still have them match. So when I saw that the Mechagorgon destroyed Danny's original costume, I thought, 'This is my chance!' It also looked better with Danny's bandages than the open chest would have.

Matt suggested we do a costume sort of like Bruce Lee's yellow track suit in 'Game of Death,' and I came up with these just to show him how crappy it would look. It's horrible.

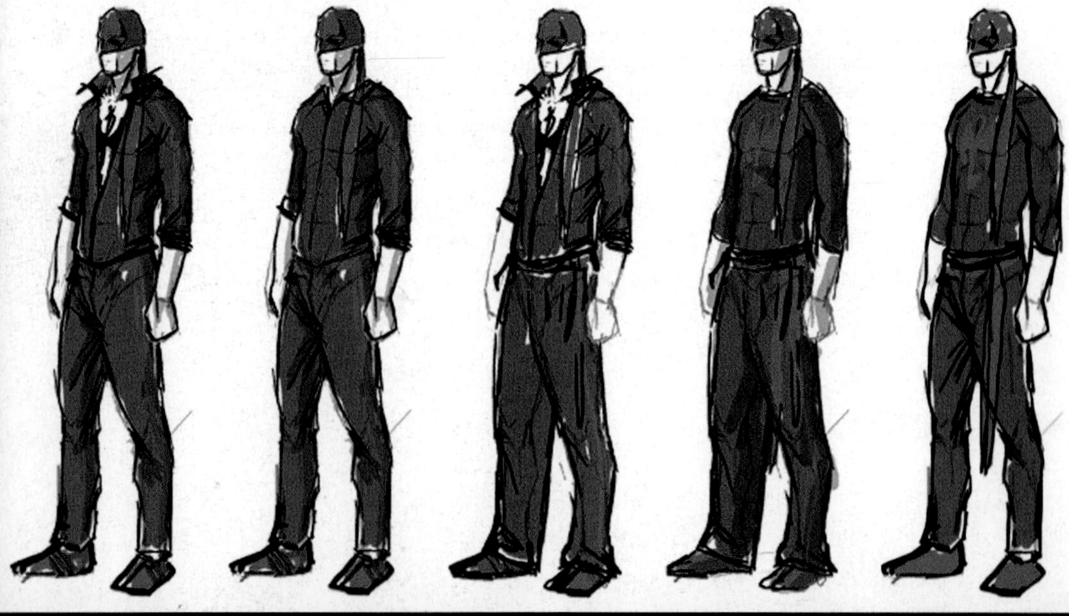

BEHIND-THE-SCENES E-MAIL EXCHANGE

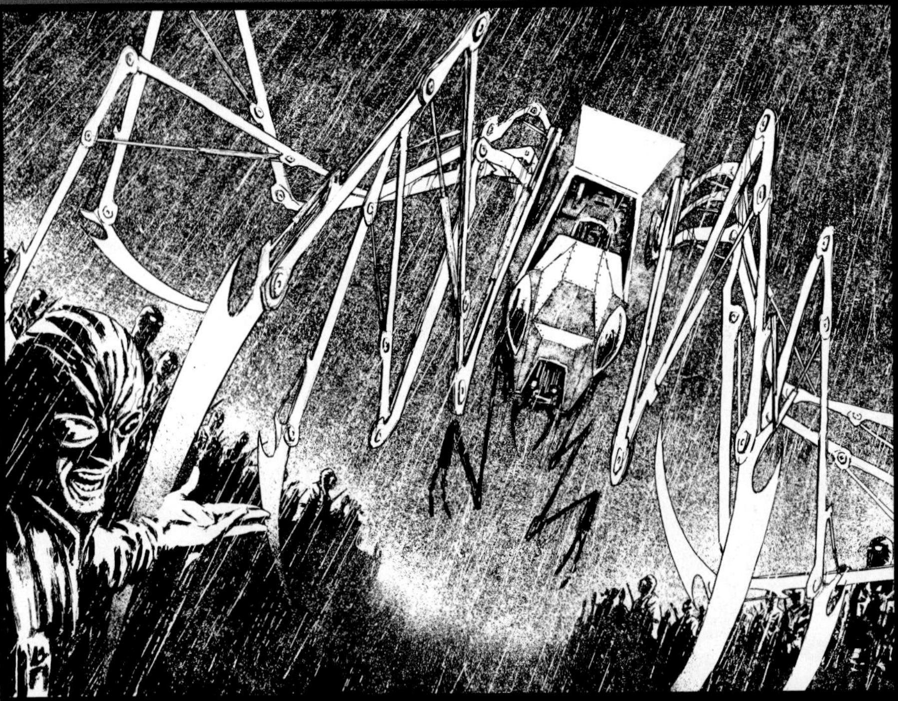

FROM "THE IMMORTAL IRON FIST" #1 SCRIPT:

The HYDRA GUYS move, revealing behind them, lying in wait, MECHAGORGON, a fearsome robot with eight arms like a mechanical spider and legs like a big-footed gazelle...in short, an Anime nightmare come to life in HYDRA colors. Nine, ten feet tall almost, each of its arms holds a long blade weapon. Go for a real "oh &$%#!" reveal here as the HYDRA GUY sorta presents it with a 'ta-daaaa!" kind of gesture.

HYDRA GUY: Mechagorgon!

From: Ed Brubaker
To: David Aja
Cc: Stefano Gaudiano; Arbona, Alejandro; Simons, Warren; Michael Lark; Matt Hollingsworth; Matt Fraction
Subject: Re: Iron Fist01 pages 15 to 19 low-res

Wow, great stuff.

I saw the mechagorgon as more of a suit someone wore, but this is awesome. It's like a giant insane spider. Brutal fight scene.

From: Matt Fraction
To: Ed Brubaker
Cc: David Aja; Stefano Gaudiano; Arbona, Alejandro; Simons, Warren; Michael Lark; Matt Hollingsworth
Subject: Re: Iron Fist01 pages 15 to 19 low-res

I know, right? I just told Warren, I thought he'd be a dude with lots of arms.

This is like some psychotic AT-AT spider nightmare. So excellent. So so excellent.

From: David Aja
To: Ed Brubaker
Cc: Matt Fraction; Stefano Gaudiano; Arbona, Alejandro; Simons, Warren; Michael Lark; Matt Hollingsworth
Subject: Re: Iron Fist01 pages 15 to 19 low-res

Thanks Ed!

I started sketching some kind of Doc Ock, more like the suit stuff you say,but at last, don't know exactly how, it finished being this.

Heh, I love the "psychotic AT-AT spider nightmare" thing

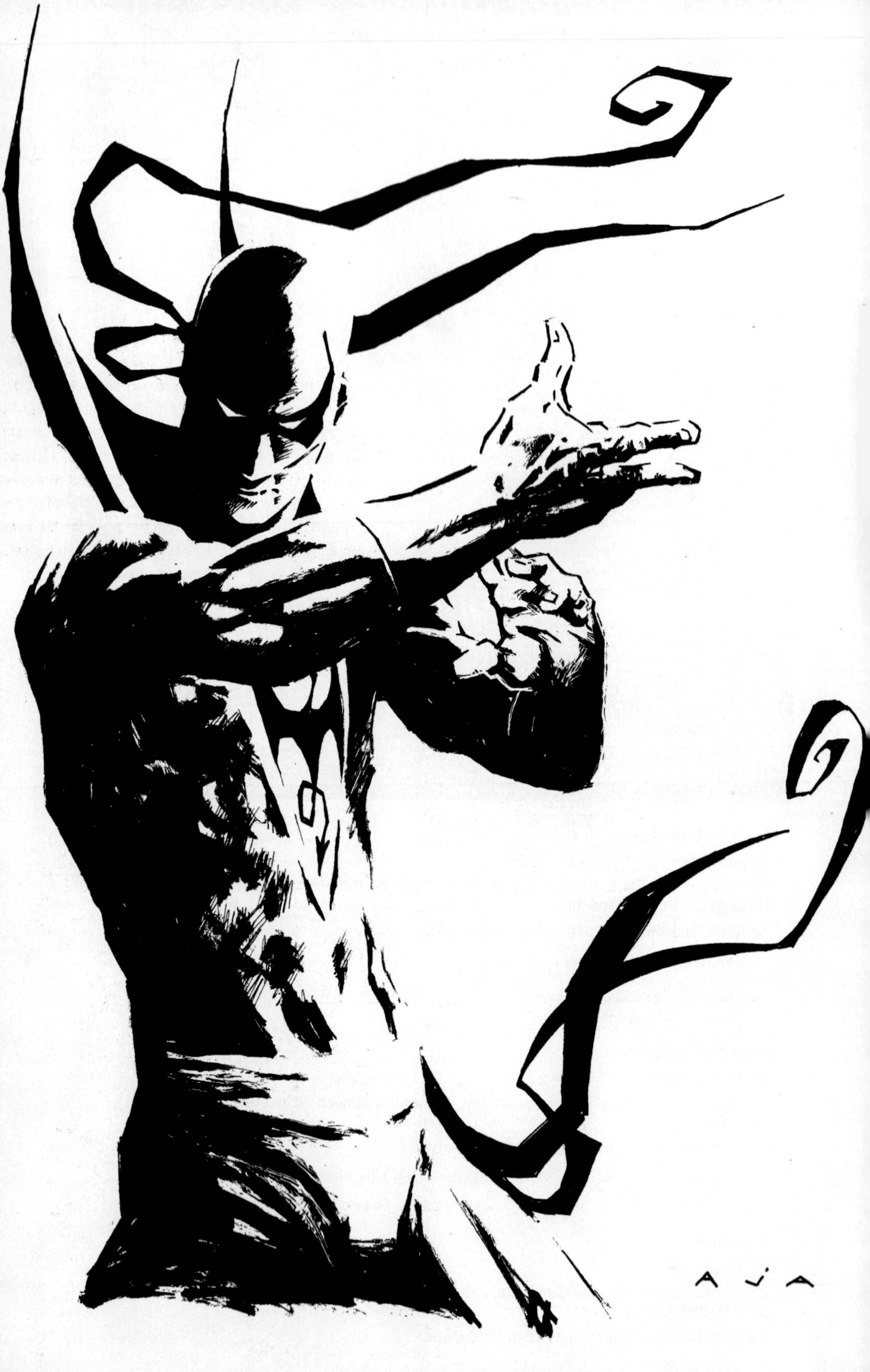
AJA

This sketch was created one morning while I worked on *Daredevil #88*. I didn't know yet that I would do [Iron Fist] and I still hadn't started to design anything. That was how I found out and agreed to do the series.

This was one of the many small ideas I had during the sketching process. In case Danny became a Hero for Hire again, this was for him to greet his clients in a more elegant costume.

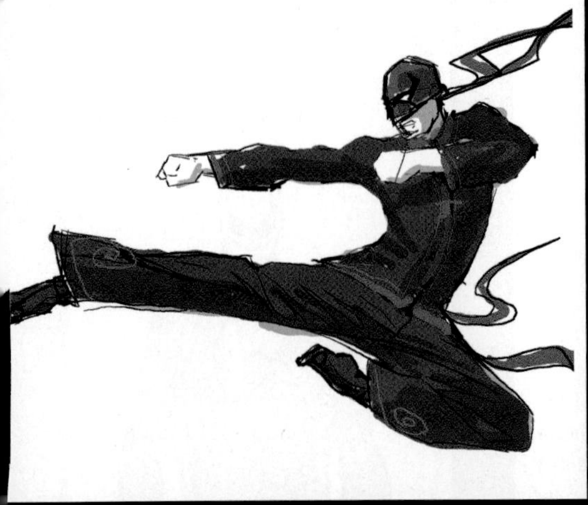

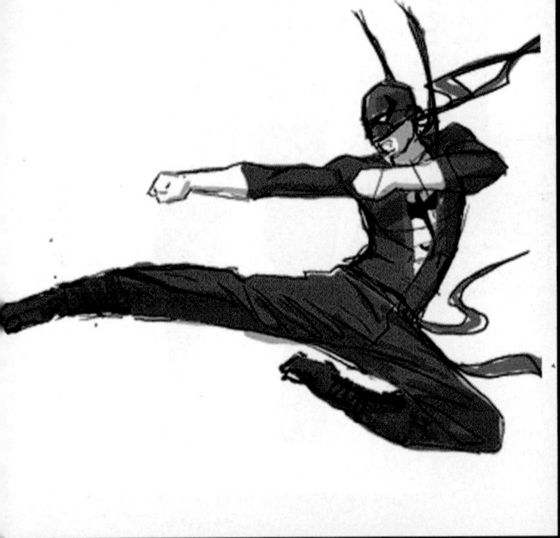

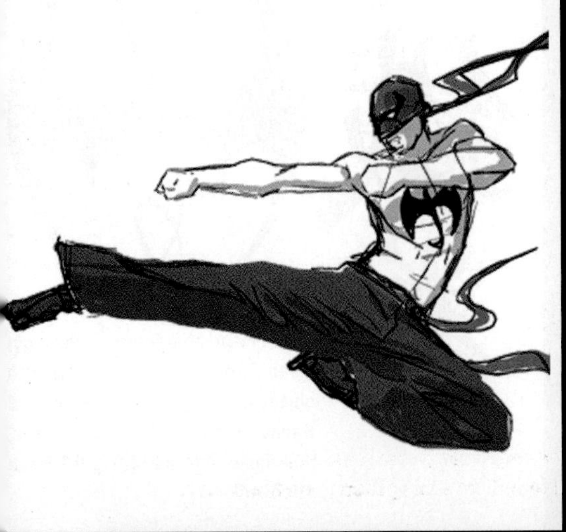

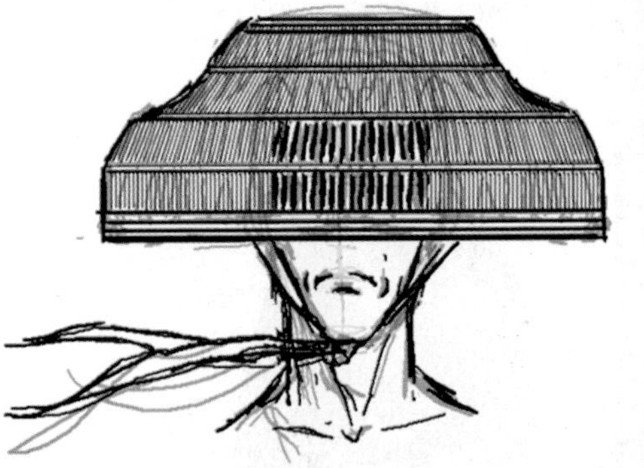

The first thing I was clear on [when designing the past Iron Fists] was that there couldn't be spandex before the 20th century, and from there on it was research, looking at old paintings and woodcuts, Hong Kong period movies, etc...I also wanted to evolve the characters' attire as a precedent to Danny's current costume. For Bei Ming-Tian, I based myself on the classic vestments of Shaolin monks. Matt and Ed wanted to add a 'ronin'-style hat, so, basing myself on the styles of Chinese straw hats, I added a mesh for his eyes more in the Japanese style. I also added a scar on his eye, possibly from his encounter with Shou-Lao.

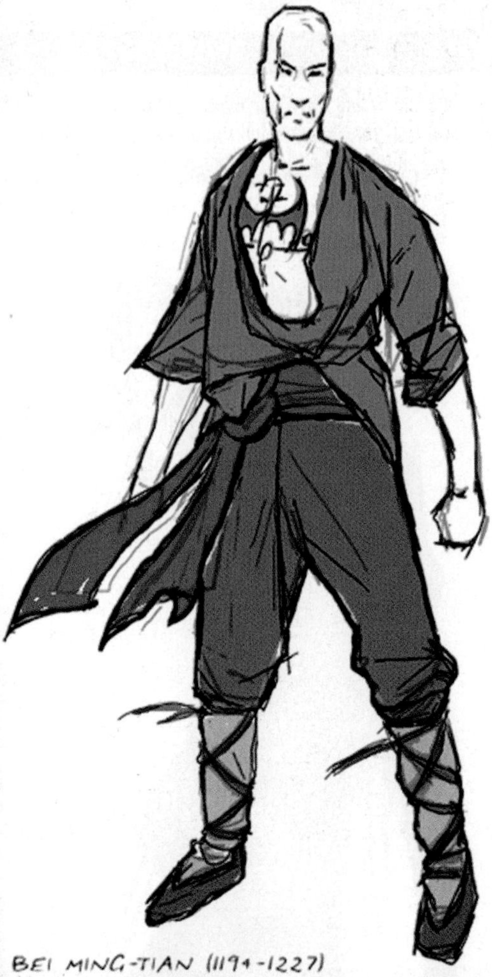

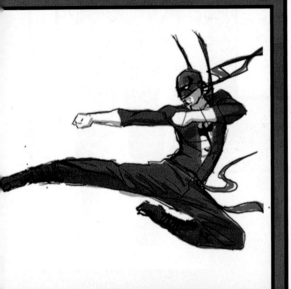

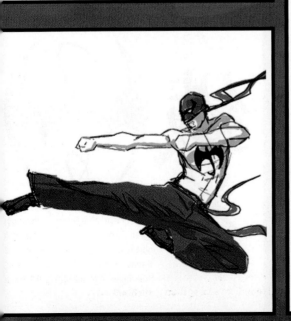

BEI MING-TIAN (1194-1227)

BEI BANG-WEN
(1827-1860)

Bei Bang-Wen is a variation of the uniforms of [19th-century Chinese revolutionaries] the Boxers. I wanted to create the feeling of a pretty "informal" costume.

For Orson Randall, the look was very clear: a little bit of [classic pulp heroes] the Phantom, Doc Savage, the Shadow and the Spider, plus the current Iron Fist mask.

ORSON RANDALL (1900-1933)

Wu Ao-Shi would have her eyes painted in honor of Bei's scar, which would later become the typical feature of the eyes of the Iron Fist mask.

WU AO-SHI (1517-1550)

The Chinese characters [in the logo] mean "iron fist"...that much was obvious, huh? I also redesigned Danny's tattoo. But as you can see, that came after designing the issue #1 cover.

THE IMMORTAL IRON FIST #1

COVER PROCESS

The idea with the cover design was to create a unifying look for the entire mini-series, which later became just the first story arc. I also tried to make the title treatment and logo another essential part of the cover, to play an important part in the design. I veered off into big, white areas mainly because it's not something you tend to see on super hero books, and would call attention to the book on the stands. Also, anybody would be able to see from far away that a new issue had come out.

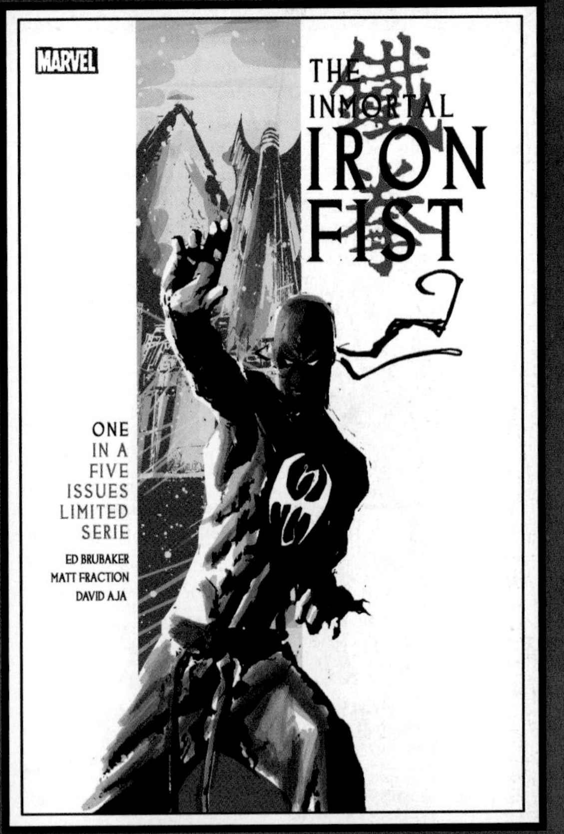
MARVEL
THE IMMORTAL
IRON FIST
ONE
IN A
FIVE
ISSUES
LIMITED
SERIE
ED BRUBAKER
MATT FRACTION
DAVID AJA

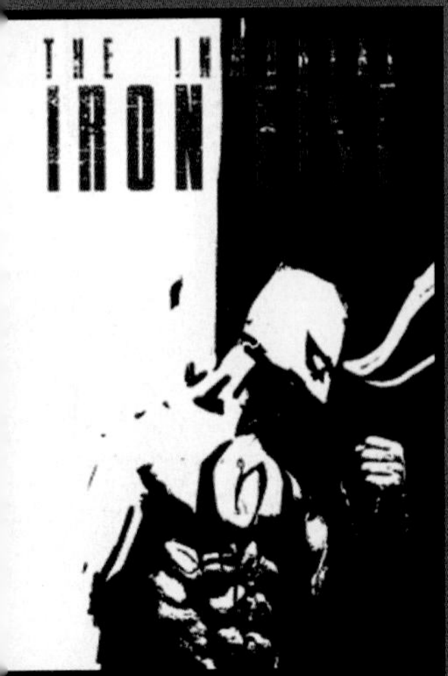

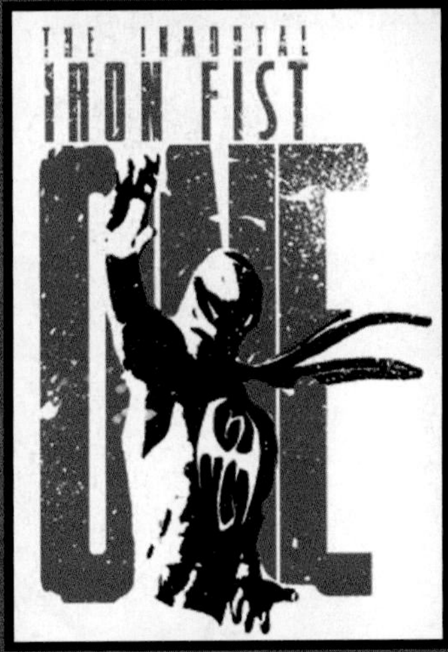
THE IMMORTAL
IRON FIST

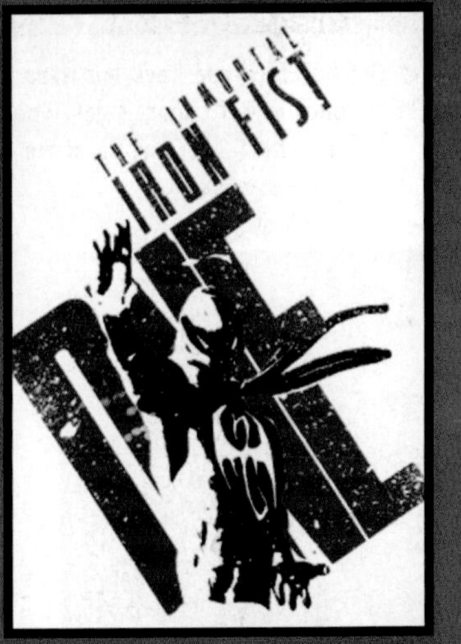
THE IMMORTAL
IRON FIST

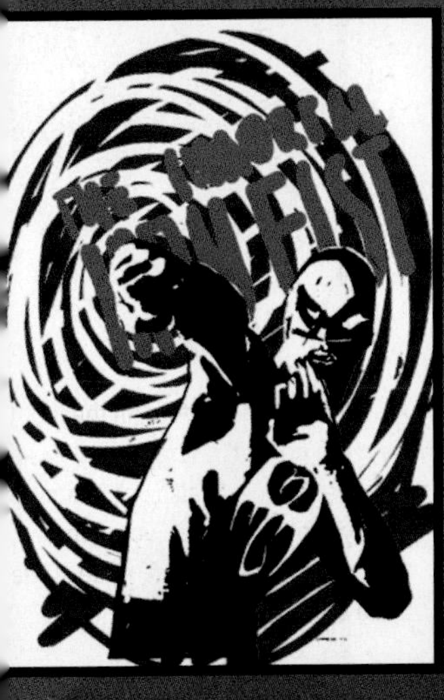

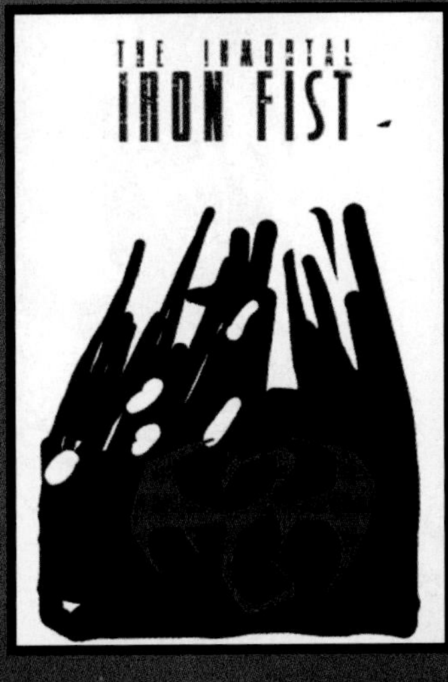
THE IMMORTAL
IRON FIST

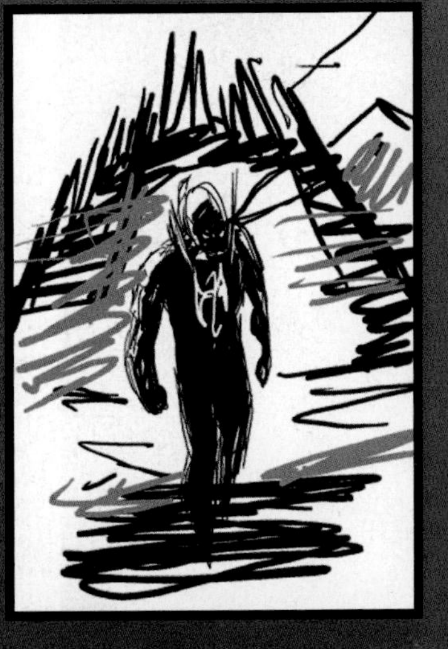

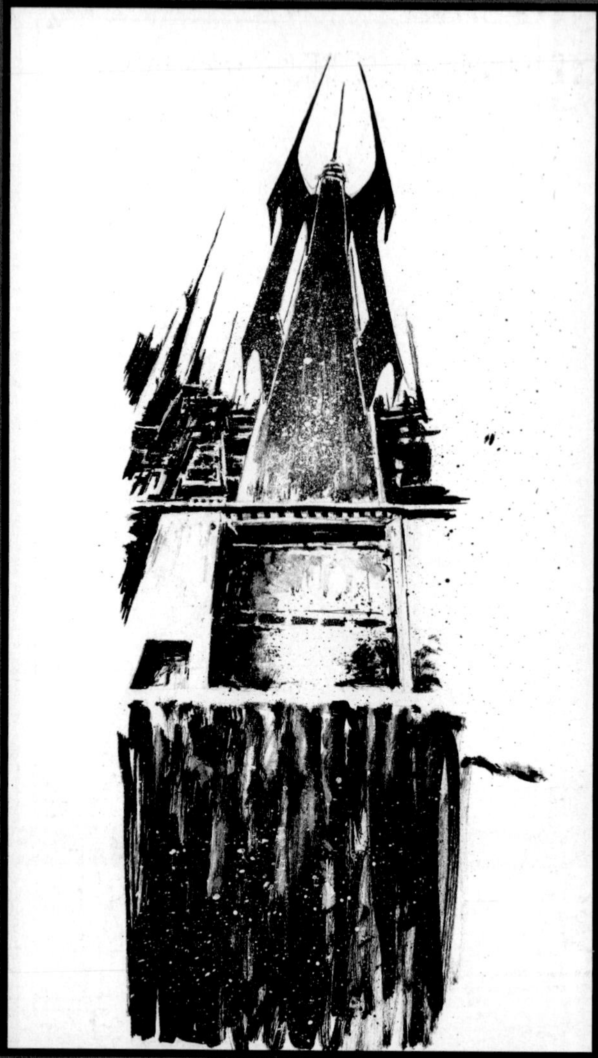
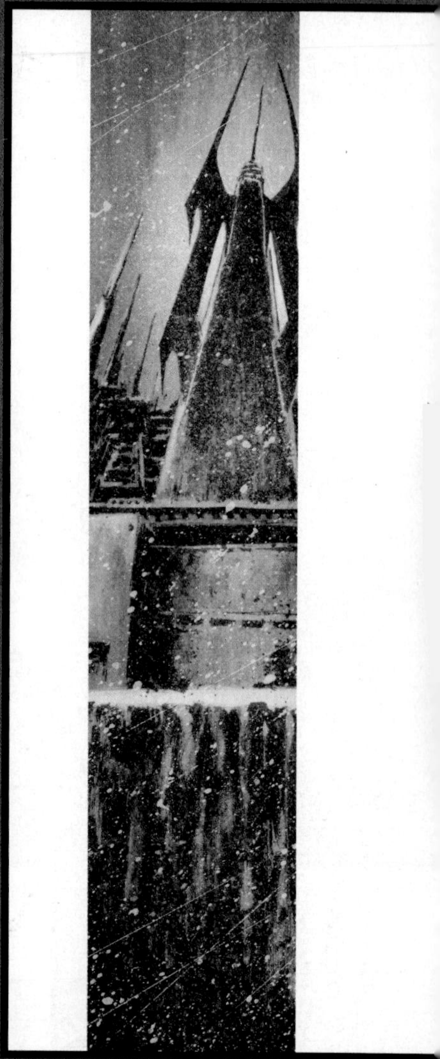
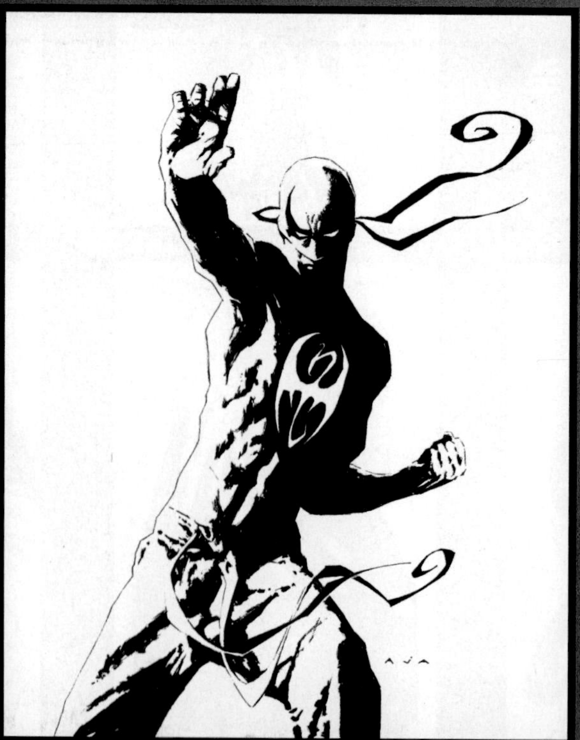

HEPTAGONAL MAP OF THE SEVEN CAPITAL CITIES OF HEAVEN
BY DAVID AJA

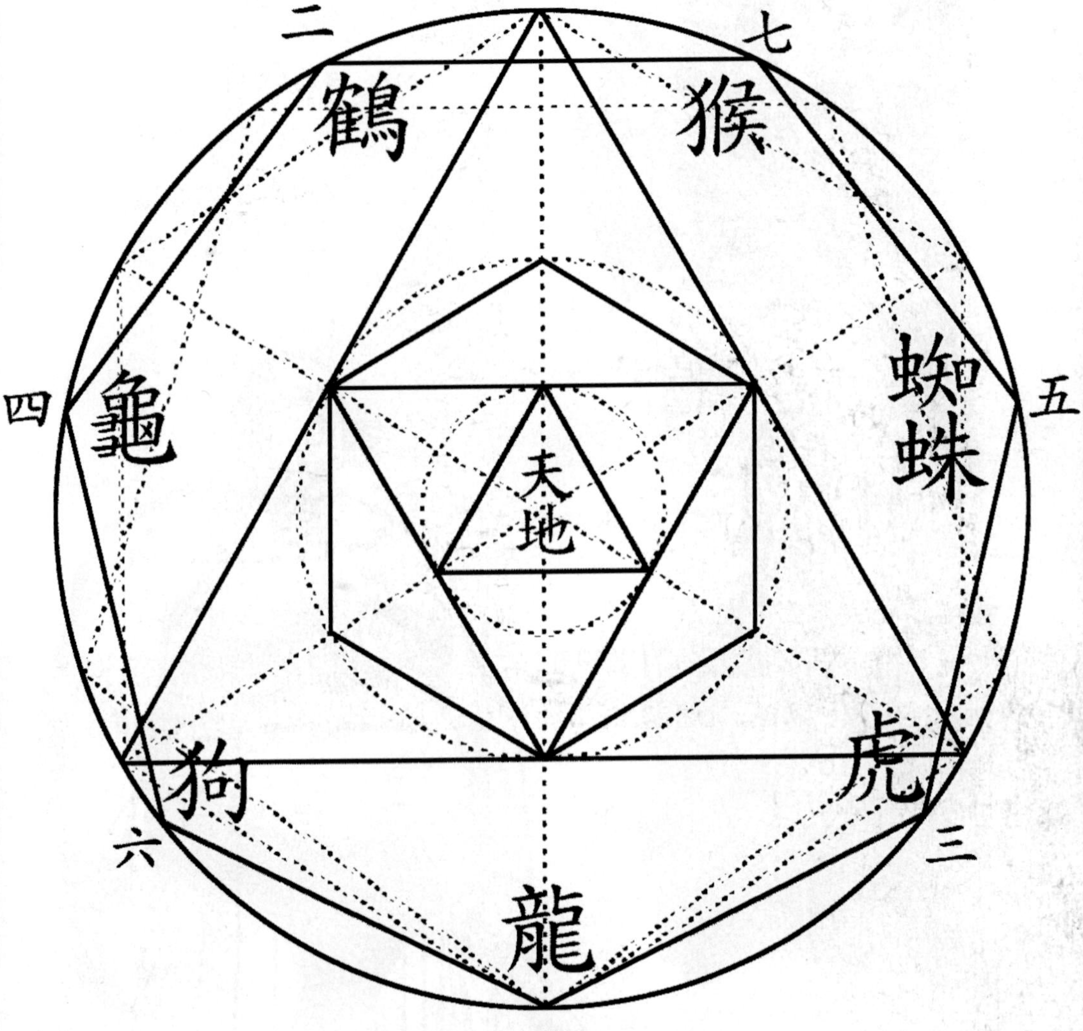

二
七
鶴
猴
四
龜
蜘
蛛
五
天
地
狗
虎
六
三
龍
一

The Seven Capital Cities of Heaven

CHARACTER SKETCHES BY DAVID AJA

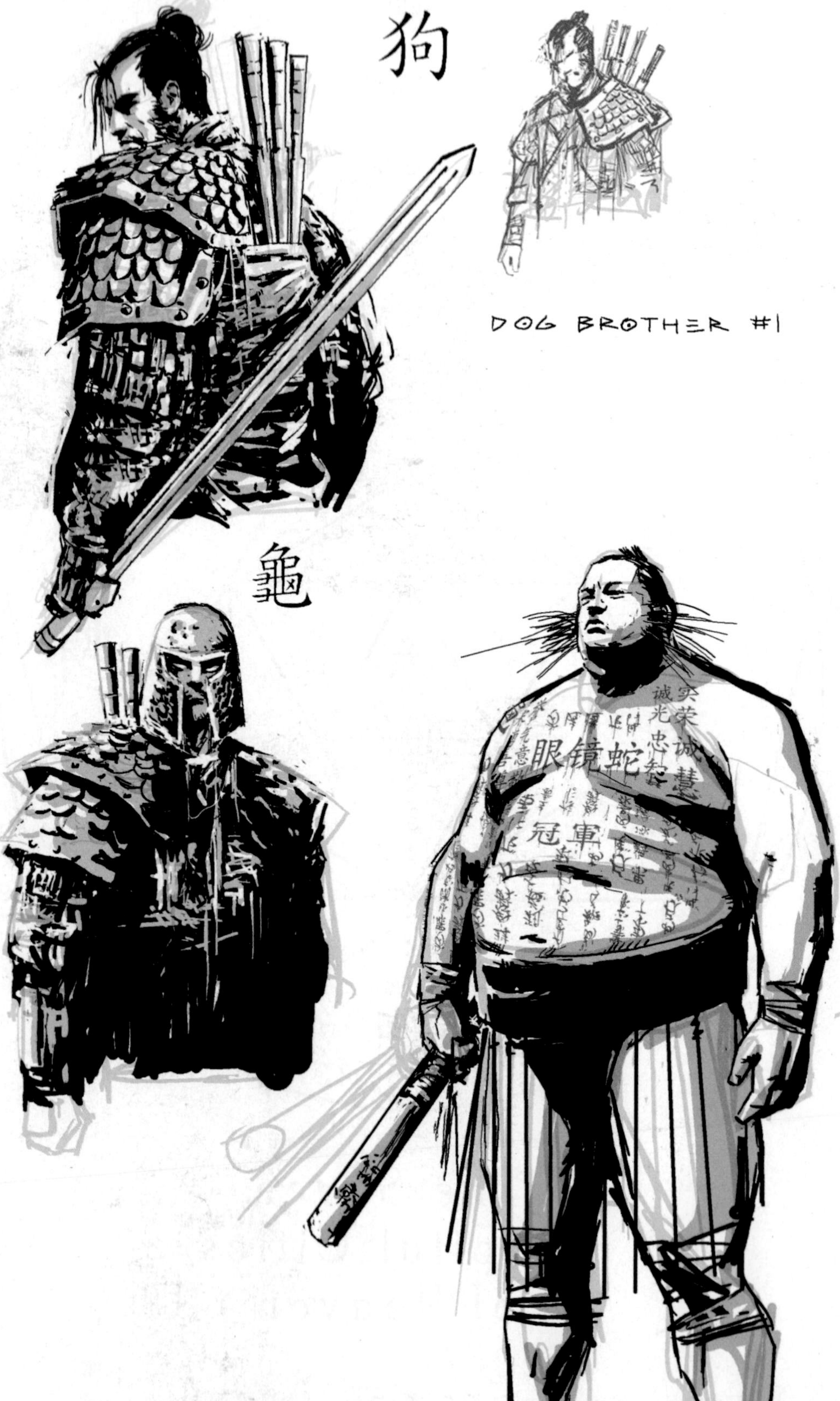

狗
DOG BROTHER #1
龜
眼镜蛇
冠軍
FAT COBRA

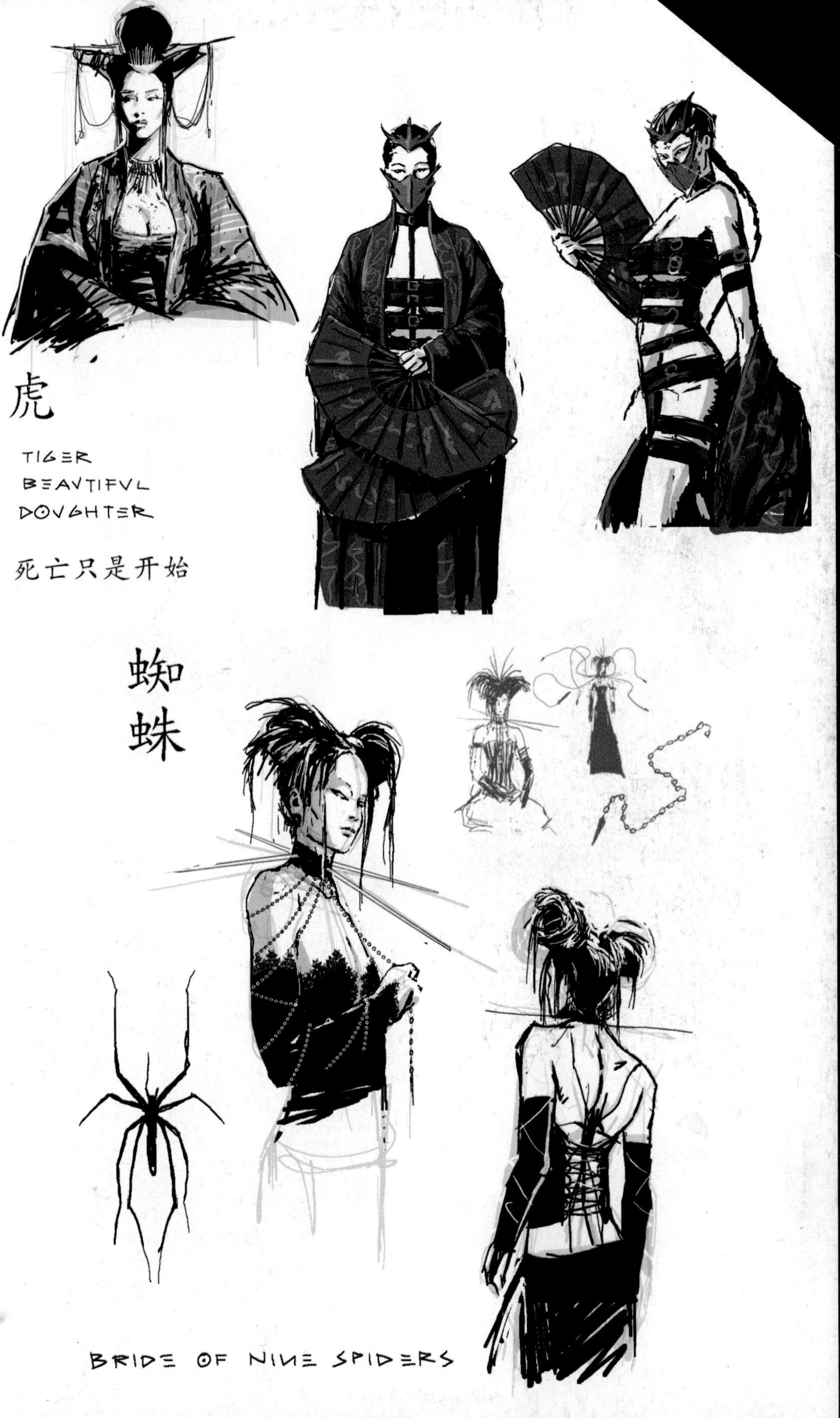

虎
TIGER
BEAUTIFUL
DOUGHTER
死亡只是开始
蜘
蛛
BRIDE OF NINE SPIDERS

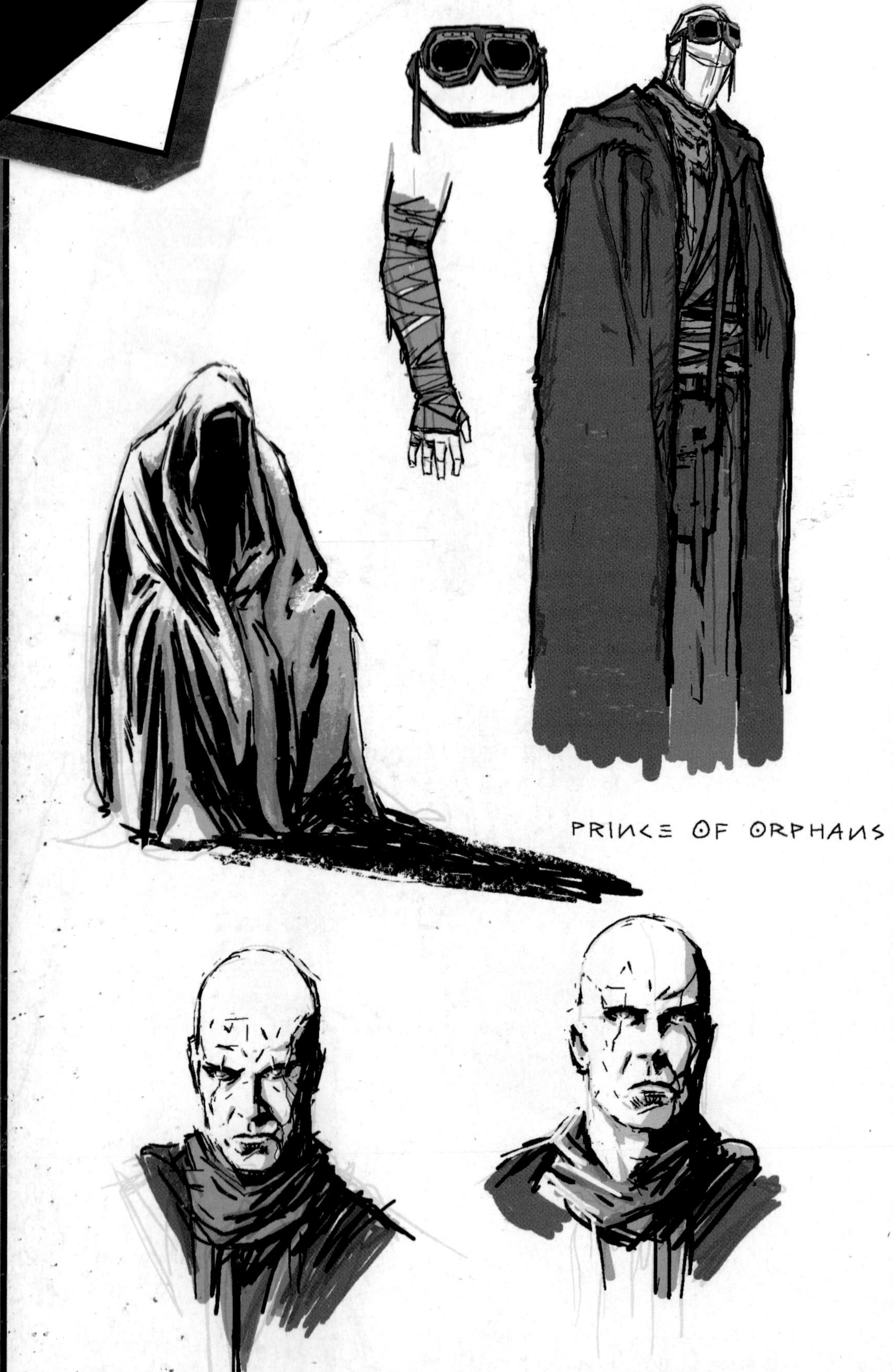

PRINCE OF ORPHANS